ITF
International Tennis Federation

the ITF year 2005

The official yearbook of the International Tennis Federation

edited by mitzi ingram evans

The ITF Year Contributors

Writers

Rachel Woodward is the ITF Administrator for the Tennis Development programme and is responsible for a range of initiatives in developing countries including touring teams, junior circuits, coaches education, the supply of tennis equipment and the ITF School Tennis Initiative.

Marta Balint is the ITF Wheelchair Tennis Silver Fund project coordinator and is responsible for the development of start-up wheelchair tennis programmes in countries around the world.

Simon Cambers is a freelance sports journalist. He has reported on global sports for the best part of a decade and has focused on tennis for the last five years. He has reported for various publications, notably *Reuters* and *The Times.*

Helen McFetridge works in the ITF Seniors Department and is responsible for the ITF Seniors World Team and Individual Championships.

Sandra Harwitt is a freelance journalist covering tennis for the past 25 years. Among the over 30 prominent media outlets she has worked for through her career are: *The New York Times, Miami Herald, Philadelphia Inquirer, USA Today, The Australian, The Guardian, ESPN.com* and *Tennis Magazine.*

John Haylett has been on the staff of four British tennis magazines. He was with *Tennis Today* from 1976-1982 and with *Serve & Volley* from 1992-1996. He has been with *Ace* since it launched in 1996 and is currently Senior Tennis Editor as well as Editor of *British Tennis.*

Jackie Nesbitt is the ITF's Head of Professional Circuits. Until 2002 she was the Manager of Juniors and Seniors tennis before moving to her current position in which she has overseen the successful launch and implementation of IPIN/Online Service, the ITF's dedicated player number and related ITF Pro Circuit online entry system.

Stuart Miller is the ITF's Head of Science & Technical. He is also Vice President of the International Society of Biomechanics in Sports, and has published academic research papers in tennis and other scientific subjects.

Eleanor Preston is a freelance tennis journalist and broadcaster. She reports on the men's and women's circuit and on junior events around the world for a number of UK publications and English language radio stations, and is also the Co-President of the International Tennis Writers' Association.

Alix Ramsay has been covering tennis for longer than she cares to remember. She was tennis correspondent of *The Times* for three years and is now a freelance for a range of publications in England, Scotland and the United States.

Douglas Robson is a freelance journalist based in San Francisco, California. He covers tennis for *USA Today* and writes for a variety of tennis, business and general interest publications.

Ossian Shine is the Tennis Correspondent for *Reuters* international news agency. Author of *The Language of Tennis*, he has reported on the sport from around the globe for the past decade and writes a weekly column for Reuters.

Photographers

Will Burgess, Sergio Carmona, Antonio Constantini, William Crabb, Corinne Dubreuil, Henk Koster, Ken Matts, Hiromaso Mano, Susan Mullane, Fabio Padilla, Martin Sidorjale, Paul Zimmer.

ISBN: 1-903013-29-1

Designed and produced by Domino 4, 01932 264550.

Contents

Abbreviations used in this book:

A alternate
abn abandoned
d defeated
def default
LL lucky loser
PR protected ranking
Q qualifier
ret retired
SE special exempt
SR special ranking
WC wildcard
w/o walkover
(I) Indoor
(O) Outdoor
BS Boys' Singles
GS Girls' Singles
BD Boys' Doubles
GD Girls' Doubles
WS Women's Singles
WD Women's Doubles
MS Men's Singles
MD Men's Doubles
QS Quad Singles
QD Quad Doubles

ITF International Tennis Federation

Contents (continued)

ITF™ International Tennis Federation

Welcome to the ITF Year

By Francesco Ricci Bitti

In my memory, there has rarely been a year as dramatic and turbulent as 2005. This year started with global tragedy, the tsunami that devastated much of Southeast Asia and killed more than a quarter of a million people. Before year's end, we suffered through many natural disasters including an agonisingly long hurricane season that affected many Caribbean nations, Mexico and the United States including the destruction of New Orleans as well as devastating earthquakes in Pakistan and in Iran, the former with great loss of life. The war in Iraq continues and terrorism around the world seems to be escalating at a frightening pace including the attacks on the London transport system that hit very close to home for our Roehampton-based staff. In many ways, viewing the issues that face our sport in this context has made it easier for us to compromise, cooperate and work towards solutions as none of our problems, however important, are as critical as the daily struggle faced by so many of our fellow citizens and let us all hope for a more peaceful and prosperous 2006 for everyone throughout the world.

With the exception of the peerless Roger Federer, the professional game this year was as unpredictable as 2005's climate. Roger's few losses were notable for only their rarity and for the quality of the people who defeated him. In the Australian Open semifinals, in what many described as the best match of the year, Roger lost to Marat Safin who went on to defeat Lleyton Hewitt to win his second Grand Slam title. Rafael Nadal ended Federer's hopes of winning Roland Garros in the semifinals and then went on to win his first (but surely not his last) Grand Slam title. Federer's other two losses came at the hands of Richard Gasquet in Monte Carlo and David Nalbandian who shocked the world No. 1 in the Tennis Masters Cup Final. Let me extend my congratulations to Roger who will be the ITF Men's World Champion for a second consecutive year.

The three Grand Slam champions plus Andy Roddick and Andre Agassi all suffered injuries that kept them off the tour for extended periods. The great season-ending championship, co-owned by the ITF, ATP and the Grand Slams, was decimated by withdrawals losing Safin, Nadal, Roddick and Lleyton Hewitt all before they hit a ball and Agassi after he lost in the opening match to the Russian Nikolay Davydenko. The organisers were rejoicing that Federer had returned to form just in time to compete in Shanghai. In addition to Roger, everyone was impressed by the class of young Nadal as he charmed the Chinese public and the tournament sponsors with an apology on court and more than three hours of meet-and-greet on the following day. Despite the set-backs, however, the Tennis Masters Cup had one of the most exciting conclusions with Nalbandian coming back from two sets down to defeat Federer in a match that I hope will be the springboard for this talented Argentine to fulfil his promise.

Men's doubles was also in foment this year after the ATP made an announcement during Wimbledon of some changes that would materially affect men's doubles players. This was not very well received by the players or the public but the new ATP Chairman, Etienne de Villiers, has taken control of this issue and found a compromise that the public will understand and most players like. He has promised to do his best to promote doubles as a speciality at ATP tournaments around the world and to put a stop to the internecine fighting that has characterised this past year and has damaged our sport. Doubles had a great show at the Tennis Masters Cup in Shanghai, with Michael Llodra and Fabrice Santoro winning this important title, but, based on their consistent performance throughout the year, Bob and Mike Bryan have been named the ITF Men's Doubles World Champions for the third consecutive year.

In the women's game, there were four different Grand Slam champions: Serena Williams in Melbourne, Justine Henin-Hardenne in Paris, Venus Williams at Wimbledon and Kim Clijsters in New York. While there is no doubt who is the best player in men's tennis, it is not so easy with the women with Lindsay Davenport ending the year ranked No. 1 and Amelie Mauresmo winning the season-ending WTA Tour Championships. It was wonderful to see the Williams sisters performing well in the Grand Slam tournaments and to see Justine triumphing over the illness that has plagued her last 18 months but my fondest memories of 2005 will be of Kim's long overdue victory at the US Open, Amelie's equally long awaited breakthrough to win a major tournament and the rejuvenated Mary Pierce who reached two Grand Slam finals and almost won the Fed Cup title for France. It was very close but, by a small margin, Kim Clijsters was named ITF Women's World Champion for 2005.

Speaking of Fed Cup, it certainly was a year to remember with the new home-and-away format now firmly established and, thanks to our friends from the French Tennis Federation, a final to remember. To see the Philippe Chatrier Court full to brimming with over 15,000 each day to see France take on the defending champions from Russia was just spectacular. On the final day, as darkness neared, the stadium was still full to see the third set of the final doubles rubber. It could have gone either way but Russia took control and retained the title for a second consecutive year. My congratulations to Shamil Tarpischev and his team, particularly Elena Dementieva, who won three points to win the Final. This Final was a huge boost for Fed Cup that also received a significant and well-deserved vote of confidence when BNP Paribas agreed to become title sponsor of this event through 2011.

BNP Paribas also reinforced its commitment to Davis Cup by extending its relationship with our flagship competition, also through 2011. NEC also continued their relationship with wheelchair tennis through 2008 and Lufthansa became the Official Airline and sponsor of junior events through 2007.

This year, Davis Cup by BNP Paribas was as surprising as it was exciting with two small nations, Slovak Republic and Croatia, defeating the defending champions from Spain and finalists from the United States in the opening round and then continuing their outstanding run to reach the Final. The 4,100 seat National Tennis Centre in Bratislava was, we believe, the smallest Final venue since the World Group was founded in 1981. But the outstanding organisation and the spirit and sense of fairness from the spectators from both Slovak Republic and Croatia made it the equal of any Final I have ever witnessed.

Like Fed Cup, the title was decided in the final fifth rubber when Mario Ancic, who had not won a live singles match all year, defeated Michal Mertinak in straight sets to give Croatia its first Davis Cup victory. However, in the view of many, the match of the weekend was Dominik Hrbaty's five set victory over Ivan Ljubicic in the first of the reverse singles on Sunday. Ljubicic will always be remembered as the Davis Cup player of the year, having won a record 11 live matches, but it will also be impossible to forget Hrbaty's commitment and passion when he plays for his country. Croatia, the first unseeded nation ever to win the Davis Cup by BNP Paribas, welcomed home their team with a rousing reception that attracted 100,000 people in Zagreb and it is clear that this victory is one of this country's greatest sporting achievements ever. My congratulations to Captain Niki Pilic, the only captain ever to win this title for two different countries, and to the Croatian team on this remarkable victory.

My congratulations to Captain Niki Pilic, the only captain ever to win this title for two different countries, and to the Croatian team on this remarkable victory.

Philippe Chatrier court during the Fed Cup final

It was a great year also for junior tennis with 318 events staged in 115 countries on the ITF Junior Circuit. Viktoria Azarenka of Belarus, a former ITF Development Team member, dominated the junior girls' rankings all year but that was not the case in the junior boys' category with Marin Cilic of Croatia and Donald Young of the United States fighting it out until the end, accepting wildcards into the last event of the year, the Yucatan Cup, in order to determine the year-end No. 1. In the end, Young won out and will join Azarenka as the 2005 ITF Junior World Champions.

The first big team event of the junior year was the World Junior Tennis Finals for 14 & under players. The French boys and the Russian girls were victorious, defeating Argentina and Japan respectively. Junior Davis Cup by BNP Paribas and Junior Fed Cup were held once again at Barcelona's beautiful Polo Club with France overcoming Czech Republic in the Junior Davis Cup and Poland defeating France to win Junior Fed Cup. The success of the French at this young level is just one more indicator of how strong their programme is and it is obvious that France will continue to perform at the highest level not only in the team competitions but also at the major tournaments for many years to come.

Senior tennis had another strong year with 153 events staged in 47 countries. The Seniors World Team Championships were staged in Perth with host nation Australia and the United States dominating the winners' table in both the team and individual events. Australia and USA won seven of the ten team cups and 14 of 20 of the individual titles at the ITF Senior World Individual Championships. In the ITF Super-Seniors Team Championships, USA also dominated, winning five of the nine Cups played and in the Super-Seniors Individual Championships won six of the 11 titles on offer.

Wheelchair tennis continues to grow with 123 events in 31 countries. Two new high-visibility events were staged in 2005, the inaugural Wheelchair Tennis Event at the US Open, a part of the NEC Wheelchair Tour, and an invitational men's doubles event at Wimbledon.

It is no surprise that, once again, Esther Vergeer, with her 55-0 record in singles,

Francesco Ricci Bitti with Roger Federer

ITF President with Francoise Durr and Christian Bimes

will be the ITF Women's Wheelchair World Champion. This is the sixth consecutive year that we will present Esther with this honour and she well deserves it. Michael Jeremiasz of France, with a 50-6 win-loss record in singles, edged David Hall to top the rankings in the men's field and will, for the first time, become ITF Men's Wheelchair World Champion.

The 14th Worldwide Coaches Workshop was another successful activity of the ITF's Development Department which works tirelessly to promote our sport worldwide. The five-day Workshop attracted 290 coaches from 90 nations, with one of the highlights being a presentation from former world No. 1 Arantxa Sanchez-Vicario. Other important Development activities included the staging of the African Junior Championships in Mauritius, the success of the International Junior Touring Team highlighted by Bahamian Ryan Sweeting's victory at the US Open and the continued growth of the International Tennis Number with currently 83 nations with ITN on-court assessors.

The activities of our Technical Department also fall under the Development umbrella, along with Juniors, Seniors and Wheelchair. It has been an exceptionally busy year for Technical adding the testing of electronic line-calling system to their long list of projects that includes ball approval, court surface testing and the development of Tennis GUT, a powerful software package which models the effects of tennis equipment and atmospheric conditions on the nature of tennis. Working with a team from ITF Officiating and the two professional tours, the Technical Department spent weeks testing electronic line-calling systems with the result that one, Hawk-Eye Officiating, was felt to have met the criteria set by the committee. The ITF's International Mixed Team Competition, Hopman Cup XVIII will be the first official event to use this technology that we believe will provide an aide to officiating for the future.

The ITF Professional Circuits continue to grow with 493 events in 69 countries for the men and 374 events in 59 countries for the women but the most important development for the Circuits in 2005 was the successful launch of the on-line entry system, IPIN. This service, which is linked to a player's International Player Identification Number (IPIN), is designed to enable players to manage their own tournament schedule online. Developed by the ITF's ICT Department in conjunction with the ITF's Pro Circuits Department, this innovation has proved popular with both players and tournaments alike and, at year's end, some 12,698 players have signed up for IPIN.

The ICT Department has also worked closely with our Communications Department to develop our website portfolio including the growth of the ITF portal and our Davis Cup by BNP Paribas and Fed Cup by BNP Paribas websites.

At the start of next year, the ITF will launch our new anti-doping weblet in conjunction with taking over from the ATP the administration of anti-doping at ATP-sanctioned events from 1 January 2006. This is one of the most important activities of the ITF and our partners, the ATP and WTA Tour. I want to thank the ATP for their confidence and support, as well as that of the Grand Slam tournaments, and we will work closely with all of our partners not only to run an effective programme but also to do a better job to educate players on the dangers that doping presents to their health and their careers. Frankly, I don't want to see one more player be convicted of a doping offence because he or she forgets to fill in their TUE (therapeutic use exemptions) or underestimates the dangers of supplements or over-the-counter medication.

The ITF staged a wonderful AGM in Prague as a part of the Centenary celebrations of the Czech Tennis Federation. Among the activities were elections for the ITF Board of Directors. Four new members, Miguel Carrizosa of Paraguay, Pierre Darmon of France, Franklin Johnson of the United States and Charles Trippe of Great Britain, plus one returning member, Ismail El Shafei of Egypt, joined the Board and we look forward to working with them. I also want to thank the outgoing members of the board, Christian Bimes of France, Paul Chingoka of Zimbabwe, Merv Heller of the United States, Ian King of Great Britain and Nelson Nastas of Brazil for their hard work on behalf of the ITF.

Awards presented by the ITF in 2005 included the Philippe Chatrier Award, which was presented to Tony Trabert of the United States whose career as a player, coach, captain, TV commentator and President of the International Hall of Fame more than qualified him to receive our most prestigious award. Francoise Durr of France received the ITF/International Tennis Hall of Fame Fed Cup Award of Excellence while Miloslav Mecir of Slovak Republic and Goran Ivanisevic of Croatia received the ITF/ITHF Davis Cup Award of Excellence. Sue Wolstenholme of the British Tennis Foundation received the Brad Parks Award. Eduardo Moline O'Connor was voted Honorary Life Counsellor of the ITF. Croatia finished the year atop the ITF Davis Cup Nations Ranking while Russia finished at the top of the ITF Fed Cup Nations Ranking.

As we approach 2006, there is much work to do but I am hopeful that there will be a fresh look at many of the problems that face our sport including the calendar and that we can all work together in a more positive fashion for the future benefit of tennis.

ITF Board of Directors

There are 14 ITF Directors, including ITF President Francesco Ricci Bitti and Executive Vice President Juan Margets. They will all serve on the Board until the 2007 AGM. A full listing of all ITF Committees can be found in the 2006 ITF Constitution.

ITF President Francesco Ricci Bitti

PERSONAL
Born 1942 in Faenza, Italy. Citizen of Italy
Languages: Italian, English, French

AWARDS
2001 Golden Racket Award (Italy)
2000 Honorary Life President of the European Tennis Federation
1999 Paul Fellow Award – Rotary International
1998 Golden Star Award – presented by CONI (Italian NOC)
1997 Honorary Life Counsellor of the International Tennis Federation

BUSINESS
Senior executive in leading multi-national information and communication technology companies for the past 30 years

OLYMPIC ACTIVITIES
2001–present Member, ASOIF Council
2000–present Chairman, ITF Olympic Committee
1997–1999 Member, Italian NOC (CONI)
1992 & 1996 ITF Board of Directors
1984 ITF Technical Delegate
1999–present Mediator, Court of Arbitration for Sport (CAS)
2001–present Member, WADA Foundation Board

TENNIS ADMINISTRATION
International Tennis Federation
1999–present President of the ITF
1997–1999 Member, Junior Competitions Committee
1987–1997 Chairman, Junior Competitions Committee
1987–1997 Member, Committee of Management
1987–1991 Member, Finance Committee
1981–1987 Member, Junior Competitions Committee
Tennis Europe
2000 Honorary Life President
1993–1999 President
1989–1993 Vice President
1981–1993 Member, Board of Management
1990–1993 Chairman, Junior Competitions Committee
1977–1990 Member, Junior Competitions Committee
Italian Tennis Federation
1997–1999 President
1997–1999 Chairman, Italian Open Tournament (Rome)
1989–1995 First Vice President
1981–1985 Vice President
1977–1989 Member, Committee of Management

TENNIS COMPETITION EXPERIENCE
1971 Quarterfinalist, Italian Singles National Championships
1970 & 1971 Member, Italian National Team Championships
1962, 1964, 1965 Winner, Italian University Championships
1960 Member, Italian National Junior Team

ITF Executive Vice President Juan Margets

PERSONAL
Born in 1954
Citizen of Spain
Languages: Spanish, English, French

BUSINESS
Qualifications: Economist (Graduate of the University of Barcelona)
Read one year of Law Studies
1978–1983 Commercial Director of family textile company
1983–1998 General Manager and Partner in Grupo Constelacion, a real estate company

TENNIS ADMINISTRATION
International Tennis Federation
1998–2007 Executive Vice President
1997–2007 Member, Board of Directors
1991–1997 Member, Committee of Management
1999–2007 Chairman, Davis Cup Committee
1999–2007 Chairman, ITF Men's Circuit Committee
1997–1999 Chairman, Wheelchair Tennis Committee
1993–1999 Member, Davis Cup Committee
1991–1993 Member, Fed Cup Committee
Tennis Europe
1996–1999 Vice President & Chairman, Development Committee
1993–1995 Chairman, Junior Committee
1990–1995 Member, Committee of Management
1987–1993 Men's Team Championship Committee
1985–1993 Member of "Coupe d'Europe de Clubs" Committee
Spanish Tennis Federation
1989–2000 Member, Committee of Management
President, Professional Tennis Committee
1986–1989 Executive Assistant to the President of the Spanish Tennis Federation

OTHER
2001–present Member, WTA Tour Board
1993–present Member, Spanish Olympic Committee
1987–1991 President, Club Tennis Bara
1983–1985 General Secretary, Federacion Catalana de Tenis

TENNIS COMPETITION EXPERIENCE
1971 Member of the Spanish Under 18 Team
1968 Under 14 Spanish Champion
ITN: 3

Jan Carlzon

PERSONAL
Born in 1941
Citizen of Sweden
Languages:
Swedish, English

BUSINESS
2003–present Chairman of the British-Swedish Chamber of Commerce
1996–present Chairman and founding partner of a venture capital organisation, listed on the Stockholm Stock Exchange
1995–1997 Executive Chairman of Fritidsresor AB, a travel company
1981–1993 President and CEO of Scandinavian Airline System (SAS)
1979–1980 President and CEO of Linjeflyg, the domestic Swedish airline
1971–1978 Marketing Director, from 1974 CEO of Vingresor, the leading Scandinavian tour operating company

TENNIS ADMINISTRATION
International Tennis Federation
2001–2007 Member, Board of Directors
2001–2007 Member, Finance Committee
2003–2007 Chairman, Wheelchair Tennis Committee
Swedish Tennis Association
1999–present President

OTHER
Author of Moments of Truth, a bestselling book on customer service, published in 17 languages
Awarded Commander with Star of the Royal Norwegian Order of Merit
Awarded King of Sweden's Medal
Holds Honorary Doctorates from Pepperdine University, California and Pacific Lutheran University, Washington

Miguel Carrizosa

PERSONAL
Born in 1955
Citizen of Paraguay
Languages: English, German, Spanish, Portuguese
Doctor in Economy & Business Administration (Sevilla University/ American University in Paraguay)
Masters in Business Administration – Denver University, Colorado

BUSINESS
2004–2005 President, Paraguayan Congress
2003–2004 Vice President, Senate Chamber
2003–2008 Paraguayan Senator
1997–2003 President, Paraguayan Federation of Production, Industry & Commerce
1992–1998 President – Paraguayan Importers Association
Family Business: DIESA S.A. – Managing Director (Vehicle Imports), SOLFRIO S.A. – Vice-President (Tyres), MAPFRE S.A. – Director (Insurance)

TENNIS ADMINISTRATION
International Tennis Federation
2005-2007 Member, Board of Directors
1992–2005 Member, Junior Competitions Committee
2005–2007 Chairman, Development Advisors Group
COSAT
1994–2005 Vice President
1992–present Director, Junior Committee
Paraguayan Tennis Association
2002–present President, International Relations
1989–2001 President
1988–1989 Vice President
1986–1988 Director
1989 World Youth Cup, Tournament Director
1990 Officiating Course – Level 2
1989–2001 Director, Davis Cup events played by Paraguayan Team

OTHER
1997–present Director, Paraguayan Olympic Committee

TENNIS COMPETITION EXPERIENCE
Up to 1989 National ranked player, "Selección and Primera"
South American ranked player
Seniors player 40+ and 45+

Pierre Darmon

PERSONAL
Born in 1934
Citizen of France
Languages: French, English, Spanish
Baccalaureate
Chevalier de la Légion d'honneur
Chevalier de l'Ordre National du Mérite

TENNIS ADMINISTRATION
International Tennis Federation
2005–2007 Member, Board of Directors
2005–2007 Member, Davis Cup Committee
French Tennis Federation
1968–1972 & 2005–present Member, Committee of Management
1969–1978 Director, Roland Garros tournament
2004–Chairman, French ILTC
2004–Chairman, "Amis du Tenniseum"

OTHER
2002–present Board Member, Monte Carlo Country Club
1979–1989 Managing Director, Proserv Europe
1982–1989 Tournament Director, Antwerp Tournament
1990–1996 Executive Vice President for Europe, ATP Tour
1972–1979 Member, Board of Directors of the ATP (founder member)
Member of MIPTC from its creation until 1979

TENNIS COMPETITION EXPERIENCE
1966–1978 No. 1 player in France
1956–67 Player, French Davis Cup team (69 matches)
44 victories in international tournaments
1963 Finalist at Roland Garros (men's singles)
1963 Finalist at Wimbledon (men's doubles)
1974–1979 Captain, French Davis Cup team

ITF Board of Directors (continued)

Ismail El Shafei

PERSONAL

Born in 1947
Citizen of Egypt
Languages: Arabic, English , French
Awarded Medals of Honour by Egyptian Presidents Nasser, Sadat and Mubarak
BA Economics, Cairo University, 1968
Elected Athlete of the Year in Egypt from 1969–1974

BUSINESS

Chairman/Managing Director, Allied Trading & Consultancy Group

TENNIS ADMINISTRATION

International Tennis Federation

2005–2007 Member, Board of Directors
1997–2001 & 2005–07 Chairman, Coaches Commission
2002 Elected ITF Honorary Life Counsellor
1998–2001 Member, Board of Directors
1997 Member, Committee of Management
1999–2001 Member, Davis Cup Committee
1997–2001 Chairman, Davis Cup African Zonal Committee
1995–1999 Member, Satellite Committee

Egyptian Tennis Federation

2005–2008 President
1994–1996 President
1988–1992 Member, Board of Directors
1984–1988 Head of Technical Committee
1980–1986 Captain Egyptian Davis Cup Team

OTHER

1972–1974 Secretary of ATP Board of Directors

TENNIS COMPETITION EXPERIENCE

1963–1980 Ranked No.1 tennis player in Egypt
1964 Winner, Junior Wimbledon and Junior Orange Bowl
1969 Finalist, US National indoors
1969, 73, 74 Winner, Men's Singles, Egyptian International Tournament
1970–1972 Professional Tour Players World Championship Tennis
1974 Wimbledon Quarterfinalist
1974 Semifinalist, Doubles Masters in Houston

Franklin R Johnson

PERSONAL

Born in 1936
Citizen of the United States of America.
B.S. (Accounting) and MBA, University of California, Los Angeles

BUSINESS

Managing Partner, Price Waterhouse LLP (retired)
Business Consultant and Expert Witness, Entertainment Industry Litigation
Member, Board of Directors and Chair of Audit Committee, Party City Corporation, Reliance Steel & Aluminium Co., and Special Value Opportunities Fund LLC.
Board Member, UCLA Foundation
Board Member, Fraternity of Friends

TENNIS ADMINISTRATION

International Tennis Federation

2005–2007 Member, Board of Directors
2005–2007 Vice President
2005–2007 Chairman, Joint Media Commission
2003–2005 Member, Junior Competitions Committee
2000, 2003-2005 USTA Delegate to AGM

United States Tennis Association

2005–present Chairman of the Board & President
2005–present Chairman, US Open
2003–2004 First Vice President
2001–2002 Secretary-Treasurer
1997–2000 Director at Large
2003–2004 Member, USTA Diversity Guide Team
2001–2002 Chair, USTA Budget Committee
1999–2002 Chair, USTA Investment Committee

OTHER

2003–present Grand Slam Committee
2003–present Member, Board of Directors, International Tennis Hall of Fame
2005–present Executive Committee, International Tennis Hall of Fame
2004–present Board Member, USTA Tennis & Education Foundation
2001–2003 Secretary-Treasurer, USTA Tennis & Education Foundation

TENNIS COMPETITION EXPERIENCE

Winner of four national titles consisting of the USTA hard court 15 & under and 18 & under championships in singles & doubles.
Varsity Team, University of California; team won conference title for three consecutive years and NCAA team championship in 1956.

Anil Kumar Khanna

PERSONAL

Born in 1953
Citizen of India
Languages: English, Hindi, Urdu & Punjabi
F.C.A. (Institute of Chartered Accountants in England & Wales since 1977)

BUSINESS

1996–present Director of a Bank in India
1995–present Managing director of a Japanese joint venture company
1990–present Chairman of DFK India, worldwide group of chartered accountants
1998–present Managing Director of Saurer India (a company of Saurer Group, Switzerland)

TENNIS ADMINISTRATION

International Tennis Federation

2003–2007 Member, Board of Directors
2005-2007 Chairman, Women's Circuit Committee
2003–2005 Chairman, Seniors Committee
2003–2007 Member, Development Advisors Group
1999–2001 Member, Davis Cup Zonal Committee
1990–present AITA delegate to AGM

Asian Tennis Federation

2003–present Hon. Secretary General and Hon. Treasurer
1998–present Vice President
1998–present Member, Board of Directors
2002–present Chairman, Finance Committee
1998–2003 Chairman Men's Tennis Committee

All India Tennis Association

2000–2008 Hon. Executive Vice President and Secretary General
1990–present Chairman, Davis Cup Management Committee

Delhi Lawn Tennis Association

2000–2004 President
1992–2000 Secretary
1989–1992 Treasurer

TENNIS COMPETITION EXPERIENCE

1966–1973 National ranked player, junior and senior
Represented Delhi State in juniors and seniors

Geoff Pollard

PERSONAL
Born in 1944
Citizen of Australia
Awarded Member of Order of Australia for Services to Tennis
MSC, AIA, FAIM, FAICD

BUSINESS
1992–2001 Director of Delfin Property Group
1974–1989 Senior Lecturer in Actuarial Studies, Demography, Statistics at Macquarie University, Sydney

TENNIS ADMINISTRATION
International Tennis Federation
1998–2007 Member, Board of Directors
1999–2007 Vice President
1991–1997 Member, Committee of Management
1999–2003 & 2005-2007 Chairman, Rules of Tennis Committee
1998–1999 Chairman, Constitutional Committee
1997–2007 Member, Finance Committee
1997–2001 Member, Olympic Committee
1993–1997 Member, Rules of ITF Committee
1991–1994 Member, Davis Cup Committee
Tennis Australia
1989–present President
1979–1989 Councillor/Director

OTHER
1991–2007 Member, Grand Slam Committee
1991–2007 Chairman, Technical Commission
1993–2005 President, Oceania Tennis Federation
1987–2000 WTA Tour representative for Rest of World
1993–1997 Australian Olympic Committee Board Member
1983–1987 Director, Australian Institute of Sport
1979–1989 President, New South Wales Tennis Association
1971–1978 Honorary Secretary, Australian Universities' Sports Association

TENNIS COMPETITION EXPERIENCE
1973 General Manager of Australian Team for World Student Games, Moscow
1967, 1970 Represented Australia in World Student Games (Tokyo and Turin)
1961 & 1962 Represented Australia in the Sunshine Cup
1962 & 1963 Runner-up in Orange Bowl Singles (18 and Under)
1961 Runner-up in Australian Junior Championships

Alan G Schwartz

PERSONAL
Born in 1931
Citizen of the United States of America
B.S. (Engineering) Yale University
MBA Harvard University

BUSINESS
Chairman of the Board – Tennis Corporation of America (Largest owner/operator of racquet sport facilities in North America)
Advisory Director US Bancorp (New York Stock Exchange)
Board member Duke University Graduate School of Business (1974–present)
Trustee Roosevelt University (1993–present)
Trustee – Institute for International Education of Students (1992–present)

TENNIS ADMINISTRATION
International Tennis Federation
2003–2007 Member, Board of Directors
2003–2005 Vice President
2003–2005 Chairman, Joint Media Commission
2003–2004 Member, Davis Cup Committee
1998–2003 USTA Delegate to AGM
United States Tennis Association
2003–2004 President and Chairman of the Board
2001–2003 First Vice President
1997–2001 Vice President
1995–2004 Member, Board of Directors
1990–1994 Member, Technical and Tennis Industry Committees
1958–1973 Director and Officer Chicago District Tennis Association

OTHER
2001–2004 Member, Grand Slam Committee
2003 Selected Tennis Industry Magazine Man of the Year
1986–1998 Board Member, Tennis Industry Association
1987 Inducted into the Club Industry Hall of Fame

TENNIS COMPETITION EXPERIENCE
Winner of eight National Public Parks Tennis Championships
Winner of seven Illinois State Tennis Championships
Captain Yale Tennis Team
USTA national junior and senior rankings

Charles Trippe

PERSONAL
Born in 1943
Citizen of Great Britain
Certified Accountant

BUSINESS
Retired director of several construction companies
Previously an economist and accountant with Unilever

TENNIS ADMINISTRATION
International Tennis Federation
2005–2007 Member, Board of Directors
2005–2007 Chairman, Constitutional Committee
2005–2007 Chairman, Seniors Committee
2000–2004 Delegate to ITF AGM
Tennis Europe
1993–2005 Member, Seniors Committee
Lawn Tennis Association
2003–2005 President & Chairman, Board of Management
1994–2005 Member, Board of Management
2000–2002 Deputy President
1998–2002 Honorary Treasurer
1994–1998 Chairman, Development Division
1990–1994 Member, Competitions & Tournaments Committee

OTHER
2002–present Hon. Treasurer, Council of International Lawn Tennis Clubs
1998–present Member, Committee of Management, Wimbledon Championships
2000–2002 Chairman, Hampshire & Isle of Wight County LTA
1977–1999 Hon Treasurer, Hampshire & Isle of Wight County LTA
Member, All England Lawn Tennis & Croquet Club
Member, International Club of Great Britain

TENNIS COMPETITION EXPERIENCE
1964 & 1965 Played Wimbledon Qualifying
1965 Represented GBR in World Student Games in Budapest
1962–1974 Played for County
1962–1965 Won various GBR Open tournaments
1960 Won North Coast, California Junior tournament

ITF Board of Directors (continued)

Georg Von Waldenfels

PERSONAL
Born in 1944
Citizen of Germany
Languages: German, English

BUSINESS
2002–present Solicitor of Counsel, Clifford Chance, Munich
2000–2002 Board Member, VIAG Telecom AG, Munich
Board Member of other German companies
1996–2000 Board Member, VIAG AG, Munich
1990–1995 Minister of Finance for the State of Bavaria
1987–1990 Minister of Federal and European Affairs for the State of Bavaria
1978–1987 Deputy Minister of Economic Affairs for the State of Bavaria
1974–1996 Member of Bavarian State Parliament
1972 Awarded law degree (Dr. jur.)

TENNIS ADMINISTRATION
International Tennis Federation
2001–2007 Member, Board of Directors
2003–2007 Chairman, Fed Cup Committee
2001–2003 Chairman, Seniors Committee
2001–2003 Member, Fed Cup Committee
German Tennis Federation
1999–present President
1983–2000 President, Bavarian Tennis Federation

TENNIS COMPETITION EXPERIENCE
Enthusiastic amateur player

Christine Ungricht

PERSONAL
Born in 1947
Citizen of Switzerland
Languages: German, French, English
Bachelor of Business Administration

BUSINESS
1983–present Director of Emil Frey Group, Switzerland

TENNIS ADMINISTRATION
International Tennis Federation
2003–2007 Member, Board of Directors
2003–2007 Chairman, Junior Competitions Committee
2003–2005 Member, Development Advisers Group
2001–2005 Member, ITF Women's Circuit Committee
1994, 1999 Swiss Tennis delegate to AGM
Tennis Europe
1999–2005 Honorary Treasurer
1999–2005 Member, Committee of Management
1999–2005 Chairman, Women's Committee
Swiss Tennis Association
1989–present President and Chairman

OTHER
1996–present Member, Swiss Olympic Committee

TENNIS COMPETITION EXPERIENCE
1973 Regional Champion
20 years as Interclub player

Honorary Treasurer David Jude

PERSONAL
Born in 1939
Citizen of Great Britain

BUSINESS
Retired Director of a City bank
Currently Non Executive Director of several companies

TENNIS ADMINISTRATION
International Tennis Federation
1998–2005 Honorary Treasurer and Member, Board of Directors
1991–2005 Chairman, Finance Committee
1991–2005 Member, Remuneration Committee
1998–2005 Chairman, Audit Committee
1998–present Director, Roehampton Investments Limited
2000–2005 Member, PILA Independent Review Panel
1977–1998 Honorary Treasurer and Member, Committee of Management
1977–1991 Member, Finance Committee
1987–1998 Director of ITF Holdings Limited
1988–1998 Trustee of ITF

OTHER
Member of The All England Lawn Tennis & Croquet Club
Member of The International Lawn Tennis Club of Great Britain

TENNIS COMPETITION EXPERIENCE
1954–1956 Played at Junior Wimbledon
1957–1979 Played for county

ITF Office Holders

The International Tennis Federation
Bank Lane, Roehampton London SW15 5XZ
Telephone: 44 208 878 6464
Fax: 44 208 878 7799
Websites:
www.itftennis.com
www.daviscup.com
www.fedcup.com

Presidential & Communications

The closeness of the Presidential and Communications areas ensures that communications and public relations are fully integrated within the decision making process. In addition, several key ITF events – the World Champions' Dinner and the AGM – have public relations considerations and implications.

President: Francesco Ricci Bitti
Executive Vice President: Juan Margets
Head of Communications: Barbara Travers

Professional Tennis

The Professional Tennis Department has wide responsibilities from the ITF's flagship competitions – the Davis Cup by BNP Paribas, Fed Cup by BNP Paribas and Olympics – through to officiating and men's and women's entry-level circuits.

Executive Director, Davis Cup & Men's Tennis: Bill Babcock
Executive Director, Fed Cup & Women's Tennis: Juan Margets
Head of Event Operations: Paul Smith
Head of Professional Circuits: Jackie Nesbitt

Tennis Development

The concentration of juniors, wheelchair tennis and seniors events, along with development activities, enables the ITF to employ key skills across all these areas for the benefit of tennis players worldwide. Product development and the ITF Technical Centre also come under the umbrella of the Tennis Development Department.

Executive Director, Tennis Development: Dave Miley
Head of Science and Technical: Dr Stuart Miller
Manager, Juniors & Seniors Tennis: Luca Santilli
Manager, Wheelchair Tennis: Ellen de Lange

Commercial

The Commercial Department maintains responsibility for the following areas: television sales, TV servicing, sponsorship sales. The Department concentrates on developing and strengthening the ITF's existing brands. It also strengthens relationships with existing and new sponsors, the tennis industry and television broadcasters.

Executive Director, Commercial: Jan Menneken
Manager, Sponsorship: James Mercer

Finance and Administration

The responsibilities of the Finance and Administration Department are broad and include human resources, staff travel, accounts and IT.

Executive Director, Finance & Administration: John Garnham
Manager, HR & Administration: Clive Painter
ICT Manager: Mat Pemble

2006 ITF Calendar of Events

Davis Cup by BNP Paribas:	World Group 1st Round: 10-12 February
	World Group Quarterfinals: 7-9 April
	World Group Semifinals: 22-24 September
	World Group Final: 1-3 December
Fed Cup by BNP Paribas:	World Group 1st Round: 22-23 April
	World Group Semifinals: 15-16 July
	World Group Final: 16-17 September
Hyundai Hopman Cup:	Perth, Australia: 30 December-6 January
Grand Slams:	Australian Open: 16-29 January
	Roland Garros: 28 May-11 June
	Wimbledon: 26 June-9 July
	US Open: 28 August-10 September
Sony Ericsson WTA Tour Championships:	Madrid, Spain: 6-12 November
Tennis Masters Cup:	Shanghai, China: 12-19 November
ITF Seniors World Team Championships:	Durban, South Africa: 17-22 April
ITF Seniors World Individual Championships:	Durban, South Africa: 23-30 April
ITF World Champions Dinner:	Paris, France: 6 June
Invacare World Team Cup (Wheelchair):	Brasilia, Brazil: 1-7 May
Nations Senior Cup:	Marbella, Spain: 13-15 July
World Junior Tennis Final (14&U):	Prostejov, Czech Republic: 7-12 August
ITF Annual General Meeting:	Seoul, Korea: 23-25 August
Junior Davis Cup and Junior Fed Cup by BNP Paribas (16&U):	Barcelona, Spain: 26 September-1 October
ITF Super-Seniors World Team Championships:	Naples, FL, USA: 23-28 October
ITF Super-Seniors World Individual Champs:	Naples, FL, USA: 29 October-5 November
Camozzi Doubles Masters (Wheelchair):	Cividino, Italy: 7-12 November
NEC Wheelchair Tennis Masters:	Amsterdam, Netherlands: 14-19 November

The 2005 ITF World Champions

Every year, the ITF honours the players who have made the biggest impact on the tennis world in that season, naming a World Champion in senior, junior and wheelchair competition. On the following pages are the biographies of the 2005 recipients of the accolade, and the honours list of past winners.

The 2005 ITF World Champions will receive their awards at the ITF World Champions Dinner, an annual event which takes place in June during Roland Garros.

Roger Federer (SUI)

The Swiss superman stayed at the top of the rankings for the whole of 2005. He is the sixth man to be named ITF World Champion in back-to-back years.

Federer's two Grand Slam titles fell short of the three he collected in 2004. He lost is Australian Open crown to Marat Safin after holding match points. This marked one of only four losses in 85 matches played which saw him win 11 titles on three different surfaces, and win a record four ATP Masters Series events.

He fulfilled his dream of winning a third consecutive Wimbledon title becoming just the eighth player in Wimbledon's 119-year history to win the men's singles title for three successive years. In an electric US Open final he defeated Andre Agassi in four sets to secure his sixth Grand Slam triumph and become just the third man in history to win both Wimbledon and the US Open in successive years.

His loss to Nadal at Roland Garros after advancing as far as the semifinals was probably his major disappointment of the year, alongside his shock loss to David Nalbandian at the Tennis Masters Cup.

Date and place of birth: 8 August 1981, Basel, Switzerland
Residence: Oberwil, Switzerland
Height: 6'1"/1.85m
Weight: 177lbs/80kg
Plays: right handed
Coach: none

Highest Entry System singles ranking: 1 (first reached 2 February 2004)
Year-end Entry System singles ranking: 2005-1; 2004–1; 2003-2; 2002-6; 2001-13; 2000-29; 1999- 64; 1998-302; 1997-T700
2005 Grand Slam singles titles: Wimbledon, US Open
Career Grand Slam singles titles: 6
Other 2005 singles titles: Doha, Rotterdam, Dubai, Indian Wells, Miami, Hamburg, Halle, Cincinnati, Bangkok
Total other singles titles: 27
2005 singles win-loss record: 81-4
Career singles win-loss record: 395-123

Kim Clijsters (BEL)

The 22-year-old battled back from a career-threatening injury in 2005 to capture the US Open title and a tour-high nine titles during the year. Clijsters won more matches than any other woman and finishing the season with a 67-9 record. Her triumph in New York came after four heartbreaking defeats in Slam finals.

A left wrist injury and subsequent surgery had sidelined Clijsters for a total of nine months from 2004 into early 2005, but on her return she hit peak form with back-to-back title victories at Tier I events Indian Wells and Miami. She made a triumphant return to Fed Cup in her hometown Bree, winning all three of her matches against Argentina to help Belgium retain its place in the World Group.

But it was on the summer hard court circuit that Clijsters really got into her stride. In four tournaments played in the lead-up to the US Open, she lost just one match to make her the clear winner of the US Open Series. Clijsters' form held at Flushing Meadows, her defeat of Mary Pierce in the final handing her a longed-for first Grand Slam title.

Date and place of birth: 8 June 1983, Bilzen, Belgium
Residence: Bree, Belgium
Height: 5'8 1/2"/1.74m
Weight: 150lbs/68kg
Plays: right handed
Coach: none

Highest Entry System singles ranking: 1 (first reached 11 August 2003)
Year-end Entry System singles ranking: 2005-2; 2004–22; 2003-2; 2002-4; 2001-5; 2000-18; 1999- 47; 1998-409.
2005 Grand Slam singles titles: US Open
Career Grand Slam singles titles: 1
Other 2005 singles titles: Indian Wells, Miami, Eastbourne, Stanford, Los Angeles, Canadian Open, Luxembourg, Hasselt
Total other singles titles: 29
2005 singles win-loss record: 67-9
Career singles win-loss record: 339-87

Bob Bryan (USA) and Mike Bryan (USA)

Bob and Mike Bryan are the first doubles partnership to be named ITF Men's Doubles Champions for three straight years, and the second men's duo after Todd Woodbridge and Mark Woodforde to receive the honour for a third time. They finished 2005 as the No. 1 doubles team for the second time in three years and continue to be great ambassadors for the doubles game.

In 2005 the Bryans became the second partnership in 50 years to reach the finals of all four majors in a season, and won their second career Grand Slam title at the US Open. They appeared in a season-best 11 doubles finals, collecting five titles to take their total haul to 26.

In Davis Cup the pair suffered their first loss in six rubbers when Croatia staged a shock 3-2 victory over USA in the first round. They regained their winning form in September's World Group Play-off tie against Belgium to help USA back to the World Group.

Bob Bryan (USA)

Date and place of birth: 29 April 1978, Camarillo, California, USA
Residence: Camarillo, California, USA
Height: 6'4"/1.93m
Weight: 202lbs/91kg
Plays: left handed
Coach: Philip Farmer
Highest doubles entry system ranking: 1= (first reached 8 September 2003)
Year-end doubles entry system rankings: 2005-1=; 2004-4=; 2003-2=; 2002-7; 2001-23; 2000-63; 1999-T64; 1998-T174; 1997-T635; 1996-T654; 1995-T1200

Mike Bryan (USA)

Date and place of birth: 29 April 1978, Camarillo, California, USA
Residence: Camarillo, California, USA
Height: 6'3"/1.91m
Weight: 192lbs/89kg
Plays: right handed
Coach: Philip Farmer
Highest doubles entry system ranking: 1= (first reached 8 September 2003)
Year-end doubles entry system rankings: 2005-1=; 2004-4=; 2003-2=; 2002-7; 2001-23; 2000-63; 1999-T64; 1998-T174; 1997-T635; 1996-T654; 1995-T1200

2005 Grand Slam team titles: US Open
Career Grand Slam team titles: 2
Other 2005 team titles: Scottsdale, Queen's, Washington, Paris Open.
Total other team titles: 24
2005 team win-loss record: 58-18
Career team win-loss record: 315-149

Lisa Raymond (USA) and Samantha Stosur (AUS)

In a year of women's doubles when, as in singles, there were four different Grand Slam champions, this new partnership edged out the competition for the ITF World Champions honour. Lisa Raymond and Samantha Stosur added victory at the WTA Tour Championships to their US Open triumph, and finished the year as the No. 1-ranked doubles team. The pair, who had never played together before 2005, won five titles in five months. They didn't team up until July, and won their first title at New Haven in August in just their fourth tournament together. A week later, they upset top-seeded Cara Black and Raymond's former partner Rennae Stubbs in the US Open quarterfinals on their way to lifting the trophy.

Raymond, the older of the two by more than ten years, is ITF World Champion for the second time, having also received the honour with Rennae Stubbs in 2001.

Lisa Raymond (USA)

Date and place of birth: 10 August 1973, Norristown, Pennsylvania, USA
Residence: Wayne, Pennsylvania, USA
Height: 5'5"/1.65m
Weight: 121lbs/55kg
Plays: right handed
Coach: Gigi Fernandez
Highest doubles entry system ranking: 1 (first reached 12 June 2000)
Year-end doubles entry system rankings: 2005-3; 2004-10; 2003-5; 2002-3; 2001-1; 2000-5; 1999-5; 1998-5; 1997-12; 1996-15; 1995-16; 1994-10; 1993-32; 1992-0; 1991-725; 1990-216.

Samantha Stosur (AUS)

Date and place of birth: 30 March 1984, Brisbane, Queensland, Australia
Residence: Gold Coast, Queensland, Australia
Height: 5'7 3/4"/1.72m
Weight: 143lbs/65kg
Plays: right handed
Coach: Gigi Fernandez
Highest doubles entry system ranking: 2 (first reached 14 November 2005)
Year-end doubles entry system rankings: 2005-2; 2004-53; 2003-141; 2002-131; 2001-291.

2005 Grand Slam team titles: US Open
Career Grand Slam team titles: 1
Other 2005 team titles: New Haven, Luxembourg, Moscow, WTA Tour Championships
Total other team titles: 4
2005 team win-loss record: 26-6
Career team win-loss record: 26-6

Donald Young (USA)

Donald Young is the youngest boy to become ITF Junior World Champion, claiming the year-end No. 1 ranking at the age of 16 years, five months – one month younger than Richard Gasquet when he topped the rankings in 2002.

The American set the standard early in 2005, winning the Grade A tournament in Mexico and his first Grand Slam trophy at the Australian Open. He took the No. 1 spot on 31 January and remained there for the rest of the season, finishing runner-up at three more singles events, and collecting two doubles titles.

Young defeated Korea's Sun-Yong Kim in the Australian Open final, and with partner Thiemo De Bakker, finished runner-up in the doubles. He advanced to the singles semifinals at Wimbledon before losing to eventual champion Jeremy Chardy, and was stopped by Kim in the quarterfinals of the US Open singles, but took the doubles title there alongside compatriot Alex Clayton.

Date and place of birth: 23 July 1989, Chicago, Illinois, USA
Residence: Atlanta, Georgia, USA
Height: 5'10"/1.78m
Weight: 145lbs/66kg
Plays: left handed
Coach: Donald Young Sr, Illonah Young
Highest ranking: 1 (first reached 31 January 2005)
Year end ranking: 2005–1; 2004–14; 2003–187; 2002-1419=

2005 Grand Slam titles: Australian Open
Other 2005 singles titles: Casablanca Cup
2005 singles win-loss record: 44.12
Career singles win-loss record: 89-29

Viktoria Azarenka (BLR)

Viktoria Azarenka becomes only the second ITF World Champion from Belarus due to an outstanding year which saw her win two Grand Slam singles titles and three Grand Slam doubles titles.

The 15-year-old got off the year off to the best possible start by winning the singles and doubles at the Australian Open. Defeat in the second round Roland Garros was somewhat compensated for by another doubles title. At Wimbledon the young Belarusian reached the singles semifinal and retaining the doubles trophy. But it was at the US Open where Azarenka cemented her hold on the World Champion title. Azarenka swept through the draw dropping only one set on route to the title. Unfortunately an historic doubles Grand Slam was made impossible when Azarenka's partner was forced to withdraw from the doubles with an injury. The Belarusian rounded off the year with her third Grade A victory at the Osaka Mayor's Cup in Japan.

Date and place of birth: 31 July 1989, Minsk, Belarus
Residence: Minsk, Belarus/Arizona, USA
Height: 5'11"/1.80m
Weight: 122lbs/55kg
Plays: right handed
Coach: Adam Altschuler, Antonio Van Grichen
Highest ranking: 1 (first reached 31 January 2005)
Year end ranking: 2005–1; 2004–4; 2003–54

2005 Grand Slam titles: Australian Open, US Open
Other 2005 singles titles: Osaka Mayor's Cup, Australian Hardcourt, Victorian Championships.
2005 singles win-loss record: 29-2
Career singles win-loss record: 90-21

Michael Jeremiasz (FRA)

Jeremiasz is a new name on the ITF Men's Wheelchair World Champion honour roll, and the second Frenchman to receive the award after Laurent Giammartini in 1992 and 1994.

The top spot in the men's NEC Wheelchair Tennis Ranking changed hands between Australia's David Hall and Robin Ammerlaan of the Netherlands for the first eight months of the year, but Jeremiasz moved up from No. 3 to reach the pinnacle in October and stayed there for the rest of the year. The 24-year-old Paris resident only started playing wheelchair tennis five years ago after a skiing accident, having played the able-bodied sport as a junior.

Jeremiasz performed consistently in both singles and doubles in 2005. He compiled a 50-6 singles record and captured eight singles titles, including the US Open in San Diego. He was runner-up at five further events, including the season-ending NEC Masters.

Date and place of birth: 15 October 1981, Paris, France
Residence: Paris, France
Weight: 162lbs/73kg
Plays: right handed
Coach: Jerome Delbert
Age began wheelchair tennis: 19

Highest singles ranking: 1 (first reached 17 October 2005)
Year-end singles ranking: 2005-1; 2004-3; 2003-8; 2002-10; 2001-31.
2005 Masters/Super Series singles titles: US Open (USTA National)
Career Masters/Super Series singles titles: 1
Other 2005 singles titles: Florida Open, Brasilia Open, Amsterdam Open, French Open, Swiss Open, Citta di Livorno, Nottingham Indoor.
Total other singles titles: 19
2005 singles win-loss record: 50-6
Career singles win-loss record: 175-54

Esther Vergeer (NED)

Esther Vergeer remains without peer in wheelchair tennis, having again dominated the season to be named ITF Women's Wheelchair World Champion for a record sixth year. No other woman has got her hands on the trophy since the Dutchwoman first finished on top in 2000.

Vergeer was undefeated in singles in 2005, compiling a remarkable 55-0 record without dropping a set and extending her two-year-ten-month unbeaten run to 172 consecutive victories through the end of the year. She had just one loss in doubles, finishing with a 36-1 record.

The 24-year-old won 16 singles and 13 doubles tournaments in 2005 despite missing the first two months of the season due to a left foot surgery. Her tally of titles includes six Masters and Super Series titles, the NEC Masters for an outstanding eighth year, and the Camozzi Doubles with Jiske Griffioen.

Date and place of birth: 18 July 1981, Woerden, Netherlands
Residence: Woerden, Netherlands
Weight: 147lbs/67kg
Plays: right handed
Coach: Aad Zwaan
Age began wheelchair tennis: 12

Highest singles ranking: 1 (first reached 6 April 1999)
Year-end singles ranking: 2005-1; 2004-1; 2003-1; 2002-1; 2001-1; 2000-1; 1999-2; 1998-2; 1997-14; 1996-21; 1995-48
2005 Masters/Super Series singles titles: Nasdaq-100, British Open, US Open, Atlanta, US Open (USTA National), NEC Wheelchair Masters.
Career Masters/Super Series singles titles: 18
Other 2005 singles titles: Florida Open, Brasicia Open, Amsterdam Open, DaimlerChrysler Open, French Open, Dutch Open, Belgian Open, Swiss Open, USTA Indoor, PTR/ROHO Championships
Total other singles titles: 77
2005 singles win-loss record: 55-0
Career singles win-loss record: 387-25

ITF World Champions Roll of Honour

ITF World Champions

	Men's Singles	Women's Singles
1978	Bjorn Borg (SWE)	Chris Evert (USA)
1979	Bjorn Borg (SWE)	Martina Navratilova (USA)
1980	Bjorn Borg (SWE)	Chris Evert (USA)
1981	John McEnroe (USA)	Chris Evert (USA)
1982	Jimmy Connors (USA)	Martina Navratilova (USA)
1983	John McEnroe (USA)	Martina Navratilova (USA))
1984	John McEnroe (USA)	Martina Navratilova (USA)
1985	Ivan Lendl (TCH)	Martina Navratilova (USA)
1986	Ivan Lendl (TCH)	Martina Navratilova (USA)
1987	Ivan Lendl (TCH)	Steffi Graf (GER)
1988	Mats Wilander (SWE)	Steffi Graf (GER)
1989	Boris Becker (GER)	Steffi Graf (GER)
1990	Ivan Lendl (TCH)	Steffi Graf (GER)
1991	Stefan Edberg (SWE)	Monica Seles (USA)
1992	Jim Courier (USA)	Monica Seles (USA)
1993	Pete Sampras (USA)	Steffi Graf (GER)
1994	Pete Sampras (USA)	Arantxa Sanchez-Vicario (ESP)
1995	Pete Sampras (USA)	Steffi Graf (GER))
1996	Pete Sampras (USA)	Steffi Graf (GER)
1997	Pete Sampras (USA)	Martina Hingis (SUI)
1998	Pete Sampras (USA)	Lindsay Davenport (USA)
1999	Andre Agassi (USA)	Martina Hingis (SUI)
2000	Gustavo Kuerten (BRA)	Martina Hingis (SUI)
2001	Lleyton Hewitt (AUS)	Jennifer Capriati (USA)
2002	Lleyton Hewitt (AUS)	Serena Williams (USA)
2003	Andy Roddick (USA)	Justine Henin-Hardenne (BEL)
2004	Roger Federer (SUI)	Anastasia Myskina (RUS)
2005	Roger Federer (SUI)	Kim Clijsters (BEL)

	Men's Doubles	Women's Doubles
1996	Todd Woodbridge/Mark Woodforde (AUS)	Lindsay Davenport/Mary Joe Fernandez (USA)
1997	Todd Woodbridge/Mark Woodforde (AUS)	Lindsay Davenport (USA)/Jana Novotna (CZE)
1998	Jacco Eltingh/Paul Haarhuis (NED)	Lindsay Davenport (USA)/Natasha Zvereva (BLR)
1999	Mahesh Bhupathi/Leander Paes (IND)	Martina Hingis (SUI)/Anna Kournikova (RUS)
2000	Todd Woodbridge/Mark Woodforde (AUS)	Julie Halard-Decugis (FRA)/Ai Sugiyama (JPN)
2001	Jonas Bjorkman (SWE)/Todd Woodbridge (AUS)	Lisa Raymond (USA)/Rennae Stubbs (AUS)
2002	Mark Knowles (BAH)/Daniel Nestor (CAN)	Virginia Ruano Pascual (ESP)/Paola Suarez (ARG)
2003	Bob Bryan/Mike Bryan (USA)	Virginia Ruano Pascual (ESP)/Paola Suarez (ARG)
2004	Bob Bryan/Mike Bryan (USA)	Virginia Ruano Pascual (ESP)/Paola Suarez (ARG)
2005	Bob Bryan/Mike Bryan (USA)	Lisa Raymond (USA)/Samantha Stosur (AUS)

ITF Junior World Champions

	Boys' Singles	Girls' Singles
1978	Ivan Lendl (TCH)	Hana Mandlikova (TCH)
1979	Raul Viver (ECU)	Mary-Lou Piatek (USA)
1980	Thierry Tulasne (FRA)	Susan Mascarin (USA)
1981	Pat Cash (AUS)	Zina Garrison (USA)
1982	Guy Forget (FRA)	Gretchen Rush (USA)
1983	Stefan Edberg (SWE)	Pascale Paradis (FRA)
1984	Mark Kratzmann (AUS)	Gabriela Sabatini (ARG)
1985	Claudio Pistolesi (ITA)	Laura Garrone (ITA)
1986	Javier Sanchez (ESP)	Patricia Tarabini (ARG)
1987	Jason Stoltenberg (AUS)	Natalia Zvereva (URS)
1988	Nicolas Pereira (VEN)	Cristina Tessi (ARG)

ITF World Champions Roll of Honour (continued)

	Boys' Singles	Girls' Singles
1989	Nicklas Kulti (SWE)	Florencia Labat (ARG)
1990	Andrea Gaudenzi (ITA)	Karina Habsudova (TCH)
1991	Thomas Enqvist (SWE)	Zdenka Malkova (TCH)l
1992	Brian Dunn (USA)	Rossana De Los Rios (PAR)
1993	Marcelo Rios (CHI)	Nino Louarsabishvili (GEO)
1994	Federico Browne (ARG)	Martina Hingis (SUI)
1995	Mariano Zabaleta (ARG)	Anna Kournikova (RUS)
1996	Sebastien Grosjean (FRA)	Amelie Mauresmo (FRA)
1997	Arnaud Di Pasquale (FRA)	Cara Black (ZIM)
1998	Roger Federer (SUI)	Jelena Dokic (AUS)
1999	Kristian Pless (DEN)	Lina Krasnoroutskaia (RUS)
2000	Andy Roddick (USA)	Maria Emilia Salerni (ARG)
2001	Gilles Muller (LUX)	Svetlana Kuznetsova (RUS)
2002	Richard Gasquet (FRA)	Barbora Strycova (CZE)
2003	Marcos Baghdatis (CYP)	Kirsten Flipkens (BEL)

	Boys' Doubles	Girls' Doubles
1982	Fernando Perez (MEX)	Beth Herr (USA)
1983	Mark Kratzmann (AUS)	Larisa Savchenko (URS)
1984	Augustin Moreno (MEX)	Mercedes Paz (ARG)
1985	Petr Korda/Cyril Suk (TCH)	Mariana Perez-Roldan/Patricia Tarabini (ARG)
1986	Tomas Carbonell (ESP)	Leila Meskhi (URS)
1987	Jason Stoltenberg (AUS)	Natalia Medvedeva (URS)
1988	David Rikl/Tomas Zdrazila (TCH)	Jo-Anne Faull (AUS)
1989	Wayne Ferreira (RSA)	Andrea Strnadova (TCH)
1990	Marten Renstroem (SWE)	Karina Habsudova (TCH)
1991	Karim Alami (MAR)	Eva Martincova (TCH)
1992	Enrique Abaroa (MEX)	Laurence Courtois/Nancy Feber (BEL)
1993	Steven Downs (NZL)	Cristina Moros (USA)
1994	Benjamin Ellwood (AUS)	Martina Nedelkova (SVK)
1995	Kepler Orellana (VEN)	Ludmila Varmuzova (CZE)
1996	Sebastien Grosjean (FRA)	Michaela Pastikova/Jitka Schonfeldova (CZE)
1997	Nicolas Massu (CHI)	Cara Black (ZIM)/Irina Selyutina (KAZ)
1998	Jose De Armas (VEN)	Eva Dyrberg (DEN)
1999	Julien Benneteau/Nicolas Mahut (FRA)	Daniela Bedanova (CZE)
2000	Lee Childs/James Nelson (GBR)	Maria Emilia Salerni (ARG)
2001	Bruno Echagaray/Santiago Gonzalez (MEX)	Petra Cetkovska (CZE)
2002	Florin Mergea/Horia Tecau (ROM)	Elke Clijsters (BEL)
2003	Scott Oudsema (USA)	Andrea Hlavackova (CZE)

The Junior World Champion Singles and Doubles award was combined in 2004.

	Boys	Girls
2004	Gael Monfils (FRA)	Michaella Krajicek (NED)
2005	Donald Young (USA)	Viktoria Azarenka (BLR)

ITF Wheelchair World Champions

	Men	Women
1991	Randy Snow (USA)	Chantal Vandierendonck (NED)
1992	Laurent Giammartini (FRA)	Monique van den Bosch (NED)
1993	Kai Schrameyer (GER)	Monique Kalkman (NED)
1994	Laurent Giammartini (FRA)	Monique Kalkman (NED)
1995	David Hall (AUS)	Monique Kalkman (NED)
1996	Ricky Molier (NED)	Chantal Vandierendonck (NED)
1997	Ricky Molier (NED)	Chantal Vandierendonck (NED)
1998	David Hall (AUS)	Daniela Di Toro (AUS)

	Men	Women
1999	Stephen Welch (USA)	Daniela Di Toro (AUS)
2000	David Hall (AUS)	Esther Vergeer (NED)
2001	Ricky Molier (NED)	Esther Vergeer (NED)
2002	David Hall (AUS)	Esther Vergeer (NED)
2003	David Hall (AUS)	Esther Vergeer (NED)
2004	David Hall (AUS)	Esther Vergeer (NED)
2005	Michael Jeremiasz (FRA)	Esther Vergeer (NED)

The Philippe Chatrier Award

Named after former ITF President Philippe Chatrier and awarded for Contributions to the Game of Tennis.

1996	Stefan Edberg (SWE)
1997	Chris Evert (USA)
1998	Rod Laver (AUS)
1999	Nicola Pietrangeli (ITA)
2000	Juan Antonio Samaranch (ESP)
2001	NEC
2002	Jack Kramer (USA)
2003	Billie Jean King (USA)
2004	Yannick Noah (FRA)
2005	Tony Trabert (USA)

Tony Trabert (USA)

croatia's dreams come true in bratislava

by douglas robson

It may be premature to conclude that the meek will inherit the Cup. But if there was a lesson to be gleaned from the 2005 Davis Cup by BNP Paribas Final pitting plucky upstarts Croatia and Slovak Republic, it was this: No longer is the Cup the sole providence of big, rich, populous lands teeming with tennis tradition.

Never in the history of the Cup had two nations so small and with so little history of independence battled for the trophy. But over three stirring days in December, Croatia and Slovak Republic both proved worthy of the right to be called the least populous and first unseeded winner of the prestigious team competition in 105 years.

Only one would prevail. Croat superhero Ivan Ljubicic entered the clinching singles match with a perfect 11-0 Davis Cup mark – one shy of John McEnroe's perfect 12-0 record in 1982.

But even Superman has his weakness. When the Croatian man of steel faltered in the face of kryptonite-bearer Dominik Hrbaty of Slovakia to advance each nation to the precipice of glory, another hero stepped out of the shadows to save the day.

With his idol, mentor and teammate Goran Ivanisevic cheering from the sidelines, Mario Ancic sealed the decisive fifth rubber over last-hour substitute Michal Mertinak in three tense, but convincing, sets. The 3-2 tie earned the Croatian team of Ljubicic, Ancic, Ivanisevic and Ivo Karlovic its first-ever title, and gave them the distinction of being just the 12th winning nation since 1900.

Dominik Hrbaty (SVK)

Croat superhero Ivan Ljubicic entered the clinching singles match with a perfect 11-0 Davis Cup mark – one shy of John McEnroe's perfect 12-0 record in 1982.

"It's an unforgettable match and an unforgettable day," said the 21-year-old nicknamed "Baby Goran," whose win in the 4,100-seat Sibamac Arena in the Slovakian capital set off a pandemonium of song, dance and flares among the healthy dose of Croat fans who had travelled to see history made. "I am not sure people realise how big it is to be at the top of the pyramid."

Mario Ancic and Ivan Ljubicic (CRO)

It was an improbable finish to an unprecedented final. Two unseeded countries had never before met to decide the Cup. Croatia, with 4.5 million people, and Slovak Republic, with 5.4 million, has between them less than 30 years of independence. Neither had been beyond the quarterfinals in the World Group before.

Independent since 1991 following the bloody break-up of Yugoslavia, Croatia has produced some notable individual sporting glories, including Iva Majoli's 1997 French Open crown, Ivanisevic's improbable 2001 Wimbledon win and skier Janica Kostelic's four medals at the 2002 Winter Olympics. But its best team performance until now was third place at the 1998 soccer World Cup.

"I knew that we could do it," said Ivanisevic, who came out of retirement to join his countrymen but did not see any action during the tie. He ranked the win second only to his Wimbledon title. "We are a brilliant team, which can play on all surfaces," he said. "We are at the top of Mount Everest. This is the pinnacle."

Among other firsts, Croat coach Niki Pilic became the only person to win the Cup at the helm for two different nations, having guided Germany to titles in 1988, 1989 and 1993. But this one was far away the sweetest.

"There is no comparison – today I won with my people," said Pilic, who like Ancic and Ivanisevic was born and raised in Split. "The Davis Cup is one of the greatest competitions in the world and I am really proud of my team."

Like Croatia, the gallant Slovak team overcame the odds mostly on the broad shoulders of one man: team leader Hrbaty. The Slovaks were down a man throughout the final when No. 2 singles player Karol Beck's injured knee forced coach Miloslav Mecir to go to his bench. Mecir nominated veteran Karol Kucera for the first singles match against Ljubicic and then Hrbaty in place of Beck in doubles.

Both decisions came up short, as the towering, bald and nearly invincible Croat easily brushed aside a rusty Kucera and the powerful team of Ljubicic and Ancic – bronze medalists in Athens – had little problem with Hrbaty and Mertinak in doubles.

But Bratislava's native-son Hrbaty kept his team in the mix, winning his opening singles match against Ancic and then stunning Ljubicic in five glorious sets in the most anticipated, and best, contest of the tie.

In the end, the inexperienced Mertinak, elected by Mecir to play Ancic one hour before the decisive match, was overmatched, despite the constant drumbeats and cheers from the

croatia's dreams come true in bratislava

by douglas robson

enthusiastic faithful who crammed into the indoor arena to see their home team triumph on the medium-fast hard court surface.

"Of course, there is no need to cry," said indomitable Hrbaty, who finished his 2005 Davis Cup campaign with a 6-1 singles record. "I am such a person that I am happy to have a medal of any kind."

Mecir added: "I can say that all the guys played very well and brought very intensive and emotional experience to all of us. So in this tie, there was no winner or loser because everybody who participated was a winner."

Befitting the tremendous strides made by both nations, the festive weekend was capped by the International Tennis Hall of Fame and the International Tennis Federation recognising Mecir and Ivanisevic with 2005 Davis Cup Awards of Excellence.

"The Davis Cup Award of Excellence represents outstanding achievement in international competition," said ITF president Francesco Ricci Bitti, who was accompanied by 1984 Hall of Famer Neale Fraser, the first-ever recipient of the award in 2001, as well as 2002 winner Pierre Darmon of France. "Goran and Miloslav have been exceptional, spirited competitors for their countries, and as they both continue to pursue excellence in tennis, we are proud to honour them as this year's Davis Cup award recipients."

Ancic may have been the man of the hour, but it was the nearly unassailable Ljubicic who played the protagonist in his team's march to the Final in Bratislava.

The journey began with a stunning defeat of the USA's "Dream Team" in Carson, California, in the opening round. After losing to Spain in last year's final, US captain Patrick McEnroe persuaded ageless wonder Andre Agassi to rejoin the powerful American squad that already included record-breaking server Andy Roddick and the world's top doubles duo, Bob and Mike Bryan.

Ljubicic handled everything the Americans threw at him. He beat Agassi, the Bryans and Roddick to account for all three of his team's points in a 3-2 win – USA's first opening round defeat at home since World Group play began. It left the Americans – title-less since 1995 – wondering what else they would have to do to add to their record 31 Davis Cup titles.

The next two contests for the versatile team were easy by comparison. With home-court advantage, the Croats selected a slick, indoor carpet surface at the cozy Dvorana SC Gripe stadium in Split, defeating Romania 4-1 in the quarterfinals and Russia 3-2 in the semifinals.

Both times, Ljubicic clinched the tie, defeating Andrei Pavel and Nikolay Davydenko in straight sets to remain unbeaten. Though he failed to match John McEnroe's 12-0 record, Ljubicic's 11 live rubber victories (four in doubles, seven in singles) is the most in World Group history.

Slovak Republic also knows something about the perks of playing at home. It did not have to travel beyond its borders in 2005. Had it defeated Croatia, it would have been the ninth country since the inception of the World Group in 1981 to capture the Davis Cup entirely on home soil.

The Slovaks kicked off their campaign with a stunner. Spain, which had knocked off the United States to win its second Davis Cup just three months prior, arrived in Bratislava without three of its top players – Carlos Moya, Tommy Robredo and Juan Carlos Ferrero.

Even though 2004 hero Moya had decided to skip Davis Cup to concentrate on Grand Slam events and Robredo and Ferrero were nursing injuries, the Spaniards were heavy favourites.

But not even Rafael Nadal, the youngest

Ancic may have been the man of the hour, but it was the nearly unassailable Ljubicic who played the protagonist in his team's march to the Final in Bratislava.

Mario Ancic (CRO)

Ivan Ljubicic (CRO)

player to have won the Davis Cup and a key player in the 2004 victory, could come to the rescue. The teenager was dropped from the first singles by captain Jordi Arrese, partially because he had little time to practice on the fast indoor court, and then lost to Hrbaty and Beck in doubles with Albert Costa.

After taking advantage of the depleted defending champions to advance 4-1, Hrbaty and company swept aside Netherlands in the quarterfinals by the same score.

Against a strong Argentine team that included top-10 players Guillermo Coria and David Nalbandian, the Slovaks proved they were no fluke. Although Hrbaty lost his only match of the season to Masters Cup champion Nalbandian, Beck captured two points with wins over Coria and in doubles with Mertinak for another 4-1 triumph.

With three players in the top-10 and four in the top-12, it seems only a matter of time before Argentina manages to surpass its best ever finish in 1981, when Guillermo Vilas led his nation to the Final.

The same could be said for the outstanding group of countries who managed to emerge from play-off ties and reaffirm their place in the elite World Group. Some will be hunting for first-time glory in 2006, while others will be looking to add another trophy to their case. Among them are the USA, Chile, Switzerland, Sweden and Austria, which all cruised into the top 16.

Spain, however, escaped with a 3-2 win over Italy only after former No. 1 Juan Carlos Ferrero beat Italy's Daniele Bracciali in straight sets at Italy's Torre del Greco.

Three-time winner Germany upset the seeded Czech Republic, which was sent to relegation play after losing 3-2 at Liberec when Tommy Haas held off Tomas Zib in the deciding fifth rubber.

Belarus, a semifinalist in 2004, came back from a 2-1 deficit to book its place when it staved off a game Canada in Toronto.

Certainly, the unlikely 2005 finalists – and the fifth different Davis Cup champion in succession – will stir hopes for the 118 other Davis Cup participants that have yet to etch their names on the Cup. If not necessarily a reordering of the natural power structure in team tennis, Croatia's inclusion in a club with the likes of the USA, Australia, France and Great Britain is a strong signal to those with less pedigree and population.

"It's great because these are new countries and they showed they have world class tennis players helping to spread the name of the sport around the world," reflected Mecir on the unparalleled final, which marked the first meeting of the neophyte Eastern European nations. "It helps other countries believe they can get into the top."

Croatia has shown that the summit is not as high as it might seem.

A dream ending for the Croatians

2005 Davis Cup by BNP Paribas Results

World Group

First Round 4-6 March

Slovak Republic defeated Spain 4-1, Bratislava, SVK; Hard (I): Karol Beck (SVK) d. Feliciano Lopez (ESP) 64 75 63; Dominik Hrbaty (SVK) d. Fernando Verdasco (ESP) 63 64 67(7) 63; Karol Beck/Michal Mertinak (SVK) d. Albert Costa/Rafael Nadal (ESP) 76(3) 64 76(8); Michal Mertinak (SVK) d. Feliciano Lopez (ESP) 60 67(3) 64; Fernando Verdasco (ESP) d. Kamil Capkovic (SVK) 62 62. **Netherlands defeated Switzerland 3-2, Fribourg, SUI; Hard (I):** Sjeng Schalken (NED) d. Marco Chiudinelli (SUI) 76(4) 46 63 57 62; Peter Wessels (NED) d. Stanislas Wawrinka (SUI) 76(12) 67(4) 76(7) 64; Yves Allegro/George Bastl (SUI) d. Dennis Van Scheppingen/Peter Wessels (NED) 57 46 76(5) 75 97; Sjeng Schalken (NED) d. Stanislas Wawrinka (SUI) 16 62 64 26 97; Marco Chiudinelli (SUI) d. Peter Wessels (NED) 46 ret. **Australia defeated Austria 5-0, Sydney, AUS; Grass (O):** Lleyton Hewitt (AUS) d. Alexander Peya (AUT) 62 63 64; Wayne Arthurs (AUS) d. Jurgen Melzer (AUT) 76(5) 62 64; Wayne Arthurs/Todd Woodbridge (AUS) d. Julian Knowle/Jurgen Melzer (AUT) 46 63 26 64 75; Todd Woodbridge (AUS) d. Marco Mirnegg (AUT) 63 46 75; Chris Guccione (AUS) d. Alexander Peya (AUT) 63 64. **Argentina defeated Czech Republic 5-0, Buenos Aires, ARG; Clay (O):** David Nalbandian (ARG) d. Jiri Novak (CZE) 46 62 63 64; Guillermo Coria (ARG) d. Tomas Berdych (CZE) 63 36 60 63; Guillermo Canas/David Nalbandian (ARG) d. Jan Hernych/Tomas Zib (CZE) 63 46 61 62; Guillermo Coria (ARG) d. Jan Hernych (CZE) 63 60; Agustin Calleri (ARG) d. Tomas Zib (CZE) 62 64. **Russia defeated Chile 4-1, Moscow, RUS; Carpet (I):** Fernando Gonzalez (CHI) d. Mikhail Youzhny (RUS) 76(4) 57 63 76(4); Marat Safin (RUS) d. Adrian Garcia (CHI) 61 36 63 76(4); Marat Safin/Mikhail Youzhny (RUS) d. Adrian Garcia/Fernando Gonzalez (CHI) 63 64 63; Marat Safin (RUS) d. Fernando Gonzalez (CHI) 76(4) 76(5) 16 67(3) 64; Nikolay Davydenko (RUS) d. Paul Capdeville (CHI) 62 61. **France defeated Sweden 3-2, Strasbourg, FRA; Clay (I);** Paul-Henri Mathieu (FRA) d. Joachim Johansson (SWE) 63 64 62; Thomas Johansson (SWE) d. Sebastien Grosjean (FRA) 64 64 76(1); Arnaud Clement/Michael Llodra (FRA) d. Simon Aspelin/Jonas Bjorkman (SWE) 76(5) 64 67(4) 64; Joachim Johansson (SWE) d. Sebastien Grosjean (FRA) 36 61 64 61; Paul-Henri Mathieu (FRA) d. Thomas Johansson (SWE) 61 64 67(4) 64. **Romania defeated Belarus 3-2, Brasov, ROM; Clay (I):** Max Mirnyi (BLR) d. Victor Hanescu (ROM) 76(6) 64 36 64; Andrei Pavel (ROM) d. Vladimir Voltchkov (BLR) 64 76(2) 76(2); Max Mirnyi/Vladimir Voltchkov (BLR) d. Andrei Pavel/Gabriel Trifu (ROM) 76(3) 63 64; Andrei Pavel (ROM) d. Max Mirnyi (BLR) 61 76(0) 46 63; Victor Hanescu (ROM) d. Vladimir Voltchkov (BLR) 76(2) 64 76(6). **Croatia defeated USA 3-2, Carson, CA, USA; Hard (O):** Ivan Ljubicic (CRO) d. Andre Agassi (USA) 63 76(0) 63; Andy Roddick (USA) d. Mario Ancic (CRO) 46 62 61 64; Mario Ancic/Ivan Ljubicic (CRO) d. Bob Bryan/Mike Bryan (USA) 36 76(8) 64 64; Ivan Ljubicic (CRO) d. Andy Roddick (USA) 46 63 76(11) 67(7) 62; Bob Bryan (USA) d. Roko Karanusic (CRO) 62 36 61.

Quarterfinals 15-17 July

Slovak Republic defeated Netherlands 4-1, Bratislava, SVK; Hard (I): Dominik Hrbaty (SVK) d. Raemon Sluiter (NED) 61 57 64 63; Peter Wessels (NED) d. Karol Beck (SVK) 67(5) 75 67(3) 64 62; Karol Beck/Michal Mertinak (SVK) d. Paul Haarhuis/Melle Van Gemerden (NED) 57 63 64 75; Dominik Hrbaty (SVK) d. Peter Wessels (NED) 63 61 30 ret.; Michal Mertinak (SVK) d. Melle Van Gemerden (NED) 46 63 64. **Argentina defeated Australia 4-1, Sydney, AUS; Grass (O):** Lleyton Hewitt (AUS) d. Guillermo Coria (ARG) 76(5) 61 16 62; David Nalbandian (ARG) d. Wayne Arthurs (AUS) 63 76(8) 57 62; David Nalbandian/Mariano Puerta (ARG) d. Wayne Arthurs/Lleyton Hewitt (AUS) 76(6) 64 63; David Nalbandian (ARG) d. Lleyton Hewitt (AUS) 62 64 64; Guillermo Coria (ARG) d. Peter Luczak (AUS) 63 76(11). **Russia defeated France 3-2, Moscow, RUS; Clay (I):** Richard Gasquet (FRA) d. Igor Andreev (RUS) 64 63 76(1); Nikolay Davydenko (RUS) d. Paul-Henri Mathieu (FRA) 75 62 75; Arnaud Clement/Michael Llodra (FRA) d. Igor Andreev/Mikhail Youzhny (RUS) 75 64 67(3) 62; Nikolay Davydenko (RUS) d. Richard Gasquet (FRA) 62 46 62 61; Igor Andreev (RUS) d. Paul-Henri Mathieu (FRA) 60 62 61. **Croatia defeated Romania 4-1, Split, CRO; Carpet (I):** Andrei Pavel (ROM) d. Mario Ancic (CRO) 16 64 46 63 64; Ivan Ljubicic (CRO) d. Victor Hanescu (ROM) 63 62 76(3); Mario Ancic/Ivan Ljubicic (CRO) d. Andrei Pavel/Gabriel Trifu (ROM) 57 64 67(9) 64 64; Ivan Ljubicic (CRO) d. Andrei Pavel (ROM) 63 64 63; Mario Ancic (CRO) d. Victor Hanescu (ROM) 76(3) 76(8).

Semifinals 23-25 September

Slovak Republic defeated Argentina 4-1, Bratislava, SVK; Hard (I): Karol Beck (SVK) d. Guillermo Coria (ARG) 75 64 64; David Nalbandian (ARG) d. Dominik Hrbaty (SVK) 36 75 75 63; Karol Beck/Michal Mertinak (SVK) d. David Nalbandian/Mariano Puerta (ARG) 76(5) 75 76(5); Dominik Hrbaty (SVK) d. Guillermo Coria (ARG) 76(2) 62 63; Karol Kucera (SVK) d. Mariano Puerta (ARG) 46 63 21 ret. **Croatia defeated Russia 3-2, Split, CRO; Carpet (I):** Nikolay Davydenko (RUS) d. Mario Ancic (CRO) 75 64 57 64; Ivan Ljubicic (CRO) d. Mikhail Youzhny (RUS) 36 63 64 46 64; Mario Ancic/Ivan Ljubicic (CRO) d. Igor Andreev/Dmitry Tursunov (RUS) 62 46 76(5) 36 64; Ivan Ljubicic (CRO) d. Nikolay Davydenko (RUS) 63 76(6) 64; Dmitry Tursunov (RUS) d. Ivo Karlovic (CRO) 64 64.

Final 2-4 December

Croatia defeated Slovak Republic 3-2; Bratislava, SVK; Hard (I): Ivan Ljubicic (CRO) d. Karol Kucera (SVK) 63 64 63; Dominik Hrbaty (SVK) d. Mario Ancic (CRO) 76(4) 63 67(4) 64; Mario Ancic/Ivan Ljubicic (CRO) d. Dominik Hrbaty/Michal Mertinak (SVK) 76(5) 63 76(5); Dominik Hrbaty (SVK) d. Ivan Ljubicic (CRO) 46 63 64 36 64; Mario Ancic (CRO) d. Michal Mertinak (SVK) 76(1) 63 64.

World Group Play-offs 23-25 September

Austria defeated Ecuador 4-1, Portschach, AUT; Hard (O): Jurgen Melzer (AUT) d. Giovanni Lapentti (ECU) 61 60 62; Nicolas Lapentti (ECU) d. Stefan Koubek (AUT) 57 46 64 76(5) 75; Julian Knowle/Jurgen Melzer (AUT) d. Giovanni Lapentti/Nicolas Lapentti (ECU) 26 64 60 63; Jurgen Melzer (AUT) d. Nicolas Lapentti (ECU) 75 64 75; Stefan Koubek (AUT) d. Carlos Avellan (ECU) 63 62. **Belarus defeated Canada 3-2, Toronto, CAN; Hard (O):** Frank Dancevic (CAN) d. Vladimir Voltchkov (BLR) 57 64 46 76(3) 63; Max Mirnyi (BLR) d. Daniel Nestor (CAN) 67(4) 75 21 ret.; Daniel Nestor/Frederic Niemeyer (CAN) d. Max Mirnyi/Vladimir Voltchkov (BLR) 75 62 36 76(6); Max Mirnyi (BLR) d. Frank Dancevic (CAN) 46 63 64 36 64; Vladimir Voltchkov (BLR) d. Frederic Niemeyer (CAN) 62 67(2) 63 64. **Chile defeated Pakistan 5-0, Santiago, CHI; Clay (O):** Fernando Gonzalez (CHI) d. Aqeel Khan (PAK) 60 60 61; Nicolas Massu (CHI) d. Aisam Qureshi (PAK) 62 76(4) 61; Fernando Gonzalez/Nicolas Massu (CHI) d. Aqeel Khan/Aisam Qureshi (PAK) 61 63 60; Paul Capdeville (CHI) d. Shahzad Khan (PAK) 60 61; Adrian Garcia (CHI) d. Aqeel Khan (PAK) 62 64. **Germany defeated Czech Republic 3-2, Liberec, CZE; Clay (I):** Tomas Berdych (CZE) d. Tommy Haas (GER) 46 46 61 76(9) 63; Nicolas Kiefer (GER) d. Tomas Zib (CZE) 76(4) 46 64 62; Tommy Haas/Alexander Waske (GER) d. Frantisek Cermak/Leos Friedl (CZE) 46 75 62 26 64; Tomas Berdych (CZE) d. Nicolas Kiefer (GER) 67(5) 63 26 64 75; Tommy Haas (GER) d. Tomas Zib (CZE) 67(3) 75 62 60. **Spain defeated Italy 3-2, Torre del Greco, ITA; Clay (O):** Andreas Seppi (ITA) d. Juan Carlos Ferrero (ESP) 57 36 60 63 62; Rafael Nadal (ESP) d. Daniele Bracciali (ITA) 63 62 61; Daniele Bracciali/Giorgio Galimberti (ITA) d. Feliciano Lopez/ Rafael Nadal (ESP) 46 64 62 46 97; Rafael Nadal (ESP) d. Andreas Seppi (ITA) 61 62 57 64; Juan Carlos Ferrero (ESP) d. Daniele Bracciali (ITA) 63 60 63. **Sweden defeated India 3-1, New Delhi, IND; Grass (O):** Jonas Bjorkman (SWE) d. Prakash Amritraj (IND) 64 64 64; Thomas Johansson (SWE) d. Rohan Bopanna (IND) 76(3) 76(2) 76(4); Mahesh Bhupathi/Leander Paes (IND) d. Simon Aspelin/Jonas Bjorkman (SWE) 36 63 64 63; Thomas Johansson (SWE) d. Prakash Amritraj (IND) 64 63 62. **Switzerland defeated Great Britain 5-0, Geneva, SUI; Clay (I):** Roger Federer (SUI) d. Alan Mackin (GBR) 60 60 62; Stanislas Wawrinka (SUI) d. Andy Murray (GBR) 63 76(5) 64; Yves Allegro/ Roger Federer (SUI) d. Andy Murray/Greg Rusedski (GBR) 75 26 76(1) 62; George Bastl (SUI) d. David Sherwood (GBR) 63 60; Stanislas Wawrinka (SUI) d. Alan Mackin (GBR) 75 76(5). **USA defeated Belgium 4-1, Leuven, BEL; Clay (I):** Olivier Rochus (BEL) d. James Blake (USA) 64 75 61; Andy Roddick (USA) d. Christophe Rochus (BEL) 61 62 63; Bob Bryan/Mike Bryan (USA) d. Olivier Rochus/ Kristof Vliegen (BEL) 63 67(2) 61 63; Andy Roddick (USA) d. Olivier Rochus (BEL) 67(4) 76(4) 76(5) 46 63; James Blake (USA) d. Steve Darcis (BEL) 75 61.

Europe/Africa Zone Group I

First Round 4-6 March

Serbia & Montenegro defeated Zimbabwe 5-0, Novi Sad, SCG; Clay (I): Novak Djokovic (SCG) d. Genius Chidzikwe (ZIM) 64 60 64; Janko Tipsarevic (SCG) d. Gwinyai Tongoona (ZIM) 63 62 61; Dusan Vemic/Nenad Zimonjic (SCG) d. Genius Chidzikwe/Gwinyai Tongoona (ZIM) 76(3) 60 63; Janko Tipsarevic (SCG) d. Zibusiso Ncube (ZIM) 60 62; Novak Djokovic (SCG) d. Pfungwa Mahefu (ZIM) 61 62.
Italy defeated Luxembourg 5-0, Luxembourg, LUX; Hard (I): Daniele Bracciali (ITA) d. Gilles Muller (LUX) 76(4) 67(4) 64 64; Potito Starace (ITA) d. Mike Scheidweiler (LUX) 63 61 62; Daniele Bracciali/Giorgio Galimberti (ITA) d. Gilles Muller/Mike Scheidweiler (LUX) 64 64 67(6) 75; Potito Starace (ITA) d. Gilles Kremer (LUX) 64 62; Andreas Seppi (ITA) d. Laurent Bram (LUX) 76(4) 63.

Second Round 4-6 March

Great Britain defeated Israel 3-2, Ramat Hasharon, ISR; Hard (O): Greg Rusedski (GBR) d. Harel Levy (ISR) 64 63 60; Noam Okun (ISR) d. Alex Bogdanovic (GBR) 76(3) 62 62; Andrew Murray/David Sherwood (GBR) d. Jonathan Erlich/Andy Ram (ISR) 64 76(5) 26 76(5); Greg Rusedski (GBR) d. Noam Okun (ISR) 63 64 62; Harel Levy (ISR) d. David Sherwood (GBR) 67(1) 64 63. **Germany defeated South Africa 3-2, Doornfontein, RSA; Hard (I):** Nicolas Kiefer (GER) d. Wesley Moodie (RSA) 46 67(3) 76(4) 63 62; Tommy Haas (GER) d. Wayne Ferreira (RSA) 63 60 76(3); Jeff Coetzee/Wesley Moodie (RSA) d. Nicolas Kiefer/Rainer Schuettler (GER) 63 76(4) 75; Wesley Moodie (RSA) d. Tommy Haas (GER) 67(5) 62 46 63 108; Rainer Schuettler (GER) d. Wayne Ferreira (RSA) 61 62 64.

- **28-30 April Italy defeated Morocco 4-1,Rome, ITA; Clay (O):** Potito Starace (ITA) d. Mounir El Aarej (MAR) 60 36 75 60; Filippo Volandri (ITA) d. Younes El Aynaoui (MAR) 62 64 61; Daniele Bracciali/Giorgio Galimberti (ITA) d. Younes El Aynaoui/Mehdi Tahiri (MAR) 75 61 62; Mounir El Aarej (MAR) d. Filippo Volandri (ITA) 63 16 61; Potito Starace (ITA) d. Mehdi Tahiri (MAR) 61 36 64.

- **29 April-1 May Belgium defeated Serbia & Montenegro 3-2, Belgrade, SCG; Clay (O):** Janko Tipsarevic (SCG) d. Christophe Rochus (BEL) 26 46 75 64 61; Olivier Rochus (BEL) d. Novak Djokovic (SCG) 16 75 67(3) 61 63; Dick Norman/Kristof Vliegen (BEL) d. Dusan Vemic/Nenad Zimonjic (SCG) 63 64 36 64; Janko Tipsarevic (SCG) d. Olivier Rochus (BEL) 67(8) 36 76(3) 62 64; Kristof Vliegen (BEL) d. Novak Djokovic (SCG) 63 63 36 62.

Belgium, Germany, Great Britain and Italy advanced to World Group Play-offs on 23-25 September 2005.

2005 Davis Cup by BNP Paribas Results (continued)

Second Round/Play-off 15-17 July

Luxembourg defeated Morocco 3-2, Esch sur Alzette, LUX; Hard (I): Mehdi Tahiri (MAR) d. Gilles Muller (LUX) 67(9) 64 76(1) 67(2) 64; Gilles Kremer (LUX) d. Mounir El Aarej (MAR) 63 75 64; Gilles Muller/Mike Scheidweiler (LUX) d. Mounir El Aarej/Mehdi Tahiri (MAR) 60 64 57 76(2); Gilles Muller (LUX) d. Mounir El Aarej (MAR) 63 64 67(4) 63; Mehdi Tahiri (MAR) d. Laurent Bram (LUX) 75 64.

Third Round/Play-off 23-25 September

Israel defeated Zimbabwe 4-1, Harare, ZIM; Hard (I): Wayne Black (ZIM) d. Dudi Sela (ISR) 61 76(4) 67(2) 63; Noam Okun (ISR) d. Genius Chidzikwe (ZIM) 62 76(3) 63; Jonathan Erlich/Andy Ram (ISR) d. Wayne Black/Gwinyai Tongoona (ZIM) 62 63 63; Dudi Sela (ISR) d. Genius Chidzikwe (ZIM) 64 64 63; Noam Okun (ISR) d. Stefan D'Almeida (ZIM) 60 62. **Morocco defeated South Africa 4-1, Khemisset, MAR; Clay (O):** Mounir El Aarej (MAR) d. Justin Bower (RSA) 64 64 36 46 86; Mehdi Tahiri (MAR) d. Rik De Voest (RSA) 26 62 64 46 62; Jeff Coetzee/Chris Haggard (RSA) d. Talal Ouahabi/Mehdi Ziadi (MAR) 76(4) 67(2) 46 63 75; Mounir El Aarej (MAR) d. Rik De Voest (RSA) 63 64 75; Mehdi Tahiri (MAR) d. Justin Bower (RSA) 75 76(2).

South Africa and Zimbabwe relegated to Europe/Africa Zone Group II in 2006.

Americas Zone Group I

First Round 4-6 March

Venezuela defeated Peru 4-1, Caracas, VEN; Hard (O): Ivan Miranda (PER) d. Jhonathan Medina (VEN) 26 75 76(4) 61; Jose De Armas (VEN) d. Sergio Rojas (PER) 61 61 63; Jose De Armas/Yohny Romero (VEN) d. Luis Horna/Ivan Miranda (PER) 63 75 62; Jose De Armas (VEN) d. Ivan Miranda (PER) 64 36 76(3) 62; Jhonathan Medina (VEN) d. Sergio Rojas (PER) 76(0) 61. **Ecuador defeated Mexico 3-2, Guanajuato, MEX; Hard (O):** Giovanni Lapentti (ECU) d. Alejandro Hernandez (MEX) 63 36 67(6) 76(4) 61; Miguel Gallardo-Valles (MEX) d. Nicolas Lapentti (ECU) 46 64 62 64; Giovanni Lapentti/Nicolas Lapentti (ECU) d. Bruno Echagaray/Santiago Gonzalez (MEX) 64 76(6) 64; Giovanni Lapentti (ECU) d. Miguel Gallardo-Valles (MEX) 63 64 36 76(5); Santiago Gonzalez (MEX) d. Carlos Avellan (ECU) 64 46 64.

Second Round 29 April-1 May

Canada defeated Venezuela 4-0, Valencia, VEN; Clay (O): Frank Dancevic (CAN) d. Yohny Romero (VEN) 64 76(4) 60; Frederic Niemeyer (CAN) d. Jose De Armas (VEN) 76(2) 61 63; Daniel Nestor/Frederic Niemeyer (CAN) d. Jose De Armas/Yohny Romero (VEN) 64 36 63 62; Robert Steckley (CAN) d. Daniel Vallverdu (VEN) 67(2) 61 64. **Ecuador defeated Paraguay 5-0, Guayaquil, ECU; Clay (O):** Giovanni Lapentti (ECU) d. Gustavo Ramirez (PAR) 60 76(3) 63; Carlos Avellan (ECU) d. Daniel Lopez (PAR) 63 60 75; Carlos Avellan/Nicolas Lapentti (ECU) d. Enzo Pigola/Juan-Carlos Ramirez (PAR) 63 64 61; Jhony De Leon (ECU) d. Juan-Carlos Ramirez (PAR) 62 61; Carlos Avellan (ECU) d. Enzo Pigola (PAR) 64 61.

Canada and Ecuador advanced to World Group Play-offs on 23-25 September 2005.

Second Round/Play-off 15-17 July

Mexico defeated Paraguay 5-0, Puebla, MEX; Hard (I): Miguel Gallardo-Valles (MEX) d. Juan-Enrique Crosa (PAR) 61 61 62; Carlos Palencia (MEX) d. Gustavo Ramirez (PAR) 64 64 62; Miguel Gallardo-Valles/Victor Romero (MEX) d. Enzo Pigola/Juan-Carlos Ramirez (PAR) 63 46 63 64; Victor Romero (MEX) d. Gustavo Ramirez (PAR) 64 64; Carlos Palencia (MEX) d. Juan-Carlos Ramirez (PAR) 62 60.

Third Round/Play-off 23-25 September

Peru defeated Paraguay 5-0, Lima, PER; Clay (O): Ivan Miranda (PER) d. Juan-Carlos Ramirez (PAR) 75 61 63; Luis Horna (PER) d. Enzo Pigola (PAR) 61 62 61; Luis Horna/Ivan Miranda (PER) d. Ricardo Gorostiaga/Juan-Carlos Ramirez (PAR) 62 61 75; Matias Silva (PER) d. Juan-Carlos Ramirez (PAR) 63 20 ret.; Mauricio Echazu (PER) d. Enzo Pigola (PAR) 64 64.

Paraguay relegated to Americas Zone Group II in 2006.

Asia/Oceania Zone Group I

First Round 4-6 March

Pakistan defeated Thailand 3-2, Lahore, PAK; Grass (O): Aisam Qureshi (PAK) d. Danai Udomchoke (THA) 62 75 67(5) 76(5); Paradorn Srichaphan (THA) d. Aqeel Khan (PAK) 64 16 76(3) 61; Aqeel Khan/Aisam Qureshi (PAK) d. Paradorn Srichaphan/Danai Udomchoke (THA) 64 57 62 76(4); Aisam Qureshi (PAK) d. Paradorn Srichaphan (THA) 75 26 64 64; Danai Udomchoke (THA) d. Shahzad Khan (PAK) 63 76(1). **Chinese Taipei defeated Japan 3-2, Tao Yuan, TPE; Hard (O):** Yen-Hsun Lu (TPE) d. Gouichi Motomura (JPN) 36 63 60 46 64; Takao Suzuki (JPN) d. Yeu-Tzuoo Wang (TPE) 64 61 61; Thomas Shimada/Takao Suzuki (JPN) d. Yen-Hsun Lu/Yeu-Tzuoo Wang (TPE) 16 76(5) 64 64; Yen-Hsun Lu (TPE) d. Takao Suzuki (JPN) 57 64 63 76(1); Yeu-Tzuoo Wang (TPE) d. Gouichi Motomura (JPN) 76(4) 75 46 76(2). **Uzbekistan defeated Indonesia 3-2, Jakarta, INA; Hard (O):** Denis Istomin (UZB) d. Suwandi Suwandi (INA) 63 62 64; Prima Simpatiaji (INA) d. Farrukh Dustov (UZB) 61 62 64; Suwandi Suwandi/Bonit Wiryawan (INA) d. Murad Inoyatov/Denis Istomin (UZB) 46 64 63 46 64; Farrukh Dustov (UZB) d. Suwandi Suwandi (INA) 75 75 46 26 63; Denis Istomin (UZB) d. Prima Simpatiaji (INA) 76(7) 76(5) 60. **India defeated China, P.R. 5-0, New Delhi, IND; Grass (O):** Harsh Mankad (IND) d. Peng Sun (CHN) 75 63 62; Prakash Amritraj (IND) d. Yu Wang (CHN) 63 64 62; Mahesh Bhupathi/Leander Paes (IND) d. Yu Wang/Ben-Qiang Zhu (CHN) 76(11) 63 36 61; Prakash Amritraj (IND) d. Peng Sun (CHN) 62 64; Harsh Mankad (IND) d. Hao Lu (CHN) 62 63.

Second Round 29 April-1 May

Pakistan defeated Chinese Taipei 4-1, Lahore, PAK; Grass (O): Aisam Qureshi (PAK) d.Yeu-Tzuoo Wang (TPE) 62 61 63; Yen-Hsun Lu (TPE) d. Aqeel Khan (PAK) 76(4) 46 75 76(5); Aqeel Khan/Aisam Qureshi (PAK) d. Yen-Hsun Lu/Yeu-Tzuoo Wang (TPE) 76(3) 62 75; Aisam Qureshi (PAK) d. Yen-Hsun Lu (TPE) 63 64 63; Aqeel Khan (PAK) d. Ti Chen (TPE) 67(5) 64 62. **India defeated Uzbekistan 5-0, Jaipur, IND; Grass (O):** Leander Paes (IND) d. Farrukh Dustov (UZB) 76(4) 62 60; Prakash Amritraj (IND) d. Denis Istomin (UZB) 63 62 62; Mahesh Bhupathi/Leander Paes (IND) d. Murad Inoyatov/Denis Istomin (UZB) 63 64 64; Prakash Amritraj (IND) d. Farrukh Dustov (UZB) 67(4) 64 62; Harsh Mankad (IND) d Murad Inoyatov (UZB) 75 61.

India and Pakistan advanced to World Group Play-offs on 23-25 September 2005.

Second Round/Play-off 15-17 July

Japan defeated Thailand 4-1, Osaka, JPN; Carpet (I): Takao Suzuki (JPN) d. Danai Udomchoke (THA) 67(5) 64 16 75 64; Paradorn Srichaphan (THA) d. Gouichi Motomura (JPN) 64 76(2) 60; Satoshi Iwabuchi/Takao Suzuki (JPN) d. Sanchai Ratiwatana/Sonchat Ratiwatana (THA) 63 64 36 76(3); Takao Suzuki (JPN) d. Paradorn Srichaphan (THA) 62 64 64; Go Soeda (JPN) d. Sanchai Ratiwatana (THA) 63 63. **China, P.R. defeated Indonesia 4-1, Tianjin, CHN; Hard (O):** Peng Sun (CHN) d. Suwandi Suwandi (INA) 63 62 64; Yu Wang (CHN) d. Prima Simpatiaji (INA) 64 60 64; Yu Wang/Xin-Yuan Yu (CHN) d. Suwandi Suwandi/Bonit Wiryawan (INA) 63 76(4) 76(2); Prima Simpatiaji (INA) d. Hao Lu (CHN) 22 ret.; Xin-Yuan Yu (CHN) d. Suwandi Suwandi (INA) 76(4) 63.

Third Round/Play-Off 23-25 September

Thailand defeated Indonesia 4-1, Bangkok, THA; Hard (O): Paradorn Srichaphan (THA) d. Sunu-Wahyu Trijati (INA) 61 64 62; Danai Udomchoke (THA) d. Prima Simpatiaji (INA) 62 63 64; Suwandi Suwandi/Bonit Wiryawan (INA) d. Sanchai Ratiwatana/Sonchat Ratiwatana (THA) 57 63 16 61 97; Paradorn Srichaphan (THA) d. Prima Simpatiaji (INA) 62 67(5) 62 76(6); Sanchai Ratiwatana (THA) d. Sunu-Wahyu Trijati (INA) 76(4) 62.

Indonesia relegated to Asia/Oceania Zone Group II in 2006.

Europe/Africa Zone Group II

First Round 4-6 March

Finland defeated Ghana 5-0, Accra, GHA; Hard (O): Jarkko Nieminen (FIN) d. Salifu Mohamed (GHA) 61 62 61; Tuomas Ketola (FIN) d. Henry Adjei-Darko (GHA) 76(4) 57 61 40 ret.; Lauri Kiiski/Jarkko Nieminen (FIN) d. Henry Adjei-Darko/Gunther Darkey (GHA) 36 76(3) 64 76(5); Jarkko Nieminen (FIN) d. Henry Adjei-Darko (GHA) 62 64; Tuomas Ketola (FIN) d. Salifu Mohamed (GHA) 61 63. **Bulgaria defeated Georgia 4-1, Sofia, BUL; Carpet (I):** Lado Chikhladze (GEO) d. Ivaylo Traykov (BUL) 76(5) 36 76(3) 63; Todor Enev (BUL) d. Irakli Ushangishvili (GEO) 62 63 62; Yordan Kanev/Ilia Kushev (BUL) d. Lado Chikhladze/Irakli Ushangishvili (GEO) 64 36 64 64; Todor Enev (BUL) d. Lado Chikhladze (GEO) 61 62 57 64; Ivaylo Traykov (BUL) d. David Kvernadze (GEO) 62 67(7) 76(0). **Hungary defeated Monaco 4-1, Hodmezovasarhely, HUN; Hard (I):** Gergely Kisgyorgy (HUN) d. Benjamin Balleret (MON) 64 26 64 46 61; Sebo Kiss (HUN) d. Emmanuel Heussner (MON) 76(8) 57 62 76(2); Gergely Kisgyorgy/Sebo Kiss (HUN) d. Benjamin Balleret/Guillaume Couillard (MON) 61 64 60; Guillaume Couillard (MON) d. Adam

2005 Davis Cup by BNP Paribas Results (continued)

Kellner (HUN) 46 64 63; Denes Lukacs (HUN) d. Thomas Drouet (MON) 64 62. **Ukraine defeated Norway 4-1, Kiev, UKR; Carpet(I):** Jan-Frode Andersen (NOR) d. Sergei Bubka (UKR) 76(5) 63 75; Orest Tereshchuk (UKR) d. Stian Boretti (NOR) 75 67(5) 64 67(4) 62; Mikhail Filima/Orest Tereshchuk (UKR) d. Jan-Frode Andersen/Stian Boretti (NOR) 61 63 67(4) 46 108; Mikhail Filima (UKR) d. Jan-Frode Andersen (NOR) 26 67(2) 62 76(6) 86; Sergei Bubka (UKR) d. Marius Tangen (NOR) 75 61. **Portugal defeated Estonia 4-1, Tallinn, EST; Carpet (I):** Frederico Gil (POR) d. Mait Kunnap (EST) 76(7) 64 62; Leonardo Tavares (POR) d. Alti Vahkal (EST) 36 26 62 76(5) 64; Frederico Gil/Leonardo Tavares (POR) d. Mait Kunnap/Alti Vahkal (EST) 63 64 64; Andrei Luzgin (EST) d. Rui Machado (POR) 57 64 63; Diogo Rocha (POR) d. Oskar Saarne (EST) 63 62. **Algeria defeated Poland 3-2, Algiers, ALG; Clay (O):** Lukasz Kubot (POL) d. Lamine Ouahab (ALG) 62 76(4) 61; Slimane Saoudi (ALG) d. Mariusz Fyrstenberg (POL) 36 63 76(2) 64; Lamine Ouahab/Slimane Saoudi (ALG) d. Mariusz Fyrstenberg/Marcin Matkowski (POL) 76(2) 64 36 63; Lukasz Kubot (POL) d. Slimane Saoudi (ALG) 57 16 62 63 60; Lamine Ouahab (ALG) d. Filip Urban (POL) 62 63 64. **Slovenia defeated Cote D'Ivoire 5-0, Kranj, SLO; Hard (I):** Grega Zemlja (SLO) d. Valentin Sanon (CIV) 64 64 75; Bostjan Osabnik (SLO) d. Claude N'Goran (CIV) 61 60 26 67(5) 62; Rok Jarc/Grega Zemlja (SLO) d. Claude N'Goran/Valentin Sanon (CIV) 62 62 ret.; Luka Gregorc (SLO) d. Valentin Sanon (CIV) 64 63; Rok Jarc (SLO) d. Terence Nugent (CIV) 62 60. **Latvia defeated Greece 4-1, Jurmala, LAT; Carpet (I):** Andis Juska (LAT) d. Konstantinos Economidis (GRE) 76(3) 76(2) 26 62; Vasilis Mazarakis (GRE) d. Ernests Gulbis (LAT) 63 64 63; Andis Juska/Deniss Pavlovs (LAT) d. Konstantinos Economidis/Vasilis Mazarakis (GRE) 57 46 63 64 64; Andis Juska (LAT) d. Vasilis Mazarakis (GRE) 62 63 75; Deniss Pavlovs (LAT) d. Alexander Jakupovic (GRE) 61 62.

Second Round 15-17 July

Bulgaria defeated Finland 3-2, Helsinki, FIN; Clay (O): Todor Enev (BUL) d. Tuomas Ketola (FIN) 36 64 61 36 86; Jarkko Nieminen (FIN) d. Radoslav Lukaev (BUL) 76(4) 63 62; Ilia Kushev/Radoslav Lukaev (BUL) d. Lauri Kiiski/Jarkko Nieminen (FIN) 75 63 67(5) 63; Jarkko Nieminen (FIN) d. Ilia Kushev (BUL) 63 75 62; Radoslav Lukaev (BUL) d. Tuomas Ketola (FIN) 76(5) 64 61. **Ukraine defeated Hungary 3-2, Donetsk, UKR; Hard (O):** Sergei Yaroshenko (UKR) d. Gergely Kisgyorgy (HUN) 63 64 67(4) 63; Orest Tereshchuk (UKR) d. Kornel Bardoczky (HUN) 64 62 36 26 63; Mikhail Filima/Orest Tereshchuk (UKR) d. Kornel Bardoczky/Gergely Kisgyorgy (HUN) 67(3) 76(2) 64 64; Kornel Bardoczky (HUN) d. Mikhail Filima (UKR) 36 76(6) 76(5); Sebo Kiss (HUN) d. Oleksandr Nedovesov (UKR) 76(4) 67(5) 64. **Portugal defeated Algeria 3-2, Lisbon, POR; Clay (O):** Slimane Saoudi (ALG) d. Rui Machado (POR) 46 60 36 76(3) 64; Lamine Ouahab (ALG) d. Frederico Gil (POR) 76(2) 64 63; Frederico Gil/Leonardo Tavares (POR) d. Abdel-Hak Hameurlaine/Slimane Saoudi (ALG) 67(3) 63 61 76(3); Rui Machado (POR) d. Lamine Ouahab (ALG) 64 62 62; Frederico Gil (POR) d. Slimane Saoudi (ALG) 46 67(5) 60 62 62. **Slovenia defeated Latvia 5-0, Kranj, SLO; Clay (O):** Marko Tkalec (SLO) d. Andis Juska (LAT) 61 63 64; Grega Zemlja (SLO) d. Ernests Gulbis (LAT) 57 63 61 64; Rok Jarc/Bostjan Osabnik (SLO) d. Ernests Gulbis/Andis Juska (LAT) 62 76(4) 46 62; Bostjan Osabnik (SLO) d. Deniss Pavlovs (LAT) 61 36 60; Rok Jarc (SLO) d. Janis Skroderis (LAT) 64 62.

Third Round 23-25 September

Ukraine defeated Bulgaria 4-1, Donetsk, UKR; Hard (O): Orest Tereshchuk (UKR) d. Todor Enev (BUL) 62 64 63; Radoslav Lukaev (BUL) d. Sergei Yaroshenko (UKR) 64 64 76(4); Mikhail Filima/Orest Tereshchuk (UKR) d. Ilia Kushev/Radoslav Lukaev (BUL) 64 62 76(3); Mikhail Filima (UKR) d. Todor Enev (BUL) 64 64 63; Sergei Bubka (UKR) d. Yordan Kanev (BUL) 67(7) 64 63. **Portugal defeated Slovenia 4-1, Estoril, POR; Clay (O):** Frederico Gil (POR) d. Bostjan Osabnik (SLO) 76(3) 61 61; Marko Tkalec (SLO) d. Rui Machado (POR) 63 46 67(5) 61 63; Frederico Gil/Leonardo Tavares (POR) d. Rok Jarc/Grega Zemlja (SLO) 64 62 64; Rui Machado (POR) d. Grega Zemlja (SLO) 63 63 26 64; Leonardo Tavares (POR) d. Marko Tkalec (SLO) 64 75.

Portugal and Ukraine promoted to Europe/Africa Zone Group I in 2006.

Play-off 15-17 July

Georgia defeated Ghana 3-2, Accra, GHA; Hard (O): Irakli Labadze (GEO) d. Gunther Darkey (GHA) 62 62 61; Henry Adjei-Darko (GHA) d. Lado Chikhladze (GEO) 76(7) 62 62; Lado Chikhladze/Irakli Labadze (GEO) d. Henry Adjei-Darko/Gunther Darkey (GHA) 46 63 63 64; Irakli Labadze (GEO) d. Henry Adjei-Darko (GHA) 64 63 61; Salifu Mohammed (GHA) d. Irakli Ushangishvili (GEO) 46 75 63. **Norway defeated Monaco 4-1, Oslo, NOR; Clay (O):** Benjamin Balleret (MON) d. Stian Boretti (NOR) 63 62 36 75; Jan Frode Andersen (NOR) d. Guillaume Couillard (MON) 62 64 67(4) 76(5); Jan Frode Andersen/Stian Boretti (NOR) d. Thomas Drouet/Emmanuel Heussner (MON) 36 62 61 62; Jan Frode Andersen (NOR) d. Benjamin Balleret (MON) 62 62 62; Stian Boretti (NOR) d. Guillaume Couillard (MON) 64 61. **Poland defeated Estonia 5-0, Gdynia, POL; Clay (O):** Lukasz Kubot (POL) d. Jaak Poldma (EST) 60 61 76(7); Adam Chadaj (POL) d. Mait Kunnap (EST) 63 63 64; Mariusz Fyrstenberg/Lukasz Kubot (POL) d. Mihkel Koppel/Mait Kunnap (EST) 63 64 63; Michal Przysiezny (POL) d. Mait Kunnap (EST) 26 63 62; Adam Chadaj (POL) d. Mikk Irdoja (EST) 62 61. **Greece defeated Cote D'Ivoire 5-0, Athens, GRE; Clay (O):** Konstantinos Economidis (GRE) d. Valentin Sanon (CIV) 64 63 62; Vasilis Mazarakis (GRE) d. Claude N'Goran (CIV) 62 76(1) 67(3) 60; Konstantinos Economidis/Vasilis Mazarakis (GRE) d. Claude N'Goran/Valentin Sanon (CIV) 36 67(8) 60 63 64; Nikos Rovas (GRE) d. Charles Irie (CIV) 61 61; Alexander Jakupovic (GRE) d. Terence Nugent (CIV) 64 36 61.

Cote d'Ivoire, Estonia, Ghana and Monaco relegated to Europe/Africa Zone Group III in 2006.

Americas Zone Group II

First Round 4-6 March

Brazil defeated Colombia 5-0, Bogota, COL; Clay (O): Flavio Saretta (BRA) d. Pablo Gonzalez (COL) 62 46 64 61; Ricardo Mello (BRA) d. Michael Quintero (COL) 63 64 63; Andre Sa/Bruno Soares (BRA) d. Pablo Gonzalez/Michael Quintero (COL) 63 64 26 61; Andre Sa (BRA) d. Oscar Rodriguez-Sanchez (COL) 63 61; Bruno Soares (BRA) d. Sergio Ramirez (COL) 06 63 63. **Netherlands Antilles defeated Bahamas 3-2, Curacao, AHO; Hard (O):** Devin Mullings (BAH) d. Rasid Winklaar (AHO) 61 63 62; Jean-Julien Rojer (AHO) d. Marvin Rolle (BAH) 62 62 75; Raoul Behr/Jean-Julien Rojer (AHO) d. Marvin Rolle/Ryan Sweeting (BAH) 64 64 64; Jean-Julien Rojer (AHO) d. Devin Mullings (BAH) 62 76(5) 63; Ryan Sweeting (BAH) d. David Josepa (AHO) 60 63. **Uruguay defeated Cuba 3-2, Havana, CUB; Hard (O):** Marcel Felder (URU) d. Edgar Hernandez-Perez (CUB) 36 75 26 64 61; Ricardo Chile-Fonte (CUB) d. Pablo Cuevas (URU) 26 63 64 67(1) 63; Ricardo Chile-Fonte/Sandor Martinez-Breijo (CUB) d Marcel Felder/Martin Vilarrubi (URU) 62 62 62; Marcel Felder (URU) d. Ricardo Chile-Fonte (CUB) 36 75 62 26 61; Pablo Cuevas (URU) d. Sandor Martinez-Breijo (CUB) 62 63 63. **Dominican Republic defeated Jamaica 3-2, Kingston, JAM; Hard (O):** Ryan Russell (JAM) d. Victor Estrella (DOM) 67(4) 62 62 61; Johnson Garcia (DOM) d. Scott Willinsky (JAM) 63 63 64; Victor Estrella/Johnson Garcia (DOM) d. Ryan Russell/Jermaine Smith (JAM) 64 76(5) 64; Ryan Russell (JAM) d. Johnson Garcia (DOM) 61 26 63 64; Victor Estrella (DOM) d. Damar Johnson (JAM) 46 36 64 62 63.

Second Round 15-17 July

Brazil defeated Netherlands Antilles 5-0, Santa Caterina, BRA; Clay (I): Ricardo Mello (BRA) d. David Josepa (AHO) 60 60 60; Gustavo Kuerten (BRA) d. Alexander Blom (AHO) 61 63 62; Andre Sa/Flavio Saretta (BRA) d. Raoul Behr/Alexander Blom (AHO) 61 61 64; Ricardo Mello (BRA) d. Alexander Blom (AHO) 63 41 ret.; Gustavo Kuerten (BRA) d. Raoul Behr (AHO) 60 62. **Uruguay defeated Dominican Republic 4-1, Montevideo, URU; Clay (O):** Marcel Felder (URU) d. Johnson Garcia (DOM) 62 61 62; Pablo Cuevas (URU) d. Victor Estrella (DOM) 76(8) 63 63; Pablo Cuevas/Martin Vilarrubi (URU) d. Victor Estrella/Johnson Garcia (DOM) 63 62 63; Marcel Felder (URU) d. Federico Rodriguez (DOM) 64 61; Henry Estrella (DOM) d. Augusto Ricciardi-Castelli (URU) 64 26 76(2).

Third Round 23-25 September

Brazil defeated Uruguay 3-2, Montevideo, URU; Clay (O): Gustavo Kuerten (BRA) d. Marcel Felder (URU) 61 60 36 64; Pablo Cuevas (URU) d. Flavio Saretta (BRA) 63 36 64 62; Gustavo Kuerten/Andre Sa (BRA) d. Pablo Cuevas/Martin Vilarrubi (URU) 36 63 64 64; Ricardo Mello (BRA) d. Marcel Felder (URU) 67(5) 61 63 62; Pablo Cuevas (URU) d. Gustavo Kuerten (BRA) 76(5) ret.

Brazil promoted to Americas Zone Group I in 2006.

Play-off 15-17 July

Colombia defeated Bahamas 5-0, Bogota, COL; Clay (O): Pablo Gonzalez (COL) d. Marvin Rolle (BAH) 36 62 62 36 62; Alejandro Falla (COL) d. Devin Mullings (BAH) 64 62 63; Alejandro Falla/Carlos Salamanca (COL) d. Marvin Rolle/Ryan Sweeting (BAH) 75 61 63; Alejandro Falla (COL) d. Ryan Sweeting (BAH) 64 64; Michael Quintero (COL) d. H'Cone Thompson (BAH) 61 61. **Jamaica defeated Cuba 3-1, Kingston, JAM; Hard (O):** Ryan Russell (JAM) d. Edgar Hernandez-Perez (CUB) 60 62 61; Damar Johnson (JAM) d. Ricardo Chile-Fonte (CUB) 63 76(6) 64; Ricardo Chile-Fonte/Sandor Martinez-Breijo (CUB) d. Damar Johnson/Ryan Russell (JAM) 63 64 36 46 63; Ryan Russell (JAM) d. Ricardo Chile-Fonte (CUB) 36 76(2) 76(6) 23 ret.

Bahamas and Cuba relegated to Americas Zone Group III in 2006.

Asia/Oceania Zone Group II

First Round 4-6 March

New Zealand defeated Kazakhstan 4-1, Auckland, NZL; Hard (I): Mark Nielsen (NZL) d. Dmitri Makeyev (KAZ) 60 62 63; GD Jones (NZL) d. Alexey Kedriouk (KAZ) 63 64 64; Mark Nielsen/Matt Prentice (NZL) d. Alexey Kedriouk/Dmitri Makeyev (KAZ) 63 62 62; Alexey Kedriouk (KAZ) d. Jose Statham (NZL) 64 75; GD Jones (NZL) d. Stanislav Buykov (KAZ) 61 60. **Kuwait defeated Iran 4-1, Tehran, IRI; Clay (O):** Abdullah Magdas (KUW) d. Ashkan Shokoofi (IRI) 76(7) 75 63; Mohammed Al Ghareeb (KUW) d. Anoosha Shahgholi (IRI) 75 76(5) 63; Mohammed Al Ghareeb/Mohamed-Khaliq Siddiq (KUW) d. Ashkan Shokoofi/Akbar Taheri (IRI) 61 64 75; Shahab Hassani-Nafez (IRI) d. Mohammad Ahmad (KUW) 62 75; Abdullah Magdas (KUW) d. Anoosha Shahgholi (IRI) 63 63. **Pacific Oceania defeated Lebanon 3-2, Lautoka, FIJ; Hard (O):** Michael Leong (POC) d. Patrick Chucri (LIB) 63 26 63 57 30 ret.; Juan Sebastien Langton (POC) d. Karim Alayli (LIB) 67(6) 63 61 75; Patrick Chucri/Jicham Zaatini (LIB) d. Brett Baudinet/Juan Sebastien Langton (POC) 63 76(0) 76(4); Michael Leong (POC)

d. Jicham Zaatini (LIB) 75 67(14) 63 46 62; Patrick Chucri (LIB) d. Brett Baudinet (POC) 64 26 62. **Korea, Rep. defeated Philippines 3-2, Manila, PHI; Clay (I):** Patrick Tierro (PHI) d. Hyun-Joon Suk (KOR) 75 75 64; Woong-Sun Jun (KOR) d. Johnny Arcilla (PHI) 64 36 76(7) 46 64; Hee-Seok Chung/Dong-Hyun Kim (KOR) d. Johnny Arcilla/Joseph Victorino (PHI) 64 60 60; Woong-Sun Jun (KOR) d. Patrick Tierro (PHI) 63 63 63; Johnny Arcilla (PHI) d. Hyun-Joon Suk (KOR) 62 75.

Second Round 15-17 July

New Zealand defeated Kuwait 3-2, Auckland, NZL; Hard (I): Mark Nielsen (NZL) d. Abdullah Magdas (KUW) 76(1) 16 64 61; GD Jones (NZL) d. Mohammed Al Ghareeb (KUW) 36 64 75 62; Daniel King-Turner/Mark Nielsen (NZL) d. Mohammed Al Ghareeb/Mohamed-Khaliq Siddiq (KUW) 76(4) 64 64; Mohammed Al Ghareeb (KUW) d. Adam Thompson (NZL) 75 63; Abdullah Magdas (KUW) d. Daniel King-Turner (NZL) 76(4) 57 63. **Korea, Rep. defeated Pacific Oceania 5-0, Seoul, KOR; Hard (O):** Sun-Yong Kim (KOR) d. Michael Leong (POC) 60 36 64 63; Woong-Sun Jun (KOR) d. West Nott (POC) 75 64 61; Woong-Sun Jun/Oh-Hee Kwon (KOR) d. Brett Baudinet/Juan Sebastien Langton (POC) 61 60 64; Jae-Sung An (KOR) d. Michael Leong (POC) 64 63; Sun-Yong Kim (KOR) d. Juan Sebastien Langton (POC) 64 63.

Third Round 23-25 September

Korea, Rep. defeated New Zealand 3-2, Auckland, NZL; Hard (I): Mark Nielsen (NZL) d. Kyu-Tae Im (KOR) 06 46 64 60 52 ret.; Hyung-Taik Lee (KOR) d. Daniel King-Turner (NZL) 61 76(5) 61; Oh-Hee Kwon/Hyung-Taik Lee (KOR) d. Daniel King-Turner/Mark Nielsen (NZL) 62 62 62; Hyung-Taik Lee (KOR) d. Mark Nielsen (NZL) 62 76(8) 63; Jose Statham (NZL) d. Sun-Yong Kim (KOR) 64 64.

Korea, Rep. promoted to Asia/Oceania Zone Group I in 2006.

Play-off 15-17 July

Kazakhstan defeated Iran 3-2, Tehran, IRI; Clay (O): Alexey Kedriouk (KAZ) d. Shahab Hassani-Nafez (IRI) 75 61 62; Ashkan Shokoofi (IRI) d. Dmitri Makeyev (KAZ) 63 64 60; Alexey Kedriouk/Anton Tsymbalov (KAZ) d. Ramin Raziyani/Ashkan Shokoofi (IRI) 64 62 76(4); Alexey Kedriouk (KAZ) d. Ashkan Shokoofi (IRI) 63 61 64; Anoosha Shahgholi (IRI) d. Dmitri Makeyev (KAZ) 63 67(5) 64. **Lebanon defeated Philippines 3-2, Beirut, LIB; Clay (O):** Patrick Chucri (LIB) d. Johnny Arcilla (PHI) 62 62 62; Patrick Tierro (PHI) d. Karim Alayli (LIB) 63 36 64 16 75; Karim Alayli/Patrick Chucri (LIB) d. Adelo Abadia/Johnny Arcilla (PHI) 26 63 46 64 64; Patrick Tierro (PHI) d. Patrick Chucri (LIB) 67(5) 67(8) 61 64 75; Karim Alayli (LIB) d. Johnny Arcilla (PHI) 62 76(5) 61.

Iran and Philippines relegated to Asia/Oceania Zone Group III in 2006.

Europe/Africa Zone Group III – Venue I

Date: 27 April-1 May
Venue: Cairo, Egypt
Surface: Clay (O)
Group A: Denmark, Kenya, Macedonia, F.Y.R., Namibia
Group B: Bosnia/Herzegovina, Egypt, Lithuania, Madagascar

- **Group A 27 April Denmark defeated Kenya 3-0:** Mik Ledvonova (DEN) d. Christian Vitulli (KEN) 63 63; Frederik Nielsen (DEN) d. Allan Cooper (KEN) 60 64; Frederik Nielsen/Morgan Thempler (DEN) d. Willis Mbandi/Christian Vitulli (KEN) 62 62. **Macedonia, F.Y.R. defeated Namibia 3-0:** Predrag Rusevski (MKD) d. Johan Theron (NAM) 60 63; Lazar Magdincev (MKD) d. Jurgens Strydom (NAM) 64 60; Lazar Magdincev/Predrag Rusevski (MKD) d. Henrico Du Plessis/Jurgens Strydom (NAM) 61 61.

- **28 April Denmark defeated Namibia 3-0:** Mik Ledvonova (DEN) d. Johan Theron (NAM) 62 62; Frederik Nielsen (DEN) d. Jurgens Strydom (NAM) 60 62; Frederik Nielsen/Morgan Thempler (DEN) d. Henrico Du Plessis/Jean-Pierre Huish (NAM) 62 62. **Macedonia, F.Y.R. defeated Kenya 3-0:** Predrag Rusevskl (MKD) d. Willis Mbandi (KEN) 60 60; Lazar Magdincev (MKD) d. Allan Cooper (KEN) 61 61; Dimitar Grabulovski/Predrag Rusevski (MKD) d. Allan Cooper/Maurice Wamukowa (KEN) 62 63.

- **29 April Macedonia, F.Y.R. defeated Denmark 3-0:** Predrag Rusevski (MKD) d. Mik Ledvonova (DEN) 57 63 62; Lazar Magdincev (MKD) d. Frederik Nielsen (DEN) 61 76(3); Lazar Magdincev/Predrag Rusevski (MKD) d. Frederik Nielsen/Morgan Thempler (DEN) 62 63. **Namibia defeated Kenya 2-1:** Christian Vitulli (KEN) d. Johan Theron (NAM) 61 46 63; Jurgens Strydom (NAM) d. Allan Cooper (KEN) 67(7) 63 63; Henrico Du Plessis/Jurgens Strydom (NAM) d. Allan Cooper/Christian Vitulli (KEN) 67(4) 62 64.

David Nalbandian (ARG)

2005 Davis Cup by BNP Paribas Results (continued)

- **Group B 27 April Egypt defeated Madagascar 3-0:** Mohamed Maamoun (EGY) d. Jacob Rasolondrazana (MAD) 61 62; Karim Maamoun (EGY) d. Germain Rasolondrazana (MAD) 62 60; Omar Hedayet/Mohamed Nashaat (EGY) d. Thierry Rajaobelina/Germain Rasolondrazana (MAD) 63 76(4). **Bosnia/Herzegovina defeated Lithuania 2-1:** Bojan Vujic (BIH) d. Rolandas Murashka (LTU) 63 36 60; Daniel Lencina (LTU) d. Ivan Dodig (BIH) 64 76(5); Ivan Dodig/Bojan Vujic (BIH) d. Daniel Lencina/Rolandas Murashka (LTU) 64 62.

- **28 April Egypt defeated Bosnia/Herzegovina 3-0:** Mohamed Maamoun (EGY) d. Bojan Vujic (BIH) 64 64; Karim Maamoun (EGY) d. Ivan Dodig (BIH) 57 62 64; Karim Maamoun/Mohamed Maamoun (EGY) d. Ivan Dodig/Bojan Vujic (BIH) 61 64. **Lithuania defeated Madagascar 3-0:** Gvidas Sabeckis (LTU) d. Thierry Rajaobelina (MAD) 61 63; Daniel Lencina (LTU) d. Germain Rasolondrazana (MAD) 63 63; Rolandas Murashka/Gvidas Sabeckis (LTU) d. Antso Rakotondramanga/Germain Rasolondrazana (MAD) 62 76(7).

- **29 April Egypt defeated Lithuania 2-1:** Rolandas Murashka (LTU) d. Mohamed Maamoun (EGY) 06 61 63; Karim Maamoun (EGY) d. Daniel Lencina (LTU) 62 76(3); Karim Maamoun/Mohamed Maamoun (EGY) d. Rolandas Murashka/Gvidas Sabeckis (LTU) 46 76(7) 64. **Bosnia/Herzegovina defeated Madagascar 2-1:** Bojan Vujic (BIH) d. Antso Rakotondramanga (MAD) 62 62; Ivan Dodig (BIH) d. Jacob Rasolondrazana (MAD) 63 36 63; Thierry Rajaobelina/Germain Rasolondrazana (MAD) d. Aleksandar Maric/Ugljesa Ostojic (BIH) 63 63.

- **Play-off for 1st-4th positions:**
  Results carried forward: Macedonia, F.Y.R. defeated Denmark 3-0; Egypt defeated Bosnia/Herzegovina 3-0
  30 April Macedonia, F.Y.R. defeated Bosnia/Herzegovina 3-0: Predrag Rusevski (MKD) d. Bojan Vujic (BIH) 62 60; Lazar Magdincev (MKD) d. Ivan Dodig (BIH) 62 62; Lazar Magdincev/Predrag Rusevski (MKD) d. Aleksandar Maric/Ugljesa Ostojic (BIH) 61 75. **Egypt defeated Denmark 2-1:** Mohamed Maamoun (EGY) d. Mik Ledvonova (DEN) 62 63; Frederik Nielsen (DEN) d. Karim Maamoun (EGY) 64 63; Karim Maamoun/Mohamed Maamoun (EGY) d. Frederik Nielsen/Morgan Thempler (DEN) 62 26 63.

- **1 May Macedonia, F.Y.R. defeated Egypt 2-1:** Omar Hedayet (EGY) d. Dimitar Grabulovski (MKD) 63 63; Predrag Rusevski (MKD) d. Mohamed Nashaat (EGY) 64 62; Lazar Magdincev/Predrag Rusevski (MKD) d. Mohamed Maamoun/Mohamed Nashaat (EGY) 26 64 63. **Denmark defeated Bosnia/Herzegovina 2-1:** Jacob Melskens (DEN) d. Aleksandar Maric (BIH) 64 26 64; Frederik Nielsen (DEN) d. Ugljesa Ostojic (BIH) 61 60; Aleksandar Maric/Bojan Vujic (BIH) d. Jacob Melskens/Morgan Thempler (DEN) 62 76(2).

- **Play-off for 5th-8th Positions:**
  Results carried forward: Namibia defeated Kenya 2-1; Lithuania defeated Madagascar 3-0
  30 April Namibia defeated Madagascar 2-1: Johan Theron (NAM) d. Thierry Rajaobelina (MAD) 75 26 63; Jurgens Strydom (NAM) d. Germain Rasolondrazana (MAD) 62 63; Antso Rakotondramanga/Germain Rasolondrazana (MAD) d. Henrico Du Plessis/Jurgens Strydom (NAM) 63 36 64. **Lithuania defeated Kenya 3-0:** Gvidas Sabeckis (LTU) d. Christian Vitulli (KEN) 63 67(4) 64; Daniel Lencina (LTU) d. Allan Cooper (KEN) 61 57 97; Arturas Gotovskis/Rolandas Murashka (LTU) d. Christian Vitulli/Maurice Wamukowa (KEN) 36 62 60.

- **1 May Lithuania defeated Namibia 2-1:** Jean-Pierre Huish (NAM) d. Arturas Gotovskis (LTU) 61 63; Rolandas Murashka (LTU) d. Jurgens Strydom (NAM) 62 62; Daniel Lencina/Rolandas Murashka (LTU) d. Jean-Pierre Huish/Jurgens Strydom (NAM) 76(6) 61. **Madagascar defeated Kenya 3-0:** Antso Rakotondramanga (MAD) d. Maurice Wamukowa (KEN) 63 75; Germain Rasolondrazana (MAD) d. Willis Mbandi (KEN) 62 61; Antso Rakotondramanga/Germain Rasolondrazana (MAD) d. Willis Mbandi/Maurice Wamukowa (KEN) 64 62.

- **Final Positions:** 1. Macedonia, F.Y.R., 2. Egypt, 3. Denmark, 4. Bosnia/Herzegovina, 5. Lithuania, 6. Namibia, 7. Madagascar, 8. Kenya.

Egypt and Macedonia, F.Y.R. promoted to Europe/Africa Zone Group II in 2006.
Kenya and Madagascar relegated to Europe/Africa Zone Group IV in 2006.

Europe/Africa Zone – Venue II

Date: 13-17 July
Venue: Dublin, Ireland
Surface: Carpet (O)
Group A: Armenia, Iceland, Ireland, Nigeria
Group B: Cyprus, San Marino, Tunisia, Turkey

- **Group A 13 July Ireland defeated Nigeria 3-0:** Louk Sorensen (IRL) d. Abdul-Mumin Babalola (NGR) 60 61; Kevin Sorensen (IRL) d. Jonathan Igbinovia (NGR) 63 63; Conor Niland/David O'Connell (IRL) d. Jonathan Igbinovia/Damisa Robinson (NGR) 62 64; **Armenia**

defeated Iceland 2-1: Harutyun Sofyan (ARM) d. Andri Jonsson (ISL) 62 64; Arnar Sigurdsson (ISL) d. Sargis Sargsian (ARM) 75 06 63; Sargis Sargsian/Harutyun Sofyan (ARM) d. Raj-Kumar Bonifacius/Arnar Sigurdsson (ISL) 61 64.

- **14 July Ireland defeated Armenia 3-0:** Louk Sorensen (IRL) d. Harutyun Sofyan (ARM) 63 61; Kevin Sorensen (IRL) d. Sargis Sargsian (ARM) 63 63; Conor Niland/David O'Connell (IRL) d. Sargis Sargsian/Harutyun Sofyan (ARM) 75 16 75. **Nigeria defeated Iceland 3-0:** Abdul-Mumin Babalola (NGR) d. Andri Jonsson (ISL) 62 60; Jonathan Igbinovia (NGR) d. Arnar Sigurdsson (ISL) 76(6) 62; Abdul-Mumin Babalola/Lawal Shehu (NGR) d. Andri Jonsson/Arnar Sigurdsson (ISL) 75 76(7).

- **15 July Ireland defeated Iceland 3-0:** Conor Niland (IRL) d. Andri Jonsson (ISL) 60 60; Kevin Sorensen (IRL) d. Raj-Kumar Bonifacius (ISL) 62 61; Conor Niland/David O'Connell (IRL) d. David Halldorsson/Andri Jonsson (ISL) 62 60. **Armenia defeated Nigeria 2-1:** Abdul-Mumin Babalola (NGR) d. Harutyun Sofyan (ARM) 57 61 64; Sargis Sargsian (ARM) d. Jonathan Igbinovia (NGR) 62 76(7); Sargis Sargsian/Harutyun Sofyan (ARM) d. Jonathan Igbinovia/Damisa Robinson (NGR) 63 63.

- **Group B 13 July Tunisia defeated San Marino 3-0:** Heithem Abid (TUN) d. Domenico Vicini (SMR) 67(6) 75 62; Malek Jaziri (TUN) d. Diego Zonzini (SMR) 60 63; Heithem Abid/Malek Jaziri (TUN) d. William Forcellini/Christian Rosti (SMR) 60 75. **Cyprus defeated Turkey 2-1:** Fotos Kallias (CYP) d. Baris Erguden (TUR) 76(7) 61; Marcos Baghdatis (CYP) d. Haluk Akkoyun (TUR) 63 61; Haluk Akkoyun/Esat Tanik (TUR) d. Fotos Kallias/Demetrios Leontis (CYP) 64 57 63.

- **14 July Cyprus defeated Tunisia 3-0:** Fotos Kallias (CYP) d. Heithem Abid (TUN) 64 61; Marcos Baghdatis (CYP) d. Malek Jaziri (TUN) 61 63; Marcos Baghdatis/Demetrios Leontis (CYP) d. Wael Kilani/Fares Zaier (TUN) 76(5) 63. **Turkey defeated San Marino 3-0:** Baris Erguden (TUR) d. Domenico Vicini (SMR) 76(3) 64; Haluk Akkoyun (TUR) d. William Forcellini (SMR) 63 62; Haluk Akkoyun/Esat Tanik (TUR) d. William Forcellini/Christian Rosti (SMR) 76(4) 62.

- **15 July Tunisia defeated Turkey 2-1:** Heithem Abid (TUN) d. Esat Tanik (TUR) 62 63; Haluk Akkoyun (TUR) d. Malek Jaziri (TUN) 63 64; Heithem Abid/Malek Jaziri (TUN) d. Haluk Akkoyun/Baris Erguden (TUR) 64 36 61. **Cyprus defeated San Marino 3-0:** Christopher Koutrouzas (CYP) d. Christian Rosti (SMR) 63 64; Fotos Kallias (CYP) d. Diego Zonzini (SMR) 60 60; Marcos Baghdatis/Demetrios Leontis (CYP) d. William Forcellini/Diego Zonzini (SMR) 61 61.

- **Play-off for 1st-4th Positions:**
  Results carried forward: Ireland defeated Armenia 3-0; Cyprus defeated Tunisia 3-0
  16 July Cyprus defeated Ireland 2-1: Conor Niland (IRL) d. Fotos Kallias (CYP) 64 36 60; Marcos Baghdatis (CYP) d. Kevin Sorensen (IRL) 62 46 60; Marcos Baghdatis/Demetrios Leontis (CYP) d. Conor Niland/David O'Connell (IRL) 46 60 61. **Armenia defeated Tunisia 2-1:** Heithem Abid (TUN) d. Harutyun Sofyan (ARM) 76(3) 75; Sargis Sargsian (ARM) d. Malek Jaziri (TUN) 64 61; Sargis Sargsian/Harutyun Sofyan (ARM) d. Malek Jaziri/Wael Kilani (TUN) 64 63.

- **17 July Ireland defeated Tunisia 3-0:** Louk Sorensen (IRL) d. Wael Kilani (TUN) 61 62; Kevin Sorensen (IRL) d. Malek Jaziri (TUN) 62 75; David O'Connell/Kevin Sorensen (IRL) d. Wael Kilani/Fares Zaier (TUN) 62 57 62. **Cyprus defeated Armenia 2-1:** Fotos Kallias (CYP) d. Harutyun Sofyan (ARM) 60 61; Marcos Baghdatis (CYP) d. Hayk Zohranyan (ARM) 63 61; Harutyun Sofyan/Hayk Zohranyan (ARM) d. Christopher Koutrouzas/Demetrios Leontis (CYP) 76(4) 62.

- **Play-off for 5th-8th Positions:**
  Results carried forward: Nigeria defeated Iceland 3-0; Turkey defeated San Marino 3-0
  16 July Nigeria defeated Turkey 2-1: Abdul-Mumin Babalola (NGR) d. Baris Erguden (TUR) 64 62; Haluk Akkoyun (TUR) d. Jonathan Igbinovia (NGR) 76(5) 16 64; Abdul-Mumin Babalola/Lawal Shehu (NGR) d. Haluk Akkoyun/Esat Tanik (TUR) 64 64. **Iceland defeated San Marino 2-1:** Domenico Vicini (SMR) d. Raj-Kumar Bonifacius (ISL) 63 76(5); Arnar Sigurdsson (ISL) d. William Forcellini (SMR) 61 60; Andri Jonsson/Arnar Sigurdsson (ISL) d. Christian Rosti/Domenico Vicini (SMR) 63 75.

- **17 July Nigeria defeated San Marino 3-0:** Abdul-Mumin Babalola (NGR) d. William Forcellini (SMR) 61 62; Jonathan Igbinovia (NGR) d. Diego Zonzini (SMR) 61 61; Abdul-Mumin Babalola/Lawal Shehu (NGR) d. Domenico Vicini/Diego Zonzini (SMR) 76(6) 75. **Turkey defeated Iceland 2-1:** Baris Erguden (TUR) d. Raj-Kumar Bonifacius (ISL) 64 76(3); Arnar Sigurdsson (ISL) d. Haluk Akkoyun (TUR) 62 76(2); Haluk Akkoyun/Baris Erguden (TUR) d. Andri Jonsson/Arnar Sigurdsson (ISL) 62 76(4).

- **Final Positions:** 1. Cyprus, 2. Ireland, 3. Armenia, 4. Tunisia, 5. Nigeria, 6. Turkey, 7. Iceland, 8. San Marino.

Cyprus and Ireland promoted to Europe/Africa Zone Group II in 2006.
Iceland and San Marino relegated to Europe/Africa Zone Group IV in 2006.

2005 Davis Cup by BNP Paribas Results (continued)

Americas Zone Group III

Date: 2-6 March
Venue: La Paz, Bolivia
Surface: Clay (O)
Group A: Bolivia, Haiti, Honduras, St. Lucia
Group B: El Salvador, Guatemala, Panama, Puerto Rico

- **Group A 2 March Haiti defeated St. Lucia 2-1:** Bertrand Madsen (HAI) d. Vernon Lewis (LCA) 63 64; Olivier Claude Sajous (HAI) d. Sirsean Arlain (LCA) 62 61; Kane Easter/Vernon Lewis (LCA) d. Gael Gaetjens/Iphton Louis (HAI) 64 64. **Bolivia defeated Honduras 3-0:** Jose Antelo (BOL) d. Jose Moncada (HON) 75 62; Mauricio Estivariz (BOL) d. Calton Alvarez (HON) 62 75; Jose Antelo/Mauricio Estivariz (BOL) d. Carlos Caceres/Jose Moncada (HON) 26 75 62.

- **3 March Bolivia defeated Haiti 3-0:** Jose Antelo (BOL) d. Bertrand Madsen (HAI) 36 63 64; Mauricio Estivariz (BOL) d. Olivier Claude Sajous (HAI) 61 76(8); Mario Salinas/Jorge Villanueva (BOL) d. Iphton Louis/Bertrand Madsen (HAI) 62 67(2) 108. **Honduras defeated St. Lucia 3-0:** Jose Moncada (HON) d. Alberton Richelieu (LCA) 64 75; Calton Alvarez (HON) d. Vernon Lewis (LCA) 61 64; Carlos Caceres/ Jose Moncada (HON) d. Kane Easter/Vernon Lewis (LCA) 63 26 75.

- **4 March Haiti defeated Honduras 3-0:** Bertrand Madsen (HAI) d. Jose Moncada (HON) 63 64; Olivier Claude Sajous (HAI) d. Calton Alvarez (HON) 76(5) 64; Gael Gaetjens/Iphton Louis (HAI) d. Carlos Caceres/Jose Moncada (HON) 63 63. **Bolivia defeated St. Lucia 3-0:** Jose Antelo (BOL) d. Kane Easter (LCA) 60 63; Mauricio Estivariz (BOL) d. Sirsean Arlain (LCA) 60 61; Mario Salinas/Jorge Villanueva (BOL) d. Sirsean Arlain/Kane Easter (LCA) 63 63.

- **Group B 2 March Guatemala defeated Panama 3-0:** Cristian Paiz (GUA) d. Alberto Gonzalez (PAN) 63 62; Jacobo Chavez (GUA) d. Augusto Alvarado (PAN) 61 62; Manuel Chavez/Luis Perez-Chete (GUA) d. Braen Aneiros-Romero/Alberto Gonzalez (PAN) 62 64. **Puerto Rico defeated El Salvador 2-1:** Jorge Rangel (PUR) d. Manuel-Antonio Tejada-Ruiz (ESA) 61 64; Rafael Arevalo-Gonzalez (ESA) d. Gabriel Montilla (PUR) 62 60; Gilberto Alvarez/Gabriel Montilla (PUR) d. Rafael Arevalo-Gonzalez/Manuel-Antonio Tejada-Ruiz (ESA) 63 64.

- **3 March Guatemala defeated Puerto Rico 2-1:** Cristian Paiz (GUA) d. Jorge Rangel (PUR) 62 61; Jacobo Chavez (GUA) d. Gabriel Montilla (PUR) 63 62; Gilberto Alvarez/Gabriel Montilla (PUR) d. Manuel Chavez/Luis Perez-Chete (GUA) 57 76(5) 64. **El Salvador defeated Panama 3-0:** Manuel-Antonio Tejada-Ruiz (ESA) d. Juan Jose Fuentes (PAN) 62 62; Rafael Arevalo-Gonzalez (ESA) d. Alberto Gonzalez (PAN) 62 61; Rafael Arevalo-Gonzalez/Manuel-Antonio Tejada-Ruiz (ESA) d. Juan Jose Fuentes/Alberto Gonzalez (PAN) 63 63.

- **4 March Guatemala defeated El Salvador 2-1:** Cristian Paiz (GUA) d. Manuel-Antonio Tejada-Ruiz (ESA) 63 64; Rafael Arevalo-Gonzalez (ESA) d. Jacobo Chavez (GUA) 63 61; Manuel Chavez/Luis Perez-Chete (GUA) d. Rafael Arevalo-Gonzalez/Manuel-Antonio Tejada-Ruiz (ESA) 64 64. **Puerto Rico defeated Panama 2-1:** Gilberto Alvarez (PUR) d. Braen Aneiros-Romero (PAN) 64 62; Alberto Gonzalez (PAN) d. Gabriel Montilla (PUR) 63 75; Gilberto Alvarez/Gabriel Montilla (PUR) d. Juan Jose Fuentes/Alberto Gonzalez (PAN) 63 62.

- **Play-off for 1st-4th Positions:**
  Results carried forward: Bolivia defeated Haiti 3-0; Guatemala defeated Puerto Rico 2-1
  5 March Bolivia defeated Puerto Rico 3-0: Jose Antelo (BOL) d. Gilberto Alvarez (PUR) 62 62; Mauricio Estivariz (BOL) d. Gabriel Montilla (PUR) 75 62; Jose Antelo/Mauricio Estivariz (BOL) d. Gilberto Alvarez/Gabriel Montilla (PUR) 57 63 62. **Guatemala defeated Haiti 3-0:** Luis Perez-Chete (GUA) d. Bertrand Madsen (HAI) 64 26 64; Cristian Paiz (GUA) d. Olivier Claude Sajous (HAI) 75 62; Jacobo Chavez/Luis Perez-Chete (GUA) d. Gael Gaetjens/Iphton Louis (HAI) 64 62

- **6 March Guatemala defeated Bolivia 3-0:** Luis Perez-Chete (GUA) d. Jose Antelo (BOL) 60 75; Cristian Paiz (GUA) d. Mauricio Estivariz (BOL) 76(4) 63; Jacobo Chavez/Manuel Chavez (GUA) d. Mario Salinas/Jorge Villanueva (BOL) 26 64 62. **Puerto Rico defeated Haiti 2-0:** Gilberto Alvarez (PUR) d. Gael Gaetjens (HAI) 60 60; Jorge Rangel (PUR) d. Olivier Claude Sajous (HAI) 63 63; Doubles not played.

- **Play-off for 5th-8th Positions:**
  Results carried forward: Honduras defeated St. Lucia 3-0; El Salvador defeated Panama 3-0
  5 March Honduras defeated Panama 2-1: Jose Moncada (HON) d. Braen Aneiros-Romero (PAN) 36 63 62; Alberto Gonzalez (PAN) d. Calton Alvarez (HON) 75 64; Carlos Caceres/Jose Moncada (HON) d. Braen Aneiros-Romero/Alberto Gonzalez (PAN) 64 76(3).
  El Salvador defeated St. Lucia 3-0: Manuel-Antonio Tejada-Ruiz (ESA) d. Vernon Lewis (LCA) 36 60 62; Rafael Arevalo-Gonzalez (ESA) d. Sirsean Arlain (LCA) 61 60; Rafael Arevalo-Gonzalez/Manuel-Antonio Tejada-Ruiz (ESA) d. Kane Easter/Alberton Richelieu (LCA) 61 64.

- **6 March Honduras defeated El Salvador 2-0:** Carlos Caceres (HON) d. Marcelo Arevalo (ESA) 61 61; Jose Moncada (HON) d. Manuel-Antonio Tejada-Ruiz (ESA) 64 67(3) 61; Doubles not played. **Panama defeated St. Lucia 2-0:** Braen Aneiros-Romero (PAN) d. Kane Easter (LCA) 76(8) 46 64; Alberto Gonzalez (PAN) d. Sirsean Arlain (LCA) 63 63; Doubles not played.

- **Final Positions:** 1. Guatemala, 2. Bolivia, 3. Puerto Rico, 4. Haiti, 5. Honduras, 6. El Salvador, 7. Panama, 8. St Lucia.

Bolivia and Guatemala promoted to Americas Zone Group II in 2006.
Panama and St. Lucia relegated to Americas Group IV in 2006.

Asia/Oceania Zone Group III

Date: 13-17 July
Venue: Causeway Bay, Hong Kong China
Surface: Hard (O)
Group A: Hong Kong China; Malaysia, Saudi Arabia, Tajikistan
Group B: Bahrain, Qatar, Sri Lanka, Vietnam

- **Group A 13 July Hong Kong China defeated Saudi Arabia 3-0:** Martin Sayer (HKG) d. Fahad Al Saad (KSA) 62 62; Hiu-Tung Yu (HKG) d. Omar Al Thagib (KSA) 61 60; Brian Hung/Martin Sayer (HKG) d. Fahad Al Saad/Bager Bokhleaf (KSA) 62 62. **Malaysia defeated Tajikistan 3-0:** Selvam Veerasingam (MAS) d. Mirkhusein Yakhyaev (TJK) 61 60; Yew-Ming Si (MAS) d. Dilshod Sharifi (TJK) 63 75; Nikesh Singh Panthlia/Adrian Tan (MAS) d. Dilshod Sharifi/Mirkhusein Yakhyaev (TJK) 64 61.

- **14 July Hong Kong China defeated Malaysia 3-0:** Wayne Wong (HKG) d. Selvam Veerasingam (MAS) 67(5) 63 64; Hiu-Tung Yu (HKG) d. Yew-Ming Si (MAS) 36 76(2) 75; Brian Hung/Martin Sayer (HKG) d. Nikesh Singh Panthlia/Adrian Tan (MAS) 61 61. **Saudi Arabia defeated Tajikistan 2-1:** Fahad Al Saad (KSA) d. Mirkhusein Yakhyaev (TJK) 62 62; Dilshod Sharifi (TJK) d. Omar Al Thagib (KSA) 60 46 63; Badar Al Megayel/Fahad Al Saad (KSA) d. Dilshod Sharifi/Mansour Yakhyaev (TJK) 62 64.

- **15 July Hong Kong China defeated Tajikistan 3-0:** Martin Sayer (HKG) d. Mirkhusein Yakhyaev (TJK) 60 62; Brian Hung (HKG) d. Dilshod Sharifi (TJK) 60 61; Brian Hung/Martin Sayer (HKG) d. Rahmatullo Rajabaliev/Mirkhusein Yakhyaev (TJK) 60 61. **Malaysia defeated Saudi Arabia 2-1;** Fahad Al Saad (KSA) d. Adrian Tan (MAS) 64 62; Yew-Ming Si (MAS) d. Omar Al Thagib (KSA) 62 64; Yew-Ming Si/Selvam Veerasingam (MAS) d. Badar Al Megayel/Fahad Al Saad (KSA) 61 63.

- **Group B 13 July Sri Lanka defeated Qatar 3-0:** Harshana Godamanne (SRI) d. Sultan-Khalfan Al Alawi (QAT) 62 61; Renouk Wijemanne (SRI) d. Mohammed Abdulla (QAT) 64 60; Harshana Godamanne/Oshada Wijemanne (SRI) d. Mohammed Abdulla/Abdulla Hajji (QAT) 61 61. **Vietnam defeated Bahrain 2-1:** Abdul-Rahman Shehab (BRN) d. Quang-Huy Ngo (VIE) 64 63; Minh-Quan Do (VIE) d. Mohammed Abdul-Latif (BRN) 60 62; Minh-Quan Do/Quoc-Khanh Le (VIE) d. Mohammed Abdul-Latif/Abdul-Rahman Shehab (BRN) 63 62.

- **14 July Vietnam defeated Qatar 3-0:** Quang-Huy Ngo (VIE) d. Sultan-Khalfan Al Alawi (QAT) 63 76(5); Minh-Quan Do (VIE) d. Mohammed Abdulla (QAT) 61 62; Quoc-Khanh Le/Thanh-Hoang Tran (VIE) d. Mohammed Abdulla/Abdulla Hajji (QAT) 62 61. **Sri Lanka defeated Bahrain 3-0:** Harshana Godamanne (SRI) d. Abdul-Rahman Shehab (BRN) 61 64; Renouk Wijemanne (SRI) d. Khaled Al Thawadi (BRN) 62 64; Rajeev Rajapakse/Oshada Wijemanne (SRI) d. Mohammed Abdul-Latif/Abdul-Latif Al Murraghi (BRN) 75 64.

- **15 July Bahrain defeated Qatar 2-1:** Abdul-Rahman Shehab (BRN) d. Sultan-Khalfan Al Alawi (QAT) 75 63; Mohammed Abdulla (QAT) d. Khaled Al Thawadi (BRN) 62 36 86; Mohammed Abdul-Latif/Abdul-Rahman Shehab (BRN) d. Mohammed Abdulla/Sultan-Khalfan Al Alawi (QAT) 64 62. **Vietnam defeated Sri Lanka 2-1:** Harshana Godamanne (SRI) d. Quang-Huy Ngo (VIE) 46 63 63; Minh-Quan Do (VIE) d. Renouk Wijemanne (SRI) 64 64; Minh-Quan Do/Quoc-Khanh Le (VIE) d. Harshana Godamanne/Rajeev Rajapakse (SRI) 63 61.

- **Play-off for 1st-4th Positions:**
Results carried forward: Hong Kong China defeated Malaysia 3-0; Vietnam defeated Sri Lanka 2-1
16 July Hong Kong China defeated Sri Lanka 3-0: Wayne Wong (HKG) d. Harshana Godamanne (SRI) 75 62; Hiu-Tung Yu (HKG) d. Renouk Wijemanne (SRI) 75 62; Brian Hung/Martin Sayer (HKG) d. Harshana Godamanne/Renouk Wijemanne (SRI) 75 61. **Malaysia defeated Vietnam 3-0:** Selvam Veerasingam (MAS) d. Quang-Huy Ngo (VIE) 64 64; Yew-Ming Si (MAS) d. Minh-Quan Do (VIE) 67(9) 64 86; Nikesh Singh Panthlia/Adrian Tan (MAS) d. Minh-Quan Do/Quoc-Khanh Le (VIE) 63 62.

2005 Davis Cup by BNP Paribas Results (continued)

- **17 July Hong Kong China defeated Vietnam 3-0:** Martin Sayer (HKG) d. Thanh-Hoang Tran (VIE) 63 61; Brian Hung (HKG) d. Minh-Quan Do (VIE) 62 64; Martin Sayer/Hiu-Tung Yu (HKG) d. Minh-Quan Do/Quoc-Khanh Le (VIE) 61 63. **Malaysia defeated Sri Lanka 3-0:** Selvam Veerasingam (MAS) d. Harshana Godamanne (SRI) 36 76(5) 75; Yew-Ming Si (MAS) d. Renouk Wijemanne (SRI) 62 61; Nikesh Singh Panthlia/Adrian Tan (MAS) d. Rajeev Rajapakse/Oshada Wijemanne (SRI) 63 26 97.

- **Play-off for 5th-8th Positions:**
  Results carried forward: Saudi Arabia defeated Tajikistan 2-1; Bahrain defeated Qatar 2-1
  16 July Saudi Arabia defeated Qatar 2-1: Fahad Al Saad (KSA) d. Sultan-Khalfan Al Alawi (QAT) 62 64; Mohammed Abdulla (QAT) d. Omar Al Thagib (KSA) 60 61; Badar Al Megayel/Fahad Al Saad (KSA) d. Mohammed Abdulla/Sultan-Khalfan Al Alawi (QAT) 06 76(6) 62. **Tajikistan defeated Bahrain 2-1:** Abdul-Rahman Shehab (BRN) d. Mansour Yakhyaev (TJK) 67(6) 63 64; Dilshod Sharifi (TJK) d. Khaled Al Thawadi (BRN) 63 63; Dilshod Sharifi/ Mirkhusein Yakhyaev (TJK) d. Mohammed Abdul-Latif/Abdul-Rahman Shehab (BRN) 64 64.

- **17 July Bahrain defeated Saudi Arabia 2-1:** Abdul-Rahman Shehab (BRN) d. Badar Al Megayel (KSA) 62 01 ret.; Fahad Al Saad (KSA) d. Khaled Al Thawadi (BRN) 62 36 63; Mohammed Abdul-Latif/Abdul-Rahman Shehab (BRN) d. Badar Al Megayel/Fahad Al Saad (KSA) 75 64. **Qatar defeated Tajikistan 2-1:** Mirkhusein Yakhyaev (TJK) d. Abdulla Hajji (QAT) 64 64; Mohammed Abdulla (QAT) d. Dilshod Sharifi (TJK) 75 36 75; Mohammed Abdulla/Sultan-Khalfan Al Alawi (QAT) d. Dilshod Sharifi/Mirkhusein Yakhyaev (TJK) 62 62.

- **Final Positions:** 1. Hong Kong China, 2. Malaysia, 3. Vietnam, 4. Sri Lanka, 5. Bahrain, 6. Saudi Arabia, 7. Qatar, 8. Tajikistan.

Hong Kong China and Malaysia promoted to Asia/Oceania Zone Group II in 2006.
Qatar and Tajikistan relegated to Asia/Oceania Group IV in 2006.

Europe/Africa Zone Group IV

Date:	1-6 March
Venue:	Kampala, Uganda
Surface:	Clay (O)
Group A:	Benin, Botswana, Djibouti, Malta, Moldova
Group B:	Andorra, Azerbaijan, Mauritius, Rwanda, Senegal, Uganda

- **Group A 2 March Botswana defeated Benin 2-1:** Bokang Setshogo (BOT) d. Romain Setomey (BEN) 62 46 63; Phenyo Matong (BOT) d. Armand Segodo (BEN) 67(12) 60 62; Alphonse Gandonou/Armand Segodo (BEN) d. Phenyo Matong/Bokang Setshogo (BOT) 62 64. **Moldova defeated Djibouti 3-0:** Evghenii Plugiarov (MDA) d. Abdi-Fatah Abdourahman Youssouf (DJI) 60 60; Andrei Ciumac (MDA) d. Kader Mohamed Mogueh (DJI) 60 60; Serghei Cuptov/Artiom Podgainii (MDA) d. Abdi-Fatah Abdourahaman Youssouf/Kadar Mogueh (DJI) 60 60.

- **3 March Moldova defeated Malta 3-0:** Evghenii Plugariov (MDA) d. Marcus Delicata (MLT) 60 61; Andrei Ciumac (MDA) d. Daniel Ceross (MLT) 62 61; Serghei Cuptov/Artiom Podgainii (MDA) d. Matthew Asciak/Marcus Delicata (MLT) 63 67(5) 61. **Benin defeated Djibouti 3-0:** Jean Segodo (BEN) d. Fahim Osman Obsien (DJI) 60 60; Armand Segodo (BEN) d. Kadar Mogueh (DJI) 60 60; Jean Segodo/Romain Setomey (BEN) d. Abdi-Fatah Abdourahman Youssouf/Fahim Osman Obsien (DJI) 60 61.

- **4 March Moldova defeated Benin 3-0:** Evghenii Plugariov (MDA) d. Romain Setomey (BEN) 75 62; Andrei Ciumac (MDA) d. Armand Segodo (BEN) 61 61; Serghei Cuptov/Artiom Podgainii (MDA) d. Alphonse Gandonou/Armand Segodo (BEN) 76(5) 76(5). **Botswana defeated Malta 3-0:** Bokang Setshogo (BOT) d. Marcus Delicata (MLT) 62 63; Phenyo Matong (BOT) d. Daniel Ceross (MLT) 36 63 64; Phenyo Matong/Bokang Setshogo (BOT) d. Matthew Asciak/Marcus Delicata (MLT) 36 63 64.

- **5 March Moldova defeated Botswana 2-1:** Evghenii Plugariov (MDA) d. Bokang Setshogo (BOT) 62 64; Andrei Ciumac (MDA) d. Phenyo Matong (BOT) 75 63; Phenyo Matong/Bokang Setshogo (BOT) d. Serghei Cuptov/Artiom Podgainii (MDA) 46 61 63. **Malta defeated Djibouti 3-0:** Marcus Delicata (MLT) d. Abdi-Fatah Abdourahman Youssouf (DJI) 61 60; Daniel Ceross (MLT) d. Kadar Mogueh (DJI) 61 61; Matthew Asciak/Daniel Ceross (MLT) d. Abdi-Fatah Abdourahman Youssouf/Kadar Mogueh (DJI) 61 61.

- **6 March Botswana defeated Djibouti 3-0:** Bino Rasedisa (BOT) d. Fahim Osman Obsien (DJI) 61 60; Bokang Setshogo (BOT) d. Kadar Mogueh (DJI) 60 60; Bino Rasedisa/Tshepang Tlhan Kane (BOT) d. Abdi-Fatah Abdourahman Youssouf/Fahim Osman Obsien (DJI) 63 61. **Benin defeated Malta 3-0:** Jean Segodo (BEN) d. Matthew Asciak (MLT) 76(4) 61; Armand Segodo (BEN) d. Daniel Ceross (MLT) 64 64; Jean Segodo/Romain Setomey (BEN) d. Daniel Ceross/Marcus Delicata (MLT) 63 64.

- **Final Positions:** 1. Moldova, 2. Botswana, 3. Benin, 4. Malta, 5. Djibouti.

Moldova and Botswana promoted to Europe/Africa Zone Group III in 2006.

- **Group B 1 March Azerbaijan defeated Uganda 2-1:** Farid Shirinov (AZE) d. Godfrey Uzunga (UGA) 76(6) 75; Patrick Olobo (UGA) d. Fakhraddin Shirinov (AZE) 76(4) 75; Fakhraddin Shirinov/Farid Shirinov (AZE) d. Cedric Babu/Patrick Olobo (UGA) 76(6) 76(2). **Rwanda defeated Senegal 2-1:** Jean-Claude Gasigwa (RWA) d. Salif Kante (SEN) 63 76(6); Eric Hagenimana (RWA) d. Youssou Berthe (SEN) 60 63; Youssou Berthe/Salif Kante (SEN) d. Eric Hagenimana/Alain Hakizimana (RWA) 16 63 63. **Andorra defeated Mauritius 3-0:** Jean-Baptiste Poux-Gautier (AND) d. Olivier Rey (MRI) 60 61; Paul Gerbaud-Farras (AND) d. Jerome Mamet (MRI) 61 60; Jean-Baptiste Poux-Gautier/Axel Rabanal (AND) d. Olivier Rey/Mathieu Vallet (MRI) 62 62.

- **2 March Andorra defeated Rwanda 2-1:** Jean-Baptiste Poux-Gautier (AND) d. Jean-Claude Gasigwa (RWA) 61 61; Eric Hagenimana (RWA) d. Paul Gerbaud-Farras (AND) 64 63; Paul Gerbaud-Farras/Jean-Baptiste Poux-Gautier (AND) d. Eric Hagenimana/Alain Hakizimana (RWA) 62 60. **Uganda defeated Mauritius 2-1:** Godfrey Uzunga (UGA) d. Olivier Rey (MRI) 63 60; Patrick Olobo (UGA) d. Mathieu Vallet (MRI) 60 62; Jerome Mamet/Olivier Rey (MRI) d. James Odongo/Godfrey Uzunga (UGA) 61 46 62. **Senegal defeated Azerbaijan 2-1:** Salif Kante (SEN) d. Talat Rahimov (AZE) 75 60; Youssou Berthe (SEN) d. Fakhraddin Shirinov (AZE) 64 16 61; Talat Rahimov/Farid Shirinov (AZE) d. Omar Ka/Mamadou Seye (SEN) 61 64.

- **3 March Azerbaijan defeated Mauritius 3-0:** Farid Shirinov (AZE) d. Mathieu Vallet (MRI) 60 62; Fakhraddin Shirinov (AZE) d. Jerome Mamet (MRI) 63 60; Ramin Hajiyev/Farid Shirinov (AZE) d. Olivier Rey/Mathieu Vallet (MRI) 63 67(3) 75. **Rwanda defeated Uganda 2-1:** Godfrey Uzunga (UGA) d. Jean-Claude Gasigwa (RWA) 16 76(5) 55 ret.; Eric Hagenimana (RWA) d. Patrick Olobo (UGA) 64 62; Eric Hagenimana/Alain Hakizimana (RWA) d. Cedric Babu/Patrick Olobo (UGA) 60 63. **Andorra defeated Senegal 3-0:** Jean-Baptiste Poux-Gautier (AND) d. Salif Kante (SEN) 60 60; Paul Gerbaud-Farras (AND) d. Youssou Berthe (SEN) 61 61; Jean-Baptiste Poux-Gautier/Axel Rabanal (AND) d. Youssou Berthe/Salif Kante (SEN) 64 26 60.

- **4 March Andorra defeated Azerbaijan 3-0:** Jean-Baptiste Poux-Gautier (AND) d. Ramin Hajiyev (AZE) 60 60; Paul Gerbaud-Farras (AND) d. Fakhraddin Shirinov (AZE) 60 60; Paul Gerbaud-Farras/Axel Rabanal (AND) d. Ramin Hajiyev/Talat Rahimov (AZE) 62 62. **Rwanda defeated Mauritius 3-0:** Eric Hagenimana (RWA) d. Olivier Rey (MRI) 63 62; Alain Hakizimana (RWA) d. Jerome Mamet (MRI) 60 61; Eric Hagenimana/Alain Hakizimana (RWA) d. Olivier Rey/Mathieu Vallet (MRI) 62 62. **Senegal defeated Uganda 2-1:** Salif Kante (SEN) d. James Odongo (UGA) 63 61; Youssou Berthe (SEN) d. Patrick Olobo (UGA) 60 63; Cedric Babu/Patrick Olobo (UGA) d. Youssou Berthe/Salif Kante (SEN) 46 63 64.

- **5 March Azerbaijan defeated Rwanda 2-1:** Farid Shirinov (AZE) d. Jean-Claude Gasigwa (RWA) 64 63; Eric Hagenimana (RWA) d. Fakhraddin Shirinov (AZE) 62 62; Fakhraddin Shirinov/Farid Shirinov (AZE) d. Eric Hagenimana/Alain Hakizimana (RWA) 67(4) 76(6) 63. **Andorra defeated Uganda 3-0:** Jean-Baptiste Poux-Gautier (AND) d. James Odongo (UGA) 61 60; Paul Gerbaud-Farras (AND) d. Patrick Olobo (UGA) 60 62; Paul Gerbaud-Farras/Axel Rabanal (AND) d. Cedric Babu/Patrick Olobo (UGA) 63 63. **Senegal defeated Mauritius 2-1:** Olivier Rey (MRI) d. Omar Ka (SEN) 60 76(3); Youssou Berthe (SEN) d. Mathieu Vallet (MRI) 61 61; Youssou Berthe/Salif Kante (SEN) d. Jerome Mamet/Olivier Rey (MRI) 62 63.

- **Final Positions:** 1. Andorra, 2. Rwanda, 3. Azerbaijan, 4. Senegal, 5. Uganda, 6. Mauritius.

Andorra and Rwanda promoted to Europe/Africa Zone Group III in 2006.

Americas Zone Group IV

Date: 13-17 July
Venue: San Jose, Costa Rica
Surface: Hard (O)
Nations: Bermuda, Costa Rica, Trinidad & Tobago, US Virgin Islands

- **13 July Costa Rica defeated Bermuda 2-1:** Janson Bascome (BER) d. Ignasi Roca (CRC) 75 62; Felipe Montenegro (CRC) d. James Collieson (BER) 60 61; Felipe Montenegro/Ignasi Roca (CRC) d. Janson Bascome/Gavin Manders (BER) 63 64. **Trinidad & Tobago defeated Barbados 3-0:** Richard Brown (TRI) d. Russell Moseley (BAR) 61 63; Shane Stone (TRI) d. Wkwesi Williams (BAR) 61 61; Shane Stone/Troy Stone (TRI) d. Russell Moseley/Wkwesi Williams (BAR) 62 63.

● **14 July Bermuda defeated US Virgin Islands 2-1:** Janson Bascome (BER) d. Christian Nelthropp (ISV) 62 64; Eugene Highfield (ISV) d. James Collieson (BER) 63 62; Janson Bascome/Gavin Manders (BER) d. Eugene Highfield/Christian Nelthropp (ISV) 75 46 61. **Barbados defeated Costa Rica 2-1:** Wkwesi Williams (BAR) d. Ignasi Roca (CRC) 64 75; Felipe Montenegro (CRC) d. Haydn Lewis (BAR) 46 61 61; Haydn Lewis/Russell Moseley (BAR) d. Felipe Montenegro/Marcos Salazar (CRC) 46 61 62.

● **15 July Trinidad & Tobago defeated US Virgin Islands 3-0:** Richard Brown (TRI) d. Christian Nelthropp (ISV) 60 62; Shane Stone (TRI) d. Eugene Highfield (ISV) 64 76(5); Shane Stone/Troy Stone (TRI) d. Eugene Highfield/Whitney Mcfarlane (ISV) 36 61 61. **Barbados defeated Bermuda 3-0:** Russell Moseley (BAR) d. Janson Bascome (BER) 62 76(3); Haydn Lewis (BAR) d. James Collieson (BER) 76(7) 63; Haydn Lewis/Russell Moseley (BAR) d. Janson Bascome/Gavin Manders (BER) 63 36 63.

● **16 July Barbados defeated US Virgin Islands 3-0:** Russell Moseley (BAR) d. Jereme Cumbermack (ISV) 60 60; Haydn Lewis (BAR) d. Eugene Highfield (ISV) 64 63; Haydn Lewis/Russell Moseley (BAR) d. Eugene Highfield/Whitney McFarlane (ISV) 62 61. **Costa Rica defeated Trinidad & Tobago 2-1:** Richard Brown (TRI) d. Marcos Salazar (CRC) 60 62; Felipe Montenegro (CRC) d. Brent Ching (TRI) 61 64; Felipe Montenegro/Ignasi Roca (CRC) d. Richard Brown/Troy Stone (TRI) 63 62.

● **17 July Costa Rica defeated US Virgin Islands 3-0:** Ignasi Roca (CRC) d. Christian Nelthropp (ISV) 61 62; Felipe Montenegro (CRC) d. Eugene Highfield (ISV) 64 63; Felipe Montenegro/Ignasi Roca (CRC) d. Whitney McFarlane/Christian Nelthropp (ISV) 64 60. **Trinidad & Tobago defeated Bermuda 3-0:** Richard Brown (TRI) d. Gavin Manders (BER) 61 60; Brent Ching (TRI) d. Jenson Bascombe (BER) 62 64; Brent Ching/Troy Stone (TRI) d. James Collieson/Romar Douglas (BER) 63 60.

● **Final Positions:** 1. Trinidad & Tobago, 2. Costa Rica, 3. Barbados, 4. Bermuda , 5. US Virgin Islands.

Costa Rica and Trinidad & Tobago promoted to Americas Zone Group III in 2006.

Asia/Oceania Zone Group IV

Date: 27 April-1 May
Venue: Yangon, Myanmar
Surface: Hard (O)
Group A: Bangladesh, Kyrgyzstan, Syria, Turkmenistan, United Arab Emirates
Group B: Iraq, Jordan, Myanmar, Oman, Singapore

● **Group A 27 April United Arab Emirates defeated Turkmenistan 3-0:** Mohamed Abdel-Aziz Al Nuaimi (UAE) d. Stanislav Naydyonov (TKM) 61 64; Omar Bahrouzyan (UAE) d. Myalikkuli Mamedkuliyev (TKM) 60 61; Mahmoud-Nader Al Balushi/Omar Bahrouzyan (UAE) d. Dovran Chagylov/Myalikkuli Mamedkuliyev (TKM) 75 64. **Bangladesh defeated Syria 2-1:** Lays Salim (SYR) d. Shibu Lal (BAN) 62 46 75; Sree-Amol Roy (BAN) d. Abrahim Ibrahim (SYR) 61 62; Shibu Lal/Sree-Amol Roy (BAN) d. Lays Salim/Yashar Sheet (SYR) 62 76(4).

● **28 April United Arab Emirates defeated Kyrgyzstan 2-1:** Mahmoud-Nader Al Balushi (UAE) d. Ruslan Eshmuhamedov (KGZ) 64 63; Omar Bahrouzyan (UAE) d. Sergey Ni (KGZ) 76(3) 60; Boris Baichorov/Anton Litvinov (KGZ) d. Ghanem Al Hassani/Mohamed Abdel-Aziz Al Nuaimi (UAE) 60 62. **Syria defeated Turkmenistan 3-0:** Lays Salim (SYR) d. Stanislav Naydyonov (TKM) 63 61; Abrahim Ibrahim (SYR) d. Myalikkuli Mamedkuliyev (TKM) 62 62; Lays Salim/Yashar Sheet (SYR) d. Dovran Chagylov/Myalikkuli Mamedkuliyev (TKM) 62 62.

● **29 April Bangladesh defeated United Arab Emirates 2-1:** Shibu Lal (BAN) d. Mahmoud-Nader Al Balushi (UAE) 36 65 ret.; Sree-Amol Roy (BAN) d. Omar Bahrouzyan (UAE) 61 64; Mohamed Abdel-Aziz Al Nuaimi/Omar Bahrouzyan (UAE) d. Shibu Lal/Sree-Amol Roy (BAN) 63 26 63. **Kyrgyzstan defeated Turkmenistan 3-0:** Boris Baichorov (KGZ) d. Dovran Chagylov (TKM) 62 63; Sergey Ni (KGZ) d. Myalikkuli Mamedkuliyev (TKM) 75 60; Ruslan Eshmuhamedov/Anton Litvinov (KGZ) d. Dovran Chagylov/Myalikkuli Mamedkuliyev (TKM) 75 61.

● **30 April Syria defeated Kyrgyzstan 3-0:** Lays Salim (SYR) d. Boris Baichorov (KGZ) 36 61 61; Abrahim Ibrahim (SYR) d. Sergey Ni (KGZ) 64 75; Hayan Maarouf/Yashar Sheet (SYR) d. Boris Baichorov/Anton Litvinov (KGZ) 76(4) 76(3). **Bangladesh defeated Turkmenistan 2-1:** Shibu Lal (BAN) d. Stanislav Naydyonov (TKM) 61 60; Sree-Amol Roy (BAN) d. Myalikkuli Mamedkuliyev (TKM) 61 62; Dovran Chagylov/Myalikkuli Mamedkuliyev (TKM) d. Alamgir Hossain/Dipu Lal (BAN) 57 63 64.

- **1 May United Arab Emirates defeated Syria 2-1:** Mohamed Abdel-Aziz Al Nuaimi (UAE) d. Lays Salim (SYR) 75 67(7) 63; Omar Bahrouzyan (UAE) d. Abrahim Ibrahim (SYR) 61 62; Hayan Maarouf/Yashar Sheet (SYR) d. Mohamed Abdel-Aziz Al Nuaimi/Omar Bahrouzyan (UAE) 36 63 62. **Bangladesh defeated Kyrgyzstan 3-0:** Shibu Lal (BAN) d. Anton Litvinov (KGZ) 63 64; Sree-Amol Roy (BAN) d. Sergey Ni (KGZ) 61 63; Alamgir Hossain/Shibu Lal (BAN) d. Anton Litvinov/Sergey Ni (KGZ) 63 67(5) 64.

- **Final Positions:** 1. Bangladesh, 2. United Arab Emirates, 3. Syria, 4. Kyrgyzstan, 5. Turkmenistan.

Bangladesh promoted to Asia/Oceania Zone Group III in 2006.

- **Group B 27 April Oman defeated Myanmar 3-0:** Mohammed Al Nabhani (OMA) d. Zaw-Zaw Latt (MYA) 67(4) 42 ret.; Khalid Al Nabhani (OMA) d. Mg Tu Maw (MYA) 67(5) 75 60; Khalid Al Nabhani/Mohammed Al Nabhani (OMA) d. Min Min/Hla Win Naing (MYA) 75 62. **Singapore defeated Iraq 3-0:** Kok-Huen Kam (SIN) d. Akram Al Karem (IRQ) 63 62; Stanley Armando (SIN) d. Nasir Hatam (IRQ) 61 36 62; Daniel Dewandaka/Ming-Chye Lim (SIN) d. Akram Al Karem/Hussain Rasheed (IRQ) 61 62.

- **28 April Oman defeated Jordan 3-0:** Mohammed Al Nabhani (OMA) d. Ahmad Al Hadid (JOR) 62 62; Khalid Al Nabhani (OMA) d. Tareq Talal Shkakwa (JOR) 62 63; Khalid Al Nabhani/Mohammed Al Nabhani (OMA) d. Mohammed Al Hadid/Ahmad Tbayshat (JOR) 62 62. **Singapore defeated Myanmar 3-0:** Kok-Huen Kam (SIN) d. Min Min (MYA) 75 64; Stanley Armando (SIN) d. Mg Tu Maw (MYA) 75 75; Daniel Dewandaka/Ming-Chye Lim (SIN) d. Zaw-Zaw Latt/Mg Tu Maw (MYA) 46 62 64.

- **29 April Oman defeated Iraq 3-0:** Mohammed Al Nabhani (OMA) d. Akram Al Karem (IRQ) 75 63; Khalid Al Nabhani (OMA) d. Nasir Hatam (IRQ) 62 76(8); Khalid Al Nabhani/Mohammed Al Nabhani (OMA) d. Akram Al Karem/Hussain Rasheed (IRQ) 63 63. **Myanmar defeated Jordan 3-0:** Zaw-Zaw Latt (MYA) d. Ahmad Al Hadid (JOR) 76(2) 60; Mg Tu Maw (MYA) d. Tareq Talal Shkakwa (JOR) 63 75; Min Min/Hla Win Naing (MYA) d. Mohammed Al Hadid/Ahmad Tbayshat (JOR) 62 46 63.

- **30 April Singapore defeated Jordan 2-1:** Ahmad Al Hadid (JOR) d. Kok-Huen Kam (SIN) 64 76(5); Stanley Armando (SIN) d. Tareq Talal Shkakwa (JOR) 63 62; Daniel Dewandaka/Ming-Chye Lim (SIN) d. Ahmad Al Hadid/Tareq Talal Shkakwa (JOR) 60 61. **Myanmar defeated Iraq 3-0:** Zaw-Zaw Latt (MYA) d. Hussain Rasheed (IRQ) 61 60; Mg Tu Maw (MYA) d. Nasir Hatam (IRQ) 62 63; Min Min/Hla Win Naing (MYA) d. Nasir Hatam/Hussain Rasheed (IRQ) 63 76(6).

- **1 May Singapore defeated Oman 2-1:** Daniel Dewandaka (SIN) d. Mohammed Al Nabhani (OMA) 64 64; Khalid Al Nabhani (OMA) d. Stanley Armando (SIN) 75 63; Stanley Armando/Daniel Dewandaka (SIN) d. Khalid Al Nabhani/Mohammed Al Nabhani (OMA) 62 26 75. **Jordan defeated Iraq 3-0:** Ahmad Al Hadid (JOR) d. Akram AL Karem (IRQ) 63 62; Tareq Talal Shkakwa (JOR) d. Nasir Hatam (IRQ) 63 61; Mohammed Al Hadid/Ahmad Tbayshat (JOR) d. Hussain A Rasheed/Mohammed Salman (IRQ) 61 67(3) 62.

- **Final Positions:** 1. Singapore, 2. Oman, 3. Myanmar, 4. Jordan, 5. Iraq.

Singapore promoted to Asia/Oceania Zone Group III in 2006.

russians rule at roland garros

by sandra harwitt

Amelie Mauresmo and Mary Pierce (FRA)

When it comes to the Fed Cup competition over the past couple of years, it seems clear that this is the time for the reign of the Russians.

The first signs of a Russian dynasty in the heralded international team event for women came in November 2004 – the 42nd year of the Fed Cup competition – when a spirited Russian team delivered a first Fed Cup title to their country in a narrow 3-2 victory over France in Moscow.

In September 2005, a Russian squad led by Anastasia Myskina and Elena Dementieva showed that their focus was dedicated to successfully defending their Fed Cup title, not only against a weightier French team than the year before with both Amelie Mauresmo and Mary Pierce playing in the final, but in front of an extremely partisan Parisien crowd packed into Court Philippe Chartrier at Roland Garros.

Often demure, Dementieva approached the Fed Cup weekends all year long with the goal being to retain the title, saying at the beginning of the year that "I think we have a very strong team and we have a good chance again this year. We had to wait a long time to win it and maybe we can win it again."

In the end, Dementieva, who was not part of the Russian's 2004 winning campaign, was the queen of the court during the final, winning both of her singles matches as well as the doubles in the best-of-five match final. On the opening day of action, Dementieva beat Pierce 76 (1) 26 61 and then on the second day she brought in a 64 46 62 victory over Mauresmo.

Dementieva, who insisted that she was not to be seen as the standout in reeling in the second straight Russian Fed Cup title, could not contain her joy at finally being a part of a winning team after also playing in the Fed Cup final against the United States in 1999 and Belgium in 2001.

"I've been waiting so long for this. I'm so happy," Dementieva said, adding, "It's not a Dementieva victory. We win as a team and lose as a team. I am not the heroine, the team won, not any individual.

"I've been waiting so long for this. I'm so happy," Dementieva said, adding, "It's not a Dementieva victory. We win as a team and lose as a team. I am not the heroine, the team won, not any individual.

"For me personally, it will remain as a great memory. I'd been waiting for a moment like this for years."

Despite Dementieva's protestations, her opponents were not shy about admitting that their fate was in the Russian's hands during the weekend.

"She carried the team this weekend," Mauresmo said after all was determined. "She was so solid. It's hard to analyze straight after a defeat but I think one of the reasons [they won] is Dementieva."

"I knew she was a great athlete," said French Captain Georges Goven. "But this time she was exceptional, gave everything she had and fought until the end."

Surprisingly, Myskina, who has always been the driving force for Russia in Fed Cup, had difficulty enforcing her will in the final. After Dementieva provided a 1-0 lead on the opening day courtesy of the win over Pierce, Myskina fell 64 62 to Mauresmo to level the competition at 1-1.

On the second day of action, Dementieva put Myskina in position to bring in the victory with a win over Mauresmo for a 2-1

Elena Dementieva (RUS)

Russian lead. But the volatile Myskina, who argued with Russian Captain Shamil Tarpischev during the match, made far too many unforced errors to be able to hold her own against Pierce, surrendering a first-set lead to lose 46 64 62.

That left the outcome of the final to the final match of the weekend.

Stepping up for doubles duty, Dementieva partnered Dinara Safina, sister of two-time Grand Slam champion Marat Safin, to deliver a 64 16 63 win over Mauresmo and Pierce to keep the Fed Cup a Russian possession for another year. But the doubles was hardly a triumph for either team with seven breaks of serve in the first set and Pierce accidentally hitting Safina in the thigh with a shot in the second set.

One exciting outgrowth of this year's Fed Cup final was that a slice of history was carved out when the final was played in front of a crowd of 15,000 fans at Roland Garros.

"I didn't try and hit her on purpose," Pierce said. "Sometimes that happens in tennis, but it was not my goal."

A gracious Dementieva insisted upon sharing credit for the successful Fed Cup defense with Myskina. Although Myskina did not shine in the final, her role in the first two ties of the year, most especially when she scored a big win over Venus Williams in the opening match of the semifinal against USA was an integral factor in the Russian victory.

"Although Anastasia lost today, if she hadn't beaten Venus Williams in the semifinal we may not have been here," said Dementieva, defending Myskina's vital role in the Russian victory.

When the final was finished, the four main stars of the weekend had once again shown themselves to be loyal participants in the Fed Cup cause. And as they head into 2006, Dementieva holds a 19-7 winning record in Fed Cup, Myskina stands at 18-6, while Mauresmo is now at 25-7 and Pierce is at 18-14.

One exciting outgrowth of this year's Fed Cup final was that a slice of history was carved out when the final was played in front of a crowd of 15,000 fans at Roland Garros. Prior to this final, Fed Cup could be viewed as the smaller sibling of it's male-oriented Davis Cup counterpart, but with fans filling the Roland Garros main stadium, the women have finally come into their own.

The 2005 Fed Cup year started with the announcement of the draw at the end of last year and it didn't take long for a potential semifinal clash between Russia and USA to come into focus. But before that encounter took take place, the preliminaries of playing the first round were a necessity.

On paper, the American first-round outing against Belgium could have been a tough battle if the Belgians arrived in Delray Beach with Justine Henin-Hardenne and Kim Clijsters in tow. Unfortunately for the Belgians, however, neither Henin-Hardenne nor Clijsters felt sufficiently physically capable of committing to Fed Cup having just recently returned to action after sitting out most of 2004.

Playing an unheralded Belgian squad with veteran Els Callens leading the team, the US squad of Lindsay Davenport, Venus Williams, and Corina Morariu, with Serena Williams on the sidelines because of injury, lived up to Captain Zina Garrison's "Dreamettes" billing by capturing an unblemished 5-0 win.

The Russians as well as the French also had easy passage to the semifinals – the Russians defeated Italy 4-1 and the French defeated Austria 4-1. The only closely contested first round was the 3-2 win by Spain over Argentina.

When fate delivered the Russia-USA semifinal tie, the pool of talent anticipated for the semifinal made this seem like a dream tie to behold. The Russians were secure at home with the likes of Myskina and Dementieva on board and the American's were expected to field a team that boasted Davenport, the Williams sisters and Morariu. But injuries ended up keeping two of the American's away – Davenport pulled a lower back muscle while losing the Wimbledon final to Venus Williams the week before, and Serena Williams was still wincing from ankle and knee problems.

So as it turned out, the "Dreamettes" were not in full force for the semifinals, leaving the job of putting USA into the final to Venus Williams. Sharing that responsibility with Williams was Morariu, a doubles specialist, and the untested Mashona Washington and Jill Craybas.

Unfortunately, the responsibility weighed too heavily on a fatigued Williams who lost 57 64 62 to Myskina in the opening match of the semifinal. That sent the

French fans

Anastasia Myskina (RUS)

American squad in a downward spiral that they could never recover from and straight out of the 2005 competition.

For Williams, the disappointed was evident: "Obviously, I was trying to give the win to USA but she was playing too well. I tried my best today. It was just a tough day."

For Myskina, who not only was playing in front of her family, most notably her mother who was battling a serious illness, but also former Russian President Boris Yeltsin, it was a victory of special importance: "It's awesome. When you're playing at home, and you win at home, and you're playing against that kind of a great player, it's unbelievable," said the Russian.

The opening day of the semifinal concluded with Dementieva beating Washington 75 64 but on the final day, she lost to Williams in the reverse singles match 61 62. It was left to Myskina to secure the semifinal in a quick 62 64 win over Craybas and then Vera Douchevina and Safina finished off the outing in style by beating Morariu and Williams 61 75 in the doubles.

For Myskina, the 2004 Roland Garros champion and the guiding force of her squad in the semifinals, delivering Russia to a second Fed Cup final was a gift to be savoured.

"I love to play team competitions," Myskina said. "I miss it since we only play it two or three times a year and for me, it's not enough. I'm always really happy when I'm back on the team. For me, team spirit is really important."

On the other side of the draw, France was busy securing their third consecutive trip to the Fed Cup final against Spain with a 3-1 victory – rain forced the abandonment of the doubles match early in the first set.

In the semifinal, Mauresmo started the outing against Spain with a 64 63 win over Anabel Medina Garrigues and Pierce ended the opening day in style with a 64 64 victory over Nuria Llagostera Vives. When Mauresmo secured an insurmountable 3-0 lead with a 63 61 win over Llagostera Vives in the first reverse singles match on the final day, the French team replaced Pierce with Severine Beltrame, who fell 64 64 to Arantxa Parra-Santonja.

The winner of the Fed Cup in 1997 and 2003, France was hoping for revenge in the final for their 3-2 loss the previous year to the Russians. They were heavily relying on the principle that a home-court advantage in a Fed Cup final for the first time ever would be a good luck charm.

"It's a great reward," said Mauresmo, looking ahead to hosting the final against Russia. "We were all dreaming about it. We have been very consistent at the highest possible level these last few years, and here it is, we are in the final for the third consecutive year.

"This proves that France is a great tennis nation. We all invested a lot in this competition. I just hope it's going to be a fantastic event."

France certainly might be a great tennis nation, but as far as Fed Cup is concerned, the message from Russia seems loud and clear – they're the dynasty in charge and the team to beat these days.

"I love to play team competitions," Myskina said. "I miss it since we only play it two or three times a year and for me, it's not enough. I'm always really happy when I'm back on the team."

And now that Russia has become the first country to win back-to-back Fed Cup trophies since USA performed the feat in 1999-2000, they have an even mightier goal ahead for 2006. If the two-time defending champions can retain the Fed Cup title in 2006, the Russians will become the first nation to win the international competition three consecutive times since Spain did the deed from 1993 to 1995.

2005 Fed Cup Results

World Group I

First Round 23-24 April

Russia defeated Italy 4-1, Brindisi, ITA, Clay (O): Francesca Schiavone (ITA) d. Dinara Safina (RUS) 75 63; Elena Dementieva (RUS) d. Tathiana Garbin (ITA) 64 63; Elena Dementieva (RUS) d. Francesca Schiavone (ITA) 46 76(2) 60; Elena Bovina (RUS) d. Maria-Elena Camerin (ITA) 63 36 62; Vera Douchevina/Dinara Safina (RUS) d. Tathiana Garbin/Mara Santangelo (ITA) 63 75. **USA defeated Belgium 5-0, Delray Beach, FL, USA, Hard (O):** Lindsay Davenport (USA) d. Eveline Vanhyfte (BEL) 60 62; Venus Williams (USA) d. Els Callens (BEL) 62 62; Lindsay Davenport (USA) d. Els Callens (BEL) 64 60; Venus Williams (USA) d. Leslie Butkiewicz (BEL) 61 64; Lindsay Davenport/Corina Morariu (USA) d. Kirsten Flipkens/Eveline Vanhyfte (BEL) 61 62. **Spain defeated Argentina 3-2, Jerez, ESP, Clay (O):** Nuria Llagostera Vives (ESP) d. Gisela Dulko (ARG) 64 46 63; Anabel Medina Garrigues (ESP) d. Maria-Emilia Salerni (ARG) 64 46 63; Gisela Dulko (ARG) d. Marta Marrero (ESP) 60 63; Mariana Diaz-Oliva (ARG) d. Nuria Llagostera Vives (ESP) 76(6) 64; Nuria Llagostera Vives/Anabel Medina Garrigues (ESP) d. Gisela Dulko/Maria-Emilia Salerni (ARG) 64 64. **France defeated Austria 4-1, Portschach, AUT, Clay (O):** Yvonne Meusburger (AUT) d. Nathalie Dechy (FRA) 76(3) 62; Virginie Razzano (FRA) d. Tamira Paszek (AUT) 63 63; Virginie Razzano (FRA) d. Yvonne Meusburger (AUT) 63 76(2); Nathalie Dechy (FRA) d. Tamira Paszek (AUT) 76(5) 62; Nathalie Dechy/Virginie Razzano (FRA) d. Daniela Klemenschits/Sandra Klemenschits (AUT) 64 75.

Semifinals 9-10 July

Russia defeated USA 4-1, Moscow, RUS, Clay (I): Anastasia Myskina (RUS) d. Venus Williams (USA) 57 64 62; Elena Dementieva (RUS) d. Mashona Washington (USA) 75 64; Venus Williams (USA) d. Elena Dementieva (RUS) 61 62; Anastasia Myskina (RUS) d. Jill Craybas (USA) 62 64; Vera Douchevina/Dinara Safina (RUS) d. Corina Morariu/Venus Williams (USA) 61 75. **France defeated Spain 3-1, Aix en Provence, FRA, Hard (O):** Amelie Mauresmo (FRA) d. Anabel Medina Garrigues (ESP) 64 63; Mary Pierce (FRA) d. Nuria Llagostera Vives (ESP) 64 64; Amelie Mauresmo (FRA) d. Nuria Llagostera Vives (ESP) 63 61; Arantxa Parra-Santonja (ESP) d. Severine Beltrame (FRA) 64 64; Amelie Mauresmo/Mary Pierce (FRA) v. Anabel Medina Garrigues/Maria Sanchez Lorenzo (ESP) 1-2 play abandoned due to rain.

Final 17-18 September

Russia defeated France 3-2, Paris, FRA, Clay (O): Elena Dementieva (RUS) d. Mary Pierce (FRA) 76(1) 26 61; Amelie Mauresmo (FRA) d. Anastasia Myskina (RUS) 64 62; Elena Dementieva (RUS) d. Amelie Mauresmo (FRA) 64 46 62; Mary Pierce (FRA) d. Anastasia Myskina (RUS) 46 64 62; Elena Dementieva/Dinara Safina (RUS) d. Amelie Mauresmo/Mary Pierce (FRA) 64 16 63.

World Group I Play-offs 9-10 July

Austria defeated Switzerland 4-1, Lausanne, SUI, Clay (O): Yvonne Meusburger (AUT) d. Stefanie Vogele (SUI) 76(4) 61; Tamira Paszek (AUT) d. Timea Bacsinszky (SUI) 63 63; Timea Bacsinszky (SUI) d. Yvonne Meusburger (AUT) 63 64; Tamira Paszek (AUT) d. Myriam Casanova (SUI) 61 63; Daniela Klemenschits/Sandra Klemenschits (AUT) d. Stefanie Vogele/Gaelle Widmer (SUI) 60 62. **Belgium defeated Argentina 3-2, Bree, BEL, Hard (O):** Kim Clijsters (BEL) d. Mariana Diaz-Oliva (ARG) 61 62; Gisela Dulko (ARG) d. Els Callens (BEL) 61 63; Kim Clijsters (BEL) d. Gisela Dulko (ARG) 64 61; Mariana Diaz-Oliva (ARG) d. Kirsten Flipkens (BEL) 62 62; Els Callens/Kim Clijsters (BEL) d. Mariana Diaz-Oliva/Gisela Dulko (ARG) 64 36 75. **Germany defeated Croatia 4-1, Bol, CRO, Clay (O):** Karolina Sprem (CRO) d. Julia Schruff (GER) 63 64; Anna-Lena Groenefeld (GER) d. Jelena Kostanic (CRO) 61 76(5); Anna-Lena Groenefeld (GER) d. Karolina Sprem (CRO) 63 67(5) 62; Sandra Kloesel (GER) d. Jelena Kostanic (CRO) 62 64; Anna-Lena Groenefeld/Julia Schruff (GER) d. Sanda Mamic/Nika Ozegovic (CRO) 46 63 63. **Italy defeated Czech Republic 3-2, Liberec, CZE, Carpet (I):** Francesca Schiavone (ITA) d. Kveta Peschke (CZE) 64 75; Nicole Vaidisova (CZE) d. Roberta Vinci (ITA) 63 64; Nicole Vaidisova (CZE) d. Francesca Schiavone (ITA) 62 75; Flavia Pennetta (ITA) d. Kveta Peschke (CZE) 64 46 62; Francesca Schiavone/Roberta Vinci (ITA) d. Kveta Peschke/Nicole Vaidisova (CZE) 64 64.

World Group II

First Round 23-24 April

Switzerland defeated Slovak Republic 3-2, Neuchatel, SUI, Hard (I): Timea Bacsinszky (SUI) d. Martina Sucha (SVK) 64 63; Lubomira Kurhajcova (SVK) d. Myriam Casanova (SUI) 60 60; Martina Sucha (SVK) d. Myriam Casanova (SUI) 60 76(5); Timea Bacsinszky (SUI) d. Lubomira Kurhajcova (SVK) 36 64 63; Timea Bacsinszky/Myriam Casanova (SUI) d. Eva Fislova/Stanislava Hrozenska (SVK) 63 62. **Germany defeated Indonesia 4-1, Essen, GER, Clay (O):** Anna-Lena Groenefeld (GER) d. Ayu-Fani Damayanti (INA) 63 61; Julia Schruff (GER) d. Wynne Prakusya (INA) 61 60; Anna-Lena Groenefeld (GER) d. Wynne Prakusya (INA) 60 62; Anca Barna (GER) d. Romana Tedjakusuma (INA) 64 63; Wynne Prakusya/Romana Tedjakusuma (INA) d. Sandra Kloesel/Julia Schruff (GER) 76(5) 64. **Croatia defeated Thailand 3-2, Phuket, THA, Hard (O):** Tamarine Tanasugarn (THA) d. Sanda Mamic (CRO) 75 61; Jelena Kostanic (CRO) d. Suchanun

Viratprasert (THA) 75 46 63; Jelena Kostanic (CRO) d. Tamarine Tanasugarn (THA) 63 62; Suchanun Viratprasert (THA) d. Sanda Mamic (CRO) 63 76(1); Jelena Kostanic/Matea Mezak (CRO) d. Tamarine Tanasugarn/Napaporn Tongsalee (THA) 64 62. **Czech Republic defeated Japan 3-2, Prague, CZE, Clay (O):** Akiko Morigami (JPN) d. Iveta Benesova (CZE) 63 76(7); Nicole Vaidisova (CZE) d. Aiko Nakamura (JPN) 63 61; Akiko Morigami (JPN) d. Nicole Vaidisova (CZE) 63 62; Kveta Peschke (CZE) d. Rika Fujiwara (JPN) 60 63; Iveta Benesova/Kveta Peschke (CZE) d. Akiko Morigami/Saori Obata (JPN) 46 63 60.

Croatia, Czech Republic, Germany and Switzerland advance to World Group I Play-offs on 9-10 July 2005.

World Group II Play-offs 9-10 July

Indonesia defeated Puerto Rico 4-1, Salinas, PUR, Hard (O): Kristina Brandi (PUR) d. Romana Tedjakusuma (INA) 64 63; Wynne Prakusya (INA) d. Vilmarie Castellvi (PUR) 63 64; Wynne Prakusya (INA) d. Kristina Brandi (PUR) 64 62; Romana Tedjakusuma (INA) d. Vilmarie Castellvi (PUR) 62 62; Ayu-Fani Damayanti/Wynne Prakusya (INA) d. Vilmarie Castellvi/Jessica Roland (PUR) 62 60. **Japan defeated Bulgaria 4-1, Tokyo, JPN, Hard (I):** Akiko Morigami (JPN) d. Sesil Karatantcheva (BUL) 26 76(4) 60; Magdalena Maleeva (BUL) d. Aiko Nakamura (JPN) 36 64 63; Akiko Morigami (JPN) d. Magdalena Maleeva (BUL) 76(3) 63; Aiko Nakamura (JPN) d. Sesil Karatantcheva (BUL) 64 76(2); Rika Fujiwara/Akiko Morigami (JPN) d. Tszvetana Pironkova/Maria Penkova (BUL) 61 62. **Thailand defeated Slovak Republic 4-1, Pathum Thani, THA, Hard (O):** Suchanun Viratprasert (THA) d. Dominika Cibulkova (SVK) 64 64; Lubomira Kurhajcova (SVK) d. Tamarine Tanasugarn (THA) 26 64 60; Tamarine Tanasugarn (THA) d. Magdalena Rybarikova (SVK) 61 62; Suchanun Viratprasert (THA) d. Lubomira Kurhajcova (SVK) 64 62; Montinee Tangphong/Napaporn Tongsalee (THA) d. Dominika Cibulkova/Magdalena Rybarikova (SVK) 36 61 75. **China, P.R. defeated Slovenia 4-1, Beijing, CHN, Hard (I):** Katarina Srebotnik (SLO) d. Jie Zheng (CHN) 76(5) 36 63; Na Li (CHN) d. Andreja Klepac (SLO) 61 63; Na Li (CHN) d. Katarina Srebotnik (SLO) 61 62; Jie Zheng (CHN) d. Andreja Klepac (SLO) 63 61; Ting Li/Tian-Tian Sun (CHN) d. Tina Krizan/Sandra Volk (SLO) 62 60.

Americas Zone Group I

Date: 20-23 April
Venue: Montevideo, Uruguay
Surface: Clay (O)
Group A: Bolivia, Mexico, Puerto Rico, Uruguay.
Group B: Brazil, Canada, Cuba, Paraguay.

- **Group A 20 April Puerto Rico defeated Uruguay 3-0:** Vilmarie Castellvi (PUR) d. Estefania Craciun (URU) 60 76(4); Kristina Brandi (PUR) d. Ana-Lucia Migliarini De Leon (URU) 63 63; Kristina Brandi/Vilmarie Castellvi (PUR) d. Ana-Lucia Migliarini De Leon/Maria-Eugenia Roca (URU) 75 64. **Mexico defeated Bolivia 2-1:** Marcela Arroyo-Vergara (MEX) d. Maria-Irene Squillaci-Sandoval (BOL) 62 76(3); Melissa Torres-Sandoval (MEX) d. Maria-Fernanda Alvarez (BOL) 62 57 61; Maria-Fernanda Alvarez/Maria-Irene Squillaci-Sandoval (BOL) d. Erika Clarke-Magana/Daniela Munoz-Gallegos (MEX) 64 36 75.

- **21 April Puerto Rico defeated Mexico 2-1:** Vilmarie Castellvi (PUR) d. Daniela Munoz-Gallegos (MEX) 62 63; Kristina Brandi (PUR) d. Melissa Torres-Sandoval (MEX) 60 62; Marcela Arroyo-Vergara/Melissa Torres-Sandoval (MEX) d. Kristina Brandi/Vilmarie Castellvi (PUR) 76(5) 64. **Uruguay defeated Bolivia 2-1:** Estefania Craciun (URU) d. Maria-Irene Squillaci-Sandoval (BOL) 61 63; Maria-Fernanda Alvarez (BOL) d. Ana-Lucia Migliarini De Leon (URU) 62 75; Estefania Craciun/Ana-Lucia Migliarini De Leon (URU) d. Maria-Fernanda Alvarez/Maria-Irene Squillaci-Sandoval (BOL) 64 64.

- **22 April Puerto Rico defeated Bolivia 3-0:** Vilmarie Castellvi (PUR) d. Celina Grissi (BOL) 60 62; Kristina Brandi (PUR) d. Maria-Fernanda Alvarez (BOL) 60 36 64; Vilmarie Castellvi/Jessica Roland (PUR) d. Celina Grissi/Maria-Irene Squillaci-Sandoval (BOL) 62 62. **Uruguay defeated Mexico 2-1:** Maria-Eugenia Roca (URU) d. Marcela Arroyo-Vergara (MEX) 64 75; Melissa Torres-Sandoval (MEX) d. Estefania Craciun (URU) 36 62 75; Estefania Craciun/Ana-Lucia Migliarini De Leon (URU) d. Marcela Arroyo-Vergara/Melissa Torres-Sandoval (MEX) 46 61 64.

- **Final Positions:** 1. Puerto Rico, 2. Uruguay, 3. Mexico, 4. Bolivia.

- **Group B 20 April Canada defeated Cuba 3-0:** Aleksandra Wozniak (CAN) d. Yanet Nunez-Mojarena (CUB) 63 62; Marie-Eve Pelletier (CAN) d. Yamile Fors-Guerra (CUB) 62 46 75; Stephanie Dubois/Aleksandra Wozniak (CAN) d. Lumais Diaz-Hernandez/Yanet Nunez-Mojarena (CUB) 63 64. **Brazil defeated Paraguay 3-0:** Larissa Carvalho (BRA) d. Amanda Melgarejo (PAR) 60 60; Jenifer Widjaja (BRA) d. Madelaine Madelaire (PAR) 61 61; Maria-Fernanda Alves/Joana Cortez (BRA) d. Paola Doldan/Sarah Tami-Masi (PAR) 60 63.

2005 Fed Cup Results (continued)

- **21 April Canada defeated Brazil 3-0:** Aleksandra Wozniak (CAN) d. Larissa Carvalho (BRA) 36 61 60; Marie-Eve Pelletier (CAN) d. Maria-Fernanda Alves (BRA) 06 64 75; Stephanie Dubois/Aleksandra Wozniak (CAN) d. Joana Cortez/Jenifer Widjaja (BRA) 61 61. **Cuba defeated Paraguay 3-0**: Yanet Nunez-Mojarena (CUB) d. Paola Doldan (PAR) 61 63; Yamile Fors-Guerra (CUB) d. Sarah Tami-Masi (PAR) 76(4) 62; Yamile Fors-Guerra/Yanet Nunez-Mojarena (CUB) d. Paola Doldan/Amanda Melgarejo (PAR) 64 60.

- **22 April Canada defeated Paraguay 3-0:** Sharon Fichman (CAN) d. Madelaine Madelaire (PAR) 61 62; Stephanie Dubois (CAN) d. Paola Doldan (PAR) 60 62; Stephanie Dubois/Aleksandra Wozniak (CAN) d. Amanda Melgarejo/Sarah Tami-Masi (PAR) 64 62. **Brazil defeated Cuba 3-0:** Larissa Carvalho (BRA) d. Yanet Nunez-Mojarena (CUB) 62 61; Jenifer Widjaja (BRA) d. Yamile Fors-Guerra (CUB) 62 62; Maria-Fernanda Alves/Joana Cortez (BRA) d. Yamile Fors-Guerra/Yanet Nunez-Mojarena (CUB) 64 63.

- **Final Positions:** 1. Canada, 2. Brazil, 3. Cuba, 4. Paraguay.

- **Promotion Play-off 23 April Puerto Rico defeated Canada 2-0:** Vilmarie Castellvi (PUR) d. Aleksandra Wozniak (CAN) 75 46 119; Kristina Brandi (PUR) d. Marie-Eve Pelletier (CAN) 64 36 86; Doubles not played.

- **Play-off for 3rd-4th Positions 23 April Brazil defeated Uruguay 3-0:** Larissa Carvalho (BRA) d. Estefania Craciun (URU) 60 61; Jenifer Widjaja (BRA) d. Ana-Lucia Migliarini De Leon (URU) 57 62 60; Maria-Fernanda Alves/Joana Cortez (BRA) d. Camila Belassi/Maria-Eugenia Roca (URU) 63 61.

- **Relegation Play-off 23 April Mexico defeated Paraguay 3-0:** Daniela Munoz-Gallegos (MEX) d. Madelaine Madelaire (PAR) 26 61 60; Melissa Torres-Sandoval (MEX) d. Sarah Tami-Masi (PAR) 36 62 63; Marcela Arroyo-Vergara/Erika Clarke-Magana (MEX) d. Amanda Melgarejo/Sarah Tami-Masi (PAR) 06 61 60. **Cuba defeated Bolivia 2-1:** Yanet Nunez-Mojarena (CUB) d. Maria-Irene Squillaci-Sandoval (BOL) 60 62; Maria-Fernanda Alvarez (BOL) d. Yamile Fors-Guerra (CUB) 26 64 64; Yamile Fors-Guerra/Yanet Nunez-Mojarena (CUB) d. Maria-Fernanda Alvarez/Maria-Irene Squillaci-Sandoval (BOL) 64 64.

- Puerto Rico advances to 2005 World Group II Play-offs on 9-10 July 2005.
  Bolivia and Paraguay relegated to Americas Zone Group II in 2006.

Asia/Oceania Zone Group I

Date: 20-23 April
Venue: New Delhi, India
Surface: Hard (O)
Group A: China, P.R., India, Kazakhstan, Singapore.
Group B: Australia, Chinese Taipei, Korea, Rep., New Zealand.

- **Group A 20 April China, P.R. defeated Kazakhstan 3-0:** Jie Zheng (CHN) d. Tatiana Ignatchenko (KAZ) 62 62; Na Li (CHN) d. Mariya Kovaleva (KAZ) 60 61; Ting Li/Tian-Tian Sun (CHN) d. Mariya Kovaleva/Yekaterina Morozova (KAZ) 61 62. **India defeated Singapore 3-0:** Ankita Bhambri (IND) d. Wei-Ping Lee (SIN) 61 75; Shikha Uberoi (IND) d. Yun-Ling Ng (SIN) 60 60; Rushmi Chakravarthi/Shikha Uberoi (IND) d. Yun-Ling Ng/Shao-Fang Ong (SIN) 61 61.

- **21 April China, P.R. defeated Singapore 3-0:** Jie Zheng (CHN) d. Wei-Ping Lee (SIN) 61 61; Na Li (CHN) d. Shao-Fang Ong (SIN) 60 60; Ting Li/Tian-Tian Sun (CHN) d. Wei-Ping Lee/Yun-Ling Ng (SIN) 60 61. **India defeated Kazakhstan 3-0:** Rushmi Chakravarthi (IND) d. Yekaterina Morozova (KAZ) 60 61; Shikha Uberoi (IND) d. Mariya Kovaleva (KAZ) 60 64; Ankita Bhambri/Shikha Uberoi (IND) d. Mariya Kovaleva/Yekaterina Morozova (KAZ) 64 64.

- **22 April China, P.R. defeated India 3-0:** Jie Zheng (CHN) d. Rushmi Chakravarthi (IND) 63 60; Na Li (CHN) d. Shikha Uberoi (IND) 61 62; Ting Li/Tian-Tian Sun (CHN) d. Ankita Bhambri/Rushmi Chakravarthi (IND) 62 63. **Kazakhstan defeated Singapore 2-1:** Wei-Ping Lee (SIN) d. Tatiana Ignatchenko (KAZ) 26 63 64; Mariya Kovaleva (KAZ) d. Shao-Fang Ong (SIN) 62 64; Mariya Kovaleva/Yekaterina Morozova (KAZ) d. Wei-Ping Lee/Yun-Ling Ng (SIN) 62 60.

- **Final Positions:** 1. China, P.R., 2. India, 3. Kazakhstan, 4. Singapore.

- **Group B 20 April Australia defeated New Zealand 3-0:** Evie Dominikovic (AUS) d. Leanne Baker (NZL) 62 63; Samantha Stosur (AUS) d. Marina Erakovic (NZL) 64 64; Evie Dominikovic/Bryanne Stewart (AUS) d. Leanne Baker/Paula Marama (NZL) 67(7) 61 64.

Korea, Rep. defeated Chinese Taipei 3-0: Ye-Ra Lee (KOR) d. Ting-Wen Wang (TPE) 62 60; Jin-Hee Kim (KOR) d. Yi Chen (TPE) 62 61; Kyung-Mi Chang/Jin-A Lee (KOR) d. Yen-Hua Lu/Hsiao-Han Chao (TPE) 64 61.

- **21 April Australia defeated Chinese Taipei 3-0:** Sophie Ferguson (AUS) d. Hsiao-Han Chao (TPE) 61 62; Samantha Stosur (AUS) d. Yi Chen (TPE) 60 62; Bryanne Stewart/Samantha Stosur (AUS) d. Yen-Hua Lu/Ting-Wen Wang (TPE) 61 63. **Korea, Rep. defeated New Zealand 2-1:** Ye-Ra Lee (KOR) d. Leanne Baker (NZL) 64 36 64; Marina Erakovic (NZL) d. Jin-Hee Kim (KOR) 61 64; Kyung-Mi Chang/Jin-Hee Kim (KOR) d. Eden Marama/Paula Marama (NZL) 26 63 75.

- **22 April Australia defeated Korea, Rep. 2-1:** Evie Dominikovic (AUS) d. Ye-Ra Lee (KOR) 60 46 63; Samantha Stosur (AUS) d. Jin-Hee Kim (KOR) 63 75; Kyung-Mi Chang/Jin-A Lee (KOR) d. Sophie Ferguson/Bryanne Stewart (AUS) 75 76(4). **New Zealand defeated Chinese Taipei 3-0:** Paula Marama (NZL) d. Yen-Hua Lu (TPE) 63 62; Marina Erakovic (NZL) d. Yi Chen (TPE) 62 63; Leanne Baker/Eden Marama (NZL) d. Hsiao-Han Chao/Ting-Wen Wang (TPE) 60 64.

- **Final Positions:** 1. Australia, 2. Korea, Rep., 3. New Zealand, 4. Chinese Taipei.

- **Promotion Play-off 23 April China, P.R. defeated Australia 2-0:** Tian-Tian Sun (CHN) d. Evie Dominikovic (AUS) 63 75; Jie Zheng (CHN) d. Samantha Stosur (AUS) 63 64; Doubles not played.

- **Play-off for 3rd-4th Positions 23 April India defeated Korea, Rep. 2-1:** Ye-Ra Lee (KOR) d. Ankita Bhambri (IND) 61 63; Shikha Uberoi (IND) d. Jin-Hee Kim (KOR) 63 61; Rushmi Chakravarthi/Shikha Uberoi (IND) d. Kyung-Mi Chang/Jin-A Lee (KOR) 63 63.

- **Relegation Play-off 23 April Chinese Taipei defeated Kazakhstan 2-0:** Hsiao-Han Chao (TPE) d. Tatiana Ignatchenko (KAZ) 64 63; Yi Chen (TPE) d. Mariya Kovaleva (KAZ) 62 60; Doubles not played. **New Zealand defeated Singapore 2-0:** Paula Marama (NZL) d. Shao-Fang Ong (SIN) 61 60; Marina Erakovic (NZL) d. Yun-Ling Ng (SIN) 60 60; Doubles not played.

- China advances to 2005 World Group II Play-offs on 9-10 July 2005.
  Kazakhstan and Singapore relegated to Asia/Oceania Zone Group II in 2006.

Europe/Africa Zone Group I

Date: 20-23 April
Venue: Manavgat, Turkey
Surface: Clay (O)
Group A: Bulgaria, Estonia, Hungary, South Africa.
Group B: Luxembourg, Netherlands, Poland, Sweden.
Group C: Denmark, Great Britain, Serbia & Montenegro, Slovenia.
Group D: Belarus, Greece, Israel, Ukraine.

- **Group A 20 April Bulgaria defeated South Africa 3-0:** Sesil Karatantcheva (BUL) d. Chanelle Scheepers (RSA) 61 62; Magdalena Maleeva (BUL) d. Natalie Grandin (RSA) 64 63; Sesil Karatantcheva/Magdalena Maleeva (BUL) d. Lizaan Du Plessis/Alicia Pillay (RSA) 63 62. **Hungary defeated Estonia 3-0:** Virag Nemeth (HUN) d. Margit Ruutel (EST) 61 64; Zsofia Gubacsi (HUN) d. Maret Ani (EST) 61 75; Barbara Pocza/Agnes Szavay (HUN) d. Anett Kaasik/Margit Ruutel (EST) 60 64,

- **21 April Bulgaria defeated Hungary 2-1:** Sesil Karatantcheva (BUL) d. Agnes Szavay (HUN) 64 63; Magdalena Maleeva (BUL) d. Zsofia Gubacsi (HUN) 76(4) 62; Virag Nemeth/Agnes Szavay (HUN) d. Sesil Karatantcheva/Magdalena Maleeva (BUL) 46 63 61. **South Africa defeated Estonia 3-0:** Chanelle Scheepers (RSA) d. Margit Ruutel (EST) 60 46 62; Natalie Grandin (RSA) d. Maret Ani (EST) 62 26 62; Natalie Grandin/Chanelle Scheepers (RSA) d. Anett Kaasik/Ilona Poljakova (EST) 63 62.

- **22 April Bulgaria defeated Estonia 3-0:** Maria Penkova (BUL) d. Anett Kaasik (EST) 62 64; Tszvetana Pironkova (BUL) d. Margit Ruutel (EST) 61 60; Maria Penkova/Tszvetana Pironkova (BUL) d. Anett Kaasik/Ilona Poljakova (EST) 63 62. **South Africa defeated Hungary 2-1:** Agnes Szavay (HUN) d. Chanelle Scheepers (RSA) 64 61; Natalie Grandin (RSA) d. Virag Nemeth (HUN) 46 63 63; Natalie Grandin/Alicia Pillay (RSA) d. Virag Nemeth/Agnes Szavay (HUN) 62 16 75.

- **Final Positions:** 1. Bulgaria, 2. South Africa, 3. Hungary, 4. Estonia.

2005 Fed Cup Results (continued)

- **Group B 20 April Sweden defeated Luxembourg 2-1:** Johanna Larsson (SWE) d. Anne Kremer (LUX) 63 36 63; Claudine Schaul (LUX) d. Sofia Arvidsson (SWE) 75 76(6); Sofia Arvidsson/Hanna Nooni (SWE) d. Anne Kremer/Claudine Schaul (LUX) 63 63. **Netherlands defeated Poland 3-0:** Elise Tamaela (NED) d. Joanna Sakowicz (POL) 64 63; Michaella Krajicek (NED) d. Karolina Kosinska (POL) 61 61; Michelle Gerards/Brenda Schultz-McCarthy (NED) d. Klaudia Jans/Alicja Rosolska (POL) 62 75.

- **21 April Luxembourg defeated Poland 2-1:** Anne Kremer (LUX) d. Joanna Sakowicz (POL) 63 63; Claudine Schaul (LUX) d. Karolina Kosinska (POL) 64 46 64; Klaudia Jans/Alicja Rosolska (POL) d. Anne Kremer/Mandy Minella (LUX) 63 36 64. **Netherlands defeated Sweden 2-1:** Johanna Larsson (SWE) d. Brenda Schultz-McCarthy (NED) 75 36 61; Michaella Krajicek (NED) d. Hanna Nooni (SWE) 64 60; Michaella Krajicek/Brenda Schultz-McCarthy (NED) d. Sofia Arvidsson/Hanna Nooni (SWE) 46 64 64.

- **22 April Netherlands defeated Luxembourg 3-0:** Elise Tamaela (NED) d. Anne Kremer (LUX) 62 61; Michaella Krajicek (NED) d. Claudine Schaul (LUX) 63 36 63; Michelle Gerards/Brenda Schultz-McCarthy (NED) d. Anne Kremer/Mandy Minella (LUX) 63 62. **Sweden defeated Poland 2-1:** Johanna Larsson (SWE) d. Joanna Sakowicz (POL) 63 63; Sofia Arvidsson (SWE) d. Karolina Kosinska (POL) 46 62 61; Klaudia Jans/Alicja Rosolska (POL) d. Sofia Arvidsson/Hanna Nooni (SWE) 06 63 60.

- **Final Positions:** 1. Netherlands, 2. Sweden, 3. Luxembourg, 4. Poland.

- **Group C 20 April Slovenia defeated Great Britain 3-0:** Tina Pisnik (SLO) d. Anne Keothavong (GBR) 63 63; Katarina Srebotnik (SLO) d. Elena Baltacha (GBR) 61 61; Andreja Klepac/Tina Krizan (SLO) d. Elena Baltacha/Jane O'Donoghue (GBR) 61 64. **Serbia & Montenegro defeated Denmark 3-0:** Ana Jovanovic (SCG) d. Caroline Wozniacki (DEN) 46 76(5) 64; Jelena Jankovic (SCG) d. Karina-Ildor Jacobsgaard (DEN) 63 60; Jelena Jankovic/Dragana Zaric (SCG) d. Karina-Ildor Jacobsgaard/Hanne Jensen (DEN) 62 62.

- **21 April Slovenia defeated Serbia & Montenegro 2-1:** Tina Pisnik (SLO) d. Ana Timotic (SCG) 60 61; Jelena Jankovic (SCG) d. Katarina Srebotnik (SLO) 16 64 86; Tina Krizan/Katarina Srebotnik (SLO) d. Jelena Jankovic/Dragana Zaric (SCG) 60 76(6). **Great Britain defeated Denmark 2-1:** Anne Keothavong (GBR) d. Caroline Wozniacki (DEN) 63 46 62; Elena Baltacha (GBR) d. Karina-Ildor Jacobsgaard (DEN) 63 75; Karina-Ildor Jacobsgaard/Hanne Jensen (DEN) d. Katie O'Brien/Jane O'Donoghue (GBR) 63 76(5).

- **22 April Denmark defeated Slovenia 2-1:** Caroline Wozniacki (DEN) d. Tina Krizan (SLO) 64 60; Andreja Klepac (SLO) d. Karina-Ildor Jacobsgaard (DEN) 46 76(3) 62; Gluay Kampookaew/Hanne Jensen (DEN) d. Andreja Klepac/Tina Krizan (SLO) 12 ret.. **Serbia & Montenegro defeated Great Britain 2-1:** Dragana Zaric (SCG) d. Anne Keothavong (GBR) 26 64 64; Ana Timotic (SCG) d. Elena Baltacha (GBR) 57 63 60; Katie O'Brien/Jane O'Donoghue (GBR) d. Ana Timotic/Dragana Zaric (SCG) 62 64.

- **Final Positions:** 1. Slovenia, 2. Serbia & Montenegro, 3. Great Britain, 4. Denmark.

- **Group D 20 April Belarus defeated Israel 2-1:** Viktoria Azarenka (BLR) d. Shahar Peer (ISR) 60 75; Anna Smashnova (ISR) d. Anastasia Yakimova (BLR) 60 61; Viktoria Azarenka/Tatiana Poutchek (BLR) d. Tzipi Obziler/Anna Smashnova (ISR) 75 62. **Ukraine defeated Greece 3-0:** Olga Savchuk (UKR) d. Anna Koumantou (GRE) 63 64; Alona Bondarenko (UKR) d. Anna Gerasimou (GRE) 61 63; Katerina Bondarenko/Valeria Bondarenko (UKR) d. Asmina Kaplani/Anna Koumantou (GRE) 61 62.

- **21 April Israel defeated Greece 3-0:** Tzipi Obziler (ISR) d. Anastasia Michail (GRE) 61 62; Anna Smashnova (ISR) d. Anna Gerasimou (GRE) 75 63; Tzipi Obziler/Shahar Peer (ISR) d. Asmina Kaplani/Anna Koumantou (GRE) 63 61. **Belarus defeated Ukraine 2-1:** Viktoria Azarenka (BLR) d. Katerina Bondarenko (UKR) 62 61; Alona Bondarenko (UKR) d. Anastasia Yakimova (BLR) 62 75; Viktoria Azarenka/Tatiana Poutchek (BLR) d. Valeria Bondarenko/Olga Savchuk (UKR) 63 60.

- **22 April Israel defeated Ukraine 3-0:** Shahar Peer (ISR) d. Valeria Bondarenko (UKR) 62 61; Anna Smashnova (ISR) d. Alona Bondarenko (UKR) 26 60 61; Tzipi Obziler/Shahar Peer (ISR) d. Alona Bondarenko/Valeria Bondarenko (UKR) 61 62. **Belarus defeated Greece 3-0:** Ekaterina Dzehalevich (BLR) d. Asmina Kaplani (GRE) 61 64; Anastasia Yakimova (BLR) d. Anna Gerasimou (GRE) 64 61; Ekaterina Dzehalevich/Tatiana Poutchek (BLR) d. Asmina Kaplani/Anna Koumantou (GRE) 76(4) 75.

- **Final Positions:** 1. Belarus, 2. Israel, 3. Ukraine, 4. Greece.

- **Play-off for 1st-4th Positions 23 April Bulgaria defeated Netherlands 2-0:** Sesil Karatantcheva (BUL) d. Elise Tamaela (NED) 61 61; Magdalena Maleeva (BUL) d. Michaella Krajicek (NED) 46 63 62; Doubles not played. **Slovenia defeated Belarus 2-1:** Viktoria Azarenka (BLR) d. Tina Pisnik (SLO) 67(2) 76(0) 62; Katarina Srebotnik (SLO) d. Anastasia Yakimova (BLR) 61 60; Tina Krizan/Katarina Srebotnik (SLO) d. Viktoria Azarenka/Tatiana Poutchek (BLR) 63 62.

Mary Pierce(FRA)

2005 Fed Cup Results (continued)

- **Play-off for 5th-8th Positions 23 April South Africa defeated Sweden 2-1:** Chanelle Scheepers (RSA) d. Sousan Massi (SWE) 60 64; Sofia Arvidsson (SWE) d. Natalie Grandin (RSA) 64 64; Natalie Grandin/Alicia Pillay (RSA) d. Johanna Larsson/Sousan Massi (SWE) 75 64. **Israel defeated Serbia & Montenegro 2-0:** Tzipi Obziler (ISR) d. Dragana Zaric (SCG) 61 64; Shahar Peer (ISR) d. Ana Timotic (SCG) 64 46 63; Doubles not played.

- **Play-off for 9th-12th Positions 23 April Luxembourg defeated Hungary 2-1:** Mandy Minella (LUX) d. Barbara Pocza (HUN) 76(5) 64; Anne Kremer (LUX) d. Zsofia Gubacsi (HUN) 57 76(8) 63; Zsofia Gubacsi/Virag Nemeth (HUN) d. Mandy Minella/Lynn Philippe (LUX) 75 64. **Ukraine defeated Great Britain 2-1:** Katie O'Brien (GBR) d. Valeria Bondarenko (UKR) 63 63; Alona Bondarenko (UKR) d. Elena Baltacha (GBR) 61 63; Alona Bondarenko/Valeria Bondarenko (UKR) d. Katie O'Brien/Jane O'Donoghue (GBR) 63 62.

- **Relegation Play-off 23 April Estonia defeated Poland 3-0:** Margit Ruutel (EST) d. Joanna Sakowicz (POL) 61 ret.; Maret Ani (EST) d. Karolina Kosinska (POL) 61 76(1); Anett Kaasik/Margit Ruutel (EST) d. Klaudia Jans/Alicja Rosolska (POL) 57 64 63. **Denmark defeated Greece 2-1:** Caroline Wozniacki (DEN) d. Anna Koumantou (GRE) 46 61 63; Anna Gerasimou (GRE) d. Karina-Ildor Jacobsgaard (DEN) 36 75 119; Hanne Jensen/Caroline Wozniacki (DEN) d. Asmina Kaplani/Anna Koumantou (GRE) 76(5) 64.

- Bulgaria and Slovenia advance to 2005 World Group II Play-offs on 9-10 July 2005.
  Greece and Poland relegated to Europe/Africa Zone Group II in 2006.

Americas Zone Group II

Date: 21-23 April
Venue: Medellin, Colombia
Surface: Clay (O)
Nations: Chile, Colombia, Dominican Republic, Venezuela

- **21 April Chile defeated Dominican Republic 3-0:** Andrea Koch (CHI) d. Chandra Capozzi (DOM) 62 62; Valentina Castro (CHI) d. Francesca Segarelli (DOM) 64 62; Andrea Koch/Melisa Miranda (CHI) d. Natalia Baez/Kristel Izquierdo (DOM) 62 61. **Colombia defeated Venezuela 3-0:** Mariana Duque (COL) d. Briggitt Marcovich (VEN) 46 60 63; Catalina Castano (COL) d. Avel-Romaly Coronado (VEN) 61 62; Catalina Castano/Mariana Duque (COL) d. Avel-Romaly Coronado/Briggitt Marcovich (VEN) 63 63.

- **22 April Chile defeated Colombia 2-1:** Andrea Koch (CHI) d. Mariana Duque-Marino (COL) 76(3) 60; Catalina Castano (COL) d. Valentina Castro (CHI) 64 62; Valentina Castro/Andrea Koch (CHI) d. Catalina Castano/Mariana Duque (COL) 62 64. **Dominican Republic defeated Venezuela 2-1:** Chandra Capozzi (DOM) d. Mariaryeni Gutierrez (VEN) 57 64 63; Francesca Segarelli (DOM) d. Avel-Romaly Coronado (VEN) 26 61 61; Avel-Romaly Coronado/Briggitt Marcovich (VEN) d. Natalia Baez/Kristel Izquierdo (DOM) 64 75.

- **23 April Chile defeated Venezuela 3-0:** Andrea Koch (CHI) d. Briggitt Marcovich (VEN) 61 62; Valentina Castro (CHI) d. Avel-Romaly Coronado (VEN) 60 61; Valentina Castro/Melisa Miranda (CHI) d. Mariaryeni Gutierrez/Briggitt Marcovich (VEN) 76(3) 76(2). **Colombia defeated Dominican Republic 3-0:** Karen-Emelia Castiblanco-Duarte (COL) d. Chandra Capozzi (DOM) 61 61; Catalina Castano (COL) d. Francesca Segarelli (DOM) 60 62; Mariana Duque/Gabriela Mejia (COL) d. Natalia Baez/Francesca Segarelli (DOM) 64 62.

- **Final Positions:** 1. Chile, 2. Colombia, 3. Dominican Republic, 4. Venezuela.

- Chile and Colombia promoted to Americas Zone Group I in 2006.

Asia/Oceania Zone Group II

Date: 19-21 April
Venue: New Delhi, India
Surface: Hard (O)
Nations: Philippines, Syria, Turkmenistan, Uzbekistan

- **19 April Uzbekistan defeated Philippines 3-0:** Ivanna Israilova (UZB) d. Anja-Vanessa Peter (PHI) 46 62 75; Akgul Amanmuradova (UZB) d. Czarina-Mae Arevalo (PHI) 60 62; Akgul Amanmuradova/Dilyara Saidkhodjaeva (UZB) d. Czarina-Mae Arevalo/Denise Dy (PHI) 64 64. **Syria defeated Turkmenistan 2-1:** Ummarahmat Alisultanova (TKM) d. Hazar Sidki (SYR) 62 62; Shaza Tinawi (SYR) d. Almira Hallyeva (TKM) 63 63; Hazar Sidki/Shaza Tinawi (SYR) d. Ummarahmat Alisultanova/Almira Hallyeva (TKM) 61 63.

- **20 April Philippines defeated Turkmenistan 3-0:** Denise Dy (PHI) d. Inna Gavrilenko (TKM) 61 60; Anja-Vanessa Peter (PHI) d. Almira Hallyeva (TKM) 61 61; Czarina-Mae Arevalo/Denise Dy (PHI) d. Ummarahmat Alisultanova/Almira Hallyeva (TKM) 61 60. **Uzbekistan defeated Syria 3-0:** Dilyara Saidkhodjaeva (UZB) d. Nivin Kezbari (SYR) 60 60; Akgul Amanmuradova (UZB) d. Shaza Tinawi (SYR) 60 60; Akgul Amanmuradova/Dilyara Saidkhodjaeva (UZB) d. Nivin Kezbari/Hazar Sidki (SYR) 61 62.

- **21 April Philippines defeated Syria 3-0:** Denise Dy (PHI) d. Hazar Sidki (SYR) 60 60; Anja-Vanessa Peter (PHI) d. Shaza Tinawi (SYR) 60 63; Czarina-Mae Arevalo/Denise Dy (PHI) d. Nivin Kezbari/Hazar Sidki (SYR) 61 61. **Uzbekistan defeated Turkmenistan 3-0:** Dilyara Saidkhodjaeva (UZB) d. Ummarahmat Alisultanova (TKM) 60 60; Akgul Amanmuradova (UZB) d. Almira Hallyeva (TKM) 60 62; Akgul Amanmuradova/Dilyara Saidkhodjaeva (UZB) d. Ummarahmat Alisultanova/Almira Hallyeva (TKM) 60 60.

- **Final Positions:** 1. Uzbekistan, 2. Philippines, 3. Syria, 4. Turkmenistan.

- Philippines and Uzbekistan promoted to Asia/Oceania Zone Group I in 2006.

Europe/Africa Zone Group II

Date: 27-30 April
Venue: Manavgat, Turkey
Surface: Clay (O)
Group A: Finland, Lithuania, Romania, Tunisia.
Group B: Georgia, Ireland, Latvia, Norway.

- **Group A 27 April Romania defeated Tunisia 3-0:** Gabriela Niculescu (ROM) d. Rym Cherni (TUN) 60 62; Simona Matei (ROM) d. Olfa Dhaoui (TUN) 60 61; Gabriela Niculescu/Monica Niculescu (ROM) d. Olfa Dhaoui/Selima Frioui (TUN) 60 60. **Finland defeated Lithuania 2-1:** Aurelia Miseviciute (LTU) d. Piia Suomalainen (FIN) 63 62; Emma Laine (FIN) d. Lina Stanciute (LTU) 64 62; Emma Laine/Piia Suomalainen (FIN) d. Aurelia Miseviciute/Lina Stanciute (LTU) 64 64 .

- **28 April Romania defeated Finland 2-1:** Monica Niculescu (ROM) d. Piia Suomalainen (FIN) 62 60; Emma Laine (FIN) d. Simona Matei (ROM) 75 63; Gabriela Niculescu/Monica Niculescu (ROM) d. Emma Laine/Piia Suomalainen (FIN) 26 63 63. **Lithuania defeated Tunisia 3-0:** Aurelia Miseviciute (LTU) d. Selima Frioui (TUN) 60 60; Lina Stanciute (LTU) d. Olfa Dhaoui (TUN) 60 61; Irina Cybina/Lina Stanciute (LTU) d. Rym Cherni/Olfa Dhaoui (TUN) 60 61.

- **29 April Romania defeated Lithuania 2-1:** Monica Niculescu (ROM) d. Aurelia Miseviciute (LTU) 36 61 62; Lina Stanciute (LTU) d. Simona Matei (ROM) 46 75 62; Gabriela Niculescu/Monica Niculescu (ROM) d. Aurelia Miseviciute/Lina Stanciute (LTU) 36 76(0) 61. **Finland defeated Tunisia 3-0:** Piia Suomalainen (FIN) d. Rym Cherni (TUN) 60 60; Emma Laine (FIN) d. Olfa Dhaoui (TUN) 61 61; Essi Laine/Maarit Nieminen (FIN) d. Olfa Dhaoui/Selima Frioui (TUN) 61 61.

- **Final Positions:** 1. Romania, 2. Finland, 3. Lithuania, 4. Tunisia.

- **Group B 27 April Ireland defeated Norway 3-0:** Yvonne Doyle (IRL) d. Ina Sartz (NOR) 36 64 63; Anne Mall (IRL) d. Karoline Borgersen (NOR) 63 63; Anne Mall/Karen Nugent (IRL) d. Karoline Borgersen/Ina Sartz (NOR) 61 76(3). **Georgia defeated Latvia 3-0:** Tinatin Kavlashvili (GEO) d. Anastasija Sevastova (LAT) 62 61; Margalita Chakhnashvili (GEO) d. Irina Kuzmina (LAT) 62 61; Tinatin Kavlashvili/Tatia Mikadze (GEO) d. Irina Kuzmina/Alise Vaidere (LAT) 60 64.

- **28 April Georgia defeated Ireland 3-0:** Tinatin Kavlashvili (GEO) d. Yvonne Doyle (IRL) 64 61; Margalita Chakhnashvili (GEO) d. Anne Mall (IRL) 64 61; Salome Chachkhunashvili/Tatia Mikadze (GEO) d. Rachael Dillon/Karen Nugent (IRL) 63 64. **Latvia defeated Norway 3-0:** Alise Vaidere (LAT) d. Ina Sartz (NOR) 61 63; Irina Kuzmina (LAT) d. Karoline Borgersen (NOR) 61 26 64; Ieva Irbe/Alise Vaidere (LAT) d. Idunn Hertzberg/Karoline Steiro (NOR) 62 62.

- **29 April Latvia defeated Ireland 2-1:** Alise Vaidere (LAT) d. Yvonne Doyle (IRL) 63 36 63; Irina Kuzmina (LAT) d. Anne Mall (IRL) 46 76(4) 63; Rachael Dillon/Karen Nugent (IRL) d. Ieva Irbe/Anastasija Sevastova (LAT) 60 63. **Georgia defeated Norway 2-1:** Tinatin Kavlashvili (GEO) d. Karoline Steiro (NOR) 60 61; Margalita Chakhnashvili (GEO) d. Idunn Hertzberg (NOR) 62 62; Karoline Borgersen/Ina Sartz (NOR) d. Salome Chachkhunashvili/Tatia Mikadze (GEO) 61 64.

- **Final Positions:** 1. Georgia, 2. Latvia, 3. Ireland, 4. Norway.

- **Promotion Play-off 30 April Romania defeated Latvia 2-1:** Monica Niculescu (ROM) d. Alise Vaidere (LAT) 60 63; Irina Kuzmina (LAT) d. Simona Matei (ROM) 64 46 64; Gabriela Niculescu/Monica Niculescu (ROM) d. Irina Kuzmina/Anastasija Sevastova (LAT) 75 63. **Finland defeated Georgia 2-1:** Tinatin Kavlashvili (GEO) d. Piia Suomalainen (FIN) 61 76(4); Emma Laine (FIN) d. Margalita Chakhnashvili (GEO) 64 61; Emma Laine/Piia Suomalainen (FIN) d. Tinatin Kavlashvili/Tatia Mikadze (GEO) 62 63.

- **Relegation Play-off 30 April Lithuania defeated Norway 2-0:** Aurelia Miseviciute (LTU) d. Idunn Hertzberg (NOR) 62 60; Lina Stanciute (LTU) d. Karoline Borgersen (NOR) 63 64; Doubles not played. **Ireland defeated Tunisia 2-0:** Yvonne Doyle (IRL) d. Selima Frioui (TUN) 61 61; Anne Mall (IRL) d. Olfa Dhaoui (TUN) 61 61; Doubles not played.

- Finland and Romania promoted to Europe/Africa Zone Group I in 2006.
Norway and Tunisia relegated to Europe/Africa Zone Group III in 2006.

Europe/Africa Zone Group III

Date: 27-30 April
Venue: Manavgat, Turkey
Surface: Clay (O)
Group A: Egypt, Malta, Turkey.
Group B: Algeria, Botswana, Iceland.
Group C: Bosnia/Herzegovina, Cyprus, Namibia.
Group D: Kenya, Moldova, Portugal.

- **Group A 27 April Egypt defeated Malta 3-0;** Aliaa Fakhry (EGY) d. Lisa Camenzuli (MLT) 52 ret.; Nihal Saleh (EGY) d. Stephanie Pace (MLT) 60 61; Miray Eshak/Aliaa Fakhry (EGY) d. Stephanie Pace/Stephanie Sullivan (MLT) 76(2) 75.

- **28 April Turkey defeated Malta 3-0:** Pemra Ozgen (TUR) d. Stephanie Pace (MLT) 60 61; Ipek Senoglu (TUR) d. Stephanie Sullivan (MLT) 64 16 62; Cagla Buyukakcay/Pemra Ozgen (TUR) d. Stephanie Pace/Stephanie Sullivan (MLT) 62 60.

- **29 April Turkey defeated Egypt 2-1:** Pemra Ozgen (TUR) d. Aliaa Fakhry (EGY) 61 62; Nihal Saleh (EGY) d. Ipek Senoglu (TUR) 60 64; Pemra Ozgen/Ipek Senoglu (TUR) d. Aliaa Fakhry/Nihal Saleh (EGY) 63 63.

- **Final Positions:** 1. Turkey, 2. Egypt, 3. Malta.

- **Group B 27 April Botswana defeated Iceland 3-0:** Lesedi Ramocha (BOT) d. Rebekka Petursdottir (ISL) 61 64; Laone Botshoma (BOT) d. Sigurlaug Sigurdardottir (ISL) 62 62; Laone Botshoma/Lesedi Ramocha (BOT) d. Rebekka Petursdottir/Sigurlaug Sigurdardottir (ISL) 61 64.

- **28 April Algeria defeated Botswana 3-0:** Sara Meghoufel (ALG) d. Puleng Tlhopane (BOT) 61 61; Samia Medjahdi (ALG) d. Laone Botshoma (BOT) 61 63; Amira Ben Aissa/Sara Meghoufel (ALG) d. Laone Botshoma/Puleng Tlhopane (BOT) 62 62.

- **29 April Algeria defeated Iceland 3-0:** Assia Halo (ALG) d. Sandra Kristjansdottir (ISL) 60 60; Samia Medjahdi (ALG) d. Sigurlaug Sigurdardottir (ISL) 62 61; Amira Ben Aissa/Sara Meghoufel (ALG) d. Sandra Kristjansdottir/Sigurlaug Sigurdardottir (ISL) 62 61.

- **Final Positions:** 1. Algeria, 2. Botswana, 3. Iceland.

- **Group C 27 April Namibia defeated Cyprus 3-0:** Suzelle Davin (NAM) d. Ilina Kroushovski (CYP) 64 63; Elrien De Villiers (NAM) d. Irina Letseva (CYP) 61 63; Ajet Boonzaaier/Suzelle Davin (NAM) d. Ilina Kroushovski/Stella Kyradji (CYP) 63 64.

- **28 April Bosnia/Herzegovina defeated Cyprus 3-0:** Selma Babic (BIH) d. Ilina Kroushovski (CYP) 62 61; Diana Stojic (BIH) d. Irina Letseva (CYP) 61 61; Sanja Racic/Nadina Secerbegovic (BIH) d. Ilina Kroushovski/Stella Kyradji (CYP) 62 62.

- **29 April Bosnia/Herzegovina defeated Namibia 2-1:** Selma Babic (BIH) d. Suzelle Davin (NAM) 64 64; Diana Stojic (BIH) d. Elrien De Villiers (NAM) 61 61; Ajet Boonzaaier/Suzelle Davin (NAM) d. Selma Babic/Nadina Secerbegovic (BIH) 26 75 86.

- **Final Positions:** 1. Bosnia/Herzegovina, 2. Namibia, 3. Cyprus.

- **Group D 27 April Moldova defeated Kenya 3-0:** Svetlana Komleva (MDA) d. Wanjika Ngaruiya (KEN) 60 61; Ina Sireteanu (MDA) d. Evelyn Otula (KEN) 60 62; Olga Cosic/Maria Melihova (MDA) d. Caroline Oduor/Tamara Orwa (KEN) 61 76(4).

- **28 April Portugal defeated Moldova 2-1:** Ana-Catarina Nogueira (POR) d. Svetlana Komleva (MDA) 46 63 61; Neuza Silva (POR) d. Ina Sireteanu (MDA) 61 61; Olga Cosic/Svetlana Komleva (MDA) d. Magali De Lattre/Carlota Plantier-Santos (POR) 63 76(5).

- **29 April Portugal defeated Kenya 3-0:** Carlota Plantier-Santos (POR) d. Wanjika Ngaruiya (KEN) 60 62; Magali De Lattre (POR) d. Evelyn Otula (KEN) 60 61; Ana-Catarina Nogueira/Neuza Silva (POR) d. Caroline Oduor/Tamara Orwa (KEN) 60 60.

- **Final Positions:** 1. Portugal, 2. Moldova, 3. Kenya.

- **Play-off for 1st-4th Positions 30 April Algeria defeated Turkey 2-1:** Pemra Ozgen (TUR) d. Assia Halo (ALG) 76(5) 61; Samia Medjahdi (ALG) d. Ipek Senoglu (TUR) 57 62 61; Assia Halo/Samia Medjahdi (ALG) d. Pemra Ozgen/Ipek Senoglu (TUR) 67(7) 75 97. **Portugal defeated Bosnia/Herzegovina 2-1:** Sanja Racic (BIH) d. Ana-Catarina Nogueira (POR) 75 61; Neuza Silva (POR) d. Selma Babic (BIH) 63 60; Ana-Catarina Nogueira/Neuza Silva (POR) d. Selma Babic/Sanja Racic (BIH) 61 63.

- **Play-off for 5th-8th Positions 30 April Egypt defeated Botswana 3-0:** Aliaa Fakhry (EGY) d. Lesedi Ramocha (BOT) 61 64; Nihal Saleh (EGY) d. Laone Botshoma (BOT) 62 60; Miray Eshak/Nihal Saleh (EGY) d. Laone Botshoma/Puleng Tlhopane (BOT) 61 62. **Namibia defeated Moldova 2-1:** Ajet Boonzaaier (NAM) d. Olga Cosic (MDA) 62 61; Ina Sireteanu (MDA) d. Elrien De Villiers (NAM) 46 76(8) 63; Ajet Boonzaaier/Suzelle Davin (NAM) d. Maria Melihova/Ina Sireteanu (MDA) 75 62.

- **Play-off for 9th-12th Positions 30 April Malta defeated Iceland 3-0:** Stephanie Pace (MLT) d. Rebekka Petursdottir (ISL) 60 60; Stephanie Sullivan (MLT) d. Sigurlaug Sigurdardottir (ISL) 63 62; Stephanie Pace/Stephanie Sullivan (MLT) d. Rebekka Petursdottir/Sigurlaug Sigurdardottir (ISL) 76(3) 63. **Kenya defeated Cyprus 3-0:** Wanjika Ngaruiya (KEN) d. Ilina Kroushovski (CYP) 63 75; Evelyn Otula (KEN) d. Irina Letseva (CYP) 62 62; Caroline Oduor/Evelyn Otula (KEN) d. Ilina Kroushovski/Irina Letseva (CYP) 64 64.

hopman cup goes to slovak republic

sweet revenge as last year's runners-up finish on top

by simon cambers

The winning Slovak Republic team with Lucy Hopman

The Slovak Republic took the spoils at the XVII edition of the Hyundai Hopman Cup in Perth in January as Dominik Hrbaty and Daniela Hantuchova upstaged the big guns to give their country their second victory in the event. Hrbaty and Hantuchova saw off Argentina in the final to gain revenge for 2004, when they were denied the title by Americans James Blake and Lindsay Davenport in a deciding mixed doubles.

Capacity crowds once again flocked to the impressive Burswood Dome to see some of the world's top players, led by former world No. 1 Marat Safin of Russia and 2004 French Open runner-up Guillermo Coria of Argentina. Mark Philippoussis and Alicia Molik led the home challenge, while Meghann Shaughnessy accepted a late call-up to replace Davenport alongside Blake as the Americans looked to become the first nation to win three successive Hopman Cup titles.

With French Open champion Anastasia Myskina joining Safin, Russia began as favourites but defeats by Germany and Argentina in their first two matches cost them any chance of making the final. While Myskina won all three of her singles matches, Safin was the surprise weak link, having arrived late after staying in Moscow to collect an award from the Russian government.

"I was so nervous watching her (Hantuchova) today, I almost had a heart attack. But I always play my best tennis in team events and played very well today," Hrbaty said.

The powerful Muscovite was understandably rusty as he was beaten by Tommy Haas and Coria, while his defeat by Italian Davide Sanguinetti saw Russia make an early exit. Nevertheless, an unruffled Safin was unconcerned with his form. "I'll be okay for the Australian Open," he said, in what would prove to be an understatement of the highest order in light of his fantastic exploits at Melbourne Park later the same month.

The disappointment of losing Russia was tempered by a strong start from the home nation as Philippoussis and Molik gave the crowd something to cheer about with a 2-1 win over Slovak Republic in their opening match. Philippoussis, back after a two-month break following yet another injury-plagued year, was equally rusty as he was beaten by Hrbaty, but Molik was on top form and she beat Hantuchova before teaming with Philippoussis to win the deciding mixed doubles.

With Molik picking up where she left off in 2004, when she won three titles to rise to 13th in the world rankings, it seemed that Australia were well placed to win its second title, Philippoussis and Jelena Dokic having lifted the Cup in 1999. Molik powered her way to three victories with more of the play which has prompted many experts to say she can become Australia's first Grand Slam singles champion since Evonne Goolagong Cawley's Wimbledon triumph in 1980.

But joy turned to disappointment in their very next match as Philippoussis's injury jinx struck again when he tore a groin muscle against Dutchman Peter Wessels. Philippoussis's subsequent withdrawal from the event left the hosts unable to qualify for the final.

The big-serving Australian wasn't the only man to suffer however as Haas, Wessels and Coria all suffered injuries during the week. Haas, who had looked in good form, suffered a groin injury in the German match against Coria, handing the Argentines a place in the final as winners of Group A.

Going into the last round-robin day, the United States, Slovak Republic and the Netherlands, who beat Zimbabwe in a play-off to make the event, all had a chance to reach the final. But though the United States beat Australia, with Paul Baccanello standing in for Philippoussis, 2-1, the Slovaks reached the final with a 3-0 win over the Dutch, helped by another injury, this time to Wessels.

Despite the absence of their favourites, the crowd was treated to a high-quality and tense final between Slovak Republic and Argentina. Gisela Dulko, who had lost all three of her group matches, stunned Hantuchova by taking the first set 61, but the former world No. 5 fought back well to claim a 16 64 64 victory. And Hrbaty, who had not dropped a set in his three previous singles wins, then sealed the Hopman Cup title with a 64 61 win over Coria, who was struggling with a stiff back.

"I was so nervous watching her (Hantuchova) today, I almost had a heart attack. But I always play my best tennis in team events and played very well today," Hrbaty said afterwards.

The nation's second win in the event built on their success seven years previously, when Karol Kucera and Karina Habsudova teamed up to defeat France 2-1. "It means such a lot for us, because we are a small country," Hantuchova said. "Now, we have won the Fed Cup (2002) and World Team Cup, which is a big achievement."

Slovak Republic's Daniela Hantuchova and Dominik Hrbaty

2005 Hyundai Hopman Cup Results

Perth, Australia, 1-8 January 2005

Seeds:
1. Russia: Anastasia Myskina/Marat Safin
2. USA: Lindsay Davenport/James Blake
3. Slovak Republic: Daniela Hantuchova/Dominik Hrbaty
4. Argentina: Gisela Dulko/Guillermo Coria

Unseeded:
Germany: Anna-Lena Groenefeld/Tommy Haas
Australia: Alicia Molik/Mark Philippoussis (substituted by Paul Baccanello)
Italy: Francesca Schiavone/Davide Sanguinetti

Alternate:
Netherlands: Michaella Krajicek/Peter Wessels
Zimbabwe: Cara Black/Wayne Black

Note: Super tiebreak was used for mixed doubles: if matches are ties at one set all, winner is first to ten. Pro sets were used in some dead doubles rubbers.

Play-off

Netherlands d. Zimbabwe 2-1: Michaella Krajicek (NED) d. Cara Black (ZIM) 36 76(5) 60; Peter Wessels (NED) d. Wayne Black (ZIM) 76(7) 75; Cara Black/Wayne Black (ZIM) d. Michaella Krajicek/Peter Wessels (NED) 87.

Group A

Argentina d. Italy 2-1: Francesca Schiavone (ITA) d. Gisela Dulko (ARG) 61 63; Guillermo Coria (ARG) d. Davide Sanguinetti (ITA) 61 76(4); Gisela Dulko/Guillermo Coria (ARG) d. Francesca Schiavone/Davide Sanguinetti (ITA) 75 60.

Germany d. Russia 2-1: Anastasia Myskina (RUS) d. Anna-Lena Groenefeld (GER) 63 63; Tommy Haas (GER) d. Marat Safin (RUS) 63 36 61; Anna-Lena Groenefeld/Tommy Haas (GER) d. Anastasia Myskina/Marat Safin (RUS) 75 16 10(6).

Germany d. Italy 2-1: Francesca Schiavone (ITA) d. Anna-Lena Groenefeld (GER) 62 26 62; Tommy Haas (GER) d. Davide Sanguinetti (ITA) 63 62; Anna-Lena Groenefeld/Tommy Haas (GER) d. Francesca Schiavone/Davide Sanguinetti (ITA) 76(6) 64.

Argentina d. Russia 2-1: Anastasia Myskina (RUS) d. Gisela Dulko (ARG) 62 61; Guillermo Coria (ARG) d. Marat Safin (RUS) 76(4) 61; Guillermo Coria/Gisela Dulko (ARG) d. Marat Safin/Anastasia Myskina (RUS) 62 60.

Italy d. Russia 2-1: Anastasia Myskina (RUS) d. Francesca Schiavone (ITA) 63 62; Davide Sanguinetti (ITA) d. Marat Safin (RUS) 76(0) 67(3) 60; Francesca Schiavone/Davide Sanguinetti (ITA) d. Anastasia Myskina/Marat Safin (RUS) 86.

Argentina d. Germany 2-1: Anna-Lena Groenefeld (GER) d. Gisela Dulko (ARG) 36 62 61; Guillermo Coria (ARG) d. Tommy Haas (GER) 57 32 ret.; Gisela Dulko/Guillermo Coria (ARG) d. Anna-Lena Groenefeld/Tommy Haas w/o.

Group B

Australia d. Slovak Republic 2-1: Alicia Molik (AUS) d. Daniela Hantuchova (SVK) 63 63; Dominik Hrbaty (SVK) d. Mark Philippoussis (AUS) 75 62; Alicia Molik/Mark Philippoussis (AUS) d. Daniela Hantuchova/Dominik Hrbaty (SVK) 67(9) 63 10(9).

USA d. Netherlands 2-1: Meghann Shaughnessy (USA) d. Michaella Krajicek (NED) 75 64; James Blake (USA) d. Peter Wessels (NED) 61 76(4); Michaella Krajicek/Peter Wessels (NED) d. Meghann Shaughnessy/James Blake (USA) 75 75.

Netherlands d. Australia 2-1: Alicia Molik (AUS) d. Michaella Krajicek (NED) 63 75; Peter Wessels (NED) d. Mark Philippoussis (AUS) 76(5) 36 62; Michaella Krajicek/Peter Wessels (NED) d. Alicia Molik/Mark Philippoussis (AUS) w/o.

Slovak Republic d. USA 2-1: Daniela Hantuchova (SVK) d. Meghann Shaughnessy (USA) 64 62; Dominik Hrbaty (SVK) d. James Blake (USA) 76(2) 64; Meghann Shaughnessy/James Blake (USA) d. Daniela Hantuchova/Dominik Hrbaty (SVK) 06 76(13) 10(7).

USA d. Australia 2-1: Alicia Molik (AUS) d. Meghann Shaughnessy (USA) 62 63; James Blake (USA) d. Paul Baccanello (AUS) 63 64; Meghann Shaughnessy/James Blake (USA) d. Alicia Molik/Paul Baccanello (AUS) 67(6) 75 10(7).

Slovak Republic d. Netherlands 3-0: Daniela Hantuchova (SVK) d. Michaella Krajicek (NED) 64 62; Dominik Hrbaty (SVK) d. Peter Wessels (NED) 52 ret.; Daniela Hantuchova/Dominik Hrbaty (SVK) d. Michaella Krajicek/Peter Wessels (NED) w/o.

Final

Slovak Republic d. Argentina 3-0: Daniela Hantuchova (SVK) d. Gisela Dulko (ARG) 16 64 64; Dominik Hrbaty (SVK) d. Guillermo Coria (ARG) 64 61; Daniela Hantuchova/Dominik Hrbaty (SVK) d. Gisela Dulko/Guillermo Coria (ARG) w/o.

Lindsay Davenport (USA)

the men's year 2005

by ossian shine

Impossibly modest, impeccably mannered but with a streak as hard as teak running through him, Roger Federer once again toyed with tennis perfection to dominate the men's game in 2005. World No. 1 for the entire 12 months, only four men were able to beat Federer – and the performances they needed to conjure those victories were each breathtaking in their excellence.

It spoke volumes for the Swiss maestro's status as being head-and-shoulders above the mortals below him that he could not hide the bitter disappointment at losing each of those four matches in an otherwise stellar season. Here is a man who does not like to lose and he is unlikely to ever need to get used to it.

The Swiss kicked off his season in Doha and romped to the title – the first of 11 he would pick up in the year. Federer did not lose a set all week – in fact he lost just 23 games in the five matches it took him to win the event.

Unbeaten since the Athens Olympics in August 2004, Federer rolled into Melbourne Park in January chasing his fourth grand slam title in 12 months having won the 2004 Australian Open, Wimbledon and US Open crowns.

He burst out of the blocks in some style in Australia and was the hottest favourite in a century to win the Australian Open after romping through his first five matches without dropping a set.

It was there that he ran into a man-mountain of tennis power, a player of almost endless ability but an all-too-often brittle brain. On a hot, steamy night in Melbourne Park, Marat Safin rekindled some of the magic that had led him to the 2000 US Open crown and, after four-and-a-half hours of scintillating drama, ended Federer's Australian dreams.

Marat Safin (RUS)

Marat Safin rekindled some of the magic that had led him to the 2000 US Open crown and, after four-and-a-half hours of scintillating drama, ended Federer's Australian dreams.

Federer had missed a match point in the fourth set as Safin produced a perfect lob to stay alive and the Swiss saved six match points in the final set before his resistance finally snapped and Safin celebrated his 25th birthday with a memorable victory that dragged the capacity crowd to their feet.

Safin had beaten the seemingly invincible world No. 1 57 64 57 76 97 in a heart-stopping semifinal that avenged his loss to the Swiss in the final 12 months earlier.

"It was one of the toughest matches I ever had in my life," Safin said. "Normally he toys with all the other players but for some reason I found the power to fight.

"I live my whole life with pressure, so this is nothing different," Federer nonchalantly said after a match which had left members of the crowd gulping for air and wide-eyed with disbelief. "It's always going to hurt, no matter how great the match was but at least you can leave the place feeling good about yourself because I thought I gave it all I had."

While Federer was left to lick his wounds, the centenary Australian Open final between Safin and Australian Lleyton Hewitt was a classic battle between one man's destiny and another's determination.

The formidable Hewitt had fantasised about winning the Australian Open since his parents introduced him to tennis as a small child. Safin believed destiny was on his side having lost two previous finals in Melbourne and it was that belief which resulted in a 16 63 64 64 victory over the local favourite.

Hewitt had struggled through to his first Melbourne final the hard way, surviving two gruelling five set matches against Rafael Nadal and David Nalbandian – two

Roger Federer (SUI)

the men's year 2005

by ossian shine

of the other three men to claim Federer's scalp in 2005 – and the effort had left him running on empty.

Safin had only to conquer his own self-doubt and victory was his. "Today was a great relief for me," he grinned after triumphing. "You can win one grand slam by mistake but not two. Now I think I can win a couple more."

While Safin headed back to Europe with a smile on his face, Federer consoled himself with four back-to-back tournament wins before the grind of the claycourt season.

He snapped up the Rotterdam crown beating his Doha final victim Ivan Ljubicic in the title match before heading back to the Middle East and Dubai to snap up that crown, crushing the unfortunate Ljubicic once again in the final.

The hapless Ljubicic was again put to the sword next time out – this time in the fourth round of the ATP Masters Series Indian Wells – and Federer went on to lift that title with wins over Nicolas Kiefer, Guillermo Canas and Hewitt.

The fading Tim Henman and the evergreen Andre Agassi numbered among Federer's victims at the Miami Masters before a glimpse in the final of what promises to be an enduring and fascinating rivalry in the years to come when Federer fought back from two sets down to beat Rafael Nadal 26 67 76 63 61.

Nadal is a youngster who appears to have been hard-wired with a winning mentality and he would have his day in the sun over Federer later in the year but not before the illustrious Swiss had his nose bloodied by another precocious youngster on Monte Carlo's slow clay. Federer suffered his second defeat of the year in the Principality when French teenager Richard Gasquet stunned him 67 62 76.

"It was a fantastic match, after I won it I didn't know where I was for a few minutes," said Gasquet, shaking his head. "It was three or four seconds before I realised I had beaten Roger Federer. It's fabulous, there's no other word I can use.

Federer, who had been aiming for a record third successive Masters Series title, was generous in defeat. "He played into this zone where you had the feeling there was nothing you could do," said Federer. "He was just hitting clean winners, he definitely played a great match. Normally I can raise the bar, today it almost happened, but you can't get out of every match like this."

Federer didn't have long to wait for revenge however. On his next outing he won the Hamburg Masters for the third time in four years with almost embarrassing ease – whipping Gasquet in the final.

On a surface said to be his weakest he did not drop a single set and he barely even broke sweat. "The toughest moment was when I looked at the draw," admitted the Swiss. "I was really worried. There were many tough opponents in my section so in the end to come through without losing a set is very nice."

> "It is the most special one for me, playing Andre in the final of the US Open. He is one of the only living legends in tennis we still have," said Federer

He had every right to be worried heading into the French Open – the only grand slam to have eluded him – having struggled at Roland Garros throughout his short career. But with the same ease with which he had dispatched opponents all year Federer eased into the semis without losing a set.

There he ran into Nadal once more.

This time the Spaniard pummelled the world No. 1 into submission as night closed in at Roland Garros. The muscular Spaniard in day-glo shirts and three-quarter-length pirate trousers like some baseline buccaneer celebrated his 19th birthday by beating the Swiss 63 46 64 63 to set up a showpiece against Argentine Mariano Puerta.

"It is a dream for me. I won today against the number one," Nadal said. "Not only the number one for tennis, but the number one as a person."

Federer must now wait another year for a crack at the only grand slam title missing from his collection after he was simply unable to live with Nadal's phenomenal power.

"I really thought I had the keys to beat him today," Federer said ruefully. "It was just unfortunate that I wasn't at my best. Simple version for me is started bad and finished bad," he smiled. "Was good in the middle and that was not good enough. That's like the short and simple version."

Nadal went on to become the first man since Mats Wilander in 1982 to win the title on his Roland Garros debut with a ferocious and fearless victory over tough Argentine Puerta.

"It's unbelievable," he said, his eyes glistening. "It's a dream come true. It is one of the best moments in my career. These are important moments. I didn't think I was going to cry, but my whole family was very emotional. In the end, I started crying also."

Puerta pushed Nadal as hard as anyone had been able to at Roland Garros although he could not halt his teenage tormentor's charge to the title. "I gave it everything I had," said the 26-year-old. "Physically, he was better than I was. I lost to an excellent player, the best player in the world on clay."

If Nadal was the best player in the world on clay, there was no doubting the best player on grass. That man Federer again.

At Wimbledon he took his place alongside Bjorn Borg and Pete Sampras as the only men to have won a hat-trick of singles titles at the All England Club since World War Two.

Federer dropped just one set all tournament – a tiebreak to tricky Nicolas Kiefer – and thrashed Andy Roddick for the title. "This is the best match maybe that I've ever played," said Federer. "Today it seemed like I was playing flawlessly. I'm very, very proud because this is the most important tournament. Sampras was one of my favourite players of all time and Borg was just fantastic. To be in that group feels very special."

Federer's victory took his tally of consecutive wins on grass to 36, five short

Andre Agassi (USA)

of Borg's record. Victory was his 21st consecutive victory in a final and clinched his fifth grand slam title overall.

There was more to come.

After flexing his muscles with victory at the Cincinnati Masters, Federer went on the rampage in New York City to bag his sixth grand slam at the US Open.

Once again Kiefer was the first man to take a set from him, in the fourth round, before Federer went on to annihilate Nalbandian and sweep aside Hewitt before seeing off Agassi in the final.

Federer played dream-wrecker at Flushing Meadows downing sentimental favourite Agassi 63 26 76 61.

"Unfortunately [for Agassi and the crowd] it happened again that I played my best in the final, as usual," said the 24-year-old Federer after deflating the New York fanatics. "It is the most special one for me, playing Andre in the final of the US Open. He is one of the only living legends in tennis we still have."

Eight-times grand slam champion Agassi, playing in his 20th US Open and the oldest finalist since 1974, said: "Roger played way too good. He is the best I have ever played against."

Compliments do not come any bigger from a man who has played with the likes of Pete Sampras, Jimmy Connors, John McEnroe, Boris Becker, Stefan Edberg and Ivan Lendl.

Federer became the first man to win back-to-back Wimbledon and US Open titles in consecutive years since the game turned professional in 1968. He also joined an elite club of only four men since records began in the 1880s to win their first six grand slam finals. In the professional era nobody has won more than their first three.

"I amaze myself that I can back it up one tournament after another," he said. "I wonder why I always play so well, especially on big occasions."

It was another big occasion which so nearly pulled from him the most staggering performance of all year, but in the end a painful, niggling injury combined with an inspired foe in the form of Nalbandian ended his season in defeat.

Nalbandian's 67 67 62 61 76 victory in the final of the season-ending Masters Cup ended Federer's 35-match winning streak and his 24-straight finals wins. It also prevented Federer from claiming a third straight Masters Cup title and matching John McEnroe's professional-era best record for a season of 82-3 set in 1984.

However, it did little to shatter Federer's aura of invincibility as he pulled out all the stops after a month off with an ankle injury.

"I thought it was going to be over in five minutes at 4-0 [in the fifth set]," said Federer, who played the tournament with a strapped right ankle after suffering a bad sprain in training. "But I almost turned it around," he shrugged. "That would have been some incredible comeback."

Nalbandian knew he had been part of something special. "It makes me feel special to win like this. I left everything on court. It's not easy to keep focused, keep going, and I made it. He never loses in finals, so to beat him is really incredible."

Nalbandian got his place in Shanghai only after Roddick withdrew with a back injury and, after losing to Federer in his first match, his progress to the final went almost unnoticed.

"I was the last guy to get into the tournament, so it's normal," he smiled. "But I think I really surprised everybody with this victory. I think I surprised all the world."

the women's year 2005

by alix ramsay

Since time began, the world has loved a good comeback story. When it comes to tales of people defying the odds, triumphing over impossible circumstances and generally doing the unthinkable by returning to the fore from the brink of oblivion, Lazarus set the standard while, two millennia later, Frank Sinatra made a career out of it. And we loved it. No, you can't beat a good comeback story for warming the cockles of the heart.

Professional sport usually turns up a good tale or two over the course of a season but 2005 was truly a remarkable time for women's tennis. This was the year of the comeback and by the time Amelie Mauresmo had done for Mary Pierce in the WTA Tour Championships in November, it seemed that only those who had survived career-threatening injury, soul-destroying loss of confidence or desperate slump in form had a chance to win anything of note. Those who spent the year fit, willing and able were finished before they had even got started.

Justine Henin-Hardenne (BEL)

It all began in January with the WTA Tour trumpeting its new $88 million deal with Sony Ericsson. Suddenly the tour had money, it had a title sponsor but, alas, it was struggling to stump up big name players. Lindsay Davenport was the world No. 1 but just six months before she had talked of retirement and the joys of going off to start a family and get a real life.

The Williams sisters had been plagued by injury and lack of form and, as the new season began, it appeared that their star had waned. Serena had not won a grand slam title since Wimbledon 2003 while Venus had not got her hands on a major piece of silverware since the US Open in 2001.

The Belgian rivals, Justine Henin-Hardenne and Kim Clijsters, had taken over where the Williamses had left off with Henin-Hardenne mopping up the grand slam titles and Clijsters winning almost everything else in 2003 and the start of 2004.

The Belgian rivals, Justine Henin-Hardenne and Kim Clijsters, had taken over where the Williamses had left off with Henin-Hardenne mopping up the grand slam titles and Clijsters winning almost everything else in 2003 and the start of 2004 but they too were out of the running back in January. Henin-Hardenne was still trying to shake off a long and debilitating bout of illness and Clijsters was hoping against hope that the doctors were wrong and the injury to her left wrist would heal well enough for her to play at the very top level once again.

As for the wave of Russian stars who had, between them, won three grand slam trophies in 2004, Anastasia Myskina and Svetlana Kuznetsova both looked stunned to have won anything at all while Maria Sharapova was still growing, developing and learning about the business of being the hunted rather than the hunter.

As the tour rolled into Melbourne for the start of the Australian Open, the pundits were muttering about an "open draw" (a great cop out for those of us who are asked to put our reputations on the line and predict a winner before a ball has been struck in earnest) and the punters did not know where to look for a possible champion. Serena Williams, though, was talking a good fight.

It is never wise to underestimate Serena and it is positively foolish to antagonise her. When one gentle soul had the temerity to suggest, with all due respect, that she and her sister were not quite the force they once were, Serena, to use a phrase from a penny dreadful, bridled visibly. She was here to win and that was that.

"I definitely wouldn't be here if I didn't think so [that I could win]," she snapped. "I'd rather stay home. I always see myself as someone that's coming here for seriousness and to win the tournament. I don't think there's a player out there who would see their name against mine and go, "Oh, my God, yes!". People always assume that I'm No. 1, and I never correct them anyway."

Once the first week was out of the way and the youngest of the Williams clan was

im Clijsters (BEL)

the women's year 2005

by alix ramsay

getting into her stride on the court, she was back to her battling best off it. Our inquisitor, a man of quiet yet persistent manner, tried again. What was Serena's response to the idea that the Williams sisters were "in decline".

"I don't appreciate that language, to be honest with you," Serena roared. "I'm tired of not saying anything, but that's not fair. We're not declining. We're here."

And just to prove it, she walloped Mauresmo in the quarterfinal, fended off three match points against Sharapova in the semifinal and went on to overcome a rib injury and Davenport in the final 26 63 60.

Only a few minutes into the final, Williams went to stretch for a backhand and suddenly felt something pop. One of her ribs had clicked out of place and for a handful of games she was in serious trouble. The trainer helped manipulate everything back into alignment but by then the first set had gone. Back in business in the second set, Williams was able to shake off the shock of the injury and by the third set, she was in charge as Davenport collapsed. Well, you would collapse when faced with the steamroller that is Serena Williams in pursuit of a grand slam trophy. Even so, Williams was not done yet.

"This is one way to decline," she announced afterwards.

"It is a very fashionable way to decline."

The lesson to learn here is: don't mess with Serena.

Meanwhile, Henin-Hardenne and Clijsters were hard at work on their plans for a return. In March 2004, Clijsters had been playing at the Pacific Life Open in Indian Wells when her left wrist started to hurt. Thinking it was no more than a spot of tendinitis, she pulled out of the tournament and took herself off to the doctors. That was when everything started to go wrong.

The medics prodded and poked at the injury and came up with the alarming news that she had a bone spur on her wrist and it was cutting into the tendon every time she hit a backhand. Just for good measure, she also had a cyst that was making an already painful condition even worse. The doctors advised rest to let nature take its course.

Venus Williams (USA)

So Clijsters rested. Then she tried playing but her wrist broke down again. So she rested some more. Still the wrist would not heal. Surgery was called for and at that point she was told that, if she was lucky, she might be able to play again but never at the same level she had played to before. From March until the end of that year, she managed to play just five and a half matches – she had to pull out of the semifinal in Hasselt in the second set against Elena Bovina – and life was very glum indeed.

At the same time, she was splitting up with her fiancé, Lleyton Hewitt, and trying to avoid the prying eyes of the journalists and the camera men. Things could not have been worse.

But Clijsters is nothing if not an optimistic soul and, once the doctors gave her the go ahead, she started to work her socks in preparation for yet another comeback. This time there was no stopping her and, mopping up the titles in Indian Wells and Miami, she was back to her best in no time. She had been forced to endure the bad times, it seemed, for a reason and now she was a better player and a stronger person as a result.

"For my career it hasn't been the best but I think for my personal life, I think it's all been good," she said. "You learn so much more about yourself and you learn about life and about things that you want and things that you don't want. I learned just about me as a person, things that I would like to see or do in the future. I don't want to go too deep into things but just it made me a stronger person and a more grown up person."

Mature, grown up and belting the ball for all she was worth, Clijsters had a new view of life. Tennis was her much-loved job and she missed it when she was injured, but now losing was not the end of the world. Winning was still fun – and she was rather good at it – but being healthy was by far the most important part of her life.

The clay court season was not a particularly profitable time for her but back on the grass, she won the title in Eastbourne and headed for the American hard court swing with a new spring in her step. She was happy, she was healthy and she was about to have the best summer of her life.

As soon as her toes touched the American cement, Clijsters was all but unstoppable. She lost just one match in two and a half months and picked up four titles. To have claimed the US Open Series by dint of winning in Stanford, Los Angeles and Toronto meant that she was on course for the biggest pay cheque in women's sport. All she had to do was win the US Open and she would walk away with $2.2million. Ah, but the Open was the sticking point.

For all that Clijsters had been able to win trophies on any surface and on any continent, the small matter of a grand slam pot eluded her. Four times she had been to a major final and four times she had come away empty handed. Sometimes it was inexperience that cost her dear – as when she lost to Jennifer Capriati at the French Open in 2001 – and sometimes it was nerves and Henin-Hardenne who had ruined her day, as at the French and US Opens in 2003 and the Australian Open in 2004. The general opinion was that Clijsters was a choker and she was never destined to win a title that mattered.

But this was the new, mature Clijsters, the woman who had defied the doctors to come back and who was going to make the most of every opportunity that came her way. She absolutely clobbered everyone in the first week, she out-hit Venus in the quarterfinal, she out-thought Sharapova in the semifinal and then, taking her courage in both hands, she beat Mary Pierce 63 61 in the final. She could not quite believe it. At last she was a grand slam champion.

"I think for everything, there's a time and a place," she said. "Maybe it wasn't my time yet in those other grand slams. But those definitely motivate you to work harder and to work on a lot of things. Maybe that's why I'm sitting here now with this trophy next to me. I definitely think it all worked out very good for me."

Life had worked out pretty good for Henin-Hardenne, too. She launched her comeback six weeks after Clijsters but came back with a similar bang. In the spring of 2004, she had been felled by a virus that left her, at times, unable to get out of bed, much less play and win matches. Apart from one memorable comeback to win gold at the Athens Olympics, her season was all but over. Then, just when she thought she was ready to launch her new year in Australia, she overdid the training and picked up a knee injury.

Easing her way back in Miami – and reaching the quarterfinals – she found her feet on the clay, setting off an unbeaten run of 24 matches that brought her the titles in Charleston, Warsaw, Berlin and Roland Garros. Despite growing fatigue and a niggling back and hamstring problem, Henin-Hardenne was the queen of the red dirt and, as she disposed of a tired and nervous Mary Pierce in the final, she knew she was back where she knew she belonged. Paris is where she won her first major title and Paris is where she proved she could win major titles again.

"It's a big satisfaction," she said, in her understated way. "It's a great achievement. It's been very difficult time last year and I didn't know if I was going to be able to be at my best level any more, and I think I proved it many times in the last few weeks. For me it's a very special tournament where I had my best emotions in my life."

But after such a monumental effort, Henin-Hardenne had nothing left for the grass court season. The other main contenders were looking out of sorts and weary while Serena was still struggling with an ankle injury. Step forward, then, Venus to reclaim past victories.

While Serena had hogged the limelight in the previous couple of years, Venus had hidden in the shadows. It was not that she did not put in the work on the practice courts, it was just that the results would not come and, just when it seemed that she was about to make the breakthrough, she would find herself injured – again – and despondent.

But Wimbledon is a special place and has a peculiar restorative effect on the good and the great. The longer the tournament went on, the better Venus looked. She did not drop a set on her way to the final, beating Pierce in the quarters and walloping Sharapova in the semis before taking on the thundering might of Davenport in the final.

This was not a showdown for the faint hearted as for three blistering sets both women knocked seven bells out of the ball – and each other – until Venus won through 46 76 97. It was the longest women's final in Wimbledon's history and, for Davenport, it was a crushing blow as she had stood one point away from the trophy until Venus belted another backhand, snatched away the match point and headed for the finish.

As for Sharapova, the pin-up girl of the tour, she may have lost out to Venus in SW19 but a handful of weeks later she had moved into the top spot in the rankings. With three semifinal finishes in the grand slams to her name and three trophies in her racket bag, she may not have had the stellar year she had in 2004, but she had proved that she more than just a pretty face.

Then there were Pierce and Davenport who reached two grand slam finals apiece. Just 18 months before, Pierce and her catalogue of injuries seemed destined for retirement but suddenly fit, determined and wiser for her 30 years on the planet, she was back as a major force on the tour. Davenport, meanwhile, clung like a limpet to the No. 1 ranking and finished the year as the best player in the world. Again.

And then there was Mauresmo who, tired, fed up and out of sorts, took a breather after the US Open and returned better than ever to win the WTA Tour Championships in Los Angeles, the first major title of her career. The year of the comeback was over – and between them, Lazarus and Sinatra could not have played it better.

This was not a showdown for the faint hearted as for three blistering sets both women knocked seven bells out of the ball – and each other – until Venus won through 46 76 97. It was the longest women's final in Wimbledon's history and, for Davenport, it was a crushing blow...

2005 Australian Open Championships, 17–30 January – Men's Singles

Australian Open
The Grand Slam of Asia/Pacific

First round draw

1 Roger FEDERER (SUI)
Fabrice SANTORO (FRA)
Q Takao SUZUKI (JPN)
Jan-Michael GAMBILL (USA)
Davide SANGUINETTI (ITA)
Jarkko NIEMINEN (FIN)
Potito STARACE (ITA)
27 Paradorn SRICHAPHAN (THA)
22 Ivan LJUBICIC (CRO)
Luis HORNA (PER)
Q Federico LUZZI (ITA)
Q Marcos BAGHDATIS (CYP)
WC Yeu-Tzuoo WANG (TPE)
Q Tomas ZIB (CZE)
PR Scott DRAPER (AUS)
13 Tommy ROBREDO (ESP)
11 Joachim JOHANSSON (SWE)
Sjeng SCHALKEN (NED)
Yen-Hsun LU (TPE)
Peter WESSELS (NED)
Sargis SARGSIAN (ARM)
David SANCHEZ (ESP)
WC Paul BACCANELLO (AUS)
24 Feliciano LOPEZ (ESP)
29 Taylor DENT (USA)
Q Florent SERRA (FRA)
Michal TABARA (CZE)
Thomas ENQVIST (SWE)
Q Olivier PATIENCE (FRA)
Rainer SCHUETTLER (GER)
Q Dieter KINDLMANN (GER)
8 Andre AGASSI (USA)
4 Marat SAFIN (RUS)
Q Novak DJOKOVIC (SCG)
Ivo KARLOVIC (CRO)
Bohdan ULIHRACH (CZE)
LL Bjorn PHAU (GER)
Albert COSTA (ESP)
Oscar HERNANDEZ (ESP)
28 Mario ANCIC (CRO)
21 Nicolas KIEFER (GER)
Olivier ROCHUS (BEL)
Robby GINEPRI (USA)
WC Gael MONFILS (FRA)
WC Todd REID (AUS)
Karol BECK (SVK)
Xavier MALISSE (BEL)
16 Tommy HAAS (GER)
10 Gaston GAUDIO (ARG)
PR Justin GIMELSTOB (USA)
Juan MONACO (ARG)
Mardy FISH (USA)
Q Janko TIPSAREVIC (SCG)
Q Daniele BRACCIALI (ITA)
Robin SODERLING (SWE)
20 Dominik HRBATY (SVK)
30 Thomas JOHANSSON (SWE)
WC Peter LUCZAK (AUS)
Agustin CALLERI (ARG)
Max MIRNYI (BLR)
Kevin KIM (USA)
Hyung-Taik LEE (KOR)
Q Guillermo GARCIA-LOPEZ (ESP)
5 Carlos MOYA (ESP)

Second round

R.FEDERER (1) 61 61 62
T.SUZUKI (Q) 64 63 63
J.NIEMINEN 36 64 63 62
P.SRICHAPHAN (27) 16 62 75 64
I.LJUBICIC (22) 64 63 63
M.BAGHDATIS (Q) 61 36 61 36 63
T.ZIB (Q) 76(5) 62 64
T.ROBREDO (13) 57 62 64 62
J.JOHANSSON (11) 76(6) 62 63
P.WESSELS 63 64 64
S.SARGSIAN 76(5) 46 16 64 62
F.LOPEZ (24) 75 75 62
T.DENT (29) 75 62 64
M.TABARA 36 62 63 63
R.SCHUETTLER 76(3) 63 62
A.AGASSI (8) 64 63 60
M.SAFIN (4) 60 62 61
B.ULIHRACH 63 67(5) 75 62
B.PHAU (LL) 63 76(4) 63
M.ANCIC (28) 63 62 61
O.ROCHUS 75 26 36 62 63
G.MONFILS (WC) 16 63 64 76(6)
K.BECK 62 62 61
T.HAAS (16) 63 62 63
G.GAUDIO (10) 76(3) 64 63
M.FISH 26 60 64 46 97
J.TIPSAREVIC (Q) 76(4) 76(6) 36 61
D.HRBATY (20) 64 62 10 RET
T.JOHANSSON (30) 76(5) 46 63 46 60
A.CALLERI 64 57 64 46 64
K.KIM 36 64 63 36 61
G.GARCIA-LOPEZ (Q) 75 63 36 63

Third round

R.FEDERER (1) 63 64 64
J.NIEMINEN 63 64 62
M.BAGHDATIS (Q) 76(1) 64 67(2) 62
T.ROBREDO (13) 64 26 62 64
J.JOHANSSON (11) 63 75 64
F.LOPEZ (24) 46 63 64 76(3)
T.DENT (29) 64 61 64
A.AGASSI (8) 63 61 60
M.SAFIN (4) 64 61 63
M.ANCIC (28) 75 62 61
O.ROCHUS 61 63 63
K.BECK 57 26 62 76(5) 63
G.GAUDIO (10) 26 64 75 76(4)
D.HRBATY (20) 62 76(1) 36 75
T.JOHANSSON (30) 64 57 63 26 75
K.KIM 62 64 62

Fourth round

R.FEDERER (1) 63 52 RET
M.BAGHDATIS (Q) 76(2) 64 61
J.JOHANSSON (11) 63 36 57 76(2) 1311
A.AGASSI (8) 75 76(3) 61
M.SAFIN (4) 64 36 63 64
O.ROCHUS 67(6) 61 64 62
D.HRBATY (20) 76(5) 67(8) 67(3) 61 63
T.JOHANSSON (30) 36 62 67(4) 62 62

Quarter-finals

R.FEDERER (1) 62 62 76(4)
A.AGASSI (8) 67(4) 76(5) 76(3) 64
M.SAFIN (4) 46 76(1) 76(5) 76(2)
D.HRBATY (20) 75 63 61

Semi-finals

R.FEDERER (1) 63 64 64
M.SAFIN (4) 62 64 62

Final

M.SAFIN (4) 57 64 57 76(6) 97

Champion

M.SAFIN (4) 16 63 64 64

6 Guillermo CORIA (ARG)
Tomas BERDYCH (CZE)
Ricardo MELLO (BRA)
Alberto MARTIN (ESP)
WC Marc KIMMICH (AUS)
Mariano ZABALETA (ARG)
Q Melle VAN GEMERDEN (NED)
31 Juan Carlos FERRERO (ESP)
23 Fernando GONZALEZ (CHI)
Jose ACASUSO (ARG)
Lars BURGSMULLER (GER)
Igor ANDREEV (RUS)
Alex CALATRAVA (ESP)
Santiago VENTURA (ESP)
David FERRER (ESP)
9 David NALBANDIAN (ARG)
15 Mikhail YOUZHNY (RUS)
Jerome HAEHNEL (FRA)
Julien BENNETEAU (FRA)
Rafael NADAL (ESP)
Q Bobby REYNOLDS (USA)
Nicolas ALMAGRO (ESP)
Olivier MUTIS (FRA)
17 Andrei PAVEL (ROM)
25 Juan Ignacio CHELA (ARG)
Wayne ARTHURS (AUS)
PR Paul-Henri MATHIEU (FRA)
Gregory CARRAZ (FRA)
Florian MAYER (GER)
James BLAKE (USA)
Arnaud CLEMENT (FRA)
3 Lleyton HEWITT (AUS)
7 Tim HENMAN (GBR)
Cyril SAULNIER (FRA)
Filippo VOLANDRI (ITA)
Victor HANESCU (ROM)
LL Christophe ROCHUS (BEL)
Albert MONTANES (ESP)
Q Roko KARANUSIC (CRO)
26 Nikolay DAVYDENKO (RUS)
19 Vince SPADEA (USA)
Radek STEPANEK (CZE)
Felix MANTILLA (ESP)
Jan HERNYCH (CZE)
Fernando VERDASCO (ESP)
Gilles MULLER (LUX)
WC Chris GUCCIONE (AUS)
12 Guillermo CANAS (ARG)
14 Sebastien GROSJEAN (FRA)
Michael LLODRA (FRA)
Q Oliver MARACH (AUT)
Q Jean-Rene LISNARD (FRA)
Kenneth CARLSEN (DEN)
Philipp KOHLSCHREIBER (GER)
Anthony DUPUIS (FRA)
18 Nicolas MASSU (CHI)
32 Jurgen MELZER (AUT)
Raemon SLUITER (NED)
Flavio SARETTA (BRA)
WC Nathan HEALEY (AUS)
Jonas BJORKMAN (SWE)
Greg RUSEDSKI (GBR)
Irakli LABADZE (GEO)
2 Andy RODDICK (USA)

G.CORIA (6) 62 64 60
R.MELLO 63 63 76(5)
M.ZABALETA 64 62 67(5) 63
J.FERRERO (31) 26 63 64 64
F.GONZALEZ (23) 36 36 63 63 75
I.ANDREEV 76(2) 61 62
S.VENTURA 36 63 63 46 64
D.NALBANDIAN (9) 76(1) 46 46 63 64
M.YOUZHNY (15) 62 62 75
R.NADAL 60 64 62
B.REYNOLDS (Q) 57 64 76(7) 76(5)
A.PAVEL (17) 64 64 60
J.CHELA (25) 64 76(4) 76(1)
G.CARRAZ 64 57 75 76(5)
J.BLAKE 61 62 60
L.HEWITT (3) 63 64 61
T.HENMAN (7) 61 62 46 63
V.HANESCU 63 64 76(1)
C.ROCHUS (LL) 62 63 63
N.DAVYDENKO (26) 62 75 62
R.STEPANEK 63 57 46 75 63
J.HERNYCH 64 67(5) 61 60
F.VERDASCO 63 60 64
G.CANAS (12) 64 62 76(4)
S.GROSJEAN (14) 63 64 63
J.LISNARD (Q) 57 57 61 64 75
P.KOHLSCHREIBER 76(2) 62 61
N.MASSU (18) 67(7) 76(2) 63 62
J.MELZER (32) 33 RET
N.HEALEY (WC) 46 46 61 50 RET
G.RUSEDSKI 26 64 60 76(7)
A.RODDICK (2) 75 62 61

G.CORIA (6) 64 67(3) 63 76(3)
J.FERRERO (31) 61 62 60
F.GONZALEZ (23) 75 62 63
D.NALBANDIAN (9) 60 63 26 62
R.NADAL 61 46 46 75 63
B.REYNOLDS (Q) 76(6) 62 62
J.CHELA (25) 76(7) 62 76(3)
L.HEWITT (3) 46 76(8) 60 63
T.HENMAN (7) 75 61 64
N.DAVYDENKO (26) 64 64 62
R.STEPANEK 76(5) 61 16 67(2) 60
G.CANAS (12) 36 75 63 60
J.LISNARD (Q) 16 46 63 64 63
P.KOHLSCHREIBER 60 20 RET
J.MELZER (32) 63 62 76(3)
A.RODDICK (2) 60 36 62 63

G.CORIA (6) 63 62 61
D.NALBANDIAN (9) 67(3) 75 62 63
R.NADAL 61 61 63
L.HEWITT (3) 62 46 61 64
N.DAVYDENKO (26) 64 62 62
G.CANAS (12) 61 62 62
P.KOHLSCHREIBER 75 63 62
A.RODDICK (2) 62 62 75

D.NALBANDIAN (9) 57 75 63 60
L.HEWITT (3) 75 36 16 76(3) 62
N.DAVYDENKO (26) 63 64 63
A.RODDICK (2) 63 76(6) 61

L.HEWITT (3) 63 62 16 36 108
A.RODDICK (2) 63 75 41 RET

L.HEWITT (3) 36 76(3) 76(4) 61

2005 Australian Open Championships, 17–30 January – Women's Singles

Australian Open
The Grand Slam of Asia/Pacific

First round

1 Lindsay DAVENPORT (USA)
Conchita MARTINEZ (ESP)
Michaela PASTIKOVA (CZE)
Anne KREMER (LUX)
Maria VENTO-KABCHI (VEN)
Nicole VAIDISOVA (CZE)
WC Casey DELL'ACQUA (AUS)
31 Jelena KOSTANIC (CRO)
18 Elena LIKHOVTSEVA (RUS)
Sanda MAMIC (CRO)
WC Evie DOMINIKOVIC (AUS)
Mara SANTANGELO (ITA)
Marlene WEINGARTNER (GER)
Tathiana GARBIN (ITA)
WC Monique ADAMCZAK (AUS)
13 Karolina SPREM (CRO)
10 Alicia MOLIK (AUS)
Anabel MEDINA GARRIGUES (ESP)
Q Angela HAYNES (USA)
Q Aiko NAKAMURA (JPN)
Antonella SERRA ZANETTI (ITA)
Tatiana PANOVA (RUS)
Nicole PRATT (AUS)
23 Jelena JANKOVIC (SCG)
27 Anna SMASHNOVA (ISR)
Maria SANCHEZ LORENZO (ESP)
Barbora STRYCOVA (CZE)
Tamarine TANASUGARN (THA)
Shuai PENG (CHN)
Maria-Elena CAMERIN (ITA)
Eleni DANIILIDOU (GRE)
8 Venus WILLIAMS (USA)
3 Anastasia MYSKINA (RUS)
Kveta PESCHKE (CZE)
Emilie LOIT (FRA)
Tzipi OBZILER (ISR)
Q Meilen TU (USA)
Klara KOUKALOVA (CZE)
Q Anastasia YAKIMOVA (BLR)
25 Lisa RAYMOND (USA)
19 Nathalie DECHY (FRA)
Emmanuelle GAGLIARDI (SUI)
Catalina CASTANO (COL)
Mashona WASHINGTON (USA)
WC Capucine ROUSSEAU (FRA)
Tatiana PEREBIYNIS (UKR)
Marta MARRERO (ESP)
14 Francesca SCHIAVONE (ITA)
12 Patty SCHNYDER (SUI)
Yuliana FEDAK (UKR)
Stephanie FORETZ (FRA)
Q Michaella KRAJICEK (NED)
Meghann SHAUGHNESSY (USA)
Abigail SPEARS (USA)
Ludmila CERVANOVA (SVK)
20 Tatiana GOLOVIN (FRA)
26 Daniela HANTUCHOVA (SVK)
Akiko MORIGAMI (JPN)
Barbara SCHETT (AUT)
WC Tiffany WELFORD (AUS)
Anna CHAKVETADZE (RUS)
Arantxa PARRA-SANTONJA (ESP)
Alyona BONDARENKO (UKR)
6 Elena DEMENTIEVA (RUS)

Second round

L.DAVENPORT (1) 61 60
M.PASTIKOVA 64 64
N.VAIDISOVA 67(4) 64 62
J.KOSTANIC (31) 36 62 62
E.LIKHOVTSEVA (18) 63 63
E.DOMINIKOVIC (WC) 67(5) 64 63
T.GARBIN 75 76(5)
K.SPREM (13) 62 63
A.MOLIK (10) 61 63
A.NAKAMURA (Q) 63 64
T.PANOVA 46 62 61
J.JANKOVIC (23) 61 63
A.SMASHNOVA (27) 46 60 60
T.TANASUGARN 60 62
S.PENG 61 62
V.WILLIAMS (8) 61 75
A.MYSKINA (3) 61 64
T.OBZILER 76(11) 64
K.KOUKALOVA 63 63
L.RAYMOND (25) 60 61
N.DECHY (19) 64 63
M.WASHINGTON 62 63
T.PEREBIYNIS 16 64 75
F.SCHIAVONE (14) 63 62
P.SCHNYDER (12) 61 61
M.KRAJICEK (Q) 62 61
A.SPEARS 16 62 62
T.GOLOVIN (20) 63 75
D.HANTUCHOVA (26) 64 75
B.SCHETT 63 16 62
A.CHAKVETADZE 63 62
E.DEMENTIEVA (6) 63 63

Third round

L.DAVENPORT (1) 26 62 62
N.VAIDISOVA 60 75
E.LIKHOVTSEVA (18) 63 26 63
K.SPREM (13) 76(5) 76(2)
A.MOLIK (10) 62 64
T.PANOVA 36 64 62
A.SMASHNOVA (27) 62 62
V.WILLIAMS (8) 63 61
A.MYSKINA (3) 64 62
L.RAYMOND (25) 60 61
N.DECHY (19) 67(2) 76(5) 62
F.SCHIAVONE (14) 26 63 60
P.SCHNYDER (12) 36 63 64
A.SPEARS 75 61
D.HANTUCHOVA (26) 64 60
E.DEMENTIEVA (6) 62 61

Fourth round

L.DAVENPORT (1) 62 64
K.SPREM (13) 64 63
A.MOLIK (10) 63 62
V.WILLIAMS (8) 63 60
A.MYSKINA (3) W/O
N.DECHY (19) 63 63
P.SCHNYDER (12) 76(4) 63
E.DEMENTIEVA (6) 75 57 64

Quarter-finals

L.DAVENPORT (1) 62 62
A.MOLIK (10) 75 76(3)
N.DECHY (19) 64 62
P.SCHNYDER (12) 67(6) 76(4) 62

Semi-finals

L.DAVENPORT (1) 64 46 97
N.DECHY (19) 57 61 75

Final

L.DAVENPORT (1) 26 76(5) 64

Champion

S.WILLIAMS (7) 26 63 60

Seed	Player
5	Svetlana KUZNETSOVA (RUS)
Q	Jessica KIRKLAND (USA)
	Claudine SCHAUL (LUX)
	Marion BARTOLI (FRA)
	Mariana DIAZ-OLIVA (ARG)
	Saori OBATA (JPN)
	Kristina BRANDI (PUR)
29	Gisela DULKO (ARG)
17	Fabiola ZULUAGA (COL)
	Selima SFAR (TUN)
	Anna-Lena GROENEFELD (GER)
	Severine BELTRAME (FRA)
	Jill CRAYBAS (USA)
	Vera DOUCHEVINA (RUS)
Q	Nan-Nan LIU (CHN)
9	Vera ZVONAREVA (RUS)
15	Silvia FARINA ELIA (ITA)
	Julia SCHRUFF (GER)
	Marta DOMACHOWSKA (POL)
Q	Ting LI (CHN)
Q	Elena BALTACHA (GBR)
	Katarina SREBOTNIK (SLO)
	Stephanie COHEN-ALORO (FRA)
24	Mary PIERCE (FRA)
28	Shinobu ASAGOE (JPN)
	Anca BARNA (GER)
	Na LI (CHN)
	Laura GRANVILLE (USA)
Q	Zsofia GUBACSI (HUN)
	Lindsay LEE-WATERS (USA)
Q	Sesil KARATANTCHEVA (BUL)
4	Maria SHARAPOVA (RUS)
7	Serena WILLIAMS (USA)
	Camille PIN (FRA)
	Dally RANDRIANTEFY (MAD)
Q	Zuzana ONDRASKOVA (CZE)
WC	Sania MIRZA (IND)
WC	Cindy WATSON (AUS)
	Petra MANDULA (HUN)
30	Flavia PENNETTA (ITA)
22	Magdalena MALEEVA (BUL)
	Magui SERNA (ESP)
	Virginia RUANO PASCUAL (ESP)
	Alina JIDKOVA (RUS)
	Nuria LLAGOSTERA VIVES (ESP)
WC	Sophie FERGUSON (AUS)
	Virginie RAZZANO (FRA)
11	Nadia PETROVA (RUS)
16	Ai SUGIYAMA (JPN)
	Martina SUCHA (SVK)
	Lubomira KURHAJCOVA (SVK)
	Evgenia LINETSKAYA (RUS)
	Denisa CHLADKOVA (CZE)
	Silvija TALAJA (CRO)
	Marissa IRVIN (USA)
21	Amy FRAZIER (USA)
32	Iveta BENESOVA (CZE)
	Ana IVANOVIC (SCG)
	Maria KIRILENKO (RUS)
	Aniko KAPROS (HUN)
	Jie ZHENG (CHN)
	Dinara SAFINA (RUS)
	Samantha STOSUR (AUS)
2	Amelie MAURESMO (FRA)

Winner	Score
S.KUZNETSOVA (5)	61 61
M.BARTOLI	61 63
M.DIAZ-OLIVA	63 64
G.DULKO (29)	63 36 63
F.ZULUAGA (17)	63 75
A.GROENEFELD	61 63
V.DOUCHEVINA	36 76(2) 64
V.ZVONAREVA (9)	64 62
S.FARINA ELIA (15)	63 64
M.DOMACHOWSKA	61 36 60
E.BALTACHA (Q)	57 64 64
S.COHEN-ALORO	62 62
S.ASAGOE (28)	64 62
N.LI	62 46 62
L.LEE-WATERS	63 75
M.SHARAPOVA (4)	63 61
S.WILLIAMS (7)	61 61
D.RANDRIANTEFY	61 61
S.MIRZA (WC)	36 63 60
P.MANDULA	36 61 63
M.MALEEVA (22)	61 61
A.JIDKOVA	46 61 64
S.FERGUSON (WC)	26 76(6) 64
N.PETROVA (11)	61 62
M.SUCHA	75 64
E.LINETSKAYA	64 61
D.CHLADKOVA	76(3) 63
A.FRAZIER (21)	75 61
A.IVANOVIC	36 76(4) 61
M.KIRILENKO	57 62 64
D.SAFINA	75 36 64
A.MAURESMO (2)	62 63

Winner	Score
S.KUZNETSOVA (5)	62 60
M.DIAZ-OLIVA	76(2) 75
A.GROENEFELD	62 76(2)
V.DOUCHEVINA	63 63
S.FARINA ELIA (15)	63 76(5)
E.BALTACHA (Q)	26 63 61
N.LI	63 64
M.SHARAPOVA (4)	46 60 63
S.WILLIAMS (7)	63 60
S.MIRZA (WC)	62 61
M.MALEEVA (22)	64 75
N.PETROVA (11)	46 60 61
E.LINETSKAYA	60 62
A.FRAZIER (21)	61 36 62
A.IVANOVIC	61 61
A.MAURESMO (2)	26 61 60

Winner	Score
S.KUZNETSOVA (5)	63 76(5)
V.DOUCHEVINA	75 64
S.FARINA ELIA (15)	61 60
M.SHARAPOVA (4)	60 62
S.WILLIAMS (7)	61 64
N.PETROVA (11)	64 64
E.LINETSKAYA	63 64
A.MAURESMO (2)	62 75

Winner	Score
S.KUZNETSOVA (5)	64 62
M.SHARAPOVA (4)	46 61 62
S.WILLIAMS (7)	61 36 63
A.MAURESMO (2)	62 64

Winner	Score
M.SHARAPOVA (4)	46 62 62
S.WILLIAMS (7)	62 62

Winner	Score
S.WILLIAMS (7)	26 75 86

2005 Australian Open Championships, 17–30 January – Men's Doubles

First Round

1 Mark KNOWLES (BAH)
1 Daniel NESTOR (CAN)
Jurgen MELZER (AUT)
Alexander WASKE (GER)
PR Michael HILL (AUS)
Tripp PHILLIPS (USA)
Martin GARCIA (ARG)
Mariano HOOD (ARG)
WC Paul BACCANELLO (AUS)
WC Raphael DUREK (AUS)
WC Yen-Hsun LU (TPE)
WC Takao SUZUKI (JPN)
Giorgio GALIMBERTI (ITA)
Filippo VOLANDRI (ITA)
14 Julian KNOWLE (AUT)
14 Petr PALA (CZE)
9 Cyril SUK (CZE)
9 Pavel VIZNER (CZE)
WC Sadik KADIR (AUS)
WC Shannon NETTLE (AUS)
Jan-Michael GAMBILL (USA)
Kevin KIM (USA)
Ashley FISHER (AUS)
Travis PARROTT (USA)
Tomas BERDYCH (CZE)
Andrei PAVEL (ROM)
Ivo KARLOVIC (CRO)
Tom VANHOUDT (BEL)
Tomas CIBULEC (CZE)
Dominik HRBATY (SVK)
8 Wayne ARTHURS (AUS)
8 Paul HANLEY (AUS)
3 Mahesh BHUPATHI (IND)
3 Todd WOODBRIDGE (AUS)
WC Chris GUCCIONE (AUS)
WC Nathan HEALEY (AUS)
Igor ANDREEV (RUS)
Nikolay DAVYDENKO (RUS)
WC Adam FEENEY (AUS)
WC Marc KIMMICH (AUS)
Albert COSTA (ESP)
Rafael NADAL (ESP)
WC Domenic MARAFIOTE (AUS)
WC Robert SMEETS (AUS)
Agustin CALLERI (ARG)
Alberto MARTIN (ESP)
15 Julien BENNETEAU (FRA)
15 Nicolas MAHUT (FRA)
11 Frantisek CERMAK (CZE)
11 Leos FRIEDL (CZE)
Irakli LABADZE (GEO)
Rogier WASSEN (NED)
Jaroslav LEVINSKY (CZE)
David SKOCH (CZE)
Alex CALATRAVA (ESP)
David FERRER (ESP)
Chris HAGGARD (RSA)
Robbie KOENIG (RSA)
PR Justin GIMELSTOB (USA)
Graydon OLIVER (USA)
Juan MONACO (ARG)
Mariano ZABALETA (ARG)
5 Wayne BLACK (ZIM)
5 Kevin ULLYETT (ZIM)

Second Round

J.MELZER / A.WASKE 63 76(5)
M.GARCIA / M.HOOD 61 61
Y.LU (WC) / T.SUZUKI (WC) 76(4) 26 64
G.GALIMBERTI / F.VOLANDRI 64 36 75
C.SUK (9) / P.VIZNER (9) 63 63
A.FISHER / T.PARROTT 62 67(3) 64
T.BERDYCH / A.PAVEL 76(2) 64
W.ARTHURS (8) / P.HANLEY (8) 62 64
M.BHUPATHI (3) / T.WOODBRIDGE (3) 75 75
I.ANDREEV / N.DAVYDENKO 64 06 64
A.COSTA / R.NADAL 62 62
J.BENNETEAU (15) / N.MAHUT (15) 63 64
I.LABADZE / R.WASSEN 76(4) 63
A.CALATRAVA / D.FERRER 62 36 63
C.HAGGARD / R.KOENIG 36 62 63
W.BLACK (5) / K.ULLYETT (5) 64 61

Third Round

J.MELZER / A.WASKE 61 75
Y.LU (WC) / T.SUZUKI (WC) 63 62
A.FISHER / T.PARROTT 76(8) 64
T.BERDYCH / A.PAVEL 76(8) 75
M.BHUPATHI (3) / T.WOODBRIDGE (3) 64 46 62
A.COSTA / R.NADAL 76(2) 46 62
A.CALATRAVA / D.FERRER 46 61 64
W.BLACK (5) / K.ULLYETT (5) 76(2) 62

Quarterfinals

J.MELZER / A.WASKE 75 76(3)
T.BERDYCH / A.PAVEL 67(7) 64 63
M.BHUPATHI (3) / T.WOODBRIDGE (3) 46 76(2) 64
W.BLACK (5) / K.ULLYETT (5) 76(2) 62

Semifinals

J.MELZER / A.WASKE 76(3) 76(8)
W.BLACK (5) / K.ULLYETT (5) 76(3) 63

Final

W.BLACK (5) / K.ULLYETT (5) 63 64

Champions

W.BLACK (5) / K.ULLYETT (5) 64 64

Seed	Player
6	Michael LLODRA (FRA)
6	Fabrice SANTORO (FRA)
	Jose ACASUSO (ARG)
	Flavio SARETTA (BRA)
	Jan HERNYCH (CZE)
	Michal TABARA (CZE)
	Jordan KERR (AUS)
	Jim THOMAS (USA)
	Wesley MOODIE (RSA)
	Nenad ZIMONJIC (SCG)
	Feliciano LOPEZ (ESP)
	Fernando VERDASCO (ESP)
	Yves ALLEGRO (SUI)
	Michael KOHLMANN (GER)
12	Xavier MALISSE (BEL)
12	Olivier ROCHUS (BEL)
16	Simon ASPELIN (SWE)
16	Todd PERRY (AUS)
	Jean-Francois BACHELOT (FRA)
	Cyril SAULNIER (FRA)
	Juan Carlos FERRERO (ESP)
	Santiago VENTURA (ESP)
	Rick LEACH (USA)
	Brian MACPHIE (USA)
WC	Stephen HUSS (AUS)
WC	Peter LUCZAK (AUS)
	Ricardo MELLO (BRA)
	Andre SA (BRA)
	Bohdan ULIHRACH (CZE)
	Tomas ZIB (CZE)
4	Jonas BJORKMAN (SWE)
4	Max MIRNYI (BLR)
7	Gaston ETLIS (ARG)
7	Martin RODRIGUEZ (ARG)
	Juan Ignacio CHELA (ARG)
	Sebastian PRIETO (ARG)
	James BLAKE (USA)
	Mardy FISH (USA)
	Mariusz FYRSTENBERG (POL)
	Marcin MATKOWSKI (POL)
	Mario ANCIC (CRO)
	Ivan LJUBICIC (CRO)
	Karsten BRAASCH (GER)
	Jeff COETZEE (RSA)
	Karol BECK (SVK)
	Sargis SARGSIAN (ARM)
10	Martin DAMM (CZE)
10	Jared PALMER (USA)
13	Jonathan ERLICH (ISR)
13	Andy RAM (ISR)
	Lars BURGSMULLER (GER)
	Philipp KOHLSCHREIBER (GER)
	Arnaud CLEMENT (FRA)
PR	Paul-Henri MATHIEU (FRA)
	Hyung-Taik LEE (KOR)
	Jarkko NIEMINEN (FIN)
A	Roko KARANUSIC (CRO)
A	Uros VICO (ITA)
	Rainer SCHUETTLER (GER)
	Mikhail YOUZHNY (RUS)
	Robby GINEPRI (USA)
	Vince SPADEA (USA)
2	Bob BRYAN (USA)
2	Mike BRYAN (USA)

M.LLODRA (6)
F.SANTORO (6)
60 RET

J.KERR
J.THOMAS
26 60 62

W.MOODIE
N.ZIMONJIC
64 63

X.MALISSE (12)
O.ROCHUS (12)
64 63

S.ASPELIN (16)
T.PERRY (16)
61 67(3) 76(5)

R.LEACH
B.MACPHIE
46 62 35 RET

S.HUSS (WC)
P.LUCZAK (WC)
64 57 76(7)

J.BJORKMAN (4)
M.MIRNYI (4)
76(2) 61

J.CHELA
S.PRIETO
64 64

J.BLAKE
M.FISH
62 46 61

K.BRAASCH
J.COETZEE
64 64

K.BECK
S.SARGSIAN
76(8) 63

J.ERLICH (13)
A.RAM (13)
76(1) 62

H.LEE
J.NIEMINEN
76(4) 64

R.KARANUSIC (A)
U.VICO (A)
76(4) 21 RET

B.BRYAN (2)
M.BRYAN (2)
62 61

M.LLODRA (6)
F.SANTORO (6)
64 64

W.MOODIE
N.ZIMONJIC
63 64

S.ASPELIN (16)
T.PERRY (16)
36 75 64

J.BJORKMAN (4)
M.MIRNYI (4)
75 61

J.BLAKE
M.FISH
63 62

K.BECK
S.SARGSIAN
64 67(2) 75

J.ERLICH (13)
A.RAM (13)
W/O

B.BRYAN (2)
M.BRYAN (2)
60 62

M.LLODRA (6)
F.SANTORO (6)
63 76(3)

J.BJORKMAN (4)
M.MIRNYI (4)
62 46 76(5)

J.BLAKE
M.FISH
63 64

B.BRYAN (2)
M.BRYAN (2)
61 46 76(8)

J.BJORKMAN (4)
M.MIRNYI (4)
76(2) 75

B.BRYAN (2)
M.BRYAN (2)
64 64

B.BRYAN (2)
M.BRYAN (2)
61 63

2005 Australian Open Championships, 17-30 January – Women's Doubles

A Maria-Fernanda ALVES (BRA)
A Vanessa HENKE (GER)
Daniela HANTUCHOVA (SVK)
Martina NAVRATILOVA (USA)
WC Trudi MUSGRAVE (AUS)
WC Christina WHEELER (AUS)
Zsofia GUBACSI (HUN)
Petra MANDULA (HUN)
Ruxandra DRAGOMIR-ILIE (ROM)
Maureen DRAKE (CAN)
Olga BLAHOTOVA (CZE)
Libuse PRUSOVA (CZE)
WC Sophie FERGUSON (AUS)
WC Jaslyn HEWITT (AUS)
14 Shinobu ASAGOE (JPN)
14 Katarina SREBOTNIK (SLO)
9 Barbara SCHETT (AUT)
9 Patty SCHNYDER (SUI)
Milagros SEQUERA (VEN)
Meilen TU (USA)
Liga DEKMEIJERE (LAT)
Nana MIYAGI (JPN)
Arantxa PARRA-SANTONJA (ESP)
Magui SERNA (ESP)
WC Anne KREMER (LUX)
WC Maria SANCHEZ LORENZO (ESP)
Maret ANI (EST)
Flavia PENNETTA (ITA)
Nathalie DECHY (FRA)
Emilie LOIT (FRA)
6 Svetlana KUZNETSOVA (RUS)
6 Alicia MOLIK (AUS)
3 Lisa RAYMOND (USA)
3 Rennae STUBBS (AUS)
Martina MULLER (GER)
Julia SCHRUFF (GER)
Maria KIRILENKO (RUS)
Lina KRASNOROUTSKAYA (RUS)
Marion BARTOLI (FRA)
Anna-Lena GROENEFELD (GER)
Tathiana GARBIN (ITA)
Tina KRIZAN (SLO)
Jill CRAYBAS (USA)
Marlene WEINGARTNER (GER)
Leanne BAKER (NZL)
Francesca LUBIANI (ITA)
16 Eleni DANIILIDOU (GRE)
16 Nicole PRATT (AUS)
10 Ting LI (CHN)
10 Tian-Tian SUN (CHN)
Marta MARRERO (ESP)
Antonella SERRA ZANETTI (ITA)
Caroline DHENIN (FRA)
Silvija TALAJA (CRO)
Denisa CHLADKOVA (CZE)
Lubomira KURHAJCOVA (SVK)
WC Su-Wei HSIEH (TPE)
WC Seiko OKAMOTO (JPN)
Bryanne STEWART (AUS)
Samantha STOSUR (AUS)
Stephanie COHEN-ALORO (FRA)
Selima SFAR (TUN)
7 Anastasia MYSKINA (RUS)
7 Vera ZVONAREVA (RUS)

D.HANTUCHOVA / M.NAVRATILOVA 61 63
T.MUSGRAVE (WC) / C.WHEELER (WC) 62 26 63
R.DRAGOMIR-ILIE / M.DRAKE 64 61
S.ASAGOE (14) / K.SREBOTNIK (14) 64 61
M.SEQUERA / M.TU 75 64
L.DEKMEIJERE / N.MIYAGI 46 75 63
M.ANI / F.PENNETTA 46 62 62
S.KUZNETSOVA (6) / A.MOLIK (6) 63 62
L.RAYMOND (3) / R.STUBBS (3) 60 46 63
M.BARTOLI / A.GROENEFELD 63 61
T.GARBIN / T.KRIZAN 63 75
E.DANIILIDOU (16) / N.PRATT (16) 64 75
T.LI (10) / T.SUN (10) 62 63
D.CHLADKOVA / L.KURHAJCOVA 63 62
B.STEWART / S.STOSUR 63 76(5)
A.MYSKINA (7) / V.ZVONAREVA (7) 76(5) 63

D.HANTUCHOVA / M.NAVRATILOVA 62 60
S.ASAGOE (14) / K.SREBOTNIK (14) 64 36 75
M.SEQUERA / M.TU 62 62
S.KUZNETSOVA (6) / A.MOLIK (6) 60 63
M.BARTOLI / A.GROENEFELD 10 RET
E.DANIILIDOU (16) / N.PRATT (16) 64 63
T.LI (10) / T.SUN (10) 36 60 63
A.MYSKINA (7) / V.ZVONAREVA (7) 76(4) 67(3) 76(4)

D.HANTUCHOVA / M.NAVRATILOVA 64 64
S.KUZNETSOVA (6) / A.MOLIK (6) 36 63 63
E.DANIILIDOU (16) / N.PRATT (16) 63 26 64
A.MYSKINA (7) / V.ZVONAREVA (7) 61 75

S.KUZNETSOVA (6) / A.MOLIK (6) 63 60
A.MYSKINA (7) / V.ZVONAREVA (7) 64 63

S.KUZNETSOVA (6) / A.MOLIK (6) 62 63

S.KUZNETSOVA (6) / A.MOLIK (6) 63 64

8 Elena DEMENTIEVA (RUS)
8 Ai SUGIYAMA (JPN)
Yuliana FEDAK (UKR)
Tatiana POUTCHEK (BLR)
WC Beti SEKULOVSKI (AUS)
WC Cindy WATSON (AUS)
Anastasia RODIONOVA (RUS)
Abigail SPEARS (USA)
Alina JIDKOVA (RUS)
Tatiana PEREBIYNIS (UKR)
Jennifer RUSSELL (USA)
Mara SANTANGELO (ITA)
Yulia BEYGELZIMER (UKR)
Ipek SENOGLU (TUR)
12 Zi YAN (CHN)
12 Jie ZHENG (CHN)
13 Francesca SCHIAVONE (ITA)
13 Roberta VINCI (ITA)
Janet LEE (TPE)
Shuai PENG (CHN)
WC Jelena JANKOVIC (SCG)
WC Aniko KAPROS (HUN)
Natalie GRANDIN (RSA)
Conchita MARTINEZ-GRANADOS (ESP)
Teryn ASHLEY (USA)
Laura GRANVILLE (USA)
Gabriela NAVRATILOVA (CZE)
Michaela PASTIKOVA (CZE)
Jennifer HOPKINS (USA)
Mashona WASHINGTON (USA)
4 Conchita MARTINEZ (ESP)
4 Virginia RUANO PASCUAL (ESP)
5 Janette HUSAROVA (SVK)
5 Elena LIKHOVTSEVA (RUS)
Casey DELL'ACQUA (AUS)
Nicole SEWELL (AUS)
Chia-Jung CHUANG (TPE)
Rika FUJIWARA (JPN)
Maria-Elena CAMERIN (ITA)
Silvia FARINA ELIA (ITA)
Anabel MEDINA GARRIGUES (ESP)
Dinara SAFINA (RUS)
Nuria LLAGOSTERA VIVES (ESP)
Galina VOSKOBOEVA (RUS)
Els CALLENS (BEL)
Lisa MCSHEA (AUS)
11 Gisela DULKO (ARG)
11 Maria VENTO-KABCHI (VEN)
15 Lindsay DAVENPORT (USA)
15 Corina MORARIU (USA)
WC Daniella DOMINIKOVIC (AUS)
WC Evie DOMINIKOVIC (AUS)
Patricia WARTUSCH (AUT)
Jasmin WOEHR (GER)
Alyona BONDARENKO (UKR)
Emmanuelle GAGLIARDI (SUI)
Eva BIRNEROVA (CZE)
Andreea VANC (ROM)
Iveta BENESOVA (CZE)
Kveta PESCHKE (CZE)
Jelena KOSTANIC (CRO)
Claudine SCHAUL (LUX)
2 Cara BLACK (ZIM)
2 Liezel HUBER (RSA)

E.DEMENTIEVA (8) / A.SUGIYAMA (8) 63 60
B.SEKULOVSKI (WC) / C.WATSON (WC) 26 63 64
J.RUSSELL / M.SANTANGELO 64 57 62
Y.BEYGELZIMER / I.SENOGLU 26 62 64
J.LEE / S.PENG 67(3) 64 62
J.JANKOVIC (WC) / A.KAPROS (WC) 76(4) 75
G.NAVRATILOVA / M.PASTIKOVA 64 67(1) 63
J.HOPKINS / M.WASHINGTON 75 64
J.HUSAROVA (5) / E.LIKHOVTSEVA (5) 63 63
C.CHUANG / R.FUJIWARA 62 75
A.MEDINA GARRIGUES / D.SAFINA 63 64
G.DULKO (11) / M.VENTO-KABCHI (11) 75 61
L.DAVENPORT (15) / C.MORARIU (15) 62 62
A.BONDARENKO / E.GAGLIARDI 62 63
E.BIRNEROVA / A.VANC 75 67(5) 62
C.BLACK (2) / L.HUBER (2) 62 60

E.DEMENTIEVA (8) / A.SUGIYAMA (8) 63 63
J.RUSSELL / M.SANTANGELO 63 67(4) 63
J.LEE / S.PENG 76(3) 63
G.NAVRATILOVA / M.PASTIKOVA 26 64 63
C.CHUANG / R.FUJIWARA 67(1) 61 75
A.MEDINA GARRIGUES / D.SAFINA 61 67(6) 64
L.DAVENPORT (15) / C.MORARIU (15) 64 62
E.BIRNEROVA / A.VANC 67(6) 75 63

J.RUSSELL / M.SANTANGELO 64 64
G.NAVRATILOVA / M.PASTIKOVA 62 46 61
A.MEDINA GARRIGUES / D.SAFINA 62 63
L.DAVENPORT (15) / C.MORARIU (15) 62 62

G.NAVRATILOVA / M.PASTIKOVA 62 63
L.DAVENPORT (15) / C.MORARIU (15) 61 36 61

L.DAVENPORT (15) / C.MORARIU (15) 36 62 63

2005 Australian Open Championships, 17–30 January – Mixed Doubles

First round

1 Daniel NESTOR (CAN)
1 Rennae STUBBS (AUS)
Petr PALA (CZE)
Roberta VINCI (ITA)
Mariano HOOD (ARG)
Maria VENTO-KABCHI (VEN)
WC Luke BOURGEOIS (AUS)
WC Sophie FERGUSON (AUS)
Andy RAM (ISR)
Conchita MARTINEZ (ESP)
A Sebastian PRIETO (ARG)
A Gisela DULKO (ARG)
Gaston ETLIS (ARG)
Emilie LOIT (FRA)
8 Leos FRIEDL (CZE)
8 Janette HUSAROVA (SVK)
A Chris HAGGARD (RSA)
A Meilen TU (USA)
WC Wayne ARTHURS (AUS)
WC Trudi MUSGRAVE (AUS)
Martin DAMM (CZE)
Els CALLENS (BEL)
Paul HANLEY (AUS)
Corina MORARIU (USA)
Mark KNOWLES (BAH)
Daniela HANTUCHOVA (SVK)
WC Scott DRAPER (AUS)
WC Samantha STOSUR (AUS)
Cyril SUK (CZE)
Lisa MCSHEA (AUS)
6 Nenad ZIMONJIC (SCG)
6 Elena LIKHOVTSEVA (RUS)
5 Bob BRYAN (USA)
5 Vera ZVONAREVA (RUS)
Martin RODRIGUEZ (ARG)
Emmanuelle GAGLIARDI (SUI)
Simon ASPELIN (SWE)
Zi YAN (CHN)
A Frantisek CERMAK (CZE)
A Katarina SREBOTNIK (SLO)
Julian KNOWLE (AUT)
Barbara SCHETT (AUT)
WC Yen-Hsun LU (TPE)
WC Nan-Nan LIU (CHN)
Todd PERRY (AUS)
Milagros SEQUERA (VEN)
4 Kevin ULLYETT (ZIM)
4 Liezel HUBER (RSA)
7 Max MIRNYI (BLR)
7 Martina NAVRATILOVA (USA)
Todd WOODBRIDGE (AUS)
Eleni DANIILIDOU (GRE)
Pavel VIZNER (CZE)
Nicole PRATT (AUS)
WC Nathan HEALEY (AUS)
WC Evie DOMINIKOVIC (AUS)
Rick LEACH (USA)
Virginia RUANO PASCUAL (ESP)
Jonathan ERLICH (ISR)
Tian-Tian SUN (CHN)
WC Peter LUCZAK (AUS)
WC Jaslyn HEWITT (AUS)
2 Wayne BLACK (ZIM)
2 Cara BLACK (ZIM)

Second round

D.NESTOR (1) / R.STUBBS (1) 46 64 10(7)
M.HOOD / M.VENTO-KABCHI 76(1) 62
A.RAM / C.MARTINEZ 57 76(8) 10(6)
L.FRIEDL (8) / J.HUSAROVA (8) 75 63
W.ARTHURS (WC) / T.MUSGRAVE (WC) 64 26 10(4)
M.DAMM / E.CALLENS 63 76(5)
S.DRAPER (WC) / S.STOSUR (WC) 63 76(2)
N.ZIMONJIC (6) / E.LIKHOVTSEVA (6) 63 61
B.BRYAN (5) / V.ZVONAREVA (5) 62 67(6) 10(8)
F.CERMAK (A) / K.SREBOTNIK (A) 63 64
Y.LU (WC) / N.LIU (WC) 46 61 10(6)
K.ULLYETT (4) / L.HUBER (4) 36 62 10(5)
M.MIRNYI (7) / M.NAVRATILOVA (7) 64 64
P.VIZNER / N.PRATT 61 64
R.LEACH / V.RUANO PASCUAL 63 76(4)
W.BLACK (2) / C.BLACK (2) 62 63

Quarterfinals

D.NESTOR (1) / R.STUBBS (1) 62 63
A.RAM / C.MARTINEZ 67(4) 61 10(6)
W.ARTHURS (WC) / T.MUSGRAVE (WC) W/O
S.DRAPER (WC) / S.STOSUR (WC) 63 64
B.BRYAN (5) / V.ZVONAREVA (5) 63 62
K.ULLYETT (4) / L.HUBER (4) W/O
M.MIRNYI (7) / M.NAVRATILOVA (7) W/O
W.BLACK (2) / C.BLACK (2) 57 76(4) 10(8)

Semifinals

A.RAM / C.MARTINEZ 75 67(3) 10(12)
S.DRAPER (WC) / S.STOSUR (WC) 62 76(7)
K.ULLYETT (4) / L.HUBER (4) 67(5) 63 10(8)
M.MIRNYI (7) / M.NAVRATILOVA (7) 75 64

Final

S.DRAPER (WC) / S.STOSUR (WC) 75 63
K.ULLYETT (4) / L.HUBER (4) 62 36 10(8)

Champions

S.DRAPER (WC) / S.STOSUR (WC) 62 26 10(6)

Serena Williams (USA)

2005 French Open Championships Roland Garros, 23 May–5 June – Men's Singles

1 Roger FEDERER (SUI)
Q Dudi SELA (ISR)
Nicolas ALMAGRO (ESP)
Philipp KOHLSCHREIBER (GER)
Christophe ROCHUS (BEL)
Q Tomas BEHREND (GER)
Michael LLODRA (FRA)
25 Fernando GONZALEZ (CHI)
17 Dominik HRBATY (SVK)
Janko TIPSAREVIC (SCG)
LL Hugo ARMANDO (USA)
Q Fernando VICENTE (ESP)
Q Robin VIK (CZE)
Kevin KIM (USA)
Alberto MARTIN (ESP)
14 Carlos MOYA (ESP)
10 David NALBANDIAN (ARG)
Marcos BAGHDATIS (CYP)
Tomas BERDYCH (CZE)
Jeff MORRISON (USA)
Oscar HERNANDEZ (ESP)
Q Daniel GIMENO-TRAVER (ESP)
Q Marcos DANIEL (BRA)
18 Mario ANCIC (CRO)
31 Juan Ignacio CHELA (ARG)
Rainer SCHUETTLER (GER)
Victor HANESCU (ROM)
Michal TABARA (CZE)
Luis HORNA (PER)
Jerome HAEHNEL (FRA)
LL Juan-Pablo BRZEZICKI (ARG)
7 Tim HENMAN (GBR)
4 Rafael NADAL (ESP)
Lars BURGSMULLER (GER)
Mardy FISH (USA)
Xavier MALISSE (BEL)
Peter WESSELS (NED)
Ricardo MELLO (BRA)
LL Daniele BRACCIALI (ITA)
30 Richard GASQUET (FRA)
23 Sebastien GROSJEAN (FRA)
Juan MONACO (ARG)
WC Thierry ASCIONE (FRA)
Davide SANGUINETTI (ITA)
Andrei PAVEL (ROM)
WC Florent SERRA (FRA)
Paradorn SRICHAPHAN (THA)
16 Radek STEPANEK (CZE)
33 Robin SODERLING (SWE)
Fernando VERDASCO (ESP)
Hyung-Taik LEE (KOR)
Alex CALATRAVA (ESP)
WC Gilles SIMON (FRA)
WC Olivier PATIENCE (FRA)
Jiri VANEK (CZE)
20 David FERRER (ESP)
26 Jiri NOVAK (CZE)
Bjorn PHAU (GER)
Felix MANTILLA (ESP)
Tomas ZIB (CZE)
PR Dmitry TURSUNOV (RUS)
Stefan KOUBEK (AUT)
Julien BENNETEAU (FRA)
5 Gaston GAUDIO (ARG)

R.FEDERER (1) 61 64 60
N.ALMAGRO 76(6) 64 63
T.BEHREND (Q) 46 62 75 62
F.GONZALEZ (25) 76(3) 63 62
J.TIPSAREVIC 67(5) 63 36 63 86
F.VICENTE (Q) 76(2) 64 26 46 63
R.VIK (Q) 64 76(6) 75
C.MOYA (14) 57 61 64 62
D.NALBANDIAN (10) 06 64 64 64
T.BERDYCH 63 62 64
O.HERNANDEZ 67(4) 60 63 64
M.ANCIC (18) 62 61 76(4)
J.CHELA (31) 36 61 64 63
V.HANESCU 62 46 62 61
L.HORNA 76(2) 75 63
T.HENMAN (7) 62 61 64
R.NADAL (4) 61 76(4) 61
X.MALISSE 62 61 61
P.WESSELS 64 61 63
R.GASQUET (30) 36 63 62 64
S.GROSJEAN (23) 75 63 61
D.SANGUINETTI 36 57 60 63 64
F.SERRA (WC) 62 62 63
R.STEPANEK (16) 36 63 61 61
R.SODERLING (33) 16 36 63 63 63
H.LEE 64 26 57 76(4) 64
O.PATIENCE (WC) 62 62 46 63
D.FERRER (20) 26 76(8) 64 60
J.NOVAK (26) 46 62 63 61
F.MANTILLA 62 61 63
D.TURSUNOV (PR) 46 61 64 61
G.GAUDIO (5) 75 60 61

R.FEDERER (1) 63 76(0) 62
F.GONZALEZ (25) 63 64 64
F.VICENTE (Q) 63 16 76(2) 63
C.MOYA (14) 76(6) 67(4) 63 61
D.NALBANDIAN (10) 63 62 61
M.ANCIC (18) 46 61 62 63
V.HANESCU 75 61 36 75
L.HORNA 75 67(2) 63 64
R.NADAL (4) 62 62 64
R.GASQUET (30) 63 76(1) 61
S.GROSJEAN (23) 60 63 62
R.STEPANEK (16) 63 64 61
H.LEE 62 63 64
D.FERRER (20) 63 76(5) 75
F.MANTILLA 62 06 36 75 63
G.GAUDIO (5) W/O

R.FEDERER (1) 76(9) 75 62
C.MOYA (14) 64 76(4) 67(3) 06 64
D.NALBANDIAN (10) 64 76(4) 63
V.HANESCU 63 64 64
R.NADAL (4) 64 63 62
S.GROSJEAN (23) 61 46 36 63 64
D.FERRER (20) 63 61 75
G.GAUDIO (5) 64 64 63

R.FEDERER (1) 61 64 63
V.HANESCU 63 46 57 61 62
R.NADAL (4) 64 36 60 63
D.FERRER (20) 26 64 76(5) 57 64

R.FEDERER (1) 62 76(3) 63
R.NADAL (4) 75 62 60

R.NADAL (4) 63 46 64 63

R.NADAL (4) 67(6) 63 61 75

8	Guillermo CORIA (ARG)	G.CORIA (8)
	Kenneth CARLSEN (DEN)	64 62 64
Q	Novak DJOKOVIC (SCG)	N.DJOKOVIC (Q)
	Robby GINEPRI (USA)	60 60 63
	Jurgen MELZER (AUT)	J.MELZER
	Wayne ARTHURS (AUS)	64 62 76(4)
	Gilles MULLER (LUX)	M.YOUZHNY (29)
29	Mikhail YOUZHNY (RUS)	64 61 60
21	Tommy HAAS (GER)	T.HAAS (21)
	Florian MAYER (GER)	61 62 64
	Vince SPADEA (USA)	V.SPADEA
	Albert COSTA (ESP)	64 76(6) 62
	Guillermo GARCIA-LOPEZ (ESP)	O.ROCHUS
	Olivier ROCHUS (BEL)	76(4) 75 46 63
Q	Sasa TUKSAR (CRO)	N.DAVYDENKO (12)
12	Nikolay DAVYDENKO (RUS)	62 64 63
15	Tommy ROBREDO (ESP)	T.ROBREDO (15)
WC	Peter LUCZAK (AUS)	46 63 63 63
LL	Dick NORMAN (BEL)	D.NORMAN (LL)
	Jean-Rene LISNARD (FRA)	61 61 64
	Gustavo KUERTEN (BRA)	D.SANCHEZ
	David SANCHEZ (ESP)	63 60 46 61
PR	Scott DRAPER (AUS)	T.JOHANSSON (19)
19	Thomas JOHANSSON (SWE)	67(5) 61 36 60 61
32	Juan Carlos FERRERO (ESP)	J.FERRERO (32)
	Karol BECK (SVK)	64 63 63
	Fabrice SANTORO (FRA)	J.HERNYCH
	Jan HERNYCH (CZE)	76(4) 36 61 46 64
	Thomas ENQVIST (SWE)	L.DLOUHY (Q)
Q	Lukas DLOUHY (CZE)	62 76(3) 61
	Raemon SLUITER (NED)	M.SAFIN (3)
3	Marat SAFIN (RUS)	61 46 64 62
6	Andre AGASSI (USA)	J.NIEMINEN (Q)
Q	Jarkko NIEMINEN (FIN)	75 46 67(6) 61 60
	Jonas BJORKMAN (SWE)	I.ANDREEV
	Igor ANDREEV (RUS)	26 62 62 75
WC	Arnaud CLEMENT (FRA)	A.CLEMENT (WC)
PR	Alexander POPP (GER)	62 64 67(1) 62
	Ivo KARLOVIC (CRO)	N.KIEFER (28)
28	Nicolas KIEFER (GER)	63 63 64
24	Feliciano LOPEZ (ESP)	P.MATHIEU
	Paul-Henri MATHIEU (FRA)	62 60 67(5) 64
Q	Chris GUCCIONE (AUS)	C.GUCCIONE (Q)
	Santiago VENTURA (ESP)	63 26 61 36 62
	Albert MONTANES (ESP)	A.MONTANES
	Sargis SARGSIAN (ARM)	61 64 60
WC	Gael MONFILS (FRA)	G.CANAS (9)
9	Guillermo CANAS (ARG)	63 61 60
13	Ivan LJUBICIC (CRO)	M.PUERTA
	Mariano PUERTA (ARG)	75 75 62
Q	Anthony DUPUIS (FRA)	K.VLIEGEN (Q)
Q	Kristof VLIEGEN (BEL)	64 61 62
Q	Tomas TENCONI (ITA)	J.BLAKE (Q)
Q	James BLAKE (USA)	62 64 76(8)
Q	Stanislas WAWRINKA (SUI)	S.WAWRINKA (Q)
22	Nicolas MASSU (CHI)	67(4) 62 62 64
27	Filippo VOLANDRI (ITA)	F.VOLANDRI (27)
	Cyril SAULNIER (FRA)	60 62 61
	Greg RUSEDSKI (GBR)	F.SARETTA (LL)
LL	Flavio SARETTA (BRA)	62 76(7) 63
	Jose ACASUSO (ARG)	J.ACASUSO
	Max MIRNYI (BLR)	64 76(9) 62
WC	Jo-Wilfried TSONGA (FRA)	A.RODDICK (2)
2	Andy RODDICK (USA)	63 62 64

G.CORIA (8) 46 62 32 RET

J.MELZER 63 64 76(5)

T.HAAS (21) 64 63 RET

N.DAVYDENKO (12) 36 75 62 63

T.ROBREDO (15) 64 62 64

D.SANCHEZ 63 36 46 76(4) 64

J.FERRERO (32) 64 64 62

M.SAFIN (3) 67(6) 63 75 61

I.ANDREEV 62 64 67(3) 62

N.KIEFER (28) 46 62 62 46 64

P.MATHIEU 63 64 64

G.CANAS (9) 61 63 64

M.PUERTA 63 75 62

S.WAWRINKA (Q) 67(9) 57 61 63 64

F.VOLANDRI (27) 64 61 62

J.ACASUSO 36 46 64 63 86

G.CORIA (8) 61 61 76(2)

N.DAVYDENKO (12) 75 60 60

T.ROBREDO (15) 64 63 61

M.SAFIN (3) 76(5) 75 16 76(2)

N.KIEFER (28) 64 76(7) 36 64

G.CANAS (9) 63 76(4) 26 67(5) 86

M.PUERTA 16 63 61 64

J.ACASUSO 30 RET

N.DAVYDENKO (12) 26 63 76(1) 62

T.ROBREDO (15) 75 16 61 46 86

G.CANAS (9) W/O

M.PUERTA 64 61 61

N.DAVYDENKO (12) 36 61 62 46 64

M.PUERTA 62 36 16 63 64

M.PUERTA 63 57 26 64 64

2005 French Open Championships Roland Garros, 23 May–5 June – Women's Singles

First round

1 Lindsay DAVENPORT (USA)
Katarina SREBOTNIK (SLO)
WC Mailyne ANDRIEUX (FRA)
Shuai PENG (CHN)
Tatiana PANOVA (RUS)
Q Clarisa FERNANDEZ (ARG)
Virginie RAZZANO (FRA)
25 Dinara SAFINA (RUS)
20 Daniela HANTUCHOVA (SVK)
Q Michaella KRAJICEK (NED)
Denisa CHLADKOVA (CZE)
Catalina CASTANO (COL)
Ludmila CERVANOVA (SVK)
Aiko NAKAMURA (JPN)
Q Meilen TU (USA)
14 Kim CLIJSTERS (BEL)
9 Vera ZVONAREVA (RUS)
Q Yvonne MEUSBURGER (AUT)
Q Eva BIRNEROVA (CZE)
Maria KIRILENKO (RUS)
Jelena KOSTANIC (CRO)
Tamarine TANASUGARN (THA)
Vera DOUCHEVINA (RUS)
21 Mary PIERCE (FRA)
32 Flavia PENNETTA (ITA)
Jill CRAYBAS (USA)
Marta DOMACHOWSKA (POL)
Stephanie COHEN-ALORO (FRA)
Q Sandra KLOESEL (GER)
Q Mara SANTANGELO (ITA)
Yoon-Jeong CHO (KOR)
8 Patty SCHNYDER (SUI)
4 Elena DEMENTIEVA (RUS)
Barbora STRYCOVA (CZE)
Sanda MAMIC (CRO)
Lisa RAYMOND (USA)
Akiko MORIGAMI (JPN)
Angela HAYNES (USA)
Maria-Elena CAMERIN (ITA)
31 Karolina SPREM (CRO)
18 Silvia FARINA ELIA (ITA)
Anne KREMER (LUX)
Shenay PERRY (USA)
Arantxa PARRA-SANTONJA (ESP)
WC Sophie FERGUSON (AUS)
Mariana DIAZ-OLIVA (ARG)
Yuliana FEDAK (UKR)
16 Elena LIKHOVTSEVA (RUS)
11 Venus WILLIAMS (USA)
Marta MARRERO (ESP)
Fabiola ZULUAGA (COL)
Q Libuse PRUSOVA (CZE)
Alyona BONDARENKO (UKR)
Sesil KARATANTCHEVA (BUL)
Julia SCHRUFF (GER)
19 Shinobu ASAGOE (JPN)
27 Amy FRAZIER (USA)
Meghann SHAUGHNESSY (USA)
Emilie LOIT (FRA)
Claudine SCHAUL (LUX)
Tatiana PEREBIYNIS (UKR)
Emmanuelle GAGLIARDI (SUI)
(10) Maria SANCHEZ LORENZO (ESP)
5 Anastasia MYSKINA (RUS)

Second round

L.DAVENPORT (1) 36 62 62
S.PENG 60 61
C.FERNANDEZ (Q) 63 62
V.RAZZANO 63 63
D.HANTUCHOVA (20) 63 61
C.CASTANO 61 62
L.CERVANOVA 46 62 61
K.CLIJSTERS (14) 61 60
V.ZVONAREVA (9) 63 61
E.BIRNEROVA (Q) 26 75 63
J.KOSTANIC 60 61
M.PIERCE (21) 62 75
F.PENNETTA (32) 63 64
M.DOMACHOWSKA 63 63
S.KLOESEL (Q) 76(5) 61
P.SCHNYDER (8) 63 64
E.DEMENTIEVA (4) 63 63
S.MAMIC 62 64
A.MORIGAMI 75 64
K.SPREM (31) 64 62
S.FARINA ELIA (18) 75 62
A.PARRA-SANTONJA 36 63 64
M.DIAZ-OLIVA 64 36 61
E.LIKHOVTSEVA (16) 26 64 64
V.WILLIAMS (11) 63 62
F.ZULUAGA 61 60
S.KARATANTCHEVA 46 75 64
S.ASAGOE (19) 75 62
A.FRAZIER (27) 75 57 75
E.LOIT 63 60
E.GAGLIARDI 36 63 75
M.SANCHEZ LORENZO 64 46 60

Third round

L.DAVENPORT (1) 36 76(4) 60
V.RAZZANO 61 61
D.HANTUCHOVA (20) 64 63
K.CLIJSTERS (14) 62 61
V.ZVONAREVA (9) 46 63 60
M.PIERCE (21) 61 60
F.PENNETTA (32) 64 63
P.SCHNYDER (8) 62 63
E.DEMENTIEVA (4) 76(7) 62
A.MORIGAMI 75 63
S.FARINA ELIA (18) 75 62
E.LIKHOVTSEVA (16) 61 76(3)
V.WILLIAMS (11) 63 36 63
S.KARATANTCHEVA 75 62
E.LOIT 64 64
E.GAGLIARDI 63 63

Fourth round

L.DAVENPORT (1) 75 46 64
K.CLIJSTERS (14) 64 62
M.PIERCE (21) 76(2) 75
P.SCHNYDER (8) 46 60 61
E.DEMENTIEVA (4) 63 46 63
E.LIKHOVTSEVA (16) 75 76(2)
S.KARATANTCHEVA 63 16 61
E.GAGLIARDI 46 63 63

Quarter-finals

L.DAVENPORT (1) 16 75 63
M.PIERCE (21) 61 16 64
E.LIKHOVTSEVA (16) 76(3) 57 75
S.KARATANTCHEVA 75 63

Semi-finals

M.PIERCE (21) 63 62
E.LIKHOVTSEVA (16) 26 64 64

Final

M.PIERCE (21) 61 61

Winner

J.HENIN-HARDENNE 61 61

Seed	First Round	Second Round
7	Nadia PETROVA (RUS)	N.PETROVA (7)
	Mashona WASHINGTON (USA)	64 62
	Abigail SPEARS (USA)	S.BELTRAME
	Severine BELTRAME (FRA)	63 61
	Kveta PESCHKE (CZE)	K.PESCHKE
	Dally RANDRIANTEFY (MAD)	61 60
	Shahar PEER (ISR)	S.PEER
28	Marion BARTOLI (FRA)	64 63
17	Tatiana GOLOVIN (FRA)	T.GOLOVIN (17)
	Lilia OSTERLOH (USA)	60 62
	Antonella SERRA ZANETTI (ITA)	A.SERRA ZANETTI
	Marlene WEINGARTNER (GER)	62 64
	Martina SUCHA (SVK)	T.GARBIN
	Tathiana GARBIN (ITA)	67(8) 61 62
	Maria VENTO-KABCHI (VEN)	E.BOVINA (12)
12	Elena BOVINA (RUS)	60 63
15	Jelena JANKOVIC (SCG)	A.SMASHNOVA
	Anna SMASHNOVA (ISR)	60 63
	Roberta VINCI (ITA)	A.GROENEFELD
	Anna-Lena GROENEFELD (GER)	75 16 64
LL	Lucie SAFAROVA (CZE)	N.VAIDISOVA
	Nicole VAIDISOVA (CZE)	46 60 64
	Jie ZHENG (CHN)	F.SCHIAVONE (22)
22	Francesca SCHIAVONE (ITA)	63 36 64
29	Ana IVANOVIC (SCG)	A.IVANOVIC (29)
	Stephanie FORETZ (FRA)	63 63
	Iveta BENESOVA (CZE)	I.BENESOVA
WC	Pauline PARMENTIER (FRA)	75 64
	Alina JIDKOVA (RUS)	A.CORNET (WC)
WC	Alize CORNET (FRA)	76(4) 63
	Evie DOMINIKOVIC (AUS)	A.MAURESMO (3)
3	Amelie MAURESMO (FRA)	62 61
6	Svetlana KUZNETSOVA (RUS)	S.KUZNETSOVA (6)
WC	Mathilde JOHANSSON (FRA)	61 61
Q	Sofia ARVIDSSON (SWE)	S.ARVIDSSON (Q)
	Eleni DANIILIDOU (GRE)	61 76(1)
	Marissa IRVIN (USA)	M.IRVIN
	Nicole PRATT (AUS)	57 64 86
	Sania MIRZA (IND)	G.DULKO (30)
30	Gisela DULKO (ARG)	63 63
24	Magdalena MALEEVA (BUL)	M.MALEEVA (24)
	Rika FUJIWARA (JPN)	64 62
Q	Petra MANDULA (HUN)	A.MEDINA GARRIGUES
	Anabel MEDINA GARRIGUES (ESP)	60 61
	Virginia RUANO PASCUAL (ESP)	V.RUANO PASCUAL
Q	Anastasia YAKIMOVA (BLR)	64 76(7)
	Conchita MARTINEZ (ESP)	J.HENIN-HARDENNE (10)
10	Justine HENIN-HARDENNE (BEL)	60 46 64
13	Nathalie DECHY (FRA)	N.DECHY (13)
	Michaela PASTIKOVA (CZE)	61 64
	Silvija TALAJA (CRO)	S.STOSUR
	Samantha STOSUR (AUS)	61 62
WC	Yulia FEDOSSOVA (FRA)	K.BRANDI
	Kristina BRANDI (PUR)	16 63 62
	Nuria LLAGOSTERA VIVES (ESP)	N.LLAGOSTERA VIVES
23	Ai SUGIYAMA (JPN)	63 46 64
26	Paola SUAREZ (ARG)	A.CHAKVETADZE
	Anna CHAKVETADZE (RUS)	75 16 60
Q	Mervana JUGIC-SALKIC (BIH)	K.KOUKALOVA
	Klara KOUKALOVA (CZE)	63 46 63
WC	Camille PIN (FRA)	A.REZAI (WC)
WC	Aravane REZAI (FRA)	26 62 62
	Eugenia LINETSKAYA (RUS)	M.SHARAPOVA (2)
2	Maria SHARAPOVA (RUS)	67(3) 62 64

N.PETROVA (7) 61 63
S.PEER 61 16 64
T.GOLOVIN (17) 60 61
E.BOVINA (12) 61 16 64
A.GROENEFELD 61 60
F.SCHIAVONE (22) 62 76(5)
A.IVANOVIC (29) 63 61
A.MAURESMO (3) 60 62
S.KUZNETSOVA (6) 63 64
M.IRVIN 64 75
A.MEDINA GARRIGUES 63 64
J.HENIN-HARDENNE (10) 61 64
N.DECHY (13) 63 63
N.LLAGOSTERA VIVES 76(2) 60
A.CHAKVETADZE 64 63
M.SHARAPOVA (2) 63 62

N.PETROVA (7) 63 61
E.BOVINA (12) 63 75
F.SCHIAVONE (22) 76(3) 75
A.IVANOVIC (29) 64 36 64
S.KUZNETSOVA (6) 61 26 60
J.HENIN-HARDENNE (10) 46 62 63
N.LLAGOSTERA VIVES 76(1) 63
M.SHARAPOVA (2) 61 64

N.PETROVA (7) 75 36 64
A.IVANOVIC (29) 64 67(3) 63
J.HENIN-HARDENNE (10) 76(6) 46 75
M.SHARAPOVA (2) 62 63

N.PETROVA (7) 62 62
J.HENIN-HARDENNE (10) 64 62

J.HENIN-HARDENNE (10) 62 63

2005 French Open Championships Roland Garros, 23 May–5 June – Men's Doubles

First round

1 Mark KNOWLES (BAH)
1 Daniel NESTOR (CAN)
A Robert LINDSTEDT (SWE)
A Tom VANHOUDT (BEL)
Tomas CIBULEC (CZE)
Mariusz FYRSTENBERG (POL)
Gilles MULLER (LUX)
Christophe ROCHUS (BEL)
Giorgio GALIMBERTI (ITA)
Paradorn SRICHAPHAN (THA)
Graydon OLIVER (USA)
Jared PALMER (USA)
WC Olivier MUTIS (FRA)
WC Olivier PATIENCE (FRA)
15 Gaston ETLIS (ARG)
15 Martin RODRIGUEZ (ARG)
12 Martin DAMM (CZE)
12 Mariano HOOD (ARG)
Jiri NOVAK (CZE)
Petr PALA (CZE)
Enzo ARTONI (ITA)
Mariano PUERTA (ARG)
Alex CALATRAVA (ESP)
Ricardo MELLO (BRA)
Kenneth CARLSEN (DEN)
Ivo KARLOVIC (CRO)
Marcin MATKOWSKI (POL)
Alexander WASKE (GER)
Davide SANGUINETTI (ITA)
Sargis SARGSIAN (ARM)
7 Michael LLODRA (FRA)
7 Fabrice SANTORO (FRA)
3 Bob BRYAN (USA)
3 Mike BRYAN (USA)
David FERRER (ESP)
Santiago VENTURA (ESP)
Rainer SCHUETTLER (GER)
Mikhail YOUZHNY (RUS)
Feliciano LOPEZ (ESP)
Fernando VERDASCO (ESP)
Rick LEACH (USA)
Travis PARROTT (USA)
WC Gregory CARRAZ (FRA)
WC Anthony DUPUIS (FRA)
Dominik HRBATY (SVK)
Andre SA (BRA)
13 Xavier MALISSE (BEL)
13 Olivier ROCHUS (BEL)
10 Frantisek CERMAK (CZE)
10 Leos FRIEDL (CZE)
Robby GINEPRI (USA)
Brian MACPHIE (USA)
Petr LUXA (CZE)
David RIKL (CZE)
Juan-Pablo BRZEZICKI (ARG)
Juan Ignacio CHELA (ARG)
Jordan KERR (AUS)
Sebastian PRIETO (ARG)
WC Nicolas DEVILDER (FRA)
WC Marc GICQUEL (FRA)
Florian MAYER (GER)
Rogier WASSEN (NED)
6 Leander PAES (IND)
6 Nenad ZIMONJIC (SCG)

Second round

M.KNOWLES (1) / D.NESTOR (1) 62 76(5)
T.CIBULEC / M.FYRSTENBERG 63 63
G.GALIMBERTI / P.SRICHAPHAN 64 67(1) 97
G.ETLIS (15) / M.RODRIGUEZ (15) 63 63
M.DAMM (12) / M.HOOD (12) 36 63 64
A.CALATRAVA / R.MELLO 26 64 86
M.MATKOWSKI / A.WASKE 63 16 108
M.LLODRA (7) / F.SANTORO (7) 60 63
B.BRYAN (3) / M.BRYAN (3) 76(7) 57 75
R.SCHUETTLER / M.YOUZHNY 63 36 64
G.CARRAZ (WC) / A.DUPUIS (WC) 64 64
X.MALISSE (13) / O.ROCHUS (13) 16 62 61
F.CERMAK (10) / L.FRIEDL (10) 75 62
J.BRZEZICKI / J.CHELA 60 60
N.DEVILDER (WC) / M.GICQUEL (WC) 46 75 119
L.PAES (6) / N.ZIMONJIC (6) 63 46 62

Third round

M.KNOWLES (1) / D.NESTOR (1) 64 63
G.GALIMBERTI / P.SRICHAPHAN 63 64
M.DAMM (12) / M.HOOD (12) 64 63
M.MATKOWSKI / A.WASKE 16 63 63
B.BRYAN (3) / M.BRYAN (3) 61 64
X.MALISSE (13) / O.ROCHUS (13) 64 64
F.CERMAK (10) / L.FRIEDL (10) 46 61 62
L.PAES (6) / N.ZIMONJIC (6) 61 63

Quarter-finals

M.KNOWLES (1) / D.NESTOR (1) 62 62
M.DAMM (12) / M.HOOD (12) 36 64 64
B.BRYAN (3) / M.BRYAN (3) 76(6) 64
L.PAES (6) / N.ZIMONJIC (6) 76(5) 64

Semi-finals

M.KNOWLES (1) / D.NESTOR (1) 76(2) 36 61
B.BRYAN (3) / M.BRYAN (3) 76(5) 63

Final

B.BRYAN (3) / M.BRYAN (3) 63 32 RET

Champions

J.BJORKMAN (2) / M.MIRNYI (2) 26 61 64

5 Wayne BLACK (ZIM)
5 Kevin ULLYETT (ZIM)
Julian KNOWLE (AUT)
Jurgen MELZER (AUT)
Paul-Henri MATHIEU (FRA)
Cyril SAULNIER (FRA)
Massimo BERTOLINI (ITA)
Filippo VOLANDRI (ITA)
Victor HANESCU (ROM)
Jan HERNYCH (CZE)
Lucas ARNOLD (ARG)
Martin GARCIA (ARG)
Richard GASQUET (FRA)
Gael MONFILS (FRA)
11 Cyril SUK (CZE)
11 Pavel VIZNER (CZE)
16 Yves ALLEGRO (SUI)
16 Michael KOHLMANN (GER)
A Karsten BRAASCH (GER)
A Jiri VANEK (CZE)
Fernando GONZALEZ (CHI)
Nicolas MASSU (CHI)
Daniele BRACCIALI (ITA)
Andrei PAVEL (ROM)
WC Jeremy CHARDY (FRA)
WC Nicolas RENAVAND (FRA)
Karol BECK (SVK)
Jaroslav LEVINSKY (CZE)
Kevin KIM (USA)
Hyung-Taik LEE (KOR)
4 Mahesh BHUPATHI (IND)
4 Todd WOODBRIDGE (AUS)
8 Wayne ARTHURS (AUS)
8 Paul HANLEY (AUS)
WC Thierry ASCIONE (FRA)
WC Jean-Rene LISNARD (FRA)
Mark MERKLEIN (BAH)
Vince SPADEA (USA)
Ashley FISHER (AUS)
Chris HAGGARD (RSA)
WC Edouard ROGER-VASSELIN (FRA)
WC Gilles SIMON (FRA)
David SKOCH (CZE)
Jim THOMAS (USA)
Jean-Francois BACHELOT (FRA)
Arnaud CLEMENT (FRA)
9 Simon ASPELIN (SWE)
9 Todd PERRY (AUS)
A Oscar HERNANDEZ (ESP)
A Alex LOPEZ-MORON (ESP)
Tomas BERDYCH (CZE)
Tomas ZIB (CZE)
Igor ANDREEV (RUS)
Nikolay DAVYDENKO (RUS)
WC Jerome HAEHNEL (FRA)
WC Florent SERRA (FRA)
Robbie KOENIG (RSA)
Alberto MARTIN (ESP)
Julien BENNETEAU (FRA)
Nicolas MAHUT (FRA)
Nicolas ALMAGRO (ESP)
Juan MONACO (ARG)
2 Jonas BJORKMAN (SWE)
2 Max MIRNYI (BLR)

J.KNOWLE
J.MELZER
75 36 62

M.BERTOLINI
F.VOLANDRI
76(5) 61

L.ARNOLD
M.GARCIA
62 64

C.SUK (11)
P.VIZNER (11)
64 63

Y.ALLEGRO (16)
M.KOHLMANN (16)
64 60

F.GONZALEZ
N.MASSU
64 36 63

K.BECK
J.LEVINSKY
76(5) 63

K.KIM
H.LEE
76(6) 46 75

W.ARTHURS (8)
P.HANLEY (8)
63 64

M.MERKLEIN
V.SPADEA
63 64

E.ROGER-VASSELIN (WC)
G.SIMON (WC)
60 63

S.ASPELIN (9)
T.PERRY (9)
64 76(5)

T.BERDYCH
T.ZIB
16 64 60

I.ANDREEV
N.DAVYDENKO
62 67(8) 62

R.KOENIG
A.MARTIN
64 76(2)

J.BJORKMAN (2)
M.MIRNYI (2)
63 64

J.KNOWLE
J.MELZER
W/O

L.ARNOLD
M.GARCIA
36 63 97

F.GONZALEZ
N.MASSU
76(4) 46 63

K.KIM
H.LEE
75 61

W.ARTHURS (8)
P.HANLEY (8)
W/O

S.ASPELIN (9)
T.PERRY (9)
61 61

I.ANDREEV
N.DAVYDENKO
62 62

J.BJORKMAN (2)
M.MIRNYI (2)
63 26 64

J.KNOWLE
J.MELZER
60 76(0)

F.GONZALEZ
N.MASSU
62 62

W.ARTHURS (8)
P.HANLEY (8)
67(4) 64 86

J.BJORKMAN (2)
M.MIRNYI (2)
76(5) 62

F.GONZALEZ
N.MASSU
57 75 64

J.BJORKMAN (2)
M.MIRNYI (2)
64 76(5)

J.BJORKMAN (2)
M.MIRNYI (2)
63 46 64

2005 French Open Championships Roland Garros, 23 May–5 June – Women's Doubles

1 Virginia RUANO PASCUAL (ESP)
1 Paola SUAREZ (ARG)
Jennifer HOPKINS (USA)
Mashona WASHINGTON (USA)
Alina JIDKOVA (RUS)
Tatiana PEREBIYNIS (UKR)
Gabriela NAVRATILOVA (CZE)
Michaela PASTIKOVA (CZE)
A Anne KREMER (LUX)
A Antonella SERRA ZANETTI (ITA)
Elena BOVINA (RUS)
Elena DEMENTIEVA (RUS)
Ludmila CERVANOVA (SVK)
Klara KOUKALOVA (CZE)
15 Iveta BENESOVA (CZE)
15 Kveta PESCHKE (CZE)
12 Emilie LOIT (FRA)
12 Nicole PRATT (AUS)
Yoon-Jeong CHO (KOR)
Akiko MORIGAMI (JPN)
Ana IVANOVIC (SCG)
Tina KRIZAN (SLO)
Stephanie COHEN-ALORO (FRA)
Selima SFAR (TUN)
Eva BIRNEROVA (CZE)
Andreea VANC (ROM)
WC Mathilde JOHANSSON (FRA)
WC Aurelie VEDY (FRA)
Jennifer RUSSELL (USA)
Mara SANTANGELO (ITA)
7 Daniela HANTUCHOVA (SVK)
7 Ai SUGIYAMA (JPN)
4 Elena LIKHOVTSEVA (RUS)
4 Vera ZVONAREVA (RUS)
Janet LEE (TPE)
Shuai PENG (CHN)
WC Severine BELTRAME (FRA)
WC Camille PIN (FRA)
Catalina CASTANO (COL)
Yuliana FEDAK (UKR)
Emmanuelle GAGLIARDI (SUI)
Jelena JANKOVIC (SCG)
Marta MARRERO (ESP)
Arantxa PARRA-SANTONJA (ESP)
Lindsay LEE-WATERS (USA)
Lisa MCSHEA (AUS)
13 Shinobu ASAGOE (JPN)
13 Katarina SREBOTNIK (SLO)
11 Gisela DULKO (ARG)
11 Maria VENTO-KABCHI (VEN)
Tatiana GOLOVIN (FRA)
Anastasia MYSKINA (RUS)
WC Martina NAVRATILOVA (USA)
WC Arantxa SANCHEZ-VICARIO (ESP)
Lourdes DOMINGUEZ-LINO (ESP)
Nuria LLAGOSTERA VIVES (ESP)
Maria-Elena CAMERIN (ITA)
Tathiana GARBIN (ITA)
Dally RANDRIANTEFY (MAD)
Anna SMASHNOVA (ISR)
Els CALLENS (BEL)
Eleni DANIILIDOU (GRE)
5 Nadia PETROVA (RUS)
5 Meghann SHAUGHNESSY (USA)

V.RUANO PASCUAL (1)
P.SUAREZ (1)
64 63

G.NAVRATILOVA
M.PASTIKOVA
67(9) 63 64

E.BOVINA
E.DEMENTIEVA
61 60

I.BENESOVA (15)
K.PESCHKE (15)
63 62

E.LOIT (12)
N.PRATT (12)
63 64

S.COHEN-ALORO
S.SFAR
64 62

E.BIRNEROVA
A.VANC
61 63

D.HANTUCHOVA (7)
A.SUGIYAMA (7)
63 61

E.LIKHOVTSEVA (4)
V.ZVONAREVA (4)
64 63

C.CASTANO
Y.FEDAK
36 63 63

M.MARRERO
A.PARRA-SANTONJA
64 63

S.ASAGOE (13)
K.SREBOTNIK (13)
62 16 119

G.DULKO (11)
M.VENTO-KABCHI (11)
36 60 62

L.DOMINGUEZ-LINO
N.LLAGOSTERA VIVES
64 36 63

M.CAMERIN
T.GARBIN
46 60 61

N.PETROVA (5)
M.SHAUGHNESSY (5)
63 62

V.RUANO PASCUAL (1)
P.SUAREZ (1)
62 62

I.BENESOVA (15)
K.PESCHKE (15)
62 61

E.LOIT (12)
N.PRATT (12)
67(4) 63 119

E.BIRNEROVA
A.VANC
63 36 61

E.LIKHOVTSEVA (4)
V.ZVONAREVA (4)
61 64

S.ASAGOE (13)
K.SREBOTNIK (13)
62 61

L.DOMINGUEZ-LINO
N.LLAGOSTERA VIVES
75 62

N.PETROVA (5)
M.SHAUGHNESSY (5)
63 64

V.RUANO PASCUAL (1)
P.SUAREZ (1)
61 62

E.LOIT (12)
N.PRATT (12)
64 46 61

S.ASAGOE (13)
K.SREBOTNIK (13)
62 64

N.PETROVA (5)
M.SHAUGHNESSY (5)
64 61

V.RUANO PASCUAL (1)
P.SUAREZ (1)
64 46 64

N.PETROVA (5)
M.SHAUGHNESSY (5)
26 63 62

V.RUANO PASCUAL (1)
P.SUAREZ (1)
62 64

V.RUANO PASCUAL (1)
P.SUAREZ (1)
46 63 63

8 Corina MORARIU (USA)
8 Patty SCHNYDER (SUI)
Caroline DHENIN (FRA)
Virginie RAZZANO (FRA)
Jill CRAYBAS (USA)
Marlene WEINGARTNER (GER)
Silvia FARINA ELIA (ITA)
Flavia PENNETTA (ITA)
Vera DOUCHEVINA (RUS)
Barbora STRYCOVA (CZE)
WC Mailyne ANDRIEUX (FRA)
WC Pauline PARMENTIER (FRA)
Milagros SEQUERA (VEN)
Meilen TU (USA)
10 Bryanne STEWART (AUS)
10 Samantha STOSUR (AUS)
14 Marion BARTOLI (FRA)
14 Anna-Lena GROENEFELD (GER)
WC Florence HARING (FRA)
WC Virginie PICHET (FRA)
Rika FUJIWARA (JPN)
Tamarine TANASUGARN (THA)
Maria KIRILENKO (RUS)
Maria-Emilia SALERNI (ARG)
Marta DOMACHOWSKA (POL)
Silvija TALAJA (CRO)
Sandrine TESTUD (FRA)
Roberta VINCI (ITA)
Mariana DIAZ-OLIVA (ARG)
Martina SUCHA (SVK)
3 Lisa RAYMOND (USA)
3 Rennae STUBBS (AUS)
6 Janette HUSAROVA (SVK)
6 Conchita MARTINEZ (ESP)
WC Kildine CHEVALIER (FRA)
WC Stephanie FORETZ (FRA)
Zuzana ONDRASKOVA (CZE)
PR Renata VORACOVA (CZE)
Svetlana KUZNETSOVA (RUS)
Mary PIERCE (FRA)
Ting LI (CHN)
Tian-Tian SUN (CHN)
Yulia BEYGELZIMER (UKR)
Julia SCHRUFF (GER)
Laura GRANVILLE (USA)
Marissa IRVIN (USA)
9 Anabel MEDINA GARRIGUES (ESP)
9 Dinara SAFINA (RUS)
16 Zi YAN (CHN)
16 Jie ZHENG (CHN)
Denisa CHLADKOVA (CZE)
Ruxandra DRAGOMIR-ILIE (ROM)
Kristina BRANDI (PUR)
Nana MIYAGI (JPN)
Anna CHAKVETADZE (RUS)
Sania MIRZA (IND)
Eugenia LINETSKAYA (RUS)
Galina VOSKOBOEVA (RUS)
WC Yulia FEDOSSOVA (FRA)
WC Violette HUCK (FRA)
Jelena KOSTANIC (CRO)
Claudine SCHAUL (LUX)
2 Cara BLACK (ZIM)
2 Liezel HUBER (RSA)

C.MORARIU (8)
P.SCHNYDER (8)
63 36 61

S.FARINA ELIA
F.PENNETTA
61 62

V.DOUCHEVINA
B.STRYCOVA
62 64

B.STEWART (10)
S.STOSUR (10)
60 63

M.BARTOLI (14)
A.GROENEFELD (14)
61 63

M.KIRILENKO
M.SALERNI
67(6) 61 61

M.DOMACHOWSKA
S.TALAJA
57 64 61

L.RAYMOND (3)
R.STUBBS (3)
62 63

J.HUSAROVA (6)
C.MARTINEZ (6)
46 63 86

S.KUZNETSOVA
M.PIERCE
61 63

T.LI
T.SUN
62 76(5)

A.MEDINA GARRIGUES (9)
D.SAFINA (9)
60 62

Z.YAN (16)
J.ZHENG (16)
61 62

A.CHAKVETADZE
S.MIRZA
62 63

E.LINETSKAYA
G.VOSKOBOEVA
64 61

C.BLACK (2)
L.HUBER (2)
62 64

C.MORARIU (8)
P.SCHNYDER (8)
63 62

B.STEWART (10)
S.STOSUR (10)
61 62

M.BARTOLI (14)
A.GROENEFELD (14)
64 46 62

L.RAYMOND (3)
R.STUBBS (3)
W/O

J.HUSAROVA (6)
C.MARTINEZ (6)
76(6) 63

T.LI
T.SUN
67(7) 75 75

Z.YAN (16)
J.ZHENG (16)
46 75 62

C.BLACK (2)
L.HUBER (2)
64 61

C.MORARIU (8)
P.SCHNYDER (8)
63 63

L.RAYMOND (3)
R.STUBBS (3)
46 64 63

T.LI
T.SUN
76(3) 62

C.BLACK (2)
L.HUBER (2)
36 63 62

C.MORARIU (8)
P.SCHNYDER (8)
64 63

C.BLACK (2)
L.HUBER (2)
63 64

C.BLACK (2)
L.HUBER (2)
64 62

2005 French Open Championships Roland Garros, 23 May–5 June – Mixed Doubles

First round draw

Seed	Player
1	Daniel NESTOR (CAN)
1	Rennae STUBBS (AUS)
WC	Arnaud CLEMENT (FRA)
WC	Camille PIN (FRA)
	Todd PERRY (AUS)
	Bryanne STEWART (AUS)
	Fabrice SANTORO (FRA)
	Daniela HANTUCHOVA (SVK)
	Martin DAMM (CZE)
	Kveta PESCHKE (CZE)
	Frantisek CERMAK (CZE)
	Conchita MARTINEZ (ESP)
	Cyril SUK (CZE)
	Janette HUSAROVA (SVK)
5	Kevin ULLYETT (ZIM)
5	Liezel HUBER (RSA)
4	Jonas BJORKMAN (SWE)
4	Anastasia MYSKINA (RUS)
WC	Gael MONFILS (FRA)
WC	Alize CORNET (FRA)
WC	Jean-Francois BACHELOT (FRA)
WC	Emilie LOIT (FRA)
	Mariano HOOD (ARG)
	Maria VENTO-KABCHI (VEN)
	Julian KNOWLE (AUT)
	Anna-Lena GROENEFELD (GER)
	Todd WOODBRIDGE (AUS)
	Katarina SREBOTNIK (SLO)
	Jonathan ERLICH (ISR)
	Virginia RUANO PASCUAL (ESP)
7	Mahesh BHUPATHI (IND)
7	Lisa RAYMOND (USA)
8	Leos FRIEDL (CZE)
8	Elena LIKHOVTSEVA (RUS)
	Paul HANLEY (AUS)
	Samantha STOSUR (AUS)
	Martin RODRIGUEZ (ARG)
	Emmanuelle GAGLIARDI (SUI)
	Mark KNOWLES (BAH)
	Nicole VAIDISOVA (CZE)
	Lucas ARNOLD (ARG)
	Jelena JANKOVIC (SCG)
WC	Marc GICQUEL (FRA)
WC	Sandrine TESTUD (FRA)
WC	Michael LLODRA (FRA)
WC	Severine BELTRAME (FRA)
3	Wayne BLACK (ZIM)
3	Cara BLACK (ZIM)
6	Leander PAES (IND)
6	Martina NAVRATILOVA (USA)
WC	Nicolas DEVILDER (FRA)
WC	Stephanie FORETZ (FRA)
	Gaston ETLIS (ARG)
	Meghann SHAUGHNESSY (USA)
	Simon ASPELIN (SWE)
	Dinara SAFINA (RUS)
	Jared PALMER (USA)
	Corina MORARIU (USA)
	Pavel VIZNER (CZE)
	Nicole PRATT (AUS)
	Nenad ZIMONJIC (SCG)
	Ana IVANOVIC (SCG)
2	Max MIRNYI (BLR)
2	Ai SUGIYAMA (JPN)

Second round

D.NESTOR (1) / R.STUBBS (1)	76(2) 63
F.SANTORO / D.HANTUCHOVA	62 64
M.DAMM / K.PESCHKE	75 67(5) 63
K.ULLYETT (5) / L.HUBER (5)	46 63 86
J.BJORKMAN (4) / A.MYSKINA (4)	36 62 62
J.BACHELOT (WC) / E.LOIT (WC)	62 63
T.WOODBRIDGE / K.SREBOTNIK	61 36 63
M.BHUPATHI (7) / L.RAYMOND (7)	63 64
P.HANLEY / S.STOSUR	63 64
M.KNOWLES / N.VAIDISOVA	64 63
M.GICQUEL (WC) / S.TESTUD (WC)	63 63
W.BLACK (3) / C.BLACK (3)	62 64
L.PAES (6) / M.NAVRATILOVA (6)	64 63
S.ASPELIN / D.SAFINA	76(7) 64
J.PALMER / C.MORARIU	46 63 64
N.ZIMONJIC / A.IVANOVIC	63 36 108

Quarter-finals

F.SANTORO / D.HANTUCHOVA	67(4) 63 63
K.ULLYETT (5) / L.HUBER (5)	64 67(1) 63
J.BJORKMAN (4) / A.MYSKINA (4)	67(5) 76(1) 64
M.BHUPATHI (7) / L.RAYMOND (7)	75 76(4)
P.HANLEY / S.STOSUR	76(2) 26 63
M.GICQUEL (WC) / S.TESTUD (WC)	63 26 63
L.PAES (6) / M.NAVRATILOVA (6)	64 60
J.PALMER / C.MORARIU	W/O

Semi-finals

F.SANTORO / D.HANTUCHOVA	62 46 61
J.BJORKMAN (4) / A.MYSKINA (4)	64 62
P.HANLEY / S.STOSUR	64 61
L.PAES (6) / M.NAVRATILOVA (6)	76(5) 46 63

Final

F.SANTORO / D.HANTUCHOVA	76(5) 60
L.PAES (6) / M.NAVRATILOVA (6)	62 63

Winners

F.SANTORO / D.HANTUCHOVA 36 63 62

Rafael Nadal (ESP)

2005 Wimbledon Championships, 20 June–3 July – Men's Singles

	Player	First round
1	Roger FEDERER (SUI)	R.FEDERER (1)
	Paul-Henri MATHIEU (FRA)	64 62 64
	Ivo MINAR (CZE)	I.MINAR
	Michal TABARA (CZE)	64 64 64
WC	Joshua GOODALL (GBR)	A.DI MAURO
	Alessio DI MAURO (ITA)	63 76(4) 63
	Julien BENNETEAU (FRA)	N.KIEFER (25)
25	Nicolas KIEFER (GER)	63 76(5) 57 36 64
23	Juan Carlos FERRERO (ESP)	J.FERRERO (23)
Q	Jamie DELGADO (GBR)	76(2) 61 64
	Thomas ENQVIST (SWE)	H.LEE
	Hyung-Taik LEE (KOR)	63 67(4) 75 64
	Florian MAYER (GER)	F.MAYER
	Santiago VENTURA (ESP)	64 75 62
	Fernando VERDASCO (ESP)	F.VERDASCO
13	Tommy ROBREDO (ESP)	61 62 75
11	Joachim JOHANSSON (SWE)	J.JOHANSSON (11)
	Albert MONTANES (ESP)	76(5) 64 75
	Alberto MARTIN (ESP)	G.RUSEDSKI
	Greg RUSEDSKI (GBR)	63 46 62 61
	Jose ACASUSO (ARG)	T.ZIB
	Tomas ZIB (CZE)	75 63 63
WC	Alan MACKIN (GBR)	F.GONZALEZ (21)
21	Fernando GONZALEZ (CHI)	63 64 64
31	Mikhail YOUZHNY (RUS)	M.YOUZHNY (31)
	Marcos BAGHDATIS (CYP)	62 36 61 64
	Oscar HERNANDEZ (ESP)	J.LISNARD
	Jean-Rene LISNARD (FRA)	64 21 RET
	Jonas BJORKMAN (SWE)	J.BJORKMAN
Q	Jeff MORRISON (USA)	63 63 46 26 62
PR	Scott DRAPER (AUS)	N.DAVYDENKO (8)
8	Nikolay DAVYDENKO (RUS)	76(4) 64 63
3	Lleyton HEWITT (AUS)	L.HEWITT (3)
	Christophe ROCHUS (BEL)	63 63 61
	Jan HERNYCH (CZE)	J.HERNYCH
WC	James BLAKE (USA)	16 64 76(6) 76(4)
LL	Justin GIMELSTOB (USA)	J.GIMELSTOB (LL)
Q	Adrian GARCIA (CHI)	63 64 76(5)
	Sargis SARGSIAN (ARM)	N.MASSU (29)
29	Nicolas MASSU (CHI)	76(7) 63 64
24	Taylor DENT (USA)	T.DENT (24)
Q	Dick NORMAN (BEL)	76(4) 76(4) 46 67(7) 61
	Kevin KIM (USA)	K.KIM
WC	Alex BOGDANOVIC (GBR)	67(4) 61 64 62
Q	Anthony DUPUIS (FRA)	T.BERDYCH
	Tomas BERDYCH (CZE)	76(5) 75 36 76(4)
	Lars BURGSMULLER (GER)	L.BURGSMULLER
16	Mariano PUERTA (ARG)	61 61 64
10	Mario ANCIC (CRO)	M.ANCIC (10)
Q	Tobias SUMMERER (GER)	63 75 61
Q	Danai UDOMCHOKE (THA)	D.UDOMCHOKE (Q)
	Stefan KOUBEK (AUT)	57 64 46 63 86
	Gael MONFILS (FRA)	G.MONFILS
Q	Noam OKUN (ISR)	36 64 64 76(14)
	Cyril SAULNIER (FRA)	D.HRBATY (22)
22	Dominik HRBATY (SVK)	76(0) 60 62
26	Feliciano LOPEZ (ESP)	F.LOPEZ (26)
	Bjorn PHAU (GER)	57 76(8) 67(5) 62 64
WC	David SHERWOOD (GBR)	D.SHERWOOD (WC)
	Ricardo MELLO (BRA)	63 64 64
	Karol BECK (SVK)	M.PHILIPPOUSSIS (WC)
WC	Mark PHILIPPOUSSIS (AUS)	75 64 62
	Paradorn SRICHAPHAN (THA)	M.SAFIN (5)
5	Marat SAFIN (RUS)	62 64 64

Second round

R.FEDERER (1) 64 64 61
N.KIEFER (25) 63 75 63
J.FERRERO (23) 64 36 46 63 63
F.MAYER 76(6) 75 63
J.JOHANSSON (11) 76(10) 36 64 76(5)
F.GONZALEZ (21) 64 76(6) 63
M.YOUZHNY (31) 16 75 63 64
J.BJORKMAN 67(4) 12 RET
L.HEWITT (3) 62 75 36 63
J.GIMELSTOB (LL) 63 46 76(5) 76(0)
T.DENT (24) 63 64 64
T.BERDYCH 63 63 61
M.ANCIC (10) 76(6) 36 63 63
G.MONFILS 63 63 26 75
F.LOPEZ (26) 62 64 62
M.SAFIN (5) 76(4) 76(4) 64

Third round

R.FEDERER (1) 62 67(5) 61 75
J.FERRERO (23) 36 62 61 61
F.GONZALEZ (21) 64 64 62
M.YOUZHNY (31) 75 63 36 76(9)
L.HEWITT (3) 76(5) 64 75
T.DENT (24) 63 76(5) 63
M.ANCIC (10) 63 63 61
F.LOPEZ (26) 64 76(4) 63

Fourth round

R.FEDERER (1) 63 64 76(6)
F.GONZALEZ (21) 76(3) 76(5) 63
L.HEWITT (3) 64 64 67(7) 63
F.LOPEZ (26) 64 64 62

Quarter-finals

R.FEDERER (1) 75 62 76(2)
L.HEWITT (3) 75 64 76(2)

Semi-final

R.FEDERER (1) 63 64 76(1)

Final

R.FEDERER (1) 62 76(2) 64

Seed	Player	First round
33	Olivier ROCHUS (BEL)	O.ROCHUS (33)
LL	Paul GOLDSTEIN (USA)	64 62 62
	Max MIRNYI (BLR)	M.MIRNYI
	Rainer SCHUETTLER (GER)	63 63 64
	Stanislas WAWRINKA (SUI)	F.SANTORO
	Fabrice SANTORO (FRA)	62 67(7) 75 61
	Peter WESSELS (NED)	J.NOVAK (28)
28	Jiri NOVAK (CZE)	76(4) 63 64
19	Tommy HAAS (GER)	J.TIPSAREVIC
	Janko TIPSAREVIC (SCG)	62 21 RET
Q	Yen-Hsun LU (TPE)	Y.LU (Q)
Q	Arnaud CLEMENT (FRA)	76(4) 06 61 36 63
	Andrei PAVEL (ROM)	A.PAVEL
Q	Roko KARANUSIC (CRO)	62 46 62 64
	Bohdan ULIHRACH (CZE)	T.JOHANSSON (12)
12	Thomas JOHANSSON (SWE)	63 62 62
14	Radek STEPANEK (CZE)	R.STEPANEK (14)
	Robby GINEPRI (USA)	67(5) 63 64 62
WC	Andrew MURRAY (GBR)	A.MURRAY (WC)
Q	George BASTL (SUI)	64 62 62
PR	Karol KUCERA (SVK)	K.KUCERA (PR)
	Luis HORNA (PER)	46 63 63 64
	Raemon SLUITER (NED)	D.NALBANDIAN (18)
18	David NALBANDIAN (ARG)	62 62 75
27	Richard GASQUET (FRA)	R.GASQUET (27)
	Philipp KOHLSCHREIBER (GER)	63 36 63 62
Q	Gilles ELSENEER (BEL)	G.ELSENEER (Q)
	Potito STARACE (ITA)	63 76(9) 63
	Felix MANTILLA (ESP)	G.MULLER
	Gilles MULLER (LUX)	54 RET
	Vince SPADEA (USA)	R.NADAL (4)
4	Rafael NADAL (ESP)	64 63 60
6	Tim HENMAN (GBR)	T.HENMAN (6)
	Jarkko NIEMINEN (FIN)	36 67(5) 64 75 62
	Nicolas ALMAGRO (ESP)	D.TURSUNOV (PR)
PR	Dmitry TURSUNOV (RUS)	76(2) 76(4) 61
PR	Alexander POPP (GER)	A.POPP (PR)
	Jerome HAEHNEL (FRA)	62 63 26 64
	Wayne ARTHURS (AUS)	W.ARTHURS
32	Filippo VOLANDRI (ITA)	63 64 64
17	David FERRER (ESP)	G.GARCIA-LOPEZ
	Guillermo GARCIA-LOPEZ (ESP)	63 62 76(7)
	Juan MONACO (ARG)	N.DJOKOVIC (Q)
Q	Novak DJOKOVIC (SCG)	63 76(5) 63
	Victor HANESCU (ROM)	V.HANESCU
	Kenneth CARLSEN (DEN)	67(2) 76(4) 63 57 64
	Michael LLODRA (FRA)	S.GROSJEAN (9)
9	Sebastien GROSJEAN (FRA)	36 75 46 76(5) 64
15	Guillermo CORIA (ARG)	G.CORIA (15)
	Tomas BEHREND (GER)	61 62 62
WC	Jonathan MARRAY (GBR)	X.MALISSE
	Xavier MALISSE (BEL)	63 36 26 61 64
	Alex CALATRAVA (ESP)	A.CALATRAVA
Q	Tuomas KETOLA (FIN)	64 76(4) 64
	Jurgen MELZER (AUT)	J.MELZER
20	Ivan LJUBICIC (CRO)	64 64 64
30	Robin SODERLING (SWE)	I.ANDREEV
	Igor ANDREEV (RUS)	67(3) 75 61 75
	Davide SANGUINETTI (ITA)	D.SANGUINETTI
Q	Andreas SEPPI (ITA)	63 62 61
LL	Daniele BRACCIALI (ITA)	D.BRACCIALI (LL)
	Ivo KARLOVIC (CRO)	67(4) 76(8) 36 76(5) 1210
	Jiri VANEK (CZE)	A.RODDICK (2)
2	Andy RODDICK (USA)	61 76(4) 62

Second round

- M.MIRNYI 76(4) 62 76(3)
- J.NOVAK (28) 61 46 76(4) 63
- J.TIPSAREVIC 26 63 62 46 75
- T.JOHANSSON (12) 36 76(4) 64 76(4)
- A.MURRAY (WC) 64 64 64
- D.NALBANDIAN (18) 62 64 63
- R.GASQUET (27) 76(7) 76(3) 67(3) 62
- G.MULLER 64 46 63 64
- D.TURSUNOV (PR) 36 62 36 63 86
- A.POPP (PR) 63 67(4) 36 76(4) 1412
- N.DJOKOVIC (Q) 36 36 76(5) 76(3) 64
- S.GROSJEAN (9) 63 64 62
- G.CORIA (15) 36 63 75 67(3) 64
- J.MELZER 64 64 61
- I.ANDREEV 64 62 36 63
- A.RODDICK (2) 75 63 67(3) 46 63

Third round

- M.MIRNYI 57 75 64 76(2)
- T.JOHANSSON (12) 62 63 61
- D.NALBANDIAN (18) 67(4) 16 60 64 61
- R.GASQUET (27) 76(3) 63 63
- D.TURSUNOV (PR) 57 76(5) 62 62
- S.GROSJEAN (9) 75 64 57 64
- G.CORIA (15) 36 36 62 62 64
- A.RODDICK (2) 62 62 76(4)

Fourth round

- T.JOHANSSON (12) 64 75 64
- D.NALBANDIAN (18) 64 76(3) 60
- S.GROSJEAN (9) 64 67(5) 63 36 61
- A.RODDICK (2) 63 67(1) 64

Quarter-finals

- T.JOHANSSON (12) 76(5) 62 62
- A.RODDICK (2) 63 26 16 63 63

Semi-final

- A.RODDICK (2) 67(6) 62 76(10) 76(5)

2005 Wimbledon Championships, 20 June–3 July – Women's Singles

Seed	Player
1	Lindsay DAVENPORT (USA)
	Alina JIDKOVA (RUS)
	Marta MARRERO (ESP)
Q	Jamea JACKSON (USA)
	Barbora STRYCOVA (CZE)
	Lilia OSTERLOH (USA)
	Sanda MAMIC (CRO)
30	Dinara SAFINA (RUS)
23	Ai SUGIYAMA (JPN)
	Roberta VINCI (ITA)
	Abigail SPEARS (USA)
	Anne KREMER (LUX)
	Marissa IRVIN (USA)
Q	Saori OBATA (JPN)
WC	Katie O'BRIEN (GBR)
15	Kim CLIJSTERS (BEL)
10	Patty SCHNYDER (SUI)
	Antonella SERRA ZANETTI (ITA)
	Tatiana PEREBIYNIS (UKR)
Q	Sofia ARVIDSSON (SWE)
	Maria KIRILENKO (RUS)
Q	Els CALLENS (BEL)
	Magdalena MALEEVA (BUL)
24	Shinobu ASAGOE (JPN)
27	Nicole VAIDISOVA (CZE)
	Jelena KOSTANIC (CRO)
	Samantha STOSUR (AUS)
	Michaela PASTIKOVA (CZE)
	Akiko MORIGAMI (JPN)
	Sania MIRZA (IND)
WC	Rebecca LLEWELLYN (GBR)
5	Svetlana KUZNETSOVA (RUS)
3	Amelie MAURESMO (FRA)
LL	Melinda CZINK (HUN)
	Maria SANCHEZ LORENZO (ESP)
	Marta DOMACHOWSKA (POL)
Q	Sarah BORWELL (GBR)
	Shenay PERRY (USA)
	Tamarine TANASUGARN (THA)
25	Karolina SPREM (CRO)
22	Silvia FARINA ELIA (ITA)
	Martina SUCHA (SVK)
	Maria VENTO-KABCHI (VEN)
	Milagros SEQUERA (VEN)
	Meghann SHAUGHNESSY (USA)
	Julia SCHRUFF (GER)
	Anna SMASHNOVA (ISR)
13	Elena LIKHOVTSEVA (RUS)
9	Anastasia MYSKINA (RUS)
Q	Katerina BOHMOVA (CZE)
	Evie DOMINIKOVIC (AUS)
	Aiko NAKAMURA (JPN)
	Mariana DIAZ-OLIVA (ARG)
WC	Anne KEOTHAVONG (GBR)
	Anna CHAKVETADZE (RUS)
17	Jelena JANKOVIC (SCG)
28	Amy FRAZIER (USA)
	Mashona WASHINGTON (USA)
	Selima SFAR (TUN)
	Emilie LOIT (FRA)
WC	Elena BALTACHA (GBR)
Q	Sabine KLASCHKA (GER)
	Iveta BENESOVA (CZE)
6	Elena DEMENTIEVA (RUS)

First round

L.DAVENPORT (1) 60 62
J.JACKSON (Q) 62 63
B.STRYCOVA 63 75
D.SAFINA (30) 63 64
R.VINCI 62 26 64
A.KREMER 60 26 62
M.IRVIN 76(4) 63
K.CLIJSTERS (15) 62 63
A.SERRA ZANETTI 64 67(7) 63
S.ARVIDSSON (Q) 63 76(5)
M.KIRILENKO 62 76(3)
M.MALEEVA 62 76(6)
N.VAIDISOVA (27) 63 36 63
M.PASTIKOVA 76(1) 64
S.MIRZA 63 36 86
S.KUZNETSOVA (5) 60 61
A.MAURESMO (3) 63 62
M.SANCHEZ LORENZO 64 46 62
S.PERRY 76(11) 63
T.TANASUGARN 62 62
S.FARINA ELIA (22) 64 62
M.VENTO-KABCHI 76(1) 46 64
M.SHAUGHNESSY 61 16 62
E.LIKHOVTSEVA (13) 62 62
A.MYSKINA (9) 57 76(4) 64
A.NAKAMURA 57 63 64
M.DIAZ-OLIVA 63 64
J.JANKOVIC (17) 64 62
M.WASHINGTON 64 46 64
S.SFAR 62 46 97
S.KLASCHKA (Q) 63 62
E.DEMENTIEVA (6) 62 63

Second round

L.DAVENPORT (1) 60 63
D.SAFINA (30) 62 62
R.VINCI 63 62
K.CLIJSTERS (15) 61 61
A.SERRA ZANETTI 75 26 75
M.MALEEVA 62 63
N.VAIDISOVA (27) 75 63
S.KUZNETSOVA (5) 64 67(4) 64
A.MAURESMO (3) 61 63
S.PERRY 76(1) 62
S.FARINA ELIA (22) 61 57 63
E.LIKHOVTSEVA (13) 63 76(4)
A.MYSKINA (9) 64 63
J.JANKOVIC (17) 63 75
M.WASHINGTON 63 36 63
E.DEMENTIEVA (6) 26 63 86

Third round

L.DAVENPORT (1) 62 61
K.CLIJSTERS (15) 63 64
M.MALEEVA 63 62
S.KUZNETSOVA (5) 75 67(5) 62
A.MAURESMO (3) 60 62
E.LIKHOVTSEVA (13) 57 64 64
A.MYSKINA (9) 60 57 108
E.DEMENTIEVA (6) 75 61

Fourth round

L.DAVENPORT (1) 63 67(4) 63
S.KUZNETSOVA (5) 64 63
A.MAURESMO (3) 64 60
A.MYSKINA (9) 16 76(9) 75

Quarter-finals

L.DAVENPORT (1) 76(1) 63
A.MAURESMO (3) 63 64

Semi-final

L.DAVENPORT (1) 67(5) 76(4) 64

V.WILLIAMS (14) 46 76(4) 97

7 Justine HENIN-HARDENNE (BEL)
Eleni DANIILIDOU (GRE)
Klara KOUKALOVA (CZE)
Laura GRANVILLE (USA)
Gisela DULKO (ARG)
Juliana FEDAK (UKR)
Emmanuelle GAGLIARDI (SUI)
26 Flavia PENNETTA (ITA)
19 Ana IVANOVIC (SCG)
Vera DOUCHEVINA (RUS)
Denisa CHLADKOVA (CZE)
Stephanie FORETZ (FRA)
Q Julia VAKULENKO (UKR)
Tathiana GARBIN (ITA)
Lucie SAFAROVA (CZE)
12 Mary PIERCE (FRA)
14 Venus WILLIAMS (USA)
LL Eva BIRNEROVA (CZE)
Nicole PRATT (AUS)
Ludmila CERVANOVA (SVK)
Q Meilen TU (USA)
Shahar PEER (ISR)
Eugenia LINETSKAYA (RUS)
20 Daniela HANTUCHOVA (SVK)
29 Marion BARTOLI (FRA)
Rika FUJIWARA (JPN)
Q Ashley HARKLEROAD (USA)
Jill CRAYBAS (USA)
Q Mara SANTANGELO (ITA)
Q Tatiana POUTCHEK (BLR)
Angela HAYNES (USA)
4 Serena WILLIAMS (USA)
8 Nadia PETROVA (RUS)
Virginia RUANO PASCUAL (ESP)
Claudine SCHAUL (LUX)
LL Severine BELTRAME (FRA)
Zuzana ONDRASKOVA (CZE)
WC Cara BLACK (ZIM)
Catalina CASTANO (COL)
32 Virginie RAZZANO (FRA)
21 Francesca SCHIAVONE (ITA)
Kristina BRANDI (PUR)
Conchita MARTINEZ (ESP)
Q Katerina BONDARENKO (UKR)
Kveta PESCHKE (CZE)
Dally RANDRIANTEFY (MAD)
Marlene WEINGARTNER (GER)
11 Vera ZVONAREVA (RUS)
16 Nathalie DECHY (FRA)
Maria-Elena CAMERIN (ITA)
WC Jane O'DONOGHUE (GBR)
Anna-Lena GROENEFELD (GER)
Tatiana PANOVA (RUS)
Lisa RAYMOND (USA)
Alyona BONDARENKO (UKR)
18 Tatiana GOLOVIN (FRA)
31 Anabel MEDINA GARRIGUES (ESP)
Katarina SREBOTNIK (SLO)
Yoon-Jeong CHO (KOR)
Arantxa PARRA-SANTONJA (ESP)
WC Amanda JANES (GBR)
Sesil KARATANTCHEVA (BUL)
Nuria LLAGOSTERA VIVES (ESP)
2 Maria SHARAPOVA (RUS)

E.DANIILIDOU 76(8) 26 75
L.GRANVILLE 61 62
G.DULKO 62 64
F.PENNETTA (26) 61 62
A.IVANOVIC (19) 64 63
S.FORETZ 63 46 61
J.VAKULENKO (Q) 62 64
M.PIERCE (12) 63 64
V.WILLIAMS (14) 62 64
N.PRATT 36 63 61
S.PEER 63 63
D.HANTUCHOVA (20) 36 62 62
M.BARTOLI (29) 62 62
J.CRAYBAS 64 46 64
M.SANTANGELO (Q) 63 62
S.WILLIAMS (4) 67(12) 64 62
N.PETROVA (8) 46 63 62
S.BELTRAME (LL) 62 61
C.BLACK (WC) 63 63
V.RAZZANO (32) 67(6) 63 64
K.BRANDI 63 36 97
C.MARTINEZ 61 76(4)
K.PESCHKE 75 61
V.ZVONAREVA (11) 26 64 60
N.DECHY (16) 76(1) 61
J.O'DONOGHUE (WC) 16 61 64
T.PANOVA 75 63
A.BONDARENKO 63 36 75
K.SREBOTNIK 63 63
Y.CHO 63 63
S.KARATANTCHEVA 75 67(6) 75
M.SHARAPOVA (2) 62 62

E.DANIILIDOU 62 60
F.PENNETTA (26) 62 64
A.IVANOVIC (19) 64 63
M.PIERCE (12) 46 76(7) 97
V.WILLIAMS (14) 75 63
D.HANTUCHOVA (20) 62 26 63
J.CRAYBAS 61 64
S.WILLIAMS (4) 26 63 62
N.PETROVA (8) 61 62
C.BLACK (WC) 64 76(5)
C.MARTINEZ 62 63
K.PESCHKE 16 64 63
N.DECHY (16) 62 61
A.BONDARENKO 63 26 63
K.SREBOTNIK 75 64
M.SHARAPOVA (2) 60 61

F.PENNETTA (26) 64 63
M.PIERCE (12) 61 64
V.WILLIAMS (14) 75 63
J.CRAYBAS 63 76(4)
N.PETROVA (8) 64 63
K.PESCHKE 64 61
N.DECHY (16) 61 64
M.SHARAPOVA (2) 62 64

M.PIERCE (12) 63 61
V.WILLIAMS (14) 60 62
N.PETROVA (8) 67(5) 76(7) 63
M.SHARAPOVA (2) 64 62

V.WILLIAMS (14) 60 76(10)
M.SHARAPOVA (2) 76(6) 63

V.WILLIAMS (14) 76(2) 61

2005 Wimbledon Championships, 20 June–3 July – Men's Doubles

Draw

1 Jonas BJORKMAN (SWE)
1 Max MIRNYI (BLR)
WC Richard BARKER (GBR)
WC William BARKER (GBR)
Jordan KERR (AUS)
Jim THOMAS (USA)
Ashley FISHER (AUS)
Chris HAGGARD (RSA)
Ivan LJUBICIC (CRO)
Uros VICO (ITA)
Victor HANESCU (ROM)
Andrei PAVEL (ROM)
Jose ACASUSO (ARG)
Alberto MARTIN (ESP)
13 Julian KNOWLE (AUT)
13 Jurgen MELZER (AUT)
11 Cyril SUK (CZE)
11 Pavel VIZNER (CZE)
Justin GIMELSTOB (USA)
Brian MACPHIE (USA)
Mariusz FYRSTENBERG (POL)
Marcin MATKOWSKI (POL)
Juan MONACO (ARG)
Fernando VERDASCO (ESP)
Jan HERNYCH (CZE)
Tomas ZIB (CZE)
Jiri NOVAK (CZE)
Petr PALA (CZE)
Rainer SCHUETTLER (GER)
Alexander WASKE (GER)
7 Wayne ARTHURS (AUS)
7 Paul HANLEY (AUS)
3 Mark KNOWLES (BAH)
3 Michael LLODRA (FRA)
Robbie KOENIG (RSA)
Sebastian PRIETO (ARG)
Giorgio GALIMBERTI (ITA)
Davide SANGUINETTI (ITA)
Q Robert LINDSTEDT (SWE)
Q Alexander PEYA (AUT)
WC Mark HILTON (GBR)
WC Jonathan MARRAY (GBR)
Julien BENNETEAU (FRA)
Nicolas MAHUT (FRA)
Ivo KARLOVIC (CRO)
Rogier WASSEN (NED)
16 Yves ALLEGRO (SUI)
16 Michael KOHLMANN (GER)
9 Frantisek CERMAK (CZE)
9 Leos FRIEDL (CZE)
Q Ramon DELGADO (PAR)
Q Andre SA (BRA)
WC Andrew BANKS (GBR)
WC Alan MACKIN (GBR)
Q Tuomas KETOLA (FIN)
Q Frederic NIEMEYER (CAN)
Cyril SAULNIER (FRA)
Tom VANHOUDT (BEL)
Q Stephen HUSS (AUS)
Q Wesley MOODIE (RSA)
Graydon OLIVER (USA)
Jared PALMER (USA)
6 Mahesh BHUPATHI (IND)
6 Todd WOODBRIDGE (AUS)

Second round

J.BJORKMAN (1) / M.MIRNYI (1) 63 62 61
A.FISHER / C.HAGGARD 64 64 76(6)
V.HANESCU / A.PAVEL 63 64 64
J.KNOWLE (13) / J.MELZER (13) 63 62 63
C.SUK (11) / P.VIZNER (11) 63 67(8) 76(6) 76(3)
M.FYRSTENBERG / M.MATKOWSKI 63 62 64
J.HERNYCH / T.ZIB 06 76(4) 76(7) 46 63
R.SCHUETTLER / A.WASKE 57 57 76(5) 75 75
M.KNOWLES (3) / M.LLODRA (3) 62 64 63
R.LINDSTEDT (Q) / A.PEYA (Q) 76(3) 62 63
M.HILTON (WC) / J.MARRAY (WC) 67(4) 64 76(3) 75
I.KARLOVIC / R.WASSEN 75 63 64
F.CERMAK (9) / L.FRIEDL (9) 76(4) 63 61
T.KETOLA (Q) / F.NIEMEYER (Q) 75 76(2) 63
S.HUSS (Q) / W.MOODIE (Q) 67(5) 63 62 63
M.BHUPATHI (6) / T.WOODBRIDGE (6) 64 62 67(5) 63

Third round

J.BJORKMAN (1) / M.MIRNYI (1) 60 63 57 46 64
J.KNOWLE (13) / J.MELZER (13) 76(2) 76(5) 75
C.SUK (11) / P.VIZNER (11) 64 57 76(8) 16 75
R.SCHUETTLER / A.WASKE 64 67(1) 67(2) 62 75
M.KNOWLES (3) / M.LLODRA (3) 64 76(1) 64
I.KARLOVIC / R.WASSEN 46 63 26 61 75
F.CERMAK (9) / L.FRIEDL (9) 36 63 76(2) 63
S.HUSS (Q) / W.MOODIE (Q) 63 76(3) 63

Quarter-finals

J.BJORKMAN (1) / M.MIRNYI (1) 67(1) 46 63 64 63
R.SCHUETTLER / A.WASKE 64 64 76(6)
M.KNOWLES (3) / M.LLODRA (3) 64 64 57 64
S.HUSS (Q) / W.MOODIE (Q) 62 63 64

Semi-finals

J.BJORKMAN (1) / M.MIRNYI (1) 75 63 62
S.HUSS (Q) / W.MOODIE (Q) 64 64 64

Final

S.HUSS (Q) / W.MOODIE (Q) 26 62 64 76(4)

Champions

S.HUSS (Q) / W.MOODIE (Q) 76(4) 63 67(2) 63

5 Leander PAES (IND)
5 Nenad ZIMONJIC (SCG)
Lucas ARNOLD (ARG)
Daniele BRACCIALI (ITA)
Jeff COETZEE (RSA)
Ricardo MELLO (BRA)
Rick LEACH (USA)
Travis PARROTT (USA)
Martin GARCIA (ARG)
Luis HORNA (PER)
Karol BECK (SVK)
Jaroslav LEVINSKY (CZE)
WC Andrew MURRAY (GBR)
WC David SHERWOOD (GBR)
10 Martin DAMM (CZE)
10 Mariano HOOD (ARG)
14 Gaston ETLIS (ARG)
14 Martin RODRIGUEZ (ARG)
Enzo ARTONI (ITA)
Mariano PUERTA (ARG)
LL Ross HUTCHINS (GBR)
LL Martin LEE (GBR)
Jean-Francois BACHELOT (FRA)
Arnaud CLEMENT (FRA)
WC Alex BOGDANOVIC (GBR)
WC Joshua GOODALL (GBR)
Tomas BERDYCH (CZE)
Florian MAYER (GER)
Massimo BERTOLINI (ITA)
Filippo VOLANDRI (ITA)
4 Wayne BLACK (ZIM)
4 Kevin ULLYETT (ZIM)
8 Simon ASPELIN (SWE)
8 Todd PERRY (AUS)
Dominik HRBATY (SVK)
Michal MERTINAK (SVK)
Feliciano LOPEZ (ESP)
Rafael NADAL (ESP)
Tomas CIBULEC (CZE)
David RIKL (CZE)
Gilles MULLER (LUX)
Christophe ROCHUS (BEL)
Xavier MALISSE (BEL)
Olivier ROCHUS (BEL)
LL Lukas DLOUHY (CZE)
LL David SKOCH (CZE)
12 Fernando GONZALEZ (CHI)
12 Nicolas MASSU (CHI)
15 Jonathan ERLICH (ISR)
15 Andy RAM (ISR)
WC Jamie DELGADO (GBR)
WC Arvind PARMAR (GBR)
Johan LANDSBERG (SWE)
Robin SODERLING (SWE)
Alex LOPEZ-MORON (ESP)
Tommy ROBREDO (ESP)
Kevin KIM (USA)
Hyung-Taik LEE (KOR)
WC James AUCKLAND (GBR)
WC Daniel KIERNAN (GBR)
David FERRER (ESP)
Santiago VENTURA (ESP)
2 Bob BRYAN (USA)
2 Mike BRYAN (USA)

L.PAES (5)
N.ZIMONJIC (5)
76(3) 67(5) 63 63

R.LEACH
T.PARROTT
63 61 67(3) 36 62

K.BECK
J.LEVINSKY
63 62 36 63

M.DAMM (10)
M.HOOD (10)
61 64 64

G.ETLIS (14)
M.RODRIGUEZ (14)
62 61 76(2)

J.BACHELOT
A.CLEMENT
63 76(2) 62

T.BERDYCH
F.MAYER
62 64 64

W.BLACK (4)
K.ULLYETT (4)
61 62 62

D.HRBATY
M.MERTINAK
26 67(6) 76(5) 63 63

F.LOPEZ
R.NADAL
63 76(3) 76(9)

X.MALISSE
O.ROCHUS
64 75 36 36 62

F.GONZALEZ (12)
N.MASSU (12)
36 64 76(5) 63

J.ERLICH (15)
A.RAM (15)
64 67(5) 64 62

J.LANDSBERG
R.SODERLING
63 62 64

J.AUCKLAND (WC)
D.KIERNAN (WC)
67(3) 16 64 63 64

B.BRYAN (2)
M.BRYAN (2)
57 63 62 60

L.PAES (5)
N.ZIMONJIC (5)
36 63 64 76(3)

K.BECK
J.LEVINSKY
76(3) 67(2) 26 64 64

G.ETLIS (14)
M.RODRIGUEZ (14)
36 64 RET

W.BLACK (4)
K.ULLYETT (4)
64 61 62

D.HRBATY
M.MERTINAK
W/O

X.MALISSE
O.ROCHUS
61 76(7) 62

J.ERLICH (15)
A.RAM (15)
W/O

B.BRYAN (2)
M.BRYAN (2)
63 36 63 64

L.PAES (5)
N.ZIMONJIC (5)
75 63 64

W.BLACK (4)
K.ULLYETT (4)
64 62 36 76(3)

D.HRBATY
M.MERTINAK
61 63 63

B.BRYAN (2)
M.BRYAN (2)
63 76(0) 63

W.BLACK (4)
K.ULLYETT (4)
75 76(8) 76(8)

B.BRYAN (2)
M.BRYAN (2)
76(1) 64 76(2)

B.BRYAN (2)
M.BRYAN (2)
46 63 64 64

2005 Wimbledon Championships, 20 June–3 July – Women's Doubles

First round

17 Els CALLENS (BEL)
17 Emmanuelle GAGLIARDI (SUI)
Silvia FARINA ELIA (ITA)
Roberta VINCI (ITA)
Mariana DIAZ-OLIVA (ARG)
Martina SUCHA (SVK)
WC Elena BALTACHA (GBR)
WC Jane O'DONOGHUE (GBR)
Jill CRAYBAS (USA)
Marlene WEINGARTNER (GER)
Vera DOUCHEVINA (RUS)
Shahar PEER (ISR)
Nathalie DECHY (FRA)
Karolina SPREM (CRO)
16 Gabriela NAVRATILOVA (CZE)
16 Michaela PASTIKOVA (CZE)
10 Shinobu ASAGOE (JPN)
10 Katarina SREBOTNIK (SLO)
Marta MARRERO (ESP)
Arantxa PARRA-SANTONJA (ESP)
Anne KREMER (LUX)
Anna SMASHNOVA (ISR)
Q Evie DOMINIKOVIC (AUS)
Q Aiko NAKAMURA (JPN)
Denisa CHLADKOVA (CZE)
Virginie RAZZANO (FRA)
Eugenia LINETSKAYA (RUS)
Nicole VAIDISOVA (CZE)
Q Rika FUJIWARA (JPN)
Q Saori OBATA (JPN)
8 Anna-Lena GROENEFELD (GER)
8 Martina NAVRATILOVA (USA)
3 Lisa RAYMOND (USA)
3 Rennae STUBBS (AUS)
Stephanie COHEN-ALORO (FRA)
Selima SFAR (TUN)
Lisa MCSHEA (AUS)
Abigail SPEARS (USA)
Q Tatiana POUTCHEK (BLR)
Q Anastasia YAKIMOVA (BLR)
Svetlana KUZNETSOVA (RUS)
Amelie MAURESMO (FRA)
Ludmila CERVANOVA (SVK)
Klara KOUKALOVA (CZE)
Laura GRANVILLE (USA)
Janet LEE (TPE)
13 Gisela DULKO (ARG)
13 Maria VENTO-KABCHI (VEN)
12 Lindsay DAVENPORT (USA)
12 Corina MORARIU (USA)
Jelena JANKOVIC (SCG)
Jelena KOSTANIC (CRO)
Maria-Elena CAMERIN (ITA)
Tathiana GARBIN (ITA)
Marion BARTOLI (FRA)
Milagros SEQUERA (VEN)
Jennifer HOPKINS (USA)
Mashona WASHINGTON (USA)
Iveta BENESOVA (CZE)
Galina VOSKOBOEVA (RUS)
Q Alyona BONDARENKO (UKR)
Q Anastasia RODIONOVA (RUS)
5 Elena LIKHOVTSEVA (RUS)
5 Vera ZVONAREVA (RUS)

Second round

E.CALLENS (17)
E.GAGLIARDI (17)
63 76(4)

E.BALTACHA (WC)
J.O'DONOGHUE (WC)
75 16 61

V.DOUCHEVINA
S.PEER
76(4) 76(9)

G.NAVRATILOVA (16)
M.PASTIKOVA (16)
76(6) 64

S.ASAGOE (10)
K.SREBOTNIK (10)
60 36 63

E.DOMINIKOVIC (Q)
A.NAKAMURA (Q)
63 36 62

D.CHLADKOVA
V.RAZZANO
64 63

A.GROENEFELD (8)
M.NAVRATILOVA (8)
63 63

S.COHEN-ALORO
S.SFAR
64 36 62

L.MCSHEA
A.SPEARS
67(4) 61 61

S.KUZNETSOVA
A.MAURESMO
75 62

L.GRANVILLE
J.LEE
36 64 60

L.DAVENPORT (12)
C.MORARIU (12)
75 63

M.BARTOLI
M.SEQUERA
60 64

J.HOPKINS
M.WASHINGTON
76(5) 61

E.LIKHOVTSEVA (5)
V.ZVONAREVA (5)
62 75

Third round

E.CALLENS (17)
E.GAGLIARDI (17)
61 62

V.DOUCHEVINA
S.PEER
62 67(7) 86

S.ASAGOE (10)
K.SREBOTNIK (10)
36 62 63

A.GROENEFELD (8)
M.NAVRATILOVA (8)
61 64

L.MCSHEA
A.SPEARS
61 62

S.KUZNETSOVA
A.MAURESMO
61 62

M.BARTOLI
M.SEQUERA
76(2) 36 64

E.LIKHOVTSEVA (5)
V.ZVONAREVA (5)
67(5) 62 61

Quarter-finals

V.DOUCHEVINA
S.PEER
57 63 75

A.GROENEFELD (8)
M.NAVRATILOVA (8)
63 63

S.KUZNETSOVA
A.MAURESMO
76(3) 62

E.LIKHOVTSEVA (5)
V.ZVONAREVA (5)
64 36 63

Semi-finals

A.GROENEFELD (8)
M.NAVRATILOVA (8)
76(5) 64

S.KUZNETSOVA
A.MAURESMO
63 67(4) 61

Final

S.KUZNETSOVA
A.MAURESMO
64 64

C.BLACK (2)
L.HUBER (2)
62 61

First Round

Seed/Status	Player
6	Janette HUSAROVA (SVK)
6	Conchita MARTINEZ (ESP)
	Eva BIRNEROVA (CZE)
	Andreea VANC (ROM)
	Nuria LLAGOSTERA VIVES (ESP)
	Maria SANCHEZ LORENZO (ESP)
	Kristina BRANDI (PUR)
	Lucie SAFAROVA (CZE)
WC	Katie O'BRIEN (GBR)
WC	Melanie SOUTH (GBR)
	Yulia BEYGELZIMER (UKR)
	Antonella SERRA ZANETTI (ITA)
WC	Amanda JANES (GBR)
WC	Anne KEOTHAVONG (GBR)
11	Bryanne STEWART (AUS)
11	Samantha STOSUR (AUS)
14	Eleni DANIILIDOU (GRE)
14	Nicole PRATT (AUS)
	Kveta PESCHKE (CZE)
	Julia SCHRUFF (GER)
	Flavia PENNETTA (ITA)
	Francesca SCHIAVONE (ITA)
	Ana IVANOVIC (SCG)
	Tina KRIZAN (SLO)
	Catalina CASTANO (COL)
	Sanda MAMIC (CRO)
	Marta DOMACHOWSKA (POL)
	Silvija TALAJA (CRO)
WC	Claire CURRAN (GBR)
WC	Natalie GRANDIN (RSA)
4	Nadia PETROVA (RUS)
4	Meghann SHAUGHNESSY (USA)
7	Daniela HANTUCHOVA (SVK)
7	Ai SUGIYAMA (JPN)
LL	Erica KRAUTH (ARG)
LL	Marie-Eve PELLETIER (CAN)
	Nana MIYAGI (JPN)
	Anastasia MYSKINA (RUS)
WC	Anna HAWKINS (GBR)
WC	Rebecca LLEWELLYN (GBR)
LL	Juliana FEDAK (UKR)
LL	Lilia OSTERLOH (USA)
	Jennifer RUSSELL (USA)
	Mara SANTANGELO (ITA)
	Sesil KARATANTCHEVA (BUL)
	Tamarine TANASUGARN (THA)
9	Anabel MEDINA GARRIGUES (ESP)
9	Dinara SAFINA (RUS)
15	Emilie LOIT (FRA)
15	Barbora STRYCOVA (CZE)
	Dally RANDRIANTEFY (MAD)
	Meilen TU (USA)
	Alina JIDKOVA (RUS)
	Tatiana PEREBIYNIS (UKR)
	Anna CHAKVETADZE (RUS)
	Sania MIRZA (IND)
	Akiko MORIGAMI (JPN)
PR	Trudi MUSGRAVE (AUS)
LL	Edina GALLOVITS (ROM)
LL	Angela HAYNES (USA)
WC	Sarah BORWELL (GBR)
WC	Emily WEBLEY-SMITH (GBR)
2	Cara BLACK (ZIM)
2	Liezel HUBER (RSA)

Second Round

J.HUSAROVA (6) / C.MARTINEZ (6) 62 16 61
N.LLAGOSTERA VIVES / M.SANCHEZ LORENZO 63 61
Y.BEYGELZIMER / A.SERRA ZANETTI 63 62
B.STEWART (11) / S.STOSUR (11) 60 63
E.DANIILIDOU (14) / N.PRATT (14) 75 64
A.IVANOVIC / T.KRIZAN 62 64
M.DOMACHOWSKA / S.TALAJA 46 62 62
N.PETROVA (4) / M.SHAUGHNESSY (4) 64 76(3)
D.HANTUCHOVA (7) / A.SUGIYAMA (7) 76(1) 61
N.MIYAGI / A.MYSKINA 64 60
J.RUSSELL / M.SANTANGELO 64 61
A.MEDINA GARRIGUES (9) / D.SAFINA (9) 64 62
E.LOIT (15) / B.STRYCOVA (15) 63 75
A.JIDKOVA / T.PEREBIYNIS 62 61
A.MORIGAMI / T.MUSGRAVE (PR) 61 75
C.BLACK (2) / L.HUBER (2) 61 62

Third Round

J.HUSAROVA (6) / C.MARTINEZ (6) 62 63
B.STEWART (11) / S.STOSUR (11) 61 61
A.IVANOVIC / T.KRIZAN 63 61
N.PETROVA (4) / M.SHAUGHNESSY (4) 63 61
D.HANTUCHOVA (7) / A.SUGIYAMA (7) 75 76(5)
A.MEDINA GARRIGUES (9) / D.SAFINA (9) 61 76(7)
E.LOIT (15) / B.STRYCOVA (15) 36 64 75
C.BLACK (2) / L.HUBER (2) 62 61

Quarter-finals

B.STEWART (11) / S.STOSUR (11) 76(8) 67(5) 61
N.PETROVA (4) / M.SHAUGHNESSY (4) 61 63
D.HANTUCHOVA (7) / A.SUGIYAMA (7) 62 61
C.BLACK (2) / L.HUBER (2) 61 75

Semi-finals

B.STEWART (11) / S.STOSUR (11) 36 64 64
C.BLACK (2) / L.HUBER (2) 63 62

Final

C.BLACK (2) / L.HUBER (2) 60 62

2005 Wimbledon Championships, 20 June–3 July – Mixed Doubles

1 Bob BRYAN (USA)
1 Rennae STUBBS (AUS)
BYE
BYE
Andrei PAVEL (ROM)
Andreea VANC (ROM)
Mariano HOOD (ARG)
Gisela DULKO (ARG)
Petr PALA (CZE)
Gabriela NAVRATILOVA (CZE)
Graydon OLIVER (USA)
Maria KIRILENKO (RUS)
BYE
BYE
14 Dominik HRBATY (SVK)
14 Elena LIKHOVTSEVA (RUS)
11 Jared PALMER (USA)
11 Corina MORARIU (USA)
BYE
BYE
Paul HANLEY (AUS)
Tatiana PEREBIYNIS (UKR)
A Robbie KOENIG (RSA)
A Silvija TALAJA (CRO)
A Gaston ETLIS (ARG)
A Lisa MCSHEA (AUS)
Simon ASPELIN (SWE)
Sania MIRZA (IND)
BYE
BYE
7 Leos FRIEDL (CZE)
7 Janette HUSAROVA (SVK)
4 Kevin ULLYETT (ZIM)
4 Liezel HUBER (RSA)
BYE
BYE
WC Arvind PARMAR (GBR)
WC Jane O'DONOGHUE (GBR)
Michael KOHLMANN (GER)
Anastasia MYSKINA (RUS)
Jim THOMAS (USA)
Jennifer RUSSELL (USA)
Cyril SUK (CZE)
Jelena JANKOVIC (SCG)
BYE
BYE
16 Andy RAM (ISR)
16 Conchita MARTINEZ (ESP)
9 Pavel VIZNER (CZE)
9 Nicole PRATT (AUS)
BYE
BYE
WC Richard BARKER (GBR)
WC Claire CURRAN (GBR)
Travis PARROTT (USA)
Amy FRAZIER (USA)
WC Andrew MURRAY (GBR)
WC Shahar PEER (ISR)
Lucas ARNOLD (ARG)
Emmanuelle GAGLIARDI (SUI)
BYE
BYE
5 Mike BRYAN (USA)
5 Martina NAVRATILOVA (USA)

B.BRYAN (1)
R.STUBBS (1)
BYE

M.HOOD
G.DULKO
57 64 119

G.OLIVER
M.KIRILENKO
63 62

D.HRBATY (14)
E.LIKHOVTSEVA (14)
BYE

J.PALMER (11)
C.MORARIU (11)
BYE

P.HANLEY
T.PEREBIYNIS
63 76(9)

S.ASPELIN
S.MIRZA
67(5) 62 75

L.FRIEDL (7)
J.HUSAROVA (7)
BYE

K.ULLYETT (4)
L.HUBER (4)
BYE

M.KOHLMANN
A.MYSKINA
75 62

C.SUK
J.JANKOVIC
16 64 75

A.RAM (16)
C.MARTINEZ (16)
BYE

P.VIZNER (9)
N.PRATT (9)
BYE

T.PARROTT
A.FRAZIER
36 63 61

L.ARNOLD
E.GAGLIARDI
63 64

M.BRYAN (5)
M.NAVRATILOVA (5)
BYE

M.HOOD
G.DULKO
64 36 75

D.HRBATY (14)
E.LIKHOVTSEVA (14)
67(6) 63 62

P.HANLEY
T.PEREBIYNIS
26 64 75

L.FRIEDL (7)
J.HUSAROVA (7)
62 64

K.ULLYETT (4)
L.HUBER (4)
W/O

A.RAM (16)
C.MARTINEZ (16)
W/O

T.PARROTT
A.FRAZIER
76(3) 63

M.BRYAN (5)
M.NAVRATILOVA (5)
W/O

M.HOOD
G.DULKO
62 61

P.HANLEY
T.PEREBIYNIS
64 52 RET

K.ULLYETT (4)
L.HUBER (4)
46 63 86

M.BRYAN (5)
M.NAVRATILOVA (5)
75 67(4) 64

P.HANLEY
T.PEREBIYNIS
63 64

K.ULLYETT (4)
L.HUBER (4)
36 64 97

P.HANLEY
T.PEREBIYNIS
63 64

M.BHUPATHI
M.PIERCE
64 62

6 Todd WOODBRIDGE (AUS)
6 Samantha STOSUR (AUS)
BYE
BYE
Martin RODRIGUEZ (ARG)
Alina JIDKOVA (RUS)
Jaroslav LEVINSKY (CZE)
Anna CHAKVETADZE (RUS)
Jordan KERR (AUS)
Eugenia LINETSKAYA (RUS)
A Brian MACPHIE (USA)
A Abigail SPEARS (USA)
BYE
BYE
10 Nenad ZIMONJIC (SCG)
10 Katarina SREBOTNIK (SLO)
13 Julian KNOWLE (AUT)
13 Anna-Lena GROENEFELD (GER)
BYE
BYE
Jonathan ERLICH (ISR)
Bryanne STEWART (AUS)
WC Jamie DELGADO (GBR)
WC Amanda JANES (GBR)
Yves ALLEGRO (SUI)
Magdalena MALEEVA (BUL)
Alex LOPEZ-MORON (ESP)
Anabel MEDINA GARRIGUES (ESP)
BYE
BYE
3 Jonas BJORKMAN (SWE)
3 Lisa RAYMOND (USA)
8 Mark KNOWLES (BAH)
8 Venus WILLIAMS (USA)
BYE
BYE
Justin GIMELSTOB (USA)
Tina KRIZAN (SLO)
Todd PERRY (AUS)
Els CALLENS (BEL)
Ashley FISHER (AUS)
Jelena KOSTANIC (CRO)
Jiri NOVAK (CZE)
Tathiana GARBIN (ITA)
BYE
BYE
12 Olivier ROCHUS (BEL)
12 Kim CLIJSTERS (BEL)
15 Martin DAMM (CZE)
15 Kveta PESCHKE (CZE)
BYE
BYE
Martin GARCIA (ARG)
Mara SANTANGELO (ITA)
Sebastian PRIETO (ARG)
Maria VENTO-KABCHI (VEN)
Mahesh BHUPATHI (IND)
Mary PIERCE (FRA)
WC David SHERWOOD (GBR)
WC Elena BALTACHA (GBR)
BYE
BYE
2 Wayne BLACK (ZIM)
2 Cara BLACK (ZIM)

T.WOODBRIDGE (6)
S.STOSUR (6)
BYE

J.LEVINSKY
A.CHAKVETADZE
62 67(5) 86

B.MACPHIE (A)
A.SPEARS (A)
64 64

N.ZIMONJIC (10)
K.SREBOTNIK (10)
BYE

J.KNOWLE (13)
A.GROENEFELD (13)
BYE

J.ERLICH
B.STEWART
64 64

A.LOPEZ-MORON
A.MEDINA GARRIGUES
75 62

J.BJORKMAN (3)
L.RAYMOND (3)
BYE

M.KNOWLES (8)
V.WILLIAMS (8)
BYE

T.PERRY
E.CALLENS
40 RET

A.FISHER
J.KOSTANIC
63 64

O.ROCHUS (12)
K.CLIJSTERS (12)
BYE

M.DAMM (15)
K.PESCHKE (15)
BYE

M.GARCIA
M.SANTANGELO
63 64

M.BHUPATHI
M.PIERCE
63 64

W.BLACK (2)
C.BLACK (2)
BYE

T.WOODBRIDGE (6)
S.STOSUR (6)
61 76(5)

N.ZIMONJIC (10)
K.SREBOTNIK (10)
62 57 64

J.KNOWLE (13)
A.GROENEFELD (13)
63 67(5) 62

J.BJORKMAN (3)
L.RAYMOND (3)
62 61

M.KNOWLES (8)
V.WILLIAMS (8)
67(6) 64 64

O.ROCHUS (12)
K.CLIJSTERS (12)
61 63

M.GARCIA
M.SANTANGELO
46 61 62

M.BHUPATHI
M.PIERCE
63 64

T.WOODBRIDGE (6)
S.STOSUR (6)
36 62 63

J.BJORKMAN (3)
L.RAYMOND (3)
62 63

O.ROCHUS (12)
K.CLIJSTERS (12)
36 63 75

M.BHUPATHI
M.PIERCE
63 76(5)

J.BJORKMAN (3)
L.RAYMOND (3)
62 76(13)

M.BHUPATHI
M.PIERCE
61 75

M.BHUPATHI
M.PIERCE
75 61

2005 US Open Championships, 29 August–11 September – Men's Singles

US OPEN 2005
A USTA EVENT

1 Roger FEDERER (SUI)
Ivo MINAR (CZE)
Fabrice SANTORO (FRA)
Jurgen MELZER (AUT)
Albert MONTANES (ESP)
Victor HANESCU (ROM)
Q Robin VIK (CZE)
27 Olivier ROCHUS (BEL)
20 Juan Carlos FERRERO (ESP)
Q Arnaud CLEMENT (FRA)
Andrei PAVEL (ROM)
Q Andrew MURRAY (GBR)
Nicolas KIEFER (GER)
Jiri VANEK (CZE)
Nicolas LAPENTTI (ECU)
16 Radek STEPANEK (CZE)
11 David NALBANDIAN (ARG)
Q Alex BOGOMOLOV (USA)
Peter WESSELS (NED)
Christophe ROCHUS (BEL)
PR Dmitry TURSUNOV (RUS)
Marcos BAGHDATIS (CYP)
Q Wesley MOODIE (RSA)
21 Fernando GONZALEZ (CHI)
31 Carlos MOYA (ESP)
Michael LLODRA (FRA)
Davide SANGUINETTI (ITA)
Wayne ARTHURS (AUS)
Paradorn SRICHAPHAN (THA)
PR Younes EL AYNAOUI (MAR)
Tomas ZIB (CZE)
6 Nikolay DAVYDENKO (RUS)
3 Lleyton HEWITT (AUS)
Albert COSTA (ESP)
Jose ACASUSO (ARG)
Luis HORNA (PER)
Kenneth CARLSEN (DEN)
Nicolas ALMAGRO (ESP)
Lars BURGSMULLER (GER)
25 Taylor DENT (USA)
17 David FERRER (ESP)
Agustin CALLERI (ARG)
WC Mark PHILIPPOUSSIS (AUS)
PR Karol KUCERA (SVK)
Q Michael LAMMER (SUI)
Kevin KIM (USA)
Andreas SEPPI (ITA)
15 Dominik HRBATY (SVK)
12 Tim HENMAN (GBR)
Fernando VERDASCO (ESP)
Paul-Henri MATHIEU (FRA)
Q Paul CAPDEVILLE (CHI)
Gael MONFILS (FRA)
Novak DJOKOVIC (SCG)
Hyung-Taik LEE (KOR)
22 Mario ANCIC (CRO)
30 Max MIRNYI (BLR)
Justin GIMELSTOB (USA)
Florent SERRA (FRA)
Stefan KOUBEK (AUT)
Jarkko NIEMINEN (FIN)
Karol BECK (SVK)
PR Alexander POPP (GER)

R.FEDERER (1) 61 61 61
F.SANTORO 62 61 63
A.MONTANES 64 36 63 21 RET
O.ROCHUS (27) 57 62 62 62
A.CLEMENT (Q) 75 75 61
A.MURRAY (Q) 63 36 36 61 64
N.KIEFER 64 62 63
R.STEPANEK (16) 75 76(5) 61
D.NALBANDIAN (11) 62 75 64
P.WESSELS 67(4) 63 64 64
D.TURSUNOV (PR) 64 63 67(7) 62
F.GONZALEZ (21) 46 64 75 75
C.MOYA (31) 64 64 21 RET
D.SANGUINETTI 63 63 76(3)
P.SRICHAPHAN 64 63 60
N.DAVYDENKO (6) 62 60 64
L.HEWITT (3) 61 62 61
J.ACASUSO 46 63 64 76(11)
N.ALMAGRO 76(4) 75 64
T.DENT (25) 63 36 61 64
D.FERRER (17) 46 64 67(4) 61 61
K.KUCERA (PR) 64 62 75
M.LAMMER (Q) 36 63 75 64
D.HRBATY (15) 62 64 67(6) 62
F.VERDASCO 64 62 62
P.CAPDEVILLE (Q) 62 46 75 62
N.DJOKOVIC 75 46 76(5) 06 75
M.ANCIC (22) 62 61 75
M.MIRNYI (30) 62 75 62
F.SERRA 61 64 46 64
J.NIEMINEN 64 26 75 06 75
B.PHAU (LL)

R.FEDERER (1) 75 75 76(2)
O.ROCHUS (27) 46 62 61 63
A.CLEMENT (Q) 62 76(2) 26 67(4) 60
N.KIEFER 46 46 64 63 63
D.NALBANDIAN (11) 76(4) 16 62 76(4)
F.GONZALEZ (21) 64 36 64 63
D.SANGUINETTI 36 61 62 64
P.SRICHAPHAN 64 75 63
L.HEWITT (3) 76(6) 76(3) 62
T.DENT (25) 63 62 46 75
D.FERRER (17) 63 60 62
D.HRBATY (15) 61 61 63
F.VERDASCO 64 62 75
N.DJOKOVIC 63 57 76(4) 63
M.MIRNYI (30) 76(5) 67(4) 64 76(4)
J.NIEMINEN 62 64 57 64

R.FEDERER (1) 63 76(6) 62
N.KIEFER 64 67(5) 64 61
D.NALBANDIAN (11) 75 63 60
D.SANGUINETTI 63 46 67(2) 76(6) 76(5)
L.HEWITT (3) 63 36 67(2) 62 75
D.HRBATY (15) 67(7) 75 75 75
F.VERDASCO 61 46 67(2) 64 64
J.NIEMINEN 63 76(5) 36 63

R.FEDERER (1) 64 67(3) 63 64
D.NALBANDIAN (11) 46 76(4) 64 62
L.HEWITT (3) 61 64 62
J.NIEMINEN 62 76(6) 63

R.FEDERER (1) 62 64 61
L.HEWITT (3) 26 61 36 63 61

R.FEDERER (1) 63 76(0) 46 63

R.FEDERER (1) 63 26 76(1) 61

8	Guillermo CORIA (ARG)	G.CORIA [8] 76(5) 61 63	G.CORIA [8] 62 63 62	G.CORIA [8] 62 67(4) 61 64	G.CORIA [8] 64 26 67(5) 62 62	R.GINEPRI 46 61 75 36 75	A.AGASSI [7] 64 57 63 46 63
	Felix MANTILLA (ESP)						
Q	Glenn WEINER (USA)	V.SPADEA 64 62 60					
	Vince SPADEA (USA)						
	Robin SODERLING (SWE)	R.SODERLING 67(3) 76(4) 63 64	R.SODERLING 62 62 76(6)				
	Juan Ignacio CHELA (ARG)						
	Filippo VOLANDRI (ITA)	F.LOPEZ [26] 62 46 76(5) 61					
26	Feliciano LOPEZ (ESP)						
23	Jiri NOVAK (CZE)	J.NOVAK [23] 64 64 62	N.MASSU W/O	N.MASSU 64 63 60			
	Dick NORMAN (BEL)						
WC	Jan-Michael GAMBILL (USA)	N.MASSU 76(4) 62 63					
	Nicolas MASSU (CHI)						
	Stanislas WAWRINKA (SUI)	S.WAWRINKA 26 64 76(6) 67(2) 75	S.WAWRINKA 36 64 63 67(4) 61				
WC	Rajeev RAM (USA)						
Q	Noam OKUN (ISR)	M.PUERTA [10] 76(4) 67(3) 64 60					
10	Mariano PUERTA (ARG)						
13	Richard GASQUET (FRA)	R.GASQUET [13] 62 63 16 67(4) 64	R.GASQUET [13] 61 36 63 32 RET	R.GASQUET [13] 36 76(6) 67(7) 63 62	R.GINEPRI 63 36 67(8) 64 60		
	Alberto MARTIN (ESP)						
Q	Giorgio GALIMBERTI (ITA)	G.GALIMBERTI (Q) 76(4) 61 62					
WC	Donald YOUNG (USA)						
	Cyril SAULNIER (FRA)	C.SAULNIER 67(7) 76(3) 64 63	I.LJUBICIC [18] 76(5) 57 64 64				
	Janko TIPSAREVIC (SCG)						
Q	Tobias SUMMERER (GER)	I.LJUBICIC [18] 63 76(4) 63					
18	Ivan LJUBICIC (CRO)						
29	Tommy HAAS (GER)	T.HAAS [29] 36 63 62 63	T.HAAS [29] 76(5) 62 60	R.GINEPRI 75 67(3) 64 26 63			
Q	Peter LUCZAK (AUS)						
	Potito STARACE (ITA)	R.SCHUETTLER 61 64 16 76(4)					
	Rainer SCHUETTLER (GER)						
	Robby GINEPRI (USA)	R.GINEPRI 63 62 76(5)	R.GINEPRI 61 61 64				
	Guillermo GARCIA-LOPEZ (ESP)						
	Gilles MULLER (LUX)	G.MULLER 76(4) 76(8) 76(1)					
4	Andy RODDICK (USA)						
7	Andre AGASSI (USA)	A.AGASSI [7] 63 63 61	A.AGASSI [7] 76(4) 76(5) 76(4)	A.AGASSI [7] 36 61 64 76(2)	A.AGASSI [7] 63 64 67(5) 46 62	A.AGASSI [7] 36 36 63 63 76(6)	
	Razvan SABAU (ROM)						
	Mardy FISH (USA)	I.KARLOVIC 76(4) 63 57 76(4)					
	Ivo KARLOVIC (CRO)						
	Juan MONACO (ARG)	R.MELLO 67(2) 62 61 64	T.BERDYCH [32] 63 62 60				
	Ricardo MELLO (BRA)						
	Philipp KOHLSCHREIBER (GER)	T.BERDYCH [32] 76(6) 76(4) 64					
32	Tomas BERDYCH (CZE)						
24	Mikhail YOUZHNY (RUS)	M.YOUZHNY [24] 61 60 62	M.YOUZHNY [24] 64 64 63	X.MALISSE 57 16 61 75 76(1)			
	Florian MAYER (GER)						
	Tomas BEHREND (GER)	J.BJORKMAN (Q) 63 63 60					
Q	Jonas BJORKMAN (SWE)						
	Jan HERNYCH (CZE)	X.MALISSE 62 75 62	X.MALISSE 67(5) 62 63 64				
	Xavier MALISSE (BEL)						
WC	Brian BAKER (USA)	B.BAKER (WC) 76(9) 62 64					
9	Gaston GAUDIO (ARG)						
14	Thomas JOHANSSON (SWE)	T.JOHANSSON [14] 63 64 63	S.GROSJEAN 63 62 46 62	T.ROBREDO [19] 64 75 67(3) 76(3)	J.BLAKE (WC) 46 75 62 63		
	Mariano ZABALETA (ARG)						
	Oscar HERNANDEZ (ESP)	S.GROSJEAN 62 63 62					
	Sebastien GROSJEAN (FRA)						
	Paul GOLDSTEIN (USA)	G.KUERTEN (PR) 62 67(5) 63 76(3)	T.ROBREDO [19] 57 76(3) 63 62				
PR	Gustavo KUERTEN (BRA)						
Q	Daniele BRACCIALI (ITA)	T.ROBREDO [19] 36 63 64 62					
19	Tommy ROBREDO (ESP)						
28	Greg RUSEDSKI (GBR)	J.BLAKE (WC) 75 76(3) 63	J.BLAKE (WC) 62 62 64	J.BLAKE (WC) 64 46 63 61			
WC	James BLAKE (USA)						
Q	Gilles ELSENEER (BEL)	I.ANDREEV 64 64 62					
	Igor ANDREEV (RUS)						
Q	George BASTL (SUI)	S.JENKINS (WC) 76(4) 60 67(1) 46 76(5)	R.NADAL [2] 64 75 64				
WC	Scoville JENKINS (USA)						
WC	Bobby REYNOLDS (USA)	R.NADAL [2] 63 63 64					
2	Rafael NADAL (ESP)						

2005 US Open Championships, 29 August–11 September – Women's Singles

US OPEN 2005
A USTA EVENT

First Round

1 Maria SHARAPOVA (RUS)
Eleni DANIILIDOU (GRE)
Dally RANDRIANTEFY (MAD)
WC Mary GAMBALE (USA)
Q Anne KREMER (LUX)
Lisa RAYMOND (USA)
Julia SCHRUFF (GER)
28 Flavia PENNETTA (ITA)
21 Dinara SAFINA (RUS)
Maria-Elena CAMERIN (ITA)
Mashona WASHINGTON (USA)
Sania MIRZA (IND)
Barbora STRYCOVA (CZE)
Marion BARTOLI (FRA)
WC Shenay PERRY (USA)
14 Alicia MOLIK (AUS)
9 Nadia PETROVA (RUS)
Eva BIRNEROVA (CZE)
Marissa IRVIN (USA)
Aiko NAKAMURA (JPN)
Nicole PRATT (AUS)
Akiko MORIGAMI (JPN)
Laura GRANVILLE (USA)
22 Silvia FARINA ELIA (ITA)
26 Nicole VAIDISOVA (CZE)
Kveta PESCHKE (CZE)
Jie ZHENG (CHN)
Iveta BENESOVA (CZE)
Q Ivana LISJAK (CRO)
Emilie LOIT (FRA)
Ekaterina BYCHKOVA (RUS)
5 Svetlana KUZNETSOVA (RUS)
4 Kim CLIJSTERS (BEL)
Q Martina MULLER (GER)
WC Ashley HARKLEROAD (USA)
Fabiola ZULUAGA (COL)
Michaela PASTIKOVA (CZE)
SR Rita GRANDE (ITA)
Alona BONDARENKO (UKR)
30 Ai SUGIYAMA (JPN)
18 Ana IVANOVIC (SCG)
Lindsay LEE-WATERS (USA)
Sanda MAMIC (CRO)
Maria VENTO-KABCHI (VEN)
Marta DOMACHOWSKA (POL)
Shahar PEER (ISR)
Q Tiffany DABEK (USA)
33 Vera DOUCHEVINA (RUS)
10 Venus WILLIAMS (USA)
Rika FUJIWARA (JPN)
Laura POUS-TIO (ESP)
Maria KIRILENKO (RUS)
Q Maria-Emilia SALERNI (ARG)
WC Jessica KIRKLAND (USA)
Camille PIN (FRA)
20 Daniela HANTUCHOVA (SVK)
25 Francesca SCHIAVONE (ITA)
Jelena KOSTANIC (CRO)
Shuai PENG (CHN)
Q Emma LAINE (FIN)
Alina JIDKOVA (RUS)
Catalina CASTANO (COL)
Q Yung-Jan CHAN (TPE)
8 Serena WILLIAMS (USA)

Second Round

M.SHARAPOVA (1)
61 61
D.RANDRIANTEFY
63 61
L.RAYMOND
64 36 62
J.SCHRUFF
64 36 75
M.CAMERIN
63 67(5) 63
S.MIRZA
76(6) 67(6) 64
M.BARTOLI
63 60
S.PERRY (WC)
64 64
N.PETROVA (9)
64 64
A.NAKAMURA
63 63
N.PRATT
67(0) 60 RET
L.GRANVILLE
62 61
N.VAIDISOVA (26)
63 61
J.ZHENG
62 36 60
I.LISJAK (Q)
16 64 63
E.BYCHKOVA
63 62
K.CLIJSTERS (4)
61 62
F.ZULUAGA
60 30 RET
M.PASTIKOVA
36 76(5) 63
A.SUGIYAMA (30)
57 64 63
A.IVANOVIC (18)
76(5) 63
M.VENTO-KABCHI
16 63 63
S.PEER
75 75
V.DOUCHEVINA (33)
61 62
V.WILLIAMS (10)
63 61
M.KIRILENKO
62 63
M.SALERNI (Q)
64 36 76(0)
D.HANTUCHOVA (20)
63 61
F.SCHIAVONE (25)
62 75
E.LAINE (Q)
36 76(4) 62
C.CASTANO
64 63
S.WILLIAMS (8)
61 63

Third Round

M.SHARAPOVA (1)
61 60
J.SCHRUFF
62 63
S.MIRZA
64 16 64
M.BARTOLI
46 61 60
N.PETROVA (9)
62 60
L.GRANVILLE
64 57 75
N.VAIDISOVA (26)
63 60
I.LISJAK (Q)
75 61
K.CLIJSTERS (4)
75 60
A.SUGIYAMA (30)
26 64 64
M.VENTO-KABCHI
36 75 61
S.PEER
75 36 63
V.WILLIAMS (10)
61 63
D.HANTUCHOVA (20)
61 60
F.SCHIAVONE (25)
62 62
S.WILLIAMS (8)
62 62

Fourth Round

M.SHARAPOVA (1)
62 64
S.MIRZA
76(4) 64
N.PETROVA (9)
62 75
N.VAIDISOVA (26)
61 76(2)
K.CLIJSTERS (4)
61 64
M.VENTO-KABCHI
75 46 63
V.WILLIAMS (10)
63 63
S.WILLIAMS (8)
63 64

Quarter-finals

M.SHARAPOVA (1)
62 61
N.PETROVA (9)
76(4) 75
K.CLIJSTERS (4)
61 60
V.WILLIAMS (10)
76(5) 62

Semi-finals

M.SHARAPOVA (1)
75 46 64
K.CLIJSTERS (4)
46 75 61

Final

K.CLIJSTERS (4)
62 67(4) 63

K.CLIJSTERS (4)
63 61

7	Justine HENIN-HARDENNE (BEL)	J.HENIN-HARDENNE (7)
	Zuzana ONDRASKOVA (CZE)	63 60
LL	Maria SANCHEZ LORENZO (ESP)	M.SANCHEZ LORENZO (LL)
WC	Angela HAYNES (USA)	75 76(6)
	Yoon-Jeong CHO (KOR)	Y.CHO
	Arantxa PARRA-SANTONJA (ESP)	64 26 64
Q	Stephanie FORETZ (FRA)	G.DULKO (27)
27	Gisela DULKO (ARG)	63 62
17	Jelena JANKOVIC (SCG)	J.JANKOVIC (17)
	Denisa CHLADKOVA (CZE)	75 63
	Juliana FEDAK (UKR)	A.GLATCH (WC)
WC	Alexa GLATCH (USA)	64 63
	Katarina SREBOTNIK (SLO)	K.SREBOTNIK
Q	Su-Wei HSIEH (TPE)	60 62
	Mara SANTANGELO (ITA)	M.PIERCE (12)
12	Mary PIERCE (FRA)	62 64
13	Anastasia MYSKINA (RUS)	A.MYSKINA (13)
	Tamarine TANASUGARN (THA)	63 61
	Amy FRAZIER (USA)	A.FRAZIER
WC	Carly GULLICKSON (USA)	64 75
LL	Emmanuelle GAGLIARDI (SUI)	M.MALEEVA
	Magdalena MALEEVA (BUL)	61 63
	Tathiana GARBIN (ITA)	E.LIKHOVTSEVA (19)
19	Elena LIKHOVTSEVA (RUS)	64 61
31	Anna-Lena GROENEFELD (GER)	A.GROENEFELD (31)
	Kristina BRANDI (PUR)	62 63
	Virginie RAZZANO (FRA)	V.RAZZANO
	Abigail SPEARS (USA)	76(6) 63
	Sesil KARATANTCHEVA (BUL)	S.KARATANTCHEVA
	Meghann SHAUGHNESSY (USA)	26 75 75
	Roberta VINCI (ITA)	A.MAURESMO (3)
3	Amelie MAURESMO (FRA)	63 62
6	Elena DEMENTIEVA (RUS)	E.DEMENTIEVA (6)
	Lucie SAFAROVA (CZE)	75 63
	Mariana DIAZ-OLIVA (ARG)	M.DIAZ-OLIVA
WC	Bethanie MATTEK (USA)	64 63
	Jill CRAYBAS (USA)	J.CRAYBAS
	Jamea JACKSON (USA)	64 26 75
Q	Viktoria KUTUZOVA (UKR)	A.CHAKVETADZE (29)
29	Anna CHAKVETADZE (RUS)	63 36 75
24	Shinobu ASAGOE (JPN)	S.ASAGOE (24)
	Stephanie COHEN-ALORO (FRA)	61 64
	Nuria LLAGOSTERA VIVES (ESP)	E.LINETSKAYA
	Eugenia LINETSKAYA (RUS)	36 64 64
	Martina SUCHA (SVK)	M.SUCHA
Q	Sybille BAMMER (AUT)	46 64 75
	Conchita MARTINEZ (ESP)	P.SCHNYDER (11)
11	Patty SCHNYDER (SUI)	46 64 62
15	Nathalie DECHY (FRA)	N.DECHY (15)
	Severine BELTRAME (FRA)	64 75
	Klara KOUKALOVA (CZE)	V.KING (Q)
Q	Vania KING (USA)	63 36 61
	Anna SMASHNOVA (ISR)	A.SMASHNOVA
Q	Sandra KLOESEL (GER)	63 63
Q	Virginia RUANO PASCUAL (ESP)	T.GOLOVIN (23)
23	Tatiana GOLOVIN (FRA)	63 26 76(5)
32	Anabel MEDINA GARRIGUES (ESP)	A.MEDINA GARRIGUES (32)
	Karolina SPREM (CRO)	62 63
Q	Tian-Tian SUN (CHN)	T.SUN (Q)
	Samantha STOSUR (AUS)	63 76(4)
	Antonella SERRA ZANETTI (ITA)	P.PARMENTIER (Q)
Q	Pauline PARMENTIER (FRA)	26 63 64
	Na LI (CHN)	L.DAVENPORT (2)
2	Lindsay DAVENPORT (USA)	64 64

J.HENIN-HARDENNE (7) 63 64
Y.CHO 64 63
J.JANKOVIC (17) 62 60
M.PIERCE (12) 63 62
A.MYSKINA (13) 63 62
E.LIKHOVTSEVA (19) 62 61
A.GROENEFELD (31) 36 63 64
A.MAURESMO (3) 60 61
E.DEMENTIEVA (6) 75 61
A.CHAKVETADZE (29) 60 62
S.ASAGOE (24) 64 64
P.SCHNYDER (11) 63 26 62
N.DECHY (15) 61 61
T.GOLOVIN (23) 64 76(6)
A.MEDINA GARRIGUES (32) 64 75
L.DAVENPORT (2) 61 61

J.HENIN-HARDENNE (7) 60 76(4)
M.PIERCE (12) 63 30 RET
E.LIKHOVTSEVA (19) 06 63 76(6)
A.MAURESMO (3) 75 63
E.DEMENTIEVA (6) 61 46 76(5)
P.SCHNYDER (11) 61 63
N.DECHY (15) 75 26 62
L.DAVENPORT (2) 63 62

M.PIERCE (12) 63 64
A.MAURESMO (3) 61 64
E.DEMENTIEVA (6) 64 63
L.DAVENPORT (2) 60 63

M.PIERCE (12) 64 61
E.DEMENTIEVA (6) 61 36 76(6)

M.PIERCE (12) 36 62 62

2005 US Open Championships, 29 August–11 September – Men's Doubles

First Round

1 Jonas BJORKMAN (SWE)
1 Max MIRNYI (BLR)
Alberto MARTIN (ESP)
Tomas ZIB (CZE)
WC Brian BAKER (USA)
WC Rajeev RAM (USA)
WC Scoville JENKINS (USA)
WC Bobby REYNOLDS (USA)
Tommy HAAS (GER)
Alexander WASKE (GER)
WC Alex KUZNETSOV (USA)
WC Scott OUDSEMA (USA)
Feliciano LOPEZ (ESP)
Fernando VERDASCO (ESP)
14 Gaston ETLIS (ARG)
14 Martin RODRIGUEZ (ARG)
12 Cyril SUK (CZE)
12 Pavel VIZNER (CZE)
Alex CALATRAVA (ESP)
David FERRER (ESP)
Yves ALLEGRO (SUI)
Daniele BRACCIALI (ITA)
PR Younes EL AYNAOUI (MAR)
Tom VANHOUDT (BEL)
Andrei PAVEL (ROM)
Rainer SCHUETTLER (GER)
Jan HERNYCH (CZE)
Vince SPADEA (USA)
Julian KNOWLE (AUT)
Jurgen MELZER (AUT)
6 Michael LLODRA (FRA)
6 Fabrice SANTORO (FRA)
4 Wayne BLACK (ZIM)
4 Kevin ULLYETT (ZIM)
Giorgio GALIMBERTI (ITA)
Paradorn SRICHAPHAN (THA)
Massimo BERTOLINI (ITA)
Filippo VOLANDRI (ITA)
WC Samuel QUERREY (USA)
WC Donald YOUNG (USA)
Juan Ignacio CHELA (ARG)
Mariano ZABALETA (ARG)
Thomas JOHANSSON (SWE)
Robbie KOENIG (RSA)
Jared PALMER (USA)
Travis PARROTT (USA)
16 Lucas ARNOLD (ARG)
16 Petr PALA (CZE)
11 Jonathan ERLICH (ISR)
11 Andy RAM (ISR)
Tomas CIBULEC (CZE)
Jiri NOVAK (CZE)
Victor HANESCU (ROM)
Razvan SABAU (ROM)
Justin GIMELSTOB (USA)
Mariano HOOD (ARG)
Jordan KERR (AUS)
Graydon OLIVER (USA)
Tomas BERDYCH (CZE)
Florian MAYER (GER)
WC Amer DELIC (USA)
WC Jeff MORRISON (USA)
5 Leander PAES (IND)
5 Nenad ZIMONJIC (SCG)

Second Round

J.BJORKMAN (1) / M.MIRNYI (1) 60 63
S.JENKINS (WC) / B.REYNOLDS (WC) 61 36 63
A.KUZNETSOV (WC) / S.OUDSEMA (WC) 76(6) 63
F.LOPEZ / F.VERDASCO 76(4) 36 76(3)
C.SUK (12) / P.VIZNER (12) 63 61
Y.ALLEGRO / D.BRACCIALI 63 63
J.HERNYCH / V.SPADEA 76(2) 62
J.KNOWLE / J.MELZER 36 76(0) 64
W.BLACK (4) / K.ULLYETT (4) 63 75
M.BERTOLINI / F.VOLANDRI 62 64
T.JOHANSSON / R.KOENIG 63 64
J.PALMER / T.PARROTT 75 64
J.ERLICH (11) / A.RAM (11) 32 RET
V.HANESCU / R.SABAU 26 75 64
J.KERR / G.OLIVER 64 64
A.DELIC (WC) / J.MORRISON (WC) 76(6) 76(2)

Third Round

J.BJORKMAN (1) / M.MIRNYI (1) 67(3) 62 61
F.LOPEZ / F.VERDASCO 67(1) 64 64
C.SUK (12) / P.VIZNER (12) 63 26 63
J.HERNYCH / V.SPADEA 76(2) 46 75
W.BLACK (4) / K.ULLYETT (4) 62 60
T.JOHANSSON / R.KOENIG 63 62
J.ERLICH (11) / A.RAM (11) 60 62
A.DELIC (WC) / J.MORRISON (WC) 75 75

Quarter-finals

J.BJORKMAN (1) / M.MIRNYI (1) 63 64
C.SUK (12) / P.VIZNER (12) 76(7) 64
W.BLACK (4) / K.ULLYETT (4) 46 60 61
J.ERLICH (11) / A.RAM (11) 76(3) 63

Semi-finals

J.BJORKMAN (1) / M.MIRNYI (1) 64 63
W.BLACK (4) / K.ULLYETT (4) 64 62

Final

J.BJORKMAN (1) / M.MIRNYI (1) 57 75 62

B.BRYAN (2) / M.BRYAN (2) 61 64

7 Mahesh BHUPATHI (IND)
7 Martin DAMM (CZE)
Gael MONFILS (FRA)
Cyril SAULNIER (FRA)
Mario ANCIC (CRO)
Ivan LJUBICIC (CRO)
David SKOCH (CZE)
Radek STEPANEK (CZE)
Christophe ROCHUS (BEL)
Stanislas WAWRINKA (SUI)
Igor ANDREEV (RUS)
Nikolay DAVYDENKO (RUS)
Ashley FISHER (AUS)
Rick LEACH (USA)
9 Simon ASPELIN (SWE)
9 Todd PERRY (AUS)
13 Stephen HUSS (AUS)
13 Wesley MOODIE (RSA)
Lars BURGSMULLER (GER)
Mikhail YOUZHNY (RUS)
WC Alex BOGOMOLOV (USA)
WC Travis RETTENMAIER (USA)
Karol BECK (SVK)
Jaroslav LEVINSKY (CZE)
WC Mykyta KRYVONOS (USA)
WC Dennis ZIVKOVIC (USA)
Jose ACASUSO (ARG)
Sebastian PRIETO (ARG)
Paul GOLDSTEIN (USA)
Jim THOMAS (USA)
3 Mark KNOWLES (BAH)
3 Daniel NESTOR (CAN)
8 Wayne ARTHURS (AUS)
8 Paul HANLEY (AUS)
Jarkko NIEMINEN (FIN)
Rogier WASSEN (NED)
Dominik HRBATY (SVK)
Michal MERTINAK (SVK)
Mariusz FYRSTENBERG (POL)
Marcin MATKOWSKI (POL)
Julien BENNETEAU (FRA)
Nicolas MAHUT (FRA)
Martin GARCIA (ARG)
Luis HORNA (PER)
Robby GINEPRI (USA)
Gilles MULLER (LUX)
10 Frantisek CERMAK (CZE)
10 Leos FRIEDL (CZE)
15 Fernando GONZALEZ (CHI)
15 Nicolas MASSU (CHI)
Philipp KOHLSCHREIBER (GER)
Olivier ROCHUS (BEL)
Kenneth CARLSEN (DEN)
Jeff COETZEE (RSA)
Enzo ARTONI (ITA)
Mariano PUERTA (ARG)
Davide SANGUINETTI (ITA)
Andreas SEPPI (ITA)
Robert LINDSTEDT (SWE)
Robin SODERLING (SWE)
Arnaud CLEMENT (FRA)
Sebastien GROSJEAN (FRA)
2 Bob BRYAN (USA)
2 Mike BRYAN (USA)

M.BHUPATHI (7)
M.DAMM (7)
61 63

M.ANCIC
I.LJUBICIC
62 76(0)

I.ANDREEV
N.DAVYDENKO
75 61

S.ASPELIN (9)
T.PERRY (9)
57 62 76(3)

L.BURGSMULLER
M.YOUZHNY
76(7) 61

K.BECK
J.LEVINSKY
62 63

J.ACASUSO
S.PRIETO
64 64

P.GOLDSTEIN
J.THOMAS
46 64 62

W.ARTHURS (8)
P.HANLEY (8)
75 63

D.HRBATY
M.MERTINAK
46 63 64

J.BENNETEAU
N.MAHUT
64 64

F.CERMAK (10)
L.FRIEDL (10)
64 63

F.GONZALEZ (15)
N.MASSU (15)
64 76(0)

K.CARLSEN
J.COETZEE
62 63

R.LINDSTEDT
R.SODERLING
63 61

B.BRYAN (2)
M.BRYAN (2)
76(5) 16 63

M.BHUPATHI (7)
M.DAMM (7)
76(3) 36 76(6)

S.ASPELIN (9)
T.PERRY (9)
61 61

L.BURGSMULLER
M.YOUZHNY
64 62

P.GOLDSTEIN
J.THOMAS
60 63

W.ARTHURS (8)
P.HANLEY (8)
63 62

J.BENNETEAU
N.MAHUT
75 76(6)

F.GONZALEZ (15)
N.MASSU (15)
64 64

B.BRYAN (2)
M.BRYAN (2)
46 62 63

S.ASPELIN (9)
T.PERRY (9)
64 67(3) 63

P.GOLDSTEIN
J.THOMAS
76(8) 62

J.BENNETEAU
N.MAHUT
64 76(6)

B.BRYAN (2)
M.BRYAN (2)
63 61

P.GOLDSTEIN
J.THOMAS
46 64 76(14)

B.BRYAN (2)
M.BRYAN (2)
63 64

B.BRYAN (2)
M.BRYAN (2)
36 61 62

2005 US Open Championships, 29 August–11 September – Women's Doubles

A USTA EVENT

First round

1 Cara BLACK (ZIM)
1 Rennae STUBBS (AUS)
Lisa MCSHEA (AUS)
Abigail SPEARS (USA)
Laura GRANVILLE (USA)
Carly GULLICKSON (USA)
Jill CRAYBAS (USA)
Meilen TU (USA)
Kristina BRANDI (PUR)
Caroline DHENIN (FRA)
Dally RANDRIANTEFY (MAD)
Anna SMASHNOVA (ISR)
Rika FUJIWARA (JPN)
Na LI (CHN)
15 Janette HUSAROVA (SVK)
15 Francesca SCHIAVONE (ITA)
10 Shinobu ASAGOE (JPN)
10 Katarina SREBOTNIK (SLO)
Jennifer HOPKINS (USA)
Mashona WASHINGTON (USA)
WC Angela HAYNES (USA)
WC Bethanie MATTEK (USA)
Elena LIKHOVTSEVA (RUS)
Magdalena MALEEVA (BUL)
Vera DOUCHEVINA (RUS)
Shahar PEER (ISR)
Marion BARTOLI (FRA)
Milagros SEQUERA (VEN)
Eleni DANIILIDOU (GRE)
Jennifer RUSSELL (USA)
6 Lisa RAYMOND (USA)
6 Samantha STOSUR (AUS)
3 Conchita MARTINEZ (ESP)
3 Virginia RUANO PASCUAL (ESP)
SR Rita GRANDE (ITA)
Tamarine TANASUGARN (THA)
Jelena KOSTANIC (CRO)
Sanda MAMIC (CRO)
Stephanie COHEN-ALORO (FRA)
Selima SFAR (TUN)
Zuzana ONDRASKOVA (CZE)
Martina SUCHA (SVK)
Denisa CHLADKOVA (CZE)
Virginie RAZZANO (FRA)
Iveta BENESOVA (CZE)
Yulia BEYGELZIMER (UKR)
16 Gisela DULKO (ARG)
16 Maria KIRILENKO (RUS)
9 Anabel MEDINA GARRIGUES (ESP)
9 Dinara SAFINA (RUS)
Zi YAN (CHN)
Jie ZHENG (CHN)
Chia-Jung CHUANG (TPE)
Akiko MORIGAMI (JPN)
WC Marissa IRVIN (USA)
WC Jamea JACKSON (USA)
Amy FRAZIER (USA)
Alina JIDKOVA (RUS)
Stephanie FORETZ (FRA)
Nicole VAIDISOVA (CZE)
WC Alexa GLATCH (USA)
WC Vania KING (USA)
5 Daniela HANTUCHOVA (SVK)
5 Ai SUGIYAMA (JPN)

Second round

C.BLACK (1) / R.STUBBS (1) 61 63
J.CRAYBAS / M.TU 63 64
D.RANDRIANTEFY / A.SMASHNOVA 75 62
R.FUJIWARA / N.LI 76(5) 63
S.ASAGOE (10) / K.SREBOTNIK (10) 60 61
E.LIKHOVTSEVA / M.MALEEVA 62 46 64
V.DOUCHEVINA / S.PEER 75 57 64
L.RAYMOND (6) / S.STOSUR (6) 62 63
C.MARTINEZ (3) / V.RUANO PASCUAL (3) 63 75
S.COHEN-ALORO / S.SFAR 67(10) 63 63
D.CHLADKOVA / V.RAZZANO 63 64
G.DULKO (16) / M.KIRILENKO (16) 64 67(3) 61
Z.YAN / J.ZHENG 62 63
C.CHUANG / A.MORIGAMI 64 63
A.FRAZIER / A.JIDKOVA 75 46 76(4)
D.HANTUCHOVA (5) / A.SUGIYAMA (5) 75 60

Third round

C.BLACK (1) / R.STUBBS (1) 64 63
R.FUJIWARA / N.LI 64 75
S.ASAGOE (10) / K.SREBOTNIK (10) 62 64
L.RAYMOND (6) / S.STOSUR (6) 63 62
C.MARTINEZ (3) / V.RUANO PASCUAL (3) 75 62
G.DULKO (16) / M.KIRILENKO (16) 62 36 64
Z.YAN / J.ZHENG 63 61
D.HANTUCHOVA (5) / A.SUGIYAMA (5) 26 63 63

Quarter-finals

C.BLACK (1) / R.STUBBS (1) 64 76(3)
L.RAYMOND (6) / S.STOSUR (6) 61 63
C.MARTINEZ (3) / V.RUANO PASCUAL (3) 46 64 62
Z.YAN / J.ZHENG 63 36 75

Semi-finals

L.RAYMOND (6) / S.STOSUR (6) 57 64 64
C.MARTINEZ (3) / V.RUANO PASCUAL (3) 63 64

Final

L.RAYMOND (6) / S.STOSUR (6) 75 46 76(2)

Champions

L.RAYMOND (6) / S.STOSUR (6) 62 57 63

Seed	Player	Round 1	Round 2	Round 3	Quarterfinal	Semifinal
8	Corina MORARIU (USA)	C.MORARIU (8) / P.SCHNYDER (8) 75 62	C.MORARIU (8) / P.SCHNYDER (8) 62 63	C.MORARIU (8) / P.SCHNYDER (8) 63 36 64	E.DEMENTIEVA (14) / F.PENNETTA (14) 63 36 63	E.DEMENTIEVA (14) / F.PENNETTA (14) 62 64
8	Patty SCHNYDER (SUI)					
	Klara KOUKALOVA (CZE)					
	Lucie SAFAROVA (CZE)					
WC	Megan BRADLEY (USA)	M.BRADLEY (WC) / K.MILLER (WC) 64 62				
WC	Kristi MILLER (USA)					
	Catalina CASTANO (COL)					
	Laura POUS-TIO (ESP)					
	Mervana JUGIC-SALKIC (BIH)	M.JUGIC-SALKIC / M.PASTIKOVA 64 63	E.LOIT (11) / N.PRATT (11) 63 62			
	Michaela PASTIKOVA (CZE)					
WC	Teryn ASHLEY (USA)					
WC	Jessica KIRKLAND (USA)					
	Sania MIRZA (IND)	E.LOIT (11) / N.PRATT (11) 62 64				
	Bryanne STEWART (AUS)					
11	Emilie LOIT (FRA)					
11	Nicole PRATT (AUS)					
14	Elena DEMENTIEVA (RUS)	E.DEMENTIEVA (14) / F.PENNETTA (14) 63 62	E.DEMENTIEVA (14) / F.PENNETTA (14) 63 64	E.DEMENTIEVA (14) / F.PENNETTA (14) 76(4) 63		
14	Flavia PENNETTA (ITA)					
	Anna CHAKVETADZE (RUS)					
	Tatiana GOLOVIN (FRA)					
	Rosa-Maria ANDRES-RODRIGUEZ (ESP)	M.MARRERO / A.SERRA ZANETTI 61 64				
	Mariana DIAZ-OLIVA (ARG)					
	Marta MARRERO (ESP)					
	Antonella SERRA ZANETTI (ITA)					
	Jelena JANKOVIC (SCG)	J.JANKOVIC / T.KRIZAN 64 57 63	N.PETROVA (4) / M.SHAUGHNESSY (4) 10 RET			
	Tina KRIZAN (SLO)					
	Liga DEKMEIJERE (LAT)					
	Sesil KARATANTCHEVA (BUL)					
	Maria-Emilia SALERNI (ARG)	N.PETROVA (4) / M.SHAUGHNESSY (4) 63 67(4) 75				
	Maria VENTO-KABCHI (VEN)					
4	Nadia PETROVA (RUS)					
4	Meghann SHAUGHNESSY (USA)					
7	Anna-Lena GROENEFELD (GER)	A.GROENEFELD (7) / M.NAVRATILOVA (7) 62 62	A.GROENEFELD (7) / M.NAVRATILOVA (7) 61 60	A.GROENEFELD (7) / M.NAVRATILOVA (7) 26 76(5) 61	A.GROENEFELD (7) / M.NAVRATILOVA (7) 67(5) 75 75	
7	Martina NAVRATILOVA (USA)					
WC	Ashley HARKLEROAD (USA)					
WC	Lindsay LEE-WATERS (USA)					
WC	Ahsha ROLLE (USA)	A.ROLLE (WC) / N.UBEROI (WC) 61 26 64				
WC	Neha UBEROI (USA)					
	Els CALLENS (BEL)					
	Mara SANTANGELO (ITA)					
	Marta DOMACHOWSKA (POL)	J.LEE / S.PENG 67(5) 64 62	T.LI (12) / T.SUN (12) 63 64			
	Silvija TALAJA (CRO)					
	Janet LEE (TPE)					
	Shuai PENG (CHN)					
	Emmanuelle GAGLIARDI (SUI)	T.LI (12) / T.SUN (12) 26 75 60				
	Marlene WEINGARTNER (GER)					
12	Ting LI (CHN)					
12	Tian-Tian SUN (CHN)					
13	Kveta PESCHKE (CZE)	M.CAMERIN / T.GARBIN 76(4) 75	S.FARINA ELIA / R.VINCI 62 60	S.KUZNETSOVA (2) / A.MOLIK (2) 63 63		
13	Barbora STRYCOVA (CZE)					
	Maria-Elena CAMERIN (ITA)					
	Tathiana GARBIN (ITA)					
	Silvia FARINA ELIA (ITA)	S.FARINA ELIA / R.VINCI 36 76(9) 62				
	Roberta VINCI (ITA)					
	Nana MIYAGI (JPN)					
	Anastasia MYSKINA (RUS)					
	Eva BIRNEROVA (CZE)	E.BIRNEROVA / A.VANC 26 63 64	S.KUZNETSOVA (2) / A.MOLIK (2) 62 62			
	Andreea VANC (ROM)					
	Lourdes DOMINGUEZ-LINO (ESP)					
	Nuria LLAGOSTERA VIVES (ESP)					
	Eugenia LINETSKAYA (RUS)	S.KUZNETSOVA (2) / A.MOLIK (2) 76(3) 62				
	Galina VOSKOBOEVA (RUS)					
2	Svetlana KUZNETSOVA (RUS)					
2	Alicia MOLIK (AUS)					

2005 US Open Championships, 29 August–11 September – Mixed Doubles

US OPEN 2005
A USTA EVENT

First Round

1 Wayne BLACK (ZIM)
1 Cara BLACK (ZIM)
WC Travis PARROTT (USA)
WC Amy FRAZIER (USA)
Andy RAM (ISR)
Dinara SAFINA (RUS)
Leos FRIEDL (CZE)
Janette HUSAROVA (SVK)
Paul HANLEY (AUS)
Samantha STOSUR (AUS)
Graydon OLIVER (USA)
Maria KIRILENKO (RUS)
Pavel VIZNER (CZE)
Jelena JANKOVIC (SCG)
8 Todd PERRY (AUS)
8 Alicia MOLIK (AUS)
3 Daniel NESTOR (CAN)
3 Elena LIKHOVTSEVA (RUS)
WC Justin GIMELSTOB (USA)
WC Meghann SHAUGHNESSY (USA)
Nenad ZIMONJIC (SCG)
Katarina SREBOTNIK (SLO)
Jonathan ERLICH (ISR)
Bryanne STEWART (AUS)
Stephen HUSS (AUS)
Virginia RUANO PASCUAL (ESP)
WC Kevin KIM (USA)
WC Lilia OSTERLOH (USA)
Fabrice SANTORO (FRA)
Tatiana GOLOVIN (FRA)
7 Leander PAES (IND)
7 Martina NAVRATILOVA (USA)
5 Kevin ULLYETT (ZIM)
5 Ai SUGIYAMA (JPN)
Martin RODRIGUEZ (ARG)
Maria-Emilia SALERNI (ARG)
Gaston ETLIS (ARG)
Anabel MEDINA GARRIGUES (ESP)
WC Rick LEACH (USA)
WC Laura GRANVILLE (USA)
Simon ASPELIN (SWE)
Tian-Tian SUN (CHN)
Mahesh BHUPATHI (IND)
Daniela HANTUCHOVA (SVK)
WC Amer DELIC (USA)
WC Shenay PERRY (USA)
4 Jonas BJORKMAN (SWE)
4 Lisa RAYMOND (USA)
6 Mike BRYAN (USA)
6 Corina MORARIU (USA)
WC Jeff MORRISON (USA)
WC Jill CRAYBAS (USA)
Frantisek CERMAK (CZE)
Anna-Lena GROENEFELD (GER)
Martin DAMM (CZE)
Kveta PESCHKE (CZE)
Cyril SUK (CZE)
Nicole PRATT (AUS)
Mark KNOWLES (BAH)
Nicole VAIDISOVA (CZE)
Mariano HOOD (ARG)
Tathiana GARBIN (ITA)
2 Bob BRYAN (USA)
2 Rennae STUBBS (AUS)

Second Round

W.BLACK (1) / C.BLACK (1) 67(7) 63 10(8)
A.RAM / D.SAFINA 61 64
P.HANLEY / S.STOSUR 75 64
T.PERRY (8) / A.MOLIK (8) 76(5) 26 10(6)
D.NESTOR (3) / E.LIKHOVTSEVA (3) 64 62
N.ZIMONJIC / K.SREBOTNIK 64 62
S.HUSS / V.RUANO PASCUAL 76(1) 76(8)
L.PAES (7) / M.NAVRATILOVA (7) 63 62
K.ULLYETT (5) / A.SUGIYAMA (5) 62 63
G.ETLIS / A.MEDINA GARRIGUES 64 63
M.BHUPATHI / D.HANTUCHOVA 46 63 10(9)
J.BJORKMAN (4) / L.RAYMOND (4) 61 75
M.BRYAN (6) / C.MORARIU (6) 63 64
F.CERMAK / A.GROENEFELD 67(5) 64 10(7)
M.KNOWLES / N.VAIDISOVA 61 16 10(9)
B.BRYAN (2) / R.STUBBS (2) 62 61

Quarter-finals

A.RAM / D.SAFINA 63 64
P.HANLEY / S.STOSUR 76(1) 64
N.ZIMONJIC / K.SREBOTNIK 76(6) 63
L.PAES (7) / M.NAVRATILOVA (7) 64 61
K.ULLYETT (5) / A.SUGIYAMA (5) 63 64
M.BHUPATHI / D.HANTUCHOVA 62 76(3)
M.BRYAN (6) / C.MORARIU (6) 26 62 10(7)
B.BRYAN (2) / R.STUBBS (2) 63 76(4)

Semi-finals

A.RAM / D.SAFINA 63 64
N.ZIMONJIC / K.SREBOTNIK 76(2) 57 10(9)
M.BHUPATHI / D.HANTUCHOVA 75 62
M.BRYAN (6) / C.MORARIU (6) 64 64

Final

N.ZIMONJIC / K.SREBOTNIK 61 75
M.BHUPATHI / D.HANTUCHOVA 76(4) 75

Winners

M.BHUPATHI / D.HANTUCHOVA 64 62

2005 Tennis Masters Cup Results

Qi Zhong Stadium, Shanghai, China 13-20 November 2005

Seeded players:
1. Roger Federer (SUI)
2. Rafael Nadal (ESP)
3. Andre Agassi (USA)
4. Guillermo Coria (ARG)
5. Nikolay Davydenko (RUS)
6. Ivan Ljubicic (CRO)
7. Gaston Gaudio (ARG)
8. David Nalbandian (ARG)

Alternate:
1. Mariano Puerta (ARG) – replaced Nadal
2. Fernando Gonzalez (CHI) – replaced Agassi
3. Thomas Johansson (SWE)

Round Robin

Red Group:

Roger Federer (SUI) d. David Nalbandian (ARG) 63 26 64
Ivan Ljubicic (CRO) d. Guillermo Coria (ARG) 62 63
Roger Federer (SUI) d. Ivan Ljubicic (CRO) 63 26 76(4)
David Nalbandian (ARG) d. Guillermo Coria (ARG) 75 64
David Nalbandian (ARG) d. Ivan Ljubicic (CRO) 62 62
Roger Federer (SUI) d. Guillermo Coria (ARG) 60 16 62

Gold Group:

Nikolay Davydenko (RUS) d. Andre Agassi (USA) 64 62
Gaudio Gaudio (ARG) d. Mariano Puerta (ARG) 63 75
Nikolay Davydenko (RUS) d. Gaston Gaudio (ARG) 63 64
Fernando Gonzalez (CHI) d. Mariano Puerta (ARG) 63 46 60
Gaston Gaudio (ARG) d. Fernando Gonzalez (CHI) 16 75 75
Nikolay Davydenko (RUS) d. Mariano Puerta (ARG) 63 62

Final Standings

Red Group: 1. Roger Federer (SUI), 2. David Nalbandian (ARG), 3. Ivan Ljubicic (CRO), 4. Guillermo Coria (ARG).
Gold Group: 1. Nikolay Davydenko (RUS), 2. Gaston Gaudio (ARG), 3. Fernando Gonzalez (CHI), 4. Mariano Puerta (ARG).

Semifinals

Roger Federer (SUI) d. Gaston Gaudio (ARG) 60 60
David Nalbandian (ARG) d. Nikolay Davydenko (RUS) 60 75

Final

David Nalbandian (ARG) d. Roger Federer (SUI) 67(4) 67(11) 62 61 76(3)

Doubles Final

Michael Llodra/Fabrice Santoro (FRA) d. Leander Paes (IND)/Nenad Zimonjic (SCG) 67(6) 63 76(4)

David Nalbandian (ARG)

2005 WTA Tour Championships Results

Staples Center, Los Angeles, California, USA 8-13 November 2005

Seeded players:
1. Lindsay Davenport (USA)
2. Kim Clijsters (BEL)
3. Maria Sharapova (RUS)
4. Amelie Mauresmo (FRA)
5. Mary Pierce (FRA)
6. Patty Schnyder (SUI)
7. Nadia Petrova (RUS)
8. Elena Dementieva (RUS)

Round Robin

Green Group:

Maria Sharapova (RUS) d. Patty Schnyder (SUI) 61 36 63
Lindsay Davenport (USA) d. Nadia Petrova (RUS) 62 76(1)
Lindsay Davenport (USA) d. Patty Schnyder (SUI) 63 75
Patty Schnyder (SUI) d. Nadia Petrova (RUS) 60 57 64
Maria Sharapova (RUS) d. Lindsay Davenport (USA) 63 57 64
Nadia Petrova (RUS) d. Maria Sharapova (RUS) 61 62

Black Group:

Mary Pierce (FRA) d. Kim Clijsters (BEL) 61 46 76(2)
Mary Pierce (FRA) d. Elena Dementieva (RUS) 62 63
Amelie Mauresmo (FRA) d. Kim Clijsters (BEL) 63 76(4)
Amelie Mauresmo (FRA) d. Elena Dementieva (RUS) 62 63
Mary Pierce (FRA) d. Amelie Mauresmo (FRA) 26 64 62
Kim Clijsters (BEL) d. Elena Dementieva (RUS) 62 63

Final Standings

Green Group: 1. Maria Sharapova (RUS), 2. Lindsay Davenport (USA), 3. Patty Schnyder (SUI), 4. Nadia Petrova (RUS).
Black Group: 1. Mary Pierce (FRA), 2. Amelie Mauresmo (FRA), 3. Kim Clijsters (BEL), 4. Elena Dementieva (RUS).

Semifinals

Mary Pierce (FRA) d. Lindsay Davenport (USA) 76(5) 76(6)
Amelie Mauresmo (FRA) d. Maria Sharapova (RUS) 76(1) 63

Final

Amelie Mauresmo (FRA) d. Mary Pierce (FRA) 57 76(3) 64

Doubles Final

Lisa Raymond (USA)/Samantha Stosur (AUS) d. Cara Black (ZIM)/Rennae Stubbs (AUS) 67(5) 75 64

France's Amelie Mauresmo and Mary Pierce

2005 Men's Professional Tournaments

Wk Comm.	Venue	Surface	Singles Final	Doubles Winners
3 Jan	**Hopman Cup**	**Hard**	**Slovak Republic d. Argentina 3-0**	
3 Jan	Doha	Hard	R. Federer (SUI) (1) d. I. Ljubicic (CRO) (6) 63 61	A. Costa/R. Nadal (ESP)
3 Jan	Chennai	Hard	C. Moya (ESP) (1) d. P. Srichaphan (THA) (2) 36 64 76(5)	R. Schuettler (GER)/Y. Lu (TPE)
3 Jan	Adelaide	Hard	J. Johansson (SWE) (2) d. T. Dent (USA) (5) 75 63	X. Malisse/O. Rochus (BEL) (3)
10 Jan	Sydney	Hard	L. Hewitt (AUS) (1) d. I. Minar (CZE) (Q) 75 60	M. Bhupathi (IND)/T. Woodbridge (AUS) (3)
10 Jan	Auckland	Hard	F. Gonzalez (CHI) (5) d. O. Rochus (BEL) 64 62	Y. Allegro (SUI)/M. Kohlmann (GER)
17 Jan	**Australian Open**	**Hard**	**M. Safin (RUS) (4) d. L. Hewitt (AUS) (3) 16 63 64 64**	**W. Black/K. Ullyett (ZIM) (5)**
31 Jan	Milan	Carpet	R. Soderling (SUI) (5) d. R. Stepanek (CZE) (4) 63 67(2) 76(5)	D. Bracciali/G. Galimberti (ITA) (WC)
31 Jan	Vina Del Mar	Clay	G. Gaudio (ARG) (1) (WC) d. F. Gonzalez (CHI) (2) 63 64	D. Ferrer/S. Ventura (ESP)
31 Jan	Delray Beach	Hard	X. Malisse (BEL) (3) d. J. Novak (CZE) (2) 76(6) 62	S. Aspelin (SWE)/T. Perry (AUS) (1)
7 Feb	Buenos Aires	Clay	G. Gaudio (ARG) (2) d. M. Puerta (ARG) (WC) 64 64	F. Cermak/L. Friedl (CZE) (3)
7 Feb	San Jose	Hard	A. Roddick (USA) (1) d. C. Saulnier (FRA) 60 64	W. Arthurs/P. Hanley (AUS) (1)
7 Feb	Marseille	Hard	J. Johansson (SWE) (3) d. I. Ljubicic (CRO) (8) 75 64	M. Damm/R. Stepanek (CZE) (4)
14 Feb	Memphis	Hard	K. Carlsen (DEN) d. M. Mirnyi (BLR) (8) 75 75	S. Aspelin (SWE)/T. Perry (AUS) (4)
14 Feb	Rotterdam	Hard	R. Federer (SUI) (1) d. I. Ljubicic (CRO) 57 75 76(5)	J. Erlich/A. Ram (ISR) (4)
14 Feb	Costa do Sauipe	Clay	R. Nadal (ESP) (6) d. A. Martin (ESP) 60 67(2) 61	F. Cermak/L. Friedl (CZE) (3)
21 Feb	Acapulco	Clay	R. Nadal (ESP) (8) d. A. Montanes (ESP) 61 60	D. Ferrer/S. Ventura (ESP)
21 Feb	Dubai	Hard	R. Federer (SUI) (1) d. I. Ljubicic (CRO) (8) 61 67(6) 63	M. Damm/R. Stepanek (CZE)
21 Feb	Scottsdale	Hard	W. Arthurs (AUS) d. M. Ancic (CRO) (3) 75 63	B. Bryan/M. Bryan (USA) (1)
7 Mar	AMS Indian Wells	Hard	R. Federer (SUI) (1) d. L. Hewitt (AUS) (2) 62 64 64	M. Knowles (BAH)/D. Nestor (CAN) (1)
21 Mar	AMS Miami	Hard	R. Federer (SUI) (1) d. R. Nadal (ESP) (29) 26 67(4) 76(5) 63 61	J. Bjorkman (SWE)/M. Mirnyi (BLR) (3)
4 Apr	Valencia	Clay	I. Andreev (RUS) (7) d. D. Ferrer (ESP) (5) 63 57 63	F. Gonzalez (CHI)/M. Rodriguez (ARG) (3)
4 Apr	Casablanca	Clay	M. Puerta (ARG) (6) d. J. Monaco (ARG) 64 61	F. Cermak/L. Friedl (CZE) (2)
11 Apr	AMS Monte Carlo	Clay	R. Nadal (ESP) (11) d. G. Coria (ARG) (6) 63 61 06 75	L. Paes (IND)/N. Zimonjic (SCG) (5)
18 Apr	Barcelona	Clay	R. Nadal (ESP) (8) d. J. Ferrero (ESP) 61 76(4) 63	L. Paes (IND)/N. Zimonjic (SCG) (2)
18 Apr	Houston	Clay	A. Roddick (USA) (1) d. S. Grosjean (FRA) 62 62 61	M. Knowles (BAH)/D. Nestor (CAN) (1)
25 Apr	Estoril	Clay	G. Gaudio (ARG) (2) d. T. Robredo (ESP) (4) (WC) 61 26 61	F. Cermak/L. Friedl (CZE) (3)
25 Apr	Munich	Clay	D. Nalbandian (ARG) (1) (WC) d. A. Pavel (ROM) (5) 64 61	M. Ancic (CRO)/J. Knowle (AUT)
2 May	AMS Rome	Clay	R. Nadal (ESP) (5) d. G. Coria (ARG) (9) 64 36 63 46 76(6)	M. Llodra/F. Santoro (FRA) (8)
9 May	AMS Hamburg	Clay	R. Federer (SUI) (1) d. R. Gasquet (FRA) (Q) 63 75 76(4)	J. Bjorkman (SWE)/M. Mirnyi (BLR) (2)
16 May	St. Polten	Clay	N. Davydenko (RUS) (1) d. J. Melzer (AUT) (4) 63 26 64	L. Arnold (ARG)/P. Hanley (AUS) (2)
23 May	**Roland Garros**	**Clay**	**R. Nadal (ESP) (4) d. M. Puerta (ARG) 67(6) 63 61 75**	**J. Bjorkman (SWE)/M. Mirnyi (BLR) (2)**
6 Jun	Halle	Grass	R. Federer (SUI) (1) d. M. Safin (RUS) (2) 64 67(6) 64	Y. Allegro/R. Federer (SUI)
6 Jun	London	Grass	A. Roddick (USA) (2) d. I. Karlovic (CRO) 76(7) 76(4)	B. Bryan/M. Bryan (USA) (2)
13 Jun	's-Hertogenbosch	Grass	M. Ancic (CRO) (3) d. M. Llodra (FRA) 75 64	C. Suk/P. Vizner (CZE) (2)
13 Jun	Nottingham	Grass	R. Gasquet (FRA) (4) d. M. Mirnyi (BLR) (8) 62 63	J. Erlich/A. Ram (ISR) (2)
20 Jun	**Wimbledon**	**Grass**	**R. Federer (SUI) (1) d. A. Roddick (USA) (2) 62 76(2) 64**	**S. Huss (AUS)/W. Moodie (RSA) (Q)**
4 Jul	Gstaad	Clay	G. Gaudio (ARG) (2) d. S. Wawrinka (SUI) 64 64	F. Cermak/L. Friedl (CZE) (2)
4 Jul	Bastad	Clay	R. Nadal (ESP) (1) d. T. Berdych (CZE) 26 62 64	J. Bjorkman/J. Johansson (SWE)
4 Jul	Newport	Grass	G. Rusedski (GBR) (3) d. V. Spadea (USA) (2) 76(3) 26 64	J. Kerr (AUS)/J. Thomas (USA) (2)
18 Jul	Stuttgart	Clay	R. Nadal (ESP) (1) d. G. Gaudio (ARG) (3) 63 63 64	J. Acasuso/S. Prieto (ARG)
18 Jul	Indianapolis	Hard	R. Ginepri (USA) d. T. Dent (USA) (4) 46 60 30 ret.	P. Hanley (AUS)/G. Oliver (USA) (2)
18 Jul	Amersfoort	Clay	F. Gonzalez (CHI) (2) d. A. Calleri (ARG) 75 63	M. Garcia (ARG)/L. Horna (PER) (4)
25 Jul	Kitzbuhel	Clay	G. Gaudio (ARG) (3) d. F. Verdasco (ESP) 26 62 64 64	L. Friedl (CZE)/A. Pavel (ROM)
25 Jul	Los Angeles	Hard	A. Agassi (USA) (1) d. G. Muller (LUX) 64 75	R. Leach/B. MacPhie (USA) (WC)
25 Jul	Umag	Clay	G. Coria (ARG) (2) d. C. Moya (ESP) (6) 62 46 62	J. Novak/P. Pala (CZE) (1)
1 Aug	Washington	Hard	A. Roddick (USA) (1) d. J. Blake (USA) 75 63	B. Bryan/M. Bryan (USA) (1)
1 Aug	Sopot	Clay	G. Monfils (FRA) d. F. Mayer (GER) 76(6) 46 75	M. Fyrstenberg/M. Matkowski (POL) (4)
8 Aug	AMS Montreal	Hard	R. Nadal (ESP) (1) d. A. Agassi (USA) (4) 63 46 62	W. Black/K. Ullyett (ZIM) (4)
15 Aug	AMS Cincinnati	Hard	R. Federer (SUI) (1) d. A. Roddick (USA) (5) 63 75	J. Bjorkman (SWE)/M. Mirnyi (BLR) (2)
22 Aug	New Haven	Hard	J. Blake (USA) (WC) d. F. Lopez (ESP (5) 36 75 61	G. Etlis/M. Rodriguez (ARG)
29 Aug	**US Open**	**Hard**	**R. Federer (SUI) (1) d. A. Agassi (USA) (7) 63 26 76(1) 61**	**B. Bryan/M. Bryan (USA) (2)**
12 Sep	Bucharest	Clay	F. Serra (FRA) d. I. Andreev (RUS) 63 64	J. Acasuso/S. Prieto (ARG) (3)
12 Sep	Beijing	Hard	R. Nadal (ESP) (1) d. G. Coria (ARG) (2) 57 61 62	J. Gimelstob (USA)/N. Healey (AUS)
26 Sep	Bangkok	Hard	R. Federer (SUI) (1) d. A. Murray (GBR) (WC) 63 75	N. Hanley (AUS)/L. Paes (IND) (1)

Wk Comm.	Venue	Surface	Singles Final	Doubles Winners
26 Sep	Palermo	Clay	I. Andreev (RUS) d. F. Volandri (ITA) (6) 06 61 63	M. Garcia/M. Hood (ARG) (3)
26 Sep	Ho Chi Minh City	Hard	J. Bjorkman (SWE) d. R. Stepanek (CZE) (3) 63 76(4)	L. Burgsmuller/P. Kohlschreiber (GER)
3 Oct	Metz	Hard	W. Moodie (RSA) d. M. Ancic (CRO) (5) 16 76(7) 64	S. Iwabuchi/T. Suzuki (JPN) (WC)
3 Oct	Tokyo	Hard	I. Ljubicic (CRO) (3) d. G. Monfils (FRA) (6) 76(7) 60	M. Llodra/F. Santoro (FRA) (1)
10 Oct	Vienna	Hard	I. Ljubicic (CRO) (4) d. J. Ferrero (ESP) (7) 62 64 76(5)	M. Knowles (BAH)/D. Nestor (CAN) (1)
10 Oct	Stockholm	Hard	J. Blake (USA) (6) d. P. Srichaphan (THA) 61 76(6)	W. Arthurs/P. Hanley (AUS) (2)
10 Oct	Moscow	Carpet	I. Andreev (RUS) (7) d. N. Kiefer (GER) (6) 57 76(3) 62	M. Mirnyi (BLR)/M. Youzhny (RUS) (3)
17 Oct	AMS Madrid	Hard	R. Nadal (ESP) (1) d. I. Ljubicic (CRO) (8) 36 26 63 64 76(3)	M. Knowles (BAH)/D. Nestor (CAN) (3)
24 Oct	Basel	Carpet	F. Gonzalez (CHI) (4) d. M. Baghdatis (CYP) (Q) 67(8) 63 75 64	A. Calleri (ARG)/F. Gonzalez (CHI)
24 Oct	St. Petersburg	Carpet	T. Johansson (SWE) (2) d. N. Kiefer (GER) (5) 64 64	J. Knowles/J. Melzer (AUT)
24 Oct	Lyon	Carpet	A. Roddick (USA) (1) d. G. Monfils (FRA) 63 62	M. Llodra/F. Santoro (FRA)
31 Oct	AMS Paris	Carpet	T. Berdych (CZE) d. I. Ljubicic (CRO) (6) 63 64 36 46 64	B. Bryan/M. Bryan (USA) (2)
7 Nov	TMC Shanghai	Hard	D. Nalbandian (ARG) d. R. Federer (SUI) (1) 67(4) 67(11) 62 61 76(3)	M. Llodra/F. Santoro (FRA)
28 Nov	**Davis Cup Final**	**Hard**	**Croatia d. Slovak Republic 3-2**	

2005 Women's Professional Tournaments

Date	Venue	Surface	Singles Final	Doubles Winners
3 Jan	**Hopman Cup**	**Hard**	**Slovak Republic d. Argentina 3-0**	
3 Jan	Gold Coast	Hard	P. Schnyder (SUI) (2) d. S. Stosur (AUS) 16 63 75	E. Likhovtseva (RUS)/M. Maleeva (BUL) (2)
3 Jan	Auckland	Hard	K. Srebotnik (SLO) d. S. Asagoe (JPN) (4) 57 75 64	K. Srebotnik (SLO)/S. Asagoe (JPN) (1)
10 Jan	Sydney	Hard	A. Molik (AUS) (6) d. S. Stosur (AUS) 64 75	B. Stewart/S. Stosur (AUS)
10 Jan	Hobart	Hard	J. Zheng (CHN) d. G. Dulko (ARG) (2) 62 60	Z. Yan/J. Zheng (CHN) (1)
10 Jan	Canberra	Hard	A. Ivanovic (SCG) (Q) d. M. Czink (HUN) (LL) 75 61	T. Garbin (ITA)/T. Krizan (SLO) (3)
17 Jan	**Australian Open**	**Hard**	**S. Williams (USA) (7) d. L. Davenport (USA) (1) 26 63 60**	**S. Kuznetsova (RUS)/A. Molik (AUS) (6)**
31 Jan	Tokyo	Carpet	M. Sharapova (RUS) (2) d. L. Davenport (USA) (1) 61 36 76(5)	J. Husarova (SVK)/E. Likhovtseva (RUS) (2)
31 Jan	Pattaya	Hard	C. Martinez (ESP) (3) d. A. Groenefeld (GER) (7) 63 36 63	M. Bartoli (FRA)/A. Groenefeld (GER) (2)
7 Feb	Paris	Carpet	D. Safina (RUS) d. A. Mauresmo (FRA) (2) 64 26 63	I. Benesova/K. Peschke (CZE)
7 Feb	Hyderabad	Hard	S. Mirza (IND) d. A. Bondarenko (UKR) (9) 64 57 63	Z. Yan/J. Zheng (CHN) (3)
14 Feb	Antwerp	Carpet	A. Mauresmo (FRA) (1) d. V. Williams (USA) (3) 46 75 64	C. Black (ZIM)/E. Callens (BEL) (1)
14 Feb	Memphis	Hard	V. Zvonareva (RUS) (1) d. M. Shaughnessy (USA) (3) 76(3) 62	M. Saeki/Y. Yoshida (JPN) (Q)
14 Feb	Bogota	Clay	F. Pennetta (ITA) (2) d. L. Dominiguez Lino (ESP) (Q) 76(4) 64	E. Gagliardi (SUI)/T. Pisnik (SLO)
21 Feb	Doha	Hard	M. Sharapova (RUS) (2) d. A. Molik (AUS) (4) 46 61 64	A. Molik (AUS)/F. Schiavone (ITA)
21 Feb	Acapulco	Clay	F. Pennetta (ITA) (1) d. L. Cervanova (SVK) 36 75 63	A. Jikova (RUS)/T. Perebiynis (UKR) (4)
28 Feb	Dubai	Hard	L. Davenport (USA) (1) d. J. Jankovic (SCG) 64 36 64	V. Ruano Pascual (ESP)/P. Suarez (ARG) (1)
7 Mar	Indian Wells	Hard	K. Clijsters (BEL) d. L. Davenport (USA) (1) 64 46 62	V. Ruano Pascual (ESP)/P. Suarez (ARG) (1)
21 Mar	Miami	Hard	K. Clijsters (BEL) d. M. Sharapova (RUS) (2) 63 75	S. Kuznetsova (RUS)/A. Molik (AUS) (3)
4 Apr	Amelia Island	Clay	L. Davenport (USA) (1) d. S. Farina Elia (ITA) (12) 75 75	B. Stewart/S. Stosur (AUS)
11 Apr	Charleston	Clay	J. Henin-Hardenne (BEL) d. E. Dementieva (RUS) (2) 75 62	C. Martinez/V. Ruano Pascual (ESP) (2)
25 Apr	Warsaw	Clay	J. Henin-Hardenne (BEL) d. S. Kuznetsova (RUS) (2) 36 62 75	T. Perebiynis (UKR)/B. Strycova (CZE)
25 Apr	Estoril	Clay	L. Safarova (CZE) (Q) d. N. Li (CHN) (4) 67(4) 64 63	T. Li/T. Sun (CHN) (3)
2 May	Berlin	Clay	J. Henin-Hardenne (BEL) (12) d. N. Petrova (RUS) (6) 63 46 63	E. Likhovtseva/V. Zvonareva (RUS) (3)
2 May	Rabat	Clay	N. Llagostera Vives (ESP) (2) d. J. Zheng (CHN) (6) 64 62	E. Loit (FRA)/B. Strycova (CZE)
9 May	Rome	Clay	A. Mauresmo (FRA) (2) d. P. Schnyder (SUI) (8) 26 63 64	C. Black (ZIM)/L. Huber (RSA) (2)
9 May	Prague	Clay	D. Safina (RUS) (1) d. Z. Ondraskova (CZE) 76(2) 63	E. Loit (FRA)/N. Pratt (AUS) (2)
16 May	Strasbourg	Clay	A. Medina Garrigues (ESP) d. M. Domachowska (POL) 64 63	R. Andres (ESP)/A. Vanc (ROM)
16 May	Istanbul	Clay	V. Williams (USA) (1) d. N. Vaidisova (CZE) (2) 63 62	M. Marrero (ESP)/An.Serra Zanetti (ITA) (4)
23 May	**Roland Garros**	**Clay**	**J. Henin-Hardenne (BEL) (10) d. M. Pierce (FRA) (21) 61 61**	**V. Ruano Pascual (ESP)/P. Suarez (ARG) (1)**
6 Jun	Birmingham	Grass	M. Sharapova (RUS) (1) d. J. Jankovic (SCG) (3) 62 46 61	D. Hantuchova (SVK)/A. Sugiyama (JPN) (2)
13 Jun	Eastbourne	Grass	K. Clijsters (BEL) (7) d. V. Douchevina (RUS) (Q) 75 61	L. Raymond (USA)/R. Stubbs (AUS) (2)
13 Jun	's-Hertogenbosch	Grass	K. Koukalova (CZE) (8) d. L. Safarova (CZE) 36 62 62	A. Medina Garrigues (ESP)/D. Safina (RUS) (3)
21 Jun	**Wimbledon**	**Grass**	**V. Williams (USA) (14) d. L. Davenport (USA) (1) 46 76(4) 97**	**C. Black (ZIM)/L. Huber (RSA) (2)**
18 Jul	Cincinnati	Hard	P. Schnyder (SUI) (1) d. A. Morigami (JPN) 64 60`	L. Granville/A. Spears (USA) (3)
18 Jul	Palermo	Clay	A. Medina Garrigues (ESP) (3) d. K. Koukalova (CZE) (5) 64 60	G. Casoni (ITA)/M. Koryttseva (UKR)

2005 Women's Professional Tournaments (continued)

Wk Comm.	Venue	Surface	Singles Final	Doubles Winners
25 Jul	Stanford	Hard	K. Clijsters (BEL) (4) d. V. Williams (USA) (2) 75 62	C. Black (ZIM)/R. Stubbs (AUS) (2)
25 Jul	Budapest	Clay	A. Smashnova (ISR) (1) d. C. Castano (COL) 62 62	E. Loit (FRA)/K. Srebotnik (SLO) (1)
1 Aug	San Diego	Hard	M. Pierce (FRA) (6) d. A. Sugiyama (JPN) 60 63	C. Martinez (ESP)/V. Ruano Pascual (ESP) (3)
8 Aug	Los Angeles	Hard	K. Clijsters (BEL) (5) d. D. Hantuchova (SVK) (9) 64 61	E. Dementieva (RUS)/F. Pennetta (ITA)
8 Aug	Stockholm	Hard	K. Srebotnik (SLO) (5) d. A. Myskina (RUS) (2) 75 62	E. Loit (FRA)/K. Srebotnik (SLO) (1)
15 Aug	Toronto	Hard	K. Clijsters (BEL) (7) d. J. Henin-Hardenne (BEL) 75 61	A. Groenefeld (GER)/M. Navratilova (USA) (6)
22 Aug	New Haven	Hard	L. Davenport (USA) (1) d. A. Mauresmo (FRA) (2) 64 64	L .Raymond (USA)/S. Stosur (AUS) (3)
22 Aug	Forest Hills	Hard	L. Safarova (CZE) d. S. Mirza (IND) (3) 36 75 64	
29 Aug	**US Open**	**Hard**	**K. Clijsters (BEL) (4) d. M. Pierce (FRA) (12) 63 61**	**L. Raymond (USA)/S. Stosur (AUS) (6)**
12 Sep	**Fed Cup Final**	**Clay**	**Russia d. France 3-2**	
12 Sep	Bali	Hard	L. Davenport (USA) (1) d. F. Schiavone (ITA) (4) 62 64	A. Groenefeld (GER)/M. Shaughnessy (USA) (1)
19 Sep	Beijing	Hard	M. Kirilenko (RUS) d. A. Groenefeld (GER) (9) 63 64	N. Llagostera Vives (ESP)/M. Vento-Kabchi (VEN)
19 Sep	Kolkata	Carpet	A. Myskina (RUS) (1) d. K. Sprem (CRO) (7) 62 62	E. Likhovtseva/A. Myskina (RUS) (1)
19 Sep	Portoroz	Hard	K. Koukalova (CZE) (4) d. K. Srebotnik (SLO) (6) 62 46 63	A. Medina Garrigues (ESP)/R. Vinci (ITA) (4)
26 Sep	Luxembourg	Hard	K. Clijsters (BEL) (1) d. A. Groenefeld (GER) 62 64	L. Raymond (USA)/S. Stosur (AUS) (2)
26 Sep	Guangzhou	Hard	Z. Yan (CHN) d. N. Llagostera Vives (ESP) 64 40 ret.	M. Camerin (ITA)/E. Gagliardi (ITA) (3)
26 Sep	Seoul	Hard	N. Vaidisova (CZE) (2) d. J. Jankovic (SCG) (1) 75 63	Y. Chan/C. Chuang (TPE)
3 Oct	Filderstadt	Hard	L. Davenport (USA) (1) d. A. Mauresmo (FRA) (3) 62 64	D. Hantuchova (SVK)/A. Myskina (RUS)
3 Oct	Tokyo	Hard	N. Vaidisova (CZE) (2) d. T. Golovin (FRA) (3) 76(4) 32 ret.	G. Dulko (ARG)/M. Kirilenko (RUS) (2)
3 Oct	Tashkent	Hard	M. Krajicek (NED) (5) d. A. Amanmuradova (UZB) (WC) 60 46 63	M. Camerin (ITA)/E. Loit (FRA) (1)
10 Oct	Moscow	Carpet	M. Pierce (FRA) (3) d. F. Schiavone (ITA) 64 63	L. Raymond (USA)/S. Stosur (AUS) (2)
10 Oct	Bangkok	Hard	N. Vaidisova (CZE) (2) d. N. Petrova (RUS) (1) 61 67(5) 75	C. Martinez/V. Ruano Pascual (ESP) (1)
17 Oct	Zurich	Hard	L. Davenport (USA) (1) d. P. Schnyder (SUI) (6) 76(5) 63	C. Black (ZIM)/R. Stubbs (AUS) (2)
24 Oct	Linz	Hard	N. Petrova (RUS) (3) d. P. Schnyder (SUI) (4) 46 63 61	G. Dulko (ARG)/K. Peschke (CZE)
24 Oct	Hasselt	Hard	K. Clijsters (BEL) (1) d. F. Schiavone (ITA) (3) 62 63	E. Loit (FRA)/K. Srebotnik (SLO) (2)
31 Oct	Philadelphia	Hard	A. Mauresmo (FRA) (3) d. E. Dementieva (RUS) (4) 75 26 75	C. Black (ZIM)/R. Stubbs (AUS) (1)
31 Oct	Quebec City	Hard	A. Frazier (USA) (6) d. S. Arvidsson (SWE) (8) 61 75	A. Rodionova/E. Vesnina (RUS)
7 Nov	WTA Championships	Hard	A. Mauresmo (FRA) (4) d. M. Pierce (5) (FRA) 57 76(3) 64	L. Raymond (USA)/S. Stosur (AUS) (2)

itf pro circuit 2005

by jackie nesbitt

Marina Erakovic (NZL)

The ITF Pro Circuit for men and women provides the first professional tennis step from the ITF Junior Circuit to ATP Tour, WTA Tour and the Grand Slams.

Women's Circuit tournaments are categorised into four levels of individual week-long tournaments offering prize money in the amount of $10,000, $25,000, $50,000 and $75,000.

Men's Circuit tournaments are categorised into two levels – individual week-long Futures Tournaments offering prize money in the amount of $10,000 and $15,000 and four week Satellite Circuits offering total prize money of $25,000, $50,000 and $75,000.

Futures Tournaments must be scheduled as a minimum of three consecutive weeks of $10,000 tournaments or two consecutive weeks of $15,000 tournaments. Satellite circuits are comprised of four Satellite legs, the final leg of which is a Masters tournament.

Each year the ITF Professional Tennis Department works in conjunction with the ITF Development Department to allocate monies to numerous Pro Circuit events through the Grand Slam Development Fund. This funding is invaluable and ensures that competitive opportunities are widespread and that players have access to tournaments within their region.

Stefano Galvani (ITA)

Marina Erakovic was unranked in January 2005, but three semifinal appearances at $25,000 tournaments and one at $50,000 level, together with two titles from three attempts at $10,000 tournaments has lifted her to 213 in the rankings.

The introduction of IPIN (International Player Identification Number) and the associated IPIN Online Service automation has enabled the further development of the ITF Pro Circuit weblets. These sites, which are part of itftennis.com, provide reports and photographs from an ever-increasing number of Circuit Tournaments, which will be welcomed by players, tournaments, media, sponsors and fans alike. A comprehensive Circuit results service is also available on the site.

Women's Circuit

The ITF Women's Circuit passed yet another landmark in 2005, offering prize money in excess of $8 million, an increase of almost $1 million on the previous year's total. The total prize money available is a direct result of the organisation by National Associations of 374 tournaments in 59 countries.

Over the past 22 years the Circuit has maintained a continual increase both in terms of the number of tournaments on the calendar and the prize money available. There are now 28,000 playing opportunities for female players who can gain valuable competitive experience, while earning the ranking points necessary to gain acceptance into Tour level events.

A glance at the distribution of Circuit tournaments throughout each region shows that the majority of tournaments (221) took place in Europe. North America continues to provide a healthy number of playing opportunities, with 45 tournaments taking place in the USA and Canada. While overall growth of the Circuit in the regions of Asia/Oceania, South and Central America and the Caribbean stabilised, China and Mexico managed to significantly increase the number of tournaments staged in their respective nations.

itf pro circuit 2005

by jackie nesbitt

Several players achieved notable advances in ranking during 2005. Lucie Safarova from the Czech Republic, who started playing Pro Circuit events in 2001, won three Circuit titles during the year at $25,000 tournaments in Italy and USA and also on home ground at the $75,000 tournament in Prostejov. These performances together with two wins on the WTA Tour helped propel Lucie into the top 50 by the end of 2005 for the first time in her career. Kristina Barrois from Germany entered her first Circuit event in 2004 at the age of 22. After playing though the qualifying, Kristina made it to the main draw where she went on to win the event – her only professional tournament in 2004. Inspired by this victory Kristina played full time on the circuit in 2005. During the year she reached eight finals, winning seven of them and, from being unranked in January, ended the year just outside the top 200 at 201.

The Junior Exempt Project, which rewards the year-end top 10 female junior singles ranked players by giving them direct acceptance into the main draw of three selected ITF $25,000, $50,000 and $75,000 events, continues to be successful. Many of the players who have benefited from the project now feature in the top 100 WTA Tour ranked players. Congratulations go to the following Junior Exempts in the 2005 programme all of whom reached either the semifinal or final rounds of at least one of their selected Junior Exempt tournaments; Michaella Krajicek (NED), Viktoria Azarenka (BLR), Yung-Jan Chan (TPE), Marina Erakovic (NZL), and Wen-Hsin Hsu (TPE).

Of the eight tournaments played in 2005 Wen-Hsin reached the quarterfinal stage or better in six outings. She was a finalist at the $25,000 events in Ho Chi Minh City in Vietnam and Ibaraki, Japan, and in September she defeated her fellow countrywoman I-Hsuan Hwang to take her first circuit title at the $10,000 event in Balikpapan, Indonesia. With a WTA ranking in January 2005 of 849, posting consistent results during the year helped Wen-Hsin move up more than 500 places on the rankings to end the year at 318. Similarly, Marina Erakovic was unranked in January 2005, but three semifinal appearances at $25,000 tournaments and one at $50,000 level, together with two titles from three attempts at $10,000 tournaments has lifted her to 213 in the rankings.

The Feed Up system continues to offer the winner of selected $25,000 ITF Women's Circuit events the opportunity of securing a spot in the qualifying draw of a designated WTA Tour tournament, while the winners of selected $50,000/$75,000 ITF Women's Circuit events have the opportunity of securing a spot in the main draw of a designated WTA Tour tournament.

Madaline Gojnea (ROM) won four ITF Women's Circuit titles

Men's Circuit

2005 was another busy and successful year on the ITF Men's Circuit with prize money on offer in the amount of $5,275,000, an increase of $375,000 on 2004.

With the elimination of Satellites due at the end of 2006, the main increase in the number of tournaments staged is at Futures level. The 2005 Calendar comprised 405 Futures Tournaments, up from 355 in 2004, while the number of Satellites weeks dropped to 88, from 116 the previous year. Overall, 493 weeks of competitive opportunities were on offer, which compares favourably with 471 weeks in 2004.

No less than 98 of the current top 100 ranked players on the singles entry ranking participated in Satellite circuits and/or Futures tournaments in previous years, which provides convincing evidence of the vital role the ITF Pro Circuit plays in supporting players through their careers from the ITF Junior Circuit through to the Grand Slams.

A total of 69 countries hosted Futures and Satellites, a slight decrease on 2004, but still up on 2003. First time hosts included Senegal and Sudan who both staged $10,000 Futures tournaments. The Senegal Futures was held in conjunction with two events in Nigeria, while Sudan joined with neighbouring Kenya and Rwanda. All tournaments were well received and offered much needed playing opportunities to players from the region.

Belarus, which staged its inaugural Futures tournament in 1999, made a welcome return to the calendar in 2005, hosting two $15,000 tournaments.

Europe, with 271 weeks of competitive opportunities offering $2,765,000 in prize

Robert Smeets (AUS) won four Futures titles in 2005

No less than 98 of the current top 100 ranked players on the singles entry ranking participated in Satellite circuits and/or Futures tournaments in previous years, which provides good evidence of the vital role the ITF Pro Circuit plays.

money, remains the most active region. Nevertheless, the situation in Asia/Oceania, North/Central America & Caribbean and South America was well balanced, with all regions hosting a similar number of tournaments in comparison to 2004. Africa achieved great progress with no less than 36 tournaments – a welcome improvement on the 25 tournaments held the previous year.

A total of 280 players achieved success in a Futures Tournament or through winning at least one leg of a Satellite Circuit. Among the players achieving notable success was Victor Crivoi, a 23 year-old from Romania, who won seven Futures tournaments, six in his home country. Venezuela's Yohny Romero managed six victories in Futures Tournaments and Satellites Circuits, all on home soil. Special mention must be made of Michal Navratil, who achieved an impressive 25 match-winning streak, starting at the Egyptian Satellite at the beginning of August and ending at the Czech Republic F4 Futures Tournament in October. Michal, aged 23 from the Czech Republic, was also the only player in 2005 to win all 4 weeks of a Satellite Circuit. Three further players put together a 20 match-winning combination – Kornel Bardockzy from Hungary, Ilija Bozoljac from Serbia & Montenegro and Stefano Galvani from Italy. At the time of publishing Galvani's run has not yet come to an end. Finally, Algeria will be pleased with the progress of Lamine Ouahab, who won five Futures titles, three of which were achieved in Morocco and two in his home country.

Several players have made impressive progress in the rankings during the year. Dominik Meffert, Germany, has moved up 950 places to 278, Latvia's Ernests Gulbis moved up 896 places and Robert Godlewski, Poland, advanced 892 places.

International Player Identification Number (IPIN)

The growth of the ITF Pro Circuit calendar brought about the need to automate entry and withdrawal procedures, particularly given the ever-increasing number of active professional players each year. An IPIN became a necessary requirement for all players wishing to compete in Circuit tournaments, and in April 2005, the IPIN Online Service was launched to allow players to manage their own tournament schedule via the internet. In return for a fee, set at a level that makes the service affordable for all, players gained easy online access to important information, including changes to tournaments entered, alterations to the Circuit Rules and their own Code of Conduct record. Importantly, the ITF now has a means to communicate easily and directly with Circuit players.

To date, an incredible 12,698 players have obtained their IPIN, including many junior players, and in only its first year it is greatly encouraging that 50% of IPIN registered players have signed up to the online service.

To facilitate the implementation of the IPIN system, the ITF became the sole entry bureau for all player entries on the Men's and Women's Circuit at the beginning of 2005. Tennis Europe and the USTA, which formerly coordinated entries, have embraced their new roles as the first contact point for players and tournament organisers, while assisting with the coordination of the ITF Pro Circuit Calendar and ensuring the ITF Referees are well prepared prior to Circuit tournaments.

The high level of player acceptance is also due in no small part to the efforts of the ITF's Regional and National Associations, which played their part in supporting the IPIN, publicising the online service, and assisting players to understand the new system.

More information is available on the dedicated IPIN website: www.itftennis.com/ipin.

ITF Men's Circuit 2005 Futures Results

- **NUSSLOCH** (GER) ($10,000+H) 3-9 JANUARY – **Singles:** Robin Vik (CZE) d. Steve Darcis (BEL) 62 63.
  Doubles: Philipp Petzschner/Lars Uebel (GER) d. David Klier/Frank Wintermantel (GER) 64 67(4) 75.

- **DUBAI** (UAE) ($15,000) 10-16 JANUARY – **Singles:** Melvyn Op Der Heijde (NED) d. Alexander Hartman (SWE) 64 60.
  Doubles: Emin Agaev (AZE)/Andrei Olhovskiy (RUS) d. Alexey Kedriouk (KAZ)/Dmitri Sitak (RUS) 67(3) 63 61.

- **LEEDS** (GBR) ($10,000) 10-16 JANUARY – **Singles:** Andrew Banks (GBR) d. Travis Rettenmaier (USA) 76(5) 16 64.
  Doubles: Eric Butorac/Travis Rettenmaier (USA) d. Frederik Nielsen/Rasmus Norby (DEN) 76(7) 64.

- **MUMBAI** (IND) ($15,000) 10-15 JANUARY – **Singles:** Simon Greul (GER) d. David Sherwood (GBR) 46 63 62.
  Doubles: Mustafa Ghouse/Vishal Uppal (IND) d. Harsh Mankad/Ajay Ramaswami (IND) 64 36 76(7).

- **SAN SALVADOR** (ESA) ($10,000) 10-16 JANUARY – **Singles:** Thiago Alves (BRA) d. Bruno Soares (BRA) 62 63.
  Doubles: Francisco Rodriguez (PAR)/Scott Schnugg (USA) d. Rogerio Silva/Marcio Torres (BRA) 63 36 62.

- **STUTTGART** (GER) ($10,000) 10-16 JANUARY – **Singles:** Zeljko Krajan (CRO) d. Benjamin Ebrahim-Zadeh (GER) 63 64.
  Doubles: Philipp Petzschner/Lars Uebel (GER) d. Komlavi Loglo (TOG)/Nicolas Tourte (FRA) 64 76(6).

- **TAMPA, FL** (USA) ($10,000) 10-16 JANUARY – **Singles:** Florin Mergea (ROM) d. Matias Boeker (USA) 62 63.
  Doubles: Alex Kuznetsov (USA)/Mihail Zverev (GER) d. Goran Dragicevic/Michael Yani (USA) 64 75.

- **DEAUVILLE** (FRA) ($10,000) 17-23 JANUARY – **Singles:** Steve Darcis (BEL) d. Olivier Vandewiele (FRA) 62 61.
  Doubles: Steve Darcis/Stefan Wauters (BEL) d. Steven Korteling/Nick Van Der Meer (NED) 64 64.

- **DELHI** (IND) ($15,000) 17-23 JANUARY – **Singles:** Simon Greul (GER) d. Sunil-Kumar Sipaeya (IND) 62 62.
  Doubles: Harsh Mankad/Ajay Ramaswami (IND) d. Ashutosh Singh (IND)/Dekel Valtzer (ISR) 64 62.

- **DEVON** (GBR) ($10,000) 17-23 JANUARY – **Singles:** Matthew Smith (GBR) d. Joshua Goodall (GBR) 64 62.
  Doubles: Scott Lipsky/Brian Wilson (USA) d. Paul Logtens/Martijn Van Haasteren (NED) 61 64.

- **DOHA** (QAT) ($10,000) 17-23 JANUARY – **Singles:** Vasilis Mazarakis (GRE) d. Stefano Galvani (ITA) 63 46 64.
  Doubles: Alexey Kedriouk (KAZ)/Dmitri Sitak (RUS) d. David Novak/Martin Vacek (CZE) 60 ret.

- **GUATEMALA** (GUA) ($10,000) 17-23 JANUARY – **Singles:** John-Paul Fruttero (USA) d. Bruno Soares (BRA) 63 63.
  Doubles: Jean-Julien Rojer (AHO)/Marcio Torres (BRA) d. Thiago Alves/Bruno Soares (BRA) 46 63 62.

- **KISSIMMEE, FL** (USA) ($10,000) 17-23 JANUARY – **Singles:** Jose De Armas (VEN) d. Alex Kuznetsov (USA) 61 64.
  Doubles: Alex Kuznetsov (USA)/Mihail Zverev (GER) d. David McNamara (AUS)/Frederic Niemeyer (CAN) 67(5) 63 76(6).

- **OBERHACHING** (GER) ($10,000) 17-23 JANUARY – **Singles:** Robin Vik (CZE) d. Andreas Beck (GER) 76(3) 46 61.
  Doubles: Adam Chadaj (POL)/Philipp Marx (GER) d. Peter Steinberger/Marcel Zimmermann (GER) 64 63.

- **ANIF BY SALZBURG** (AUT) ($10,000) 24-30 JANUARY – **Singles:** Igor Zelenay (SVK) d. Bostjan Osabnik (SLO) 63 61.
  Doubles: Markus Krenn/Wolfgang Schranz (AUT) d. Martin Fafl/Lukas Rosol (CZE) 64 62.

- **CARTAGENA** (COL) ($15,000) 24-30 JANUARY – **Singles:** Thiago Alves (BRA) d. Agustin Tarantino (ARG) 76(2) 60.
  Doubles: Shuon Madden (USA)/Ruben-Dario Torres (COL) d. Sebastian Decoud (ARG)/Pablo Gonzalez (COL) 75 64.

- **DOHA** (QAT) ($10,000) 24-30 JANUARY – **Singles:** Stefano Galvani (ITA) d. Slimane Saoudi (ALG) 64 64.
  Doubles: Stephane Bohli/Michael Lammer (SUI) d. Boris Borgula/Jan Stancik (SVK) 67(4) 75 76(3).

- **FEUCHEROLLES** (FRA) ($10,000+H) 24-30 JANUARY – **Singles:** Steve Darcis (BEL) d. Jean-Michel Pequery (FRA) 64 76(1).
  Doubles: Josselin Ouanna/Jean-Michel Pequery (FRA) d. Patrice Atias/Jonathan Hilaire (FRA) 76(1) 63.

- **KAARST** (GER) ($10,000) 24-30 JANUARY – **Singles:** Lars Uebel (GER) d. Evgueni Korolev (RUS) 64 76(5).
  Doubles: Bastian Knittel/Peter Mayer-Tischer (GER) d. Floris Kilian (NED)/Komlavi Loglo (TOG) 64 63.

- **KEY BISCAYNE, FL** (USA) ($10,000) 24-30 JANUARY - **Singles:** Horia Tecau (ROM) d. Henry Adjei-Darko (GHA) 63 67(13) 63.
Doubles: Mykyta Kryvonos/Dennis Zivkovic (USA) d. Henry Adjei-Darko (GHA)/Jonathan Igbinovia (NGR) 75 75.

- **SAN JOSE** (CRC) ($10,000) 24-30 JANUARY - **Singles:** Jean-Julien Rojer (AHO) d. Miguel Gallardo-Valles (MEX) 62 61.
Doubles: Matthew Hanlin (GBR)/David Martin (USA) d. Phillip King/Chris Kwon (USA) 63 36 62.

- **BERGHEIM** (AUT) ($10,000) 31 JANUARY-6 FEBRUARY - **Singles:** Ladislav Chramosta (CZE) d. Marco Pedrini (ITA) 62 76(1).
Doubles: Nikolai Dyachok (UKR)/Evgueni Smirnov (RUS) d. Andrei Stoliarov (RUS)/Alexander Yarmola (UKR) 61 36 61.

- **BERIMBAU NAUCALPAN** (MEX) ($15,000) 31 JANUARY-6 FEBRUARY - **Singles:** Darko Madjarovski (SCG) d. Juan-Martin Del Potro (ARG) 36 64 64.
Doubles: Santiago Gonzalez/Alejandro Hernandez (MEX) d. Miguel-Angel Reyes-Varela/Victor Romero (MEX) 64 62.

- **BRESSUIRE** (FRA) ($10,000+H) 31 JANUARY-6 FEBRUARY - **Singles:** Andis Juska (LAT) d. Stefan Wauters (BEL) 64 36 63.
Doubles: Francesco Caputo (ITA)/Martijn Van Haasteren (NED) d. Baptiste Bayet/Jean-Baptiste Dupuy (FRA) 64 46 64.

- **BUCARAMANGA** (COL) ($15,000) 31 JANUARY-6 FEBRUARY - **Singles:** Thiago Alves (BRA) d. Emiliano Redondi (ARG) 62 62.
Doubles: Alexandre Bonatto/Marcelo Melo (BRA) d. Sebastian Decoud (ARG)/Pablo Gonzalez (COL) 64 64.

- **DOHA** (QAT) ($10,000) 31 JANUARY-6 FEBRUARY - **Singles:** Slimane Saoudi (ALG) d. Philipp Mukhometov (RUS) 62 62.
Doubles: Alexey Kedriouk (KAZ)/Dmitri Sitak (RUS) d. Woong-Sun Jun (KOR)/Jaco Mathew (IND) 64 67(5) 61.

- **METTMANN** (GER) ($10,000+H) 31 JANUARY-6 FEBRUARY - **Singles:** Markus Hantschk (GER) d. Sebastian Rieschick (GER) 16 63 64.
Doubles: Lars Uebel/Marcel Zimmermann (GER) d. Josef Nesticky (CZE)/Deniss Pavlovs (LAT) 63 64.

- **MURCIA** (ESP) ($10,000) 31 JANUARY-6 FEBRUARY - **Singles:** Fabio Fognini (ITA) d. Mario Radic (CRO) 26 75 60.
Doubles: Antonio Baldellou-Esteva/German Puentes-Alcaniz (ESP) d. Jordi Marse-Vidri/Alberto Soriano-Maldonado (ESP) 64 61.

- **BERGHEIM** (AUT) ($10,000) 7-13 FEBRUARY - **Singles:** Lado Chikhladze (GEO) d. Bostjan Osabnik (SLO) 26 76(3) 76(4).
Doubles: Lars Uebel (GER)/Roman Valent (SUI) d. Jaroslav Pospisil/Radim Zitko (CZE) 62 76(2).

- **CASABLANCA SATELITE** (MEX) ($15,000) 7-13 FEBRUARY - **Singles:** Marcel Felder (URU) d. Tobias Clemens (GER) 62 62.
Doubles: Daniel Langre/Victor Romero (MEX) d. Daniel Garza/Marco Osorio (MEX) 64 46 63.

- **MURCIA** (ESP) ($10,000) 7-13 FEBRUARY - **Singles:** Gorka Fraile-Exteberria (ESP) d. Ivan Navarro-Pastor (ESP) 61 62.
Doubles: Antonio Baldellou-Esteva/German Puentes-Alcaniz (ESP) d. Gerald Bremond (FRA)/Artem Sitak (RUS) 63 75.

- **HAMILTON** (NZL) ($15,000) 14-20 FEBRUARY - **Singles:** Vasilis Mazarakis (GRE) d. Mark Nielsen (NZL) 75 26 76(5).
Doubles: Alexander Hartman (SWE)/Scott Lipsky (USA) d. Satoshi Iwabuchi/Hiroyasu Sato (JPN) 76(5) 63.

- **LA HABANA** (CUB) ($10,000) 14-20 FEBRUARY - **Singles:** Ricardo Chile-Fonte (CUB) d. Yohny Romero (VEN) 76(2) 64.
Doubles: Marcel Felder/Martin Vilarrubi (URU) d. Ricardo Chile-Fonte/Sandor Martinez-Breijo (CUB) 62 63.

- **TOTANA** (ESP) ($10,000) 14-20 FEBRUARY - **Singles:** Ivan Navarro-Pastor (ESP) d. Gorka Fraile-Exteberria (ESP) 64 61.
Doubles: Marc Fornell-Mestres/Marcel Granollers-Pujol (ESP) d. Filip Urban (POL)/Marius Zay (GER) 62 63.

- **WOLLONGONG, NSW** (AUS) ($15,000) 14-20 FEBRUARY - **Singles:** Ti Chen (TPE) d. Todd Reid (AUS) 63 60.
Doubles: Adam Feeney/Joel Kerley (AUS) d. Adam Chadaj (POL)/Rameez Junaid (AUS) 57 63 10(11).

- **ZAGREB** (CRO) ($15,000) 14-20 FEBRUARY - **Singles:** Robin Vik (CZE) d. Evgeny Kirillov (RUS) 61 61.
Doubles: Jakub Hasek/Robin Vik (CZE) d. Konstantin Kravchuk/Alexander Pavlioutchenkov (RUS) 26 76(2) 76(5).

- **BROWNSVILLE, TX** (USA) ($15,000) 21-27 FEBRUARY - **Singles:** Eric Nunez (USA) d. Petr Kralert (CZE) 76(3) 36 75.
Doubles: Lester Cook (USA)/Robert Steckley (CAN) d. Tres Davis/Eric Nunez (USA) w/o.

- **CALDAS NOVAS** (BRA) ($15,000) 21-27 FEBRUARY - **Singles:** Francisco Costa (BRA) d. Franco Ferreiro (BRA) 60 36 63.
Doubles: Brian Dabul/Damian Patriarca (ARG) d. Diego Junqueira (ARG)/Gabriel Trujillo-Soler (ESP) 64 76(4).

- **CARTAGENA** (ESP) ($10,000) 21-27 FEBRUARY – **Singles:** Gorka Fraile-Exteberria (ESP) d. Mariano Albert-Ferrando (ESP) 67(7) 61 64.
  Doubles: Marc Fornell-Mestres/Alberto Soriano-Maldonado (ESP) d. Mariano Albert-Ferrando/Francisco Mendez-Garcia (ESP) 64 63.

- **FARO** (POR) ($10,000) 21-27 FEBRUARY – **Singles:** Frederico Gil (POR) d. Marcel Granollers-Pujol (ESP) 62 67(3) 63.
  Doubles: Agustin Tarantino/Horacio Zeballos (ARG) d. Marcos Conde-Jackson/Daniel Monedero-Gonzalez (ESP) 75 61.

- **GOSFORD, NSW** (AUS) ($15,000) 21-27 FEBRUARY – **Singles:** Dudi Sela (ISR) d. Sadik Kadir (AUS) 61 61.
  Doubles: Sadik Kadir/Robert Smeets (AUS) d. Brodie Stewart/Peter Tramacchi (AUS) 64 63.

- **NORTH SHORE** (NZL) ($15,000) 21-27 FEBRUARY – **Singles:** Alexander Hartman (SWE) d. John-Paul Fruttero (USA) 76(4) 75.
  Doubles: Mark Nielsen/Matthew Prentice (NZL) d. Benjamin Stapp/Clinton Thomson (AUS) 62 67(5) 75.

- **TRENTO** (ITA) ($15,000) 21-27 FEBRUARY – **Singles:** Giorgio Galimberti (ITA) d. Lado Chikhladze (GEO) 76(7) 75.
  Doubles: Stefano Galvani/Daniele Giorgini (ITA) d. Fabio Colangelo/Alessandro Da Col (ITA) 67(3) 63 61.

- **ZAGREB** (CRO) ($15,000) 21-27 FEBRUARY – **Singles:** Vjekoslav Skenderovic (CRO) d. Rok Jarc (SLO) 63 64.
  Doubles: Rok Jarc/Bostjan Osabnik (SLO) d. Marin Cilic/Ante Nakic-Alfirevic (CRO) 76(3) 62.

- **GUARULHOS** (BRA) ($10,000+H) 28 FEBRUARY-6 MARCH – **Singles:** Franco Ferreiro (BRA) d. Marcos Daniel (BRA) 61 63.
  Doubles: Julio Silva/Rogerio Silva (BRA) d. Henrique Pinto-Silva/Gabriel Pitta (BRA) 62 64.

- **HARLINGEN, TX** (USA) ($15,000) 28 FEBRUARY-6 MARCH – **Singles:** Eric Nunez (USA) d. Ryan Newport (USA) 63 76(2).
  Doubles: Scott Lipsky/David Martin (USA) d. Josh Goffi (BRA)/Wayne Odesnik (USA) 64 76(5).

- **LAGOS** (POR) ($10,000) 28 FEBRUARY-6 MARCH – **Singles:** David Guez (FRA) d. Marcel Granollers-Pujol (ESP) 62 64.

- **ROMA CASTELGANDOLFO** (ITA) ($10,000) 28 FEBRUARY-6 MARCH – **Singles:** Adrian Ungur (ROM) d. Marko Neunteibl (AUT) 67(4) 63 61.

- **LAGOS** (POR) ($10,000) 7-13 MARCH – **Singles:** Frederico Gil (POR) d. Marcel Granollers-Pujol (ESP) 61 63.
  Doubles: Rickard Holmstrom/Christian Johansson (SWE) d. Frederico Gil/Leonardo Tavares (POR) w/o.

- **LILLE** (FRA) ($15,000+H) 7-13 MARCH – **Singles:** Steve Darcis (BEL) d. Roman Valent (SUI) 75 63.
  Doubles: Mustafa Ghouse (IND)/David Sherwood (GBR) d. Patrice Atias/Frederic Jeanclaude (FRA) 64 67(4) 76(3).

- **MCALLEN, TX** (USA) ($15,000) 7-13 MARCH – **Singles:** Todd Reid (AUS) d. Michael Russell (USA) 63 60.
  Doubles: Scott Lipsky/David Martin (USA) d. Alexander Hartman (SWE)/Philip Stolt (USA) 64 75.

- **SIRACUSA** (ITA) ($10,000) 7-13 MARCH – **Singles:** Adrian Ungur (ROM) d. Fabio Fognini (ITA) 75 16 61.
  Doubles: Flavio Cipolla/Alessandro Motti (ITA) d. Cristian Brandi/Simone Vagnozzi (ITA) 75 64.

- **SUNDERLAND** (GBR) ($10,000) 7-13 MARCH – **Singles:** Frederik Nielsen (DEN) d. Mark Hilton (GBR) 64 76(9).
  Doubles: Roman Kukal/Jan Stancik (SVK) d. Frederik Nielsen (DEN)/Petar Popovic (SCG) 63 36 64.

- **BOLTON** (GBR) ($15,000) 14-20 MARCH – **Singles:** Philipp Hammer (GER) d. Petr Kralert (CZE) 63 75.
  Doubles: Henry Adjei-Darko (GHA)/Valentin Sanon (CIV) d. Roman Kukal/Jan Stancik (SVK) 75 76(4).

- **CALTANISSETTA** (ITA) ($10,000) 14-20 MARCH – **Singles:** Stefano Galvani (ITA) d. Pablo Andujar-Alba (ESP) 63 60.
  Doubles: Konstantinos Economidis/Alexander Jakupovic (GRE) d. Pablo Andujar-Alba (ESP)/Matteo Volante (ITA) 62 36 76(4).

- **KOLKATA** (IND) ($10,000) 14-20 MARCH – **Singles:** Vinod Sridhar (IND) d. Adam Fass (USA) 63 63.
  Doubles: Ajay Ramaswami/Vishal Uppal (IND) d. Karan Rastogi/Ashutosh Singh (IND) 62 63.

- **POITIERS** (FRA) ($15,000+H) 14-20 MARCH – **Singles:** Adam Chadaj (POL) d. Denis Gremelmayr (GER) 63 61.
  Doubles: Nicolas Renavand/Nicolas Tourte (FRA) d. Denis Gremelmayr/Philipp Marx (GER) 61 57 63.

● **BEAUMARIS, VIC** (AUS) ($15,000) 21-27 MARCH – **Singles:** Vasilis Mazarakis (GRE) d. Paul Logtens (NED) 63 63.
Doubles: Chris Guccione/Ryan Henry (AUS) d. Alun Jones (AUS)/Paul Logtens (NED) 75 62.

● **CATANIA** (ITA) ($10,000) 21-27 MARCH – **Singles:** Agustin Tarantino (ARG) d. Diego Alvarez (ARG) 76(3) 62.
Doubles: Flavio Cipolla/Francesco Piccari (ITA) d. Stefano Ianni (ITA)/Yordan Kanev (BUL) 63 64.

● **CHENNAI** (IND) ($15,000+H) 21-27 MARCH – **Singles:** Harsh Mankad (IND) d. Kamil Capkovic (SVK) 62 61.
Doubles: Rohan Bopanna/Vijay Kannan (IND) d. Ivan Cerovic (CRO)/Konstantin Gruber (AUT) 64 36 76(5).

● **OUJDA** (MAR) ($15,000) 21-27 MARCH – **Singles:** Mounir El Aarej (MAR) d. Gabriel Trujillo-Soler (ESP) 61 76(4).
Doubles: Ivo Klec (GER)/Jaroslav Pospisil (CZE) d. Fabian Roetschi/Jean-Claude Scherrer (SUI) 64 64.

● **BANGALORE** (IND) ($15,000+H) 28 MARCH-3 APRIL – **Singles:** Simon Greul (GER) d. Ivan Cerovic (CRO) 62 64.
Doubles: Fred Hemmes/Jasper Smit (NED) d. Harsh Mankad/Sunil-Kumar Sipaeya (IND) 61 63.

● **BENIN CITY** (NGR) ($15,000) 28 MARCH-3 APRIL – **Singles:** Henry Adjei-Darko (GHA) d. Luka Gregorc (SLO) 76(3) 63.
Doubles: Raven Klaasen (RSA)/Komlavi Loglo (TOG) d. Josef Nesticky/Radim Zitko (CZE) 76(1) 76(6).

● **FRANKSTON, VIC** (AUS) ($15,000) 28 MARCH-3 APRIL – **Singles:** Paolo Lorenzi (ITA) d. Vasilis Mazarakis (GRE) 64 76(4).
Doubles: Rameez Junaid/Jay Salter (AUS) d. Sadik Kadir/Robert Smeets (AUS) 64 76(4).

● **FRASCATI** (ITA) ($10,000) 28 MARCH-3 APRIL – **Singles:** Agustin Tarantino (ARG) d. Marco Mirnegg (AUT) 76(1) 62.
Doubles: Stefano Cobolli/Vincenzo Santopadre (ITA) d. Flavio Cipolla/Alessandro Motti (ITA) 26 75 75.

● **GRASSE** (FRA) ($15,000) 28 MARCH-3 APRIL – **Singles:** Jeremy Chardy (FRA) d. Stefan Wauters (BEL) 63 62.
Doubles: Lesley Joseph (USA)/Evgueni Korolev (RUS) d. Mathieu Montcourt/Jean-Baptiste Robin (FRA) 61 67(3) 62.

● **RABAT** (MAR) ($15,000) 28 MARCH-3 APRIL – **Singles:** Ivo Klec (GER) d. Adam Chadaj (POL) 64 67(4) 64.
Doubles: Ivo Klec (GER)/Jaroslav Pospisil (CZE) d. Adam Chadaj/Filip Urban (POL) 62 36 64.

● **BATH** (GBR) ($15,000) 29 MARCH-2 APRIL – **Singles:** Petr Kralert (CZE) d. Jean-Michel Pequery (FRA) 76(2) 62.
Doubles: Mark Hilton/Jonathan Marray (GBR) d. Mustafa Ghouse (IND)/Scott Lipsky (USA) 64 64.

● **ANGERS** (FRA) ($15,000) 4-10 APRIL – **Singles:** Evgueni Korolev (RUS) d. Mathieu Montcourt (FRA) 57 63 76(3).
Doubles: Marc Fornell-Mestres/Daniel Monedero-Gonzalez (ESP) d. Nicolas Renavand/Nicolas Tourte (FRA) 76(7) 16 64.

● **BENIN CITY** (NGR) ($15,000) 4-10 APRIL – **Singles:** Jonathan Igbinovia (NGR) d. Vadim Davletshin (RUS) 75 64.
Doubles: Raven Klaasen (RSA)/Komlavi Loglo (TOG) d. Josef Nesticky/Radim Zitko (CZE) 46 76(5) 64.

● **COLOMBO** (SRI) ($10,000) 4-10 APRIL – **Singles:** Peter Mayer-Tischer (GER) d. Rohan Bopanna (IND) 76(2) 62.
Doubles: Ashutosh Singh/Vishal Uppal (IND) d. Rohan Bopanna/Vijay Kannan (IND) 63 64.

● **LITTLE ROCK, AR** (USA) ($15,000) 4-10 APRIL – **Singles:** Zbynek Mlynarik (AUT) d. Fritz Wolmarans (RSA) 63 75.
Doubles: Tres Davis/Scott Lipsky (USA) d. Michael Johnson/Mykyta Kryvonos (USA) 63 16 63.

● **NAPOLI AVERNO** (ITA) ($10,000) 4-10 APRIL – **Singles:** Victor Ionita (ROM) d. Leonardo Azzaro (ITA) 36 63 64.
Doubles: Leonardo Azzaro/Giancarlo Petrazzuolo (ITA) d. Marco Di Vuolo/Nicola Vitiello (ITA) w/o.

● **SANTIAGO** (CHI) ($10,000) 4-10 APRIL – **Singles:** Juan-Martin Del Potro (ARG) d. Jorge Aguilar (CHI) 64 76(6).
Doubles: Brian Dabul/Damian Patriarca (ARG) d. Juan-Martin Aranguren/Patricio Rudi (ARG) 62 46 62.

● **BATH** (GBR) ($10,000) 5-9 APRIL – **Singles:** Mark Hilton (GBR) d. Igor Zelenay (SVK) 63 64.
Doubles: Ross Hutchins/Martin Lee (GBR) d. Lee Childs (GBR)/Alexander Flock (GER) 76(4) 63.

● **CREMONA** (ITA) ($10,000) 11-17 APRIL – **Singles:** Kevin Sorensen (IRL) d. Alessandro Piccari (ITA) 61 64.
Doubles: Max Raditschnigg (AUT)/Alexander Satschko (GER) d. Fabio Colangelo/Alessandro Da Col (ITA) 76(8) 64.

ITF Men's Circuit 2005 Futures Results (continued)

- **KALAMATA** (GRE) ($15,000) 11-17 APRIL – **Singles:** Todor Enev (BUL) d. Konstantinos Economidis (GRE) 63 62.
Doubles: Jean-Francois Bachelot/Gary Lugassy (FRA) d. Petr Kralert (CZE)/Jonathan Marray (GBR) 75 64.

- **KARSHI** (UZB) ($15,000) 11-17 APRIL – **Singles:** Denis Istomin (UZB) d. Akmal Sharipov (UZB) 63 62.
Doubles: Sergei Demekhine/Igor Kunitsyn (RUS) d. Murad Inoyatov/Denis Istomin (UZB) 64 57 64.

- **KOFU** (JPN) ($10,000) 11-17 APRIL – **Singles:** Satoshi Iwabuchi (JPN) d. Kyu-Tae Im (KOR) 62 76(6).
Doubles: Kyu-Tae Im/Oh-Hee Kwon (KOR) d. Mark Nielsen (NZL)/Hiroyasu Sato (JPN) 46 76(3) 63.

- **MOBILE, AL** (USA) ($15,000) 11-17 APRIL – **Singles:** Todd Widom (USA) d. Wayne Odesnik (USA) 46 64 62.
Doubles: Andrew Anderson/Roger Anderson (RSA) d. Richard Barker/William Barker (GBR) 63 75.

- **SANTIAGO** (CHI) ($10,000) 11-17 APRIL – **Singles:** Juan-Martin Del Potro (ARG) d. Thiago Alves (BRA) 61 61.
Doubles: Brian Dabul/Damian Patriarca (ARG) d. Pablo Cuevas (URU)/Horacio Zeballos (ARG) 64 62.

- **BERGAMO** (ITA) ($15,000) 18-24 APRIL – **Singles:** Fabio Fognini (ITA) d. Marco Mirnegg (AUT) 26 63 64.
Doubles: Flavio Cipolla/Alessandro Motti (ITA) d. Diego Alvarez/Diego Junqueira (ARG) 63 62.

- **GUADALAJARA SAN JAVIER** (MEX) ($10,000) 18-24 APRIL – **Singles:** Marcelo Melo (BRA) d. Philip Gubenco (CAN) 61 64.
Doubles: Andrew Anderson/Roger Anderson (RSA) d. Pablo Martinez/Carlos Palencia (MEX) 64 61.

- **GULISTAN** (UZB) ($15,000) 18-24 APRIL – **Singles:** Alexey Kedriouk (KAZ) d. Kirill Ivanov-Smolenski (RUS) 63 62.
Doubles: Alexey Kedriouk (KAZ)/Sunil-Kumar Sipaeya (IND) d. Artem Sitak/Dmitri Sitak (RUS) 63 16 63.

- **HOKUTO** (JPN) ($10,000) 18-24 APRIL – **Singles:** Satoshi Iwabuchi (JPN) d. David Martin (USA) 63 75.
Doubles: David Martin (USA)/Mark Nielsen (NZL) d. Hao Lu/Xin-Yuan Yu (CHN) 64 61.

- **MISHREF** (KUW) ($15,000) 18-24 APRIL – **Singles:** Florin Mergea (ROM) d. Mohammed Al Ghareeb (KUW) 46 63 75.
Doubles: Florin Mergea (ROM)/Ryan Russell (JAM) d. Jakub Hasek/Josef Nesticky (CZE) 61 30 ret.

- **SANTIAGO** (CHI) ($10,000) 18-24 APRIL – **Singles:** Damian Patriarca (ARG) d. Brian Dabul (ARG) 36 63 61.
Doubles: Jorge Aguilar/Felipe Parada (CHI) d. Pablo Cuevas (URU)/Horacio Zeballos (ARG) 63 64.

- **SYROS** (GRE) ($15,000) 18-24 APRIL – **Singles:** Konstantinos Economidis (GRE) d. Todor Enev (BUL) 63 61.
Doubles: Konstantinos Economidis/Alexander Jakupovic (GRE) d. Daniel Monedero-Gonzalez/Carlos Poch-Gradin (ESP) 46 76(2) 62.

- **BUDAPEST** (HUN) ($10,000) 25 APRIL-1 MAY – **Singles:** Sebo Kiss (HUN) d. Grega Zemlja (SLO) 61 62.
Doubles: Amir Hadad/Harel Levy (ISR) d. Nikola Martinovic/Josko Topic (CRO) 57 62 61.

- **CALI** (COL) ($15,000) 25 APRIL-1 MAY – **Singles:** Carlos Salamanca (COL) d. Bruno Soares (BRA) 62 62.
Doubles: Lucas Engel/Andre Ghem (BRA) d. Pablo Gonzalez/Michael Quintero (COL) 64 64.

- **CELAYA** (MEX) ($10,000) 25 APRIL-1 MAY – **Singles:** Jamie Baker (GBR) d. Marcelo Melo (BRA) 63 57 63.
Doubles: Pablo Martinez/Carlos Palencia (MEX) d. David Loewenthal/Nick Monroe (USA) 64 64.

- **CORDOBA** (ARG) ($10,000) 25 APRIL-1 MAY – **Singles:** Juan-Martin Del Potro (ARG) d. Damian Patriarca (ARG) 60 32 ret.
Doubles: Pablo Cuevas (URU)/Horacio Zeballos (ARG) d. Matias Niemiz/Cristian Villagran (ARG) 62 62.

- **LLEIDA** (ESP) ($10,000) 25 APRIL-1 MAY – **Singles:** David Marrero-Santana (ESP) d. Javier Genaro-Martinez (ESP) 76(5) 76(6).
Doubles: Pablo Andujar-Alba/Marc Fornell-Mestres (ESP) d. Rafael Arevalo-Gonzalez (ESA)/Komlavi Loglo (TOG) 62 46 63.

- **MISHREF** (KUW) ($15,000) 25 APRIL-1 MAY – **Singles:** Rohan Bopanna (IND) d. Victor Bruthans (SVK) 76(4) 64.
Doubles: Patrick Chucri (LIB)/Jasper Smit (NED) d. Motaz Abou-El Khair (EGY)/Xavier Audouy (FRA) 63 64.

- **PADOVA** (ITA) ($10,000) 25 APRIL-1 MAY – **Singles:** Massimo Ocera (ITA) d. Steven Korteling (NED) 75 63.
Doubles: Alberto Brizzi (ITA)/Steven Korteling (NED) d. Massimo Ocera/Marco Pedrini (ITA) 46 61 63.

- **SHIZUOKA** (JPN) ($10,000) 25 APRIL-1 MAY – **Singles:** Mark Nielsen (NZL) d. Go Soeda (JPN) 60 46 63.
Doubles: David Martin/Michael Yani (USA) d. Woong-Sun Jun/Sun-Yong Kim (KOR) 26 61 64.

- **BUCHAREST** (ROM) ($10,000) 2-8 MAY – **Singles:** Victor Crivoi (ROM) d. Gabriel Moraru (ROM) 62 64.
Doubles: Adrian Cruciat/Adrian Gavrila (ROM) d. Adrian Barbu/Gabriel Moraru (ROM) 76(4) 67(6) 62.

- **CHETUMAL** (MEX) ($10,000+H) 2-8 MAY – **Singles:** Felipe Lemos (BRA) d. Santiago Gonzalez (MEX) 62 61.
Doubles: Nick Rainey/Brian Wilson (USA) d. Juan-Manuel Elizondo/Daniel Langre (MEX) 46 63 62.

- **CORDOBA** (ARG) ($10,000) 2-8 MAY – **Singles:** Jonathan Gonzalia (ARG) d. Leandro Migani (ARG) 63 64.
Doubles: Pablo Cuevas (URU)/Horacio Zeballos (ARG) d. Diego Cristin (ARG)/Martin Vilarrubi (URU) 75 26 76(5).

- **MISKOLC** (HUN) ($10,000) 2-8 MAY – **Singles:** Frantisek Polyak (SVK) d. Laurent Recouderc (FRA) 63 64.
Doubles: Amir Hadad/Harel Levy (ISR) d. Bastian Knittel/Marius Zay (GER) 61 60.

- **NAMANGAN** (UZB) ($15,000) 2-8 MAY – **Singles:** Denis Istomin (UZB) d. Alexander Markin (RUS) 64 76(5).
Doubles: Raven Klaasen (RSA)/Konstantin Kravchuk (RUS) d. Sergei Demekhine/Andrei Stoliarov (RUS) 62 67(5) 76(4).

- **PEREIRA** (COL) ($15,000) 2-8 MAY – **Singles:** Bruno Soares (BRA) d. Diego Hartfield (ARG) 62 67(3) 63.
Doubles: Daniel Garza (MEX)/Diego Hartfield (ARG) d. Pablo Gonzalez (COL)/Bruno Soares (BRA) 76(4) 76(1).

- **PHUKET** (THA) ($10,000) 2-8 MAY – **Singles:** Alun Jones (AUS) d. Patrick Schmolzer (AUT) 61 61.
Doubles: Patrick Knobloch/Dominik Meffert (GER) d. Josh Goffi (BRA)/Trevor Spracklin (USA) 36 76(4) 64.

- **SEOGWIPO** (KOR) ($15,000) 2-8 MAY – **Singles:** Robert Smeets (AUS) d. James Auckland (GBR) 75 63.
Doubles: Luka Gregorc (SLO)/Marcos Ondruska (RSA) d. Kyu-Tae Im (KOR)/Mark Nielsen (NZL) 75 36 62.

- **VALDENGO** (ITA) ($10,000) 2-8 MAY – **Singles:** Michael Lammer (SUI) d. Alberto Brizzi (ITA) 63 61.
Doubles: Marco Crugnola/Stefano Ianni (ITA) d. Mattia Livraghi/Giuseppe Menga (ITA) 62 61.

- **VERO BEACH, FL** (USA) ($10,000) 2-8 MAY – **Singles:** Ryan Newport (USA) d. Brendan Evans (USA) 63 76(6).
Doubles: Henry Adjei-Darko (GHA)/Francisco Rodriguez (PAR) d. Anthony Lee/Damiisa Robinson (USA) 63 64.

- **VIC** (ESP) ($10,000) 2-8 MAY – **Singles:** Didac Perez-Minarro (ESP) d. Daniel Gimeno-Traver (ESP) 75 67(3) 76(5).
Doubles: Javier Foronda-Bolanos/Daniel Monedero-Gonzalez (ESP) d. Guillem Burniol-Teixido/Miguel-Angel Lopez-Jaen (ESP) 36 64 76(5).

- **ANDIJAN** (UZB) ($15,000) 9-15 MAY – **Singles:** Denis Istomin (UZB) d. Peng Sun (CHN) 75 63.
Doubles: Evgueni Smirnov/Andrei Stoliarov (RUS) d. Orest Tereshchuk/Sergei Yaroshenko (UKR) 06 64 61.

- **BUCHAREST** (ROM) ($10,000) 9-15 MAY – **Singles:** David Guez (FRA) d. Slimane Saoudi (ALG) 61 62.
Doubles: Adrian Cruciat/Adrian Gavrila (ROM) d. Adrian Barbu/Gabriel Moraru (ROM) w/o.

- **CORDOBA** (ARG) ($10,000) 9-15 MAY – **Singles:** Diego Hartfield (ARG) d. Rodolfo Daruich (ARG) 67(4) 61 64.
Doubles: Diego Cristin (ARG)/Martin Vilarrubi (URU) d. Pablo Cuevas (URU)/Horacio Zeballos (ARG) 46 76(5) 64.

- **HODMEZOVASARHELY** (HUN) ($10,000) 9-15 MAY – **Singles:** Boris Pashanski (SCG) d. Amir Hadad (ISR) 76(2) 61.
Doubles: Norbert Pakai/Tibor Szathmary (HUN) d. Boris Pashanski/Viktor Troicki (SCG) 63 63.

- **LLEIDA** (ESP) ($10,000) 9-15 MAY – **Singles:** Daniel Gimeno-Traver (ESP) d. Marcel Granollers-Pujol (ESP) 64 61.
Doubles: Guillem Burniol-Teixido/Miguel-Angel Lopez-Jaen (ESP) d. Israel Matos-Gil/Jose-Antonio Sanchez-De Luna (ESP) 62 63.

- **ORANGE PARK, FL** (USA) ($10,000) 9-15 MAY – **Singles:** Jose De Armas (VEN) d. Alex Kuznetsov (USA) 64 75.
Doubles: Nick Monroe/Jeremy Wurtzman (USA) d. Henry Adjei-Darko (GHA)/Francisco Rodriguez (PAR) 63 63.

- **PHUKET** (THA) ($10,000) 9-15 MAY – **Singles:** Simon Stadler (GER) d. Suwandi Suwandi (INA) 63 62.
Doubles: Josh Goffi (BRA)/Trevor Spracklin (USA) d. Suwandi Suwandi/Bonit Wiryawan (INA) 46 63 75.

ITF Men's Circuit 2005 Futures Results (continued)

- **RECIFE** (BRA) ($10,000) 9-15 MAY – **Singles:** Caio Zampieri (BRA) d. Felipe Lemos (BRA) 76(2) 64.
Doubles: Marcelo Melo/Alexandre Simoni (BRA) d. Lucas Engel/Andre Ghem (BRA) 76(5) 64.

- **SEOGWIPO** (KOR) ($15,000) 9-15 MAY – **Singles:** Satoshi Iwabuchi (JPN) d. Kyu-Tae Im (KOR) 26 62 63.
Doubles: Hee-Seok Chung/Kyu-Tae Im (KOR) d. James Auckland/Ross Hutchins (GBR) 76(3) 36 63.

- **VICENZA** (ITA) ($10,000) 9-15 MAY – **Singles:** Guillermo Carry (ARG) d. Steven Korteling (NED) 62 76(4).
Doubles: Guillermo Carry (ARG)/Giuseppe Menga (ITA) d. Anze Kapun/Andrej Kracman (SLO) 76(1) 64.

- **AGADIR** (MAR) ($10,000) 16-22 MAY – **Singles:** Lamine Ouahab (ALG) d. Tres Davis (USA) 61 62.
Doubles: Tres Davis (USA)/Marcio Torres (BRA) d. Frederico Marques (POR)/Adam Vejmelka (CZE) 62 63.

- **AGUASCALIENTES** (MEX) ($10,000) 16-22 MAY – **Singles:** Raphael Durek (AUS) d. Carlos Palencia (MEX) 76(4) 63.
Doubles: Sanjin Sadovich (CAN)/Carl Thorsen (USA) d. Joseph Schmulian (USA)/Benjamin Stapp (AUS) 75 76(5).

- **BACAU** (ROM) ($10,000) 16-22 MAY – **Singles:** Victor Crivoi (ROM) d. Adrian Cruciat (ROM) 76(2) 67(3) 63.
Doubles: Adrian Barbu (ROM)/Marc Ijzermann (NED) d. Artemon Apostu-Efremov/Teodor Bolanu (ROM) 64 36 61.

- **BALAGUER** (ESP) ($10,000) 16-22 MAY – **Singles:** Bartolome Salva-Vidal (ESP) d. Pere Riba-Madrid (ESP) 75 75.
Doubles: David Marrero-Santana/Carlos Rexach-Itoiz (ESP) d. Miguel-Angel Lopez-Jaen/Pablo Santos-Gonzalez (ESP) 76(4) 63.

- **BEIJING** (CHN) ($10,000) 16-22 MAY – **Singles:** Ben-Qiang Zhu (CHN) d. Matthew Hanlin (GBR) 64 62.
Doubles: Xin-Yuan Yu/Ben-Qiang Zhu (CHN) d. Josh Goffi (BRA)/Philip Stolt (USA) 64 75.

- **GDYNIA** (POL) ($10,000) 16-22 MAY – **Singles:** Bartlomiej Dabrowski (POL) d. Maciej Dilaj (POL) 60 46 63.
Doubles: Maciej Dilaj/Dawid Olejniczak (POL) d. Robert Godlewski/Przemyslaw Stec (POL) 60 61.

- **GROTTAGLIE** (ITA) ($10,000) 16-22 MAY – **Singles:** Andrey Golubev (RUS) d. Malek Jaziri (TUN) 63 76(3).
Doubles: Stefano Mocci/Alessandro Piccari (ITA) d. Giuseppe Menga/Marco Pedrini (ITA) 26 61 75.

- **MOST** (CZE) ($10,000) 16-22 MAY – **Singles:** Ladislav Chramosta (CZE) d. Rameez Junaid (AUS) 63 62.
Doubles: Jakub Hasek/Josef Nesticky (CZE) d. David Novak/Petr Olsak (CZE) 10 ret.

- **PHUKET** (THA) ($10,000) 16-22 MAY – **Singles:** Alun Jones (AUS) d. Phillip King (USA) 63 61.
Doubles: Domenic Marafiote (AUS)/Michael Yani (USA) d. Phillip King/Trevor Spracklin (USA) 67(4) 64 64.

- **PIRACICABA** (BRA) ($10,000) 16-22 MAY – **Singles:** Bruno Rosa (BRA) d. Lucas Engel (BRA) 57 76(6) 63.
Doubles: Lucas Engel/Andre Ghem (BRA) d. Marcelo Melo/Alexandre Simoni (BRA) 63 67(3) 76(3).

- **SARAJEVO** (BIH) ($10,000) 16-22 MAY – **Singles:** Ilia Bozoljac (SCG) d. Grega Zemlja (SLO) 64 63.
Doubles: Ilia Bozoljac/Goran Tosic (SCG) d. Rok Jarc/Grega Zemlja (SLO) 63 75.

- **TAMPA, FL** (USA) ($10,000) 16-22 MAY – **Singles:** Jose De Armas (VEN) d. Diego Alvarez (ARG) 26 63 75.
Doubles: Cody Conley/Ryan Newport (USA) d. Nick Monroe/Jeremy Wurtzman (USA) 62 75.

- **BRCKO** (BIH) ($10,000) 23-29 MAY – **Singles:** Ilia Bozoljac (SCG) d. Lazar Magdincev (MKD) 64 62.
Doubles: Lazar Magdincev/Predrag Rusevski (MKD) d. Nikola Ciric/Goran Tosic (SCG) 26 64 61.

- **BUCHAREST** (ROM) ($10,000) 23-29 MAY – **Singles:** Gabriel Moraru (ROM) d. Adrian Ungur (ROM) 46 63 63.
Doubles: Adrian Barbu/Gabriel Moraru (ROM) d. Artemon Apostu-Efremov/Teodor Bolanu (ROM) 76(5) 76(4).

- **FLORIANOPOLIS** (BRA) ($10,000) 23-29 MAY – **Singles:** Damian Patriarca (ARG) d. Felipe Lemos (BRA) 64 62.
Doubles: Lucas Engel/Andre Ghem (BRA) d. Rafael Farias/Rodrigo Guidolin (BRA) 64 64.

- **JABLONEC NAD NISOU** (CZE) ($10,000) 23-29 MAY – **Singles:** Jan Hajek (CZE) d. Tomas Jecminek (CZE) 64 62.
Doubles: Daniel Lustig/Josef Nesticky (CZE) d. Dusan Hajatko/Roman Jebavy (CZE) 64 62.

- **KEDZIERZYN KOZLE** (POL) ($10,000) 23-29 MAY – **Singles:** Rainer Eitzinger (AUT) d. Maciej Dilaj (POL) 63 61.
Doubles: Maciej Dilaj/Dawid Olejniczak (POL) d. Jordi Marse-Vidri/Alberto Soriano-Maldonado (ESP) 76(4) 62.

- **MARRAKECH** (MAR) ($10,000) 23-29 MAY – **Singles:** Lamine Ouahab (ALG) d. Lukas Lacko (SVK) 46 63 62.
Doubles: Romano Frantzen/Floris Kilian (NED) d. Jun Kato (JPN)/Igor Muguruza (VEN) 36 76(2) 75.

- **MORELIA** (MEX) ($10,000) 23-29 MAY – **Singles:** Carlos Palencia (MEX) d. Santiago Gonzalez (MEX) 63 26 64.
Doubles: Pablo Martinez/Carlos Palencia (MEX) d. Alfonso Perez-Villegas/Rolando Vargas (MEX) 61 63.

- **MUNAKATA** (JPN) ($15,000) 23-29 MAY – **Singles:** Simon Stadler (GER) d. Phillip King (USA) 76(6) 64.
Doubles: Phillip King/Michael Yani (USA) d. Katsushi Fukuda/Yuichi Ito (JPN) 64 64.

- **OXFORD** (GBR) ($10,000) 23-29 MAY – **Singles:** Nathan Healey (AUS) d. Harsh Mankad (IND) 64 75.
Doubles: Robert Green/Jim May (GBR) d. Sadik Kadir (AUS)/Frederik Nielsen (DEN) 63 63.

- **REUS** (ESP) ($10,000) 23-29 MAY – **Singles:** Marco Mirnegg (AUT) d. Hector Ruiz-Cadenas (ESP) 36 61 60.
Doubles: Marc Fornell-Mestres (ESP)/Komlavi Loglo (TOG) d. David Marrero-Santana/Pablo Santos-Gonzalez (ESP) 57 75 61.

- **TERAMO** (ITA) ($10,000) 23-29 MAY – **Singles:** Andrey Golubev (RUS) d. Alessandro Accardo (ITA) 63 61.
Doubles: Giuseppe Menga (ITA)/Juan-Francisco Spina (ARG) d. Yuri Bezeruk (AUS)/Kiantki Thomas (USA) 64 76(5).

- **TIANJIN** (CHN) ($10,000) 23-29 MAY – **Singles:** Xin-Yuan Yu (CHN) d. Hao Lu (CHN) 16 63 60.
Doubles: Xin-Yuan Yu/Ben-Qiang Zhu (CHN) d. Josh Goffi (BRA)/Philip Stolt (USA) 64 26 64.

- **BUCHAREST** (ROM) ($10,000) 30 MAY-5 JUNE – **Singles:** Adrian Ungur (ROM) d. Carlos Poch-Gradin (ESP) 62 75.
Doubles: Pablo Cuevas/Martin Vilarrubi (URU) d. Adrian Cruciat/Adrian Gavrila (ROM) 76(5) 62.

- **CESENA** (ITA) ($10,000) 30 MAY-5 JUNE – **Singles:** Alessandro Piccari (ITA) d. Alessandro Accardo (ITA) 63 63.
Doubles: Guillermo Carry (ARG)/Jhonathan Medina (VEN) d. Alessandro Motti/Marco Pedrini (ITA) 64 64.

- **KARLOVY VARY** (CZE) ($10,000) 30 MAY-5 JUNE – **Singles:** Jan Mertl (CZE) d. Cesar Ferrer-Victoria (ESP) 61 46 61.
Doubles: Jan Mertl/Michal Navratil (CZE) d. Tomas Jecminek/Daniel Lustig (CZE) 10 ret.

- **KHEMISSET** (MAR) ($10,000) 30 MAY-5 JUNE – **Singles:** Lamine Ouahab (ALG) d. Talal Ouahabi (MAR) 76(4) 61.
Doubles: Jun Kato (JPN)/Igor Muguruza (VEN) d. Christophe Dournes/Bastien Lobbrecht (FRA) 63 60.

- **KOSZALIN** (POL) ($10,000) 30 MAY-5 JUNE – **Singles:** Filip Urban (POL) d. Dawid Olejniczak (POL) 62 67(4) 64.
Doubles: Maciej Dilaj/Dawid Olejniczak (POL) d. Jakub Nijaki/Filip Urban (POL) 75 62.

- **KRANJ** (SLO) ($10,000) 30 MAY-5 JUNE – **Singles:** Grega Zemlja (SLO) d. Roman Kutac (CZE) 76(4) 63.
Doubles: Rok Jarc/Grega Zemlja (SLO) d. Fabio Colangelo/Alessandro Da Col (ITA) 26 76(6) 63.

- **MASPALOMAS** (ESP) ($10,000) 30 MAY-5 JUNE – **Singles:** Alun Jones (AUS) d. Ignasi Villacampa-Roses (ESP) 61 62.
Doubles: Marcos Conde-Jackson (ESP)/Denis Matsukevitch (RUS) d. Alun Jones/Nathan Price (AUS) 60 75.

- **MUNAKATA** (JPN) ($15,000) 30 MAY-5 JUNE – **Singles:** Michael Yani (USA) d. Go Soeda (JPN) 76(2) 76(6).
Doubles: Kyu-Tae Im/Woong-Sun Jun (KOR) d. Tasuku Iwami/Go Soeda (JPN) 36 63 76(5).

- **PRIJEDOR** (BIH) ($10,000) 30 MAY-5 JUNE – **Singles:** Ilia Bozoljac (SCG) d. Carlos Rexach-Itoiz (ESP) w/o.
Doubles: Lazar Magdincev/Predrag Rusevski (MKD) d. Ilia Bozoljac (SCG)/Milos Drakulic (CRO) 62 36 64.

- **TUNIS** (TUN) ($10,000) 30 MAY-5 JUNE – **Singles:** Heithem Abid (TUN) d. Frederic Jeanclaude (FRA) 63 46 63.
Doubles: Heithem Abid/Malek Jaziri (TUN) d. Colin Fleming (GBR)/Alexander Satschko (GER) 64 62.

- **WUHAN** (CHN) ($10,000) 30 MAY-5 JUNE – **Singles:** Robert Smeets (AUS) d. Ishay Hadash (ISR) 76(4) 63.
Doubles: Hao Lu/Xin-Yuan Yu (CHN) d. Hsin-Han Lee/Tai-Wei Liu (TPE) 76(4) 63.

ITF Men's Circuit 2005 Futures Results (continued)

- **ANKARA** (TUR) ($10,000) 6-12 JUNE – **Singles:** Victor Crivoi (ROM) d. Charles Villeneuve (FRA) 60 46 62.
Doubles: Evgueni Smirnov (RUS)/Sergei Yaroshenko (UKR) d. Cyril Baudin/Charles Villeneuve (FRA) 62 76(5).

- **BELGRADE** (SCG) ($10,000) 6-12 JUNE – **Singles:** Ilia Bozoljac (SCG) d. Ilia Kushev (BUL) 64 46 60.

- **BYTOM** (POL) ($10,000) 6-12 JUNE – **Singles:** Filip Urban (POL) d. Maciej Dilaj (POL) 57 62 63.
Doubles: Maciej Dilaj/Dawid Olejniczak (POL) d. Jakub Hasek/Josef Nesticky (CZE) 10 ret.

- **HAMMAMET** (TUN) ($10,000) 6-12 JUNE – **Singles:** Alexander Satschko (GER) d. Mehdi Ziadi (MAR) 62 16 76(5).
Doubles: Wael Kilani/Fares Zaier (TUN) d. Heithem Abid/Malek Jaziri (TUN) 62 46 75.

- **IASI** (ROM) ($10,000) 6-12 JUNE – **Singles:** Martin Alund (ARG) d. Pablo Cuevas (URU) 75 64.

- **MARIBOR** (SLO) ($10,000) 6-12 JUNE – **Singles:** Grega Zemlja (SLO) d. Vilim Visak (CRO) 61 75.
Doubles: Vincent Baudat (FRA)/Alessandro Motti (ITA) d. Fotos Kallias (CYP)/Bastian Knittel (GER) 76(5) 61.

- **SAN FLORIANO – VERONA** (ITA) ($10,000) 6-12 JUNE – **Singles:** Mario Radic (CRO) d. Marco Pedrini (ITA) 57 64 63.
Doubles: Luca Bonati/Flavio Cipolla (ITA) d. Jose-Maria Arnedo (ARG)/Mario Radic (CRO) 63 61.

- **TENERIFE** (ESP) ($15,000) 6-12 JUNE – **Singles:** Rafael Moreno-Negrin (ESP) d. Luke Bourgeois (AUS) 62 62.
Doubles: Tres Davis (USA)/Jean-Julien Rojer (AHO) d. German Puentes-Alcaniz (ESP)/Daniel Vallverdu (VEN) 62 64.

- **WOODLAND, CA** (USA) ($15,000) 6-12 JUNE – **Singles:** Jose De Armas (VEN) d. Ivan Miranda (PER) 46 64 61.
Doubles: Nick Rainey/Brian Wilson (USA) d. Ryler De Heart/Scoville Jenkins (USA) 75 64.

- **ALDIANA** (TUN) ($10,000) 13-19 JUNE – **Singles:** Malek Jaziri (TUN) d. Petar Popovic (SCG) 16 62 63.
Doubles: Oualid Jallali (TUN)/Philip Stolt (USA) d. Yassine Idmbarek/Omar-Mohamed Laalej (MAR) 62 63.

- **AUBURN, CA** (USA) ($15,000) 13-19 JUNE – **Singles:** Ryan Newport (USA) d. Wayne Odesnik (USA) 62 63.
Doubles: Nick Rainey/Brian Wilson (USA) d. Raphael Durek/Robert Smeets (AUS) 63 62.

- **BASSANO** (ITA) ($10,000) 13-19 JUNE – **Singles:** Massimo Ocera (ITA) d. Guillermo Carry (ARG) 62 76(7).
Doubles: Guillermo Carry (ARG)/Giuseppe Menga (ITA) d. Artemon Apostu-Efremov (ROM)/Mattia Livraghi (ITA) 63 76(4).

- **BELGRADE** (SCG) ($10,000) 13-19 JUNE – **Singles:** Kamil Capkovic (SVK) d. Max Raditschnigg (AUT) 62 62.
Doubles: Fabio Colangelo/Marco Crugnola (ITA) d. Jerome Becker/Peter Mayer-Tischer (GER) 46 63 61.

- **BLOIS** (FRA) ($15,000+H) 13-19 JUNE – **Singles:** Edouard Roger-Vasselin (FRA) d. Nicolas Renavand (FRA) 46 64 62.
Doubles: Bart Beks/Matwe Middelkoop (NED) d. Esteban Carril-Caso (ESP)/Stephane Robert (FRA) 46 62 63.

- **BUCHAREST** (ROM) ($10,000) 13-19 JUNE – **Singles:** Adrian Ungur (ROM) d. Victor Crivoi (ROM) 63 75.
Doubles: Pablo Cuevas/Martin Vilarrubi (URU) d. Pablo Andujar-Alba (ESP)/Igor Muguruza (VEN) 57 61 64.

- **ISTANBUL** (TUR) ($10,000) 13-19 JUNE – **Singles:** Amir Hadad (ISR) d. Sergei Yaroshenko (UKR) 36 62 60.
Doubles: Frank Moser/Bernard Parun (GER) d. Konstantin Kravchuk/Alexander Pavlioutchenkov (RUS) 36 76(2) 64.

- **KOPER** (SLO) ($10,000) 13-19 JUNE – **Singles:** Grega Zemlja (SLO) d. Marco Pedrini (ITA) 67(2) 64 64.
Doubles: Marko Neunteibl/Christoph Palmanshofer (AUT) d. Matic Omerzel/Bostjan Osabnik (SLO) 76(1) 61.

- **KUSATSU** (JPN) ($10,000) 13-19 JUNE – **Singles:** Atsuo Ogawa (JPN) d. Satoshi Iwabuchi (JPN) 76(5) 76(3).
Doubles: David Martin (USA)/Mark Nielsen (NZL) d. Phillip King (USA)/Hiroyasu Sato (JPN) 63 76(4).

- **LA PALMA** (ESP) ($10,000) 13-19 JUNE – **Singles:** Marcel Granollers-Pujol (ESP) d. Carlos Rexach-Itoiz (ESP) 75 67(5) 63.
Doubles: Artem Sitak/Dmitri Sitak (RUS) d. Javier Genaro-Martinez (ESP)/Daniel Vallverdu (VEN) 76(6) 76(4).

● **SAVITAIPALE** (FIN) ($10,000) 13-19 JUNE – **Singles:** Tommi Lenho (FIN) d. Dominik Meffert (GER) 61 75.
Doubles: Juan-Manuel Elizondo/Alfonso Perez-Villegas (MEX) d. Lauri Kiiski/Tommi Lenho (FIN) 63 36 75.

● **ALKMAAR** (NED) ($15,000) 20-26 JUNE – **Singles:** Melvyn Op Der Heijde (NED) d. Thorsten Popp (GER) 46 76(5) 60.
Doubles: Dominique Coene/Stefan Wauters (BEL) d. Denis Gremelmayr/Philipp Marx (GER) 75 61.

● **BELGRADE** (SCG) ($10,000) 20-26 JUNE – **Singles:** Viktor Troicki (SCG) d. Fabio Colangelo (ITA) 62 61.
Doubles: Darko Madjarovski/Aleksander Slovic (SCG) d. Fabio Colangelo (ITA)/Goran Tosic (SCG) 36 63 75.

● **BUCHAREST** (ROM) ($10,000) 20-26 JUNE – **Singles:** Victor Crivoi (ROM) d. Jorge Aguilar (CHI) 61 62.
Doubles: Adrian Barbu/Ion Moldovan (ROM) d. Jorge Aguilar (CHI)/Julien Maes (FRA) 36 75 62.

● **CASTELFRANCO** (ITA) ($10,000) 20-26 JUNE – **Singles:** Massimo Ocera (ITA) d. Matteo Viola (ITA) 64 60.
Doubles: Flavio Cipolla/Simone Vagnozzi (ITA) d. Stefan Kilchhofer/Benjamin Rufer (SUI) 76(1) 63.

● **CHICO, CA** (USA) ($15,000) 20-26 JUNE – **Singles:** Lesley Joseph (USA) d. Jeremy Wurtzman (USA) 64 62.
Doubles: Sam Warburg/Jeremy Wurtzman (USA) d. Patrick Briaud (USA)/Aleksander Vlaski (SCG) 16 64 63.

● **ISTANBUL** (TUR) ($10,000) 20-26 JUNE – **Singles:** Radoslav Lukaev (BUL) d. Predrag Rusevski (MKD) 62 63.
Doubles: Lazar Magdincev/Predrag Rusevski (MKD) d. Alexey Kedriouk (KAZ)/Orest Tereshchuk (UKR) w/o.

● **KARUIZAWA** (JPN) ($10,000) 20-26 JUNE – **Singles:** Oh-Hee Kwon (KOR) d. Jae-Sung An (KOR) 62 75.
Doubles: David Martin (USA)/Mark Nielsen (NZL) d. Tetsuya Chaen (JPN)/Dong-Hyun Kim (KOR) 64 64.

● **LANZAROTE** (ESP) ($15,000+H) 20-26 JUNE – **Singles:** Yeu-Tzuoo Wang (TPE) d. Artem Sitak (RUS) 63 63.
Doubles: Komlavi Loglo (TOG)/Rafael Moreno-Negrin (ESP) d. Ti Chen/Yeu-Tzuoo Wang (TPE) 75 67(8) 64.

● **TOULON** (FRA) ($15,000) 20-26 JUNE – **Singles:** Jan Mertl (CZE) d. Trystan Meniane (FRA) 60 26 76(1).
Doubles: Jan Mertl (CZE)/Giancarlo Petrazzuolo (ITA) d. Patrice Atias/Jonathan Hilaire (FRA) 64 61.

● **VIERUMAKI** (FIN) ($10,000) 20-26 JUNE – **Singles:** Benedikt Dorsch (GER) d. Mait Kunnap (EST) 61 63.
Doubles: Mait Kunnap (EST)/Janne Ojala (FIN) d. Benedikt Dorsch/Mihail Zverev (GER) 63 63.

● **BUFFALO, NY** (USA) ($10,000) 27 JUNE-3 JULY – **Singles:** Alexandre Simoni (BRA) d. Robert Steckley (CAN) 64 64.
Doubles: Treat Huey (USA)/Izak Van Der Merwe (RSA) d. Tres Davis/Nick Monroe (USA) 63 64.

● **HEERHUGOWAARD** (NED) ($15,000) 27 JUNE-3 JULY – **Singles:** Denis Gremelmayr (GER) d. Nicolas Todero (ARG) 64 62.
Doubles: Pablo Gonzalez (COL)/Nicolas Todero (ARG) d. Dominique Coene (BEL)/Jasper Smit (NED) 26 63 62.

● **HUNEDOARA** (ROM) ($10,000) 27 JUNE-3 JULY – **Singles:** Kornel Bardoczky (HUN) d. Victor Anagnastopol (ROM) 63 57 64.
Doubles: Adrian Cruciat/Adrian Gavrila (ROM) d. Shuon Madden (USA)/Leandro Migani (ARG) 64 36 63.

● **PESCARA** (ITA) ($10,000) 27 JUNE-3 JULY – **Singles:** Marco Pedrini (ITA) d. Horacio Zeballos (ARG) 75 26 62.
Doubles: Alvaro Loyola/Juan-Felipe Yanez (CHI) d. Fotos Kallias (CYP)/Adam Vejmelka (CZE) 62 64.

● **TOKYO** (JPN) ($10,000) 27 JUNE-3 JULY – **Singles:** Go Soeda (JPN) d. Jose Statham (NZL) 64 63.
Doubles: K.C. Corkery/James Pade (USA) d. Minh Le (USA)/Hiroyasu Sato (JPN) 76(4) 75.

● **TRIER** (GER) ($10,000) 27 JUNE-3 JULY – **Singles:** Andreas Beck (GER) d. Trystan Meniane (FRA) 63 60.
Doubles: Rameez Junaid (AUS)/Markus Schiller (GER) d. Dustin Brown (JAM)/Sebastian Rieschick (GER) 60 64.

● **ALICANTE** (ESP) ($15,000) 4-10 JULY – **Singles:** David Marrero-Santana (ESP) d. Bartolome Salva-Vidal (ESP) 61 46 63.
Doubles: David Marrero-Santana/Pablo Santos-Gonzalez (ESP) d. Pablo Andujar-Alba (ESP)/Jun Kato (JPN) 36 75 62.

● **BOLOGNA** (ITA) ($10,000) 4-10 JULY – **Singles:** Mario Radic (CRO) d. Matteo Colla (ITA) 61 63.
Doubles: Juan-Pablo Amado/Jonathan Gonzalia (ARG) d. Tommaso Sanna/Enrico Wellenfeld (ITA) 63 76(5).

ITF Men's Circuit 2005 Futures Results (continued)

- **BOURG-EN-BRESSE** (FRA) ($15,000+H) 4-10 JULY – **Singles:** Diego Junqueira (ARG) d. Slimane Saoudi (ALG) 36 64 63.
Doubles: Diego Junqueira/Damian Patriarca (ARG) d. Xavier Audouy/Alexandre Sidorenko (FRA) 62 64.

- **FELIXSTOWE** (GBR) ($10,000) 4-10 JULY – **Singles:** Nicolas Tourte (FRA) d. Niels Desein (BEL) 67(5) 75 63.

- **FOSCANI** (ROM) ($10,000) 4-10 JULY – **Singles:** Victor Crivoi (ROM) d. Adrian Cruciat (ROM) 76(7) 16 63.
Doubles: Jorge Aguilar (CHI)/Caio Zampieri (BRA) d. Nikolai Dyachok/Aleksandr Nedovesov (UKR) 64 60.

- **KASSEL** (GER) ($15,000+H) 4-10 JULY – **Singles:** Denis Gremelmayr (GER) d. Sascha Kloer (GER) 62 61.
Doubles: Kevin Deden/Sascha Kloer (GER) d. Marc Leimbach (GER)/Marko Neunteibl (AUT) 63 36 63.

- **PITTSBURGH, PA** (USA) ($10,000) 4-10 JULY – **Singles:** Catalin Gard (ROM) d. Michael Quintero (COL) 67(5) 62 62.
Doubles: Robert Smeets/Daniel Wendler (AUS) d. Tres Davis (USA)/Catalin Gard (ROM) w/o.

- **TELFS** (AUT) ($10,000) 4-10 JULY – **Singles:** Rok Jarc (SLO) d. Johannes Ager (AUT) 64 64.
Doubles: Bastian Knittel/Christopher Koderisch (GER) d. Benedikt Dorsch/Mihail Zverev (GER) 21 ret.

- **ANIF** (AUT) ($10,000) 11-17 JULY – **Singles:** Jaroslav Pospisil (CZE) d. Johannes Ager (AUT) 64 26 61.
Doubles: Fabian Roetschi/Benjamin Rufer (SUI) d. Werner Eschauer/Marko Neunteibl (AUT) 76(5) 64.

- **CARPI** (ITA) ($10,000) 11-17 JULY – **Singles:** Marco Pedrini (ITA) d. Flavio Cipolla (ITA) 36 75 76(6).
Doubles: Alberto Soriano-Maldonado (ESP)/Adam Vejmelka (CZE) d. Marco Crugnola/Alessandro Da Col (ITA) 63 26 75.

- **DUSSELDORF** (GER) ($10,000) 11-17 JULY – **Singles:** Jacob Adaktusson (SWE) d. Julian Reister (GER) 46 62 75.
Doubles: Dominique Coene (BEL)/Evgueni Korolev (RUS) d. Tobias Clemens/Ralph Grambow (GER) 36 62 60.

- **ELCHE** (ESP) ($15,000) 11-17 JULY – **Singles:** Pablo Andujar-Alba (ESP) d. Gabriel Trujillo-Soler (ESP) 63 36 63.
Doubles: Pablo Andujar-Alba (ESP)/Jun Kato (JPN) d. Daniel Munoz-De La Nava/Pablo Santos-Gonzalez (ESP) 75 41 ret.

- **FRINTON ON SEA** (GBR) ($10,000) 11-17 JULY – **Singles:** Neil Bamford (GBR) d. Nicolas Tourte (FRA) 63 64.
Doubles: Neil Bamford/David Corrie (GBR) d. Colin Fleming/Jamie Murray (GBR) 75 64.

- **PEORIA, IL** (USA) ($10,000) 11-17 JULY – **Singles:** Catalin Gard (ROM) d. Michael Yani (USA) 63 64.
Doubles: Pierre-Ludovic Duclos (CAN)/Alexandre Simoni (BRA) d. David Martin/Jeremy Wurtzman (USA) 63 76(7).

- **PITESTI** (ROM) ($10,000) 11-17 JULY – **Singles:** Andrei Mlendea (ROM) d. Adrian Cruciat (ROM) 76(5) 63.
Doubles: Shuon Madden/Philip Stolt (USA) d. Vladislav Bondarenko (UKR)/Sergei Krotiouk (RUS) 75 60.

- **SAINT-GERVAIS** (FRA) ($15,000) 11-17 JULY – **Singles:** Marc Gicquel (FRA) d. Xavier Audouy (FRA) 63 61.
Doubles: Patrice Atias/Antoine Benneteau (FRA) d. Diego Alvarez (ARG)/Xavier Audouy (FRA) 63 67(5) 75.

- **BUCHAREST** (ROM) ($10,000) 18-24 JULY – **Singles:** Adrian Cruciat (ROM) d. Felipe Parada (CHI) 75 63.
Doubles: Jorge Aguilar/Felipe Parada (CHI) d. Adrian Barbu/Ion Moldovan (ROM) 76(1) 67(5) 76(6).

- **CARACAS** (VEN) ($10,000) 18-24 JULY – **Singles:** Yohny Romero (VEN) d. Dejan Cvetkovic (CAN) 63 62.
Doubles: Piero Luisi/David Navarrete (VEN) d. Ryan Russell (JAM)/Marcio Torres (BRA) 63 64.

- **GANDIA** (ESP) ($10,000) 18-24 JULY – **Singles:** Hector Ruiz-Cadenas (ESP) d. Daniel Vallverdu (VEN) 62 62.
Doubles: Marc Fornell-Mestres/Jordi Marse-Vidri (ESP) d. David Marrero-Santana/Pablo Santos-Gonzalez (ESP) 46 63 76(4).

- **JOPLIN, MO** (USA) ($10,000) 18-24 JULY – **Singles:** Alexandre Simoni (BRA) d. Michael Yani (USA) 67(4) 63 75.
Doubles: John Isner/Jeremy Wurtzman (USA) d. Andrew Anderson/Stephen Mitchell (RSA) 67(3) 64 76(4).

- **KRAMSACH** (AUT) ($10,000) 18-24 JULY – **Singles:** Evgueni Korolev (RUS) d. Armin Sandbichler (AUT) 76(1) 60.
Doubles: Marko Neunteibl/Christoph Palmanshofer (AUT) d. Andreas Haider-Maurer/Christian Magg (AUT) 64 60.

- **PALAZZOLO** (ITA) ($10,000) 18-24 JULY – **Singles:** Diego Junqueira (ARG) d. Adam Vejmelka (CZE) 62 60.
Doubles: Daniele Giorgini/Matteo Volante (ITA) d. Vincent Baudat/Nicolas Tourte (FRA) 75 67(2) 61.

- **TIANJIN** (CHN) ($15,000) 18-24 JULY – **Singles:** Oh-Hee Kwon (KOR) d. Yi-Ning Wang (CHN) 60 60.
Doubles: Zhe Li/Yu Wang (CHN) d. David To/Marcus Walker (AUS) 61 62.

- **BEIJING** (CHN) ($15,000) 25-31 JULY – **Singles:** Ti Chen (TPE) d. Oh-Hee Kwon (KOR) 36 61 61.
Doubles: Xin-Yuan Yu/Yu Zhang (CHN) d. Kai-Lung Chang/Wang-Cheng Hsieh (TPE) 46 75 61.

- **CARACAS** (VEN) ($10,000) 25-31 JULY – **Singles:** Jimy Szymanski (VEN) d. Dejan Cvetkovic (CAN) 67(5) 64 62.
Doubles: Piero Luisi/David Navarrete (VEN) d. Ryan Russell (JAM)/Marcio Torres (BRA) 63 75.

- **DENIA** (ESP) ($10,000) 25-31 JULY – **Singles:** Guillem Burniol-Teixido (ESP) d. Ivan Esquerdo-Andreu (ESP) 75 26 76(5).
Doubles: Rafael Arevalo-Gonzalez (ESA)/Ben-Qiang Zhu (CHN) d. Jose-Carlos Garcia-Sanchez/Miquel Perez-Puig Domenech (ESP) 16 63 62.

- **FOLIGNO** (ITA) ($10,000) 25-31 JULY – **Singles:** Alberto Brizzi (ITA) d. Frederic Nussbaum (SUI) 61 62.
Doubles: Filippo Figliomeni/Matteo Marrai (ITA) d. Marco Crugnola (ITA)/Ismar Gorcic (BIH) 75 62.

- **GODFREY, IL** (USA) ($10,000) 25-31 JULY – **Singles:** Sam Warburg (USA) d. Jamie Baker (GBR) 76(6) 63.
Doubles: Philip Stolt/Sam Warburg (USA) d. Andrew Anderson (RSA)/Daniel King-Turner (NZL) 64 64.

- **JOUNIEH** (LIB) ($15,000) 25-31 JULY – **Singles:** Benjamin Balleret (MON) d. Dusan Karol (CZE) 62 60.

- **LEUN** (GER) ($10,000) 25-31 JULY – **Singles:** Maximilian Abel (GER) d. Sascha Kloer (GER) 75 64.
Doubles: Andre Begemann/Bastian Knittel (GER) d. Ralph Grambow/Florian Kunth (GER) 63 75.

- **TARGU MURES** (ROM) ($10,000) 25-31 JULY – **Singles:** Cesar Ferrer-Victoria (ESP) d. Jorge Aguilar (CHI) 64 36 63.
Doubles: Jorge Aguilar/Felipe Parada (CHI) d. Nikolai Dyachok/Aleksandr Nedovesov (UKR) 61 62.

- **BALS** (ROM) ($10,000) 1-7 AUGUST – **Singles:** Nikolai Dyachok (UKR) d. Felipe Parada (CHI) 57 75 63.
Doubles: Teodor-Dacian Craciun/Adrian Gavrila (ROM) d. Shuon Madden (USA)/Eric Scherer (GER) w/o.

- **CARACAS** (VEN) ($10,000) 1-7 AUGUST – **Singles:** Yohny Romero (VEN) d. Lionel Noviski (ARG) 57 63 75.
Doubles: Jhonathan Medina/Roman Recarte (VEN) d. Juan De Armas (VEN)/Marcio Torres (BRA) w/o.

- **DAKAR** (SEN) ($10,000) 1-7 AUGUST – **Singles:** Henry Adjei-Darko (GHA) d. Johar-Mubarak Saeed (QAT) 62 61.
Doubles: Candy Idoko/Lawal Shehu (NGR) d. Dennis Biggemann (GER)/Amadeus Fulford-Jones (GBR) 67(4) 76(6) 63.

- **DECATUR, IL** (USA) ($10,000) 1-7 AUGUST – **Singles:** Michael Yani (USA) d. Sam Warburg (USA) 75 64.
Doubles: Brandon Davis/Tres Davis (USA) d. Sadik Kadir/Daniel Wendler (AUS) 64 76(4).

- **INGOLSTADT** (GER) ($10,000) 1-7 AUGUST – **Singles:** Sebastian Rieschick (GER) d. Sascha Kloer (GER) 76(4) 62.
Doubles: Bastian Knittel (GER)/Louk Sorensen (IRL) d. Dominik Meffert/Sebastian Rieschick (GER) w/o.

- **JOUNIEH** (LIB) ($15,000) 1-7 AUGUST – **Singles:** Benjamin Balleret (MON) d. Laurent Recouderc (FRA) 63 75.
Doubles: Patrick Chucri (LIB)/Alexander Hartman (SWE) d. Benjamin Balleret (MON)/Clement Morel (FRA) 67(3) 76(2) 10 ret.

- **JURMALA** (LAT) ($10,000) 1-7 AUGUST – **Singles:** Stian Boretti (NOR) d. Robert Godlewski (POL) 63 63.
Doubles: Rick Schalkers/Bas Van Der Valk (NED) d. Stian Boretti (NOR)/Lauri Kiiski (FIN) 76(1) 57 61.

- **L'AQUILA** (ITA) ($10,000) 1-7 AUGUST – **Singles:** Benjamin Rufer (SUI) d. Alberto Brizzi (ITA) 75 63.
Doubles: Robin Haase/Igor Sijsling (NED) d. Frederic Nussbaum/Benjamin Rufer (SUI) 64 76(8).

- **NOVI SAD** (SCG) ($10,000) 1-7 AUGUST – **Singles:** Lazar Magdincev (MKD) d. Viktor Troicki (SCG) 64 63.
Doubles: Peter Miklusicak (SVK)/Lukas Rosol (CZE) d. Aleksander Slovic/Viktor Troicki (SCG) 64 64.

ITF Men's Circuit 2005 Futures Results (continued)

- **XATIVA** (ESP) ($10,000) 1-7 AUGUST – **Singles:** Augustin Gensse (FRA) d. Jose-Antonio Sanchez-De Luna (ESP) 75 62.
Doubles: German Puentes-Alcaniz/Javier Ramos-Martinez (ESP) d. Gordan Peranec (CRO)/Carlos Rexach-Itoiz (ESP) 46 61 64.

- **YOGYAKARTA** (INA) ($10,000) 1-7 AUGUST – **Singles:** Guilherme Ochiai (BRA) d. Chu-Huan Yi (TPE) 36 75 63.
Doubles: Suwandi Suwandi/Bonit Wiryawan (INA) d. Christopher Rungkat/Febi Widhiyanto (INA) 64 62.

- **AVEZZANO** (ITA) ($10,000) 8-14 AUGUST – **Singles:** Flavio Cipolla (ITA) d. Carlos Poch-Gradin (ESP) 63 62.
Doubles: Fabio Colangelo/Alessandro Da Col (ITA) d. Daniel Monedero-Gonzalez/Carlos Poch-Gradin (ESP) 46 76(3) 76(3).

- **BUENOS AIRES** (ARG) ($10,000) 8-14 AUGUST – **Singles:** Maximo Gonzalez (ARG) d. Lionel Noviski (ARG) 46 64 63.
Doubles: Emiliano Massa/Leonardo Mayer (ARG) d. Diego Cristin/Maximo Gonzalez (ARG) 61 57 64.

- **CHIAPAS** (MEX) ($10,000) 8-14 AUGUST – **Singles:** Luis-Manuel Flores (MEX) d. Daniel Garza (MEX) 61 64.
Doubles: Joseph Schmulian (USA)/Benjamin Stapp (AUS) d. Marcelo Amador/Daniel Garza (MEX) 75 63.

- **CRAIOVA** (ROM) ($10,000) 8-14 AUGUST – **Singles:** Pablo Galdon (ARG) d. Cesar Ferrer-Victoria (ESP) 62 61.
Doubles: Adrian Barbu/Ion Moldovan (ROM) d. Pablo Cuevas (URU)/Eric Scherer (GER) 76(3) 62.

- **ESSEN** (GER) ($10,000) 8-14 AUGUST – **Singles:** Benjamin Kohlloeffel (GER) d. Ilia Bozoljac (SCG) 26 76(4) 62.
Doubles: Sebastian Rieschick/Benedikt Stronk (GER) d. Vytis Balsiukas (LTU)/Adrian Simon (ROM) 62 62.

- **KENOSHA, WI** (USA) ($10,000) 8-14 AUGUST – **Singles:** Ryan Newport (USA) d. Brendan Evans (USA) 26 63 63.
Doubles: Cody Conley/Ryan Newport (USA) d. Eric Butorac/Chris Drake (USA) 64 75.

- **LAGOS** (NGR) ($10,000) 8-14 AUGUST – **Singles:** Henry Adjei-Darko (GHA) d. Victor Kolik (ISR) 63 60.
Doubles: Henry Adjei-Darko/Gunther Darkey (GHA) d. Abdul-Mumin Babalola/Sunday Maku (NGR) 36 61 64.

- **SEMARANG** (INA) ($10,000) 8-14 AUGUST – **Singles:** Oh-Hee Kwon (KOR) d. Hee-Seok Chung (KOR) 76(4) 61.
Doubles: Kai-Lung Chang/Chu-Huan Yi (TPE) d. Suwandi Suwandi/Bonit Wiryawan (INA) 63 64.

- **SERGIEV POSAD** (RUS) ($10,000) 8-14 AUGUST – **Singles:** Alexey Kedriouk (KAZ) d. Valeri Rudnev (RUS) 61 64.
Doubles: Mikhail Elgin (RUS)/Mikhail Filima (UKR) d. Alexey Kedriouk (KAZ)/Alexander Kudryavtsev (RUS) 62 64.

- **TEHRAN** (IRI) ($15,000) 8-14 AUGUST – **Singles:** Philipp Mullner (AUT) d. Malek Jaziri (TUN) 63 76(5).
Doubles: Benjamin Balleret (MON)/Clement Morel (FRA) d. Aqeel Khan/Asim Shafik (PAK) 62 75.

- **VILNIUS** (LTU) ($10,000) 8-14 AUGUST – **Singles:** Stian Boretti (NOR) d. Trystan Meniane (FRA) 75 64.
Doubles: Stian Boretti/Frederick Sundsten (NOR) d. Vincent Baudat (FRA)/Vince Mellino (AUS) 67(4) 53 ret.

- **VINKOVCI** (CRO) ($10,000) 8-14 AUGUST – **Singles:** Marin Cilic (CRO) d. Lukas Lacko (SVK) 63 61.
Doubles: Marin Cilic (CRO)/Ivan Dodig (BIH) d. Daniel Lustig/Karel Triska (CZE) 36 64 63.

- **ZAJECAR** (SCG) ($10,000) 8-14 AUGUST – **Singles:** Aleksander Slovic (SCG) d. Stefan Wiespeiner (AUT) 62 62.
Doubles: Dusan Mihailovic/Goran Tosic (SCG) d. Lazar Magdincev (MKD)/David Savic (SCG) 64 76(4).

- **ARAD** (ROM) ($10,000) 15-21 AUGUST – **Singles:** Victor Crivoi (ROM) d. Angelo Niculescu (ROM) 62 60.
Doubles: Adrian Barbu/Ion Moldovan (ROM) d. Bogdan Victor Leonte (ROM)/Philipp Oswald (AUT) 64 62.

- **BELCHATOW** (POL) ($10,000) 15-21 AUGUST – **Singles:** Herbert Wiltschnig (AUT) d. Dawid Olejniczak (POL) 16 61 60.
Doubles: Tomasz Bednarek (POL)/Felipe Parada (CHI) d. Maciej Dilaj/Dawid Olejniczak (POL) 62 64.

- **BOLZANO** (ITA) ($15,000) 15-21 AUGUST – **Singles:** Alberto Brizzi (ITA) d. Guillermo Carry (ARG) 64 63.
Doubles: Manuel Jorquera/Federico Torresi (ITA) d. Dusan Karol (CZE)/Damian Patriarca (ARG) 57 63 61.

- **BUENOS AIRES** (ARG) ($10,000) 15-21 AUGUST – **Singles:** Lionel Noviski (ARG) d. Juan-Martin Aranguren (ARG) 61 63.
Doubles: Diego Cristin/Maximo Gonzalez (ARG) d. Leandro Migani/Horacio Zeballos (ARG) 36 63 64.

- **CAKOVEC** (CRO) ($10,000) 15-21 AUGUST – **Singles:** Gordan Peranec (CRO) d. Thomas Holzmann (AUT) 63 26 76(3).
Doubles: Ivan Dodig (BIH)/Filip Siladi (CRO) d. Nikola Martinovic/Josko Topic (CRO) 61 62.

- **CALDAS NOVAS** (BRA) ($15,000) 15-21 AUGUST – **Singles:** Alexandre Simoni (BRA) d. Gabriel Pitta (BRA) 63 62.
Doubles: Alexandre Bonatto/Henrique Pinto-Silva (BRA) d. Eric Gomes/Pertti Vesantera (BRA) 63 75.

- **IRUN** (ESP) ($15,000) 15-21 AUGUST – **Singles:** Slimane Saoudi (ALG) d. Augustin Gensse (FRA) 64 67(3) 63.
Doubles: Marc Fornell-Mestres/Daniel Monedero-Gonzalez (ESP) d. Augustin Gensse/Julien Jeanpierre (FRA) 64 64.

- **LAGOS** (NGR) ($10,000) 15-21 AUGUST – **Singles:** Valentin Sanon (CIV) d. Henry Adjei-Darko (GHA) 76(2) 63.
Doubles: Abdul-Mumin Babalola/Sunday Maku (NGR) d. Henry Adjei-Darko/Gunther Darkey (GHA) 64 62.

- **MAKASSAR** (INA) ($10,000) 15-21 AUGUST – **Singles:** Oh-Hee Kwon (KOR) d. Tetsuya Chaen (JPN) 63 63.
Doubles: Suwandi Suwandi/Bonit Wiryawan (INA) d. Wang-Cheng Hsieh/Hsin-Han Lee (TPE) 62 76(4).

- **MONTERREY** (MEX) ($10,000) 15-21 AUGUST – **Singles:** Daniel Langre (MEX) d. Hamid Mirzadeh (USA) 64 62.
Doubles: Sanjin Sadovich (CAN)/Carl Thorsen (USA) d. Chris Kwon (USA)/Carlos Palencia (MEX) 63 26 76(3).

- **NOGINSK** (RUS) ($10,000) 15-21 AUGUST – **Singles:** Oscar Burrieza-Lopez (ESP) d. Alexander Markin (RUS) 75 60.
Doubles: Mikhail Elgin (RUS)/Mikhail Filima (UKR) d. Konstantin Kravchuk/Alexander Pavlioutchenkov (RUS) 62 62.

- **SOMBOR** (SCG) ($10,000) 15-21 AUGUST – **Singles:** Stefan Wiespeiner (AUT) d. David Savic (SCG) 62 64.
Doubles: Dusan Mihailovic/David Savic (SCG) d. Christoph Palmanshofer (AUT)/Aleksander Slovic (SCG) w/o.

- **TEHRAN** (IRI) ($15,000) 15-21 AUGUST – **Singles:** Benjamin Balleret (MON) d. Malek Jaziri (TUN) 64 30 ret.
Doubles: Anoosha Shahgholi/Ashkan Shokoofi (IRI) d. Aqeel Khan/Asim Shafik (PAK) 64 64.

- **VILNIUS** (LTU) ($10,000) 15-21 AUGUST – **Singles:** Simon Stadler (GER) d. Trystan Meniane (FRA) 46 75 60.
Doubles: Rolandas Murashka (LTU)/Dekel Valtzer (ISR) d. Johan Brunstrom (SWE)/Lauri Kiiski (FIN) 63 26 63.

- **ZILINA** (SVK) ($10,000) 15-21 AUGUST – **Singles:** Jaroslav Pospisil (CZE) d. Stefano Ianni (ITA) 26 76(4) 64.
Doubles: Jaroslav Pospisil (CZE)/Adrian Sikora (SVK) d. Daniel Lustig/Lukas Rosol (CZE) 62 36 60.

- **BUCHAREST** (ROM) ($10,000) 22-28 AUGUST – **Singles:** Victor Crivoi (ROM) d. Artemon Apostu-Efremov (ROM) 46 62 64.
Doubles: Catalin Gard/Andrei Mlendea (ROM) d. Artemon Apostu-Efremov/Alin Alexandru Simion (ROM) 64 61.

- **BUENOS AIRES** (ARG) ($10,000) 22-28 AUGUST – **Singles:** Maximo Gonzalez (ARG) d. Sebastian Decoud (ARG) 63 36 64.
Doubles: Matias O'Neille/Emiliano Redondi (ARG) d. Leandro Migani/Horacio Zeballos (ARG) 62 61.

- **CANELA** (BRA) ($10,000) 22-28 AUGUST – **Singles:** Lucas Engel (BRA) d. Andre Ghem (BRA) 76(7) 46 64.
Doubles: Lucas Engel/Andre Ghem (BRA) d. Alexandre Bonatto/Henrique Pinto-Silva (BRA) 75 61.

- **GUAYAQUIL** (ECU) ($10,000) 22-28 AUGUST – **Singles:** Jesse Witten (USA) d. Marcel Felder (URU) 64 64.
Doubles: Brian Dabul (ARG)/Marcel Felder (URU) d. Nick Monroe/Sam Warburg (USA) 75 57 62.

- **KAPOSVAR** (HUN) ($10,000) 22-28 AUGUST – **Singles:** Kornel Bardoczky (HUN) d. Jaroslav Pospisil (CZE) 75 63.
Doubles: Alessandro Da Col (ITA)/Lukas Rosol (CZE) d. Jose-Carlos Garcia-Sanchez/Miquel Perez-Puig Domenech (ESP) 75 46 64.

- **KOROLEV** (RUS) ($10,000) 22-28 AUGUST – **Singles:** Artem Sitak (RUS) d. Pavel Chekhov (RUS) 46 64 64.
Doubles: Artem Sitak/Dmitri Sitak (RUS) d. Victor Kozin/Alexei Miller (RUS) 64 76(4).

- **MUNCHEN-UNTERFOHRING** (GER) ($10,000) 22-28 AUGUST – **Singles:** Jesse Huta-Galung (NED) d. Dominik Meffert (GER) 76(3) 06 63.
Doubles: Martin Slanar/Herbert Wiltschnig (AUT) d. Aleksandar Bajin/Mike Steinherr (GER) 76(2) 63.

- **POZNAN** (POL) ($10,000) 22-28 AUGUST – **Singles:** Robert Godlewski (POL) d. Felipe Parada (CHI) 60 ret.
Doubles: Felipe Parada (CHI)/Benedikt Stronk (GER) d. Michal Domanski/Radoslav Nijaki (POL) 76(0) 64.

- **SAN BENEDETTO DEL TRONTO** (ITA) ($10,000) 22-28 AUGUST – **Singles:** Daniele Giorgini (ITA) d. Manuel Jorquera (ITA) 63 61. **Doubles:** Josef Nesticky (CZE)/Federico Torresi (ITA) d. Martin Fischer/Thomas Weindorfer (AUT) 62 62.

- **SANTANDER** (ESP) ($15,000) 22-28 AUGUST – **Singles:** Jose Checa-Calvo (ESP) d. Jose-Antonio Sanchez-De Luna (ESP) 76(5) 46 76(6). **Doubles:** Esteban Carril-Caso/Gabriel Trujillo-Soler (ESP) d. Guillem Burniol-Teixido/Jose-Antonio Sanchez-De Luna (ESP) 63 75.

- **TIJUANA** (MEX) ($15,000) 22-28 AUGUST – **Singles:** Jason Marshall (USA) d. Carlos Palencia (MEX) 62 75. **Doubles:** Eric Butorac/Chris Drake (USA) d. Chris Kwon/Jason Marshall (USA) 46 76(2) 62.

- **ZAGREB** (CRO) ($10,000) 22-28 AUGUST – **Singles:** Ivan Cinkus (CRO) d. Carlos Rexach-Itoiz (ESP) 46 64 61. **Doubles:** Zlatan Kadric/Aldin Setkic (BIH) d. Ivan Cinkus/Adnan Mesic (CRO) 63 75.

- **ALPHEN AAN DEN RIJN** (NED) ($15,000) 29 AUGUST-4 SEPTEMBER – **Singles:** Jesse Huta-Galung (NED) d. Max Raditschnigg (AUT) 76(2) 76(4). **Doubles:** Diego Alvarez (ARG)/Mait Kunnap (EST) d. Alessandro Motti (ITA)/Jasper Smit (NED) 46 64 62.

- **BUENOS AIRES** (ARG) ($10,000) 29 AUGUST-4 SEPTEMBER – **Singles:** Juan-Martin Aranguren (ARG) d. Agustin Tarantino (ARG) 76(4) 16 61. **Doubles:** Rodolfo Daruich/Lionel Noviski (ARG) d. Martin Alund/Diego Cristin (ARG) w/o.

- **FORTALEZA** (BRA) ($10,000) 29 AUGUST-4 SEPTEMBER – **Singles:** Alessandro Camarco (BRA) d. Marcelo Melo (BRA) 64 26 61. **Doubles:** Marcelo Melo/Antonio Prieto (BRA) d. Alessandro Camarco/Ronaldo Carvalho (BRA) 63 76(8).

- **GUAYAQUIL** (ECU) ($10,000) 29 AUGUST-4 SEPTEMBER – **Singles:** Jesse Witten (USA) d. Brian Dabul (ARG) 76(5) 62. **Doubles:** Jhonathan Medina (VEN)/Martin Vilarrubi (URU) d. Rahim Esmail (CAN)/Jesse Witten (USA) 62 62.

- **KASHIWA** (JPN) ($15,000) 29 AUGUST-4 SEPTEMBER – **Singles:** Toshihide Matsui (JPN) d. Michael Yani (USA) 76(6) 63. **Doubles:** David Martin/Michael Yani (USA) d. Kai-Lung Chang/Chu-Huan Yi (TPE) 64 64.

- **KHARTOUM** (SUD) ($10,000) 29 AUGUST-4 SEPTEMBER – **Singles:** Bogdan Victor Leonte (ROM) d. Marcel Miron (ROM) 64 57 63. **Doubles:** Andemir Karanashev/Timur Lomtatidze (RUS) d. Bogdan Victor Leonte/Marcel Miron (ROM) 63 62.

- **MALI LOSINJ** (CRO) ($10,000) 29 AUGUST-4 SEPTEMBER – **Singles:** Bostjan Osabnik (SLO) d. Ivan Dodig (BIH) 63 64. **Doubles:** Boris Borgula (SVK)/Jaroslav Pospisil (CZE) d. Gordan Peranec (CRO)/Carlos Rexach-Itoiz (ESP) 64 63.

- **NOTTINGHAM** (GBR) ($10,000) 29 AUGUST-4 SEPTEMBER – **Singles:** Jean-Francois Bachelot (FRA) d. Colin Fleming (GBR) 62 61. **Doubles:** Colin Fleming/Jamie Murray (GBR) d. Olivier Charroin (FRA)/Frederick Sundsten (NOR) 76(4) 63.

- **NUERNBERG** (GER) ($10,000) 29 AUGUST-4 SEPTEMBER – **Singles:** Marcel Zimmermann (GER) d. Matthias Bachinger (GER) 62 61. **Doubles:** Matthias Bachinger/Philipp Piyamongkol (GER) d. Dustin Brown (JAM)/Tobias Klein (GER) 64 64.

- **OVIEDO** (ESP) ($15,000) 29 AUGUST-4 SEPTEMBER – **Singles:** Gabriel Trujillo-Soler (ESP) d. Marc Fornell-Mestres (ESP) 75 75. **Doubles:** Esteban Carril-Caso/Gabriel Trujillo-Soler (ESP) d. Cesar Ferrer-Victoria/Daniel Munoz-De La Nava (ESP) 62 62.

- **PUERTO VALLARTA** (MEX) ($10,000) 29 AUGUST-4 SEPTEMBER – **Singles:** Stephen Mitchell (RSA) d. Chris Kwon (USA) 76(2) 76(3). **Doubles:** Daniel Garza/Victor Romero (MEX) d. Scott Doerner (AUS)/Jason Zimmermann (USA) 64 76(5).

- **SZCZECIN** (POL) ($10,000) 29 AUGUST-4 SEPTEMBER – **Singles:** Dawid Olejniczak (POL) d. Felipe Parada (CHI) 62 62. **Doubles:** Maciej Dilaj/Dawid Olejniczak (POL) d. Felipe Parada (CHI)/Benedikt Stronk (GER) 63 60.

- **SZOLNOK** (HUN) ($10,000) 29 AUGUST-4 SEPTEMBER – **Singles:** Kornel Bardoczky (HUN) d. Lukas Rosol (CZE) 62 61. **Doubles:** Kornel Bardoczky/Gergely Kisgyorgy (HUN) d. Alessandro Da Col (ITA)/Lukas Rosol (CZE) 62 61.

- **TIMISOARA** (ROM) ($10,000) 29 AUGUST-4 SEPTEMBER – **Singles:** Teodor-Dacian Craciun (ROM) d. Cosmin Cotet (ROM) 75 26 64. **Doubles:** Artemon Apostu-Efremov (ROM)/Thomas Gilner (GER) d. Catalin Gard/Andrei Mlendea (ROM) 76(5) 64.

- **ALGIERS** (ALG) ($10,000) 5-11 SEPTEMBER – **Singles:** Lamine Ouahab (ALG) d. Filip Polasek (SVK) 63 60. **Doubles:** Dusan Karol (CZE)/Filip Polasek (SVK) d. Oualid Jallali (TUN)/Alexander Satschko (GER) 46 62 64.

- **BAGNERES DE BIGORRE** (FRA) ($15,000+H) 5-11 SEPTEMBER – **Singles:** Dominik Meffert (GER) d. Philipp Hammer (GER) 76(6) 75. **Doubles:** Philipp Hammer/Dominik Meffert (GER) d. Augustin Gensse/Jonathan Hilaire (FRA) 16 61 61.

- **BUDAPEST** (HUN) ($10,000) 5-11 SEPTEMBER – **Singles:** Kornel Bardoczky (HUN) d. Sebo Kiss (HUN) 46 62 75. **Doubles:** Aleksander Slovic/Viktor Troicki (SCG) d. Kornel Bardoczky/Gergely Kisgyorgy (HUN) 46 76(0) 63.

- **COMO** (ITA) ($10,000) 5-11 SEPTEMBER – **Singles:** Marco Crugnola (ITA) d. Fabio Colangelo (ITA) 67(3) 63 62. **Doubles:** Marco Crugnola/Alessandro Da Col (ITA) d. Luca Bonati/Giancarlo Petrazzuolo (ITA) 64 64.

- **ENSCHEDE** (NED) ($15,000) 5-11 SEPTEMBER – **Singles:** Jesse Huta-Galung (NED) d. Thorsten Popp (GER) 60 20 ret. **Doubles:** Ralph Grambow/Sascha Kloer (GER) d. Jesse Huta-Galung/Igor Sijsling (NED) w/o.

- **GLIWICE** (POL) ($10,000) 5-11 SEPTEMBER – **Singles:** Michal Navratil (CZE) d. Andreu Guilera-Jover (ESP) 63 62. **Doubles:** Daniel Lustig (CZE)/Michal Varsanyi (SVK) d. Maciej Dilaj/Dawid Olejniczak (POL) 63 76(5).

- **GUAYAQUIL** (ECU) ($10,000) 5-11 SEPTEMBER – **Singles:** Brian Dabul (ARG) d. Martin Vilarrubi (URU) 64 62. **Doubles:** Brian Dabul (ARG)/Michael Quintero (COL) d. Jhonathan Medina (VEN)/Martin Vilarrubi (URU) 63 64.

- **KEMPTEN** (GER) ($10,000) 5-11 SEPTEMBER – **Singles:** Louk Sorensen (IRL) d. Zeljko Krajan (CRO) 46 63 75. **Doubles:** Jerome Becker/Julian Reister (GER) d. Dustin Brown (JAM)/Tobias Klein (GER) 46 64 63.

- **MADRID** (ESP) ($10,000) 5-11 SEPTEMBER – **Singles:** Frederik Nielsen (DEN) d. Daniel Munoz-De La Nava (ESP) 64 26 76(4). **Doubles:** Frederik Nielsen/Rasmus Norby (DEN) d. Jorge Jimenez-Letrado/Marcos Jimenez-Letrado (ESP) 62 64.

- **MINSK** (BLR) ($15,000) 5-11 SEPTEMBER – **Singles:** Darko Madjarovski (SCG) d. Deniss Pavlovs (LAT) 62 61. **Doubles:** Sergei Demekhine/Alexander Krasnorutskiy (RUS) d. Konstantin Kravchuk/Denis Matsukevitch (RUS) 76(8) 76(5).

- **MOMBASA** (KEN) ($10,000) 5-11 SEPTEMBER – **Singles:** Andrew Anderson (RSA) d. Genius Chidzikwe (ZIM) 61 63. **Doubles:** Andrew Anderson (RSA)/Myles Blake (GBR) d. Bogdan Victor Leonte/Marcel Miron (ROM) 64 64.

- **NOTTINGHAM** (GBR) ($10,000) 5-11 SEPTEMBER – **Singles:** Joshua Goodall (GBR) d. Richard Bloomfield (GBR) 76(5) 76(4). **Doubles:** Olivier Charroin (FRA)/Frederick Sundsten (NOR) d. Lee Childs/Martin Lee (GBR) 63 36 63.

- **ROSAIRO** (ARG) ($10,000) 5-11 SEPTEMBER – **Singles:** Pablo Cuevas (URU) d. Maximo Gonzalez (ARG) 64 61. **Doubles:** Maximo Gonzalez/Damian Patriarca (ARG) d. Pablo Cuevas (URU)/Horacio Zeballos (ARG) 76(5) 46 62.

- **SAO BERNARDO DO CAMPO** (BRA) ($10,000) 5-11 SEPTEMBER – **Singles:** Alessandro Camarco (BRA) d. Lucas Engel (BRA) 26 64 64. **Doubles:** Alexandre Bonatto/Marcelo Melo (BRA) d. Rodrigo-Antonio Grilli/Caio Zampieri (BRA) 75 76(2).

- **TOKYO** (JPN) ($15,000) 5-11 SEPTEMBER – **Singles:** Mark Nielsen (NZL) d. Tasuku Iwami (JPN) 63 76(6). **Doubles:** Jonathan Chu/David Martin (USA) d. Naoki Arimoto/Yasuo Miyazaki (JPN) 62 64.

- **ALGIERS** (ALG) ($10,000) 12-18 SEPTEMBER – **Singles:** Lamine Ouahab (ALG) d. Slimane Saoudi (ALG) 64 63. **Doubles:** Abdel-Hak Hameurlaine/Slimane Saoudi (ALG) d. Filip Polasek (SVK)/Filip Zeman (CZE) 64 64.

- **BUENOS AIRES** (ARG) ($10,000) 12-18 SEPTEMBER – **Singles:** Maximo Gonzalez (ARG) d. Lionel Noviski (ARG) 63 76(1). **Doubles:** Maximo Gonzalez/Damian Patriarca (ARG) d. Brian Dabul/Alejandro Fabbri (ARG) 62 60.

- **CLAREMONT, CA** (USA) ($10,000) 12-18 SEPTEMBER – **Singles:** Benedikt Dorsch (GER) d. Tyler Cleveland (USA) 62 63. **Doubles:** K.C. Corkery/William James Pade (USA) d. Troy Hahn/Hamid Mirzadeh (USA) 64 46 62.

- **FLORIANOPOLIS** (BRA) ($10,000+H) 12-18 SEPTEMBER – **Singles:** Bruno Rosa (BRA) d. Rogerio Silva (BRA) 26 63 61. **Doubles:** Franco Ferreiro/Marcelo Melo (BRA) d. Pierre-Ludovic Duclos (CAN)/Adam Vejmelka (CZE) 62 62.

- **FRIEDBERG** (GER) ($10,000) 12-18 SEPTEMBER – **Singles:** Ernests Gulbis (LAT) d. Marcel Zimmermann (GER) 64 60. **Doubles:** Jerome Becker/Julian Reister (GER) d. Dustin Brown (JAM)/Tobias Klein (GER) 64 63.

ITF Men's Circuit 2005 Futures Results (continued)

- **GOTHENBURG** (SWE) ($10,000) 12-18 SEPTEMBER – **Singles:** Johan Settergren (SWE) d. Rickard Holmstrom (SWE) 75 62.
Doubles: Rickard Holmstrom/Christian Johansson (SWE) d. Johan Brunstrom/Alexander Hartman (SWE) 64 62.

- **KIGALI** (RWA) ($10,000) 12-18 SEPTEMBER – **Singles:** Idan Rosenberg (ISR) d. Jacob Melskens (DEN) 62 64.
Doubles: Genius Chidzikwe/Gwinyai Tongoona (ZIM) d. Andrew Anderson (RSA)/Myles Blake (GBR) w/o.

- **MADRID** (ESP) ($15,000) 12-18 SEPTEMBER – **Singles:** Marco Pedrini (ITA) d. Trystan Meniane (FRA) 64 75.
Doubles: Michel Koning/Jasper Smit (NED) d. Massimo Ocera/Marco Pedrini (ITA) 36 64 63.

- **MINSK** (BLR) ($15,000) 12-18 SEPTEMBER – **Singles:** Pavel Ivanov (RUS) d. Stian Boretti (NOR) 76(5) 67(2) 64.
Doubles: Sergei Demekhine/Alexander Krasnorutskiy (RUS) d. Konstantin Kravchuk/Denis Matsukevitch (RUS) 62 46 61.

- **MONTEVIDEO** (URU) ($10,000) 12-18 SEPTEMBER – **Singles:** Juan-Martin Aranguren (ARG) d. Pablo Cuevas (URU) 62 62.
Doubles: Pablo Cuevas/Martin Vilarrubi (URU) d. Matias O'Neille/Emiliano Redondi (ARG) 76(4) 64.

- **MULHOUSE** (FRA) ($15,000+H) 12-18 SEPTEMBER – **Singles:** Evgueni Korolev (RUS) d. Philipp Hammer (GER) 64 63.
Doubles: James Auckland (GBR)/Kirill Ivanov-Smolenski (RUS) d. Cyril Spanelis/Marc Steger (FRA) 76(3) 64.

- **SASSARI** (ITA) ($15,000) 12-18 SEPTEMBER – **Singles:** Stefano Galvani (ITA) d. Uros Vico (ITA) 64 75.
Doubles: Adriano Biasella (ITA)/Andrey Golubev (RUS) d. Farrukh Dustov (UZB)/Manuel Gasbarri (ITA) 76(6) 61.

- **TEHRAN** (IRI) ($15,000) 12-18 SEPTEMBER – **Singles:** Herbert Wiltschnig (AUT) d. Philipp Mullner (AUT) 36 64 64.
Doubles: Philipp Mullner/Herbert Wiltschnig (AUT) d. Anoosha Shahgholi/Ashkan Shokoofi (IRI) 62 64.

- **ALGIERS** (ALG) ($10,000) 19-25 SEPTEMBER – **Singles:** Slimane Saoudi (ALG) d. Lamine Ouahab (ALG) 64 36 62.
Doubles: Abdel-Hak Hameurlaine/Slimane Saoudi (ALG) d. Mattia Livraghi (ITA)/Alexander Satschko (GER) 76(2) 26 62.

- **BUENOS AIRES** (ARG) ($10,000) 19-25 SEPTEMBER – **Singles:** Juan-Martin Aranguren (ARG) d. Agustin Tarantino (ARG) 62 60.
Doubles: Emiliano Massa/Leonardo Mayer (ARG) d. Lucas Arnold/Diego Cristin (ARG) 76(4) 63.

- **COSTA MESA, CA** (USA) ($10,000) 19-25 SEPTEMBER – **Singles:** Sam Warburg (USA) d. Wayne Odesnik (USA) 75 64.
Doubles: Scott Lipsky/David Martin (USA) d. Raphael Durek/Daniel Wendler (AUS) 64 64.

- **GLASGOW** (GBR) ($10,000) 19-25 SEPTEMBER – **Singles:** Matthew Smith (GBR) d. Martin Lee (GBR) 64 36 61.
Doubles: Colin Fleming/Jamie Murray (GBR) d. David Corrie/Jim May (GBR) 64 64.

- **GOTHENBURG** (SWE) ($10,000) 19-25 SEPTEMBER – **Singles:** Johan Settergren (SWE) d. Frederik Nielsen (DEN) 64 64.
Doubles: Ervin Eleskovic/Johan Settergren (SWE) d. Rickard Holmstrom/Christian Johansson (SWE) 75 67(5) 76(5).

- **MADRID** (ESP) ($15,000) 19-25 SEPTEMBER – **Singles:** Michel Koning (NED) d. David Marrero-Santana (ESP) 46 63 62.
Doubles: Michel Koning/Jasper Smit (NED) d. Rasmus Norby (DEN)/Joseph Schmulian (USA) 57 62 76(5).

- **ORISTANO** (ITA) ($15,000) 19-25 SEPTEMBER – **Singles:** Stefano Galvani (ITA) d. Alessandro Da Col (ITA) 63 60.
Doubles: Stefano Galvani (ITA)/Ismar Gorcic (BIH) d. Fabio Colangelo/Alessandro Da Col (ITA) 76(8) 76(5).

- **PLAISIR** (FRA) ($15,000+H) 19-25 SEPTEMBER – **Singles:** Roman Valent (SUI) d. Philipp Marx (GER) 64 76(4).
Doubles: Rameez Junaid (AUS)/Philipp Marx (GER) d. Eric Butorac/Chris Drake (USA) 75 64.

- **PORTE ALEGRE** (BRA) ($10,000) 19-25 SEPTEMBER – **Singles:** Lucas Engel (BRA) d. Andre Ghem (BRA) 26 62 62.
Doubles: Rodrigo-Antonio Grilli/Caio Zampieri (BRA) d. Franco Ferreiro/Andre Ghem (BRA) 76(5) 64.

- **ROCKHAMPTON, QLD** (AUS) ($10,000) 19-25 SEPTEMBER – **Singles:** Robert Smeets (AUS) d. Luke Bourgeois (AUS) 76(3) 26 64.
Doubles: Luke Bourgeois/Steven Goh (AUS) d. Sadik Kadir/Joel Kerley (AUS) 63 63.

- **TEHRAN** (IRI) ($15,000) 19-25 SEPTEMBER – **Singles:** Herbert Wiltschnig (AUT) d. Jan Mertl (CZE) 75 63.
Doubles: Jan Mertl (CZE)/Nils Muschiol (GER) d. Manuel Jorquera (ITA)/Sascha Ruckelshausen (GER) 63 63.

● **BARRANQUILLA** (COL) ($15,000) 26 SEPTEMBER-2 OCTOBER – **Singles:** Brian Dabul (ARG) d. Horacio Zeballos (ARG) 64 76(4).
Doubles: Luciano Vitullo/Horacio Zeballos (ARG) d. Brian Dabul (ARG)/Ivan Miranda (PER) 57 76(4) 64.

● **BRISBANE, QLD** (AUS) ($15,000) 26 SEPTEMBER-2 OCTOBER – **Singles:** Aleksander Vlaski (SCG) d. Luke Bourgeois (AUS) 62 30 ret.
Doubles: Sadik Kadir/Joel Kerley (AUS) d. Ben Rocavert/Nick Trkulja (AUS) 75 64.

● **CARACAS** (VEN) ($10,000) 26 SEPTEMBER-2 OCTOBER – **Singles:** Yohny Romero (VEN) d. Matthew Behrmann (USA) 46 63 64.
Doubles: Marcelo Melo/Marcio Torres (BRA) d. Martin Fischer/Philipp Oswald (AUT) 62 36 64.

● **COCHABAMBA** (BOL) ($15,000) 26 SEPTEMBER-2 OCTOBER – **Singles:** Agustin Tarantino (ARG) d. Juan-Martin Aranguren (ARG) 64 64.
Doubles: Alejandro Fabbri (ARG)/Martin Vilarrubi (URU) d. Juan-Pablo Amado/Agustin Tarantino (ARG) 26 62 61.

● **EDINBURGH** (GBR) ($10,000) 26 SEPTEMBER-2 OCTOBER – **Singles:** Mark Hilton (GBR) d. Jamie Baker (GBR) 63 63.
Doubles: Colin Fleming/Jamie Murray (GBR) d. Matthew Lott/Gary Thomson (GBR) 63 63.

● **FALUN** (SWE) ($10,000) 26 SEPTEMBER-2 OCTOBER – **Singles:** Johan Settergren (SWE) d. Carl-Henrik Hansen (SWE) 62 64.
Doubles: Stian Boretti (NOR)/Lauri Kiiski (FIN) d. Rickard Holmstrom/Christian Johansson (SWE) 36 62 75.

● **GORLOVKA** (UKR) ($10,000) 26 SEPTEMBER-2 OCTOBER – **Singles:** Fotos Kallias (CYP) d. Laurent Recouderc (FRA) 75 64.
Doubles: Alexander Markin (RUS)/Deniss Pavlovs (LAT) d. Alexander Aksyonov/Vladimir Levin (UKR) 61 63.

● **IRVINE, CA** (USA) ($10,000) 26 SEPTEMBER-2 OCTOBER – **Singles:** Tyler Cleveland (USA) d. Augustin Gensse (FRA) 46 61 63.
Doubles: Tyler Cleveland/Dave Lingman (USA) d. Raphael Durek/Daniel Wendler (AUS) 63 75.

● **MARTOS** (ESP) ($15,000) 26 SEPTEMBER-2 OCTOBER – **Singles:** Marcel Granollers-Pujol (ESP) d. Steven Korteling (NED) 62 63.
Doubles: Michel Koning/Jasper Smit (NED) d. Oscar Burrieza-Lopez (ESP)/Nikolai Nesterov (RUS) 61 75.

● **OLBIA** (ITA) ($10,000) 26 SEPTEMBER-2 OCTOBER – **Singles:** Lukas Lacko (SVK) d. Tobias Koeck (AUT) 61 63.
Doubles: Ivan Cerovic (CRO)/Farrukh Dustov (UZB) d. Filippo Figliomeni/Matteo Marrai (ITA) 62 63.

● **SARREGUEMINES** (FRA) ($10,000) 26 SEPTEMBER-2 OCTOBER – **Singles:** Benjamin Ebrahim-Zadeh (GER) d. Julien Maes (FRA) 64 76(4).
Doubles: Patrice Atias/Antoine Benneteau (FRA) d. Frank Moser (GER)/Radim Zitko (CZE) 26 64 63.

● **ARZACHENA** (ITA) ($10,000) 3-9 OCTOBER – **Singles:** Tony Holzinger (GER) d. Alessandro Accardo (ITA) 64 62.
Doubles: Alessandro Accardo/Adriano Biasella (ITA) d. Andreas Fasching/Konstantin Gruber (AUT) 63 63.

● **BOLTON** (GBR) ($10,000) 3-9 OCTOBER – **Singles:** Jamie Baker (GBR) d. Ladislav Chramosta (CZE) 63 62.
Doubles: Ross Hutchins/Jamie Murray (GBR) d. Roman Herold/Benedikt Stronk (GER) 46 76(2) 64.

● **CARACAS** (VEN) ($10,000) 3-9 OCTOBER – **Singles:** Frederico Gil (POR) d. Piero Luisi (VEN) 75 62.
Doubles: Ricardo Chile-Fonte/Sandor Martinez-Breijo (CUB) d. Martin Fischer/Philipp Oswald (AUT) 67(5) 76(3) 63.

● **CHERKASSY** (UKR) ($10,000) 3-9 OCTOBER – **Singles:** Lukas Lacko (SVK) d. Sascha Kloer (GER) 26 63 61.
Doubles: Mikhail Filima/Orest Tereshchuk (UKR) d. Fotos Kallias (CYP)/Laurent Recouderc (FRA) 64 62.

● **EL EJIDO** (ESP) ($15,000) 3-9 OCTOBER – **Singles:** David Marrero-Santana (ESP) d. Jesse Huta-Galung (NED) 63 64.
Doubles: Marcel Granollers-Pujol/David Marrero-Santana (ESP) d. Marcos Jimenez-Letrado/Juan-Miguel Such-Perez (ESP) 64 64.

● **KAWANA, QLD** (AUS) ($15,000) 3-9 OCTOBER – **Singles:** Gero Kretschmer (GER) d. Sadik Kadir (AUS) 76(5) 63.
Doubles: Robert Smeets (AUS)/Aleksander Vlaski (SCG) d. Alun Jones/Joseph Sirianni (AUS) 67(4) 62 10(4).

● **LAGUNA NIGUEL, CA** (USA) ($10,000) 3-9 OCTOBER – **Singles:** Benjamin Becker (GER) d. Zack Fleishman (USA) 63 64.
Doubles: Erik Chvojka/Philip Gubenco (CAN) d. Lester Cook (USA)/Robert Steckley (CAN) 76(4) 46 61.

● **MEDELLIN** (COL) ($15,000) 3-9 OCTOBER – **Singles:** Santiago Giraldo (COL) d. Luciano Vitullo (ARG) 26 64 75.
Doubles: Felipe Parada (CHI)/Luciano Vitullo (ARG) d. Michael Quintero/Sergio Ramirez (COL) 63 75.

ITF Men's Circuit 2005 Futures Results (continued)

- **NEVERS** (FRA) ($15,000+H) 3-9 OCTOBER – **Singles:** Florin Mergea (ROM) d. Jean-Michel Pequery (FRA) 76(4) 67(2) 62.
Doubles: Julien Jeanpierre/Jean-Michel Pequery (FRA) d. David Sherwood/Kyle Spencer (GBR) 64 67(7) 75.

- **SANTA CRUZ** (BOL) ($15,000) 3-9 OCTOBER – **Singles:** Antonio Pastorino (ARG) d. Martin Vilarrubi (URU) 76(6) 61.
Doubles: Alejandro Fabbri (ARG)/Martin Vilarrubi (URU) d. Maximo Gonzalez/Damian Patriarca (ARG) 76(4) 64.

- **TORREON** (MEX) ($10,000) 3-9 OCTOBER – **Singles:** Dawid Olejniczak (POL) d. Antonio Ruiz-Rosales (MEX) 75 62.
Doubles: Michal Domanski/Dawid Olejniczak (POL) d. Bruno Echagaray/Carlos Palencia (MEX) 64 64.

- **CORDOBA** (ESP) ($10,000) 10-16 OCTOBER – **Singles:** Alessandro Da Col (ITA) d. Fabio Colangelo (ITA) 61 26 64.
Doubles: Fabio Colangelo/Alessandro Da Col (ITA) d. Antonio Ochoa-Collado/Alejandro Vargas-Garcia (ESP) 64 64.

- **GABORONE** (BOT) ($10,000) 10-16 OCTOBER – **Singles:** Andrew Anderson (RSA) d. Genius Chidzikwe (ZIM) 76(4) 26 62.
Doubles: Nick Monroe (USA)/Izak Van Der Merwe (RSA) d. Genius Chidzikwe/Gwinyai Tongoona (ZIM) 64 63.

- **ILLYICHOVSK** (UKR) ($10,000) 10-16 OCTOBER – **Singles:** Fotos Kallias (CYP) d. Lukas Lacko (SVK) 63 57 61.
Doubles: Sergei Bubka/Mikhail Filima (UKR) d. Nikolai Dyachok/Aleksandr Nedovesov (UKR) 61 63.

- **JERSEY** (GBR) ($10,000) 10-16 OCTOBER – **Singles:** Matthew Smith (GBR) d. Simon Harston (GBR) 63 64.
Doubles: David Corrie (GBR)/Philip Stolt (USA) d. Eric Butorac/Chris Drake (USA) 75 67(5) 76(3).

- **LAGOS** (NGR) ($15,000+H) 10-16 OCTOBER – **Singles:** Henry Adjei-Darko (GHA) d. Valentin Sanon (CIV) 57 64 76(1).
Doubles: Rafael Arevalo-Gonzalez (ESA)/Alexander Satschko (GER) d. Colin Beecher/Ross Hutchins (GBR) 67(3) 64 64.

- **MONTERREY** (MEX) ($10,000) 10-16 OCTOBER – **Singles:** Bruno Echagaray (MEX) d. Victor Romero (MEX) 76(8) 62.
Doubles: Zach Dailey/Troy Hahn (USA) d. Yaoki Ishii/Joji Miyao (JPN) 64 57 76(4).

- **BRISBANE, QLD** (AUS) ($15,000) 10-16 OCTOBER – **Singles:** Robert Smeets (AUS) d. Mark Nielsen (NZL) 75 63.
Doubles: Adam Feeney/Robert Smeets (AUS) d. Scott Doerner (AUS)/Aleksander Vlaski (SCG) w/o.

- **SAINT-DIZIER** (FRA) ($15,000) 10-16 OCTOBER – **Singles:** Jo-Wilfried Tsonga (FRA) d. Thorsten Popp (GER) 60 76(8).
Doubles: Rok Jarc/Grega Zemlja (SLO) d. Olivier Charroin/Gary Lugassy (FRA) 36 76(4) 60.

- **SASSARI** (ITA) ($10,000) 10-16 OCTOBER – **Singles:** Stefano Galvani (ITA) d. Tony Holzinger (GER) 63 67(6) 63.
Doubles: Farrukh Dustov (UZB)/Manuel Gasbarri (ITA) d. Giancarlo Petrazzuolo/Federico Torresi (ITA) 75 36 76(4).

- **VALENCIA** (VEN) ($10,000) 10-16 OCTOBER – **Singles:** Matthew Behrmann (USA) d. Piero Luisi (VEN) 63 57 62.
Doubles: Piero Luisi/David Navarrete (VEN) d. Ricardo Chile-Fonte/Sandor Martinez-Breijo (CUB) 67(3) 76(4) 75.

- **ARLINGTON, TX** (USA) ($15,000) 17-23 OCTOBER – **Singles:** Michael Russell (USA) d. Benedikt Dorsch (GER) 61 63.
Doubles: Kelly Jones/Pete Stroer (USA) d. Bo Hodge/Hamid Mirzadeh (USA) 60 36 61.

- **BARCELONA** (ESP) ($10,000) 17-23 OCTOBER – **Singles:** Stephane Robert (FRA) d. Pablo Andujar-Alba (ESP) 75 63.
Doubles: Antonio Baldellou-Esteva/German Puentes-Alcaniz (ESP) d. David Marrero-Santana/Gabriel Trujillo-Soler (ESP) 76(4) 64.

- **BULAWAYO** (ZIM) ($10,000) 17-23 OCTOBER – **Singles:** Izak Van Der Merwe (RSA) d. Andrew Anderson (RSA) 46 64 63.
Doubles: Nick Monroe (USA)/Izak Van Der Merwe (RSA) d. Andrew Anderson/Stephen Mitchell (RSA) 46 63 60.

- **OBREGON** (MEX) ($10,000) 17-23 OCTOBER – **Singles:** Rodrigo-Antonio Grilli (BRA) d. Roman Borvanov (USA) 61 76(5).
Doubles: Jonathan Chu/Alberto Francis (USA) d. Bruno Echagaray/Carlos Palencia (MEX) 26 76(5) 62.

- **LA ROCHE SUR YON** (FRA) ($15,000+H) 17-23 OCTOBER – **Singles:** Olivier Vandewiele (FRA) d. Florin Mergea (ROM) 76(2) 36 64.
Doubles: Julien Jeanpierre/Nicolas Renavand (FRA) d. Darko Madjarovski/Petar Popovic (SCG) 06 63 64.

- **LAGOS** (NGR) ($15,000+H) 17-23 OCTOBER – **Singles:** Komlavi Loglo (TOG) d. Johar-Mubarak Saeed (QAT) 64 36 63.
Doubles: Komlavi Loglo (TOG)/Valentin Sanon (CIV) d. Rafael Arevalo-Gonzalez (ESA)/Alexander Satschko (GER) 36 64 61.

- **LECCE** (ITA) ($10,000) 17-23 OCTOBER – **Singles:** Eric Prodon (FRA) d. Farrukh Dustov (UZB) 36 64 64.
Doubles: Leonardo Azzaro/Giancarlo Petrazzuolo (ITA) d. Daniele Giorgini/Matteo Volante (ITA) 60 64.

- **PRAGUE** (CZE) ($10,000) 17-23 OCTOBER – **Singles:** Max Raditschnigg (AUT) d. Karel Triska (CZE) 61 61.
Doubles: Daniel Lustig (CZE)/Filip Polasek (SVK) d. Michal Navratil/Mirko Zapletal (CZE) 64 62.

- **SANTIAGO** (CHI) ($10,000) 17-23 OCTOBER – **Singles:** Maximo Gonzalez (ARG) d. Simone Vagnozzi (ITA) 75 16 63.
Doubles: Alejandro Fabbri (ARG)/Martin Vilarrubi (URU) d. Juan-Pablo Amado/Agustin Tarantino (ARG) 61 62.

- **MAZATLAN, SINALOA** (MEX) ($10,000) 24-30 OCTOBER – **Singles:** Bruno Echagaray (MEX) d. Pierre-Ludovic Duclos (CAN) 63 64.
Doubles: Richard Irwin (GBR)/Dawid Olejniczak (POL) d. Bruno Echagaray/Daniel Langre (MEX) 76(4) 60.

- **OPAVA** (CZE) ($10,000) 24-30 OCTOBER – **Singles:** Jan Vacek (CZE) d. Victor Crivoi (ROM) 63 63.
Doubles: Daniel Lustig (CZE)/Filip Polasek (SVK) d. Evgeny Kirillov/Alexander Krasnorutskiy (RUS) 64 61.

- **PRETORIA** (RSA) ($10,000) 24-30 OCTOBER – **Singles:** Nick Monroe (USA) d. Stephen Mitchell (RSA) 64 76(4).
Doubles: Andrew Anderson/Stephen Mitchell (RSA) d. Nick Monroe (USA)/Izak Van Der Merwe (RSA) 67(4) 64 62.

- **RODEZ** (FRA) ($10,000+H) 24-30 OCTOBER – **Singles:** Mathieu Montcourt (FRA) d. Tobias Clemens (GER) 63 62.
Doubles: Xavier Audouy/Jean-Francois Bachelot (FRA) d. Jesse Huta-Galung/Melvyn Op Der Heijde (NED) 76(3) 64.

- **SANT CUGAT** (ESP) ($10,000) 24-30 OCTOBER – **Singles:** Gorka Fraile-Exteberria (ESP) d. Xavier Pujo (FRA) 75 63.
Doubles: Diego Alvarez/Guillermo Carry (ARG) d. Antonio Baldellou-Esteva/German Puentes-Alcaniz (ESP) 46 62 64.

- **WACO, TX** (USA) ($15,000) 24-30 OCTOBER – **Singles:** Benjamin Becker (GER) d. Scott Oudsema (USA) 76(4) 61.
Doubles: Benjamin Becker (GER)/Jason Marshall (USA) d. Johan Brunstrom (SWE)/Philip Stolt (USA) 63 76(4).

- **FRYDLANT NAD OSTRAVICI** (CZE) ($10,000) 31 OCTOBER-6 NOVEMBER – **Singles:** Jan Hajek (CZE) d. Lukas Lacko (SVK) 16 75 64.
Doubles: Daniel Lustig (CZE)/Filip Polasek (SVK) d. Roman Kutac/Karel Triska (CZE) 63 64.

- **LEON, GUANAJUATO** (MEX) ($10,000) 31 OCTOBER-6 NOVEMBER – **Singles:** Victor Romero (MEX) d. Riccardo Ghedin (ITA) 63 75.
Doubles: Daniel Garza (MEX)/Michael Quintero (COL) d. Mikael Ekman/Carl-Henrik Hansen (SWE) 36 61 76(10).

- **PRETORIA** (RSA) ($10,000) 31 OCTOBER-6 NOVEMBER – **Singles:** Andrew Anderson (RSA) d. Stephen Mitchell (RSA) 62 36 63.
Doubles: Andrew Anderson/Stephen Mitchell (RSA) d. James Cerretani (USA)/Jason Pieters (RSA) 63 64.

- **SANTIAGO** (CHI) ($10,000) 31 OCTOBER-6 NOVEMBER – **Singles:** Guillermo Hormazabal (CHI) d. Pablo Galdon (ARG) 76(4) 75.
Doubles: Emiliano Redondi/Patricio Rudi (ARG) d. Thomaz Bellucci (BRA)/Filip Urban (POL) 76(1) 63.

- **SINT-KATELIJNE-WAVER** (BEL) ($15,000) 31 OCTOBER-6 NOVEMBER – **Singles:** Richard Bloomfield (GBR) d. Gary Lugassy (FRA) 63 63.
Doubles: Kirill Ivanov-Smolensky/Denis Matsukevitch (RUS) d. Richard Bloomfield/David Sherwood (GBR) 75 62.

- **TORONTO** (CAN) ($10,000) 31 OCTOBER-6 NOVEMBER – **Singles:** Matthew Behrmann (USA) d. Philip Stolt (USA) 67(3) 63 75.
Doubles: Benjamin Becker (GER)/Philip Stolt (USA) d. Marco Crugnola (ITA)/Yordan Kanev (BUL) 76(4) 46 64.

- **VILAFRANCA** (ESP) ($10,000) 31 OCTOBER-6 NOVEMBER – **Singles:** Pablo Andujar-Alba (ESP) d. Nick Van Der Meer (NED) 26 63 75.
Doubles: Diego Alvarez/Guillermo Carry (ARG) d. Andreu Guilera-Jover/Jordi Marse-Vidri (ESP) 61 61.

- **ABERFOYLE PARK, SA** (AUS) ($15,000) 7-13 NOVEMBER – **Singles:** Marc Kimmich (AUS) d. Frederik Nielsen (DEN) 63 62.
Doubles: Carsten Ball/Andrew Coelho (AUS) d. Adam Feeney/Joel Kerley (AUS) 67(9) 64 10(13).

- **JIANGMEN** (CHN) ($15,000) 7-13 NOVEMBER – **Singles:** Kyu-Tae Im (KOR) d. Melvyn Op Der Heijde (NED) 57 63 60.
Doubles: Alexander Peya (AUT)/Lars Uebel (GER) d. Kyu-Tae Im/Sun-Yong Kim (KOR) 76(4) 75.

- **MARACAY** (VEN) ($15,000) 7-13 NOVEMBER – **Singles:** Jhonathan Medina (VEN) d. Yohny Romero (VEN) 63 64.
Doubles: Brian Dabul (ARG)/Marcel Felder (URU) d. Pablo Cuevas (URU)/Horacio Zeballos (ARG) 75 64.

ITF Men's Circuit 2005 Futures Results (continued)

- **QUERETARO** (MEX) ($10,000) 7-13 NOVEMBER – **Singles:** Rodrigo-Antonio Grilli (BRA) d. Martin Fischer (AUT) 64 06 63.
  Doubles: Mikael Ekman/Carl-Henrik Hansen (SWE) d. Miguel-Angel Reyes-Varela/Bruno Rodriguez (MEX) 63 62.

- **RIMOUSKI** (CAN) ($10,000) 7-13 NOVEMBER – **Singles:** Benjamin Becker (GER) d. Lee Childs (GBR) 36 63 64.
  Doubles: Ross Hutchins/Jamie Murray (GBR) d. Lee Childs (GBR)/Frederick Sundsten (NOR) 76(5) 76(6).

- **SANTIAGO** (CHI) ($10,000) 7-13 NOVEMBER – **Singles:** Leonardo Mayer (ARG) d. Emiliano Redondi (ARG) 63 64.
  Doubles: Guillermo Hormazabal/Luis Hormazabal (CHI) d. Borja Malo/Hans Podlipnik (CHI) 62 46 64.

- **WAIKOLOA, HI** (USA) ($15,000) 7-13 NOVEMBER – **Singles:** Wayne Odesnik (USA) d. Scott Lipsky (USA) 61 61.
  Doubles: Scott Lipsky/David Martin (USA) d. Tyler Cleveland/Dave Lingman (USA) 75 62.

- **WATERLOO** (BEL) ($15,000) 7-13 NOVEMBER – **Singles:** Stephane Bohli (SUI) d. Andrey Golubev (RUS) 63 64.
  Doubles: Maxime Authom/Frederic De Fays (BEL) d. Maxime Braeckman/Jeroen Masson (BEL) 76(5) 61.

- **ANTOFAGASTA** (CHI) ($10,000) 14-20 NOVEMBER – **Singles:** Leandro Migani (ARG) d. Ricardo Hocevar (BRA) 62 62.
  Doubles: Guillermo Hormazabal/Luis Hormazabal (CHI) d. Hermes Gamonal/Roberto Lau (CHI) 63 64.

- **BERRI** (AUS) ($15,000) 14-20 NOVEMBER – **Singles:** Luke Bourgeois (AUS) d. Joseph Sirianni (AUS) 61 36 63.
  Doubles: Carsten Ball/Andrew Coelho (AUS) d. Rohan Bopanna (IND)/Horia Tecau (ROM) 57 63 10(5).

- **GRAN CANARIA** (ESP) ($15,000) 14-20 NOVEMBER – **Singles:** Ivo Klec (GER) d. Rui Machado (POR) 63 63.
  Doubles: Marcel Granollers-Pujol/David Marrero-Santana (ESP) d. Antonio Baldellou-Esteva (ESP)/Jose Luis Muguruza (ARU) 61 63.

- **HONOLULU, HI** (USA) ($15,000) 14-20 NOVEMBER – **Singles:** Wayne Odesnik (USA) d. Samuel Querrey (USA) 64 63.
  Doubles: Marco Crugnola/Stefano Ianni (ITA) d. Brendan Evans/Pete Stroer (USA) 16 63 76(4).

- **JIANGMEN** (CHN) ($15,000) 14-20 NOVEMBER – **Singles:** Lars Uebel (GER) d. Melvyn Op Der Heijde (NED) 63 62.
  Doubles: Alexander Peya (AUT)/Lars Uebel (GER) d. Yu Wang/Xin-Yuan Yu (CHN) 76(7) 64.

- **MARACAY** (VEN) ($15,000) 14-20 NOVEMBER – **Singles:** Pablo Cuevas (URU) d. Yohny Romero (VEN) 62 30 ret.
  Doubles: Brian Dabul (ARG)/Marcel Felder (URU) d. Piero Luisi/David Navarrete (VEN) 75 64.

- **MONTREAL** (CAN) ($10,000) 14-20 NOVEMBER – **Singles:** Benjamin Becker (GER) d. Ross Hutchins (GBR) 64 64.
  Doubles: Clay Donato (CAN)/Jesse Levine (USA) d. Peter Polansky/Adil Shamasdin (CAN) 62 67(5) 63.

- **SFAX** (TUN) ($10,000) 14-20 NOVEMBER – **Singles:** Tony Holzinger (GER) d. Benjamin Balleret (MON) 16 61 75.
  Doubles: Rok Jarc/Blaz Kavcic (SLO) d. Gordan Peranec (CRO)/Carlos Rexach-Itoiz (ESP) 76(8) 61.

- **ASHKELON** (ISR) ($10,000) 21-27 NOVEMBER – **Singles:** Robin Haase (NED) d. Dekel Valtzer (ISR) 61 36 62.
  Doubles: Roman Kutac/Michal Navratil (CZE) d. Robin Haase/Igor Sijsling (NED) 76(2) 36 62.

- **BARMERA** (AUS) ($15,000) 21-27 NOVEMBER – **Singles:** Horia Tecau (ROM) d. Luke Bourgeois (AUS) 36 62 75.
  Doubles: Samuel Groth/Joseph Sirianni (AUS) d. Callum Beale/Joel Kerley (AUS) 62 57 10(4).

- **GRAN CANARIA** (ESP) ($15,000) 21-27 NOVEMBER – **Singles:** Rui Machado (POR) d. Ivo Klec (GER) 26 63 63.
  Doubles: David De Miguel-Lapiedra (ESP)/Rui Machado (POR) d. Pablo Andujar-Alba (ESP)/Dusan Karol (CZE) 46 64 64.

- **MONASTIR** (TUN) ($10,000) 21-27 NOVEMBER – **Singles:** Tony Holzinger (GER) d. Lamine Ouahab (ALG) 76(1) 64.
  Doubles: Mikhail Elgin/Denis Matsukevitch (RUS) d. Martin Emmrich/Tony Holzinger (GER) 63 60.

- **COLOMBO** (SRI) ($10,000) 28 NOVEMBER-4 DECEMBER – **Singles:** Go Soeda (JPN) d. Toshihide Matsui (JPN) 46 75 75.
  Doubles: Ravi-Shankar Pathanjali/Vinod Sridhar (IND) d. Hsin-Han Lee/Chu-Huan Yi (TPE) 63 63.

- **MENZAH** (TUN) ($10,000) 28 NOVEMBER-4 DECEMBER – **Singles:** Farrukh Dustov (UZB) d. Frederic Jeanclaude (FRA) 64 61.
  Doubles: Mohammed Al Ghareeb (KUW)/Oualid Jallali (TUN) d. Pawel Dilaj/Robert Godlewski (POL) 62 64.

- **PONTEVEDRA** (ESP) ($10,000) 28 NOVEMBER-4 DECEMBER – **Singles:** Gorka Fraile-Exteberria (ESP) d. Rui Machado (POR) 61 67(1) 76(3).
Doubles: Antonio Baldellou-Esteva/Jordi Marse-Vidri (ESP) d. Gorka Fraile-Exteberria/Hector Ruiz-Cadenas (ESP) 63 62.

- **RAMAT HASHARON** (ISR) ($10,000) 28 NOVEMBER-4 DECEMBER – **Singles:** Lazar Magdincev (MKD) d. Aleksandr Nedovesov (UKR) 76(3) 76(2).
Doubles: Victor Kolik/Dudi Sela (ISR) d. Aleksandr Nedovesov (UKR)/Deniss Pavlovs (LAT) 63 63.

- **CHANDIGARH** (IND) ($10,000) 5-11 DECEMBER – **Singles:** Aisam Qureshi (PAK) d. Frank Moser (GER) 76(6) 67(5) 64.
Doubles: Karan Rastogi/Ashutosh Singh (IND) d. Frank Moser (GER)/Vishal Uppal (IND) 76(5) 63.

- **RAANANA** (ISR) ($10,000) 5-11 DECEMBER – **Singles:** Sebastian Rieschick (GER) d. Amir Hadad (ISR) 64 67(1) 63.
Doubles: Nick Monroe/Sam Warburg (USA) d. Ivan Cerovic (CRO)/Lazar Magdincev (MKD) 63 76(4).

- **DELHI** (IND) ($10,000+H) 12-18 DECEMBER – **Singles:** Sanam Singh (IND) d. Radoslav Nijaki (POL) 62 62.
Doubles: Ravi-Shankar Pathanjali/Vinod Sridhar (IND) d. Vijay Kannan/Ashutosh Singh (IND) 63 36 63.

Lamine Ouahab (ALG)

ITF Men's Circuit 2005 Satellite Results

Circuit (US$ Value)	Start date	Singles winner(s) (pts)	Doubles winner(s) (pts)
Spain 1 ($25,000)	3 Jan	David Marrero-Santana (ESP) (24)	Javier Garcia-Sintes (ESP) (33), German Puentes-Alcaniz (ESP) (33)
Portugal 1 ($25,000)	24 Jan	Rui Machado (POR) (33)	Marin Bradaric (CRO) (33), Nikola Martinovic (CRO) (33)
Great Britain 1 ($50,000)	31 Jan	Harsh Mankad (IND) (39)	Eric Butorac (USA) (41), Harsh Mankad (IND) (41)
Switzerland 1 ($25,000)	7 Feb	Michel Koning (NED) (35)	Matteo Galli (ITA) (29), Giuseppe Menga (ITA) (29)
Spain 2 ($25,000)	28 Feb	Mariano Albert-Ferrando (ESP) (34)	David Marrero-Santana (ESP) (31), Carlos Rexach-Itoiz (ESP) (31)
Croatia 1 ($25,000)	7 Mar	Gorka Fraile-Exteberria (ESP) (33)	Nikola Martinovic (CRO) (32)
Israel 1 ($25,000)	14 Mar	David Guez (FRA) (33)	Daniel Lustig (CZE) (34), Filip Polasek (SVK) (34)
Sweden/Denmark 1 ($25,000)	28 Mar	Philipp Marx (GER) (36)	Colin Fleming (GBR) (33), Jamie Murray (GBR) (33)
Turkey 1 ($25,000)	4 Apr	Carlos Cuadrado-Quero (ESP) (35)	Adrian Barbu (ROM) (30), Adrian Cruciat (ROM) (30)
Great Britain 2 ($25,000)	25 Apr	Flavio Cipolla (ITA) (35)	Flavio Cipolla (ITA) (36), Alessandro Motti (ITA) (36)
Bulgaria 1 ($25,000)	2 May	Frederico Gil (POR) (33), Ilia Kushev (BUL) (33)	Ilia Kushev (BUL) (33), Dimo Tolev (BUL) (33)
Venezuela 1 ($25,000)	2 May	Yohny Romero (VEN) (35)	Eric Butorac (USA) (34), Chris Drake (USA) (34)
India 1 ($25,000+H)	30 May	Peter Clarke (IRL) (45)	Jaco Mathew (IND) (43), Ashutosh Singh (IND) (43)
Great Britain 3 ($50,000)	25 Jul	Alun Jones (AUS) (43)	Joshua Goodall (GBR) (46), Ross Hutchins (GBR) (46)
China 1 ($25,000)	1 Aug	Yu Wang (CHN) (36)	Kamala Kannan (IND) (31)
Egypt 1 ($25,000)	1 Aug	Michal Navratil (CZE) (36)	Michal Navratil (CZE) (35), Filip Polasek (SVK) (35)
Switzerland 2 ($25,000)	29 Aug	Simone Vagnozzi (ITA) (35)	Bastian Knittel (GER) (33), Christopher Koderisch (GER) (33) Jordi Marse-Vidri (ESP) (33), Matteo Volante (ITA) (33)
Egypt 2 ($25,000)	12 Sep	Karim Maamoun (EGY) (33)	Karim Maamoun (EGY) (36), Mohamed Maamoun (EGY) (36)
Indonesia 1 ($25,000)	12 Sep	Chris Kwon (USA) (33)	Suwandi Suwandi (INA) (33), Bonit Wiryawan (INA) (33)
India 2 ($25,000+H)	19 Sep	Karan Rastogi (IND) (43)	Mustafa Ghouse (IND) (43), Vishal Uppal (IND) (43)
Germany 1 ($25,000)	3 Oct	Ernests Gulbis (LAT) (33)	Lado Chikhladze (GEO) (26), David Klier (GER) (26), Lukas Rosol (CZE) (26)
Great Britain 4 ($25,000)	24 Oct	Martin Lee (GBR) (33)	David Corrie (GBR) (33), Martin Lee (GBR) (33)

ITF Women's Circuit 2005 Results

- **$10,000 DUBAI** (UAE) 10-16 JANUARY – **Singles:** Sandra Klemenschits (AUT) d. Kyra Nagy (HUN) 64 61.
  Doubles: Daniela Klemenschits/Sandra Klemenschits (AUT) d. Kristina Grigorian (RUS)/Oxana Lyubtsova (UKR) 75 61.

- **$10,000 STUTTGART** (GER) 10-16 JANUARY – **Singles:** Mervana Jugic-Salkic (BIH) d. Sabine Klaschka (GER) 62 62.
  Doubles: Mervana Jugic-Salkic (BIH)/Darija Jurak (CRO) d. Danielle Harmsen/Eva Pera (NED) 63 75.

- **$10,000 TAMPA, FL** (USA) 10-16 JANUARY – **Singles:** Anda Perianu (ROM) d. Yan-Ze Xie (CHN) 75 57 64.
  Doubles: Julie Ditty (USA)/Vladimira Uhlirova (CZE) d. Cory-Ann Avants/Kristen Schlukebir (USA) 61 62.

- **$10,000 GRENOBLE** (FRA) 17-23 JANUARY – **Singles:** Mervana Jugic-Salkic (BIH) d. Karen Paterson (GBR) 63 61.
  Doubles: Mervana Jugic-Salkic (BIH)/Darija Jurak (CRO) d. Emilie Bacquet/Anais Laurendon (FRA) 62 62.

- **$10,000 MIAMI, FL** (USA) 17-23 JANUARY – **Singles:** Clarisa Fernandez (ARG) d. Yan-Ze Xie (CHN) 64 62.
  Doubles: Julie Ditty (USA)/Vladimira Uhlirova (CZE) d. Melanie Marois (CAN)/Sarah Riske (USA) 63 26 76(3).

- **$10,000 OBERHACHING** (GER) 17-23 JANUARY – **Singles:** Kristina Barrois (GER) d. Sabine Klaschka (GER) 75 64.
  Doubles: Kristina Barrois/Korina Perkovic (GER) d. Lucie Hradecka/Zuzana Zalabska (CZE) 63 57 76(6).

- **$10,000 TIPTON** (GBR) 17-23 JANUARY – **Singles:** Irina Bulykina (RUS) d. Katie O'Brien (GBR) 67(5) 62 64.
  Doubles: Surina De Beer (RSA)/Jane O'Donoghue (GBR) d. Katie O'Brien/Melanie South (GBR) 64 62.

- **$10,000 CLEARWATER, FL** (USA) 24-30 JANUARY – **Singles:** Ahsha Rolle (USA) d. Anda Perianu (ROM) 64 63.
  Doubles: Lauren Fisher/Amanda Johnson (USA) d. Anna Bastrikova (RUS)/Natalia Dziamidzenka (BLR) 46 64 63.

- **$10,000 HULL** (GBR) 24-30 JANUARY – **Singles:** Katie O'Brien (GBR) d. Ivanna Israilova (UZB) 64 64.
  Doubles: Irina Bulykina/Vasilisa Davydova (RUS) d. Katie O'Brien/Melanie South (GBR) 46 63 75.

- **$25,000 BELFORT** (FRA) 24-30 JANUARY – **Singles:** Sandra Kleinova (CZE) d. Tszvetana Pironkova (BUL) 64 63.
  Doubles: Michelle Gerards/Anouska Van Exel (NED) d. Daniela Klemenschits/Sandra Klemenschits (AUT) 61 42 ret.

- **$50,000 WAIKOLOA, HI** (USA) 24-30 JANUARY – **Singles:** Marie-Eve Pelletier (CAN) d. Hana Sromova (CZE) 46 61 64.
  Doubles: Natalie Grandin (RSA)/Kaysie Smashey (USA) d. Lauren Breadmore (AUS)/Ayami Takase (JPN) 63 64.

- **$10,000 VALE DO LOBO** (POR) 31 JANUARY-6 FEBRUARY – **Singles:** Madalina Gojnea (ROM) d. Lucia Jimenez-Almendros (ESP) 64 46 60.
  Doubles: Madalina Gojnea/Gabriela Niculescu (ROM) d. Irina Buryachok (UKR)/Olga Panova (RUS) 63 64.

- **$10,000 WELLINGTON** (NZL) 31 JANUARY-6 FEBRUARY – **Singles:** Leanne Baker (NZL) d. Mirielle Dittmann (AUS) 26 61 61.
  Doubles: Maki Arai (JPN)/Kyung-Mi Chang (KOR) d. Beti Sekulovski (AUS)/Aleksandra Srndovic (SWE) 36 64 64.

- **$25,000 ROCKFORD, IL** (USA) 31 JANUARY-6 FEBRUARY – **Singles:** Stephanie Dubois (CAN) d. Hana Sromova (CZE) 61 62.
  Doubles: Julie Ditty (USA)/Vladimira Uhlirova (CZE) d. Joana Cortez (BRA)/Svetlana Krivencheva (BUL) 36 75 75.

- **$25,000 SUNDERLAND** (GBR) 31 JANUARY-6 FEBRUARY – **Singles:** Sofia Arvidsson (SWE) d. Irina Bulykina (RUS) 61 61.
  Doubles: Sofia Arvidsson (SWE)/Martina Muller (GER) d. Katarina Misic/Dragana Zaric (SCG) 62 63.

- **$75,000 ORTISEI** (ITA) 31 JANUARY-6 FEBRUARY – **Singles:** Michaella Krajicek (NED) d. Sandra Kloesel (GER) 63 63.
  Doubles: Tina Pisnik (SLO)/Barbora Strycova (CZE) d. Mervana Jugic-Salkic (BIH)/Darija Jurak (CRO) 62 36 76(1).

- **$10,000 BLENHEIM** (NZL) 7-13 FEBRUARY – **Singles:** Kyung-Mi Chang (KOR) d. Mirielle Dittmann (AUS) 57 63 76(2).
  Doubles: Maki Arai (JPN)/Kyung-Mi Chang (KOR) d. Beti Sekulovski (AUS)/Aleksandra Srndovic (SWE) 64 76(3).

- **$10,000 MALLORCA** (ESP) 7-13 FEBRUARY – **Singles:** Christina Schiechtl (AUT) d. Matilde Munoz-Gonzalves (ESP) 63 61.
  Doubles: Adriana Gonzalez-Penas (ESP)/Romina Oprandi (ITA) d. Olga Brozda (POL)/Christina Schiechtl (AUT) 63 75.

- **$10,000 MONTECHORO** (POR) 7-13 FEBRUARY – **Singles:** Kristina Barrois (GER) d. Lisanne Balk (NED) 62 62.
  Doubles: Lenka Broosova/Jana Juricova (SVK) d. Emilie Bacquet/Anais Laurendon (FRA) 64 26 62.

- **$25,000 CAPRIOLO** (ITA) 7-13 FEBRUARY – **Singles:** Lucie Safarova (CZE) d. Mervana Jugic-Salkic (BIH) 64 61.
Doubles: Mariya Koryttseva (UKR)/Emma Laine (FIN) d. Klaudia Jans/Alicja Rosolska (POL) 36 64 75.

- **$25,000 REDBRIDGE** (GBR) 7-13 FEBRUARY – **Singles:** Nika Ozegovic (CRO) d. Elena Baltacha (GBR) 60 63.
Doubles: Giulia Casoni/Francesca Lubiani (ITA) d. Daria Kustava (BLR)/Ekaterina Makarova (RUS) 64 63.

- **$75,000 MIDLAND, MI** (USA) 7-13 FEBRUARY – **Singles:** Laura Granville (USA) d. Yoon-Jeong Cho (KOR) 63 36 76(6).
Doubles: Yulia Beygelzimer (UKR)/Kelly McCain (USA) d. Anna Bastrikova (RUS)/Iryna Kuryanovich (BLR) 62 64.

- **$10,000 BIBERACH** (GER) 14-20 FEBRUARY – **Singles:** Kristina Barrois (GER) d. Lucie Hradecka (CZE) 75 64.
Doubles: Lucie Hradecka/Sandra Zahlavova (CZE) d. Kristina Barrois/Stefanie Weis (GER) 57 62 75.

- **$10,000 MALLORCA** (ESP) 14-20 FEBRUARY – **Singles:** Romina Oprandi (ITA) d. Anna Floris (ITA) 63 60.
Doubles: Olga Brozda (POL)/Petra Cetkovska (CZE) d. Adriana Gonzalez-Penas (ESP)/Romina Oprandi (ITA) 63 64.

- **$10,000 PORTIMAO** (POR) 14-20 FEBRUARY – **Singles:** Lucia Jimenez-Almendros (ESP) d. Rebecca Llewellyn (GBR) 76(6) 64.
Doubles: Irina Buryachok (UKR)/Olga Panova (RUS) d. Anais Laurendon (FRA)/Linda Smolenakova (SVK) 64 62.

- **$25,000 BROMMA** (SWE) 14-20 FEBRUARY – **Singles:** Olga Savchuk (UKR) d. Emma Laine (FIN) 61 62.
Doubles: Michelle Gerards/Anouska Van Exel (NED) d. Ryoko Fuda/Rika Fujiwara (JPN) w/o.

- **$10,000 MELILLA** (ESP) 21-27 FEBRUARY – **Singles:** Sara Errani (ITA) d. Lucia Jimenez-Almendros (ESP) 61 64.
Doubles: Sara Errani (ITA)/Maria-Jose Martinez-Sanchez (ESP) d. Sheng-Nan Sun/Shu-Jing Yang (CHN) 67(2) 60 75.

- **$25,000 TAIPEI** (TPE) 21-27 FEBRUARY – **Singles:** Yung-Jan Chan (TPE) d. Seiko Okamoto (JPN) 63 62.
Doubles: Chia-Jung Chuang/Su-Wei Hsieh (TPE) d. Ryoko Fuda/Seiko Okamoto (JPN) 63 62.

- **$50,000 BENDIGO** (AUS) 21-27 FEBRUARY – **Singles:** Ye-Ra Lee (KOR) d. Shayna McDowell (AUS) 63 62.
Doubles: Casey Dell'Acqua/Trudi Musgrave (AUS) d. Beti Sekulovski/Cindy Watson (AUS) 64 76(2).

- **$50,000 ST PAUL, MN** (USA) 21-27 FEBRUARY – **Singles:** Laura Granville (USA) d. Akiko Morigami (JPN) 62 67(6) 62.
Doubles: Yulia Beygelzimer (UKR)/Sandra Kloesel (GER) d. Melanie Marois (CAN)/Sarah Riske (USA) 62 61.

- **$10,000 BUCHEN** (GER) 28 FEBRUARY-6 MARCH – **Singles:** Mervana Jugic-Salkic (BIH) d. Eva Hrdinova (CZE) 62 20 ret.
Doubles: Mervana Jugic-Salkic (BIH)/Darija Jurak (CRO) d. Korina Perkovic/Andrea Petkovic (GER) 62 62.

- **$10,000 GRAND CANARY** (ESP) 28 FEBRUARY-6 MARCH – **Singles:** Carla Suarez-Navarro (ESP) d. Petra Cetkovska (CZE) 26 64 63.
Doubles: Petra Cetkovska (CZE)/Katia Sabate-Orera (ESP) d. Bibiane Schoofs (NED)/Laura Vallverdu-Zaira (ESP) 67(5) 63 61.

- **$10,000 WARRNAMBOOL** (AUS) 28 FEBRUARY-6 MARCH – **Singles:** Marina Erakovic (NZL) d. Daniella Dominikovic (AUS) 62 46 63.
Doubles: Hye-Mi Kim (KOR)/Keiko Taguchi (JPN) d. Lucia Gonzalez/Christina Horiatopoulos (AUS) 76(7) 75.

- **$10,000 BENALLA** (AUS) 7-13 MARCH – **Singles:** Meng Yuan (CHN) d. Marina Erakovic (NZL) 64 64.
Doubles: Julia Vorobeva (RUS)/Meng Yuan (CHN) d. Lauren Cheung/Lisa D'Amelio (AUS) 64 63.

- **$10,000 GRAND CANARY** (ESP) 7-13 MARCH – **Singles:** Romina Oprandi (ITA) d. Christina Schiechtl (AUT) 63 62.
Doubles: Romina Oprandi (ITA)/Vanessa Wellauer (SUI) d. Irina Kotkina (RUS)/Charlene Vanneste (FRA) 75 62.

- **$10,000 NAPOLI** (ITA) 7-13 MARCH – **Singles:** Anna Floris (ITA) d. Raffaella Bindi (ITA) 62 63.
Doubles: Alberta Brianti (ITA)/Stefanie Haidner (AUT) d. Anna Floris/Giulia Meruzzi (ITA) 64 63.

- **$10,000 ROGASKA SLATINA** (SLO) 7-13 MARCH – **Singles:** Lucie Hradecka (CZE) d. Kristina Andlovic (SWE) 64 62.
Doubles: Lucie Hradecka/Zuzana Zalabska (CZE) d. Kristina Czafikova (SVK)/Andrea Hlavackova (CZE) 75 60.

- **$10,000 SUNDERLAND** (GBR) 7-13 MARCH – **Singles:** Kristina Barrois (GER) d. Anett Kaasik (EST) 76(2) 63.
Doubles: Verena Amesbauer (AUT)/Veronika Chvojkova (CZE) d. Lizaan Du Plessis (RSA)/Rebecca Llewellyn (GBR) 63 64.

- **$10,000 TOLUCA** (MEX) 7-13 MARCH – **Singles:** Larissa Carvalho (BRA) d. Julia Cohen (USA) 62 62.
Doubles: Valentina Castro (CHI)/Ana-Lucia Migliarini De Leon (URU) d. Lauren Fisher/Christina Fusano (USA) 62 46 75.

- **$10,000 AMIENS** (FRA) 14-20 MARCH – **Singles:** Renata Voracova (CZE) d. Karla Mraz (FRA) 46 62 63.
Doubles: Tatsiana Kapshay (BLR)/Renata Voracova (CZE) d. Sanne Van Den Biggelaar/Suzanne Van Hartingsveldt (NED) 26 76(5) 64.

- **$10,000 BOLTON** (GBR) 14-20 MARCH – **Singles:** Anne Keothavong (GBR) d. Veronika Chvojkova (CZE) 36 61 61.
Doubles: Lisanne Balk/Leonie Mekel (NED) d. Katarzyna Siwosz (POL)/Linda Smolenakova (SVK) 75 64.

- **$10,000 CAIRO** (EGY) 14-20 MARCH – **Singles:** Monica Niculescu (ROM) d. Galina Fokina (RUS) 64 62.
Doubles: Gabriela Niculescu/Monica Niculescu (ROM) d. Hanna Andreyeva/Valeria Bondarenko (UKR) 62 63.

- **$10,000 FUERTEVENTURA** (ESP) 14-20 MARCH – **Singles:** Laura Zelder (GER) d. Charlene Vanneste (FRA) 63 64.
Doubles: Annette Kolb/Laura Zelder (GER) d. Nuria Roig-Tost/Astrid Waernes-Garcia (ESP) 62 46 61.

- **$10,000 MORELIA** (MEX) 14-20 MARCH – **Singles:** Jenifer Widjaja (BRA) d. Frederica Piedade (POR) 16 64 75.
Doubles: Jorgelina Cravero/Veronica Spiegel (ARG) d. Daniela Klemenschits/Sandra Klemenschits (AUT) 64 62.

- **$10,000 ROME – BORGHESIANA** (ITA) 14-20 MARCH – **Singles:** Aravane Rezai (FRA) d. Maria Penkova (BUL) 62 63.
Doubles: Valentina Sulpizio (ITA)/Sandra Zahlavova (CZE) d. Raffaella Bindi/Stefania Chieppa (ITA) 75 64.

- **$10,000 YARRAWONGA** (AUS) 14-20 MARCH – **Singles:** Marina Erakovic (NZL) d. Emily Hewson (AUS) 63 46 64.
Doubles: Lara Picone (AUS)/Julia Vorobeva (RUS) d. Emily Hewson/Nicole Kriz (AUS) 64 63.

- **$50,000 ORANGE, CA** (USA) 14-20 MARCH – **Singles:** Yoon-Jeong Cho (KOR) d. Julia Schruff (GER) 76(3) 61.
Doubles: Carly Gullickson/Jennifer Hopkins (USA) d. Leanne Baker (NZL)/Francesca Lubiani (ITA) 63 64.

- **$10,000 AIN ALSOUKHNA** (EGY) 21-27 MARCH – **Singles:** Monica Niculescu (ROM) d. Magdalena Rybarikova (SVK) 63 64.
Doubles: Gabriela Niculescu/Monica Niculescu (ROM) d. Laura Husaru (ROM)/Sarah Raab (GER) 61 61.

- **$10,000 ATHENS** (GRE) 21-27 MARCH – **Singles:** Madalina Gojnea (ROM) d. Anna Gerasimou (GRE) 61 63.
Doubles: Lauren Breadmore (AUS)/Aurelie Vedy (FRA) d. Madalina Gojnea/Lenore Lazaroiu (ROM) 63 75.

- **$10,000 ROME – PARIOLI** (ITA) 21-27 MARCH – **Singles:** Romina Oprandi (ITA) d. Ana Jovanovic (SCG) 64 76(4).
Doubles: Valentina Sulpizio (ITA)/Sandra Zahlavova (CZE) d. Ivana Abramovic (CRO)/Stefanie Haidner (AUT) 75 57 61.

- **$25,000 REDDING, CA** (USA) 21-27 MARCH – **Singles:** Lucie Safarova (CZE) d. Ivana Lisjak (CRO) 62 63.
Doubles: Yulia Beygelzimer (UKR)/Stephanie Dubois (CAN) d. Leanne Baker (NZL)/Francesca Lubiani (ITA) 64 67(1) 63.

- **$25,000 SAN LUIS POTOSI** (MEX) 21-27 MARCH – **Singles:** Yvonne Meusburger (AUT) d. Kyra Nagy (HUN) 75 57 63.
Doubles: Lourdes Dominguez-Lino (ESP)/Clarisa Fernandez (ARG) d. Joana Cortez (BRA)/Tomoko Yonemura (JPN) 62 62.

- **$25,000 ST. PETERSBURG** (RUS) 21-27 MARCH – **Singles:** Ekaterina Bychkova (RUS) d. Emma Laine (FIN) 61 62.
Doubles: Nina Bratchikova/Ekaterina Makarova (RUS) d. Ekaterina Kosminskaya/Alla Kudryavtseva (RUS) 76(2) 62.

- **$10,000 BATH** (GBR) 28 MARCH-3 APRIL – **Singles:** Anne Keothavong (GBR) d. Claire Peterzan (GBR) 61 61.
Doubles: Surina De Beer (RSA)/Melanie South (GBR) d. Ekaterina Kozhokhina (RUS)/Trudi Musgrave (AUS) 62 75.

- **$10,000 BENIN CITY** (NGR) 28 MARCH-3 APRIL – **Singles:** Rebecca Dandeniya (GBR) d. Diana Vranceanu (GER) 46 64 76(3).
Doubles: Chantal Coombs (GBR)/Khushchehr Italia (IND) d. Karin Schlapbach (SUI)/Diana Vranceanu (GER) 63 62.

- **$10,000 CAIRO** (EGY) 28 MARCH-3 APRIL – **Singles:** Magdalena Rybarikova (SVK) d. Sarah Raab (GER) 61 63.
Doubles: Galina Fokina/Raissa Gourevitch (RUS) d. Katerina Avdiyenko/Marina Khomenko (UKR) 62 61.

- **$10,000 PATRAS** (GRE) 28 MARCH-3 APRIL – **Singles:** Madalina Gojnea (ROM) d. Antonia Tout (ROM) 75 62.
Doubles: Madalina Gojnea/Lenore Lazaroiu (ROM) d. Asmina Kaplani/Anna Koumantou (GRE) 63 62.

ITF Women's Circuit 2005 Results (continued)

- **$10,000 ROME – TIRO A VOLO** (ITA) 28 MARCH-3 APRIL – **Singles:** Romina Oprandi (ITA) d. Magda Mihalache (ROM) 64 64.
Doubles: Adriana Gonzalez-Penas (ESP)/Romina Oprandi (ITA) d. Greta Arn (GER)/Janette Bejlkova (CZE) 63 63.

- **$25,000 AUGUSTA, GA** (USA) 28 MARCH-3 APRIL – **Singles:** Saori Obata (JPN) d. Viktoria Azarenka (BLR) 62 62.
Doubles: Tatiana Poutchek (BLR)/Anastasia Rodionova (RUS) d. Rika Fujiwara/Saori Obata (JPN) 76(3) 60.

- **$25,000 POZA RICA** (MEX) 28 MARCH-3 APRIL – **Singles:** Mara Santangelo (ITA) d. Ryoko Fuda (JPN) 36 62 60.
Doubles: Seda Noorlander (NED)/Mara Santangelo (ITA) d. Daniela Klemenschits/Sandra Klemenschits (AUT) 62 46 63.

- **$10,000 MINSK** (BLR) 4-10 APRIL – **Singles:** Arina Rodionova (RUS) d. Aleksandra Malyarchikova (BLR) 60 62.
Doubles: Alexandra Panova/Olga Panova (RUS) d. Olga Govortsova (BLR)/Katerina Polunina (UKR) 75 63.

- **$10,000 BATH** (GBR) 4-10 APRIL – **Singles:** Melanie South (GBR) d. Anne Keothavong (GBR) 64 46 64.
Doubles: Anna Hawkins/Rebecca Llewellyn (GBR) d. Vanessa Pinto (GER)/Verdiana Verardi (ITA) 36 61 64.

- **$10,000 BENIN CITY** (NGR) 4-10 APRIL – **Singles:** Diana Vranceanu (GER) d. Carolina-Magalhaes Malheiros (BRA) 61 62.
Doubles: Chantal Coombs (GBR)/Khushchehr Italia (IND) d. Karin Schlapbach (SUI)/Diana Vranceanu (GER) 76(3) 26 63.

- **$10,000 MAKARSKA** (CRO) 4-10 APRIL – **Singles:** Sanja Ancic (CRO) d. Emilie Bacquet (FRA) 64 63.
Doubles: Aleksandra Lukic/Patricia Vollmeier (SLO) d. Melanie Hafner (GER)/Meta Sevsek (SLO) 64 62.

- **$10,000 MUMBAI** (IND) 4-10 APRIL – **Singles:** Chin-Wei Chan (TPE) d. Montinee Tangphong (THA) 62 63.
Doubles: Chin-Wei Chan (TPE)/Julia Vorobeva (RUS) d. Sanaa Bhambri (IND)/Mihaela Buzarnescu (ROM) 62 61.

- **$10,000 PORTO SANTO** (POR) 4-10 APRIL – **Singles:** Maria-Jose Argeri (ARG) d. Maraike Biglmaier (GER) 63 61.
Doubles: Maria-Jose Argeri (ARG)/Leticia Sobral (BRA) d. Annette Kolb/Laura Zelder (GER) 76(6) 61.

- **$10,000 RAMAT HASHARON** (ISR) 4-10 APRIL – **Singles:** Iveta Gerlova (CZE) d. Irina Buryachok (UKR) 36 64 61.
Doubles: Irina Buryachok (UKR)/Charlene Vanneste (FRA) d. Jessie De Vries (BEL)/Pemra Ozgen (TUR) 61 62.

- **$10,000 WUHAN** (CHN) 4-10 APRIL – **Singles:** Sheng-Nan Sun (CHN) d. Chen Liang (CHN) 63 46 63.
Doubles: Chun-Mei Ji/Dan Yu (CHN) d. Ayu-Fani Damayanti/Septi Mende (INA) 62 64.

- **$25,000 COATZACOALCOS** (MEX) 4-10 APRIL – **Singles:** Yvonne Meusburger (AUT) d. Shiho Hisamatsu (JPN) 36 64 63.
Doubles: Mariya Koryttseva (UKR)/Rita Kuti Kis (HUN) d. Kildine Chevalier (FRA)/Jorgelina Cravero (ARG) 62 63.

- **$25,000 ROME – EUR** (ITA) 4-10 APRIL – **Singles:** Tszvetana Pironkova (BUL) d. Magda Mihalache (ROM) 75 75.
Doubles: Alice Canepa/Emily Stellato (ITA) d. Adriana Barna (GER)/Andreea Vanc (ROM) 64 60.

- **$25,000 TUNICA, MS** (USA) 4-10 APRIL – **Singles:** Edina Gallovits (ROM) d. Varvara Lepchenko (UZB) 63 46 63.
Doubles: Tatiana Poutchek (BLR)/Anastasia Rodionova (RUS) d. Edina Gallovits (ROM)/Varvara Lepchenko (UZB) 62 64.

- **$75,000 DINAN** (FRA) 4-10 APRIL – **Singles:** Roberta Vinci (ITA) d. Zuzana Ondraskova (CZE) 75 75.
Doubles: Michaella Krajicek (NED)/Agnes Szavay (HUN) d. Yulia Beygelzimer (UKR)/Sandra Kloesel (GER) 75 75.

- **$10,000 CHANGSHA** (CHN) 11-17 APRIL – **Singles:** Yan-Ze Xie (CHN) d. Ying Yu (CHN) 61 61.
Doubles: Shu-Jing Yang/Ying Yu (CHN) d. Ayu-Fani Damayanti/Septi Mende (INA) 61 67(5) 62.

- **$10,000 HVAR** (CRO) 11-17 APRIL – **Singles:** Sanja Ancic (CRO) d. Masa Zec-Peskiric (SLO) 46 62 64.
Doubles: Wynne Prakusya/Romana Tedjakusuma (INA) d. Lucie Kriegsmannova/Darina Sedenkova (CZE) 16 60 63.

- **$10,000 PORTO SANTO** (POR) 11-17 APRIL – **Singles:** Surina De Beer (RSA) d. Laura Zelder (GER) 64 63.
Doubles: Maria-Jose Argeri (ARG)/Leticia Sobral (BRA) d. Lisanne Balk (NED)/Surina De Beer (RSA) 64 46 76(13).

- **$10,000 TAMPICO** (MEX) 11-17 APRIL – **Singles:** Lauren Barnikow (USA) d. Kildine Chevalier (FRA) 63 63.
Doubles: Kildine Chevalier (FRA)/Jorgelina Cravero (ARG) d. Andrea Benitez/Flavia Mignola (ARG) 76(6) 26 75.

- **$25,000 BIARRITZ** (FRA) 11-17 APRIL – **Singles:** Martina Muller (GER) d. Timea Bacsinszky (SUI) 46 76(2) 62.
Doubles: Stephanie Cohen-Aloro (FRA)/Selima Sfar (TUN) d. Timea Bacsinszky (SUI)/Aurelie Vedy (FRA) 62 61.

- **$25,000 CIVITAVECCHIA** (ITA) 11-17 APRIL – **Singles:** Magda Mihalache (ROM) d. Maret Ani (EST) 16 75 64.
Doubles: Lucie Hradecka/Sandra Zahlavova (CZE) d. Gabriela Niculescu/Monica Niculescu (ROM) 64 63.

- **$25,000 JACKSON, MS** (USA) 11-17 APRIL – **Singles:** Varvara Lepchenko (UZB) d. Ahsha Rolle (USA) 63 62.
Doubles: Anastasia Rodionova (RUS)/Kristen Schlukebir (USA) d. Ahsha Rolle (USA)/Milagros Sequera (VEN) 61 36 62.

- **$25,000 MUMBAI** (IND) 11-17 APRIL – **Singles:** Chin-Wei Chan (TPE) d. Rushmi Chakravarthi (IND) 64 62.
Doubles: Nina Bratchikova (RUS)/Francesca Lubiani (ITA) d. Rushmi Chakravarthi/Sai-Jayalakshmy Jayaram (IND) 63 64.

- **$10,000 BOL** (CRO) 18-24 APRIL – **Singles:** Sanja Ancic (CRO) d. Ivana Lisjak (CRO) 75 64.
Doubles: Mari Andersson/Kristina Andlovic (SWE) d. Sanja Ancic/Ivana Lisjak (CRO) 63 62.

- **$10,000 PORTO SANTO** (POR) 18-24 APRIL – **Singles:** Surina De Beer (RSA) d. Annette Kolb (GER) 60 61.
Doubles: Lisanne Balk (NED)/Surina De Beer (RSA) d. Maraike Biglmaier/Annette Kolb (GER) 63 36 63.

- **$10,000 YAMAGUCHI** (JPN) 18-24 APRIL – **Singles:** Lauren Breadmore (AUS) d. Erika Takao (JPN) 63 62.
Doubles: Maki Arai/Kumiko Iijima (JPN) d. Lisa D'Amelio/Christina Horiatopoulos (AUS) 63 76(6).

- **$25,000 BARI** (ITA) 18-24 APRIL – **Singles:** Darija Jurak (CRO) d. Olga Blahotova (CZE) 63 62.
Doubles: Stefanie Haidner (AUT)/Mervana Jugic-Salkic (BIH) d. Stefania Chieppa/Romina Oprandi (ITA) 63 76(3).

- **$25,000 VALENCIA – ROCAFORT** (ESP) 18-24 APRIL – **Singles:** Stephanie Foretz (FRA) d. Anna Floris (ITA) 63 60.
Doubles: Kildine Chevalier/Stephanie Foretz (FRA) d. Rosa-Maria Andres-Rodriguez/Arantxa Parra-Santonja (ESP) 46 76(5) 62.

- **$75,000 DOTHAN, AL** (USA) 18-24 APRIL – **Singles:** Milagros Sequera (VEN) d. Varvara Lepchenko (UZB) 26 62 64.
Doubles: Carly Gullickson (USA)/Galina Voskoboeva (RUS) d. Julie Ditty (USA)/Vladimira Uhlirova (CZE) 46 61 62.

- **$10,000 BOURNEMOUTH** (GBR) 25 APRIL-1 MAY – **Singles:** Gaelle Widmer (SUI) d. Georgie Stoop (GBR) 63 62.
Doubles: Claire Peterzan/Melanie South (GBR) d. Anna Hawkins/Holly Richards (GBR) 57 64 63.

- **$10,000 CAVTAT** (CRO) 25 APRIL-1 MAY – **Singles:** Darina Sedenkova (CZE) d. Kristina Andlovic (SWE) 60 57 62.
Doubles: Ivana Lisjak (CRO)/Korina Perkovic (GER) d. Meta Sevsek/Ana Skafar (SLO) 64 76(2).

- **$10,000 HERCEG NOVI** (SCG) 25 APRIL-1 MAY – **Singles:** Raluca Olaru (ROM) d. Miljana Adanko (HUN) 75 76(2).
Doubles: Raluca Olaru/Antonia Tout (ROM) d. Aleksandra Lukic/Patricia Vollmeier (SLO) 64 41 ret.

- **$10,000 JAKARTA** (INA) 25 APRIL-1 MAY – **Singles:** Ayu-Fani Damayanti (INA) d. Nudnida Luangnam (THA) 64 60.
Doubles: Ayu-Fani Damayanti/Septi Mende (INA) d. Orawan Lamangthong (THA)/Wukirasih Sawondari (INA) 61 63.

- **$10,000 RABAT** (MAR) 25 APRIL-1 MAY – **Singles:** Andreja Klepac (SLO) d. Dominika Cibulkova (SVK) 61 36 64.
Doubles: Anett Kaasik (EST)/Andreja Klepac (SLO) d. Meryem El Haddad/Habiba Ifrakh (MAR) 60 62.

- **$25,000 HAMANAKO** (JPN) 25 APRIL-1 MAY – **Singles:** Ryoko Fuda (JPN) d. Casey Dell'Acqua (AUS) 41 ret.
Doubles: Ryoko Fuda/Seiko Okamoto (JPN) d. Shiho Hisamatsu/Ayami Takase (JPN) 75 64.

- **$25,000 TARANTO** (ITA) 25 APRIL-1 MAY – **Singles:** Mara Santangelo (ITA) d. Kyra Nagy (HUN) 61 60.
Doubles: Mervana Jugic-Salkic (BIH)/Darija Jurak (CRO) d. Nadejda Ostrovskaya/Tatiana Poutchek (BLR) 63 67(3) 63.

- **$25,000 TORRENT** (ESP) 25 APRIL-1 MAY – **Singles:** Paula Garcia (ESP) d. Natalia Gussoni (ARG) 63 57 60.
Doubles: Sara Errani (ITA)/Paula Garcia (ESP) d. Nuria Roig-Tost/Gabriela Velasco-Andreu (ESP) 67(5) 64 62.

- **$50,000 LAFAYETTE, LA** (USA) 25 APRIL-1 MAY – **Singles:** Edina Gallovits (ROM) d. Olga Lazarchuk (UKR) 62 76(6).
Doubles: Beti Sekulovski/Cindy Watson (AUS) d. Maria-Fernanda Alves (BRA)/Marie-Eve Pelletier (CAN) 46 64 63.

ITF Women's Circuit 2005 Results (continued)

- **$75,000 CAGNES SUR MER** (FRA) 25 APRIL-1 MAY – **Singles:** Laura Pous-Tio (ESP) d. Ekaterina Bychkova (RUS) 76(4) 64. **Doubles:** Yulia Beygelzimer (UKR)/Sandra Kloesel (GER) d. Caroline Dhenin (FRA)/Andreea Vanc (ROM) 63 36 61.

- **$10,000 ANTALYA** (TUR) 2-8 MAY – **Singles:** Gabriela Niculescu (ROM) d. Aurelie Vedy (FRA) 57 62 62. **Doubles:** Gabriela Niculescu/Monica Niculescu (ROM) d. Irina Buryachok (UKR)/Olga Panova (RUS) 63 64.

- **$10,000 DUBROVNIK** (CRO) 2-8 MAY – **Singles:** Vanja Corovic (SCG) d. Evgeniya Rodina (RUS) 64 60. **Doubles:** Natalia Bogdanova (UKR)/Evgeniya Rodina (RUS) d. Tina Obrez/Meta Sevsek (SLO) 46 64 64.

- **$10,000 EDINBURGH** (GBR) 2-8 MAY – **Singles:** Ekaterina Kozhokhina (RUS) d. Melanie South (GBR) 64 63. **Doubles:** Rebecca Llewellyn/Melanie South (GBR) d. Leonie Mekel/Bibiane Schoofs (NED) 60 36 63.

- **$10,000 OBREGON** (MEX) 2-8 MAY – **Singles:** Daniela Munoz-Gallegos (MEX) d. Lauren Barnikow (USA) 76(5) 26 60. **Doubles:** Lauren Barnikow/Kelly Schmandt (USA) d. Lorena Arias-Rodriguez/Erika Clarke-Magana (MEX) 60 62.

- **$10,000 TARAKAN** (INA) 2-8 MAY – **Singles:** Wynne Prakusya (INA) d. Romana Tedjakusuma (INA) 64 62. **Doubles:** Wynne Prakusya/Romana Tedjakusuma (INA) d. Maya Rosa/Eny Sulistyowati (INA) 75 62.

- **$10,000 TORTOSA** (ESP) 2-8 MAY – **Singles:** Adriana Gonzalez-Penas (ESP) d. Anna Font-Estrada (ESP) 46 63 60. **Doubles:** Claire De Gubernatis (FRA)/Adriana Gonzalez-Penas (ESP) d. Anna Font-Estrada/Lourdes Pascual-Rodriguez (ESP) w/o.

- **$25,000 CATANIA** (ITA) 2-8 MAY – **Singles:** Jarmila Gajdosova (SVK) d. Ivana Abramovic (CRO) 63 75. **Doubles:** Alberta Brianti/Giulia Casoni (ITA) d. Giulia Gabba/Valentina Sulpizio (ITA) 63 63.

- **$25,000 WARSAW** (POL) 2-8 MAY – **Singles:** Tatiana Poutchek (BLR) d. Oxana Lyubtsova (UKR) 60 46 62. **Doubles:** Karolina Kosinska/Alicja Rosolska (POL) d. Tatiana Poutchek (BLR)/Anastasia Rodionova (RUS) 46 62 76(3).

- **$50,000 GIFU** (JPN) 2-8 MAY – **Singles:** Saori Obata (JPN) d. Shiho Hisamatsu (JPN) 61 26 64. **Doubles:** Rika Fujiwara/Saori Obata (JPN) d. Ryoko Fuda/Seiko Okamoto (JPN) 61 62.

- **$75,000 RALEIGH, NC** (USA) 2-8 MAY – **Singles:** Olga Lazarchuk (UKR) d. Mary Gambale (USA) 63 61. **Doubles:** Ashley Harkleroad/Lindsay Lee-Waters (USA) d. Maria-Fernanda Alves (BRA)/Stephanie Dubois (CAN) 62 06 63.

- **$10,000 AHMEDABAD** (IND) 9-15 MAY – **Singles:** Sheng-Nan Sun (CHN) d. Ankita Bhambri (IND) 62 62. **Doubles:** Ankita Bhambri/Sai-Jayalakshmy Jayaram (IND) d. Sanaa Bhambri/Shruti Dhawan (IND) 62 75.

- **$10,000 BUCHAREST** (ROM) 9-15 MAY – **Singles:** Alexandra Dulgheru (ROM) d. Liana Balaci (ROM) 62 62. **Doubles:** Bianca Bonifate/Madalina Gojnea (ROM) d. Asmina Kaplani/Anna Koumantou (GRE) 62 76(3).

- **$10,000 CASALE** (ITA) 9-15 MAY – **Singles:** Romina Oprandi (ITA) d. Sandra Zahlavova (CZE) 62 60. **Doubles:** Joana Cortez/Roxane Vaisemberg (BRA) d. Katalin Marosi (HUN)/Gloria Pizzichini (ITA) 62 60.

- **$10,000 FALKENBERG** (SWE) 9-15 MAY – **Singles:** Johanna Larsson (SWE) d. Sofia Arvidsson (SWE) 61 63. **Doubles:** Mari Andersson/Johanna Larsson (SWE) d. Natalia Kolat/Monika Schneider (POL) 61 61.

- **$10,000 LOS MOCHIS** (MEX) 9-15 MAY – **Singles:** Flavia Mignola (ARG) d. Jorgelina Cravero (ARG) 61 67(5) 64. **Doubles:** Jorgelina Cravero/Flavia Mignola (ARG) d. Lorena Arias-Rodriguez/Erika Clarke-Magana (MEX) 63 60.

- **$10,000 MOSTAR** (BIH) 9-15 MAY – **Singles:** Vanja Corovic (SCG) d. Agnes Szatmari (ROM) 64 61. **Doubles:** Daniela Krejsova/Michaela Michalkova (SVK) d. Jessie De Vries (BEL)/Agnes Szatmari (ROM) 67(5) 75 61.

- **$25,000 ANTALYA** (TUR) 9-15 MAY – **Singles:** Monica Niculescu (ROM) d. Ekaterina Dzehalevich (BLR) 62 62. **Doubles:** Gabriela Niculescu/Monica Niculescu (ROM) d. Renata Kucerkova (CZE)/Kathrin Woerle (GER) 67(0) 60 60.

- **$25,000 MONZON** (ESP) 9-15 MAY – **Singles:** Olena Antypina (UKR) d. Angelique Kerber (GER) 63 63. **Doubles:** Olena Antypina (UKR)/Surina De Beer (RSA) d. Petra Cetkovska (CZE)/Gabriela Velasco-Andreu (ESP) 75 75.

- **$50,000 CHARLOTTESVILLE, VA** (USA) 9-15 MAY – **Singles:** Carly Gullickson (USA) d. Varvara Lepchenko (UZB) 64 64.
Doubles: Ashley Harkleroad/Lindsay Lee-Waters (USA) d. Samantha Reeves (USA)/Christina Wheeler (AUS) 64 75.

- **$50,000 FUKUOKA** (JPN) 9-15 MAY – **Singles:** Yung-Jan Chan (TPE) d. Ayumi Morita (JPN) 63 62.
Doubles: Ryoko Fuda/Seiko Okamoto (JPN) d. Yung-Jan Chan/Chia-Jung Chuang (TPE) 62 76(1).

- **$50,000 SAINT GAUDENS** (FRA) 9-15 MAY – **Singles:** Aravane Rezai (FRA) d. Stephanie Gehrlein (GER) 64 26 62.
Doubles: Claire Curran (GBR)/Natalie Grandin (RSA) d. Maria-Jose Argeri (ARG)/Leticia Sobral (BRA) 63 61.

- **$10,000 EL PASO, TX** (USA) 16-22 MAY – **Singles:** Anda Perianu (ROM) d. Raquel Kops-Jones (USA) 36 76(2) 62.
Doubles: Beau Jones (USA)/Anda Perianu (ROM) d. Krista Damico/Cristina Moros (USA) 75 63.

- **$10,000 INDORE** (IND) 16-22 MAY – **Singles:** Isha Lakhani (IND) d. Sanaa Bhambri (IND) 61 67(3) 64.
Doubles: Ankita Bhambri/Sanaa Bhambri (IND) d. Isha Lakhani/Megha Vakharia (IND) 57 63 62.

- **$10,000 MAZATLAN** (MEX) 16-22 MAY – **Singles:** Anna Bastrikova (RUS) d. Lauren Barnikow (USA) 64 76(4).
Doubles: Jorgelina Cravero/Flavia Mignola (ARG) d. Lauren Barnikow/Kelly Schmandt (USA) 64 63.

- **$10,000 PITESTI** (ROM) 16-22 MAY – **Singles:** Alexandra Sere (ROM) d. Alexandra Dulgheru (ROM) 75 62.
Doubles: Madalina Gojnea/Gabriela Niculescu (ROM) d. Vojislava Lukic/Andrea Popovic (SCG) 64 63.

- **$10,000 ZADAR** (CRO) 16-22 MAY – **Singles:** Sarah Raab (GER) d. Josipa Bek (CRO) 57 62 63.
Doubles: Josipa Bek/Jelena Stanivuk (CRO) d. Bernadett Birkas (SCG)/Sayaka Yoshino (JPN) 60 60.

- **$25,000 CASERTA** (ITA) 16-22 MAY – **Singles:** Ivana Lisjak (CRO) d. Olga Blahotova (CZE) 63 75.
Doubles: Olga Blahotova (CZE)/Soledad Esperon (ARG) d. Ivana Lisjak/Nadja Pavic (CRO) 75 75.

- **$25,000 CHANGWON** (KOR) 16-22 MAY – **Singles:** Jin-Hee Kim (KOR) d. Chia-Jung Chuang (TPE) 46 63 64.
Doubles: Chia-Jung Chuang (TPE)/Seiko Okamoto (JPN) d. Chin-Wei Chan/Su-Wei Hsieh (TPE) 62 75.

- **$25,000 HO CHI MINH CITY** (VIE) 16-22 MAY – **Singles:** Wynne Prakusya (INA) d. Wen-Hsin Hsu (TPE) 64 61.
Doubles: Wynne Prakusya/Romana Tedjakusuma (INA) d. Akgul Amanmuradova (UZB)/Napaporn Tongsalee (THA) 64 60.

- **$25,000 TENERIFE** (ESP) 16-22 MAY – **Singles:** Petra Cetkovska (CZE) d. Carla Suarez-Navarro (ESP) 67(0) 63 61.
Doubles: Amanda Janes/Anne Keothavong (GBR) d. Julia Babilon/Adriana Barna (GER) 76(5) 36 63.

- **$10,000 BALS** (ROM) 23-29 MAY – **Singles:** Andrea Popovic (SCG) d. Lenka Dlhopolcova (SVK) 60 76(4).
Doubles: Bianca Bonifate/Gabriela Niculescu (ROM) d. Lenka Dlhopolcova (SVK)/Alexandra Iacob (ROM) 62 75.

- **$10,000 HOUSTON, TX** (USA) 23-28 MAY – **Singles:** Anda Perianu (ROM) d. Raquel Kops-Jones (USA) 62 63.
Doubles: Anda Perianu (ROM)/Kaysie Smashey (USA) d. Raquel Kops-Jones/Aleke Tsoubanos (USA) 46 62 64.

- **$10,000 KIEV** (UKR) 23-28 MAY – **Singles:** Alexandra Panova (RUS) d. Oxana Lyubtsova (UKR) 36 76(4) 20 ret.
Doubles: Alexandra Panova/Olga Panova (RUS) d. Vasilisa Davydova/Kristina Grigorian (RUS) 62 60.

- **$10,000 LA PALMA** (ESP) 23-28 MAY – **Singles:** Sara Del Barrio-Aragon (ESP) d. Teresa Ferrer-Lopez Cuervo (ESP) 61 57 63.
Doubles: Martina Pavelec/Andrea Sieveke (GER) d. Diana Aroutiounova (RUS)/Anett Kaasik (EST) 62 61.

- **$10,000 LEON** (MEX) 23-29 MAY – **Singles:** Mari Tanaka (JPN) d. Micaela Moran (ARG) 64 61.
Doubles: Andrea Benitez (ARG)/Daniela Munoz-Gallegos (MEX) d. Biffy Kaufman (USA)/Mari Tanaka (JPN) 64 16 61.

- **$10,000 OLECKO** (POL) 23-28 MAY – **Singles:** Darina Sedenkova (CZE) d. Radana Holusova (CZE) 75 61.
Doubles: Olga Brozda/Natalia Kolat (POL) d. Irina Kuzmina/Alise Vaidere (LAT) 57 61 61.

- **$10,000 OXFORD** (GBR) 23-27 MAY – **Singles:** Rebecca Llewellyn (GBR) d. Surina De Beer (RSA) 06 63 63.
Doubles: Anna Hawkins/Rebecca Llewellyn (GBR) d. Melissa Berry/Holly Richards (GBR) 61 64.

ITF Women's Circuit 2005 Results (continued)

- **$25,000 CAMPOBASSO** (ITA) 23-28 MAY – **Singles:** Mariya Koryttseva (UKR) d. Zuzana Kucova (SVK) 57 61 75.
Doubles: Giulia Casoni (ITA)/Bahia Mouhtassine (MAR) d. Katarina Kachlikova/Lenka Tvaroskova (SVK) 60 75.

- **$25,000 NAGANO** (JPN) 23-28 MAY – **Singles:** Mayumi Yamamoto (JPN) d. Seiko Okamoto (JPN) 62 62.
Doubles: Ryoko Takemura/Tomoko Yonemura (JPN) d. Hye-Mi Kim (KOR)/Keiko Taguchi (JPN) 61 76(5).

- **$25,000 PHUKET** (THA) 23-28 MAY – **Singles:** Ryoko Fuda (JPN) d. Montinee Tangphong (THA) 61 64.
Doubles: Akgul Amanmuradova (UZB)/Napaporn Tongsalee (THA) d. Monique Adamczak (AUS)/Annette Kolb (GER) 61 61.

- **$25,000 SHANGHAI** (CHN) 23-28 MAY – **Singles:** Daniela Kix (AUT) d. Suchanun Viratprasert (THA) 76(6) 63.
Doubles: Chia-Jung Chuang (TPE)/Remi Tezuka (JPN) d. Wan-Ting Liu/Sheng-Nan Sun (CHN) 46 64 61.

- **$10,000 HILTON HEAD, SC** (USA) 30 MAY-5 JUNE – **Singles:** Ansley Cargill (USA) d. Ekaterina Afinogenova (RUS) 46 63 76(8).
Doubles: Shadisha Robinson/Robin Stephenson (USA) d. Ansley Cargill/Aleke Tsoubanos (USA) 63 75.

- **$10,000 MONTERREY** (MEX) 30 MAY-5 JUNE – **Singles:** Andrea Benitez (ARG) d. Daniela Munoz-Gallegos (MEX) 61 62.
Doubles: Andrea Benitez (ARG)/Daniela Munoz-Gallegos (MEX) d. Lorena Arias-Rodriguez/Erika Clarke-Magana (MEX) 75 63.

- **$25,000 GALATINA** (ITA) 30 MAY-5 JUNE – **Singles:** Mariya Koryttseva (UKR) d. Elena Vesnina (RUS) 63 62.
Doubles: Casey Dell'Acqua/Lucia Gonzalez (AUS) d. Jarmila Gajdosova (SVK)/Tatiana Poutchek (BLR) 64 63.

- **$25,000 GUNMA** (JPN) 30 MAY-5 JUNE – **Singles:** Su-Wei Hsieh (TPE) d. Seiko Okamoto (JPN) 61 62.
Doubles: Chin-Wei Chan/Su-Wei Hsieh (TPE) d. Ayami Takase/Mayumi Yamamoto (JPN) 62 11 ret.

- **$25,000 NANJING** (CHN) 30 MAY-5 JUNE – **Singles:** Yan-Ze Xie (CHN) d. Daniela Kix (AUT) 62 62.
Doubles: Chia-Jung Chuang (TPE)/Yan-Ze Xie (CHN) d. Maria-Jose Argeri (ARG)/Leticia Sobral (BRA) 63 67(5) 62.

- **$25,000 RAANANA** (ISR) 30 MAY-5 JUNE – **Singles:** Tzipi Obziler (ISR) d. Margalita Chakhnashvili (GEO) 60 62.
Doubles: Tzipi Obziler/Shahar Peer (ISR) d. Daniela Klemenschits/Sandra Klemenschits (AUT) 76(2) 16 62.

- **$25,000 SURBITON** (GBR) 30 MAY-5 JUNE – **Singles:** Kristina Brandi (PUR) d. Laura Granville (USA) 63 61.
Doubles: Rika Fujiwara/Saori Obata (JPN) d. Jennifer Hopkins/Mashona Washington (USA) 46 64 62.

- **$75,000 PROSTEJOV** (CZE) 30 MAY-5 JUNE – **Singles:** Lucie Safarova (CZE) d. Tathiana Garbin (ITA) 64 36 63.
Doubles: Yulia Beygelzimer (UKR)/Mara Santangelo (ITA) d. Daja Bedanova/Barbora Strycova (CZE) 61 46 62.

- **$10,000 NAZARE** (POR) 6-12 JUNE – **Singles:** Florencia Molinero (ARG) d. Joana Cortez (BRA) 75 36 60.
Doubles: Joana Cortez (BRA)/Silvia Disderi (ITA) d. Pemra Ozgen (TUR)/Nana Urotadze (GEO) 67(3) 61 64.

- **$10,000 NUEVA SAN SALVADOR** (ESA) 6-12 JUNE – **Singles:** Andrea Benitez (ARG) d. Andrea Koch (CHI) 63 60.
Doubles: Andrea Benitez/Flavia Mignola (ARG) d. Patricia Holzman (ARG)/Andrea Koch (CHI) w/o.

- **$10,000 STARE SPLAVY** (CZE) 6-12 JUNE – **Singles:** Petra Novotnikova (CZE) d. Veronika Raimrova (CZE) 63 63.
Doubles: Iveta Gerlova/Lucie Kriegsmannova (CZE) d. Petra Novotnikova/Veronika Raimrova (CZE) 46 64 62.

- **$10,000 TOKYO** (JPN) 6-12 JUNE – **Singles:** Kanae Hisami (JPN) d. Mari Tanaka (JPN) 63 63.
Doubles: Natsuko Kurita/Ayumi Oka (JPN) d. Nozomi Aiba/Kana Okawa (JPN) 63 64.

- **$10,000 WARSAW** (POL) 6-12 JUNE – **Singles:** Agnieszka Radwanska (POL) d. Oksana Teplyakova (UKR) 61 63.
Doubles: Olga Brozda/Natalia Kolat (POL) d. Veronika Kapshay (UKR)/Elena Tchalova (RUS) 61 64.

- **$25,000 ALLENTOWN, PA** (USA) 6-12 JUNE – **Singles:** Varvara Lepchenko (UZB) d. Lindsay Lee-Waters (USA) 76(3) 64.
Doubles: Ansley Cargill/Julie Ditty (USA) d. Cory-Ann Avants/Kristen Schlukebir (USA) 62 63.

- **$25,000 GRADO** (ITA) 6-12 JUNE – **Singles:** Tatsiana Uvarova (BLR) d. Meng Yuan (CHN) 64 64.
Doubles: Maria Kondratieva (RUS)/Tatsiana Uvarova (BLR) d. Daniella Dominikovic (AUS)/Daria Kustava (BLR) 61 36 75.

- **$25,000 SEOUL** (KOR) 6-11 JUNE – **Singles:** Su-Wei Hsieh (TPE) d. Jin-Hee Kim (KOR) 62 26 63.
Doubles: Chin-Wei Chan/Su-Wei Hsieh (TPE) d. Maki Arai (JPN)/Eun-Jeong Lee (KOR) 62 61.

- **$50,000 BEIJING** (CHN) 6-12 JUNE – **Singles:** Ting Li (CHN) d. Zi Yan (CHN) 61 63.
Doubles: Zi Yan/Jie Zheng (CHN) d. Ting Li/Tian-Tian Sun (CHN) 61 75.

- **$50,000+H MARSEILLE** (FRA) 6-12 JUNE – **Singles:** Conchita Martinez-Granados (ESP) d. Marie-Eve Pelletier (CAN) 61 61.
Doubles: Liga Dekmeijere (LAT)/Caroline Dhenin (FRA) d. Maria-Fernanda Alves (BRA)/Marie-Eve Pelletier (CAN) 62 16 62.

- **$75,000 ZAGREB** (CRO) 6-12 JUNE – **Singles:** Zuzana Ondraskova (CZE) d. Tszvetana Pironkova (BUL) 46 64 63.
Doubles: Lucie Hradecka/Vladimira Uhlirova (CZE) d. Daniela Klemenschits/Sandra Klemenschits (AUT) 62 62.

- **$10,000 BUCHAREST** (ROM) 13-19 JUNE – **Singles:** Corina Corduneanu (ROM) d. Mihaela Moldovan (ROM) 62 60.
Doubles: Corina Corduneanu/Diana Enache (ROM) d. Alexandra Dulgheru/Mihaela Moldovan (ROM) 22 ret.

- **$10,000 FORT WORTH, TX** (USA) 13-19 JUNE – **Singles:** Tara Snyder (USA) d. Story Tweedie-Yates (USA) 63 63.
Doubles: Ansley Cargill/Tara Snyder (USA) d. Sabrina Capannolo/Jessica Leitch (USA) 63 76(2).

- **$10,000 LENZERHEIDE** (SUI) 13-19 JUNE – **Singles:** Danica Krstajic (SCG) d. Karin Knapp (ITA) 62 75.
Doubles: Petra Cetkovska (CZE)/Martina Lautenschlager (SUI) d. Eva-Maria Hoch (AUT)/Diana Vranceanu (GER) 60 63.

- **$10,000 LES FRANQUESES DEL VALLES** (ESP) 13-19 JUNE – **Singles:** Estrella Cabeza-Candela (ESP) d. Justine Ozga (GER) 76(3) 46 62.
Doubles: Hannah Kuervers/Justine Ozga (GER) d. Sandhya Nagaraj (IND)/Svenja Weidemann (GER) 62 62.

- **$10,000 MONTEMOR-O-NOVO** (POR) 13-19 JUNE – **Singles:** Ana Salas-Lozano (ESP) d. Laura Zelder (GER) 75 46 62.
Doubles: Marina Tavares/Carla Tiene (BRA) d. Sarah Raab/Laura Zelder (GER) 64 63.

- **$25,000 GORIZIA** (ITA) 13-19 JUNE – **Singles:** Ivana Lisjak (CRO) d. Alice Canepa (ITA) 62 63.
Doubles: Giulia Casoni/Valentina Sulpizio (ITA) d. Olena Antypina (UKR)/Nina Bratchikova (RUS) 62 60.

- **$25,000 INCHEON** (KOR) 13-19 JUNE – **Singles:** Su-Wei Hsieh (TPE) d. Mi Lyoo (KOR) 61 62.
Doubles: Chin-Wei Chan/Su-Wei Hsieh (TPE) d. Jin-Young Choi/Ye-Ra Lee (KOR) 62 76(4).

- **$10,000 ALCOBACA** (POR) 20-26 JUNE – **Singles:** Laura Zelder (GER) d. Andrea Sieveke (GER) 63 63.
Doubles: Joana Cortez (BRA)/Laura Zelder (GER) d. Rebecca Fong/Kirsty Woolley (GBR) w/o.

- **$10,000 ALKMAAR** (NED) 20-26 JUNE – **Singles:** Lia Jikia (GEO) d. Marrit Boonstra (NED) 64 61.
Doubles: Kelly De Beer (NED)/Jessie De Vries (BEL) d. Kristina Grigorian (RUS)/Liuodmila Nikoian (ARM) 36 63 64.

- **$10,000 BUCHAREST** (ROM) 20-26 JUNE – **Singles:** Ekaterina Ivanova (RUS) d. Corina Corduneanu (ROM) 46 63 75.
Doubles: Corina Corduneanu/Gabriela Niculescu (ROM) d. Ekaterina Ivanova/Elena Tchalova (RUS) 62 64.

- **$10,000 DAVOS** (SUI) 20-26 JUNE – **Singles:** Andrea Petkovic (GER) d. Janette Bejlkova (CZE) 64 62.
Doubles: Zuzana Hejdova (CZE)/Andrea Petkovic (GER) d. Petra Cetkovska (CZE)/Sandra Martinovic (BIH) 63 62.

- **$10,000 EDMOND, OK** (USA) 20-26 JUNE – **Singles:** Sarah Riske (USA) d. Anda Perianu (ROM) 36 63 64.
Doubles: Tamara Encina/Daron Moore (USA) d. Sarah Riske/Robin Stephenson (USA) 76(6) 64.

- **$10,000 ORESTIADA** (GRE) 20-26 JUNE – **Singles:** Claire De Gubernatis (FRA) d. Christine Sperling (GER) 64 67(4) 61.
Doubles: Claire De Gubernatis (FRA)/Christine Sperling (GER) d. Klara Jagosova (CZE)/Katerina Polunina (UKR) 75 62.

- **$10,000 OSLO** (NOR) 20-26 JUNE – **Singles:** Mari Andersson (SWE) d. Johanna Larsson (SWE) 64 64.
Doubles: Johanna Larsson/Nadja Roma (SWE) d. Kristina Andlovic (SWE)/Karoline Borgersen (NOR) 64 64.

- **$25,000 FONTANAFREDDA** (ITA) 20-26 JUNE – **Singles:** Sybille Bammer (AUT) d. Alice Canepa (ITA) 76(3) 62.
Doubles: Mervana Jugic-Salkic (BIH)/Darija Jurak (CRO) d. Eva Fislova/Stanislava Hrozenska (SVK) 57 63 64.

- **$25,000 PERIGUEUX** (FRA) 20-26 JUNE – **Singles:** Virginie Pichet (FRA) d. Ekaterina Dzehalevich (BLR) 63 76(8).
  Doubles: Katarina Kachlikova/Lenka Tvaroskova (SVK) d. Akgul Amanmuradova (UZB)/Antonia Matic (GER) 75 61.

- **$10,000 GALATI** (ROM) 27 JUNE-3 JULY – **Singles:** Corina Corduneanu (ROM) d. Anna Bastrikova (RUS) 63 57 64.
  Doubles: Corina Corduneanu/Gabriela Niculescu (ROM) d. Vasilisa Davydova/Olga Panova (RUS) 64 57 61.

- **$10,000 HEERHUGOWAARD** (NED) 27 JUNE-3 JULY – **Singles:** Kelly De Beer (NED) d. Marrit Boonstra (NED) 62 61.
  Doubles: Kristina Antoniychuk (UKR)/Ana Veselinovic (SCG) d. Marrit Boonstra/Nicole Thyssen (NED) 16 62 75.

- **$10,000 PADOVA** (ITA) 27 JUNE-3 JULY – **Singles:** Sandra Martinovic (BIH) d. Agnese Zucchini (ITA) 64 62.
  Doubles: Giulia Meruzzi/Nancy Rustignoli (ITA) d. Aleksandra Lukic/Tina Obrez (SLO) 57 61 62.

- **$10,000 SOUTH LAKE, TX** (USA) 27 JUNE-3 JULY – **Singles:** Megan Bradley (USA) d. Story Tweedie-Yates (USA) 64 62.
  Doubles: Anne Smith/Tara Snyder (USA) d. Megan Bradley/Shadisha Robinson (USA) 36 76(4) 76(4).

- **$25,000 BASTAD** (SWE) 27 JUNE-3 JULY – **Singles:** Hanna Nooni (SWE) d. Erica Krauth (ARG) 60 62.
  Doubles: Olena Antypina (UKR)/Nadejda Ostrovskaya (BLR) d. Erica Krauth (ARG)/Hanna Nooni (SWE) 75 36 63.

- **$25,000 MONT DE MARSAN** (FRA) 27 JUNE-3 JULY – **Singles:** Mathilde Johansson (FRA) d. Natalia Gussoni (ARG) 36 64 64.
  Doubles: Natalia Gussoni (ARG)/Frederica Piedade (POR) d. Emilie Bacquet/Violette Huck (FRA) 61 76(5).

- **$25,000 VAIHINGEN** (GER) 27 JUNE-3 JULY – **Singles:** Vanessa Henke (GER) d. Kyra Nagy (HUN) 62 06 64.
  Doubles: Yulia Beygelzimer (UKR)/Vanessa Henke (GER) d. Kristina Barrois/Kathrin Woerle (GER) 76(5) 61.

- **$50,000 LOS GATOS, CA** (USA) 27 JUNE-3 JULY – **Singles:** Lindsay Lee-Waters (USA) d. Carly Gullickson (USA) 64 60.
  Doubles: Teryn Ashley/Carly Gullickson (USA) d. Lindsay Lee-Waters/Kaysie Smashey (USA) 64 46 61.

- **$75,000 FANO** (ITA) 27 JUNE-3 JULY – **Singles:** Kaia Kanepi (EST) d. Melinda Czink (HUN) 36 61 75.
  Doubles: Gabriela Navratilova/Michaela Pastikova (CZE) d. Stefanie Haidner (AUT)/Valentina Sulpizio (ITA) 62 60.

- **$10,000 DAEGU** (KOR) 4-10 JULY – **Singles:** Mi-Ok Kim (KOR) d. Eun-Jeong Lee (KOR) 62 60.
  Doubles: Jeong-A Cho/Ji-Young Kim (KOR) d. Kazusa Ito/Yukiko Yabe (JPN) 76(1) 64.

- **$10,000 GETXO** (ESP) 4-10 JULY – **Singles:** Stefania Chieppa (ITA) d. Magali De Lattre (POR) 61 63.
  Doubles: Estrella Cabeza-Candela/Nuria Roig-Tost (ESP) d. Anna Gil-Mares (ESP)/Tara Wigan (GBR) 61 60.

- **$10,000 KRASNOARMEISK** (RUS) 4-9 JULY – **Singles:** Elena Tchalova (RUS) d. Irina Bulykina (RUS) 64 60.
  Doubles: Anna Bastrikova/Julia Vorobeva (RUS) d. Ekaterina Ivanova/Elena Tchalova (RUS) 62 76(3).

- **$10,000 LE TOUQUET** (FRA) 4-10 JULY – **Singles:** Karina-Ildor Jacobsgaard (DEN) d. Diana Brunel (FRA) 60 60.
  Doubles: Julie Coin/Alice Hall (FRA) d. Karla Mraz/Virginie Pichet (FRA) 75 76(5).

- **$25,000 DARMSTADT** (GER) 4-10 JULY – **Singles:** Vanessa Henke (GER) d. Eva Fislova (SVK) 76(4) 61.
  Doubles: Vanessa Henke/Laura Siegemund (GER) d. Vasilisa Bardina/Yaroslava Shvedova (RUS) 64 62.

- **$25,000 FELIXSTOWE** (GBR) 4-10 JULY – **Singles:** Jarmila Gajdosova (SVK) d. Alla Kudryavtseva (RUS) 75 61.
  Doubles: Leanne Baker (NZL)/Francesca Lubiani (ITA) d. Jarmila Gajdosova (SVK)/Alla Kudryavtseva (RUS) 61 46 32 ret.

- **$25,000 TORUN** (POL) 4-10 JULY – **Singles:** Ana Timotic (SCG) d. Joanna Sakowicz (POL) 61 62.
  Doubles: Nadejda Ostrovskaya (BLR)/Yevgenia Savransky (ISR) d. Zuzana Hejdova (CZE)/Joanna Sakowicz (POL) 61 75.

- **$50,000 COLLEGE PARK, MD** (USA) 4-10 JULY – **Singles:** Camille Pin (FRA) d. Ashley Harkleroad (USA) 26 62 63.
  Doubles: Maria-Jose Argeri (ARG)/Leticia Sobral (BRA) d. Ashley Harkleroad (USA)/Svetlana Krivencheva (BUL) 64 36 76(1).

- **$50,000 CUNEO** (ITA) 4-10 JULY – **Singles:** Laura Pous-Tio (ESP) d. Conchita Martinez-Granados (ESP) 63 62.
  Doubles: Mariya Koryttseva (UKR)/Galina Voskoboeva (RUS) d. Sara Errani/Giulia Gabba (ITA) 63 75.

Gabriela Niculescu (ROM)

- **$10,000 BALTIMORE, MD** (USA) 11-17 JULY – **Singles:** Madison Brengle (USA) d. Beau Jones (USA) 64 61.
Doubles: Beau Jones (USA)/Petra Rampre (SLO) d. Tarakaa Bertrand/Amanda Fish (USA) 63 75.

- **$10,000 BRUSSELS** (BEL) 11-17 JULY – **Singles:** Leslie Butkiewicz (BEL) d. Claire De Gubernatis (FRA) 57 61 64.
Doubles: Iveta Gerlova (CZE)/Carmen Klaschka (GER) d. Leslie Butkiewicz/Caroline Maes (BEL) 75 62.

- **$10,000 GARCHING** (GER) 11-17 JULY – **Singles:** Josipa Bek (CRO) d. Korina Perkovic (GER) 57 61 61.
Doubles: Zuzana Hejdova (CZE)/Eva-Maria Hoch (AUT) d. Lenka Dlhopolcova (SVK)/Laura Siegemund (GER) 46 64 63.

- **$10,000 ISTANBUL** (TUR) 11-17 JULY – **Singles:** Pemra Ozgen (TUR) d. Radana Holusova (CZE) 64 63.
Doubles: Pemra Ozgen (TUR)/Gabriela Velasco-Andreu (ESP) d. Irina Buryachok (UKR)/Vasilisa Davydova (RUS) 62 63.

- **$10,000 MONTERONI** (ITA) 11-17 JULY – **Singles:** Corinna Dentoni (ITA) d. Verdiana Verardi (ITA) 60 57 64.
Doubles: Giulia Meruzzi/Verdiana Verardi (ITA) d. Silvia Disderi/Giorgia Mortello (ITA) 76(4) 76(1).

- **$10,000 SEOGWIPO** (KOR) 11-17 JULY – **Singles:** Mi Yoo (KOR) d. Mi-Ok Kim (KOR) 62 63.
Doubles: Kyung-Yee Chae/Mi Yoo (KOR) d. Kyung-Mi Chang/Mi-Ok Kim (KOR) 62 61.

- **$25,000 HAMILTON** (CAN) 11-17 JULY – **Singles:** Aleksandra Wozniak (CAN) d. Maria-Jose Argeri (ARG) 61 62.
Doubles: Kumiko Iijima/Junri Namigata (JPN) d. Lauren Barnikow (USA)/Lauren Breadmore (AUS) 67(4) 62 62.

- **$50,000 LOUISVILLE, KY** (USA) 11-17 JULY – **Singles:** Ashley Harkleroad (USA) d. Severine Bremond (FRA) 46 75 60.
Doubles: Natalia Dziamidzenka (BLR)/Anda Perianu (ROM) d. Teryn Ashley/Julie Ditty (USA) 75 26 64.

- **$50,000 VITTEL** (FRA) 11-17 JULY – **Singles:** Hanna Nooni (SWE) d. Mathilde Johansson (FRA) 62 62.
Doubles: Hana Sromova/Renata Voracova (CZE) d. Stanislava Hrozenska (SVK)/Lenka Nemeckova (CZE) 64 64.

- **$10,000 ANCONA** (ITA) 18-24 JULY – **Singles:** Claudia Ivone (ITA) d. Verdiana Verardi (ITA) 63 64.
Doubles: Alesa Bagola/Tina Obrez (SLO) d. Eleonora Iannozzi/Stella Menna (ITA) 61 60.

- **$10,000 BUCHAREST** (ROM) 18-24 JULY – **Singles:** Raluca Olaru (ROM) d. Anna Bastrikova (RUS) 63 63.
Doubles: Madalina Gojnea/Gabriela Niculescu (ROM) d. Agnes Szatmari (ROM)/Oksana Teplyakova (UKR) 63 62.

- **$10,000 DUSSELDORF** (GER) 18-24 JULY – **Singles:** Danica Krstajic (SCG) d. Franziska Etzel (GER) 62 76(4).
Doubles: Olga Brozda/Monika Schneider (POL) d. Danica Krstajic (SCG)/Elena Tchalova (RUS) 16 61 62.

- **$10,000 EVANSVILLE, IN** (USA) 18-24 JULY – **Singles:** Sarah Taylor (USA) d. Kristi Miller (USA) 76(8) 61.
Doubles: Wynne Prakusya/Romana Tedjakusuma (INA) d. Kristi Miller/Christian Tara (USA) 60 61.

- **$10,000 PALIC** (SCG) 18-24 JULY – **Singles:** Miljana Adanko (HUN) d. Ana Jovanovic (SCG) 75 61.
Doubles: Karolina Jovanovic/Natasa Zoric (SCG) d. Tatjana Jecmenica (SCG)/Anna-Maria Zubori (FRA) 61 64.

- **$10,000 ZWEVEGEM** (BEL) 18-24 JULY – **Singles:** Petra Cetkovska (CZE) d. Stefania Chieppa (ITA) 64 62.
Doubles: Leslie Butkiewicz/Caroline Maes (BEL) d. Petra Cetkovska (CZE)/Gabriela Velasco-Andreu (ESP) 63 62.

- **$25,000 CAMPOS DO JORDAO** (BRA) 18-24 JULY – **Singles:** Maria-Fernanda Alves (BRA) d. Maria-Jose Argeri (ARG) 63 75.
Doubles: Maria-Jose Argeri (ARG)/Leticia Sobral (BRA) d. Maria-Fernanda Alves (BRA)/Frederica Piedade (POR) 60 62.

- **$25,000 HAMMOND, LA** (USA) 18-24 JULY – **Singles:** Miho Saeki (JPN) d. Anda Perianu (ROM) 63 26 61.
Doubles: Mary Gambale/Kelley Hyndman (USA) d. Christina Fusano/Ahsha Rolle (USA) 26 63 75.

- **$25,000 KURUME** (JPN) 18-24 JULY – **Singles:** Su-Wei Hsieh (TPE) d. Erika Takao (JPN) 62 63.
Doubles: Chin-Wei Chan/Su-Wei Hsieh (TPE) d. Ayumi Morita/Erika Sema (JPN) 64 63.

- **$25,000 LES CONTAMINES** (FRA) 18-24 JULY – **Singles:** Julie Coin (FRA) d. Dominika Nociarova (SVK) 67(5) 62 64.
Doubles: Nadejda Ostrovskaya (BLR)/Yevgenia Savransky (ISR) d. Nina Bratchikova/Ekaterina Kosminskaya (RUS) 61 26 64.

- **$50,000 PETANGE** (LUX) 18-24 JULY – **Singles:** Viktoria Azarenka (BLR) d. Viktoria Kutuzova (UKR) 64 62.
Doubles: Yulia Beygelzimer (UKR)/Sandra Kloesel (GER) d. Claire Curran (GBR)/Kim Kilsdonk (NED) 64 60.

- **$10,000 ARAD** (ROM) 25-31 JULY – **Singles:** Madalina Gojnea (ROM) d. Oksana Karyshkova (RUS) 61 63.
Doubles: Corina Corduneanu/Raluca Olaru (ROM) d. Anna Bastrikova/Vasilisa Davydova (RUS) 61 64.

- **$10,000 DUBLIN** (IRL) 25-31 JULY – **Singles:** Suzanne Van Hartingsveldt (NED) d. Emily Hewson (AUS) 63 62.
Doubles: Sanne Van Den Biggelaar/Suzanne Van Hartingsveldt (NED) d. Sarah Coles/Elizabeth Thomas (GBR) 61 63.

- **$10,000 HORB** (GER) 25-31 JULY – **Singles:** Kristina Barrois (GER) d. Andrea Hlavackova (CZE) 75 63.
Doubles: Lucie Kriegsmannova/Zuzana Zalabska (CZE) d. Ivanna Israilova (UZB)/Elena Tchalova (RUS) 64 63.

- **$10,000 PONTEVEDRA** (ESP) 25-31 JULY – **Singles:** Anais Laurendon (FRA) d. Marina Cossou (FRA) 62 60.
Doubles: Anna Font-Estrada/Laura Vallverdu-Zaira (ESP) d. Olivia Lukaszewicz (AUS)/Galina Semenova (RUS) 63 67(2) 64.

- **$10,000 SEZZE** (ITA) 25-31 JULY – **Singles:** Aurelie Vedy (FRA) d. Claudia Ivone (ITA) 61 62.
Doubles: Sonia Iacovacci/Nancy Rustignoli (ITA) d. Maraike Biglmaier (GER)/Nana Urotadze (GEO) 64 63.

- **$10,000 ST. JOSEPH, MD** (USA) 25-31 JULY – **Singles:** Wynne Prakusya (INA) d. Sarah Riske (USA) 62 64.
Doubles: Wynne Prakusya/Romana Tedjakusuma (INA) d. Lauren Barnikow/Raquel Kops-Jones (USA) 62 63.

- **$50,000 LEXINGTON, KY** (USA) 25-31 JULY – **Singles:** Natalie Grandin (RSA) d. Stephanie Dubois (CAN) 64 63.
Doubles: Vilmarie Castellvi (PUR)/Samantha Reeves (USA) d. Kumiko Iijima/Junri Namigata (JPN) 62 61.

- **$10,000 BAD SAULGAU** (GER) 1-7 AUGUST – **Singles:** Darija Jurak (CRO) d. Vanja Corovic (SCG) 61 60.
Doubles: Ivanna Israilova (UZB)/Elena Tchalova (RUS) d. Darija Jurak (CRO)/Sandra Martinovic (BIH) 64 46 64.

- **$10,000 BUCHAREST** (ROM) 1-7 AUGUST – **Singles:** Raluca Olaru (ROM) d. Madalina Gojnea (ROM) 76(3) 75.
Doubles: Corina Corduneanu/Raluca Olaru (ROM) d. Bianca Bonifate/Sorana Cirstea (ROM) 61 61.

- **$10,000 GARDONE VAL TROMPIA** (ITA) 1-7 AUGUST – **Singles:** Mandy Minella (LUX) d. Sandra Zahlavova (CZE) 64 63.
Doubles: Maria-Belen Corbalan (ARG)/Sonia Iacovacci (ITA) d. Petra Cetkovska (CZE)/Mandy Minella (LUX) w/o.

- **$10,000 PUERTO ORDAZ** (VEN) 1-7 AUGUST – **Singles:** Yamile Fors-Guerra (CUB) d. Yanet Nunez-Mojarena (CUB) 75 64.
Doubles: Yamile Fors-Guerra/Yanet Nunez-Mojarena (CUB) d. Lumais Diaz-Hernandez (CUB)/Marina Giral (VEN) 61 62.

- **$10,000 VIGO** (ESP) 1-7 AUGUST – **Singles:** Maria-Jose Martinez-Sanchez (ESP) d. Annette Kolb (GER) 67(5) 75 76(4).
Doubles: Anna Font-Estrada/Maria-Jose Martinez-Sanchez (ESP) d. Estrella Cabeza-Candela/Matilde Munoz-Gonzalves (ESP) 62 63.

- **$10,000 WREXHAM** (GBR) 1-7 AUGUST – **Singles:** Laura Peterzan (GBR) d. Alexandra Kulikova (RUS) 60 36 64.
Doubles: Rebecca Llewellyn/Anna Smith (GBR) d. Rushmi Chakravarthi (IND)/Paula Marama (NZL) 63 75.

- **$25,000 VANCOUVER** (CAN) 1-7 AUGUST – **Singles:** Ansley Cargill (USA) d. Melanie Gloria (CAN) 64 62.
Doubles: Sarah Borwell (GBR)/Sarah Riske (USA) d. Lauren Barnikow (USA)/Antonia Matic (GER) 64 36 76(0).

- **$50,000 MARTINA FRANCA** (ITA) 1-7 AUGUST – **Singles:** Nathalie Vierin (ITA) d. Maret Ani (EST) 63 64.
Doubles: Zsofia Gubacsi (HUN)/Mariya Koryttseva (UKR) d. Lourdes Dominguez-Lino/Conchita Martinez-Granados (ESP) 61 63.

- **$75,000 WASHINGTON, DC** (USA) 1-7 AUGUST – **Singles:** Ashley Harkleroad (USA) d. Olga Poutchkova (RUS) 62 61.
Doubles: Olena Antypina (UKR)/Tatiana Poutchek (BLR) d. Jennifer Hopkins (USA)/Zi Yan (CHN) 64 64.

- **$10,000 GDYNIA** (POL) 8-14 AUGUST – **Singles:** Petra Cetkovska (CZE) d. Agnieszka Radwanska (POL) 63 64.
Doubles: Agnieszka Radwanska/Urszula Radwanska (POL) d. Katerina Avdiyenko/Natalia Bogdanova (UKR) 61 61.

- **$10,000 LONDON** (GBR) 8-14 AUGUST – **Singles:** Julie Coin (FRA) d. Claire Peterzan (GBR) 64 16 63.
Doubles: Ankita Bhambri/Sanaa Bhambri (IND) d. Sarah Coles/Elizabeth Thomas (GBR) 63 63.

ITF Women's Circuit 2005 Results (continued)

- **$10,000 MOSCOW** (RUS) 8-14 AUGUST – **Singles:** Anastasia Pivovarova (RUS) d. Olga Panova (RUS) 76(1) 76(4).
Doubles: Ekaterina Ivanova/Olga Panova (RUS) d. Anna Bastrikova/Vasilisa Davydova (RUS) 75 63.

- **$10,000 REBECQ** (BEL) 8-14 AUGUST – **Singles:** Elena Tchalova (RUS) d. Noemie Scharle (FRA) 61 ret.
Doubles: Leslie Butkiewicz/Jessie De Vries (BEL) d. Kim Kilsdonk (NED)/Neda Kozic (SCG) w/o.

- **$25,000 HECHINGEN** (GER) 8-14 AUGUST – **Singles:** Kirsten Flipkens (BEL) d. Magdalena Rybarikova (SVK) 64 63.
Doubles: Kristina Barrois/Jasmin Woehr (GER) d. Renata Voracova/Sandra Zahlavova (CZE) 46 76(3) 64.

- **$25,000 WUXI** (CHN) 8-14 AUGUST – **Singles:** Miho Saeki (JPN) d. Sheng-Nan Sun (CHN) 62 76(1).
Doubles: Mi-Ra Jeon (KOR)/Wynne Prakusya (INA) d. Casey Dell'Acqua/Sophie Ferguson (AUS) 62 76(6).

- **$50,000 RIMINI** (ITA) 8-14 AUGUST – **Singles:** Lourdes Dominguez-Lino (ESP) d. Mariya Koryttseva (UKR) 06 60 63.
Doubles: Giulia Casoni (ITA)/Mariya Koryttseva (UKR) d. Daria Kustava (BLR)/Ekaterina Makarova (RUS) 62 64.

- **$10,000 GUAYAQUIL** (ECU) 15-21 AUGUST – **Singles:** Angelina Gabueva (RUS) d. Nicole Clerico (ITA) 62 46 64.
Doubles: Andrea Koch (CHI)/Veronica Spiegel (ARG) d. Kit Carson (USA)/Dragana Jakovljevic (AUS) 61 62.

- **$10,000 JESI** (ITA) 15-21 AUGUST – **Singles:** Leanne Baker (NZL) d. Vanessa Pinto (GER) 62 76(6).
Doubles: Silvia Disderi/Giulia Gabba (ITA) d. Leanne Baker (NZL)/Francesca Lubiani (ITA) 62 26 64.

- **$10,000 KOKSIJDE** (BEL) 15-21 AUGUST – **Singles:** Caroline Maes (BEL) d. Nadege Vergos (FRA) 62 60.
Doubles: Iveta Gerlova (CZE)/Carmen Klaschka (GER) d. Jessie De Vries (BEL)/Samia Medjahdi (ALG) 61 60.

- **$10,000 NOTTINGHAM** (GBR) 15-21 AUGUST – **Singles:** Lindsay Cox (GBR) d. Rebecca Fong (GBR) 64 36 63.
Doubles: Jade Curtis (GBR)/Rachael Dillon (IRL) d. Marie-Perrine Baudouin (FRA)/Claire Peterzan (GBR) 62 63.

- **$25,000 COIMBRA** (POR) 15-21 AUGUST – **Singles:** Monica Niculescu (ROM) d. Aravane Rezai (FRA) 63 61.
Doubles: Maria-Jose Martinez-Sanchez (ESP)/Ana-Catarina Nogueira (POR) d. Angelique Kerber/Tatjana Priachin (GER) 64 76(1).

- **$25,000 HELSINKI** (FIN) 15-21 AUGUST – **Singles:** Emma Laine (FIN) d. Irina Kuzmina (LAT) 60 62.
Doubles: Maria Geznenge (BUL)/Stefanie Haidner (AUT) d. Emma Laine/Essi Laine (FIN) 75 26 64.

- **$25,000 KEDZIERZYN KOZLE** (POL) 15-21 AUGUST – **Singles:** Petra Cetkovska (CZE) d. Natalia Gussoni (ARG) 36 64 63.
Doubles: Agnieszka Radwanska/Urszula Radwanska (POL) d. Renata Voracova/Sandra Zahlavova (CZE) 61 64.

- **$25,000 NANJING** (CHN) 15-21 AUGUST – **Singles:** Miho Saeki (JPN) d. Wen-Hsin Hsu (TPE) 62 62.
Doubles: Julia Vorobeva (RUS)/Yan-Ze Xie (CHN) d. Tomoko Sugano/Akiko Yonemura (JPN) 64 63.

- **$50,000 BRONX, NY** (USA) 15-21 AUGUST – **Singles:** Sybille Bammer (AUT) d. Camille Pin (FRA) 36 64 64.
Doubles: Ting Li/Tian-Tian Sun (CHN) d. Tatiana Poutchek/Anastasia Yakimova (BLR) 26 62 64.

- **$10,000 AMARANTE** (POR) 22-28 AUGUST – **Singles:** Dominika Cibulkova (SVK) d. Paula Fondevila-Castro (ESP) 60 62.
Doubles: Joana Cortez (BRA)/Neuza Silva (POR) d. Flavia Mignola (ARG)/Gabriela Velasco-Andreu (ESP) 62 63.

- **$10,000 BIELEFELD** (GER) 22-28 AUGUST – **Singles:** Sandra Zahlavova (CZE) d. Franziska Etzel (GER) 36 61 75.
Doubles: Kristina Barrois/Korina Perkovic (GER) d. Justine Ozga/Andrea Sieveke (GER) 76(1) 63.

- **$10,000 BOGOTA** (COL) 22-28 AUGUST – **Singles:** Carla Tiene (BRA) d. Andrea Koch (CHI) 64 60.
Doubles: Estefania Balda (ECU)/Mariana Muci (VEN) d. Maria Irigoyen/Luciana Sarmenti (ARG) 75 63.

- **$10,000 BUCHAREST** (ROM) 22-28 AUGUST – **Singles:** Simona Matei (ROM) d. Diana Enache (ROM) 63 60.
Doubles: Corina Corduneanu/Agnes Szatmari (ROM) d. Liana Balaci/Simona Matei (ROM) w/o.

- **$10,000 MARIBOR** (SLO) 22-28 AUGUST – **Singles:** Mari Andersson (SWE) d. Dia Evtimova (BUL) 75 63.
Doubles: Mari Andersson/Kristina Andlovic (SWE) d. Katalin Marosi (HUN)/Marina Tavares (BRA) 76(2) 63.

- **$10,000 TRECASTAGNII** (ITA) 22-28 AUGUST – **Singles:** Regina Kulikova (RUS) d. Giulia Meruzzi (ITA) 61 46 64.
Doubles: Leanne Baker (NZL)/Francesca Lubiani (ITA) d. Regina Kulikova/Marina Shamayko (RUS) 62 46 63.

- **$10,000 WESTENDE** (BEL) 22-28 AUGUST – **Singles:** Diana Brunel (FRA) d. Claire De Gubernatis (FRA) 64 36 61.
Doubles: Leslie Butkiewicz/Eveline Vanhyfte (BEL) d. Claire De Gubernatis (FRA)/Anna Font-Estrada (ESP) 64 62.

- **$25,000 MOSCOW** (RUS) 22-28 AUGUST – **Singles:** Alisa Kleybanova (RUS) d. Vasilisa Bardina (RUS) 62 62.
Doubles: Ekaterina Kozhokhina (RUS)/Daria Kustava (BLR) d. Nadejda Ostrovskaya (BLR)/Yevgenia Savransky (ISR) 62 64.

- **$10,000 ALPHEN A/D RIJN** (NED) 29 AUGUST-4 SEPTEMBER – **Singles:** Andrea Petkovic (GER) d. Eva Pera (NED) 75 75.
Doubles: Mireille Bink/Susanne Trik (NED) d. Veronika Raimrova (CZE)/Aleksandra Srndovic (SWE) 62 36 62.

- **$10,000 BUCHAREST** (ROM) 29 AUGUST-4 SEPTEMBER – **Singles:** Corina Corduneanu (ROM) d. Maria Penkova (BUL) 62 63.
Doubles: Corina Corduneanu/Lenore Lazaroiu (ROM) d. Antonia-Xenia Tout (ROM)/Emily Webley-Smith (GBR) 61 62.

- **$10,000 GLIWICE** (POL) 29 AUGUST-4 SEPTEMBER – **Singles:** Katalin Marosi (HUN) d. Natalia Kolat (POL) 61 63.
Doubles: Lucie Kriegsmannova/Zuzana Zalabska (CZE) d. Olga Brozda/Natalia Kolat (POL) 75 46 62.

- **$10,000 MOLLERUSA** (ESP) 29 AUGUST-4 SEPTEMBER – **Singles:** Kildine Chevalier (FRA) d. Maria-Jose Martinez-Sanchez (ESP) 62 57 62.
Doubles: Larissa Carvalho (BRA)/Nuria Roig-Tost (ESP) d. Anna Boada-Plade Llorens/Rebeca Bou-Nogueiro (ESP) 60 61.

- **$10,000 NOTTINGHAM** (GBR) 29 AUGUST-4 SEPTEMBER – **Singles:** Anne Keothavong (GBR) d. Karen Paterson (GBR) 16 76(4) 64.
Doubles: Anne Keothavong/Claire Peterzan (GBR) d. Lindsay Cox/Rebecca Fong (GBR) 61 61.

- **$10,000 SAITAMA** (JPN) 29 AUGUST-4 SEPTEMBER – **Singles:** Beti Sekulovski (AUS) d. Mari Tanaka (JPN) 36 64 63.
Doubles: Biffy Kaufman (USA)/Mari Tanaka (JPN) d. Hye-Mi Kim (KOR)/Eriko Mizuno (JPN) 64 63.

- **$10,000 SANTA CRUZ DE LA SIERRA** (BOL) 29 AUGUST-4 SEPTEMBER – **Singles:** Natalia Garbellotto (ARG) d. Jenifer Widjaja (BRA) 67(1) 63 63.
Doubles: Andrea Koch (CHI)/Veronica Spiegel (ARG) d. Dominika Dieskova (SVK)/Courtney Nagle (USA) 63 63.

- **$10,000 VITTORIA** (ITA) 29 AUGUST-4 SEPTEMBER – **Singles:** Anna Floris (ITA) d. Carla Suarez-Navarro (ESP) 64 75.
Doubles: Lauren Fisher (USA)/Carla Suarez-Navarro (ESP) d. Silvia Disderi/Giorgia Mortello (ITA) 62 63.

- **$25,000 BALASHIKHA** (RUS) 29 AUGUST-4 SEPTEMBER – **Singles:** Alla Kudryavtseva (RUS) d. Vasilisa Bardina (RUS) 26 75 64.
Doubles: Anna Bastrikova/Nina Bratchikova (RUS) d. Ekaterina Ivanova/Olga Panova (RUS) 62 62.

- **$10,000 CIMPINA** (ROM) 5-11 SEPTEMBER – **Singles:** Alexandra Orasanu (ROM) d. Alexandra Sere (ROM) 06 64 63.
Doubles: Maria-Luiza Craciun/Ioana Ivan (ROM) d. Agnes Szatmari/Antonia-Xenia Tout (ROM) 67(6) 64 64.

- **$10,000 ENSCHEDE** (NED) 5-11 SEPTEMBER – **Singles:** Veronika Raimrova (CZE) d. Marlot Meddens (NED) 61 60.
Doubles: Kelly De Beer/Eva Pera (NED) d. Danielle Harmsen/Nicole Thyssen (NED) 64 64.

- **$10,000 KYOTO** (JPN) 5-11 SEPTEMBER – **Singles:** Beti Sekulovski (AUS) d. Lei Huang (CHN) 62 30 ret.
Doubles: Hye-Mi Kim (KOR)/Keiko Taguchi (JPN) d. Eriko Mizuno/Tomoyo Takagishi (JPN) 46 60 61.

- **$10,000 SANTIAGO** (CHI) 5-11 SEPTEMBER – **Singles:** Natalia Garbellotto (ARG) d. Estefania Craciun (URU) 62 64.
Doubles: Dominika Dieskova (SVK)/Courtney Nagle (USA) d. Estefania Craciun (URU)/Florencia Salvadores (ARG) 61 63.

- **$10,000 VESSY** (SUI) 5-11 SEPTEMBER – **Singles:** Tanja Ostertag (GER) d. Stephanie Rizzi (FRA) 64 76(17).
Doubles: Alexandra Kiesl/Justine Ozga (GER) d. Geraldine Roma (SWE)/Vanessa Wellauer (SUI) 62 62.

- **$25,000 DURMERSHEIM** (GER) 5-11 SEPTEMBER – **Singles:** Yevgenia Savransky (ISR) d. Adriana Barna (GER) 26 75 61.
Doubles: Danica Krstajic (SCG)/Elena Tchalova (RUS) d. Adriana Barna/Caroline Schneider (GER) 46 64 64.

- **$25,000 MADRID** (ESP) 5-11 SEPTEMBER – **Singles:** Matilde Munoz-Gonzalves (ESP) d. Olga Blahotova (CZE) 63 62.
Doubles: Andreja Klepac (SLO)/Nika Ozegovic (CRO) d. Kelly Liggan (IRL)/Seda Noorlander (NED) 63 63.

ITF Women's Circuit 2005 Results (continued)

- **$25,0000 MESTRE** (ITA) 5-11 SEPTEMBER – **Singles:** Magdalena Rybarikova (SVK) d. Kyra Nagy (HUN) 62 75.
  Doubles: Rita Kuti Kis/Kyra Nagy (HUN) d. Elisa Balsamo/Emily Stellato (ITA) 75 64.

- **$50,000 BEIJING** (CHN) 5-11 SEPTEMBER – **Singles:** Meng Yuan (CHN) d. Vilmarie Castellvi (PUR) 46 64 64.
  Doubles: Maki Arai (JPN)/So-Jung Kim (KOR) d. Yung-Jan Chan/I-Hsuan Hwang (TPE) 64 60.

- **$75,000 DENAIN** (FRA) 5-11 SEPTEMBER – **Singles:** Liudmila Skavronskaia (RUS) d. Arantxa Parra-Santonja (ESP) 76(5) 60.
  Doubles: Lucie Hradecka/Vladimira Uhlirova (CZE) d. Zsofia Gubacsi (HUN)/Mariya Koryttseva (UKR) 60 75.

- **$10,000 HIROSHIMA** (JPN) 12-18 SEPTEMBER – **Singles:** Tomoyo Takagishi (JPN) d. Kanae Hisami (JPN) 63 76(4).
  Doubles: Etsuko Kitazaki/Tomoko Taira (JPN) d. Eriko Mizuno/Tomoyo Takagishi (JPN) 64 06 62.

- **$10,000 LLEIDA** (ESP) 12-18 SEPTEMBER – **Singles:** Elena Tchalova (RUS) d. Nuria Roig-Tost (ESP) 62 36 76(1).
  Doubles: Anna Font-Estrada/Nuria Roig-Tost (ESP) d. Marlene Ryan/Melissa Ryan (USA) 62 62.

- **$10,000 MATAMOROS** (MEX) 12-18 SEPTEMBER – **Singles:** Daniela Munoz-Gallegos (MEX) d. Raquel Kops-Jones (USA) 46 62 64.
  Doubles: Daniela Munoz-Gallegos (MEX)/Paula Zabala-Alvarez (COL) d. Ana Cetnik (SCG)/Story Tweedie-Yates (USA) 64 64.

- $10,000 **TBILISI** (GEO) 12-18 SEPTEMBER – **Singles:** Margalita Chakhnashvili (GEO) d. Manana Shapakidze (GEO) 62 61.
  Doubles: Irina Kotkina/Olga Panova (RUS) d. Vasilisa Davydova (RUS)/Pemra Ozgen (TUR) 62 36 64.

- **$10,000 TORRE DEL GRECO** (ITA) 12-18 SEPTEMBER – **Singles:** Corinna Dentoni (ITA) d. Jana Juricova (SVK) 63 62.
  Doubles: Maraike Biglmaier (GER)/Jana Juricova (SVK) d. Stefanie Haidner (AUT)/Valentina Sulpizio (ITA) 62 46 63.

- **$25,000 SOFIA** (BUL) 12-18 SEPTEMBER – **Singles:** Tamira Paszek (AUT) d. Kristina Barrois (GER) 76(5) 63.
  Doubles: Sanja Ancic (CRO)/Tamira Paszek (AUT) d. Joana Cortez (BRA)/Karolina Kosinska (POL) 67(9) 62 64.

- **$75,000 BORDEAUX** (FRA) 12-18 SEPTEMBER – **Singles:** Stephanie Foretz (FRA) d. Liudmila Skavronskaia (RUS) 61 62.
  Doubles: Conchita Martinez-Granados/Maria-Jose Martinez-Sanchez (ESP) d. Julia Schruff/Jasmin Woehr (GER) 75 62.

- **$10,000 BUENOS AIRES** (ARG) 19-25 SEPTEMBER – **Singles:** Natalia Garbellotto (ARG) d. Estefania Craciun (URU) 64 61.
  Doubles: Flavia Mignola/Veronica Spiegel (ARG) d. Patricia Holzman/Mariana Lopez-Terribile (ARG) 61 76(5).

- **$10,000 CIAMPINO** (ITA) 19-25 SEPTEMBER – **Singles:** Jana Juricova (SVK) d. Emily Stellato (ITA) 62 62.
  Doubles: Lenka Broosova/Lenka Wienerova (SVK) d. Raffaella Bindi/Annalisa Bona (ITA) 64 64.

- **$10,000 JAKARTA** (INA) 19-25 SEPTEMBER – **Singles:** Nudnida Luangnam (THA) d. Lu-Ling Chen (TPE) 64 64.
  Doubles: Yi Chen/Shao-Yuan Kao (TPE) d. Lutfiana-Aris Budiharto/Vivien Silvany-Tony (INA) 63 60.

- **$25,000 GLASGOW** (GBR) 19-25 SEPTEMBER – **Singles:** Kristina Barrois (GER) d. Greta Arn (GER) 63 36 64.
  Doubles: Elena Baltacha (GBR)/Margit Ruutel (EST) d. Anne Keothavong/Karen Paterson (GBR) 63 67(2) 62.

- **$25,000 IBARAKI** (JPN) 19-25 SEPTEMBER – **Singles:** Petra Cetkovska (CZE) d. Erika Takao (JPN) 26 75 63.
  Doubles: Ryoko Takemura/Tomoko Yonemura (JPN) d. Mi-Ra Jeon (KOR)/Ayami Takase (JPN) 62 64.

- **$25,000 MACKAY, QLD** (AUS) 19-25 SEPTEMBER – **Singles:** Casey Dell'Acqua (AUS) d. Maria-Jose Argeri (ARG) 16 63 60.
  Doubles: Casey Dell'Acqua/Daniella Dominikovic (AUS) d. Monique Adamczak/Olivia Lukaszewicz (AUS) 76(6) 76(2).

- **$25,000 TBILISI** (GEO) 19-25 SEPTEMBER – **Singles:** Sandra Zahlavova (CZE) d. Ana Timotic (SCG) 60 63.
  Doubles: Ekaterina Dzehalevich/Tatsiana Kapshay (BLR) d. Karolina Kosinska (POL)/Tatsiana Uvarova (BLR) 60 75.

- **$75,000 ALBUQUERQUE, NM** (USA) 19-25 SEPTEMBER – **Singles:** Anastasia Rodionova (RUS) d. Maureen Drake (CAN) 62 63.
  Doubles: Julie Ditty (USA)/Milagros Sequera (VEN) d. Romana Tedjakusuma (INA)/Napaporn Tongsalee (THA) 63 67(6) 76(2).

- **$75,000 JOUNIEH** (LIB) 19-25 SEPTEMBER – **Singles:** Mariya Koryttseva (UKR) d. Lourdes Dominguez-Lino (ESP) 75 75.
  Doubles: Mariya Koryttseva (UKR)/Anastasia Yakimova (BLR) d. Olena Antypina (UKR)/Hana Sromova (CZE) 75 62.

- **$10,000 BALIKPAPAN** (INA) 26 SEPTEMBER-2 OCTOBER – **Singles:** Wen-Hsin Hsu (TPE) d. I-Hsuan Hwang (TPE) 63 76(4).
Doubles: Yi Chen/Shao-Yuan Kao (TPE) d. Wen-Hsin Hsu/I-Hsuan Hwang (TPE) 63 75.

- **$10,000 BENEVENTO** (ITA) 26 SEPTEMBER-2 OCTOBER – **Singles:** Sandra Martinovic (BIH) d. Anna Korzeniak (POL) 64 61.
Doubles: Dorota Hibental (POL)/Alexandra Karavaeva (RUS) d. Marrit Boonstra/Nicole Thyssen (NED) w/o.

- **$10,000 MORELIA** (MEX) 26 SEPTEMBER-2 OCTOBER – **Singles:** Katie Ruckert (USA) d. Valeria Pulido-Velasco (MEX) 63 63.
Doubles: Daniela Munoz-Gallegos/Valeria Pulido-Velasco (MEX) d. Olga Brozda (POL)/Jessica Williams (USA) 62 60.

- **$10,000 PODGORICA** (SCG) 26 SEPTEMBER-2 OCTOBER – **Singles:** Diana Stojic (BIH) d. Neda Kozic (SCG) 46 75 63.
Doubles: Ani Mijacika (CRO)/Diana Stojic (BIH) d. Neda Kozic (SCG)/Vesna Manasieva (RUS) 16 63 64.

- **$10,000 VOLOS** (GRE) 26 SEPTEMBER-3 OCTOBER – **Singles:** Patricia Mayr (AUT) d. Dia Evtimova (BUL) 64 76(5).
Doubles: Nicole Clerico (ITA)/Katarina Tuohimaa (FIN) d. Katalin Marosi (HUN)/Marina Tavares (BRA) 64 62.

- **$25,000 OPORTO** (POR) 26 SEPTEMBER-3 OCTOBER – **Singles:** Tina Schiechtl (AUT) d. Lourdes Dominguez-Lino (ESP) 76(4) 76(2).
Doubles: Simona Matei (ROM)/Lina Stanciute (LTU) d. Kelly De Beer/Eva Pera (NED) 26 64 64.

- **$25,000 PELHAM, AL** (USA) 26 SEPTEMBER-2 OCTOBER – **Singles:** Soledad Esperon (ARG) d. Aleksandra Wozniak (CAN) 75 62.
Doubles: Kristina Czafikova (SVK)/Tetiana Luzhanska (UKR) d. Raquel Kops-Jones/Kristen Schlukebir (USA) 76(2) 64.

- **$25,000 ROCKHAMPTON, QLD** (AUS) 26 SEPTEMBER-2 OCTOBER – **Singles:** Casey Dell'Acqua (AUS) d. Beti Sekulovski (AUS) 61 64.
Doubles: Casey Dell'Acqua/Daniella Dominikovic (AUS) d. Beti Sekulovski (AUS)/Aleksandra Srndovic (SWE) 64 62.

- **$50,000 ASHLAND, KY** (USA) 26 SEPTEMBER-2 OCTOBER – **Singles:** Napaporn Tongsalee (THA) d. Kristina Brandi (PUR) 64 26 64.
Doubles: Teryn Ashley/Amy Frazier (USA) d. Maria-Fernanda Alves (BRA)/Ahsha Rolle (USA) 61 64.

- **$50,000 BATUMI** (GEO) 26 SEPTEMBER-2 OCTOBER – **Singles:** Anastasia Yakimova (BLR) d. Ana Timotic (SCG) 64 61.
Doubles: Nadejda Ostrovskaya/Anastasia Yakimova (BLR) d. Anna Bastrikova/Nina Bratchikova (RUS) 26 62 76(9).

- **$50,000 BIELLA** (ITA) 26 SEPTEMBER-2 OCTOBER – **Singles:** Yulia Beygelzimer (UKR) d. Giulia Gabba (ITA) 62 64.
Doubles: Lucie Hradecka/Renata Voracova (CZE) d. Maret Ani (EST)/Mervana Jugic-Salkic (BIH) 64 76(4).

- **$10,000 CORDOBA** (ARG) 3-9 OCTOBER – **Singles:** Estefania Craciun (URU) d. Jorgelina Cravero (ARG) 64 63.
Doubles: Maria Irigoyen/Luciana Sarmenti (ARG) d. Fernanda Hermenegildo (BRA)/Sarah Tami-Masi (PAR) 63 36 62.

- **$10,000 HERCEG NOVI** (SCG) 3-9 OCTOBER – **Singles:** Tina Obrez (SLO) d. Natasa Zoric (SCG) 76(4) 26 64.
Doubles: Vanja Corovic/Natasa Zoric (SCG) d. Miljana Adanko (HUN)/Tina Obrez (SLO) 57 64 62.

- **$10,000 ROME** (ITA) 3-9 OCTOBER – **Singles:** Anna Korzeniak (POL) d. Annalisa Bona (ITA) 64 62.
Doubles: Katalin Marosi (HUN)/Marina Tavares (BRA) d. Giulia Meruzzi/Nancy Rustignoli (ITA) w/o.

- **$25,000 BOLTON** (GBR) 3-9 OCTOBER – **Singles:** Sandra Kleinova (CZE) d. Yaroslava Shvedova (RUS) 06 63 63.
Doubles: Daniela Kix (AUT)/Neuza Silva (POR) d. Veronika Chvojkova (CZE)/Claire Peterzan (GBR) 60 62.

- **$25,000 NANTES** (FRA) 3-9 OCTOBER – **Singles:** Kristina Barrois (GER) d. Alberta Brianti (ITA) 64 62.
Doubles: Mailyne Andrieux (FRA)/Renata Voracova (CZE) d. Marie-Eve Pelletier (CAN)/Aurelie Vedy (FRA) 67(3) 75 62.

- **$50,000 JUAREZ** (MEX) 3-9 OCTOBER – **Singles:** Olga Blahotova (CZE) d. Frederica Piedade (POR) 76(2) 62.
Doubles: Maria-Jose Argeri (ARG)/Leticia Sobral (BRA) d. Olga Blahotova (CZE)/Soledad Esperon (ARG) 76(1) 63.

- **$50,000 TROY, AL** (USA) 3-9 OCTOBER – **Singles:** Ahsha Rolle (USA) d. Maria Kondratieva (RUS) 61 75.
Doubles: Julie Ditty (USA)/Milagros Sequera (VEN) d. Salome Devidze (GEO)/Mandy Minella (LUX) 62 62.

- **$75,000 BARCELONA** (ESP) 3-9 OCTOBER – **Singles:** Katerina Bohmova (CZE) d. Maria Sanchez Lorenzo (ESP) 36 63 75.
Doubles: Lourdes Dominguez-Lino/Maria Sanchez Lorenzo (ESP) d. Conchita Martinez-Granados/Maria-Jose Martinez-Sanchez (ESP) 75 67(4) 76(3).

- **$10,000 BENICARLO** (ESP) 10-16 OCTOBER – **Singles:** Patricia Mayr (AUT) d. Berta Morata-Flaquer (ESP) 64 62.
Doubles: Sofia Brun (SWE)/Patricia Mayr (AUT) d. Elena Caldes-Marques/Mariona Gallifa-Puig Desens (ESP) 75 16 62.

- **$10,000 CASTEL GANDOLFO** (ITA) 10-16 OCTOBER – **Singles:** Anna Korzeniak (POL) d. Giulia Gatto-Monticone (ITA) 63 60.
Doubles: Alena Bayarchyk (BLR)/Alexandra Karavaeva (RUS) d. Stefania Chieppa/Nicole Clerico (ITA) 62 62.

- **$10,000 PORTO SANTO** (POR) 10-16 OCTOBER – **Singles:** Nicole Thyssen (NED) d. Justine Ozga (GER) 76(4) 64.
Doubles: Sorana Cirstea/Alexandra Orasanu (ROM) d. Diana Eriksson/Nadja Roma (SWE) 57 75 64.

- **$10,000 TUCUMAN** (ARG) 10-16 OCTOBER – **Singles:** Jorgelina Cravero (ARG) d. Estefania Craciun (URU) 61 46 64.
Doubles: Agustina Lepore (ARG)/Bibiane Schoofs (NED) d. Lucia Jara-Lozano/Denise Kirbijikian (ARG) 61 75.

- **$25,000 JERSEY** (GBR) 10-16 OCTOBER – **Singles:** Elena Baltacha (GBR) d. Daniela Kix (AUT) 64 64.
Doubles: Veronika Chvojkova (CZE)/Stanislava Hrozenska (SVK) d. Kelly Liggan (IRL)/Nadejda Ostrovskaya (BLR) 46 62 75.

- **$25,000 LAGOS** (NGR) 10-16 OCTOBER – **Singles:** Petra Cetkovska (CZE) d. Anne Keothavong (GBR) 36 63 62.
Doubles: Surina De Beer (RSA)/Gabriela Velasco-Andreu (ESP) d. Lisa Sabino (ITA)/Masa Zec-Peskiric (SLO) 64 62.

- **$25,000 LYNEHAM, ACT** (AUS) 10-16 OCTOBER – **Singles:** Lauren Breadmore (AUS) d. Beti Sekulovski (AUS) 75 64.
Doubles: Casey Dell'Acqua/Daniella Dominikovic (AUS) d. Alison Bai/Jenny Swift (AUS) 64 63.

- **$25,000 VICTORIA** (MEX) 10-16 OCTOBER – **Singles:** Aleksandra Wozniak (CAN) d. Olga Blahotova (CZE) 26 60 64.
Doubles: Maria-Jose Argeri (ARG)/Leticia Sobral (BRA) d. Soledad Esperon (ARG)/Valentina Sassi (ITA) 63 64.

- **$50,000 JOUE LES TOURS** (FRA) 10-16 OCTOBER – **Singles:** Emilie Loit (FRA) d. Jelena Kostanic (CRO) 62 61.
Doubles: Jelena Kostanic/Matea Mezak (CRO) d. Zsofia Gubacsi (HUN)/Daria Kustava (BLR) 64 64.

- **$50,000 SAN FRANCISCO, CA** (USA) 10-16 OCTOBER – **Singles:** Kristina Brandi (PUR) d. Lilia Osterloh (USA) 57 64 64.
Doubles: Ansley Cargill/Tara Snyder (USA) d. Angela Haynes (USA)/Francesca Lubiani (ITA) 76(2) 75.

- **$10,000 ASUNCION** (PAR) 17-23 OCTOBER – **Singles:** Jorgelina Cravero (ARG) d. Estefania Craciun (URU) 64 76(7).
Doubles: Karen-Emelia Castiblanco-Duarte (COL)/Maria Irigoyen (ARG) d. Albertina Gandara/Sheila Guerberg (ARG) 64 64.

- **$10,000 DUBROVNIK** (CRO) 17-23 OCTOBER – **Singles:** Tina Obrez (SLO) d. Ani Mijacika (CRO) 61 75.
Doubles: Vanja Corovic (SCG)/Tina Obrez (SLO) d. Lenka Broosova/Lenka Wienerova (SVK) 64 62.

- **$10,000 PORTO SANTO** (POR) 17-23 OCTOBER – **Singles:** Magali De Lattre (POR) d. Chayenne Ewijk (NED) 75 61.
Doubles: Sorana Cirstea/Alexandra Orasanu (ROM) d. Hannah Kuervers/Imke Kusgen (GER) 67(2) 64 60.

- **$10,000 SETTIMO SAN PIETRO** (ITA) 17-23 OCTOBER – **Singles:** Anna Floris (ITA) d. Regina Kulikova (RUS) 64 41 ret.
Doubles: Alice Balducci/Nancy Rustignoli (ITA) d. Simona Dobra/Renata Kucerkova (CZE) 62 64.

- **$25,000 LAGOS** (NGR) 17-23 OCTOBER – **Singles:** Anne Keothavong (GBR) d. Masa Zec-Peskiric (SLO) 63 76(7).
Doubles: Ankita Bhambri/Sanaa Bhambri (IND) d. Rushmi Chakravarthi/Punam Reddy (IND) w/o.

- **$25,000 MAKINOHARA** (JPN) 17-23 OCTOBER – **Singles:** Alisa Kleybanova (RUS) d. Akiko Yonemura (JPN) 60 61.
Doubles: Ryoko Takemura/Tomoko Yonemura (JPN) d. Seiko Okamoto/Ayami Takase (JPN) 64 63.

- **$25,000 MEXICO CITY** (MEX) 17-23 OCTOBER – **Singles:** Maria-Jose Argeri (ARG) d. Aleksandra Wozniak (CAN) 64 40 ret.
Doubles: Maria-Jose Argeri (ARG)/Leticia Sobral (BRA) d. Soledad Esperon (ARG)/Kelly Liggan (IRL) 76(2) 26 60.

- **$25,000 SEVILLE** (ESP) 17-23 OCTOBER – **Singles:** Conchita Martinez-Granados (ESP) d. Ana Timotic (SCG) 62 62.
Doubles: Sara Errani (ITA)/Maria-Jose Martinez-Sanchez (ESP) d. Gabriela Niculescu/Monica Niculescu (ROM) 62 76(5).

- **$50,000 HOUSTON, TX** (USA) 17-23 OCTOBER – **Singles:** Amy Frazier (USA) d. Anda Perianu (ROM) 63 36 64.
Doubles: Christina Fusano/Raquel Kops-Jones (USA) d. Angela Haynes/Bethanie Mattek (USA) 64 63.

- **$50,000 ST. RAPHAEL** (FRA) 17-23 OCTOBER – **Singles:** Maret Ani (EST) d. Mara Santangelo (ITA) 63 75.
Doubles: Lucie Hradecka/Sandra Zahlavova (CZE) d. Maria-Emilia Salerni (ARG)/Meilen Tu (USA) 46 64 75.

- **$10,000 DUBROVNIK** (CRO) 24-30 OCTOBER – **Singles:** Ani Mijacika (CRO) d. Andrea Popovic (SCG) 64 75.
Doubles: Josipa Bek/Ani Mijacika (CRO) d. Polona Rebersak/Patricia Vollmeier (SLO) 76(3) 76(2).

- **$10,000 PORTO SANTO** (POR) 24-30 OCTOBER – **Singles:** Sorana Cirstea (ROM) d. Pauline Wong (NED) 62 76(3).
Doubles: Danielle Brown/Elizabeth Thomas (GBR) d. Diana Aroutiounova/Natalia Orlova (RUS) 75 64.

- **$10,000 QUARTU SANT ELENA** (ITA) 24-30 OCTOBER – **Singles:** Eva Fernandez-Brugues (ESP) d. Renata Kucerkova (CZE) 61 61.
Doubles: Kika Hogendoorn (NED)/Samantha Murray (GBR) d. Simona Dobra/Renata Kucerkova (CZE) 64 46 75.

- **$10,000 TOKYO** (JPN) 24-30 OCTOBER – **Singles:** Hye-Mi Kim (KOR) d. Lauren Breadmore (AUS) 63 63.

- **$25,000 ISTANBUL** (TUR) 24-30 OCTOBER – **Singles:** Oxana Lyubtsova (UKR) d. Mariya Koryttseva (UKR) 26 61 61.
Doubles: Zsofia Gubacsi (HUN)/Mariya Koryttseva (UKR) d. Agnieszka Radwanska/Urszula Radwanska (POL) 63 63.

- **$25,000 MEXICO CITY** (MEX) 24-30 OCTOBER – **Singles:** Mathilde Johansson (FRA) d. Florence Haring (FRA) w/o.
Doubles: Soledad Esperon (ARG)/Kelly Liggan (IRL) d. Yamile Fors-Guerra/Yanet Nunez-Mojarena (CUB) 16 64 63.

- **$25,000 ST. CUGAT** (ESP) 24-30 OCTOBER – **Singles:** Lourdes Dominguez-Lino (ESP) d. Rita Kuti Kis (HUN) 46 60 62.
Doubles: Lourdes Dominguez-Lino/Arantxa Parra-Santonja (ESP) d. Conchita Martinez-Granados/Maria-Jose Martinez-Sanchez (ESP) 64 63

- **$10,000 PRETORIA** (RSA) 31 OCTOBER-6 NOVEMBER – **Singles:** Alicia Pillay (RSA) d. Lizaan Du Plessis (RSA) 62 62.
Doubles: Anna De Bruyn (RSA)/Julia Paetow (GER) d. Alicia Pillay (RSA)/Diana Vranceanu (GER) 75 16 76(2).

- **$10,000 PUNE** (IND) 31 OCTOBER-6 NOVEMBER – **Singles:** Naomi Cavaday (GBR) d. Isha Lakhani (IND) 64 61.
Doubles: Nicole Clerico (ITA)/Ksenia Palkina (KGZ) d. Rushmi Chakravarthi/Sai-Jayalakshmy Jayaram (IND) 75 76(7).

- **$10,000 SAO PAULO** (BRA) 31 OCTOBER-6 NOVEMBER – **Singles:** Florencia Molinero (ARG) d. Joana Cortez (BRA) 75 76(3).
Doubles: Ana-Clara Duarte/Roxane Vaisemberg (BRA) d. Vanessa Menga/Andrea Vieira (BRA) 36 75 64.

- **$10,000 STOCKHOLM** (SWE) 31 OCTOBER-6 NOVEMBER – **Singles:** Carmen Klaschka (GER) d. Johanna Larsson (SWE) 63 63.
Doubles: Eva-Maria Hoch (AUT)/Martina Pavelec (GER) d. Mari Andersson/Johanna Larsson (SWE) 64 63.

- **$25,000 MINSK** (BLR) 31 OCTOBER-6 NOVEMBER – **Singles:** Yulia Beygelzimer (UKR) d. Agnieszka Radwanska (POL) 76(1) 61.
Doubles: Ekaterina Dzehalevich/Daria Kustava (BLR) d. Agnieszka Radwanska/Urszula Radwanska (POL) 63 63.

- **$25,000 SUTAMA** (JPN) 31 OCTOBER-6 NOVEMBER – **Singles:** Alisa Kleybanova (RUS) d. Shiho Hisamatsu (JPN) 63 75.
Doubles: Maki Arai/Kumiko Iijima (JPN) d. Tomoko Dokei/Yukiko Yabe (JPN) 61 62.

- **$50,000 BUSAN** (KOR) 31 OCTOBER-6 NOVEMBER – **Singles:** So-Jung Kim (KOR) d. Alla Kudryavtseva (RUS) 36 61 62.
Doubles: Wynne Prakusya (INA)/Julia Vorobyeva (RUS) d. Seiko Okamoto/Ayami Takase (JPN) 64 67(6) 61.

- **$10,000 LE HAVRE** (FRA) 7-13 NOVEMBER – **Singles:** Leslie Butkiewicz (BEL) d. Emilie Bacquet (FRA) 75 63.
Doubles: Janette Bejlkova/Renata Voracova (CZE) d. Emilie Bacquet/Louise Doutrelant (FRA) 63 63.

- **$10,000 MALLORCA** (ESP) 7-13 NOVEMBER – **Singles:** Nuria Roig-Tost (ESP) d. Estrella Cabeza-Candela (ESP) 63 63.

- **$10,000 MANILA** (PHI) 7-13 NOVEMBER – **Singles:** Wing-Yau Chan (HKG) d. Czarina-Mae Arevalo (PHI) 61 64.
Doubles: Yi Chen/Shao-Yuan Kao (TPE) d. Jin-A Lee/Sae-Mi Lim (KOR) 64 61.

- **$10,000 PUNE** (IND) 7-13 NOVEMBER – **Singles:** Ankita Bhambri (IND) d. Parul Goswami (IND) 61 63.
Doubles: Geeta Manohar/Archana Venkataraman (IND) d. Parul Goswami/Sandhya Nagaraj (IND) 62 76(5).

ITF Women's Circuit 2005 Results (continued)

- **$25,000 JAKARTA** (INA) 7-13 NOVEMBER – **Singles:** Wynne Prakusya (INA) d. Chia-Jung Chuang (TPE) 64 46 61.
Doubles: Ryoko Fuda (JPN)/Wynne Prakusya (INA) d. Yung-Jan Chan/Chia-Jung Chuang (TPE) 64 64.

- **$25,000 MEXICO CITY** (MEX) 7-13 NOVEMBER – **Singles:** Romina Oprandi (ITA) d. Kyra Nagy (HUN) 63 60.
Doubles: Carla Tiene/Jenifer Widjaja (BRA) d. Francesca Lubiani/Valentina Sassi (ITA) 76(5) 63.

- **$25,000 PORT PIRIE** (AUS) 7-13 NOVEMBER – **Singles:** Casey Dell'Acqua (AUS) d. Cindy Watson (AUS) 63 75.
Doubles: Greta Arn (GER)/Sunitha Rao (USA) d. Monique Adamczak/Christina Horiatopoulos (AUS) 64 36 62.

- **$25,000 TORONTO** (CAN) 7-13 NOVEMBER – **Singles:** Aleksandra Wozniak (CAN) d. Olena Antypina (UKR) 64 63.
Doubles: Olena Antypina (UKR)/Martina Muller (GER) d. Lauren Barnikow/Kristen Schlukebir (USA) 63 61.

- **$50,000 SHENZHEN** (CHN) 7-13 NOVEMBER – **Singles:** Tamarine Tanasugarn (THA) d. Miho Saeki (JPN) 62 64.
Doubles: Su-Wei Hsieh (TPE)/Zi Yan (CHN) d. Chin-Wei Chan/Wen-Hsin Hsu (TPE) 60 62.

- **$75,000 PITTSBURGH, PA** (USA) 7-13 NOVEMBER – **Singles:** Lilia Osterloh (USA) d. Galina Voskoboeva (RUS) 76(5) 64.
Doubles: Teryn Ashley/Carly Gullickson (USA) d. Ashley Harkleroad/Bethanie Mattek (USA) 61 60.

- **$10,000 GIZA** (EGY) 14-20 NOVEMBER – **Singles:** Galina Fokina (RUS) d. Biliana Pavlova (BUL) 62 75.
Doubles: Galina Fokina/Raissa Gourevitch (RUS) d. Lizaan Du Plessis (RSA)/Leonie Mekel (NED) 63 61.

- **$10,000 MALLORCA** (ESP) 14-20 NOVEMBER – **Singles:** Julia Parasyuk (RUS) d. Sandra Martinovic (BIH) 67(4) 64 60.
Doubles: Gianna Doz (CRO)/Stefanie Haidner (AUT) d. Cristina Bala-Abella/Berta Morata-Flaquer (ESP) 64 60.

- **$10,000 MANILA** (PHI) 14-20 NOVEMBER – **Singles:** Riza Zalameda (USA) d. Wing-Yau Chan (HKG) 63 62.
Doubles: Denise Dy (PHI)/Riza Zalameda (USA) d. Yi Chen/Shao-Yuan Kao (TPE) 62 63.

- **$25,000 NURIOOTPA** (AUS) 14-20 NOVEMBER – **Singles:** Anastasia Rodionova (RUS) d. Greta Arn (GER) 63 61.
Doubles: Greta Arn (GER)/Anastasia Rodionova (RUS) d. Casey Dell'Acqua/Trudi Musgrave (AUS) 64 16 75.

- **$25,000 PRUHONICE** (CZE) 14-20 NOVEMBER – **Singles:** Lucie Hradecka (CZE) d. Agnieszka Radwanska (POL) 46 61 76(8).
Doubles: Lucie Hradecka/Libuse Prusova (CZE) d. Olga Blahotova/Eva Hrdinova (CZE) 63 36 63.

- **$25,000 PUEBLA** (MEX) 14-20 NOVEMBER – **Singles:** Romina Oprandi (ITA) d. Jenifer Widjaja (BRA) 61 61.
Doubles: Ivana Abramovic/Maria Abramovic (CRO) d. Bettina Jozami/Veronica Spiegel (ARG) 46 64 76(4).

- **$50,000 DEAUVILLE** (FRA) 14-20 NOVEMBER – **Singles:** Viktoria Kutuzova (UKR) d. Tszvetana Pironkova (BUL) 64 76(2).
Doubles: Stephanie Cohen-Aloro (FRA)/Selima Sfar (TUN) d. Alona Bondarenko/Katerina Bondarenko (UKR) 63 61.

- **$75,000 TUCSON, AZ** (USA) 14-20 NOVEMBER – **Singles:** Juliana Fedak (UKR) d. Vania King (USA) 75 60.
Doubles: Viktoria Azarenka/Tatiana Poutchek (BLR) d. Maria-Fernanda Alves (BRA)/Melinda Czink (HUN) 46 76(3) 61.

- **$10,000 ASHKELON** (ISR) 21-27 NOVEMBER – **Singles:** Sharon Fichman (CAN) d. Pemra Ozgen (TUR) 61 61.
Doubles: Marrit Boonstra/Nicole Thyssen (NED) d. Verena Amesbauer (AUT)/Mariella Greschik (GER) 63 62.

- **$10,000 GIZA** (EGY) 21-27 NOVEMBER – **Singles:** Leonie Mekel (NED) d. Stella Menna (ITA) 26 63 76(1).
Doubles: Galina Fokina/Raissa Gourevitch (RUS) d. Emilia Desiderio (ITA)/Stefanie Haidner (AUT) 64 63.

- **$10,000 SUNDERLAND** (GBR) 21-27 NOVEMBER – **Singles:** Margit Ruutel (EST) d. Piia Suomalainen (FIN) 75 60.
Doubles: Sarah Coles (GBR)/Katerina Vankova (CZE) d. Melissa Berry/Lindsay Cox (GBR) 26 61 64.

- **$25,000 MOUNT GAMBIER** (AUS) 21-27 NOVEMBER – **Singles:** Ryoko Fuda (JPN) d. Anastasia Rodionova (RUS) 62 63.
Doubles: Ryoko Fuda (JPN)/Sunitha Rao (USA) d. Greta Arn (GER)/Anastasia Rodionova (RUS) 61 ret.

- **$25,000 OPOLE** (POL) 21-27 NOVEMBER – **Singles:** Oxana Lyubtsova (UKR) d. Joanna Sakowicz (POL) 61 36 61.
Doubles: Timea Bacsinszky (SUI)/Nadejda Ostrovskaya (BLR) d. Lucie Hradecka/Gabriela Navratilova (CZE) 64 76(5).

- **$25,000 SAN LUIS POTOSI** (MEX) 21-27 NOVEMBER – **Singles:** Frederica Piedade (POR) d. Jorgelina Cravero (ARG) 63 61.
Doubles: Francesca Lubiani/Valentina Sassi (ITA) d. Olga Brozda (POL)/Jenifer Widjaja (BRA) 63 46 75.

- **$75,000 POITIERS** (FRA) 21-27 NOVEMBER – **Singles:** Viktoria Kutuzova (UKR) d. Maret Ani (EST) 63 36 64.
Doubles: Maret Ani (EST)/Mervana Jugic-Salkic (BIH) d. Akgul Amanmuradova (UZB)/Nina Bratchikova (RUS) 76(0) 61.

- **$10,000 GIZA** (EGY) 28 NOVEMBER-4 DECEMBER – **Singles:** Galina Fokina (RUS) d. Stefanie Haidner (AUT) 62 64.
Doubles: Galina Fokina/Raissa Gourevitch (RUS) d. Lenore Lazaroiu (ROM)/Biliana Pavlova (BUL) 63 75.

- **$10,000 HAVANA** (CUB) 28 NOVEMBER-4 DECEMBER – **Singles:** Florencia Molinero (ARG) d. Yamile Fors-Guerra (CUB) 64 63.
Doubles: Yamile Fors-Guerra/Yanet Nunez-Mojarena (CUB) d. Julianna Gates/Chrissie Seredni (USA) 63 62.

- **$10,000 RAMAT HASHARON** (ISR) 28 NOVEMBER-4 DECEMBER – **Singles:** Margalita Chakhnashvili (GEO) d. Sharon Fichman (CAN) 63 76(4).
Doubles: Marrit Boonstra/Nicole Thyssen (NED) d. Pemra Ozgen (TUR)/Gabriela Velasco-Andreu (ESP) 62 63.

- **$50,000 PALM BEACH GARDENS, FL** (USA) 28 NOVEMBER-4 DECEMBER – **Singles:** Bethanie Mattek (USA) d. Melinda Czink (HUN) 46 64 64.
Doubles: Chin-Wei Chan/Su-Wei Hsieh (TPE) d. Olga Blahotova/Katerina Bohmova (CZE) 76(2) 75.

- **$10,000 RAANANA** (ISR) 5-11 DECEMBER – **Singles:** Margalita Chakhnashvili (GEO) d. Tzipi Obziler (ISR) 63 75.
Doubles: Marrit Boonstra/Nicole Thyssen (NED) d. Aleksandra Kulikova/Natalia Orlova (RUS) 75 63.

- **$25,000 PREROV** (CZE) 5-11 DECEMBER – **Singles:** Joanna Sakowicz (POL) d. Lucie Hradecka (CZE) 64 64.
Doubles: Lucie Hradecka/Gabriela Navratilova (CZE) d. Greta Arn (GER)/Margit Ruutel (EST) 36 64 64.

- **$25,000 VALASSKE MEZIRICI** (CZE) 12-18 DECEMBER – **Singles:** Margit Ruutel (EST) d. Eva Hrdinova (CZE) 60 62.
Doubles: Darija Jurak (CRO)/Renata Voracova (CZE) d. Lucie Hradecka/Sandra Zahlavova (CZE) 63 63.

- **$50,000 BERGAMO** (ITA) 12-18 DECEMBER – **Singles:** Ekaterina Bychkova (RUS) d. Mervana Jugic-Salkic (BIH) 63 60.
Doubles: Ekaterina Bychkova/Marina Shamayko (RUS) d. Francesca Lubiani/Valentina Sassi (ITA) 61 63.

- **$75,000 DUBAI** (UAE) 12-18 DECEMBER – **Singles:** Marion Bartoli (FRA) d. Kaia Kanepi (EST) 62 60.
Doubles: Gabriela Navratilova/Hana Sromova (CZE) d. Ekaterina Makarova/Olga Panova (RUS) 75 64.

tennis development in 2005

by rachel woodward

In 2005, the ITF Development Department continued with its work to help raise the level of tennis worldwide and increase the number of countries competing in mainstream international tennis. Through a variety of different programmes, the ITF Development Department works with more than 150 national associations of developing tennis nations on a range of initiatives from the grass roots to high-level player development. The ITF development programme is funded by the ITF and through the Grand Slam Development Fund. In 2005, US$3.4million was spent on tennis development, with US$2million being provided by the ITF and US$1.4million by the Grand Slam nations.

Arantxa Sanchez-Vicario (ESP) at the Worldwide Coaches Workshop

The implementation of many of the ITF development initiatives relies on the work of the nine full-time development officers who are 'out in the field' helping nations to put in place and monitor the development initiatives. The development officers are the eyes and ears of the development programme and in order to truly be able to advise and assist national associations on their activities – the development officers each spend an average of 30 weeks on the road attending events and visiting the nations in their region.

In October of this year, two new development officers joined the ITF development team – Amine Ben Makhlouf of Morocco and Karim Saadallah of Algeria. Amine is the new ITF Development Officer for West & Central Africa and is based in Accra, Ghana. Karim is the new ITF Development Officer for West Asia and is based in Qatar. In addition, Doug MacCurdy was appointed ITF Development Officer for China on a one-year contract which commenced in May 2005. The project is jointly funded by the ITF and Olympic Solidarity and allows Doug to work closely with the Chinese Tennis Association in the areas of high-level player training and coaches' education.

Speakers at this year's event included: former world No 1. Arantxa Sanchez-Vicario, Gustavo Luza, Georges Goven, Louis Cayer, Antoni Girod, Rohan Goetzke, Per Renstrom, Craig Tiley and Ann Quinn.

The development officers provide an essential link between national associations and the ITF and one of their main areas of activity continues to be coaches education. With many national associations currently without a coaches education programme of its own, the ITF assists national associations with the creation of their own coaches education programme and also works to improve the level of tennis coaching throughout the world. National associations and coaches are able to access a variety of ITF resources including the ITF recommended Level 1, 2 and 3 syllabi and it is encouraging to see an increasing number of ITF member nations working with the ITF to put in place their own certification programme. In 2005 alone, 47 courses were held including 23 Level 1 courses, 11 Level 2 courses and 1 Level 3 course.

The ITF's coaches education flagship event – the 14th ITF Worldwide Coaches Workshop was held in Antalya, Turkey from 17–23 October. Hosted by the ITF and the Turkish Tennis Federation, more than 280 coaches from 85 countries gathered to attend the biennial event which also attracted a large field of speakers including some of the world's top coaches, national technical directors and international experts in the various areas of tennis sport science. The theme of this year's Workshop was "Quality Coaching for the Future" and the programme for the week consisted of five days of lecture room and on-court presentations as well as some shorter sessions involving three presentations taking place simultaneously. Speakers at this year's event included: former world No 1. Arantxa Sanchez-Vicario, Gustavo Luza, Georges Goven, Louis Cayer, Antoni Girod, Rohan Goetzke, Per Renstrom, Craig Tiley and Ann Quinn.

It is important to acknowledge the continued support the ITF and its member nations receive from Olympic Solidarity (OS). OS is the part of the International Olympic Committee that distributes television income from the Olympic Games to National Olympic Committees and since the reintroduction of tennis into the Olympic family in Seoul in 1988, the ITF through the Development Department has collaborated closely with OS on a variety of programmes designed to help tennis grow around the world.

In 2005, in addition to technical course grants, OS has also provided Olympic scholarships for six coaches to undergo a three-month intensive course of high-level training, practical experience and theoretical study in Valencia, Spain. In

US Open Champion Ryan Sweeting (BAH)

tennis development in 2005

by rachel woodward

2005, George Oyoo (KEN), Noah Bukari (GHA), Juan Pino (CUB), Rodrigo Vallejo (DOM), Kevin Yarde (BAH) and Elena Mitrofanova (UZB) all benefited from the OS scholarship programme.

Noah Bukari said, "We have had the opportunity to enrich our coaching profession by studying and working with great coaches and players. This coupled with travelling with players to Futures tournaments has made a lot difference, especially considering the part of the world I come from."

In addition to courses, coaches all over the world are now able to keep up-to-date on the latest coaching news by visiting the ITF coaching website (www.itftennis.com/coaching). The website, which was launched in July 2004, contains information on the ITF Coach Education programme, upcoming courses and also allows coaches to access the latest issue of Coaching & Sports Science Review and ITF publications. It is also a resource centre with information on injury prevention, ethics and tennis academies. May saw the launch of the eLearning presentations on the ITF coaching weblet which allow coaches to not only log onto the website to see powerpoint presentations from renowned speakers but also to hear the experts present their work. With further development of the coaching website scheduled for 2006 it looks set to be one of the most useful and invaluable tools of the ITF Coaches Education programme.

For any tennis nation, developed or otherwise, equipment and facilities are at the core of its development plan. Many of the ITF member nations still find it difficult to obtain equipment for its tennis programmes. The ITF's Equipment Distribution programme is able to help nations by providing ITF branded equipment (rackets, balls, strings), free of charge, for use by national associations. In 2005 alone, 6,851 rackets, 10,208 mini-tennis bats and 178,642 balls were sent out to nations.

This equipment is one of the main sources of support for the ITF Junior Tennis Initiative (JTI). This programme encompasses mini-tennis (School Tennis Initiative), performance player training and tournaments (Performance Tennis Initiative) and provision of equipment (Equipment Distribution Programme).

Countries involved are expected to put together in conjunction with our development officers, their own Junior Tennis Initiative (in effect a 14 & Under player development plan), ensuring that there is a logical link between the various 14 & Under programmes operating at national level. ITF support for mini-tennis, player training, new tournaments, equipment and any coordinator subsidies is based on the totality of the Junior Tennis Initiative plan in place in a particular nation.

Now operating in more than 80 countries, the Junior Tennis Initiative not only gives children their first taste of tennis but a large proportion of competitors who now take part in ITF funded regional competitions and training camps have come through the School Tennis Initiative and Performance Tennis Initiative programmes, demonstrating that the Junior Tennis Initiative is starting to show results.

In 2005, 25 regional junior events (18, 16 and 14 & Under) took place across five continents with ITF or GSDF financial assistance. The competitions provide the opportunity for the players from each country to test themselves against the best in their region.

In Asia, Tajikistan became the fourth Central Asian nation to organise the ITF 13 & Under Central Asia Junior Championships – Zone 3. The event was held in the capital Dushanbe in September and saw players from Afghanistan, Kazakhstan, Kyrgyzstan, Turkmenistan and Uzbekistan participating in the event. Also in September, the Federación Salvadoreña de Tenis played host to the 8th ITF Central American 14 & Under Development Championships. The event, which is organised in conjunction with COTECC, attracted 29 players from the Central American countries of Costa Rica, Guatemala, Honduras and Panama with the players from Guatemala proving too strong for the rest of the draw, clinching both the boys' and girls' singles titles.

In the Pacific, the team from the West Pacific continued its domination of the Pacific Oceania Junior Championships (POJC) as its 16-player team clinched the regional title for the fifth consecutive year. The annual event, which plays host to the best 18 & Under and 14 & Under players from throughout the Pacific region was held at the ITF Regional Training Centre in Lautoka, Fiji in August of this year.

One of the more established junior events on the development calendar is the ITF/CAT African Junior Championships (AJC) which this year saw Mauritius hosting the 28th edition of the event in March. The Championships offers competition in three age groups at the 14 & Under, 16 & Under and 18 & Under levels. In addition two regional qualifying events, one for the West/Central Africa and one for East/Southern Africa took place earlier in the year. From these events, the best players were selected to join an ITF team, which also took part in the Championships.

The ITF's Equipment Distribution programme is able to help nations by providing ITF branded equipment (rackets, balls, strings), free of charge, for use by national associations. In 2005 alone, 6,851 rackets, 10,208 mini-tennis bats and 178,642 balls were sent out to nations.

POJC winners Michelle Pang (GUM) and Johnson Taliki (SOL)

Alex Ferrauti (GER) demonstrates elite children's tennis training

With Cyclone Hennie waiting in the wings and heavy rains delaying play, the format of the event had to modified slightly in order to allow the tournament to finish on time which was a relief to the 151 players from 27 different African countries that had travelled to Mauritius for the event.

Anas Fattar (MAR) defeated Kevin Kerr (RSA) in the boys' 18 & Under event while in the girls' event Ola Abu Zekri from Egypt defeated fellow compatriot Magy Nader Aziz to clinch the girls' 18 & Under singles title. Players gained points for their country according to their placing, and the team with the highest aggregate won the Team Trophy. This year, South Africa fought back to take the silverware from Morocco who had broken South Africa's 8-year unbroken run the previous year.

Based on performances at regional junior circuits, players have the opportunity to win a place on an ITF touring team to play higher-level events outside their region, with the ITF coach and expenses during the tour financed by the Development programme. The ITF touring team programme is probably the ITF's most well-known development initiative. Paradorn Srichaphan (THA), Gustavo Kuerten (BRA), Cara Black (ZIM), Eleni Daniilidou (GRE) and Marcos Baghdatis (CYP) have all been ITF touring team members in the past. In 2005 there were 19 ITF touring teams involving 165 players from 78 different countries.

The flagship team of the programme is undoubtedly the ITF 18 & Under Team, which plays a series of Grade 1 and Grade A events including junior Roland Garros and junior Wimbledon. In 2005, the team consisted of 13 players from 11 different countries. Raluca Olaru of Romania was one of the best performers of the team, winning the girls' singles title at the Astrid Bowl and reaching two singles finals at Milan and Roland Garros. On the boys' side, Ryan Sweeting of the Bahamas had some good results reaching the singles semifinals in Santa Croce, Milan and Roehampton. He then went on to win the US Open Juniors event as a member of the ITF 18 & Under Team to North America, bringing the Bahamas their first ever Junior Grand Slam title.

Training is also an essential part of any tennis players' programme. The ITF organises training camps on a regional basis, which enables some of the best players in the region to not only practice together, but also to educate and update coaches from the region in high-level training methods.

In addition the ITF continued to operate three training centres in 2005 with players from less developed tennis nations attending on a full-time or part-time basis. Those attending on a full-time basis still continue their schooling at local schools and many of the players attending the ITF centres are benefiting from ITF or Olympic Solidarity scholarships as a result of their performance at regional competitions.

The ITF/SATA African Training Centre is based in Pretoria, South Africa with players using the facilities at the University of Pretoria while continuing their education at local schools. In 2005, 15 players attended the centre on a full-time basis.

The ITF/OTF Pacific Oceania Regional Training Centre is based in Lautoka, Fiji. In 2005, there were 12 players from the region on full-time scholarships residing at the centre.

As mentioned above, Olympic Solidarity also supports the Development programme through Olympic Scholarships for Athletes, awarding athletes who have the potential to compete in future Olympic Games with scholarships to train at high-level training centres. The ITF Spanish Training Centre, which has been open since July 2000 accepted several recipients of these scholarships in 2005. The centre operates in Barcelona in conjunction with the Spanish and Catalan Tennis Federations. One of the principle aims is to allow players who have graduated from the junior circuit access to high level training and easy access to professional tournaments, of which there are over 30 weeks in Spain.

Tournament play is essential to the development of any tennis player and many players have problems financing their travel to events. This is where the ITF can help players through the GSDF travel grants. Grants are awarded based on applications received from developing tennis nations, which are considered by the GSDF committee. Grants are also awarded as a form of follow-up assistance to players that have performed well at ITF Junior Circuit events. In 2005, travel grants were provided to 31 players from 12 countries to play a specific programme of tournaments.

The GSDF also continues to provide prize-money grants to assist less developed tennis nations with the hosting of entry-level professional events for men and women, to help provide competitive opportunities through the world. In 2005, the fund provided grants for 42 weeks of men's professional events (ITF Satellites and Futures) and 28 weeks of ITF Women's Circuit events.

The ITF is also able to help national associations without their own tennis centres to build or refurbish their own facilities by awarding facility grants. Although grants are only a small percentage of the overall building cost, the ITF grant often acts as an endorsement and catalyst to enable associations to attract other funding whether from the government or private sector.

Looking forward to next year with five ITF Regional Workshops on the calendar in addition to the current schedule of events, 2006 looks set to be just as busy as this year.

APAN

Marketing the Game

A Marketing the Game Summit held in 2000, attended by the established tennis nations and all constituencies of the game, identified a number of projects to increase interest and participation in tennis. Projects have included a joint marketing campaign, where the ITF has matched funds provided by other partners and a Schools Tennis website, a curriculum based teaching aid which is now available for nations to adapt to their home market. An individual tennis rating system, known as the International Tennis Number (ITN) has now been successfully launched in 37 countries and task forces are working on a number of projects designed to attract and retain players.

Team Identification

The Team Identification project was introduced in 2002 as a way to improve the look of ITF team events, to increase enjoyment for TV audiences and mirror the patriotism of the spectators. The project's long term aim is to bring the flagship events, Davis Cup and Fed Cup, into line with other international sports, requiring that players be dressed in a consistent manner, reflecting their national team colours. The regulation has been mandatory in the Davis Cup and Fed Cup World Groups since 2004 and from 2006 will also be mandatory in Zone Group I of each competition.

In response to feedback, the doubles rule has been tightened up to make the matches more visually appealing and from 2006 both players of the doubles team in Davis Cup and Fed Cup must either display the nation's name on the back of their shirts and wear substantially the same colours, or both members of the team must dress in national colours.

International Tennis Number (ITN)

The ITN Manual is now available on the new ITN weblet (www.itftennis.com/itn) along with comparison charts, calculation formula and description of standards. It provides nations with all the tools needed to implement the ITN on a national and club level.

An ITN On Court Assessment has also been developed which is an objective method of initially rating recreational players who do not play competitions on a regular basis. A demonstration of the On Court Assessment is also available online, with a booklet in English, French and Spanish. Coaches can log on at www.oncourtassessment.com and enter assessment results of all their players. Players can chart their own development, compare their scores to other players and print out their own ITN Certificate.

To date 37 countries have officially launched the ITN on a national basis with coaches in over 70 countries using the On Court Assessment website to enter scores.

Intro to Tennis project

A task force composed of tennis participation experts from some of the world's leading tennis nations has been researching how tennis is currently introduced to juniors and adults worldwide and ways in which it could be done more effectively. The group has encouraged the exchange of best practice between countries including the production of DVDs and tennis manuals on adult tennis.

A number of additional projects were identified for further development in 2005, including:

Coaches' education

A new practical 4-day "Play Tennis" course has been written for coaches working with starter players, which encourages the use of game-based tuition and rotation of groups of players to ensure starter players benefit from stimulating sessions which involves match play. The course is being piloted in South Africa and will be available to nations worldwide early in 2006.

Competition formats

A sub-group has been formed with the objective of devising simple competition formats for different ages and standards of players. The formats will be showcased on a new competition website.

Research into ball perception

- This research forms part of a wider objective to promote greater use of modified balls which make tennis easier to play. The ITF continues to promote different types of balls through its Coaches' Education programme.
- Research has started to determine which colour of modified ball is best suited to adult beginner play.
- An ITF ball approval scheme for Mini Tennis orange and green balls is now in operation and the ITF intends to invite ball manufacturers to submit their products for approval.

Fit for Tennis

Initial discussions have been held on devising a 'Fit for Tennis' template which can be used by coaches worldwide in their lessons. The examples of the USTA's "Cardio Tennis" and the Australian Open's "Tennis Workout" are being studied.

Health benefits of tennis

The Sport Science and Medicine Commission is engaged in research to establish the physiological requirements of play at different levels, the physiological effects of using modified balls, and in the collation of research studies relating to the health benefits of exercise in general, and tennis in particular.

Japan's Kurumi Nara competing at the World Junior Tennis Finals in Prostejov, Czech Republic

young brings junior year full circle

by eleanor preston

Such is the attention and speculation which surrounds 16-year-old Donald Young that perhaps no-one should be surprised that the prodigy from Chicago made the news at both the beginning and the end of 2005, punctuating the season with eye-catching performances.

In girls' competition, Belarusian Viktoria Azarenka outstripped Young by securing the Australian Open and US Open singles titles and the year-end world No.1 position, and excelling in doubles by winning the Australian Open (with Marina Erakovic), Wimbledon and Roland Garros (with Hungarian Agnes Szavay), and only missing out on the grand slam when, after reuniting with Erakovic, she was forced to withdraw from the US Open doubles in the quarterfinals when the New Zealander got injured.

Yet despite all Azarenka's success and the successful transition to the women's game she had begun to affect by the time the year drew to a close, Young was by far the most talked about teenager in tennis, a new hope both for US tennis and those who long for another African American role model to bring more ethnic diversity to the sport. The 16-year-old shrugged off the onerous burden of expectation to win his first junior grand slam at January's Australian Open (when he was still only 15) and the Grade A Casablanca Cup in Mexico. Young put his seal on 2005 by winning a tight race with Marin Cilic to end the year as world No.1.

Cilic lifted the boys' trophy at Roland Garros in May and the Croatian, who trains in Zagreb with members of Croatia's victorious Davis Cup by BNP Paribas team, was one of the year's most consistent performers and was thus a worthy rival to Young. Cilic, thanks partly to a purple patch of form in November which saw him win both the Osaka Mayor's Cup and the Eddie Herr International, pushed the American all the way in the race to No. 1, and even took a late decision to play the Yucatan Cup in Mexico a week before Christmas in the hope of taking a last tilt at Young's lead in the rankings. In the end it was the unlikely figure of Romanian Petru-Alexandru Luncanu, ranked outside the world's top hundred, who had the ultimate say in the destiny of the 2005 year-end No. 1 ranking. By beating Cilic in three sets in the semifinals in Mexico, he ensured that Young could not be caught, even though Luncanu managed to beat the American to take the title.

It's not as though we weren't warned of Young's ambition to be the world's best junior player for he revealed, after beating Korea's Sun-Yong Kim in straight sets in the Australian Open final, that his feat in becoming, at 15, the youngest ever World No. 1 was actually a long-cherished dream of his. "Being No. 1 is awesome. I've wanted to be No. 1 since I started playing tournaments," Young told those listening in the press theatrette at Melbourne Park.

European clay was always going to be a challenge for Young, who feels most at home with hardcourt beneath his feet and Roland Garros proved beyond him. Instead the title went to Cilic, who proved himself deserving of the silverware when he beat the then reigning US Open junior champion

Donald Young (USA)

Young was by far the most talked about teenager in tennis, a new hope both for US tennis and those who long for another African American role model to bring more ethnic diversity to the sport.

Viktoria Azarenka (BLR)

young brings junior year full circle

by eleanor preston

Andy Murray (GBR) in the semifinals before easing past Antal Van Der Duim (NED) to take the title. When Murray went on to surge up the men's ATP Rankings, reaching no. 66 by the end of the year, it proved what a big victory Cilic's was and the Croatian said after winning he title that he knew when he had beaten the Scot that he was ready to win his first junior grand slam.

Grass didn't suit Young either, partly because, as even his most ardent admirers would admit, his lack of serving power put him at an immediate disadvantage at Wimbledon. Instead it was France's Jeremy Chardy would took the honours, beating Robin Haase (NED) in the final to emulate his compatriot Gael Monfils, who had beaten him in the quarterfinals the previous year and provided Chardy with inspiration.

"After I lost that match Gael said to me, 'you will come back next year and win the title, I promise you'," revealed Chardy after beating Haase.

Chardy went on to reach the US Open boys' final as well, though his quest to win back-to-back junior grand slams ended in disappointment when 18-year-old Bahamian Ryan Sweeting exceeded even his own expectations by taking his debut junior major at Flushing Meadows.

"I didn't even think I was capable of winning this tournament," said Sweeting, who had to save five match-points in his first round match against Australia's Carsten Ball. "My goal coming in wasn't to win, it was just to give 100% and play my best, because that's the only thing you can do on the court. I mean, you want to win, obviously. But that's not really something you can control. The only thing you can control is playing your best, and that's what I did. It worked this week, and I'm just so happy."

"After I lost that match Gael said to me, 'you will come back next year and win the title, I promise you'," revealed Chardy after beating Haase.

Jeremy Chardy (FRA)

Sweeting was a member of the ITF's Development Touring Team during 2005 and also plays Davis Cup for the Bahamas alongside veteran Bahamian doubles specialist Mark Knowles, an experience he said helped him when it came to playing the biggest match of his junior career.

"It's a great advantage playing Davis Cup," said Sweeting, who was also a contender for the year-end world No. 1 ranking, at least until he lost at the Orange Bowl. "You get the experience of hitting with the big guys, with the pros, playing matches with them, seeing how they act, how they behave on the court. You're there with them; you're one of them during those weeks. It's helped me so much handling myself on the court, behaving, staying calm, focused, acting professional, you know, not like a kid. I've been playing Davis Cup for a while now, so I'm kind of used to that with the crowds and everything but the US Open junior final was probably the most important match of my life right now, and I'm just really, really excited how I handled it."

With Azarenka dominating the season in girls' junior tennis, others did well to get a look in, notably her sometime doubles partner Szavay, who, having endured the bitter experience of losing to Azarenka in the Australian Open final, won the singles title at Roland Garros with a 61 61 win over Romania's Raluca-Ioana Olaru (another ITF Development Touring Team member).

Agnieska Radwanska (POL)

"It was a grand slam final but because it was the second time for me I was relaxed," said Szavay. "I think maybe she was more nervous than me. I hope this is a big step for me. It's a really good feeling and now I know all the other juniors will be looking at me, saying, 'she won Roland Garros'."

They will be saying similar things about Agnieska Radwanska of Poland, who beat Timea Paszek (AUT) 63 64 to win the Wimbledon girls' title. Radwanska admitted afterwards that she had been "afraid of the grass" before the tournament began and succeeded chiefly with the tactical advice of her coach and father Robert Radwanski.

Radwanski and his daughter joined forces again in Barcelona during the Junior Fed Cup final at the Real Club de Polo, where Radwanska, her sister Urszula and team-mate Maksymiliana Wandel were captained to victory by Radwanski. The Polish team skipped through the round robin phase and the semifinals but was severely tested by France in the final, with Agnieska and Alizé Cornet serving up a contender for junior match of the year in the second singles rubber of the tie.

"Of course my wife and I are very proud parents and I'm very proud of the team," he said afterwards. "This is very big for tennis in Poland because the sport there is not so good. When my daughters win it is great for sport in our country."

There was better news for France's boys in Barcelona after they won the Junior Davis Cup by BNP Paribas, beating Czech Republic in the final. According to French coach Alois Beust, the French team, who finished the season unbeaten, epitomised the spirit of team competition in tennis. "I'm so proud of my players," said Beust. "They've played very well. It's been a very, very long road and this is an incredibly tough competition, very long and lots of hours on court. This team has a wonderful spirit because they've played together all year, they've been through a lot together and they've become good friends. That's what is so great about these competitions – it allows them to form strong bonds with each other. It paid off."

There was plenty of motivation for all those involved on the final weekend in Barcelona, whether they were challenging for the title or simply trying to improve their position in the final standings. In a new ITF initiative those that finished in the top three of Junior Davis Cup (France, Czech Republic and Ecuador) and Junior Fed Cup (Poland, France and Czech Republic) received 16 & under team competition feed-up exempt positions for their players – effectively a free pass into selected junior tournaments next season.

There was plenty to play for until the last ball for all teams, not least those battling for the lower placings. Thailand finished in the 16th and final position of the Junior Davis Cup and therefore Asia will have one less place in the final for the 2006 competition. South Africa's finish in 16th spot in the Junior Fed Cup means Africa will lose a final place for that competition next year.

France also emerged victorious from the season's boys' 14 & under ITF junior team competition, World Junior Tennis, with victory over Argentina in the final in Prostejov in August. Russia, led by the talented Anastasia Pavlyuchenkova, beat Japan to win the girls' event whilst teams from Africa – Algeria's girls and South Africa's boys, finished in 16th spot.

Radwanska, meanwhile finished at no. 3 in the girls' rankings, behind Azarenka and Szavay and ahead of 2005 Orange Bowl champion, Caroline Wozniacki of Denmark. Switzerland's Robin Roshart, the surprise winner of the boys' Orange Bowl title, finished the season as world no. 7, with Young, Cilic, Sweeting, Chardy, Leonardo Mayer and Haase ahead of him.

Radwanska admitted afterwards that she had been "afraid of the grass" before the tournament began and succeeded chiefly with the tactical advice of her coach and father Robert Radwanski.

As ever, though, it was Young who had the last word on 2005, a season which saw him make history in Melbourne and finish up in Mexico an older, wiser and, arguably, more complete player than he had been in January. Young's race with Cilic was so close in the end that the Croatian actually ended up with more singles points than the American, who owed his victory to his achievements in doubles, notably winning the US Open doubles title with compatriot Alex Clayton.

With both Young and Cilic eligible to play junior events in 2006, their rivalry could develop further in the coming months. As the past year proved, it pays to pay attention to Young.

ITF Junior World Rankings 2005 Points Explanation

The ITF Junior Circuit is a world-wide points-linked circuit of 318 tournaments, including eight continental championships and two team competitions in 115 countries under the management of the International Tennis Federation. There are ten separate points categories covering the three types of events. The best six singles results and one quarter of the best six doubles results from tournaments (Grade A and 1-5), continental championships (Grade B1-B3) and team competitions (Grade C) count towards a player's Junior Ranking. To qualify for a year-end ranking a player must have competed in at least six events, including at least three Grade A tournaments and at least three outside his or her own home country.

Tournaments and Continental Championships

Singles

Grade	A	1	2	3	4	5	B1	B2	B3
Winner	250	150	100	60	40	30	180	120	80
Runner-up	180	100	75	45	30	20	120	80	50
Semifinalists	120	80	50	30	20	15	80	60	30
Quarterfinalists	80	60	30	20	15	10	60	40	15
Losers in last 16	50	30	20	15	10	5	30	25	5
Losers in last 32	30	20	–	–	–	–	20	10	–

Doubles

Grade	A	1	2	3	4	5	B1	B2	B3
Winners	180	100	75	50	30	20	120	80	50
Runners-up	120	75	50	30	20	15	80	60	30
Semifinalists	80	50	30	20	15	10	60	40	15
Quarterfinalists	50	30	20	15	10	5	30	25	5
Losers in last 16	30	20	–	–	–	–	20	10	–

Grade A Super Series Bonus Points

	Singles	Doubles
Winner of three or more Grade A events	250	180

Grand Slam Bonus Points

	Singles	Doubles
Winner	250	180

Qualifying players losing in the first round of the main draw will receive 25 ranking points
Players losing in the final round of qualifying will receive 20 ranking points

Grade C Team Competition – Regional Qualifying

	No. 1 Singles Player Win	No. 2 Singles Player Win	Doubles Win Each Player
Final	80	60	60
Semifinal	60	40	40
Quarterfinal	40	20	20

Points are to be given to a player for one result only (their best) in the competition.
Only players from the best eight teams will be considered for the allocation of World Ranking Points.

ITF Junior World Rankings 2005

End of year positions

Only those players who qualifed for a year-end ranking are listed. The minimum requirements for this were having played six events, three of which were outside their own country and three of which were Group A status.

Boys

1	Donald Young (USA)
2	Marin Cilic (CRO)
3	Ryan Sweeting (BAH)
4	Jeremy Chardy (FRA)
5	Leonardo Mayer (ARG)
6	Robin Haase (NED)
7	Robin Roshardt (SUI)
8	Niels Desein (BEL)
9	Thiemo De Bakker (NED)
10	Andre Miele (BRA)
11	Carsten Ball (AUS)
12	Sun-Jong Kim (KOR)
13	Piero Luisi (VEN)
14	Raony Carvalho (BRA)
15	Antal van der Duim (NED)
16	Dusan Lojda (CZE)
17	Samuel Querrey (USA)
18	Evgeny Kirillov (RUS)
19	Petar Jelenic (CRO)
20	Andreas Haider-Maurer (AUT)

Girls

1	Viktoria Azarenka (BLR)
2	Agnes Szavay (HUN)
3	Agnieszka Radwanska (POL)
4	Caroline Wozniacki (DEN)
5	Dominika Cibulkova (SVK)
6	Raluca-Ioana Olaru (ROM)
7	Alexandra Dulgheru (ROM)
8	Alexa Glatch (USA)
9	Yung-Jan Chan (TPE)
10	Mihaela Buzarnescu (ROM)
11	Alisa Kleybanova (RUS)
12	Ayumi Morita (JPN)
13	Aleksandra Wozniak (CAN)
14	Vania King (USA)
15	Bibiane Schoofs (NED)
16	Sharon Fichman (CAN)
17	Sorana-Mihaela Cirstea (ROM)
18	Yaroslava Shvedova (RUS)
19	Amina Rakhim (KAZ)
20	Marina Erakovic (NZL)

Viktoria Azarenka (BLR) and Agnes Szavay (HUN)

ITF Junior Circuit 2005 Results

- **TLALNEPANTLA** (MEX) (Grade A) 27 DECEMBER-2 JANUARY – **GS:** Aleksandra Wozniak (CAN) d. Dominika Cibulkova (SVK) 63 36 61. **GD:** Yung-Jan Chan (TPE)/Aleksandra Wozniak (CAN) d. Bibiane Schoofs (NED)/Agnes Szatmari (ROM) 61 60. **BS:** Donald Young (USA) d. Juan-Martin Del Potro (ARG) 75 75. **BD:** Juan-Martin Del Potro (ARG)/David Navarrete (VEN) d. Robin Haase/Antal Van Der Duim (NED) 63 63.

- **STOCKHOLM** (SWE) (Grade 4) 1-6 JANUARY – **GS:** Eugenia Vertesheva (RUS) d. Jelena Kulikova (RUS) 64 76. **GD:** Diana Eriksson/ Johanna Larsson (SWE) d. Mathilda Engstrom/Mona Mansour (SWE) 61 64. **BS:** Tim Goransson (SWE) d. Dean Jackson (GER) 62 61. **BD:** Blazej Koniusz/Piotr Zielinski (POL) d. Marcin Gawron/Mateusz Szmigiel (POL) 62 57 75.

- **COTONOU** (BEN) (Grade 4) 2-6 JANUARY – **GS:** Xenia Samoilova (RUS) d. Nicole Rottmann (AUT) 61 62. **GD:** Nicole Rottmann (AUT)/ Xenia Samoilova (RUS) d. Kate Coleman/Emma Kodjoe (GHA) 75 76(6). **BS:** Loic Didavi (BEN) d. Jean Segodo (BEN) 63 62. **BD:** Emmanuel Mensah/Menford Owusu (GHA) d. Mlapa Tingou Akomlo/Komlan Dziwonou (TOG) 62 62.

- **SAN JOSE** (CRC) (Grade 1) 3-8 JANUARY – **GS:** Aleksandra Wozniak (CAN) d. Irena Pavlovic (FRA) 63 76(6). **GD:** Mihaela Buzarnescu (ROM)/Bibiane Schoofs (NED) d. Yung-Jan Chan (TPE)/Aleksandra Wozniak (CAN) 64 60. **BS:** Robin Haase (NED) d. Juan-Martin Del Potro (ARG) 63 36 63. **BD:** Robin Haase/Antal Van Der Duim (NED) d. Juan-Martin Del Potro/Francisco Pozzi-Romanazzi (ARG) w/o.

- **DHAKA** (BAN) (Grade 4) 4-8 JANUARY – **GS:** Elena Chernyakova (RUS) d. Waratchaya Wongteanchai (THA) 63 60. **GD:** Elina Hasanova (AZE)/Elena Chernyakova (RUS) d. Parichart Charoensukploypho/Kamonthip Saovana (THA) 62 62. **BS:** Kittipong Wachiramanowong (THA) d. Sumit Prakash Gupta (IND) 62 60. **BD:** Ranjan Ram/Sree-Amol Roy (BAN) d. Sumit Prakash Gupta (IND)/Oshada Wijemanne (SRI) 36 62 61.

- **TRARALGON** (AUS) (Grade 1) 7-12 JANUARY – **GS:** Magdalena Rybarikova (SVK) d. Jarmila Gajdosova (SVK) w/o. **GD:** Michaela Johansson/Nadja Roma (SWE) d. Sara Errani/Stella Menna (ITA) 63 16 64. **BS:** Carsten Ball (AUS) d. Todd Ley (AUS) 76(4) 61. **BD:** Pavol Cervenak/Lukas Lacko (SVK) d. Richard Ruckelshausen (AUT)/Jurgens Strydom (NAM) 64 67(4) 75.

- **VASTERAS** (SWE) (Grade 4) 7-12 JANUARY – **GS:** Jelena Kulikova (RUS) d. Marina Yudanov (SWE) 64 76(5). **GD:** Viktoriya Agryutenkova/ Jelena Kulikova (RUS) d. Yana Kireeva/Maria Mosolova (RUS) 60 ret. **BS:** Tim Goransson (SWE) d. Piotr Zielinski (POL) 64 63. **BD:** Marcin Gawron/Mateusz Szmigiel (POL) d. Simon Bekker/Victor Kozin (RUS) 63 62.

- **LOME** (TOG) (Grade 4) 8-12 JANUARY – **GS:** Xenia Samoilova (RUS) d. Nicole Rottmann (AUT) 60 61. **GD:** Nicole Rottmann (AUT)/ Xenia Samoilova (RUS) d. Kate Coleman (GHA)/Emma Cudjoe (GUA) 64 61. **BS:** Loic Didavi (BEN) d. Emmanuel Mensah (GHA) 64 75. **BD:** Loic Didavi (BEN)/Arnaud Jousselin (FRA) d. Emmanuel Mensah/Menford Owusu (GHA) 46 62 64.

- **CARACAS** (VEN) (Grade 1) 10-16 JANUARY – **GS:** Giulia Gabba (ITA) d. Bibiane Schoofs (NED) 67(9) 61 63. **GD:** Marrit Boonstra/Renee Reinhard (NED) d. Fernanda Hermenegildo (BRA)/Irina Matiychyk (UKR) 63 75. **BS:** Piero Luisi (VEN) d. David Navarrete (VEN) 67(0) 63 63. **BD:** Piero Luisi/David Navarrete (VEN) d. Luis-Henrique Grangeiro/Andre Miele (BRA) 63 76(4).

- **BERGHEIM** (AUT) (Grade 4) 10-15 JANUARY – **GS:** Astrid Besser (ITA) d. Karin Knapp (ITA) 57 75 63. **GD:** Astrid Besser/Karin Knapp (ITA) d. Klaudia Malenovska/Lenka Wienerova (SVK) 64 63. **BS:** Kristofer Wachter (AUT) d. Paul-Mihai Puscasu (ROM) 16 63 60. **BD:** Marc Meigel (GER)/Nikola Mektic (CRO) d. Petru-Alexandru Luncanu/Paul-Mihai Puscasu (ROM) 57 63 62.

- **RAJSHAHI** (BAN) (Grade 3) 11-15 JANUARY – **GS:** Elena Chernyakova (RUS) d. Waratchaya Wongteanchai (THA) 62 64. **GD:** Elina Hasanova (AZE)/Elena Chernyakova (RUS) d. Ratchaya Chaichanachaicharn/Waratchaya Wongteanchai (THA) 36 76(8) 75. **BS:** Huai-En Chang (TPE) d. Oshada Wijemanne (SRI) 62 75. **BD:** Min Fu Ko/Hsin-Han Lee (TPE) d. Tetta Oyama (JPN)/Kittipong Wachiramanowong (THA) 63 61.

- **GLEN WAVERLEY** (AUS) (Grade 1) 16-22 JANUARY – **GS:** Viktoria Azarenka (BLR) d. Timea Bacsinszky (SUI) 62 64. **GD:** Nikola Frankova (CZE)/Agnes Szavay (HUN) d. Viktoria Azarenka (BLR)/Alisa Kleybanova (RUS) 63 62. **BS:** Sun-Yong Kim (KOR) d. Dusan Lojda (CZE) 62 61. **BD:** Timothy Neilly/Tim Smyczek (USA) d. Marin Cilic (CRO)/Luka Ocvirk (SLO) 67(5) 64 63.

- **BARRANQUILLA** (COL) (Grade 1) 17-23 JANUARY – **GS:** Giulia Gabba (ITA) d. Estefania Balda (ECU) 46 63 61. **GD:** Bibiane Schoofs (NED)/ Roxane Vaisemberg (BRA) d. Estefania Balda (ECU)/Florencia Molinero (ARG) w/o. **BS:** Santiago Giraldo (COL) d. Luis-Henrique Grangeiro (BRA) 64 60. **BD:** Chris Chirico (USA)/Branko Kuzmanovic (SCG) d. Joaquin Guillier/Borja Malo (CHI) 76(5) 64.

- **BRATISLAVA** (SVK) (Grade 2) 17-23 JANUARY – **GS:** Agnieszka Radwanska (POL) d. Urszula Radwanska (POL) 62 76(1). **GD:** Agnieszka Radwanska/Urszula Radwanska (POL) d. Claudia Smolders/Aude Vermoezen (BEL) 61 60. **BS:** Denes Lukacs (HUN) d. Aljoscha Thron (GER) 64 46 76(4). **BD:** Pavel Chekhov (RUS)/Dmitry Novikov (BLR) d. Roman Jebavy/Vaclav Kucera (CZE) 76(5) 64.

- **DHAKA** (BAN) (Grade 3) 18-22 JANUARY – **GS:** Waratchaya Wongteanchai (THA) d. Elena Chernyakova (RUS) 46 64 63. **GD:** Elina Hasanova (AZE)/Elena Chernyakova (RUS) d. Ratchaya Chaichanachaicharn/Waratchaya Wongteanchai (THA) 64 62. **BS:** Faisal Aidil (INA) d. Tejesvi Rao (IND) 63 63. **BD:** Peerakit Siributwong/Kittipong Wachiramanowong (THA) d. Sumit Prakash Gupta/Tejesvi Rao (IND) 61 61.

- **HAMBURG** (GER) (Grade 4) 18-23 JANUARY – **GS:** Anna Gerasimou (GRE) d. Alize Cornet (FRA) 60 36 63. **GD:** Melissa Ravestein/Steffi Weterings (NED) d. Marlot Coolen/Marcella Koek (NED) 60 63. **BS:** Dimitar Kutrovsky (BUL) d. Yannick Mertens (BEL) 62 61. **BD:** Dimitar Kutrovsky (BUL)/Denis Molcianov (MDA) d. Cesare Gallo/Nicola Remedi (ITA) 61 62.

- **ABU DHABI** (UAE) (Grade 5) 24-28 JANUARY – **GS:** Viktoriya Agryutenkova (RUS) d. Oxana Kalashnikova (GEO) 26 62 63. **GD:** Maria Kalashnikova/Oxana Kalashnikova (GEO) d. Jessica-Marie Agra (PHI)/Aya Mochizuki (JPN) 62 63. **BS:** Ahmed Rabeea (KUW) d. Alexander Seleznev (KGZ) 61 61. **BD:** Thomas Gilner (GER)/Alexander Seleznev (KGZ) d. Ali Ismail/Ahmed Rabeea (KUW) 61 64.

- **MELBOURNE** (AUS) (Grade A) 24-30 JANUARY – **GS:** Viktoria Azarenka (BLR) d. Agnes Szavay (HUN) 62 62. **GD:** Viktoria Azarenka (BLR)/Marina Erakovic (NZL) d. Nikola Frankova (CZE)/Agnes Szavay (HUN) 60 62. **BS:** Donald Young (USA) d. Sun-Yong Kim (KOR) 62 64. **BD:** Sun-Yong Kim (KOR)/Chu-Huan Yi (TPE) d. Thiemo De Bakker (NED)/Donald Young (USA) 63 64.

- **KOLKATA** (IND) (Grade 3) 24-29 JANUARY – **GS:** Sandhya Nagaraj (IND) d. Dominice Ripoll (GER) 64 64. **GD:** Denise Dy (PHI)/He-Wen-Fei Li (CHN) d. Dominice Ripoll (GER)/Eleonora Sidjemileva (UZB) 75 62. **BS:** Jeevan Nedunchezhiyan (IND) d. Xiao-Peng Lai (HKG) 62 64. **BD:** Rupesh Roy/Vivek Shokeen (IND) d. Jeevan Nedunchezhiyan/Sanam Singh (IND) 63 67(7) 62.

- **CUENCA** (ECU) (Grade 2) 24-30 JANUARY – **GS:** Bibiane Schoofs (NED) d. Liset Brito (CHI) 62 62. **GD:** Estefania Balda (ECU)/Roxane Vaisemberg (BRA) d. Anna Bartenstein (AUT)/Florencia Molinero (ARG) 36 63 64. **BS:** Luis-Henrique Grangeiro (BRA) d. Andre Miele (BRA) 67(5) 61 62. **BD:** Emiliano Massa/Leonardo Mayer (ARG) d. Luis-Henrique Grangeiro/Andre Miele (BRA) 76(3) 76(5).

- **PREROV** (CZE) (Grade 1) 24-30 JANUARY – **GS:** Anastasia Pavlyuchenkova (RUS) d. Agnieszka Radwanska (POL) 63 64. **GD:** Kristina Antoniychuk (UKR)/Anastasia Pavlyuchenkova (RUS) d. Daniela Pernetova/Katerina Vankova (CZE) 64 63. **BS:** Aljoscha Thron (GER) d. Jiri Kosler (CZE) 26 64 63. **BD:** Pavel Chekhov/Valeri Rudnev (RUS) d. Tomas Josefus/Ondrej Kacmar (CZE) 63 63.

- **SHATIN** (HKG) (Grade 5) 30 JANUARY-5 FEBRUARY – **GS:** Ling Zhang (HKG) d. Chang Xu (CHN) 63 60. **GD:** Zi-Jun Yang/Ling Zhang (HKG) d. Rumi Abe/Hirono Yoshikawa (JPN) 67(5) 62 60. **BS:** Tetta Oyama (JPN) d. Kyle Joshua Dandan (PHI) 62 46 64. **BD:** Alvin-Putra Kurniawan/Lenz Theodor (INA) d. Taiki Kato/Toshiya Suzuki (JPN) w/o.

- **NEW DELHI** (IND) (Grade 2) 31 JANUARY-5 FEBRUARY – **GS:** Amina Rakhim (KAZ) d. Madura Ranganathan (IND) 62 60. **GD:** Ksenia Palkina (KGZ)/Amina Rakhim (KAZ) d. Laura-Ioana Andrei (ROM)/Justina Derungs (SUI) 62 61. **BS:** Vivek Shokeen (IND) d. Jeevan Nedunchezhiyan (IND) 75 63. **BD:** Jeevan Nedunchezhiyan/Sanam Singh (IND) d. Sumit Prakash Gupta/Vivek Shokeen (IND) 76(3) 76(5).

- **LIMA** (PER) (Grade 2) 31 JANUARY-6 FEBRUARY – **GS:** Florencia Molinero (ARG) d. Emiko Ito (JPN) 64 62. **GD:** Jade Curtis (GBR)/Chelsey Gullickson (USA) d. Yvette Hyndman (USA)/Maria Mokh (RUS) 63 61. **BS:** Leonardo Mayer (ARG) d. Emiliano Massa (ARG) 63 62. **BD:** Johnny Hamui (USA)/Kei Nishikori (JPN) d. Juan-Andres Gomez/Jose Zunino (ECU) 76(5) 62.

- **RADENCI** (SLO) (Grade 5) 2-6 FEBRUARY – **GS:** Taja Mohorcic (SLO) d. Jasmina Kajtazovic (SLO) 61 62. **GD:** Aleksandra Lukic/Patricia Vollmeier (SLO) d. Lisa Summerer/Janina Toljan (AUT) 61 61. **BS:** Petru-Alexandru Luncanu (ROM) d. Boran Poljancic (CRO) 63 61. **BD:** Vedran Siljegovic/Tibor Simic (CRO) d. Alen Haluzan/Bojan Kovac (CRO) 46 63 61.

- **AUCKLAND** (NZL) (Grade 4) 4-9 FEBRUARY – **GS:** Jenny Swift (AUS) d. Ayumi Okuma (JPN) 76(7) 62. **GD:** Emelyn Starr/Jenny Swift (AUS) d. Ayumi Okuma/Natsumi Yokota (JPN) 62 63. **BS:** Chu-Huan Yi (TPE) d. Mehdi Bouabbane (ALG) 63 64. **BD:** Matthew Stark (NZL)/Chu-Huan Yi (TPE) d. Jackson Bodle/Austin Childs (NZL) 62 63.

- **LA PAZ** (BOL) (Grade 2) 7-12 FEBRUARY – **GS:** Tereza Mrdeza (CRO) d. Liset Brito (CHI) 61 06 63. **GD:** Emiko Ito/Maya Kato (JPN) d. Liset Brito (CHI)/Jessica Sweeting (BAH) 36 62 61. **BS:** Raony Carvalho (BRA) d. Andre Miele (BRA) 75 76(6). **BD:** Raony Carvalho (BRA)/Johnny Hamui (USA) d. Peter Aarts (USA)/Luis-Javier Cuellar-Contreras (CUB) 76(3) 61.

- **CHANDIGARH** (IND) (Grade 3) 7-12 FEBRUARY – **GS:** Amina Rakhim (KAZ) d. Martina Lautenschlager (SUI) 62 64. **GD:** Goele Lemmens/Yanina Wickmayer (BEL) d. Sandhya Nagaraj/Madura Ranganathan (IND) 60 16 75. **BS:** Jeevan Nedunchezhiyan (IND) d. Xiao-Peng Lai (HKG) 63 60. **BD:** Jeevan Nedunchezhiyan/Vivek Shokeen (IND) d. Vaja Uzakov (UZB)/Stas Zhuravski (RUS) 63 63.

- **FRYDLANT NAD OSTRAVICI** (CZE) (Grade 4) 9-13 FEBRUARY – **GS:** Daniela Pernetova (CZE) d. Madlen Kadur (GER) 64 63. **GD:** Tereza Hladikova/Martina Ondrackova (CZE) d. Andrea Berkova/Daniela Pernetova (CZE) 62 60. **BS:** Martin Kamenik (CZE) d. Denes Lukacs (HUN) 62 62. **BD:** Siarhei Betau (BLR)/Maros Horny (SVK) d. Roman Jebavy/Michal Kozerovsky (CZE) 63 57 62.

- **CANTERBURY** (NZL) (Grade 4) 12-16 FEBRUARY – **GS:** Sacha Jones (NZL) d. Ayumi Okuma (JPN) 60 63. **GD:** Emelyn Starr/Jenny Swift (AUS) d. Ayumi Okuma/Natsumi Yokota (JPN) 36 64 75. **BS:** Marcel Goodman (USA) d. Mehdi Bouabbane (ALG) 75 76(7). **BD:** Ryan Bellamy/Greg Jones (AUS) d. Dae Jin Kim/Dae Young Kim (KOR) 76(4) 62.

- **CONTRERAS** (MEX) (Grade 5) 14-20 FEBRUARY – **GS:** Stefanie Nunic (USA) d. Paulina Luquin (MEX) 62 63. **GD:** Bianca Aboubakare/Carissa Aboubakare (USA) d. Thalia Diaz Barriga/Paulina Luquin (MEX) 62 63. **BS:** Wil Spencer (USA) d. Guillaume St Maurice (CAN) 76(7) 62. **BD:** Alejandro Moreno (MEX)/Shan Sondhu (USA) d. Bruno Berruti/Gustavo Loza (MEX) 76(3) 36 61.

- **COLOMBO** (SRI) (Grade 5) 14-20 FEBRUARY – **GS:** Justina Derungs (SUI) d. Vandana Murali (IND) 26 75 63. **GD:** Justina Derungs (SUI)/Vandana Murali (IND) d. Kai-Chen Chang/Yun Ku (TPE) 62 36 64. **BS:** Hsin-Han Lee (TPE) d. Oshada Wijemanne (SRI) 63 36 63. **BD:** Tsung Hua Yang/Yen Te Li (TPE) d. Hsin-Han Lee/Terence Wong (TPE) 75 62.

- **SANTIAGO** (CHI) (Grade 2) 14-20 FEBRUARY – **GS:** Anna Tatishvili (GEO) d. Ana-Clara Duarte (BRA) 75 62. **GD:** Irina Matiychyk (UKR)/Stephanie Wetmore (CAN) d. Sharon Fichman (CAN)/Anna Tatishvili (GEO) 76(4) 26 63. **BS:** Joao Souza (BRA) d. Nicolas Santos (BRA) 46 76(8) 63. **BD:** Peter Aarts/Jonathon Boym (USA) d. Nicolas Santos/Joao Souza (BRA) 62 63.

- **RUNGSTED KYST** (DEN) (Grade 4) 14-19 FEBRUARY – **GS:** Stefania Boffa (SUI) d. Maria Mosolova (RUS) 64 67(3) 63. **GD:** Ksenia Pervak/Elena Chernyakova (RUS) d. Ieva Irbe (LAT)/Maria Mosolova (RUS) 62 62. **BS:** Andy Chirita (SWE) d. Robert Varga (UKR) 62 76(4). **BD:** Cesare Gallo (ITA)/Robert Varga (UKR) d. Nikolas Holzen/Mauro Piras (GER) 67(4) 64 76(4).

- **WELLINGTON** (NZL) (Grade 5) 19-23 FEBRUARY – **GS:** Yoon-Young Jeong (KOR) d. Therese Tisseverasinghe (AUS) 64 61. **GD:** Yoon-Young Jeong (KOR)/Natsumi Yokota (JPN) d. Emelyn Starr/Jenny Swift (AUS) 64 57 63. **BS:** Soon-Sung Park (KOR) d. Austin Childs (NZL) 64 63. **BD:** Robert Foy/Adam Siddall (NZL) d. Michael Bartlett/James Pilbro (NZL) 62 75.

- **MAR DEL PLATA** (ARG) (Grade 2) 21-27 FEBRUARY – **GS:** Anna Tatishvili (GEO) d. Florencia Molinero (ARG) 60 60. **GD:** Sharon Fichman (CAN)/Anna Tatishvili (GEO) d. Fernanda Hermenegildo (BRA)/Florencia Molinero (ARG) 75 64. **BS:** Joao Souza (BRA) d. Leonardo Mayer (ARG) 76(5) 06 63. **BD:** Emiliano Massa/Leonardo Mayer (ARG) d. Ravid Hezi (ISR)/Bryan Koniecko (USA) 62 67(4) 61.

- **HELSINKI** (FIN) (Grade 4) 21-25 FEBRUARY – **GS:** Johanna Larsson (SWE) d. Katarina Tuohimaa (FIN) 64 64. **GD:** Idunn Hertzberg/Nina Munch-Soegaard (NOR) d. Julia Bone/Samantha Murray (GBR) 62 61. **BS:** Rasmus Moller (DEN) d. Victor Kozin (RUS) 63 64. **BD:** Vladimir Ivanov (EST)/Victor Kozin (RUS) d. Martin Kildahl/Carl Sundberg (NOR) 62 61.

- **JALISCO** (MEX) (Grade 5) 21-27 FEBRUARY – **GS:** Valentina Fauviau (FRA) d. Paulina Luquin (MEX) 75 61. **GD:** Thalia Diaz Barriga/Paulina Luquin (MEX) d. Yi-Xi Liu (CHN)/Stefanie Nunic (USA) 61 64. **BS:** Guillaume St Maurice (CAN) d. Keziel Juneau (CAN) 26 61 64. **BD:** Bradley Cox/Wil Spencer (USA) d. Keziel Juneau/Guillaume St Maurice (CAN) 46 63 63.

- **SARAWAK** (MAS) (Grade 3) 22-27 FEBRUARY – **GS:** Shao-Yuan Kao (TPE) d. Yurina Koshino (JPN) 76(7) 63. **GD:** Yurina Koshino/Chie Moriuchi (JPN) d. Shao-Yuan Kao/Su-Han Yang (TPE) 57 64 63. **BS:** Hsin-Han Lee (TPE) d. Shuhei Uzawa (JPN) 62 63. **BD:** Elbert Sie (INA)/Shuhei Uzawa (JPN) d. Ronald Chow/Xiao-Peng Lai (HKG) 62 62.

- **ALMERE** (NED) (Grade 4) 23-26 FEBRUARY – **GS:** Marrit Boonstra (NED) d. Stefania Boffa (SUI) 76(1) 61. **GD:** Marlot Meddens/Arantxa Rus (NED) d. Stefania Boffa (SUI)/Tatiana Cutrona (BEL) 63 61. **BS:** Danny Heidecker (GER) d. Florian Stephan (GER) 63 61. **BD:** Danny Heidecker/Dean Jackson (GER) d. Jan Hoekzema/Florian Stephan (GER) 62 60.

- **IZHEVSK** (RUS) (Grade 3) 28 FEBRUARY-6 MARCH – **GS:** Yaroslava Shvedova (RUS) d. Anastasia Petukhova (RUS) 36 63 64. **GD:** Alexandra Panova/Yaroslava Shvedova (RUS) d. Maria Mosolova/Anastasia Petukhova (RUS) 62 75. **BS:** Andrei Levine (RUS) d. Alexei Nikolaev (RUS) 76(4) 63. **BD:** Victor Kozin/Stas Zhuravski (RUS) d. Dmitri Perevoschikov/Eugeni Slesarev (RUS) 62 64.

- **ADELAIDE** (AUS) (Grade 4) 28 FEBRUARY-5 MARCH – **GS:** Benita Milenkiewicz (AUS) d. Jessica Moore (AUS) 61 63. **GD:** Shiho Akita/Ai Yamamoto (JPN) d. Ashlee Brown (AUS)/Jawariah Noordin (MAS) 64 36 62. **BS:** Samuel Groth (AUS) d. Lachlan Reed (AUS) 63 75. **BD:** Edward Bourchier/Lachlan Reed (AUS) d. Austin Childs (NZL)/Patrick Szacinski (AUS) 76(3) 46 ret.

● **OSLO** (NOR) (Grade 4) 28 FEBRUARY-5 MARCH – **GS:** Katarina Tuohimaa (FIN) d. Nina Munch-Soegaard (NOR) 76(8) 46 62. **GD:** Idunn Hertzberg/Nina Munch-Soegaard (NOR) d. Maya Pitenina (RUS)/Katarina Tuohimaa (FIN) 75 26 63. **BS:** Andy Chirita (SWE) d. Carl Sundberg (NOR) 64 63. **BD:** Martin Kildahl/Carl Sundberg (NOR) d. Andy Chirita (SWE)/Philip Therp (DEN) 64 62.

● **ANNABA** (ALG) (Grade 5) 28 FEBRUARY-4 MARCH – **GS:** Sona Novakova (CZE) d. Sara Meghoufel (ALG) 62 76(5). **GD:** Sona Novakova/Zora Vlckova (CZE) d. Lisa Summerer/Janina Toljan (AUT) 54(0) 40. **BS:** Hicham Laalej (MAR) d. Mehdi Bouabbane (ALG) 62 76(5). **BD:** Abdelkrim Ben Osman/Mehdi Bouabbane (ALG) d. Mehdi Bouras (ALG)/Maximilien Genuini (FRA) 40 54(4).

● **LA LIBERTAD** (ESA) (Grade 4) 28 FEBRUARY-5 MARCH – **GS:** Liset Brito (CHI) d. Alena Bayarchyk (BLR) 64 26 63. **GD:** Alena Bayarchyk (BLR)/Stefanie Nunic (USA) d. Thalia Diaz Barriga/Paulina Luquin (MEX) 64 64. **BS:** Istvan Bolgar (USA) d. Ricardo Hernandez (VEN) 64 63. **BD:** Bruno Berruti/Jaime Clark (MEX) d. Alejandro Argumedo (ESA)/Ricardo Hernandez (VEN) 36 62 76(2).

● **PUNTA DEL ESTE** (URU) (Grade 2) 28 FEBRUARY-5 MARCH – **GS:** Anna Tatishvili (GEO) d. Raluca Olaru (ROM) 62 60. **GD:** Alexandra Dulgheru/Raluca Olaru (ROM) d. Anna Bartenstein (AUT)/Florencia Molinero (ARG) 46 64 75. **BS:** Leonardo Mayer (ARG) d. Emiliano Massa (ARG) 75 63. **BD:** Emiliano Massa/Leonardo Mayer (ARG) d. Borja Malo/Guillermo Rivera (CHI) 76(4) ret.

● **JALAN BERAKAS** (BRU) (Grade 4) 1-6 MARCH – **GS:** Shao-Yuan Kao (TPE) d. Nicha Lertpitasinchai (THA) 64 62. **GD:** Shao-Yuan Kao/Yun Ku (TPE) d. Naoko Ueshima (JPN)/Varanya Vijuksanaboon (THA) 26 64 64. **BS:** Xiao-Peng Lai (HKG) d. Huai-En Chang (TPE) 64 60. **BD:** Hsin-Han Lee/Cheng Hsun Yang (TPE) d. Ronald Chow/Xiao-Peng Lai (HKG) 62 57 63.

● **NURNBERG** (GER) (Grade 2) 1-6 MARCH – **GS:** Ekaterina Makarova (RUS) d. Evgeniya Rodina (RUS) 62 75. **GD:** Agnieszka Radwanska/Urszula Radwanska (POL) d. Ekaterina Makarova/Evgeniya Rodina (RUS) 64 76(2). **BS:** Andrea Arnaboldi (ITA) d. Alexander Krasnorutskiy (RUS) 64 62. **BD:** Christoph Hodl (AUT)/Grzegorz Panfil (POL) d. Marc Meigel/Tobias Wernet (GER) 63 62.

● **SIAULIAI** (LTU) (Grade 4) 2-6 MARCH – **GS:** Julija Gotovskyte (LTU) d. Yulia Solonitskaya (RUS) w/o. **GD:** Irina Cybina/Julija Gotovskyte (LTU) d. Yulia Solonitskaya (RUS)/Ksenia Tokareva (UKR) w/o. **BS:** Konstantinos Kalaitzis (GBR) d. Mikk Irdoja (EST) 61 36 76(5). **BD:** Andre Rizzoli (ITA)/Robert Varga (UKR) d. Ricardas Berankis/Simas Kucas (LTU) 64 46 62.

● **LAMBARE** (PAR) (Grade 1) 7-13 MARCH – **GS:** Nikola Frankova (CZE) d. Alexandra Dulgheru (ROM) 64 63. **GD:** Nikola Frankova/Katerina Kramperova (CZE) d. Irena Pavlovic (FRA)/Roxane Vaisemberg (BRA) 76(5) 76(5). **BS:** Leonardo Mayer (ARG) d. Dusan Lojda (CZE) 61 62. **BD:** Dusan Lojda/Jan Marek (CZE) d. Luis-Henrique Grangeiro/Andre Miele (BRA) 60 75.

● **SAN JOSE** (CRC) (Grade 3) 7-12 MARCH – **GS:** Lyndsay Burdette (USA) d. Kimberly Couts (USA) 61 62. **GD:** Kimberly Couts/Kristen McVitty (USA) d. Lyndsay Burdette/Mallory Burdette (USA) 64 64. **BS:** David Simon (AUT) d. Dominic Pagon (JAM) 57 63 62. **BD:** Branko Kuzmanovic (SCG)/Alberton Richelieu (LCA) d. Edward Kelly (USA)/David Simon (AUT) 61 16 64.

● **GOSFORD** (AUS) (Grade 4) 7-12 MARCH – **GS:** Jessica Moore (AUS) d. Tyra Calderwood (AUS) 62 64. **GD:** Shiho Akita/Ai Yamamoto (JPN) d. Tyra Calderwood/Jessica Moore (AUS) 64 36 63. **BS:** Samuel Groth (AUS) d. James Pilbro (NZL) 61 64. **BD:** Samuel Groth/Joel Lindner (AUS) d. Edward Bourchier/Lachlan Reed (AUS) 76(5) 63.

● **ORAN** (ALG) (Grade 4) 7-11 MARCH – **GS:** Sona Novakova (CZE) d. Sara Meghoufel (ALG) 62 64. **GD:** Sona Novakova/Zora Vlckova (CZE) d. Tegan Edwards/Lisa Levenberg (RSA) 61 61. **BS:** Mehdi Bouabbane (ALG) d. Stefan Nikolic (SCG) 63 76(2). **BD:** Abdelkrim Ben Osman/Mehdi Bouabbane (ALG) d. Hicham Laalej (MAR)/Mahar Zeidan (FRA) 06 75 63.

● **KRAMFORS** (SWE) (Grade 3) 8-13 MARCH – **GS:** Anastasia Revzina (RUS) d. Ksenia Pervak (RUS) 63 75. **GD:** Ieva Irbe/Trina Slapeka (LAT) d. Diana Eriksson/Sandra Hribar (SWE) 64 62. **BS:** Daniel Danilovic (SWE) d. Karl Norberg (SWE) 75 63. **BD:** Blazej Koniusz/Piotr Zielinski (POL) d. Andy Chirita (SWE)/Christoph Hodl (AUT) 61 64.

● **JAKARTA** (INA) (Grade 2) 8-13 MARCH – **GS:** Yung-Jan Chan (TPE) d. Elena Chernyakova (RUS) 63 60. **GD:** Yung-Jan Chan (TPE)/Nicole Thyssen (NED) d. Ayu-Fani Damayanti (INA)/Maya Gaverova (RUS) 63 62. **BS:** Robin Roshardt (SUI) d. Kellen Damico (USA) 76(5) 41 ret. **BD:** Hsin-Han Lee/Chia-Chu Lien (TPE) d. Robin Roshardt/Alexander Sadecky (SUI) 64 61.

● **CHISINAU** (MDA) (Grade 3) 8-13 MARCH – **GS:** Maria Mosolova (RUS) d. Yana Kireeva (RUS) 61 62. **GD:** Yulia Solonitskaya (RUS)/Ksenia Tokareva (UKR) d. Yuliya Hnateyko/Yuliya Trubachova (UKR) 46 76(4) 63. **BS:** Oleksandr Nedovesov (UKR) d. Denis Molcianov (MDA) 67(3) 76(5) 64. **BD:** Achim Ceban/Denis Molcianov (MDA) d. Oleksandr Nedovesov/Ivan Sergeyev (UKR) 62 64.

- **RIGA** (LAT) (Grade 5) 9-13 MARCH – **GS:** Farida Karaeva (UKR) d. Alessandra Ferrazzi (ITA) 46 64 62. **GD:** Anja Maskaljun (EST)/Alise Razina (LAT) d. Tuule Tani/Julia Zubkova (EST) 64 64. **BS:** Mikk Irdoja (EST) d. Ricardas Berankis (LTU) 64 76(5). **BD:** Matiss Libietis/Peteris Vinogradovs (LAT) d. Tomasz Krzyszkowski/Pawel Turzanski (POL) w/o.

- **SAO PAULO** (BRA) (Grade A) 14-20 MARCH – **GS:** Sharon Fichman (CAN) d. Alexandra Dulgheru (ROM) 36 60 75. **GD:** Bianca Bonifate (ROM)/Sharon Fichman (CAN) d. Dominika Cibulkova (SVK)/Nikola Frankova (CZE) 64 64. **BS:** Leonardo Mayer (ARG) d. Andre Miele (BRA) 61 60. **BD:** Piero Luisi/David Navarrete (VEN) d. Raony Carvalho (BRA)/Ryan Sweeting (BAH) 63 64.

- **KUALA LUMPUR** (MAS) (Grade 1) 14-19 MARCH – **GS:** Alexa Glatch (USA) d. Vania King (USA) 63 62. **GD:** Wen-Hsin Hsu (TPE)/Amina Rakhim (KAZ) d. Mihaela Buzarnescu (ROM)/Erika Sema (JPN) 60 61. **BS:** Kellen Damico (USA) d. Andrew Kennaugh (GBR) 57 76(3) 76(3). **BD:** Philip Bester/Peter Polansky (CAN) d. Kellen Damico/Nathaniel Schnugg (USA) 64 30 ret.

- **KRAMFORS** (SWE) (Grade 4) 14-19 MARCH – **GS:** Nina Munch-Soegaard (NOR) d. Ieva Irbe (LAT) 64 46 63. **GD:** Ieva Irbe/Trina Slapeka (LAT) d. Diana Eriksson/Sandra Hribar (SWE) 64 76(5). **BS:** Marcin Gawron (POL) d. Blazej Koniusz (POL) 75 62. **BD:** Blazej Koniusz/Piotr Zielinski (POL) d. Marcin Gawron/Mateusz Szmigiel (POL) 64 57 62.

- **LEUGGERN** (SUI) (Grade 5) 14-19 MARCH – **GS:** Stefania Boffa (SUI) d. Carolin Weikard (GER) 63 60. **GD:** Stefania Boffa (SUI)/Olivia Lilien (BEL) d. Ramona Erb/Amra Sadikovic (SUI) 75 46 75. **BS:** Tobias Wernet (GER) d. Kristofer Wachter (AUT) 76(2) 75. **BD:** Jonathan Eysseric (FRA)/Dylan Sessagesimi (SUI) d. Felix Grabs/Nico Hegge (GER) 62 36 62.

- **LLANOS DE CURUNDU** (PAN) (Grade 4) 14-20 MARCH – **GS:** Melanie Klaffner (AUT) d. Efrat Mishor (ISR) 61 60. **GD:** Melanie Klaffner/Jeaninne Prentner (AUT) d. Alena Bayarchyk (BLR)/Natalia Ryjonkova (RUS) 64 62. **BS:** Francisco Franco (COL) d. Vittorio Belletini (ECU) 62 62. **BD:** Francisco Franco (COL)/Carlos Galvez (ECU) d. Gian Hodgson (ARU)/Dominic Pagon (JAM) 64 76(2).

- **ALGIERS** (ALG) (Grade 4) 14-18 MARCH – **GS:** Nikola Hofmanova (AUT) d. Sona Novakova (CZE) 46 63 61. **GD:** Sona Novakova/Zora Vlckova (CZE) d. Tegan Edwards (RSA)/Rebekka Seipel (AUT) 62 62. **BS:** Artem Gramma (UKR) d. Yannick Weihs (AUT) 06 62 76(5). **BD:** Marc Rath/Yannick Weihs (AUT) d. Mehdi Bouras (ALG)/Julien Dubail (BEL) w/o.

- **UMAG** (CRO) (Grade 1) 15-20 MARCH – **GS:** Karin Knapp (ITA) d. Sara Errani (ITA) 63 76(2). **GD:** Sara Errani/Stella Menna (ITA) d. Kristina Antoniychuk (UKR)/Ana Veselinovic (SCG) 61 64. **BS:** Niels Desein (BEL) d. Andrea Arnaboldi (ITA) 46 64 63. **BD:** Andrea Arnaboldi (ITA)/Niels Desein (BEL) d. Nikola Mektic/Tibor Simic (CRO) 62 64.

- **PHOENIX** (MRI) (Grade 3) 15-19 MARCH – **GS:** Else Potgieter (RSA) d. Fatima El Allami (MAR) 60 60. **BS:** Kevin Kerr (RSA) d. Jurgens Strydom (NAM) 62 61.

- **PORTO ALEGRE** (BRA) (Grade 1) 21-27 MARCH – **GS:** Alexandra Dulgheru (ROM) d. Raluca Olaru (ROM) 60 61. **GD:** Nikola Frankova/Katerina Kramperova (CZE) d. Giulia Gabba (ITA)/Fernanda Hermenegildo (BRA) 62 64. **BS:** Raony Carvalho (BRA) d. Leonardo Mayer (ARG) 67(4) 60 64. **BD:** Raony Carvalho (BRA)/Ryan Sweeting (BAH) d. Roberto Maytin/Roman Recarte (VEN) 64 76(5).

- **PHOENIX** (MRI) (Grade B2) 21-26 MARCH – **GS:** Ola Abou Zekri (EGY) d. Magy Aziz (EGY) 57 75 62. **BS:** Anas Fattar (MAR) d. Kevin Kerr (RSA) 57 64 75.

- **SUPHANBURI** (THA) (Grade 1) 21-27 MARCH – **GS:** Vania King (USA) d. Alexa Glatch (USA) w/o. **GD:** Alexa Glatch/Vania King (USA) d. Ayumi Morita/Erika Sema (JPN) 63 63. **BS:** Alexander Sadecky (SUI) d. Martin Sayer (HKG) 64 36 64. **BD:** Tristan Farron-Mahon (IRL)/Alexander Sadecky (SUI) d. Philip Bester/Peter Polansky (CAN) w/o.

- **COLLEGE STATION, TX** (USA) (Grade 5) 22-27 MARCH – **GS:** Kristy Frilling (USA) d. Yi-Xi Liu (CHN) 64 60. **GD:** Yi-Xi Liu (CHN)/Lauren Lui (USA) d. Christala Andrews/Krista Damico (USA) 64 75. **BS:** Mateusz Kecki (USA) d. Shan Sondhu (USA) 61 57 75. **BD:** Bradley Cox/Jeff Dadamo (USA) d. Jarmere Jenkins/Andy Magee (USA) 64 60.

- **ASUNCION** (PAR) (Grade 4) 23-27 MARCH – **GS:** Amanda Melgarejo (PAR) d. Lisa Marshall (RSA) 60 75. **GD:** Daniela Leyria/Candelaria Rizzuto (ARG) d. Fiorella Salierno/Paulina Salierno (ARG) 63 61. **BS:** Juan-Carlos Ramirez (PAR) d. Guido Sola (ARG) 26 75 61. **BD:** Martin Di Mella/Juan-Manuel Romanazzi (ARG) d. Juan Maunel Arganaras/Guillermo Duran (ARG) 64 64.

- **FLORENCE** (ITA) (Grade 2) 23-28 MARCH – **GS:** Renee Reinhard (NED) d. Sara Errani (ITA) 75 61. **GD:** Marrit Boonstra/Renee Reinhard (NED) d. Sara Errani/Karin Knapp (ITA) 62 64. **BS:** Andrea Arnaboldi (ITA) d. Luka Belic (CRO) 63 63. **BD:** Thiemo De Bakker/Leander Van Der Vaart (NED) d. Mikhail Pavlov/Valeri Rudnev (RUS) 63 61.

- **MENDOZA** (ARG) (Grade 5) 28 MARCH-2 APRIL – **GS:** Lucia Huber (ARG) d. Maria-Dolores Pazo (ARG) 63 64. **GD:** Paulina Jorquera/ Paulina Ojeda (CHI) d. Maria-Dolores Pazo/Candelaria Rizzuto (ARG) 64 63. **BS:** Federico Cavallero (ARG) d. Martin Di Mella (ARG) 75 62. **BD:** Gabriel Gomez/Andres Molteni (ARG) d. Joaquin Guillier/Andres Nunez (CHI) 61 64.

- **PORT OF SPAIN** (TRI) (Grade 4) 28 MARCH-2 APRIL – **GS:** Ekaterina Rybakova (USA) d. Yolande Leacock (TRI) 61 46 63. **GD:** Victoria Brook/Abbie Probert (GBR) d. Yolande Leacock (TRI)/Ekaterina Rybakova (USA) 62 36 64. **BS:** Ricardas Berankis (LTU) d. Gian Hodgson (ARU) 61 61. **BD:** Gian Hodgson (ARU)/Dominic Pagon (JAM) d. Elias Gastao/Joao Sousa (POR) w/o.

- **MARSA** (MLT) (Grade 5) 28 MARCH-3 APRIL – **GS:** Madlen Kadur (GER) d. Naomi Cavaday (GBR) 62 64. **GD:** Nikola Hofmanova (AUT)/ Zuzana Linhova (CZE) d. Valeria Makarycheva/Eugeniya Pashkova (RUS) 75 36 63. **BS:** Oscar Podlewski (GBR) d. Arsenije Zlatanovic (SCG) 63 16 64. **BD:** Michael Garthoffner (GER)/Korneel Sanders (BEL) d. Artem Kuznetsov (RUS)/Alexei Milner (ISR) 57 62 62.

- **MANILA** (PHI) (Grade 1) 29 MARCH-3 APRIL – **GS:** Yung-Jan Chan (TPE) d. Wen-Hsin Hsu (TPE) 36 62 63. **GD:** Yung-Jan Chan/I-Hsuan Hwang (TPE) d. Amina Rakhim (KAZ)/Caroline Wozniacki (DEN) 64 61. **BS:** Abdullah Magdas (KUW) d. Martin Sayer (HKG) 64 63. **BD:** Vivek Shokeen/Sanam Singh (IND) d. Hsin-Han Lee (TPE)/Christopher Llewellyn (GBR) 67(6) 61 64.

- **SFAX** (TUN) (Grade 3) 29 MARCH-2 APRIL – **GS:** Irina Khatsko (UKR) d. Elizaveta Tochilovskaya (RUS) 64 62. **GD:** Irina Khatsko/ Mariya Malkhasyan (UKR) d. Nelli Dzidzishvili/Ksenia Lykina (RUS) 76(6) 62. **BS:** Pedro Sousa (POR) d. Ahmed Rabeea (KUW) 62 60. **BD:** Graeme Dyce (GBR)/Michal Konecny (CZE) d. Vedran Siljegovic/Tibor Simic (CRO) 76(3) 62.

- **SINJHUANG CITY** (TPE) (Grade 4) 29 MARCH-3 APRIL – **GS:** Shayna McDowell (AUS) d. Lu-Ling Chen (TPE) 61 60. **GD:** Chi Fan Liu/ Pei-Ling Wu (TPE) d. Yi-Ching Chen/Wen-Ling Wang (TPE) 61 61. **BS:** Chu-Huan Yi (TPE) d. Patrick Nicholls (AUS) 76(3) 26 62. **BD:** Ting Lung Chang-Chien/Tung Han Lee (TPE) d. Yen Te Li/Chu-Huan Yi (TPE) 76(7) 63.

- **CAP D'AIL** (FRA) (Grade 2) 4-10 APRIL – **GS:** Tamira Paszek (AUT) d. Astrid Besser (ITA) 61 62. **GD:** Eva Kadlecova (CZE)/Tamira Paszek (AUT) d. Kristina Antoniychuk (UKR)/Jelena Kulikova (RUS) 63 57 76(4). **BS:** Niels Desein (BEL) d. Alexander Krasnorutskiy (RUS) 62 62. **BD:** Alexander Krasnorutskiy/Valeri Rudnev (RUS) d. Adrian Mannarino/Boris Obama (FRA) 61 62.

- **ST. FRANCOIS** (GUD) (Grade 4) 4-9 APRIL – **GS:** Jade Curtis (GBR) d. Francesca Kinsella (GBR) 63 76(3). **GD:** Marianne Eelens (ARU)/ Francesca Kinsella (GBR) d. Jade Curtis (GBR)/Alanna Rodgers (BAH) 46 13 ret. **BS:** Ricardas Berankis (LTU) d. Joao Sousa (POR) 75 63. **BD:** Elias Gastao/Joao Sousa (POR) d. Ricardas Berankis (LTU)/Corey Huggins (ECA) 57 63 76.

- **CARSON, CA** (USA) (Grade 1) 4-10 APRIL – **GS:** Vania King (USA) d. Alexa Glatch (USA) 64 64. **GD:** Vania King/Yasmin Schnack (USA) d. Jennifer-Lee Heinser/Elizabeth Plotkin (USA) 63 60. **BS:** Samuel Querrey (USA) d. Pavel Chekhov (RUS) 75 62. **BD:** Philip Bester (CAN)/ Holden Seguso (USA) d. Jesse Levine/Michael Shabaz (USA) 63 62.

- **MONASTIR** (TUN) (Grade 3) 5-9 APRIL – **GS:** Ksenia Lykina (RUS) d. Mariya Malkhasyan (UKR) 61 36 63. **GD:** Nelli Dzidzishvili/Ksenia Lykina (RUS) d. Irina Khatsko/Mariya Malkhasyan (UKR) 01 ret. **BS:** Michal Konecny (CZE) d. Wael Kilani (TUN) 64 57 31 ret. **BD:** Andy Chirita (SWE)/Ahmed Rabeea (KUW) d. Ivan Galic (AUT)/Cristian Hodel (ROM) w/o.

- **NAGOYA** (JPN) (Grade 1) 5-10 APRIL – **GS:** Caroline Wozniacki (DEN) d. Ayumi Morita (JPN) 62 06 64. **GD:** Yung-Jan Chan (TPE)/ Veronica Ruo-Qi Li (USA) d. Amina Rakhim (KAZ)/Caroline Wozniacki (DEN) 62 63. **BS:** Andreas Haider-Maurer (AUT) d. Jeevan Nedunchezhiyan (IND) 76(2) 67(4) 62. **BD:** Huai-En Chang/Hsin-Han Lee (TPE) d. Jeevan Nedunchezhiyan/Sanam Singh (IND) 63 46 62.

- **SEOUL** (KOR) (Grade B1) 11-17 APRIL – **GS:** Yung-Jan Chan (TPE) d. Amina Rakhim (KAZ) 64 60. **GD:** Yung-Jan Chan/I-Hsuan Hwang (TPE) d. Wen-Hsin Hsu (TPE)/Amina Rakhim (KAZ) 62 62. **BS:** Sanam Singh (IND) d. Abdullah Magdas (KUW) 64 62. **BD:** Jeevan Nedunchezhiyan/Sanam Singh (IND) d. Elbert Sie (INA)/Shuhei Uzawa (JPN) 63 62.

- **PALM SPRINGS, CA** (USA) (Grade B1) 11-17 APRIL – **GS:** Alexa Glatch (USA) d. Jennifer-Lee Heinser (USA) 67(1) 60 63. **GD:** Lyndsay Burdette/Alexa Glatch (USA) d. Jennifer-Lee Heinser/Elizabeth Plotkin (USA) 61 64. **BS:** Samuel Querrey (USA) d. Carsten Ball (AUS) 63 63. **BD:** Dylan Arnould/Marcus Fugate (USA) d. Carsten Ball (AUS)/Michael Venus (USA) 62 76(8).

- **ST MICHAEL** (BAR) (Grade 4) 11-16 APRIL – **GS:** Jade Curtis (GBR) d. Yolande Leacock (TRI) 64 63. **GD:** Jade Curtis/Francesca Kinsella (GBR) d. Yolande Leacock (TRI)/Ashley Spicer (USA) 63 64. **BS:** Ricardas Berankis (LTU) d. Alberton Richelieu (LCA) 63 64. **BD:** Alberton Richelieu (LCA)/Matthew Sands (BAH) d. Akshay Bajoria (IND)/Harry Skinner (GBR) 64 64.

- **MIRAMAS** (FRA) (Grade 2) 11-17 APRIL – **GS:** Alize Cornet (FRA) d. Estelle Guisard (FRA) 61 62. **GD:** Kristina Antoniychuk (UKR)/Bianca Bonifate (ROM) d. Laura-Ioana Andrei (ROM)/Ksenia Palkina (KGZ) 64 61. **BS:** Javier Garrapiz-Borderias (ESP) d. Robin Roshardt (SUI) 61 61. **BD:** Evgeny Kirillov (RUS)/Oleksandr Nedovesov (UKR) d. Dmitry Novikov (BLR)/Valeri Rudnev (RUS) 62 75.

- **MOSTAR** (BIH) (Grade 5) 13-17 APRIL – **GS:** Alja Zec-Peskiric (SLO) d. Taja Mohorcic (SLO) 75 63. **GD:** Taja Mohorcic/Alja Zec-Peskiric (SLO) d. Katarina Milinkovic (SCG)/Vana Sutalo (CRO) 64 62. **BS:** Goran Rozic (CRO) d. Igor Skoric (CRO) 63 64. **BD:** Ivan Skaro/Igor Skoric (CRO) d. Silvio Dadic (CRO)/Ivo Mijic (GER) 62 63.

- **BEAULIEU SUR MER** (FRA) (Grade 1) 18-24 APRIL – **GS:** Alexandra Dulgheru (ROM) d. Kristina Antoniychuk (UKR) 62 75. **GD:** Sorana Cirstea/Alexandra Dulgheru (ROM) d. Dominika Cibulkova (SVK)/Agnes Szatmari (ROM) 06 60 75. **BS:** Evgeny Kirillov (RUS) d. Gianluca Naso (ITA) 57 76(4) 62. **BD:** Tristan Farron-Mahon (IRL)/Alexander Sadecky (SUI) d. Pavel Chekhov/Valeri Rudnev (RUS) 63 63.

- **PIESTANY** (SVK) (Grade 2) 19-24 APRIL – **GS:** Jana Juricova (SVK) d. Natasa Zoric (SCG) 26 63 64. **GD:** Jana Juricova/Magdalena Rybarikova (SVK) d. Klaudia Boczova/Nikola Vajdova (SVK) 63 62. **BS:** Vaclav Kucera (CZE) d. Peter Paulenka (SVK) 06 62 75. **BD:** Jiri Kosler (CZE)/Grzegorz Panfil (POL) d. Blazej Koniusz/Piotr Zielinski (POL) 62 36 63.

- **ALICANTE** (ESP) (Grade 5) 19-23 APRIL – **GS:** Michaela Ince (GBR) d. Katarina Tuohimaa (FIN) 64 63. **GD:** Zuzana Linhova (CZE)/Lisa Summerer (AUT) d. Anastasiya Solomko (KAZ)/Tatsiana Teterina (BLR) 61 63. **BS:** Goncalo Falcao (POR) d. Iain Atkinson (GBR) 64 62. **BD:** Conrado Lopez-Carbajo/Hugo Taracido-loureiro (ESP) d. Goncalo Falcao (POR)/Christian Serrano-Garcia (ESP) 64 63.

- **SEOUL** (KOR) (Grade 4) 20-24 APRIL – **GS:** Cho-Won Lee (KOR) d. Hae-Sung Kim (KOR) 75 60. **GD:** Seul-Ki Chin/So-Yeon Kim (KOR) d. Hae-Youm Bae/Bo-Ra Kwak (KOR) 67(5) 60 64. **BS:** Sho Aida (JPN) d. Shuhei Uzawa (JPN) 64 67(3) 64. **BD:** Faisal Aidil/Agung-Bagus Dewantoro (INA) d. Christopher Rungkat (INA)/Shuhei Uzawa (JPN) 46 76(4) 60.

- **BURLINGTON** (CAN) (Grade 5) 25-30 APRIL – **GS:** Jessica Zok (CAN) d. Laura Pola (CAN) 67(5) 76(2) 60. **GD:** Taylor Ormond/Laura Pola (CAN) d. Mia Gordon/Steffi Wong (CAN) 64 75. **BS:** Keziel Juneau (CAN) d. Kirill Sinitsyn (RUS) 62 60. **BD:** Bradley Cox (USA)/Peter Marrack (CAN) d. Zack Radetzky/Mark Rutherford (CAN) 75 76(4).

- **SALSOMAGGIORE** (ITA) (Grade 2) 25 APRIL-1 MAY – **GS:** Alexandra Dulgheru (ROM) d. Anna Gerasimou (GRE) 62 62. **GD:** Alexandra Dulgheru/Agnes Szatmari (ROM) d. Vesna Manasieva (RUS)/Dominice Ripoll (GER) 75 63. **BS:** Gianluca Naso (ITA) d. Alexander Sadecky (SUI) 62 75. **BD:** Grzegorz Panfil (POL)/Jurgen Zopp (EST) d. Tristan Farron-Mahon (IRL)/Alexander Sadecky (SUI) 62 36 62.

- **ALICANTE** (ESP) (Grade 3) 26-30 APRIL – **GS:** Zuzana Linhova (CZE) d. Michaela Ince (GBR) 75 63. **GD:** Sara Celma-Boix/Clara Schuhmacher-Terron (ESP) d. Jade Curtis (GBR)/Katarina Tuohimaa (FIN) 67(2) 63 64. **BS:** Mikhail Karpol (CRO) d. Joao Sousa (POR) 57 75 61. **BD:** Matthew Taylor/Bruce Wagstaff (GBR) d. Goncalo Falcao/Joao Sousa (POR) 64 64.

- **BATON ROUGE, LA** (USA) (Grade 5) 26 APRIL-1 MAY – **GS:** Sarah Guzick (USA) d. Melanie Oudin (USA) 75 64. **GD:** Sarah Guzick/Simone Templeton (USA) d. Brooke Bolender/Connie Hsu (USA) 63 63. **BS:** Rupesh Roy (IND) d. Jason McNaughton (USA) 75 63. **BD:** Diego Machuca/Oscar Machuca (ECU) d. Geoffrey Barton (CRC)/Jose Moncada (HON) 60 46 64.

- **BALS** (ROM) (Grade 5) 26 APRIL-1 MAY – **GS:** Lenore Lazaroiu (ROM) d. Olga Duko (BLR) 64 60. **GD:** Maria-Luiza Craciun/Ioana Ivan (ROM) d. Camelia-Elena Hristea/Lenore Lazaroiu (ROM) 63 61. **BS:** Paul-Mihai Puscasu (ROM) d. Emanuel Brighiu (ROM) 61 46 61. **BD:** Emanuel Brighiu/Victor Alexandru Caliciu (ROM) d. Petru-Alexandru Luncanu/Paul-Mihai Puscasu (ROM) 46 61 64.

- **BAT YAM** (ISR) (Grade 4) 26-30 APRIL – **GS:** Julia Glushko (ISR) d. Chen Astrugo (ISR) 63 63. **GD:** Margarita Spicin/Victoria Tseitlin (ISR) d. Hila Elster/Keren Shlomo (ISR) 64 63. **BS:** Victor Kolik (ISR) d. Omri Hasin (ISR) 63 61. **BD:** Almog Mashiach/Sahar Shimiel (ISR) d. Ravid Hezi/Victor Kolik (ISR) 64 63.

- **PRATO** (ITA) (Grade 2) 2-7 MAY – **GS:** Nina Henkel (GER) d. Corinna Dentoni (ITA) 61 46 64. **GD:** Vesna Manasieva (RUS)/Dominice Ripoll (GER) d. Martina Lautenschlager/Stefanie Vogele (SUI) 61 60. **BS:** Andrea Arnaboldi (ITA) d. Andreas Haider-Maurer (AUT) 64 62. **BD:** Denis Molcianov (MDA)/Serguei Tarasevitch (BLR) d. Andreas Haider-Maurer (AUT)/Jiri Skoloudik (CZE) 76(0) 63.

- **MAMAIA** (ROM) (Grade 4) 3-8 MAY – **GS:** Laura-Ioana Andrei (ROM) d. Simona Halep (ROM) 63 63. **GD:** Maria-Luiza Craciun/Ioana Ivan (ROM) d. Laura-Ioana Andrei/Andrada Dinu (ROM) 12 ret. **BS:** Ivan Sergeyev (UKR) d. Dmytro Petrov (UKR) 76(4) 64. **BD:** Ionut-Mihai Beleleu/Mihai Nichifor (ROM) d. Vladyslav Klymenko/Ivan Sergeyev (UKR) 62 64.

- **DESTIN, FL** (USA) (Grade 5) 3-8 MAY – **GS:** Maria Mokh (RUS) d. Christina Liles (USA) 46 62 63. **GD:** Maria Mokh/Natalia Ryjonkova (RUS) d. Xenia Schneider (GER)/Caitlin Whoriskey (USA) 76(4) 61. **BS:** Attila Bucko (SCG) d. Oscar Machuca (ECU) 64 64. **BD:** Jeff Dadamo/ Bradley Mixson (USA) d. Bradley Cox/Calvin Kemp (USA) 57 64 64.

- **HAIFA** (ISR) (Grade 4) 3-7 MAY – **GS:** Ksenia Milevskaya (BLR) d. Nicolette Van Uitert (NED) 62 64. **GD:** Ima Bogush/Ksenia Milevskaya (BLR) d. Maria Kalashnikova/Oxana Kalashnikova (GEO) 61 64. **BS:** Danila Arsenov (RUS) d. Almog Mashiach (ISR) 64 16 63. **BD:** Almog Mashiach/Sahar Shimiel (ISR) d. Ravid Hezi/Shay Sagie (ISR) 67(3) 64 60.

- **SANTA CROCE** (ITA) (Grade 1) 9-15 MAY – **GS:** Yaroslava Shvedova (RUS) d. Stefania Boffa (SUI) 46 76(5) 61. **GD:** Sorana Cirstea (ROM)/ Barbora Hodinarova (CZE) d. Vania King/Yasmin Schnack (USA) 36 63 64. **BS:** Sergei Bubka (UKR) d. Thiemo De Bakker (NED) 63 16 63. **BD:** Evgeny Kirillov (RUS)/Denis Molcianov (MDA) d. Piero Luisi (VEN)/Ryan Sweeting (BAH) 63 36 62.

- **ST. POLTEN** (AUT) (Grade 2) 10-15 MAY – **GS:** Tamira Paszek (AUT) d. Stephanie Herz (NED) 76(4) 36 62. **GD:** Agnieszka Radwanska/ Urszula Radwanska (POL) d. Katerina Kramperova (CZE)/Tamira Paszek (AUT) 61 62. **BS:** Nikola Mektic (CRO) d. Kevin Botti (FRA) 63 63. **BD:** Ruben Bemelmans (BEL)/Jaak Poldma (EST) d. Boris Obama (FRA)/David Simon (AUT) 60 76(5).

- **BEER SHIVA** (ISR) (Grade 4) 10-14 MAY – **GS:** Ksenia Milevskaya (BLR) d. Nadine Fahoum (ISR) 76(5) 75. **GD:** Ima Bogush/Ksenia Milevskaya (BLR) d. Farida Karaeva (UKR)/Monika Sirilova (SVK) 63 60. **BS:** Almog Mashiach (ISR) d. Ravid Hezi (ISR) 64 75. **BD:** Almog Mashiach/Sahar Shimiel (ISR) d. Wesley Baptiste/Tucker Vorster (RSA) 63 76(5).

- **PLOVDIV** (BUL) (Grade 5) 10-15 MAY – **GS:** Anja Maskaljun (EST) d. Huliya Velieva (BUL) 62 57 61. **GD:** Lora Stancheva/Tania Stoimanova (BUL) d. Anja Maskaljun/Carolyn Saan (EST) 64 75. **BS:** Vassil Mladenov (BUL) d. Plamen Avramov (BUL) 60 61. **BD:** Valentin Dimov (BUL)/Maxim Filippov (KAZ) d. Arsel Kumdereli/Adem Ozmeral (TUR) 46 62 64.

- **SANTIAGO** (CHI) (Grade 5) 16-22 MAY – **GS:** Giannina Minieri (CHI) d. Catalina Arancibia (CHI) 06 62 62. **GD:** Daniela Leyria/Candelaria Rizzuto (ARG) d. Renata Barchiesi (CHI)/Lara Rafful (BRA) 75 67 62. **BS:** Guillermo Rivera (CHI) d. Marcos Linconir (CHI) 16 76(0) 62. **BD:** Alejandro Breve/Ricardo Urzua (CHI) d. Francisco Olivares/Guillermo Rivera (CHI) 64 64.

- **MILAN** (ITA) (Grade A) 16-22 MAY – **GS:** Dominika Cibulkova (SVK) d. Raluca Olaru (ROM) 62 64. **GD:** Ekaterina Makarova/Evgeniya Rodina (RUS) d. Sharon Fichman (CAN)/Caroline Wozniacki (DEN) 61 64. **BS:** Petar Jelenic (CRO) d. Niels Desein (BEL) 67(3) 64 75. **BD:** Evgeny Kirillov (RUS)/Denis Molcianov (MDA) d. Alex Clayton/Donald Young (USA) 57 64 64.

- **ISTANBUL** (TUR) (Grade 5) 16-22 MAY – **GS:** Nikki Prosser (GBR) d. Huliya Velieva (BUL) 61 76(4). **GD:** Huliya Velieva/Lyutfya Velieva (BUL) d. Eylul Benli (TUR)/Valeria Savinykh (RUS) 76(5) 46 64. **BS:** Marsel Khamdamov (UZB) d. Sami Beceren (TUR) 63 76(3). **BD:** Sami Beceren/Orcun Seyrek (TUR) d. Arsel Kumdereli/Eren Turkmenler (TUR) .

- **PODGORICA** (SCG) (Grade 4) 16-21 MAY – **GS:** Ana Veselinovic (SCG) d. Katarina Milinkovic (SCG) 63 64. **GD:** Ivana Milutinovic/Ana Veselinovic (SCG) d. Aleksandra Markovic (SCG)/Katarina Poljakova (SVK) 63 64. **BS:** Ilija Martinoski (MKD) d. Ivan Skaro (CRO) 36 62 64. **BD:** Milan Zekic/Arsenije Zlatanovic (SCG) d. Atila Kulhanek (SCG)/Alexander Somogyi (SVK) 75 61.

- **TOGLIATTI** (RUS) (Grade 4) 16-21 MAY – **GS:** Natalia Orlova (RUS) d. Augusta Tsybycheva (RUS) 62 62. **GD:** Yulia Parasyuk/Elizaveta Titova (RUS) d. Marina Melnikova/Maria Skvortsova (RUS) 63 63. **BS:** Artur Chernov (RUS) d. Yury Shirshov (RUS) 64 63. **BD:** Artur Chernov/Alexei Filonov (RUS) d. Alexander Seleznev (KGZ)/Stas Zhuravski (RUS) 64 61.

- **VILLACH** (AUT) (Grade 2) 17-21 MAY – **GS:** Johanna Larsson (SWE) d. Michaela Pochabova (SVK) 60 61. **GD:** Johanna Larsson/ Nadja Roma (SWE) d. Klaudia Boczova/Michaela Pochabova (SVK) 63 60. **BS:** Jonathan Dahan (FRA) d. Jaak Poldma (EST) 76(4) 61. **BD:** Nikola Mektic/Vedran Siljegovic (CRO) d. Ruben Bemelmans (BEL)/Ahmed Rabeea (KUW) 64 75.

- **LOVERVAL** (BEL) (Grade 1) 23-28 MAY – **GS:** Raluca Olaru (ROM) d. Ayumi Morita (JPN) 26 61 76(4). **GD:** Alisa Kleybanova/Evgeniya Rodina (RUS) d. Vania King/Yasmin Schnack (USA) 60 26 63. **BS:** Niels Desein (BEL) d. Donald Young (USA) 63 60. **BD:** Carsten Ball (AUS)/Piero Luisi (VEN) d. Luis-Henrique Grangeiro/Andre Miele (BRA) 26 76(5) 76(4).

- **SAMARA** (RUS) (Grade 3) 23-29 MAY – **GS:** Yulia Parasyuk (RUS) d. Natalia Orlova (RUS) 64 62. **GD:** Ekaterina Krylova/Marina Melnikova (RUS) d. Yulia Solonitskaya/Augusta Tsybycheva (RUS) 64 63. **BS:** Yury Shirshov (RUS) d. Victor Kozin (RUS) 63 64. **BD:** Victor Kozin/Stas Zhuravski (RUS) d. Artur Chernov/Alexei Filonov (RUS) 67(5) 75 75.

- **BUDAPEST** (HUN) (Grade 4) 24-29 MAY – **GS:** Michaela Pochabova (SVK) d. Lucia Batta (HUN) 60 61. **GD:** Michaela Pochabova/Patricia Veresova (SVK) d. Elena Chernyakova (RUS)/Katarina Poljakova (SVK) 76(10) 63. **BS:** Joel Lindner (AUS) d. Balazs Novak (HUN) 61 62. **BD:** Attila Balazs/Bence-Gyula Toth (HUN) d. Brydon Klein/Joel Lindner (AUS) 76(1) 46 75.

- **PARIS** (FRA) (Grade A) 29 MAY-5 JUNE – **GS:** Agnes Szavay (HUN) d. Raluca Olaru (ROM) 62 61. **GD:** Viktoria Azarenka (BLR)/Agnes Szavay (HUN) d. Raluca Olaru (ROM)/Amina Rakhim (KAZ) 46 64 60. **BS:** Marin Cilic (CRO) d. Antal Van Der Duim (NED) 63 61. **BD:** Emiliano Massa/Leonardo Mayer (ARG) d. Sergei Bubka (UKR)/Jeremy Chardy (FRA) 26 63 64.

- **TASHKENT** (UZB) (Grade 3) 30 MAY-4 JUNE – **GS:** Dilyara Saidkhodjaeva (UZB) d. Lutfiana Aris Budiharto (INA) 60 63. **GD:** Vlada Ekshibarova/Albina Khabibulina (UZB) d. Elina Arutyunova (UZB)/Yekaterina Morozova (KAZ) 60 63. **BS:** Faisal Aidil (INA) d. Akmal Sharipov (UZB) 62 63. **BD:** Akmal Sharipov/Vaja Uzakov (UZB) d. Gursher Singh Harika (IND)/Alexey Tikhonov (RUS) 63 16 63.

- **MONTERREY** (MEX) (Grade 5) 30 MAY-5 JUNE – **GS:** Pamela Montez (MEX) d. Mcall Jones (USA) 36 76(4) 60. **GD:** Clarisse Baca/Alejandra Guerra (MEX) d. Alicia Aguilar/Maria Bayon (MEX) 76(5) 63. **BS:** Eduardo Meza (MEX) d. Daniel Sanchez (MEX) 63 63. **BD:** Eduardo Peralta/Daniel Sanchez (MEX) d. Eduardo Meza/Hector Nieto (MEX) 61 57 64.

- **TANGER** (MAR) (Grade 5) 30 MAY-4 JUNE – **GS:** Fatima El Allami (MAR) d. Tegan Edwards (RSA) 60 61. **GD:** Majdouline Akrate/Fatima El Allami (MAR) d. Ana Beltran-Trigueros (ESP)/Zineb Hilali (MAR) 60 76(3). **BS:** Houssam Yassine (MAR) d. Wassim Derbel (TUN) 26 63 63. **BD:** Kevin Kerr (RSA)/Bokang Setshogo (BOT) d. Christian Vitulli (KEN)/Bradwin Williams (RSA) 64 36 62.

- **TALLINN** (EST) (Grade 4) 31 MAY-5 JUNE – **GS:** Katarzyna Piter (POL) d. Sandra Hribar (SWE) 62 62. **GD:** Barbara Sobaszkiewicz/Sylwia Zagorska (POL) d. Melinda Akerbrandt-Bengtsson/Mona Mansour (SWE) 63 62. **BS:** Jaak Poldma (EST) d. Vladimir Ivanov (EST) 63 62. **BD:** Vladimir Ivanov/Jurgen Zopp (EST) d. Jaak Poldma/Fredi Voormann (EST) 76(6) 46 62.

- **BUDAPEST** (HUN) (Grade 2) 1-5 JUNE – **GS:** Jelena Kulikova (RUS) d. Andrea Berkova (CZE) 62 64. **GD:** Michaela Pochabova/Patricia Veresova (SVK) d. Klaudia Boczova/Nikola Vajdova (SVK) 62 63. **BS:** Ivan Sergeyev (UKR) d. Stephen Donald (AUS) 63 46 62. **BD:** Roman Jebavy/Jiri Kosler (CZE) d. Petru-Alexandru Luncanu/Paul-Mihai Puscasu (ROM) 67(3) 76(12) 62.

- **TAMPICO** (MEX) (Grade 5) 6-11 JUNE – **GS:** Alejandra Guerra (MEX) d. Alicia Aguilar (MEX) 63 75. **GD:** Clarisse Baca/Alejandra Guerra (MEX) d. Brooke Bolender/Cristina McHale (USA) 64 62. **BS:** Daniel Sanchez (MEX) d. Eduardo Peralta (MEX) 64 60. **BD:** Eduardo Meza/Cesar Ramirez (MEX) d. Eduardo Peralta/Daniel Sanchez (MEX) 67(3) 75 76(1).

- **MOSCOW** (RUS) (Grade 3) 6-12 JUNE – **GS:** Alexandra Panova (RUS) d. Anastasia Pivovarova (RUS) 62 62. **GD:** Alexandra Panova/Anastasia Revzina (RUS) d. Maria Mosolova/Anastasia Pivovarova (RUS) 36 64 62. **BS:** Mikhail Pavlov (RUS) d. Artur Chernov (RUS) 63 63. **BD:** Vladimir Karusevich/Vladimir Zinyakov (RUS) d. Artur Chernov/Alexei Filonov (RUS) 63 63.

- **RABAT** (MAR) (Grade 3) 6-11 JUNE – **GS:** Chelsey Gullickson (USA) d. Anastasia Petukhova (RUS) 62 62. **GD:** Krista Damico/Chelsey Gullickson (USA) d. Jessica Moore/Therese Tisseverasinghe (AUS) 64 61. **BS:** Marcin Gawron (POL) d. Blazej Koniusz (POL) 60 63. **BD:** Nathaniel Schnugg (USA)/Bruce Wagstaff (GBR) d. Christian Vitulli (KEN)/Bradwin Williams (RSA) 75 57 64.

- **OFFENBACH/MAIN** (GER) (Grade 1) 7-12 JUNE – **GS:** Yaroslava Shvedova (RUS) d. Kristina Kucova (SVK) 61 61. **GD:** Magdalena Kiszczynska (POL)/Katerina Kramperova (CZE) d. Magy Aziz (EGY)/Amina Rakhim (KAZ) 63 62. **BS:** Jochen Schottler (GER) d. James Lemke (AUS) 62 63. **BD:** Javier Garrapiz-Borderias/Albert Ramos-Vinolas (ESP) d. Dean Jackson (GER)/Ahmed Rabeea (KUW) 76(3) 57 64.

- **NAMANGAN** (UZB) (Grade 3) 7-11 JUNE – **GS:** Waratchaya Wongteanchai (THA) d. Nigora Sirojiddinova (UZB) 60 64. **GD:** Dilyara Saidkhodjaeva (UZB)/Waratchaya Wongteanchai (THA) d. Vlada Ekshibarova (UZB)/Irina Matiychyk (UKR) 61 67(3) 75. **BS:** Faisal Aidil (INA) d. Peraklat Siriluethaiwattana (THA) 62 26 63. **BD:** Faisal Aidil/Ayrton Wibowo (INA) d. Alexander Chen/Vaja Uzakov (UZB) 63 75.

- **CARIARI** (CRC) (Grade 5) 13-18 JUNE – **GS:** Pamela Duran-Vinueza (ECU) d. Anne Christine Voicu (CAN) 63 75. **GD:** Olivia Bennett (TRI)/Anne Christine Voicu (CAN) d. Pamela Duran-Vinueza (ECU)/Marianne Eelens (ARU) 64 06 61. **BS:** Ricardo Hernandez (VEN) d. Christian Saravia (GUA) 63 63. **BD:** Andres Bucaro (GUA)/Santiago Gruter (ESA) d. Alessandro Di Palma/Eduardo Pinto (CRC) 67(3) 63 63.

- **DONETSK** (UKR) (Grade 4) 13-18 JUNE – **GS:** Mariya Malkhasyan (UKR) d. Eugeniya Pashkova (RUS) 61 75. **GD:** Eugeniya Pashkova/Augusta Tsybycheva (RUS) d. Yevgenia Nudga/Ksenia Tokareva (UKR) 64 64. **BS:** Artem Smirnov (UKR) d. Sergey Rudenko (UKR) 60 62. **BD:** Illya Marchenko/Sergey Rudenko (UKR) d. Dmitry Brichek/Vladyslav Klymenko (UKR) 63 62.

● **BISHKEK** (KGZ) (Grade 5) 13-17 JUNE – **GS:** Nigora Sirojiddinova (UZB) d. Yekaterina Morozova (KAZ) 61 61. **GD:** Diana Narzykulova/Nigora Sirojiddinova (UZB) d. Olga Ippolitova/Yekaterina Morozova (KAZ) 63 63. **BS:** Alexander Seleznev (KGZ) d. Maxim Filippov (KAZ) 64 60. **BD:** Maxim Filippov (KAZ)/Alexander Seleznev (KGZ) d. Anton Litvinov/Sergey Ni (KGZ) 75 75.

● **MOHAMMEDIA** (MAR) (Grade 2) 13-18 JUNE – **GS:** Ksenia Milevskaya (BLR) d. Yanina Wickmayer (BEL) 16 62 63. **GD:** Krista Damico/Chelsey Gullickson (USA) d. Stephanie Herz/Anouk Tigu (NED) 60 60. **BS:** Kevin Botti (FRA) d. Valeri Rudnev (RUS) 57 61 63. **BD:** Christian Vitulli (KEN)/Bradwin Williams (RSA) d. Michal Konecny (CZE)/Blazej Koniusz (POL) 16 63 76(4).

● **PHILADELPHIA, PA** (USA) (Grade 3) 13-18 JUNE – **GS:** Madison Brengle (USA) d. Lyndsay Burdette (USA) 63 63. **GD:** Sanaz Marand/Ashley Weinhold (USA) d. Jelena Durisic (SLO)/Stefanie Nunic (USA) 63 64. **BS:** Rupesh Roy (IND) d. Wil Spencer (USA) 61 62. **BD:** Bradley Cox (USA)/Rupesh Roy (IND) d. Clint Bowles/Michael Sroczynski (USA) 67(8) 75 62.

● **HALLE** (GER) (Grade 3) 14-18 JUNE – **GS:** Marina Erakovic (NZL) d. Agnieszka Radwanska (POL) 63 36 64. **GD:** Agnieszka Radwanska/Urszula Radwanska (POL) d. Julia Goerges (GER)/Lia Jikia (GEO) 64 62. **BS:** Alexander Sadecky (SUI) d. Robin Roshardt (SUI) 75 62. **BD:** Robin Roshardt/Alexander Sadecky (SUI) d. Christoph Hodl (AUT)/Jiri Kosler (CZE) 75 63.

● **GDYNIA** (POL) (Grade 4) 15-19 JUNE – **GS:** Karolina Filipiak (POL) d. Barbara Sobaszkiewicz (POL) 63 67(1) 63. **GD:** Barbara Sobaszkiewicz/Sylwia Zagorska (POL) d. Petra Mokra/Alena Nogolova (CZE) 62 64. **BS:** Mateusz Kowalczyk (POL) d. Jakub Lustyk (CZE) 76(2) 63. **BD:** Mateusz Kowalczyk/Dawid Piatkowski (POL) d. Sven Kasper/Jurgen Zopp (EST) 64 62.

● **LONDON** (GBR) (Grade 1) 19-24 JUNE – **GS:** Caroline Wozniacki (DEN) d. Marina Erakovic (NZL) 60 63. **GD:** Alexa Glatch/Vania King (USA) d. Raluca Olaru (ROM)/Amina Rakhim (KAZ) 63 64. **BS:** Marin Cilic (CRO) d. Petar Jelenic (CRO) 63 63. **BD:** Marin Cilic (CRO)/Tristan Farron-Mahon (IRL) d. Robin Roshardt/Alexander Sadecky (SUI) 26 76(5) 119.

● **LA HABANA** (CUB) (Grade 5) 20-26 JUNE – **GS:** Paulina Luquin (MEX) d. Alicia Aguilar (MEX) 63 62. **GD:** Misleidis Diaz-Gonzalez/Maibel Quintana (CUB) d. Alicia Aguilar (MEX)/Odalis Sardinas (CUB) 36 63 62. **BS:** Luis-Javier Cuellar-Contreras (CUB) d. Alejandro De Mucha (MEX) 61 63. **BD:** Luis-Javier Cuellar-Contreras/Alexander Pelaez-Herrera (CUB) d. Ricardo Andrei Campos (MEX)/Pablo Crespo (CUB) 61 62.

● **PEMBROKE** (BER) (Grade 5) 20-25 JUNE – **GS:** Pamela Duran-Vinueza (ECU) d. Carolyn McVeigh (USA) 75 75. **GD:** Manijee Ashrafi (PUR)/Yolande Leacock (TRI) d. Analy Guzman (GUA)/Megan Jones (USA) 63 36 61. **BS:** Andrew Sharnov (USA) d. Alberton Richelieu (LCA) 26 63 64. **BD:** Michael Clarke (TRI)/Alberton Richelieu (LCA) d. Jack Boling (USA)/Corey Huggins (ECA) 63 75.

● **KIEV** (UKR) (Grade 3) 20-26 JUNE – **GS:** Alexandra Panova (RUS) d. Maria Mosolova (RUS) 64 41 ret. **GD:** Olga Duko/Tatsiana Kapshay (BLR) d. Ima Bogush/Katsarina Zheltova (BLR) 64 61. **BS:** Ivan Sergeyev (UKR) d. Denis Molcianov (MDA) 64 63. **BD:** Victor Kozin (RUS)/Denis Molcianov (MDA) d. Ivan Anikanov/Dmitry Brichek (UKR) 63 63.

● **NOUVELLE-CALEDONIE** (CAL) (Grade 5) 20-24 JUNE – **GS:** Kairangi Vano (NZL) d. Tammi Patterson (AUS) 75 76(1). **GD:** Hannah Fick/Kairangi Vano (NZL) d. Tomoko Iyori/Marina Sato (JPN) 64 64. **BS:** Edward Bourchier (AUS) d. Brenton Dumbrell (AUS) 61 62. **BD:** Edward Bourchier/John Peers (AUS) d. Jonathon Dixon/Troy Smith (AUS) 63 62.

● **CASABLANCA** (MAR) (Grade 2) 20-26 JUNE – **GS:** Ksenia Milevskaya (BLR) d. Chelsey Gullickson (USA) 46 61 64. **GD:** Natalia Orlova (RUS)/Anouk Tigu (NED) d. Lauren Albanese/Gail Brodsky (USA) 64 61. **BS:** Stephen Donald (AUS) d. Karl Norberg (SWE) 61 62. **BD:** Michal Konecny (CZE)/Blazej Koniusz (POL) d. Brydon Klein/Joel Lindner (AUS) 63 64.

● **JAKARTA** (INA) (Grade 4) 20-27 JUNE – **GS:** Ling Zhang (HKG) d. Zi-Jun Yang (HKG) 63 60. **GD:** Wing-Yau Chan/Yi-Ching Yang (HKG) d. Lutfiana Aris Budiharto/Jessy Rompies (INA) 63 75. **BS:** Faisal Aidil (INA) d. Xiao-Long Yin (CHN) 26 63 62. **BD:** Sumit Prakash Gupta (IND)/Oshada Wijemanne (SRI) d. Faisal Aidil/Ayrton Wibowo (INA) 16 75 63.

● **LONDON** (GBR) (Grade A) 25 JUNE-3 JULY – **GS:** Agnieszka Radwanska (POL) d. Tamira Paszek (AUT) 63 64. **GD:** Viktoria Azarenka (BLR)/Agnes Szavay (HUN) d. Marina Erakovic (NZL)/Monica Niculescu (ROM) 67(5) 62 60. **BS:** Jeremy Chardy (FRA) d. Robin Haase (NED) 64 63. **BD:** Jesse Levine/Michael Shabaz (USA) d. Samuel Groth (AUS)/Andrew Kennaugh (GBR) 64 61.

● **BRUCHKOEBEL** (GER) (Grade 4) 27 JUNE-3 JULY – **GS:** Martina Balogova (SVK) d. Barbara Sobaszkiewicz (POL) 64 64. **GD:** Barbara Sobaszkiewicz/Sylwia Zagorska (POL) d. Marina Melnikova/Anna Vavrik (RUS) 63 26 63. **BS:** Andres Arango (ECU) d. Marc Meigel (GER) 06 64 63. **BD:** Radu Albot/Achim Ceban (MDA) d. Marc Meigel/Tobias Wernet (GER) 76(5) 62.

ITF Junior Circuit 2005 Results (continued)

- **NASSAU** (BAH) (Grade 5) 27 JUNE-2 JULY – **GS:** Pamela Duran-Vinueza (ECU) d. Alanna Rodgers (BAH) 26 62 63. **GD:** Alanna Rodgers (BAH)/Ekaterina Rybakova (USA) d. Pamela Duran-Vinueza (ECU)/Analy Guzman (GUA) 62 61. **BS:** Arnaldo Lovera (VEN) d. Miguel Cicenia (VEN) 75 75. **BD:** Michael Clarke (TRI)/Matthew Sands (BAH) d. Waylon Chin/Andy Magee (USA) w/o.

- **CASTRICUM** (NED) (Grade 2) 27 JUNE-3 JULY – **GS:** Katerina Vankova (CZE) d. Lynn Philippe (LUX) 26 64 63. **GD:** Marlot Meddens/Anouk Tigu (NED) d. Roxana Vaideanu/Erika Zanchetta (ITA) 63 64. **BS:** Stephen Donald (AUS) d. Antonio Veic (CRO) 75 76. **BD:** Luka Belic/Antonio Veic (CRO) d. Kevin Botti/Stephane Piro (FRA) 46 64 61.

- **AARHUS** (DEN) (Grade 5) 27 JUNE-3 JULY – **GS:** Mona Barthel (GER) d. Petra Mokra (CZE) 62 75. **GD:** Mona Barthel/Mara Nowak (GER) d. Annemieke Hoekman/Manon Veldhorst (NED) 75 36 64. **BS:** David Rice (GBR) d. Rasmus Moller (DEN) 76(2) 62. **BD:** David Rice/Darren Walsh (GBR) d. Christoffer Konigsfeldt/Soren Wedege (DEN) w/o.

- **BANDUNG** (INA) (Grade 4) 28 JUNE-3 JULY – **GS:** Wing-Yau Chan (HKG) d. Lu-Ling Chen (TPE) 64 36 61. **GD:** Mai Iwasaki/Machiko Shigefuji (JPN) d. Yoon-Young Jeong/So-Yeon Kim (KOR) 46 62 64. **BS:** Faisal Aidil (INA) d. Junn Mitsuhashi (JPN) 61 63. **BD:** Faisal Aidil/Ayrton Wibowo (INA) d. Sumit Prakash Gupta (IND)/Oshada Wijemanne (SRI) 61 61.

- **LAUTOKA** (FIJ) (Grade 4) 28 JUNE-2 JULY – **GS:** Tammi Patterson (AUS) d. Hayley Ericksen (AUS) 62 62. **GD:** Hannah Fick/Kairangi Vano (NZL) d. Ashlee Brown/Tammi Patterson (AUS) 76(4) 75. **BS:** Austin Childs (NZL) d. Ryan Bellamy (AUS) 63 64. **BD:** Ryan Bellamy/Greg Jones (AUS) d. Edward Bourchier/Lachlan Reed (AUS) 76(3) 75.

- **TUNIS** (TUN) (Grade 3) 29 JUNE-3 JULY – **GS:** Fadzai Mawisire (ZIM) d. Ola Abou Zekri (EGY) 61 64. **GD:** Ola Abou Zekri (EGY)/Fadzai Mawisire (ZIM) d. Engela Olivier/Jane Pringle (RSA) 26 62 64. **BS:** Christian Vitulli (KEN) d. Slah Mbarek (TUN) 63 61. **BD:** Christian Vitulli (KEN)/Bradwin Williams (RSA) d. Emmanuel Mensah (GHA)/Dominic Pagon (JAM) 67(5) 63 61.

- **ORANJESTAD** (ARU) (Grade 4) 4-9 JULY – **GS:** Pamela Duran-Vinueza (ECU) d. Briggitt Marcovich (VEN) 67(4) 63 62. **GD:** Natalia Baez (DOM)/Briggitt Marcovich (VEN) d. Analy Guzman (GUA)/Arielle Von Strolley (JAM) 46 63 63. **BS:** Eduardo Meza (MEX) d. Gian Hodgson (ARU) 64 62. **BD:** Eduardo Meza/Daniel Sanchez (MEX) d. Graeme Dyce (GBR)/Takashi Yoshii (JPN) w/o.

- **BANGKOK** (THA) (Grade 5) 4-10 JULY – **GS:** Varanya Vijuksanaboon (THA) d. Zi-Jun Yang (HKG) 67(5) 76(11) 63. **GD:** Sophia Mulsap (THA)/Zi-Jun Yang (HKG) d. Penporn Chantawannop/Varanya Vijuksanaboon (THA) 63 64. **BS:** Yuya Tomisaki (JPN) d. Kittipong Wachiramanowong (THA) 62 63. **BD:** Sang-Gyun Kim/Hyun-Soo Lim (KOR) d. Tadayuki Longhi/Yuya Tomisaki (JPN) 75 57 76(3).

- **HANNIBAL** (TUN) (Grade 4) 4-9 JULY – **GS:** Fadzai Mawisire (ZIM) d. Engela Olivier (RSA) 76(4) 64. **GD:** Zuzana Linhova (CZE)/Lisa Summerer (AUT) d. Fadzai Mawisire (ZIM)/Jenna-May Osborne (RSA) 61 62. **BS:** Christian Vitulli (KEN) d. Corrado Pricone (ITA) 62 06 63. **BD:** Emmanuel Mensah (GHA)/Dominic Pagon (JAM) d. Antonio Comporto/Corrado Pricone (ITA) 63 46 62.

- **ST. PETERSBURG** (RUS) (Grade 4) 4-10 JULY – **GS:** Arina Rodionova (RUS) d. Natalia Ryjonkova (RUS) 60 63. **GD:** Arina Rodionova/Augusta Tsybycheva (RUS) d. Yulia Parasyuk/Elizaveta Titova (RUS) 61 63. **BS:** Artur Chernov (RUS) d. Mikhail Pavlov (RUS) 75 63. **BD:** Vladimir Karusevich/Vladimir Zinyakov (RUS) d. Ivan Anikanov (UKR)/Dmitri Suslov (RUS) 62 62.

- **OSLO** (NOR) (Grade 5) 4-10 JULY – **GS:** Idunn Hertzberg (NOR) d. Amanda Cunningham (GBR) 64 26 62. **GD:** Idunn Hertzberg/Karoline Steiro (NOR) d. Mathilda Engstrom/Johanna Forsberg (SWE) 61 60. **BS:** Carl Sundberg (NOR) d. Milos Sekulic (SWE) w/o. **BD:** Martin Kildahl/Carl Sundberg (NOR) d. Stefan Nikolic (SCG)/Milos Sekulic (SWE) 63 64.

- **OSTROG** (UKR) (Grade 5) 4-10 JULY – **GS:** Mariya Ryzhova (UKR) d. Yevgenia Nudga (UKR) 76(4) 64. **GD:** Maria Melihova (MDA)/Yevgenia Nudga (UKR) d. Oksana Khomyk (UKR)/Valeria Savinykh (RUS) 63 67(5) 63. **BS:** Illya Marchenko (UKR) d. Anton Bobytskyy (UKR) 62 62. **BD:** Anton Bobytskyy/Artem Smirnov (UKR) d. Dmytro Badanov (UKR)/Artiom Podgainii (MDA) 64 63.

- **ESSEN** (GER) (Grade 1) 5-10 JULY – **GS:** Sorana Cirstea (ROM) d. Erika Zanchetta (ITA) 62 67(2) 63. **GD:** Katerina Kramperova (CZE)/Polona Rebersak (SLO) d. Daniela Pernetova/Katerina Vankova (CZE) 76(5) 76(3). **BS:** Javier Garrapiz-Borderias (ESP) d. Ivan Sergeyev (UKR) 63 67(4) 75. **BD:** Luka Belic/Antonio Veic (CRO) d. Stephen Donald (AUS)/Hans Podlipnik (CHI) 75 36 64.

- **LEIDSCHENDAM** (NED) (Grade 4) 5-10 JULY – **GS:** Arantxa Rus (NED) d. Kim Van Der Horst (NED) 63 61. **GD:** Babs Van Kampen/Nicolette Van Uitert (NED) d. Suzelle Davin (NAM)/Tuule Tani (EST) 60 75. **BS:** Dragos Mirtea (ROM) d. Bart Brons (NED) 46 63 76(0). **BD:** Mikk Irdoja/Jurgen Zopp (EST) d. Bart Brons/Tim Van Terheijden (NED) 62 61.

Marin Cilic (CRO)

ITF Junior Circuit 2005 Results (continued)

- **DARWIN** (AUS) (Grade 3) 6-11 JULY – **GS:** Sacha Jones (NZL) d. Jenny Swift (AUS) 61 61. **GD:** Tyra Calderwood/Jessica Moore (AUS) d. Yurina Koshino/Ayumi Okuma (JPN) 64 62. **BS:** Lachlan Reed (AUS) d. Brydon Klein (AUS) 64 76(8). **BD:** John Peers/John-Patrick Smith (AUS) d. Ryan Bellamy/Greg Jones (AUS) 62 64.

- **VILNIUS** (LTU) (Grade 5) 6-10 JULY – **GS:** Alise Razina (LAT) d. Mariya Kovaliova (BLR) 64 76(0). **GD:** Julia Korsunova/Alise Razina (LAT) d. Kristina Jonutyte/Juste Kubiliute (LTU) 62 61. **BS:** Pawel Glodkowski (POL) d. Halvar Dil (NED) 75 40 ret. **BD:** Maksim Beliankou/Anton Khadasevich (BLR) d. Matiss Libietis (LAT)/Morten Ritslaid (EST) 61 36 62.

- **VANCOUVER** (CAN) (Grade 5) 11-15 JULY – **GS:** Stefi Gjine (CAN) d. Alexandra Odell-Michels (CAN) 63 61. **GD:** Stefi Gjine/Alexandra Odell-Michels (CAN) d. Marie-Pier Huet/Casey Kennedy (CAN) 36 63 63. **BS:** Graeme Kassautzki (CAN) d. Vasek Pospisil (CAN) 60 63. **BD:** Graeme Kassautzki/Vasek Pospisil (CAN) d. Matt Manasse (USA)/Philip Nemec (CAN) 62 62.

- **BANGKOK** (THA) (Grade 4) 11-17 JULY – **GS:** Zi-Jun Yang (HKG) d. Yoon-Young Jeong (KOR) 64 75. **GD:** Penporn Chantawannop/Nungnadda Wannasuk (THA) d. Porntip Mulsap/Kamonthip Saovana (THA) 75 36 63. **BS:** Ronald Chow (HKG) d. Peerakit Siributwong (THA) 75 63. **BD:** Junn Mitsuhashi/Takao Ohno (JPN) d. Tadayuki Longhi/Yuya Tomisaki (JPN) 62 67(5) 76(5).

- **VESSY** (SUI) (Grade 5) 11-16 JULY – **GS:** Nicole Riner (SUI) d. Madeleine Geibert (GER) 57 63 62. **GD:** Solange Baumesiter/Nicole Riner (SUI) d. Mahault De Claviere (SUI)/Madeleine Geibert (GER) 61 75. **BS:** Alexander Somogyi (SVK) d. Julian Dehn (GER) 64 61. **BD:** Pascal Krauth/Stephen Schwarz (GER) d. Patrick Mettler/Nicolas Pisecky (SUI) 63 63.

- **DAMASCUS** (SYR) (Grade 4) 11-16 JULY – **GS:** Wing-Yau Chan (HKG) d. Jaklin Alawi (BUL) 61 64. **GD:** Wing-Yau Chan (HKG)/Rana El Derwy (EGY) d. Jaklin Alawi (BUL)/Tejaswini Datta (IND) 62 61. **BS:** Marc Abdelnour (SYR) d. Akshay Bajoria (IND) 63 60. **BD:** Akshay Bajoria (IND)/Neil Rajpal (CAN) d. Marc Abdelnour/Nawar Baram (SYR) 36 63 63.

- **HELSINKI** (FIN) (Grade 5) 11-15 JULY – **GS:** Karoline Steiro (NOR) d. Maya Pitenina (RUS) 62 64. **GD:** Anja Maskaljun/Carolyn Saan (EST) d. Emma Helisten/Ina Kauppila (FIN) 36 62 64. **BS:** Patrik Rosenholm (SWE) d. Halvar Dil (NED) w/o. **BD:** Harri Heliovaara/Antti Vallila (FIN) d. Stefan Nikolic (SCG)/Krisjanis Stabins (LAT) 62 63.

- **ST. MAARTEN** (AHO) (Grade 4) 11-16 JULY – **GS:** Kai-Chen Chang (TPE) d. Gabriela Mejia (COL) 75 62. **GD:** Natalia Baez (DOM)/Briggitt Marcovich (VEN) d. Pamela Duran-Vinueza (ECU)/Analy Guzman (GUA) 36 63 62. **BS:** Graeme Dyce (GBR) d. Daniel Sanchez (MEX) 67(3) 75 64. **BD:** Eduardo Meza/Daniel Sanchez (MEX) d. Bradley Cox (USA)/Peter Marrack (CAN) w/o.

- **WINCHESTER** (GBR) (Grade 4) 11-16 JULY – **GS:** Alexandra Kulikova (RUS) d. Lauren Dossor (GBR) 61 64. **GD:** Nikki Prosser/Amy Sargeant (GBR) d. Yasmin Clarke/Rachael Hall (GBR) 62 64. **BS:** Iain Atkinson (GBR) d. Simon Ferguson (GBR) 36 62 64. **BD:** Iain Atkinson/Sean Galpin (GBR) d. Konstantinos Kalaitzis (GBR)/Nikita Zotov (RUS) 76(2) 06 63.

- **BERLIN** (GER) (Grade 4) 12-16 JULY – **GS:** Ksenia Pervak (RUS) d. Syna Kayser (GER) 64 62. **GD:** Karolyn Grymel (GER)/Kristina Pejkovic (AUS) d. Ana Beltran-Trigueros (ESP)/Efrat Mishor (ISR) 64 64. **BS:** Nico Hegge (GER) d. Peter Frank (GER) 60 63. **BD:** Julien Dubail (BEL)/Mikhail Fufygin (RUS) d. Johannes Pulsfort/Willi Wolfer (GER) 50 ret.

- **HILLEGOM** (NED) (Grade 4) 12-17 JULY – **GS:** Anouk Tigu (NED) d. Nicolette Van Uitert (NED) 63 62. **GD:** Marlot Meddens/Anouk Tigu (NED) d. Babs Van Kampen/Nicolette Van Uitert (NED) 76(11) 64. **BS:** Michiel Antheunis (BEL) d. Arjan Pastoors (NED) 63 61. **BD:** Kristof De Leeuw/Nikolas Zogaj (BEL) d. Bart Brons/Tim Van Terheijden (NED) 76(6) 67(4) 60.

- **DARWIN** (AUS) (Grade 3) 12-17 JULY – **GS:** Sacha Jones (NZL) d. Shona Lee (NZL) 61 63. **GD:** Tyra Calderwood/Jessica Moore (AUS) d. Lisa Miller/Maria Sorbello (AUS) 63 76(3). **BS:** Brydan Klein (AUS) d. Troy Smith (AUS) 61 64. **BD:** Ryan Bellamy/Greg Jones (AUS) d. Brydan Klein/Kenneth Prajoga (AUS) 76(5) ret.

- **WELS** (AUT) (Grade 1) 12-17 JULY – **GS:** Agnieszka Radwanska (POL) d. Urszula Radwanska (POL) 62 63. **GD:** Agnieszka Radwanska/Urszula Radwanska (POL) d. Marrit Boonstra/Renee Reinhard (NED) 75 62. **BS:** Luka Belic (CRO) d. Yannick Mertens (BEL) 61 63. **BD:** Luka Belic/Antonio Veic (CRO) d. Nikola Mektic/Vedran Siljegovic (CRO) 63 64.

- **PRAHA** (CZE) (Grade 4) 13-17 JULY – **GS:** Tereza Belbova (CZE) d. Naomi Cavaday (GBR) 46 64 75. **GD:** Ksenia Lykina (RUS)/Sona Novakova (CZE) d. Tereza Belbova/Hana Birnerova (CZE) 64 61. **BS:** Harry Skinner (GBR) d. Andrei Martin (SVK) w/o. **BD:** Petr Michniev/Tomas Urban (CZE) d. Martin Durdik/Adrian Sikora (SVK) 62 62.

- **ASTANA CITY** (KAZ) (Grade 5) 16-21 JULY – **GS:** Mariya Kovaleva (KAZ) d. Yekaterina Morozova (KAZ) 46 75 61. **GD:** Mariya Kovaleva/Yekaterina Morozova (KAZ) d. Olga Ippolitova/Maya Maralbayeva (KAZ) 60 62. **BS:** Stanislav Buykov (KAZ) d. Alexander Chen (UZB) 64 62. **BD:** Stanislav Buykov/Maxim Filippov (KAZ) d. Danjil Braun (KAZ)/Anton Litvinov (KGZ) 63 75.

- **DAMASCUS** (SYR) (Grade 4) 18-23 JULY – **GS:** Petra Mokra (CZE) d. Jaklin Alawi (BUL) 46 63 61. **GD:** Jaklin Alawi (BUL)/Ashmitha Easwaramurthi (IND) d. Shivika Burman/Tejaswini Datta (IND) 76(2) 75. **BS:** Marc Abdelnour (SYR) d. Akshay Bajoria (IND) 75 64. **BD:** Martin Dalton/Zack Goldsmith (GBR) d. Marc Abdelnour/Nawar Baram (SYR) 64 57 76(6).

- **KINGSTON** (JAM) (Grade 4) 18-24 JULY – **GS:** Ekaterina Rybakova (USA) d. Victoria Brook (GBR) 62 57 63. **GD:** Victoria Brook/Abbie Probert (GBR) d. Natalia Baez (DOM)/Briggitt Marcovich (VEN) 62 64. **BS:** Gregory Gumbs (FRA) d. Eduardo Meza (MEX) 76(6) 63. **BD:** Eduardo Meza/Daniel Sanchez (MEX) d. Gregory Gumbs (FRA)/Dominic Pagon (JAM) 63 62.

- **KLOSTERS** (SUI) (Grade B1) 18-24 JULY – **GS:** Agnes Szavay (HUN) d. Monica Niculescu (ROM) 61 62. **GD:** Alla Kudryavtseva/Ekaterina Makarova (RUS) d. Mihaela Buzarnescu/Monica Niculescu (ROM) 46 61 64. **BS:** Thiemo De Bakker (NED) d. Alexandre Sidorenko (FRA) 76(3) 63. **BD:** Dusan Lojda/Jan Marek (CZE) d. David Klier/Jochen Schoettler (GER) 36 63 76(4).

- **CORK** (IRL) (Grade 5) 18-22 JULY – **GS:** Amanda Elliott (GBR) d. Mona Barthel (GER) 63 64. **GD:** Rachael Hall/Sophie Wilkinson (GBR) d. Mona Barthel (GER)/Ilse Hulskes (NED) 63 62. **BS:** Paul Fitzgerald (IRL) d. Joshua Milton (GBR) 62 61. **BD:** David Rice/Darren Walsh (GBR) d. Austen Childs (NZL)/Paul Fitzgerald (IRL) 63 62.

- **GIZA** (EGY) (Grade 3) 18-24 JULY – **GS:** Maya Gaverova (RUS) d. Ksenia Milevskaya (BLR) 63 75. **GD:** Zuzana Linhova (CZE)/Ksenia Milevskaya (BLR) d. Ola Abou Zekri/Magy Aziz (EGY) 62 63. **BS:** Houssam Yassine (MAR) d. Ahmed Rabeea (KUW) 63 63. **BD:** Ivan Anikanov/Igor Nikitin (UKR) d. Sumit Prakash Gupta (IND)/Ahmed Rabeea (KUW) 62 64.

- **TALLINN** (EST) (Grade 4) 19-23 JULY – **GS:** Ekaterina Jeritsheva (EST) d. Maya Pitenina (RUS) 62 62. **GD:** Anja Maskaljun (EST)/Alise Razina (LAT) d. Maya Pitenina (RUS)/Carolyn Saan (EST) 62 64. **BS:** Mikk Irdoja (EST) d. Fredi Voormann (EST) 60 63. **BD:** Mikk Irdoja/Markus Pops (EST) d. Vladimir Karusevich (RUS)/Mikhail Trukshanin (BLR) 63 63.

- **AUCKLAND** (NZL) (Grade 4) 19-24 JULY – **GS:** Kairangi Vano (NZL) d. Tyra Calderwood (AUS) 75 67(8) 64. **GD:** Hannah Fick/Kairangi Vano (NZL) d. Shona Lee (NZL)/Johanna Morrison (AUS) 46 76(3) 10 ret. **BS:** Andrew Allan (NZL) d. Greg Jones (AUS) 67(2) 63 63. **BD:** Robert Foy (NZL)/John Peers (AUS) d. Jared Easton/Hugh McDonald (AUS) 64 61.

- **HATFIELD** (RSA) (Grade 2) 19-24 JULY – **GS:** Stephanie Herz (NED) d. Jade Curtis (GBR) 64 61. **GD:** Jade Curtis (GBR)/Stephanie Herz (NED) d. Farida Karaeva (UKR)/Maria Mosolova (RUS) 62 63. **BS:** Christian Vitulli (KEN) d. David Simon (AUT) 75 36 63. **BD:** Brad Brinkhause Williams/Charl Wolmarans (RSA) d. Johnny Hamui (USA)/Jiri Kosler (CZE) 75 76(5).

- **PLZEN** (CZE) (Grade 3) 20-24 JULY – **GS:** Sona Novakova (CZE) d. Michaela Pochabova (SVK) 64 67(3) 64. **GD:** Magdalena Kiszczynska/Joanna Matuszczyk (POL) d. Tereza Belbova/Hana Birnerova (CZE) 46 64 63. **BS:** Martin Kamenik (CZE) d. Michal Kozerovsky (CZE) 06 62 63. **BD:** Michal Kozerovsky/Tomas Urban (CZE) d. Blazej Koniusz/Pawel Turzanski (POL) 46 62 76(4).

- **SANTO DOMINGO** (DOM) (Grade 4) 24-30 JULY – **GS:** Alexandra Anghelescu (USA) d. Gabriela Mejia (COL) 62 60. **GD:** Gabriela Mejia (COL)/Jo-Ann Van Aerde (SUR) d. Jessica Sweeting (BAH)/Kirsten-Andrea Weedon (GUA) 61 64. **BS:** Eduardo Meza (MEX) d. Luis-Javier Cuellar-Contreras (CUB) 61 61. **BD:** Bruno Berruti/Gustavo Loza (MEX) d. Jamaal Adderley (BAH)/Yohansey Williams (TRI) 36 61 75.

- **ALMATY CITY** (KAZ) (Grade 4) 25-30 JULY – **GS:** Ksenia Palkina (KGZ) d. Mariya Kovaleva (KAZ) 62 62. **GD:** Ksenia Palkina (KGZ)/Nigora Sirojiddinova (UZB) d. Diana Narzykulova/Eleonora Sidjemileva (UZB) 63 62. **BS:** Alexander Seleznev (KGZ) d. Stanislav Buykov (KAZ) 75 60. **BD:** Alexander Seleznev (KGZ)/Vaja Uzakov (UZB) d. Stanislav Buykov/Maxim Filippov (KAZ) 57 76(4) 64.

- **LUXEMBOURG** (LUX) (Grade 2) 25-30 JULY – **GS:** Anastasia Pavlyuchenkova (RUS) d. Anastasia Pivovarova (RUS) 62 64. **GD:** Nina Henkel (GER)/Elena Kulikova (RUS) d. Hana Birnerova/Barbora Hodinarova (CZE) 61 61. **BS:** Frederic De Fays (BEL) d. Blazej Koniusz (POL) 63 36 76(5). **BD:** Maxime Authom/Frederic De Fays (BEL) d. Wael Kilani (TUN)/Ahmed Rabeea (KUW) 64 62.

- **DUBLIN** (IRL) (Grade 5) 25-29 JULY – **GS:** Amanda Elliott (GBR) d. Sophie Wilkinson (GBR) 75 75. **GD:** Evelien Strijker/Marlies Vermeulen (NED) d. Niamh Coveney (IRL)/Mariana Levova (BUL) 63 61. **BS:** Paul Fitzgerald (IRL) d. Johannes Pulsfort (GER) 76 41 ret. **BD:** David Rice/Darren Walsh (GBR) d. Paul Morrisey (IRL)/Johannes Pulsfort (GER) w/o.

- **HATFIELD** (RSA) (Grade 2) 25-30 JULY – **GS:** Maria Mosolova (RUS) d. Wing-Yau Chan (HKG) 61 61. **GD:** Farida Karaeva (UKR)/Maria Mosolova (RUS) d. Goele Lemmens/Yanina Wickmayer (BEL) 06 62 61. **BS:** Christian Vitulli (KEN) d. Keith-Patrick Crowley (RSA) 76(3) 63. **BD:** Faisal Aidil/Ayrton Wibowo (INA) d. Jiri Kosler (CZE)/Rupesh Roy (IND) 62 67(4) 64.

- **CAIRO** (EGY) (Grade 3) 25-31 JULY – **GS:** Dilyara Saidkhodjaeva (UZB) d. Sandhya Nagaraj (IND) 64 63. **GD:** Mai El Wardany/Nihal Saleh (EGY) d. Majdouline Akrate/Fatima El Allami (MAR) 64 76(3). **BS:** Houssam Yassine (MAR) d. Bassam Beidas (LIB) 62 36 64. **BD:** Hicham Laalej/Houssam Yassine (MAR) d. Sumit Prakash Gupta (IND)/Mahmoud Kamel (EGY) w/o.

- **MADRID** (ESP) (Grade 5) 27-30 JULY – **GS:** Ling Zhang (HKG) d. Paloma Diaz-Sada (ESP) 60 61. **GD:** Anastasia Kontratevidi (GRE)/ Ling Zhang (HKG) d. Rocio De La Torre-Sanchez/Paloma Diaz-Sada (ESP) 60 60. **BS:** Francisco Javier De La Torre-Sanchez (ESP) d. Conrado Lopez-Carbajo (ESP) 64 62. **BD:** Ivan Arenas-Gualda/Rodrigo Figueroa-Vazquez (ESP) d. Conrado Lopez-Carbajo/Hugo Taracido-loureiro (ESP) w/o.

- **LA ROCHELLE** (FRA) (Grade C) 31 JULY-2 AUGUST – **Germany d. Russia 2-1:** Matthias Bachinger (GER) d. Valeri Rudnev (RUS) 63 61; Mihail Zverev (GER) d. Evgeny Kirillov (RUS) 75 62; Matthias Bachinger/Mihail Zverev (GER) d. Pavel Chekhov/Evgeny Kirillov (RUS) 64 61.

- **GRANVILLE** (FRA) (Grade C) 31 JULY-2 AUGUST – **Russia d. Spain 3-0:** Alla Kudryavtseva (RUS) d. Silvia Soler-Espinosa (ESP) 46 61 62; Ekaterina Makarova (RUS) d. Carla Suarez-Navarro (ESP) 36 61 62; Alla Kudryavtseva/Yaroslava Shvedova (RUS) d. Sara Del Barrio-Aragon/ Carla Suarez-Navarro (ESP) 62 60.

- **BISHKEK** (KGZ) (Grade 4) 1-6 AUGUST – **GS:** Ksenia Palkina (KGZ) d. Nigora Sirojiddinova (UZB) 61 63. **GD:** Ksenia Palkina (KGZ)/ Nigora Sirojiddinova (UZB) d. Diana Narzykulova/Eleonora Sidjemileva (UZB) 63 62. **BS:** Alexander Seleznev (KGZ) d. Vaja Uzakov (UZB) 64 63. **BD:** Maxim Filippov (KAZ)/Alexander Seleznev (KGZ) d. Alexander Chen/Vaja Uzakov (UZB) 64 26 63.

- **WINDHOEK** (NAM) (Grade 4) 1-5 AUGUST – **GS:** Justine-Kelly Sutherland (RSA) d. Marne Roos (RSA) 61 62. **GD:** Abigail Olivier/ Justine-Kelly Sutherland (RSA) d. Engela Olivier/Jane Pringle (RSA) 63 61. **BS:** Rupesh Roy (IND) d. Jurgens Strydom (NAM) 63 63. **BD:** Wesley Baptiste/Tucker Vorster (RSA) d. Lofo Ramiaramanan (MAD)/Bokang Setshogo (BOT) 61 75.

- **SANTO DOMINGO** (DOM) (Grade B3) 1-7 AUGUST – **GS:** Liset Brito (CHI) d. Valeria Pulido-Velasco (MEX) 64 61. **GD:** Liset Brito (CHI)/ Valeria Pulido-Velasco (MEX) d. Yolande Leacock (TRI)/Alanna Rodgers (BAH) 61 62. **BS:** Ryan Sweeting (BAH) d. Alberto Gonzalez (PAN) 63 76(1). **BD:** Eduardo Meza/Daniel Sanchez (MEX) d. Bruno Berruti/Gustavo Loza (MEX) 63 64.

- **LEIRIA** (POR) (Grade 4) 2-6 AUGUST – **GS:** Julia Glushko (ISR) d. Nadine Fahoum (ISR) 75 62. **GD:** Ana Beltran-Trigueros (ESP)/Marlot Coolen (NED) d. Rita Gouveia (POR)/Charlotte Rodier (FRA) 61 62. **BS:** Austen Childs (NZL) d. Victor Andrei Ion (ROM) 63 63. **BD:** Elias Gastao/Joao Sousa (POR) d. Goncalo Falcao (POR)/Artem Kuznetsov (RUS) 63 64.

- **DOMZALE** (SLO) (Grade 3) 3-7 AUGUST – **GS:** Arina Rodionova (RUS) d. Michaela Pochabova (SVK) 64 76(3). **GD:** Arina Rodionova/Julia Semeneko (RUS) d. Taja Mohorcic/Alja Zec-Peskiric (SLO) 62 63. **BS:** Evthimios Karaliolios (NED) d. Calin Paar (GER) 63 62. **BD:** Marcin Gawron/Piotr Zielinski (POL) d. Ivan Anikanov (UKR)/Danila Arsenov (RUS) 60 75.

- **GABORONE** (BOT) (Grade 4) 7-11 AUGUST – **GS:** Justine-Kelly Sutherland (RSA) d. Abigail Olivier (RSA) 63 76(1). **GD:** Chane Hines/ Marne Roos (RSA) d. Abigail Olivier/Justine-Kelly Sutherland (RSA) 67(4) 64 63. **BS:** Rupesh Roy (IND) d. Jurgens Strydom (NAM) 16 64 75. **BD:** Keith-Patrick Crowley (RSA)/Rupesh Roy (IND) d. Lofo Ramiaramanan (MAD)/Bokang Setshogo (BOT) 63 64.

- **IBAGUE-TOLIMA** (COL) (Grade 5) 8-14 AUGUST – **GS:** Giannina Minieri (CHI) d. Rebeca Neves (BRA) 75 61. **GD:** Gabriela Mejia (COL)/ Giannina Minieri (CHI) d. Karen-Natalia Martinez-Bernal/Juanita Munoz (COL) 60 63. **BS:** German Sole (URU) d. Luis Rovira (VEN) 62 64. **BD:** Ariel Behar/German Sole (URU) d. Alejandro Gonzalez/Sergio Velez (COL) 62 64.

- **PORTO** (POR) (Grade 4) 8-13 AUGUST – **GS:** Keren Shlomo (ISR) d. Joana Pangaio (POR) 75 64. **GD:** Maria Guerreiro (POR)/Marlot Meddens (NED) d. Elana Agranovich/Chen Astrugo (ISR) 76(5) 64. **BS:** Wael Kilani (TUN) d. Elias Gastao (POR) 36 62 64. **BD:** Wael Kilani/Slah Mbarek (TUN) d. Goncalo Falcao (POR)/Artem Kuznetsov (RUS) 62 26 62.

- **TAMPICO** (MEX) (Grade 4) 8-13 AUGUST – **GS:** Victoria Brook (GBR) d. Danielle Mills (USA) 67(1) 76(5) 62. **GD:** Clarisse Baca/Ana-Laura Ochoa-Magana (MEX) d. Alicia Aguilar/Chloe Mielgo (MEX) 76(4) 62. **BS:** Cesar Ramirez (MEX) d. Eduardo Peralta (MEX) 64 61. **BD:** Alejandro Moreno/Eduardo Peralta (MEX) d. Ramiro Alexis Campos/Cesar Ramirez (MEX) 46 60 75.

● **ZABRZE** (POL) (Grade 4) 10-14 AUGUST – **GS:** Sylwia Zagorska (POL) d. Patricia Veresova (SVK) 62 57 64. **GD:** Katarina Poljakova/ Patricia Veresova (SVK) d. Barbara Sobaszkiewicz/Sylwia Zagorska (POL) 64 63. **BS:** Blazej Koniusz (POL) d. Marcin Gawron (POL) 63 62. **BD:** Marcin Gawron/Blazej Koniusz (POL) d. Simon Bekker (RUS)/Vladyslav Klymenko (UKR) 75 76(5).

● **MARIBOR** (SLO) (Grade 4) 10-14 AUGUST – **GS:** Petra Mokra (CZE) d. Aleksandra Lukic (SLO) 64 62. **GD:** Aleksandra Lukic/Patricia Vollmeier (SLO) d. Petra Mokra (CZE)/Katharina Negrin (AUT) 61 61. **BS:** Boran Poljancic (CRO) d. Alexander Somogyi (SVK) 36 76(5) 61. **BD:** Andrei Martin/Alexander Somogyi (SVK) d. Iztok Kukec/Grega Teraz (SLO) 64 75.

● **BULAWAYO** (ZIM) (Grade 4) 13-17 AUGUST – **GS:** Chane Hines (RSA) d. Justine-Kelly Sutherland (RSA) 62 46 63. **GD:** Abigail Olivier/ Justine-Kelly Sutherland (RSA) d. Chane Hines/Jane Pringle (RSA) 61 57 64. **BS:** Jurgens Strydom (NAM) d. Brad Brinkhause Williams (RSA) 57 63 76(3). **BD:** Wesley Baptiste/Tucker Vorster (RSA) d. Johan De Wet/Jurgens Strydom (NAM) 64 62.

● **CASTRIES** (LCA) (Grade 5) 15-20 AUGUST – **GS:** Yolande Leacock (TRI) d. Nachell Proctor (USA) 63 64. **GD:** Breanna Atkinson/Nachell Proctor (USA) d. Carlista Mohammed/Shenelle Mohammed (TRI) 60 64. **BS:** Alberton Richelieu (LCA) d. Rasid Winklaar (AHO) 63 63. **BD:** Alberton Richelieu (LCA)/Rasid Winklaar (AHO) d. Michael Clarke/Yohansey Williams (TRI) 63 62.

● **CALI** (COL) (Grade 5) 15-21 AUGUST – **GS:** Giannina Minieri (CHI) d. Catalina Robles (COL) 75 61. **GD:** Giannina Minieri (CHI)/Gabriela Paz (VEN) d. Yessica Medina/Catalina Robles (COL) 61 64. **BS:** Edgar Rodriguez (COL) d. Magin Ortiga (COL) 64 62. **BD:** Francisco Franco/ Diego Medrano (COL) d. Boris Barrios (VEN)/Sergio Velez (COL) 63 76(5).

● **CAMPO DE MARTE** (GUA) (Grade 4) 15-21 AUGUST – **GS:** Victoria Brook (GBR) d. Paulina Luquin (MEX) 60 63. **GD:** Analy Guzman/ Kirsten-Andrea Weedon (GUA) d. Victoria Brook (GBR)/Danielle Mills (USA) 64 26 61. **BS:** Alejandro Moreno (MEX) d. Viju George (USA) 62 16 63. **BD:** Alejandro Argumedo (ESA)/Sebastian Vidal (GUA) d. Andres Bucaro/Tulio Davila (GUA) 36 76(2) 76(2).

● **TAIWAN** (TPE) (Grade 4) 16-21 AUGUST – **GS:** Wing-Yau Chan (HKG) d. Nungnadda Wannasuk (THA) 46 63 62. **GD:** Wing-Yau Chan (HKG)/Shao-Yuan Kao (TPE) d. Lu-Ling Chen/Wen-Ling Wang (TPE) 61 62. **BS:** Ronald Chow (HKG) d. Tung Han Lee (TPE) 61 64. **BD:** Chu Ping Chiu/Hsien-Yin Peng (TPE) d. Tung Han Lee/Chien Chih Wu (TPE) 76(2) 62.

● **CORFU** (GRE) (Grade 5) 16-21 AUGUST – **GS:** Eylul Benli (TUR) d. Alexandra Sakalaridi (GRE) 46 63 61. **GD:** Eylul Benli/Gozde Unkaya (TUR) d. Alexandra Sakalaridi/Agni Stefanou (GRE) 36 61 62. **BS:** George Balafoytas (GRE) d. Nikos Spyrou (GRE) 62 75. **BD:** Paris Gemouchidis/Nikos Spyrou (GRE) d. Dimitris Kouramas (GRE)/Dimitrios Loucareas (USA) 75 63.

● **LEIDSCHENDAM** (NED) (Grade 4) 16-21 AUGUST – **GS:** Florence De Vrye (BEL) d. Romana Janshen (NED) 63 61. **GD:** Babs Van Kampen/ Nicolette Van Uitert (NED) d. Syna Kayser/Ellen Linsenbolz (GER) 64 76(6). **BS:** Tim Goransson (SWE) d. Phillippe Brand (NED) 63 67(5) 62. **BD:** Remi Groenendaal/Arjan Pastoors (NED) d. Evthimios Karaliolios/Kevin Schimmel (NED) w/o.

● **VILA DO CONDE** (POR) (Grade 3) 16-21 AUGUST – **GS:** Nikola Hofmanova (AUT) d. Melanie Klaffner (AUT) 64 62. **GD:** Olga Duko (BLR)/ Kristina Ufimtseva (RUS) d. Julia Glushko (ISR)/Joana Pangaio (POR) 62 64. **BS:** Elias Gastao (POR) d. Niels Desein (BEL) 60 76(6). **BD:** Goncalo Falcao (POR)/Artem Kuznetsov (RUS) d. Irakli Dshandshgava (AUT)/Kiryl Harbatsiuk (BLR) 63 63.

● **BRATISLAVA** (SVK) (Grade 4) 17-21 AUGUST – **GS:** Lenka Jurikova (SVK) d. Zuzana Zlochova (SVK) 63 63. **GD:** Katarina Poljakova/ Zuzana Zlochova (SVK) d. Monika Kochanova/Katarina Mlcochova (SVK) 64 64. **BS:** Martin Klizan (SVK) d. Maros Horny (SVK) 76(7) 06 62. **BD:** Maros Horny/Martin Klizan (SVK) d. Andrei Martin/Tomas Sevcov (SVK) 64 64.

● **SOFIA** (BUL) (Grade 5) 17-21 AUGUST – **GS:** Elitsa Kostova (BUL) d. Delia Damaschin (ROM) w/o. **GD:** Lora Stancheva/Tania Stoimanova (BUL) d. Alexandra Cadantu/Ioana Oprea (ROM) 63 64. **BS:** Ilija Martinoski (MKD) d. Wesley Koolhof (NED) 63 60. **BD:** Dragomir Aleksandrov/Nikola Petrov (BUL) d. Nikola Bubnic/Predrag Nedeljkovic (SCG) w/o.

● **WARSAW** (POL) (Grade 4) 17-21 AUGUST – **GS:** Ima Bogush (BLR) d. Alena Nogolova (CZE) 62 61. **GD:** Eugeniya Pashkova (RUS)/ Katarzyna Piter (POL) d. Barbara Sobaszkiewicz/Sylwia Zagorska (POL) 64 67(4) 62. **BS:** Artem Smirnov (UKR) d. Marcin Gawron (POL) 76(3) 76(6). **BD:** Marcin Gawron/Mateusz Szmigiel (POL) d. Simon Bekker (RUS)/Vladyslav Klymenko (UKR) 62 62.

● **LAUTOKA** (FIJ) (Grade B2) 21-25 AUGUST – **GS:** Sacha Jones (NZL) d. Ellen Barry (NZL) 46 62 63. **GD:** Tyra Calderwood/Jessica Moore (AUS) d. Michelle Brycki (AUS)/Kairangi Vano (NZL) w/o. **BS:** Brydan Klein (AUS) d. Greg Jones (AUS) 62 61. **BD:** Jason Lee (AUS)/James Pilbro (NZL) d. Brydan Klein/Joel Lindner (AUS) 67(0) 76(5) 62.

- **AMMAN** (JOR) (Grade 5) 22-26 AUGUST – **GS:** Rana Tharwat-Hafez (EGY) d. Line Ghannam (SYR) 62 63. **GD:** Mai El Wardany/Rana Tharwat-Hafez (EGY) d. Lara Al Samman (SYR)/Jordane Dobbins (GBR) 62 62. **BS:** Marc Abdelnour (SYR) d. Issam Al Taweel (SYR) 64 75. **BD:** Marc Abdelnour/Nawar Baram (SYR) d. Mohammed Al Hadid/Ahmed Tabyshat (JOR) 62 64.

- **CLERMONT-FERRAND** (FRA) (Grade 4) 22-28 AUGUST – **GS:** Adeline Goncalves (FRA) d. Ondine Trompette (FRA) 75 62. **GD:** Cindy Chala/Marie Menacer (FRA) d. Kelly Couturier/Valentina Fauviau (FRA) 76(0) 75. **BS:** Jerome Inzerillo (FRA) d. Kiryl Harbatsiuk (BLR) 36 64 62. **BD:** Jerome Inzerillo/Stephane Piro (FRA) d. Dorian Descloix/Luka Karabatic (FRA) 62 62.

- **ALLENWOOD, NJ** (USA) (Grade 3) 22-27 AUGUST – **GS:** Hilary Barte (USA) d. Ksenia Lykina (RUS) 63 64. **GD:** Ksenia Lykina (RUS)/Trina Slapeka (LAT) d. Maria Mokh (RUS)/Stefanie Nunic (USA) 63 26 62. **BS:** Nikola Mektic (CRO) d. Jaak Poldma (EST) 62 46 64. **BD:** Clint Bowles/Michael Sroczynski (USA) d. Attila Bucko (SCG)/Christopher Racz (USA) 75 46 63.

- **CIUDAD MERLIOT** (ESA) (Grade 4) 22-27 AUGUST – **GS:** Liset Brito (CHI) d. Paulina Luquin (MEX) 63 62. **GD:** Liset Brito (CHI)/Paulina Luquin (MEX) d. Analy Guzman/Kirsten-Andrea Weedon (GUA) 63 64. **BS:** Alejandro Moreno (MEX) d. Santiago Gruter (ESA) 75 64. **BD:** Andres Bucaro (GUA)/Santiago Gruter (ESA) d. Jaime Clark/Alejandro Moreno (MEX) 64 75.

- **ST. KATELIJNE WAVER** (BEL) (Grade 3) 23-28 AUGUST – **GS:** Arantxa Rus (NED) d. Petra Mokra (CZE) 64 60. **GD:** Marlot Meddens/Anouk Tigu (NED) d. Babs Van Kampen/Nicolette Van Uitert (NED) 63 61. **BS:** Tim Goransson (SWE) d. Yannick Thomet (SUI) 46 60 63. **BD:** Frederic De Fays/Yannick Mertens (BEL) d. Dylan Sessagesimi/Yannick Thomet (SUI) 60 61.

- **SKOPJE** (MKD) (Grade 5) 24-28 AUGUST – **GS:** Lyutfya Velieva (BUL) d. Huliya Velieva (BUL) 62 20 ret. **GD:** Huliya Velieva/Lyutfya Velieva (BUL) d. Nives Pavlovic/Nevena Selakovic (SCG) 64 61. **BS:** Ilija Martinoski (MKD) d. Ilija Vucic (SCG) 60 62. **BD:** Philip Barlow (GBR)/Kaan Yaylali (TUR) d. Strate Krstevski/Dimitar Labudovik (MKD) 60 36 62.

- **MINSK** (BLR) (Grade 5) 24-28 AUGUST – **GS:** Tatsiana Kapshay (BLR) d. Ima Bogush (BLR) 60 62. **GD:** Tatsiana Kapshay/Katsarina Zheltova (BLR) d. Ima Bogush/Ekaterina Lukomskaya (BLR) 64 63. **BS:** Dmitry Novikov (BLR) d. Anton Stryhas (BLR) 76(1) 61. **BD:** Siarhei Betau/Dmitry Novikov (BLR) d. Alexei Bessonov/Pavel Katliarou (BLR) 62 62.

- **STOBREC** (CRO) (Grade 5) 24-28 AUGUST – **GS:** Veronika Ciganikova (SVK) d. Antea Huljev-Ajlin (SLO) 64 33 ret. **GD:** Veronika Ciganikova/Nina Gajdosikova (SVK) d. Petra Bohm (AUT)/Antea Huljev-Ajlin (SLO) 63 63. **BS:** Marko Mijacevic (CRO) d. Deni Zmak (CRO) 62 16 76(6). **BD:** Bojan Kovac/Goran Rozic (CRO) d. Duje Janjic/Ivan Skaro (CRO) 60 64.

- **JEJU** (KOR) (Grade 5) 24-28 AUGUST – **GS:** Zi-Jun Yang (HKG) d. Sung-Hee Han (KOR) 62 63. **GD:** Seul-Ki Chin/Yoon-Young Jeong (KOR) d. Ji-Hee Lee/Ji-Hyun Oh (KOR) 61 60. **BS:** Dae Soung Oh (KOR) d. Daniel Yoon (KOR) 63 61. **BD:** Dae Jin Kim/Dae Young Kim (KOR) d. Soong-Jae Cho/Soon-Sung Park (KOR) 61 76(5).

- **HASKOVO** (BUL) (Grade 5) 24-28 AUGUST – **GS:** Elitsa Kostova (BUL) d. Jaklin Alawi (BUL) 62 62. **GD:** Lora Stancheva/Tania Stoimanova (BUL) d. Jaklin Alawi/Evlin Barbutova (BUL) 64 64. **BS:** Valentin Dimov (BUL) d. Gueorgui Roumenov-Payakov (BUL) 16 62 63. **BD:** Valentin Dimov/Gueorgui Roumenov-Payakov (BUL) d. Andrei Daraban/Costin Paval (ROM) w/o.

- **MISKOLC** (HUN) (Grade 3) 24-28 AUGUST – **GS:** Tereza Mrdeza (CRO) d. Petra Martic (CRO) 61 63. **GD:** Michaela Pochabova/Patricia Veresova (SVK) d. Klaudia Boczova/Monika Kochanova (SVK) 46 75 61. **BS:** Attila Balazs (HUN) d. Adrian Sikora (SVK) 63 60. **BD:** Ivan Anikanov/Vladyslav Klymenko (UKR) d. Anton Bobytskyy/Artem Smirnov (UKR) 62 63.

- **TEHRAN** (IRI) (Grade 5) 29 AUGUST-2 SEPTEMBER – **BS:** Martin Dalton (GBR) d. Hami Darvishi Omrani (IRI) 61 62. **BD:** Samriddh Burman (IND)/Martin Dalton (GBR) d. Afshin Bayati/Reza Kohastani (IRI) 61 76(6).

- **REPENTIGNY** (CAN) (Grade 1) 29 AUGUST-3 SEPTEMBER – **GS:** Yaroslava Shvedova (RUS) d. Lauren Albanese (USA) 75 63. **GD:** Alexandra Panova/Yaroslava Shvedova (RUS) d. Jade Curtis (GBR)/Sharon Fichman (CAN) 75 63. **BS:** Leonardo Mayer (ARG) d. Philip Bester (CAN) 75 61. **BD:** Piero Luisi (VEN)/Ryan Sweeting (BAH) d. Leonardo Mayer (ARG)/Andre Miele (BRA) 62 63.

- **HELIOPOLIS** (EGY) (Grade 5) 29 AUGUST-4 SEPTEMBER – **GS:** Charlotte Rodier (FRA) d. Victoria Larriere (FRA) 60 46 62. **GD:** Victoria Larriere/Charlotte Rodier (FRA) d. Yasmin Hamza/Rana Ramez (EGY) 60 63. **BS:** Mahmoud Kamel (EGY) d. Hassan Abdel Fatah (EGY) 61 63. **BD:** Ali Abdelaziz/Mahmoud Kamel (EGY) d. Ahmed Ali/Abdullah Hashim (KUW) 63 61.

- **ISLAMABAD** (PAK) (Grade 5) 29 AUGUST-4 SEPTEMBER – **GS:** Jawariah Noordin (MAS) d. Karina Ahuja (IND) 36 63 64. **GD:** Inayat Khosla (IND)/Jawariah Noordin (MAS) d. Karina Ahuja/Tejaswini Datta (IND) 62 62. **BS:** Sumit Prakash Gupta (IND) d. Kinshuk Sharma (IND) 61 64. **BD:** Anshuman Dutta/Sumit Prakash Gupta (IND) d. Khunpol Issara (THA)/Kinshuk Sharma (IND) 63 64.

- **KRAMFORS** (SWE) (Grade 5) 29 AUGUST-3 SEPTEMBER – **GS:** Sandra Tworek (DEN) d. Annie Goransson (SWE) 63 60. **GD:** Jessica Gardefjord/Annie Goransson (SWE) d. Sabina Gunnarsson/Mona Mansour (SWE) 62 61. **BS:** Patrik Rosenholm (SWE) d. Anders Lindstrom (SWE) 75 62. **BD:** Patrik Rosenholm/Fredric Sandberg (SWE) d. Robin Akser/Nicklas Szymanski (SWE) 64 64.

- **RIGA** (LAT) (Grade 5) 29 AUGUST-2 SEPTEMBER – **GS:** Anastasija Sevastova (LAT) d. Viktoria Yemialyanava (BLR) 60 63. **GD:** Ieva Irbe/Alise Razina (LAT) d. Justyna Jegiolka/Sylwia Zagorska (POL) 62 63. **BS:** Vladimir Ivanov (EST) d. Jurgen Zopp (EST) 75 60. **BD:** Vladimir Ivanov/Jurgen Zopp (EST) d. Ricards Opmanis (LAT)/Alex Vasin (USA) 63 60.

- **YARACUY** (VEN) (Grade 5) 29 AUGUST-4 SEPTEMBER – **GS:** Mariaryeni Gutierrez (VEN) d. Gabriela Mejia (COL) 62 60. **GD:** Oriana Escalante/Josymar Escalona (VEN) d. Gabriela Mejia (COL)/Giannina Minieri (CHI) w/o. **BS:** Alejandro Gonzalez (COL) d. Ricardo Urzua (CHI) 46 61 64. **BD:** Jhonny Figueroa/Luis David Martinez (VEN) d. Filippo Baronti/Ricardo Urzua (CHI) 63 26 76(1).

- **TIMISOARA** (ROM) (Grade 4) 31 AUGUST-4 SEPTEMBER – **GS:** Maria-Luiza Craciun (ROM) d. Alice Radu (ROM) 61 62. **GD:** Maria-Luiza Craciun/Ioana Ivan (ROM) d. Camelia-Elena Hristea/Ionela-Andreea Iova (ROM) 60 64. **BS:** Vassil Mladenov (BUL) d. Maksim Bakunin (UKR) 64 46 76(4). **BD:** Radu Albot/Achim Ceban (MDA) d. Alexandru Frangulea/Alexandru Joitoiu (ROM) 62 63.

- **HYOGO** (JPN) (Grade 5) 31 AUGUST-4 SEPTEMBER – **GS:** Shiho Akita (JPN) d. Yuka Matoba (JPN) 60 62. **GD:** Shiho Akita/Ai Yamamoto (JPN) d. Akari Inoue/Yumi Nakano (JPN) 57 63 64. **BS:** Tatsuma Ito (JPN) d. Tadayuki Longhi (JPN) 63 63. **BD:** Tomohiro Shinokawa/Kousuke Sugimoto (JPN) d. Shinta Fujii/Genki Tomita (JPN) 62 61.

- **SKOPJE** (MKD) (Grade 5) 31 AUGUST-4 SEPTEMBER – **GS:** Katarina Milinkovic (SCG) d. Michaela Ince (GBR) 63 60. **GD:** Aleksandra Markovic/Katarina Milinkovic (SCG) d. Nives Pavlovic/Nevena Selakovic (SCG) 63 64. **BS:** Ilija Martinoski (MKD) d. Dimitar Labudovik (MKD) 63 76(5). **BD:** Aleksandar Elezovic/Milos Romic (SCG) d. Nikola Bubnic/Milan Zekic (SCG) 64 64.

- **MARIBOR** (SLO) (Grade 5) 31 AUGUST-4 SEPTEMBER – **GS:** Selma Babic (BIH) d. Stephanie Vogt (LIE) 57 61 62. **GD:** Aleksandra Lukic/Patricia Vollmeier (SLO) d. Katharina Negrin/Lisa Summerer (AUT) 60 64. **BS:** Janez Semrajc (SLO) d. Grega Teraz (SLO) 46 63 76(2). **BD:** Iztok Kukec/Grega Teraz (SLO) d. Petr Dostal/Martin Studeny (CZE) 64 57 61.

- **BUDAPEST** (HUN) (Grade 5) 31 AUGUST-4 SEPTEMBER – **GS:** Vivien Laszloffy (HUN) d. Sinika Jezkova (CZE) 64 62. **GD:** Katarina Poljakova/Zuzana Zlochova (SVK) d. Monika Hadvigerova (SVK)/Alenka Hubacek (AUS) 61 62. **BS:** Artem Smirnov (UKR) d. Andrei Martin (SVK) 64 64. **BD:** Anton Bobytskyy/Artem Smirnov (UKR) d. Marton Bots/Akos Torok (HUN) 61 61.

- **FLUSHING, NY** (USA) (Grade A) 4-11 SEPTEMBER – **GS:** Viktoria Azarenka (BLR) d. Alexa Glatch (USA) 63 64. **GD:** Nikola Frankova (CZE)/Alisa Kleybanova (RUS) d. Alexa Glatch/Vania King (USA) 75 76(3). **BS:** Ryan Sweeting (BAH) d. Jeremy Chardy (FRA) 64 64. **BD:** Alex Clayton/Donald Young (USA) d. Carsten Ball (AUS)/Thiemo De Bakker (NED) 76(3) 46 75.

- **NASER CITY** (EGY) (Grade 5) 5-11 SEPTEMBER – **GS:** Victoria Larriere (FRA) d. Charlotte Rodier (FRA) 64 36 63. **GD:** Victoria Larriere/Charlotte Rodier (FRA) d. Mai El Wardany/Injie Fawzy (EGY) 62 62. **BS:** Mahmoud Ezz (EGY) d. Marawan Osama (EGY) 62 76(2). **BD:** Mohamed Kassem/Marawan Osama (EGY) d. Mahmoud Ezz/Mina Nasser (EGY) 63 64.

- **JURMALA** (LAT) (Grade 4) 5-9 SEPTEMBER – **GS:** Ieva Irbe (LAT) d. Anja Maskaljun (EST) 61 46 63. **GD:** Ieva Irbe/Alise Razina (LAT) d. Maria Babanova/Elizaveta Tochilovskaya (RUS) 63 62. **BS:** Jurgen Zopp (EST) d. Vladimir Karusevich (RUS) 63 26 62. **BD:** Vladimir Ivanov/Jurgen Zopp (EST) d. Simon Bekker (RUS)/Pawel Turzanski (POL) 63 60.

- **BEIRUT** (LIB) (Grade 5) 5-10 SEPTEMBER – **GS:** Lara Al Samman (SYR) d. Yasmine Sahyoun (LIB) 62 63. **GD:** Line Ghannam/Ranim Mkahal (SYR) d. Fatma Alnabhani (OMA)/Yasmine Sahyoun (LIB) 76(4) 46 64. **BS:** Bassam Beidas (LIB) d. Marc Abdelnour (SYR) 61 64. **BD:** Georgio Bedran/Bassam Beidas (LIB) d. Marc Abdelnour/Nawar Baram (SYR) 63 64.

- **LAHORE** (PAK) (Grade 5) 5-11 SEPTEMBER – **GS:** Khunpak Issara (THA) d. Prerna-Mythri Appineni (IND) 57 75 76(8). **BS:** Sumit Prakash Gupta (IND) d. Kinshuk Sharma (IND) 36 63 63.

- **VALENCIA** (VEN) (Grade 5) 5-11 SEPTEMBER – **GS:** Mariaryeni Gutierrez (VEN) d. Gabriela Paz (VEN) 63 63. **GD:** Gabriela Mejia (COL)/Giannina Minieri (CHI) d. Mariaryeni Gutierrez (VEN)/Catalina Robles (COL) 63 64. **BS:** Alejandro Gonzalez (COL) d. Leonel Vivas (VEN) 63 61. **BD:** Alfred Martinez/Claudio Romano (VEN) d. Adrian Donoso (SWE)/Joshua Scholl (USA) 46 62 64.

- **NICOSIA** (CYP) (Grade 4) 6-10 SEPTEMBER – **GS:** Daria Gutsevich (RUS) d. Petra Mokra (CZE) 63 64. **GD:** Zuzana Linhova/Petra Mokra (CZE) d. Elizaveta Ezhova/Daria Gutsevich (RUS) 63 60. **BS:** Rasmus Moller (DEN) d. Evthimios Karaliolios (NED) 64 64. **BD:** Sergey Belov (RUS)/Rasmus Moller (DEN) d. Dusan Miljevic/Filip Miljevic (SCG) 61 63.

- **SANXENXO** (ESP) (Grade 5) 6-11 SEPTEMBER – **GS:** Eugenia Yordanova (BUL) d. Olga Kirpicheva (RUS) 62 51 ret. **GD:** Julia Kalabina/Olga Kirpicheva (RUS) d. Ana Beltran-Trigueros/Maria Garcia-Planas (ESP) 62 63. **BS:** Roberto Bautista-Agut (ESP) d. Yury Shirshov (RUS) 63 63. **BD:** Roberto Bautista-Agut/Pablo Martin-Adalia (ESP) d. Conrado Lopez-Carbajo/Hugo Taracido-loureiro (ESP) 64 64.

- **HYOGO** (JPN) (Grade 5) 7-11 SEPTEMBER – **GS:** Shiho Akita (JPN) d. Saori Karikomi (JPN) 61 75. **GD:** Chinami Ogi/Kotomi Takahata (JPN) d. Akari Inoue/Mai Iwasaki (JPN) 63 62. **BS:** Tatsuma Ito (JPN) d. Jun Ito (JPN) 62 62. **BD:** Tatsuma Ito/Junn Mitsuhashi (JPN) d. Shota Iino/Yuki Matsuo (JPN) 63 61.

- **CHENNAI** (IND) (Grade 5) 12-17 SEPTEMBER – **GS:** Poojashree Venkatesh (IND) d. Vandana Murali (IND) 62 63. **GD:** Vandana Murali/Gangothri Sandri (IND) d. Gayatri Krishnan/Poojashree Venkatesh (IND) 62 63. **BS:** Rohan Gide (IND) d. Ashwin Vijayragavan (IND) 76(5) 64. **BD:** Anshuman Dutta/Gursher Singh Harika (IND) d. Ryan Cheung/Tsz-Chun Gilbert Wong (HKG) 16 62 64.

- **CARACAS** (VEN) (Grade 5) 12-18 SEPTEMBER – **GS:** Gabriela Mejia (COL) d. Giannina Minieri (CHI) 62 76(6). **GD:** Gabriela Mejia (COL)/Giannina Minieri (CHI) d. Mariaryeni Gutierrez (VEN)/Catalina Robles (COL) 62 76(1). **BS:** Alejandro Gonzalez (COL) d. Luis David Martinez (VEN) 61 62. **BD:** Luis Rovira (VEN)/Ricardo Urzua (CHI) d. Alfred Martinez/Claudio Romano (VEN) 64 63.

- **LEXINGTON, KY** (USA) (Grade 1) 12-18 SEPTEMBER – **GS:** Alisa Kleybanova (RUS) d. Amina Rakhim (KAZ) 64 75. **GD:** Alisa Kleybanova/Ekaterina Kosminskaya (RUS) d. Julia Cohen (USA)/Anastasia Pavlyuchenkova (RUS) 75 76(2). **BS:** Philip Bester (CAN) d. Andre Miele (BRA) 67(6) 62 62. **BD:** Piero Luisi/Roberto Maytin (VEN) d. Rupesh Roy/Vivek Shokeen (IND) 36 63 76(3).

- **CHYMKENT** (KAZ) (Grade 5) 12-17 SEPTEMBER – **GS:** Mariya Kovaleva (KAZ) d. Ekaterina Morozova (RUS) 64 64. **GD:** Mariya Kovaleva (KAZ)/Ekaterina Morozova (RUS) d. Tatiana Ignatchenko (KAZ)/Nigora Sirojiddinova (UZB) 64 75. **BS:** Andrey Boldarev (UZB) d. Victor Kim (UZB) 64 46 62. **BD:** Andrey Boldarev (UZB)/Danjil Braun (KAZ) d. Rynat Khusainov/Ivan Lidzar (KAZ) 61 60.

- **BEIJING** (CHN) (Grade 2) 13-18 SEPTEMBER – **GS:** Ling Zhang (HKG) d. Wing-Yau Chan (HKG) 76(8) 75. **GD:** Yi-Fan Xu/Yi Yang (CHN) d. Zi-Jun Yang/Ling Zhang (HKG) 63 75. **BS:** Jason Jung (USA) d. Jun-Chao Xu (CHN) 26 61 76(5). **BD:** Sho Aida/Fumiaki Kita (JPN) d. Ronald Chow/Xiao-Peng Lai (HKG) 62 60.

- **PANCEVO** (SCG) (Grade 3) 13-17 SEPTEMBER – **GS:** Natasa Zoric (SCG) d. Anastasia Poltoratskaya (RUS) 62 75. **GD:** Irina Khatsko/Yevgenia Nudga (UKR) d. Farida Karaeva (UKR)/Anastasia Poltoratskaya (RUS) 62 36 64. **BS:** Tim Goransson (SWE) d. Petru-Alexandru Luncanu (ROM) 60 76(0). **BD:** Simon Bekker (RUS)/Mateusz Szmigiel (POL) d. Ivan Anikanov/Vladyslav Klymenko (UKR) 75 67(1) 76(2).

- **MOSTAR** (BIH) (Grade 5) 14-18 SEPTEMBER – **GS:** Mika Urbancic (SLO) d. Ana Savic (CRO) 67(3) 61 62. **GD:** Caterina Marusic (ITA)/Mika Urbancic (SLO) d. Jasmina Kajtazovic/Anja Poglajen (SLO) w/o. **BS:** Ante Pavic (CRO) d. Igor Skoric (CRO) 63 62. **BD:** Alexander Lobkov (RUS)/Luka Somen (CRO) d. Tomislav Brkic (BIH)/Robert Raguz (CRO) 16 60 61.

- **PRAGUE** (CZE) (Grade 2) 14-18 SEPTEMBER – **GS:** Anna Korzeniak (POL) d. Eugenia Vertesheva (RUS) 62 64. **GD:** Michaela Pochabova/Patricia Veresova (SVK) d. Tyra Calderwood/Jessica Moore (AUS) 76(7) 63. **BS:** Blazej Koniusz (POL) d. Michal Konecny (CZE) 62 61. **BD:** Stephen Donald/Patrick Nicholls (AUS) d. Roman Jebavy/Lubomir Majsajdr (CZE) 46 63 75.

- **RIYADH** (KSA) (Grade 4) 19-23 SEPTEMBER – **BS:** Martin Dalton (GBR) d. Kaan Yaylali (TUR) 63 63. **BD:** Tuna Altuna/Kaan Yaylali (TUR) d. Tamer Antabi (KSA)/Zeyad Montasser (EGY) 61 61.

- **MANILA** (PHI) (Grade 4) 19-25 SEPTEMBER – **GS:** Denise Dy (PHI) d. Katharina Negrin (AUT) 76(5) 63. **GD:** Edilyn Balanga-Margate (ESP)/Denise Dy (PHI) d. An Jie Lee/Yuilynn Miao (TPE) 62 62. **BS:** Tung Han Lee (TPE) d. Pablo Olivarez (PHI) 63 16 63. **BD:** Ting Lung Chang-Chien/Zzu-Ming Huang (TPE) d. Miguel Narvaez/Pablo Olivarez (PHI) 75 75.

● **HYDERABAD** (IND) (Grade 5) 19-24 SEPTEMBER – **GS:** Poojashree Venkatesh (IND) d. Ashmitha Easwaramurthi (IND) 61 60. **GD:** Shweta Kakhandki/Gangothri Sandri (IND) d. Gayatri Krishnan/Poojashree Venkatesh (IND) 46 62 61. **BS:** Rohan Gide (IND) d. Kinshuk Sharma (IND) 64 46 63. **BD:** Siddarth Hande/Kinshuk Sharma (IND) d. Siddharth Alapati/Rohan Gide (IND) 64 63.

● **TASHKENT** (UZB) (Grade 4) 19-24 SEPTEMBER – **GS:** Dilyara Saidkhodjaeva (UZB) d. Vlada Ekshibarova (UZB) 60 64. **GD:** Yekaterina Morozova (KAZ)/Dilyara Saidkhodjaeva (UZB) d. Tatiana Ignatchenko (KAZ)/Nigora Sirojiddinova (UZB) 61 63. **BS:** Andrei Plotniy (RUS) d. Achim Ceban (MDA) 76(4) 62. **BD:** Giorgi Chantouria/George Khrikadze (GEO) d. Achim Ceban (MDA)/Gennady Yakubovsky (RUS) 57 63 64.

● **SOCHI** (RUS) (Grade 5) 19-25 SEPTEMBER – **GS:** Elizaveta Titova (RUS) d. Elizaveta Tochilovskaya (RUS) 64 46 64. **GD:** Nadejda Guskova/Elizaveta Titova (RUS) d. Eugeniya Pashkova/Elizaveta Tochilovskaya (RUS) 76(4) 26 61. **BS:** Dmitry Rachev (RUS) d. Alexey Tikhonov (RUS) 64 62. **BD:** Andrei Levine/Dmitry Rachev (RUS) d. Igor Rud/Alexey Tikhonov (RUS) 36 60 61.

● **VIÑA DEL MAR** (CHI) (Grade 4) 20-24 SEPTEMBER – **GS:** Soledad Podlipnik (CHI) d. Paulina Jorquera (CHI) 62 75. **GD:** Mailen Auroux/Daniela Leyria (ARG) d. Mallory Burdette/Alexa Guarachi (USA) 61 62. **BS:** German Sole (URU) d. Pedro Graber (CHI) 62 76(6). **BD:** Pedro Graber (CHI)/German Sole (URU) d. Diego Orellana/Mario Zavala (CHI) 62 63.

● **NOVI SAD** (SCG) (Grade 2) 20-24 SEPTEMBER – **GS:** Anastasia Pivovarova (RUS) d. Ksenia Pervak (RUS) 76(2) 16 75. **GD:** Michaela Pochabova/Patricia Veresova (SVK) d. Klaudia Boczova/Monika Kochanova (SVK) 75 61. **BS:** Paul-Mihai Puscasu (ROM) d. Tim Goransson (SWE) 63 62. **BD:** Stephen Donald/Patrick Nicholls (AUS) d. Petru-Alexandru Luncanu/Paul-Mihai Puscasu (ROM) 63 63.

● **ATLANTA, GA** (USA) (Grade 4) 20-25 SEPTEMBER – **GS:** Sanaz Marand (USA) d. Naoko Ueshima (JPN) 61 57 60. **GD:** Kristy Frilling/Sanaz Marand (USA) d. Olivia Janowicz/Melanie Oudin (USA) 61 63. **BS:** Attila Bucko (SCG) d. Andrew Thomas (AUS) 76(3) 62. **BD:** Attila Bucko (SCG)/Mike Motyka (SVK) d. Devin Britton/Rhyne Williams (USA) 61 62.

● **HUZHOU** (CHN) (Grade 3) 20-25 SEPTEMBER – **GS:** Seul-Ki Chin (KOR) d. Keren Shlomo (ISR) 75 67(4) 61. **GD:** Shao-Zhuo Liu/Shuai Zhang (CHN) d. Chu Chu/Yi Yang (CHN) 46 63 64. **BS:** Jun-Chao Xu (CHN) d. Hsin-Han Lee (TPE) 64 64. **BD:** Hsin-Han Lee/Hsien-Yin Peng (TPE) d. Yan Bai/Jun-Chao Xu (CHN) 64 36 62.

● **SANTIAGO** (CHI) (Grade 4) 26 SEPTEMBER-2 OCTOBER – **GS:** Mallory Burdette (USA) d. Mailen Auroux (ARG) 76(8) 62. **GD:** Mallory Burdette/Alexa Guarachi (USA) d. Paulina Jorquera/Giannina Minieri (CHI) 62 63. **BS:** Guillermo Duran (ARG) d. Guillermo Rivera (CHI) 63 76(6). **BD:** Pedro Graber (CHI)/German Sole (URU) d. Guillermo Duran/Juan-Manuel Romanazzi (ARG) 63 57 61.

● **MANILA** (PHI) (Grade 5) 26 SEPTEMBER-2 OCTOBER – **GS:** Stephanie Vogt (LIE) d. Natasha Bredl (AUT) 61 63. **GD:** Edilyn Balanga-Margate (ESP)/Denise Dy (PHI) d. Katharina Negrin (AUT)/Stephanie Vogt (LIE) 75 62. **BS:** Miguel Narvaez (PHI) d. Nico-Riego De Dios (PHI) 75 46 20 ret. **BD:** Fendy Gunawan (INA)/Miguel Narvaez (PHI) d. Hugh McDonald/William McNamee (AUS) 62 76(6).

● **RIYADH** (KSA) (Grade 4) 26-30 SEPTEMBER – **BS:** Martin Dalton (GBR) d. Ahmed Sharaf (EGY) 62 64. **BD:** Hamad Abbas (UAE)/Martin Dalton (GBR) d. Tuna Altuna/Kaan Yaylali (TUR) w/o.

● **FERGANA** (UZB) (Grade 4) 27 SEPTEMBER-1 OCTOBER – **GS:** Albina Khabibulina (UZB) d. Diana Narzykulova (UZB) 61 46 61. **GD:** Albina Khabibulina (UZB)/Yekaterina Morozova (KAZ) d. Tatiana Ignatchenko (KAZ)/Nigora Sirojiddinova (UZB) 62 61. **BS:** Achim Ceban (MDA) d. Alexander Seleznev (KGZ) 61 75. **BD:** Andrei Plotniy (RUS)/Alexander Seleznev (KGZ) d. Achim Ceban (MDA)/Evgeny Donskoy (RUS) 62 26 64.

● **MIJAS** (ESP) (Grade 5) 28 SEPTEMBER-1 OCTOBER – **GS:** Anastasia Kontratevidi (GRE) d. Sina Ladage (GER) 64 63. **GD:** Elle Carney (AUS)/Cristina Valladares (ESP) d. Marlene Mesgarzadeh (GER)/Efrat Mishor (ISR) 57 64 63. **BS:** Roberto Bautista-Agut (ESP) d. Francisco Lourenco (POR) 60 62. **BD:** Goncalo Falcao (POR)/Artem Pudovkin (RUS) d. Pierre Clad (GBR)/Halvar Dil (NED) 46 63 60.

● **DOWNSVIEW** (CAN) (Grade 4) 3-8 OCTOBER – **GS:** Tara Moore (USA) d. Alexandra Odell-Michels (CAN) 63 64. **GD:** Alexandra Odell-Michels/Natalie Toporowski (CAN) d. Natalie Araya/Marie-Pier Huet (CAN) 76(6) 36 62. **BS:** Christopher Racz (USA) d. Kirill Sinitsyn (RUS) 64 61. **BD:** Mark Rutherford (CAN)/Kirill Sinitsyn (RUS) d. Alexandre Labrosse/Zack Radetzky (CAN) 62 36 62.

● **PORTO SEGURO** (BRA) (Grade 5) 3-9 OCTOBER – **GS:** Isabela Kulaif (BRA) d. Barbara Oliveira (BRA) 61 61. **GD:** Fernanda Ferreira/Barbara Oliveira (BRA) d. Fabiana Chiaparini/Natasha Lotuffo (BRA) 26 64 64. **BS:** Vitor Requiao (BRA) d. Andre Pinheiro (BRA) 62 10 ret. **BD:** Alain Michel/Vitor Requiao (BRA) d. Bernardo Dias/Pier-Marco Pieracciani (BRA) 75 64.

- **COLOMBO** (SRI) (Grade 5) 3-9 OCTOBER – **GS:** Sweta Solanki (IND) d. Gangothri Sandri (IND) 36 63 63. **GD:** Niroshita Madanala/ Gangothri Sandri (IND) d. Martina Gregoric (CRO)/Vishakha Sheroan (IND) 61 46 63. **BS:** Tsung Hua Yang (TPE) d. Hsu-Chun Huang (TPE) 63 60. **BD:** Dae-Hee Lee/Hyo Dong Woo (KOR) d. Kohulan Ravindrakumar/Dinusha Wijesuriya (SRI) 62 62.

- **URBANA, IL** (USA) (Grade 4) 4-9 OCTOBER – **GS:** Irina Falconi (USA) d. Melanie Oudin (USA) 62 63. **GD:** Joanna Mather/Melanie Oudin (USA) d. Kirsten Flower/Mcall Jones (USA) w/o. **BS:** Attila Bucko (SCG) d. Jonathan Wong (USA) 64 75. **BD:** Geoffrey Barton (CRC)/ Bradley Mixson (USA) d. Attila Bucko (SCG)/Mike Motyka (SVK) 67(6) 64 75.

- **MALI LOSINJ** (CRO) (Grade 4) 5-9 OCTOBER – **GS:** Petra Martic (CRO) d. Jasmina Kajtazovic (SLO) 64 62. **GD:** Vivien Laszloffy (HUN)/ Taja Mohorcic (SLO) d. Petra Martic/Petra Viskovic (CRO) w/o. **BS:** Antonio Sancic (CRO) d. Mario Jukic (CRO) 64 67(1) 62. **BD:** Bojan Kovac/Antonio Sancic (CRO) d. Karlo Pintaric (SLO)/Luka Somen (CRO) 63 62.

- **ASHGABAT** (TKM) (Grade 5) 5-9 OCTOBER – **GS:** Nigora Sirojiddinova (UZB) d. Anastasia Rukavyshnykova (UKR) 62 60. **GD:** Valeriy Petrovich/Anastasia Rukavyshnykova (UKR) d. Zainab Djalilova/Nigora Sirojiddinova (UZB) 62 63. **BS:** Gursher Singh Harika (IND) d. Kiryl Barysenka (BLR) 16 63 63. **BD:** Sergey Dulin (UZB)/Kiril Karchmit (BLR) d. Gursher Singh Harika (IND)/Neil Rajpal (CAN) 64 36 76(5).

- **CURACAO** (AHO) (Grade 5) 10-15 OCTOBER – **GS:** Natasha Vieira (VEN) d. Jo-Ann Van Aerde (SUR) 62 63. **GD:** Natalia Guevara (PUR)/ Natasha Vieira (VEN) d. Tiffany Testing (AHO)/Jo-Ann Van Aerde (SUR) 26 63 64. **BS:** Luis Rovira (VEN) d. Rasid Winklaar (AHO) 62 61. **BD:** Jose Chavez/Luis Rovira (VEN) d. Lawrence Carpio (USA)/Uriel Oquendo (COL) 61 61.

- **CAUSEWAY BAY** (HKG) (Grade 4) 10-15 OCTOBER – **GS:** Zi-Jun Yang (HKG) d. Lutfiana-Aris Budiharto (INA) 62 64. **GD:** Xuan-Yu Guo/ Yi-Miao Zhou (CHN) d. Chang Liu/Meng Liu (CHN) 63 64. **BS:** Yan Bai (CHN) d. Simon Childs (GBR) 62 64. **BD:** Yan Bai/Chauan Jiang (CHN) d. Xiao-Long Yin/Zhuo-Qing Zhou (CHN) 64 64.

- **COLOMBO** (SRI) (Grade 5) 10-16 OCTOBER – **GS:** Shweta Solanki (IND) d. Ksenia Sidorova (RUS) 26 61 75. **BS:** Tsung Hua Yang (TPE) d. Prajnesh Gunneswaran (IND) 61 61.

- **LONDRINA** (BRA) (Grade 5) 10-16 OCTOBER – **GS:** Gabriela Rangel (BRA) d. Barbara Oliveira (BRA) 75 67(5) 75. **GD:** Loriane Favoretto/ Lorena Valente (BRA) d. Alana Muller/Mariana Pagan (BRA) 64 75. **BS:** Victor Melo (BRA) d. Vitor Requiao (BRA) 76(5) 62. **BD:** Caio Burjaili/Andre Pinheiro (BRA) d. Bernardo Dias/Vitor Requiao (BRA) 64 75.

- **OSAKA CITY** (JPN) (Grade A) 10-16 OCTOBER – **GS:** Viktoria Azarenka (BLR) d. Ayumi Morita (JPN) 64 62. **GD:** Ayumi Morita/Erika Sema (JPN) d. Akari Inoue/Yurina Koshino (JPN) 63 61. **BS:** Marin Cilic (CRO) d. Jeremy Chardy (FRA) 64 64. **BD:** Jeremy Chardy (FRA)/Marin Cilic (CRO) d. Roman Jebavy/Jiri Kosler (CZE) 75 63.

- **DOHA** (QAT) (Grade 5) 10-17 OCTOBER – **GS:** Charlotte Rodier (FRA) d. Adeline Goncalves (FRA) 61 63. **GD:** Aliaa Fakhry (EGY)/Gozde Unkaya (TUR) d. Linda Abu Mushraf (BRN)/Martina Gregoric (CRO) 75 62. **BS:** Stefano Valenti (ITA) d. Alberto Via (ITA) 61 61. **BD:** Stefano Valenti/Alberto Via (ITA) d. Mohamed Dawoudi/Mohamed Kassem (EGY) 62 60.

- **TULSA, OK** (USA) (Grade B1) 11-16 OCTOBER – **GS:** Valerie Tetreault (CAN) d. Julia Cohen (USA) 57 64 60. **GD:** Sanaz Marand/Ashley Weinhold (USA) d. Kristy Frilling/Lena Litvak (USA) 63 64. **BS:** Ryan Sweeting (BAH) d. Donald Young (USA) 16 76 64. **BD:** Peter Polansky (CAN)/Donald Young (USA) d. Jamie Hunt/Holden Seguso (USA) 62 26 62.

- **CONCEPCIÓN** (CHI) (Grade 5) 17-23 OCTOBER – **GS:** Javiera Colignon (CHI) d. Gabriela Roux (CHI) 76(5) 62. **GD:** Javiera Colignon/ Gabriela Roux (CHI) d. Paulina Jorquera/Soledad Podlipnik (CHI) 57 62 62. **BS:** Francisco Olivares (CHI) d. Edgar Rodriguez (COL) 75 60. **BD:** Andres Nunez/Thomas Zamora (CHI) d. Francisco Olivares/Pablo Varas (CHI) 62 75.

- **DUBAI** (UAE) (Grade 4) 17-23 OCTOBER – **GS:** Charlotte Rodier (FRA) d. Jaklin Alawi (BUL) 61 62. **GD:** Adeline Goncalves/Charlotte Rodier (FRA) d. Linda Abu Mushraf (BRN)/Klaudia Mansfeldova (SVK) 67(3) 62 63. **BS:** Andrei Plotniy (RUS) d. Stas Zhuravski (RUS) 64 62. **BD:** Evgeny Donskoy/Stas Zhuravski (RUS) d. Ned Boone (GBR)/Andrei Plotniy (RUS) 75 62.

- **MONTREAL** (CAN) (Grade 3) 17-21 OCTOBER – **GS:** Valerie Tetreault (CAN) d. Alexandra Odell-Michels (CAN) 63 61. **GD:** Tania Rice/ Valerie Tetreault (CAN) d. Victoria Brook (GBR)/Lena Litvak (USA) 64 36 63. **BS:** Michael Sroczynski (USA) d. Christopher Racz (USA) 76(7) 62. **BD:** Peter Marrack/Peter Polansky (CAN) d. Milos Raonic (CAN)/Kirill Sinitsyn (RUS) 75 62.

- **BANGKAPI** (THA) (Grade 2) 17-23 OCTOBER – **GS:** Maya Gaverova (RUS) d. Dilyara Saidkhodjaeva (UZB) 75 64. **GD:** Tyra Calderwood/Jessica Moore (AUS) d. Farida Karaeva (UKR)/Katarina Tuohimaa (FIN) 61 46 61. **BS:** Dylan Sessagesimi (SUI) d. Roman Jebavy (CZE) 62 62. **BD:** Christopher Rungkat (INA)/Shuhei Uzawa (JPN) d. Austen Childs (NZL)/Yann Marti (SUI) 76(5) 46 76(6).

- **EL PASO, TX** (USA) (Grade 5) 17-22 OCTOBER – **GS:** Courtney Clayton (USA) d. Sarah Woestmann (GER) 63 62. **GD:** Saori Karikomi/Kurumi Nara (JPN) d. Daisha Hill Hurtado/Keri Wong (USA) 64 76. **BS:** Bradley Klahn (USA) d. JT Sundling (USA) 61 64. **BD:** Christopher Price/Peter Rispoli (USA) d. Eduardo Peralta/Alberto Rojas (MEX) 63 61.

- **COPENHAGEN** (DEN) (Grade 4) 18-22 OCTOBER – **GS:** Ksenia Pervak (RUS) d. Sandra Roma (SWE) 64 62. **GD:** Ieva Irbe/Trina Slapeka (LAT) d. Amanda Elliott/Nikki Prosser (GBR) 76(6) 26 60. **BS:** Daniel Kumlin (SWE) d. Graeme Dyce (GBR) 64 67(5) 61. **BD:** Marc Baghdadi (FRA)/Milos Sekulic (SWE) d. Christoffer Konigsfeldt/Soren Wedege (DEN) 76(4) 64.

- **BANGKOK** (THA) (Grade B1) 25-30 OCTOBER – **GS:** Ellen Barry (NZL) d. Sanaa Bhambri (IND) 61 62. **GD:** Tyra Calderwood/Jessica Moore (AUS) d. Jessy Rompies (INA)/Dilyara Saidkhodjaeva (UZB) 75 64. **BS:** Sanam Singh (IND) d. Hsin-Han Lee (TPE) w/o. **BD:** Sho Aida/Shuhei Uzawa (JPN) d. Jeevan Nedunchezhiyan/Sanam Singh (IND) 76(6) 76(2).

- **BUENOS AIRES** (ARG) (Grade 5) 26-28 OCTOBER – **GS:** Mailen Auroux (ARG) d. Barbara Rush (ARG) 64 76(6). **GD:** Agustina Ametrano/Mailen Auroux (ARG) d. Maria Sol Mezio/Maria-Dolores Pazo (ARG) 75 64. **BS:** Guido Sola (ARG) d. Guillermo Duran (ARG) 62 67(2) 62. **BD:** Juan-Manuel Romanazzi/Guido Sola (ARG) d. Juan-Manuel Arganaras/Guillermo Duran (ARG) 60 62.

- **VIERUMAKI** (FIN) (Grade 4) 26-30 OCTOBER – **GS:** Ieva Irbe (LAT) d. Eugeniya Pashkova (RUS) 63 75. **GD:** Julia Bone (GBR)/Katarina Tuohimaa (FIN) d. Ieva Irbe/Trina Slapeka (LAT) 64 75. **BS:** Jurgen Zopp (EST) d. Carl Sundberg (NOR) 16 64 63. **BD:** Harri Heliovaara/Antti Vallila (FIN) d. Artem Kuznetsov/Alexey Tikhonov (RUS) 64 36 64.

- **ANDORRA LA VELLA** (AND) (Grade 5) 31 OCTOBER-5 NOVEMBER – **BS:** Roberto Bautista-Agut (ESP) d. Dorian Descloix (FRA) 62 61. **BD:** Marc Abdel Nour (SYR)/Dorian Descloix (FRA) d. Anton Khadasevich/Dzmitry Zhyrmont (BLR) 46 63 62.

- **NONTHABURI** (THA) (Grade 4) 31 OCTOBER-6 NOVEMBER – **GS:** Denise Dy (PHI) d. Zi-Jun Yang (HKG) 61 60. **GD:** Denise Dy/Anja-Vanessa Peter (PHI) d. Noppawan Lertcheewaka/Nicha Lertpitasinchai (THA) 76(5) 57 62. **BS:** Genki Tomita (JPN) d. Yan Bai (CHN) 64 63. **BD:** Kirati Siributwong/Peerakit Siributwong (THA) d. Khunpol Issara/Kittipong Wachiramanowong (THA) 63 63.

- **LEXINGTON, KY** (USA) (Grade 2) 1-6 NOVEMBER – **GS:** Lauren Albanese (USA) d. Madison Brengle (USA) 75 61. **GD:** Kimberly Couts/Ellah Nze (USA) d. Kristy Frilling/Lena Litvak (USA) 61 64. **BS:** Clint Bowles (USA) d. Mateusz Kecki (USA) 64 64. **BD:** Roberto Maytin (VEN)/Bradley Mixson (USA) d. Branko Kuzmanovic (SCG)/Alberton Richelieu (LCA) 64 61.

- **TAMPERE** (FIN) (Grade 4) 1-5 NOVEMBER – **GS:** Eugeniya Pashkova (RUS) d. Ieva Irbe (LAT) 63 26 62. **GD:** Augusta Tsybycheva/Maria Zharkova (RUS) d. Eugeniya Pashkova/Elizaveta Tochilovskaya (RUS) 62 64. **BS:** Jurgen Zopp (EST) d. Carl Sundberg (NOR) 76(2) 62. **BD:** Ivan Anikanov (UKR)/Sergey Belov (RUS) d. Danila Arsenov/Evgeny Donskoy (RUS) 63 62.

- **YANGON** (MYA) (Grade 5) 7-12 NOVEMBER – **GS:** Chit Su Yee (MYA) d. Khunpak Issara (THA) 61 46 76(3). **GD:** Arisa Furihata/Marina Sato (JPN) d. Shivika Burman (IND)/Satjaporn Mahajaroenkul (THA) 62 64. **BS:** Seuk Ki Um (KOR) d. Khunpol Issara (THA) 36 64 40 ret. **BD:** Ryan Cheung/Tse-Chun Wong (HKG) d. Kyawzaw Naing/Phyo Min Thar (MYA) 62 75.

- **BOCA RATON, FL** (USA) (Grade 4) 8-13 NOVEMBER – **GS:** Lyndsay Burdette (USA) d. Courtney Clayton (USA) 75 64. **GD:** Saori Karikomi/Kurumi Nara (JPN) d. Nina Pantic (CAN)/Reka Zsilinszka (USA) 46 62 60. **BS:** Attila Bucko (SCG) d. David Simon (AUT) 64 76(3). **BD:** Clint Bowles/Michael Sroczynski (USA) d. Vlad Mavropulos Stolyarenko (GRE)/Herbert Weirather (AUT) 62 64.

- **SANTA CRUZ** (BOL) (Grade 5) 14-20 NOVEMBER – **GS:** Alexandra Akhmedjanova (ARG) d. Andrea Rivera (PER) 60 63. **GD:** Ivanova Mercado/Marcela Rivero (BOL) d. Alexandra Akhmedjanova (ARG)/Nataly Yoo (USA) 57 63 64. **BS:** Juan-Manuel Romanazzi (ARG) d. Guido Sola (ARG) 61 60. **BD:** Juan-Manuel Romanazzi/Guido Sola (ARG) d. Martin Arguello (BRA)/Mateo Fortuny (ARG) 64 62.

- **CENTRAL JAVA** (INA) (Grade 4) 15-20 NOVEMBER – **GS:** Lutfiana-Aris Budiharto (INA) d. Abigail Olivier (RSA) 61 61. **GD:** Jessy Rompies/Vivien Silvany-Tony (INA) d. Augusta Tsybycheva/Anna Vavrik (RUS) 60 61. **BS:** Christopher Rungkat (INA) d. Agung-Bagus Dewantoro (INA) 63 60. **BD:** Christopher Rungkat/Aditya Hari Sasongko (INA) d. Agung-Bagus Dewantoro/Ayrton Wibowo (INA) 62 57 61.

- **LIMA** (PER) (Grade 5) 21-27 NOVEMBER – **GS:** Ingrid Vargas (PER) d. Claudine Paulson (ECU) 75 64. **GD:** S. Herrera/Maria Ines Noya (PER) d. Alexandra Akhmedjanova (ARG)/Nataly Yoo (USA) w/o. **BS:** Edgar Rodriguez (COL) d. Ismael Rodrigo (PER) 62 36 64. **BD:** Mauricio Echazu/Juan Pedro Torres (PER) d. Martin Cevasco/Mateo Fortuny (ARG) 76(5) 61.

- **SURABAYA** (INA) (Grade 4) 22-27 NOVEMBER – **GS:** Lutfiana-Aris Budiharto (INA) d. Vivien Silvany-Tony (INA) 62 61. **GD:** Jessy Rompies/Vivien Silvany-Tony (INA) d. Lutfiana-Aris Budiharto/Beatrice Gumulya (INA) 62 62. **BS:** Faisal Aidil (INA) d. Agung-Bagus Dewantoro (INA) 63 64. **BD:** Faisal Aidil/Ayrton Wibowo (INA) d. Agung-Bagus Dewantoro/Christopher Rungkat (INA) 67(3) 62 ret.

- **KIGALI** (RWA) (Grade 4) 27 NOVEMBER-1 DECEMBER – **GS:** Nicole Smith (RSA) d. Suzelle Davin (NAM) 64 61. **GD:** Suzelle Davin (NAM)/Nicole Smith (RSA) d. Samia Mohamed (SUD)/Martina Vitulli (KEN) 61 64. **BS:** Lofo Ramiaramanan (MAD) d. Tomer Hodorov (ISR) 61 61. **BD:** Lofo Ramiaramanan (MAD)/Bokang Setshogo (BOT) d. Emmanuel Mensah (GHA)/Gelawdios Mesfin (ETH) 63 26 64.

- **GUAYAQUIL** (ECU) (Grade 5) 28 NOVEMBER-4 DECEMBER – **GS:** Claudia Razzeto (PER) d. Andrea Rivera (PER) 62 76(2). **GD:** Lorena Aviles/Claudine Paulson (ECU) d. Claudia Hidalgo (ECU)/Andrea Rivera (PER) 62 61. **BS:** Juan-Andres Gomez (ECU) d. Andrew Brasseaux (USA) 63 62. **BD:** Diego Machuca/Oscar Machuca (ECU) d. Alberto Diaz/Carlos Galvez (ECU) 63 75.

- **BRADENTON, FL** (USA) (Grade 1) 28 NOVEMBER-4 DECEMBER – **GS:** Dominika Cibulkova (SVK) d. Sorana Cirstea (ROM) 63 46 60. **GD:** Ayumi Morita (JPN)/Caroline Wozniacki (DEN) d. Sorana Cirstea/Raluca Olaru (ROM) 63 57 76(3). **BS:** Marin Cilic (CRO) d. Nikola Mektic (CRO) 63 75. **BD:** Dusan Lojda (CZE)/Ryan Sweeting (BAH) d. Clay Donato (CAN)/Jesse Levine (USA) 64 64.

- **MUMBAI** (IND) (Grade 4) 28 NOVEMBER-4 DECEMBER – **GS:** Sanaa Bhambri (IND) d. Julia Goloborodko (UKR) 61 62. **GD:** Sanaa Bhambri/Gangothri Sandri (IND) d. Julia Goloborodko/Anastasiya Vasylyeva (UKR) 26 60 61. **BS:** Rohan Gide (IND) d. Siddharth Alapati (IND) 26 62 76(3). **BD:** Rohan Gide/Tejesvi Rao (IND) d. Arnav Jain/Kinshuk Sharma (IND) 76(5) 75.

- **KUCHING** (MAS) (Grade 3) 30 NOVEMBER-4 DECEMBER – **GS:** Stefanie Vogele (SUI) d. Stephanie Vogt (LIE) 46 76(0) 60. **GD:** Anastasia Petukhova/Anastasia Revzina (RUS) d. Shiho Otake/Mayumi Seki (JPN) 64 62. **BS:** Rasmus Moller (DEN) d. Attila Balazs (HUN) 64 60. **BD:** John Peers/Lachlan Reed (AUS) d. Ivan Anikanov (UKR)/Sumit Prakash Gupta (IND) 64 63.

- **KAMPALA** (UGA) (Grade 4) 3-7 DECEMBER – **GS:** Veronika Studena (CZE) d. Nicole Smith (RSA) 63 60. **GD:** Anahita Jagtiani (IND)/Veronika Studena (CZE) d. Suzelle Davin (NAM)/Nicole Smith (RSA) 64 64. **BS:** Lofo Ramiaramanan (MAD) d. Emmanuel Mensah (GHA) 76(4) 76(4). **BD:** Emmanuel Mensah (GHA)/Gelawdios Mesfin (ETH) d. Tomer Hodorov/Guy Michelevitz (ISR) 61 64.

- **GURGAON** (IND) (Grade 4) 5-11 DECEMBER – **GS:** Poojashree Venkatesh (IND) d. Shweta Solanki (IND) 60 61. **GD:** Parija Maloo/Poojashree Venkatesh (IND) d. Julia Goloborodko/Anastasiya Vasylyeva (UKR) 76(8) 61. **BS:** Rohan Gide (IND) d. Tejesvi Rao (IND) 75 36 64. **BD:** Vikram Reddy/Ashwin Vijayragavan (IND) d. Arnav Jain/Christopher Marquis (IND) 64 63.

- **KEY BISCAYNE, FL** (USA) (Grade A) 5-11 DECEMBER – **GS:** Caroline Wozniacki (DEN) d. Mihaela Buzarnescu (ROM) 61 64. **GD:** Jennifer-Lee Heinser/Elizabeth Plotkin (USA) d. Anna Tatishvili (GEO)/Caroline Wozniacki (DEN) 62 26 64. **BS:** Robin Roshardt (SUI) d. Paris Gemouchidis (GRE) 61 60. **BD:** Emiliano Massa/Leonardo Mayer (ARG) d. Marin Cilic/Nikola Mektic (CRO) 64 76(3).

- **BURSWOOD** (AUS) (Grade 5) 6-11 DECEMBER – **GS:** Bridget Healy (AUS) d. Anna Wishink (AUS) 64 63. **GD:** Janelle Cuthbertson/Rachel Houpapa (AUS) d. Tiarne Ettingshausen/Bridget Healy (AUS) 61 63. **BS:** James Rigg (AUS) d. Jared Easton (AUS) 64 16 76(7). **BD:** Marcus Daniell (NZL)/Jared Easton (AUS) d. Justin Astri/Edward Bourchier (AUS) 63 26 63.

- **KUALA LUMPUR** (MAS) (Grade 3) 7-11 DECEMBER – **GS:** Anastasia Revzina (RUS) d. Stefanie Vogele (SUI) 64 61. **GD:** Shiho Otake/Ai Yamamoto (JPN) d. Stefanie Vogele (SUI)/Stephanie Vogt (LIE) 64 64. **BS:** Dylan Sessagesimi (SUI) d. Fumiaki Kita (JPN) 62 61. **BD:** Jason Lee/John-Patrick Smith (AUS) d. Ivan Anikanov (UKR)/Sumit Prakash Gupta (IND) 62 46 76(5).

- **NAIROBI** (KEN) (Grade 5) 9-13 DECEMBER – **GS:** Aziza Butoyi (BDI) d. Suzelle Davin (NAM) 62 64. **GD:** Suzelle Davin (NAM)/Nicole Smith (RSA) d. Samia Mohamed (SUD)/Martina Vitulli (KEN) 64 62. **BS:** Emmanuel Mensah (GHA) d. Lofo Ramiaramanan (MAD) 26 62 64. **BD:** Lofo Ramiaramanan (MAD)/Bokang Setshogo (BOT) d. Duncan Mugabe/Patrick Ochan (UGA) 63 62.

- **MIAMI, FL** (USA) (Grade 4) 12-16 DECEMBER – **GS:** Kristina Antoniychuk (UKR) d. Arina Rodionova (RUS) 64 75. **GD:** Kristina Antoniychuk (UKR)/Eleonora Sidjemileva (UZB) d. Arina Rodionova/Julia Semeneko (RUS) 46 64 63. **BS:** Axel Michon (FRA) d. Artem Smirnov (UKR) 57 63 75. **BD:** Vladyslav Klymenko/Artem Smirnov (UKR) d. Rikus De Villiers/James Monroe (RSA) 62 62.

- **SINGAPORE** (SIN) (Grade 5) 12-18 DECEMBER – **GS:** Yui-Lynn Miao (TPE) d. Shiho Otake (JPN) 64 64. **GD:** Shiho Otake/Mayumi Seki (JPN) d. Mu-Ying Chen/Ting-Fei Juan (TPE) 62 62. **BS:** Hyun-Soo Lim (KOR) d. Khunpol Issara (THA) 61 62. **BD:** Aditya Hari Sasongko/ Ganang Surya-Atmaja (INA) d. Yong-Kyu Lim (KOR)/Mohammed-Ashaari Zainal (MAS) w/o.

- **MERIDA** (MEX) (Grade 1) 12-17 DECEMBER – **GS:** Mihaela Buzarnescu (ROM) d. Sorana-Mihaela Cirstea (ROM) 63 62. **GD:** Agnieszka Radwanska (POL)/Natasa Zoric (SCG) d. Bibiane Schoofs (NED)/Caroline Wozniacki (DEN) 40 54(4). **BS:** Petru-Alexandru Luncanu (ROM) d. Donald Young (USA) 63 63. **BD:** Marin Cilic (CRO)/Robin Roshardt (SUI) d. Dennis Lajola (USA)/Roberto Maytin (VEN) 63.

- **PORT ELIZABETH** (RSA) (Grade 5) 15-18 DECEMBER – **GS:** Bronwyn Davidson (RSA) d. Lisa Levenberg (RSA) 46 61 75. **GD:** Marne Roos/ Hedda Wolmarans (RSA) d. Engela Olivier/Jane Pringle (RSA) 76(2) 76(1). **BS:** Jean Andersen (RSA) d. Keith-Patrick Crowley (RSA) 75 62. **BD:** Jean Andersen/Wesley Baptiste (RSA) d. Matthew Fawcett/Mpiloenhle Migogo (RSA) 63 61.

- **SINT-KATELIJNE-WAVER** (BEL) (Grade 4) 27-31 DECEMBER – **GS:** Aude Vermoezen (BEL) d. Scherazad Ben Amar (FRA) 63 64. **GD:** Julie Lamont/Aude Vermoezen (BEL) d. Zuzana Linhova (CZE)/Zuzana Zlochova (SVK) 61 26 63. **BS:** Ruben Bemelmans (BEL) d. Frederic De Fays (BEL) 46 76(5) 63. **BD:** Michiel Antheunis (BEL)/Roberto Bautista-Agut (ESP) d. Elias Gastao (POR)/Harry Skinner (GBR) 57 62 76(5).

RUSSIA

World Junior Tennis Finals 2005

ITF Junior Team Championships for boys and girls of 14 & Under

Prostejov, Czech Republic, 8-13 August 2005

BOYS' FINAL STANDINGS:

1. France, 2. Argentina, 3. Australia, 4. USA, 5. Japan, 6. Belgium, 7. Chinese Taipei, 8. Russia, 9. Brazil, 10. Czech Republic, 11. Ecuador, 12. Korea, Rep., 13. Bulgaria, 14. Mexico, 15. Portugal, 16. South Africa.

Semifinals:

France d. Australia 2-1: Constantin Belot (FRA) d. Jake Eames (AUS) 63 61; Mark Verryth (AUS) d. Adrien Puget (FRA) 64 75; Constantin Belot/Adrien Puget (FRA) d. Jake Eames/Mark Verryth (AUS) 63 64. **Argentina d. USA 2-1:** Guido Andreozzi (ARG) d. Devin Britton (USA) 64 76(12); Chase Buchanan (USA) d. Juan Vazquez (ARG) 26 76(5) 63; Nicolas Pastor/Juan Vazquez (ARG) d. Devin Britton/Chase Buchanan (USA) 75 36 64.

Final:

France d. Argentina 2-1: Guido Andreozzi (ARG) d. Constantin Belot (FRA) 62 64; Adrien Puget (FRA) d. Juan Vazquez (ARG) 64 75; Constantin Belot/Adrien Puget (FRA) d. Nicolas Pastor/Juan Vazquez (ARG) 63 76(5).

GIRLS' FINAL STANDINGS:

1. Russia, 2. Japan, 3. Croatia, 4. Slovenia, 5. China, P.R., 6. Czech Republic, 7. Australia, 8. Ukraine, 9. USA, 10. Mexico, 11. Germany, 12. Peru, 13. Chile, 14. Ecuador, 15. Korea, Rep., 16. Algeria.

Semifinals:

Russia d. Croatia 3-0: Elena Kulikova (RUS) d. Indire Akiki (CRO) 67(2) 62 75; Anastasia Pavlyuchenkova (RUS) d. Petra Martic (CRO) 36 60 63; Elena Pavlyuchenkova/Elena Kulikova (RUS) d. Indire Akiki/Petra Martic (CRO) 67(3) 62 75. **Japan d. Slovenia 2-1:** Chihiro Takayama (JPN) d. Masa Grgan (SLO) 63 64; Kurumi Nara (JPN) d. Polona Hercog (SLO) 61 62; Masa Grgan/Polona Hercog (SLO) d. Misaki Doi/Chihiro Takayama (JPN) 64 62.

Final:

Russia d. Japan 3-0: Elena Kulikova (RUS) d. Chihiro Takayama (JPN) 61 76(0); Anastasia Pavlyuchenkova (RUS) d. Kurumi Nara (JPN) 60 61; Anastasia Pavlyuchenkova/Marta Sirotkina (RUS) d. Misaki Doi/Kurumi Nara (JPN) 62 62.

Above: France's Constantin Belot and Adrien Puget
Left: Russia's winning girls' team

BNP P

Junior Davis Cup by BNP Paribas Final 2005

ITF Junior Team Championships for boys of 16 & Under; prior to 2002 the competition was known as the NEC World Youth Cup.

Barcelona, Spain, 27 September–2 October 2005

FINAL STANDINGS:
1. France, 2. Czech Republic, 3. Ecuador, 4. Italy, 5. Japan, 6. USA, 7. Australia, 8. Brazil, 9. Mexico, 10. Austria, 11. Spain, 12. Bulgaria, 13. Philippines, 14. Tunisia, 15. South Africa, 16. Thailand.

Semifinals:
France d. Ecuador 3-0: Jerome Inzerillo (FRA) d. Escobar Gonzalo (ECU) 62 46 62; Kevin Botti (FRA) d. Patricio Alvarado (ECU) 63 67(5) 62; Kevin Botti/Stephane Piro (FRA) d. Patricio Alvarado/Escobar Gonzalo (ECU) 64 62. **Czech Republic d. Italy 2-1:** Matteo Trevisan (ITA) d. Roman Jebavy (CZE) 63 63; Michael Konecny (CZE) d. Thomas Fabbiano (ITA) 63 63; Roman Jebavy/Michael Konecny (CZE) d. Thomas Fabbiano/Andrea Volpini (ITA) 76(2) 64.

Final:
France d. Czech Republic 2-0: Jerome Inzerillo (FRA) d. Roman Jebavy (CZE) 57 64 61; Kevin Botti (FRA) d. Michael Konecny (CZE) 46 63 62; Doubles not played.

Junior Fed Cup Final 2005

ITF Junior Team Championships for girls of 16 & Under; prior to 2002 the competition was known as the NEC World Youth Cup.

FINAL STANDINGS:
1. Poland, 2. France, 3. Czech Republic, 4. Spain, 5. Brazil, 6. Russia, 7. Australia, 8. USA, 9. Netherlands, 10. China, 11. Hong Kong, 12. Canada, 13. Venezuela, 14. Argentina, 15. Morocco, 16. South Africa.

Semifinals:
France d. Spain 2-1: Estelle Guisard (FRA) d. Leticia Costas (ESP) 61 64; Alize Cornet (FRA) d. Maite Gabarrus (ESP) 63 62; Leticia Costas/Maite Gabarrus (ESP) d. Estelle Guisard/Noemie Scharle (FRA) 61 61. **Poland d. Czech Republic 2-1:** Urszula Radwanska (POL) d. Eva Kadlecova (CZE) 61 64; Agnieszka Radwanska (POL) d. Katerina Vankova (CZE) 75 60; Eva Kadlecova/Katerina Vankova (CZE) d. Urszula Radwanska/Maksymilia Wandel (POL) 62 36 62.

Final:
Poland d. France 2-0: Urszula Radwanska (POL) d. Estelle Guisard (FRA) 62 61; Agnieszka Radwanska (POL) d. Alize Cornet (FRA) 76(5) 63; Doubles not played.

2005 Australian Open Junior Championships, 24–30 January – Boys' Singles

Australian Open
The Grand Slam of Asia/Pacific

1	Sun-Yong KIM (KOR)	S.KIM (1)
	Jesse LEVINE (USA)	67(6) 75 62
Q	Elbert SIE (INA)	A.VAN DER DUIM (Q)
LL	Antal VAN DER DUIM (NED)	63 76(6)
	Petar JELENIC (CRO)	P.JELENIC
	Jiri SKOLOUDIK (CZE)	63 26 62
	Peter POLANSKY (CAN)	M.PEDERSEN (16)
16	Martin PEDERSEN (DEN)	62 62
11	Pavol CERVENAK (SVK)	P.CERVENAK (11)
WC	Joel LINDNER (AUS)	64 62
	Andrea ARNABOLDI (ITA)	A.ARNABOLDI
	Michael LOOK (AUS)	76(4) 76(6)
	Serguei TARASEVITCH (BLR)	C.BALL
	Carsten BALL (USA)	63 64
	Abdullah MAGDAS (KUW)	C.YI (5)
5	Chu-Huan YI (TPE)	76(2) 64
4	Robin HAASE (NED)	R.HAASE (4)
Q	Richard RUCKELSHAUSEN (AUT)	64 57 62
Q	Paris GEMOUCHIDIS (GRE)	J.MAREK
	Jan MAREK (CZE)	75 16 75
Q	Thomas KROMANN (DEN)	T.LEY (WC)
WC	Todd LEY (AUS)	63 76(1)
	Benedict HALBROTH (GER)	F.SKUGOR (14)
14	Franco SKUGOR (CRO)	75 62
12	Alexandr DOLGOPOLOV (UKR)	A.DOLGOPOLOV (12)
	Miguel-Angel REYES-VARELA (MEX)	75 63
Q	Martin COLENBRANDER (NZL)	J.STRYDOM (Q)
Q	Jurgens STRYDOM (NAM)	67(5) 76(5) 64
	Marcus FUGATE (USA)	M.FUGATE
	Tristan FARRON-MAHON (IRL)	64 75
WC	James LEMKE (AUS)	T.NEILLY (7)
7	Timothy NEILLY (USA)	76(3) 76(5)
6	Sergei BUBKA (UKR)	S.BUBKA (6)
	Bryan KONIECKO (USA)	62 63
WC	Stephen DONALD (AUS)	J.GRUBISIC
	Jurica GRUBISIC (CRO)	26 63 61
	Andrew COELHO (AUS)	A.COELHO
	Luka OCVIRK (SLO)	46 76(4) 86
	Ryan SWEETING (BAH)	R.SWEETING
10	Tim SMYCZEK (USA)	63 26 62
15	Jochen SCHOTTLER (GER)	J.SCHOTTLER (15)
	Myles BLAKE (GBR)	16 63 62
	Jamie HUNT (USA)	F.SILADI (Q)
Q	Filip SILADI (CRO)	67(8) 61 61
	Michael JOHNSON (USA)	M.JOHNSON
	Weerapat DOAKMAIKLEE (THA)	63 63
	Dylan ARNOULD (USA)	L.LACKO (3)
3	Lukas LACKO (SVK)	62 62
8	Dusan LOJDA (CZE)	D.LOJDA (8)
	Alex CLAYTON (USA)	62 75
WC	Nick LINDAHL (AUS)	N.LINDAHL (WC)
Q	Jose STATHAM (NZL)	46 64 63
	Marin CILIC (CRO)	M.CILIC
	Steven GOH (AUS)	63 61
	Martin SAYER (HKG)	J.CHARDY (9)
9	Jeremy CHARDY (FRA)	61 76(4)
13	Thiemo DE BAKKER (NED)	T.DE BAKKER (13)
WC	Tomas HABSUDA (AUS)	57 63 63
	Michael SHABAZ (USA)	M.SHABAZ
WC	Ben ROCAVERT (AUS)	63 63
	Takanobu FUJII (JPN)	P.NICHOLLS (WC)
WC	Patrick NICHOLLS (AUS)	64 76(8)
	Philip BESTER (CAN)	D.YOUNG (2)
2	Donald YOUNG (USA)	76(2) 61

S.KIM (1) 62 76(3)
P.JELENIC 46 76(1) 63
P.CERVENAK (11) 61 36 63
C.BALL 64 75
R.HAASE (4) 64 61
F.SKUGOR (14) 61 76(4)
J.STRYDOM (Q) 46 76(5) 62
T.NEILLY (7) 62 64
S.BUBKA (6) 75 60
R.SWEETING 75 46 1412
J.SCHOTTLER (15) 64 75
L.LACKO (3) 60 64
D.LOJDA (8) 67(4) 63 62
M.CILIC 76(7) 64
M.SHABAZ 62 46 62
D.YOUNG (2) 63 57 62

S.KIM (1) 67(2) 64 43 RET
C.BALL 36 64 60
R.HAASE (4) 63 75
T.NEILLY (7) 64 62
S.BUBKA (6) 64 76(1)
L.LACKO (3) 63 62
M.CILIC 64 62
D.YOUNG (2) 62 64

S.KIM (1) 57 63 62
R.HAASE (4) 63 62
S.BUBKA (6) 75 75
D.YOUNG (2) 63 75

S.KIM (1) 57 62 75
D.YOUNG (2) 62 64

D.YOUNG (2) 62 64

2005 Australian Open Junior Championships, 24-30 January – Girls' Singles

Australian Open
The Grand Slam of Asia/Pacific

First round draw

Seed/Entry	Player
1	Viktoria AZARENKA (BLR)
	Ekaterina SHULAEVA (CAN)
Q	Alison BAI (AUS)
WC	Olivia LUKASZEWICZ (AUS)
	Sorana CIRSTEA (ROM)
	Punam REDDY (IND)
	Ye-Ra LEE (KOR)
13	Alisa KLEYBANOVA (RUS)
9	Marina ERAKOVIC (NZL)
	Elizabeth PLOTKIN (USA)
	Michelle BRYCKI (AUS)
WC	Megan PRICE (AUS)
	Irena PAVLOVIC (FRA)
LL	Porntip MULSAP (THA)
	Nadja ROMA (SWE)
5	Yung-Jan CHAN (TPE)
3	Angelique KERBER (GER)
	Alexa GLATCH (USA)
Q	Sara ERRANI (ITA)
	Daniella DOMINIKOVIC (AUS)
Q	Therese TISSEVERASINGHE (AUS)
	Nudnida LUANGNAM (THA)
	Ayumi MORITA (JPN)
14	Magdalena RYBARIKOVA (SVK)
11	Caroline WOZNIACKI (DEN)
	Nicole THYSSEN (NED)
	Katerina KRAMPEROVA (CZE)
	Agnes SZATMARI (ROM)
	Shona LEE (NZL)
	I-Hsuan HWANG (TPE)
WC	Jessica MOORE (AUS)
6	Aleksandra WOZNIAK (CAN)
8	Dominika CIBULKOVA (SVK)
	Erika SEMA (JPN)
	Elizabeth KOBAK (USA)
	Ekaterina KOSMINSKAYA (RUS)
	Mirna MARINOVIC (CRO)
	Nikola FRANKOVA (CZE)
Q	Jessica ENGELS (AUS)
12	Agnes SZAVAY (HUN)
16	Pichittra THONGDACH (THA)
	Ellen BARRY (NZL)
Q	Holly CAO (AUS)
	Tamira PASZEK (AUT)
WC	Lia TAPPER (AUS)
Q	Karolina WLODARCZAK (AUS)
	Michaela JOHANSSON (SWE)
4	Olga SAVCHUK (UKR)
7	Monica NICULESCU (ROM)
	Shayna MCDOWELL (AUS)
	Barbora HODINAROVA (CZE)
Q	Francesca KINSELLA (GBR)
WC	Bridget HEALY (AUS)
	Anastasia POLTORATSKAYA (RUS)
	Josipa BEK (CRO)
10	Wen-Hsin HSU (TPE)
15	Jennifer-Lee HEINSER (USA)
Q	Stella MENNA (ITA)
WC	Tammi PATTERSON (AUS)
	Valerie TETREAULT (CAN)
WC	Jenny SWIFT (AUS)
WC	Tyra CALDERWOOD (AUS)
	Andrea PETKOVIC (GER)
2	Timea BACSINSZKY (SUI)

Second round

Winner	Score
V.AZARENKA (1)	62 61
O.LUKASZEWICZ (WC)	61 64
S.CIRSTEA	75 46 64
A.KLEYBANOVA (13)	46 61 61
M.ERAKOVIC (9)	64 63
M.BRYCKI	60 62
I.PAVLOVIC	60 64
Y.CHAN (5)	61 63
A.GLATCH	64 36 64
S.ERRANI (Q)	62 61
T.TISSEVERASINGHE (Q)	63 36 86
A.MORITA	26 62 64
C.WOZNIACKI (11)	62 62
A.SZATMARI	62 76(1)
I.HWANG	63 61
A.WOZNIAK (6)	62 61
D.CIBULKOVA (8)	61 61
E.KOSMINSKAYA	75 61
N.FRANKOVA	63 64
A.SZAVAY (12)	57 61 61
E.BARRY	61 64
T.PASZEK	61 61
K.WLODARCZAK (Q)	36 63 62
O.SAVCHUK (4)	62 63
M.NICULESCU (7)	75 64
F.KINSELLA (Q)	46 63 60
A.POLTORATSKAYA	64 62
W.HSU (10)	61 63
J.HEINSER (15)	60 61
V.TETREAULT	63 63
T.CALDERWOOD (WC)	63 62
T.BACSINSZKY (2)	62 62

Third round

Winner	Score
V.AZARENKA (1)	62 61
A.KLEYBANOVA (13)	63 75
M.ERAKOVIC (9)	75 64
Y.CHAN (5)	76(5) 63
S.ERRANI (Q)	63 63
A.MORITA	63 62
C.WOZNIACKI (11)	63 57 62
A.WOZNIAK (6)	61 61
D.CIBULKOVA (8)	62 62
A.SZAVAY (12)	60 57 64
T.PASZEK	46 61 62
O.SAVCHUK (4)	61 63
M.NICULESCU (7)	62 62
W.HSU (10)	64 62
V.TETREAULT	75 75
T.BACSINSZKY (2)	60 61

Quarterfinals

Winner	Score
V.AZARENKA (1)	61 61
M.ERAKOVIC (9)	63 64
S.ERRANI (Q)	62 61
A.WOZNIAK (6)	16 76(7) 61
A.SZAVAY (12)	62 61
T.PASZEK	63 62
M.NICULESCU (7)	61 36 61
T.BACSINSZKY (2)	46 76(6) 61

Semifinals

Winner	Score
V.AZARENKA (1)	61 63
A.WOZNIAK (6)	61 63
A.SZAVAY (12)	63 63
T.BACSINSZKY (2)	76(3) 64

Final

Winner	Score
V.AZARENKA (1)	60 64
A.SZAVAY (12)	62 62

Champion

V.AZARENKA (1)
62 62

2005 Australian Open Junior Championships, 24-30 January – Boys' Doubles

Seed	Player	First round	Second round	Quarter-finals	Semi-finals	Final
1	Sun-Yong KIM (KOR)	S.KIM (1) / C.YI (1) 76(2) 62	S.KIM (1) / C.YI (1) 67(3) 62 63	S.KIM (1) / C.YI (1) 63 62	S.KIM (1) / C.YI (1) 61 64	S.KIM (1) / C.YI (1) 63 64
1	Chu-Huan YI (TPE)					
WC	Stephen DONALD (AUS)					
WC	Ben ROCAVERT (AUS)					
	Syrym ABDUKHALIKOV (KAZ)	P.BESTER / P.POLANSKY 64 64				
	Todd LEY (AUS)					
	Philip BESTER (CAN)					
	Peter POLANSKY (CAN)					
	Richard RUCKELSHAUSEN (AUT)	R.RUCKELSHAUSEN / J.STRYDOM 64 64	A.ARNABOLDI (8) / M.PEDERSEN (8) 61 60			
	Jurgens STRYDOM (NAM)					
	Jurica GRUBISIC (CRO)					
	Petar JELENIC (CRO)					
	Dylan ARNOULD (USA)	A.ARNABOLDI (8) / M.PEDERSEN (8) 57 75 62				
	Marcus FUGATE (USA)					
8	Andrea ARNABOLDI (ITA)					
8	Martin PEDERSEN (DEN)					
4	Pavol CERVENAK (SVK)	J.LEVINE / M.SHABAZ 63 64	J.LEVINE / M.SHABAZ 36 61 64	J.LEVINE / M.SHABAZ 76(5) 62		
4	Lukas LACKO (SVK)					
	Jesse LEVINE (USA)					
	Michael SHABAZ (USA)					
	Miguel-Angel REYES-VARELA (MEX)	M.REYES-VARELA / R.SWEETING 63 63				
	Ryan SWEETING (BAH)					
WC	Matthew EBDEN (AUS)					
WC	Luke WEIGHTMAN (AUS)					
	Andrew COELHO (AUS)	A.COELHO / S.GOH W/O	R.HAASE (7) / A.VAN DER DUIM (7) 62 63			
	Steven GOH (AUS)					
	Victor KOLICK (ISR)					
	Bryan KONIECKO (USA)					
	Paris GEMOUCHIDIS (GRE)	R.HAASE (7) / A.VAN DER DUIM (7) 61 61				
	Thomas KROMANN (DEN)					
7	Robin HAASE (NED)					
7	Antal VAN DER DUIM (NED)					
5	Timothy NEILLY (USA)	M.LOOK (WC) / P.NICHOLLS (WC) 76(2) 75	T.HABSUDA / J.SKOLOUDIK 61 76(5)	T.DE BAKKER (3) / D.YOUNG (3) 61 63	T.DE BAKKER (3) / D.YOUNG (3) 67(7) 75 75	
5	Tim SMYCZEK (USA)					
WC	Michael LOOK (AUS)					
WC	Patrick NICHOLLS (AUS)					
	Tomas HABSUDA (AUS)	T.HABSUDA / J.SKOLOUDIK 76(0) 64				
	Jiri SKOLOUDIK (CZE)					
	Benedict HALBROTH (GER)					
	Abdullah MAGDAS (KUW)					
	Takanobu FUJII (JPN)	M.CILIC / L.OCVIRK 76(3) 62	T.DE BAKKER (3) / D.YOUNG (3) 62 63			
	Yuichi SUGITA (JPN)					
	Marin CILIC (CRO)					
	Luka OCVIRK (SLO)					
	Weerapat DOAKMAIKLEE (THA)	T.DE BAKKER (3) / D.YOUNG (3) 64 36 76(3)				
	Tristan FARRON-MAHON (IRL)					
3	Thiemo DE BAKKER (NED)					
3	Donald YOUNG (USA)					
6	Dusan LOJDA (CZE)	D.LOJDA (6) / J.MAREK (6) 61 64	F.SILADI / F.SKUGOR 76(1) 36 64	A.CLAYTON / M.JOHNSON 63 64		
6	Jan MAREK (CZE)					
	Martin COLENBRANDER (NZL)					
	Jochen SCHOTTLER (GER)					
	Filip SILADI (CRO)	F.SILADI / F.SKUGOR 63 63				
	Franco SKUGOR (CRO)					
	Alexandr DOLGOPOLOV (UKR)					
	Serguei TARASEVITCH (BLR)					
	Carsten BALL (USA)	A.CLAYTON / M.JOHNSON 63 63	A.CLAYTON / M.JOHNSON W/O			
	Jamie HUNT (USA)					
	Alex CLAYTON (USA)					
	Michael JOHNSON (USA)					
WC	Samuel GROTH (AUS)	S.BUBKA (2) / J.CHARDY (2) 61 61				
WC	Joel LINDNER (AUS)					
2	Sergei BUBKA (UKR)					
2	Jeremy CHARDY (FRA)					

2005 Australian Open Junior Championships, 24-30 January – Girls' Doubles

Seed	Player
1	Timea BACSINSZKY (SUI)
1	Angelique KERBER (GER)
WC	Jessica MOORE (AUS)
WC	Lia TAPPER (AUS)
	Punam REDDY (IND)
	Erika SEMA (JPN)
	Alexa GLATCH (USA)
	Ekaterina KOSMINSKAYA (RUS)
WC	Bridget HEALY (AUS)
WC	Megan PRICE (AUS)
	Elizabeth KOBAK (USA)
	Stella MENNA (ITA)
	Barbora HODINAROVA (CZE)
	Nicole THYSSEN (NED)
6	Nikola FRANKOVA (CZE)
6	Agnes SZAVAY (HUN)
4	Yung-Jan CHAN (TPE)
4	Alisa KLEYBANOVA (RUS)
	Michelle BRYCKI (AUS)
	Shayna MCDOWELL (AUS)
	Irena PAVLOVIC (FRA)
	Andrea PETKOVIC (GER)
	Katerina KRAMPEROVA (CZE)
	Tamira PASZEK (AUT)
	Michaela JOHANSSON (SWE)
	Nadja ROMA (SWE)
	Ellen BARRY (NZL)
	Anastasia POLTORATSKAYA (RUS)
	Josipa BEK (CRO)
	Mirna MARINOVIC (CRO)
8	Wen-Hsin HSU (TPE)
8	I-Hsuan HWANG (TPE)
5	Dominika CIBULKOVA (SVK)
5	Magdalena RYBARIKOVA (SVK)
	Jennifer-Lee HEINSER (USA)
	Elizabeth PLOTKIN (USA)
	Sara ERRANI (ITA)
	Agnes SZATMARI (ROM)
	Jessica ENGELS (AUS)
	Bianca SMITH (AUS)
	Daniella DOMINIKOVIC (AUS)
	Olivia LUKASZEWICZ (AUS)
	Johanna KONTA (AUS)
	Karolina WLODARCZAK (AUS)
	Alenka HUBACEK (AUS)
	Therese TISSEVERASINGHE (AUS)
3	Caroline WOZNIACKI (DEN)
3	Aleksandra WOZNIAK (CAN)
7	Sorana CIRSTEA (ROM)
7	Monica NICULESCU (ROM)
	Ekaterina SHULAEVA (CAN)
	Valerie TETREAULT (CAN)
WC	Tyra CALDERWOOD (AUS)
WC	Jenny SWIFT (AUS)
	Francesca KINSELLA (GBR)
	Ewa LOSINSKI (AUS)
	Ye-Ra LEE (KOR)
	Ayumi MORITA (JPN)
WC	Marija MIRKOVIC (AUS)
WC	Kristina PEJKOVIC (AUS)
	Shona LEE (NZL)
	Pichittra THONGDACH (THA)
2	Viktoria AZARENKA (BLR)
2	Marina ERAKOVIC (NZL)

First round

- T.BACSINSZKY (1) / A.KERBER (1) 60 61
- A.GLATCH / E.KOSMINSKAYA 61 61
- B.HEALY (WC) / M.PRICE (WC) 63 64
- N.FRANKOVA (6) / A.SZAVAY (6) 62 62
- Y.CHAN (4) / A.KLEYBANOVA (4) 64 61
- I.PAVLOVIC / A.PETKOVIC 63 36 63
- E.BARRY / A.POLTORATSKAYA 64 36 63
- W.HSU (8) / I.HWANG (8) 75 46 64
- J.HEINSER / E.PLOTKIN 62 63
- J.ENGELS / B.SMITH 16 63 63
- D.DOMINIKOVIC / O.LUKASZEWICZ 64 62
- C.WOZNIACKI (3) / A.WOZNIAK (3) 60 62
- S.CIRSTEA (7) / M.NICULESCU (7) 63 61
- T.CALDERWOOD (WC) / J.SWIFT (WC) 60 75
- Y.LEE / A.MORITA 63 62
- V.AZARENKA (2) / M.ERAKOVIC (2) 62 62

Second round

- T.BACSINSZKY (1) / A.KERBER (1) 64 62
- N.FRANKOVA (6) / A.SZAVAY (6) 60 62
- Y.CHAN (4) / A.KLEYBANOVA (4) 61 64
- W.HSU (8) / I.HWANG (8) 61 36 62
- J.ENGELS / B.SMITH 46 64 64
- D.DOMINIKOVIC / O.LUKASZEWICZ 76(5) 64
- S.CIRSTEA (7) / M.NICULESCU (7) 62 60
- V.AZARENKA (2) / M.ERAKOVIC (2) 62 63

Quarterfinals

- N.FRANKOVA (6) / A.SZAVAY (6) 63 60
- W.HSU (8) / I.HWANG (8) 63 46 64
- D.DOMINIKOVIC / O.LUKASZEWICZ 76(5) 36 62
- V.AZARENKA (2) / M.ERAKOVIC (2) 62 36 64

Semifinals

- N.FRANKOVA (6) / A.SZAVAY (6) 63 61
- V.AZARENKA (2) / M.ERAKOVIC (2) 61 61

Final

- V.AZARENKA (2) / M.ERAKOVIC (2) 60 62

2005 International Junior Championships of France, 29 May-5 June – Boys' Singles

Seed	Player	First round
1	Andrew MURRAY (GBR)	A.MURRAY (1)
	Piero LUISI (VEN)	64 26 63
	Kellen DAMICO (USA)	J.DASNIERES DE VEIGY (WC)
WC	Jonathan DASNIERES DE VEIGY (FRA)	75 64
	Gianluca NASO (ITA)	G.NASO
	Sanam SINGH (IND)	61 63
Q	Jamie HUNT (USA)	C.BALL (13)
13	Carsten BALL (AUS)	60 64
11	Dusan LOJDA (CZE)	P.BESTER
	Philip BESTER (CAN)	63 62
	Marcus FUGATE (USA)	A.KRASNORUTSKIY
	Alexander KRASNORUTSKIY (RUS)	75 64
	Luis-Henrique GRANGEIRO (BRA)	S.GIRALDO (Q)
Q	Santiago GIRALDO (COL)	63 64
WC	Alexandre SIDORENKO (FRA)	J.DEL POTRO (6)
6	Juan-Martin DEL POTRO (ARG)	62 60
3	Sun-Yong KIM (KOR)	S.KIM (3)
	Robin ROSHARDT (SUI)	64 62
	Jochen SCHOTTLER (GER)	J.SCHOTTLER
	Vivek SHOKEEN (IND)	67(6) 75 63
	Thiemo DE BAKKER (NED)	M.CILIC
	Marin CILIC (CRO)	64 63
WC	Yannick THIVANT (FRA)	Y.THIVANT (WC)
16	Timothy NEILLY (USA)	63 62
9	Raony CARVALHO (BRA)	R.CARVALHO (9)
WC	Adrian MANNARINO (FRA)	46 63 61
Q	Andrew COELHO (AUS)	M.BRUCH (Q)
Q	Matt BRUCH (USA)	36 75 64
	Pavel CHEKHOV (RUS)	P.CERVENAK
	Pavol CERVENAK (SVK)	36 62 60
	Alex CLAYTON (USA)	S.BUBKA (5)
5	Sergei BUBKA (UKR)	64 60
8	Andreas HAIDER-MAURER (AUT)	V.RUDNEV (Q)
Q	Valeri RUDNEV (RUS)	62 75
Q	Andrew KENNAUGH (GBR)	A.KENNAUGH (Q)
WC	Jonathan DAHAN (FRA)	63 67(2) 63
WC	Laurent ROCHETTE (FRA)	S.QUERREY
	Samuel QUERREY (USA)	60 64
Q	Todd LEY (AUS)	T.LEY (Q)
12	Andre MIELE (BRA)	61 63
15	David NAVARRETE (VEN)	T.RAJAOBELINA (WC)
WC	Tony RAJAOBELINA (FRA)	63 61
	Andrea ARNABOLDI (ITA)	J.LEVINE
	Jesse LEVINE (USA)	75 76(4)
	Tim SMYCZEK (USA)	L.LACKO
	Lukas LACKO (SVK)	62 61
	Martin SAYER (HKG)	M.SAYER
4	Leonardo MAYER (ARG)	63 64
7	Niels DESEIN (BEL)	P.POLANSKY (Q)
Q	Peter POLANSKY (CAN)	63 64
	Alexander SADECKY (SUI)	M.SHABAZ
	Michael SHABAZ (USA)	64 62
	Aljoscha THRON (GER)	A.VAN DER DUIM
	Antal VAN DER DUIM (NED)	75 60
	Ryan SWEETING (BAH)	J.CHARDY (10)
10	Jeremy CHARDY (FRA)	62 61
14	Evgeny KIRILLOV (RUS)	E.KIRILLOV (14)
LL	Petar JELENIC (CRO)	76(3) 76(4)
WC	Boris OBAMA (FRA)	B.OBAMA (WC)
LL	Roman RECARTE (VEN)	46 75 62
	Alexandr DOLGOPOLOV (UKR)	A.DOLGOPOLOV
	Jeevan NEDUNCHEZHIYAN (IND)	76(4) 26 61
	Abdullah MAGDAS (KUW)	D.YOUNG (2)
2	Donald YOUNG (USA)	63 63

Second round

- A.MURRAY (1) 63 76(4)
- G.NASO 62 61
- A.KRASNORUTSKIY 36 62 62
- J.DEL POTRO (6) 61 64
- S.KIM (3) 76(7) 46 63
- M.CILIC 46 60 64
- M.BRUCH (Q) 26 63 64
- S.BUBKA (5) 63 36 62
- A.KENNAUGH (Q) 62 76(5)
- S.QUERREY 64 62
- J.LEVINE 63 64
- L.LACKO 64 62
- P.POLANSKY (Q) 75 63
- A.VAN DER DUIM 36 63 86
- E.KIRILLOV (14) 60 64
- A.DOLGOPOLOV 46 62 62

Third round

- A.MURRAY (1) 62 62
- J.DEL POTRO (6) 61 64
- M.CILIC 61 63
- S.BUBKA (5) 76(6) 62
- S.QUERREY 60 60
- L.LACKO 64 76(5)
- A.VAN DER DUIM 46 75 86
- A.DOLGOPOLOV 62 64

Quarter-finals

- A.MURRAY (1) 64 62
- M.CILIC 76(5) 62
- L.LACKO 67(5) 63 63
- A.VAN DER DUIM 46 64 61

Semi-finals

- M.CILIC 75 63
- A.VAN DER DUIM 64 46 75

Final

- M.CILIC 63 61

2005 International Junior Championships of France, 29 May-5 June – Girls' Singles

Seed/Status	Player	First round
1	Jessica KIRKLAND (USA)	J.KIRKLAND (1) 60 62
LL	Dominice RIPOLL (GER)	
WC	Laurene FAYOL (FRA)	B.SCHOOFS 60 64
	Bibiane SCHOOFS (NED)	
	Sharon FICHMAN (CAN)	R.VAISEMBERG 63 63
	Roxane VAISEMBERG (BRA)	
	Katerina KRAMPEROVA (CZE)	O.GOVORTSOVA (13) 26 61 64
13	Olga GOVORTSOVA (BLR)	
9	Alexandra DULGHERU (ROM)	A.DULGHERU (9) 63 61
WC	Gracia RADOVANOVIC (FRA)	
	Elizabeth PLOTKIN (USA)	A.MORITA 62 61
	Ayumi MORITA (JPN)	
	Andrea REMYNSE (USA)	L.DOUTRELANT (WC) 76(3) 62
WC	Louise DOUTRELANT (FRA)	
	Amina RAKHIM (KAZ)	E.MAKAROVA (6) 67(5) 62 75
6	Ekaterina MAKAROVA (RUS)	
4	Aleksandra WOZNIAK (CAN)	M.ANDRIEUX (WC) 46 64 64
WC	Mailyne ANDRIEUX (FRA)	
	Alla KUDRYAVTSEVA (RUS)	A.KUDRYAVTSEVA 64 63
	Yasmin SCHNACK (USA)	
	Irena PAVLOVIC (FRA)	I.PAVLOVIC 36 64 64
	Polona REBERSAK (SLO)	
	Karin KNAPP (ITA)	R.OLARU (14) 63 64
14	Raluca OLARU (ROM)	
12	Caroline WOZNIACKI (DEN)	C.WOZNIACKI (12) 63 26 64
	Mihaela BUZARNESCU (ROM)	
Q	Shayna MCDOWELL (AUS)	A.CORNET (WC) 76(3) 62
WC	Alize CORNET (FRA)	
	Krystina MARCIO (USA)	A.RADWANSKA 60 62
	Agnieszka RADWANSKA (POL)	
Q	Yaroslava SHVEDOVA (RUS)	T.BACSINSZKY (5) 61 36 62
5	Timea BACSINSZKY (SUI)	
8	Agnes SZAVAY (HUN)	A.SZAVAY (8) 46 63 63
WC	Violette HUCK (FRA)	
	Tamira PASZEK (AUT)	A.TATISHVILI 64 36 64
	Anna TATISHVILI (GEO)	
	Valerie TETREAULT (CAN)	V.TETREAULT 75 61
Q	Olivia LUKASZEWICZ (AUS)	
Q	Anastasia PAVLYUCHENKOVA (RUS)	A.GLATCH (10) 62 62
10	Alexa GLATCH (USA)	
15	Madalina GOJNEA (ROM)	M.GOJNEA (15) 63 61
	Sara ERRANI (ITA)	
	Kristina ANTONIYCHUK (UKR)	K.ANTONIYCHUK 63 63
	Maria-Fernanda ALVAREZ (BOL)	
WC	Estelle GUISARD (FRA)	E.RODINA 64 63
	Evgeniya RODINA (RUS)	
LL	Ellah NZE (USA)	Y.CHAN (3) 75 64
3	Yung-Jan CHAN (TPE)	
7	Monica NICULESCU (ROM)	M.NICULESCU (7) 36 75 75
	Eugenia GREBENYUK (RUS)	
WC	Yulia FEDOSSOVA (FRA)	Y.FEDOSSOVA (WC) 64 76(5)
Q	Jennifer STEVENS (USA)	
	Jennifer-Lee HEINSER (USA)	J.HEINSER 63 57 64
Q	Marta LESNIAK (POL)	
Q	Melanie GLORIA (CAN)	M.GLORIA (Q) 36 62 64
11	Aravane REZAI (FRA)	
16	Vania KING (USA)	V.KING (16) 62 62
Q	Alice BELLICHA (FRA)	
	Sorana CIRSTEA (ROM)	F.MOLINERO 62 63
	Florencia MOLINERO (ARG)	
	Julia COHEN (USA)	A.KLEYBANOVA 46 63 75
	Alisa KLEYBANOVA (RUS)	
	Magdalena RYBARIKOVA (SVK)	V.AZARENKA (2) 62 76(10)
2	Viktoria AZARENKA (BLR)	

Second round

- B.SCHOOFS 67(4) 61 97
- O.GOVORTSOVA (13) 46 62 63
- A.MORITA 63 62
- E.MAKAROVA (6) 63 62
- M.ANDRIEUX (WC) 61 64
- R.OLARU (14) 62 75
- C.WOZNIACKI (12) 57 62 62
- T.BACSINSZKY (5) 36 62 63
- A.SZAVAY (8) 63 62
- A.GLATCH (10) 62 60
- M.GOJNEA (15) 60 61
- E.RODINA 64 63
- Y.FEDOSSOVA (WC) 36 61 64
- J.HEINSER 36 64 63
- V.KING (16) 76(2) 76(5)
- A.KLEYBANOVA 76(7) 46 86

Third round

- B.SCHOOFS 64 76(5)
- A.MORITA 76(3) 64
- R.OLARU (14) 63 63
- T.BACSINSZKY (5) 46 75 63
- A.SZAVAY (8) 63 75
- E.RODINA 26 62 62
- Y.FEDOSSOVA (WC) 61 67(5) 62
- A.KLEYBANOVA 63 61

Quarter-finals

- A.MORITA 46 63 64
- R.OLARU (14) 62 63
- A.SZAVAY (8) 61 63
- A.KLEYBANOVA 64 63

Semi-finals

- R.OLARU (14) 46 60 62
- A.SZAVAY (8) 61 63

Final

- A.SZAVAY (8) 62 61

2005 International Junior Championships of France, 29 May-5 June – Boys' Doubles

First Round

Seed	Players
1	Dusan LOJDA (CZE)
1	Donald YOUNG (USA)
	Robin ROSHARDT (SUI)
	Alexander SADECKY (SUI)
	Emiliano MASSA (ARG)
	Leonardo MAYER (ARG)
	Martin PEDERSEN (DEN)
	Jochen SCHOTTLER (GER)
WC	Kevin BOTTI (FRA)
WC	Jerome INZERILLO (FRA)
	Jeevan NEDUNCHEZHIYAN (IND)
	Sanam SINGH (IND)
	Matt BRUCH (USA)
	Marcus FUGATE (USA)
5	Raony CARVALHO (BRA)
5	Ryan SWEETING (BAH)
3	Sun-Yong KIM (KOR)
3	Aljoscha THRON (GER)
WC	Jonathan DASNIERES DE VEIGY (FRA)
WC	Boris OBAMA (FRA)
	Evgeny KIRILLOV (RUS)
	Alexander KRASNORUTSKIY (RUS)
	Jesse LEVINE (USA)
	Michael SHABAZ (USA)
	Andrew COELHO (AUS)
	Todd LEY (AUS)
	Thiemo DE BAKKER (NED)
	Antal VAN DER DUIM (NED)
	Marin CILIC (CRO)
	Abdullah MAGDAS (KUW)
6	Timothy NEILLY (USA)
6	Tim SMYCZEK (USA)
7	Carsten BALL (AUS)
7	Samuel QUERREY (USA)
WC	Jonathan DAHAN (FRA)
WC	Yannick THIVANT (FRA)
	Juan-Martin DEL POTRO (ARG)
	David NAVARRETE (VEN)
	Pavel CHEKHOV (RUS)
	Valeri RUDNEV (RUS)
	Kellen DAMICO (USA)
	Jamie HUNT (USA)
	Andrew KENNAUGH (GBR)
	Andrew MURRAY (GBR)
	Alexandr DOLGOPOLOV (UKR)
	Serguei TARASEVITCH (BLR)
4	Andrea ARNABOLDI (ITA)
4	Niels DESEIN (BEL)
8	Sergei BUBKA (UKR)
8	Jeremy CHARDY (FRA)
	Pavol ČERVENAK (SVK)
	Lukas LACKO (SVK)
	Martin SAYER (HKG)
	Vivek SHOKEEN (IND)
	Philip BESTER (CAN)
	Peter POLANSKY (CAN)
WC	Adrian MANNARINO (FRA)
WC	Alexandre SIDORENKO (FRA)
	Alex CLAYTON (USA)
	Piero LUISI (VEN)
	Luis-Henrique GRANGEIRO (BRA)
	Andre MIELE (BRA)
2	Andreas HAIDER-MAURER (AUT)
2	Petar JELENIC (CRO)

Second Round

- R.ROSHARDT / A.SADECKY 64 62
- E.MASSA / L.MAYER 61 63
- K.BOTTI (WC) / J.INZERILLO (WC) 36 75 75
- R.CARVALHO (5) / R.SWEETING (5) 63 62
- S.KIM (3) / A.THRON (3) 61 62
- J.LEVINE / M.SHABAZ 46 64 63
- T.DE BAKKER / A.VAN DER DUIM 64 46 64
- T.NEILLY (6) / T.SMYCZEK (6) 63 57 62
- C.BALL (7) / S.QUERREY (7) 63 36 61
- P.CHEKHOV / V.RUDNEV 75 76(6)
- A.KENNAUGH / A.MURRAY 46 75 61
- A.DOLGOPOLOV / S.TARASEVITCH 76(1) 67(2) 75
- S.BUBKA (8) / J.CHARDY (8) 64 62
- P.BESTER / P.POLANSKY 63 64
- A.CLAYTON / P.LUISI 61 75
- A.HAIDER-MAURER (2) / P.JELENIC (2) 26 62 108

Third Round

- E.MASSA / L.MAYER 76(3) 46 86
- R.CARVALHO (5) / R.SWEETING (5) 62 64
- S.KIM (3) / A.THRON (3) 63 63
- T.DE BAKKER / A.VAN DER DUIM 62 61
- P.CHEKHOV / V.RUDNEV 76(4) 63
- A.KENNAUGH / A.MURRAY 63 64
- S.BUBKA (8) / J.CHARDY (8) 57 64 1311
- A.HAIDER-MAURER (2) / P.JELENIC (2) 64 63

Quarter-finals

- E.MASSA / L.MAYER 62 62
- S.KIM (3) / A.THRON (3) 63 64
- P.CHEKHOV / V.RUDNEV 64 16 86
- S.BUBKA (8) / J.CHARDY (8) 63 62

Semi-finals

- E.MASSA / L.MAYER 76(3) 63
- S.BUBKA (8) / J.CHARDY (8) 64 36 61

Final

- E.MASSA / L.MAYER 26 63 64

2005 International Junior Championships of France, 29 May-5 June – Girls' Doubles

First round

- 1 Yung-Jan CHAN (TPE) / 1 Aleksandra WOZNIAK (CAN)
- Timea BACSINSZKY (SUI) / Tamira PASZEK (AUT)
- Ellah NZE (USA) / Jennifer STEVENS (USA)
- Alice BELLICHA (FRA) / Estelle GUISARD (FRA)
- Olivia LUKASZEWICZ (AUS) / Shayna MCDOWELL (AUS)
- Anastasia PAVLYUCHENKOVA (RUS) / Yaroslava SHVEDOVA (RUS)
- Agnieszka RADWANSKA (POL) / Urszula RADWANSKA (POL)
- 5 Mihaela BUZARNESCU (ROM) / 5 Bibiane SCHOOFS (NED)
- 3 Viktoria AZARENKA (BLR) / 3 Agnes SZAVAY (HUN)
- Katerina KRAMPEROVA (CZE) / Ekaterina MAKAROVA (RUS)
- Vania KING (USA) / Yasmin SCHNACK (USA)
- Mailyne ANDRIEUX (FRA) / Louise DOUTRELANT (FRA)
- Florencia MOLINERO (ARG) / Roxane VAISEMBERG (BRA)
- Yulia FEDOSSOVA (FRA) / Violette HUCK (FRA)
- Yvette HYNDMAN (USA) / Anna TATISHVILI (GEO)
- 6 Sorana CIRSTEA (ROM) / 6 Alexandra DULGHERU (ROM)
- 7 Madalina GOJNEA (ROM) / 7 Monica NICULESCU (ROM)
- Kristina ANTONIYCHUK (UKR) / Magdalena RYBARIKOVA (SVK)
- Maria-Fernanda ALVAREZ (BOL) / Dominice RIPOLL (GER)
- Jennifer-Lee HEINSER (USA) / Elizabeth PLOTKIN (USA)
- Julia COHEN (USA) / Andrea REMYNSE (USA)
- Ayumi MORITA (JPN) / Erika SEMA (JPN)
- Alize CORNET (FRA) / Aravane REZAI (FRA)
- 4 Sharon FICHMAN (CAN) / 4 Caroline WOZNIACKI (DEN)
- 8 Raluca OLARU (ROM) / 8 Amina RAKHIM (KAZ)
- Eugenia GREBENYUK (RUS) / Krystina MARCIO (USA)
- Gracia RADOVANOVIC (FRA) / Charlotte RODIER (FRA)
- Melanie GLORIA (CAN) / Valerie TETREAULT (CAN)
- Alisa KLEYBANOVA (RUS) / Evgeniya RODINA (RUS)
- Sara ERRANI (ITA) / Karin KNAPP (ITA)
- WC Charlotte DOUWMA (FRA) / WC Laurene FAYOL (FRA)
- 2 Alexa GLATCH (USA) / 2 Olga GOVORTSOVA (BLR)

Second round

- Y.CHAN (1) / A.WOZNIAK (1) 61 57 62
- E.NZE / J.STEVENS 36 60 61
- A.PAVLYUCHENKOVA / Y.SHVEDOVA 46 62 75
- M.BUZARNESCU (5) / B.SCHOOFS (5) 75 63
- V.AZARENKA (3) / A.SZAVAY (3) 57 61 60
- V.KING / Y.SCHNACK 63 63
- F.MOLINERO / R.VAISEMBERG 63 62
- Y.HYNDMAN / A.TATISHVILI 63 26 97
- M.GOJNEA (7) / M.NICULESCU (7) 61 62
- M.ALVAREZ / D.RIPOLL 63 16 75
- A.MORITA / E.SEMA 63 76(3)
- S.FICHMAN (4) / C.WOZNIACKI (4) W/O
- R.OLARU (8) / A.RAKHIM (8) 75 46 64
- M.GLORIA / V.TETREAULT 61 61
- A.KLEYBANOVA / E.RODINA 64 62
- A.GLATCH (2) / O.GOVORTSOVA (2) 60 62

Quarter-finals

- Y.CHAN (1) / A.WOZNIAK (1) 62 61
- M.BUZARNESCU (5) / B.SCHOOFS (5) 64 63
- V.AZARENKA (3) / A.SZAVAY (3) 61 63
- F.MOLINERO / R.VAISEMBERG 61 62
- M.GOJNEA (7) / M.NICULESCU (7) 64 60
- S.FICHMAN (4) / C.WOZNIACKI (4) 46 75 62
- R.OLARU (8) / A.RAKHIM (8) 61 61
- A.GLATCH (2) / O.GOVORTSOVA (2) 62 36 108

Semi-finals

- Y.CHAN (1) / A.WOZNIAK (1) 36 61 75
- V.AZARENKA (3) / A.SZAVAY (3) 75 64
- S.FICHMAN (4) / C.WOZNIACKI (4) 36 64 64
- R.OLARU (8) / A.RAKHIM (8) 62 61

Final

- V.AZARENKA (3) / A.SZAVAY (3) 75 46 61
- R.OLARU (8) / A.RAKHIM (8) 64 61

Winners

- V.AZARENKA (3) / A.SZAVAY (3) 46 64 60

2005 Junior Championships, Wimbledon, 25 June–3 July – Boys' Singles

	Player	First round	Second round	Third round	Quarter-finals	Semi-finals	Final
17	Thiemo DE BAKKER (NED)	T.DE BAKKER (17) 62 64	T.DE BAKKER (17) 75 46 61	J.LEVINE 26 75 64	T.SMYCZEK 64 63	R.HAASE (14) 76(5) 67(4) 64	J.CHARDY 64 63
Q	Mikhail KARPOL (CRO)						
	Robin ROSHARDT (SUI)	V.SHOKEEN 36 60 63					
	Vivek SHOKEEN (IND)						
	Alexandr DOLGOPOLOV (UKR)	J.LEVINE 63 62	J.LEVINE 63 36 64				
	Jesse LEVINE (USA)						
	Martin SAYER (HKG)	D.NAVARRETE (16) 64 64					
16	David NAVARRETE (VEN)						
12	Raony CARVALHO (BRA)	I.SIJSLING 63 62	T.SMYCZEK 67(2) 76(4) 64	T.SMYCZEK 16 63 60			
	Igor SIJSLING (NED)						
	Tim SMYCZEK (USA)	T.SMYCZEK 63 61					
LL	Anas FATTAR (MAR)						
Q	Christoph HODL (AUT)	E.KIRILLOV 61 46 97	N.DESEIN (6) 76(1) 75				
	Evgeny KIRILLOV (RUS)						
	Jochen SCHOTTLER (GER)	N.DESEIN (6) 76(1) 60					
6	Niels DESEIN (BEL)						
3	Leonardo MAYER (ARG)	L.MAYER (3) 64 57 64	L.MAYER (3) 62 76(5)	R.HAASE (14) 61 75	R.HAASE (14) 76(4) 57 63		
Q	Jurgens STRYDOM (NAM)						
Q	Jiri KOSLER (CZE)	M.SHABAZ 75 76(4)					
	Michael SHABAZ (USA)						
WC	Faris KHATIB (GBR)	F.KHATIB (WC) 64 76(2)	R.HAASE (14) 63 76(5)				
	Luis-Henrique GRANGEIRO (BRA)						
	Philip BESTER (CAN)	R.HAASE (14) 64 67(3) 63					
14	Robin HAASE (NED)						
10	Samuel QUERREY (USA)	S.QUERREY (10) 46 63 62	S.QUERREY (10) 26 63 61	M.CILIC (5) 64 67(1) 64			
WC	Scott DICKSON (GBR)						
Q	Patrick NICHOLLS (AUS)	R.SWEETING 75 64					
	Ryan SWEETING (BAH)						
Q	Bryan KONIECKO (USA)	B.KONIECKO (Q) 75 57 62	M.CILIC (5) 75 61				
WC	Andrew KENNAUGH (GBR)						
	Elbert SIE (INA)	M.CILIC (5) 63 63					
5	Marin CILIC (CRO)						
8	Petar JELENIC (CRO)	E.MASSA (LL) 64 52 RET	J.CHARDY 63 61	J.CHARDY 64 64	J.CHARDY 61 62	J.CHARDY 64 76(4)	
LL	Emiliano MASSA (ARG)						
	Serguei TARASEVITCH (BLR)	J.CHARDY 75 26 75					
	Jeremy CHARDY (FRA)						
	Jeevan NEDUNCHEZHIYAN (IND)	M.BLAKE 57 64 61	M.BLAKE 64 64				
	Myles BLAKE (GBR)						
	Kellen DAMICO (USA)	K.DAMICO 46 62 64					
11	Andre MIELE (BRA)						
15	Timothy NEILLY (USA)	T.NEILLY (15) 62 16 64	T.NEILLY (15) 62 64	T.NEILLY (15) 63 61			
Q	Kei NISHIKORI (JPN)						
	Andrea ARNABOLDI (ITA)	A.ARNABOLDI 76(4) 67(6) 63					
WC	Matthew TAYLOR (GBR)						
	Andrew COELHO (AUS)	A.MAGDAS 75 75	A.MAGDAS 76(4) 36 63				
	Abdullah MAGDAS (KUW)						
Q	Peter POLANSKY (CAN)	S.KIM (4) 64 63					
4	Sun-Yong KIM (KOR)						
7	Sergei BUBKA (UKR)	D.LOJDA (WC) 64 64	D.LOJDA (WC) 64 75	A.VAN DER DUIM 64 62	D.YOUNG (2) 63 62		
WC	Dusan LOJDA (CZE)						
	Aljoscha THRON (GER)	D.ARNOULD 75 76(1)					
	Dylan ARNOULD (USA)						
	Sanam SINGH (IND)	S.SINGH 60 62	A.VAN DER DUIM 62 63				
WC	Christopher LLEWELLYN (GBR)						
	Antal VAN DER DUIM (NED)	A.VAN DER DUIM 76(10) 36 62					
9	Carsten BALL (AUS)						
13	Andreas HAIDER-MAURER (AUT)	P.LUISI 63 63	P.LUISI 64 64	D.YOUNG (2) 76(8) 62			
	Piero LUISI (VEN)						
	Alexander SADECKY (SUI)	A.SADECKY 63 64					
	Jamie HUNT (USA)						
	Pavel CHEKHOV (RUS)	T.FARRON-MAHON 63 63	D.YOUNG (2) 61 64				
	Tristan FARRON-MAHON (IRL)						
WC	Chris EATON (GBR)	D.YOUNG (2) 61 75					
2	Donald YOUNG (USA)						

2005 Junior Championships, Wimbledon, 25 June–3 July – Girls' Singles

	Player	First round	Second round	Third round	Quarter-finals	Semi-finals	Final
1	Viktoria AZARENKA (BLR)	V.AZARENKA (1) 62 75	V.AZARENKA (1) 63 61	V.AZARENKA (1) 46 61 63	V.AZARENKA (1) 64 61	T.PASZEK 75 46 63	A.RADWANSKA 63 64
	Irena PAVLOVIC (FRA)						
	Amina RAKHIM (KAZ)	A.RAKHIM 76(5) 46 62					
	Yaroslava SHVEDOVA (RUS)						
	Anna TATISHVILI (GEO)	A.TATISHVILI 62 64	A.TATISHVILI 64 64				
	Erika SEMA (JPN)						
WC	Julia BONE (GBR)	V.KING (15) 61 62					
15	Vania KING (USA)						
9	Yung-Jan CHAN (TPE)	Y.CHAN (9) 46 62 60	Y.CHAN (9) 61 60	D.CIBULKOVA (5) 67(4) 64 61			
Q	Sabine LISICKI (GER)						
Q	Anastasia REVZINA (RUS)	M.GOJNEA 64 76(4)					
	Madalina GOJNEA (ROM)						
	Magy AZIZ (EGY)	M.AZIZ 62 75	D.CIBULKOVA (5) 61 63				
LL	Ana-Clara DUARTE (BRA)						
	Elizabeth PLOTKIN (USA)	D.CIBULKOVA (5) 60 63					
5	Dominika CIBULKOVA (SVK)						
3WC	Jessica KIRKLAND (USA)	J.KIRKLAND (3) (WC) 64 62	J.KIRKLAND (3) (WC) 67(6) 64 62	J.KIRKLAND (3) (WC) 26 60 62	T.PASZEK 63 61		
	Eugenia GREBENYUK (RUS)						
Q	Aude VERMOEZEN (BEL)	A.VERMOEZEN (Q) 61 61					
Q	Shayna MCDOWELL (AUS)						
	Florencia MOLINERO (ARG)	F.MOLINERO 61 76(7)	K.KRAMPEROVA 61 60				
WC	Georgie STOOP (GBR)						
	Katerina KRAMPEROVA (CZE)	K.KRAMPEROVA 36 76(2) 63					
16	Bibiane SCHOOFS (NED)						
11	Marina ERAKOVIC (NZL)	M.ERAKOVIC (11) 63 60	M.ERAKOVIC (11) 63 63	T.PASZEK 64 62			
WC	Samantha MURRAY (GBR)						
	Evgeniya RODINA (RUS)	E.RODINA 64 62					
	Valerie TETREAULT (CAN)						
	Polona REBERSAK (SLO)	T.PASZEK 62 36 63	T.PASZEK 62 62				
	Tamira PASZEK (AUT)						
Q	Urszula RADWANSKA (POL)	R.OLARU (8) 36 63 64					
8	Raluca OLARU (ROM)						
6	Aleksandra WOZNIAK (CAN)	A.WOZNIAK (6) 75 62	A.WOZNIAK (6) 63 62	A.WOZNIAK (6) 57 64 62	A.RADWANSKA 60 46 62	A.RADWANSKA 76(1) 62	
	Jennifer-Lee HEINSER (USA)						
WC	Jade CURTIS (GBR)	O.LUKASZEWICZ 64 63					
	Olivia LUKASZEWICZ (AUS)						
	Ekaterina KOSMINSKAYA (RUS)	E.KOSMINSKAYA 61 63	N.FRANKOVA 64 64				
	Dominice RIPOLL (GER)						
	Nikola FRANKOVA (CZE)	N.FRANKOVA 63 36 63					
10	Caroline WOZNIACKI (DEN)						
14	Monica NICULESCU (ROM)	M.NICULESCU (14) 63 61	A.RADWANSKA 60 75	A.RADWANSKA 61 75			
	Maria-Fernanda ALVAREZ (BOL)						
	Agnieszka RADWANSKA (POL)	A.RADWANSKA 64 62					
LL	Corinna DENTONI (ITA)						
WC	Claire PETERZAN (GBR)	E.BARRY (Q) 46 62 63	A.KLEYBANOVA 60 62				
Q	Ellen BARRY (NZL)						
	Alisa KLEYBANOVA (RUS)	A.KLEYBANOVA 63 76(6)					
LL	Ellah NZE (USA)						
7	Jarmila GAJDOSOVA (SVK)	J.GAJDOSOVA (7) 62 60	J.GAJDOSOVA (7) 62 61	E.MAKAROVA (12) 46 76(3) 60	A.SZAVAY (2) 60 67(6) 61		
	Renee REINHARD (NED)						
Q	Maya GAVEROVA (RUS)	N.KHAN (WC) 64 26 64					
WC	Natasha KHAN (GBR)						
	Olga GOVORTSOVA (BLR)	M.BUZARNESCU 64 62	E.MAKAROVA (12) 75 64				
	Mihaela BUZARNESCU (ROM)						
Q	Melanie GLORIA (CAN)	E.MAKAROVA (12) 63 64					
12	Ekaterina MAKAROVA (RUS)						
13	Alexa GLATCH (USA)	A.GLATCH (13) 57 76(3) 1311	A.GLATCH (13) 46 75 64	A.SZAVAY (2) 64 64			
	Alla KUDRYAVTSEVA (RUS)						
WC	Laura PETERZAN (GBR)	L.PETERZAN (WC) 36 75 64					
	Agnes SZATMARI (ROM)						
	Astrid BESSER (ITA)	A.BESSER 76(4) 63	A.SZAVAY (2) 64 57 61				
	Jessica SWEETING (BAH)						
	Ayumi MORITA (JPN)	A.SZAVAY (2) 64 76(5)					
2	Agnes SZAVAY (HUN)						

2005 Junior Championships, Wimbledon, 25 June–3 July – Boys' Doubles

Seed	First Round Players	First Round	Second Round	Quarter-Finals	Semi-Finals	Final
9	Luis-Henrique GRANGEIRO (BRA)	R.HAASE				
9	Andre MIELE (BRA)	I.SIJSLING				
	Robin HAASE (NED)	76(4) 64	A.COELHO			
	Igor SIJSLING (NED)		P.NICHOLLS			
	Andrew COELHO (AUS)	A.COELHO	76(6) 64			
	Patrick NICHOLLS (AUS)	P.NICHOLLS				
	Pavel CHEKHOV (RUS)	63 64		S.GROTH (WC)		
	Evgeny KIRILLOV (RUS)			A.KENNAUGH (WC)		
	Abdullah MAGDAS (KUW)	A.MAGDAS		76(5) 63		
	Vivek SHOKEEN (IND)	V.SHOKEEN				
	Christoph HODL (AUT)	46 63 97	S.GROTH (WC)			
	Jochen SCHOTTLER (GER)		A.KENNAUGH (WC)			
WC	Samuel GROTH (AUS)	S.GROTH (WC)	63 62			
WC	Andrew KENNAUGH (GBR)	A.KENNAUGH (WC)				
5	Andreas HAIDER-MAURER (AUT)	57 64 75			S.GROTH (WC)	
5	Dusan LOJDA (CZE)				A.KENNAUGH (WC)	
4	Andrea ARNABOLDI (ITA)	J.CHARDY			63 36 1513	
4	Niels DESEIN (BEL)	D.NAVARRETE				
	Jeremy CHARDY (FRA)	26 63 64	R.ROSHARDT			
	David NAVARRETE (VEN)		A.SADECKY			
	Robin ROSHARDT (SUI)	R.ROSHARDT	64 63			
	Alexander SADECKY (SUI)	A.SADECKY				
	Myles BLAKE (GBR)	76(4) 63		T.DE BAKKER (6)		
	Todd LEY (AUS)			A.VAN DER DUIM (6)		
	Raony CARVALHO (BRA)	R.CARVALHO		64 64		
	Kei NISHIKORI (JPN)	K.NISHIKORI				
	Elbert SIE (INA)	63 63	T.DE BAKKER (6)			
	Shuhei UZAWA (JPN)		A.VAN DER DUIM (6)			
	Bryan KONIECKO (USA)	T.DE BAKKER (6)	36 62 63			
	Martin SAYER (HKG)	A.VAN DER DUIM (6)				
6	Thiemo DE BAKKER (NED)	64 64				J.LEVINE
6	Antal VAN DER DUIM (NED)					M.SHABAZ
7	Emiliano MASSA (ARG)	D.ARNOULD				64 61
7	Leonardo MAYER (ARG)	J.HUNT				
	Dylan ARNOULD (USA)	61 64	C.LLEWELLYN (WC)			
	Jamie HUNT (USA)		J.STRYDOM (WC)			
	Ali EL SHERBINI (EGY)	C.LLEWELLYN (WC)	76(3) 76(5)			
	Anas FATTAR (MAR)	J.STRYDOM (WC)				
WC	Christopher LLEWELLYN (GBR)	46 76(5) 64		C.LLEWELLYN (WC)		
WC	Jurgens STRYDOM (NAM)			J.STRYDOM (WC)		
	Petar JELENIC (CRO)	C.EATON (WC)		63 76(4)		
	Mikhail KARPOL (CRO)	F.KHATIB (WC)				
WC	Chris EATON (GBR)	64 61	K.DAMICO			
WC	Faris KHATIB (GBR)		T.SMYCZEK			
	Kellen DAMICO (USA)	K.DAMICO	63 64			
	Tim SMYCZEK (USA)	T.SMYCZEK				
3	Sun-Yong KIM (KOR)	46 63 64			J.LEVINE	
3	Aljoscha THRON (GER)				M.SHABAZ	
8	Piero LUISI (VEN)	P.BESTER			76(4) 63	
8	Ryan SWEETING (BAH)	P.POLANSKY				
	Philip BESTER (CAN)	57 64 64	P.BESTER			
	Peter POLANSKY (CAN)		P.POLANSKY			
	Sho AIDA (JPN)	J.NEDUNCHEZHIYAN	75 76(4)			
	Jiri KOSLER (CZE)	S.SINGH				
	Jeevan NEDUNCHEZHIYAN (IND)	63 64		J.LEVINE		
	Sanam SINGH (IND)			M.SHABAZ		
	Jesse LEVINE (USA)	J.LEVINE		57 64 62		
	Michael SHABAZ (USA)	M.SHABAZ				
	Marin CILIC (CRO)	63 64	J.LEVINE			
	Tristan FARRON-MAHON (IRL)		M.SHABAZ			
	Alexandr DOLGOPOLOV (UKR)	A.DOLGOPOLOV	63 64			
	Serguei TARASEVITCH (BLR)	S.TARASEVITCH				
2	Timothy NEILLY (USA)	36 63 64				
2	Samuel QUERREY (USA)					

2005 Junior Championships, Wimbledon, 25 June–3 July – Girls' Doubles

Seed	Player
1	Viktoria AZARENKA (BLR)
1	Agnes SZAVAY (HUN)
	Corinna DENTONI (ITA)
	Anastasia REVZINA (RUS)
	Ekaterina KOSMINSKAYA (RUS)
	Alla KUDRYAVTSEVA (RUS)
	Agnieszka RADWANSKA (POL)
	Urszula RADWANSKA (POL)
	Maria-Fernanda ALVAREZ (BOL)
	Ana-Clara DUARTE (BRA)
	Mihaela BUZARNESCU (ROM)
	Madalina GOJNEA (ROM)
	Yvette HYNDMAN (USA)
	Jennifer STEVENS (USA)
6	Yung-Jan CHAN (TPE)
6	Nikola FRANKOVA (CZE)
4	Alexa GLATCH (USA)
4	Vania KING (USA)
	Olga GOVORTSOVA (BLR)
	Alisa KLEYBANOVA (RUS)
	Magy AZIZ (EGY)
	Jessica SWEETING (BAH)
	Tamira PASZEK (AUT)
	Renee REINHARD (NED)
	Florencia MOLINERO (ARG)
	Irena PAVLOVIC (FRA)
WC	Jade CURTIS (GBR)
WC	Sabine LISICKI (GER)
	Melanie GLORIA (CAN)
	Valerie TETREAULT (CAN)
7	Dominika CIBULKOVA (SVK)
7	Anna TATISHVILI (GEO)
5	Raluca OLARU (ROM)
5	Amina RAKHIM (KAZ)
	Astrid BESSER (ITA)
	Polona REBERSAK (SLO)
WC	Claire PETERZAN (GBR)
WC	Laura PETERZAN (GBR)
	Katerina KRAMPEROVA (CZE)
	Agnes SZATMARI (ROM)
	Ellah NZE (USA)
	Anastasia PIVOVAROVA (RUS)
	Jarmila GAJDOSOVA (SVK)
	Aude VERMOEZEN (BEL)
	Ekaterina MAKAROVA (RUS)
	Evgeniya RODINA (RUS)
3	Bibiane SCHOOFS (NED)
3	Caroline WOZNIACKI (DEN)
8	Jennifer-Lee HEINSER (USA)
8	Elizabeth PLOTKIN (USA)
WC	Julia BONE (GBR)
WC	Samantha MURRAY (GBR)
WC	Natasha KHAN (GBR)
WC	Georgie STOOP (GBR)
	Olivia LUKASZEWICZ (AUS)
	Shayna MCDOWELL (AUS)
	Eugenia GREBENYUK (RUS)
	Yaroslava SHVEDOVA (RUS)
	Ellen BARRY (NZL)
	Maya GAVEROVA (RUS)
	Ayumi MORITA (JPN)
	Erika SEMA (JPN)
2	Marina ERAKOVIC (NZL)
2	Monica NICULESCU (ROM)

First round

Winners	Score
V.AZARENKA (1) / A.SZAVAY (1)	61 62
A.RADWANSKA / U.RADWANSKA	64 26 61
M.BUZARNESCU / M.GOJNEA	63 60
Y.CHAN (6) / N.FRANKOVA (6)	62 62
O.GOVORTSOVA / A.KLEYBANOVA	64 57 64
T.PASZEK / R.REINHARD	64 61
F.MOLINERO / I.PAVLOVIC	61 64
D.CIBULKOVA (7) / A.TATISHVILI (7)	63 62
R.OLARU (5) / A.RAKHIM (5)	60 62
K.KRAMPEROVA / A.SZATMARI	63 61
J.GAJDOSOVA / A.VERMOEZEN	63 62
B.SCHOOFS (3) / C.WOZNIACKI (3)	46 62 75
J.HEINSER (8) / E.PLOTKIN (8)	63 63
O.LUKASZEWICZ / S.MC DOWELL	63 64
E.GREBENYUK / Y.SHVEDOVA	62 64
M.ERAKOVIC (2) / M.NICULESCU (2)	63 63

Second round

Winners	Score
V.AZARENKA (1) / A.SZAVAY (1)	46 61 60
M.BUZARNESCU / M.GOJNEA	46 64 61
O.GOVORTSOVA / A.KLEYBANOVA	64 61
F.MOLINERO / I.PAVLOVIC	61 62
R.OLARU (5) / A.RAKHIM (5)	46 64 63
B.SCHOOFS (3) / C.WOZNIACKI (3)	61 62
J.HEINSER (8) / E.PLOTKIN (8)	46 61 63
M.ERAKOVIC (2) / M.NICULESCU (2)	64 62

Quarter-finals

Winners	Score
V.AZARENKA (1) / A.SZAVAY (1)	60 61
O.GOVORTSOVA / A.KLEYBANOVA	64 60
B.SCHOOFS (3) / C.WOZNIACKI (3)	63 36 62
M.ERAKOVIC (2) / M.NICULESCU (2)	63 62

Semi-finals

Winners	Score
V.AZARENKA (1) / A.SZAVAY (1)	62 63
M.ERAKOVIC (2) / M.NICULESCU (2)	64 64

Final

Winners	Score
V.AZARENKA (1) / A.SZAVAY (1)	67(5) 62 60

2005 US Open Junior Championships, 4-11 September – Boys' Singles

	Player	First round
1	Donald YOUNG (USA)	D.YOUNG (1)
	Philip BESTER (CAN)	36 61 63
	David NAVARRETE (VEN)	D.NAVARRETE
	Vivek SHOKEEN (IND)	63 57 62
WC	Nathaniel SCHNUGG (USA)	R.ROY (LL)
LL	Rupesh ROY (IND)	63 64
Q	Matt BRUCH (USA)	M.BRUCH (Q)
15	Andre MIELE (BRA)	64 46 61
11	Petar JELENIC (CRO)	C.VITULLI
	Christian VITULLI (KEN)	64 16 61
	Michael SHABAZ (USA)	M.SHABAZ
	Valeri RUDNEV (RUS)	57 75 63
	Kellen DAMICO (USA)	J.SCHOTTLER
	Jochen SCHOTTLER (GER)	64 46 63
WC	Dylan ARNOULD (USA)	S.KIM (6)
6	Sun-Yong KIM (KOR)	62 63
3	Leonardo MAYER (ARG)	L.MAYER (3)
	Javier GARRAPIZ-BORDERIAS (ESP)	62 60
WC	Jamie HUNT (USA)	D.LOJDA
	Dusan LOJDA (CZE)	64 76(4)
	Luka BELIC (CRO)	L.BELIC
Q	Kevin BOTTI (FRA)	62 64
	Martin SAYER (HKG)	S.QUERREY (13)
13	Samuel QUERREY (USA)	64 62
12	Carsten BALL (AUS)	R.SWEETING
	Ryan SWEETING (BAH)	26 63 76(1)
	Andrea ARNABOLDI (ITA)	A.ARNABOLDI
	Andrew KENNAUGH (GBR)	63 16 61
	Lukas LACKO (SVK)	L.LACKO
Q	Kento TAKEUCHI (JPN)	63 64
WC	Holden SEGUSO (USA)	H.SEGUSO (WC)
8	Niels DESEIN (BEL)	64 64
5	Alex KUZNETSOV (USA)	A.KUZNETSOV (5)
	Nikola MEKTIC (CRO)	67(3) 64 63
	Dennis LAJOLA (USA)	D.LAJOLA
Q	Sho AIDA (JPN)	63 61
	Tim SMYCZEK (USA)	T.SMYCZEK
	Pavel CHEKHOV (RUS)	63 16 64
	Abdullah MAGDAS (KUW)	T.DE BAKKER (9)
9	Thiemo DE BAKKER (NED)	61 76(3)
16	Jesse LEVINE (USA)	J.LEVINE (16)
	Jeevan NEDUNCHEZHIYAN (IND)	64 64
Q	Miguel-Angel REYES-VARELA (MEX)	P.LUISI
	Piero LUISI (VEN)	62 64
	James LEMKE (AUS)	A.VEIC
	Antonio VEIC (CRO)	75 62
Q	Peter POLANSKY (CAN)	S.GIRALDO (4)
4	Santiago GIRALDO (COL)	62 62
7	Jeremy CHARDY (FRA)	J.CHARDY (7)
Q	Alberto GONZALEZ (PAN)	61 63
WC	Johnny HAMUI (USA)	K.NORBERG (Q)
Q	Karl NORBERG (SWE)	64 62
	Pavol CERVENAK (SVK)	K.NISHIKORI (LL)
LL	Kei NISHIKORI (JPN)	62 63
LL	Jaak POLDMA (EST)	T.NEILLY (10)
10	Timothy NEILLY (USA)	75 76(3)
14	Evgeny KIRILLOV (RUS)	E.KIRILLOV (14)
	Tristan FARRON-MAHON (IRL)	76(5) 63
	Alex CLAYTON (USA)	A.CLAYTON
	Ivan SERGEYEV (UKR)	57 63 63
WC	Wil SPENCER (USA)	W.SPENCER (WC)
	Stephen DONALD (AUS)	75 46 41 RET
WC	Michael MCCLUNE (USA)	M.CILIC (2)
2	Marin CILIC (CRO)	62 62

Second round

D.YOUNG (1) 46 62 60
M.BRUCH (Q) 36 64 63
C.VITULLI 46 64 75
S.KIM (6) 63 64
L.MAYER (3) 75 64
S.QUERREY (13) 63 63
R.SWEETING 63 36 61
H.SEGUSO (WC) 76(5) 61
A.KUZNETSOV (5) 63 62
T.SMYCZEK 61 76(0)
P.LUISI 46 64 60
S.GIRALDO (4) 64 62
J.CHARDY (7) 63 63
K.NISHIKORI (LL) 64 60
E.KIRILLOV (14) 46 64 76(4)
M.CILIC (2) 76(3) 64

Third round

D.YOUNG (1) 67(4) 76(4) 62
S.KIM (6) 75 64
L.MAYER (3) 76(4) 76(3)
R.SWEETING 61 62
T.SMYCZEK 76(3) 64
S.GIRALDO (4) 62 75
J.CHARDY (7) 75 61
M.CILIC (2) 76(5) 64

Quarter-finals

S.KIM (6) 76(1) 26 76(2)
R.SWEETING 64 75
S.GIRALDO (4) 61 36 62
J.CHARDY (7) 46 64 62

Semi-finals

R.SWEETING 64 60
J.CHARDY (7) 76(5) 62

Final

R.SWEETING 64 64

US OPEN 2005

A USTA EVENT

2005 US Open Junior Championships, 4-11 September – Girls' Singles

A USTA EVENT

Seed	Player	First round
1	Viktoria AZARENKA (BLR)	V.AZARENKA (1)
SE	Alexandra PANOVA (RUS)	62 61
Q	Jennifer STEVENS (USA)	K.KRAMPEROVA
	Katerina KRAMPEROVA (CZE)	63 62
	Renee REINHARD (NED)	R.REINHARD
	Anastasia PAVLYUCHENKOVA (RUS)	63 76(4)
	Julia COHEN (USA)	J.COHEN
16	Amina RAKHIM (KAZ)	61 75
10	Vania KING (USA)	V.KING (10)
Q	Jillian O'NEILL (CAN)	60 60
WC	Madison BRENGLE (USA)	M.BRENGLE (WC)
	Urszula RADWANSKA (POL)	60 36 61
WC	Gail BRODSKY (USA)	G.BRODSKY (WC)
	Dominice RIPOLL (GER)	61 64
	Yasmin SCHNACK (USA)	M.ERAKOVIC (6)
6	Marina ERAKOVIC (NZL)	63 62
4	Caroline WOZNIACKI (DEN)	J.HAMPTON (WC)
WC	Jamie HAMPTON (USA)	62 26 64
WC	Lauren ALBANESE (USA)	Y.SHVEDOVA
	Yaroslava SHVEDOVA (RUS)	16 63 61
	Stephanie HERZ (NED)	A.TATISHVILI
	Anna TATISHVILI (GEO)	67(4) 62 62
Q	Anna BARTENSTEIN (AUT)	M.BUZARNESCU (14)
14	Mihaela BUZARNESCU (ROM)	61 64
12	Ayumi MORITA (JPN)	O.GOVORTSOVA (Q)
Q	Olga GOVORTSOVA (BLR)	64 64
WC	Lyndsay BURDETTE (USA)	J.LARSSON (Q)
Q	Johanna LARSSON (SWE)	63 61
	Roxane VAISEMBERG (BRA)	S.FICHMAN
	Sharon FICHMAN (CAN)	61 62
	Liset BRITO (CHI)	M.GAMBALE (8)
8	Mary GAMBALE (USA)	76(2) 63
7	Alexa GLATCH (USA)	A.GLATCH (7)
	Olivia LUKASZEWICZ (AUS)	63 61
	Astrid BESSER (ITA)	V.TETREAULT
	Valerie TETREAULT (CAN)	64 63
LL	Erika SEMA (JPN)	E.SEMA (LL)
SE	Jade CURTIS (GBR)	76(8) 63
Q	Kristen MCVITTY (USA)	E.MAKAROVA (9)
9	Ekaterina MAKAROVA (RUS)	63 75
13	Bibiane SCHOOFS (NED)	B.SCHOOFS (13)
	Ana-Clara DUARTE (BRA)	62 64
	Ellah NZE (USA)	K.VANKOVA
	Katerina VANKOVA (CZE)	61 63
WC	Lyndsay KINSTLER (USA)	M.JOHANSSON
	Michaela JOHANSSON (SWE)	61 61
WC	Chelsey GULLICKSON (USA)	D.CIBULKOVA (3)
3	Dominika CIBULKOVA (SVK)	75 63
5	Alexandra DULGHERU (ROM)	A.KLEYBANOVA
	Alisa KLEYBANOVA (RUS)	46 76(6) 64
	Nina HENKEL (GER)	N.HENKEL
Q	Ksenia MILEVSKAYA (BLR)	62 61
Q	Ashley WEINHOLD (USA)	S.CIRSTEA
	Sorana CIRSTEA (ROM)	76(3) 63
	Andrea REMYNSE (USA)	W.HSU (11)
11	Wen-Hsin HSU (TPE)	61 62
15	Jennifer-Lee HEINSER (USA)	N.FRANKOVA
	Nikola FRANKOVA (CZE)	62 75
WC	Sarah FANSLER (USA)	E.KOSMINSKAYA (Q)
Q	Ekaterina KOSMINSKAYA (RUS)	75 36 62
	Elizabeth PLOTKIN (USA)	E.PLOTKIN
	Marrit BOONSTRA (NED)	76(2) 76(3)
LL	Megan ALEXANDER (USA)	A.RADWANSKA (2)
2	Agnieszka RADWANSKA (POL)	61 60

Second round	Third round	Quarter-finals	Semi-finals	Final
V.AZARENKA (1) 61 62	V.AZARENKA (1) 60 60	V.AZARENKA (1) 52 RET	V.AZARENKA (1) 36 62 62	V.AZARENKA (1) 63 64
R.REINHARD 16 64 60	M.ERAKOVIC (6) 63 36 76(2)	M.BUZARNESCU (14) 62 76(3)	A.GLATCH (7) 61 75	
V.KING (10) 61 60	M.BUZARNESCU (14) 63 63	A.GLATCH (7) 60 64		
M.ERAKOVIC (6) 61 61	O.GOVORTSOVA (Q) 64 64	N.HENKEL 75 75		
Y.SHVEDOVA 36 63 60	A.GLATCH (7) 76(2) 16 63			
M.BUZARNESCU (14) 62 64	D.CIBULKOVA (3) 63 75			
O.GOVORTSOVA (Q) 76(6) 64	N.HENKEL 75 16 75			
S.FICHMAN 06 75 64	E.PLOTKIN 63 64			
A.GLATCH (7) 62 61				
E.MAKAROVA (9) 61 62				
B.SCHOOFS (13) 76(2) 57 63				
D.CIBULKOVA (3) 36 63 63				
N.HENKEL 63 64				
W.HSU (11) 64 46 64				
E.KOSMINSKAYA (Q) 64 63				
E.PLOTKIN 64 64				

2005 US Open Junior Championships, 4–11 September – Boys' Doubles

US OPEN 2005
A USTA EVENT

First Round Draw

1 Leonardo MAYER (ARG)
1 Andre MIELE (BRA)
BYE
BYE
Kellen DAMICO (USA)
Tim SMYCZEK (USA)
Rupesh ROY (IND)
David SIMON (AUT)
Alberto GONZALEZ (PAN)
Kei NISHIKORI (JPN)
Andrew KENNAUGH (GBR)
Jochen SCHOTTLER (GER)
Luka BELIC (CRO)
Antonio VEIC (CRO)
8 Alex CLAYTON (USA)
8 Donald YOUNG (USA)
3 Petar JELENIC (CRO)
3 Evgeny KIRILLOV (RUS)
Kevin BOTTI (FRA)
Jeremy CHARDY (FRA)
Matt BRUCH (USA)
Holden SEGUSO (USA)
Sho AIDA (JPN)
Kento TAKEUCHI (JPN)
Tyler HOCHWALT (USA)
Dennis NEVOLO (USA)
Stephen DONALD (AUS)
Javier GARRAPIZ-BORDERIAS (ESP)
Waylon CHIN (USA)
Johnny HAMUI (USA)
5 Timothy NEILLY (USA)
5 Ryan SWEETING (BAH)
6 Andrea ARNABOLDI (ITA)
6 Niels DESEIN (BEL)
Pavol CERVENAK (SVK)
Lukas LACKO (SVK)
Michael MC CLUNE (USA)
Samuel QUERREY (USA)
Jeevan NEDUNCHEZHIYAN (IND)
Vivek SHOKEEN (IND)
Jesse LEVINE (USA)
Michael SHABAZ (USA)
Pavel CHEKHOV (RUS)
Valeri RUDNEV (RUS)
Philip BESTER (CAN)
Peter POLANSKY (CAN)
4 Sun-Yong KIM (KOR)
4 Dusan LOJDA (CZE)
7 Piero LUISI (VEN)
7 David NAVARRETE (VEN)
Jaak POLDMA (EST)
Wil SPENCER (USA)
Nikola MEKTIC (CRO)
Ivan SERGEYEV (UKR)
James LEMKE (AUS)
Miguel-Angel REYES-VARELA (MEX)
Dylan ARNOULD (USA)
Jamie HUNT (USA)
Marin CILIC (CRO)
Tristan FARRON-MAHON (IRL)
Dennis LAJOLA (USA)
Nathaniel SCHNUGG (USA)
2 Carsten BALL (AUS)
2 Thiemo DE BAKKER (NED)

Second Round

L.MAYER (1) / A.MIELE (1) — BYE
K.DAMICO / T.SMYCZEK 63 60
A.KENNAUGH / J.SCHOTTLER 76(6) 64
A.CLAYTON (8) / D.YOUNG (8) 64 62
P.JELENIC (3) / E.KIRILLOV (3) 63 76(3)
M.BRUCH / H.SEGUSO 61 64
S.DONALD / J.GARRAPIZ-BORDERIAS 46 61 61
T.NEILLY (5) / R.SWEETING (5) 62 60
P.CERVENAK / L.LACKO 63 64
M.MCCLUNE / S.QUERREY 62 76(6)
J.LEVINE / M.SHABAZ 63 63
P.BESTER / P.POLANSKY 75 64
P.LUISI (7) / D.NAVARRETE (7) 61 62
N.MEKTIC / I.SERGEYEV 64 76(6)
M.CILIC / T.FARRON-MAHON 63 63
C.BALL (2) / T.DE BAKKER (2) 63 63

Third Round

K.DAMICO / T.SMYCZEK 63 64
A.CLAYTON (8) / D.YOUNG (8) 76(2) 57 64
P.JELENIC (3) / E.KIRILLOV (3) 26 64 64
T.NEILLY (5) / R.SWEETING (5) 62 46 62
P.CERVENAK / L.LACKO 62 75
J.LEVINE / M.SHABAZ 75 62
N.MEKTIC / I.SERGEYEV 36 76(2) 64
C.BALL (2) / T.DE BAKKER (2) 75 46 63

Quarter-finals

A.CLAYTON (8) / D.YOUNG (8) 61 76(5)
P.JELENIC (3) / E.KIRILLOV (3) 64 16 76(2)
J.LEVINE / M.SHABAZ 62 76(2)
C.BALL (2) / T.DE BAKKER (2) 26 76(3) 76(5)

Semi-finals

A.CLAYTON (8) / D.YOUNG (8) 62 63
C.BALL (2) / T.DE BAKKER (2) 61 63

Final

A.CLAYTON (8) / D.YOUNG (8) 76(3) 46 75

2005 US Open Junior Championships, 4–11 September – Girls' Doubles

First round

Seed	Player
1	Viktoria AZARENKA (BLR)
1	Marina ERAKOVIC (NZL)
	Andrea REMYNSE (USA)
	Yasmin SCHNACK (USA)
	Dominika CIBULKOVA (SVK)
	Ekaterina KOSMINSKAYA (RUS)
	Marrit BOONSTRA (NED)
	Renee REINHARD (NED)
	Julia COHEN (USA)
	Mary GAMBALE (USA)
	Olga GOVORTSOVA (BLR)
	Bibiane SCHOOFS (NED)
	Liset BRITO (CHI)
	Roxane VAISEMBERG (BRA)
6	Jennifer-Lee HEINSER (USA)
6	Elizabeth PLOTKIN (USA)
3	Mihaela BUZARNESCU (ROM)
3	Alexandra DULGHERU (ROM)
	Lauren ALBANESE (USA)
	Jennifer STEVENS (USA)
	Yvette HYNDMAN (USA)
	Jillian O'NEILL (CAN)
	Anna BARTENSTEIN (AUT)
	Ellah NZE (USA)
	Katerina KRAMPEROVA (CZE)
	Katerina VANKOVA (CZE)
	Bianca BONIFATE (ROM)
	Ana-Clara DUARTE (BRA)
WC	Brittany AUGUSTINE (USA)
WC	Madison BRENGLE (USA)
7	Nikola FRANKOVA (CZE)
7	Alisa KLEYBANOVA (RUS)
5	Wen-Hsin HSU (TPE)
5	Amina RAKHIM (KAZ)
WC	Jamie HAMPTON (USA)
WC	Lyndsay KINSTLER (USA)
	Veronica Ruo-Qi LI (USA)
	Valerie TETREAULT (CAN)
	Michaela JOHANSSON (SWE)
	Johanna LARSSON (SWE)
WC	Gail BRODSKY (USA)
WC	Ksenia MILEVSKAYA (BLR)
	Nina HENKEL (GER)
	Dominice RIPOLL (GER)
WC	Lyndsay BURDETTE (USA)
WC	Mallory BURDETTE (USA)
4	Anna TATISHVILI (GEO)
4	Caroline WOZNIACKI (DEN)
8	Agnieszka RADWANSKA (POL)
8	Urszula RADWANSKA (POL)
	Ayumi MORITA (JPN)
	Erika SEMA (JPN)
	Megan ALEXANDER (USA)
	Chelsey GULLICKSON (USA)
	Sorana CIRSTEA (ROM)
	Anastasia PAVLYUCHENKOVA (RUS)
	Kristen MCVITTY (USA)
	Ashley WEINHOLD (USA)
	Astrid BESSER (ITA)
	Stephanie HERZ (NED)
	Jade CURTIS (GBR)
	Sharon FICHMAN (CAN)
2	Alexa GLATCH (USA)
2	Vania KING (USA)

Second round

- V.AZARENKA (1) / M.ERAKOVIC (1) 62 61
- M.BOONSTRA / R.REINHARD 63 60
- O.GOVORTSOVA / B.SCHOOFS 46 61 61
- L.BRITO / R.VAISEMBERG 75 75
- M.BUZARNESCU (3) / A.DULGHERU (3) 64 63
- Y.HYNDMAN / J.O'NEILL 64 62
- K.KRAMPEROVA / K.VANKOVA 62 63
- N.FRANKOVA (7) / A.KLEYBANOVA (7) 62 61
- W.HSU (5) / A.RAKHIM (5) 63 64
- M.JOHANSSON / J.LARSSON 26 64 64
- N.HENKEL / D.RIPOLL 62 63
- A.TATISHVILI (4) / C.WOZNIACKI (4) 26 62 76(5)
- A.MORITA / E.SEMA 46 61 75
- S.CIRSTEA / A.PAVLYUCHENKOVA 62 60
- K.MCVITTY / A.WEINHOLD 26 64 61
- A.GLATCH (2) / V.KING (2) 63 46 62

Quarterfinals

- V.AZARENKA (1) / M.ERAKOVIC (1) 61 61
- O.GOVORTSOVA / B.SCHOOFS 75 46 64
- M.BUZARNESCU (3) / A.DULGHERU (3) 46 64 63
- N.FRANKOVA (7) / A.KLEYBANOVA (7) 46 64 63
- W.HSU (5) / A.RAKHIM (5) 60 60
- A.TATISHVILI (4) / C.WOZNIACKI (4) 62 63
- A.MORITA / E.SEMA 61 64
- A.GLATCH (2) / V.KING (2) 62 64

Semifinals

- O.GOVORTSOVA / B.SCHOOFS W/O
- N.FRANKOVA (7) / A.KLEYBANOVA (7) 63 75
- W.HSU (5) / A.RAKHIM (5) 57 60 75
- A.GLATCH (2) / V.KING (2) 64 63

Final

- N.FRANKOVA (7) / A.KLEYBANOVA (7) 76(6) 63
- A.GLATCH (2) / V.KING (2) 63 62

Winners

N.FRANKOVA (7) / A.KLEYBANOVA (7) 75 76(3)

US OPEN 2005
A USTA EVENT

the wheelchair tennis year 2005

by marta balint

With the Paralympics having so noticeably dominated the wheelchair tennis season last year, it was almost unavoidable that 2005 would be a slightly quieter year. Nonetheless significant progress was made in the promotion and growth of the sport and the year also saw the crowning of a new men's World Champion, while Esther Vergeer (NED) continued to impress and took the highest honours again.

The formidable Dutchwoman maintained her unparalleled march to finish at the top of the women's ranking for the sixth consecutive year. Her extraordinary dominance saw Vergeer emerge from yet another season undefeated and, moreover, without dropping a single set. Having been the year-end No. 1 in doubles for the last two years, this time Vergeer conceded the spot to a gifted and determined player from France, Florence Gravellier who had won three of the four Super Series doubles titles.

Esther Vergeer (NED)

The race for the top position in the men's competition was much closer. Having clinched last year's title in his last match of the season at the NEC Masters, Australia's David Hall had the advantage of starting in the pole position this year. His supremacy was quickly challenged by old-time nemesis Robin Ammerlaan (NED) who overthrew the six-time World Champion in February to temporarily dominate the game. But Hall, having won two of the Super Series, the Australian and Japan Opens in the first half of the year, quickly regained composure. He was back in his usual form and at the top of the ranking by May, doing his best to watch out not only for Ammerlaan but also for a remarkable Michael Jeremiasz (FRA), on the rise for the last two years. A junior player before his accident six years ago, as soon as he started playing wheelchair tennis it was clear that Jeremiasz would not be just a passing flame. Three and a half years after he came on the rankings, Jeremiasz was already No. 3 at the end of last year and a finalist at the NEC Masters.

As soon as he started playing wheelchair tennis it was clear that Jeremiasz would not be just a passing flame. Three and a half years after he came on the rankings, Jeremiasz was already No. 3 at the end of last year and a finalist at the NEC Masters.

Jeremiasz's rise to the No. 1 position this year meant successfully by-passing both Hall and Ammerlaan at the crucial moments. He took a number of ITF 1 Series titles this season, including the French Open in his home-town Paris and topped an already impressive record with winning his first Super Series tournament at the US Open in San Diego. This decisive win sealed the fate of the World Champion title as Jeremiasz rose to the top in October and no losses or wins by his two rivals could oust him from this spot thereafter.

The rivalry between the three was set to continue at the 2005 NEC Masters, the last one to be hosted by the city of Amersfoort before the event moves to a new venue in Amsterdam next year. After Hall withdrew with a shoulder injury two days before the start the wide open men's field was completed by Shingo Kunieda of Japan. A lucky, last minute addition to the draw, the Japanese 21-year old produced some of the most thrilling matches of the week and inscribed his name among the most

Michael Jeremiasz (FRA)

the wheelchair tennis year 2005

by marta balint

promising stars of the game. Jeremiasz, with his year-end title safely secured, was clearly aiming for the trophy this year. He survived two tight matches in the round robin phase and saved seven match points against Kunieda in the semifinal, eventually defeating the Japanese in the third set tiebreak. At the same time, Ammerlaan emerged from his pool undefeated and continued his impressive run in the final, dismissing Jeremiasz 62 63 to claim the fourth Masters title of his career.

The women's Masters produced no real shocks, though Florence Gravellier managed to steal the headlines as she became the first woman since 1996 to break the all-Dutch line-up for the final. The Frenchwoman finished first in her pool after an indomitable sequence, securing her advance into the final with a three-set victory over last year's finalist Jiske Griffioen (NED) in the semis. Meanwhile, Vergeer marched into her eighth consecutive final unchallenged and she ultimately triumphed over Gravellier with a 64 62 victory.

Robin Ammerlaan (NED)

Ammerlaan emerged from his pool undefeated and continued his impressive run in the final, dismissing Jeremiasz 62 63 to claim the fourth Masters title of his career.

David Wagner (USA) successfully defended his Masters title in the quad division with a 62 61 win over countryman Nick Taylor in the final, indisputably living up to his year-end No.1 ranking.

A week before the NEC Masters, Wagner and Taylor also won their first Camozzi Doubles Masters title after a close battle with Italian duo Giuseppe Polidori and Antonio Raffaele which the Americans clinched 63 67(5) 75. The 2005 men's title went to the runners-up for the past two years, top seeds Jeremiasz and Jayant Mistry (GBR) having finally overcome two-time champions Satoshi Saida (JPN) and Martin Legner (AUT) in straight sets. In the women's final, Griffioen and Vergeer completed a dominant week as they eased to a comfortable 61 62 win over top seeds Gravellier and Maaike Smit (NED).

The NEC wheelchair tennis tour this year was further enriched by two inaugural wheelchair tennis competitions at Wimbledon and the US Open. Given that grass is not an easy surface for wheelchair tennis, a men's doubles tournament was found to be the most appropriate format for showcasing the game at Wimbledon. Eight of the world's top ranked players wowed the crowds on Court 14 for two days while the BBC provided extensive TV coverage. Top seeds Jayant Mistry (GBR) and Jeremiasz took second seeds Hall and Martin Legner (AUT) to a thrilling final clash which they narrowly won 46 63 76(8).

"I don't think I've got the words right now to describe this feeling," said a visibly delighted Mistry afterwards. "I've been playing wheelchair tennis for 20 years and to be a Briton and win at my home Grand Slam is just astounding." Mistry and Jeremiasz received the winners' silver cup from former Wimbledon champion Ann Jones. In another landmark event that day, Paralympic quad singles gold medallist Peter Norfolk (GBR) conducted the coin toss ahead of the men's singles final between Andy Roddick and Roger Federer.

At the first wheelchair tennis competition at the US Open, with a men's and women's draw of eight, Ammerlaan and Vergeer dominated in their respective fields, with wins in the finals over Jeremiasz and Korie Homan (NED), respectively. With the fourth Classic 8's at the Australian Open held in January and a second exhibition hosted at Roland Garros in June, wheelchair tennis was for the second time fully represented at all four Grand Slams. These types of exhibitions and full-scale competitions at the able-bodied Grand Slams are crucial for the promotion and development of the sport. Bringing wheelchair tennis into the full view of the mainstream tennis world raises awareness not only about the sport in particular but also about people and athletes with a disability in general.

And if so far the Dutch dominance of wheelchair tennis, especially among the women, has not been obvious, their supremacy was confirmed, this time on home soil, at the 2005 Invacare World Team Cup in Groningen. In the women's event, top seeds the Netherlands and seventh seeds Korea reached the last round, making this the 18th time for the mighty Dutch team and the first time for the Asian nation. Griffioen and Vergeer won both singles rubbers against Park Ju Yeon and Hong Young Suk (KOR) in straight sets to give Netherlands its six consecutive title.

USA's Nick Taylor and David Wagner

Israel and USA are the only two countries to have won the quad title three times in the eight years that the division has been part of the Invacare World Team Cup.

In the final of the men's World Group 1, Ammerlaan and Ronald Vink outclassed the Japanese duo of Kunieda and Saida in the deciding doubles to clinch a 75 76(4) triumph over the 2004 Paralympic gold doubles medallists. In World Group 2 Hungary overcame Italy 2-1 in the final and both countries have thus earned promotion to World Group 1 for next year's competition.

In the quad event, defending champions Israel and USA progressed to the final in which Taylor and Wagner both dominated their singles rubbers. Israel and USA are the only two countries to have won the quad title three times in the eight years that the division has been part of the Invacare World Team Cup.

The junior title was fiercely contested by two round-robin pools of four nations, in which Belgium and Australia finished top of their respective groups. In the final the Belgian boys outclassed their Australian rivals in the singles rubbers, to the delight of a tearful but joyous crowd of family and friends.

The junior programme has received a significant boost in 2005 when the Cruyff Foundation, already a significant Silver Fund supporter, came on board as a partner to sponsor the extension of competitive and training opportunities available to the youngest wheelchair tennis players. Through this programme, four international junior camps and more than ten national camps were held across the globe. The junior World Team Cup competition, the Cruyff Foundation Junior Masters at Les Petits As in France and several junior draws at NEC Tour events constituted the elite levels of the programme. For all of these, the ambitious juniors were rewarded with ranking points that were ultimately translated into a Cruyff Foundation junior ranking, now at its tenth edition. "Having 48 boys and 18 girls on the rankings at the end of the year has exceeded most of our expectations. The junior ranking and the junior programme as a whole has been an extraordinary success and we are pleased that the Cruyff Foundation decided to support it again in 2006" says the ITF's Wheelchair Tennis Development Officer Mark Bullock.

The development of the game has continued on other fronts as well, particularly the wheelchair tennis Silver Fund which was set up in 2001 to celebrate the 25th anniversary of wheelchair tennis. The Fund aims to establish sustainable wheelchair tennis programmes in developing nations through the provision of tennis equipment, technical expertise and the identification of local partners who will take the programme to self-supporting levels. With 11 successful countries on the record already and four new ones starting next year (Thailand, Malaysia, Nigeria and Tanzania), the Silver Fund can pride itself on the remarkable achievement of taking the game to many places around the world where resources are scarce but where the enthusiasm of players, coaches and administrators abounds.

Aad Zwaan (NED) coaching in Colombia

NEC Wheelchair Tennis Tour 2005 Results

- **QUEENSLAND OPEN** (AUS) (ITFFS) ($1,500) 27-30 JANUARY – **MS:** Lee Hinson (USA) d. Michael Esler (AUS) 60 64. **MD:** Lee Hinson (USA)/ David Johnson (AUS) d. Pedro Kruemmel (GER)/Thomas Suter (SUI) 62 60.

- **WHEELCHAIR CLASSIC 8'S AT AUSTRALIAN OPEN** (AUS) (ITFMS) 28-30 JANUARY – **WS:** Mie Yaosa (JPN) d. Maaike Smit (NED) 76 61. **WD:** Florence Gravellier (FRA)/Maaike Smit (NED) d. Yuka Chokyu (CAN)/Mie Yaosa (JPN) 63 63. **MS:** David Hall (AUS) d. Robin Ammerlaan (NED) 75 36 61. **MD:** Robin Ammerlaan (NED)/Martin Legner (AUT) d. Anthony Bonaccurso/David Hall (AUS) 64 63.

- **SYDNEY INTERNATIONAL** (AUS) (ITF1S) ($15,000) 2-6 FEBRUARY – **WS:** Florence Gravellier (FRA) d. Jiske Griffioen (NED) 63 63. **WD:** Yuka Chokyu (CAN)/Karin Suter-Erath (SUI) d. Britta Siegers (GER)/Sharon Walraven (NED) 61 63. **MS:** Robin Ammerlaan (NED) d. Satoshi Saida (JPN) 75 26 63. **MD:** Jayant Mistry (GBR)/Peter Wikstrom (SWE) d. Robin Ammerlaan (NED)/Martin Legner (AUT) 63 75.

- **AUSTRALIAN OPEN** (AUS) (ITFSS) ($27,600) 9-13 FEBRUARY – **WS:** Sharon Walraven (NED) d. Korie Homan (NED) 76(3) 61. **WD:** Florence Gravellier (FRA)/Maaike Smit (NED) d. Yuka Chokyu (CAN)/Jiske Griffioen (NED) 64 16 61. **MS:** David Hall (AUS) d. Robin Ammerlaan (NED) 57 63 63. **MD:** Robin Ammerlaan (NED)/Martin Legner (AUT) d. Frederic Cazeaudumec (FRA)/Satoshi Saida (JPN) 61 60.

- **SION INDOOR** (SUI) (ITF3S) ($7,500) 10-13 FEBRUARY – **WS:** Agnieszka Bartczak (POL) d. Janet McMorran (GBR) 63 64. **WD:** Sandra Kalt/Karin Suter-Erath (SUI) d. Janet McMorran/Lucy Shuker (GBR) 75 60. **MS:** Miroslav Brychta (CZE) d. Jozef Felix (SVK) 62 63. **MD:** Miroslav Brychta (CZE)/Jozef Felix (SVK) d. Frederic Cattaneo (FRA)/Gert Vos (BEL) 61 61.

- **NEW ZEALAND OPEN** (NZL) (ITF3S) ($7,500) 16-19 FEBRUARY – **MS:** Michael Esler (AUS) d. Yoshinobu Fujimoto (JPN) 76 75. **MD:** Glenn Barnes/Travis Moffat (NZL) d. Yoshinobu Fujimoto/Masaaki Taga (JPN) 64 63.

- **VASTERHANINGE CUP** (SWE) (ITFFS) ($1,500) 25-27 FEBRUARY – **MS:** Peter Wikstrom (SWE) d. Stefan Olsson (SWE) 63 46 62. **MD:** Niclas Larsson/Peter Wikstrom (SWE) d. Alexander Hansson/Stefan Olsson (SWE) 62 62.

- **USTA NATIONAL SOUTHWEST DESERT WHEELCHAIR CLASSICS** (USA) (ITFFS) ($5,000) 3-6 MARCH – **MS:** Regino Espinoza (USA) d. Eddie Medel (USA) 61 62. **MD:** Alex Anguiano/Regino Espinoza (USA) d. David Buck/Russell Rodriguez (USA) 64 61. **QS:** David Wagner (USA) d. Bryan Barten (USA) 63 60.

- **WINDSOR CLASSIC INDOOR GAMES** (CAN) (ITFFS) ($1,500) 4-6 MARCH – **WS:** Helene Simard (CAN) d. Tami Saj (CAN) 62 60. **MS:** Paul Walker (USA) d. Phillip Rowe (CAN) 63 36 64. **MD:** Phillip Rowe (CAN)/Paul Walker (USA) d. Colin McKeage/Frank Peter (CAN) 65 ret.

- **LES SYSTEMES ACCI** (CAN) (ITFFS) ($1,500) 4-6 MARCH – **MS:** Christoph Trachsel (CAN) d. Yann Mathieu (CAN) 63 76. **MD:** Claude Brunet/Jeff McBride (CAN) d. Yann Mathieu/Christoph Trachsel (CAN) 76 64.

- **BIEL-BIENNE INDOORS** (SUI) (ITF3S) ($7,500) 10-13 MARCH – **WS:** Jiske Griffioen (NED) d. Brigitte Ameryckx (BEL) 62 60. **WD:** Jiske Griffioen (NED)/Karin Suter-Erath (SUI) d. Brigitte Ameryckx (BEL)/Sandra Kalt (SUI) 63 62. **MS:** Tadeusz Kruszelnicki (POL) d. Martin Legner (AUT) 64 61. **MD:** Miroslav Brychta (CZE)/Martin Legner (AUT) d. Maikel Scheffers/Ronald Vink (NED) 63 60.

- **TAIWAN LION'S CUP** (TPE) (ITF3S) ($7,500) 10-13 MARCH – **WS:** Sakhorn Khanthasit (THA) d. Chiyoko Ohmae (JPN) 63 61. **WD:** Kanako Domori/Yuko Okabe (JPN) d. Rieko Iida/Keiko Nitta (JPN) 36 34 ret. **MS:** Shingo Kunieda (JPN) d. Shinichi Nakamuta (JPN) 62 60. **MD:** Sumrerng Kruamai/Wittaya Peem-Mee (THA) d. Shingo Kunieda/Katsuaki Mitsugi (JPN) 63 76(4).

- **LES INTERNATIONAUX SAVARIA** (CAN) (ITFFS) ($1,750) 11-13 MARCH – **MS:** Stefane Goudou (FRA) d. Yann Mathieu (CAN) 63 63. **MD:** Stefane Goudou (FRA)/Yann Mathieu (CAN) d. Lee Carter/Christoph Trachsel (CAN) 60 61.

- **TASMANIAN WHEELCHAIR OPEN** (AUS) (ITFFS) ($1,500) 11-13 MARCH – **MS:** Michael Esler (AUS) d. Lee Hinson (USA) 63 75.

- **ALPI DEL MARE** (ITA) (ITF3S) ($8,000) 17-20 MARCH – **WS:** Sharon Walraven (NED) d. Sandra Kalt (SUI) 64 26 61. **MS:** Ronald Vink (NED) d. Martin Legner (AUT) 60 60. **MD:** Maikel Scheffers/Ronald Vink (NED) d. Jozef Felix (SVK)/Martin Legner (AUT) 75 61.

- **NORTH EAST WHEELCHAIR TENNIS TOURNAMENT** (GBR) (ITF3S) ($7,600) 17-20 MARCH – **WS:** Kimberly Blake (GBR) d. Janet McMorran (GBR) 76(2) 64. **WD:** Janet McMorran/Lucy Shuker (GBR) d. Kimberly Blake/Jenny Dalgleish (GBR) 62 62. **MS:** Frederic Cazeaudumec (FRA) d. Miroslav Brychta (CZE) 62 76(5). **MD:** Lahcen Majdi (FRA)/Jayant Mistry (GBR) d. Frederic Cazeaudumec/Stefane Goudou (FRA) 63 62.

- **WAIKATO CHAMPIONSHIPS** (NZL) (ITFFS) ($1,500) 18-20 MARCH – **WS:** Tiffiney Perry (NZL) d. Gabriel Bateman (NZL) 63 60. **WD:** Gabriel Bateman/Tiffiney Perry (NZL) d. Janice Greenem/Rosie McLeod (NZL) 60 60. **MS:** Glenn Barnes (NZL) d. Dave Venter (NZL) 60 64. **MD:** Glenn Barnes/Cameron Hastings (NZL) d. Danny McBride/Dave Venter (NZL) 64 64. **QS:** James McLeod (NZL) d. Richard Page (NZL) 62 16 64.

- **YAFO OPEN--NEW DATES** (ISR) (ITFFS) ($1,500) 29 MARCH-1 APRIL – **MS:** Avi Weinberg (ISR) d. Genadi Kohanov (ISR) 60 63. **MD:** Moshe Bar Hen/Arik Lewin (ISR) d. Genadi Kohanov/Haim Lev (ISR) 63 60.

- **NASDAQ-100 OPEN** (USA) (ITFMS) 30 MARCH-2 APRIL – **WS:** Esther Vergeer (NED) d. Jiske Griffioen (NED) 63 63. **MS:** Robin Ammerlaan (NED) d. David Hall (AUS) 64 26 64. **MD:** David Hall (AUS)/Martin Legner (AUT) d. Robin Ammerlaan (NED)/Michael Jeremiasz (FRA) 64 63.

- **PENSACOLA OPEN** (USA) (ITF3S) ($12,000) 1-3 APRIL – **WS:** Beth Ann Arnoult-Ritthaler (USA) d. Armelle Fabre (FRA) 60 36 62. **WD:** Armelle Fabre (FRA)/Aniek Van Koot (NED) d. Beth Ann Arnoult-Ritthaler (USA)/Helene Simard (CAN) 64 63. **MS:** Peter Wikstrom (SWE) d. Maikel Scheffers (NED) 62 76(6). **MD:** Maikel Scheffers/Ronald Vink (NED) d. Derek Bolton/Larry Quintero (USA) 36 75 62. **QS:** David Wagner (USA) d. Brian McPhate (CAN) 62 61. **QD:** Marc McLean/David Wagner (USA) d. Roy Humphreys (GBR)/Brian McPhate (CAN) 62 76(2).

- **FLORIDA OPEN** (USA) (ITF1S) ($15,000) 6-10 APRIL – **WS:** Esther Vergeer (NED) d. Sharon Walraven (NED) 63 64. **WD:** Jiske Griffioen/Esther Vergeer (NED) d. Florence Gravellier (FRA)/Maaike Smit (NED) 75 75. **MS:** Michael Jeremiasz (FRA) d. David Hall (AUS) 63 64. **MD:** Robin Ammerlaan (NED)/Michael Jeremiasz (FRA) d. David Hall (AUS)/Martin Legner (AUT) 46 63 64. **QS:** Peter Norfolk (GBR) d. David Wagner (USA) 36 64 64. **QD:** Nicholas Taylor/David Wagner (USA) d. Peter Norfolk (GBR)/Sarah Hunter (CAN) 61 63.

- **BRASILIA OPEN** (BRA) (ITF1S) ($15,000) 13-17 APRIL – **WS:** Esther Vergeer (NED) d. Jiske Griffioen (NED) 75 62. **MS:** Michael Jeremiasz (FRA) d. Robin Ammerlaan (NED) 64 64. **MD:** Robin Ammerlaan (NED)/Michael Jeremiasz (FRA) d. Miroslav Brychta (CZE)/Jozef Felix (SVK) 61 63.

- **CAJUN CLASSIC** (USA) (ITF2S) ($12,000) 14-17 APRIL – **WS:** Florence Gravellier (FRA) d. Sharon Walraven (NED) 63 64. **WD:** Florence Gravellier (FRA)/Sharon Walraven (NED) d. Karin Korb/Hope Lewellen (USA) 63 63. **MS:** Stephen Welch (USA) d. Frederic Cazeaudumec (FRA) 64 61. **MD:** Derek Bolton/Stephen Welch (USA) d. Frederic Cazeaudumec (FRA)/Larry Quintero (USA) 62 61. **QS:** David Wagner (USA) d. Sarah Hunter (CAN) 63 63. **QD:** David Jordan/David Wagner (USA) d. Brent Poppen (USA)/Sarah Hunter (CAN) 63 63.

- **CHILEAN OPEN** (CHI) (ITF3S) ($6,000) 21-24 APRIL – **WS:** Maria-Antonieta Ortiz (CHI) d. Ofelia Bonifacio (ARG) 61 61. **WD:** Ofelia Bonifacio/Andrea Medrano (ARG) d. Maria-Antonieta Ortiz/Zapata (CHI) 63 63. **MS:** Miroslav Brychta (CZE) d. Stefane Goudou (FRA) 61 61. **MD:** Miroslav Brychta (CZE)/Jozef Felix (SVK) d. Stefane Goudou (FRA)/Yann Mathieu (CAN) 62 62.

- **VICTORIAN HARDCOURT CHAMPIONSHIPS** (AUS) (ITFFS) ($1,500) 23-24 APRIL – **WS:** Alana Duncombe (AUS) d. Marny Cringle (AUS) 60 61. **MS:** Anthony Bonaccurso (AUS) d. Ben Weekes (AUS) 63 60. **MD:** Anthony Bonaccurso/Michael Esler (AUS) d. David Latham/Ben Weekes (AUS) 61 62.

- **ARGENTINA OPEN** (ARG) (ITFFS) ($7,500) 26-29 APRIL – **WS:** Samanta Almeida (BRA) d. Andrea Medrano (ARG) 76 60. **WD:** Ofelia Bonifacio/Andrea Medrano (ARG) d. Lourdes Castillo/Estela Santana (PER) 61 63. **MS:** Jozef Felix (SVK) d. Oscar Diaz (ARG) 75 64. **MD:** Oscar Diaz (ARG)/Jozef Felix (SVK) d. Niclas Larsson (SWE)/Carlo Tresch (SUI) 64 61.

- **KOBE OPEN** (JPN) (ITF3S) ($7,500) 28 APRIL-1 MAY – **WS:** Mie Yaosa (JPN) d. Yuka Chokyu (CAN) 36 60 63. **WD:** Chiyoko Ohmae/Mie Yaosa (JPN) d. Naomi Ishimoto/Yuko Okabe (JPN) 60 61. **MS:** Shingo Kunieda (JPN) d. Satoshi Saida (JPN) 46 64 62. **MD:** Shingo Kunieda/Satoshi Saida (JPN) d. Yoshinobu Fujimoto/Masaaki Taga (JPN) 60 60. **QS:** Sadahiro Kimura (JPN) d. Hiroshi Toma (JPN) 76(5) 61.

- **OPEN DE LA ROCHE SUR YON** (FRA) (ITFFS) ($1,500) 5-7 MAY – **WS:** Armelle Fabre (FRA) d. Muriel Ellissalde (FRA) 63 63. **MS:** Lahcen Majdi (FRA) d. Frederic Cattaneo (FRA) 62 60. **MD:** Frederic Cattaneo/Stefane Goudou (FRA) d. Pierre Fusade/Lahcen Majdi (FRA) 62 61.

- **JAPAN OPEN** (JPN) (ITFSS) ($25,000) 17-22 MAY – **WS:** Jiske Griffioen (NED) d. Maaike Smit (NED) 61 36 60. **WD:** Florence Gravellier (FRA)/Jiske Griffioen (NED) d. Yuka Chokyu (CAN)/Karin Suter-Erath (SUI) 62 63. **MS:** David Hall (AUS) d. Michael Jeremiasz (FRA) 62 76(0). **MD:** David Hall (AUS)/Michael Jeremiasz (FRA) d. Shingo Kunieda/Satoshi Saida (JPN) 64 46 62. **QS:** Peter Norfolk (GBR) d. Sarah Hunter (CAN) 62 62. **QD:** Peter Norfolk (GBR)/Sarah Hunter (CAN) d. Ryuji Kakinokihara/Sadahiro Kimura (JPN) 63 61.

- **KOREA OPEN** (KOR) (ITF2S) ($12,000) 24-27 MAY – **WS:** Jiske Griffioen (NED) d. Florence Gravellier (FRA) 62 36 64. **WD:** Florence Gravellier (FRA)/Jiske Griffioen (NED) d. Naomi Ishimoto/Yuko Okabe (JPN) 60 60. **MS:** Shingo Kunieda (JPN) d. Frederic Cazeaudumec (FRA) 75 75. **MD:** Shingo Kunieda/Satoshi Saida (JPN) d. Frederic Cazeaudumec (FRA)/Ha-Gel Lee (KOR) 61 61.

- **ATLANTA OPEN** (USA) (ITF1S) ($15,000) 25-29 MAY – **WS:** Beth Ann Arnoult-Ritthaler (USA) d. Sharon Walraven (NED) 64 64. **WD:** Karin Korb (USA)/Helene Simard (CAN) d. Simone Blaauw/Sharon Walraven (NED) 60 61. **MS:** Stephen Welch (USA) d. Ronald Vink (NED) 60 64. **MD:** Derek Bolton/Stephen Welch (USA) d. Larry Quintero (USA)/Ronald Vink (NED) 64 46 64. **QS:** David Wagner (USA) d. Nicholas Taylor (USA) 63 62. **QD:** Nicholas Taylor/David Wagner (USA) d. Brian McPhate/Sarah Hunter (CAN) 63 62.

- **TOURNOI INDOORS BULLE** (SUI) (ITFFS) ($1,500) 27-29 MAY – **WS:** Sandra Kalt (SUI) d. Ludmila Bubnova (RUS) 60 62. **MS:** Leonid Shevchik (RUS) d. Laurent Fischer (FRA) 76(4) 64. **MD:** Martin Erni/Daniel Pellegrina (SUI) d. Laurent Fischer/Sebastien Husser (FRA) 46 75 75.

- **DAEGU OPEN** (KOR) (ITF2S) ($12,000) 30 MAY-2 JUNE – **WS:** Young-Suk Hong (KOR) d. Ilanit Fridman (ISR) 62 61. **WD:** Young-Suk Hong/Myung-Hee Hwang (KOR) d. Ilanit Fridman (ISR)/Ju-Yeon Park (KOR) 62 62. **MS:** Satoshi Saida (JPN) d. Shingo Kunieda (JPN) 26 75 64. **MD:** Shingo Kunieda/Satoshi Saida (JPN) d. Michael Esler (AUS)/Ha-Gel Lee (KOR) 63 62.

- **ISRAEL OPEN** (ISR) (ITF3S) ($7,500) 31 MAY-3 JUNE – **MS:** Laszlo Farkas (HUN) d. Miroslav Brychta (CZE) 75 63. **MD:** Miroslav Brychta (CZE)/Frederic Cattaneo (FRA) d. Laszlo Farkas (HUN)/Gert Vos (BEL) 63 61. **QS:** Shraga Weinberg (ISR) d. Ido Fridman (ISR) 61 75.

- **TROFEO DELLA MOLE** (ITA) (ITF3S) ($11,000) 1-5 JUNE – **MS:** Tadeusz Kruszelnicki (POL) d. Martin Legner (AUT) 64 64. **MD:** Martin Legner (AUT)/Kai Schrameyer (GER) d. Jozef Felix (SVK)/Tadeusz Kruszelnicki (POL) 76(3) 60.

- **10TH ANTIBES OPEN** (FRA) (ITFFS) ($1,500) 2-5 JUNE – **WS:** Arlette Racineux (FRA) d. Susan Paisley (GBR) 60 64. **WD:** Christine Gontard/Arlette Racineux (FRA) d. Armelle Fabre/Christine Schoenn-Anchling (FRA) 62 64. **MS:** Eric Stuurman (NED) d. Lahcen Majdi (FRA) 76 62. **MD:** Laurent Giammartini (FRA)/Eric Stuurman (NED) d. Bernard Fasanelli/Lahcen Majdi (FRA) 62 57 75.

- **CANADIAN OPEN** (CAN) (ITF2S) ($15,000) 2-5 JUNE – **WS:** Yuka Chokyu (CAN) d. Helene Simard (CAN) 06 62 62. **MS:** Ronald Vink (NED) d. Jayant Mistry (GBR) 64 63. **MD:** Jayant Mistry (GBR)/Ronald Vink (NED) d. Derek Bolton/Paul Walker (USA) 61 63. **QS:** Sarah Hunter (CAN) d. David Jordan (USA) 76 67 62. **QD:** Brian McPhate/Sarah Hunter (CAN) d. Bryan Barten/David Jordan (USA) 76 67 62.

- **BIRKESDORF OPEN** (GER) (ITFFS) ($1,500) 3-5 JUNE – **WS:** Aniek Van Koot (NED) d. Dorrie Timmermans Van Hall (NED) 76 63. **WD:** Natalia Bakhmatova/Ludmila Bubnova (RUS) d. Dorrie Timmermans Van Hall/Mette Van Dongen (NED) 26 64 63. **MS:** Peter Seidl (GER) d. Steffen Sommerfeld (GER) 76 63. **MD:** Peter Seidl/Steffen Sommerfeld (GER) d. Sven Hiller/Pedro Kruemmel (GER) 61 61.

- **WHEELCHAIR CZECH OPEN** (CZE) (ITF1S) ($16,000) 8-12 JUNE – **WS:** Sharon Walraven (NED) d. Maaike Smit (NED) 63 62. **MS:** Robin Ammerlaan (NED) d. Martin Legner (AUT) 76(4) 75. **MD:** Robin Ammerlaan (NED)/Peter Wikstrom (SWE) d. Miroslav Brychta (CZE)/Martin Legner (AUT) 36 64 64.

- **ALBARELLA OPEN** (ITA) (ITFFS) ($5,000) 9-12 JUNE – **MS:** Laszlo Farkas (HUN) d. Leonid Shevchik (RUS) 60 64. **MD:** Laszlo Farkas/Csaba Prohaszka (HUN) d. Mirko Gerotto/Gerardo Riccardi (ITA) 63 61.

- **JANA HUNSAKER MEMORIAL** (USA) (ITF3S) ($7,500) 9-12 JUNE – **WS:** Yuka Chokyu (CAN) d. Beth Ann Arnoult-Ritthaler (USA) 61 62.

- **CARINTHIAN OPEN** (AUT) (ITFFS) ($1,500) 9-12 JUNE – **MS:** Manfred Sing (GER) d. Peter Seidl (GER) 63 61. **MD:** Herwig Pellosch (AUT)/Manfred Sing (GER) d. Thomas Mossier/Harald Pfundner (AUT) w/o.

- **TOURNOI HANDISPORT DE CAGNES SUR MER** (FRA) (ITFFS) ($1,500) 10-12 JUNE – **WS:** Christine Schoenn-Anchling (FRA) d. Cathy Portier (FRA) 64 62. **MS:** Bernard Fasanelli (FRA) d. Francois Xavier Morille (FRA) 63 57 75. **MD:** Sebastien Husser/Francois Xavier Morille (FRA) d. Bernard Fasanelli/Laurent Leseguillon (FRA) 62 64.

- **MUSIC CITY CLASSIC** (USA) (ITF3S) ($7,500) 10-12 JUNE – **MS:** Stephen Welch (USA) d. Derek Bolton (USA) 61 64. **MD:** Derek Bolton/Russell Rodriguez (USA) d. John Becker/Hunter Groce (USA) 26 62 55 ret. **QS:** David Jordan (USA) d. Marc McLean (USA) 60 64. **QD:** David Jordan/Marc McLean (USA) d. David Harrison/Troy Weise (USA) 75 60.

- **SLOVAKIA OPEN** (SVK) (ITF2S) ($11,000) 15-19 JUNE – **WS:** Sharon Walraven (NED) d. Karin Suter-Erath (SUI) 60 62. **MS:** Miroslav Brychta (CZE) d. Jozef Felix (SVK) 76(6) 64. **MD:** Jozef Felix (SVK)/Tadeusz Kruszelnicki (POL) d. Miroslav Brychta (CZE)/Martin Legner (AUT) w/o.

- **MERWEDE AMSTERDAM OPEN** (NED) (ITF2S) ($11,000) 16-19 JUNE – **WS:** Esther Vergeer (NED) d. Florence Gravellier (FRA) 62 60. **WD:** Jiske Griffioen/Esther Vergeer (NED) d. Korie Homan/Sonja Peters (NED) 62 61. **MS:** Michael Jeremiasz (FRA) d. Robin Ammerlaan (NED) 62 61. **MD:** Michael Jeremiasz/Lahcen Majdi (FRA) d. Robin Ammerlaan/Eric Stuurman (NED) 64 67(3) 62. **QS:** Nicholas Taylor (USA) d. David Wagner (USA) 64 63. **QD:** Nicholas Taylor/David Wagner (USA) d. Monique De Beer/Dorrie Timmermans Van Hall (NED) 63 60.

- **SARREGUEMINES HANDISPORT OPEN** (FRA) (ITF3S) ($10,000) 16-19 JUNE – **WS:** Arlette Racineux (FRA) d. Meliha Karic (FRA) 75 63. **WD:** Christine Gontard/Arlette Racineux (FRA) d. Parmila Grangie (SUI)/Meliha Karic (FRA) 60 63. **MS:** Frederic Cattaneo (FRA) d. Regis Harel (FRA) 63 63. **MD:** Frederic Cattaneo/Regis Harel (FRA) d. Laurent Fischer/Christian Gross (FRA) 46 61 76.

- **PITE CUPEN** (SWE) (ITFFS) ($1,500) 17-19 JUNE – **MS:** Peter Wikstrom (SWE) d. Niclas Larsson (SWE) 61 64.

- **ORLEN POLISH OPEN** (POL) (ITF2S) ($11,000) 28 JUNE-2 JULY – **WS:** Agnieszka Bartczak (POL) d. Anna Alenas (SWE) 62 76(1). **MS:** Peter Wikstrom (SWE) d. Tadeusz Kruszelnicki (POL) 76(4) 62. **MD:** Niclas Larsson/Peter Wikstrom (SWE) d. Jozef Felix (SVK)/ Tadeusz Kruszelnicki (POL) 61 75.

- **DAIMLERCHRYSLER OPEN** (NED) (ITF2S) ($12,000) 29 JUNE-3 JULY – **WS:** Esther Vergeer (NED) d. Korie Homan (NED) 62 61. **WD:** Jiske Griffioen/Esther Vergeer (NED) d. Chiyoko Ohmae/Mie Yaosa (JPN) 60 61. **MS:** Satoshi Saida (JPN) d. Robin Ammerlaan (NED) 75 60. **MD:** Shingo Kunieda/Satoshi Saida (JPN) d. Stefan Olsson (SWE)/Eric Stuurman (NED) 61 61. **QS:** David Wagner (USA) d. Sarah Hunter (CAN) 60 61.

- **BIRRHARD OPEN** (SUI) (ITFFS) ($1,500) 1-3 JULY – **WS:** Sandra Kalt (SUI) d. Parmila Grangier (SUI) 60 60. **MS:** Daniel Pellegrina (SUI) d. Laurent Fischer (FRA) 75 60. **MD:** Daniel Pellegrina/Thomas Suter (SUI) d. Konstantin Schmaeh (SUI)/Manfred Sing (GER) 61 64.

- **BNP PARIBAS FRENCH OPEN** (FRA) (ITF1S) ($20,000) 5-10 JULY – **WS:** Esther Vergeer (NED) d. Jiske Griffioen (NED) 61 60. **WD:** Jiske Griffioen/Esther Vergeer (NED) d. Florence Gravellier (FRA)/Maaike Smit (NED) 61 61. **MS:** Michael Jeremiasz (FRA) d. David Hall (AUS) 57 63 76(0). **MD:** Shingo Kunieda/Satoshi Saida (JPN) d. David Hall (AUS)/Michael Jeremiasz (FRA) 62 76(5). **QS:** David Wagner (USA) d. Andre Rousset (FRA) 62 60. **QD:** Guiseppe Polidori/Antonio Raffaele (ITA) d. Andre Rousset (FRA)/Monique De Beer (NED) 64 63.

- **DUTCH OPEN** (NED) (ITF2S) ($20,000) 12-17 JULY – **WS:** Esther Vergeer (NED) d. Jiske Griffioen (NED) 63 63. **WD:** Jiske Griffioen/ Esther Vergeer (NED) d. Korie Homan/Sonja Peters (NED) 60 61. **MS:** Robin Ammerlaan (NED) d. David Hall (AUS) 61 62. **MD:** Robin Ammerlaan/Eric Stuurman (NED) d. Maikel Scheffers/Ronald Vink (NED) 64 63. **QS:** David Wagner (USA) d. Monique De Beer (NED) 64 64. **QD:** Giuseppe Polidori/Antonio Raffaele (ITA) d. David Jordan/David Wagner (USA) 36 76 63.

- **BC OPEN** (CAN) (ITFFS) ($1,500) 15-17 JULY – **MS:** Christoph Trachsel (CAN) d. Anthony Anderson (USA) 61 26 63. **MD:** Anthony Anderson (USA)/Phillip Rowe (CAN) d. Yann Mathieu/Christoph Trachsel (CAN) 64 16 61.

- **BELGIAN OPEN** (BEL) (ITF2S) ($15,000) 19-24 JULY – **WS:** Esther Vergeer (NED) d. Sharon Walraven (NED) 61 76(2). **WD:** Maaike Smit/Esther Vergeer (NED) d. Korie Homan/Sonja Peters (NED) 61 61. **MS:** David Hall (AUS) d. Maikel Scheffers (NED) 63 61. **MD:** Michael Jeremiasz (FRA)/Gert Vos (BEL) d. David Hall (AUS)/Lee Hinson (USA) 62 64. **QS:** David Wagner (USA) d. Dorrie Timmermans Van Dall (NED) 62 63.

- **MIDWEST REGIONAL CHAMPIONSHIPS** (USA) (ITF3S) ($7,500) 22-24 JULY – **WS:** Helene Simard (CAN) d. Karin Korb (USA) 64 16 64. **WD:** Yuka Chokyu (CAN)/Jan Proctor (USA) d. Annie Morissette/Helene Simard (CAN) 63 61. **MS:** Stefane Goudou (FRA) d. Derek Bolton (USA) 36 63 63. **MD:** Derek Bolton/Daniel Lachman (USA) d. Stefane Goudou (FRA)/Yann Mathieu (CAN) 76(6) 64. **QS:** David Jordan (USA) d. Bryan Barten (USA) 76(6) 63. **QD:** David Jordan/Marc McLean (USA) d. Bryan Barten/Eric Daniels (USA) 62 46 63.

- **ROGERS OPEN AT STANLEY PARK** (CAN) (ITFFS) ($1,500) 22-24 JULY – **MS:** Robinson Mendez (CHI) d. Anthony Anderson (USA) w/o. **MD:** Robinson Mendez (CHI)/Phillip Rowe (CAN) d. Anthony Anderson (USA)/Christoph Trachsel (CAN) w/o.

- **BRITISH OPEN** (GBR) (ITFSS) ($22,000) 26-31 JULY – **WS:** Esther Vergeer (NED) d. Sharon Walraven (NED) 61 63. **WD:** Florence Gravellier (FRA)/Maaike Smit (NED) d. Esther Vergeer/Sharon Walraven (NED) 36 63 76(4). **MS:** David Hall (AUS) d. Michael Jeremiasz (FRA) 63 62. **MD:** David Hall (AUS)/Michael Jeremiasz (FRA) d. Robin Ammerlaan (NED)/Jayant Mistry (GBR) 62 64. **QS:** Peter Norfolk (GBR) d. David Wagner (USA) 76(3) 63. **QD:** Ido Fridman/Shraga Weinberg (ISR) d. Giuseppe Polidori/Antonio Raffaele (ITA) 64 64.

NEC Wheelchair Tennis Tour 2005 Results (continued)

- **BC INTERNATIONAL TENNIS FESTIVAL** (CAN) (ITFFS) ($1,000) 29-31 JULY – **MS:** Robinson Mendez (CHI) d. Phillip Rowe (CAN) 62 64. **MD:** Anthony Anderson (USA)/Christoph Trachsel (CAN) d. Jerome Bouvier (CAN)/Robinson Mendez (CHI) 75 75.

- **AUSTRIAN OPEN** (AUT) (ITF2S) ($17,000) 3-7 AUGUST – **WS:** Maaike Smit (NED) d. Agnieszka Bartczak (POL) 61 62. **MS:** Tadeusz Kruszelnicki (POL) d. Martin Legner (AUT) 63 75. **MD:** Miroslav Brychta (CZE)/Piotr Jaroszewski (POL) d. Niclas Larsson (SWE)/Steffen Sommerfeld (GER) 61 64.

- **SWISS OPEN** (SUI) (ITF1S) ($22,000) 9-14 AUGUST – **WS:** Esther Vergeer (NED) d. Florence Gravellier (FRA) 61 62. **WD:** Esther Vergeer/Sharon Walraven (NED) d. Korie Homan/Maaike Smit (NED) 64 64. **MS:** Michael Jeremiasz (FRA) d. Ronald Vink (NED) 61 61. **MD:** Michael Jeremiasz (FRA)/Jayant Mistry (GBR) d. Martin Legner (AUT)/Peter Wikstrom (SWE) 63 61. **QS:** David Wagner (USA) d. Andre Rousset (FRA) 60 63.

- **FLANDERS OPEN** (BEL) (ITF3S) ($7,500) 10-14 AUGUST – **WS:** Jiske Griffioen (NED) d. Brigitte Ameryckx (BEL) 62 76. **WD:** Brigitte Ameryckx (BEL)/Jiske Griffioen (NED) d. Agnieszka Bartczak (POL)/Lucy Shuker (GBR) 61 64. **MS:** Eric Stuurman (NED) d. Lahcen Majdi (FRA) 63 62. **MD:** Serge Biron/Lahcen Majdi (FRA) d. Eric Stuurman (NED)/Gert Vos (BEL) 60 46 76.

- **SSZ CUP** (CZE) (ITFFS) ($2,000) 12-14 AUGUST – **MS:** Miroslav Brychta (CZE) d. Jozef Felix (SVK) 64 60. **MD:** Miroslav Brychta/Michal Stefanu (CZE) d. Jozef Felix/Tomas Masaryk (SVK) 62 62.

- **CAPITAL CITY CLASSIC** (CAN) (ITFFS) ($1,500) 12-14 AUGUST – **MS:** Yann Mathieu (CAN) d. Claude Brunet (CAN) 64 64. **MD:** Yann Mathieu/Christoph Trachsel (CAN) d. Claude Brunet/Jeff McBride (CAN) 64 61.

- **BAVARIAN OPEN** (GER) (ITF2S) ($11,000) 18-21 AUGUST – **WS:** Sharon Walraven (NED) d. Karin Suter-Erath (SUI) 76 63. **MS:** Robin Ammerlaan (NED) d. Stephen Welch (USA) 61 64. **MD:** Miroslav Brychta (CZE)/Martin Legner (AUT) d. Robin Ammerlaan (NED)/Steffen Sommerfeld (GER) 46 62 75.

- **ATH OPEN** (BEL) (ITF3S) ($7,500) 18-21 AUGUST – **WS:** Jiske Griffioen (NED) d. Brigitte Ameryckx (BEL) 62 60. **WD:** Brigitte Ameryckx (BEL)/Jiske Griffioen (NED) d. Nadege Carlier/Louisa Van Der Wallen (BEL) 61 60. **MS:** Frederic Cazeaudumec (FRA) d. Lahcen Majdi (FRA) 26 61 63. **MD:** Frederic Cazeaudumec/Lahcen Majdi (FRA) d. Robinson Mendez (CHI)/Francesc Tur (ESP) w/o.

- **SZINVANET CUP** (HUN) (ITFFS) ($1,850) 19-21 AUGUST – **MS:** Jozef Felix (SVK) d. Laszlo Farkas (HUN) 63 36 75. **MD:** Jozef Felix/Tomas Masaryk (SVK) d. Laszlo Farkas/Csaba Prohaszka (HUN) 75 76(5).

- **SALZBURG OPEN** (AUT) (ITF2S) ($11,000) 25-28 AUGUST – **WS:** Annick Sevenans (BEL) d. Karin Suter-Erath (SUI) 64 62. **MS:** Stephen Welch (USA) d. Martin Legner (AUT) 61 64. **MD:** Miroslav Brychta (CZE)/Martin Legner (AUT) d. Piotr Jaroszewski/Tadeusz Kruszelnicki (POL) 64 75.

- **KANAGAWA OPEN** (JPN) (ITFFS) ($1,000) 25-28 AUGUST – **WS:** Mie Yaosa (JPN) d. Yuko Okabe (JPN) 62 60. **WD:** Naomi Ishimoto/Yuko Okabe (JPN) d. Rieko Iida/Keiko Nitta (JPN) 64 67(3) 62. **MS:** Hidekazu Nakano (JPN) d. Yoshinobu Fujimoto (JPN) 75 75. **MD:** Yoshinobu Fujimoto/Hiroyuki Takeda (JPN) d. Mizuhito Kawakami/Yasuaki Nagao (JPN) 62 36 64. **QS:** Masao Takashima (JPN) d. Hiroshi Toma (JPN) 46 63 62. **QD:** Sadahiro Kimura/Hiroshi Toma (JPN) d. Takahiro Koga/Masao Takashima (JPN) 62 61.

- **PACIFIC NORTHWEST SECTIONAL CHAMPS** (USA) (ITFFS) ($1,500) 26-28 AUGUST – **MS:** Anthony Anderson (USA) d. Claude Brunet (CAN) 36 62 63. **MD:** Phillip Rowe (CAN)/David Wagner (USA) d. Anthony Anderson/Patrick Jacobson (USA) 63 36 61.

- **INAIL CITTA DI LIVORNO** (ITA) (ITF1S) ($15,000) 30 AUGUST-4 SEPTEMBER – **WS:** Sharon Walraven (NED) d. Florence Gravellier (FRA) 64 36 63. **WD:** Florence Gravellier (FRA)/Sharon Walraven (NED) d. Annick Sevenans (BEL)/Karin Suter-Erath (SUI) 60 62. **MS:** Michael Jeremiasz (FRA) d. Martin Legner (AUT) 63 61. **MD:** Martin Legner (AUT)/Peter Wikstrom (SWE) d. Michael Jeremiasz (FRA)/Jayant Mistry (GBR) 26 75 64. **QS:** Monique De Beer (NED) d. Antonio Raffaele (ITA) 63 36 64. **QD:** Giuseppe Polidori/Antonio Raffaele (ITA) d. Patrick Sappino (FRA)/Monique De Beer (NED) 63 61.

- **JESOLO EURO BEACH CUP** (ITA) (ITF2S) ($16,000) 6-10 SEPTEMBER – **WS:** Sharon Walraven (NED) d. Karin Suter-Erath (SUI) 62 61. **WD:** Karin Suter-Erath (SUI)/Aniek Van Koot (NED) d. Janet McMorran/Lucy Shuker (GBR) 60 63. **MS:** Tadeusz Kruszelnicki (POL) d. Martin Legner (AUT) 60 62. **MD:** Miroslav Brychta (CZE)/Martin Legner (AUT) d. Frederic Cazeaudumec (FRA)/Tadeusz Kruszelnicki (POL) 62 62.

- **US OPEN** (USA) (ITFMS) 8-11 SEPTEMBER – **WS:** Esther Vergeer (NED) d. Korie Homan (NED) 62 61. **WD:** Korie Homan/Esther Vergeer (NED) d. Beth Ann Arnoult-Ritthaler/Jan Proctor (USA) 63 61. **MS:** Robin Ammerlaan (NED) d. Michael Jeremiasz (FRA) 61 63. **MD:** Robin Ammerlaan (NED)/Michael Jeremiasz (FRA) d. David Hall (AUS)/Jayant Mistry (GBR) 61 62.

- **WROCLAW CUP** (POL) (ITF3S) ($7,500) 9-11 SEPTEMBER – **WS:** Agnieszka Bartczak (POL) d. Agniezska Gidzinska (POL) 62 60. **MS:** Peter Wikstrom (SWE) d. Piotr Jaroszewski (POL) 75 63. **MD:** Piotr Jaroszewski (POL)/Peter Wikstrom (SWE) d. Jozef Felix (SVK)/ Michal Stefanu (CZE) 61 64.

- **PELLIKAAN WHEELS TOURNAMENT** (NED) (ITFFS) ($8,700) 9-11 SEPTEMBER – **WS:** Willemien Smits (NED) d. Rianka Timmermans (NED) 61 63. **WD:** Rianka Timmermans/Yolanda Van Raay Baarends (NED) d. Willemien Smits/Ingrid Van Steen (NED) 64 60. **MS:** Maikel Scheffers (NED) d. Jasper Touw (NED) 60 60. MD: Koen Meerwijk/Maikel Scheffers (NED) d. Gert Dogger/Tom Egberink (NED) 61 61.

- **BANGKOK CUP** (THA) (ITFFS) ($1,500) 9-11 SEPTEMBER – **MS:** Wittaya Peem-Mee (THA) d. Suwitchai Muangprom (THA) 62 62. **MD:** Suwitchai Muangprom/Wittaya Peem-Mee (THA) d. Suthi Khlongrua/Sumrerng Kruamai (THA) 62 63.

- **USTA NATIONAL INDOOR ROHO GATEWAY CLASSIC** (USA) (ITF2S) ($15,000) 13-17 SEPTEMBER – **WS:** Esther Vergeer (NED) d. Korie Homan (NED) 61 63. **WD:** Korie Homan/Esther Vergeer (NED) d. Beth Ann Arnoult-Ritthaler (USA)/Yuka Chokyu (CAN) 64 64. **MS:** Stephen Welch (USA) d. Jayant Mistry (GBR) 64 60. **MD:** Derek Bolton/Stephen Welch (USA) d. Thomas Mossier/Harald Pfundner (AUT) 64 63. **QS:** David Wagner (USA) d. David Jordan (USA) 60 64. **QD:** Nicholas Taylor/David Wagner (USA) d. David Jordan/Marc McLean (USA) 62 62.

- **CESENATICO OPEN** (ITA) (ITF2S) ($10,000) 14-18 SEPTEMBER – **WS:** Ilanit Fridman (ISR) d. Stefania Galletti (ITA) 61 60. **MS:** Tadeusz Kruszelnicki (POL) d. Martin Legner (AUT) 76(4) 62. **MD:** Miroslav Brychta (CZE)/Martin Legner (AUT) d. Tadeusz Kruszelnicki (POL)/ Ben Weekes (AUS) 61 61.

- **SENDAI OPEN** (JPN) (ITFFS) ($1,500) 16-19 SEPTEMBER – **WS:** Kanako Domori (JPN) d. Naomi Ishimoto (JPN) 63 46 61. **WD:** Kanako Domori/Chie Ito (JPN) d. Kaori Nakagawa/Keiko Nitta (JPN) 62 62. **MS:** Hidekazu Nakano (JPN) d. Kazutaka Katou (JPN) 64 76(5). **MD:** Kazutaka Katou/Hidekazu Nakano (JPN) d. Toshio Ikenoya/Takao Ishii (JPN) 61 57 64. **QS:** Masao Takashima (JPN) d. Koki Terui (JPN) 60 60.

- **TAIPEI OPEN** (TPE) (ITFFS) ($1,500) 16-19 SEPTEMBER – **WS:** Hsiao-Yun Hsu (TPE) d. Hui-Ying Wu (TPE) 64 64. **WD:** Miew-Kuan Chung (SIN)/Hsiao-Yun Hsu (TPE) d. Yi-Shan Wu/Shu-Chin Yu (TPE) 64 63. **MS:** Han Tsung Cheng (TPE) d. Isamu Yamane (JPN) 63 67(3) 62. **MD:** Han Tsung Cheng (TPE)/Yasin Onasie (INA) d. Hiroyuki Takeda/Isamu Yamane (JPN) 64 62.

- **SOUTH PACIFIC WHEELCHAIR TENNIS OPEN** (AUS) (ITFFS) ($2,500) 16-18 SEPTEMBER – **MS:** Anthony Bonaccurso (AUS) d. Mick Connell (AUS) 64 60. **MD:** Anthony Bonaccurso/Mick Connell (AUS) d. Michael Esler/Jerry Markoja (AUS) 60 61.

- **SARDINIA OPEN** (ITA) (ITF2S) ($13,000) 20-24 SEPTEMBER – **WS:** Ilanit Fridman (ISR) d. Lucy Shuker (GBR) 26 62 63. **WD:** Janet McMorran/Lucy Shuker (GBR) d. Marianna Lauro/Monica Quassinti (ITA) 62 63. **MS:** Peter Wikstrom (SWE) d. Martin Legner (AUT) 64 76(6). **MD:** Miroslav Brychta (CZE)/Martin Legner (AUT) d. Ben Weekes (AUS)/Peter Wikstrom (SWE) 60 63.

- **ARAG GERMAN OPEN** (GER) (ITF3S) ($7,500) 21-25 SEPTEMBER – **WS:** Aniek Van Koot (NED) d. Agnieszka Bartczak (POL) 60 62. **WD:** Agnieszka Bartczak (POL)/Katharina Kruger (GER) d. Nora Sommerfeld (GER)/Aniek Van Koot (NED) 62 64. **MS:** Maikel Scheffers (NED) d. Frederic Cazeaudumec (FRA) 67 76 63. **MD:** Maikel Scheffers/Eric Stuurman (NED) d. Frederic Cattaneo (FRA)/Jozef Felix (SVK) 63 64.

- **PTR/ROHO CHAMPIONSHIPS** (USA) (ITF1S) ($15,000) 21-25 SEPTEMBER – **WS:** Esther Vergeer (NED) d. Jiske Griffioen (NED) 62 64. **MS:** David Hall (AUS) d. Jayant Mistry (GBR) 61 36 62. **MD:** David Hall (AUS)/Jayant Mistry (GBR) d. Derek Bolton/Daniel Lachman (USA) 60 62. **QS:** David Wagner (USA) d. David Jordan (USA) 60 61. **QD:** David Jordan/Chris Studwell (USA) d. Marc McLean/David Wagner (USA) 62 75.

- **OSAKA OPEN** (JPN) (ITFFS) ($2,500) 22-25 SEPTEMBER – **WS:** Fuli Dong (CHN) d. Kanako Domori (JPN) 61 64. **WD:** Kanako Domori/ Rieko Iida (JPN) d. Chie Ito/Keiko Nitta (JPN) 63 62. **MS:** Takahiro Hirate (JPN) d. Hidekazu Nakano (JPN) 75 63. **MD:** Hidekazu Nakano/ Hiroyuki Takeda (JPN) d. Mizuhito Kawakami/Masaaki Taga (JPN) 62 75. **QS:** Sadahiro Kimura (JPN) d. Hiroshi Toma (JPN) 26 61 62. **QD:** Sadahiro Kimura/Hiroshi Toma (JPN) d. Ryuji Kakinokihara/Kazumi Ohashi (JPN) 64 46 75.

NEC Wheelchair Tennis Tour 2005 Results (continued)

- **SACRAMENTO CAPITALS** (USA) (ITFFS) ($1,500) 23-25 SEPTEMBER – **MD:** Yann Mathieu/Phillip Rowe (CAN) d. Donald Bearden/Michael Pruitt-Yousefi (USA) 61 61.

- **TAHOE DONNER INTERNATIONAL CHAMPIONSHIPS** (USA) (ITF3S) ($8,000) 29 SEPTEMBER-2 OCTOBER – **WS:** Yuka Chokyu (CAN) d. Ilanit Fridman (ISR) 63 61. **WD:** Yuka Chokyu (CAN)/Ilanit Fridman (ISR) d. Jan Proctor (USA)/Helene Simard (CAN) 62 67(5) 62. **MS:** Robinson Mendez (CHI) d. Jeff McBride (CAN) 61 60. **MD:** Anthony Anderson (USA)/Lee Carter (CAN) d. Francisco Cayulef/Robinson Mendez (CHI) 64 63. **QS:** Jim Carlton (USA) d. Patrick Sappino (FRA) 62 62.

- **GIRONA COSTA BRAVA OPEN** (ESP) (ITF3S) ($7,500) 29 SEPTEMBER-2 OCTOBER – **WS:** Karin Suter-Erath (SUI) d. Janet McMorran (GBR) 63 16 63. **WD:** Janet McMorran (GBR)/Karin Suter-Erath (SUI) d. Anna Alenas (SWE)/Nadege Carlier (BEL) 60 60. **MS:** Ben Weekes (AUS) d. Frederic Cattaneo (FRA) 63 64. **MD:** Frederic Cattaneo (FRA)/Ben Weekes (AUS) d. Francesc Tur (ESP)/Gert Vos (BEL) 64 61.

- **ATLANTA WHEELCHAIR TENNIS MASTERS SERIES** (USA) (ITFMS) ($50,000) 30 SEPTEMBER-2 OCTOBER – **WS:** Esther Vergeer (NED) d. Jiske Griffioen (NED) 63 60. **WD:** Jiske Griffioen/Esther Vergeer (NED) d. Korie Homan/Maaike Smit (NED) 61 75. **MS:** David Hall (AUS) d. Michael Jeremiasz (FRA) 62 75. **MD:** Robin Ammerlaan (NED)/Martin Legner (AUT) d. Shingo Kunieda/Satoshi Saida (JPN) 67 60 64. **QS:** David Wagner (USA) d. Nicholas Taylor (USA) 64 63. **QD:** Nicholas Taylor/David Wagner (USA) d. Giuseppe Polidori/Antonio Raffaele (ITA) 63 63.

- **US OPEN (USTA NATIONAL WHEELCHAIR CHAMPIONSHIPS)** (USA) (ITFSS) ($22,000) 4-9 OCTOBER – **WS:** Esther Vergeer (NED) d. Jiske Griffioen (NED) 62 62. **WD:** Jiske Griffioen/Esther Vergeer (NED) d. Florence Gravellier (FRA)/Maaike Smit (NED) 64 75. **MS:** Michael Jeremiasz (FRA) d. Satoshi Saida (JPN) 75 63. **MD:** Shingo Kunieda/Satoshi Saida (JPN) d. David Hall (AUS)/Michael Jeremiasz (FRA) 46 61 61. **QS:** Nicholas Taylor (USA) d. David Wagner (USA) 62 64. **QD:** Nicholas Taylor/David Wagner (USA) d. Giuseppe Polidori/Antonio Raffaele (ITA) 60 60.

- **KOREA CUP** (KOR) (ITFFS) ($1,500) 11-13 OCTOBER – **WS:** Young-Suk Hong (KOR) d. Ju-Yeon Park (KOR) 60 61. **WD:** Young-Suk Hong/Myung-Hee Hwang (KOR) d. Young-Sil Cho/Ju-Yeon Park (KOR) 60 60. **MS:** Ha-Gel Lee (KOR) d. Seung-Jin Kim (KOR) 64 62. **MD:** Dong-Ju Kwak/Ha-Gel Lee (KOR) d. Sam-Ju Kim/Seung-Jin Kim (KOR) 61 75.

- **HAWAII PACIFIC OPEN WHEELCHAIR CHAMPIONSHIPS** (USA) (ITFFS) ($3,000) 12-16 OCTOBER – **MS:** Robinson Mendez (CHI) d. Richard Julian (USA) 61 62. **MD:** Richard Julian (USA)/Robinson Mendez (CHI) d. Francisco Cayulef (CHI)/Fabio Padilla (COL) 60 75.

- **GRENOBLE OPEN** (FRA) (ITF3S) ($9,000) 13-16 OCTOBER – **WS:** Karin Suter-Erath (SUI) d. Janet McMorran (GBR) 63 63. **WD:** Katharina Kruger (GER)/Karin Suter-Erath (SUI) d. Christine Gontard/Arlette Racineux (FRA) 64 64. **MS:** Frederic Cazeaudumec (FRA) d. Laszlo Farkas (HUN) 60 61. **MD:** Frederic Cattaneo (FRA)/Laszlo Farkas (HUN) d. Frederic Cazeaudumec/Lahcen Majdi (FRA) w/o. **QS:** Andre Rousset (FRA) d. Adam Field (GBR) 61 62.

- **VICTORIAN WHEELCHAIR OPEN** (AUS) (ITFFS) ($1,500) 15-16 OCTOBER – **WS:** Alana Duncombe (AUS) d. Anne Wells (AUS) 61 61. **WD:** Alana Duncombe/Rosalie Turnbull (AUS) d. Narelle Henderson/Anne Wells (AUS) 64 76. **MS:** Ben Weekes (AUS) d. Lee Hinson (USA) 76 64. **MD:** Dylan Alcott/Ben Weekes (AUS) d. Michael Esler/David Latham (AUS) 61 62.

- **PEACE CUP** (JPN) (ITF3S) ($7,500) 19-23 OCTOBER – **WS:** Mie Yaosa (JPN) d. Young-Suk Hong (KOR) 16 61 61. **WD:** Young-Suk Hong/Myung-Hee Hwang (KOR) d. Yuka Chokyu (CAN)/Ju-Yeon Park (KOR) 60 63. **MS:** Shingo Kunieda (JPN) d. Ha-Gel Lee (KOR) 61 64. **MD:** Seung-Jin Kim/Ha-Gel Lee (KOR) d. Yasuaki Nagao/Koji Niitani (JPN) 61 62. **QS:** Tzu-Hsuan Huang (TPE) d. Masao Takashima (JPN) 64 64. **QD:** Tzu-Hsuan Huang (TPE)/Masao Takashima (JPN) d. Sadahiro Kimura/Hiroshi Toma (JPN) 64 76(2).

- **ESPORTA CARDIFF** (GBR) (ITFFS) ($1,500) 21-23 OCTOBER – **WS:** Debbie Thomas (GBR) d. Debbie Brazier (GBR) 63 61. **WD:** Susan Paisley/Debbie Thomas (GBR) d. Gill James/Jordanne Whiley (GBR) 64 60. **MS:** Matthew Faucher (GBR) d. Kevin Plowman (GBR) 26 64 64. **MD:** Kevin Plowman/Paul Simmons (GBR) d. Matthew Faucher/James Robinson (GBR) 64 75.

- **TOURNOI DE MONTFERMEIL** (FRA) (ITFFS) ($3,000) 21-23 OCTOBER – **WS:** Arlette Racineux (FRA) d. Christine Schoenn-Anchling (FRA) 61 63. **MS:** Frederic Cattaneo (FRA) d. Francois Xavier Morille (FRA) 64 63. **MD:** Laurent Fischer/Francois Xavier Morille (FRA) d. Frederic Cattaneo/Pascal Chessel (FRA) 57 60 61.

- **LILLACUPEN** (SWE) (ITFFS) ($1,500) 28-30 OCTOBER – **MS:** Peter Wikstrom (SWE) d. Stefan Olsson (SWE) 63 63. **MD:** Stefan Olsson/Peter Wikstrom (SWE) d. Martin Kallberg/Niclas Larsson (SWE) 61 75.

- **NOTTINGHAM INDOOR TOURNAMENT** (GBR) (ITF2S) ($11,000) 3-6 NOVEMBER – **WS:** Jiske Griffioen (NED) d. Lucy Shuker (GBR) 60 60. **WD:** Jiske Griffioen/Aniek Van Koot (NED) d. Janet McMorran/Lucy Shuker (GBR) 60 64. **MS:** Michael Jeremiasz (FRA) d. Peter Wikstrom (SWE) 61 60. **MD:** Michael Jeremiasz (FRA)/Jayant Mistry (GBR) d. Stefan Olsson/Peter Wikstrom (SWE) 63 75. **QS:** Peter Norfolk (GBR) d. Shraga Weinberg (ISR) 63 64. **QD**: Peter Norfolk (GBR)/Monique De Beer (NED) d. Giuseppe Polidori/Antonio Raffaele (ITA) 60 60.

- **NSW WHEELCHAIR TENNIS OPEN** (AUS) (ITFFS) ($2,500) 4-6 NOVEMBER – **MS:** Mick Connell (AUS) d. Lee Hinson (USA) 63 67 62. **MD:** Mick Connell/Errol Hyde (AUS) d. Ben Baker/David Coulston (AUS) 61 60.

- **CAMOZZI WHEELCHAIR TENNIS DOUBLES MASTERS** (ITA) (ITFMS) ($40,000) 8-13 NOVEMBER – **WD:** Jiske Griffioen/Esther Vergeer (NED) d. Florence Gravellier (FRA)/Maaike Smit (NED) 61 62. **MD:** Ammerlaan/Eric Stuurman (NED) d. Tadeusz Kruszelnicki (POL)/ Peter Wikstrom (SWE) 63 63. **QD:** Patrick Sappino (FRA)/Dorrie Timmermans Van Hall (NED) d. David Jordan/Marc McLean (USA) 61 75.

- **CIS MARIN INDOOR** (SUI) (ITFFS) ($1,500) 11-13 NOVEMBER – **WS:** Parmila Grangier (SUI) d. Susanne Bertschy (SUI) 60 46 60. **MS:** Sebastien Husser (FRA) d. Daniel Pellegrina (SUI) 61 62. **MD:** Bernard Fasanelli/Sebastien Husser (FRA) d. Daniel Pellegrina (SUI)/ Harald Pfundner (AUT) 76 76.

- **NEC WHEELCHAIR TENNIS MASTERS** (NED) (ITFMS) ($40,000) 15-20 NOVEMBER – **WS:** Mie Yaosa (JPN) d. Agnieszka Bartczak (POL) 62 67(4) 60. **MS:** Tadeusz Kruszelnicki (POL) d. Martin Legner (AUT) 63 64. **QS:** Monique De Beer (NED) d. David Jordan (USA) 61 60.

- **HUNGARIAN OPEN** (HUN) (ITF2S) ($8,000) 23-26 NOVEMBER – **MS:** Tadeusz Kruszelnicki (POL) d. Martin Legner (AUT) 26 63 62. **MD:** Miroslav Brychta (CZE)/Martin Legner (AUT) d. Piotr Jaroszewski/Tadeusz Kruszelnicki (POL) 75 63.

- **LA CLASSIQUE INTERNATIONALE OPHQ** (CAN) (ITF2S) ($11,000) 1-4 DECEMBER – **WS:** Florence Gravellier (FRA) d. Helene Simard (CAN) 61 64. **MS:** Maikel Scheffers (NED) d. Gert Vos (BEL) 61 61. **MD:** Maikel Scheffers (NED)/Gert Vos (BEL) d. Frederic Cazeaudumec/ Stefane Goudou (FRA) def. **QS:** Patrick Sappino (FRA) d. Adrian Dieleman (CAN) 61 63.

- **PRAGUE CUP CZECH INDOOR** (CZE) (ITF3S) ($7,900) 1-4 DECEMBER – **WS:** Lola Ochoa (ESP) d. Lucy Shuker (GBR) 62 75. **WD:** Janet McMorran/Lucy Shuker (GBR) d. Agnieszka Bartczak/Lucyna Skorupinska (POL) 75 63. **MS**: Tadeusz Kruszelnicki (POL) d. Stefan Olsson (SWE) 61 63. **MD:** Frederic Cattaneo (FRA)/Jozef Felix (SVK) d. Miroslav Brychta (CZE)/Martin Legner (AUT) 64 61. **QS:** Christer Jansson (SWE) d. Adam Field (GBR) 64 63.

- **CENTRAL COAST OPEN** (AUS) (ITFFS) ($1,500) 2-4 DECEMBER – **MS:** Ben Weekes (AUS) d. Justin Pryor (AUS) 64 62. **MD:** Michael Dobbie/ Ben Weekes (AUS) d. Mick Connell (AUS)/Lee Hinson (USA) 64 64.

- **AUCKLAND CHAMPS** (NZL) (ITFFS) ($1,500) 10-12 DECEMBER – **WS:** Jacqueline Courtier (NZL) d. Tiffiney Perry (NZL) 62 63. **MS:** Glenn Barnes (NZL) d. Dave Venter (NZL) 76(4) 60. **MD:** Glenn Barnes/Cameron Hastings (NZL) d. Danny McBride/Dave Venter (NZL) 60 76(3).

Invacare World Team Cup 2005

Groningen, Netherlands, 21-26 June 2005

Men's World Group 1 final standings: 1. Netherlands, 2. Japan, 3. France, 4. Australia, 5. Sweden, 6. Poland, 7. Czech Republic, 8. Great Britain, 9. Austria, 10. Slovak Republic, 11. Germany, 12. Korea, Rep. 13. Spain, 14. USA, 15. Brazil, 16. Argentina.

Final: Netherlands d. Poland 2-0: Shingo Kunieda (JPN) d. Eric Stuurman (NED) 60 63; Robin Ammerlaan (NED) d. Satoshi Saida (JPN) 62 60; Robin Ammerlaan/Ronald Vink (NED) d. Shingo Kunieda/Satoshi Saida (JPN) 75 76(4).

Men's World Group 2 final standings: 1. Hungary, 2. Italy, 3. Chile, 4. Switzerland, 5. Belgium, 6. Canada, 7. Israel, 8. Chinese Taipei, 9. Russia, 10. Sri Lanka, 11. Croatia, 12. Finland, 13. Denmark, 14. China, P.R. 15. Greece, 16. South Africa.

Final: Hungary d. Italy 2-1: Fabian Mazzei (ITA) d. Sandor Navratyil (HUN) 60 60; Laszlo Farkas (HUN) d. Diego Amadori (ITA) 60 60; Laszlo Farkas/Csaba Prohaszka (HUN) d. Fabian Mazzei/Luca Spano (ITA) 62 64.

Women's final standings: 1. Netherlands, 2. Korea, Rep. 3. Switzerland, 4. Canada, 5. USA, 6. France, 7. Japan, 8. Belgium, 9. Russia, 10. Poland, 11. Spain, 12. Chinese Taipei, 13. China, P.R. 14. Italy, 15. Great Britain.

Final: Netherlands d. Korea, Rep. 2-0: Esther Vergeer (NED) d. Young-Suk Hong (KOR) 61 62; Jiske Griffioen (NED) d. Ju-Yeon Park (KOR) 61 60.

Quad's final standings: 1. USA, 2. Israel, 3. Netherlands, 4. Italy, 5. Canada, 6. Great Britain, 7. Japan, 8. Sweden.

Final: USA d. Israel 2-0: Nick Taylor (USA) d. Ido Fridman (ISR) 63 46 60; David Wagner (USA) d. Shraga Weinberg (ISR) 61 63.

Juniors' final standings: 1. Belgium, 2. Australia, 3. Netherlands, 4. USA, 5. France, 6. Germany, 7. Great Britain, 8. Poland.

Final: Belgium d. Australia 2-0: Mike Denayer (BEL) d. Richard Engles (AUS) 62 75; Joachim Gerard (BEL) d. Michael Esler (AUS) 75 63.

ITF Wheelchair Tennis World Rankings 2005

Men's Singles

Rank	Name	Points	Played
1	Michael Jeremiasz (FRA)	2095	14
2	David Hall (AUS)	1950	14
3	Robin Ammerlaan (NED)	1821	16
4	Tadeusz Kruszelnicki (POL)	1301	17
5	Satoshi Saida (JPN)	1227	11
6	Martin Legner (AUT)	1227	24
7	Stephen Welch (USA)	1196	11
8	Shingo Kunieda (JPN)	1077	11
9	Peter Wikstrom (SWE)	1036	18
10	Ronald Vink (NED)	1019	14

Men's Doubles

Rank	Name	Points	Played
1	Michael Jeremiasz (FRA)	1961	15
2	Robin Ammerlaan (NED)	1776	15
3	David Hall (AUS)	1714	15
4	Martin Legner (AUT)	1689	24
5	Jayant Mistry (GBR)	1631	17
6	Satoshi Saida (JPN)	1626	11
7	Peter Wikstrom (SWE)	1485	18
8	Miroslav Brychta (CZE)	1451	18
9	Shingo Kunieda (JPN)	1442	10
10	Tadeusz Kruszelnicki (POL)	1168	17

Women's Singles

Rank	Name	Points	Played
1	Esther Vergeer (NED)	2009	16
2	Sharon Walraven (NED)	1576	18
3	Jiske Griffioen (NED)	1468	21
4	Florence Gravellier (FRA)	1347	17
5	Maaike Smit (NED)	1144	15
6	Korie Homan (NED)	949	16
7	Mie Yaosa (JPN)	818	11
8	Karin Suter-Erath (SUI)	782	12
9	Agnieszka Bartczak (POL)	634	12
10	Yuka Chokyu (CAN)	634	15

Women's Doubles

Rank	Name	Points	Played
1	Florence Gravellier (FRA)	1770	15
2	Jiske Griffioen (NED)	1767	19
3	Esther Vergeer (NED)	1688	14
4	Maaike Smit (NED)	1601	14
5	Sharon Walraven (NED)	1415	12
6	Yuka Chokyu (CAN)	1219	12
7	Karin Suter-Erath (SUI)	1163	10
8	Korie Homan (NED)	1071	13
9	Janet McMorran (GBR)	883	11
10	Lucy Shuker (GBR)	856	9

Quads Singles

Rank	Name	Points	Played
1	David Wagner (USA)	1224	17
2	Nicholas Taylor (USA)	1002	7
3	Peter Norfolk (GBR)	938	4
4	David Jordan (USA)	763	15
5	Sarah Hunter (CAN)	745	7
6	Monique De Beer (NED)	736	9
7	Giuseppe Polidori (ITA)	580	8
8	Patrick Sappino (FRA)	465	9
9	Andre Rousset (FRA)	448	4
10	Antonio Raffaele (ITA)	440	9

Quads Doubles

Rank	Name	Points	Played
1	David Wagner (USA)	1191	14
2	Nicholas Taylor (USA)	1188	7
3=	Antonio Raffaele (ITA)	1031	9
3=	Giuseppe Polidori (ITA)	1031	9
5	David Jordan (USA)	813	14
6	Sarah Hunter (CAN)	783	6
7	Marc McLean (USA)	696	10
8	Monique de Beer (NED)	566	6
9	Peter Norfolk (GBR)	544	4
10	Brian McPhate (CAN)	527	7

the seniors year 2005

by helen mcfetridge

Tennis is often described as a game for those aged eight to 80, but for some of the players on the ITF Seniors Circuit, 80 is only the beginning. Three players in their ninth decade became World Champions for the very first time this year, and none of them plan to stop there.

Jo Louis (GBR)

These days, players are remaining fitter and able to play competitive tennis for longer than ever, and the ITF endeavours to cater for these older players as far as possible in the events we provide. For this reason, a competition for women aged 80 and over was held for the first time this year at the Super-Seniors World Individual Championships in Antalya, Turkey. Dorothy Knode (USA) was the inaugural 80s World Champion, claiming her first ever ITF Seniors world title a full half-century after reaching her first Grand Slam final in 1955. Other octogenarians to become singles world champions for the first time were Graydon Nichols (USA) in the men's 80s and Gerry Ells (GBR) in the men's 85s. Donna Fales (USA) also won her first world championship in the women's 65 singles, while Petro Kruger (RSA) ended an 11-year wait for a second singles crown when she upset world No. 1 Heide Orth (GER) to take the women's 60s title.

Lorne Main (CAN) broke his own record for the most world championship wins when he claimed an incredible ninth singles title and tenth doubles crown in 19 years of seniors competition, this in the men's 75s event. Other world champions crowned in Antalya were a trio of Americans who successfully defended their titles from last year, Jimmy Parker in the men's 60s, King Van Nostrand in the men's 70s and Louise Russ in the women's 75s. Peter Pokorny (AUT) in the men's 65s and Margaret Robinson (AUS) in the women's 70s complete the list of winners, both reclaiming the world titles they won in the same venue two years ago.

> Lorne Main (CAN) broke his own record for the most world championship wins when he claimed an incredible ninth singles title and 10th doubles crown in 19 years of seniors competition.

As usual, the Super-Seniors World Team Championships were held the week prior to the individuals, with the USA just as dominant in the first as they were in the second. In fact, the Americans won five of the nine cups on offer, equalling their haul of last year and underlining their dominance in the older age categories.

The United States teams, who were top seeds in seven of the nine events, and with several world No.1s and past world champions in their squads, were heavily favoured to be the big winners of the week. They went on to capture the Von Cramm Cup (men's 60), Jack Crawford Cup (men's 70), Gardnar Mulloy (men's 80), Althea Gibson Cup (women's 70) and Queens' Cup (women's 75), and also picked up silver medals in the Britannia Cup (men's 65) and Bitsy Grant Cup (men's 75). The Americans have an almost unbreakable hold on the oldest age categories, having won the Gardnar Mulloy Cup nine times in the competition's ten-year history and the Queens' Cup all four years that it has been in existence.

The Britannia Cup was won for the second time by second seeded Austria with USA taking second place and France picking up the bronze medal. France also took the silver medal in the Kitty Godfree Cup (women's 65), losing to Australia in a reverse of last year's final result. The French did manage to take home one trophy however, as they defeated Germany to clinch the Alice Marble Cup (women's 60) in the most dramatic final of the week. Gail Lovera (FRA) saved match points against Heide Orth (GER) in the No.1 singles to level the final at one rubber apiece and then teamed up with Michele Bichon to win the doubles and claim the cup for France.

The Bitsy Grant Cup (men's 75) was won for the first time by the Lorne Main-led Canadian team, who defeated the Americans in an exciting final which went down to the third set of the deciding doubles.

Earlier in the year, the younger seniors (age categories 35 to 55) had their World Championships in the sunshine of Perth, Australia. As with the Super-Seniors, both Team and Individual events were hotly contested by players in some cases just a few years off the ATP and WTA Tours.

In the team competitions, home advantage proved to be key for the Australians, who made the most of some of their opponents' discomfort on grass to win four of the ten cups. They retained the Fred Perry Cup (men's 50) and Maureen Connolly Cup (women's 55), and also won the Austria Cup (men's 55) and Margaret Court Cup (women's 45). It was particularly fitting that the Australians managed to win the cup named after their nation's most successful ever female player, as Court actually lives in Perth and had spoken at the championships' opening ceremony.

Lorne Main (CAN)

the seniors year 2005

by will fletcher and helen mcfetridge

The home team also took silver medals in the Maria Esther Bueno Cup (women's 50), going down 2-1 to the Netherlands in a tight match but confirming that in the 45-55 age categories, they are very much the nation to beat.

If Australia dominated the oldest age categories in Perth, USA did the same in the 40-45 age groups, winning the Tony Trabert Cup (men's 40), Dubler Cup (men's 45) and Young Cup (women's 40), and losing 2-1 to Australia in the final of the Margaret Court Cup. And in the 35s age category, France and Great Britain were a cut above the rest, contesting both finals with the French coming out on top each time. Both results were a surprise, with the French ladies having been unseeded in the Suzanne Lenglen Cup and their male counterparts, seeded second, overcoming the top seeded British team in the Italia Cup final.

As in the team events, the Americans and Australians were the big winners in the Individual Championships the following week, between them capturing 14 of the 20 titles on offer. For the USA, Mario Tabares and Bob Litwin took their first ever Seniors world titles in the men's 40s and 55s respectively, while Val Wilder came agonisingly close to defending his 45s singles title before falling to Australian Patrick Serret in the week's closest final 67(3) 75 76(6). Other Australian singles winners were Ros Balodis in the women's 45s and Elizabeth Craig-Allan in the women's 55s, although perhaps Craig-Allan's greatest achievement came in the doubles where she recorded an amazing thirteenth successive win, the last five with countrywoman Kerry Ballard.

Most of the women's singles finals were surprisingly one-sided affairs, with Florence Boucard defeating her French Suzanne Lenglen Cup team-mate Marie-Dominique Bahu 63 61 in the women's 35s and Elly Appel (NED) dropping just two games to Sherri Bronson (USA) in the 50 age category. However, there was one final which went the distance as South Africa's Rene Plant took her first world title with a 61 36 64 win over Sylvie Mattel (FRA) in the women's 40s.

There was a similarly close final in the men's 50s, as Alan Rasmussen (DEN) overcame local favourite Wayne Pascoe 62 57 64 to disappoint the home fans.

There was a similarly close final in the men's 50s, as Alan Rasmussen (DEN) overcame local favourite Wayne Pascoe 62 57 64 to disappoint the home fans. And in the men's 35s, top seed Chris Wilkinson (GBR) claimed the title at his first attempt when defending champion Sander Groen (NED) was forced to retire when trailing 64 41.

Although the World Championships are undoubtedly the most important feature of the ITF Seniors calendar, the circuit continues throughout the year with many players travelling the globe with just as much intensity as in their professional days. Peter Adrigan, who finished 2005 as world No. 1 in the men's 60s category, played in 14 tournaments to edge out Peter Pokorny for the top spot. The two actually finished with the same number of points, but Adrigan finished on top due to his runner-up finish in the World Championships, where Pokorny had only competed in the 65s event. Pokorny did however claim the top spot in the 65s, where he lost just one set throughout the entire year.

As in the 60s, the men's 80s category finished the year with two players tied on the same number of points, Oskar Jirkovsky (AUT) and Fred Kovaleski of the USA. And again as in the 60s, a runner-up finish in the World Championships was the deciding factor, this time in favour of Jirkovsky.

If the 60s and 80s were closely fought, the other men's super-seniors categories were all one-horse races. King Van Nostrand didn't come close to dropping a set all year in the 70s, with none of his opponents able to get anywhere near him. In the 75s, world champion Lorne Main was similarly dominant, winning all his matches with ease and finishing an incredible 190 points ahead of his nearest challenger in the rankings. This feat was almost matched by Bob Sherman (USA) in the 85s, who ended the year 180 points ahead of second placed compatriot Marvin Henderson. Sherman ends the year at No. 1 for the ninth time in the last 11 years, an outstanding record.

The younger men's age categories were all relatively closely fought, with Nicolas

Alan Rasmussen (DEN)

Chris Wilkinson (GBR)

Becerra's (ARG) 85-point lead over Sander Groen the widest gap at the top in the year-end rankings. In contrast, Manfred Hundstorfer (AUT) finished with exactly the same number of points as Russia's Alexey Karpenko in the men's 40s, but his quarterfinal showing at the World Championships guaranteed him the top spot.

Val Wilder led the men's 45 rankings throughout the year, his strong showings in the USA national clay, grass and hard championships keeping him ahead of his European challengers. In the 50s, Denmark's Alan Rasmussen's first world title helped him end the year as No. 1, while in the 55s Jorge Camina Borda (ESP) took the top spot, his solid performance in Grade 1 events throughout the year making up for his non-appearance in the World Individual Championships.

The women's year-end rankings are notable by the lack of world champions in the top spots – along with Dorothy Knode, whose world championship was the only sanctioned event in the women's 80s, only Louise Russ in the 75 category took both the world title and the year-end No. 1 spot. Florence Boucard in the 35s, Ros Balodis in the 45s and Donna Fales in the 65s may have managed it had they played the minimum four events, but with only three events played each they finished behind Pastur Fernandez (ARG), Diane Fishburne (USA) and Elisabeth Van Boemmel (GER) respectively.

After losing in the semifinals of the World Championships, Olga Shaposhnikova (RUS) remained undefeated through four tournaments until October to clinch her place as year-end No. 1 in the women's 40s. In the 50s, Italy's Eugenia Birukova didn't play the World Championships but reached the final of every tournament she did play, winning five of them, to secure the top spot. And in the 55s, Germany's Heidi Eisterlehner held off the challenge of her compatriot Heide Orth to finish ahead, putting together an amazing 27-0 record during 2005. There was some consolation for Orth however as she topped the 60s age category, despite losing her world title. It extends her amazing record of topping the world rankings for five consecutive years, and eight years in the last nine, a record which surpasses even Eisterlehner's five No. 1 finishes in the last six years.

In the women's 70s, USA's Dorothy Matthiessen's 23-1 record for 2005, including a clean sweep of all four USTA national titles, helped her to the top in her first year in this age category.

There is precious little time for this year's world champions to rest on their laurels, however, as the 2006 circuit gets underway at the beginning of January and the race starts up again. Next year the seniors will head to Durban, South Africa in April for their World Championships, while the super-seniors' event will take place in Naples, Florida at the end of the year.

There is precious little time for this year's world champions to rest on their laurels, however, as the 2006 circuit gets underway at the beginning of January and the race starts up again.

Elly Appel (NED)

25th ITF Seniors World Individual Championships

Perth, Australia, 2–9 April 2005

MEN

35 Singles – Final: Chris Wilkinson (GBR) d. Sander Groen (NED) 64 41 ret..
35 Doubles – Final: Matthias Huning/Frank Potthoff (GER) d. Daniel Ahl (GBR)/Glen Philp (AUS) 75 64.
40 Singles – Final: Mario Tabares (USA) d. Stefan Heckmanns (GER) 62 64.
40 Doubles – Final: Glenn Erickson/Mario Tabares (USA) d. Robert Kilborn/Neil Smith (AUS) 67(1) 64 62.
45 Singles – Final: Patrick Serret (AUS) d. Val Wilder (USA) 67(4) 75 76(6).
45 Doubles – Final: Mike Fedderly/Val Wilder (USA) d. Tres Cushing (USA)/Pierre Godfroid (BEL) 64 64.
50 Singles – Final: Alan Rasmussen (DEN) d. Wayne Pascoe (AUS) 62 57 64.
50 Doubles – Final: Bruce Osborne/Andrew Rae (AUS) d. Wayne Pascoe (AUS)/Heiner Seuss (GER) 64 76(5).
55 Singles – Final: Bob Litwin (USA) d. Lito Alvarez (AUS) 62 30 ret..
55 Doubles – Final: Neal Newman/Larry Turville (USA) d. Lito Alvarez/Peter Rigg (AUS) 26 64 63.

WOMEN

35 Singles – Final: Florence Boucard (FRA) d. Marie-Dominique Bahu (FRA) 63 61.
35 Doubles – Final: Mary Dailey/Renata Marcinkowska (USA) d. Jo Louis/Siobhan Nicholson (GBR) 06 63 63.
40 Singles – Final: Rene Plant (RSA) d. Sylvie Mattel (FRA) 61 36 64.
40 Doubles – Final: Rosanne Duke (AUS)/Rene Plant (RSA) d. Mary Dailey/Diane Fishburne (USA) 63 46 63.
45 Singles – Final: Ros Balodis (AUS) d. Diane Fishburne (USA) 60 63.
45 Doubles – Final: Ros Balodis/Kaye Nealon (AUS) d. Yukie Koizumi (JPN)/Beatriz Villaverde (ARG) 63 64.
50 Singles – Final: Elisabeth Appel (NED) d. Sherri Bronson (USA) 60 62.
50 Doubles – Final: Lyn Mortimer/Susanne Walter (AUS) d. Frances Candy/Pauline Fisher (GBR) 62 75.
55 Singles – Elizabeth Craig-Allan (AUS) d. Adrienne Avis (AUS) 64 60.
55 Doubles – Kerry Ballard/Elizabeth Craig-Allan (AUS) d. Carol Campling/Dianne Zelinski (AUS) 63 46 62.

25th ITF Super-Seniors World Individual Championships

Antalya, Turkey, 23-30 October 2005

MEN

60 Singles – Final: Jimmy Parker (USA) d. Peter Adrigan (GER) 76(4) 26 61
60 Doubles – Final: Jimmy Parker/Ken Robinson (USA) d. Leland Housman/Hugh Thomson (USA) 60 63
65 Singles – Final: Peter Pokorny (AUT) d. Michel Leclercq (FRA) 60 76(5)
65 Doubles – Final: Henry Leichtfried/George Sarantos (USA) d. Joseph Bachmann (USA)/Gordon Waygood (AUS) 61 75
70 Singles – Final: King Van Nostrand (USA) d. Gordon Davis (USA) 61 62
70 Doubles – Final: Gordon Davis/Richard Doss (USA) d. Hector Arellano/Miguel Cravioto (MEX) 62 64
75 Singles – Final: Lorne Main (CAN) d. Ken Sinclair (CAN) 62 64
75 Doubles – Final: Lorne Main/Ken Sinclair (CAN) d. William Davis/Charles Devoe (USA) 62 06 62
80 Singles – Final: Graydon Nichols (USA) d. Oskar Jirkovsky (AUT) 76(1) 62
80 Doubles – Final: Anthony Franco/Graydon Nichols (USA) d. Neville Halligan/Richard Wilson (AUS) 62 64
85 Singles – Final: Gerry Ells (GBR) d. Franz Kornfeld (AUT) 61 62
85 Doubles – Final: Gerry Ells (GBR)/Franz Kornfeld (AUT) d. Martin Brink (RSA)/Raul Fernandez Rangel (MEX) 60 61

WOMEN

60 Singles – Final: Petro Kruger (RSA) d. Heide Orth (GER) 61 57 75
60 Doubles – Final: Charleen Hillebrand (USA)/Frances Maclennan (GBR) d. Petro Kruger/Mariette Viljoen (RSA) 61 67(6) 62
65 Singles – Final: Donna Fales (USA) d. Rosie Darmon (FRA) 67(4) 61 64
65 Doubles – Final: Susanne Clark/Dori DeVries (USA) d. Inger Delamare (FRA)/Donna Fales (USA) 64 63
70 Singles – Final: Margaret Robinson (AUS) d. Ann Fotheringham (AUS) 60 64
70 Doubles – Final: Mary Boswell/Belmar Gunderson (USA) d. Ann Fotheringham/Margaret Robinson (AUS) 06 64 75
75 Singles – Final: Louise Russ (USA) d. Diane Hoffman (USA) 63 60
75 Doubles – Final: Diane Hoffman/Louise Russ (USA) d. Rosemarie Asch/Joyce Jones (CAN) 75 46 10(6)
80 Singles – Final: Dorothy Knode (USA) d. Ingeborg Knuth (GER) 60 75
80 Doubles – Final: Marlies Jennis/Christa Uhlmann (GER) d. Carmen Christlieb (MEX)/Dorothy Knode (USA) 61 60

2005 ITF Seniors World Team Championships

Australia, 27 March–April 2005

- **ITALIA CUP (MEN'S 35) – PERTH (AUS); Final: France d. Great Britain 2-0:** Guillaume Drach (FRA) d. Daniel Ahl (GBR) 60 76(8); Lionel Barthez (FRA) d. Chris Wilkinson (GBR) 64 63.
- **TONY TRABERT CUP (MEN'S 40) – PERTH (AUS); Final: USA d. Netherlands 2-0:** Glen Erickson (USA) d. Bart Theelen (NED) 67(3) 62 64; Mario Tabares (USA) d. Remko Jansen (NED) 2-0 ret..
- **DUBLER CUP (MEN'S 45) – PERTH (AUS); Final: USA d. Germany 2-1:** Holger Prehn (GER) d. Sal Castillo (USA) 67(6) 64 75; Val Wilder (USA) d. Norbert Henn (GER) 63 62; Mike Fedderly/Val Wilder (USA) d. Norbert Henn/Holger Prehn (GER) 64 63.
- **FRED PERRY CUP (MEN'S 50) – PERTH (AUS); Final: Australia d. USA 3-0:** Andrew Rae (AUS) d. John Peckskamp (USA) 62 64; Wayne Pascoe (AUS) d. Bob Wright (USA) 63 64; Bruce Osborne/Rodney Wurtz (AUS) d. Phil Landauer/Geoff Cykman (USA) 76(4) 46 75.
- **AUSTRIA CUP (MEN'S 55) – PERTH (AUS); Final: Australia d. Spain 2-1:** Jorge Camina Borda (ESP) d. Max Bates (AUS) 63 62; Lito Alvarez (AUS) d. Jairo Velasco Ramirez (ESP) 64 61; Lito Alvarez/Peter Rigg (AUS) d. Jorge Camina Borda/Jairo Velasco Ramirez (ESP) 46 61 62.
- **SUZANNE LENGLEN CUP (WOMEN'S 35) – PERTH (AUS); Final: France d. Great Britain 2-0:** Florence Boucard (FRA) d. Siobhan Nicholson (GBR) 36 76(4) 62; Valerie LeDroff (FRA) d. Jo Louis (GBR) 75 62.
- **YOUNG CUP (WOMEN'S 40) – PERTH (AUS); Final: USA d. France 2-1:** Sylvie Mattel (FRA) d. Marianna Hollmann (USA) 76(4) 63; Gretchen Magers (USA) d. Marielle Roux Lapadu (FRA) 61 63; Gretchen Magers/Renata Marcinkowska (USA) d. Sylvie Mattel/ Marielle Roux Lapadu (FRA) 62 63.
- **MARGARET COURT CUP (WOMEN'S 45) – PERTH (AUS); Final: Australia d. USA 2-1:** Susan Wright (USA) d. Gwen Weightman (AUS) 57 63 62; Ros Balodis (AUS) d. Diane Fishburne (USA) 36 60 63; Ros Balodis/Kaye Nealon (AUS) d. Susan Wright/Diane Fishburne (USA) 76(3) 64.
- **MARIA ESTHER BUENO CUP (WOMEN'S 50) – PERTH (AUS); Final: Netherlands d. Australia 2-1:** Nora Blom (NED) d. Helen Worland (AUS) 62 63; Elly Appel (NED) d. Lyn Mortimer (AUS) 63 64; Sue Walter/Lyn Mortimer (AUS) d. Elly Appel/Nora Blom (NED) 60 60.
- **MAUREEN CONNOLLY CUP (WOMEN'S 55) – PERTH (AUS); Final: Australia d. USA 2-1:** Elizabeth Craig-Allan (AUS) d. Mary Wilson (USA) 76(4) 64; Carol Campling (AUS) d. Brenda Carter (USA) 76(4) 64; Kerry Ballard/Elizabeth Craig-Allan (AUS) d. Judy Louie/Marilyn McComb (USA) 62 75.

2005 ITF Super-Seniors World Team Championships

Antalya, Turkey, 17–22 October 2005

- **VON CRAMM CUP (MEN'S 60) – ANTALYA (TUR); Final: USA d. Germany 2-1:** Leland Housman (USA) d. Stepan Koudelka (GER) 60 62; Peter Adrigan (GER) d. Jim Parker (USA) 75 63; Jim Parker/Ken Robinson (USA) d. Peter Adrigan/Stepan Koudelka (GER) 64 63.
- **BRITANNIA CUP (MEN'S 65) – ANTALYA (TUR); Final: Austria d. USA 2-1:** Eberhard Madlsperger (AUT) d. Rudy Hernando (USA) 06 63 61; Peter Pokorny (AUT) d. Joseph Bachmann (USA) 62 62; Henry Leichtfried/George Sarantos (USA) d. Hans Gradischnig/Peter Pokorny (AUT) 75 63.
- **JACK CRAWFORD CUP (MEN'S 70) – ANTALYA (TUR); Final: USA d. France 2-0:** Gordon Davis (USA) d. Thadee Polak (FRA) 60 61; King Van Nostrand (USA) d. Joseph Mateo (FRA) 64 63.
- **BITSY GRANT CUP (MEN'S 75) – ANTALYA (TUR); Final: Canada d. USA 2-1:** Russell Seymour (USA) d. Ken Sinclair (CAN) 64 16 63; Lorne Main (CAN) d. Clement Hopp (USA) 64 61; Lorne Main/Ken Sinclair (CAN) d. Bill Davis/Chuck Devoe (USA) 64 46 60.
- **GARDNAR MULLOY CUP (MEN'S 80) – ANTALYA (TUR); Final: USA d. Great Britain 3-0:** Tony Franco (USA) d. Gerry Ells (GBR) 60 60; Graydon Nichols (USA) d. Robert Caruana (GBR) 62 60; Vincent Fotre/Newton Meade (USA) d. Tony Biggs/Mervyn Brown (GBR) 36 63 61.
- **ALICE MARBLE CUP (WOMEN'S 60) – ANTALYA (TUR); Final: France d. Germany 2-1:** Renate Schroeder (GER) d. Sylvie Galfard-Kirsten (FRA) 63 63; Gail Lovera (FRA) d. Heide Orth (GER) 67(6) 76(4) 75; Michele Bichon/Gail Lovera (FRA) d. Brigitte Hoffmann/Alena Klein (GER) 62 46 62.
- **KITTY GODFREE CUP (WOMEN'S 65) – ANTALYA (TUR); Final: Australia d. France 2-1:** Inger Delamare (FRA) d. Nola Collins (AUS) 61 62; Margaret Wayte (AUS) d. Rosie Darmon (FRA) 75 63; Lesley Heumiller/Margaret Wayte (AUS) d. Rosie Darmon/Inger Delamare (FRA) 63 63.
- **ALTHEA GIBSON CUP (WOMEN'S 70) – ANTALYA (TUR); Final: USA d. Australia 2-1:** Ann Fotheringham (AUS) d. Yvonne Van Nostrand (USA) 63 46 64; Dorothy Matthiessen (USA) d. Margaret Robinson (AUS) 61 60; Dorothy Matthiessen/Belmar Gundersen (USA) d. Lorice Forbes/Alison Ide (AUS) 61 61.
- **QUEENS' CUP (WOMEN'S 75) – ANTALYA (TUR); Final: USA d. Canada 2-1:** Olga Mahaney (USA) d. Eva Barbiero (CAN) 61 61; Louise Russ (USA) d. Rosemarie Asch (CAN) 75 76(3); Eva Barbiero/Joyce Jones (CAN) d. Diane Hoffman/Doris Jane Lutz (USA) 63 63.

ITF Seniors World Rankings 2005

Men's 35

Rank	Name	Points	Played
1	Nicolas Becerra (ARG)	500	7
2	Sander Groen (NED)	415	3
3	Daniel Ahl (GBR)	410	6
4	Chris Wilkinson (GBR)	405	3
5	Igor Tsirkun (RUS)	375	6
6	Andrew Lake (USA)	360	3
7	Paul Kleverlaan (AUS)	355	7
8	Narck Rodrigues Da Silva Filho (BRA)	340	4
9	Dinko Gudelj (CRO)	315	3
10	Miguel Kelbert (BRA)	315	3

Men's 40

Rank	Name	Points	Played
1	Manfred Hundstorfer (AUT)	600	9
2	Alexey Karpenko (RUS)	600	11
3	Glenn Erickson (USA)	450	5
4	Mario Tabares (USA)	440	2
5	Stefan Fasthoff (GER)	425	4
6	Steve Casey (AUS)	410	4
7	Dean Pedersen (DEN)	400	5
8	Stefan Eggmayer (GER)	380	3
9	Nicholas Fulwood (GBR)	380	5
10	Richard Schmidt (USA)	380	4

Men's 45

Rank	Name	Points	Played
1	Val Wilder (USA)	600	6
2	Norbert Henn (GER)	560	9
3	Pierre Godfroid (BEL)	540	9
4	Reinhold Walgram (AUT)	485	10
5	Zdenko Hoppe (CRO)	440	4
6	Stefano Barbarossa (ITA)	425	6
7	Mike Fedderly (USA)	390	7
8	Gerd Wilde (GER)	380	9
9	Michael Maldoner (AUT)	380	4
10	Adriano Da Ponte (ITA)	370	5

Men's 50

Rank	Name	Points	Played
1	Alan Rasmussen (DEN)	700	4
2	Andrew Rae (AUS)	660	9
3	Wayne Pascoe (AUS)	610	4
4	Radovan Cizek (CZE)	600	6
5	Paul French (GBR)	510	7
6	Olivera Garcia (ARG)	500	8
7	Franco Brino (ITA)	470	7
8	Augusto Possenti (ITA)	440	6
9	Fred Robinson (USA)	400	5
10	Roberto Yunis (CHI)	390	11

Women's 35

Rank	Name	Points	Played
1	Pastur C Fernandez (ARG)	480	6
2	Jo Louis (GBR)	460	5
3	Florence Boucard (FRA)	370	3
4	Monica Yanagi (BRA)	335	4
5	Stephanie Bowler (AUS)	300	2
6	Jamie Patterson (USA)	295	5
7	Andrea Jakimczuk (ARG)	270	5
8	Marianne Groat (CAN)	260	6
9	Luciene Sapienza Muro (BRA)	260	3
10	Julie Cass (USA)	260	3

Women's 40

Rank	Name	Points	Played
1	Olga Shaposhnikova (RUS)	600	6
2	Simone Vasconcellos-Calves (BRA)	480	3
3	Sylvie Mattel (FRA)	470	4
4	Marisa Ferrero (ARG)	460	7
5	Rene Plant (RSA)	430	3
6	Natascha Faschingbauer (GER)	405	4
7	Gretchen Magers (USA)	370	3
8	Francesca Ciardi (ITA)	360	3
9	Maria Goni (ARG)	305	6
10	Luisa Gouveia (POR)	305	6

Women's 45

Rank	Name	Points	Played
1	Diane Fishburne (USA)	720	7
2	Ros Balodis (AUS)	580	3
3	Barbara Koutna (CZE)	540	6
4	Maira Brenner-Feier (BRA)	450	4
5	Susan Wright (USA)	435	7
6	Gerda Preissing-Sigel (GER)	435	4
7	Reinhild Ferlemann (GER)	410	6
8	Marcela De Gregorio (ARG)	400	6
9	Christine French (GBR)	390	6
10	Julia Smutny (AUT)	380	6

Women's 50

Rank	Name	Points	Played
1	Eugenia Birukova (ITA)	600	8
2	Sherri Bronson (USA)	510	9
3	Beatrice Chrystman (BRA)	510	5
4	Katalin Fagyas (HUN)	495	5
5	Luisa Figueroa (ARG)	440	5
6	Gabriele Leinen (GER)	435	4
7	Elly Appel (NED)	400	2
8	Carolyn Nichols (USA)	400	5
9	Mary Ginnard (USA)	395	5
10	Pauline Fisher (GBR)	390	5

Men's 55

Rank	Name	Points	Played
1	Jorge Camina-Borda (ESP)	600	10
2	Larry Turville (USA)	540	6
3	Bruno Renoult (FRA)	470	5
4	Julio Lavagno (ARG)	470	8
5	Hermann Fahrnberger (AUT)	430	11
6	Robert Litwin (USA)	420	3
7	Bojan Miklavcic (SLO)	410	9
8	Reinhold Bahe (GER)	405	12
9	Max Bates (AUS)	395	4
10	Brian Cheney (USA)	370	6

Women's 55

Rank	Name	Points	Played
1	Heidi Eisterlehner (GER)	720	5
2	Heide Orth (GER)	660	7
3	Elizabeth Craig-Allan (AUS)	485	3
4	Sylvia Bauwens (GER)	480	5
5	Heidemarie Oehlsen (GER)	420	11
6	Sara Kelbert (BRA)	410	6
7	Miriam Borali (ITA)	410	7
8	Luise Moser (AUT)	410	4
9	Sandra Libman (BRA)	390	5
10	Marjory Love (GBR)	380	4

Men's 60

Rank	Name	Points	Played
1	Peter Adrigan (GER)	720	14
2	Peter Pokorny (AUT)	720	5
3	James Parker (USA)	670	6
4	Hugh Thomson (USA)	510	4
5	Hannes Futterknecht (AUT)	510	5
6	Daniel Harms (ARG)	500	5
7	Alan Walsh (AUS)	480	6
8	Michael Hepker (GBR)	480	14
9	Petr Kolacek (SUI)	420	6
10	Leland Housman (USA)	400	5

Women's 60

Rank	Name	Points	Played
1	Heide Orth (GER)	720	7
2	Alena Klein (GER)	600	11
3	Mary Wilson-Mclean (USA)	570	6
4	Frances Maclennan (GBR)	545	6
5	Sylvie Galfard-Kirsten (FRA)	520	8
6	Renate Schroeder (GER)	510	6
7	Zsofia Garaguly (AUT)	510	8
8	Mariana Karolyi (HUN)	480	5
9	Suella Steel (USA)	450	5
10	Charlene Hillebrand (USA)	435	6

Men's 65

Rank	Name	Points	Played
1	Peter Pokorny (AUT)	740	5
2	Joseph Bachmann (USA)	660	7
3	Rudy Hernando (USA)	600	6
4	Eberhard Madlsperger (AUT)	600	7
5	Hans Peter Kruck (AUT)	540	7
6	Vittorio Monaco (ITA)	510	7
7	Horst Heider (GER)	450	19
8	Ilio Santos (BRA)	450	8
9	Michel Leclercq (FRA)	425	5
10	Donald Shears (GBR)	425	5

Women's 65

Rank	Name	Points	Played
1	Elisabeth Van Boemmel (GER)	570	5
2	Marika Stock (GER)	530	7
3	Nanda Fischer (GER)	510	9
4	Donna Fales (USA)	490	3
5	Dorothy De Vries (USA)	480	8
6	Susanne Clark (USA)	460	5
7	Rosie Darmon (FRA)	435	3
8	Margaret Wayte (AUS)	430	3
9	Renate Mayer-Zdralek (GER)	405	6
10	Renate Castellucci (GER)	385	4

Men's 70

Rank	Name	Points	Played
1	King Van Nostrand (USA)	740	8
2	Gordon Davis (USA)	720	7
3	John Powless (USA)	590	5
4	David William Garman (GBR)	550	7
5	Damir Novak (CRO)	540	11
6	Gerhard Coldewey (GER)	520	6
7	Hans Jell (AUT)	480	12
8	Gerhard Zogoll (GER)	455	7
9	Gunther Herrmann (GER)	440	6
10	Hans Busch (GER)	435	7

Women's 70

Rank	Name	Points	Played
1	Dorothy Matthiessen (USA)	730	5
2	Brigitte Jung (GER)	660	7
3	Ann Fotheringham (AUS)	575	4
4	Clelia Mazzoleni (ITA)	570	4
5	Yvonne Van Nostrand (USA)	510	7
6	Ilse Michael (GER)	465	7
7	Margaret Robinson (AUS)	460	3
8	June Pearce (GBR)	455	7
9	Marie-France Pelissier (FRA)	440	8
10	Mary Boswell (USA)	420	7

ITF Seniors World Rankings 2005 (continued)

Men's 75

Rank	Name	Points	Played
1	Lorne Main (CAN)	790	8
2	Adolfo Ibarrondo (ARG)	600	7
3	Kenneth Sinclair (CAN)	540	6
4	Jean Desmet (BEL)	540	11
5	Clem Hopp (USA)	540	9
6	George Ghidrai (ROM)	500	7
7	Russell Seymour (USA)	470	4
8	Joseph Russell (USA)	450	5
9	Charles Devoe (USA)	435	6
10	Andre Desselas (FRA)	435	6

Men's 80

Rank	Name	Points	Played
1	Oskar Jirkovsky (AUT)	720	6
2	Frederick Kovaleski (USA)	720	4
3	Graydon Nichols (USA)	680	8
4	Laszlo Lenart (HUN)	570	6
5	Cornelis Marre (NED)	540	14
6	Tony Franco (USA)	460	4
7	Richard Wilson (AUS)	450	5
8	Robert Caruana (GBR)	445	6
9	Henri Kerouredan (FRA)	370	9
10	Elias Del Cano (ARG)	350	3

Men's 85

Rank	Name	Points	Played
1	Robert Sherman (USA)	720	6
2	Marvin Henderson (USA)	540	4
3	Kenneth Hayes (USA)	420	6
4	Alex Swetka (USA)	375	4
5	Franz Kornfeld (AUT)	360	4
6	Gerald Ells (GBR)	340	2
7	John Benn (USA)	315	4
8	Jim Carleton (USA)	305	6
9	Howard William Kuntz (USA)	285	4
10	Howard F. Moffett (USA)	260	5

Women's 75

Rank	Name	Points	Played
1	Louise Russ (USA)	730	9
2	Erzsebet Szentirmay (HUN)	495	6
3	Diane Hoffman (USA)	395	4
4	Lucette Moreau (FRA)	385	4
5	Ilse Jacob (GER)	360	5
6	Louise Owen (USA)	345	3
7	Anita Fischer (GER)	335	6
8	Rita Caputi-Price (USA)	305	5
9	Suzanne Ryerson (USA)	300	4
10	Nancy Stout (USA)	290	4

Women's 80

Rank	Name	Points	Played
1	Dorothy Knode (USA)	250	1
2	Ingeborg Knuth (GER)	180	1
3=	Lieselotte Carstens (GER)	120	1
3=	Nadine Matton (FRA)	120	1
5=	Helene Feneau (FRA)	90	1
5=	Christa Uhlmann (GER)	90	1

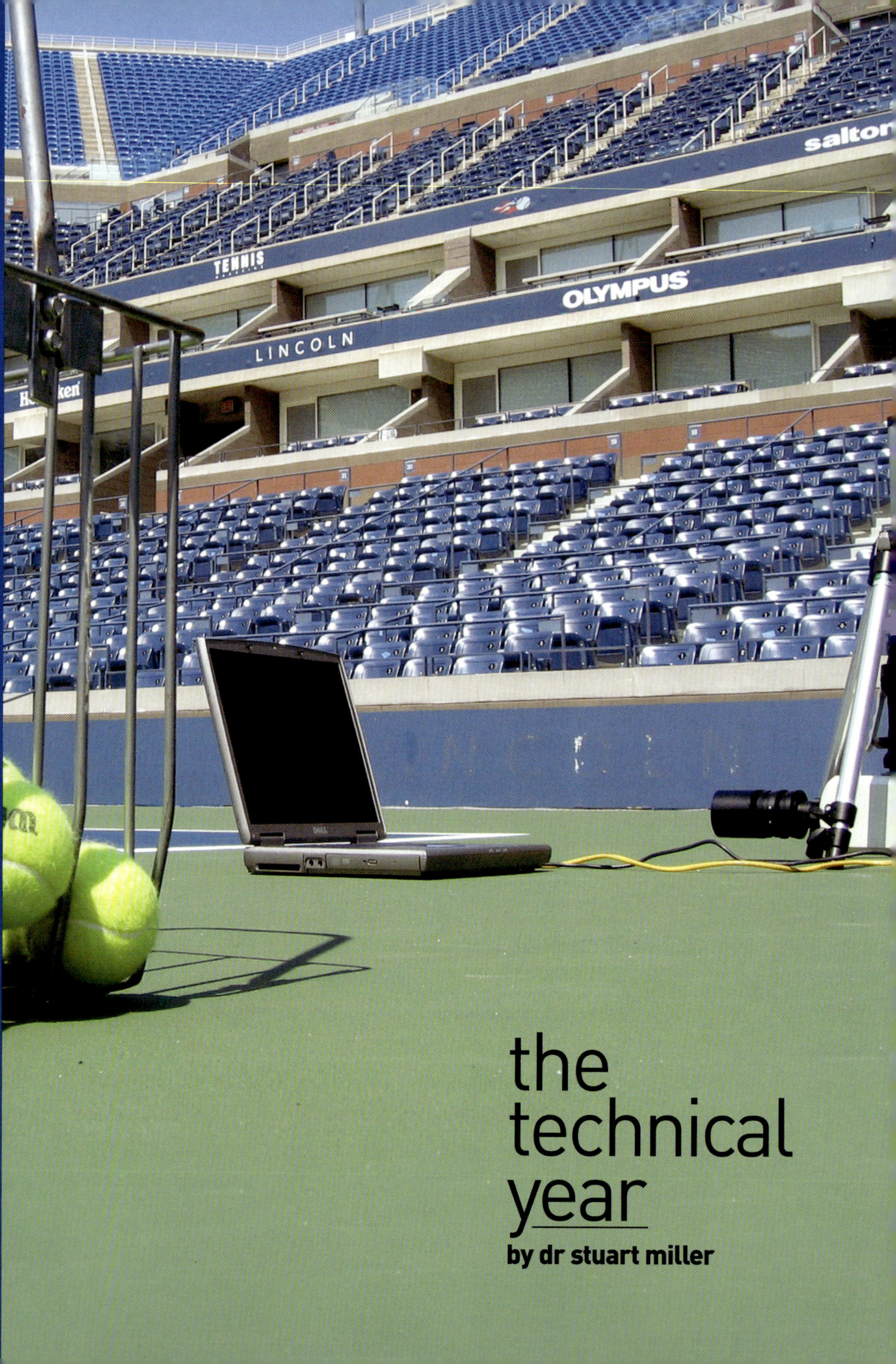

the technical year

by dr stuart miller

In 2005, the Technical Department continued to demonstrate its leadership in the field of tennis technology, and confirmed its position as the key provider of testing, approval and research of tennis equipment. The introduction of several new projects and the continuation of existing work demonstrated both the strength and breadth of its remit. In addition, the Technical Centre has led the introduction into professional tennis of electronic line-calling as an aid to on-court officials. Investment in the Technical Centre has helped to retain its position as the world's leading tennis-specific research and testing facility.

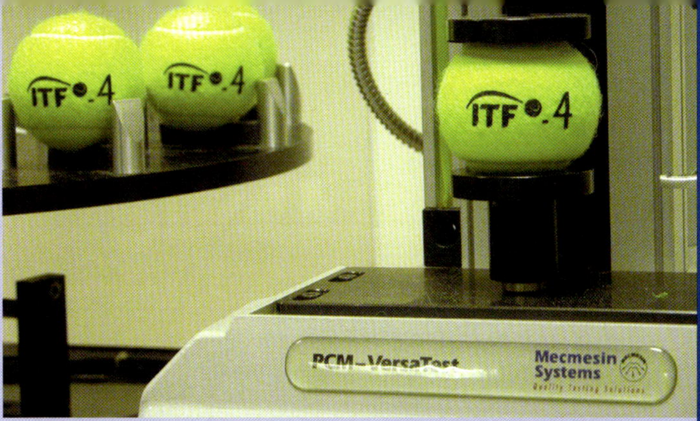

Ball deformation test

ITF Technical Centre

Fulfilment of the Technical Centre's mission to protect the nature of tennis by 'actively preserving the skills traditionally required to play the game, and, to encourage innovation and improvements which maintain the challenge of the game and make it more exciting to play and watch' requires it to be proactive. Thus, by undertaking research and testing programmes, and developing predictive models and simulations, the ITF is an effective guardian of the technical and technological aspects of the game. This work is crucial in preventing a reactive approach to the regulation of tennis equipment, which history has shown to be potentially hazardous.

Testing of the aerodynamic characteristics of tennis balls – the property that determines their trajectories through the air – is ongoing. A database of ball aerodynamics for all approved brands will be collected during 2006, and presentations relating to this project have been made at international scientific conferences. Improvements to the system continue to be made to enhance its capabilities.

The racket power machine ("MYO") has also undergone considerable use throughout 2005. An improved method of measuring power has been added and validated, and rackets are being tested to establish a benchmark of racket performance. A systematic evaluation of all rackets on the market will take place in 2006.

The ITF spin project was started in 2005 and aims to establish the spin-generating characteristics of tennis racket and string combinations. An automated data collection and analysis system has been installed in the ITF Technical Centre, and a systematic evaluation of several variables, including tension, type, and gauge, is ongoing.

The ITF Sports Shoe Tester has undergone considerable development in 2005 to improve both its realism and capacity for measuring the frictional and impact-absorbing characteristics of different shoe/surface combinations. Specifically, a more realistic 'foot' and 'ankle' has been added, and further development is planned.

Version 1 of 'Tennis GUT', the software package that quantifies the combined effects of all tennis equipment on the nature of tennis, is now complete, and has exceeded expectations in terms of its power and versatility. In addition to simulating the effects of different combinations of equipment and atmospheric conditions, the software allows experimentation with changes in equipment to establish the future effects of current trends or to test any proposed changes in the relevant Rules of Tennis.

Considerable time has been devoted to the introduction of electronic line-calling systems into professional tennis as an aid to on-court officials. In 2005, 11 evaluations were undertaken, and, in October, 'Hawk-Eye Officiating' became the first system to meet the required standards for accuracy and reliability.

Ball testing

As the sole worldwide testing and approval centre for tennis balls that are used in tournament play according to the Rules of Tennis, the ITF Technical Centre continued with its expanded programme of testing in the last year:

1. Ball Approval. In 2004, 225 brands of ball were approved for the 2005 calendar year, a record number for the ninth consecutive year. The Technical Centre published its annual official list of approved balls in January (the list is also available on the ITF website). Ball approval testing for 2006 has been ongoing since June, and a similar number of brands are expected to be approved.

2. Market testing. This continues to form a significant volume of the Technical Centre's ball testing programme. Continued cooperation with the ATP and WTA tours has resulted in a similar number of samples being received from tournaments in 2005 as compared to approval tests. The results of this testing will again be used to inform future ITF ball

Version 1 of 'Tennis GUT', the software package that quantifies the combined effects of all tennis equipment on the nature of tennis, is now complete, and has exceeded expectations in terms of its power and versatility.

Line-calling evaluation

the technical year

by dr stuart miller

testing policy and strategy and to provide feedback to the ball manufacturing industry and interested members of the ITF Foundation.

Further development of the testing and analysis processes has been undertaken to facilitate the increased volume of testing.

Quality assurance of testing standards forms a key part of the Technical Centre's philosophy. Following a British Standards Institute audit in February, the Technical Centre retained its ISO 9001:2000 quality assurance standard in 2005.

Court Surface Classification

The ITF Court Surface Classification Scheme continues to expand, with over 70 surfaces now having an ITF classification. The Technical Centre is working in collaboration with the Davis Cup Committee in the incorporation of surface pace rating into the competition's rules. A draft revision of the Initial ITF Study on Performance Standards for Tennis Court Surfaces was presented to key members of the court surface industry in October.

Microscope image of acrylic tennis surface

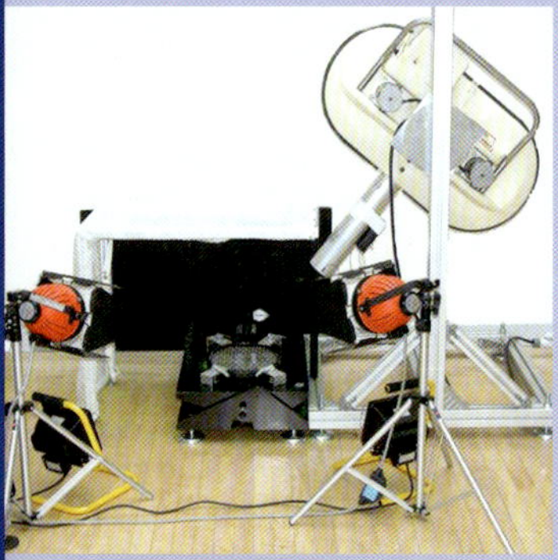

Ball spin test rig

Sport Science & Medicine Commission

Quality assurance of testing standards forms a key part of the Technical Centre's philosophy. Following a British Standards Institute audit in February, the Technical Centre retained its ISO 9001:2000 quality assurance standard in 2005.

ITF Foundation

It is through the ITF Foundation that the Technical Centre enjoys an open and productive relationship with the tennis industry. In 2005 the ITF Foundation had 33 member companies, the largest number for several years.

A major benefit of Foundation membership is exclusive access to the ITF attitude and participation survey. Research was conducted in six nations in 2005 at Davis Cup and Fed Cup ties. The countries were Belgium, Canada, Croatia, Mexico, Switzerland, and Venezuela. The data continues to be well received by Foundation members.

ITF Technical Commission

The Technical Commission has again been active throughout the year. Supplementing the membership with representatives from ITF Officiating and both the ATP and WTA tours facilitated a more complete discussion of technical issues, which has covered all areas of tennis equipment.

ITF Sport Science & Medicine Commission

Two meetings have taken place in 2005, which have focused on the development of materials for the Commission's website, which will be its primary vehicle for the distribution of information. Among its key projects is the development of an injury registration system, which will allow the recording, monitoring and analysis of player health in professional tennis, including the junior level and professional tours. This project, which is being conducted in collaboration with the ATP and WTA, will be the largest and most comprehensive source of information relating to health and injury of players ever conducted in tennis.

In summary, the Technical Department has again reinforced its role as the leading regulatory, research, testing and approval body for tennis equipment. In addition, the ongoing projects and initiatives will continue to enhance the ITF's governance of tennis, and facilitate informed decision-making on any equipment-related changes to the Rules of Tennis. The challenge of protecting the nature of tennis is a key role of the ITF, and one which the Technical Department has successfully met in 2005.

Goran Ivanisevic (CRO) and Miroslav Mecir (SVK), recipients of the ITF/ITHF Davis Cup Award of Excellence in 2005

reference section

The greatest players, historic records, addresses of National Associations and other tennis organisations, obituaries.

The Greatest

Biographies of leading players

Written by John Haylett.

The Men

ANDRE AGASSI (USA)

One of five players who have won all four Grand Slam titles at least once. Has invented a new style of tennis, attacking from the baseline.

Born:	Las Vegas, Nevada, USA, April 29, 1970.
Grand Slam titles:	Australian 1995, 2000-01, 2003. French 1999. Wimbledon 1992. United States 1994, 1999.
Olympics:	Gold medal, singles, 1996.
Davis Cup winning teams:	USA 1990, 1992.

Agassi is the most exciting and charismatic tennis player of the current era. A powerhouse of energy and a vigorous shotmaker, he is one of only five men to take all four Grand Slam singles titles. He burst upon the scene in 1986 and became instantly recognisable, not only for his relentless go-for-broke baseline hitting, but also his flamboyant image.

He rapidly shot into the top five but it was five years before he won his first Grand Slam title. Having lost finals at the 1990 and 1991 Roland Garros, and 1990 US Open, and stated an avowed dislike of grass, Agassi surprised most experts by defeating Goran Ivanisevic in a pulsating five set final at Wimbledon in 1992. From then on he established himself as a leading contender, winning the 1994 US Open title. He developed a terrific rivalry with Pete Sampras, winning the final of the 1995 Australian Open and losing to him at the same stage at Flushing Meadows.

In 1997 he married the actress Brooke Shields and his form declined steeply – his ranking plummeted to 141 in the autumn and he was reduced to playing in Challenger events. But having engaged the former top ten player, Brad Gilbert, as his coach, Agassi rediscovered his enthusiasm for the game and achieved the finest sequence of his career. He defeated Andrei Medvedev in the final of the 1999 French Open then lost to Sampras in the Wimbledon final. He won the next two Slams, at Flushing Meadows and Melbourne, to claim an undisputed status as the world's top player at the age of 30. He captured the Australian Open title for a second consecutive year in 2001 and narrowly lost to Pete Sampras in the 2002 US Open Final. Agassi was forced to miss Melbourne in 2002 due to injury but returned to win his fourth title in 2003 to become the oldest Grand Slam Champion for 28 years. Later in 2003 he became the oldest holder of the No. 1 Entry Ranking in the history of the rankings (since 1973) when he took over the top spot for the fifth time in his career. He married Steffi Graff in 2001, the couple have two children Jaden Gil (born October 01) and Jaz Elle (born October 2003).

ARTHUR ASHE (USA)

Style, elegance and consistency. The first black player to win a Grand Slam title. A great example for his sport and for his race.

Born:	Richmond, Virginia, USA, July 10, 1943.
Died:	New York, New York, USA, February 6, 1993.
Grand Slam titles:	Australian 1970. Wimbledon 1975. United States 1968. Two men's doubles titles.
Davis Cup winning teams:	USA 1968-70.

Ashe was the first and, to date, only African-American man to win any of the game's major titles, and such is the esteem in which he is held, when the new main stadium at Flushing Meadows was built in 1997 it was named after him. Born in the Deep South at a time when racial attitudes made it extremely difficult for any black player to make progress in tennis, Ashe overcame considerable obstacles to reach back-to-back Australian singles finals in 1966-67 while also serving in the US armed forces. He had a fast, accurate serve, impeccable volleys and a fine overhead, and he also had one of the best brains of any tennis player in history.

In 1968, the year the game went Open, he achieved the unique feat of winning both the US Nationals (an event confined to amateurs and registered players) at Boston and then the inaugural US Open at Forest Hills. As an amateur he was obliged to forfeit the prize money. He turned professional soon afterwards and would be one of the world's leading players for the next decade, winning the Australian Open in 1970 and Wimbledon in 1975. In the latter year he achieved the No. 1 ranking, and his Wimbledon final defeat of the holder, Jimmy Connors, by 61 61 57 64, was regarded as possibly the most astute and intelligent tactical display ever seen on the Centre Court. With clever changes of pace and spin, and slicing his serve wide to his opponent's double-handed backhand, Ashe bewildered the hitherto dominant Connors to claim a famous upset victory.

Ashe's style, elegance and consistency, coupled with his perceptive comments on the developing Open sport and his leadership of the fledgling Association of Tennis Professionals, made him a respected statesman of the game. Although he was almost 32 when he won Wimbledon he continued to play at a high level until 1979, when his career was terminated by a heart attack. Having represented the United States in the Davis Cup from 1963 to 1978, he assumed the captaincy for five years and led his country to victory in 1981 and 1982. Tragically, in 1988 he contracted AIDS through a blood transfusion and he died before his 50th birthday.

BORIS BECKER (GER)

Youngest player to win the men's singles title at Wimbledon and first unseeded champion.

Born: Leimen, Germany, November 22, 1967.
Grand Slam titles: Australian 1991, 1996. Wimbledon 1985-86, 1989. United States 1989.
Olympics: Gold medal, doubles: 1992.
Davis Cup winning teams: Germany 1988-89.

Boris Becker, a big, powerful, redhead with battering-ram serves and crunching volleys, set three simultaneous records when he won Wimbledon at the age of 17 in 1985. He was the youngest-ever winner, the first unseeded champion and the first player from Germany to capture the world's premier grass court championship. In an astonishing display of courage and determination, Becker overcame the eighth-seeded South African, Kevin Curren, 63 67 76 64 in the final, literally hurling himself around the court. He become a great player, but he failed to achieve the domination of other champions like Laver, Borg and Sampras. There were two reasons for this: he had a suspect temperament, and occasionally imploded, as he did when losing to his compatriot, Michael Stich, in the 1991 Wimbledon final; and he lacked the patience to succeed on slower surfaces. He never won a professional singles title on clay.

Becker burst upon the world stage in 1984, when he reached the quarterfinals of the Australian Open as a 16-year-old. When he came to England for the grass court season in June 1985 he provided a portent of things to come by winning the title at Queen's Club, then came his momentous first Wimbledon triumph. Later that year he led West Germany (as it still was) to the final of the Davis Cup and beat both Edberg and Wilander, although he could not prevent Sweden winning the tie overall.

He retained his Wimbledon title in 1986 but the following year, in an astonishing upset, lost in the second round to a little-known Australian, Peter Doohan. But that was his only bad result in over a decade at the Championships. He contested three finals in a row against Edberg from 1988 to 1990, winning in 1989, the same year he overcame Ivan Lendl for his only US Open title. In 1991 came the surprise loss to Stich. There would be one further Wimbledon final (losing to Sampras in 1995) and one more Grand Slam title – the Australian in 1996, after which he reached the No. 1 ranking for the first time in his career. But from the mid-1990s his form went into decline. He announced his retirement in 1997, but returned for another season in 1999. He reached the fourth round at Wimbledon but after a decisive loss to Patrick Rafter finally called it a day.

BJORN BORG (SWE)

Great athletic talent. Proved everybody wrong by winning, as a clay court specialist, five consecutive Wimbledon titles.

Born: Sodertaljie, Sweden, June 6, 1956.
Grand Slam titles: French 1974-75, 1978-81. Wimbledon 1976-80.
Davis Cup winning team: Sweden 1975.

Probably the best baseliner the world has ever seen, Bjorn Borg rewrote the coaching manuals by proving that it was possible to win consistently on grass without a conventional serve and volley game. Blessed with broad shoulders and tremendous upper body strength, Borg had a great serve, blistering topspin groundstrokes (double-handed on the backhand) and the ability to run down every shot. Whilst he was capable of playing the serve and volley, he relied chiefly on his superb fitness and great strength off the ground to win Wimbledon five years running – a feat unsurpassed since the abolition of the Challenge Round.

Selected to play for Sweden in the Davis Cup in 1972, when he was still only 15, Borg was a very young achiever. He won the Wimbledon junior title that year and 12 months later extended Britain's experienced Roger Taylor to a dramatic five set quarterfinal in the senior event. His dashing looks made him tennis's first ever teenybop heart-throb, idolised by an army of young girls who stormed the Centre Court and made him an icon comparable to contemporary pop stars like Donny Osmond and David Cassidy. Borg, who was basically shy, continued to make progress despite the attentions of his fans. In 1974 he became the youngest-ever winner of the French Open (at the time) and retained the title the following year, when he also led Sweden to its first ever triumph in the Davis Cup.

He won the first of his Wimbledon titles without dropping a set, and held onto it for four more years, despite a determined challenge from John McEnroe in the 1980 final, which has gone down in history as perhaps the best ever. But in 1981 McEnroe had his revenge, and Borg's motivation began to fade. He never managed to win the US Open, losing in four finals, and he did not play in Australia after his one appearance in 1974. But he lost only one match at Roland Garros after 1973, winning his sixth title there on his last appearance in 1981.

In 1982, in dispute with the authorities over the number of events he wished to play, he walked away from the game. He made an ill-judged comeback in the early 1990s, still using his by now obsolete wooden racket, but was unable to make any impression on a sport that had moved on during his decade away from the courts.

JEAN BOROTRA (FRA)

The third best of the Four Musketeers by results, his flamboyant personality always making him a leader both on and off the court.

Born:	Arbonne, France, August 13, 1898.
Died:	Arbonne, France, July 17, 1994.
Grand Slam titles:	Australian 1928. French 1931. Wimbledon 1924, 1926. Nine men's doubles titles; five mixed doubles titles.
Olympics:	Bronze medal, doubles, 1924.
Davis Cup winning teams:	France 1927-32.

'The Bounding Basque', as Jean Borotra was known, was the most successful of the 'Four Musketeers' – a quartet of highly talented Frenchmen (the others were Henri Cochet, Rene Lacoste and Jacques Brugnon) who, along with the American, Bill Tilden, dominated men's tennis from the mid-1920s to the early 1930s. They won the Davis Cup for France for six consecutive years from 1927 to 1932 and between them gathered 18 Grand Slam singles titles.

Borotra, as Gallic as the actor Maurice Chevalier, was instantly recognisable not only for his trademark blue beret but also his explosive style of play. Although slight in physique he possessed extraordinary energy and would hurtle around the court, always eager to attack but equally capable of running down any drop shot or lob an opponent gave him. He was a consummate volleyer – a skill rewarded with a career total of 14 Grand Slam doubles and mixed doubles titles, and his backhand return of serve was a potent weapon. Not only was Borotra an exciting and entertaining player, but he was debonair and charming – an inveterate ladies' man who never missed an opportunity to kiss the hand of an attractive female spectator.

As a winner of all the major titles except the American, where he was runner-up in 1926, Borotra proved he could play well on all surfaces. But his unparalleled net game was particularly effective on wood, then the principal surface indoors. He won 11 British Covered Court singles championships – the last as late as 1949, when he was 53 years old – and four US Indoor singles titles. In the Davis Cup he represented France with huge distinction every year from 1922 to 1937 and again in 1947, compiling a 19-12 win-loss record in singles and 17-6 in doubles. Perhaps his greatest feat was retaining the Cup for France against the Americans in 1932. With the French leading 2-1 on rubbers in the Challenge Round, Borotra, then 33, lost the first two sets against Wilmer Allison and saved four match points before going on to triumph 16 36 64 62 75.

During World War II he served as a minister in the Vichy government. He was also president of the French Tennis Federation for many years. Borotra played more matches at Wimbledon than any other player (223 between 1922 and 1964) and took part in every International Club match between France and Great Britain from 1929 to 1985.

DONALD BUDGE (USA)

The first man to achieve the Grand Slam. One of the best backhands ever. His career was shortened by turning professional at 23.

Born:	Oakland, California, USA, June 13, 1915.
Died:	Scranton, Pennsylvania, USA, January 26, 2000.
Grand Slam titles:	Australian 1938. French 1938. Wimbledon 1937-38. United States 1937-38. Four men's doubles titles; four mixed doubles titles.
Davis Cup winning teams:	USA 1937-38.

Donald Budge had one of the shortest careers in major competition of any tennis champion, but in the space of two years he won six major singles titles, plus four men's doubles and four mixed doubles championships. Until his total domination of the 1938 season the concept of the Grand Slam was unheard of. The Grand Slam was originally a term borrowed from the game of bridge by American journalist Allison Danzig and now denotes the winning of all four of tennis's greatest titles, the Australian, French, Wimbledon and United States Championships, by the same player in the same calendar year. Only one other man (Rod Laver in 1962 and 1969) and three women – Maureen Connolly (1953), Margaret Court (1970) and Steffi Graf (1988) have followed in Budge's footsteps.

The son of a Scottish immigrant who played professional football for Paisley, Donald Budge was a strapping 6ft 1in redhead who had a commanding all-round game, with a ferocious service and one of the best backhands the sport has ever seen. He was first selected to the US Davis Cup team at the age of 19 in 1935, and in September 1936 he defeated Fred Perry, the world No. 1, to win the important Pacific Southwest tournament in Los Angeles. When Perry turned professional shortly afterwards Budge was ready to succeed him as the world's leading player.

In 1937 he won all three titles at Wimbledon – the singles, beating Germany's Gottfried von Cramm in straight sets, the men's doubles with fellow-American Gene Mako and the mixed with Alice Marble. The same month he beat von Cramm again in the deciding rubber of the Davis Cup Inter-Zone Final at Wimbledon. This was one of the greatest matches of all time. Budge won 68 57 64 62 86 from 1-4 down in the final set, and the Americans went on to take the Cup from Great Britain in the Challenge Round. In 1938 he won the Australian title, the French, Wimbledon and Forest Hills. He also won the men's doubles and mixed doubles at Wimbledon and the US Championships. After a successful US defence of the Davis Cup he signed a professional contract and swiftly conquered the pro game as well.

HENRI COCHET (FRA)

A master of strategy. Able to play inside the baseline with great anticipation, taking the ball early. Staged a great recovery against Bill Tilden to win the 1927 Wimbledon semifinal.

Born:	Lyon, France, December 14, 1901.
Died:	St Germain-en-Laye, France, April 1, 1987.
Grand Slam titles:	French 1926, 1928, 1930, 1932. Wimbledon 1927, 1929. United States 1928. Five men's doubles titles, three mixed doubles titles.
Olympics:	Silver medals, singles and doubles, 1924.
Davis Cup winning teams:	France 1927-32.

Henri Cochet was an extraordinarily talented player who defied the usual precepts of the game. He could create winners from seemingly impossible situations, taking the ball early, with fantastic volleys and half-volleys even when apparently out of position. Reluctant to work hard, he nevertheless relied on marvellous strategic ability and ease of shot to beat stronger and more technically orthodox opponents.

The Frenchman was a mainstay of his country's Davis Cup team, winning 10 consecutive Challenge Round singles rubbers after he and the other Musketeers (Jean Borotra, Rene Lacoste and Jacques Brugnon) captured the trophy for the first time from the United States in 1927. His victory over William Johnston in Philadelphia sealed the historic victory, and he continued the sequence with wins over John Hennessey, Bill Tilden (thrice), George Lott (twice), Bunny Austin, Fred Perry and Wilmer Allison, plus doubles wins with Borotra and Brugnon.

He was also a highly successful performer in Grand Slam events, where his greatest triumph was probably at Wimbledon in 1927. In the semifinals he trailed Tilden by two sets to love and 1-5 in the third, yet managed to recover to win 26 46 75 64 63. He went on to defeat Borotra in the final. The following year he won the French and American titles and began a four year run as world No. 1. He won the French championship for the first time in 1922, when it was restricted to French nationals, and took the title four more times – in 1926 and 1928 (beating Lacoste in the final), in 1930 (over Tilden) and in 1932 (over Giorgio de Stefani). He was also runner-up the following year to Jack Crawford. At Wimbledon his victim in both winning finals (1927 and 1929) was Borotra. In the 1927 final Cochet made a thrilling recovery from 2-5 in the final set, saving six match points. He was runner-up in 1928 to Lacoste. He won the US title in 1928 against Francis Hunter and was losing finalist to Ellsworth Vines in 1932.

In 1933 France lost its grip on the Davis Cup despite Cochet's win over Austin in the fourth rubber, having earlier lost to Perry. After this he turned professional, but did not have a particularly successful career as a paid performer. In 1945 he was reinstated as an amateur.

JIMMY CONNORS (USA)

The greatest fighter of them all. Won the US Open at 31 and reached the semis there at 39. Won the three Grand Slam tournaments he played in 1974.

Born:	Belleville, Illinois, USA, September 2, 1952.
Grand Slam titles:	Australian 1974. Wimbledon 1974, 1982. United States 1974, 1976, 1978, 1982-83. Two men's doubles titles.

Jimmy Connors was one of four players – the others were Bjorn Borg, Ilie Nastase and John McEnroe – who were largely responsible for turning tennis from a minority sport into a huge, multi-million dollar entertainment industry in the late 1970s. He was a tremendously exciting player – feisty, jocular, controversial, hard-hitting, dogged and a marvel of longevity. He was a leading contender and a top box office attraction for a span of two decades.

Connors was a streetfighter who knew how to milk a crowd and orchestrate it into a frenzy of excitement as he waged winning battles against opponents who knew that he was capable of beating them from seemingly impossible positions. He was often uncouth and unsporting, but such was his charisma that audiences forgave his excesses and applauded his sheer guts and fighting qualities. His style was all-out attrition from the baseline. His serve was not a major weapon, and he could volley and smash efficiently, but it was his groundstrokes, especially his double-handed backhand, that were the hallmark of his success. It was a physically demanding mode of play that made his longevity as a top flight player all the more remarkable. He was very fast, able to cover the court so well that it was extremely difficult to put a winner past him. Even more remarkable was his loyalty to the Wilson T-2000 – a steel frame racket that he used from the late 1960s (when still a junior) into the 1980s, long after all other players had discarded it as unusable.

Connors' first major success was winning the Wimbledon doubles with Nastase in 1973, but after that he concentrated on singles. He won three of the four Grand Slam titles in 1974, overwhelming the 39-year-old Ken Rosewall in the finals at Wimbledon and Forest Hills, and might have taken the French as well had he not been barred because he was under contract to the World Team Tennis league. He holds the unique distinction of winning the US Open on three different surfaces – on grass in 1974, on clay in 1976 and on hard courts in 1978, 1982 and 1983. During his career he had many memorable battles against Borg, McEnroe and Ivan Lendl, and he reached the semifinals of the US Open at the age of 39 in 1991.

JIM COURIER (USA)

Reached the finals of all four Slam tournaments and triumphed on vastly different surfaces to win the Australian and French twice.

Born: Sanford, Florida, USA, August 17, 1970.
Grand Slam titles: Australian 1992-93. French 1991-92.
Davis Cup winning teams: USA 1992, 1995.

A rugged athlete with a brutally physical style, Jim Courier relied on his supreme fitness and relentless work ethic to reach the pinnacle of the game in the early 1990s. A product of the Nick Bollettieri Academy in Bradenton, Florida – breeding ground for such stars as Andre Agassi, Monica Seles and David Wheaton – Courier was an exponent of the powerhitting baseline style which virtually took over tennis. His chief weapons were his ferocious double-handed backhand and devastating inside-out forehand with which he would slug endless shots deep into his opponent's court. Courier toiled long hours on the practice court as a junior and became a feared adversary because his stamina and determination ensured that he could usually last longer than most other men in marathon baseline battles.

One of a batch of top American prospects to burst upon the scene in the late 1980s – others included Agassi, Wheaton, Pete Sampras and Michael Chang – Courier established an early ascendancy with his back-to-back French titles in 1991-92 and Australian victories in 1992-93. He achieved the No. 1 ranking in 1992 and looked set for a long reign, but after losing the 1993 finals at Roland Garros (to Sergi Bruguera) and Wimbledon (to Sampras) he went into a slow decline. He never won the US Open, having lost to Stefan Edberg in the 1991 final, and his loss to Cedric Pioline in the fourth round at Flushing Meadows in 1993 marked a turning point in his career from which he never recovered.

Somewhat of an individualist, Courier was admired for the way he refused to behave like a celebrity and his crowd-pleasing gestures. But at the 1993 ATP World Championships in Frankfurt he raised eyebrows by abandoning his trademark baseball cap and reading a novel during changeovers. From 1994 until his abrupt retirement in May 2000, Courier never again advanced beyond a Grand Slam quarterfinal and slid inexorably down the rankings. He would have become almost unnoticeable but for his continuing heroic exploits in the Davis Cup. He is the only American player to win two five set deciding fifth rubbers – against Marat Safin in 1998 and against Greg Rusedski in 1999.

JACK CRAWFORD (AUS)

By winning the three major titles in 1933 and losing the final of the fourth, he first raised the concept of the Grand Slam in tennis.

Born: Albury, New South Wales, Australia, March 22, 1908.
Died: Cessnock, New South Wales, Australia, September 10, 1991.
Grand Slam titles: Australian 1931-33, 1935. French 1933. Wimbledon 1933. Six men's doubles titles, five mixed doubles titles.

Jack Crawford came within one set of winning the Grand Slam five years before Donald Budge took the four major singles titles in 1938. He won the 1933 Australian, French and Wimbledon championships and advanced to the final at Forest Hills, where he faced Britain's Fred Perry. The Briton won the first set 63 but lost the next two 1113 46, so the Australian stood on the brink of an historic feat. But he had been suffering from asthma and insomnia, and his strength evaporated. Perry won the last two sets 60 61, denying Crawford an achievement which up until then had never been considered possible, far less given a name which, through Budge, would become the ultimate goal for any top class tennis player.

Crawford was a hugely admired player in his time, dubbed by one contemporary "the most popular Wimbledon winner in history". Impeccably sporting, he was regarded as a throwback to the pre-World War I era, not only in his attire – he always wore long-sleeved cricket shirts, buttoned at the wrist, but also his equipment – he used an old-fashioned flat-topped racket, and his style of play – from the back of the court, with fluent, accurate ground strokes rather than bludgeoning power. His hair was parted in the middle and he was every inch a courteous Edwardian gentleman. Between sets on a hot day he customarily revived himself by sipping hot tea.

His winning Wimbledon final against Ellsworth Vines in 1933 is regarded as one of the greatest of all time. Vines, a hard-hitting American in a peaked cap, renowned for his devastating serve, was expected to retain his title. But Crawford, for all his outdated characteristics, had the guile to beat him. He nullified the power of Vines's forehand by feeding him a succession of high-bouncing shots to the forehand side and then preventing Vines from getting into a groove by switching to low, sliced shots to his weaker backhand flank.

Crawford lost to Perry in the 1934 Australian final but gained his revenge the following year. He lost two further Australian finals to Adrian Quist in 1936 and 1940. He was easily beaten by Perry in the 1934 Wimbledon final. His only appearance for Australia in the Davis Cup Challenge Round resulted in defeats by both Perry and Bunny Austin in 1936.

STEFAN EDBERG (SWE)

His backhand volley was one of the best shots the game has ever seen. A five-set loss to Michael Chang in the 1989 Roland Garros final prevented him from winning all four Slam tournaments.

Born:	Vastervik, Sweden, January 19, 1966.
Grand Slam titles:	Australian 1985, 1987. Wimbledon 1988, 1990. United States 1991-92. Three men's doubles titles.
Olympics:	Gold medal, singles, 1984. Bronze medals, singles and doubles, 1988.
Davis Cup winning teams:	Sweden 1984-85, 1994.

Stefan Edberg was the third of a triumvirate of Swedish players – the others were Bjorn Borg and Mats Wilander – to achieve the No. 1 ranking. He is the only man apart from John McEnroe to reach No. 1 at both singles and doubles. He appeared in 54 consecutive Grand Slams between 1983 and 1996, a record only recently surpassed.

Unlike Borg and Wilander, he played a classic serve and volley game, with a style that was almost an anachronism in an era when power hitting from the baseline became the norm. He had a beautifully timed serve, elegant ground strokes, single-handed on the backhand, and the best net game of his generation. He was an exponent of chip and charge tactics to gain the net whenever possible. He could dispatch exquisitely angled volleys to all parts of the court and put away lobs with crunching smashes.

It was clear that he would become an outstanding player when, in 1983, he won a Grand Slam of major junior singles titles. Edberg wasted little time in beginning his collection of senior Grand Slam titles. At the age of 19 he captured the 1985 Australian Open – then played on grass in December – outplaying Wilander in straight sets in the final. Thirteen months later, in January 1987, he retained the title over that year's Wimbledon champion, Pat Cash. He was runner-up three more times in Melbourne.

He appeared in three consecutive Wimbledon finals against Boris Becker between 1988 and 1990, winning the first and third of these encounters. And at the US Open he triumphed in 1991 and 1992, winning the former final over Jim Courier 62 64 60 in one of the most perfect displays of aggressive tennis ever seen. When he retained the title against Pete Sampras while still only 26 it seemed that many more successes would come his way.

However, Edberg would reach only one more Grand Slam final – the 1993 Australian, where he lost to Courier. In his only French Open final, in 1989, he was frustrated by the dogged returning of Michael Chang. The final four years of his career saw a decline, although he could still delight audiences with his skills and impeccable sportsmanship. He was a staunch member of the Swedish Davis Cup team and in the victorious teams of 1984, 1985 and 1994.

ROY EMERSON (AUS)

Took advantage of Lew Hoad, Ken Rosewall and Rod Laver turning professional; however 12 Slam titles is still a great achievement. Won all the Grand Slam tournaments at least twice.

Born:	Blackbutt, Queensland, Australia, November 3, 1936.
Grand Slam titles:	Australian 1961, 1963-67. French 1963, 1967. Wimbledon 1964-65. United States 1961, 1964. 16 men's doubles titles.
Davis Cup winning teams:	Australia 1959-62, 1964-67.

Although Roy Emerson's record of 12 Grand Slam singles titles was overtaken by Pete Sampras in 2000, the Australian's total of 28 major singles and doubles championships is still unsurpassed in the men's game. It is, however, important to note that his six Australian titles were won at a time when the tournament did not attract a similar quality of entry as the other three Slam events. Emerson was one of the greatest of a long line of superlative Australian players trained by the country's Davis Cup captain, Harry Hopman, in the 1950s and 1960s. A country boy reared on a dairy farm about 100 miles north of Brisbane, he developed exceptionally strong wrists by milking large numbers of cows every day. He was also an outstanding athlete, running the 100 yards in 10.6 seconds at the age of 14. But "Emmo" decided at an early age to concentrate on tennis, because he saw a greater future in it. That he became such a good player was due in no small part to the very high standard of fitness he maintained throughout his 20-year top class tennis career.

He was a gregarious fellow and partied as hard as he played, but he was always prepared for major events. He had an all-out attacking game with a vicious serve prefaced by a unique corkscrew wind-up, but he could adapt his game to survive on any surface, as proved by his two French championships. He won them in 1963, when he defeated Pierre Darmon in the final, and 1967, when he dethroned his compatriot Tony Roche.

In those days the other three Grand Slams were all played on grass. Emerson began his conquest of the major prizes in 1961, when he beat Rod Laver in both the Australian and American finals. After Laver turned professional in 1962 Emerson was almost unbeatable in his own country, winning the championship for the next five years. He also took back-to-back Wimbledons in 1964-65 and a further US title in 1964.

In 1967 he played on a record eighth winning Australian Davis Cup team, crushing his great rival Manuel Santana in the opening rubber of the Challenge Round. He resisted the temptation to turn professional until the eve of Open tennis in 1968, but by this time he was 31 and on the wane. Emerson continued to compete until 1979.

ROGER FEDERER (SUI)

Roger Federer is the rarest of tennis players – a genius who only comes along perhaps once in a generation. The Swiss player is already being mentioned in the same breath as Pete Sampras, John McEnroe and Rod Laver.

Born: Basel, Switzerland, August 8, 1981.
Grand Slam titles: Australian 2004. Wimbledon 2003-04. United States 2004-05.

The great Laver says of Federer: "I would be honoured to even be compared with Roger. He is such an unbelievable talent and is capable of anything. Roger could be the greatest tennis player of all time." McEnroe is equally enthusiastic. "When he plays his best tennis there is no player that plays better than him," he says. "He's one of the best players that ever played, already."

Federer has a complete game and is equally awesome on all surfaces, having won titles on clay, hard courts, grass and carpet. His service, though not as fast as Andy Roddick's, is powerful and varied. His forehand is heavy and accurate, whilst his backhand, one-handed and struck with supreme elegance, is infinitely versatile, both in attack and defence. His volley and overhead are perfectly timed, and his movement, courtcraft and anticipation so good that opponents are often demoralised, such is his brilliance.

Federer was an outstanding junior, winning the boys' singles at Wimbledon in 1998, and in the same year he reached the quarterfinals of only his second ATP Tour event, at Toulouse. He was ranked inside the world's top 100 by mid-1999, improving 248 positions from the previous year. In 2000 he was in two ATP finals and reached the semifinals at the Sydney Olympics, losing the bronze medal play-off to Arnaud di Pasquale. In 2001 he vaulted into the top 20, winning his first ATP title at Milan, leading Switzerland to an upset victory over the USA in the Davis Cup and stunning Sampras in the fourth round at Wimbledon. In 2002 he established himself in the top 10 and won his first Masters Series title, in Hamburg. In winning his first Wimbledon title in 2003, Federer dropped only one set – to Mardy Fish in the third round. He reached No.2 that summer but, despite also winning the Masters Cup in Houston, was held off the top position by Roddick.

In 2004, however, Federer lifted himself to a position of complete domination. He won three of the four Grand Slams, failing only in Paris where he was beaten by Gustavo Kuerten, and won a total of 11 titles (the most since Muster in 1995). In 2005 he almost emulated John McEnroe's open era win-loss record of 82-3. He lost his Australian Open title to Marat Safin in the semifinals and went out to Rafael Nadal at the French Open at the same stage, but retained Wimbledon and the US Open and again collected 11 titles in all. Despite missing most of the autumn because of a foot injury he reached the final of the Masters Cup in Shanghai and served for the title before losing a fifth set tiebreak to an inspired David Nalbandian. This left Federer with a record of 81-4 for the year and snapped a sequence of 24 consecutive winning finals (an open era record) going back to July 2003.

NEALE FRASER (AUS)

The last player to win, in 1960, the US Championships without the loss of a set. Part of a Davis Cup winning team four times as a player, four times as a captain.

Born: Melbourne, Victoria, Australia, October 3, 1933.
Grand Slam titles: Wimbledon 1960. United States 1959-60. 11 men's doubles titles, five mixed doubles titles.
Davis Cup winning teams: Australia 1959-62.

Neale Fraser, a rugged left-hander who exemplified the sort of attacking, all-court player with a perfect serve and volley game that came out of the Harry Hopman champion production line in the 1950s and 1960s, is perhaps more closely associated with the Davis Cup than any other player. He was on four winning teams between 1959 and 1962, and captained the Australian side for a record 22 years from 1970 to 1993, receiving the trophy four times in this capacity (1973, 1977, 1983 and 1986). So it was entirely appropriate that when the ITF honoured a select number of distinguished players as Davis Cup Ambassadors on the competition's centenary in 1999, he was included.

Fraser was the son of a judge, and although his parents did not play tennis, he and his brother John were encouraged to take up the game because they lived near courts in the Melbourne suburb of South Yarra. He developed an almost unreturnable repertoire of serves – a hard flat one, a swinging slice and a vicious twister, which was especially effective against right-handers. It was this that enabled him to beat the reigning Wimbledon champion, Alex Olmedo, in Fraser's debut Challenge Round singles rubber against the United States at Forest Hills in 1959. He repeated this win in the final of the US Championships shortly afterwards, and retained the title the following year without dropping a set – the last man to do so. At Wimbledon he was runner-up to fellow-Australian Ashley Cooper in 1958, then in 1960 he defeated another compatriot, Rod Laver, in the final. Apart from the US Championships later that year Fraser won no more big singles titles, although he and his brother John were both Wimbledon semifinalists in 1962. Unlike Cooper, Laver and all the other great Aussie champions, he never turned professional because he was employed in part-time jobs by Slazenger and tobacco company WD & HO Wills and preferred this financial security to the tough, roadshow existence of the contract pros in those days.

Fraser was even more successful in doubles than singles. He formed a highly effective partnership with Emerson that won seven Grand Slam titles, and he also acquired five major mixed doubles championships. An occasional competitor right up to the mid-1970s, he reached the Wimbledon doubles final in 1973 with John Cooper, younger brother of Ashley, with whom he won three Grand Slam titles.

PANCHO GONZALES (USA)

Along with Ken Rosewall, the best player never to have won Wimbledon. Played his best tennis as a professional.

Born:	Los Angeles, USA, May 9, 1928.
Died:	Las Vegas, USA, July 3, 1995.
Grand Slam titles:	United States 1948-49. Two men's doubles titles.
Davis Cup winning team:	USA 1949.

An imposing 6ft 2in tall Mexican-American who played with pantherish elegance and glowered menacingly at opponents, court officials and spectators, Ricardo 'Pancho' Gonzales had personality with a capital 'P' and bestrode the international scene like a colossus for nearly four decades. Regarded as one of the two finest players (along with Ken Rosewall) who never won Wimbledon, he was a contract professional in the pre-Open Era for most of his career and as such unable to take part in the major championships.

Originating in a large and poor family of Mexican immigrants in a tough district of Los Angeles, he was a problem child and his early life was tainted with delinquency. But when he took up tennis at 12 he developed a commanding game, with one of the purest service actions ever seen. Such was the quality of his stylish, aggressive method of play that he was good enough to win the US Championship at the age of 20, sweeping past Eric Sturgess 62 63 1412 in the final, and he retained the title by outlasting Wimbledon champion Ted Schroeder in five sets in 1949. In his one and only Wimbledon appearance as an amateur in the same year he lost in the fourth round to Geoff Brown but won the doubles with Frank Parker.

After helping the United States retain the Davis Cup he turned professional, though still only 21. For much of the next 18 years he dominated the pro tour, and when Open tennis arrived he was still a leading contender despite the fact he was 40. At Wimbledon in 1969 he won the longest match (in terms of games) ever played at the Championships, recovering from two sets down and saving seven match points against 25-year-old Charlie Pasarell, 2224 16 1614 63 119. Later that year he beat John Newcombe, Rosewall, Stan Smith and Arthur Ashe to win a big-money tournament in Las Vegas. In 1972, three months before his 44th birthday, he became the oldest winner of a tour-level event in Open history when he beat Georges Goven in the final at Des Moines, Iowa.

He was a top box-office draw not only for his enduring skills but also his explosive personality. At Queen's Club in 1972 he stormed off the court after shoving the female referee, Bea Seal, in a disagreement over a line call.

LEW HOAD (AUS)

Turning professional at 23 and problems with his back limited his successes. At his best he was probably the greatest player ever.

Born:	Sydney, New South Wales, Australia, November 23, 1934.
Died:	Fuengirola, Spain, July 3, 1994.
Grand Slam titles:	Australian 1956. French 1956. Wimbledon 1956-57. Eight men's doubles titles, one mixed doubles title.
Davis Cup winning teams:	Australia 1953, 1955-56.

At his best, Lew Hoad possibly played tennis better than any other man in history. This blond Adonis, whose striking good looks and muscular physique were matched by the breathtaking strength and command of his shots, would have been even more successful had he not been struck down by a cruel and chronic back injury when he was at the height of his powers. Like his compatriot Jack Crawford, Hoad came within one match of winning the Grand Slam. In 1956, already holding the Australian, French and Wimbledon titles, he faced his friend and Davis Cup partner, Ken Rosewall, in the final of the US Championship. Hoad lost a match of superlative quality in four sets and was thus denied the chance to become only the second man to hold all four majors at the same time.

Hoad was a flamboyant player, always preferring to attempt a big shot rather than play safe, and when his huge, aggressive game was on song he was irresistible. He and Rosewall emerged at the same time as Australia's Davis Cup heroes, brought in for the 1953 Challenge Round after Frank Sedgman and Ken McGregor had turned professional. They were trailing the USA 2-1 when Hoad won a dramatic five set rubber against US champion Tony Trabert and Rosewall clinched victory for Australia by defeating Wimbledon champion Vic Seixas.

Hoad and Rosewall, though sharply contrasting in appearance and playing styles, were known as 'The Twins' and were Australia's leading players for the next three years. They won three Grand Slam doubles together in 1953 and 1956, and contested three Slam singles finals in 1956, with Hoad triumphing at Brisbane and Wimbledon. Before the final of the French he partied all night and got over his hangover by running all the way from his hotel in central Paris to Roland Garros, where he demolished Sven Davidson in straight sets.

Whereas Rosewall turned professional at the start of 1957, Hoad remained amateur and retained his Wimbledon title with a devastating display in the final against Ashley Cooper. After this he too signed a pro contract, but he had already begun to suffer severe back pain and rarely again attained the force of his earlier years. He played spasmodically into the Open Era and faded out in the early 1970s.

YEVGENY KAFELNIKOV (RUS)

After Andre Agassi, Kafelnikov is the only winner of the French Open in the last ten years who has also been able to win a Slam title on another surface. His talent has been tested more than his consistency. The busiest player on the circuit, from 1994-2001 Kafelnikov was never ranked lower than No. 12, reaching No. 1 in 1999.

Born:	Sochi, Russia, February 18, 1974.
Grand Slam titles:	Australian 1999. French 1996. Four doubles titles.
Olympics:	Gold medal, singles, 2000.
Davis Cup winning team:	Russia 2002.

Still the most successful Russian player in the history of tennis, Yevgeny Kafelnikov was an indefatigable competitor who played more matches, in singles and doubles, than anyone else on the ATP circuit in the 1990s. His total of 26 singles and 27 doubles titles, accumulated over a professional career beginning in 1992, was a testament to his busy and fruitful activity, although it has to be said that Kafelnikov's effort level varied from week to week.

He was a thoroughly modern player, his game characterised by hard hitting from the baseline (double-handed on the backhand), a powerful serve and a competent volleying ability, as evidenced by his success in doubles. Kafelnikov won titles on all four surfaces, although his record at Wimbledon, where he only once reached the quarterfinals, was far inferior to his showing in the other three Grand Slam events.

He was the first of a new generation of Russian players to benefit from the fall of communism. Under the Soviet regime, athletes' movements were controlled and their prizemoney forfeited to the government. Kafelnikov was able to enjoy unrestricted travel (although he continued to live in the Black Sea resort where he was born) and the lifestyle of a multi-millionaire, having earned over $22 million from the sport. He was staunchly patriotic and extended his career in order to achieve his final ambition – to win the Davis Cup for Russia. This was accomplished in 2002, and he carried on playing for one more year before retiring.

In 1996 he won both the singles and doubles (with Daniel Vacek) at the French Open, the first man to do so since Ken Rosewall in 1968, and made the top five of both singles and doubles rankings. His 1997 was less successful, the highlights being the French and US Open doubles titles (with Vacek) and reaching the final of the ATP World Championship, where he lost to Sampras.

After a poor year in 1998, when he dropped out of the top ten, Kafelnikov stormed back to top form at the 1999 Australian Open, beating Thomas Enqvist in a four set final. Soon afterwards he reached No.1 in the world and held this position for 16 weeks. He reached the final at Melbourne the following year but found Andre Agassi in irresistible mood. Apart from the Olympic title in 2000 and a US Open semifinal in 2001, the Russian shone less brightly in major events in later years.

JACK KRAMER (USA)

Nobody has dominated tennis like he did in 1946-47. In 1947 he won Wimbledon for the loss of only 37 games in seven matches, a record.

Born:	Las Vegas, USA, August 5, 1921.
Grand Slam titles:	Wimbledon 1947. United States 1946-47. Six men's doubles titles, one mixed doubles title.
Davis Cup winning teams:	USA 1946-47.

Jack Kramer was a principal player on the amateur circuit for just two years, yet his influence on the game was greater than just about anyone else for almost 40 years. He was indisputably the world's top amateur in 1947, then he dominated the professional tour for five seasons. Even before his enforced retirement as a player because of an arthritic back he had taken over as the pro tour's promoter and was responsible for arranging the tour and recruiting its star performers into the 1960s. He worked tirelessly to help bring about Open tennis in 1968, which brought all the world's best players – professional and amateur – into the same events. He devised the Grand Prix – a points-linked system which was the precursor of today's ATP tour, and was instrumental in forming the Association of Tennis Professionals, which eventually took over the running of the top level of men's tennis. He was the world's leading television commentator. And by striking a deal with Wilson Sporting Goods in 1947 his name was perpetuated on the world's top-selling racket, earning himself a fortune in the process.

Kramer is credited with inventing 'The Big Game' – a style of play that was adopted by the vast majority of players who won Grand Slam titles on grass (which in those days excluded only the French Championships) until tennis began to move back to the baseline in the 1970s. The Big Game comprised a blistering serve and a decisive first volley, while returns consisted of a chip-and-charge strategy to gain the net. Kramer perfected this style on the high-bouncing cement courts of California and readily adapted it to grass, on which he was virtually unbeatable.

He made his international debut in the 1939 Davis Cup Challenge Round when he was selected to play doubles at the age of 18. Because of World War II, during which he served in the US Coastguards and played a restricted schedule, Kramer had to wait until 1946 for his Wimbledon debut. Suffering from severe blisters on his racket hand, he lost in the fourth round to Jaroslav Drobny, but the following year he won for the loss of only 37 games in seven rounds – a record. He finished his amateur career with a flourish, retaining the US title and the Davis Cup for Uncle Sam.

RENE LACOSTE (FRA)

Physical problems shortened his career and forced him to retire in 1929 having won seven Grand Slam titles and two Davis Cup championships as part of the French team.

Born:	Paris, France, July 2, 1904.
Died:	St Jean de Luz, France, October 12, 1996.
Grand Slam titles:	French 1925, 1927, 1929. Wimbledon 1925, 1928. United States 1926-27. Three men's doubles titles.
Olympics:	Bronze medal, doubles, 1924.
Davis Cup winning teams:	France 1927-28.

Chemise Lacoste is a brand name as famous as Fred Perry and Sergio Tacchini, and its logo, the crocodile, was adopted from its founder, Rene Lacoste, so nicknamed because he tended to gobble up his opponents. He was a self-made champion who did not take up tennis until he was 15, but by working assiduously on his game he made up for lost time and was a champion by the time he was 21. A slight man with pronounced Gallic features, Lacoste was frail of physique and did not suffer good health, but his determination compensated for these shortcomings. He played chiefly from the baseline and was a master of strategy, hitting to an impeccable length, rarely making an error, in order to wait for a mistake from his opponent or to score with a lob or passing shot.

In 1923 he made his debut for France in Davis Cup and in 1924 he reached the Wimbledon final. In 1925 he won Wimbledon, avenging his loss to Jean Borotra in the previous year's final, and also triumphed in the French championship, trouncing Borotra in straight sets. He would win a total of two Wimbledon and three French singles titles during his brief career, but it was his achievement in taking back-to-back US championships in 1926-27, being the first non-English speaker to do so, that established him as the top player in the world. Only one non-American had ever won the title, which for six consecutive years had been the personal property of the great Bill Tilden. With Tilden losing early in the 1926 championship Lacoste swept to the title, brushing aside Borotra 64 60 64 after a much harder five set defeat of the third great Frenchman, Henri Cochet. The following year Lacoste met Tilden in the final and again came through, 119 63 119.

Even more sensationally, he beat Tilden on the latter's home court in Philadelphia to help win the Davis Cup for France for the first time. When the French defended the trophy at the newly-built Stade Roland Garros in 1928 Lacoste lost to Tilden but clinched the tie by overcoming John Hennessy. Sadly, after winning the French title for the third time in 1929 his health began to deteriorate and he abruptly retired. But he would live on another 67 years, make his clothing brand one of the most famous in sport, and outlive the other three Musketeers.

ROD LAVER (AUS)

How many Grand Slam titles would he have won if had not been ruled out of competition as a professional for the best five years of his life? Won 31 consecutive matches at Wimbledon between 1961 and 1970.

Born:	Rockhampton, Queensland, Australia, August 9, 1938.
Grand Slam titles:	Australian 1960, 1962, 1969. French 1962, 1969. Wimbledon 1961-62, 1968-69. United States 1962, 1969. Six men's doubles titles, three mixed doubles titles.
Davis Cup winning teams:	Australia 1959-62, 1973.

Rod Laver stands joint third with Bjorn Borg in the all-time pantheon of men's Grand Slam champions with 11 titles, behind Pete Sampras (14) and Roy Emerson (12) but many experts rate him the greatest player of all. His career spanned the final years of the pre-Open Era, when contract professionals were barred from the traditional championships, and the first few years of the Open game, after which he was able to return to the major arenas and take up where he had left off. Who knows how many more top titles he would have won if he had been able to compete in the events he was denied access to between 1963 and 1967, when he dominated the pro tour?

Laver did not cut an imposing figure, but his left arm produced the most magnificent tennis ever seen. He had a complete game, with a devastating serve, penetrating ground strokes, beautifully timed volleys, a decisive smash and exquisite half-volleys. His topspin backhand, a shot rarely seen before but later adopted by such champions as Borg (albeit with two hands) and Guillermo Vilas, drew gasps from observers and sighs of despair from opponents.

Laver stands alone as the only tennis player – male or female – to achieve the Grand Slam twice. He did so in 1962, as an amateur, and in 1969 as a professional. Born just before Don Budge became the first Slammer in 1938, 'Rocket' took time to mature as a champion. He reached his first major final at Wimbledon in 1959, losing to Alex Olmedo, and would fail again at the same stage in 1960 at the hands of Neale Fraser. But by this time he had beaten Fraser for the Australian title and was on his way to the pinnacle of the sport.

He won his first Wimbledon singles title in 1961, crushing Chuck McKinley for the loss of eight games, and would never lose again there until 1970, when he lost in the fourth round to Britain's Roger Taylor. The greatest threat to his 1962 Slam came in Paris, where he was match point down to Australia's Martin Mulligan in the quarterfinals, but he more easily beat the same player to retain his Wimbledon crown. His toughest match during the 1969 campaign was a 90-game marathon against Tony Roche at the Australian Open. He won no more major titles after 1969 but played on at a high level until 1977.

IVAN LENDL (CZE/USA)

Hard-working with obsessive, methodic preparation. He played eight consecutive finals at the US Open and won there three times in a row, losing only three of 66 sets played.

Born:	Ostrava, Czechoslovakia, March 7, 1960.
Grand Slam titles:	Australian 1989-90. French 1984, 1986-87. United States 1985-87.
Davis Cup winning team:	Czechoslovakia 1980.

Ivan Lendl introduced a brand of tennis which is very much still with us now: a strong, deep serve and extremely powerful ground strokes, struck like missiles. In his time the grass court season shrank to a few weeks around Wimbledon and for a few years he didn't bother to play there, but when he made a serious bid to compete at Wimbledon he never quite got to grips with the need to volley and did not succeed despite twice reaching the final. He was tall, well built and super fit, and his heavy forehand reaped a huge reward on all surfaces other than grass (although he did win at Queen's Club in 1989 and 1990).

His first big success was in the 1980 Davis Cup, when he won all three of his rubbers against Italy to secure Czechoslovakia's sole triumph in the competition. For the next three years he readily gathered minor titles but seemed to waver on the brink of Grand Slam success. Lendl's most remarkable feat was reaching the final of the US Open eight years in succession – a record he shares with Bill Tilden. He lost the first three in 1982-84, but took the next three in a row against John McEnroe, Miroslav Mecir and Mats Wilander. Then he lost to Wilander in 1988 and to Boris Becker in 1989. His first Grand Slam title was in Paris in 1984, when he recovered from two sets down to defeat McEnroe, then the undisputed world No. 1. Lendl had himself achieved the No. 1 ranking in February 1983 despite his lack of Grand Slam titles at that stage and would eventually become the longest incumbent in that position, with 270 weeks at the top, until Pete Sampras overtook him for this record in 1999.

He lost to Wilander in the 1985 French final but won it back in 1986 over Mikael Pernfors and over Wilander in 1987. Having lost to Wilander in the 1983 Australian final, when it was still played on grass, he captured the title Down Under on hard courts over Mecir (1989) and Stefan Edberg (1990). He surrendered the title in the 1991 final to Becker. He failed to win a set in either of his Wimbledon finals, crashing to Becker in 1986 and to Pat Cash in 1987.

Lendl moved to the US in 1984 and became a US citizen in 1992. A chronic back injury obliged him to retire in 1994.

JOHN MCENROE (USA)

Greatest artist to ever play the game. His talent made everybody forgive his outrageous behaviour on court.

Born:	Wiesbaden, Germany, February 16, 1959.
Grand Slam titles:	Wimbledon 1981, 1983-84. United States: 1979-81, 1984. Nine men's doubles titles, one mixed doubles title.
Davis Cup winning teams:	USA 1978-79, 1981-82, 1992.

John McEnroe is probably the most naturally gifted player ever to step onto a tennis court, and the most controversial. Crowds gasped with admiration at the sheer brilliance of his shotmaking and were appalled by the extremes of his behaviour. He waged a one man war against the tennis establishment for most of his turbulent career and came close to being thrown out of the sport long before he was finally disqualified at the Australian Open in 1990. But he never shirked his responsibilities in the Davis Cup and played with great distinction for 12 years, five times on the winning team. He always said that he did not need to practise very much because he played as much doubles as singles, ending his career with 77 singles and 77 doubles titles on his record. He won nine Grand Slam doubles championships, including seven with his fellow-American Peter Fleming.

The foundation of his game was a left-handed service that he could vary as required, whether a swinging slice that drew his opponent well out of the court or a fast missile down the middle. He could play awesome volleys, struck hard or with feather-like touch, at breathtaking angles. And when he lost his temper with umpires and line judges he usually played even better. His matches were often stormy – most notably the 1982 Wimbledon final, which he lost to Jimmy Connors in deplorable circumstances. But with his other great rival, Bjorn Borg, whom he played in two classic Wimbledon finals in 1980 and 1981, there was a strong mutual respect.

He burst onto the scene in 1977, when he reached the semifinal at his first Wimbledon as an 18-year-old qualifier. The following year he made his Davis Cup debut in the final against Great Britain, winning both of his rubbers. He won his first US Open in 1979 and his first Wimbledon in 1981, reversing the previous year's titanic battle against Borg. His greatest year was 1984, when he came within a few games of winning the French Open (ultimately submitting to Ivan Lendl) and won Wimbledon for the third time. In the final against Connors he gave one of the most devastatingly ruthless displays ever seen on the Centre Court, destroying the former champion 61 61 62 in 80 minutes. McEnroe retired in 1992 after reaching the semifinals at Wimbledon and winning the doubles with Michael Stich.

ILIE NASTASE (ROM)

Won many less titles than he should, but his style on court will never be equalled. Played an unpredictable, new style of tennis.

Born: Bucharest, Romania, July 19, 1946.
Grand Slam titles: French 1973. United States 1972. Three men's doubles titles, two mixed doubles titles.

Ilie Nastase was a supremely talented artist who could dazzle galleries with his skills and showmanship, but he could never resist the temptation to show off, create a diversion and infuriate an opponent with mischievous pranks. As a result he fell short of fulfilling his potential – he should have won many more major titles and lifted the Davis Cup for his country. Nastase had the ability to play every shot in the book to perfection, and he was an innovator, always coming up with the unexpected and toying with an opponent before delivering the coup de grace. But his temperament was fragile, and he would waste energy arguing with officials and performing outrageous antics that delighted crowds but derailed his own aims.

A stalwart in the Davis Cup – he played more rubbers than any other player except Italy's Nicola Pietrangeli – Nastase and his mentor Ion Tiriac took Romania to the Challenge Round in the United States in 1969 and 1971, then in the first year of the Final, in 1972, missed a golden opportunity to win the trophy on home soil. Overwhelmed with nerves, Nastase lost in straight sets to Stan Smith in the opening rubber and the chance was gone.

In individual play he was top-seeded in the 1970 French Open but flopped against America's Cliff Richey in the quarterfinals, and at 1973 Wimbledon, the year of the ATP boycott, he was the strong favourite but crashed out to another American, Sandy Mayer, in the fourth round. He narrowly lost to Smith in a magnificent Wimbledon final in 1972 but at the same stage four years later was outplayed by Bjorn Borg in straight sets.

Against those failures, Nastase had a spectacular success at the 1972 US Open, where he recovered from two sets to one and 4-2 down in the fourth to beat Arthur Ashe for the title. The following year he won the French Open without dropping a set and became the first man to be ranked No. 1 when the ATP introduced its computerised world ranking list. Apart from these two Grand Slam titles he was four times the winner of the Grand Prix Masters (precursor of today's Tennis Masters Cup) and won two Italian Opens. During a playing career that lasted from 1966 to 1985 he had 57 singles and 51 doubles tournament victories.

JOHN NEWCOMBE (AUS)

He never won the French, but in Rome they will never forget the way he played and won the Italian Open in 1969, beating Jan Kodes in five sets in the semis and Tony Roche in the finals.

Born: Sydney, New South Wales, Australia, May 23, 1944.
Grand Slam titles: Australian 1973, 1975. Wimbledon 1967, 1970-71. United States 1967, 1973. 17 men's doubles titles, two mixed doubles title.
Davis Cup winning teams: Australia 1965-67, 1973.

John Newcombe was the last of the line of great Australian champions who ruled tennis throughout the 1950s and 1960s, and he was the last amateur champion of Wimbledon, easily defeating Germany's Wilhelm Bungert 63 61 61 in a final that lasted only 71 minutes. Open tennis came at exactly the right time for him – he was 23 and the clear world No. 1 when he turned professional at the end of 1967, when the signs were that the distinction between amateurs and pros was about to be abolished.

Even with the pros on the scene he was good enough to reach the Wimbledon final in 1969, where he had to settle for a supporting role in Rod Laver's Grand Slam victory parade, but he regained the title in 1970 over another veteran Aussie, Ken Rosewall, and held onto it the following year against a determined challenge from America's Stan Smith.

Newcombe was an all-out, no-frills attacking player whose aim was always to deliver a fast, swinging first serve, get straight into the net and put away the volley. He was devastating in the air and overhead, and his game was ideally suited to grass, on which he won all his major titles. But he was so fit and ready to run that he achieved some success on clay as well, winning the German Open in 1968 and the Italian in 1969. He made few attempts on the French Open, where his best result was a 1969 quarterfinal.

His two United States championships – one as an amateur and one as a pro – were six years apart and widely differing in the manner of their achievement. In 1967 he dropped only four sets in seven rounds, while in 1973 he was pushed all the way in the final by Jan Kodes, who beat him in the first round in 1971. He won his first Australian Open in a fairly weak field, because the event was staged between Christmas and the New Year, beating New Zealander Onny Parun in a four set final, and he took the title back from Jimmy Connors in the 1975 decider.

He was even more successful in doubles, winning 12 Grand Slam championships with Tony Roche and a grand total of 26 Slam trophies in singles, doubles and mixed – more than any other man except Roy Emerson. His top class playing career lasted from 1960 to 1978.

FRED PERRY (GBR)

Everybody knows (especially Tim Henman) that he was the last British man to win Wimbledon, in 1936. He was also the last one to win any Grand Slam tournament.

Born:	Stockport, Cheshire, Great Britain, May 18, 1909.
Died:	Melbourne, Australia, February 2, 1995.
Grand Slam titles:	Australian 1934. French 1935. Wimbledon 1934-36. United States 1933-34, 1936. Two men's doubles titles, four mixed doubles titles.
Davis Cup winning teams:	Great Britain 1933-36.

Fred Perry was the greatest British player of all time and the last to date to win any Grand Slam men's singles titles. He was the first player to win all four majors (although not all in the same year) and his name is universally known today not only because he was such a successful player but through the sports clothes company he founded and which is still a prestigious brand. He became a world champion at two sports – at table tennis, whose world championship he won in 1929, and at tennis, at which he was the dominant player from 1934 to 1936.

He was a supremely confident and self-assured person and had the iron willpower and determination, that all champions need, in abundance. Considering that he did not take up tennis until he was 18, he mastered the game extraordinarily quickly. Benefiting from the competitive edge he had already acquired as a top table tennis player, Perry assembled a formidable array of shots, the best of which was his running forehand, hit early with a continental grip, which overwhelmed his opponents because he struck the ball as soon as it rose from the court.

He was good enough to make the world's top ten in 1931, just four years after he had taken up the game, and reached the semifinals at Wimbledon that year. In 1933 he spearheaded Great Britain's first triumph in the Davis Cup for 21 years, beating Wilmer Allison and Ellsworth Vines of the USA in the Inter-Zone Final and Henri Cochet and Andre Merlin of France in the Challenge Round. Both of these ties were on clay in Paris. Later that summer he won the United States Championship, overcoming Jack Crawford 86 in the fifth set of the final.

At Wimbledon he won three consecutive finals in straight sets – against Jack Crawford in 1934 and Gottfried von Cramm in 1935 and 1936. He beat Crawford again for the 1934 Australian title and von Cramm in the 1935 Roland Garros final. He played a pivotal role in retaining the Davis Cup for Britain in 1934-36, winning all his Challenge Round rubbers. In taking his third US crown he defeated Don Budge, who took over as world No. 1 when Perry turned professional at the end of 1936. Perry also won the US pro championship in 1938 and 1941.

BOBBY RIGGS (USA)

Known mostly for the match he lost to Billie Jean King in 1973 but don't forget that he won Wimbledon and the US Championships just before the outbreak of the war in 1939.

Born:	Los Angeles, California, USA, February 25, 1918.
Died:	Leucadia, California, USA, October 25, 1995.
Grand Slam titles:	Wimbledon 1939. United States 1939, 1941. One men's doubles titles, two mixed doubles titles.
Davis Cup winning team:	USA 1938.

Although Bobby Riggs has the rare distinction of winning all three titles open to him – singles, doubles and mixed – at his one and only attempt, in his appearance at Wimbledon in 1939, he is best remembered as the self-appointed 'Male Chauvinist Pig' of 1973 who played two highly publicised mixed singles matches against Margaret Court and Billie Jean King. The latter encounter, at the Houston Astradome, attracted more spectators (30,472) and a bigger television audience (50 million) than any other match in the history of tennis.

Riggs, an inveterate gambler who made a fortune by betting on his matches and arranging bizarre gimmick events, placed a wager with a London bookmaker before his Wimbledon campaign, backing himself at very long odds to win the triple crown. As he had just lost the final of the Queen's Club tournament 61 60 to Gottfried von Cramm, the likelihood of his losing his stake seemed great. But he went on to win the singles, beating his fellow-American Elwood Cooke in a five set singles final, joining Cooke to defeat Charles Hare and Frank Wilde for the men's doubles title, and taking the mixed doubles with Alice Marble over Wilde and Nina Brown. From his stake of £100 he netted £21,600 – a considerable sum in those days.

He didn't hit with great power, but he was a very clever strategist who could outmanoeuvre big hitters with subtlety and cunning. His lobs and drop shots were well disguised and uncannily accurate. Add to these qualities a boundless self-confidence and you have a very capable player, able to make the most of his opportunities. When Don Budge turned professional at the end of 1938 Riggs was ready to take over the amateur game. With war looming he followed up his Wimbledon victory by taking the United States title, demolishing Welby Van Horn in a straight set final. He lost the title to Don McNeill in 1940 but regained it the following year over Frank Kovacs.

He enjoyed a successful career as a pro throughout the 1940s, becoming a promoter at the end of the decade. Then over 20 years later he emerged from obscurity in the age of Women's Lib to challenge first Court, whom he beat 61 62 and then King, who made him look his age, winning 64 63 63. But he was believed to have made $1 million out of it.

TONY ROCHE (AUS)

On grass, his best surface, he always found Rod Laver or John Newcombe in his path, but he did win the French Open on clay. One of the best doubles players ever.

Born:	Wagga Wagga, New South Wales, Australia, May 17, 1945.
Grand Slam titles:	French 1966. 13 men's doubles titles, two mixed doubles titles.
Davis Cup winning teams:	Australia 1965-67, 1977.

For a player who had a formidable left-handed serve and volleying skills second to none, it was a strange quirk of fate that Tony Roche never won a major singles title on grass. He was runner-up to Rod Laver at Wimbledon in 1968 and at Forest Hills in 1969, and to Ken Rosewall at Forest Hills in 1970. Then he won 15 Grand Slam doubles and mixed doubles titles during an 12-year stretch. But his only big singles victory was at the French Championships in 1966, a few weeks after he had lifted the next most important clay court title, the Italian. He won both the semifinal (against Francois Jauffret) and the final at Roland Garros (against Istvan Gulyas) in straight sets, tempering the power of his serve and volley game with well-struck, accurate ground strokes.

At the end of 1967 he turned professional a few months before the arrival of Open tennis. At Wimbledon 1968 he swept past the second seeded Rosewall on his way to the final, but once there he was no match for Laver. In 1969 at Forest Hills he defeated John Newcombe 86 in the fifth set of a thrilling semifinal, but could only play a supporting role in Laver's historic progress to a second Grand Slam. And in 1970 he could not prevent Rosewall from turning back the years to win the US Open 14 years after his previous triumph.

Not long afterwards, Roche began to suffer from shoulder trouble and tennis elbow. He tried numerous cures, eventually turning to a faith healer in the Philippines in 1974 who performed an operation by acupuncture. Although he never completely recovered from the injury he was able to resume competition and continued to acquire major doubles titles. His partnership with Newcombe garnered five Wimbledon championships – a record in the post-World War I period until overtaken by Todd Woodbridge and Mark Woodforde in 2000.

Roche was included in the Australian Davis Cup team for nine years between 1964 and 1978 and had his finest hour in 1977 when he was selected to play singles in the final against Italy in Sydney and beat Adriano Panatta in the opening rubber. He retired in 1979 and would later coach Ivan Lendl and Patrick Rafter, as well as coaching the Australian Davis Cup team from 1997 to 2000.

KEN ROSEWALL (AUS)

Both the youngest and the oldest winner of the Australian Championships. Won his four titles there spanning 19 years and appeared in Wimbledon finals 20 years apart.

Born:	Sydney, New South Wales, Australia, November 2, 1934.
Grand Slam titles:	Australian 1953, 1955, 1971-72. French 1953, 1968. United States 1956, 1970. Nine men's doubles titles, one mixed doubles title.
Davis Cup winning teams:	Australia, 1953, 1955-56.

Ken Rosewall is the ultimate long haul tennis champion: his international playing career lasted an amazing 25 years, from 1952 to 1977, and he won Grand Slam titles over a span of 19 years. He played his last Wimbledon final 20 years after his first, making him the oldest Grand Slam finalist in the post-war era. Ironically nicknamed 'Muscles', Rosewall was slight for a phenomenal athlete at only 5ft 7in tall and 135 pounds. He could not generate the power of his stablemate Lew Hoad, with whom he took the world by storm as a 17-year-old in 1952, but he used his brain and a matchless array of wonderful strokes to stay amongst the world's best 20 players for all of his quarter-century in the world class game.

Rosewall was, perhaps more than any other player, equally good on any surface. He could play the serve and volley game with magnificent panache because his serve, though not especially strong, was well placed and delivered with admirable technique. His net game was exemplary and his agility second to none. Similarly, he had such fine groundstrokes – including possibly the most beautifully hit backhand the world has ever seen – that he was as much a master on clay as grass. Blessed with an unflappable temperament and impeccable sportsmanship, you can understand the world's dismay that he never won Wimbledon despite reaching the final four times.

His career falls into three phases. From 1952 to 1956 he was one of the top amateurs, winning two Australian, one French and one US championship (plus the doubles at all four Grand Slams) and losing two Wimbledon finals – to Jaroslav Drobny in 1954 and to Hoad in 1956. Then he turned professional, and spent the next 12 years barred from the traditional events. When Open tennis arrived in 1968 he was 33 but still the world's No. 2 player, and for 10 more years he regularly won big titles, taking two more Australian, one French and one US Open.

He won the first ever Open tournament, beating Rod Laver in the final at Bournemouth, but his most remarkable feat was reaching the finals both at Wimbledon and Forest Hills in 1974 at the age of 39. Sadly, he was humiliated in both matches by Jimmy Connors, 18 years his junior. He also took part in the Davis Cup in years as far apart as 1953 and 1975.

PETE SAMPRAS (USA)

They shouldn't wait five years for his induction into the International Tennis Hall of Fame. Seven Wimbledons and seven other Grand Slam titles make up for the one he has not claimed in Paris.

Born:	Washington DC, USA, August 12, 1971.
Grand Slam titles:	Australian 1994, 1997. Wimbledon 1993-95, 1997-2000. United States 1990, 1993, 1995-96, 2002.
Davis Cup winning teams:	USA 1992, 1995.

With 14 Grand Slam titles to his name, Sampras is the all-time No. 1 men's Grand Slam champion, including two Australian and five US Opens in his tally. But those who argue that Rod Laver, with two calendar Slams was the greater player, point to an inescapable blemish on Sampras's record. He never, in 13 attempts, managed to take the French Open, and on only one occasion went further than the quarterfinals. Although he won the Italian Open on clay in 1994, Sampras always found the demands of the red clay Grand Slam event beyond his ability to conquer.

This great champion, regarded with awe and respect by all his fellow-players, proved himself over and over again on all surfaces other than clay by his peerless command of the game. A dynamic, beautifully constructed service action, crunching forehand, precision volleys and, above all, his famous 'slam dunk' jumping smash made him the winner of 64 career singles titles and a supreme status at No. 1 on the ATP rankings for 286 weeks, including a record six consecutive year-end finishes in pole position. This achievement is the one cited by those who insist he was better than Laver, disregarding the fact that Laver's career spanned the pre-Open and Open Eras, with all-player rankings impossible to determine before 1968. Against that, it must be acknowledged that the overall quality of the sport was much weaker in Laver's day.

Sampras became the youngest-ever US Open champion in 1990, when he was 19, and his unparalleled run of success at Wimbledon between 1993 and 2000 was broken only by a quarterfinal defeat by Richard Krajicek in 1996. At Flushing Meadows he was runner-up in 1992 (to Stefan Edberg), in 2000 (to Marat Safin) and in 2001 (to Lleyton Hewitt). Winning the 2002 US Open delivering a resounding response to those who had said his career was over. He defeated old rival Andre Agassi in a high-quality final, claiming his first title in 34 tournaments and winning his first event since claiming his record breaking 13th Grand Slam title at Wimbledon in 2000. The US Open win turned out to be his last professional match. After taking time off for the birth of his first child with his actress wife Bridgette Wilson, a son born in November 2002, Sampras officially announced his retirement a year later at the 2003 US Open.

MANUEL SANTANA (ESP)

The only Spanish player to win a Grand Slam title on grass, and he did it twice – at the US Championships in 1965 and at Wimbledon a year later. He introduced the passing lifted lob to tennis.

Born:	Madrid, Spain, May 10, 1938.
Grand Slam titles:	French 1961, 1964. Wimbledon 1966. United States 1965. One men's doubles title.

Manuel Santana remains the greatest Spanish player in the history of tennis despite the recent resurgence of the game in his country. Not only did he twice win the French championship on clay, the surface on which he learnt the game, but he captured two Grand Slam titles on grass, at Forest Hills and Wimbledon. A cheerful and popular character with a trademark gap-tooth smile, Santana was an impeccably good-mannered player and a consummate stylist. Not only did he hit the ball with both power and touch, but his exceptional racket control enabled him to produce amazing winners when least expected. This magician could improvise and dig himself out of seemingly impossible situations with clever drop shots, topspin lobs and half-volleys. During his career his rivalry with Roy Emerson enthralled galleries with the contrast between the irresistible force of the net-rushing Australian and the immovable object of the ever-resourceful Spaniard.

Santana reached the quarterfinals of the French Championship in 1960 and first won it the following year, scoring five-set victories over Rod Laver and Nicola Pietrangeli in the last two rounds. In 1962 and 1963 he was a semifinalist, losing to Emerson and Pierre Darmon, but he was champion again in 1964, avenging the previous year's defeat by Darmon in the semis and repeating his 1961 final victory over Pietrangeli. He also won the doubles in 1963 with Emerson. At Forest Hills he never made the later stages before 1965, when he overcame Arthur Ashe in the semis and Cliff Drysdale in the final. The following year he succumbed in the semis to John Newcombe. At Wimbledon he was in the last eight of 1962 and the last four of 1963, when he failed to win a set against Fred Stolle, but in 1966, seeded fourth, he was in the best form of his career. Santana survived two five set epics against Ken Fletcher in the quarters and Owen Davidson in the semis, both at 75 in the fifth, before outmanoeuvring Dennis Ralston 64 119 64 for the title.

In 1967 he became the first men's champion at Wimbledon ever to surrender his title in the first round, at the hands of Charlie Pasarell. He led Spain to two Davis Cup Challenge Rounds (1965, 1967) and between 1958 and 1973 played more times in the event than anyone in history except Pietrangeli and Ilie Nastase.

FRANK SEDGMAN (AUS)

The best player in the most difficult zone of the court – between the service line and the baseline – giving him spectacular coverage. Turned professional at 25 after winning five Grand Slam titles and three Davis Cups for Australia.

Born:	Mount Albert, Victoria, Australia, October 29, 1927.
Grand Slam titles:	Australian 1949-50. Wimbledon 1952. United States 1951-52. Nine men's doubles titles, eight mixed doubles titles.
Davis Cup winning teams:	Australia 1950-52.

No other player ever accumulated so many Grand Slam singles, doubles and mixed doubles titles within a four year period as Frank Sedgman, who totted up 22 between 1949 and 1952, placing him third in the all-time men's list behind Roy Emerson (28) and John Newcombe (25). Who knows how many more Sedgman would have won had he not turned professional at the age of 25 and ruled himself out of contention. Sedgman was the first of a long line of Australian champions who ruled the game for 25 years. A fitness fanatic, he worked assiduously in the gym and in outdoor training to build up an enviable athletic physique and reserves of stamina that enabled him to compete, week after week, at tournaments around the world. He was a staunch disciple of the serve and volley game, and lived at the net, from whence he rarely needed to play a second volley.

His five singles, nine men's doubles and eight mixed doubles Grand Slam titles are a testament to his desire to compete to the full. He was the third and last man to win the triple crown at Wimbledon (Don Budge and Bobby Riggs were the others) and with fellow-Australian Ken McGregor he achieved the only Grand Slam in men's doubles in 1951. (They came within a whisker of repeating the sweep the following year but lost 86 in the fifth set of the US final to Mervyn Rose and Vic Seixas.)

Sedgman began his international career in 1947, and in 1949 he won the Australian championship, battering his more experienced compatriot John Bromwich in straight sets. The following year he overcame McGregor in four sets for the title. In the French singles, the only Grand Slam title (including doubles) to elude him, he was runner-up to Jaroslav Drobny in 1952. At Wimbledon he lost the 1950 final to Budge Patty but won in 1952, avenging his Roland Garros loss to Drobny. He won the US championships in 1951 and 1952, against Seixas and Gardnar Mulloy.

He embarked on a glorious professional career at the end of 1952 and kept himself in such great shape that he was able to return to Wimbledon and the other traditional events after tennis went Open. Even in his mid-forties he was good enough to reach the third round at Wimbledon in 1971 and at Melbourne in 1972.

FRED STOLLE (AUS)

Lost three Wimbledon finals in a row but won the French and the US titles, the latter unseeded in 1966. He was a great doubles player.

Born:	Hornsby, New South Wales, Australia, October 8, 1938.
Grand Slam titles:	French 1965. United States 1966. Ten men's doubles titles, six mixed doubles titles.
Davis Cup winning teams:	Australia 1964-66.

Such was the plethora of tennis talent that came out of Australia in the 1950s and 1960s that Fred Stolle tends to be overshadowed by the likes of Rod Laver, Ken Rosewall, Roy Emerson and John Newcombe. But he was a highly successful player, reaching the finals of all four Grand Slam events and winning all four doubles titles at these championships. A tall (6ft 3in) and rangy player, Stolle had an impressive serve and volley style but an excellent baseline game as well, enabling him to win the French and German titles on continental clay. Although he played in the Davis Cup for only three seasons he was on the winning team all three times and managed a commanding 13-3 win-loss record in the competition.

His singles record is one of enviable consistency over a long period, although he never reached the very pinnacle of the sport and his best world ranking was No. 2 for 1964 and 1966. His two Grand Slam singles titles came shortly before the arrival of Open tennis, and because he turned professional at the beginning of 1967 he missed only one year of traditional competition.

At the French Championships in 1965 he beat Cliff Drysdale in five sets in the semifinals and Tony Roche in four sets in the final. He also reached the last eight at Roland Garros in 1966 and 1969. In the Australian Championships he lost to Emerson in the finals of 1964 and 1965 – the first time easily and the second in five gruelling sets. At Wimbledon he had the misfortune to lose three consecutive finals – against Chuck McKinley in 1963 and against Emerson in 1964 and 1965. His finest hour came at Forest Hills in 1966. Despite having lost to Emerson in the 1964 final and having just won the German championship, he found himself unseeded and, stung by the slight, proceeded to win the title. At last he beat his old nemesis, Emerson, in a stunningly one-sided 64 61 61 semifinal and got the better of Newcombe, also unseeded, in a tough 46 1210 63 64 final.

He also reached the quarterfinals at the US Open in 1969 and 1972, when at the age of 33 he beat Emerson, Newcombe and Drysdale before submitting to Ilie Nastase in four sets.

BILL TILDEN (USA)

A legend. Old-time experts considered him the best ever, but the success of the Four Musketeers against him puts a question mark over that. Won his first and last Wimbledon title ten years apart, in 1920 and 1930.

Born:	Philadelphia, Pennsylvania, USA, February 10, 1893.
Died:	Los Angeles, USA, June 5, 1953.
Grand Slam titles:	Wimbledon 1920-21, 1930. United States 1920-25, 1929. Six men's doubles titles, five mixed doubles titles.
Davis Cup winning teams:	USA 1920-26.

Historians generally agree that Bill Tilden was one of the three greatest players of all time, along with Rod Laver and Pete Sampras. He was virtually unbeatable between 1920 and 1926, and achieved a level of dominance unsurpassed by any other man. He won seven US and three Wimbledon singles titles, the third ten years after the first, and at 37 he was one of the oldest champions. An imposing figure at over 6ft tall with broad shoulders, Tilden was a master of every shot in the game, with a cannonball first serve and vicious, kicking American twist second serve, an extraordinary deployment of spin, slice and chop and devastatingly effective drop shots. He played chiefly from the back of the court and operated his matches like a game of chess, using innovative strategies to confound all but the most able of opponents.

Tilden lost half of one of his fingers in an accident early in his career but modified his grip and the handicap never affected him. There are stories of poor personal hygiene and homosexuality, which later caused him to be ostracised in tennis circles, but he had a very forceful personality, coloured by strong likes and dislikes. He was also constantly at loggerheads with his national association.

Tilden lost his first two US finals in 1918 and 1919 but began his reign as champion in 1920 when he won the first of six consecutive finals against his compatriot Bill Johnston. Also in 1920 he made his first appearance at Wimbledon and defeated the holder, Gerald Patterson, in the Challenge Round. In defending the title in 1921 he saved match points against the young South African, Brian Norton. In the late 1920s he was eclipsed by the Frenchmen Henri Cochet and Rene Lacoste at major championships but in 1930 at Wimbledon he squeezed past Jean Borotra in the last four and regained the title against Wilmer Allison in the final.

At Forest Hills he won for the last time in 1929, over Frank Hunter. Tilden was twice runner-up for the French Championship and won 13 consecutive rubbers in the Challenge Round of the Davis Cup between 1920 and 1927. He turned professional in 1931 and continued playing right up to his death at the age of 60.

TONY TRABERT (USA)

Won five Grand Slam titles, three of them without losing a single set. He turned professional in 1955 at the age of 25.

Born:	Cincinnati, Ohio, USA, August 16, 1930.
Grand Slam titles:	French 1954-55. Wimbledon 1955. United States 1953, 1955. Five men's doubles titles.
Davis Cup winning team:	USA 1954.

Tony Trabert, the archetypal 1950s American athlete with a strong physique, crewcut and pugnacious personality, is known to tennis fans today as former tournament director of the US Open, and he still introduces the finalists for the trophy presentations in Arthur Ashe Stadium. But in 1955 he achieved a stranglehold over men's tennis, winning three of the four Grand Slam championships and capturing 18 singles and 12 doubles titles at the 23 tournaments he entered. Unusually for a player in that era he was equally good on all surfaces, because in addition to an attacking game with firm volleys he owned superb ground strokes – particularly on the backhand. Between 1950, when he won the French doubles, and his annus mirabilis of 1955, he was a stalwart of the US Davis Cup team, joining Vic Seixas in his country's only victory over Australia in an eight year stretch in 1954.

His Grand Slam singles parade began in 1953, when he won his first US title without losing a set, brushing aside French champion Ken Rosewall in the last four and finishing with a decisive 63 62 63 victory over Seixas, the reigning Wimbledon champion. In 1954 and 1955 he was unbeaten at Roland Garros, trouncing Art Larsen and Sven Davidson in the two finals. No other American won the title until Michael Chang in 1989.

Trabert went on to win Wimbledon in 1955 without dropping a set, taking out Jaroslav Drobny, the holder, in the quarterfinals, Budge Patty, the 1950 champion, in the semifinals and crushing Kurt Nielsen 63 75 61 in the final. He repeated the feat at Forest Hills, allowing Lew Hoad only seven games in the semifinals and avenging his one blemish of the year against Ken Rosewall in the title round. Rosewall had wrecked Trabert's chances of winning the Grand Slam in the semifinals of the Australian Championships.

Trabert also had a strong doubles record. Partnering Seixas, he won the Australian title in 1955, the French in 1954 and 1955 and the US Nationals at Boston in 1954 as well as the 1950 French with Bill Talbert. He turned professional in 1956 but was unable to match the skills of Pancho Gonzales, then at the height of his powers. When his playing career ended in the early 1960s he became a coach and a television commentator and served as the US Davis Cup captain from 1976 to 1980, leading the team to victory in 1978 and 1979.

GUILLERMO VILAS (ARG)

A clay court specialist who was able to win the Australian Open twice on grass. The first man from Argentina to win a Grand Slam title.

Born: Mar del Plata, Argentina, August 17, 1952.
Grand Slam titles: Australian 1978-79. French 1977. United States 1977.

South America has produced a string of fine male players over the years, but none has had as much success as Argentina's Guillermo Vilas, a relentless winning machine who achieved an Open Era record of 46 consecutive match wins and claimed two Grand Slam titles in his best year, 1977. A thick-set, muscular athlete with thighs like tree trunks, Vilas was a distinctive, head-banded figure with flowing brown hair and the strength of an ox. A left-hander with a dangerous, swinging serve, he could rally forever with heavy, topspun ground strokes on both sides and a heartbreakingly cruel lob. But though his game was ideally suited to clay he proved his versatility by winning three major titles on grass at Melbourne. He also had a social conscience. He wore two bracelets that once belonged to unidentified American soldiers killed in the Vietnam War, and he composed poetry which indicated a sensitivity towards the world beyond the existence of the touring tennis professional.

Although his main tour career lasted from 1970 to 1989, the most productive stage was from 1973 to 1983, during which time he gathered 62 titles. Given the clear suitability of his game for clay, it was an extraordinary surprise that he won his first big title, the Grand Prix Masters, on grass. He beat John Newcombe, Bjorn Borg and Onny Parun in his group, then Raul Ramirez in the semifinals and Ilie Nastase in the final. He returned to Melbourne in 1977 and lost the Australian Open final to Roscoe Tanner, but he took the title in 1978 over John Marks and in 1979 over John Sadri.

But Vilas's forte was really on clay, and his monumental run in 1977 included victory at Roland Garros, where he destroyed Brian Gottfried 60 63 60 in the shortest final on record, and at Forest Hills, in the US Open's third staging on clay and last time at the West Side Club. He beat holder Jimmy Connors in a thrilling four set final and by rights should have overtaken the American as No. 1 in the world. However, the ATP's computer never raised him higher than No. 2. Vilas's last big final was at the 1982 French Open, where he lost to Mats Wilander, and in the Davis Cup he and Jose Luis Clerc took Argentina to the 1981 final but could not overcome the United States.

ELLSWORTH VINES (USA)

In 1933 he lost one of the best Wimbledon finals ever to Jack Crawford. He turned professional at the age of 22.

Born: Los Angeles, California, USA, September 28, 1911.
Died: La Quinta, California, USA, March 17, 1994.
Grand Slam titles: Wimbledon 1932. United States 1931-32. Two men's doubles titles, one mixed doubles title.

Nicknamed "The Californian Comet", Henry Ellsworth Vines Jr appeared at Wimbledon for the first time in 1932 and blazed to the title, losing just one set in seven matches. He briefly lost his way against Iwao Aoki of Japan in the fourth round, but then demolished Enrique Maier of Spain 62 63 62, Jack Crawford of Australia 62 61 63 and, in the final, Britain's Bunny Austin 64 62 60 in a devastating 50 minutes. His winning shot, an ace, was so fast that Austin never even saw it.

Vines was less overwhelming at Forest Hills, where he won in 1931 by overcoming Fred Perry in five sets in the semifinals and George Lott in a tough 79 63 97 75 final. He retained the title with even more difficulty, extended to 46 810 1210 108 61 by Charles Sutter in the semis and Henri Cochet 64 64 64 in the final. But the Comet really lived up to his name. In 1933 he lost both to Perry and Austin in the Davis Cup, was outmanoeuvred by the wily Crawford in the Wimbledon final and stunned by a less exalted American, Bitsy Grant, in the fourth round at Forest Hills. Shortly afterwards, at the age of only 22, he turned professional and won a series against Bill Tilden, but by the end of the 1930s he had lost interest in tennis and turned to golf, at which sport he became good enough to reach the semifinals of the 1951 US PGA Championship.

What made this phenomenal talent so good for such a short space of time? Vines had a thunderbolt serve, probably the fastest struck by any player in the wooden racket era, with very little spin, a fast and no holds barred forehand, deadly volleys and a smash that never came back. He had little margin for error, going for broke on everything, so that when he was on song he was unplayable, but if his timing was off he would perpetrate suicidal errors.

Vines's amateur career was so short – he first played Forest Hills as an 18-year-old in 1929 and turned pro just four years later – that it is difficult to assess his standing among the all-time greats. But Jack Kramer rated Vines the second greatest player he ever saw, after Don Budge. "On his best days, Vines played the best tennis ever," he wrote. "Hell, when Elly was on, you'd be lucky to get your racket on the ball once you served it."

MATS WILANDER (SWE)

Shook the tennis world by winning the French Open age 17 in 1982. In 1988 won three of the four Grand Slam titles, finishing the year as No. 1.

Born:	Vaxjo, Sweden, August 22, 1964.
Grand Slam titles:	Australian 1983-84, 1988. French 1982, 1985, 1988. United States 1988. One men's doubles title.
Davis Cup winning teams:	Sweden 1984-85, 1987.

A baseline metronome who won 33 professional titles during a 15-year pro career, Mats Wilander was often criticised for being dull and unenterprising. But he developed his game from simply grinding out endless backcourt rallies with his relentless topspinning ground strokes, double-handed on the backhand, to an all-court attacking mode which gained him two Australian singles titles on grass and the Wimbledon doubles crown with his fellow Swede, Joakim Nystrom.

No man in the open era ever made such a huge leap from the juniors to the pros as Wilander, who won the boys' singles at Roland Garros in 1981 and the men's singles the following year. He was only 17 years and nine months old at the time, and it was his first professional title. In an extraordinary series of upsets the skinny boy wonder took out Ivan Lendl, Vitas Gerulaitis, Jose Luis Clerc and Guillermo Vilas and made a mockery of the theory that the French Open is the most difficult title to win and requires the most experience.

Wilander had infinite patience and was always prepared to keep on slugging away until his opponents capitulated. It took him 4 hours, 42 minutes to outlast the similarly indefatigable Vilas, and in two Davis Cup rubbers the Swede battled for over six hours against John McEnroe (in 1982) and Austria's Horst Skoff in 1989 (though he lost both of these). He won two Australian Opens on grass, subduing Lendl in 1983 and Kevin Curren in 1984, and he vanquished Lendl to win again in Paris in 1985. But his great year was 1988, when he won three of the four Grand Slams and took over the No. 1 ranking for 20 weeks. He defeated Pat Cash at Melbourne, Henri Leconte in Paris and Lendl at Flushing Meadows, although at Wimbledon he never got further than the quarterfinals. He played in every Davis Cup from 1981 to 1990, finishing on the winning team three times. He returned to the team in 1995 for Sweden's semifinal tie against the United States.

After 1988 he lost motivation and slid down the rankings, taking a long break from the tour between June 1991 and May 1993. His last four years in competition were undistinguished compared with his performances throughout the 1980s and he did not get further than the last 16 at Melbourne and the low 40s in the rankings. Since then however, he has carved out a career as a coach, including a stint with Marat Safin, and in 2002 he was appointed Sweden's Davis Cup captain.

TODD WOODBRIDGE (AUS)

The younger member of the fantastically successful Woodies, he went on to further victories with the Swede, Jonas Bjorkman.

Born:	Sydney, New South Wales, Australia, April 2, 1971.
Grand Slam titles:	16 men's doubles, six mixed doubles titles.
Olympics:	Gold medal, doubles: 1996. Silver medal, doubles: 2000.
Davis Cup winning team:	Australia 1999, 2003.

Woodbridge is the younger half of the famous 'Woodies' – the most successful men's doubles partnership of the open era and possibly of all time. Woodbridge and Mark Woodforde won a record 61 pro titles together, which is four more than Peter Fleming/John McEnroe and Bob Hewitt/Frew McMillan. During their 10 years in partnership they won every major title in the game. They shared 11 Grand Slam titles, which is one less than another Australian pair, John Newcombe and Tony Roche. They played together in 16 Davis Cup ties and lost only twice; they were in the winning team of 1999. And they landed two ATP Tour World Championships. Perhaps their only major disappointment was their very last match, the Sydney Olympic final of 2000, when they failed to retain the gold medal against Canadians Sebastien Lareau and Daniel Nestor.

The son of a policeman, Woodbridge took up tennis at the age of four and was coached by Ray Ruffels. He had an outstanding junior career, reaching the final of the Australian boys' singles in 1987 and 1989 and the Wimbledon boys' singles in 1989. He won seven junior Grand Slam doubles titles. He had already earned an ATP ranking at the age of 15 and was playing in the main draws of Grand Slam men's singles events at 17. Although comparatively short for a tennis pro (5ft 10ins), Woodbridge was always a fit, dedicated and highly competitive player. In 1989 he beat Pete Sampras at Wimbledon and in 1997 he reached the semifinals at the same event, beating Michael Chang and Patrick Rafter. But like Woodforde, this was the only time he survived beyond the last 16 at a Grand Slam singles event. He won two ATP singles titles (Coral Springs 1995 and Adelaide 1997) and he was runner-up at Toronto, a Super Nine (now Masters Series) event in 1996.

After Woodforde's retirement Woodbridge formed a highly fruitful partnership with Sweden's Jonas Bjorkman. They gathered five Grand Slam titles together, the last at Wimbledon in 2004 when the victory gave Woodbridge a record ninth crown at the grass court event, breaking a 99-year-old record held by Laurie and Reggie Doherty, who won their eighth title in 1905. It was also with Bjorkman that Woodbridge broke Tom Okker's open era record of 78 doubles titles. The pair have amassed 14 titles with the Australian holding a record 83 in all. Woodbridge's Davis Cup career spanned 14 years, he played more years, more ties and had the most wins of any Australian in doubles. At his retirement in July 2005 he held a 25-7 Davis Cup doubles record.

MARK WOODFORDE (AUS)

Red-headed left-hander whose doubles partnership with Todd Woodbridge was one of the most successful of all time.

Born:	Adelaide, South Australia, September 23, 1965.
Grand Slam titles:	12 men's doubles, five mixed doubles titles.
Olympics:	Gold medal, doubles: 1996. Silver medal, doubles: 2000.
Davis Cup winning team:	Australia 1999.

Mark Woodforde is the older of the Woodies by six years. As a youngster, the Adelaide left-hander was coached by Barry Phillips-Moore, an old friend of his father. He turned pro in 1983, the year he earned his first world ranking, but took several years to work his way through the Satellite and Challenger circuits, winning his first ATP Tour singles at Auckland in 1986, when he was 20. In 1987 he reached the fourth round at the US Open and established a place in the top 100, a level at which he stayed inside, or very close to, for the next 11 years.

In the early part of his career Woodforde was equally successful in singles and doubles. He memorably beat John McEnroe in consecutive events (Toronto, US Open) in 1988 and won three more Tour singles titles – Adelaide (1988-89) and Philadelphia (1993). But in a Grand Slam singles career that stretched from 1985 to 2000 he only once got further than the fourth round – as a semifinalist at the 1996 Australian Open, where he beat Mark Philippoussis and Thomas Enqvist before falling to Boris Becker.

Before forming his doubles partnership with Woodbridge, Woodforde successfully played with a number of different partners, including John McEnroe, with whom he won the 1989 US Open, and Thomas Smid, fellow-winner at the 1989 Monte Carlo Open.

His doubles partnership with Woodbridge, which began in 1991 and was virtually constant until the end of 2000 (they occasionally partnered other players in Davis Cup ties) was probably the greatest of all time. Before the open era, many top players enjoyed successful careers in singles and doubles, but since John McEnroe, very few headlining stars have regularly taken part in both disciplines. The Woodies won five consecutive doubles titles at Wimbledon – a unique feat since the abolition of the Challenge Round in 1922 (only the Doherty brothers, who did not have to play through, had won it that many times consecutively). After years of disappointment, the two Australians completed a full set of Grand Slam titles when they won the French in 2000, Woodforde's farewell season.

Since retiring from competitive tennis at the end of 2000 Woodforde has become a television commentator and coach to the Australian Fed Cup team.

Todd Woodbridge and Mark Woodforde winning Olympic Gold, Atlanta 1996

LOUISE BROUGH (USA)

For three years she dominated Wimbledon more completely than any player before or since by reaching nine finals and winning eight of them. In 1949 she played the singles, doubles and mixed doubles finals on the same day, playing 117 games in eight sets.

Born: Oklahoma City, Oklahoma, USA, March 11, 1923.
Grand Slam titles: Australian 1950. Wimbledon 1948-50, 1955. United States 1947. 21 women's doubles titles, eight mixed doubles titles.

As a multiple title winner, Louise Brough was the fifth most successful woman tennis player of all time. She won a remarkable 35 Grand Slam titles – six singles, 21 women's doubles and eight mixed doubles – during a stretch of 16 years, 1942-1957. This indefatigable champion, who also had an unblemished 22-0 win-loss record in the Wightman Cup, was a disciple of the serve and volley game pioneered amongst women by Alice Marble. She had a strong, kicking serve and splendid hands for volleying. Her style was always to get to the net at every opportunity, which was ideal for grass but less so on clay – a surface that proved fairly barren ground for her.

Strong and successful though she was, Brough would have been even more prominent in the history of the game had her career not coincided with the golden age of American women's tennis. Whilst competitive tennis ground to a halt in Europe during the war, it continued in the USA, and a legion of amazons emerged to dominate the sport for the first decade after hostilities ceased. In addition to Brough, there was Pauline Betz, Margaret Osborne DuPont, Doris Hart, Shirley Fry, Maureen Connolly, Pat Todd and Althea Gibson – all exceptional players and all Grand Slam singles champions between 1946 and 1958.

Of all these champions, Brough gathered the most titles. Early on, she was regularly thwarted by Betz, who beat her in two US finals (1942, 1943) and at Wimbledon in 1946. She defeated Osborne for the US title in 1947 and then won three consecutive Wimbledons – over Hart in 1948 and over DuPont in 1949 and 1950. She also beat Hart for the 1950 Australian title. The arrival of the near-invincible Connolly put her singles ambitions on hold for three years in the early Fifties, but after Connolly's retirement she took one last Wimbledon in 1955, over Beverly Fleitz. In the women's doubles Brough was even more prolific. Her partnership with DuPont was one of the best of all time. They won 20 major titles together, including 12 US Championships.

At Wimbledon in 1948-1950 she won eight of the nine titles available to her. During the course of finals day in 1949 she played a record 117 games, winning the singles over DuPont 108 16 108, joining DuPont to beat Gussie Moran and Pat Todd 86 75, and with John Bromwich narrowly failing against Eric Sturgess and Sheila Summers of South Africa 97 911 75.

MARIA BUENO (BRA)

Between 1958-1967, the Brazilian with rare grace and artistry won 115 matches at Wimbledon, including 49 in singles, winning the title three times. Won the US singles four times before illness and injury prematurely ended her career.

Born: Sao Paulo, Brazil, October 11, 1939.
Grand Slam titles: Wimbledon 1959-60, 1964. United States 1959, 1963-64, 1966. 11 women's doubles titles, one mixed doubles title.

The best female player ever to come out of Latin America, Maria Bueno lit up the tennis scene and enthralled audiences around the world with her graceful, artistic and attacking style of tennis. She was an entirely natural player whose appeal was as much due to her decorative and exotic appearance as her arsenal of lovely shots. Although she learned the game on clay she was at her best on grass, with an elegant, fluid service and daring, penetrating volleys. Safe shots were not for her: she loved to take risks and dazzle the gallery with exquisitely constructed winners. When on form, she was magnificent. But she had little margin for error.

Bueno made her first European tour in 1958 and made an immediate impact, winning the Italian championship and the Wimbledon doubles with Althea Gibson. The following year she swept through Wimbledon, outclassing US No. 1 Darlene Hard 64 63 in the final. She added the US championship, dismissing Hard and Christine Truman in identical 61 64 scorelines in the last two rounds.

She retained the Wimbledon title in 1960 and came within a match point of the triple crown, although she lost in the quarterfinals of the Australian championship to the teenage sensation Margaret Smith, and to Hard in Paris (semis) and Forest Hills (final).

Then things began to turn sour for the balletic Brazilian. She missed most of the 1961 season because of hepatitis, and for the rest of her career she was afflicted with a variety of ailments, including jaundice, shoulder trouble and acute tennis elbow. She did not regain her best form until 1963, when she beat Smith for the US title, and then enjoyed a fine 1964, losing to Smith in a three set French final, gaining revenge in a marvellous final at Wimbledon and humiliating Carole Graebner 61 60 for a third US championship.

Bueno lost the 1965 Wimbledon final to Smith and the 1966 Wimbledon decider to Billie Jean King but claimed one last Forest Hills crown in 1966, over Nancy Richey. After that her injuries and poor health reduced her effectiveness and she retired in early 1969.
But she made a comeback in the mid-1970s, winning the Japan Open in 1974 and reaching the fourth round at Wimbledon in 1976. She was a superb doubles player, netting 11 Grand Slam titles in women's doubles and her partnership with Hard was one of the best in tennis history.

JENNIFER CAPRIATI (USA)

Age 13, she won her first match for the United States in Wightman Cup. At 14 became the youngest to reach the top ten; at 15, the youngest Wimbledon semifinalist. In 2001, her rehabilitation complete, she won the Australian and French Open titles and gained the No. 1 ranking.

Born:	New York, New York, USA, March 29, 1976.
Grand Slam titles:	Australian 2001-02. French 2001.
Olympics:	Gold medal, singles, 1992.
Fed Cup winning teams:	USA 1990, 2000.

Jennifer Capriati holds a unique place in tennis history. In an era of teenage prodigies she was the youngest achiever, reaching the semifinals of her first French Open at the age of 14. At 18 she was branded a victim of 'burn-out', had several brushes with the law and underwent rehabilitation for drug abuse. At 20 she returned to tennis but struggled to regain her early form. Then in 2001 she had a glorious year, winning two Grand Slam titles and reaching the No. 1 spot for the first time. Like most champions of the new millennium, Capriati is a baseline power-hitter, armed with a strong serve, bullet-like ground strokes (double-handed on the backhand) and the well-toned physique of a champion athlete.

As a 13-year-old winner of the French and US Open junior titles in 1989 she was selected to play for the United States in the last Wightman Cup. In 1990 she reached the final of her first pro tournament and became the first 14 year-old to claim a place in the world's top ten. Capriati marched on, reaching the semifinals at Wimbledon and the US Open in 1991, and in 1992 she dethroned Steffi Graf in the final of the Olympics at Barcelona. But there was trouble at home: her parents separated and she began to perform listlessly. After a disastrous first round loss at Flushing Meadows in 1993 she walked away from the game. She continued to make headlines, but for the wrong reasons, and did not return to tennis until 1996.

She finally won a title in Strasbourg in 1999, six years after her last success, and in 2000 she reached the semifinals at the Australian Open. Then came the fulfilment of her talent. She won the 2001 Australian Open and at Paris she battled past Kim Clijsters 16 64 1210 in a thrilling final. The following year, in 2002, Capriati defended her Australian Open title, fighting off four match points to beat three-time champ Martina Hingis in the final. Back down under in 2003 Capriati became the first defending champion to lose in the opening round in the open era. Later that year she narrowly missed out in the US Open semifinals, losing to eventual champion Justine Henin-Hardenne in an epic match that lasted just over three hours. History repeated itself in the following year, when Capriati again served for a place in the US Open final before succumbing to Svetlana Kuznetsova. She missed the entire 2005 season with a shoulder injury.

MAUREEN CONNOLLY (USA)

2003 marked the 50th anniversary of her achievement in becoming the first woman to complete the Grand Slam in 1953. This natural left-hander, who was persuaded to play tennis right-handed, was forced to retire after an accident just before her 20 birthday..

Born:	San Diego, California, USA, September 17, 1934.
Died:	Dallas, USA, June 21, 1969.
Grand Slam titles:	Australian 1953. French 1953-54. Wimbledon 1952-54. United States 1951-53. Two women's doubles titles, one mixed doubles title.

Maureen Connolly ranks among the elite of women's tennis champions, although her career lasted no longer than her teenage years, and she died at an age when she might have still been playing. Compact and diminutive at a mere 5ft 5in tall, she was an implacable baseliner, pounding deep, penetrating ground strokes to an impeccable length and humbling the regiment of amazon-like warriors that faced her with merciless precision. Her serve was average and she rarely volleyed, but when attacked by net-rushers she had the perfect solution: razor-sharp passing shots that hardly ever missed. Blessed with astonishing determination and concentration, Connolly ruled because she never gave an opponent a weak return to exploit.

Guided by Eleanor 'Teach' Tennant, who had also coached Alice Marble, Connolly was left-handed but advised to switch to the right. She won the US girls' championship in 1949 and 1950 and also made her debut in the Nationals at Forest Hills in the those years. Her two losses there were the only Grand Slam singles defeats of her career. In 1951 she became the youngest (at that time) winner of the title at 16 years, 11 months.

In 1952 she won Wimbledon, escaping seemingly certain defeat against a British player, Susan Partridge, in the fourth round but thereafter not losing a set. She defeated the four-time champion Louise Brough for the title. At Forest Hills she beat Hart for her second US championship. In 1953 she became the first woman to win the Grand Slam, dropping only one set in 20 matches played (in Paris, again to Partridge). Hart was her victim in three of the four finals.

In 1954 she retained the French and Wimbledon crowns but shortly before the US Championships, whilst out riding, her horse was hit by a truck and her leg was badly injured. It ended her competitive career. In four years on the circuit she was beaten just four times – twice by Hart, once by Fry and once by Beverly Baker. She had a 9-0 record in the Wightman Cup. Maureen Connolly married Norman Brinker, an Olympic showjumper, in 1955 and had two daughters. She died of ovarian cancer at the age of 34 in 1969.

MARGARET COURT (AUS)

It is doubtful whether her haul of 64 Grand Slam titles will ever be surpassed. The first woman to complete the Grand Slam in Open tennis, she was regarded as one of the hardest hitters the game had ever seen.

Born:	Albury, New South Wales, Australia, July 16, 1942.
Grand Slam titles:	Australian 1960-66, 1969-71, 1973. French 1962, 1964, 1969-70, 1973. Wimbledon 1963, 1965, 1970. United States 1962, 1965, 1969-70, 1973. 19 women's doubles titles, 21 mixed doubles titles.
Fed Cup winning teams:	Australia 1964-65, 1968-69, 1971.

Margaret Court (who was Margaret Smith until her marriage in 1967) is the all-time supreme winner in tennis, with 62 Grand Slam titles – 24 in singles, 19 in women's doubles and 21 in mixed doubles. She won two calendar Grand Slams – in singles in 1970 and in mixed doubles (with Ken Fletcher) in 1963, took three of the four Slams in four other years and was ranked No. 1 seven times – yet few experts would judge her the greatest player in history. The reason for this is because, despite her unsurpassed record over 14 years of international competition, she was sometimes prone to nerves, and would then play badly. She never enjoyed invincible runs like Suzanne Lenglen, Helen Wills Moody, Maureen Connolly and Martina Navratilova, and defeats by more inspired rivals like Maria Bueno and Billie Jean King when she was at the height of her powers marred her reputation. Even in 1970, when she won 21 tournaments, she lost six times, including defeats by such lesser players as Joyce Williams, Patti Hogan and the then 15-year-old Chris Evert. Worst of all, she allowed herself to be totally intimidated by Bobby Riggs in their 1973 Battle of the Sexes, although Riggs was subsequently humiliated by King.

Nevertheless, at her best Court was a majestic and awesome performer. The first woman tennis player to train in the gym, she was tall, strong and athletic, with exceptionally long arms, giving her great reach at the net. She could play all the shots and was equally good on all surfaces. In mixed doubles opponents faced a woman who could play as well as half of a men's doubles partnership.

Her 11 Australian singles titles – a record for any Grand Slam event – were achieved over a period of 14 years, but in the majority of those the field she overcame was predominantly Australian. She suffered the indignity of becoming the first female top seed at a Grand Slam event to lose in her opening match at Wimbledon in 1962, when she was beaten by Billie Jean Moffitt, but she avenged this the following year in the final. Moffitt (later Mrs King) was the principal adversary of her career, and Court would get the better of their duel with a 22-10 head-to-head record. Their greatest battle was in the 1970 Wimbledon final, when, with both players injured, Court won a tremendous encounter 1412 119 – the longest women's final ever in that championship.

LINDSAY DAVENPORT (USA)

Holder of three Grand Slam titles, her successes made this tall and powerful player the first American-born Grand Slam champion since Chris Evert.

Born:	Palos Verdes, California, USA, June 8, 1976.
Grand Slam titles:	Australian 2000. Wimbledon 1999. United States 1998. Three women's doubles titles.
Olympics:	Gold medal, singles, 1996.
Fed Cup winning teams:	USA 1996, 1999, 2000.

One of the tallest and strongest players on the women's tour, Davenport has been ranked in, or just outside, the top ten for the past 12 years, but her ascent to the pinnacle of the sport was steady rather than meteoric. Apart from one notable early success, when she won the Olympic Gold in Atlanta at the age of 20, she was considered an underachiever. She broke into the top ten in June 1994 and had already won 11 tour singles titles before she reached her first Grand Slam semifinal at the 1997 US Open.

One of the reasons for this delay in her reaching the highest level was a lack of discipline when it came to fitness and training. She was always a powerful, commanding player, who hit the ball harder than almost anyone else on the tour, but she was overweight and comparatively slow.

In 1997 Davenport adopted a rigorous training regime, shed her excess weight and transformed herself from a top ten player into a Grand Slam champion. She won the US Open in 1998, outclassing Venus Williams in the semis and Martina Hingis 63 75 in the final. Soon afterwards she reached No. 1 in the world rankings. The following year she won Wimbledon, avenging a French Open loss to Steffi Graf and bringing down the curtain on the German's fabulous career. A third Slam success came in Australia in 2000, when she battered Hingis into submission, 61 75. In fact, she did not drop a set en route to any of her three Grand Slam triumphs.

Davenport regained the No. 1 ranking at the end of 2001 after taking seven Tour titles, although a second major injury on her right knee took her out of competition for the next eight months. This injury plus surgery on a long-standing left foot injury disrupted her 2002 and 2003 seasons. Despite considering retirement throughout 2004 Davenport's form returned. She clinched seven titles and regained the No. 1 ranking for the sixth time in her career in October, and finished the year on top for the third time. 2005 continued in the same vein with six titles, appearances in two Grand Slam finals and ending the year at No.1. Her most disappointing loss was to Venus Williams at Wimbledon after holding Championship point, in what was the longest women's final in Wimbledon history. Davenport married Jon Leach, the brother of her former coach in April 2003.

LOTTIE DOD (GBR)

No-one has yet beaten Charlotte (Lottie) Dod's record as the youngest Grand Slam singles champion, man or women. She was 15 years 285 days old when she won the Wimbledon title for the first of five times in 1887.

Born:	Bebington,Great Britain, June 8, 1871.
Died:	Sway, Great Britain, June 27, 1960.
Grand Slam titles:	Wimbledon 1887-88, 1891-93.

Lottie Dod was the youngest ever Wimbledon singles champion, winning the title at the age of 15 years, 285 days in 1887, although Martina Hingis took the women's doubles at 15 years, 282 days in 1996. But Dod was also unbeaten in five appearances at the championships and was probably the greatest all-round sportswoman the world has ever seen, reaching the highest level of ice-skating, archery, field hockey and golf as well. In an age when female tennis players were restricted by tight collars, cuffs, stays and petticoats, because of her tender years she was allowed to play in shorter skirts, giving her greater freedom of movement than her opponents. She served underarm, as did most women in the nineteenth century, but she had a powerful forehand drive, could volley capably and had a forceful smash.

Her first notable victory was over the first Wimbledon champion, Maud Watson, at Bath in 1886. Watson had won 55 consecutive matches dating back to the Edgbaston tournament in 1881, but she was disconcerted by the way her 15-year-old opponent ran to the net to volley whenever possible. In 1887 Dod made her debut at Wimbledon, where the entry numbered just five women. After a bye she beat Miss James 61 61 in the semifinals and Edith Cole 62 63 in the allcomers' final. Then she trounced the holder, Blanche Bingley 62 60 in the Challenge Round. As champion, Dod was not required to play through the following year. Despite the lack of matchplay she again beat Mrs Hillyard 63 63 to retain the title.

Because of her other sporting interests, Dod didn't bother to enter in either 1889 or 1890, when she was representing Britain in hockey and doing a spot of yachting, but she returned in 1891. She beat Mrs Parsons 60 60, Miss Steedman 63 61 and Mrs Hillyard 62 61, then regained the title because the holder, Helena Rice, did not defend it. In 1892 she once again sent Hillyard packing, 61 61 in the Challenge Round, and in 1893 Hillyard came through and this time actually managed to wrest a set before going down 68 61 64.

After this, at the grand old age of 20, Dod decided there was nothing left for her to achieve in tennis. (She had also won the Irish title in 1887). Deserting the sport for good, she conquered golf, winning the British women's championship at Troon in 1904, and won an Olympic silver medal at archery in 1908.

CHRIS EVERT (USA)

Won at least one Grand Slam title every year between 1974 and 1986, and inspired a whole generation of youngsters to play with a double-handed backhand. Supreme in dictating the pattern of matches from the back of the court.

Born:	Fort Lauderdale, Florida, USA, December 21, 1954.
Grand Slam titles:	Australian 1982, 1984. French 1974-75, 1979-80, 1983, 1985-86. Wimbledon 1974, 1976, 1981. United States 1975-78, 1980, 1982. Three women's doubles titles.
Fed Cup winning teams:	USA 1977-82, 1986, 1989.

Chris Evert won at least one Grand Slam title for 13 consecutive years – a record – and in 56 Grand Slam title attempts over 19 years she only four times failed to reach the semifinals. No other player in history has performed so constantly and consistently over such a long period. From September 1970, when as a 15-year-old she stunned Margaret Court in her Grand Slam year at Charlotte, North Carolina, until October 1989, when she was unbeaten in her swansong at the Federation Cup in Tokyo, Evert was a winner. She was ranked No. 1 in the world for 262 weeks, won a total of 154 professional singles titles and was runner-up for 72 more, reaching the final at 76 per cent of the 303 tournaments she entered. Evert, who was married to British player John Lloyd from 1979 to 1987, gained a total of 21 Grand Slam titles, including three in doubles.

Between 1973 and 1979 she won 125 consecutive matches on clay, her formative and best surface, including the three years that the US Open was a clay court event. Nevertheless, such was her control and accuracy that she was equally strong on grass, carpet and hard courts. She changed the course of the sport inasmuch as at the time she came to the fore, top class women's tennis was mainly played from the net. Evert's metronomic consistency from the back of the court, her crushing forehands and line-splitting double-handed backhands, allied to devastating finesse on drop shots and lobs, broke the mould and spawned a generation of imitators. Although she did not hit the ball as hard as some players, Evert had an acutely shrewd brain and her mental strength was her greatest asset.

She was also the perfect professional – immaculate in appearance and demeanour, always sporting and respected by all with whom she came into contact. Early on, Wimbledon crowds found her less appealing than her sunnier rival, Evonne Goolagong, but eventually she became as popular there and elsewhere as she always was in America. She won 55 consecutive matches in 1974, taking in the Italian, French and Wimbledon titles, but perhaps her greatest triumphs were in 1985 and 1986, when she beat Martina Navratilova in two classic French Open finals. Her rivalry with Navratilova was one of the greatest in sport. They played 80 times between 1973 and 1988, with Navratilova gaining the edge 43-37.

ALTHEA GIBSON (USA)

Overcame racial barriers to become the first black woman to achieve major success, winning five Grand Slam titles. She won the Wimbledon singles twice; the doubles three times plus the French Championship once and US title twice. Tall, hard hitter.

Born:	Silver, South Carolina, USA, August 25, 1927.
Died:	New Jersey, USA, September 28, 2003.
Grand Slam titles:	French 1956. Wimbledon 1957-58. United States 1957-58. Five women's doubles titles, one mixed doubles title.

Renowned as the first black player of either sex to win a major title, Althea Gibson rose from the humblest of origins and overcame the most disadvantaged of circumstances to reach the pinnacle of the sport when she was 30 years old. The child of poverty-stricken sharecroppers in the Deep South, Gibson moved with her family to Harlem when she was three years old. Abused by a brutal father, she ran away from home at 11 and lived in a hostel, surviving on a series of menial jobs. At 13 she was spotted playing paddle tennis by Buddy Walker, director of the Harlem Society Orchestra, who bought her a tennis racket and paid for her to have lessons at a New York club. At 18 she came under the patronage of Dr Walter Johnson, who was later to help Arthur Ashe, who took her into his home in Wilmington, North Carolina, and helped her develop her evident talent for tennis.

Gibson was a formidably tall and athletic performer who used her height to pound down powerful serves and volleys, but she played mainly from the back of the court. In 1950 she won the American Tennis Association's championship for black players and was grudgingly allowed to become the first player of African-American race ever to take part in the National Championships at Forest Hills. She nearly caused a sensational upset, leading Wimbledon champion Louise Brough 76 in the final set before the No. 3 seed profited from a rain break to escape.

Gibson had to endure endless obstacles, but she overcame massive prejudice to persevere in the white-dominated sport and make her first European tour in 1956, when she won the Italian and French championships and the French and Wimbledon doubles with a British player, Angela Buxton. She was also runner-up to Shirley Fry at Forest Hills. In 1957 she won the Wimbledon singles title without dropping a set, plus the doubles with Darlene Hard, then she went to Forest Hills and routed Brough 63 62 for the title and added the mixed doubles with Kurt Nielsen.

In 1958 she retained her Wimbledon singles and doubles (with Maria Bueno) and her US singles, beating Hard. After this she turned professional but there was little opposition in that field and she soon turned to golf, at which sport she played fairly successfully from 1963 to 1977.

EVONNE GOOLAGONG CAWLEY (AUS)

Few players radiated greater joy and enchantment even when she went 'walkabout' mentally. Won the French on her first visit in 1971 and four weeks later beat Billie Jean King and Margaret Court to win her first of two Wimbledon crowns.

Born:	Griffith, New South Wales, Australia, July 31, 1951.
Grand Slam titles:	Australian 1974-76, 1977 (Dec). French 1971. Wimbledon 1971, 1980. Six women's doubles titles, one mixed doubles title.
Fed Cup winning teams:	Australia 1971, 1973-74.

The only tennis player of Aboriginal extraction to reach greatness in the sport, Evonne Goolagong (who married Englishman Roger Cawley in 1975) was also unique in that she brought a freshness, joie de vivre and effortless talent that had never been seen before. She entranced Wimbledon by gliding to victory in 1971 at only her second attempt, and nine years later she won again – the first mother to win the title since Dorothea Lambert Chambers in 1914. Spectators were enchanted by the sight of this happy girl who weaved a gossamer web of magic on the Centre Court, delighting them with glorious winners and delicate touch shots, then laughing off careless mistakes.

Goolagong began life on a sheep farm in the Australian outback and only took up tennis when a local resident saw her peering through the fence at local courts and encouraged her to play. Her extraordinary natural ability was reported to a Sydney coach, Vic Edwards, who took her into his home and coached her to international standard. A serve and volleyer who caressed rather than pounded the ball, she made a strong impact on her first overseas tour in 1970, and after helping Australia to win the Federation Cup in Perth in December of that year she swiftly moved into the top stratum. She won the French Open in 1971, defeating her compatriot, Helen Gourlay, and then conquered Wimbledon, stunning the two best players in the world, Billie Jean King and Margaret Court, in straight sets in the last two rounds.

For the next seven years (plus one year out to have her first child) Goolagong lost some of her inspiration and became inconsistent. She lost two Wimbledon finals to King in 1972 and 1975, and the 1976 final to Evert. And she was losing finalist at Forest Hills for four consecutive years – against Court in 1973, King in 1974 and Evert in 1975 and 1976. Her four Australian titles in weaker fields were small consolation. But in 1980 she rolled back the years and regained her Wimbledon title, overcoming Evert in two sets. She retired in 1983 with 68 singles and 11 doubles titles to her credit. She won six Grand Slam women's doubles championships including Wimbledon with Peggy Michel in 1974.

STEFFI GRAF (GER)

The blonde German with a sledgehammer forehand won all four Grand Slam titles and the singles gold medal in Seoul in 1988 when tennis returned to the Olympic Games as a full medal sport.

Born:	Mannheim, Germany, June 14, 1969.
Grand Slam titles:	Australian 1988-90, 1994. French 1987-88, 1993, 1995-96, 1999. Wimbledon 1988-89, 1991-93, 1995-96. United States 1988-89, 1993, 1995-96. One women's doubles title.
Olympics:	Gold medal, singles, 1984, 1988. Silver medal, singles, 1992. Bronze medal, doubles, 1988.
Fed Cup winning teams:	Germany 1987,1992.

A player of the highest stature in the game, Stefanie Maria Graf is regarded by many as a champion without equal. She won a unique Golden Slam of all four majors plus the Olympic gold medal in 1988 and is the only player of either sex to win all four Grand Slam titles at least four times. Graf introduced a new style of play that has been imitated but never bettered. A splendid athlete who once ran an Olympic qualifying time for the 800 metres, she could cover the court with amazing speed and intimidate her opponents with her rushing, impatient eagerness. Her service toss was unusually high, but the stroke was well hit, and although she seldom ventured to the net her volleys and overheads were effective. But it was from the baseline that this aggressive player really scored. Her sledgehammer forehand drive was probably the finest the game has ever seen, and her single-fisted backhand was sure when sliced – as it usually was – and devastating when hit with topspin.

Graf secured a WTA ranking at the age of 13 and was a precocious star, winning the exhibition Los Angeles Olympic Gold medal (restricted to players aged 20 and under) at 15. She made the world's top ten in 1985 and reached the top in August 1987. She held the premier spot for a record 377 weeks, including 186 consecutive weeks between 1987 and 1991. She rose to her zenith at the same time that Martina Navratilova and Chris Evert were beginning to wane, and she beat them both to win her first big title, the Lipton at Key Biscayne, in March 1987. She won her first Grand Slam title, the French Open, over Navratilova in June 1987 and established an edge over the same player to take her first Wimbledon in 1988. But her dominance was eventually usurped by a new star, Monica Seles, who overtook her in the rankings in 1991.

With Seles out of the game after being stabbed in 1993, Graf regained her pre-eminence in the mid-Nineties, but a succession of serious injuries forced her into a long time-out in 1997-1998. She returned falteringly, but in 1999 had her last and perhaps greatest triumph – a dramatic victory over Martina Hingis for the French title. Graf retired in July 1999 after losing to Lindsay Davenport in only her second unsuccessful Wimbledon final. She married Andre Agassi in October 2001 and has two children, Jaden Gil (born October 2001) and Jaz Elle (born October 2003).

DORIS HART (USA)

Took up tennis aged six as a remedial exercise for an illness which might have crippled her. Won the triple crown at Wimbledon in 1951 and was twice singles champion in France and the United States.

Born:	St Louis, Missouri, USA, June 20, 1925.
Grand Slam titles:	Australian 1949. French 1950, 1952. Wimbledon 1951. United States 1954-55.14 women's doubles titles, 15 mixed doubles titles.

Doris Hart is the only player apart from Margaret Court to win the singles, doubles and mixed doubles at all four Grand Slam championships, and her total of 35 majors ties her at fifth with Louise Brough in the all-time list, behind Margaret Court, Martina Navratilova, Billie Jean King and Margaret DuPont. Hart was a swift and graceful player, equally at home at the back of the court and at the net, and was unfailingly gracious and sporting. She was even more successful at doubles than singles. Her seven-year partnership with her fellow-American Shirley Fry amassed 11 Grand Slam titles, and their rivalry with Brough and DuPont was a feature of many exciting finals. The most notable was in the 1953 US Championships at Boston when Fry and Hart recovered from 2-5 and two match points down in the third set to win 62 79 97. In the same year they crushed Maureen Connolly and Julie Sampson 60 60 in Wimbledon's only 'double bagel' doubles final.

Hart's athleticism and fluidity of movement was all the more remarkable because as a child she almost died from an infected knee and took up tennis as a form of therapy. She recovered so well that her legs, albeit thin and bowed, carried her surely around the court to despatch stylish winners. She also had no lack of stamina, reaching the finals of all three events at tournaments on many occasions and taking the triple crown at Wimbledon in 1951. In doing so, she dropped only one set in 17 matches – in the mixed with Frank Sedgman. In the singles final she overwhelmed Shirley Fry 61 60 in 35 minutes, giving possibly the most devastating display of attacking tennis ever seen from a woman on the Centre Court. Only a month before, Fry had beaten her in the French final.

She was ranked in the world's top four each year she competed on the international circuit (1946 to 1955). Her highest position was No. 1, in 1951. Her six Grand Slam singles titles were scant reward for such consistency, but she played in an era of exceptional quality. She was runner-up in one Australian, three French, three Wimbledon and five US championships. Hart retired to become a coach in 1955, but returned to Forest Hills in 1969 to reach the quarterfinals of the mixed doubles with her former co-champion, Vic Seixas.

JUSTINE HENIN-HARDENNE (BEL)

Though slight in stature, she has rightly earned the reputation as one of the sternest competitors in women's tennis who already has three Grand Slam titles and an Olympic Gold medal.

Born:	Liege, Belgium, June 1, 1982.
Grand Slam titles:	Australian 2004. French 2003, 2005. United States 2003.
Olympics:	Gold medal, singles, 2004
Fed Cup winning team:	Belgium 2001.

The arrival of not one but two Belgians at the top of women's tennis is something that could never have been predicted. But the simultaneous rise of two Belgian players – one Flemish, the other Walloon, and only a year apart in age, has been the most striking feature of the sport in the early years of the 21st century.

Justine Henin-Hardenne, who is a year older than her compatriot Kim Clijsters, is physically very slight (5ft 5ins tall and 126 lbs) and is dwarfed by most of the other women on the tour. But she possesses exceptional drive, dedication and determination. She has a single-handed backhand drive that is generally agreed to be one of the best the sport has ever seen, and she has worked very hard at building up her strength and fitness during the off-season. She has had a meteoric rise in the game. In 1999, aged 17, she received a wild card into the WTA Tour event in Antwerp and won the title.

After a largely inactive 2000, during which she suffered a variety of injuries, Henin came storming back in 2001 and improved her world ranking from 48 to No. 7. There was a less spectacular 2002, in which her highlight was the Wimbledon semifinals, but in 2003 Henin, by now married to Pierre-Yves Hardenne, was treading on Clijsters' heals every step of the way as the two Belgians took over leadership of the game from the ailing Williams sisters. Henin-Hardenne overwhelmed Clijsters in a historic first all-Belgian Grand Slam final in Paris. The Williams temporarily restored their pre-eminence at Wimbledon, but at Flushing Meadow in another Belgian battle the Walloon once again triumphed. After holding the World No. 1 ranking for just one week in October 2003, Henin-Hardenne regained the top position for the end of year. Her dominance over Clijsters continued in 2004 with another victory in the Australian Open final. A lingering viral illness interrupted much of the rest of the year but she recovered enough to take Belgian's first tennis medal in singles when she beat Amelie Mauresmo for Gold at the Athens Olympic Games. 2005 was another injury-disrupted year the highlight of which was a 24-match winning streak, taking in three tour titles en route to her second victory at Roland Garros.

MARTINA HINGIS (SUI)

The youngest player ever to reach No.1 in the world, Hingis dominated the sport as a teenager but failed to fend off the challenge of stronger players like the Williams sisters.

Born:	Kosice, Czechoslovakia, September 30, 1980.
Grand Slam titles:	Australian 1997-99. Wimbledon 1997. United States 1997. Nine women's doubles titles.

Martina Hingis was a truly exceptional champion in that she reached the peak of her career whilst still technically a junior. Having dominated women's tennis as a 16-year-old, she remained at the top of the rankings for most of the next four years but was unable to resist the advancing threat of more powerful rivals.

Like the Williams sisters, Hingis was bred to be a champion. Her mother, Melanie Molitor – herself a top 20 Czech player in the 1970s – named Martina after the great Navratilova and introduced her to tennis when she was two years old. Hingis spent her first eight years in what is now the Slovak Republic, but when her parents divorced and her mother married a Swiss, Andreas Zog, she moved with Melanie to Trubbach in Switzerland.

As a child, Hingis was a phenomenally precocious player. She won the French Open junior title at the age of 12 in 1993 and won her first professional title, a $10,000 event in Langenthal, Switzerland, the same year. In October 1994 she won her first match at a WTA Tour event in Zurich. Her progress in pro tennis was meteoric: first WTA final (Hamburg) in May 1995; the Wimbledon doubles title (with Helena Sukova) in 1996, making her the youngest player ever to win a Grand Slam title, and her first major singles title, the Australian Open, in January 1997.

Hingis did not succeed in tennis by hitting the ball harder than anyone else. She was better than anyone else at anticipating where her opponent was going to hit the ball, and finding a place from whence the opponent was least likely to return it. She possessed an amazingly mature brain for someone so young, but she would occasionally explode – most memorably in the 1999 French Open final which she lost to Steffi Graf after serving for the match. Roland Garros remained the one Grand Slam singles event she never won.

She won three of the four majors in 1997 and achieved the top spot in the world ranking three months into that year. She was only 16 and a half at the time and remains the youngest ever No.1. She won the Australian Open singles and doubles three years running and the Grand Slam of women's doubles in 1998, but as the new Millennium dawned, her best was behind her. She was gradually overpowered and overtaken by the Williams sisters and Jennifer Capriati and was also troubled by ankle injuries which she blamed on her footwear manufacturer.

Hingis announced her retirement from tennis in January 2003, but she retains a high profile as an ambassador for the World Health Organisation and a television presenter.

HELEN JACOBS (USA)

So often overshadowed by Helen Wills Moody but she won the US title four consecutive years. She also won the US doubles three times and the Wimbledon singles title in 1936.

Born: Globe, Arizona, USA, August 6, 1908.
Died: Easthampton, New York, USA, June 2, 1997.
Grand Slam titles: Wimbledon 1936. United States 1932-35. Three women's doubles titles, one mixed doubles title.

Helen Jacobs' name is inextricably linked with that of another Helen – Wills Moody – whom she played in one French, four Wimbledon and two United States finals. Moody won each time except the 1933 US showdown, when she retired at 0-3 in the final set. The media built up a feud between them that was probably exaggerated, but they were certainly not friends. This despite the fact that they lived on the same street in Berkeley, California, played at the same club and had the same coach.

The two Helens contrasted in personality and playing style. Whereas Moody was reserved and aloof, Jacobs was cheerful, outgoing and generous. When Moody told the umpire in that 1933 Forest Hills final that she was in pain, Jacobs tried to comfort her but was rebuffed. When they met again in the 1938 Wimbledon final Jacobs was almost lame with an Achilles tendon injury, but Moody ignored her plight. Their most dramatic showdown came in the 1935 Wimbledon final. Jacobs had all but completed the job when she led Moody 5-2 and match point in the final set. Presented with an easy smash, a gust of wind deflected the ball and Jacobs netted it. The chance was gone.

Jacobs did not hit the ball as hard as Moody, but she had a tremendous competitive instinct and always fought to the last ditch. She had a poor forehand and adopted a slice which was merely defensive, but her backhand was positive and aggressive, and she had exceptional volleying skills. She was a Grand Slam finalist more often than a winner, and all her major titles were achieved (with the exception of her 1933 US victory) in the absence of Moody. She lost two French, five Wimbledon and four Forest Hills finals in a span from 1928 to 1940. But her four consecutive US titles, from 1932 to 1935, and her one Wimbledon in 1936 were just reward for years of enthusiastic application. In Moody's absence at the 1936 Wimbledon, Jacobs won through a strong field to beat Germany's Hilde Sperling (the reigning French champion) 62 46 75 in a desperately close final.

Jacobs won three US doubles titles, with Sarah Palfrey Fabyan, in 1932, 1934 and 1935, and the 1934 mixed doubles with George Lott, thereby taking the triple crown. She played in 12 Wightman Cup matches, every year between 1927 and 1939 except 1938, and had a 19-11 winning record.

BILLIE JEAN KING (USA)

Few have contributed more to the popularity and growth of women's tennis. Best known for her exuberant serve and volley style. Won singles titles at all four Slams and her 'Battle of the Sexes' victory over Bobby Riggs drew a world record crowd of more than 30,000.

Born: Long Beach, California, USA, November 22, 1943.
Grand Slam titles: Australian 1968. French 1972. Wimbledon 1966-68, 1972-73, 1975. United States 1967, 1971-72, 1974. 16 women's doubles titles, 11 mixed doubles titles.
Fed Cup winning teams: USA 1963, 1966-67, 1976-79.

Probably the most important individual in the history of women's tennis, Billie Jean Moffitt (who married Larry King in 1968) competed valiantly on the world circuit from 1961 to 1983, amassing an all-time third best 39 Grand Slam titles, and fought ferociously for the women's professional game. Feisty, uncompromising and sometimes controversial, she rebelled against the amateur establishment to improve the lot of female players. As a player, King was one of the most accomplished serve-volleyers ever. No woman was ever technically better or hit a superior backhand drive, volley and half-volley, and although her game was markedly suited to fast surfaces she improved her baseline game to succeed on clay as well.

She won a record 20 Wimbledon titles – six singles, ten doubles and four mixed doubles – and appeared in a total of 28 finals. She was triple champion in 1967 and 1973, and her partners on both occasions were Rosie Casals and Owen Davidson. Her greatest rivalry was with Margaret Court, to whom she lost in the 1963 and 1970 finals but beat in the second round in 1962 and the semifinals in 1966. After Court had been trounced by Bobby Riggs in a battle of the sexes in 1973, King agreed to play Riggs and won, resoundingly, 64 63 63 at Houston.

Having established herself as world No. 1 in 1967, when she triumphed both at Wimbledon and Forest Hills, King entered the Open era as one of four women professionals (the others were Casals, Ann Jones and Francoise Durr). In the early years of Open tennis there was a huge disparity in prize money between men and women, and in 1970 King was in the forefront of a campaign to set up an independent women's tour, offering more appropriate rewards. In 1971 she spearheaded the Virginia Slims tour and became the first female athlete to win more than $100,000 in prize money in a single year.

King was also a magnificent team player. She was a forceful member of seven winning Federation Cup teams and of nine successful Wightman Cup sides between 1961 and 1978. Towards the end of her career, when she was a Wimbledon semifinalist at 39, King was sued for 'palimony' by a former female lover but achieved worldwide respect for the dignified way she endured the ordeal. She served as captain of the United States Fed Cup team for eight years between 1995 and 2003.

SUZANNE LENGLEN (FRA)

Won a staggering 81 singles titles, 73 in doubles and 87 in mixed. Three times she won the triple crown at Wimbledon. It was her success and notoriety – generated by her fiery temper and choice of dress – which prompted Wimbledon's move to a larger site.

Born: Paris, France, May 24, 1899.
Died: Paris, France, July 4, 1938.
Grand Slam titles: French 1920-23, 1925-26. Wimbledon 1919, 1920-23, 1925. Eight women's doubles titles, five mixed doubles titles.
Olympics: Gold medals, singles and mixed doubles, 1920. Bronze medal, doubles, 1920.

Suzanne Lenglen achieved a greater degree of invincibility than any other player in the history of tennis. During a top class career that spanned nine seasons she suffered only two singles defeats. The first, against her compatriot Marguerite Broquedis, in the 1914 French Championship, was when she was 15 years old. The second, her only competitive match in the United States, in 1921, was when she was ill and retired after losing the first set against Molla Mallory. Despite suffering chronic ill-health, Lenglen had a unique talent for the game, and her uncanny powers of anticipation enabled her to prepare for her opponents' shots almost before they had been struck. She was one of the first women to play an all-court game, able to reach seemingly impossible volleys and to smash with unanswerable finality. She moved like a ballerina and had enormous charisma. Lenglen was also a pioneer of modern tennis clothing. Until she arrived on the scene, female players wore long skirts, long-sleeved blouses fastened at the neck, and stays; Lenglen turned out in loose, one-piece dresses that reached just below her knees.

She won a total of 241 titles, including 81 in singles, 73 in women's doubles and 87 in mixed. Her partnership with Elizabeth Ryan was undefeated. Having won her first major title, the World Hard Court Championship, in Paris in 1914, Lenglen was obliged to sit out the war before launching her international career in 1919. At her first Wimbledon she won one of the greatest finals of all time – a 108 46 97 classic against the 40-year-old holder, Dorothea Lambert Chambers, saving two match points. The Wimbledon spectators were thrilled by her skills, her flamboyance and her dramatic personality, and her popularity attracted far greater crowds than ever before, necessitating a move by the All England Club to larger grounds at Church Road in 1922.

In 1926 she pulled out of Wimbledon in a state of distress because of a misunderstanding over scheduling, and shortly afterwards she turned professional. Earlier that year she won her only meeting with the other great player of her time, Helen Wills Moody, at Cannes. She died of pernicious anemia at the age of 39 in 1938.

HANA MANDLIKOVA (CZE/AUS)

A superb athlete, she progressed from being world junior champion to winning three of the four Grand Slam singles titles and probably would have amassed rather more had her career not coincided with that of Chris Evert and Martina Navratilova.

Born: Prague, Czechoslovakia, February 19, 1962.
Grand Slam titles: Australian 1980, 1987. French 1981. United States 1985. One women's doubles title.
Fed Cup winning teams: Czechoslovakia 1983-85.

During the long reigns of Chris Evert and Martina Navratilova as joint queens of the game between 1978 and 1987, three players made incursions into their duopoly: Tracy Austin, Hana Mandlikova and Steffi Graf. Mandlikova, who memorably beat both Evert and Navratilova to win the 1985 US Open, was snapping at their heels for a long time, but never managed to lift herself above them in the world rankings. A richly talented player, she was a consistently successful competitor throughout the 1980s but her form fell away sharply in the last year of the decade.

Her father was an Olympic sprinter, and Mandlikova herself was a superb athlete, able to cover the court with lightning speed and superb footwork. She had an aggressive all-court game and had tremendous flair both off the ground and in the air. At the age of 16 she became the ITF's first World Junior Champion, winning the Italian and French girls' titles and losing the Wimbledon girls' final to Tracy Austin. She wasted no time in making an impact on the senior game, and in 1980 she won the Australian Open, trouncing Wendy Turnbull 60 75 in the final, and reaching the last round of the US Open, where she beat Navratilova and Andrea Jaeger before submitting in three sets to Evert.

In 1981 she rose to No. 4 in the world, winning the French Open with a straight sets victory over Evert in the semifinals, followed by an easy 62 64 verdict over Germany's Sylvia Hanika. Her march continued as far as the final at Wimbledon, where she outvolleyed Navratilova in the semis but flopped against Evert, who won 62 62. Instead of building on her already impressive record, the Czech faltered and did not reach another Grand Slam final until the 1982 US Open, where once again she gleaned but four games from Evert. Her apotheosis at Flushing Meadows in 1985, another Wimbledon final in 1986, when she beat Evert and lost to Navratilova, and a final Grand Slam title in Melbourne in 1987 were the other highpoints in her career.

Mandlikova led Czechoslovakia to three consecutive Federation Cup wins (1983-85) but married an Australian of Czech origin, Jan Sedlak, in 1986 and became an Australian citizen in 1988. In 2001, her marriage long over, she gave birth to twins which were biologically fathered by a male friend but would be brought up by Mandlikova with her female partner, Liz Resseguie.

ALICE MARBLE (USA)

Despite her trim figure, she was one of the most aggressive American players before the Second World War as she took serve and volley tennis to new heights. Recovered from tuberculosis to win the US title in 1936 and Wimbledon three years later.

Born: Plumas County, California, USA, September 28, 1913.
Died: Palm Springs, California, USA, December 13, 1990.
Grand Slam titles: Wimbledon 1939. United States 1936, 1938-40. Six women's doubles titles, seven mixed doubles titles.

A trim, pretty blonde who always sported shorts and a peaked cap, Alice Marble was a dynamic and well-loved champion who, but for a life-threatening illness in mid-career and the advent of World War II, might have won many more major titles. She is credited with being the first exponent of the 'big game' among women, playing the same way as such aggressive male players as Ellsworth Vines, Donald Budge and Jack Kramer to dominate from the net. Marble, born into a family of modest means from a rural part of Northern California, moved to San Francisco as a child and her abundant talent at racket sports was quickly noticed. Something of a tomboy, she developed her skills by frequently practising and playing with men, and this was how she perfected her exceptionally strong American twist serve – a shot few other women ever attempted. Taking the ball on the rise, her ground strokes were risky, with a short backswing, but her momentum was always to reach the net, and from there her volleying ability was sensational.

Already a US top ten player by the time she was 19, Marble had to play four matches in one day at a tournament in East Hampton, New York, in 1933. After playing 108 games in scorching heat she collapsed. The following year she was again taken ill when playing in Paris and was diagnosed first with pleurisy, then with tuberculosis. She was desperately ill and was unable to play again until late in 1935. Helped and inspired by her coach, Eleanor 'Teach' Tennant, who would later guide Maureen Connolly, Marble ended Helen Jacobs' four year reign as champion at Forest Hills in 1936.

She lost in the quarterfinals there in 1937 but won three more US titles in 1938, 1939 and 1940, overcoming Australia's Nancy Wynne in the first and Jacobs in the other two finals. At Wimbledon in 1939 she swept to the triple crown, taking the singles without losing a set and demolishing Britain's Kay Stammers 62 60 in the final and adding the women's doubles with Sarah Fabyan and the mixed with Bobby Riggs. She did not lose a match of any importance in either 1939 or 1940, after which she retired, turned professional and toured with Budge, Bill Tilden and Mary Hardwick. During World War II she served in US military intelligence.

MARTINA NAVRATILOVA (USA)

The finest female player in the game's history. She has won 58 Grand Slam titles – including two in 2003, at the age of 46 – and is the all-time Wimbledon record-holder. During her extraordinary career she has inspired moves towards added power and greater athleticism in women's tennis.

Born: Prague, Czechoslovakia, October 18, 1956.
Grand Slam titles: Australian 1981, 1983, 1985. French 1982, 1984. Wimbledon 1978-79, 1982-87, 1990. United States 1983-84, 1986-87. 31 women's doubles titles, nine mixed doubles titles.

Martina Navratilova achieved more success than any other player in history during the main part of her career, which lasted from 1973 to 1994. But in 2003, in the fourth year of a doubles-only comeback career on the professional tour, the Czech-born American extended her record with two more Grand Slam mixed doubles titles and seven WTA doubles titles – although she was in her late forties.

With her 58 Grand Slam titles, Navratilova is still three short of the record held by Margaret Court, but in every other respect she should be regarded as the greatest female player in the history of the sport. In 2003 she equalled Billie Jean King's record of 20 Wimbledon titles, she also became the oldest player of either sex to win a Grand Slam title, beating a mark set by Margaret DuPont 41 years earlier. Navratilova competed in her first Olympic Games in 2004 and continued her Fed Cup career, suffering her first loss in 41 matches.

But more than any of these magnificent achievements, Navratilova will be remembered for her heyday in the 1980s when she won six consecutive Wimbledon singles titles (her total of nine is the most achieved by any player) and for several years made herself almost unbeatable. She was defeated only once in the whole of 1983, and in 1984 she went for 74 matches without loss. (Her doubles partnership with Pam Shriver at the same time was also invincible.)

Her abundant natural talent, nurtured on clay in her native Czechoslovakia, enabled Navratilova to enjoy sporadic success in her early years on the tour, but a realisation that she could turn herself into the best tennis player the world had ever seen raised her to levels never previously achieved. She worked intensively on her fitness, technique and nutrition and made herself into the complete player. This gave other women players a model to emulate and overall increased standards of playing and athleticism.

Her rivalry with Chris Evert was one of the greatest ever seen in sport, and their finals at Wimbledon and the French Open are regarded as classics of the women's game.

MARGARET OSBORNE DUPONT (USA)

A regular title winner before the days of Open tennis, she accumulated 37 Grand Slam wins in singles, doubles and mixed. Outstanding in doubles, she and Louise Brough won 20 major titles.

Born:	Joseph, Oregon, USA, March 4, 1918.
Grand Slam titles:	French 1946, 1949. Wimbledon 1947. United States 1948-50. 21 women's doubles titles, 10 mixed doubles titles.

A prolific collector of major titles whose top class career lasted a remarkable 24 years, from 1938 to 1962, Margaret Osborne (who married William DuPont, from the multinational industrial dynasty, in 1947) was a class act in an era of strong female players. Although her contemporaries Pauline Betz, Louise Brough and Doris Hart are generally regarded as superior players, DuPont was ranked No. 1 in the world for four straight years from 1947 to 1950. She used guile and skill rather than power to win 37 titles in three of the four Grand Slam championships (she never travelled to Australia). She had a good serve and crisp volleys, whilst her forehand drive, hit with a heavy chop, and a lethal cocktail of spins and slices on both sides, bamboozled opponents and negated their efforts to overpower her with pace. Her fabulous doubles partnership with Brough racked up 12 American, five Wimbledon and three French titles, while in mixed doubles she assembled nine US championships playing with Bill Talbert, Ken McGregor, Ken Rosewall and Neale Fraser. Always taking the right court, DuPont was the mistress of doubles arts, and age did not wither her effectiveness. By winning the 1962 Wimbledon mixed doubles with Fraser she became the oldest ever women's Grand Slam champion at 44 (she has since been overtaken by Martina Navratilova).

Her singles title haul was not quite so fruitful, but during her peak years she was a vigorous and resolute competitor. She reached the first of her five Forest Hills finals in 1944, when she was beaten by Betz, and then succumbed to Brough at the same stage in 1947. The following year she turned the tables on her close friend and doubles partner, winning a titanic battle 46 64 1513. She retained the title in both 1949 and 1950 in straight sets against Hart.

At Wimbledon, DuPont was champion in 1947, defeating Hart, and she lost the 1949 and 1950 finals to Brough. On the former occasion they played out a marathon 108 16 108 before teaming up to retain the doubles. She won twice at Roland Garros, a shock 16 86 75 winner over Betz, at the time the world's dominant player, in 1946, and again in 1949 over Frenchwoman Nelly Adamson. Although she reached no more major singles finals after 1950, DuPont remained a redoubtable force in doubles for another dozen years (albeit interrupting her career in 1952 to have a son). In nine Wightman Cup matches between 1946 and 1962 she was never beaten, winning 10 singles and nine doubles rubbers.

ELIZABETH RYAN (USA)

Probably the best woman player never to win a Grand Slam singles title. In doubles she collected 26, including a record 19 at Wimbledon, during a career spanning 22 years. Her insatiable love of tennis flourished especially in 1924 when she won 75 singles and doubles titles.

Born:	Anaheim, California, USA, February 8, 1892.
Died:	London, England, July 8, 1979.
Grand Slam titles:	17 women's doubles titles, nine mixed doubles titles.

Elizabeth Ryan, always known as 'Bunny', was probably the best woman player never to win a Grand Slam singles title, and with 26 major championships in doubles and mixed doubles won over 20 years she was perhaps the outstanding doubles player of all time.

Although American by nationality she settled in England before World War I and seldom returned to the US. Ryan was tirelessly active in tournaments from 1912 to 1914 and, when competition resumed in Europe, from 1919 to 1934. During the playing season she was constantly engaged in singles, doubles and mixed tournament draws and is estimated to have won a total of 659 titles. In her peak year of 1924 she was successful in 75 events.

Ryan, who won the majority of her titles in her thirties, was perhaps a little too stout and slow to challenge the top players of her time, who included Suzanne Lenglen and Helen Wills Moody. She had a trademark chopped forehand, a wicked drop shot and the most reliable of volleys, and in doubles her tactical ability was unparalleled. Her first notable singles title was the Russian Championship in 1914, and she went on to win the British Covered Courts in 1920, the British Hard Courts in 1924-25, the Irish in 1919-23, the Italian in 1933, Beckenham seven times between 1919 and 1928, the Welsh in 1924 and Queen's in 1923-25 and 1929. She was runner-up at Wimbledon in 1921 and 1930, and at Forest Hills in 1926, when she led 42-year-old Molla Mallory 40 in the final set and had a match point at 76 only to lose 46 64 97.

Perhaps her nearest miss at Wimbledon came in 1924, when she became the first player to wrest a set from Lenglen in five years and lost a desperately close quarterfinal 62 68 64 only for Lenglen to scratch in the following round. In doubles, however, Ryan was supreme, and her greatest partnership, with Lenglen, was invincible. They won Wimbledon six times, and when the French Federation insisted on Lenglen partnering another Frenchwoman, Didi Vlasto, in 1926, Ryan and Mary K. Browne beat Lenglen and Vlasto 36 97 62, saving two match points.

Ryan won her other Wimbledon doubles titles with Agnes Morton, Browne, Wills Moody and Simone Mathieu. Her total of 19 Wimbledon titles was a record until overtaken by Billie Jean King in 1979. Ryan collapsed and died at Wimbledon the day before her record fell.

ARANTXA SANCHEZ-VICARIO (ESP)

Between 1989-1999, this diminutive but always doughty competitor never dropped out of the world top ten. Her competitive longevity was underlined by the way her three triumphs at the French Open also spanned ten years, while she also won the US Open and was runner-up at eight other Grand Slam tournaments.

Born:	Barcelona, Spain, December 18, 1971.
Grand Slam titles:	French 1989, 1994, 1998. United States 1994. Six women's doubles titles and four mixed doubles titles.
Olympics:	Silver medals, singles, 1996, doubles, 1992. Bronze medals, singles, 1992, doubles, 1996.
Fed Cup winning team:	Spain 1991, 1993-95, 1998.

Arantxa Sanchez-Vicario is the most successful woman player ever produced by Spain and the only one of her nationality to be ranked No.1 in the world. From a family of tennis achievers – her brothers Emilio and Javier were both Davis Cup players – she reached her peak in the mid-1990s. This was, admittedly, a time when women's tennis was in a slight trough. Monica Seles took two and a half years to recover from her stabbing, Jennifer Capriati was also out of the game and Davenport, Hingis and the Williams sisters had yet to emerge. Sanchez-Vicario was not a powerful player but she was strong (both mentally and physically) and very persistent. She was capable of running down most balls that would be winners against most other players and any opponent would expect to be involved in long, uncompromising rallies.

The 'Barcelona Bumblebee' (so dubbed by tennis writer Bud Collins) became the youngest player to win the French Open at 17 years, five months in 1989 when she shocked reigning Golden Slammer Steffi Graf 76(6) 36 75 in a compelling final. (Her record was broken the following year by the even younger Seles.) It would be another five years until the sizzling senorita would strike again. This time, also at Roland Garros, she stunned Mary Pierce and 15,000 French spectators by winning her second major and made her final assault on the WTA's No.1 ranking. Adding the US Open, with another battling victory over Graf, the top position was hers by February 1995. She held it for a total of 12 weeks.

Sanchez-Vicario's last great achievement was a third French Open title in 1998, when she surprised everyone to deny Seles the title after the American had easily dispatched Hingis in the semifinals. She was also a finalist at the Australian Open (1994-95) and Wimbledon (1995-96). There were two near misses in major finals against Graf: at Wimbledon, Sanchez Vicario lost by a whisker to the German in 1995 and at Roland Garros in 1996 she served for the match at 5-4 in the final set, only to lose an epic encounter 63 67(4)108.

With her compatriot Conchita Martinez, Sanchez-Vicario won the Fed Cup for Spain five times and reached a further five finals. One of the most active players in history, she accumulated 29 singles and 67 doubles titles during her 17-year professional career.

MONICA SELES (YUG/USA)

Until she was stabbed by a crazed spectator in Hamburg in 1993, she was firmly established as world No. 1, with many predicting she could be the best ever. Her powerful double-handed drives off both flanks had won her seven of the previous eight Grand Slams played.

Born:	Novi Sad, Yugoslavia, December 2, 1973.
Grand Slam titles:	Australian 1991-93, 1996. French 1990-92. United States 1991-92.
Olympics:	Bronze medal, singles, 2000.
Fed Cup winning teams:	USA 1996, 2000.

Monica Seles is almost indisputably the greatest female player not to have won Wimbledon. She captured the other three Grand Slam titles in both 1991 and 1992 and during her peak years she was almost unbeatable. In her only Wimbledon final – 1992 – she was trounced 62 61 by Steffi Graf after a concerted media campaign against her loud exhalation of air every time she hit the ball.

There is no question that Seles could have established herself as the most dominant player of all time had she not been stabbed in the back by a crazed spectator at Hamburg on April 30, 1993. At that point she was the queen of the courts, having overtaken Graf as world No. 1 in September 1991. The physical damage was slight, but the psychological impact on Seles was devastating: she did not return to competition for two and a half years. When she reappeared in the late summer of 1995 she lost to Graf in a spellbinding US Open final and won the following year's Australian Open, but this remains her only Grand Slam success since her tragic hiatus.

A left-hander, Seles plays double-handed on both sides. Taking the ball on the rise, she hits with tremendous power and penetration. Her serve is also an effective weapon, but since her return she has had to contend with weight and fitness problems and a succession of injuries. Also, whereas in the early part of her career she had no real rival except Graf, she struggled to keep pace with the guile of Martina Hingis and the brutal power of the Williams sisters and Lindsay Davenport.

Born in Yugoslavia but resident in Florida from an early age (a US citizen since 1994), Seles exploded onto the tour as a 15-year-old in 1989, when she beat Chris Evert to win her first pro title in Houston. She was a semifinalist at Roland Garros in 1989 and became the youngest ever French Open champion at 16 years, 6 months in 1990. Between the 1990 and 1995 US Opens her 1992 loss to Graf at Wimbledon was her only defeat in eight Grand Slam appearances. Having lost to Graf in the US Open finals of 1995 and 1996 her only subsequent Grand Slam final has been at Roland Garros in 1998, when after beating Hingis in the semifinals she lost to Arantxa Sanchez-Vicario.

VIRGINIA WADE (GBR)

Won the very first Open tournament at Bournemouth in 1968, a few months before claiming the US Open title. An attacking player, who won titles all round the world, she added Wimbledon to the list at her 16th attempt during the Championship's emotional centenary year.

Born:	Bournemouth, England, July 10, 1945.
Grand Slam titles:	Australian 1972. Wimbledon 1977. United States 1968. Four women's doubles titles.

A passionate, dramatic and exciting player, Virginia Wade was arguably the most successful of all British women in tennis – certainly in the Open era. In addition to three Grand Slam singles titles she won four doubles championships – all with Margaret Court – the Australian and French in 1973 and the US Open in 1973 and 1975. She was in the world's top ten for 13 consecutive years – 1967 to 1979 – and reached No. 2 in 1968 and 1975. Moreover, she was a dedicated Wightman Cup and Federation Cup player for her country.

Wade was a fiery and aggressive player who had one of the best serves in women's tennis, a heavily sliced but effective backhand, strong forehand and fine volley and overhead. Over an exceptionally long top class career – 23 years from 1962 to 1985 – she tottered for years on a rollercoaster ranging between glorious victories and ignominious defeats. It was only from the mid-1970s, when she placed her destiny in the hands of an American coach, Jerry Teeguarden, that she largely eradicated her technical deficiencies and formulated a strategic sense that had hitherto been missing.

Winner of the world's first Open tournament at Bournemouth in 1968, Wade achieved an early career milestone in the same year when she trounced world No. 1 Billie Jean King 64 64 in the final of the first US Open. She achieved other successes, in the 1971 Italian Open and the 1972 Australian Open, but at Wimbledon, where the crowds were desperate for her to do justice to her undoubted talent, she suffered a succession of early shock defeats. In 1974 she at last made the semifinals but crashed out 16 75 64 after looking certain to beat Russia's Olga Morozova.

In 1977, days short of her 32nd birthday, Wade chose a unique occasion – the centenary Wimbledon championships, coinciding with the Queen's Silver Jubilee – to finally take the title. She played the match of her life to dethrone Chris Evert 62 46 61 in the semifinals and then willed herself to beat Betty Stove 46 63 61 in the final. To the accompaniment of deafening applause, she received the trophy from the Queen (a rare visitor to Wimbledon) and made herself the heroine of the tournament's greatest patriotic spectacle since the British glory days of the 1930s. Wade battled on and reached the Wimbledon quarterfinals as late as 1983, when she was nearly 38.

SERENA WILLIAMS (USA)

Just as her father Richard predicted, Serena has become even more successful than older sister Venus, sweeping to No. 1 during 2002 when she won the French, Wimbledon and US Open titles.

Born:	Saginaw, Michigan, USA, September 26, 1981.
Grand Slam titles:	Australian 2003, 2005. French 2002. Wimbledon 2002-03. United States 1999, 2002. Six women's doubles titles, two mixed doubles titles.
Olympics:	Gold medal, doubles, 2000.
Fed Cup winning team:	USA 1999.

The younger of the two sensational sisters, Serena surged to the top of the sport in 2002, winning three out of the four Grand Slam championships and five other titles. The 21 year-old set a notable record, rising from No. 9 in the world in March to No. 1 in July – a feat unsurpassed since the WTA Tour rankings began in 1975. Serena is unquestionably one of the strongest women's champions in physical terms. Although her height (5ft 9ins) and weight (135 lbs) are average among professional women tennis players, she has a highly-toned physique and muscle bulk of a track and field athlete. This is reflected in her game, which is extremely powerful. She has one of the best serves in the game and plays chiefly from the baseline, although her volleying ability is considerable.

Like her elder sister Venus, Serena was withdrawn from junior competition by her father and coach, Richard Williams. Apart from a one-off appearance as a 14-year-old in qualifying at Quebec City in the autumn of 1995, she made her debut on the WTA Tour in October 1997. In only her second tournament, at Chicago, she beat two seeds to reach the semifinals. This launched her very swift rise to the upper levels of the game. Her first Grand Slam singles title came in 1999, when she won the US Open. Few would have expected Serena to win a Grand Slam crown before Venus. She won four other titles that year and ended the season at No. 4 in the rankings.

Serena might have reached the very top sooner had she not suffered a series of niggling injuries in 2000 and 2001. During those two years she reached only one Grand Slam final – the 2001 US Open, losing to Venus.

In 2002, after missing the Australian Open because of injury, she took off on a procession of victories, gathering the French, Wimbledon and US Open titles (beating Venus in all three finals). Her first Australian Open title came at the start of 2003 when she became the fifth woman of all-time to hold all four Grand Slam titles at once. Also that year she partnered James Blake to the Hopman Cup title and successfully defended her Wimbledon crown, both 2003 Grand Slam finals were contested against her sister. Wimbledon turned out to be her last tournament of the season when a left knee injury required surgery and a long rehabilitation. The following two years were injury-plagued. In 2004 she lost her Wimbledon crown to Maria Sharapova but regained her Australian Open title in 2005, overcoming Lindsay Davenport in the final.

VENUS WILLIAMS (USA)

Capped a memorable year in 2000 by winning Wimbledon, the US Open and Olympic gold in singles and doubles (with sister Serena). Tall and powerful, she hits serves harder than many men and her forehand is also a ruthless matchwinner.

Born:	Lynwood, California, USA, June 17, 1980.
Grand Slam titles:	Wimbledon 2000-01, 2005. United States 2000-01. Six women's doubles titles, two mixed doubles titles.
Olympics:	Gold medals, singles and doubles, 2000.
Fed Cup winning team:	USA 1999.

Venus Williams has been one of the most successful woman players of the new Millennium. In 2000 and 2001 she blazed a trail of success across the globe with barely a serious challenger in sight. Then her younger sister Serena, previously rather in her shadow, burst through in 2002 and supplanted her sibling at the top of the world rankings. They played in four consecutive Grand Slam finals starting at the 2002 French Open, Serena got the better of her sister on each occasion. Because, understandably, the sisters prefer not to face each other in singles match, the only tournaments they both enter are the very biggest – the Grand Slams and other top events such as Miami and the WTA Tour Championships.

Venus, a tall, athletic player who hits with great power and has the strongest (although not the most consistent) service in the women's game, made an immediate impact. She reached the final of the US Open the first time she played (1997) and ended her debut season just outside the top 20. The following year she won in Miami, defeating Martina Hingis and Anna Kournikova in the last two rounds. She retained this title in 1999, beating Serena in the first major final between sisters, and was also successful in Hamburg and Rome.

Suffering from tendonitis in both wrists, Venus did not play at all between November 1999 and May 2000 but after a shaky start to her season she hit a 35-match winning streak, taking in Wimbledon, US Open, Sydney Olympics and three other tournaments. In 2001 she regained the Miami title and held on to both Wimbledon and the US Open. Mainly due to insufficient activity she did not attain the world No. 1 ranking until February 2002. She held it for a total of 11 weeks until Serena took over mid-July. Even so, Venus picked up seven titles during the year. She lost the Wimbledon final to her sister in 2003 after which an abdominal strain ended her season. After an indifferent year in 2004 Venus returned to form in 2005 regaining the Wimbledon title after saving a championships point against Lindsay Davenport. At two hours and 45 minutes it was the longest women's singles final in The Championships' history.

HELEN WILLS MOODY (USA)

This hard-hitting Californian, famous for wearing a white eyeshade and known as 'Little Miss Poker Face' because of her total focus, won 19 Grand Slam singles titles including eight at Wimbledon in only nine visits.

Born:	Centerville, California, USA, October 6, 1905.
Died:	Carmel, California, USA, January 1, 1998.
Grand Slam titles:	French 1928-30, 1932. Wimbledon 1927-30, 1932-33, 1935, 1938. United States 1923-25, 1927-29, 1931. Nine women's doubles titles, three mixed doubles titles.
Olympics:	Gold medals, singles and doubles, 1924.

Famously dubbed with such epithets as 'Little Miss Poker Face' and 'Venus with a headache', Helen Wills (who married Freddie Moody in 1929 and Aiden Roark in 1939, but divorced twice) was the undisputed queen of tennis from 1927 to 1933, when she did not yield a single set. Apart from a retirement, she was unbeaten for eight years. No other player, male or female, has ever achieved such dominance. Her total of 19 Grand Slam singles titles is bettered only by Margaret Court and Steffi Graf, and her eight Wimbledon crowns stood as a record until overtaken by Martina Navratilova in 1990. A strikingly beautiful woman who shunned the company of fellow-players and socialised with the rich and famous, she was a notable painter and writer as well as an exceptionally gifted tennis player. Her success was borne of iron determination, extreme mental strength and utter concentration. Inscrutable under a white eyeshade, Moody never showed any emotion on court, and because of her icy demeanour crowds never warmed to her.

Technically, her game was sound and as free from error as anyone who has ever played. Having practised against men in her native California she hit with great power and penetration, concentrating on hard, accurate ground strokes but able to volley and smash when necessary. Her sliced serve broke wide, pulling the receiver out of the court. Her only weakness was poor footwork, but such was the remorseless strength of her driving that this was hardly a handicap.

Over a long career, stretching from 1919 to 1938, she won 52 of 92 tournaments, but at her peak she was totally invincible. She lost only once at Wimbledon, to Britain's Kitty McKane in the 1924 final, from 4-1 in the final set, and was beaten 63 86 in her only meeting with Suzanne Lenglen, at Cannes in 1926. At Forest Hills she won seven times, but in the 1933 final she retired against Helen Jacobs at 0-3 in the final set – her only technical defeat against the other Helen in 11 encounters. She missed several Wimbledons due to illness or injury, but in five of her victories there she did not drop a set. Her doubles titles included four with Elizabeth Ryan and three with Hazel Wightman.

Davis Cup

Established in 1900. Until 1971 the defending champion did not play through, meeting the winner of a knock-out competition in the Challenge Round to decide the title, and having choice of venue. In 1972 the Challenge Round was abolished, the defending champion having to play the whole competition for a chance to reach the Final Round. The 16-nation World Group was introduced in 1981.

Challenge Round

1900 USA d. British Isles 3-0, Longwood Cricket Club, Boston, MA, USA (Grass)
(Winning Captain: Dwight Davis, losing Captain: Arthur Gore) M. Whitman (USA) d. A. Gore (GBR) 61 63 62; D. Davis (USA) d. E. Black (GBR) 46 62 64 64; D. Davis/H. Ward (USA) d. H. Barrett/E. Black (GBR) 64 64 64; D. Davis (USA) vs. A. Gore (GBR) 97 99 unfinished.

1901 Not held

1902 USA d. British Isles 3-2, Crescent Athletic Club, Brooklyn, NY, USA (Grass)
(Winning Captain: Malcolm Whitman, losing Captain: William Collins) R. Doherty (GBR) d. W. Larned (USA) 26 36 63 64 64; M. Whitman (USA) d. J. Pim (GBR) 61 61 16 60; L. Doherty/R. Doherty (GBR) d. D. Davis/H. Ward (USA) 36 108 63 64; W. Larned (USA) d. J. Pim (GBR) 63 62 63; M. Whitman (USA) d. R. Doherty (GBR) 61 75 64.

1903 British Isles d. USA 4-1, Longwood Cricket Club, Boston, MA, USA (Grass)
(Winning Captain: William Collins, losing Captain: William Larned) L. Doherty (GBR) d. R. Wrenn (USA) 60 63 64; W. Larned (USA) d. R. Doherty (GBR) ret; L. Doherty/R. Doherty (GBR) d. G. Wrenn/R. Wrenn (USA) 75 97 26 63; L. Doherty (GBR) d. W. Larned (USA) 63 68 60 26 75; R. Doherty (GBR) d. R. Wrenn (USA) 64 36 63 68 64.

1904 British Isles d. Belgium 5-0, Worple Road, Wimbledon, London, Great Britain (Grass)
(Winning Captain: William Collins, losing Captain: Paul de Borman) L. Doherty (GBR) d. L. de Borman (BEL) 64 61 61; F. Riseley (GBR) d. W. Lemaire de Warzee (BEL) 61 64 62; L. Doherty/R. Doherty (GBR) d. L. de Borman/W. Lemaire de Warzee (BEL) 60 61 63; L. Doherty (GBR) d. W. Lemaire de Warzee (BEL) w/o; F. Riseley (GBR) d. L. de Borman (BEL) 46 62 86 75.

1905 British Isles d. USA 5-0, Worple Road, Wimbledon, London, Great Britain (Grass)
(Winning Captain: William Collins, losing Captain: Paul Dashiel) L. Doherty (GBR) d. H. Ward (USA) 79 46 61 62 60; S. Smith (GBR) d. W. Larned (USA) 64 64 57 64; L. Doherty/R. Doherty (GBR) d. H. Ward/B. Wright (USA) 810 62 62 46 86; S. Smith (GBR) d. W. Clothier (USA) 46 61 64 63; L. Doherty (GBR) d. W. Larned (USA) 64 26 68 64 62.

1906 British Isles d. USA 5-0, Worple Road, Wimbledon, London, Great Britain (Grass)
(Winning Captain: William Collins, losing Captain: Beals Wright) S. Smith (GBR) d. R. Little (USA) 64 64 61; L. Doherty (GBR) d. H. Ward (USA) 62 86 63; L. Doherty/R. Doherty (GBR) d. R. Little/H. Ward (USA) 36 119 97 61; S. Smith (GBR) d. H. Ward (USA) 61 60 64; L. Doherty (GBR) d. R. Little (USA) 36 63 68 61 63.

1907 Australasia d. British Isles 3-2, Worple Road, Wimbledon, London, Great Britain (Grass)
(Winning Captain: Norman Brookes, losing Captain: Alfred Hickson) N. Brookes (AUS) d. A. Gore (GBR) 75 61 75; A. Wilding (AUS) d. H. Barrett (GBR) 16 64 63 75; H. Barrett/A. Gore (GBR) d. N. Brookes/A. Wilding (AUS) 36 46 75 62 1311; A. Gore (GBR) d. A. Wilding (AUS) 36 63 75 62; N. Brookes (AUS) d. H. Barrett (GBR) 62 60 63.

1908 Australasia d. USA 3-2, Albert Ground, Melbourne, VIC, Australia (Grass)
(Winning Captain: Norman Brookes, losing Captain: Beals Wright) N. Brookes (AUS) d. F. Alexander (USA) 57 97 62 46 63; B. Wright (USA) d. A. Wilding (AUS) 36 75 63 61; N. Brookes/A. Wilding (AUS) d. F. Alexander/B. Wright (USA) 64 62 57 16 64; B. Wright (USA) d. N. Brookes (AUS) 06 36 75 62 1210; A. Wilding (AUS) d. F. Alexander (USA) 63 64 61.

1909 Australasia d. USA 5-0, Double Bay Grounds, Sydney, NSW, Australia (Grass)
(Winning Captain: Norman Brookes, losing Captain: Maurice McLoughlin) N. Brookes (AUS) d. M. McLoughlin (USA) 62 62 64; A. Wilding (AUS) d. M. Long (USA) 62 75 61; N. Brookes/A. Wilding (AUS) d. M. Long/M. McLoughlin (USA) 1210 97 63; N. Brookes (AUS) d. M. Long (USA) 64 75 86; A. Wilding (AUS) d. M. McLoughlin (USA) 36 86 62 63.

1910 Not held

1911 Australasia d. USA 5-0, Hagley Park, Christchurch, New Zealand (Grass)
(Winning Captain: Norman Brookes, losing Captain: William Larned) N. Brookes (AUS) d. B. Wright (USA) 64 26 63 63; R. Heath (AUS) d. W. Larned (USA) 26 61 75 62; N. Brookes/A. Dunlop (AUS) d. M. McLoughlin/B. Wright (USA) 64 57 75 64; N. Brookes (AUS) d. M. McLoughlin (USA) 64 36 46 63 64; R. Heath (AUS) d. B. Wright (USA) w/o.

1912 British Isles d. Australasia 3-2, Albert Ground, Melbourne, VIC, Australia (Grass)
(Winning Captain: Charles Dixon, losing Captain: Norman Brookes) J. Parke (GBR) d. N. Brookes (AUS) 86 63 57 62; C. Dixon (GBR) d. R. Heath (AUS) 57 64 64 64; N. Brookes/A. Dunlop (AUS) d. A. Beamish/J. Parke (GBR) 64 61 57; N. Brookes (AUS) d. C. Dixon (GBR) 62 64 64; J. Parke (GBR) d. R. Heath (AUS) 62 64 64.

1913 USA d. British Isles 3-2, Worple Road, Wimbledon, London, Great Britain (Grass)
(Winning Captain: Harold Hackett, losing Captain: Roger McNair) J. Parke (GBR) d. M. McLoughlin (USA) 810 75 64 16 75; R. Williams (USA) d. C. Dixon (GBR) 86 36 62 16 75; H. Hackett/M. McLoughlin (USA) d. H. Barrett/C. Dixon (GBR) 57 61 26 75 64; M. McLoughlin (USA) d. C. Dixon (GBR) 86 63 62; J. Parke (GBR) d. R. Williams (USA) 62 57 57 64 62.

1914 Australasia d. USA 3-2, West Side Tennis Club, New York, NY, USA (Grass)
(Winning Captain: Norman Brookes, losing Captain: Maurice McLoughlin) A. Wilding (AUS) d. R. Williams (USA) 75 62 63; M. McLoughlin (USA) d. N. Brookes (AUS) 1715 63 63; N. Brookes/A. Wilding (AUS) d. T. Bundy/M. McLoughlin (USA) 63 86 97; N. Brookes (AUS) d. R. Williams (USA) 61 62 810 63; M. McLoughlin (USA) d. A. Wilding (AUS) 62 63 26 62.

1915-18 Not held

1919 Australasia d. British Isles 4-1, Double Bay Grounds, Sydney, NSW, Australia (Grass)
(Winning Captain: Norman Brookes, losing Captain: Algernon Kingscote) G. Patterson (AUS) d. A. Lowe (GBR) 64 63 26 63; A. Kingscote (GBR) d. J. Anderson (AUS) 75 62 64; N. Brookes/G. Patterson (AUS) d. A. Beamish/A. Kingscote (GBR) 60 60 62; G. Patterson (AUS) d. A. Kingscote (GBR) 64 64 86; J. Anderson (AUS) d. A. Lowe (GBR) 64 57 63 46 1210.

1920 USA d. Australasia 5-0, Domain Cricket Club, Auckland, New Zealand (Grass)
(Winning Captain: Sam Hardy, losing Captain: Norman Brookes) B. Tilden (USA) d. N. Brookes (AUS) 108 64 16 64; W. Johnston (USA) d. G. Patterson (AUS) 63 61 61; W. Johnston/B. Tilden (USA) d. N. Brookes/G. Patterson (AUS) 46 64 60 64; W. Johnston (USA) d. N. Brookes (AUS) 57 75 63 63; B. Tilden (USA) d. G. Patterson (AUS) 57 62 63 63.

1921 USA d. Japan 5-0, West Side Tennis Club, New York, NY, USA (Grass)
(Winning Captain: Norris Williams, losing Captain: Ichiya Kumagae) W. Johnston (USA) d. I. Kumagai (JPN) 62 64 62; B. Tilden (USA) d. Z. Shimizu (JPN) 57 46 75 62 61; W. Washburn/R. Williams (USA) d. I. Kumagai/Z. Shimizu (JPN) 62 75 46 75; B. Tilden (USA) d. I. K. (JPN) 97 64 61; W. Johnston (USA) d. Z. Shimizu (JPN) 63 57 62 64.

1922 USA d. Australasia 4-1, West Side Tennis Club, New York, NY, USA (Grass)
(Winning Captain: Norris Williams, losing Captain: James Anderson) B. Tilden (USA) d. G. Patterson (AUS) 75 108 60; W. Johnston (USA) d. J. Anderson (AUS) 61 62 63; P. O'Hara-Wood/G. Patterson (AUS) d. V. Richards/B. Tilden (USA) 64 60 63; W. Johnston (USA) d. G. Patterson (AUS) 62 62 61; B. Tilden (USA) d. J. Anderson (AUS) 64 57 36 64 62.

1923 USA d. Australia 4-1, West Side Tennis Club, Forest Hills, NY, USA (Grass)
(Winning Captain: Norris Williams, losing Captain: Gerald Patterson) J. Anderson (AUS) d. W. Johnston (USA) 46 62 26 75 62; B. Tilden (USA) d. J. Hawkes (AUS) 64 62 61; B. Tilden/R. Williams (USA) d. J. Anderson/J. Hawkes (AUS) 1715 1113 26 63 62; W. Johnston (USA) d. J. Hawkes (AUS) 60 62 61; B. Tilden (USA) d. J. Anderson (AUS) 62 63 16 75.

1924 USA d. Australia 5-0, Germantown Cricket Club, Philadelphia, PA, USA (Grass)
(Winning Captain: Norris Williams, losing Captain: Gerald Patterson) B. Tilden (USA) d. G. Patterson (AUS) 64 62 63; V. Richards (USA) d. P. O'Hara-Wood (AUS) 63 62 64; W. Johnston/B. Tilden (USA) d. P. O'Hara-Wood/G. Patterson (AUS) 57 63 64 61; B. Tilden (USA) d. P. O'Hara-Wood (AUS) 62 61 61; V. Richards (USA) d. G. Patterson (AUS) 63 75 64.

1925 USA d. France 5-0, Germantown Cricket Club, Philadelphia, PA, USA (Grass)
(Winning Captain: Norris Williams, losing Captain: Max Decugis) B. Tilden (USA) d. J. Borotra (FRA) 46 60 26 97 64; W. Johnston (USA) d. R. Lacoste (FRA) 61 61 68 63; R. Richards/V. Williams (USA) d. J. Borotra/R. Lacoste (FRA) 64 64 63; B. Tilden (USA) d. R. Lacoste (FRA) 36 1012 86 75 62; W. Johnston (USA) d. J. Borotra (FRA) 61 64 60.

1926 USA d. France 4-1, Germantown Cricket Club, Philadelphia, PA, USA (Grass)
(Winning Captain: Norris Williams, losing Captain: Pierre Gillou) W. Johnston (USA) d. R. Lacoste (FRA) 60 64 06 60; B. Tilden (USA) d. J. Borotra (FRA) 62 63 63; R. Richards/V. Williams (USA) d. J. Brugnon/H. Cochet (FRA) 64 64 62; W. Johnston (USA) d. J. Borotra (FRA) 86 64 97; R. Lacoste (FRA) d. B. Tilden (USA) 46 64 86 86.

1927 France d. USA 3-2, Germantown Cricket Club, Philadelphia, PA, USA (Grass)
(Winning Captain: Pierre Gillou, losing Captain: Charles Garland) R. Lacoste (FRA) d. W. Johnston (USA) 63 62 62; B. Tilden (USA) d. H. Cochet (FRA) 64 26 62 86; F. Hunter/B. Tilden (USA) d. J. Borotra/J. Brugnon (FRA) 36 63 63 46 60; R. Lacoste (FRA) d. B. Tilden (USA) 64 46 63 63; H. Cochet (FRA) d. W. Johnston (USA) 64 46 62 64.

1928 France d. USA 4-1, Stade Roland Garros, Paris, France (Red Clay)
(Winning Captain: Pierre Gillou, losing Captain: Joseph Wear) B. Tilden (USA) d. R. Lacoste (FRA) 16 64 64 26 63; H. Cochet (FRA) d. J. Hennessey (USA) 57 97 63 60; J. Borotra/H. Cochet (FRA) d. F. Hunter/B. Tilden (USA) 64 68 75 46 62; R. Lacoste (FRA) d. J. Hennessey (USA) 46 61 75 63; H. Cochet (FRA) d. B. Tilden (USA) 97 86 64.

1929 France d. USA 3-2, Stade Roland Garros, Paris, France (Red Clay)
(Winning Captain: Pierre Gillou, losing Captain: Fitz-Eugene Dixon) H. Cochet (FRA) d. B. Tilden (USA) 63 61 62; J. Borotra (FRA) d. G. Lott (USA) 61 36 64 75; W. Allison/J. Van Ryn (USA) d. J. Borotra/H. Cochet (FRA) 61 86 64; H. Cochet (FRA) d. G. Lott (USA) 61 36 60 63; B. Tilden (USA) d. J. Borotra (FRA) 46 61 64 75.

1930 France d. USA 4-1, Stade Roland Garros, Paris, France (Red Clay)
(Winning Captain: Pierre Gillou, losing Captain: Fitz-Eugene Dixon) B. Tilden (USA) d. J. Borotra (FRA) 26 75 64 75; H. Cochet (FRA) d. G. Lott (USA) 64 62 62; J. Brugnon/H. Cochet (FRA) d. W. Allison/J. Van Ryn (USA) 63 75 16 62; J. Borotra (FRA) d. G. Lott (USA) 57 63 26 62 86; H. Cochet (FRA) d. B. Tilden (USA) 46 63 61 75.

1931 France d. Great Britain 3-2, Stade Roland Garros, Paris, France (Red Clay)
(Winning Captain: Rene Lacoste, losing Captain: Herbert Barrett) H. Cochet (FRA) d. B. Austin (GBR) 36 119 62 64; F. Perry (GBR) d. J. Borotra (FRA) 46 108 60 46 64; J. Brugnon/H. Cochet (FRA) d. P. Hughes/C. Kingsley (GBR) 61 57 63 86; H. Cochet (FRA) d. F. Perry (GBR) 64 16 97 63; B. Austin (GBR) d. J. Borotra (FRA) 75 63 36 75.

1932 France d. USA 3-2, Stade Roland Garros, Paris, France (Red Clay)
(Winning Captain: Rene Lacoste, losing Captain: Bernon Prentice) H. Cochet (FRA) d. W. Allison (USA) 57 75 36 75 62; J. Borotra (FRA) d. E. Vines (USA) 64 62 26 64; W. Allison/J. Van Ryn (USA) d. J. Brugnon/H. Cochet (FRA) 63 1113 75 46 64; J. Borotra (FRA) d. W. Allison (USA) 16 36 64 62 75; E. Vines (USA) d. H. Cochet (FRA) 46 06 75 86 62.

1933 Great Britain d. France 3-2, Stade Roland Garros, Paris, France (Red Clay)
(Winning Captain: Herbert Barrett, losing Captain: Rene Lacoste) B. Austin (GBR) d. A. Merlin (FRA) 63 64 60; F. Perry (GBR) d. H. Cochet (FRA) 810 64 86 36 61; J. Borotra/J. Brugnon (FRA) d. P. Hughes/H. Lee (GBR) 63 86 62; H. Cochet (FRA) d. B. Austin (GBR) 57 64 46 64 64; F. Perry (GBR) d. A. Merlin (FRA) 46 86 62 75.

1934 Great Britain d. USA 4-1, Centre Court, Wimbledon, London, Great Britain (Grass)
(Winning Captain: Herbert Barrett, losing Captain: Norris Williams) F. Perry (GBR) d. S. Wood (USA) 61 46 57 60 63; B. Austin (GBR) d. F. Shields (USA) 64 64 61; G. Lott/L. Stoefen (USA) d. P. Hughes/H. Lee (GBR) 75 60 46 97; F. Perry (GBR) d. F. Shields (USA) 64 46 62 1513; B. Austin (GBR) d. S. Wood (USA) 64 60 68 63.

1935 Great Britain d. USA 5-0, Centre Court, Wimbledon, London, Great Britain (Grass)
Winning Captain: Herbert Barrett, losing Captain: Joseph Wear) F. Perry (GBR) d. D. Budge (USA) 60 68 63 64; B. Austin (GBR) d. W. Allison (USA) 62 26 46 63 75; P. Hughes/R. Tuckey (GBR) d. W. Allison/J. Van Ryn (USA) 62 16 68 63 63; F. Perry (GBR) d. W. Allison (USA) 46 64 75 63; B. Austin (GBR) d. D. Budge (USA) 62 64 68 75.

1936 Great Britain d. Australia 3-2, Centre Court, Wimbledon, London, Great Britain (Grass)
(Winning Captain: Herbert Barrett, losing Captain: Cliff Sproule) B. Austin (GBR) d. J. Crawford (AUS) 46 63 61 61; F. Perry (GBR) d. A. Quist (AUS) 61 46 75 62; J. Crawford/A. Quist (AUS) d. P. Hughes/R. Tuckey (GBR) 64 26 75 108; A. Quist (AUS) d. B. Austin (GBR) 64 36 75 62; F. Perry (GBR) d. J. Crawford (AUS) 62 63 63.

1937 USA d. Great Britain 4-1, Centre Court, Wimbledon, London, Great Britain (Grass)
(Winning Captain: Walter Pate, losing Captain: Herbert Barrett) B. Austin (GBR) d. F. Parker (USA) 63 62 75; D. Budge (USA) d. C. Hare (GBR) 1513 61 62; D. Budge/G. Mako (USA) d. R. Tuckey/F. Wilde (GBR) 63 75 79 1210; F. Parker (USA) d. C. Hare (GBR) 62 64 62; D. Budge (USA) d. B. Austin (GBR) 86 36 64 63.

1938 USA d. Australia 3-2, Germantown Cricket Club, Philadelphia, PA, USA (Grass)
(Winning Captain: Walter Pate, losing Captain: Harry Hopman) B. Riggs (USA) d. A. Quist (AUS) 46 60 86 61; D. Budge (USA) d. J. Bromwich (AUS) 62 63 46 75; J. Bromwich/A. Quist (AUS) d. D. Budge/G. Mako (USA) 06 63 64 62; D. Budge (USA) d. A. Quist (AUS) 86 61 62; J. Bromwich (AUS) d. B. Riggs (USA) 64 46 60 62.

1939 Australia d. USA 3-2, Merion Cricket Club, Haverford, PA, USA (Grass)
(Winning Captain: Harry Hopman, losing Captain: Walter Pate) B. Riggs (USA) d. J. Bromwich (AUS) 64 60 75; F. Parker (USA) d. A. Quist (AUS) 63 26 64 16 75; J. Bromwich/A. Quist (AUS) d. J. Hunt/J. Kramer (USA) 57 62 75 62; A. Quist (AUS) d. B. Riggs (USA) 61 64 36 36 64; J. Bromwich (AUS) d. F. Parker (USA) 60 63 61.

1940-45 Not held

1946 USA d. Australia 5-0, Kooyong Stadium, Melbourne, VIC, Australia (Grass)
(Winning Captain: Walter Pate, losing Captain: Gerald Patterson) T. Schroeder (USA) d. J. Bromwich (AUS) 36 61 62 06 63; J. Kramer (USA) d. D. Pails (AUS) 86 62 97; J. Kramer/T. Schroeder (USA) d. J. Bromwich/A. Quist (AUS) 62 75 64; J. Kramer (USA) d. J. Bromwich (AUS) 86 64 62 64; G. Mulloy (USA) d. D. Pails (AUS) 63 63 64.

1947 USA d. Australia 4-1, West Side Tennis Club, Forest Hills, NY, USA (Grass
(Winning Captain: Alrick Man, losing Captain: Roy Cowling) J. Kramer (USA) d. D. Pails (AUS) 62 61 62; T. Schroeder (USA) d. J. Bromwich (AUS) 64 57 63 63; J. Bromwich/C. Long (AUS) d. J. Kramer/T. Schroeder (USA) 64 26 62 64; T. Schroeder (USA) d. D. Pails (AUS) 63 86 46 911 108; J. Kramer (USA) d. J. Bromwich (AUS) 63 62 62.

1948 USA d. Australia 5-0, West Side Tennis Club, Forest Hills, NY, USA (Grass)
(Winning Captain: Alrick Man, losing Captain: Adrian Quist) F. Parker (USA) d. B. Sidwell (AUS) 64 64 64; T. Schroeder (USA) d. A. Quist (AUS) 63 46 60 60; G. Mulloy/B. Talbert (USA) d. C. Long/B. Sidwell (AUS) 86 97 26 75; F. Parker (USA) d. A. Quist (AUS) 62 62 63; T. Schroeder (USA) d. B. Sidwell (AUS) 62 61 61.

1949 USA d. Australia 4-1, West Side Tennis Club, Forest Hills, NY, USA (Grass)
(Winning Captain: Alrick Man, losing Captain: John Bromwich) T. Schroeder (USA) d. B. Sidwell (AUS) 61 57 46 62 63; P. Gonzales (USA) d. F. Sedgman (AUS) 86 64 97; J. Bromwich/B. Sidwell (AUS) d. G. Mulloy/B. Talbert (USA) 36 46 108 97 97; T. Schroeder (USA) d. F. Sedgman (AUS) 64 63 63; P. Gonzales (USA) d. B. Sidwell (AUS) 61 63 63.

1950 Australia d. USA 4-1, West Side Tennis Club, Forest Hills, NY, USA (Grass)
(Winning Captain: Harry Hopman, losing Captain: Alrick Man) F. Sedgman (AUS) d. T. Brown (USA) 60 86 97; K. McGregor (AUS) d. T. Schroeder (USA) 1311 63 64; J. Bromwich/F. Sedgman (AUS) d. G. Mulloy/T. Schroeder (USA) 46 64 62 46 64; F. Sedgman (AUS) d. T. Schroeder (USA) 62 62 62; T. Brown (USA) d. K. McGregor (AUS) 911 810 119 61 64.

1951 Australia d. USA 3-2, White City Stadium, Sydney, NSW, Australia (Grass)
(Winning Captain: Harry Hopman, losing Captain: Frank Shields) V. Seixas (USA) d. M. Rose (AUS) 63 64 97; F. Sedgman (AUS) d. T. Schroeder (USA) 64 63 46 64; K. McGregor/F. Sedgman (AUS) d. T. Schroeder/T. Trabert (USA) 62 97 63; T. Schroeder (USA) d. M. Rose (AUS) 64 1311 75; F. Sedgman (AUS) d. V. Seixas (USA) 64 62 62.

1952 Australia d. USA 4-1, Memorial Drive, Adelaide, SA, Australia (Grass)
(Winning Captain: Harry Hopman, losing Captain: Vic Seixas) F. Sedgman (AUS) d. V. Seixas (USA) 63 64 63; K. McGregor (AUS) d. T. Trabert (USA) 119 64 61; K. McGregor/F. Sedgman (AUS) d. V. Seixas/T. Trabert (USA) 63 64 16 63; F. Sedgman (AUS) d. T. Trabert (USA) 75 64 108; V. Seixas (USA) d. K. McGregor (AUS) 63 86 68 63.

1953 Australia d. USA 3-2, Kooyong Stadium, Melbourne, VIC, Australia (Grass)
(Winning Captain: Harry Hopman, losing Captain: Bill Talbert) L. Hoad (AUS) d. V. Seixas (USA) 64 62 63; T. Trabert (USA) d. K. Rosewall (AUS) 63 64 64; V. Seixas/T. Trabert (USA) d. R. Hartwig/L. Hoad (AUS) 62 64 64; L. Hoad (AUS) d. T. Trabert (USA) 1311 63 26 36 75; K. Rosewall (AUS) d. V. Seixas (USA) 62 26 63 64.

1954 USA d. Australia 3-2, White City Stadium, Sydney, NSW, Australia (Grass)
(Winning Captain: Bill Talbert, losing Captain: Harry Hopman) T. Trabert (USA) d. L. Hoad (AUS) 64 26 1210 63; V. Seixas (USA) d. K. Rosewall (AUS) 86 68 64 63; V. Seixas/T. Trabert (USA) d. L. Hoad/K. Rosewall (AUS) 62 46 62 108; K. Rosewall (AUS) d. T. Trabert (USA) 97 75 63; R. Hartwig (AUS) d. V. Seixas (USA) 46 63 62 63.

1955 Australia d. USA 5-0, West Side Tennis Club, Forest Hills, NY, USA (Grass)
(Winning Captain: Harry Hopman, losing Captain: Bill Talbert) K. Rosewall (AUS) d. V. Seixas (USA) 63 108 46 62; L. Hoad (AUS) d. T. Trabert (USA) 46 63 63 86; R. Hartwig/L. Hoad (AUS) d. V. Seixas/T. Trabert (USA) 1214 64 63 36 75; K. Rosewall (AUS) d. H. Richardson (USA) 64 36 61 64; L. Hoad (AUS) d. V. Seixas (USA) 79 61 64 64.

1956 Australia d. USA 5-0, Memorial Drive, Adelaide, SA, Australia (Grass)
(Winning Captain: Harry Hopman, losing Captain: Bill Talbert) L. Hoad (AUS) d. H. Flam (USA) 62 63 63; K. Rosewall (AUS) d. V. Seixas (USA) 62 75 63; L. Hoad/K. Rosewall (AUS) d. S. Giammalva/V. Seixas (USA) 16 61 75 64; L. Hoad (AUS) d. V. Seixas (USA) 62 75 63; K. Rosewall (AUS) d. S. Giammalva (USA) 46 61 86 75.

1957 Australia d. USA 3-2, Kooyong Stadium, Melbourne, VIC, Australia (Grass)
(Winning Captain: Harry Hopman, losing Captain: Bill Talbert) A. Cooper (AUS) d. V. Seixas (USA) 36 75 61 16 63; M. Anderson (AUS) d. B. MacKay (USA) 63 75 36 79 63; M. Anderson/M. Rose (AUS) d. B. MacKay/V. Seixas (USA) 64 64 86; B. MacKay (USA) d. A. Cooper (AUS) 64 16 46 64 63; V. Seixas (USA) d. M. Anderson (AUS) 63 46 63 06 1311.

1958 USA d. Australia 3-2, Milton Courts, Brisbane, QLD, Australia (Grass)
(Winning Captain: Perry Jones, losing Captain: Harry Hopman) A. Olmedo (USA) d. M. Anderson (AUS) 86 26 97 86; A. Cooper (AUS) d. B. MacKay (USA) 46 63 62 64; A. Olmedo/H. Richardson (USA) d. M. Anderson/N. Fraser (AUS) 1012 36 1614 63 75; A. Olmedo (USA) d. A. Cooper (AUS) 63 46 64 86; M. Anderson (AUS) d. B. MacKay (USA) 75 1311 119.

1959 Australia d. USA 3-2, West Side Tennis Club, Forest Hills, NY, USA (Grass)
(Winning Captain: Harry Hopman, losing Captain: Perry Jones) N. Fraser (AUS) d. A. Olmedo (USA) 86 68 64 86; B. MacKay (USA) d. Rod Laver (AUS) 75 64 61; R. Emerson/N. Fraser (AUS) d. B. Buchholz/A. Olmedo (USA) 75 75 64; A. Olmedo (USA) d. R. Laver (AUS) 97 46 108 1210; N. Fraser (AUS) d. B. MacKay (USA) 86 36 62 64.

1960 Australia d. Italy 4-1, White City Stadium, Sydney, NSW, Australia (Grass)
(Winning Captain: Harry Hopman, losing Captain: Vanni Canapele) N. Fraser (AUS) d. O. Sirola (ITA) 46 63 63 63; R. Laver (AUS) d. N. Pietrangeli (ITA) 86 64 63; R. Emerson/N. Fraser (AUS) d. N. Pietrangeli/O. Sirola (ITA) 108 57 63 64; R. Laver (AUS) d. O. Sirola (ITA) 97 62 63; N. Pietrangeli (ITA) d. N. Fraser (AUS) 119 63 16 62.

1961 Australia d. Italy 5-0, Kooyong Stadium, Melbourne, VIC, Australia (Grass)
(Winning Captain: Harry Hopman, losing Captain: Vanni Canapele) R. Emerson (AUS) d. N. Pietrangeli (ITA) 86 64 60; R. Laver (AUS) d. O. Sirola (ITA) 61 64 63; R. Emerson/N. Fraser (AUS) d. N. Pietrangeli/O. Sirola (ITA) 62 63 64; R. Emerson (AUS) d. O. Sirola (ITA) 62 63 46 62; R. Laver (AUS) d. N. Pietrangeli (ITA) 63 36 46 63 86.

1962 Australia d. Mexico 5-0, Milton Courts, Brisbane, QLD, Australia (Grass)
(Winning Captain: Harry Hopman, losing Captain: Francisco Contreras) N. Fraser (AUS) d. T. Palafox (MEX) 79 63 64 119; R. Laver (AUS) d. R. Osuna (MEX) 62 61 75; R. Emerson/R. Laver (AUS) d. R. Osuna/T. Palafox (MEX) 75 62 64; N. Fraser (AUS) d. R. Osuna (MEX) 36 119 61 36 64; R. Laver (AUS) d. T. Palafox (MEX) 61 46 64 86.

1963 USA d. Australia 3-2, Memorial Drive, Adelaide, SA, Australia (Grass)
(Winning Captain: Robert Kelleher, losing Captain: Harry Hopman) D. Ralston (USA) d. J. Newcombe (AUS) 64 61 36 46 75; R. Emerson (AUS) d. C. McKinley (USA) 63 36 75 75; C. McKinley/D. Ralston (USA) d. R. Emerson/N. Fraser (AUS) 63 46 119 119; R. Emerson (AUS) d. D. Ralston (USA) 62 63 36 62; C. McKinley (USA) d. J. Newcombe (AUS) 1012 62 97 62.

1964 Australia d. USA 3-2, Harold Clark Courts, Cleveland, OH, USA (Clay)
(Winning Captain: Harry Hopman, losing Captain: Vic Seixas) C. McKinley (USA) d. F. Stolle (AUS) 61 97 46 62; R. Emerson (AUS) d. D. Ralston (USA) 63 61 63; C. McKinley/D. Ralston (USA) d. R. Emerson/F. Stolle (AUS) 64 46 46 63 64; F. Stolle (AUS) d. D. Ralston (USA) 75 63 36 911 64; R. Emerson (AUS) d. C. McKinley (USA) 36 62 64 64.

1965 Australia d. Spain 4-1, White City Stadium, Sydney, NSW, Australia (Grass)
(Winning Captain: Harry Hopman, losing Captain: Jaime Bartroli) F. Stolle (AUS) d. M. Santana (ESP) 1012 36 61 64 75; R. Emerson (AUS) d. J. Gisbert (ESP) 63 62 62; J. Newcombe/T. Roche (AUS) d. J. Arilla/M. Santana (ESP) 63 46 75 62; M. Santana (ESP) d. R. Emerson (AUS) 26 63 64 1513; F. Stolle (AUS) d. J. Gisbert (ESP) 62 64 86.

1966 Australia d. India 4-1, Kooyong Stadium, Melbourne, VIC, Australia (Grass)
(Winning Captain: Harry Hopman, losing Captain: Raj Khanna) F. Stolle (AUS) d. R. Krishnan (IND) 63 62 64; R. Emerson (AUS) d. J. Mukerjea (IND) 75 64 62; R. Krishnan/J. Mukerjea (IND) d. J. Newcombe/T. Roche (AUS) 46 75 64 64; R. Emerson (AUS) d. R. Krishnan (IND) 60 62 108; F. Stolle (AUS) d. J. Mukerjea (IND) 75 68 63 57 63.

1967 Australia d. Spain 4-1, Milton Courts, Brisbane, QLD, Australia (Grass)
(Winning Captain: Harry Hopman, losing Captain: Jaime Bartroli) R. Emerson (AUS) d. M. Santana (ESP) 64 61 61; J. Newcombe (AUS) d. M. Orantes (ESP) 63 63 62; J. Newcombe/T. Roche (AUS) d. M. Orantes/M. Santana (ESP) 64 64 64; M. Santana (ESP) d. J. Newcombe (AUS) 75 64 62; R. Emerson (AUS) d. M. Orantes (ESP) 61 61 26 64.

1968 USA d. Australia 4-1, Memorial Drive, Adelaide, SA, Australia (Grass)
(Winning Captain: Donald Dell, losing Captain: Harry Hopman) C. Graebner (USA) d. B. Bowrey (AUS) 810 64 86 36 61; A. Ashe (USA) d. R. Ruffels (AUS) 68 75 63 63; B. Lutz/S. Smith (USA) d. J. Alexander/R. Ruffels (AUS) 64 64 62; C. Graebner (USA) d. R. Ruffels (AUS) 36 86 26 63 61; B. Bowrey (AUS) d. A. Ashe (USA) 26 63 119 86.

1969 USA d. Romania 5-0, Harold Clark Courts, Cleveland, OH, USA (Hard)
(Winning Captain: Donald Dell, losing Captain: Georgy Cobzucs) A. Ashe (USA) d. I. Nastase (ROM) 62 1513 75; S. Smith (USA) d. I. Tiriac (ROM) 68 63 57 64 64; B. Lutz/S. Smith (USA) d. I. Nastase/I. Tiriac (ROM) 86 61 119; S. Smith (USA) d. I. Nastase (ROM) 46 46 64 61 119; A. Ashe (USA) d. I. Tiriac (ROM) 63 86 36 40 ret.

1970 USA d. West Germany 5-0, Harold Clark Courts, Cleveland, OH, USA (Hard)
(Winning Captain: Edward Turville, losing Captain: Ferdinand Henkel) A. Ashe (USA) d. W. Bungert (FRG) 62 108 62; C. Richey (USA) d. C. Kuhnke (FRG) 63 64 62; B. Lutz/S. Smith (USA) d. W. Bungert/C. Kuhnke (FRG) 63 75 64; C. Richey (USA) d. W. Bungert (FRG) 64 64 75; A. Ashe (USA) d. C. Kuhnke (FRG) 68 1012 97 1311 64.

1971 USA d. Romania 3-2, Olde Providence Racquet Club, Charlotte, NC, USA (Hard)
(Winning Captain: Edward Turville, losing Captain: Stefan Georgescu) S. Smith (USA) d. I. Nastase (ROM) 75 63 61; F. Froehling (USA) d. I. Tiriac (ROM) 36 16 61 63 86; I. Nastase/I. Tiriac (ROM) d. S. Smith/E. Van Dillen (USA) 75 64 86; S. Smith (USA) d. I. Tiriac (ROM) 86 63 60; I. Nastase (ROM) d. F. Froehling (USA) 63 61 16 64.

Final Round

1972 USA d. Romania 3-2, Progresul Club, Bucharest, Romania (Red Clay)
(Winning Captain: Dennis Ralston, losing Captain: Stefan Georgescu) S. Smith (USA) d. I. Nastase (ROM) 119 62 63; I. Tiriac (ROM) d. T. Gorman (USA) 46 26 64 63 62; S. Smith/E. Van Dillen (USA) d. I. Nastase/I. Tiriac (ROM) 62 60 63; S. Smith (USA) d. I. Tiriac (ROM) 46 62 64 26 60; I. Nastase (ROM) d. T. Gorman (USA) 61 62 57 108.

1973 Australia d. USA 5-0, Public Auditorium, Cleveland, OH, USA (Carpet)
(Winning Captain: Neale Fraser, losing Captain: Dennis Ralston) J. Newcombe (AUS) d. S. Smith (USA) 61 36 63 36 64; R. Laver (AUS) d. T. Gorman (USA) 810 86 68 63 61; R. Laver/J. Newcombe (AUS) d. S. Smith/E. Van Dillen (USA) 61 62 64; J. Newcombe (AUS) d. T. Gorman (USA) 62 61 63; R. Laver (AUS) d. S. Smith (USA) 63 64 36 62.

1974 South Africa d. India w/o.

1975 Sweden d. Czechoslovakia 3-2, Kungliga Tennishallen, Stockholm, Sweden (Carpet)
(Winning Captain: Lennart Bergelin, losing Captain: Antonin Bolardt) J. Kodes (TCH) d. O. Bengtsson (SWE) 64 26 75 64; B. Borg (SWE) d. J. Hrebec (TCH) 61 63 60; O. Bengtsson/B. Borg (SWE) d. J. Kodes/V. Zednik (TCH) 64 64 64; B. Borg (SWE) d. J. Kodes (TCH) 64 62 62; J. Hrebec (TCH) d. O. Bengtsson (SWE) 16 63 61 64.

1976 Italy d. Chile 4-1, Estadio Nacional, Santiago, Chile (Red Clay)
(Winning Captain: Nicola Pietrangeli, losing Captain: Luis Ayala) C. Barazzutti (ITA) d. J. Fillol (CHI) 75 46 75 61; A. Panatta (ITA) d. P. Cornejo (CHI) 63 61 63; P. Bertolucci/A. Panatta (ITA) d.. P. Cornejo/J. Fillol (CHI) 36 62 97 63; A. Panatta (ITA) d. J. Fillol (CHI) 86 64 36 108; B. Prajoux (CHI) d. A. Zugarelli (ITA) 64 64 62.

1977 Australia d. Italy 3-1, White City Stadium, Sydney, NSW, Australia (Grass)
(Winning Captain: Neale Fraser, losing Captain: Nicola Pietrangeli) T. Roche (AUS) d. A. Panatta (ITA) 63 64 64; J. Alexander (AUS) d. C. Barazzutti (ITA) 62 86 46 62; P. Bertolucci/A. Panatta (ITA) d. J. Alexander/P. Dent (AUS) 64 64 75; J. Alexander (AUS) d. A. Panatta (ITA) 64 46 26 86 119; T. Roche (AUS) vs. C. Barazzutti (ITA) 1212 unfinished.

1978 USA d. Great Britain 4-1, Mission Hills C.C., Rancho Mirage, CA, USA (Hard)
(Winning Captain: Tony Trabert, losing Captain: Paul Hutchins) J. McEnroe (USA) d. J. Lloyd (GBR) 61 62 62; B. Mottram (GBR) d. B. Gottfried (USA) 46 26 108 64 63; B. Lutz/S. Smith (USA) d. M. Cox/D. Lloyd (GBR) 62 62 63; J. McEnroe (USA) d. B. Mottram (GBR) 62 62 61; B. Gottfried (USA) d. J. Lloyd (GBR) 61 62 64.

1979 USA d. Italy 5-0, Civic Auditorium, San Francisco, CA, USA (Carpet)
(Winning Captain: Tony Trabert, losing Captain: Vittorio Crotta) V. Gerulaitis (USA) d. C. Barazzutti (ITA) 63 32 ret; J. McEnroe (USA) d. A. Panatta (ITA) 62 63 64; B. Lutz/S. Smith (USA) d. P. Bertolucci/A. Panatta (ITA) 64 1210 62; J. McEnroe (USA) d. A. Zugarelli (ITA) 64 63 61; V. Gerulaitis (USA) d. A. Panatta (ITA) 61 63 63.

1980 Czechoslovakia d. Italy 4-1, Sportovni Hala, Prague, Czechoslovakia (Carpet)
(Winning Captain: Antonin Bolardt, losing Captain: Vittorio Crotta) T. Smid (TCH) d. A. Panatta (ITA) 36 36 63 64 64; I. Lendl (TCH) d. C. Barazzutti (ITA) 46 61 61 62; I. Lendl/T. Smid (TCH) d. P. Bertolucci/A. Panatta (ITA) 36 63 36 63 64; C. Barazzutti (ITA) d. T. Smid (TCH) 36 63 62; I. Lendl (TCH) d. G. Ocleppo (ITA) 63 63.

World Group Final Round

1981 USA d. Argentina 3-1, Riverfront Coliseum, Cincinnati, OH, USA (Carpet)
(Winning Captain: Arthur Ashe, losing Captain: Carlos Junquet) J. McEnroe (USA) d. G. Vilas (ARG) 63 62 62; J. Clerc (ARG) d. R. Tanner (USA) 75 63 86; P. Fleming/J. McEnroe (USA) d. J. Clerc/G. Vilas (ARG) 63 46 64 46 119; J. McEnroe (USA) d. J. Clerc (ARG) 75 57 63 36 63; R. Tanner (USA) vs. G. Vilas (ARG) 1110 unfinished.

1982 USA d. France 4-1, Palais des Sports, Grenoble, France (Red Clay)
(Winning Captain: Arthur Ashe, losing Captain: Jean-Paul Loth) J. McEnroe (USA) d. Y. Noah (FRA) 1210 16 36 62 63; G. Mayer (USA) d. H. Leconte (FRA) 62 62 79 64; P. Fleming/J. McEnroe (USA) d. H. Leconte/Y. Noah (FRA) 63 64 97; Y. Noah (FRA) d. G. Mayer (USA) 61 60; J. McEnroe (USA) d. H. Leconte (FRA) 62 63.

1983 Australia d. Sweden 3-2, Kooyong Stadium, Melbourne, VIC, Australia (Grass)
(Winning Captain: Neale Fraser, losing Captain: Hans Olsson) M. Wilander (SWE) d. P. Cash (AUS) 63 46 97 63; J. Fitzgerald (AUS) d. J. Nystrom (SWE) 64 62 46 64; M. Edmondson/P. McNamee (AUS) d. A. Jarryd/H. Simonsson (SWE) 64 64 62; P. Cash (AUS) d. J. Nystrom (SWE) 64 61 61; M. Wilander (SWE) d. J. Fitzgerald (AUS) 68 60 61.

1984 Sweden d. USA 4-1, The Scandinavium, Gothenburg, Sweden (Red Clay)
(Winning Captain: Hans Olsson, losing Captain: Arthur Ashe) M. Wilander (SWE)) d. J. Connors (USA) 61 63 63; H. Sundstrom (SWE) d. J. McEnroe (USA) 1311 64 63; S. Edberg/A. Jarryd (SWE) d. P. Fleming/J. McEnroe (USA) 75 57 62 75; J. McEnroe (USA) d. M. Wilander (SWE) 63 67 63; H. Sundstrom (SWE) d. J. Arias (USA) 36 86 63.

1985 Sweden d. West Germany 3-2, Olympiahalle, Munich, West Germany (Carpet)
(Winning Captain: Hans Olsson, losing Captain: Wilhelm Bungert) M. Wilander (SWE) d. M. Westphal (FRG) 63 64 108; B. Becker (FRG) d. S. Edberg (SWE) 63 36 75 86; M. Wilander/J. Nystrom (SWE) d. B. Becker/A. Maurer (FRG) 64 62 61; B. Becker (FRG) d. M. Wilander (SWE) 63 26 63 36; S. Edberg (SWE) d. M. Westphal (FRG) 36 75 64 63.

1986 Australia d. Sweden 3-2, Kooyong Stadium, Melbourne, VIC, Australia (Grass)
(Winning Captain: Neale Fraser, losing Captain: Hans Olsson) P. Cash (AUS) d. S. Edberg (SWE) 1311 1311 64; M. Pernfors (SWE) d. P. McNamee (AUS) 63 61 63; P. Cash/J. Fitzgerald (AUS) d. S. Edberg/A. Jarryd (SWE) 63 64 46 61; P. Cash (AUS) d. M. Pernfors (SWE) 26 46 63 64 63; S. Edberg (SWE) d. P. McNamee (AUS) 108 64.

1987 Sweden d. India 5-0, The Scandinavium, Gothenburg, Sweden (Red Clay)
(Winning Captain: Hans Olsson, losing Captain: Vijay Amritraj) M. Wilander (SWE) d. R. Krishnan (IND) 64 61 63; A. Jarryd (SWE) d. V. Amritraj (IND) 63 63 61; J. Nystrom/M. Wilander (SWE) d. A. Amritraj/V. Amritraj (IND) 62 36 61 62; A. Jarryd (SWE) d. R. Krishnan (IND) 64 63; M. Wilander (SWE) d. V. Amritraj (IND) 62 60.

1988 West Germany d. Sweden 4-1, The Scandinavium, Gothenburg, Sweden (Red Clay)
(Winning Captain: Niki Pilic, losing Captain: Hans Olsson) C. Steeb (FRG) d. M. Wilander (SWE) 810 16 62 64 86; B. Becker (FRG) d. S. Edberg (SWE) 63 61 64; B. Becker/E. Jelen (FRG) d. S. Edberg/A. Jarryd (SWE) 36 26 75 63 62; S. Edberg (SWE) d. C. Steeb (FRG) 64 86; P. Kuhnen (FRG) d. K. Carlsson (SWE) w/o.

1989 West Germany d. Sweden 3-2, Schleyer Halle, Stuttgart, Germany (Carpet)
(Winning Captain: Niki Pilic, losing Captain: John-Anders Sjogren) M.Wilander (SWE) d. C. Steeb (FRG) 57 76 67 62 63; B. Becker (FRG) d. S. Edberg (SWE) 62 62 64; B. Becker/E. Jelen (FRG) d. J. Gunnarsson/A. Jarryd (SWE) 76 64 36 67 64; B. Becker (FRG) d. M. Wilander (SWE) 62 60 62; S. Edberg (SWE) d. C. Steeb (FRG) 62 64.

1990 USA d. Australia 3-2, Suncoast Dome, St. Petersburg, FL, USA (Red Clay)
(Winning Captain: Tom Gorman, losing Captain: Neale Fraser) A. Agassi (USA) d. R. Fromberg (AUS) 46 62 46 62 64; M. Chang (USA) d. D. Cahill (AUS) 62 76 60; R. Leach/J. Pugh (USA) d. P. Cash/J. Fitzgerald (AUS) 64 62 36 76; D. Cahill (AUS) d. A. Agassi (USA) 64 46 ret; R. Fromberg (AUS) d. M. Chang (USA) 75 26 63.

1991 France d. USA 3-1, Palais des Sports Gerland, Lyon, France (Carpet)
(Winning Captain: Yannick Noah, losing Captain: Tom Gorman) A. Agassi (USA) d. G. Forget (FRA) 67 62 61 62; H. Leconte (FRA) d. P. Sampras (USA) 64 75 64; G. Forget/H. Leconte (FRA) d. K. Flach/R. Seguso (USA) 61 64 46 62; G. Forget (FRA) d. P. Sampras (USA) 76 36 63 64; H. Leconte (FRA) vs. A. Agassi (USA) not played.

1992 USA d. Switzerland 3-1, Tarrant County Center, Ft. Worth, TX, USA (Hard)
(Winning Captain: Tom Gorman, losing Captain: Dimitri Sturdza) A. Agassi (USA) d. J. Hlasek (SUI) 61 62 62; M. Rosset (SUI) d. J. Courier (USA) 63 67 36 64 64; J. McEnroe/P. Sampras (USA) d. J. Hlasek/M. Rosset (SUI) 67 67 75 61 62; J. Courier (USA) d. J. Hlasek (SUI) 63 36 63 64; A. Agassi (USA) vs. M. Rosset (SUI) not played.

1993 Germany d. Australia 4-1, Messe Dusseldorf, Dusseldorf, Germany (Clay)
(Winning Captain: Niki Pilic, losing Captain: Neale Fraser) M. Stich (GER) d. J. Stoltenberg (AUS) 67 63 61 46 63; R. Fromberg (AUS) d. M. Goellner (GER) 36 57 76 62 97; P. Kuhnen/M. Stich (GER) d. T. Woodbridge/M. Woodforde (AUS) 76 46 63 76; M. Stich (GER) d. R. Fromberg (AUS) 64 62 62; M. Goellner (GER) d. J. Stoltenberg (AUS) 61 67 76.

1994 Sweden d. Russia 4-1, Olympic Stadium, Moscow, Russia (Carpet)
(Winning Captain: John-Anders Sjogren, losing Captain: Vadim Borisov) S. Edberg (SWE) d. A. Volkov (RUS) 64 62 67 06 86; M. Larsson (SWE) d. Y. Kafelnikov (RUS) 60 62 36 26 63; J. Apell/J. Bjorkman (SWE) d. Y. Kafelnikov/A. Olhovskiy(RUS) 67 62 63 16 86; Y. Kafelnikov (RUS) d. S. Edberg (SWE) 46 64 60; M. Larsson (SWE) d. A. Volkov (RUS) 76 64.

1995 USA d. Russia 3-2, Olympic Stadium, Moscow, Russia (Red Clay)
(Winning Captain: Tom Gullikson, losing Captain: Anatoly Lepeshin) P. Sampras (USA) d. A. Chesnokov (RUS) 36 64 63 67 64; Y. Kafelnikov (RUS) d. J. Courier (USA) 76 75 63; T. Martin/P. Sampras (USA) d. Y. Kafelnikov/A. Olhovskiy (RUS) 75 64 63; P. Sampras (USA) d. Y. Kafelnikov (RUS) 62 64 76; A. Chesnokov (RUS) d. J. Courier (USA) 67 75 60.

1996 France d. Sweden 3-2, Malmomassan, Malmo, Sweden (Hard)
(Winning Captain: Yannick Noah, losing Captain: Carl-Axel Hageskog) C. Pioline (FRA) d. S. Edberg (SWE) 63 64 63; T. Enqvist (SWE) d. A. Boetsch (FRA) 64 63 76; G. Forget/G. Raoux (FRA) d. J. Bjorkman/N. Kulti (SWE) 63 16 63 63; T. Enqvist (SWE) d. C. Pioline (FRA) 36 67 64 64 97; A. Boetsch (FRA) d. N. Kulti (SWE) 76 26 46 76 108.

1997 Sweden d. USA 5-0, The Scandinavium, Gothenburg, Sweden (Carpet)
(Winning Captain: Carl-Axel Hageskog, losing Captain: Tom Gullikson) J. Bjorkman (SWE) d. M. Chang (USA) 75 16 63 63; M. Larsson (SWE) d. P. Sampras (USA) 36 76 21 ret; J. Bjorkman/N. Kulti (SWE) d. T. Martin/J. Stark (USA) 64 64 64; J. Bjorkman (SWE) d. J. Stark (USA) 61 61; M. Larsson (SWE) d. M. Chang (USA) 76 67 64.

1998 Sweden d. Italy 4-1, The Forum, Milan, Italy (Red Clay)
(Winning Captain: Carl-Axel Hageskog, losing Captain: Paolo Bertolucci) M. Norman (SWE) d. A. Gaudenzi (ITA) 67 76 46 63 66 ret; M. Gustafsson (SWE) d. D. Sanguinetti (ITA) 61 64 60; J. Bjorkman/N. Kulti (SWE) d. D. Nargiso/D. Sanguinetti (ITA) 76 61 63; M. Gustafsson (SWE) d. G. Pozzi (ITA) 64 62; D. Nargiso (ITA) d. M. Norman (SWE) 62 63.

1999 Australia d. France 3-2, Nice Acropolis, Nice, France (Red Clay)
(Winning Captain: John Newcombe, losing Captain: Guy Forget) M. Philippoussis (AUS) d. S. Grosjean (FRA) 64 62 64; C. Pioline (FRA) d. L. Hewitt (AUS) 76 76 75; T. Woodbridge/M. Woodforde (AUS) d. O. Delaitre/F. Santoro (FRA) 26 75 62 62; M. Philippoussis (AUS) d. C. Pioline (FRA) 63 57 61 62; S. Grosjean (FRA) d. L. Hewitt (AUS) 64 63.

2000 Spain d. Australia 3-1, Palau Sant Jordi, Barcelona, Spain (Red Clay)
(Winning Captain: Javier Duarte, losing Captain: John Newcombe) L. Hewitt (AUS) d. A. Costa (ESP) 36 61 26 64 64; J. Ferrero (ESP) d. P. Rafter (AUS) 67 76 62 31 ret; J. Barcells/A. Corretja (ESP) d. S. Stolle/M. Woodforde (AUS) 64 64 64; J. Ferrero (ESP) d. L. Hewitt (AUS) 62 76 46 64; A. Corretja (ESP) vs. P. Rafter (AUS) not played.

2001 France d. Australia 3.2 Melbourne Park, Melbourne, VIC, Australia (Grass)
(Winning Captain: Guy Forget, losing Captain: John Fitzgerald) N. Escude (FRA) d. L Hewitt (AUS) 46 63 36 63 64; P. Rafter (AUS) d. S. Grosjean (FRA) 63 76 75; C. Pioline/F. Santoro (FRA) d. L. Hewitt/P. Rafter (AUS) 26 63 76 61; L. Hewitt (AUS) d. S Grosjean (FRA) 63 62 63; N. Escude (FRA) d. W. Arthurs (AUS) 76 67 63 63.

2002 Russia d. France 3-2, Palais Omnisports Paris Bercy, Paris, France (Red Clay)
(Winning Captain: Shamil Tarpischev, losing Captain: Guy Forget) M. Safin (RUS) d. P. Mathieu (FRA) 64 36 61 64; S. Grosjean (FRA) d. Y. Kafelnikov (RUS) 76 63 60; N. Escude/F. Santoro (FRA) d. Y. Kafelnikov/M. Safin (RUS) 63 36 57 63 64; M. Safin (RUS) d. S. Grosjean (FRA) 63 62 76; M. Youzhny (RUS) d. P. Mathieu (FRA) 36 26 63 75 64.

2003 Australia d. Spain 3-1, Melbourne Park, Melbourne, VIC, Australia, (Grass)
(Winning Captain: John Fitzgerald, losing Captain: Jordi Arrese) L. Hewitt (AUS) d. J. Ferrero (ESP) 36 63 36 76 62; C. Moya (ESP) d. M. Philippoussis (AUS) 64 64 46 76; W. Arthurs/T. Woodbridge (AUS) d. A. Corretja/F. Lopez (ESP) 63 61 63; M. Philippoussis (AUS) d. J. Ferrero (ESP) 75 63 16 26 60; L. Hewitt (AUS) vs. C. Moya (ESP) not played.

2004 Spain d. USA 3-2, Estadio Olimpico de Sevilla, Seville, Spain (Red Clay)
(Winning Captain: Jordi Arrese, losing Captain: Patrick McEnroe) C. Moya (ESP) d. M. Fish (USA) 64 62 63; R. Nadal (ESP) d. A. Roddick (USA) 67 62 76 62; B. Bryan/M. Bryan (USA) d. J. Ferrero/T. Robredo (ESP) 60 63 62; C. Moya (ESP) d. A. Roddick (USA) 62 76 76; M. Fish (USA) d. T. Robredo (ESP) 76 62.

2005 Croatia d. Slovak Republic 3-2, Sibamac Arena National Tennis Centre, Bratislava, Slovak Republic (Hard)
(Winning Captain: Nikola Pilic, losing Captain: Miroslav Mecir) I. Ljubicic (CRO) d. K. Kucera (SVK) 63 64 63; D. Hrbaty (SVK) d. M. Ancic (CRO) 76 63 67 64; M. Ancic/I. Ljubicic (CRO) d. D. Hrbaty/M. Mertinak (SVK) 76 63 76; D. Hrbaty (SVK) d. I. Ljubicic (CRO) 46 63 64 36 64; M. Ancic (CRO) d. M. Mertinak (SVK) 76 63 64.

Fed Cup

Launched in 1963 as The Federation Cup. Renamed the Fed Cup in 1995.

1963 USA d. Australia 2-1, Queen's Club, London, Great Britain (Grass)
(Winning Captain: William Kellogg, losing Captain: Nell Hopman) M. Smith (AUS) d. D. Hard (USA) 63 60; B. Moffitt (USA) d. L. Turner (AUS) 57 60 63; D. Hard/B. Moffitt (USA) d. M. Smith/L. Turner (AUS) 36 1311 63.

1964 Australia d. USA 2-1, Germantown Cricket Club, Philadelphia, PA, USA (Grass)
(Winning Captain: Brian Tobin, losing Captain: Madge Vosters) M. Smith (AUS) d. B. Moffitt (USA) 62 63; L. Turner (AUS) d. N. Richey (USA) 75 61; K. Hantze Susman/B. Moffitt (USA) d. M. Smith/L. Turner (AUS) 46 75 61.

1965 Australia d. USA 2-1, Kooyong Tennis Club, Melbourne, VIC, Australia (Grass)
(Winning Captain: Margaret Smith, losing Captain: Billie Jean Moffitt) L. Turner (AUS) d. C. Graebner (USA) 63 26 63; M. Smith (AUS) d. B. Moffitt (USA) 64 86; C. Graebner/B. Moffitt (USA) d. M. Smith/J. Tegart (AUS) 75 46 64.

1966 USA d. West Germany 3-0, Press Sporting Club, Turin, Italy (Clay)
(Winning Captain: Ros Greenwood, losing Captain: Edda Buding) J. Heldman (USA) d. H. Niessen (FRG) 46 75 61; B. King (USA) d. E. Buding (FRG) 63 36 61; C. Graebner/B. King (USA) d. E. Buding/H. Schulz (FRG) 64 62.

1967 USA d. Great Britain 2-0, Blau Weiss Club, Berlin, Germany (Clay)
(Winning Captain: Donna Fales, losing Captain: Angela Mortimer Barrett) R. Casals (USA) d. V. Wade (GBR) 97 86; B. King (USA) d. A. Jones (GBR) 63 64; R. Casals/B. King (USA) v. A. Jones/V. Wade (GBR) 68 97 play abandoned.

1968 Australia d. Netherlands 3-0, Stade Roland Garros, Paris, France (Clay)
(Winning Captain: Margaret Court, losing Captain: Jenny Ridderhof) K. Melville (AUS) d. M. Jansen (NED) 46 75 63; M. Court (AUS) d. A. Suurbeek (NED) 61 63; M. Court/K. Melville (AUS) d. L. Jansen Venneboer/A. Suurbeek (NED) 63 68 75.

1969 USA d. Australia 2-1, Athens Tennis Club, Athens, Greece
(Winning Captain: Donna Fales, losing Captain: Wayne Reid) N. Richey (USA) d. K. Melville (AUS) 64 63; M. Court (AUS) d. J. Heldman (USA) 61 86; P. Bartkowicz/N. Richey (USA) d. M. Court/J. Tegart (AUS) 64 64.

1970 Australia d. West Germany 3-0, Freiburg Tennis Club, Freiburg, Germany (Clay)
(Winning Captain: Alf Chave, losing Captain: Edward Dorrenberg) K. Krantzcke (AUS) d. H. Schultz Hoesl (FRG) 62 63; J. Dalton (AUS) d. H. Niessen (FRG) 46 63 63; K. Krantzcke/J. Dalton (AUS) d. H. Schultz Hoesl/H. Niessen (FRG) 62 75.

1971 Australia d. Great Britain 3-0, Royal King's Park Tennis Club, Perth, Australia (Grass)
(Winning Captain: Margaret Court, losing Captain: Ann Jones) M. Court (AUS) d. A. Jones (GBR) 68 63 62; E. Goolagong (AUS) d. V. Wade (GBR) 64 61; M. Court/L. Hunt (AUS) d. W. Shaw/V. Wade (GBR) 64 64.

1972 South Africa d. Great Britain 2-1, Ellis Park, Johannesburg, South Africa (Grass)
(Winning Captain: Dr. Jackie Du Toit, losing Captain: Virginia Wade) V. Wade (GBR) d. P. Waldken Pretorius (RSA) 63 62; B. Kirk (RSA) d. W. Shaw (GBR) 46 75 60; B. Kirk/P. Waldken Pretorius (RSA) d. V. Wade/J. Williams (GBR) 61 75.

1973 Australia d. South Africa 3-0, Bad Homburg Tennis Club, Bad Homburg, Germany (Clay)
(Winning Captain: Vic Edwards, losing Captain: Dr. Jackie Du Toit) E. Goolagong (AUS) d. P. Waldken Pretorius (RSA) 60 62; P. Coleman (AUS) d. B. Kirk (RSA) 108 60; E. Goolagong/J. Young (AUS) d. B. Kirk/P. Waldken Pretorius (RSA) 61 62.

1974 Australia d. USA 2-1, Tennis Club of Naples, Naples, Italy (Clay)
(Winning Captain: Vic Edwards, losing Captain: Donna Fales) E. Goolagong (AUS) d. J. Heldman (USA) 61 75; J. Evert (USA) d. D. Fromholtz (AUS) 26 75 64; E. Goolagong/J. Young (AUS) d. J. Heldman/S. Walsh (USA) 75 86.

1975 Czechoslovakia d. Australia 3-0, Aixoise Country Club, Aix-en-Provence, France (Clay)
(Winning Captain: Vera Sukova, losing Captain: Vic Edwards) M. Navratilova (TCH) d. E. Goolagong Cawley (AUS) 63 64; R. Tomanova (TCH) d. H. Gourlay (AUS) 64 62; M. Navratilova/R. Tomanova (TCH) d. D. Fromholtz/H. Gourlay (AUS) 63 61.

1976 USA d. Australia 2-1, The Spectrum, Philadelphia, PA, USA (Carpet)
(Winning Captain: Billie Jean King, losing Captain: Neale Fraser) K. Reid (AUS) d. R. Casals (USA) 16 63 75; B. King (USA) d. E. Goolagong Cawley (AUS) 76 64; R. Casals/B. King (USA) d. E. Goolagong Cawley/K. Reid (AUS) 75 63.

1977 USA d. Australia 2-1, Devonshire Park, Eastbourne, Great Britain (Grass)
(Winning Captain: Vicky Berner, losing Captain: Neale Fraser) B. King (USA) d. D. Fromholtz (AUS) 61 26 62; C. Evert (USA) d. K. Reid (AUS) 75 63; K. Reid/W. Turnbull (AUS) d. R. Casals/C. Evert (USA) 63 63.

1978 USA d. Australia 2-1, Kooyong Stadium, Melbourne, VIC, Australia (Grass)
(Winning Captain: Vicky Berner, losing Captain: Neale Fraser) K. Reid (AUS) d. T. Austin (USA) 63 63; C. Evert (USA) d. W. Turnbull (AUS) 36 61 61; C. Evert/B. King (USA) d. K. Reid/W. Turnbull (AUS) 46 61 64.

1979 USA d. Australia 3-0, R.S.H.E. Club de Campo, Madrid, Spain (Clay)
(Winning Captain: Vicky Berner, losing Captain: Neale Fraser) T. Austin (USA) d. K. Reid (AUS) 63 60; C. Evert (USA) d. D. Fromholtz (AUS) 26 63 86; R. Casals/B. King (USA) d. K. Reid/W. Turnbull (AUS) 36 63 86.

1980 USA d. Australia 3-0, Rot-Weiss Tennis Club, Berlin, Germany (Clay)
(Winning Captain: Vicky Berner, losing Captain: Mary Hawton) C. Evert (USA) d. D. Fromholtz (AUS) 46 61 61; T. Austin (USA) d. W. Turnbull (AUS) 62 63; R. Casals/K. Jordan (USA) d. D. Fromholtz/S. Leo (AUS) 26 64 64.

1981 USA d. Great Britain 3-0, Tamagawa-en Racquet Club, Tokyo, Japan (Clay)
(Winning Captain: Chris Evert, losing Captain: Sue Mappin) C. Evert (USA) d. S. Barker (GBR) 62 61; A. Jaeger (USA) d. V. Wade (GBR) 63 61; R. Casals/K. Jordan (USA) d. S. Barker/V. Wade (GBR) 64 75.

1982 USA d. West Germany 3-0, Decathlon Club, Santa Clara, CA, USA (Hard)
(Winning Captain: Judy Dalton, losing Captain: Klaus Hofsass) C. Evert (USA) d. C. Kohde (FRG) 26 61 63; M. Navratilova (USA) d. B. Bunge (FRG) 64 64; C. Evert/M. Navratilova (USA) d. B. Bunge/C. Kohde (FRG) 36 61 62.

1983 Czechoslovakia d. West Germany 2-1, Albisguetli Tennis Complex, Zurich, Switzerland (Clay)
(Winning Captain: Jan Kukal, losing Captain: Klaus Hofsass) H. Sukova (TCH) d. C. Kohde (FRG) 64 26 62; H. Mandlikova (TCH) d. B. Bunge (FRG) 62 30 ret; C. Kohde/E. Pfaff (FRG) d. I. Budarova/M. Skuherska (TCH) 36 62 61.

1984 Czechoslovakia d. Australia 2-1, Esporte Clube Pinheiros, Sao Paulo, Brazil (Clay)
(Winning Captain: Jan Kukal, losing Captain: Judy Dalton) A. Minter (AUS) d. H. Sukova (TCH) 75 75; H. Mandlikova (TCH) d. E. Sayers (AUS) 61 60; H. Mandlikova/H. Sukova (TCH) d. E. Sayers/W. Turnbull (AUS) 62 62.

1985 Czechoslovakia d. USA 2-1, Nagoya Green Tennis Club, Nagoya, Japan (Hard)
(Winning Captain: Jiri Medonos, losing Captain: Tom Gorman) H. Mandlikova (TCH) d. K. Jordan (USA) 75 61; H. Sukova (TCH) d. E. Burgin (USA) 63 67 64; E. Burgin/S. Walsh (USA) d. A. Holikova/R. Marsikova (TCH) 62 63.

1986 USA d. Czechoslovakia 3-0, Stvanice Stadium, Prague, Czechoslovakia (Clay)
(Winning Captain: Marty Riessen, losing Captain: Jiri Medonos) C. Evert (USA) d. H. Sukova (TCH) 75 76; M. Navratilova (USA) d. H. Mandlikova (TCH) 75 61; M. Navratilova/P. Shriver (USA) d. H. Mandlikova/H. Sukova (TCH) 64 62.

1987 West Germany d. USA 2-1, Hollyburn Country Club, Vancouver, Canada (Hard)
(Winning Captain: Klaus Hofsass, losing Captain: Marty Riessen) P. Shriver (USA) d. C. Kohde-Kilsch (FRG) 60 76; S. Graf (FRG) d. C. Evert (USA) 62 61; S. Graf/C. Kohde-Kilsch (FRG) d. C. Evert/P. Shriver (USA) 16 75 64.

1988 Czechoslovakia d. USSR 2-1, Flinders Park, Melbourne, VIC, Australia (Hard)
(Winning Captain: Jiri Medonos, losing Captain: Olga Morozova) R. Zrubakova (TCH) d. L. Savchenko (URS) 61 76; H. Sukova (TCH) d. N. Zvereva (URS) 63 64; L. Savchenko/N. Zvereva (URS) d. J. Novotna/J. Pospisilova (TCH) 76 75.

1989 USA d. Spain 3-0, Ariake Tennis Centre, Tokyo, Japan (Hard)
(Winning Captain: Marty Riessen, losing Captain: Juan Alvarino) C. Evert (USA) d. C. Martinez (ESP) 63 62; M. Navratilova (USA) d. A. Sanchez Vicario (ESP) 06 63 64; Z. Garrison/P. Shriver (USA) d. C. Martinez/A. Sanchez Vicario (ESP) 75 61.

1990 USA d. USSR 2-1, Peachtree World of Tennis, Atlanta, GA, USA (Hard)
(Winning Captain: Marty Riessen, losing Captain: Olga Morozova) J. Capriati (USA) d. L. Meskhi (URS) 76 62; N. Zvereva (URS) d. Z. Garrison (USA) 63 75; G. Fernandez/Z. Garrison (USA) d. L. Savchenko/N. Zvereva (URS) 64 63.

1991 Spain d. USA 2-1, City of Nottingham Tennis Centre, Nottingham, Great Britain (Hard)
(Winning Captain: Juan Alvarino, losing Captain: Marty Riessen) J. Capriati (USA) d. C. Martinez (ESP) 46 76 61; A. Sanchez Vicario (ESP) d. M. Fernandez 63 64; C. Martinez/A. Sanchez Vicario (ESP) d. G. Fernandez/Z. Garrison (USA) 36 61 61.

1992 Germany d. Spain 2-1, Waldstadion, Frankfurt, Germany (Clay)
(Winning Captain: Klaus Hofsass, losing Captain: Juan Alvarino) A. Huber (GER) d. C. Martinez (ESP) 63 67 61; S. Graf (GER) d. A. Sanchez Vicario (ESP) 64 62; C. Martinez/A. Sanchez Vicario (ESP) d. A. Huber/B. Rittner (GER) 61 62.

1993 Spain d. Australia 3-0, Waldstadion, Frankfurt, Germany (Clay)
(Winning Captain: Miguel Margets, losing Captain: Wendy Turnbull) C. Martinez (ESP) d. M. Jaggard-Lai (AUS) 60 62; A. Sanchez Vicario (ESP) d. N. Provis (AUS) 62 63; C. Martinez/A. Sanchez Vicario (ESP) d. L. Smylie/R. Stubbs (AUS) 36 61 63.

1994 Spain d. USA 3-0, Waldstadion, Frankfurt, Germany (Clay)
(Winning Captain: Miguel Margets, losing Captain: Marty Riessen) C. Martinez (ESP) d. M. Fernandez (USA) 62 62; A. Sanchez Vicario (ESP) d. L. Davenport (USA) 62 61; C. Martinez/A. Sanchez Vicario (ESP) d. G. Fernandez/M. Fernandez (USA) 63 64.

1995 Spain d. USA 3-2, Club Tenis de Valencia, Valencia, Spain (Clay)
(Winning Captain: Miguel Margets, losing Captain: Billie Jean King) C. Martinez (ESP) d. C. Rubin (USA) 75 76; A. Sanchez Vicario (ESP) d. M. Fernandez 63 62; C. Martinez (ESP) d. M. Fernandez (USA) 63 64; C. Rubin (USA) d. A. Sanchez Vicario (ESP) 16 64 64; L. Davenport/ G. Fernandez (USA) d. V. Ruano Pascual/M. Sanchez Lorenzo (ESP) 63 76.

1996 USA d. Spain 5-0, Atlantic City Convention Center, Atlantic City, NJ, USA (Carpet)
(Winning Captain: Billie Jean King, losing Captain: Miguel Margets) M. Seles (USA) d. C. Martinez (ESP) 62 64; L. Davenport (USA) d. A. Sanchez Vicario (ESP) 75 61; M. Seles (USA) d. A. Sanchez Vicario (ESP) 36 63 61; L. Davenport (USA) d. G. Leon Garcia (ESP) 75 62; M. Fernandez/L. Wild (USA) d. G. Leon Garcia/V. Ruano Pascual (ESP) 61 64.

1997 France d. Netherlands 4-1, Brabanthallen, s'Hertogenbosch, Netherlands (Carpet)
(Winning Captain: Yannick Noah, losing Captain: Fred Hemmes) S. Testud (FRA) d B. Schultz-McCarthy (NED) 64 46 63; M. Pierce (FRA) d M. Oremans (NED) 64 61; B. Schultz-McCarthy (NED) d M. Pierce (FRA) 46 63 64; S. Testud (FRA) d M. Oremans (NED) 06 63 63; A. Fusai/ N. Tauziat (FRA) d M. Bollegraf/C. Vis (NED) 63 64.

1998 Spain d. Switzerland 3-2, Palexpo Hall, Geneva, Switzerland (Hard)
(Winning Captain: Miguel Margets, losing Captain: Melanie Molitor) A. Sanchez-Vicario (ESP) d. P. Schnyder (SUI) 62 36 62; M. Hingis (SUI) d. C. Martinez (ESP) 64 64; M. Hingis (SUI) d. A. Sanchez -Vicario (ESP) 76(5) 63; C. Martinez (ESP) d. P. Schnyder (SUI) 63 26 97; C. Martinez/A. Sanchez-Vicario (ESP) d. M. Hingis/P. Schnyder (SUI) 60 62.

1999 USA d. Russia 4-1, Taube Tennis Stadium, Stanford, CA, USA (Hard)
(Winning Captain: Billie Jean King, losing Captain: Konstantin Bogoroditsky) V. Williams (USA) d. E. Likhovtseva (RUS) 63 64; L. Davenport (USA) d. E. Dementieva (RUS) 64 60; L. Davenport (USA) d. E. Likhovtseva (RUS) 64 64; E. Dementieva (RUS) d. V. Williams (USA) 16 63 76; S. Williams/V. Williams (USA) d. E. Dementieva/E. Makarova (RUS) 62 61.

2000 USA d. Spain 5-0, Mandalay Bay Resort, Las Vegas, NV, USA (Carpet)
(Winning Captain: Billie Jean King, losing Captain: Miguel Margets) M. Seles (USA) d. C. Martinez (ESP) 62 63; L. Davenport (USA) d. A. Sanchez-Vicario (ESP) 62 16 63; L. Davenport (USA) d. C. Martinez (ESP) 61 62; J. Capriati (USA) d. A. Sanchez-Vicario (ESP) 61 10 ret; J. Capriati/L. Raymond (USA) d. V. Ruano Pascual/M. Serna (ESP) 46 64 62.

2001 Belgium d. Russia 2-1, Parque Ferial Juan Carlos I, Madrid, Spain (Clay)
(Winning Captain: Ivo Van Aken, losing Captain: Shamil Tarpischev) J. Henin (BEL) d. N. Petrova (RUS) 60 63; K. Clijsters (BEL) d. E. Dementieva (RUS) 60 64; E. Likhovtseva/N. Petrova (RUS) d. E. Callens/L. Courtois (BEL) 75 76.

2002 Slovak Republic d. Spain 3-1, Palacio de Congresos de Maspalomas, Maspalomas, Gran Canaria (Hard)
(Winning Captain: Tomas Malik, losing Captain: Miguel Margets) C. Martinez (ESP) d. J. Husarova (SVK) 64 76; D. Hantuchova (SVK) d. M. Serna (ESP) 62 61; D. Hantuchova (SVK) d. C. Martinez (ESP) 67 75 64; J. Husarova (SVK) d. A. Sanchez-Vicario (ESP) 60 62; doubles not played.

2003 France d. USA 4-1, Olympic Stadium, Moscow, Russia (Carpet)
(Winning Captain: Guy Forget, losing Captain: Billie Jean King) A. Mauresmo (FRA) d. L. Raymond (USA) 64 63; M. Pierce (FRA) d. M. Shaughnessy (USA) 63 36 86; A. Mauresmo (FRA) d. M. Shaughnessy (USA) 62 61; E. Loit (FRA) d. A. Stevenson (USA) 64 62; M. Navratilova/ L. Raymond (USA) d. S. Cohen-Aloro/E. Loit (FRA) 64 60.

Fed Cup (continued)

2004 Russia d. France 3-2, Ice Stadium "Krylatskoe", Moscow, Russia (Carpet)
(Winning Captain: Shamil Tarpischev, losing Captain: Guy Forget) N. Dechy (FRA) d. S. Kuznetsova (RUS) 36 76 86; A. Myskina (RUS) d. T. Golovin (FRA) 64 76; A. Myskina (RUS) d. N. Dechy (FRA) 63 64; T. Golovin (FRA) d. S. Kuznetsova (RUS) 64 61; A. Myskina/V. Zvonareva (RUS) d. M. Bartoli/E. Loit (FRA) 76 75.

2005 Russia d. France 3-2, Roland Garros, Paris, France (Clay)
(Winning Captain: Shamil Tarpischev, losing Captain: Georges Goven) E. Dementieva (RUS) d. M. Pierce (FRA) 76 26 61; A. Mauresmo (FRA) d. A. Myskina (RUS) 64 62; E. Dementieva (RUS) d. A. Mauresmo (FRA) 64 46 62; M. Pierce (FRA) d. A. Myskina (RUS) 46 64 62; E. Dementieva/D. Safina (RUS) d. A. Mauresmo/M. Pierce (FRA) 64 16 63.

Carole Caldwell is also Carole Graebner
Evonne Goolagong is also Evonne Goolagong Cawley
Claudia Kohde is also Claudia Kohde-Kilsch
Kerry Melville is also Kerry Reid
Billie Jean Moffitt is also Billie Jean King
Margaret Smith is also Margaret Court
Judy Tegart is also Judy Dalton.

Hopman Cup

A mixed team event first played in 1989, Hopman Cup has been an official event of the ITF since 1997. It is played every January in Perth, Australia.

1989 Czechoslovakia d. Australia 2-0: H. Sukova (TCH) d. H. Mandlikova (AUS) 64 63; M. Mecir/H. Sukova (TCH) d. P. Cash/H. Mandlikova (AUS) 62 64.

1990 Spain d. USA 2-1: E. Sanchez (ESP) d. J. McEnroe (USA) 57 75 75; J. McEnroe/P. Shriver (USA) d. E. Sanchez/A. Sanchez-Vicario (ESP) 63 62; A. Sanchez-Vicario (ESP) d. P. Shriver (USA) 63 63.

1991 Yugoslavia d. USA 3-0: M. Seles (YUG) d. Z. Garrison (USA) 61 61; G. Prpic (YUG) d. D. Wheaton (USA) 46 63 75; G. Prpic/M. Seles (YUG) d. D. Wheaton/Z. Garrison (USA) 83 (pro set).

1992 Switzerland d. Czechoslovakia 2-1: M. Maleeva-Fragniere (SUI) d. H. Sukova (TCH) 62 64; J. Hlasek (SUI) d. K. Novacek (TCH) 64 64; K. Novacek/H. Sukova (TCH) d. J. Hlasek/M. Maleeva-Fragniere (SUI) 84 (pro set).

1993 Germany d. Spain 2-1: S. Graf (GER) d. A. Sanchez-Vicario (ESP) 64 63; M. Stich (GER) d. E. Sanchez (ESP) 75 63; E. Sanchez/A. Sanchez-Vicario (ESP) d. M. Stich/S. Graf (GER) w/o.

1994 Czech Republic d. Germany 2-1: J. Novotna (CZE) d. A. Huber (GER) 16 64 63; P. Korda (CZE) d. B. Karbacher (GER) 63 63; B. Karbacher/A. Huber (GER) d. P. Korda/J. Novotna (CZE) 83 (pro set).

1995 Germany d. Ukraine 3-0: A. Huber (GER) d. N. Medvedeva (UKR) 64 36 64; B. Becker (GER) d. A. Medvedev (UKR) 63 67 63; B. Becker/A. Huber (GER) d. A. Medvedev/N. Medvedeva (UKR) w/o.

1996 Croatia d. Switzerland 2-1: M. Hingis (SUI) d. I. Majoli (CRO) 63 60; G. Ivanisevic (CRO) d. M. Rosset (SUI) 76 75; G. Ivanisevic/I. Majoli (CRO) d. M. Rosset/M. Hingis (SUI) 36 76 55 ret.

1997 USA d. South Africa 2-1: C. Rubin (USA) d. A. Coetzer (RSA) 75 62; W. Ferreira (RSA) d. J. Gimelstob (USA) 64 76; J. Gimelstob/C. Rubin (USA) d. W. Ferreira/A. Coetzer (RSA) 36 62 75.

1998 Slovak Republic d. France 2-1: M. Pierce (FRA) d. K. Habsudova (SVK) 64 75; K. Kucera (SVK) d. C. Pioline (FRA) 76 64; K. Kucera/K. Habsudova (SVK) d. C. Pioline/M. Pierce (FRA) 63 64.

1999 Australia d. Sweden 2-1: J. Dokic (AUS) d. A. Carlsson (SWE) 62 76; M. Philippoussis (AUS) d. J. Bjorkman (SWE) 63 76; J. Bjorkman/A. Carlsson (SWE) d. M. Philippoussis/J. Dokic (AUS) 86 (pro set).

2000 South Africa d. Thailand 3-0: A. Coetzer (RSA) d. T. Tanasugarn (THA) 36 64 64; W. Ferreira (RSA) d. P. Srichaphan (THA) 76 63; W. Ferreira/A. Coetzer (RSA) d. P. Srichaphan/T. Tanasugarn (THA) 81 (pro set).

2001 Switzerland d. USA 2-1: M. Hingis (SUI) d. M. Seles (USA) 75 64; R. Federer (SUI) d. J. Gambill (USA) 64 63; J. Gambill/M. Seles (USA) d. R. Federer/M. Hingis (SUI) 26 64 76.

2002 Spain d. USA 2-1: M. Seles (USA) d. A. Sanchez-Vicario (ESP) 61 76; T. Robredo (ESP) d. J. Gambill (USA) 63 26 76; T. Robredo/A. Sanchez-Vicario (ESP) d. J. Gambill/M. Seles (USA) 64 62.

2003 USA d. Australia 3-0: S. Williams (USA) d. A. Molik (AUS) 62 63; J. Blake (USA) d. L. Hewitt (AUS) 63 64; J. Blake/S.Williams (USA) d. L. Hewitt/A. Molik ((AUS) 63 62.

2004 USA d. Slovak Republic 2-1: L. Davenport (USA) d. D. Hantuchova (SVK) 63 61; K. Kucera (SVK) d. J. Blake (USA) 46 64 76; J. Blake/L. Davenport (USA) d. K. Kucera/D. Hantuchova (SVK) 62 63.

2005 Slovak Republic d. Argentina 3-0: D. Hantuchova (SVK) d. G. Dulko (ARG) 16 64 64; D. Hrbaty (SVK) d. G. Coria (ARG) 64 61; D. Hrbaty/D. Hantuchova (SVK) d. G. Coria/G. Dulko (ARG) w/o.

Olympic Tennis Event

Tennis was one of the original sports at the first modern Olympiad in Athens in 1896, but was withdrawn after the 1924 Paris Games. It returned as a full medal sport at Seoul in 1988.

Year/Venue	Event	Gold	Silver	Bronze
1896 Athens, Greece	Men's Singles	John Boland (IRL)	Dionysios Kasdaglis (GRE)	Konstantinos Paspatis (GRE) Momcilo Tapavica (HUN)
	Men's Doubles	John Boland (IRL)/ Freidrich Traun (GER)	Dionysios Kasdaglis/ Dimitrios Petrokokkinos (GRE)	A. Akratopoulos/ K. Akratopoulos (GRE) Edwin Flack (AUS)/ George Robertson (GBR)
1900 Paris, France	Men's Singles	Laurence Doherty (GBR)	Harold Mahony (IRL)	Reginald Doherty (GBR) Arthur Norris (GBR)
	Men's Doubles	Laurence Doherty/ Reginald Doherty (GBR)	Maxime Decugis (FRA)/ Basil De Garmendia (USA)	Georges De La Chapelle/ Andre Prevost (FRA) Harold Mahony (IRL)/ Arthur Norris (GBR)
	Women's Singles	Charlotte Cooper (GBR)	Helene Prevost (FRA)	Marion Jones (USA) Hedwig Rosenbaum (BOH)
	Mixed Doubles	Reginald Doherty/ Charlotte Cooper (GBR)	Harold Mahony (IRL)/ Helene Prevost (FRA)	Laurence Doherty (GBR)/ Marion Jones (USA) Archibald Warden (GBR)/ Hedwig Rosenbaum (BOH)
1904 St. Louis, USA	Men's Singles	Beals Wright (USA)	Robert Le Roy (USA)	Alphonzo Bell (USA) Edgar Leonard (USA)
	Men's Doubles	Edgar Leonard/ Beals Wright (USA)	Alphonzo Bell/ Robert Le Roy (USA)	Clarence Gamble/ Arthur Wear (USA) Joseph Wear/ Allen West (USA)
1906 Athens, Greece (Demonstration)	Men's Singles	Maxime Decugis (FRA)	Maurice Germot (FRA)	Zdenek Zemla (BOH)
	Men's Doubles	Maxime Decugis/ Maurice Germot (FRA)	Joannis Ballis/ Xenophon Kasdaglis (GRE)	Ladislav Zemla/ Zdenek Zemla (BOH)
	Women's Singles	Esmee Simirioti (GRE)	Sophia Marinou (GRE)	Euphrosine Paspati (GRE)
	Mixed Doubles	Maxime Decugis/ Marie Decugis (FRA)	Georgios Simiriotis/ Sophia Marinou (GRE)	Xenophon Kasdaglis/ Aspasia Matsa (GRE)
1908 London Indoor, England	Men's Singles	Arthur Gore (GBR)	George Caridia (GBR)	Josiah Ritchie (GBR)
	Mixed Doubles	Herbert Roper Barrett/ Arthur Gore (GBR)	George Caridia/ George Simond (GBR)	Wollmar Bostrom/ Gunnar Setterwall (SWE)
	Women's Singles	Gladys Eastlake-Smith (GBR)	Alice Greene (GBR)	Martha Adlerstrahle (SWE)
1908 London Outdoor, England	Men's Singles	Josiah Ritchie (GBR)	Otto Froitzheim (GBR)	Wilberforce Eaves (GBR)
	Men's Doubles	Reginald Doherty/ George Hillyard (GBR)	James Parke (IRL)/ Josiah Ritchie (GBR)	Clement Cazalet/ Charles Dixon (GBR)
	Women's Singles	Dorothea Lambert-Chambers (GBR)	Dora Boothby (GBR)	Ruth Winch (GBR)
1912 Stockholm Indoor, Sweden	Men's Singles	Andre Gobert (FRA)	Charles Dixon (GBR)	Anthony Wilding (NZL)
	Men's Doubles	Maurice Germot/ Andre Gobert (FRA)	Carl Kempe/ Gunnar Setterwall (SWE)	Alfred Beamish/ Charles Dixon (GBR)
	Women's Singles	Edith Hannam (GBR)	Sofie Castenschiold (DEN)	Mabel Parton (GBR)
	Mixed Doubles	Charles Dixon/ Edith Hannam (GBR)	Herbert Roper Barrett/ Helen Aitchison (GBR)	Gunnar Setterwall/ Sigrid Fick (SWE)

Year/Venue	Event	Gold	Silver	Bronze
1912 Stockholm Outdoor, Sweden	Men's Singles	Charles Winslow (RSA)	Harold Kitson (RSA)	Oskar Kreuzer (GER)
	Men's Doubles	Harold Kitson/ Charles Winslow (RSA)	Felix Pipes/ Arthur Zborzil (AUT)	Albert Canet/ Eduard Meny De Marangue (FRA)
	Women's Singles	Marguerite Broquedis (FRA)	Dorothea Koring (GER)	Margrethe Bjurstedt (NOR)
	Mixed Doubles	Heinrich Schomburgk/ Dorothea Koring (GER)	Gunnar Setterwall/ Sigrid Fick (SWE)	Albert Canet/ Marguerite Broquedis (FRA)
1920 Antwerp, Belgium	Men's Singles	Louis Raymond (RSA)	Ichiya Kumagai (JPN)	Charles Winslow (RSA)
	Men's Doubles	Noel Turnbull/ Maxwell Woosnam (GBR)	Seiichiro Kashio/ Ichiya Kumagai (JPN)	Pierre Albarran/ Maxime Decugis (FRA)
	Women's Singles	Suzanne Lenglen (FRA)	Dorothy Holman (GBR)	Kathleen McKane (GBR)
	Women's Doubles	Kathleen McKane/ Winifred McNair (GBR)	Geraldine Beamish/ Dorothy Holman (GBR)	Elisabeth D'Ayen/ Suzanne Lenglen (FRA)
	Mixed Doubles	Maxime Decugis/ Suzanne Lenglen (FRA)	Maxwell Woosnam/ Kathleen McKane (GBR)	Ladislav Zemla/ Milada Skrobkova (TCH)
1924 Paris, France	Men's Singles	Vincent Richards (USA)	Henri Cochet (FRA)	Umberto De Morpurgo (ITA)
	Men's Doubles	Francis Hunter/ Vincent Richards (USA)	Jacques Brugnon/ Henri Cochet (FRA)	Jean Borotra/ Rene Lacoste (FRA)
	Women's Singles	Helen Wills (USA)	Julie Vlasto (FRA)	Kathleen McKane (GBR)
	Women's Doubles	Hazel Wightman/ Helen Wills (USA)	Phyllis Covell/ Kathleen McKane (GBR)	Evelyn Colyer/ Dorothy Shepherd-Barron (GBR)
	Mixed Doubles	Richard Williams/ Hazel Wightman (USA)	Vincent Richards/ Marion Jessup (USA)	Hendrik Timmer/ Kornelia Bouman (NED)
1968 Guadalajara, Mexico (Demonstration)	Men's Singles	Manuel Santana (ESP)	Manuel Orantes (ESP)	Herbert Fitzgibbon (USA)
	Men's Doubles	Rafael Osuna/ Vicente Zarazua (MEX)	Juan Gisbert/ Manuel Santana (ESP)	Pierre Darmon (FRA)/ Joaquin Loyo-Mayo (MEX)
	Women's Singles	Helga Niessen (FRG)	Jane Bartkowicz (USA)	Julie Heldman (USA)
	Women's Doubles	Edda Buding/ Helga Niessen (FRG)	Rosa-Maria Darmon (FRA)/ Julie Heldman (USA)	Jane Bartkowicz/ Valerie Ziegenfuss (USA)
	Mixed Doubles	Herbert Fitzgibbon/ Julie Heldman (USA)	Jurgen Fassbender/ Helga Niessen (FRG)	James Osborne/ Jane Bartkowicz (USA)
1968 Mexico City, Mexico (Exhibition)	Men's Singles	Rafael Osuna (MEX)	Inge Buding (FRG)	Vladimir Korotkov (URS) Nicola Pietrangeli (ITA)
	Men's Doubles	Rafael Osuna/ Vicente Zarazua (MEX)	Pierre Darmon (FRA)/ Joaquin Loyo-Mayo (MEX)	Francisco Guzman (ECU)/ Teimuraz Kakulia (URS) Vladimir Korotkov/ Anatoly Volkov (URS)
	Women's Singles	Jane Bartkowicz (USA)	Julie Heldman (USA)	Maria-Eugenia Guzman (ECU) Suzana Petersen (BRA)
	Women's Doubles	Rosa-Maria Darmon (FRA)/ Julie Heldman (USA)	Jane Bartkowicz/ Valerie Ziegenfuss (USA)	Maria-Eugenia Guzman (ECU)/ Suzana Petersen (BRA) Cecilia Rosado (MEX)/ Zaiga Yansone (URS)
	Mixed Doubles	Vladimir Korotkov/ Zaiga Yansone (URS)	Inge Buding (FRG)/ Jane Bartkowicz (USA)	Pierre Darmon/ Rosa-Maria Darmon (FRA) Teimuraz Kakulia (URS)/ Suzana Petersen (BRA)
1984 Los Angeles, USA (Demonstration)	Men's Singles	Stefan Edberg (SWE)	Francisco Maciel (MEX)	James Arias (USA) Paolo Cane (ITA)
	Women's Singles	Steffi Graf (FRG)	Sabrina Goles (YUG)	Raffaella Reggi (ITA) Catherine Tanvier (FRA)

Olympic Tennis Event (continued)

Year/Venue	Event	Gold	Silver	Bronze
1988 Seoul, Korea	Men's Singles	Miloslav Mecir (TCH)	Timothy Mayotte (USA)	Stefan Edberg (SWE) Brad Gilbert (USA)
	Men's Doubles	Ken Flach/ Robert Seguso (USA)	Sergio Casal/ Emilio Sanchez (ESP)	Stefan Edberg/ Anders Jarryd (SWE) Miloslav Mecir Milan Srejber (TCH)
	Women's Singles	Steffi Graf (FRG)	Gabriela Sabatini (ARG)	Zina Garrison (USA) Manuela Maleeva (BUL)
	Women's Doubles	Zina Garrison/ Pamela Shriver (USA)	Jana Novotna/ Helena Sukova (TCH)	Steffi Graf/ Claudia Kohde-Kilsch (FRG) Elizabeth Smylie/ Wendy Turnbull (AUS)
1992 Barcelona, Spain	Men's Singles	Marc Rosset (SUI)	Jordi Arrese (ESP)	Andrei Cherkasov (EUN) Goran Ivanisevic (CRO)
	Men's Doubles	Boris Becker/ Michael Stich (GER)	Wayne Ferreira/ Piet Norval (RSA)	Javier Frana/ Cristian Miniussi (ARG) Goran Ivanisevic/ Goran Prpic (CRO)
	Women's Singles	Jennifer Capriati (USA)	Steffi Graf (GER)	Mary Joe Fernandez (USA) Arantxa Sanchez-Vicario (ESP)
	Women's Doubles	Gigi Fernandez/ Mary Joe Fernandez (USA)	Conchita Martinez/ A. Sanchez-Vicario (ESP)	Rachel McQuillan/ Nicole Provis (AUS) Leila Meskhi/ Natalia Zvereva (EUN)
1996 Atlanta, USA	Men's Singles	Andre Agassi (USA)	Sergi Bruguera (ESP)	Leander Paes (IND)
	Men's Doubles	Todd Woodbridge/ Mark Woodforde (AUS)	Neil Broad/ Tim Henman (GBR)	Marc-Kevin Goellner/ David Prinosil (GER)
	Women's Singles	Lindsay Davenport (USA)	A. Sanchez-Vicario (ESP)	Jana Novotna (CZE)
	Women's Doubles	Gigi Fernandez/ Mary Joe Fernandez (USA)	Jana Novotna/ Helena Sukova (CZE)	Conchita Martinez/ Arantxa Sanchez-Vicario (ESP)
2000 Sydney, Australia	Men's Singles	Yevgeny Kafelnikov (RUS)	Tommy Haas (GER)	Arnaud Di Pasquale (FRA)
	Men's Doubles	Sebastien Lareau/ Daniel Nestor (CAN)	Tood Woodbridge/ Mark Woodforde (AUS)	Alex Corretja/ Albert Costa (ESP)
	Women's Singles	Venus Williams (USA)	Elena Dementieva (RUS)	Monica Seles (USA)
	Women's Doubles	Serena Williams/ Venus Williams (USA)	Kristie Boogert/ Miriam Oremans (NED)	Els Callens/ Dominique Van Roost (BEL)
2004 Athens, Greece	Men's Singles	Nicolas Massu (CHI)	Mardy Fish (USA)	Fernando Gonzalez (CHI)
	Men's Doubles	Fernando Gonzalez/ Nicolas Massu (CHI)	Nicolas Kiefer/ Rainer Schuettler (GER)	Mario Ancic/ Ivan Ljubicic (CRO)
	Women's Singles	Justine Henin-Hardenne (BEL)	Amelie Mauresmo (FRA)	Alicia Molik (AUS)
	Women's Doubles	Ting Li/ Tian Tian Sun (CHN)	Conchita Martinez/ Virginia Ruano Pascual (ESP)	Paola Suarez/ Patricia Tarabini (ARG)

Australian Championships

Men's Singles

Year	Champion	Runner-up	Score
1905	R. Heath (AUS)	A. Curtis (AUS)	46 63 64 64
1906	A. Wilding (NZL)	F. Fisher (AUS)	60 64 64
1907	H. Rice (AUS)	H. Parker (AUS)	63 64 64
1908	F. Alexander (USA)	A. Dunlop (AUS)	36 36 60 62 63
1909	A. Wilding (NZL)	E. Parker (AUS)	61 75 62
1910	R. Heath (AUS)	H. Rice (AUS)	64 63 62
1911	N. Brookes (AUS)	H. Rice (AUS)	61 62 63
1912	J. Parke (GBR)	A. E. Beamish (AUS)	36 63 16 61 75
1913	E. Parker (AUS)	H. Parker (AUS)	26 61 63 62
1914	A. O'Hara Wood (AUS)	G. Patterson (AUS)	64 63 57 61
1915	G. Lowe (GBR)	H. Rice (AUS)	46 61 61 64
1916-18 not played			
1919	A. Kingscote (GBR)	E. Pockley (AUS)	64 60 63
1920	P. O'Hara Wood (AUS)	R. Thomas (AUS)	63 46 68 61 63
1921	R. Gemmell (AUS)	A. Hedeman (AUS)	75 61 64
1922	J. Anderson (AUS)	G. Patterson (AUS)	60 36 36 63 62
1923	P. O'Hara Wood (AUS)	C. St John (AUS)	61 61 63
1924	J. Anderson (AUS)	R. Schlesinger (AUS)	63 64 36 57 63
1925	J. Anderson (AUS)	G. Patterson (AUS)	119 26 62 63
1926	J. Hawkes (AUS)	J. Willard (AUS)	61 63 61
1927	G. Patterson (AUS)	J. Hawkes (AUS)	36 64 36 1816 63
1928	J. Borotra (FRA)	R. Cummings (AUS)	64 61 46 57 63
1929	J. Gregory (GBR)	R. Schlesinger (AUS)	62 62 57 75
1930	E. Moon (AUS)	H. Hopman (AUS)	63 61 63
1931	J. Crawford (AUS)	H. Hopman (AUS)	64 62 26 61
1932	J. Crawford (AUS)	H. Hopman (AUS)	46 63 36 63 61
1933	J. Crawford (AUS)	K. Gledhill (AUS)	26 75 63 62
1934	F. Perry (GBR)	J. Crawford (AUS)	63 75 61
1935	J. Crawford (AUS)	F. Perry (GBR)	26 64 64 64
1936	A. Quist (AUS)	J. Crawford (AUS)	62 63 46 36 97
1937	V. McGrath (AUS)	J. Bromwich (AUS)	63 16 60 26 61
1938	D. Budge (USA)	J. Bromwich (AUS)	64 62 61
1939	J. Bromwich (AUS)	A. Quist (AUS)	64 61 63
1940	A. Quist (AUS)	J. Crawford (AUS)	63 61 62
1941-45 not played			
1946	J. Bromwich (AUS)	D. Pails (AUS)	57 63 75 36 62
1947	D. Pails (AUS)	J. Bromwich (AUS)	46 64 36 75 86
1948	A. Quist (AUS)	J. Bromwich (AUS)	64 36 63 26 63
1949	F. Sedgman (AUS)	J. Bromwich (AUS)	63 62 62
1950	F. Sedgman (AUS)	K. McGregor (AUS)	63 64 46 61
1951	D. Savitt (USA)	K. McGregor (AUS)	63 26 63 61
1952	K. McGregor (AUS)	F. Sedgman (AUS)	75 1210 26 62
1953	K. Rosewall (AUS)	M. Rose (AUS)	60 63 64
1954	M. Rose (AUS)	R. Hartwig (AUS)	62 06 64 62
1955	K. Rosewall (AUS)	L. Hoad (AUS)	97 64 64
1956	L. Hoad (AUS)	K. Rosewall (AUS)	64 36 64 75
1957	A. Cooper (AUS)	N. Fraser (AUS)	63 911 64 62
1958	A. Cooper (AUS)	M. Anderson (AUS)	75 63 64
1959	A. Olmedo (USA)	N. Fraser (AUS)	61 62 36 63
1960	R. Laver (AUS)	N. Fraser (AUS)	57 36 63 86 86
1961	R. Emerson (AUS)	R. Laver (AUS)	16 63 75 64
1962	R. Laver (AUS)	R. Emerson (AUS)	86 06 64 64
1963	R. Emerson (AUS)	K. Fletcher (AUS)	63 63 61
1964	R. Emerson (AUS)	F. Stolle (AUS)	63 64 62

Australian Championships (continued)

Year	Champion	Runner-up	Score
1965	R. Emerson (AUS)	F. Stolle (AUS)	79 26 64 75 61
1966	R. Emerson (AUS)	A. Ashe (USA)	64 68 62 63
1967	R. Emerson (AUS)	A. Ashe (USA)	64 61 64
1968	W. Bowrey (AUS)	J. Gisbert (ESP)	75 26 97 64
1969	R. Laver (AUS)	A. Gimeno (ESP)	63 64 75
1970	A. Ashe (USA)	R. Crealy (AUS)	64 97 62
1971	K. Rosewall (AUS)	A. Ashe (USA)	61 75 63
1972	K. Rosewall (AUS)	M. Anderson (AUS)	76 63 75
1973	J. Newcombe (AUS)	O. Parun (NZL)	63 67 75 61
1974	J. Connors (USA)	P. Dent (AUS)	76 64 46 63
1975	J. Newcombe (AUS)	J. Connors (USA)	75 36 64 76
1976	M. Edmondson (AUS)	J. Newcombe (AUS)	67 63 76 61
1977 (Jan)	R. Tanner (USA)	G. Vilas (ARG)	63 63 63
1977 (Dec)	V. Gerulaitis (USA)	J. Lloyd (GBR)	63 76 57 36 62
1978	G. Vilas (ARG)	J. Marks (AUS)	64 64 36 63
1979	G. Vilas (ARG)	J. Sadri (USA)	76 63 62
1980	B. Teacher (USA)	K. Warwick (AUS)	75 76 63
1981	J. Kriek (RSA)	S. Denton (USA)	62 76 67 64
1982	J. Kriek (USA)	S. Denton (USA)	63 63 62
1983	M. Wilander (SWE)	I. Lendl (TCH)	61 64 64
1984	M. Wilander (SWE)	K. Curren (RSA)	67 64 76 62
1985 (Nov)	S. Edberg (SWE)	M. Wilander (SWE)	64 63 63
1986 not played			
1987 (Jan)	S. Edberg (SWE)	P. Cash (AUS)	63 64 36 57 63
1988	M. Wilander (SWE)	P. Cash (AUS)	63 67 36 61 86
1989	I. Lendl (TCH)	M. Mecir (TCH)	62 62 62
1990	I. Lendl (TCH)	S. Edberg (SWE)	46 76 52 ret.
1991	B. Becker (GER)	I. Lendl (TCH)	16 64 64 64
1992	J. Courier (USA)	S. Edberg (SWE)	63 36 64 62
1993	J. Courier (USA)	S. Edberg (SWE)	62 61 26 75
1994	P. Sampras (USA)	T. Martin (USA)	76 64 64
1995	A. Agassi (USA)	P. Sampras (USA)	46 61 76 64
1996	B. Becker (GER)	M. Chang (USA)	62 64 26 62
1997	P. Sampras (USA)	C. Moya (ESP)	62 63 63
1998	P. Korda (CZE)	M. Rios (CHI)	62 62 62
1999	Y. Kafelnikov (RUS)	T. Enqvist (SWE)	46 60 63 76
2000	A. Agassi (USA)	Y. Kafelnikov (RUS)	36 63 62 64
2001	A. Agassi (USA)	A. Clement (FRA)	64 62 62
2002	T. Johansson (SWE)	M. Safin (RUS)	36 64 64 76
2003	A. Agassi (USA)	R. Schuettler (GER)	62 62 61
2004	R. Federer (SUI)	M. Safin (RUS)	76 64 62
2005	M. Safin (RUS)	L. Hewitt (AUS)	16 63 64 64

Women's Singles

Year	Champion	Runner-up	Score
1922	M. Molesworth (AUS)	E. Boyd (AUS)	63 108
1923	M. Molesworth (AUS)	E. Boyd (AUS)	61 75
1924	S. Lance (AUS)	E. Boyd (AUS)	63 36 86
1925	D. Akhurst (AUS)	E. Boyd (AUS)	16 86 64
1926	D. Akhurst (AUS)	E. Boyd (AUS)	61 63
1927	E. Boyd (AUS)	S. Harper (AUS)	57 61 62
1928	D. Akhurst (AUS)	E. Boyd (AUS)	75 62
1929	D. Akhurst (AUS)	L. Bickerton (AUS)	61 57 62
1930	D. Akhurst (AUS)	S. Harper (AUS)	108 26 75
1931	C. Buttsworth (AUS)	M. Crawford (AUS)	16 63 64

Lleyton Hewitt (AUS)

Australian Championships (continued)

Year	Champion	Runner-up	Score
1932	C. Buttsworth (AUS)	K. Le Mesurier (AUS)	97 64
1933	J. Hartigan (AUS)	C. Buttsworth (AUS)	64 63
1934	J. Hartigan (AUS)	M. Molesworth (AUS)	61 64
1935	D. Round (GBR)	N. Lyle (AUS)	16 61 63
1936	J. Hartigan (AUS)	N. Wynne (AUS)	64 64
1937	N. Wynne (AUS)	E. Westacott (AUS)	63 57 64
1938	D. Bundy (USA)	D. Stevenson (AUS)	63 62
1939	E. Westacott (AUS)	N. Hopman (AUS)	61 62
1940	N. Bolton (AUS) (nee Wynne)	T. Coyne (AUS)	57 64 60
1941-45 not played			
1946	N. Bolton (AUS)	J. Fitch (AUS)	64 64
1947	N. Bolton (AUS)	N. Hopman (AUS)	63 62
1948	N. Bolton (AUS)	M. Toomey (AUS)	63 61
1949	D. Hart (USA)	N. Bolton (AUS)	63 64
1950	L. Brough (USA)	D. Hart (USA)	64 36 64
1951	N. Bolton (AUS)	T. Long (AUS)	61 75
1952	T. Long (AUS)	H. Angwin (AUS)	62 63
1953	M. Connolly (USA)	J. Sampson (USA)	63 62
1954	T. Long (AUS)	J. Staley (AUS)	63 64
1955	B. Penrose (AUS)	T. Long (AUS)	64 63
1956	M. Carter (AUS)	T. Long (AUS)	36 62 97
1957	S. Fry (USA)	A. Gibson (USA)	63 63
1958	A. Mortimer (GBR)	L. Coghlan (AUS)	63 64
1959	M. Reitano (AUS)	R. Schuurman (RSA)	62 63
1960	M. Smith (AUS)	J. Lehane (AUS)	75 62
1961	M. Smith (AUS)	J. Lehane (AUS)	61 64
1962	M. Smith (AUS)	J. Lehane (AUS)	60 62
1963	M. Smith (AUS)	J. Lehane (AUS)	62 62
1964	M. Smith (AUS)	L. Turner (AUS)	63 62
1965	M. Smith (AUS)	M. Bueno (BRA)	57 64 52 ret.
1966	M. Smith (AUS)	N. Richey (USA)	w/o
1967	N. Richey (USA)	L. Turner (AUS)	61 64
1968	B. King (USA)	M. Court (AUS) (nee Smith)	61 62
1969	M. Court (AUS)	B. King (USA)	64 61
1970	M. Court (AUS)	K. Melville (AUS)	63 61
1971	M. Court (AUS)	E. Goolagong (AUS)	26 76 75
1972	V. Wade (GBR)	E. Goolagong (AUS)	64 64
1973	M. Court (AUS)	E. Goolagong (AUS)	64 75
1974	E. Goolagong (AUS)	C. Evert (USA)	76 46 60
1975	E. Goolagong (AUS)	M. Navratilova (TCH)	63 62
1976	E. Goolagong Cawley (AUS)	R. Tomanova (TCH)	62 62
1977 (Jan)	K. Reid (AUS) (nee Melville)	D. Balestrat (AUS)	75 62
1977 (Dec)	E. Goolagong Cawley (AUS)	H. Cawley (AUS)	63 60
1978	C. O'Neil (AUS)	B. Nagelsen (USA)	63 76
1979	B. Jordan (USA)	S. Walsh (USA)	63 63
1980	H. Mandlikova (TCH)	W. Turnbull (AUS)	60 75
1981	M. Navratilova (USA)	C. Evert Lloyd (USA)	67 64 75
1982	C. Evert Lloyd (USA)	M. Navratilova (USA)	63 26 63
1983	M. Navratilova (USA)	K. Jordan (USA)	62 76
1984	C. Evert Lloyd (USA)	H. Sukova (TCH)	67 61 63
1985 (Nov)	M. Navratilova (USA)	C. Evert Lloyd (USA)	62 46 62
1986 not played			
1987 (Jan)	H. Mandlikova (TCH)	M. Navratilova (USA)	75 76
1988	S. Graf (FRG)	C. Evert (USA)	61 76
1989	S. Graf (FRG)	H. Sukova (TCH)	64 64

Year	Champion	Runner-up	Score
1990	S. Graf (GER)	M. Fernandez (USA)	63 64
1991	M. Seles (YUG)	J. Novotna (TCH)	57 63 61
1992	M. Seles (YUG)	M. Fernandez (USA)	62 63
1993	M. Seles (YUG)	S. Graf (GER)	46 63 62
1994	S. Graf (GER)	A. Sanchez Vicario (ESP)	60 62
1995	M. Pierce (FRA)	A. Sanchez Vicario (ESP)	63 62
1996	M. Seles (USA)	A. Huber (GER)	64 61
1997	M. Hingis (SUI)	M. Pierce (FRA)	62 62
1998	M. Hingis (SUI)	C. Martinez (ESP)	63 63
1999	M. Hingis (SUI)	A. Mauresmo (FRA)	62 63
2000	L. Davenport (USA)	M. Hingis (SUI)	61 75
2001	J. Capriati (USA)	M. Hingis (SUI)	64 63
2002	J. Capriati (USA)	M. Hingis (SUI)	46 76 62
2003	S. Williams (USA)	V. Williams (USA)	76 36 64
2004	J. Henin-Hardenne (BEL)	K. Clijsters (BEL)	62 76
2005	S. Williams (USA)	L. Davenport (USA)	26 63 60

	Men's Doubles	**Women's Doubles**	**Mixed Doubles**
Year	**Champions**	**Champions**	**Champions**
1905	R. Lycett/T. Tachell		
1906	R. Heath/A. Wilding		
1907	W. Gregg/H. Parker		
1908	F. Alexander/A. Dunlop		
1909	J. Keane/E. Parker		
1910	A. Campbell/H. Rice		
1911	R. Heath/R. Lycett		
1912	C. Dixon/J. Parke		
1913	A. Hedemann/E. Parker		
1914	A. Campbell/G. Patterson		
1915	H. Rice/C. Todd		
1916-1918 not played			
1919	P. O'Hara Wood/R. Thomas		
1920	P. O'Hara Wood/R. Thomas		
1921	S. Eaton/R. Gemmell		
1922	J. Hawkes/G. Patterson	E. Boyd/M. Mountain	J. Hawkes/E. Boyd
1923	P. O'Hara Wood/C. St John	E. Boyd/S. Lance	H. Rice/S. Lance
1924	J. Anderson/N. Brookes	D. Akhurst/S. Lance	J. Willard/D. Akhurst
1925	P. O'Hara Wood/G. Patterson	D. Akhurst/R. Harper	J. Willard/D. Akhurst
1926	J. Hawkes/G. Patterson	E. Boyd/M. O'Hara Wood	J. Hawkes/E. Boyd
1927	J. Hawkes/G. Patterson	L. Bickerton/M. O'Hara Wood	J. Hawkes/E. Boyd
1928	J. Borotra/J. Brugnon	D. Akhurst/E. Boyd	J. Borotra/D. Akhurst
1929	J. Crawford/H. Hopman	D. Akhurst/L. Bickerton	E. Moon/D. Akhurst
1930	J. Crawford/H. Hopman	E. Hood/M. Molesworth	H. Hopman/N. Hall
1931	C. Donohoe/R. Dunlop	L. Bickerton/R. Cozens	J. Crawford/M. Crawford
1932	J. Crawford/E. Moon	C. Buttsworth/M. Crawford	J. Crawford/M. Crawford
1933	K. Gledhill/E. Vines	M. Molesworth/E. Westacott	J. Crawford/M. Crawford
1934	G. Hughes/F. Perry	M. Molesworth/E. Westacott	E. Moon/J. Hartigan
1935	J. Crawford/V. McGrath	E. Dearman/N. Lyle	C. Boussus/L. Bickerton
1936	A. Quist/P. Turnbull	T. Coyne/N. Wynne	H. Hopman/N. Hopman
1937	A. Quist/P. Turnbull	T. Coyne/N. Wynne	H. Hopman/N. Hopman
1938	J. Bromwich/A. Quist	T. Coyne/N. Wynne	J. Bromwich/J. Wilson
1939	J. Bromwich/A. Quist	T. Coyne/N. Wynne	H. Hopman/N. Hopman
1940	J. Bromwich/A. Quist	T. Coyne/N. Bolton	C. Long/N. Bolton
1941-1945 not played			
1946	J. Bromwich/A. Quist	M. Bevis/J. Fitch	C. Long/N. Bolton

Australian Championships (continued)

Year	Champions	Champions	Champions
1947	J. Bromwich/A. Quist	N. Bolton/T. Long	C. Long/N. Bolton
1948	J. Bromwich/A. Quist	N. Bolton/T. Long	C. Long/N. Bolton
1949	J. Bromwich/A. Quist	N. Bolton/T. Long	F. Sedgman/D. Hart
1950	J. Bromwich/A. Quist	L. Brough/D. Hart	F. Sedgman/D. Hart
1951	K. McGregor/F. Sedgman	N. Bolton/T. Long	G. Worthington/T. Long
1952	K. McGregor/F. Sedgman	N. Bolton/T. Long	G. Worthington/T. Long
1953	L. Hoad/K. Rosewall	M. Connolly/J. Sampson	R. Hartwig/J. Sampson
1954	R. Hartwig/M. Rose	M. Hawton/B. Penrose	R. Hartwig/T. Long
1955	V. Seixas/T. Trabert	M. Hawton/B. Penrose	G. Worthington/T. Long
1956	L. Hoad/K. Rosewall	M. Hawton/T. Long	N. Fraser/B. Penrose
1957	N. Fraser/L. Hoad	S. Fry/A. Gibson	M. Anderson/F. Muller
1958	A. Cooper/N. Fraser	M. Hawton/T. Long	R. Howe/M. Hawton
1959	R. Laver/R. Mark	S. Reynolds/R. Schuurman	R. Mark/S. Reynolds
1960	R. Laver/R. Mark	M. Bueno/C. Truman	T. Fancutt/J. Lehane
1961	R. Laver/R. Mark	M. Reitano/M. Smith	R. Hewitt/J. Lehane
1962	R. Emerson/N. Fraser	R. Ebbern/M. Smith	F. Stolle/L. Turner
1963	R. Hewitt/F. Stolle	R. Ebbern/M. Smith	K. Fletcher/M. Smith
1964	R. Hewitt/F. Stolle	J. Tegart/L. Turner	K. Fletcher/M. Smith
1965	J. Newcombe/T. Roche	M. Smith/L. Turner	J. Newcombe/M. Smith & O. Davidson/R. Ebbern
1966	R. Emerson/F. Stolle	C. Graebner/N. Richey	A. Roche/J. Tegart
1967	J. Newcombe/T. Roche	J. Tegart/L. Turner	O. Davidson/L. Turner
1968	R. Crealy/A. Stone	K. Krantzcke/K. Melville	R. Crealy/B. King
1969	R. Emerson/R. Laver	M. Court/J. Tegart	M. Riessen/M. Court & F. Stolle/A. Jones
1970	R. Lutz/S. Smith	M. Court/J. Dalton	1970-1986 not played
1971	J. Newcombe/T. Roche	M. Court/E. Goolagong	
1972	O. Davidson/K. Rosewall	H. Gourlay/K. Harris	
1973	M. Anderson/J. Newcombe	M. Court/V. Wade	
1974	R. Case/G. Masters	E. Goolagong/M. Michel	
1975	J. Alexander/P. Dent	E. Goolagong/M. Michel	
1976	J. Newcombe/T. Roche	E. Goolagong Cawley/H. Gourlay	
1977 (Jan)	A. Ashe/T. Roche	D. Fromholtz/H. Gourlay	
1977 (Dec)	A. Stone/R. Ruffels	E. Goolagong Cawley/H. Cawley (nee Gourlay)	
1978	W. Fibak/K. Warwick	B. Nagelsen/R. Tomanova	
1979	P. McNamara/P. McNamee	J. Chaloner/R. Evers	
1980	M. Edmondson/K. Warwick	B. Nagelsen/M. Navratilova	
1981	M. Edmondson/K. Warwick	K. Jordan/A. Smith	
1982	J. Alexander/J. Fitzgerald	M. Navratilova/P. Shriver	
1983	M. Edmondson/P. McNamee	M. Navratilova/P. Shriver	
1984	M. Edmondson/S. Stewart	M. Navratilova/P. Shriver	
1985 (Nov)	P. Annacone/C. Van Rensburg	M. Navratilova/P. Shriver	
1986 not played			
1987 (Jan)	S. Edberg/A. Jarryd	M. Navratilova/P. Shriver	S. Stewart/Z. Garrison
1988	R. Leach/J. Pugh	M. Navratilova/P. Shriver	J. Pugh/J. Novotna
1989	R. Leach/J. Pugh	M. Navratilova/P. Shriver	J. Pugh/J. Novotna
1990	P. Aldrich/D. Visser	J. Novotna/H. Sukova	J. Pugh/N. Zvereva
1991	S. Davis/D. Pate	P. Fendick/M. Fernandez	J. Bates/J. Durie
1992	T. Woodbridge/M. Woodforde	A. Sanchez Vicario/H. Sukova	M. Woodforde/N. Provis
1993	D. Visser/L. Warder	G. Fernandez/N. Zvereva	T. Woodbridge/A. Sanchez Vicario
1994	J. Eltingh/P. Haarhuis	G. Fernandez/N. Zvereva	A. Olhovskiy/L. Neiland
1995	J. Palmer/R. Reneberg	J. Novotna/A. Sanchez Vicario	R. Leach/N. Zvereva
1996	S. Edberg/P. Korda	C. Rubin/A. Sanchez Vicario	M. Woodforde/L. Neiland
1997	T. Woodbridge/M. Woodforde	M. Hingis/N. Zvereva	R. Leach/M. Bollegraf
1998	J. Bjorkman/J. Eltingh	M. Hingis/M. Lucic	J. Gimelstob/V. Williams
1999	J. Bjorkman/P. Rafter	M. Hingis/A. Kournikova	D. Adams/M. De Swardt
2000	E. Ferreira/R. Leach	L. Raymond/R. Stubbs	J. Palmer/R. Stubbs

Year	Champions	Champions	Champions
2001	J. Bjorkman/T. Woodbridge	S. Williams/V. Williams	E. Ferreira/C. Morariu
2002	M. Knowles/D. Nestor	M. Hingis/A. Kournikova	K. Ullyett/D. Hantuchova
2003	M. Llodra/F. Santoro	S. Williams/V. Williams	L. Paes/M. Navratilova
2004	M. Llodra/F. Santoro	V. Ruano Pascual/P. Suarez	N. Zimonjic/E. Bovina
2005	W. Black/K. Ullyett	S. Kuznetsova/A. Molik	S. Draper/S. Stosur

French Championships Roland Garros

Men's Singles

Year	Champion	Runner-up	Score
1925	R. Lacoste (FRA)	J. Borotra (FRA)	75 61 64
1926	H. Cochet (FRA)	R. Lacoste (FRA)	62 64 63
1927	R. Lacoste (FRA)	W. Tilden (USA)	64 46 57 63 119
1928	H. Cochet (FRA)	R. Lacoste (FRA)	57 63 61 63
1929	R. Lacoste (FRA)	J. Borotra (FRA)	63 26 60 26 86
1930	H. Cochet (FRA)	W. Tilden (USA)	36 86 63 61
1931	J. Borotra (FRA)	C. Boussus (FRA)	26 64 75 64
1932	H. Cochet (FRA)	G. De Stefani (ITA)	60 64 46 63
1933	J. Crawford (AUS)	H. Cochet (FRA)	86 61 63
1934	G. Von Cramm (GER)	J. Crawford (AUS)	64 79 36 75 63
1935	F. Perry (GBR)	G. Von Cramm (GER)	63 36 61 63
1936	G. Von Cramm (GER)	F. Perry (GBR)	60 26 62 26 60
1937	H. Henkel (GER)	H. Austin (USA)	61 64 63
1938	D. Budge (USA)	R. Menzel (TCH)	63 62 64
1939	W. McNeill (USA)	R. Riggs (USA)	75 60 63
1940-1945 not played			
1946	M. Bernard (FRA)	J. Drobny (TCH)	36 26 61 64 63
1947	J. Asboth (HUN)	E. Sturgess (RSA)	86 75 64
1948	F. Parker (USA)	J. Drobny (TCH)	64 75 57 86
1949	F. Parker (USA)	B. Patty (USA)	63 16 61 64
1950	B. Patty (USA)	J. Drobny (TCH)	61 62 36 57 75
1951	J. Drobny (TCH)	E. Sturgess (RSA)	63 63 63
1952	J. Drobny (TCH)	F. Sedgman (AUS)	62 60 36 64
1953	K. Rosewall (AUS)	V. Seixas (USA)	63 64 16 62
1954	T. Trabert (USA)	A. Larsen (USA)	64 75 61
1955	T. Trabert (USA)	S. Davidson (SWE)	26 61 64 62
1956	L. Hoad (AUS)	S. Davidson (SWE)	64 86 63
1957	S. Davidson (SWE)	H. Flam (USA)	63 64 64
1958	M. Rose (AUS)	L. Ayala (CHI)	63 64 64
1959	N. Pietrangeli (ITA)	I. Vermaak (RSA)	36 63 64 61
1960	N. Pietrangeli (ITA)	L. Ayala (CHI)	36 63 64 46 63
1961	M. Santana (ESP)	N. Pietrangeli (ITA)	46 61 36 60 62
1962	R. Laver (AUS)	R. Emerson (AUS)	36 26 63 97 62
1963	R. Emerson (AUS)	P. Darmon (FRA)	36 61 64 64
1964	M. Santana (ESP)	N. Pietrangeli (ITA)	63 61 46 75
1965	F. Stolle (AUS)	T. Roche (AUS)	36 60 62 63
1966	T. Roche (AUS)	I. Gulyas (HUN)	61 64 75
1967	R. Emerson (AUS)	T. Roche (AUS)	61 64 26 62
1968	K. Rosewall (AUS)	R. Laver (AUS)	63 61 26 62
1969	R. Laver (AUS)	K. Rosewall (AUS)	64 63 64
1970	J. Kodes (TCH)	Z. Franulovic (YUG)	62 64 60
1971	J. Kodes (TCH)	I. Nastase (ROM)	86 62 26 75
1972	A. Gimeno (ESP)	P. Proisy (FRA)	46 63 61 61
1973	I. Nastase (ROM)	N. Pilic (YUG)	63 63 60

French Championships Roland Garros (continued)

Year	Champion	Runner-up	Score
1974	B. Borg (SWE)	M. Orantes (ESP)	26 67 60 61 61
1975	B. Borg (SWE)	G. Vilas (ARG)	62 63 64
1976	A. Panatta (ITA)	H. Solomon (USA)	61 64 46 76
1977	G. Vilas (ARG)	B. Gottfried (USA)	60 63 60
1978	B. Borg (SWE)	G. Vilas (ARG)	61 61 63
1979	B. Borg (SWE)	V. Pecci (PAR)	63 61 67 64
1980	B. Borg (SWE)	V. Gerulaitis (USA)	64 61 62
1981	B. Borg (SWE)	I. Lendl (TCH)	61 46 62 36 61
1982	M. Wilander (SWE)	G. Vilas (ARG)	16 76 60 64
1983	Y. Noah (FRA)	M. Wilander (SWE)	62 75 76
1984	I. Lendl (TCH)	J. McEnroe (USA)	36 26 64 75 75
1985	M. Wilander (SWE)	I. Lendl (TCH)	36 64 62 62
1986	I. Lendl (TCH)	M. Pernfors (SWE)	63 62 64
1987	I. Lendl (TCH)	M. Wilander (SWE)	75 62 36 76
1988	M. Wilander (SWE)	H. Leconte (FRA)	75 62 61
1989	M. Chang (USA)	S. Edberg (SWE)	61 36 46 64 62
1990	A. Gomez (ECU)	A. Agassi (USA)	63 26 64 64
1991	J. Courier (USA)	A. Agassi (USA)	36 64 26 61 64
1992	J. Courier (USA)	P. Korda (TCH)	75 62 61
1993	S. Bruguera (ESP)	J. Courier (USA)	64 26 62 36 63
1994	S. Bruguera (ESP)	A. Berasategui (ESP)	63 75 26 61
1995	T. Muster (AUT)	M. Chang (USA)	75 62 64
1996	Y. Kafelnikov (RUS)	M. Stich (GER)	76 75 76
1997	G. Kuerten (BRA)	S. Bruguera (ESP)	63 64 62
1998	C. Moya (ESP)	A. Corretja (ESP)	63 75 63
1999	A. Agassi (USA)	A. Medvedev (UKR)	16 26 64 63 64
2000	G. Kuerten (BRA)	M. Norman (SWE)	62 63 26 76
2001	G. Kuerten (BRA)	A. Corretja (ESP)	67 75 62 60
2002	A. Costa (ESP)	J. Ferrero (ESP)	61 60 46 63
2003	J. Ferrero (ESP)	M. Verkerk (NED)	61 63 62
2004	G. Gaudio (ARG)	G. Coria (ARG)	06 36 64 61 86
2005	R. Nadal (ESP)	M. Puerta (ARG)	67 63 61 75

Women's Singles

Year	Champion	Runner-up	Score
1925	S. Lenglen (FRA)	K. McKane (GBR)	61 62
1926	S. Lenglen (FRA)	M. Browne (USA)	61 60
1927	K. Bouman (NED)	I. Peacock (RSA)	62 64
1928	H. Wills (USA)	E. Bennett (GBR)	61 62
1929	H. Wills (USA)	S. Mathieu (FRA)	63 64
1930	H. Wills Moody (USA)	H. Jacobs (USA)	62 61
1931	C. Aussem (GER)	B. Nuthall (GBR)	86 61
1932	H. Wills Moody (USA)	S. Mathieu (FRA)	75 61
1933	M. Scriven (GBR)	S. Mathieu (FRA)	62 46 64
1934	M. Scriven (GBR)	H. Jacobs (USA)	75 46 61
1935	H. Sperling (GER)	S. Mathieu (FRA)	62 61
1936	H. Sperling (GER)	S. Mathieu (FRA)	63 64
1937	H. Sperling (GER)	S. Mathieu (FRA)	62 64
1938	S. Mathieu (FRA)	N. Landry (FRA)	60 63
1939	S. Mathieu (FRA)	J. Jedrzejowska (POL)	63 86
1940-1945 not played			
1946	M. Osborne (USA)	P. Betz (USA)	16 86 75
1947	P. Todd (USA)	D. Hart (USA)	63 36 64
1948	N. Landry (FRA)	S. Fry (USA)	62 06 60
1949	M. Osborne DuPont (USA)	N. Adamson-Landry (FRA)	75 62

Year	Champion	Runner-up	Score
1950	D. Hart (USA)	P. Todd (USA)	64 46 62
1951	S. Fry (USA)	D. Hart (USA)	63 36 63
1952	D. Hart (USA)	S. Fry (USA)	64 64
1953	M. Connolly (USA)	D. Hart (USA)	62 64
1954	M. Connolly (USA)	G. Bucaille (FRA)	64 61
1955	A. Mortimer (GBR)	D. Knode (USA)	26 75 108
1956	A. Gibson (USA)	A. Mortimer (GBR)	60 1210
1957	S. Bloomer (GBR)	D. Knode (USA)	61 63
1958	Z. Kormoczy (HUN)	S. Bloomer (GBR)	64 16 62
1959	C. Truman (GBR)	Z. Kormoczy (HUN)	64 75
1960	D. Hard (USA)	Y. Ramirez (MEX)	63 64
1961	A. Haydon (GBR)	Y. Ramirez (MEX)	62 61
1962	M. Smith (AUS)	L. Turner (AUS)	63 36 75
1963	L. Turner (AUS)	A. Jones (GBR) (nee Haydon)	26 63 75
1964	M. Smith (AUS)	M. Bueno (BRA)	57 61 62
1965	L. Turner (AUS)	M. Smith (AUS)	63 64
1966	A. Jones (GBR)	N. Richey (USA)	63 61
1967	F. Durr (FRA)	L. Turner (AUS)	46 63 64
1968	N. Richey (USA)	A. Jones (GBR)	57 64 61
1969	M. Court (AUS) (nee Smith)	A. Jones (GBR)	61 46 63
1970	M. Court (AUS)	H. Niessen (FRG)	62 64
1971	E. Goolagong (AUS)	H. Gourlay (AUS)	63 75
1972	B. King (USA)	E. Goolagong (AUS)	63 63
1973	M. Court (AUS)	C. Evert (USA)	67 76 64
1974	C. Evert (USA)	O. Morozova (URS)	61 62
1975	C. Evert (USA)	M. Navratilova (TCH)	26 62 61
1976	S. Barker (GBR)	R. Tomanova (TCH)	62 06 62
1977	M. Jausovec (YUG)	F. Mihai (ROM)	62 67 61
1978	V. Ruzici (ROM)	M. Jausovec (YUG)	62 62
1979	C. Evert Lloyd (USA)	W. Turnbull (AUS)	62 60
1980	C. Evert Lloyd (USA)	V. Ruzici (ROM)	60 63
1981	H. Mandlikova (TCH)	S. Hanika (FRG)	62 64
1982	M. Navratilova (USA)	A. Jaeger (USA)	76 61
1983	C. Evert Lloyd (USA)	M. Jausovec (YUG)	61 62
1984	M. Navratilova (USA)	C. Evert Lloyd (USA)	63 61
1985	C. Evert Lloyd (USA)	M. Navratilova (USA)	63 67 75
1986	C. Evert Lloyd (USA)	M. Navratilova (USA)	26 63 63
1987	S. Graf (FRG)	M. Navratilova (USA)	64 46 86
1988	S. Graf (FRG)	N. Zvereva (URS)	60 60
1989	A. Sanchez (ESP)	S. Graf (FRG)	76 36 75
1990	M. Seles (YUG)	S. Graf (GER)	76 64
1991	M. Seles (YUG)	A. Sanchez Vicario (ESP)	63 64
1992	M. Seles (YUG)	S. Graf (GER)	62 36 108
1993	S. Graf (GER)	M. Fernandez (USA)	46 62 64
1994	A. Sanchez Vicario (ESP)	M. Pierce (FRA)	64 64
1995	S. Graf (GER)	A. Sanchez Vicario (ESP)	75 46 60
1996	S. Graf (GER)	A. Sanchez Vicario (ESP)	63 67 108
1997	I. Majoli (CRO)	M. Hingis (SUI)	64 62
1998	A. Sanchez-Vicario (ESP)	M. Seles (USA)	76 06 62
1999	S. Graf (GER)	M. Hingis (SUI)	46 75 62
2000	M. Pierce (FRA)	C. Martinez (ESP)	62 75
2001	J. Capriati (USA)	K. Clijsters (BEL)	16 64 1210
2002	S. Williams (USA)	V. Williams (USA)	75 63
2003	J. Henin-Hardenne (BEL)	K. Clijsters (BEL)	60 64
2004	A. Myskina (RUS)	E. Dementieva (RUS)	61 62
2005	J. Henin-Hardenne (BEL)	M. Pierce (FRA)	61 61

French Championships Roland Garros (continued)

Year	Men's Doubles Champions	Women's Doubles Champions	Mixed Doubles Champions
1925	J. Borotra/R. Lacoste	S. Lenglen/D. Vlasto	J. Brugnon/S. Lenglen
1926	H. Kinsey/V. Richards	S. Lenglen/D. Vlasto	J. Brugnon/S. Lenglen
1927	J. Brugnon/H. Cochet	B. Heine/I. Peacock	J. Borotra/M. Broquedis
1928	J. Borotra/J. Brugnon	E. Bennett/P. Watson	H. Cochet/E. Bennett
1929	J. Borotra/R. Lacoste	L. De Alvarez/K. Bouman	H. Cochet/E. Bennett
1930	J. Brugnon/H. Cochet	H. Moody/E. Ryan	W. Tilden/C. Aussem
1931	G. Lott/J. Van Ryn	B. Nuthall/E. Bennett Whitingstall	P. Spense/B. Nuthall
1932	J. Brugnon/H. Cochet	H. Moody/E. Ryan	F. Perry/B. Nuthall
1933	P. Hughes/F. Perry	S. Mathieu/E. Ryan	J. Crawford/M. Scriven
1934	J. Borotra/J. Brugnon	S. Mathieu/E. Ryan	J. Borotra/C. Rosambert
1935	J. Crawford/A. Quist	M. Scriven/K. Stammers	M. Bernard/L. Payot
1936	M. Bernard/J. Borotra	S. Mathieu/A. Yorke	M. Bernard/A. Yorke
1937	G. Von Cramm/H. Henkel	S. Mathieu/A. Yorke	Y. Petra/S. Mathieu
1938	B. Destremau/Y. Petra	S. Mathieu/A. Yorke	D. Mitic/S. Mathieu
1939	C. Harris/W. McNeill	J. Jedrzejowska/S. Mathieu	E. Cooke/S. Palfrey Fabyan
1940-1945 not played			
1946	M. Bernard/Y. Petra	L. Brough/M. Osborne	B. Patty/P. Betz
1947	E. Fannin/E. Sturgess	L. Brough/M. Osborne	E. Sturgess/S. Summers
1948	L. Bergelin/J. Drobny	D. Hart/P. Todd	J. Drobny/P. Todd
1949	R. Gonzales/F. Parker	L. Brough/M. Osborne DuPont	E. Sturgess/S. Summers
1950	W. Talbert/T. Trabert	S. Fry/D. Hart	E. Morea/B. Scofield
1951	K. McGregor/F. Sedgman	S. Fry/D. Hart	F. Sedgman/D. Hart
1952	K. McGregor/F. Sedgman	S. Fry/D. Hart	F. Sedgman/D. Hart
1953	L. Hoad/K. Rosewall	S. Fry/D. Hart	V. Seixas/D. Hart
1954	V. Seixas/T. Trabert	M. Connolly/N. Hopman	L. Hoad/M. Connolly
1955	V. Seixas/T. Trabert	B. Fleitz/D. Hard	G. Forbes/D. Hard
1956	D. Candy/R. Perry	A. Buxton/A. Gibson	L. Ayala/T. Long
1957	M. Anderson/A. Cooper	S. Bloomer/D. Hard	J.Javorsky/V. Puzejova
1958	A. Cooper/N. Fraser	Y. Ramirez/R. Reyes	N. Pietrangeli/S. Bloomer
1959	N. Pietrangeli/O. Sirola	S. Reynolds/R. Schuurman	W. Knight/Y. Ramirez
1960	R. Emerson/N. Fraser	M. Bueno/D. Hard	R. Howe/M. Bueno
1961	R. Emerson/R. Laver	S. Reynolds/R. Schuurman	R. Laver/D. Hard
1962	R. Emerson/N. Fraser	S. Reynolds/R. Schuurman	R. Howe/R. Schuurmann
1963	R. Emerson/M. Santana	A. Jones/R. Schuurman	K. Fletcher/M. Smith
1964	R. Emerson/K. Fletcher	M. Smith/L. Turner	K. Fletcher/M. Smith
1965	R. Emerson/F. Stolle	M. Smith/L. Turner	K. Fletcher/M. Smith
1966	C. Graebner/D. Ralston	M. Smith/J. Tegart	F. McMillan/A. Van Zyl
1967	J. Newcombe/T. Roche	F. Durr/G. Sheriff	O. Davidson/B. King
1968	K. Rosewall/F. Stolle	F. Durr/A. Jones	J. Barclay/F. Durr
1969	J. Newcombe/T. Roche	F. Durr/A. Jones	M. Riessen/M. Court
1970	I. Nastase/I. Tiriac	G. Sheriff Chanfreau/F. Durr	R. Hewitt/B. King
1971	A. Ashe/M. Riessen	G. Sheriff Chanfreau/F. Durr	J. Barclay/F. Durr
1972	R. Hewitt/F. McMillan	B. King/B. Stove	K. Warwick/E. Goolagong
1973	J. Newcombe/T. Okker	M. Court/V. Wade	J. Barclay/F. Durr
1974	R. Crealy/O. Parun	C. Evert/O. Morozova	I. Molina/M. Navratilova
1975	B. Gottfried/R. Ramirez	C. Evert/M. Navratilova	T. Koch/F. Bonicelli
1976	F. McNair/S. Stewart	F. Bonicelli/G. Sheriff Lovera	K. Warwick/I. Kloss
1977	B. Gottfried/R. Ramirez	R. Marsikova/P. Teeguarden	J. McEnroe/M. Carillo
1978	G. Mayer/H. Pfister	M. Jausovec/V. Ruzici	P. Slozil/R. Tomanova
1979	S. Mayer/G. Mayer	B. Stove/W. Turnbull	R. Hewitt/W. Turnbull
1980	V. Amaya/H. Pfister	K. Jordan/A. Smith	W. Martin/A. Smith
1981	H. Gunthardt/B. Taroczy	R. Fairbank/T. Harford	J. Arias/A. Jaeger
1982	S. Stewart/F. Taygan	M. Navratilova/A. Smith	J. Lloyd/W. Turnbull
1983	A. Jarryd/H. Simonsson	R. Fairbank/C. Reynolds	E. Teltscher/B. Jordan

1984	Y. Noah/H. Leconte	M. Navratilova/P. Shriver	D. Stockton/A. Smith
1985	M. Edmonson/K. Warwick	M. Navratilova/P. Shriver	H. Gunthardt/M. Navratilova
1986	J. Fitzgerald/T. Smid	M. Navratilova/A. Temesvari	K. Flach/K. Jordan
1987	A. Jarryd/R. Seguso	M. Navratilova/P. Shriver	E. Sanchez/P. Shriver
1988	A. Gomez/E. Sanchez	M. Navratilova/P. Shriver	J. Lozano/L. McNeil
1989	J. Grabb/P. McEnroe	L. Savchenko/N. Zvereva	T. Nijssen/M. Bollegraf
1990	S. Casal/E. Sanchez	J. Novotna/H. Sukova	J. Lozano/A. Sanchez Vicario
1991	J. Fitzgerald/A. Jarryd	G. Fernandez/J. Novotna	C. Suk/H. Sukova
1992	J. Hlasek/M. Rosset	G. Fernandez/N. Zvereva	T. Woodbridge/A. Sanchez Vicario
1993	L. Jensen/M. Jensen	G. Fernandez/N. Zvereva	A. Olhovskiy/E. Maniokova
1994	B. Black/J. Stark	G. Fernandez/N. Zvereva	M. Oosting/K. Boogert
1995	J. Eltingh/P. Haarhuis	G. Fernandez/N. Zvereva	M. Woodforde/L. Neiland
1996	Y. Kafelnikov/D. Vacek	L. Davenport/M. Fernandez	J. Frana/P. Tarabini
1997	Y. Kafelnikov/D. Vacek	G. Fernandez/N. Zvereva	M. Bhupathi/R. Hiraki
1998	J. Eltingh/P. Haarhuis	M. Hingis/J. Novotna	J. Gimelstob/V. Williams
1999	M. Bhupathi/L. Paes	V. Williams/S. Williams	P. Norval/K. Srebotnik
2000	M. Woodforde/T. Woodbridge	M. Hingis/M. Pierce	D. Adams/M. De Swardt
2001	M. Bhupathi/L. Paes	V. Ruano Pascual/P. Suarez	T. Carbonell/V. Ruano Pascual
2002	P. Haarhuis/Y. Kafelnikov	V. Ruano Pascual/P. Suarez	W. Black/C. Black
2003	B. Bryan/M. Bryan	K. Clijsters/A. Sugiyama	M. Bryan/L. Raymond
2004	X. Malisse/O. Rochus	V. Ruano Pascual/P. Suarez	R. Gasquet/T. Golovin
2005	J. Bjorkman/M. Mirnyi	V. Ruano Pascual/P. Suarez	F. Santoro/D. Hantuchova

The Championships, Wimbledon

Men's Singles

Year	Champion	Runner-up	Score
1877	S. Gore (GBR)	W. Marshall (GBR)	61 62 64
1878	P. Hadow (GBR)	S. Gore (GBR)	75 61 97
1879	J. Hartley (GBR)	V. St L. Goold (GBR)	62 64 62
1880	J. Hartley (GBR)	H. Lawford (GBR)	63 62 26 63
1881	W. Renshaw (GBR)	J. Hartley (GBR)	60 61 61
1882	W. Renshaw (GBR)	E. Renshaw (GBR)	61 26 46 62 62
1883	W. Renshaw (GBR)	E. Renshaw (GBR)	26 63 63 46 63
1884	W. Renshaw (GBR)	H. Lawford (GBR)	60 64 97
1885	W. Renshaw (GBR)	H. Lawford (GBR)	75 62 46 75
1886	W. Renshaw (GBR)	H. Lawford (GBR)	60 57 63 64
1887	H. Lawford (GBR)	E. Renshaw (GBR)	16 63 36 64 64
1888	E. Renshaw (GBR)	H. Lawford (GBR)	63 75 60
1889	W. Renshaw (GBR)	E. Renshaw (GBR)	64 61 36 60
1890	W. Hamilton (GBR)	W. Renshaw (GBR)	68 62 36 61 61
1891	W. Baddeley (GBR)	J. Pim (GBR)	64 16 75 60
1892	W. Baddeley (GBR)	J. Pim (GBR)	46 63 63 62
1893	J. Pim (GBR)	W. Baddeley (GBR)	36 61 63 62
1894	J. Pim (GBR)	W. Baddeley (GBR)	108 62 86
1895	W. Baddeley (GBR)	W. Eaves (GBR)	46 26 86 62 63
1896	H. Mahony (GBR)	W. Baddeley (GBR)	62 68 57 86 63
1897	R. Doherty (GBR)	H. Mahony (GBR)	64 64 63
1898	R. Doherty (GBR)	H. Doherty (GBR)	63 63 26 57 61
1899	R. Doherty (GBR)	A. Gore (GBR)	16 46 63 63 63
1900	R. Doherty (GBR)	S. Smith (GBR)	68 63 61 62
1901	A. Gore (GBR)	R. Doherty (GBR)	46 75 64 64
1902	H. Doherty (GBR)	A. Gore (GBR)	64 63 36 60
1903	H. Doherty (GBR)	F. Riseley (GBR)	75 63 60
1904	H. Doherty (GBR)	F. Riseley (GBR)	61 75 86

The Championships, Wimbledon (continued)

Year	Champion	Runner-up	Score
1905	H. Doherty (GBR)	N. Brookes (AUS)	86 62 64
1906	H. Doherty (GBR)	F. Riseley (GBR)	64 46 62 63
1907	N. Brookes (AUS)	A. Gore (GBR)	64 62 62
1908	A. Gore (GBR)	H. Roper Barrett (GBR)	63 62 46 36 64
1909	A. Gore (GBR)	M. Ritchie (GBR)	68 16 62 62 62
1910	A. Wilding (NZL)	A. Gore (GBR)	64 75 46 62
1911	A. Wilding (NZL)	H. Roper Barrett (GBR)	64 46 26 62 ret.
1912	A. Wilding (NZL)	A. Gore (GBR)	64 64 46 64
1913	A. Wilding (NZL)	M. McLoughlin (USA)	86 63 108
1914	N. Brookes (AUS)	A. Wilding (NZL)	64 64 75
1915-18 not played			
1919	G. Patterson (AUS)	N. Brookes (AUS)	63 75 62
1920	W. Tilden (USA)	G. Patterson (AUS)	26 62 62 64
1921	W. Tilden (USA)	B. Norton (RSA)	46 26 61 60 75
1922	G. Patterson (AUS)	R. Lycett (GBR)	63 64 62
1923	W. Johnston (USA)	F. Hunter (USA)	60 63 61
1924	J. Borotra (FRA)	R. Lacoste (FRA)	61 36 61 36 64
1925	R. Lacoste (FRA)	J. Borotra (FRA)	63 63 46 86
1926	J. Borotra (FRA)	H. Kinsey (USA)	86 61 63
1927	H. Cochet (FRA)	J. Borotra (FRA)	46 46 63 64 75
1928	R. Lacoste (FRA)	H. Cochet (FRA)	61 46 64 62
1929	H. Cochet (FRA)	J. Borotra (FRA)	64 63 64
1930	W. Tilden (USA)	W. Allison (USA)	63 97 64
1931	S. Wood (USA)	F. Shields (USA)	w/o
1932	E. Vines (USA)	H. Austin (GBR)	62 62 60
1933	J. Crawford (AUS)	E. Vines (USA)	46 119 62 26 64
1934	F. Perry (GBR)	J. Crawford (AUS)	63 60 75
1935	F. Perry (GBR)	G. Von Cramm (GER)	62 64 64
1936	F. Perry (GBR)	G. Von Cramm (GER)	61 61 60
1937	D. Budge (USA)	G. Von Cramm (GER)	63 64 62
1938	D. Budge (USA)	H. Austin (GBR)	61 60 63
1939	R. Riggs (USA)	E. Cooke (USA)	26 86 36 63 62
1940-45 not played			
1946	Y. Petra (FRA)	G. Brown (AUS)	62 64 79 57 64
1947	J. Kramer (USA)	T. Brown (USA)	61 63 62
1948	R. Falkenburg (USA)	J. Bromwich (AUS)	75 06 62 36 75
1949	F. Schroeder (USA)	J. Drobny (TCH)	36 60 63 46 64
1950	B. Patty (USA)	F. Sedgman (AUS)	61 810 62 63
1951	R. Savitt (USA)	K. McGregor (AUS)	64 64 64
1952	F. Sedgman (AUS)	J. Drobny (EGY)	46 62 63 62
1953	V. Seixas (USA)	K. Nielsen (DEN)	97 63 64
1954	J. Drobny (EGY)	K. Rosewall (AUS)	1311 46 62 97
1955	T. Trabert (USA)	K. Nielsen (DEN)	63 75 61
1956	L. Hoad (AUS)	K. Rosewall (AUS)	62 46 75 64
1957	L. Hoad (AUS)	A. Cooper (AUS)	62 61 62
1958	A. Cooper (AUS)	N. Fraser (AUS)	36 63 64 1311
1959	A. Olmedo (USA)	R. Laver (AUS)	64 63 64
1960	N. Fraser (AUS)	R. Laver (AUS)	64 36 97 75
1961	R. Laver (AUS)	C. McKinley (USA)	63 61 64
1962	R. Laver (AUS)	M. Mulligan (AUS)	62 62 61
1963	C. McKinley (USA)	F. Stolle (AUS)	97 61 64
1964	R. Emerson (AUS)	F. Stolle (AUS)	64 1210 46 63
1965	R. Emerson (AUS)	F. Stolle (AUS)	62 64 64
1966	M. Santana (ESP)	R. Ralston (USA)	64 119 64
1967	J. Newcombe (AUS)	W. Bungert (FRG)	63 61 61

Year	Champion	Runner-up	Score
1968	R. Laver (AUS)	T. Roche (AUS)	63 64 62
1969	R. Laver (AUS)	J. Newcombe (AUS)	64 57 64 64
1970	J. Newcombe (AUS)	K. Rosewall (AUS)	57 63 62 36 61
1971	J. Newcombe (AUS)	S. Smith (USA)	63 57 26 64 64
1972	S. Smith (USA)	I. Nastase (ROM)	46 63 63 46 75
1973	J. Kodes (TCH)	A. Metreveli (URS)	61 98 63
1974	J. Connors (USA)	K. Rosewall (AUS)	61 61 64
1975	A. Ashe (USA)	J. Connors (USA)	61 61 57 64
1976	B. Borg (SWE)	I. Nastase (ROM)	64 62 97
1977	B. Borg (SWE)	J. Connors (USA)	36 62 61 57 64
1978	B. Borg (SWE)	J. Connors (USA)	62 62 63
1979	B. Borg (SWE)	R. Tanner (USA)	67 61 36 63 64
1980	B. Borg (SWE)	J. McEnroe (USA)	16 75 63 67 86
1981	J. McEnroe (USA)	B. Borg (SWE)	46 76 76 64
1982	J. Connors (USA)	J. McEnroe (USA)	36 63 67 76 64
1983	J. McEnroe (USA)	C. Lewis (NZL)	62 62 62
1984	J. McEnroe (USA)	J. Connors (USA)	61 61 62
1985	B. Becker (FRG)	K. Curren (USA)	63 67 76 64
1986	B. Becker (FRG)	I. Lendl (TCH)	64 63 75
1987	P. Cash (AUS)	I. Lendl (TCH)	76 62 75
1988	S. Edberg (SWE)	B. Becker (FRG)	46 76 64 62
1989	B. Becker (FRG)	S. Edberg (SWE)	60 76 64
1990	S. Edberg (SWE)	B. Becker (GER)	62 62 36 36 64
1991	M. Stich (GER)	B. Becker (GER)	64 76 64
1992	A. Agassi (USA)	G. Ivanisevic (CRO)	67 64 64 16 64
1993	P. Sampras (USA)	J. Courier (USA)	76 76 36 63
1994	P. Sampras (USA)	G. Ivanisevic (CRO)	76 76 60
1995	P. Sampras (USA)	B. Becker (GER)	67 62 64 62
1996	R. Krajicek (NED)	M. Washington (USA)	63 64 63
1997	P. Sampras (USA)	C. Pioline (FRA)	64 62 64
1998	P. Sampras (USA)	G. Ivanisevic (CRO)	67 76 64 36 62
1999	P. Sampras (USA)	A. Agassi (USA)	63 64 75
2000	P. Sampras (USA)	P. Rafter (AUS)	67 76 64 62
2001	G. Ivanisevic (CRO)	P. Rafter (AUS)	63 36 63 26 97
2002	L. Hewitt (AUS)	D. Nalbandian (ARG)	61 63 62
2003	R. Federer (SUI)	M. Philippoussis (AUS)	76 62 76
2004	R. Federer (SUI)	A. Roddick (USA)	46 75 76 64
2005	R. Federer (SUI)	A. Roddick (USA)	62 76 64

Women's Singles

Year	Champion	Runner-up	Score
1884	M. Watson (GBR)	L. Watson (GBR)	68 63 63
1885	M. Watson (GBR)	B. Bingley (GBR)	61 75
1886	B. Bingley (GBR)	M. Watson (GBR)	63 63
1887	C. Dod (GBR)	B. Bingley (GBR)	62 60
1888	C. Dod (GBR)	B. Bingley Hillyard (GBR)	63 63
1889	B. Bingley Hillyard (GBR)	H. Rice (GBR)	46 86 64
1890	H. Rice (GBR)	M. Jacks (GBR)	64 61
1891	C. Dod (GBR)	B. Bingley Hillyard (GBR)	62 61
1892	C. Dod (GBR)	B. Bingley Hillyard (GBR)	61 61
1893	C. Dod (GBR)	B. Bingley Hillyard (GBR)	68 61 64
1894	B. Bingley Hillyard (GBR)	L. Austin (GBR)	61 61
1895	C. Cooper (GBR)	H. Jackson (GBR)	75 86
1896	C. Cooper (GBR)	A. Pickering (GBR)	62 63
1897	B. Bingley Hillyard (GBR)	C. Cooper (GBR)	57 75 62

The Championships, Wimbledon (continued)

Year	Champion	Runner-up	Score
1898	C. Cooper (GBR)	L. Martin (GBR)	64 64
1899	B. Bingley Hillyard (GBR)	C. Cooper (GBR)	62 63
1900	B. Bingley Hillyard (GBR)	C. Cooper (GBR)	46 64 64
1901	C. Sterry (GBR) (nee Cooper)	B. Bingley Hillyard (GBR)	62 62
1902	M. Robb (GBR)	C. Sterry (GBR)	75 61
1903	D. Douglass (GBR)	E. Thomson (GBR)	46 64 62
1904	D. Douglass (GBR)	C. Sterry (GBR)	60 63
1905	M. Sutton (USA)	D. Douglass (GBR)	63 64
1906	D. Douglass (GBR)	M. Sutton (USA)	63 97
1907	M. Sutton (USA)	D. Douglass Lambert Chambers (GBR)	61 64
1908	C. Sterry (GBR)	A. Morton (GBR)	64 64
1909	D. Boothby (GBR)	A. Morton (GBR)	64 46 86
1910	D. Douglass Lambert Chambers (GBR)	D. Boothby (GBR)	62 62
1911	D. Douglass Lambert Chambers (GBR)	D. Boothby (GBR)	60 60
1912	E. Larcombe (GBR)	C. Sterry (GBR)	63 61
1913	D. Douglass Lambert Chambers (GBR)	W. McNair (GBR)	60 64
1914	D. Douglass Lambert Chambers (GBR)	E. Larcombe (GBR)	75 64
1915-18 not played			
1919	S. Lenglen (FRA)	D. Douglass Lambert Chambers (GBR)	108 46 97
1920	S. Lenglen (FRA)	D. Douglass Lambert Chambers (GBR)	63 60
1921	S. Lenglen (FRA)	E. Ryan (USA)	62 60
1922	S. Lenglen (FRA)	M. Mallory (USA)	62 60
1923	S. Lenglen (FRA)	K. McKane (GBR)	62 62
1924	K. McKane (GBR)	H. Wills (USA)	46 64 64
1925	S. Lenglen (FRA)	J. Fry (GBR)	62 60
1926	K. Godfree (GBR) (nee McKane)	E. De Alvarez (ESP)	62 46 63
1927	H. Wills (USA)	E. De Alvarez (ESP)	62 64
1928	H. Wills (USA)	E. De Alvarez (ESP)	62 63
1929	H. Wills (USA)	H. Jacobs (USA)	61 62
1930	H. Wills Moody (USA)	E. Ryan (USA)	62 62
1931	C. Aussem (GER)	H. Krahwinkel (GER)	62 75
1932	H. Wills Moody (USA)	H. Jacobs (USA)	63 61
1933	H. Wills Moody (USA)	D. Round (GBR)	64 68 63
1934	D. Round (GBR)	H. Jacobs (USA)	62 57 63
1935	H. Wills Moody (USA)	H. Jacobs (USA)	63 36 75
1936	H. Jacobs (USA)	H. Sperling (GER)	62 46 75
1937	D. Round (GBR)	J. Jedrzejowska (POL)	62 26 75
1938	H. Wills Moody (USA)	H. Jacobs (USA)	64 60
1939	A. Marble (USA)	K. Stammers (GBR)	62 60
1940-45 not played			
1946	P. Betz (USA)	L. Brough (USA)	62 64
1947	M. Osborne (USA)	D. Hart (USA)	62 64
1948	L. Brough (USA)	D. Hart (USA)	63 86
1949	L. Brough (USA)	M. Osborne DuPont (USA)	108 16 108
1950	L. Brough (USA)	M. Osborne DuPont (USA)	61 36 61
1951	D. Hart (USA)	S. Fry (USA)	61 60
1952	M. Connolly (USA)	L. Brough (USA)	75 63
1953	M. Connolly (USA)	D. Hart (USA)	86 75
1954	M. Connolly (USA)	L. Brough (USA)	62 75
1955	L. Brough (USA)	B. Fleitz (USA)	75 86
1956	S. Fry (USA)	A. Buxton (GBR)	63 61
1957	A. Gibson (USA)	D. Hard (USA)	63 62
1958	A. Gibson (USA)	A. Mortimer (GBR)	86 62
1959	M. Bueno (BRA)	D. Hard (USA)	64 63
1960	M. Bueno (BRA)	S. Reynolds (RSA)	86 60

Year	Champion	Runner-up	Score
1961	A. Mortimer (GBR)	C. Truman (GBR)	46 64 75
1962	K. Susman (USA)	V. Sukova (TCH)	64 64
1963	M. Smith (AUS)	B. Moffitt (USA)	63 64
1964	M. Bueno (BRA)	M. Smith (AUS)	64 79 63
1965	M. Smith (AUS)	M. Bueno (BRA)	64 75
1966	B. King (USA) (nee Moffitt)	M. Bueno (BRA)	63 36 61
1967	B. King (USA)	A. Jones (GBR)	63 64
1968	B. King (USA)	J. Tegart (AUS)	97 75
1969	A. Jones (GBR)	B. King (USA)	36 63 62
1970	M. Court (AUS) (nee Smith)	B. King (USA)	1412 119
1971	E. Goolagong (AUS)	M. Court (AUS)	64 61
1972	B. King (USA)	E. Goolagong (AUS)	63 63
1973	B. King (USA)	C. Evert (USA)	60 75
1974	C. Evert (USA)	O. Morozova (URS)	60 64
1975	B. King (USA)	E. Goolagong Cawley (AUS)	60 61
1976	C. Evert (USA)	E. Goolagong Cawley (AUS)	63 46 86
1977	V. Wade (GBR)	B. Stove (NED)	46 63 61
1978	M. Navratilova (USA)	C. Evert (USA)	26 64 75
1979	M. Navratilova (USA)	C. Evert Lloyd (USA)	64 64
1980	E. Goolagong Cawley (AUS)	C. Evert Lloyd (USA)	61 76
1981	C. Evert Lloyd (USA)	H. Mandlikova (TCH)	62 62
1982	M. Navratilova (USA)	C. Evert Lloyd (USA)	61 36 62
1983	M. Navratilova (USA)	A. Jaeger (USA)	60 63
1984	M. Navratilova (USA)	C. Evert Lloyd (USA)	76 62
1985	M. Navratilova (USA)	C. Evert Lloyd (USA)	46 63 62
1986	M. Navratilova (USA)	H. Mandlikova (TCH)	76 63
1987	M. Navratilova (USA)	S. Graf (FRG)	75 63
1988	S. Graf (FRG)	M. Navratilova (USA)	57 62 61
1989	S. Graf (FRG)	M. Navratilova (USA)	62 67 61
1990	M. Navratilova (USA)	Z. Garrison (USA)	64 61
1991	S. Graf (GER)	G. Sabatini (ARG)	64 36 86
1992	S. Graf (GER)	M. Seles (YUG)	62 61
1993	S. Graf (GER)	J. Novotna (TCH)	76 16 64
1994	C. Martinez (ESP)	M. Navratilova (USA)	64 36 63
1995	S. Graf (GER)	A. Sanchez Vicario (ESP)	46 61 75
1996	S. Graf (GER)	A. Sanchez Vicario (ESP)	63 75
1997	M. Hingis (SUI)	J. Novotna (CZE)	26 63 63
1998	J. Novotna (CZE)	N. Tauziat (FRA)	64 76
1999	L. Davenport (USA)	S. Graf (GER)	64 75
2000	V. Williams (USA)	L. Davenport (USA)	63 76
2001	V. Williams (USA)	J. Henin (BEL)	61 36 60
2002	S. Williams (USA)	V. Williams (USA)	76 63
2003	S. Williams (USA)	V. Williams (USA)	46 64 62
2004	M. Sharapova (RUS)	S. Williams (USA)	61 64
2005	V. Williams (USA)	L. Davenport (USA)	46 76 97

	Men's Doubles	**Women's Doubles**	**Mixed Doubles**
Year	Champions	Champions	Champions
1884	E. Renshaw/W. Renshaw		
1885	E. Renshaw/W. Renshaw		
1886	E. Renshaw/W. Renshaw		
1887	P. Lyon/W. Wilberforce		
1888	E. Renshaw/W. Renshaw		
1889	E. Renshaw/W. Renshaw		
1890	J. Pim/F. Stoker		

Year	Champions	Champions	Champions
1891	H. Baddeley/W. Baddeley		
1892	H. Barlow/E. Lewis		
1893	J. Pim/F. Stoker		
1894	H. Baddeley/W. Baddeley		
1895	H. Baddeley/W. Baddeley		
1896	H. Baddeley/W. Baddeley		
1897	H. Doherty/R. Doherty		
1898	H. Doherty/R. Doherty		
1899	H. Doherty/R. Doherty		
1900	H. Doherty/R. Doherty		
1901	H. Doherty/R. Doherty		
1902	F. Riseley/S. Smith		
1903	H. Doherty/R. Doherty		
1904	H. Doherty/R. Doherty		
1905	H. Doherty/R. Doherty		
1906	F. Riseley/S. Smith		
1907	N. Brookes/A. Wilding		
1908	M. Ritchie/A. Wilding		
1909	A. Gore/H. Roper Barrett		
1910	M. Ritchie/A. Wilding		
1911	M. Decugis/A. Gobert		
1912	C. Dixon/H. Roper Barrett		
1913	C. Dixon/H. Roper Barrett	P. Boothby/W. McNair	H. Crisp/A. Tuckey
1914	N. Brookes/A. Wilding	A. Morton/E. Ryan	J. Parke/E. Larcombe
1915-1918 not played			
1919	P. O'Hara Wood/R. Thomas	S. Lenglen/E. Ryan	R. Lycett/E. Ryan
1920	C. Garland/R. Williams	S. Lenglen/E. Ryan	G. Patterson/S. Lenglen
1921	R. Lycett/M. Woosnam	S. Lenglen/E. Ryan	R. Lycett/E. Ryan
1922	J. Anderson/R. Lycett	S. Lenglen/E. Ryan	P. O'Hara Wood/S. Lenglen
1923	L. Godfree/R. Lycett	S. Lenglen/E. Ryan	R. Lycett/E. Ryan
1924	F. Hunter/V. Richards	H. Hotchkiss Wightman/H. Wills	J. Gilbert/K. McKane
1925	J. Borotra/R. Lacoste	S. Lenglen/E. Ryan	J. Borotra/S. Lenglen
1926	J. Brugnon/H. Cochet	M. Browne/E. Ryan	L. Godfree/K. Godfree
1927	F. Hunter/W. Tilden	E. Ryan/H. Wills	F. Hunter/E. Ryan
1928	J. Brugnon/H. Cochet	M. Saunders/P. Watson	P. Spence/E. Ryan
1929	W. Allison/J. Van Ryn	M. Mitchell/P. Watson	F. Hunter/H. Wills
1930	W. Allison/J. Van Ryn	H. Wills Moody/E. Ryan	J. Crawford/E. Ryan
1931	G. Lott/J. Van Ryn	P. Mudford/D. Shepherd-Barron	G. Lott/A. Harper
1932	J. Borotra/J. Brugnon	D. Metaxa/J. Sigart	E. Maier/E. Ryan
1933	J. Borotra/J. Brugnon	S. Mathieu/E. Ryan	G. Von Cramm/H. Krahwinkel
1934	G. Lott/L. Stoefen	S. Mathieu/E. Ryan	R. Miki/D. Round
1935	J. Crawford/A. Quist	W. James/K. Stammers	F. Perry/D. Round
1936	G. Hughes/C. Tuckey	W. James/K. Stammers	F. Perry/D. Round
1937	D. Budge/G. Mako	S. Mathieu/A. Yorke	D. Budge/A. Marble
1938	D. Budge/G. Mako	A. Marble/S. Palfrey Fabyan	D. Budge/A. Marble
1939	E. Cooke/R. Riggs	A. Marble/S. Palfrey Fabyan	R. Riggs/A. Marble
1940-45 not played			
1946	T. Brown/J. Kramer	L. Brough/M. Osborne	T. Brown/L. Brough
1947	R. Falkenburg/J. Kramer	D. Hart/P. Todd	J. Bromwich/L. Brough
1948	J. Bromwich/F. Sedgman	L. Brough/M. Osborne DuPont	J. Bromwich/L. Brough
1949	R. Gonzales/F. Parker	L. Brough/M. Osborne DuPont	E. Sturgess/S. Summers
1950	J. Bromwich/A. Quist	L. Brough/M. Osborne DuPont	E. Sturgess/L. Brough
1951	K. McGregor/F. Sedgman	S. Fry/D. Hart	F. Sedgman/D. Hart
1952	K. McGregor/F. Sedgman	S. Fry/D. Hart	F. Sedgman/D. Hart
1953	L. Hoad/K. Rosewall	S. Fry/D. Hart	V. Seixas/D. Hart

Year	Champions	Champions	Champions
1954	R. Hartwig/M. Rose	L. Brough/M. Osborne DuPont	V. Seixas/D. Hart
1955	R. Hartwig/L. Hoad	A. Mortimer/J. Shilcock	V. Seixas/D. Hart
1956	L. Hoad/K. Rosewall	A. Buxton/A. Gibson	V. Seixas/S. Fry
1957	G. Mulloy/J. Patty	A. Gibson/D. Hard	M. Rose/D. Hard
1958	S. Davidson/U. Schmidt	M. Bueno/A. Gibson	R. Howe/L. Coghlan
1959	R. Emerson/N. Fraser	J. Arth/D. Hard	R. Laver/D. Hard
1960	R. Osuna/R. Ralston	M. Bueno/D. Hard	R. Laver/D. Hard
1961	R. Emerson/N. Fraser	K. Hantze/B. Moffitt	F. Stolle/L. Turner
1962	R. Hewitt/F. Stolle	B. Moffitt/K. Susman	N. Fraser/M. Osborne DuPont
1963	R. Osuna/A. Palafox	M. Bueno/D. Hard	K. Fletcher/M. Smith
1964	R. Hewitt/F. Stolle	M. Smith/L. Turner	F. Stolle/L. Turner
1965	J. Newcombe/T. Roche	M. Bueno/B. Moffitt	K. Fletcher/M. Smith
1966	K. Fletcher/J. Newcombe	M. Bueno/N. Richey	K. Fletcher/M. Smith
1967	R. Hewitt/F. McMillan	R. Casals/B. King	O. Davidson/B. King
1968	J. Newcombe/T. Roche	R. Casals/B. King	K. Fletcher/M. Court
1969	J. Newcombe/T. Roche	M. Court/J. Tegart	F. Stolle/A. Jones
1970	J. Newcombe/T. Roche	R. Casals/B. King	I. Nastase/R. Casals
1971	R. Emerson/R. Laver	R. Casals/B. King	O. Davidson/B. King
1972	R. Hewitt/F. McMillan	B. King/B. Stove	I. Nastase/R. Casals
1973	J. Connors/I. Nastase	R. Casals/B. King	O. Davidson/B. King
1974	J. Newcombe/T. Roche	E. Goolagong/M. Michel	O. Davidson/B. King
1975	V. Gerulaitis/A. Mayer	A. Kiyomura/K. Sawamatsu	M. Riessen/M. Court
1976	B. Gottfried/R. Ramirez	C. Evert/M. Navratilova	T. Roche/F. Durr
1977	R. Case/G. Masters	H. Cawley/J. Russell	R. Hewitt/G. Stevens
1978	R. Hewitt/F. McMillan	K. Reid/W. Turnbull	F. McMillan/B. Stove
1979	P. Fleming/J. McEnroe	B. King/M. Navratilova	R. Hewitt/G. Stevens
1980	P. McNamara/P. McNamee	K. Jordan/A. Smith	J. Austin/T. Austin
1981	P. Fleming/J. McEnroe	M. Navratilova/P. Shriver	F. McMillan/B. Stove
1982	P. McNamara/P. McNamee	M. Navratilova/P. Shriver	K. Curren/A. Smith
1983	P. Fleming/J. McEnroe	M. Navratilova/P. Shriver	J. Lloyd/W. Turnbull
1984	P. Fleming/J. McEnroe	M. Navratilova/P. Shriver	J. Lloyd/W. Turnbull
1985	H. Gunthardt/B. Taroczy	K. Jordan/L. Smylie	P. McNamee/M. Navratilova
1986	J. Nystrom/M. Wilander	M. Navratilova/P. Shriver	K. Flach/K. Jordan
1987	K. Flach/R. Seguso	C. Kohde-Kilsch/H. Sukova	J. Bates/J. Durie
1988	K. Flach/R. Seguso	S. Graf/G. Sabatini	S. Stewart/Z. Garrison
1989	J. Fitzgerald/A. Jarryd	J. Novotna/H. Sukova	J. Pugh/J. Novotna
1990	R. Leach/J. Pugh	J. Novotna/H. Sukova	R. Leach/Z. Garrison
1991	J. Fitzgerald/A. Jarryd	L. Savchenko/N. Zvereva	J. Fitzgerald/L. Smylie
1992	J. McEnroe/M. Stich	G. Fernandez/N. Zvereva	C. Suk/L. Neiland
1993	T. Woodbridge/M. Woodforde	G. Fernandez/N. Zvereva	M. Woodforde/M. Navratilova
1994	T. Woodbridge/M. Woodforde	G. Fernandez/N. Zvereva	T. Woodbridge/H. Sukova
1995	T. Woodbridge/M. Woodforde	J. Novotna/A. Sanchez Vicario	J. Stark/M. Navratilova
1996	T. Woodbridge/M. Woodforde	M. Hingis/H. Sukova	C. Suk/H. Sukova
1997	T. Woodbridge/M. Woodforde	G. Fernandez/N. Zvereva	C. Suk/H. Sukova
1998	J. Eltingh/P. Haarhuis	M. Hingis/J. Novotna	M. Miryni/S. Williams
1999	M. Bhupathi/L. Paes	L. Davenport/C. Morariu	L. Paes/L. Raymond
2000	T. Woodbridge/M. Woodforde	S. Williams/V. Williams	D. Johnson/K. Po
2001	D. Johnson/J. Palmer	L. Raymond/R. Stubbs	L. Friedl/D. Hantuchova
2002	J. Bjorkman/T. Woodbridge	S. Williams/V. Williams	M. Bhupathi/E. Likhovtseva
2003	J. Bjorkman/T. Woodbridge	K. Clijsters/A. Sugiyama	L. Paes/M. Navratilova
2004	J. Bjorkman/T. Woodbridge	C. Black/R. Stubbs	W. Black/C. Black
2005	S. Huss/W. Moodie	C. Black/L. Huber	M. Bhupathi/M. Pierce

US Championships

Men's Singles

Year	Champion	Runner-up	Score
1881	R. Sears (USA)	W. Glyn (USA)	60 63 62
1882	R. Sears (USA)	C. Clark (USA)	61 64 60
1883	R. Sears (USA)	J. Dwight (USA)	62 60 97
1884	R. Sears (USA)	H. Taylor (USA)	60 16 60 62
1885	R. Sears (USA)	G. Brinley (USA)	63 46 60 63
1886	R. Sears (USA)	L. Beeckman (USA)	46 61 63 64
1887	R. Sears (USA)	H. Slocum (USA)	61 63 62
1888	H. Slocum (USA)	H. Taylor (USA)	64 61 60
1889	H. Slocum (USA)	Q. Shaw (USA)	63 61 46 62
1890	O. Campbell (USA)	H. Slocum (USA)	62 46 63 61
1891	O. Campbell (USA)	C. Hobart (USA)	26 75 79 61 62
1892	O. Campbell (USA)	F. Hovey (USA)	75 36 63 75
1893	R. Wrenn (USA)	F. Hovey (USA)	64 36 64 64
1894	R. Wrenn (USA)	M. Goodbody (GBR)	68 61 64 64
1895	F. Hovey (USA)	R. Wrenn (USA)	63 62 64
1896	R. Wrenn (USA)	F. Hovey (USA)	75 36 60 16 61
1897	R. Wrenn (USA)	W. Eaves (GBR)	46 86 63 26 62
1898	M. Whitman (USA)	D. Davis (USA)	36 62 62 61
1899	M. Whitman (USA)	P. Paret (USA)	61 62 36 75
1900	M. Whitman (USA)	W. Larned (USA)	64 16 62 62
1901	W. Larned (USA)	B. Wright (USA)	62 68 64 64
1902	W. Larned (USA)	R. Doherty (GBR)	46 62 64 86
1903	H. Doherty (GBR)	W. Larned (USA)	60 63 108
1904	H. Ward (USA)	W. Clothier (USA)	108 64 97
1905	B. Wright (USA)	H. Ward (USA)	62 61 119
1906	W. Clothier (USA)	B. Wright (USA)	63 60 64
1907	W. Larned (USA)	R. LeRoy (USA)	62 62 64
1908	W. Larned (USA)	B. Wright (USA)	61 62 86
1909	W. Larned (USA)	W. Clothier (USA)	61 62 57 16 61
1910	W. Larned (USA)	T. Bundy (USA)	61 57 60 68 61
1911	W. Larned (USA)	M. McLoughlin (USA)	64 64 62
1912	M. McLoughlin (USA)	W. Johnson (USA)	36 26 62 64 62
1913	M. McLoughlin (USA)	R. Williams (USA)	64 57 63 61
1914	R. Williams (USA)	M. McLoughlin (USA)	63 86 108
1915	W. Johnston (USA)	M. McLoughlin (USA)	16 60 75 108
1916	R. Williams (USA)	W. Johnston (USA)	46 64 06 62 64
1917	L. Murray (USA)	N. Niles (USA)	57 86 63 63
1918	L. Murray (USA)	W. Tilden (USA)	63 61 75
1919	W. Johnston (USA)	W. Tilden (USA)	64 64 63
1920	W. Tilden (USA)	W. Johnston (USA)	61 16 75 57 63
1921	W. Tilden (USA)	W. Johnston (USA)	61 63 61
1922	W. Tilden (USA)	W. Johnston (USA)	46 36 62 63 64
1923	W. Tilden (USA)	W. Johnston (USA)	64 61 64
1924	W. Tilden (USA)	W. Johnston (USA)	61 97 62
1925	W. Tilden (USA)	W. Johnston (USA)	46 119 63 46 63
1926	R. Lacoste (FRA)	J. Borotra (FRA)	64 60 64
1927	R. Lacoste (FRA)	W. Tilden (USA)	119 63 119
1928	H. Cochet (FRA)	F. Hunter (USA)	46 64 36 75 63
1929	W. Tilden (USA)	F. Hunter (USA)	36 63 46 62 64
1930	J. Doeg (USA)	F. Shields (USA)	108 16 64 1614
1931	E. Vines (USA)	G. Lott (USA)	79 63 97 75
1932	E. Vines (USA)	H. Cochet (FRA)	64 64 64
1933	F. Perry (GBR)	J. Crawford (AUS)	63 1113 46 60 61
1934	F. Perry (GBR)	W. Allison (USA)	64 63 16 86

Year	Champion	Runner-up	Score
1935	W. Allison (USA)	S. Wood (USA)	62 62 63
1936	F. Perry (GBR)	D. Budge (USA)	26 62 86 16 108
1937	D. Budge (USA)	G. Von Cramm (GER)	61 79 61 36 61
1938	D. Budge (USA)	G. Mako (USA)	63 68 62 61
1939	R. Riggs (USA)	S. Van Horn (USA)	64 62 64
1940	D. McNeill (USA)	R. Riggs (USA)	46 68 63 63 75
1941	R. Riggs (USA)	F. Kovacs (USA)	57 61 63 63
1942	F. Schroeder (USA)	F. Parker (USA)	86 75 36 46 62
1943	J. Hunt (USA)	J. Kramer (USA)	63 68 108 60
1944	F. Parker (USA)	W. Talbert (USA)	64 36 63 63
1945	F. Parker (USA)	W. Talbert (USA)	1412 61 62
1946	J. Kramer (USA)	T. Brown (USA)	97 63 60
1947	J. Kramer (USA)	F. Parker (USA)	46 26 61 60 63
1948	R. Gonzales (USA)	E. Sturgess (RSA)	62 63 1412
1949	R. Gonzales (USA)	F. Schroeder (USA)	1618 26 61 62 64
1950	A. Larsen (USA)	H. Flam (USA)	63 46 57 64 63
1951	F. Sedgman (AUS)	V. Seixas (USA)	64 61 61
1952	F. Sedgman (AUS)	G. Mulloy (USA)	61 62 63
1953	T. Trabert (USA)	V. Seixas (USA)	63 62 63
1954	V. Seixas (USA)	R. Hartwig (AUS)	36 62 64 64
1955	T. Trabert (USA)	K. Rosewall (AUS)	97 63 63
1956	K. Rosewall (AUS)	L. Hoad (AUS)	46 62 63 63
1957	M. Anderson (AUS)	A. Cooper (AUS)	108 75 64
1958	A. Cooper (AUS)	M. Anderson (AUS)	62 36 46 108 86
1959	N. Fraser (AUS)	A. Olmedo (PER)	63 57 62 64
1960	N. Fraser (AUS)	R. Laver (AUS)	64 64 97
1961	R. Emerson (AUS)	R. Laver (AUS)	75 63 62
1962	R. Laver (AUS)	R. Emerson (AUS)	62 64 57 64
1963	R. Osuna (MEX)	F. Froehling (USA)	75 64 62
1964	R. Emerson (AUS)	F. Stolle (AUS)	64 62 64
1965	M. Santana (ESP)	C. Drysdale (RSA)	62 79 75 61
1966	F. Stolle (AUS)	J. Newcombe (AUS)	46 1210 63 64
1967	J. Newcombe (AUS)	C. Graebner (USA)	64 64 86
1968	A. Ashe (USA)	T. Okker (NED)	1412 57 63 36 63
1969	R. Laver (AUS)	T. Roche (AUS)	79 61 62 62
1970	K. Rosewall (AUS)	T. Roche (AUS)	26 64 76 63
1971	S. Smith (USA)	J. Kodes (TCH)	36 63 62 76
1972	I. Nastase (ROM)	A. Ashe (USA)	36 63 67 64 63
1973	J. Newcombe (AUS)	J. Kodes (TCH)	64 16 46 62 62
1974	J. Connors (USA)	K. Rosewall (AUS)	61 60 61
1975	M. Orantes (ESP)	J. Connors (USA)	64 63 63
1976	J. Connors (USA)	B. Borg (SWE)	64 36 76 64
1977	G. Vilas (ARG)	J. Connors (USA)	26 63 76 60
1978	J. Connors (USA)	B. Borg (SWE)	64 62 62
1979	J. McEnroe (USA)	V. Gerulaitis (USA)	75 63 63
1980	J. McEnroe (USA)	B. Borg (SWE)	76 61 67 57 64
1981	J. McEnroe (USA)	B. Borg (SWE)	46 62 64 63
1982	J. Connors (USA)	I. Lendl (TCH)	63 62 46 64
1983	J. Connors (USA)	I. Lendl (TCH)	63 67 75 60
1984	J. McEnroe (USA)	I. Lendl (TCH)	63 64 61
1985	I. Lendl (TCH)	J. McEnroe (USA)	76 63 64
1986	I. Lendl (TCH)	M. Mecir (TCH)	64 62 60
1987	I. Lendl (TCH)	M. Wilander (SWE)	67 60 76 64
1988	M. Wilander (SWE)	I. Lendl (TCH)	64 46 63 57 64
1989	B. Becker (FRG)	I. Lendl (TCH)	76 16 63 76

Year	Champion	Runner-up	Score
1990	P. Sampras (USA)	A. Agassi (USA)	64 63 62
1991	S. Edberg (SWE)	J. Courier (USA)	62 64 60
1992	S. Edberg (SWE)	P. Sampras (USA)	36 64 76 62
1993	P. Sampras (USA)	C. Pioline (FRA)	64 64 63
1994	A. Agassi (USA)	M. Stich (GER)	61 76 75
1995	P. Sampras (USA)	A. Agassi (USA)	64 63 46 75
1996	P. Sampras (USA)	M. Chang (USA)	61 64 76
1997	P. Rafter (AUS)	G. Rusedski (GBR)	63 62 46 75
1998	P. Rafter (AUS)	M. Philippoussis (AUS)	63 36 62 60
1999	A. Agassi (USA)	T. Martin (USA)	64 67 67 63 62
2000	M. Safin (RUS)	P. Sampras (USA)	64 63 63
2001	L. Hewitt (AUS)	P. Sampras (USA)	76 61 61
2002	P. Sampras (USA)	A. Agassi (USA)	63 64 57 64
2003	A. Roddick (USA)	J. Ferrero (ESP)	63 76 63
2004	R. Federer (SUI)	L. Hewitt (AUS)	60 76 60
2005	R. Federer (SUI)	A. Agassi (USA)	63 26 76 61

Women's Singles

Year	Champion	Runner-up	Score
1887	E. Hansell (USA)	L. Knight (USA)	61 60
1888	B. Townsend (USA)	E. Hansell (USA)	63 65
1889	B. Townsend (USA)	L. Voorhes (USA)	75 62
1890	E. Roosevelt (USA)	B. Townsend (USA)	62 62
1891	M. Cahill (USA)	E. Roosevelt (USA)	64 61 46 63
1892	M. Cahill (USA)	E. Moore (USA)	57 63 64 46 62
1893	A. Terry (USA)	A. Schultz (USA)	61 63
1894	H. Hellwig (USA)	A. Terry (USA)	75 36 60 36 63
1895	J. Atkinson (USA)	H. Hellwig (USA)	64 62 61
1896	E. Moore (USA)	J. Atkinson (USA)	64 46 62 62
1897	J. Atkinson (USA)	E. Moore (USA)	63 63 46 36 63
1898	J. Atkinson (USA)	M. Jones (USA)	63 57 64 26 75
1899	M. Jones (USA)	M. Banks (USA)	61 61 75
1900	M. McAteer (USA)	E. Parker (USA)	62 62 60
1901	E. Moore (USA)	M. McAteer (USA)	64 36 75 26 62
1902	M. Jones (USA)	E. Moore (USA)	61 10 ret.
1903	E. Moore (USA)	M. Jones (USA)	75 86
1904	M. Sutton (USA)	E. Moore (USA)	61 62
1905	E. Moore (USA)	H. Homans (USA)	64 57 61
1906	H. Homans (USA)	M. Barger-Wallach (USA)	64 63
1907	E. Sears (USA)	C. Neely (USA)	63 62
1908	M. Barger-Wallach (USA)	E. Sears (USA)	63 16 63
1909	H. Hotchkiss (USA)	M. Barger-Wallach (USA)	60 61
1910	H. Hotchkiss (USA)	L. Hammond (USA)	64 62
1911	H. Hotchkiss (USA)	F. Sutton (USA)	810 61 97
1912	M. Browne (USA)	E. Sears (USA)	64 62
1913	M. Browne (USA)	D. Green (USA)	62 75
1914	M. Browne (USA)	M. Wagner (USA)	62 16 61
1915	M. Bjurstedt (NOR)	H. Hotchkiss Wightman (USA)	46 62 60
1916	M. Bjurstedt (NOR)	L. Hammond Raymond (USA)	60 61
1917	M. Bjurstedt (NOR)	M. Vanderhoef (USA)	46 60 62
1918	M. Bjurstedt (NOR)	E. Goss (USA)	64 63
1919	H. Hotchkiss Wightman (USA)	M. Zinderstein (USA)	61 62
1920	M. Mallory (USA) (nee Bjurstedt)	M. Zinderstein (USA)	63 61
1921	M. Mallory (USA)	M. Browne (USA)	46 64 62
1922	M. Mallory (USA)	H. Wills (USA)	63 61

Year	Champion	Runner-up	Score
1923	H. Wills (USA)	M. Mallory (USA)	62 61
1924	H. Wills (USA)	M. Mallory (USA)	61 63
1925	H. Wills (USA)	K. McKane (GBR)	36 60 62
1926	M. Mallory (USA)	E. Ryan (USA)	46 64 97
1927	H. Wills (USA)	B. Nuthall (GBR)	61 64
1928	H. Wills (USA)	H. Jacobs (USA)	62 61
1929	H. Wills (USA)	P. Holcroft Watson (GBR)	64 62
1930	B. Nuthall (GBR)	A. McCune Harper (USA)	61 64
1931	H. Wills Moody (USA)	E. Bennett Whitingstall (GBR)	64 61
1932	H. Jacobs (USA)	C. Babcock (USA)	62 62
1933	H. Jacobs (USA)	H. Wills Moody (USA)	86 36 30 ret.
1934	H. Jacobs (USA)	S. Palfrey (USA)	61 64
1935	H. Jacobs (USA)	S. Palfrey Fabyan (USA)	62 64
1936	A. Marble (USA)	H. Jacobs (USA)	46 63 62
1937	A. Lizana (CHI)	J. Jedrzejowska (POL)	64 62
1938	A. Marble (USA)	N. Wynne (AUS)	60 63
1939	A. Marble (USA)	H. Jacobs (USA)	60 810 64
1940	A. Marble (USA)	H. Jacobs (USA)	62 63
1941	S. Palfrey Cooke (USA)	P. Betz (USA)	75 62
1942	P. Betz (USA)	L. Brough (USA)	46 61 64
1943	P. Betz (USA)	L. Brough (USA)	63 57 63
1944	P. Betz (USA)	M. Osborne (USA)	63 86
1945	S. Palfrey Cooke (USA)	P. Betz (USA)	36 86 64
1946	P. Betz (USA)	D. Hart (USA)	119 63
1947	L. Brough (USA)	M. Osborne (USA)	86 46 61
1948	M. Osborne DuPont (USA)	L. Brough (USA)	46 64 1513
1949	M. Osborne DuPont (USA)	D. Hart (USA)	64 61
1950	M. Osborne DuPont (USA)	D. Hart (USA)	63 63
1951	M. Connolly (USA)	S. Fry (USA)	63 16 64
1952	M. Connolly (USA)	D. Hart (USA)	63 75
1953	M. Connolly (USA)	D. Hart (USA)	62 64
1954	D. Hart (USA)	L. Brough (USA)	68 61 86
1955	D. Hart (USA)	P. Ward (GBR)	64 62
1956	S. Fry (USA)	A. Gibson (USA)	63 64
1957	A. Gibson (USA)	L. Brough (USA)	63 62
1958	A. Gibson (USA)	D. Hard (USA)	36 61 62
1959	M. Bueno (BRA)	C. Truman (GBR)	61 64
1960	D. Hard (USA)	M. Bueno (BRA)	64 1012 64
1961	D. Hard (USA)	A. Haydon (GBR)	63 64
1962	M. Smith (AUS)	D. Hard (USA)	97 64
1963	M. Bueno (BRA)	M. Smith (AUS)	75 64
1964	M. Bueno (BRA)	C. Graebner (USA)	61 60
1965	M. Smith (AUS)	B. Moffitt (USA)	86 75
1966	M. Bueno (BRA)	N. Richey (USA)	63 61
1967	B. King (USA) (nee Moffitt)	A. Jones (GBR) (nee Haydon)	119 64
1968	V. Wade (GBR)	B. King (USA)	64 64
1969	M. Court (AUS) (nee Smith)	N. Richey (USA)	62 62
1970	M. Court (AUS)	R. Casals (USA)	62 26 61
1971	B. King (USA)	R. Casals (USA)	64 76
1972	B. King (USA)	K. Melville (AUS)	63 75
1973	M. Court (AUS)	E. Goolagong (AUS)	76 57 62
1974	B. King (USA)	E. Goolagong (AUS)	36 63 75
1975	C. Evert (USA)	E. Goolagong Cawley (AUS)	57 64 62
1976	C. Evert (USA)	E. Goolagong Cawley (AUS)	63 60
1977	C. Evert (USA)	W. Turnbull (AUS)	76 62
1978	C. Evert (USA)	P. Shriver (USA)	75 64
1979	T. Austin (USA)	C. Evert Lloyd (USA)	64 63

Year	Champion	Runner-up	Score
1980	C. Evert Lloyd (USA)	H. Mandlikova (TCH)	57 61 61
1981	T. Austin (USA)	M. Navratilova (USA)	16 76 76
1982	C. Evert Lloyd (USA)	H. Mandlikova (TCH)	63 61
1983	M. Navratilova (USA)	C. Evert Lloyd (USA)	61 63
1984	M. Navratilova (USA)	C. Evert Lloyd (USA)	46 64 64
1985	H. Mandlikova (TCH)	M. Navratilova (USA)	76 16 76
1986	M. Navratilova (USA)	H. Sukova (TCH)	63 62
1987	M. Navratilova (USA)	S. Graf (FRG)	76 61
1988	S. Graf (FRG)	G. Sabatini (ARG)	63 36 61
1989	S. Graf (FRG)	M. Navratilova (USA)	36 75 61
1990	G. Sabatini (ARG)	S. Graf (GER)	62 76
1991	M. Seles (YUG)	M. Navratilova (USA)	76 61
1992	M. Seles (YUG)	A. Sanchez Vicario (ESP)	63 63
1993	S. Graf (GER)	H. Sukova (TCH)	63 63
1994	A. Sanchez Vicario (ESP)	S. Graf (GER)	16 76 64
1995	S. Graf (GER)	M. Seles (USA)	76 06 63
1996	S. Graf (GER)	M. Seles (USA)	75 64
1997	M. Hingis (SUI)	V. Williams (USA)	60 64
1998	L. Davenport (USA)	M. Hingis (SUI)	63 75
1999	S. Williams (USA)	M. Hingis (SUI)	63 76
2000	V. Williams (USA)	L. Davenport (USA)	64 75
2001	V. Williams (USA)	S. Williams (USA)	62 64
2002	S. Williams (USA)	V. Williams (USA)	64 63
2003	J. Henin-Hardenne (BEL)	K. Clijsters (BEL)	75 61
2004	S. Kuznetsova (RUS)	E. Dementieva (RUS)	63 75
2005	K. Clijsters (BEL)	M. Pierce (FRA)	63 61

Year	Men's Doubles Champions	Women's Doubles Champions	Mixed Doubles Champions
1881	C. Clark/F. Taylor		
1882	J. Dwight/R. Sears		
1883	J. Dwight/R. Sears		
1884	J. Dwight/R. Sears		
1885	J. Clark/R. Sears		
1886	J. Dwight/R. Sears		
1887	J. Dwight/R. Sears		
1888	O. Campbell/V. Hall		
1889	H. Slocum/H. Taylor	M. Ballard/B. Townsend	
1890	V. Hall/C. Hobart	E. Roosevelt/G. Roosevelt	
1891	O. Campbell/R. Huntington	M. Cahill/Mrs W. Fellowes Morgan	
1892	O. Campbell/R. Huntington	M. Cahill/A. McKinlay	C. Hobart/M. Cahill
1893	C. Hobart/F. Hovey	H. Butler/A. Terry	C. Hobart/E. Roosevelt
1894	C. Hobart/F. Hovey	J. Atkinson/H. Hellwig	E. Fischer/J. Atkinson
1895	M. Chace/R. Wrenn	J. Atkinson/H. Hellwig	E. Fischer/J. Atkinson
1896	C. Neel/G. Sheldon	J. Atkinson/E. Moore	E. Fischer/J. Atkinson
1897	G. Sheldon/L. Ware	J. Atkinson/K. Atkinson	D. Magruder/L. Henson
1898	G. Sheldon/L. Ware	J. Atkinson/K. Atkinson	E. Fischer/C. Neely
1899	D. Davis/H. Ward	J. Craven/M. McAteer	A. Hoskins/E. Rastall
1900	D. Davis/H. Ward	H. Champlin/E. Parker	A. Codman/M. Hunnewell
1901	D. Davis/H. Ward	J. Atkinson/M. McAteer	R. Little/M. Jones
1902	H. Doherty/R. Doherty	J. Atkinson/M. Jones	W. Grant/E. Moore
1903	H. Doherty/R. Doherty	E. Moore/C. Neely	H. Allen/H. Chapman
1904	H. Ward/B. Wright	M. Hall/M. Sutton	W. Grant/E. Moore
1905	H. Ward/B. Wright	H. Homans/C. Neely	C. Hobart/A. Hobart
1906	H. Ward/B. Wright	A. Coe/E. Platt	E. Dewhurst/S. Coffin

Year	Champions	Champions	Champions
1907	F. Alexander/H. Hackett	C. Neely/M. Wimer	W. Johnson/M. Sayres
1908	F. Alexander/H. Hackett	M. Curtis/E. Sears	N. Niles/E. Rotch
1909	F. Alexander/H. Hackett	H. Hotchkiss/E. Rotch	W. Johnson/H. Hotchkiss
1910	F. Alexander/H Hackett	H. Hotchkiss/E. Rotch	J. Carpenter/H. Hotchkiss
1911	R. Little/G. Touchard	H. Hotchkiss/E. Sears	W. Johnson/H. Hotchkiss
1912	T. Bundy/M. McLoughlin	M. Browne/D. Green	R. Williams/M. Browne
1913	T. Bundy/M. McLoughlin	M. Browne/L. Williams	W. Tilden/M. Browne
1914	T. Bundy/M. McLoughlin	M. Browne/L. Williams	W. Tilden/M. Browne
1915	C. Griffin/W. Johnston	H. Hotchkiss Wightman/E. Sears	H. Johnson/H. Hotchkiss Wightman
1916	C. Griffin/W. Johnston	M. Bjurstedt/E. Sears	W. Davis/E. Sears
1917	F. Alexander/H. Throckmorton	M. Bjurstedt/E. Sears	I. Wright/M. Bjurstedt
1918	V. Richards/W. Tilden	E. Goss/M. Zinderstein	I. Wright/H. Hotchkiss Wightman
1919	N. Brookes/G. Patterson	E. Goss/M. Zinderstein	V. Richards/M. Zinderstein
1920	C. Griffin/W. Johnston	E. Goss/M. Zinderstein	W. Johnson/H. Hotchkiss Wightman
1921	V. Richards/W. Tilden	M. Browne/L. Williams	W. Johnston/M. Browne
1922	V. Richards/W. Tilden	M. Jessup/H. Wills	W. Tilden/M. Browne
1923	B. Norton/W. Tilden	P. Covell/K. McKane	W. Tilden/M. Mallory
1924	H. Kinsey/R. Kinsey	H. Hotchkiss Wightman/H. Wills	V. Richards/H. Wills
1925	V. Richards/R. Williams	M. Browne/H. Wills	J. Hawkes/K. McKane
1926	V. Richards/R. Williams	E. Goss/E. Ryan	J. Borotra/E. Ryan
1927	F. Hunter/W. Tilden	K. Godfree/E. Harvey	H. Cochet/E. Bennett
1928	J. Doeg/G. Lott	H. Hotchkiss Wightman/H. Wills	J. Hawkes/H. Wills
1929	J. Doeg/G. Lott	P. Mitchell/P. Watson	G. Lott/B. Nuthall
1930	J. Doeg/G. Lott	B. Nuthall/S. Palfrey	W. Allison/E. Cross
1931	W. Allison/J. Van Ryn	B. Nuthall/E. Bennett Whitingstall	G. Lott/B. Nuthall
1932	K. Gledhill/E. Vines	H. Jacobs/S. Palfrey	F. Perry/S. Palfrey
1933	G. Lott/L. Stoefen	F. James/B. Nuthall	E. Vines/E. Ryan
1934	G. Lott/L. Stoefen	H. Jacobs/S. Palfrey	G. Lott/H. Jacobs
1935	W. Allison/J. Van Ryn	H. Jacobs/S. Palfrey Fabyan	E. Maier/S. Palfrey Fabyan
1936	D. Budge/G. Mako	C. Babcock/M. Van Ryn	G. Mako/A. Marble
1937	G. Von Cramm/H. Henkel	A. Marble/S. Palfrey Fabyan	D. Budge/S. Palfrey Fabyan
1938	D. Budge/G. Mako	A. Marble/S. Palfrey Fabyan	D. Budge/A. Marble
1939	J. Bromwich/A. Quist	A. Marble/S. Palfrey Fabyan	H. Hopman/A. Marble
1940	J. Kramer/F. Schroeder	A. Marble/S. Palfrey Fabyan	R. Riggs/A. Marble
1941	J. Kramer/F. Schroeder	M. Osborne/S. Palfrey Cooke	J. Kramer/S. Palfrey Cooke
1942	G. Mulloy/W. Talbert	L. Brough/M. Osborne	F. Schroeder/L. Brough
1943	J. Kramer/F. Parker	L. Brough/M. Osborne	W. Talbert/M. Osborne
1944	R. Falkenburg/D. McNeill	L. Brough/M. Osborne	W. Talbert/M. Osborne
1945	G. Mulloy/W. Talbert	L. Brough/M. Osborne	W. Talbert/M. Osborne
1946	G. Mulloy/W. Talbert	L. Brough/M. Osborne	W. Talbert/M. Osborne
1947	J. Kramer/F. Schroeder	L. Brough/M. Osborne	J. Bromwich/L. Brough
1948	G. Mulloy/W. Talbert	L. Brough/M. Osborne DuPont	T. Brown/L. Brough
1949	J. Bromwich/W. Sidwell	L. Brough/M. Osborne DuPont	E. Sturgess/L. Brough
1950	J. Bromwich/F. Sedgman	L. Brough/M. Osborne DuPont	K. McGregor/M. Osborne DuPont
1951	K. McGregor/F. Sedgman	S. Fry/D. Hart	F. Sedgman/D. Hart
1952	M. Rose/V. Seixas	S. Fry/D. Hart	F. Sedgman/D. Hart
1953	R. Hartwig/M. Rose	S. Fry/D. Hart	V. Seixas/D. Hart
1954	V. Seixas/T. Trabert	S. Fry/D. Hart	V. Seixas/D. Hart
1955	K. Kamo/A. Miyagi	L. Brough/M. Osborne DuPont	V. Seixas/D. Hart
1956	L. Hoad/K. Rosewall	L. Brough/M. Osborne DuPont	K. Rosewell/M. Osborne DuPont
1957	A. Cooper/N. Fraser	L. Brough/M. Osborne DuPont	K. Nelson/A. Gibson
1958	A. Olmedo/H. Richardson	J. Arth/D. Hard	N. Fraser/M. Osborne DuPont
1959	R. Emerson/N. Fraser	J. Arth/D. Hard	N. Fraser/M. Osborne DuPont
1960	R. Emerson/N. Fraser	M. Bueno/D. Hard	N. Fraser/M. Osborne DuPont
1961	C. McKinley/D. Ralston	D. Hard/L. Turner	R. Mark/M. Smith
1962	R. Osuna/A. Palafox	M. Bueno/D. Hard	F. Stolle/M. Smith
1963	C. McKinley/D. Ralston	R. Ebbern/M. Smith	K. Fletcher/M. Smith

Year	Champions	Champions	Champions
1964	C. McKinley/D. Ralston	B. Moffitt/K. Susman	J. Newcombe/M. Smith
1965	R. Emerson/F. Stolle	C. Graebner/N. Richey	F. Stolle/M. Smith
1966	R. Emerson/F. Stolle	M. Bueno/N. Richey	O. Davidson/D. Fales
1967	J. Newcombe/T. Roche	R. Casals/B. King	O. Davidson/B. King
1968	R. Lutz/S. Smith	M. Bueno/M. Court	Not held
1969	K. Rosewall/F. Stolle	F. Durr/D. Hard	M. Riessen/M. Court
1970	P. Barthes/N. Pilic	M. Court/J. Dalton	M. Riessen/M. Court
1971	J. Newcombe/R. Taylor	R. Casals/J. Dalton	O. Davidson/B. King
1972	C. Drysdale/R. Taylor	F. Durr/B. Stove	M. Riessen/M. Court
1973	O. Davidson/J. Newcombe	M. Court/V. Wade	O. Davidson/B. King
1974	R. Lutz/S. Smith	R. Casals/B. King	G. Masters/P. Teeguarden
1975	J. Connors/I. Nastase	M. Court/V. Wade	R. Stockton/R. Casals
1976	T. Okker/M. Riessen	D. Boshoff/I. Kloss	P. Dent/B. King
1977	R. Hewitt/F. McMillan	M. Navratilova/B. Stove	F. McMillan/B. Stove
1978	R. Lutz/S. Smith	B. King/M. Navratilova	F. McMillan/B. Stove
1979	P. Fleming/J. McEnroe	B. Stove/W. Turnbull	R. Hewitt/G. Stevens
1980	R. Lutz/S. Smith	B. King/M. Navratilova	M. Riessen/W. Turnbull
1981	P. Fleming/J. McEnroe	K. Jordan/A. Smith	K. Curren/A. Smith
1982	K. Curren/S. Denton	R. Casals/W. Turnbull	K. Curren/A. Smith
1983	P. Fleming/J. McEnroe	M. Navratilova/P. Shriver	J. Fitzgerald/E. Sayers
1984	J. Fitzgerald/T. Smid	M. Navratilova/P. Shriver	T. Gullikson/M. Maleeva
1985	K. Flach/R. Seguso	C. Kohde-Kilsch/H. Sukova	H. Gunthardt/M. Navratilova
1986	A. Gomez/S. Zivojinovic	M. Navratilova/P. Shriver	S. Casal/R. Reggi
1987	S. Edberg/A. Jarryd	M. Navratilova/P. Shriver	E. Sanchez/M. Navratilova
1988	S. Casal/E. Sanchez	G. Fernandez/R. White	J. Pugh/J. Novotna
1989	J. McEnroe/M. Woodforde	H. Mandlikova/M. Navratilova	S. Cannon/R.White
1990	P. Aldrich/D. Visser	G. Fernandez/M. Navratilova	T. Woodbridge/E. Smylie
1991	J. Fitzgerald/A. Jarryd	P. Shriver/N. Zvereva	T. Nijssen/M. Bollegraf
1992	J. Grabb/R. Reneberg	G. Fernandez/N. Zvereva	M. Woodforde/N. Provis
1993	K. Flach/R. Leach	A. Sanchez Vicario/H. Sukova	T. Woodbridge/H. Sukova
1994	J. Eltingh/P. Haarhuis	J. Novotna/A. Sanchez Vicario	E. Reinach/P. Galbraith
1995	T. Woodbridge/M. Woodforde	G. Fernandez/N. Zvereva	M. Lucena/M. McGrath
1996	T. Woodbridge/M. Woodforde	G. Fernandez/N. Zvereva	P. Galbraith/L. Raymond
1997	Y. Kafelnikov/D. Vacek	L. Davenport/J. Novotna	R. Leach/M. Bollegraf
1998	S. Stolle/C. Suk	M. Hingis/J. Novotna	M. Mirnyi/S. Williams
1999	S. Lareau/A. O'Brien	S. Williams/V. Williams	M. Bhupathi/A. Sugiyama
2000	L. Hewitt/M. Mirnyi	J. Halard-Decugis/A. Sugiyama	J. Palmer/A. Sanchez-Vicario
2001	W. Black/K. Ullyett	L. Raymond/R. Stubbs	T. Woodbridge/R. Stubbs
2002	M. Bhupathi/M. Mirnyi	V. Ruano Pascual/P. Suarez	M. Bryan/L. Raymond
2003	J. Bjorkman/T. Woodbridge	V. Ruano Pascual/P. Suarez	B. Bryan/K. Srebotnik
2004	M. Knowles/D. Nestor	V. Ruano Pascual/P. Suarez	B. Bryan/V. Zvonareva
2005	B. Bryan/M. Bryan	L. Raymond/S. Stosur	M. Bhupathi/D. Hantuchova

Name Changes

Eileen Bennett is also Eileen Bennett Whitingstall
Blanche Bingley is also Blanche Bingley Hillyard
Carole Caldwell is also Carole Graebner
Dorothea Douglass is also Dorothea Douglass Lambert Chambers
Chris Evert is also Chris Evert Lloyd
Evonne Goolagong is also Evonne Goolagong Cawley
Helen Gourlay is also Helen Cawley
Ann Haydon is also Ann Jones
Justine Henin is also Justine Henin-Hardenne
Hazel Hotchkiss is also Hazel Hotchkiss Wightman
Claudia Kohde is also Claudia Kohde-Kilsch
Kitty McKane is also Kitty Godfree
Kerry Melville is also Kerry Reid
Billie Jean Moffitt is also Billie Jean King
Larissa Neiland is also Larissa Savchenko
Margaret Osborne is also Margaret Osborne DuPont
Sarah Palfrey is also Sarah Palfrey Fabyan and Sarah Palfrey Cooke
Gail Sheriff Chanfreau is also Gail Sheriff Lovera
Margaret Smith is also Margaret Court
Charlotte Sterry is also Charlotte Cooper
Judy Tegart is also Judy Dalton
Helen Wills is also Helen Wills Moody
Nancy Wynne is also Nancy Bolton

The Grand Slam

To achieve the Grand Slam, a player must win the Australian, French, Wimbledon and US Championships in the same calendar year.

Men's Singles

1938	Donald Budge (USA)	
1962	Rod Laver (AUS)	
1969	Rod Laver (AUS)	

Women's Singles

1953	Maureen Connolly (USA)	
1970	Margaret Court (AUS)	
1988	Steffi Graf (GER)*	*Achieved a unique 'Golden Slam', also winning gold at the 1988 Olympics in Seoul

Men's Doubles

1951	Ken McGregor/Frank Sedgman (AUS)	

Women's Doubles

1960	Maria Bueno (BRA)	Australian with Christine Truman (GBR) French, Wimbledon and US Championships with Darlene Hard (USA)
1984	Martina Navratilova (TCH)	Pam Shriver (USA)
1998	Martina Hingis (SUI)	Australian with Mirjana Lucic (CRO) French, Wimbledon and US Championships with Jana Novotna (CZE)

Mixed Doubles

1963	Ken Fletcher (AUS)	Margaret Smith (AUS)
1967	Owen Davidson (AUS)	Australian with Lesley Turner (AUS) French, Wimbledon and US Championships with Billie Jean King (USA)

Juniors

1983	Stefan Edberg (SWE)	

Greatest Grand Slam Singles Winners

Below are lists of all those players who have won five or more singles titles at the four Grand Slam championships in Australia, France, Great Britain and USA. Listed separately are their combined doubles and mixed doubles totals at the four events to give a final overall total of Grand Slam titles won.

The Australian Championships started in 1905 with men's singles and doubles. Women's singles was added in 1922 along with women's doubles and mixed doubles. The tournament was played on grass until 1988 when it moved to the hard courts at Melbourne Park. The French Championships were open only to national players until 1924 therefore international records did not begin until 1925. The tournament has always been played on red clay. The first meeting of The Championships, Wimbledon was held in 1877 for men's singles. Women's singles and men's doubles were included in 1884 and in 1913 women's doubles and mixed doubles completed the line-up of events. This grass court tournament moved to the All England Lawn Tennis and Croquet Club in 1922. The US Championships started in 1881 for men's singles and doubles. Women's singles was added in 1887; two years later women's doubles was included with mixed doubles starting in 1892. The tournament was played on grass until 1975 when it moved to the clay courts of the West Side Tennis Club. The move to the tournament's current venue in Flushing Meadows took place in 1978 when the surface was switched to hard court.

World War I and II interrupted Grand Slam tournaments in Australia, France and Great Britain from 1915-1918, and 1940-45 (Australia held tournaments in 1915 and 1940).

Professional players were excluded from completing in the Grand Slam tournaments until the Open Era began in April 1968.

Men **Name (winning singles span)**	**Total Singles**	**AUS**	**FRA**	**WIM**	**USA**	**Dbls**	**Mxd**	**TOTAL**
Pete Sampras (1990-2002)	14	2	0	7	5	0	0	14
Roy Emerson (1961-67)	12	6	2	2	2	16	0	28
Rod Laver (1960-69)	11	3	2	4	2	6	3	20
Bjorn Borg (1974-81)	11	0	6	5	0	0	0	11

Greatest Grand Slam Singles Winners (continued)

Men

Name (winning singles span)	Total Singles	AUS	FRA	WIM	USA	Dbls	Mxd	TOTAL
Bill Tilden (1920-30)	10	0	0	3	7	6	5	21
Ken Rosewall (1953-72)	8	4	2	0	2	9	1	18
Fred Perry (1933-36)	8	1	1	3	3	2	4	14
Jimmy Connors (1974-83)	8	1	0	2	5	2	0	10
Andre Agassi (1992-2003)	8	4	1	1	2	0	0	8
Ivan Lendl (1984-90)	8	2	3	0	3	0	0	8
John Newcombe (1967-75)	7	2	0	3	2	17	2	26
John McEnroe (1979-84)	7	0	0	3	4	9	1	17
Henri Cochet (1926-32)	7	0	4	2	1	5	3	15
Richard Sears (1881-87)	7	0	0	0	7	6	0	13
William Renshaw (1881-89)	7	0	0	7	0	5	0	12
Rene Lacoste (1925-29)	7	0	3	2	2	3	0	10
Mats Wilander (1982-88)	7	3	3	0	1	1	0	8
William Larned (1901-11)	7	0	0	0	7	0	0	7
Jack Crawford (1931-35)	6	4	1	1	0	6	5	17
Laurence Doherty (1902-06)	6	0	0	5	1	10	0	16
Don Budge (1937-38)	6	1	1	2	2	4	4	14
Anthony Wilding (1906-13)	6	2	0	4	0	5	0	11
Stefan Edberg (1985-92)	6	2	0	2	2	3	0	9
Boris Becker (1985-96)	6	2	0	3	1	0	0	6
Roger Federer (2003-05)	6	1	0	3	2	0	0	6
Frank Sedgman (1949-52)	5	2	0	1	2	9	8	22
Tony Trabert (1953-55)	5	0	2	1	2	5	0	10

Women

Name (winning singles span)	Total Singles	AUS	FRA	WIM	USA	Dbls	Mxd	TOTAL
Margaret Court (1960-73)	24	11	5	3	5	19	21	64
Steffi Graf (1987-99)	22	4	6	7	5	1	0	23
Helen Wills Moody (1923-38)	19	0	4	8	7	9	3	31
Martina Navratilova (1978-90)	18	3	2	9	4	31	9	58
Chris Evert (1974-86)	18	2	7	3	6	3	0	21
Billie Jean King (1966-75)	12	1	1	6	4	16	11	39
Maureen Connolly (1951-54)	9	1	2	3	3	2	1	12
Monica Seles (1990-96)	9	4	3	0	2	0	0	9
Suzanne Lenglen (1919-26)	8	0	2	6	0	8	5	21
Molla Bjurstedt Mallory (1915-26)	8	0	0	0	8	2	2	12
Maria Bueno (1959-66)	7	0	0	3	4	11	1	19
Serena Williams (1999-2005)	7	2	1	2	2	6	2	15
Evonne Goolagong Cawley (1971-80)	7	4	1	2	0	6	1	14
Dorothea Douglass Chambers (1903-14)	7	0	0	7	0	0	0	7
Margaret Osborne DuPont (1946-50)	6	0	2	1	3	21	10	37
Louise Brough (1947-55)	6	1	0	4	1	21	8	35
Doris Hart (1949-55)	6	1	2	1	2	14	15	35
Nancy Wynne Bolton (1937-51)	6	6	0	0	0	10	4	20
Blanche Bingley Hillyard (1886-1900)	6	0	0	6	0	0	0	6
Alice Marble (1936-40)	5	0	0	1	4	6	7	18
Daphne Akhurst (1925-30)	5	5	0	0	0	5	4	14
Martina Hingis (1997-99)	5	3	0	1	1	9	0	14
Venus Williams (2000-05)	5	0	0	3	2	6	2	13
Althea Gibson (1956-58)	5	0	1	2	2	5	1	11
Helen Jacobs (1932-36)	5	0	0	1	4	3	1	9
Pauline Betz (1942-46)	5	0	0	1	4	0	1	6
Charlotte Cooper Sterry (1895-1908)	5	0	0	5	0	0	0	5
Lottie Dod (1887-93)	5	0	0	5	0	0	0	5

Tennis Masters Cup

The end of season men's event, jointly owned by the ATP, ITF and the Grand Slams tournaments, began in 2000 and replaced the ATP Tour World Championship and the Grand Slam Cup. Records of both previous events are shown.

Singles

Year	Venue	Champion	Runner-up	Score
2000	Lisbon, Portugal	G. Kuerten (BRA)	A. Agassi (USA)	64 64 64
2001	Sydney, Australia	L. Hewitt (AUS)	S. Grosjean (FRA)	63 63 64
2002	Shanghai, China	L. Hewitt (AUS)	J. Ferrero (ESP)	75 75 26 26 64
2003	Houston, TX, USA	R. Federer (SUI)	A. Agassi (USA)	63 60 64
2004	Houston, TX, USA	R. Federer (SUI)	L. Hewitt (AUS)	63 62
2005	Shanghai, China	D. Nalbandian (ARG)	R. Federer (SUI)	67 67 62 61 76

Doubles

Year	Venue	Champion	Runner-up	Score
2003	Houston, TX, USA	B. Bryan/M. Bryan (USA)	M. Llodra/F. Santoro (FRA)	67 63 36 76 64
2004	Houston, TX, USA	B. Bryan/M. Bryan (USA)	W. Black/K. Ullyett (ZIM)	46 75 64 62
2005	Shanghai, China	M. Llodra/F. Santoro (FRA)	L. Paes (IND)/N. Zimonjic (SCG)	67 63 76

WTA Tour Championships

Singles

Year	Venue	Champion	Runner-up	Score
1972	Boca Raton, FL, USA	C. Evert (USA)	K. Melville (AUS)	75 64
1973	Boca Raton, FL, USA	C. Evert (USA)	N. Richey (USA)	63 63
1974	Los Angeles, CA, USA	E. Goolagong (AUS)	C. Evert (USA)	63 64
1975	Los Angeles, CA, USA	C. Evert (USA)	M. Navratilova (TCH)	64 62
1976	Los Angeles, CA, USA	E. Goolagong Cawley (AUS)	C. Evert (USA)	63 57 63
1977	New York, NY, USA	C. Evert (USA)	S. Barker (GBR)	26 61 61
1978	Oakland, CA, USA	M. Navratilova (TCH)	E. Goolagong Cawley (AUS)	76 64
1979	New York, NY, USA	M. Navratilova (TCH)	T. Austin (USA)	63 36 62
1980	New York, NY, USA	T. Austin (USA)	M. Navratilova (TCH)	62 26 62
1981	New York, NY, USA	M. Navratilova (USA)	A. Jaeger (USA)	63 76
1982	New York, NY, USA	S. Hanika (GER)	M. Navratilova (USA)	16 63 64
1983	New York, NY, USA	M. Navratilova (USA)	C. Evert (USA)	62 60
1984	New York, NY, USA	M. Navratilova (USA)	C. Evert (USA)	63 75 61
1985	New York, NY, USA	M. Navratilova (USA)	H. Sukova (TCH)	63 75 64
1986 (Mar)	New York, NY, USA	M. Navratilova (USA)	H. Mandlikova (TCH)	62 60 36 61
1986 (Nov)	New York, NY, USA	M. Navratilova (USA)	S. Graf (GER)	76 63 62
1987	New York, NY, USA	S. Graf (GER)	G. Sabatini (ARG)	46 64 60 64
1988	New York, NY, USA	G. Sabatini (ARG)	P. Shriver (USA)	75 62 62
1989	New York, NY, USA	S. Graf (GER)	M. Navratilova (USA)	64 75 26 62
1990	New York, NY, USA	M. Seles (YUG)	G. Sabatini (ARG)	64 57 36 64 62
1991	New York, NY, USA	M. Seles (YUG)	M. Navratilova (USA)	64 36 75 60
1992	New York, NY, USA	M. Seles (YUG)	M. Navratilova (USA)	75 63 61
1993	New York, NY, USA	S. Graf (GER)	A. Sanchez-Vicario (ESP)	61 64 36 61
1994	New York, NY, USA	G. Sabatini (ARG)	L. Davenport (USA)	63 62 64
1995	New York, NY, USA	S. Graf (GER)	A. Huber (GER)	61 26 61 46 63
1996	New York, NY, USA	S. Graf (GER)	M. Hingis (SUI)	63 46 60 46 60
1997	New York, NY, USA	J. Novotna (CZE)	M. Pierce (FRA)	76 62 63
1998	New York, NY, USA	M. Hingis (SUI)	L. Davenport (USA)	75 64 46 62
1999	New York, NY, USA	L. Davenport (USA)	M. Hingis (SUI)	64 62
2000	New York, NY, USA	M. Hingis (SUI)	M. Seles (USA)	67 64 64
2001	Munich, GER	S. Williams (USA)	L. Davenport (USA)	w/o
2002	Los Angeles, CA, USA	K. Clijsters (BEL)	S. Williams (USA)	75 63
2003	Los Angeles, CA, USA	K. Clijsters (BEL)	A. Mauresmo (FRA)	62 60

WTA Tour Championships (continued)

Year	Venue	Champion	Runner-up	Score
2004	Los Angeles, CA, USA	M. Sharapova (RUS)	S. Williams (USA)	46 62 64
2005	Los Angeles, CA, USA	A. Mauresmo (FRA)	M. Pierce (FRA)	57 76 64

Doubles

Year	Venue	Champion	Runner-up	Score
1973	Boca Raton, FL, USA	R. Casals (USA)/M. Court (AUS)	F. Durr (FRA)/B. Stove (NED)	62 64
1974	Los Angeles, CA, USA	B. King/R. Casals (USA)	F. Durr (FRA)/B. Stove (NED)	61 67 75
1975-78 not played				
1979	New York, NY, USA	F. Durr (FRA)/B. Stove (NED)	S. Barker (GBR)/A. Kiyomura (USA)	64 62
1980	New York, NY, USA	B. King (USA)/M. Navratilova (TCH)	R. Casals (USA)/W. Turnbull (AUS)	63 46 63
1981	New York, NY, USA	M. Navratilova/P. Shriver (USA)	B. Potter/S. Walsh (USA)	60 76
1982	New York, NY, USA	M. Navratilova/P. Shriver (USA)	K. Jordan/A. Smith (USA)	64 63
1983	New York, NY, USA	M. Navratilova/P. Shriver (USA)	C. Kohde-Kilsch/E. Pfaff (GER)	75 62
1984	New York, NY, USA	M. Navratilova/P. Shriver (USA)	J. Durie (GBR)/A. Kiyomura (USA)	63 61
1985	New York, NY, USA	M. Navratilova/P. Shriver (USA)	C. Kohde-Kilsch (GER)/H. Sukova (TCH)	67 64 76
1986 (Mar)	New York, NY, USA	H. Mandlikova (TCH)/W. Turnbull (AUS)	C. Kohde-Kilsch (GER)/H. Sukova (TCH)	64 67 63
1986 (Nov)	New York, NY, USA	M. Navratilova/P. Shriver (USA)	C. Kohde-Kilsch (GER)/H. Sukova (TCH)	76 63
1987	New York, NY, USA	M. Navratilova/P. Shriver (USA)	C. Kohde-Kilsch (GER)/H. Sukova (TCH)	61 61
1988	New York, NY, USA	M. Navratilova/P. Shriver (USA)	L. Neiland/N. Zvereva (URS)	63 64
1989	New York, NY, USA	M. Navratilova/P. Shriver (USA)	L. Neiland/N. Zvereva (URS)	63 62
1990	New York, NY, USA	K. Jordan (USA)/E. Smylie (AUS)	M. Paz (ARG)/A. Sanchez-Vicario (ESP)	76 64
1991	New York, NY, USA	M. Navratilova/P. Shriver (USA)	G. Fernandez (USA)/J. Novotna (TCH)	46 75 64
1992	New York, NY, USA	A. Sanchez-Vicario (ESP)/H. Sukova (TCH)	L. Neiland (URS)/J. Novotna (TCH)	76 61
1993	New York, NY, USA	G. Fernandez (USA)/N. Zvereva (BLR)	L. Neiland (LAT)/J. Novotna (CZE)	63 75
1994	New York, NY, USA	G. Fernandez (USA)/N. Zvereva (BLR)	J. Novotna (CZE)/A. Sanchez-Vicario (ESP)	63 67 63
1995	New York, NY, USA	J. Novotna (CZE)/A. Sanchez-Vicario (ESP)	G. Fernandez (USA)/N. Zvereva (BLR)	62 61
1996	New York, NY, USA	L. Davenport/M. Fernandez (USA)	J. Novotna (CZE)/A. Sanchez-Vicario (ESP)	63 62
1997	New York, NY, USA	L. Davenport (USA)/J. Novotna (CZE)	A. Fusai/N. Tauziat (FRA)	67 63 62
1998	New York, NY, USA	L. Davenport (USA)/N. Zvereva (BLR)	A. Fusai/N. Tauziat (FRA)	67 75 63
1999	New York, NY, USA	M. Hingis (SUI)/A. Kournikova (RUS)	L. Neiland (LAT)/A. Sanchez-Vicario (ESP)	64 64
2000	New York, NY, USA	M. Hingis (SUI)/A. Kournikova (RUS)	N. Arendt (USA)/M. Bollegraf (NED)	62 63
2001	Munich, GER	L. Raymond (USA)/R. Stubbs (AUS)	C. Black (ZIM)/E. Likhovtseva (RUS)	75 36 63
2002	Los Angeles, CA, USA	E. Dementieva (RUS)/J. Husarova (SVK)	C. Black (ZIM)/E. Likhovtseva (RUS)	46 64 63
2003	Los Angeles, CA, USA	V. Ruano Pascual (ESP)/P. Suarez (ARG)	K. Clijsters (BEL)/A. Sugiyama (JPN)	64 36 63
2004	Los Angeles, CA, USA	N. Petrova (RUS)/M. Shaughnessy (USA)	C. Black (ZIM)/R. Stubbs (AUS)	75 62
2005	Los Angeles, CA, USA	L. Raymond (USA)/S. Stosur (AUS)	C. Black (ZIM)/R. Stubbs (AUS)	67 75 64

ATP Tour World Championships

Held 1970-1999.

Year	Venue	Champion	Runner-up	Score
1970	Tokyo, Japan	S. Smith (USA)	R. Laver (AUS)	Round robin
1971	Paris, France	I. Nastase (ROM)	S. Smith (USA)	Round robin
1972	Barcelona, Spain	I. Nastase (ROM)	S. Smith (USA)	63 62 36 26 63
1973	Boston, MA, USA	I. Nastase (ROM)	T. Okker (NED)	63 75 46 63
1974	Melbourne, Australia	G. Vilas (ARG)	I. Nastase (ROM)	76 62 36 36 64
1975	Stockholm, Sweden	I. Nastase (ROM)	B. Borg (SWE)	62 62 61
1976	Houston, TX, USA	M. Orantes (ESP)	W. Fibak (POL)	57 62 06 76 61
1977	New York, NY, USA	J. Connors (USA)	B. Borg (SWE)	64 16 64
1978	New York, NY, USA	J. McEnroe (USA)	A. Ashe (USA)	67 63 75
1979	New York, NY, USA	B. Borg (SWE)	V. Gerulaitis (USA)	62 62
1980	New York, NY, USA	B. Borg (SWE)	I. Lendl (TCH)	64 62 62
1981	New York, NY, USA	I. Lendl (TCH)	V. Gerulaitis (USA)	67 26 76 62 64
1982	New York, NY, USA	I. Lendl (TCH)	J. McEnroe (USA)	64 64 62
1983	New York, NY, USA	J. McEnroe (USA)	I. Lendl (TCH)	63 64 64
1984	New York, NY, USA	J. McEnroe (USA)	I. Lendl (TCH)	75 60 64
1985	New York, NY, USA	I. Lendl (TCH)	B. Becker (GER)	62 76 63
1986	New York, NY, USA	I. Lendl (TCH)	B. Becker (GER)	64 64 64
1987	New York, NY, USA	I. Lendl (TCH)	M. Wilander (SWE)	62 62 63
1988	New York, NY, USA	B. Becker (GER)	I. Lendl (TCH)	57 76 36 62 76
1989	New York, NY, USA	S. Edberg (SWE)	B. Becker (GER)	46 76 63 61
1990	Frankfurt, Germany	A. Agassi (USA)	S. Edberg (SWE)	57 76 75 62
1991	Frankfurt, Germany	P. Sampras (USA)	J. Courier (USA)	36 76 63 64
1992	Frankfurt, Germany	B. Becker (GER)	J. Courier (USA)	64 63 75
1993	Frankfurt, Germany	M. Stich (GER)	P. Sampras (USA)	76 26 76 62
1994	Frankfurt, Germany	P. Sampras (USA)	B. Becker (GER)	46 63 75 64
1995	Frankfurt, Germany	B. Becker (GER)	M. Chang (USA)	76 60 76
1996	Hannover, Germany	P. Sampras (USA)	B. Becker (GER)	36 76 76 67 64
1997	Hannover, Germany	P. Sampras (USA)	Y. Kafelnikov (RUS)	63 62 62
1998	Hannover, Germany	A. Corretja (ESP)	C. Moya (ESP)	36 36 75 63 75
1999	Hannover, Germany	P. Sampras (USA)	A. Agassi (USA)	61 75 64

Grand Slam Cup

Held 1990-1999 in Munich, Germany. A women's event was added for the last two years.

Men

Year	Champion	Runner-up	Score
1990	P. Sampras (USA)	B. Gilbert (USA)	63 64 62
1991	D. Wheaton (USA)	M. Chang (USA)	75 62 64
1992	M. Stich (GER)	M. Chang (USA)	62 63 62
1993	P. Korda (TCH)	M. Stich (GER)	26 64 76 26 119
1994	M. Larsson (SWE)	P. Sampras (USA)	76 46 76 64
1995	G. Ivanisevic (CRO)	T. Martin (USA)	76 63 64
1996	B. Becker (GER)	G. Ivanisevic (CRO)	63 64 64
1997	P. Sampras (USA)	P. Rafter (AUS)	62 64 75
1998	M. Rios (CHI)	A. Agassi (USA)	64 26 76 57 63
1999	G. Rusedski (GBR)	T. Haas (GER)	63 64 67 76

Women

Year	Champion	Runner-up	Score
1998	V. Williams (USA)	P. Schnyder (SUI)	62 36 62
1999	S. Williams (USA)	V. Williams (USA)	61 36 63

Australian Junior Championships

Boys' Singles

Year	Champion	Runner-up	Score
1922	A. Yeldham (AUS)		
1923	L. Cryle (AUS)		
1924	H. Coldham (AUS)		
1925	H. Coldham (AUS)		
1926	J. Crawford (AUS)		
1927	J. Crawford (AUS)		
1928	J. Crawford (AUS)		
1929	J. Crawford (AUS)		
1930	D. Turnbull (AUS)		
1931	B. Moore (AUS)		
1932	V. McGrath (AUS)		
1933	A. Quist (AUS)		
1934	N. Ennis (AUS)		
1935	J. Bromwich (AUS)		
1936	J. Bromwich (AUS)		
1937	J. Bromwich (AUS)		
1938	M. Newcombe (AUS)		
1939	W. Sidwell (AUS)		
1940	D. Pails (AUS)		
1941-45 not played			
1946	F. Sedgman (AUS)		
1947	D. Candy (AUS)		
1948	K. McGregor (AUS)	K. Johnstone (AUS)	60 61
1949	C. Wilderspin (AUS)		
1950	K. Rosewall (AUS)	P. Cawthorn (AUS)	64 46 75
1951	L. Hoad (AUS)	K. Rosewall (AUS)	63 62
1952	K. Rosewall (AUS)	L. Hoad (AUS)	108 62
1953	W. Gilmour (AUS)		
1954	W. Knight (GBR)	R. Emerson (AUS)	63 61
1955	G. Moss (USA)	M. Green (USA)	108 62
1956	R. Mark (AUS)	M. Collins (AUS)	63 86
1957	R. Laver (AUS)	J. Pearce (AUS)	1113 75 62
1958	M. Mulligan (AUS)	R. Hewitt (AUS)	64 63
1959	E. Buchholz (USA)	M. Mulligan (AUS)	36 63 63
1960	W. Coghlan (AUS)	G. Pares (AUS)	64 61
1961	J. Newcombe (AUS)	G. Pollard (AUS)	63 63
1962	J. Newcombe (AUS)	O. Davidson (AUS)	61 46 64
1963	J. Newcombe (AUS)	G. Stilwell (GBR)	64 64
1964	A. Roche (AUS)	G. Stilwell (GBR)	1210 63
1965	G. Goven (FRA)	J. Walker (AUS)	75 26 63
1966	K. Coombes (AUS)	G. Olsson (AUS)	64 46 86
1967	B. Fairlie (NZL)	D. Smith (AUS)	60 63
1968	P. Dent (AUS)	R. Giltinan (AUS)	62 64
1969	A. McDonald (AUS)	A. Wijono (INA)	60 61
1970	J. Alexander (AUS)	P. Dent (AUS)	46 63 86
1971	C. Letcher (AUS)		
1972	P. Kronk (AUS)		
1973	P. McNamee (AUS)		
1974	H. Brittain (AUS)	J. Haillet (FRA)	108 75
1975	B. Drewett (AUS)		
1976	R. Kelly (AUS)	J. Dilouie (USA)	62 64
1977 (Jan)	B. Drewett (AUS)	T. Wilkison (USA)	64 76
1977 (Dec)	R. Kelly (AUS)		
1978	P. Serrett (AUS)	C. Johnstone (AUS)	64 63

Year	Champion	Runner-up	Score
1979	G. Whitecross (AUS)	C. Miller (AUS)	64 63
1980	C. Miller (AUS)	W. Masur (AUS)	76 62
1981	J. Windahl (SWE)	P. Cash (AUS)	64 64
1982	M. Kratzmann (AUS)	S. Youl (AUS)	63 75
1983	S. Edberg (SWE)	S. Youl (AUS)	64 64
1984	M. Kratzmann (AUS)	P. Flyn (AUS)	64 61
1985 (Nov)	S. Barr (AUS)	S. Furlong (AUS)	76 67 63
1986 not played			
1987 (Jan)	J. Stoltenberg (AUS)	T. Woodbridge (AUS)	62 76
1988	J. Anderson (AUS)	A. Florent (AUS)	75 76
1989	N. Kulti (SWE)	T. Woodbridge (AUS)	62 60
1990	D. Dier (GER)	L. Paes (IND)	64 76
1991	T. Enqvist (SWE)	S. Gleeson (AUS)	76 67 61
1992	G. Doyle (AUS)	B. Dunn (USA)	62 60
1993	J. Baily (GBR)	S. Downs (NZL)	63 62
1994	B. Ellwood (AUS)	A. Ilie (AUS)	57 63 63
1995	N. Kiefer (GER)	J. Lee (KOR)	64 64
1996	B. Rehnqvist (SWE)	M. Hellstrom (SWE)	26 62 75
1997	D. Elsner (GER)	W. Whitehouse (RSA)	76 62
1998	J. Jeanpierre (FRA)	A. Vinciguerra (SWE)	46 64 63
1999	K. Pless (DEN)	M. Youzhny (RUS)	64 63
2000	A. Roddick (USA)	M. Ancic (CRO)	76 63
2001	J. Tipsarevic (YUG)	Y. Wang (TPE)	36 75 60
2002	C. Morel (FRA)	T. Reid (AUS)	64 64
2003	M. Baghdatis (CYP)	F. Mergea (ROM)	64 64
2004	G. Monfils (FRA)	J. Ouanna (FRA)	60 63
2005	D. Young (USA)	S. Kim (KOR)	62 64

Girls' Singles

Year	Champion	Runner-up	Score
1930	E. Hood (AUS)	N. Hall (AUS)	64 57 119
1931	J. Hartigan (AUS)		
1932	N. Lewis (AUS)		
1933	N. Lewis (AUS)		
1934	M. Blick (AUS)		
1935	T. Coyne (AUS)		
1936	T. Coyne (AUS)		
1937	M. Wilson (AUS)		
1938	J. Wood (AUS)		
1939	J. Wood (AUS)		
1940	J. Wood (AUS)		
1941-45 not played			
1946	S. Grant (AUS)		
1947	J. Tuckfield (AUS)		
1948	B. Penrose (AUS)		
1949	J. Warnock (AUS)		
1950	B. McIntyre (AUS)	H. Angwin (AUS)	46 64 64
1951	M. Carter (AUS)	H. Astley (AUS)	36 64 64
1952	M. Carter (AUS)		
1953	J. Staley (AUS)	M. Carter (AUS)	61 64
1954	E. Orton (AUS)	M. McCalman (AUS)	63 64
1955	E. Orton (AUS)	M. Hellyer (AUS)	60 75
1956	L. Coghlan (AUS)	M. Hellyer (AUS)	60 75
1957	M. Rayson (AUS)	J. Lehane (AUS)	57 62 62

Australian Junior Championships (continued)

Year	Champion	Runner-up	Score
1958	J. Lehane (AUS)	B. Holstein (AUS)	75 61
1959	J. Lehane (AUS)	M. Smith (AUS)	60 61
1960	L. Turner (AUS)	M. Smith (AUS)	26 62 62
1961	R. Ebbern (AUS)	F. Toyne (AUS)	46 86 60
1962	R. Ebbern (AUS)	M. Schacht (AUS)	64 63
1963	R. Ebbern (AUS)	K. Dening (AUS)	75 63
1964	K. Dening (AUS)	K. Melville (AUS)	26 63 97
1965	K. Melville (AUS)	H. Gourlay (AUS)	61 61
1966	A. Krantzcke (AUS)	K. Melville (AUS)	63 63
1967	A. Kenny (AUS)	J. Young (AUS)	63 46 61
1968	L. Hunt (AUS)	K. Harris (AUS)	26 63 86
1969	L. Hunt (AUS)	J. Young (AUS)	46 61 75
1970	E. Goolagong (AUS)	J. Young (AUS)	61 61
1971	P. Coleman (AUS)		
1972	P. Coleman (AUS)		
1973	C. O'Neill (AUS)	J. Walker (AUS)	26 62 86
1974	J. Walker (AUS)		
1975	S. Barker (GBR)	C. O'Neill (AUS)	62 76
1976	S. Saliba (AUS)	J. Fenwick (AUS)	26 63 64
1977 (Jan)	P. Bailey (AUS)	A. Tobin (AUS)	62 63
1977 (Dec)	A. Tobin (AUS)	L. Harrison (AUS)	61 62
1978	E. Little (AUS)	S. Leo (AUS)	61 62
1979	A. Minter (AUS)	S. Leo (AUS)	64 63
1980	A. Minter (AUS)	E. Sayers (AUS)	64 62
1981	A. Minter (AUS)	C. Vanier (FRA)	64 62
1982	A. Brown (GBR)	P. Paradis (FRA)	63 64
1983	A. Brown (GBR)	B. Randall (AUS)	76 63
1984	A. Croft (GBR)	H. Dahlstrom (SWE)	60 61
1985	J. Byrne (AUS)	L. Field (AUS)	61 63
1986 not played			
1987	M. Jaggard (AUS)	N. Provis (AUS)	62 64
1988	J. Faull (AUS)	E. Derly (FRA)	64 64
1989	J. Kessaris (AUS)	A. Farley (USA)	61 62
1990	M. Maleeva (BUL)	L. Stacey (AUS)	75 67 61
1991	N. Pratt (AUS)	K. Godridge (AUS)	64 63
1992	J. Limmer (AUS)	L. Davenport (USA)	75 62
1993	H. Rusch (GER)	A. Glass (GER)	61 62
1994	T. Musgrave (AUS)	B. Schett (AUT)	46 64 62
1995	S. Drake-Brockman (AUS)	A. Elwood (AUS)	63 46 75
1996	M. Grzybowska (POL)	N. Dechy (FRA)	61 46 61
1997	M. Lucic (CRO)	M. Weingartner (GER)	62 62
1998	J. Kostanic (CRO)	W. Prakusya (INA)	60 75
1999	V. Razzano (FRA)	K. Basternakova (SVK)	61 61
2000	A. Kapros (HUN)	M. Martinez (ESP)	62 36 62
2001	J. Jankovic (YUG)	S. Arvidsson (SWE)	62 61
2002	B. Strycova (CZE)	M. Sharapova (RUS)	60 75
2003	B. Strycova (CZE)	V. Kutuzova (UKR)	06 62 62
2004	S. Peer (ISR)	N. Vaidisova (CZE)	61 64
2005	V. Azarenka (BLR)	A. Szavay (HUN)	62 62

	Boys' Doubles	**Girls' Doubles**
Year	**Champions**	**Champions**
1922	C. Grogan/L. Roche	
1923	E. Moon/L. Roche	
1924	A. Berckelman/R. Dunlop	

Year	Champions	Champions
1925	J. Crawford/H. Hopman (AUS)	
1926	J. Crawford/H.Hopman (AUS)	
1927	J. Crawford/H. Hopman (AUS)	
1928	J. Crawford/C. Whiteman	
1929	C. Cropper/W. Walker	
1930	A. Quist/D. Turnbull (AUS)	N. Hall/E. Hood (AUS)
1931	J. Purcell/B. Tonkin	S. Moon/E. Westacott (AUS)
1932	A. Quist/L. Schwartz (AUS)	F. Francisco/J. Williams (AUS)
1933	J. Purcell/B. Tonkin	D. Stevenson/G. Stevenson (AUS)
1934	N. Ennis/C. McKenzie	E. Chrystal/E. McColl (AUS)
1935	J. Bromwich/A. Huxley	D. Stevenson/N. Wynne (AUS)
1936	J. Gilchrist/H. Lindo (AUS)	M. Carter/M. Wilson (AUS)
1937	J. Bromwich/D. Pails (AUS)	J. Prior/I. Webb (AUS)
1938	D. Pails/W. Sidwell (AUS)	A. Burton/J. Wood (AUS)
1939	R. Felan/H. Impey (AUS)	A. Burton/J. Wood (AUS)
1940	W. Edwards/D. Pails (AUS)	A. Burton/J. Wood (AUS)
1941-45 not played		
1946	F. Herringe/G. Worthington (AUS)	N. Reid/H. Utz (AUS)
1947	R. Hartwig/A. Kendall (AUS)	S. Jackson/V. Linehan (AUS)
1948	D. Candy/K. McGregor (AUS)	G. Blair/B. Bligh (AUS)
1949	J. Blacklock/C. Wilderspin (AUS)	B. Penrose/J. Robbins (AUS)
1950	L. Hoad/K. Rosewall (AUS)	C. Borelli/P. Southcombe (AUS)
1951	L. Hoad/K. Rosewall (AUS)	J. Staley/M. Wallis (AUS)
1952	L. Hoad/K. Rosewall (AUS)	M. Carter/B. Holstein (AUS)
1953	W. Gilmor/W. Woodcock (AUS)	M. Carter/B. Warby (AUS)
1954	M. Anderson/R. Emerson (AUS)	B. Holstein/B. Jones (AUS)
1955	M. Green/G. Moss (USA)	E. Orton/P. Parmenter (AUS)
1956	P. Hearnden/B. Mark (AUS)	S. Armstrong (GBR)/L. Coghlan (AUS)
1957	F. Gorman/R. Laver (AUS)	M. Rayson/V. Roberts (AUS)
1958	R. Hewitt/M. Mulligan (AUS)	B. Holstein/J. Lehane (AUS)
1959	J. Arilla (ESP)/E. Buchholz (USA)	J. Lehane/D. Robberds (AUS)
1960	G. Hughes/J. Shepherd (AUS)	D. Robberds/L. Turner (AUS)
1961	R. Brent/J. Newcombe (AUS)	R. Ebbern/M. Schacht (AUS)
1962	W. Bowrey/G. Knox (AUS)	H. Ross/J. Star (AUS)
1963	R. Brien/J. Cotterill (AUS)	P. McClenaughan/G. Sherriff (AUS)
1964	S. Matthews/G. Stilwell (GBR)	K. Dening/H. Gourlay (AUS)
1965	T. Musgrave/J. Walker (AUS)	H. Gourlay/K. Melville (AUS)
1966	R. Layton/P. McCumstie (AUS)	K. Krantzcke/P. Turner (AUS)
1967	J. Bartlett (AUS)/S. Ginman (SWE)	S. Alexander/C. Cooper (AUS)
1968	P. Dent/W. Lloyd (AUS)	L. Hunt/V. Lancaster (AUS)
1969	N. Higgins/J. James (AUS)	P. Edwards/E. Goolagong (AUS)
1970	A. McDonald/G. Perkins (AUS)	J. Fallis/J. Young (AUS)
1971	S. Marks/M. Phillips (AUS)	P. Edwards/J. Whyte (AUS)
1972	W. Durham/S. Myers (AUS)	S. Irvine/P. Whytcross (AUS)
1973	T. Saunders/G. Thoroughgood (AUS)	J. Dimond/D. Fromholtz (AUS)
1974	D. Carter/T. Little (AUS)	N. Gregory/J. Hanrahan (AUS)
1975	G. Busby/W. Maher (AUS)	D. Evers/N. Gregory (AUS)
1976	C. Fancutt/P. McCarthy (AUS)	J. Morton/J. Wilton (AUS)
1977 (Jan)	P. Davies/P. Smylie (AUS)	K. Pratt/A. Tobin (AUS)
1977 (Dec)	R. Kelly/G. Thams (AUS)	K. Pratt/A. Tobin (AUS)
1978	M. Fancutt/W. Gilmour (AUS)	D. Freeman/K. Mantle (AUS)
1979	M. Fancutt/G. Whitecross (AUS)	L. Cassell/S. Leo (AUS)
1980	C. Miller/W. Masur (AUS)	A. Minter/M. Yates (AUS)
1981	D. Lewis (NZL)/T. Withers (AUS)	M. Booth/S. Hodgkin (AUS)
1982	B. Burke/M. Hartnett (AUS)	A. Gulley/K. Staunton (AUS)

Australian Junior Championships (continued)

Year	Champions	Champions
1983	J. Harty/D. Tyson (AUS)	B. Randall/K. Staunton (AUS)
1984	M. Baroch/M. Kratzmann (AUS)	L. Field (AUS)/L. Savchenko (URS)
1985	B. Custer/D. Macpherson (AUS)	J. Byrne/J. Thompson (AUS)
1986 not played		
1987	J. Stoltenberg/T. Woodbridge (AUS)	A. Devries (BEL)/N. Provis (AUS)
1988	J. Stoltenberg/T. Woodbridge (AUS)	J. Faull/R. McQuillan (AUS)
1989	J. Anderson/T. Woodbridge (AUS)	A. Strnadova/E. Sviglerova (TCH)
1990	R. Petterson/M. Renstroem (SWE)	R. Mayer/L. Zaltz (ISR)
1991	G. Doyle/J. Eagle (AUS)	K. Habsudova (TCH)/B. Rittner (GER)
1992	G. Doyle/B. Sceney (AUS)	L. Davenport/N. London (USA)
1993	L. Rehmann/C. Tambue (GER)	J. Manta (SUI)/L. Richterova (TCH)
1994	B. Ellwood/M. Philippoussis (AUS)	C. Morariu (USA)/L. Varmuzova (CZE)
1995	L. Bourgeois (AUS)/J. Lee (KOR)	C. Morariu (USA)/L. Varmuzova (CZE)
1996	D. Bracciali (ITA)/J. Robichaud (CAN)	M. Pastikova/J. Schonfeldova (CZE)
1997	D. Sherwood/J. Trotman (GBR)	M. Lucic (CRO)/J. Wohr (GER)
1998	J. Haehnel/J. Jeanpierre (FRA)	E. Dominikovic/A. Molik (AUS)
1999	J. Melzer (AUT)/K. Pless (DEN)	E. Daniilidou (GRE)/V. Razzano (FRA)
2000	N. Mahut (FRA)/T. Robredo (ESP)	A. Kapros (HUN)/C. Wheeler (AUS)
2001	Y. Abougzir (USA)/L. Vitullo (ARG)	P. Cetkovska/B. Strycova (CZE)
2002	R. Henry/T. Reid (AUS)	G. Dulko (ARG)/A.Widjaja (INA)
2003	S. Oudsema/P. Simmonds (USA)	C. Dell'Acqua/A.Szili (AUS)
2004	B. Evans/S. Oudsema (USA)	Y. Chan (TPE)/S. Sun (CHN)
2005	S. Kim (KOR)/C. Yi (TPE)	V. Azarenka (BLR)/M. Erakovic (NZL)

French Junior Championships – Roland Garros

Boys' Singles

Year	Champion	Runner-up	Score
1947	J. Brichant (BEL)	A. Roberts (GBR)	63 46 75
1948	K. Nielsen (DEN)	J. Brichant (BEL)	36 63 64
1949	J. Molinari (FRA)	R. Haillet (FRA)	62 79 86
1950	R. Dubuisson (FRA)	G. Pilet (FRA)	1012 61 63
1951	H. Richardson (USA)	G. Mezzi (BEL)	63 62
1952	K. Rosewall (AUS)	J. Grinda (FRA)	62 62
1953	J. Grinda (FRA)	F. Andries (BEL)	61 62
1954	R. Emerson (AUS)	J. Grinda (FRA)	61 68 64
1955	A. Gimeno (ESP)	M. Belkhodja (TUN)	62 46 75
1956	M. Belkhodja (TUN)	R. Laver (AUS)	46 64 63
1957	A. Arilla (ESP)	J. Renavand (FRA)	68 63 64
1958	E. Buchholz (USA)	A. Bresson (FRA)	68 64 62
1959	I. Buding (GER)	E. Mandarino (BRA)	60 06 64
1960	I. Buding (GER)	J. Gisbert (ESP)	63 86
1961	J. Newcombe (AUS)	D. Contet (FRA)	67 15-15 ret
1962	J. Newcombe (AUS)	T. Koch (BRA)	46 64 86
1963	N. Kalogeropoulos (GRE)	T. Koch (BRA)	26 97 63
1964	C. Richey (USA)	G. Goven (FRA)	64 62
1965	G. Battrick (GBR)	G. Goven (FRA)	75 64
1966	V. Korotkov (URS)	J. Guerrero (ESP)	63 62
1967	P. Proisy (FRA)	J. Tavares (BRA)	63 86
1968	P. Dent (AUS)	J. Alexander (AUS)	63 36 75
1969	A. Munoz (ESP)	J. Thamin (FRA)	62 46 64
1970	J. Herrera (ESP)	J. Thamin (FRA)	46 62 64
1971	C. Barazzutti (ITA)	S. Warboys (GBR)	26 63 61
1972	C. Mottram (GBR)	U. Pinner (FRG)	62 26 75

Year	Champion	Runner-up	Score
1973	V. Pecci (PAR)	P. Slozil (TCH)	64 64
1974	C. Casa (FRA)	U. Marten (FRG)	16 64 61
1975	C. Roger-Vasselin (FRA)	P. Elter (FRG)	61 62
1976	H. Gunthardt (SUI)	J. Clerc (ARG)	46 76 64
1977	J. McEnroe (USA)	R. Kelly (AUS)	61 61
1978	I. Lendl (TCH)	P. Hjertquist (SWE)	76 64
1979	R. Krishnan (IND)	B. Testerman (USA)	26 61 60
1980	H. Leconte (FRA)	A. Tous (ESP)	76 63
1981	M. Wilander (SWE)	J. Brown (USA)	75 61
1982	T. Benhabiles (FRA)	L. Courteau (FRA)	76 62
1983	S. Edberg (SWE)	F. Fevrier (FRA)	26 62 61
1984	K. Carlsson (SWE)	M. Kratzmann (AUS)	63 63
1985	J. Yzaga (PER)	T. Muster (AUT)	26 63 60
1986	G. Perez-Roldan (ARG)	S. Grenier (FRA)	46 63 62
1987	G. Perez-Roldan (ARG)	J. Stoltenberg (AUS)	63 36 61
1988	N. Pereira (VEN)	M. Larsson (SWE)	76 63
1989	F. Santoro (FRA)	J. Palmer (USA)	63 36 97
1990	A. Gaudenzi (ITA)	T. Enqvist (SWE)	26 76 64
1991	A. Medvedev (UKR)	T. Enqvist (SWE)	64 76
1992	A. Pavel (ROM)	M. Navarra (ITA)	61 36 63
1993	R. Carretero (ESP)	A. Costa (ESP)	60 76
1994	J. Diaz (ESP)	G. Galimberti (ITA)	63 76
1995	M. Zabaleta (ARG)	M. Puerta (ARG)	62 63
1996	A. Martin (ESP)	B. Rehnquist (SWE)	63 76
1997	D. Elsner (GER)	L. Horna (PER)	64 64
1998	F. Gonzalez (CHI)	J. Ferrero (ESP)	46 64 63
1999	G. Coria (ARG)	D. Nalbandian (ARG)	64 63
2000	P. Mathieu (FRA)	T. Robredo (ESP)	36 76 62
2001	C. Cuadrado (ESP)	B. Dabul (ARG)	61 60
2002	R. Gasquet (FRA)	L. Recouderc (FRA)	60 61
2003	S. Wawrinka (SUI)	B. Baker (USA)	75 46 63
2004	G. Monfils (FRA)	A. Kuznetsov (USA)	62 62
2005	M. Cilic (CRO)	A. Van der Duim (NED)	63 61

Girls' Singles

Year	Champion	Runner-up	Score
1953	C. Brunon (FRA)	B. De Chambure (FRA)	26 62 60
1954	B. De Chambure (FRA)	C. Monnot (FRA)	64 86
1955	M. Reidl (ITA)	C. Baumgarten (FRA)	64 60
1956	E. Launay (FRA)	J. Lieffrig (FRA)	61 64
1957	I. Buding (GER)	C. Seghers (FRA)	62 75
1958	F. Gordigiani (ITA)	S. Galtier (FRA)	63 26 62
1959	J. Cross (RSA)	M. Rucquoy (BEL)	61 64
1960	F. Durr (FRA)	M. Rucquoy (BEL)	60 61
1961	R. Ebbern (AUS)	F. Courteix (FRA)	61 63
1962	K. Dening (AUS)	R. Ebbern (AUS)	16 61 63
1963	M. Salfati (FRA)	A. Van Zyl (RSA)	62 46 61
1964	N. Seghers (FRA)	E. Subirats (MEX)	63 63
1965	E. Emanuel (RSA)	E. Subirats (MEX)	64 62
1966	O. De Roubin (FRA)	M. Cristiani (FRA)	64 63
1967	C. Molesworth (GBR)	P. Montano (MEX)	36 64 64
1968	L. Hunt (AUS)	E. Izopajtyse (URS)	64 62
1969	K. Sawamatsu (JPN)	A. Cassaigne (FRA)	62 60
1970	V. Burton (GBR)	R. Tomanova (TCH)	64 64
1971	E. Granatourova (URS)	F. Guedy (FRA)	26 64 75

Year	Champion	Runner-up	Score
1972	R. Tomanova (TCH)	M. Jausovec (YUG)	62 63
1973	M. Jausovec (YUG)	R. Marsikova (TCH)	63 62
1974	M. Simionescu (ROM)	S. Barker (GBR)	63 63
1975	R. Marsikova (TCH)	L. Mottram (GBR)	63 57 62
1976	M. Tyler (GBR)	M. Zoni (ITA)	61 63
1977	A. Smith (USA)	H. Strachonova (TCH)	63 76
1978	H. Mandlikova (TCH)	M. Rothschild (USA)	60 61
1979	L. Sandin (SWE)	M. Piatek (USA)	63 61
1980	K. Horvath (USA)	K. Henry (USA)	62 62
1981	B. Gadusek (USA)	H. Sukova (TCH)	67 61 64
1982	M. Maleeva (BUL)	P. Barg (USA)	75 62
1983	P. Paradis (FRA)	D. Spence (USA)	76 63
1984	G. Sabatini (ARG)	K. Maleeva (BUL)	63 57 63
1985	L. Garrone (ITA)	D. Van Rensburg (RSA)	61 63
1986	P. Tarabini (ARG)	N. Provis (AUS)	63 63
1987	N. Zvereva (URS)	J. Pospisilova (TCH)	61 60
1988	J. Halard (FRA)	A. Farley (USA)	62 46 75
1989	J. Capriati (USA)	E. Sviglerova (TCH)	64 60
1990	M. Maleeva (BUL)	T. Ignatieva (URS)	62 63
1991	A. Smashnova (ISR)	I. Gorrochategui (ARG)	26 75 61
1992	R. De Los Rios (PAR)	P. Suarez (ARG)	64 60
1993	M. Hingis (SUI)	L. Courtois (BEL)	75 75
1994	M. Hingis (SUI)	S. Jeyaseelan (CAN)	63 61
1995	A. Cocheteux (FRA)	M. Weingartner (GER)	75 64
1996	A. Mauresmo (FRA)	M. Shaughnessy (USA)	60 64
1997	J. Henin (BEL)	C. Black (ZIM)	46 64 64
1998	N. Petrova (RUS)	J. Dokic (AUS)	63 63
1999	L. Dominguez Lino (ESP)	S. Foretz (FRA)	64 64
2000	V. Razzano (FRA)	M. Salerni (ARG)	57 64 86
2001	K. Kanepi (EST)	S. Kuznetsova (RUS)	63 16 62
2002	A. Widjaja (INA)	A. Harkleroad (USA)	36 61 64
2003	A. Groenefeld (GER)	V. Douchevina (RUS)	64 64
2004	S. Karatantcheva (BUL)	M. Gojnea (ROM)	64 60
2005	A. Szavay (HUN)	R. Olaru (ROM)	61 61

	Boys' Doubles	Girls' Doubles
Year	Champions	Champions
1981	B. Moir/M. Robertson (RSA)	S. Amiach/C. Vanier (FRA)
1982	P. Cash/J. Frawley (AUS)	B. Herr/J. Lagasse (USA)
1983	M. Kratzmann/S. Youl (AUS)	C. Anderholm/H. Olsson (SWE)
1984	L. Jensen/P. McEnroe (USA)	D. Ketelaar/S. Schilder (NED)
1985	P. Korda/C. Suk (TCH)	M. Perez-Roldan/P. Tarabini (ARG)
1986	F. Davin/G. Perez-Roldan (ARG)	L. Meskhi/N. Zvereva (URS)
1987	J. Courier/J. Stark (USA)	N. Medvedeva/N. Zvereva (URS)
1988	J. Stoltenberg/T. Woodbridge (AUS)	A. Dechaume/E. Derly (FRA)
1989	J. Anderson/T. Woodbridge (AUS)	N. Pratt (AUS)/S. Wang (TPE)
1990	S. Leblanc/S. Lareau (CAN)	R. Dragomir/I. Spirlea (ROM)
1991	T. Enqvist/M. Martinelle (SWE)	E. Bes (ESP)/I. Gorrochategui (ARG)
1992	E. Abaroa (MEX)/G. Doyle (AUS)	L. Courtois/N. Feber (BEL)
1993	S. Downs/J. Greenhalgh (NZL)	L. Courtois/N. Feber (BEL)
1994	G. Kuerten (BRA)/N. Lapentti (ECU)	M. Hingis (SUI)/H. Nagyova (SVK)
1995	R. Sluiter/P. Wessels (NED)	C. Morariu (USA)/L. Varmuzova (CZE)
1996	S. Grosjean/O. Mutis (FRA)	A. Canepa/G. Casoni (ITA)
1997	J. de Armas (VEN)/L. Horna (PER)	C. Black (ZIM)/I. Selyutina (KAZ)
1998	J. de Armas (VEN)/F. Gonzalez (CHI)	K. Clijsters (BEL)/J. Dokic (AUS)

Year	Champions	Champions
1999	I. Labadze (GEO)/L. Zovko (CRO)	F. Pennetta/R. Vinci (ITA)
2000	M. Lopez/T. Robredo (ESP)	M. Martinez/A. Medina (ESP)
2001	A. Falla/C. Salamanca (COL)	P. Cetkovska/R. Voracova (CZE)
2002	M. Bayer/P. Petzschner (GER)	A. Groenefeld (GER)/B. Strycova (CZE)
2003	G. Balazs (HUN)/D. Sela (ISR)	M. Fraga-Perez/A. Gonzalez-Penas (ESP)
2004	P. Andujar-Alba/M. Granollers-Pujol (ESP)	K. Bohmova (CZE)/M. Krajicek (NED)
2005	E. Massa/L. Mayer (ARG)	V. Azarenka(BLR)/A. Szavay (HUN)

The Junior Championships, Wimbledon

Boys' Singles

Year	Champion	Runner-up	Score
1947	K. Nielsen (DEN)	S. Davidson (SWE)	86 61 97
1948	S. Stockenberg (SWE)	D. Vad (HUN)	60 68 57 64 62
1949	S. Stockenberg (SWE)	J. Horn (GBR)	62 61
1950	J. Horn (GBR)	K. Mobarek (EGY)	60 62
1951	J. Kupferburger (RSA)	K. Mobarek (EGY)	86 64
1952	B. Wilson (GBR)	T. Fancutt (RSA)	63 63
1953	B. Knight (GBR)	R. Krishnan (IND)	75 64
1954	R. Krishnan (IND)	A. Cooper (AUS)	62 75
1955	M. Hann (GBR)	J. Lundquist (SWE)	60 119
1956	R. Holmberg (USA)	R. Laver (AUS)	61 61
1957	J. Tattershall (GBR)	I. Ribeiro (BRA)	62 61
1958	E. Buchholz (USA)	P. Lall (IND)	61 63
1959	T. Lejus (URS)	R. Barnes (BRA)	62 64
1960	R. Mandelstam (RSA)	J. Mukerjea (IND)	16 86 64
1961	C. Graebner (USA)	E. Blanke (AUT)	63 97
1962	S. Matthews (GBR)	A. Metreveli (URS)	108 36 64
1963	N. Kalogeropoulos (GRE)	I. El Shafei (EGY)	64 63
1964	I. El Shafei (EGY)	V. Korotkov (URS)	62 63
1965	V. Korotkov (URS)	G. Goven (FRA)	62 36 63
1966	V. Korotkov (URS)	B. Fairlie (NZL)	63 119
1967	M. Orantes (ESP)	M. Estep (USA)	62 60
1968	J. Alexander (AUS)	J. Thamin (FRA)	61 62
1969	B. Bertram (RSA)	J. Alexander (AUS)	75 57 64
1970	B. Bertram (RSA)	F. Gebert (FRG)	60 63
1971	R. Kreiss (USA)	S. Warboys (GBR)	26 64 63
1972	B. Borg (SWE)	C. Mottram (GBR)	63 46 75
1973	B. Martin (USA)	C. Dowdeswell (ZIM)	62 64
1974	B. Martin (USA)	A. Amritraj (IND)	62 61
1975	C. Lewis (NZL)	R. Ycaza (ECU)	61 64
1976	H. Gunthardt (SUI)	P. Elter (FRG)	64 75
1977	V. Winitsky (USA)	T. Teltscher (USA)	61 16 86
1978	I. Lendl (TCH)	J. Turpin (USA)	63 64
1979	R. Krishnan (IND)	D. Siegler (USA)	60 62
1980	T. Tulasne (FRA)	H. Beutel (FRG)	64 36 64
1981	M. Anger (USA)	P. Cash (AUS)	76 75
1982	P. Cash (AUS)	H. Sundstrom (SWE)	64 67 63
1983	S. Edberg (SWE)	J. Frawley (AUS)	63 76
1984	M. Kratzmann (AUS)	S. Kruger (RSA)	64 46 63
1985	L. Lavalle (MEX)	E. Velez (MEX)	64 64
1986	E. Velez (MEX)	J. Sanchez (ESP)	63 75
1987	D. Nargiso (ITA)	J. Stoltenberg (AUS)	76 64
1988	N. Pereira (VEN)	G. Raoux (FRA)	76 62

The Junior Championships, Wimbledon (continued)

Year	Champion	Runner-up	Score
1989	N. Kulti (SWE)	T. Woodbridge (AUS)	64 63
1990	L. Paes (IND)	M. Ondruska (RSA)	75 26 64
1991	T. Enqvist (SWE)	M. Joyce (USA)	64 63
1992	D. Skoch (TCH)	B. Dunn (USA)	64 63
1993	R. Sabau (ROM)	J. Szymanski (VEN)	61 63
1994	S. Humphries (USA)	M. Philippoussis (AUS)	76 36 64
1995	O. Mutis (FRA)	N. Kiefer (GER)	62 62
1996	V. Voltchkov (BLR)	I. Ljubicic (CRO)	36 62 63
1997	W. Whitehouse (RSA)	D. Elsner (GER)	63 76
1998	R. Federer (SUI)	I. Labadze (GEO)	64 64
1999	J. Melzer (AUT)	K. Pless (DEN)	76 63
2000	N. Mahut (FRA)	M Ancic (CRO)	36 63 75
2001	R. Valent (SUI)	G. Muller (LUX)	36 75 63
2002	T. Reid (AUS)	L. Ouahab (ALG)	76 64
2003	F. Mergea (ROM)	C. Guccione (AUS)	62 76
2004	G. Monfils (FRA)	M. Kasiri (GBR)	75 76
2005	J. Chardy (FRA)	R. Haase (NED)	64 63

Girls' Singles

Year	Champion	Runner-up	Score
1947	G. Domken (BEL)	B. Wallen (SWE)	61 64
1948	O. Miskova (TCH)	V. Rigollet (SUI)	64 62
1949	C. Mercelis (BEL)	J. Partridge (GBR)	64 62
1950	L. Cornell (GBR)	A. Winter (NOR)	62 64
1951	L. Cornell (GBR)	S. Lazzarino (ITA)	63 64
1952	F. ten Bosch (NED)	R. Davar (IND)	57 61 75
1953	D. Killan (RSA)	V. Pitt (GBR)	64 46 61
1954	V. Pitt (GBR)	C. Monnot (FRA)	57 63 62
1955	S. Armstrong (GBR)	B. De Chambure (FRA)	62 64
1956	A. Haydon (GBR)	I. Buding (GER)	63 64
1957	M. Arnold (USA)	E. Reyes (MEX)	86 62
1958	S. Moore (USA)	A. Dmitrieva (URS)	62 64
1959	J. Cross (RSA)	D. Schuster (AUT)	61 61
1960	K. Hantze (USA)	L. Hutchings (RSA)	64 64
1961	G. Baksheeva (URS)	K. Chabot (USA)	64 86
1962	G. Baksheeva (URS)	E. Terry (NZL)	64 62
1963	M. Salfati (FRA)	K. Dening (AUS)	64 61
1964	P. Bartkowicz (USA)	E. Subirats (MEX)	63 61
1965	O. Morozova (URS)	R. Giscafre (ARG)	63 63
1966	B. Lindstrom (FIN)	J. Congdon (GBR)	75 63
1967	J. Salome (NED)	E. Strandberg (SWE)	64 62
1968	K. Pigeon (USA)	L. Hunt (AUS)	64 63
1969	K. Sawamatsu (JPN)	B. Kirk (RSA)	61 16 75
1970	S. Walsh (USA)	M. Kroshina (URS)	86 64
1971	M. Kroshina (URS)	S. Minford (GBR)	64 64
1972	I. Kloss (RSA)	G. Coles (GBR)	64 46 64
1973	A. Kiyomura (USA)	M. Navratilova (TCH)	64 75
1974	M. Jausovec (YUG)	M. Simionescu (ROM)	75 64
1975	N. Chmyreva (URS)	R. Marsikova (TCH)	64 63
1976	N. Chmyreva (URS)	M. Kruger (RSA)	63 26 61
1977	L. Antonoplis (USA)	M. Louie (USA)	75 61
1978	T. Austin (USA)	H. Mandlikova (TCH)	60 36 64
1979	M. Piatek (USA)	A. Moulton (USA)	61 63
1980	D. Freeman (AUS)	S. Leo (AUS)	76 75
1981	Z. Garrison (USA)	R. Uys (RSA)	64 36 60

Year	Champion	Runner-up	Score
1982	C. Tanvier (FRA)	H. Sukova (TCH)	62 75
1983	P. Paradis (FRA)	P. Hy (HKG)	62 61
1984	A. Croft (GBR)	E. Reinach (RSA)	36 63 62
1985	A. Holikova (TCH)	J. Byrne (AUS)	75 61
1986	N. Zvereva (URS)	L. Meskhi (URS)	26 62 97
1987	N. Zvereva (URS)	J. Halard (FRA)	64 64
1988	B. Schultz (NED)	E. Derly (FRA)	76 61
1989	A. Strnadova (TCH)	M. McGrath (USA)	62 63
1990	A. Strnadova (TCH)	K. Sharpe (AUS)	62 64
1991	B. Rittner (GER)	E. Makarova (URS)	67 62 63
1992	C. Rubin (USA)	L. Courtois (BEL)	62 75
1993	N. Feber (BEL)	R. Grande (ITA)	76 16 62
1994	M. Hingis (SUI)	M. Jeon (KOR)	75 64
1995	A. Olsza (POL)	T. Tanasugarn (THA)	75 76
1996	A. Mauresmo (FRA)	M. Serna (ESP)	46 63 64
1997	C. Black (ZIM)	A. Rippner (USA)	63 75
1998	K. Srebotnik (SLO)	K. Clijsters (BEL)	76 63
1999	I. Tulyaganova (UZB)	L. Krasnoroutskaya (RUS)	76 64
2000	M. Salerni (ARG)	T. Perebiynis (UKR)	64 75
2001	A. Widjaja (INA)	D. Safina (RUS)	64 06 75
2002	V. Douchevina (RUS)	M. Sharapova (RUS)	46 61 62
2003	K. Flipkens (BEL)	A. Tchakvetadze (RUS)	64 36 63
2004	K. Bondarenko (UKR)	A. Ivanovic (SCG)	64 67 62
2005	A. Radwanska (POL)	T. Paszek (AUT)	63 64

	Boys' Doubles	**Girls' Doubles**
Year	**Champions**	**Champions**
1982	P. Cash/J. Frawley (AUS)	P. Barg/B. Herr (USA)
1983	M. Kratzmann/S. Youl (AUS)	P. Fendick (USA)/P. Hy (HKG)
1984	R. Brown/R. Weiss (USA)	C. Kuhlman/S. Rehe (USA)
1985	A. Moreno (MEX)/J. Yzaga (PER)	L. Field/J. Thompson (AUS)
1986	T. Carbonell (ESP)/P. Korda (TCH)	M. Jaggard/L. O'Neill (AUS)
1987	J. Stoltenberg/T. Woodbridge (AUS)	N. Medvedeva/N. Zvereva (URS)
1988	J. Stoltenberg/T. Woodbridge (AUS)	J. Faull/R. McQuillan (AUS)
1989	J. Palmer/J. Stark (USA)	J. Capriati/M. McGrath (USA)
1990	S. Lareau/S. Leblanc (CAN)	K. Habsudova/A. Strnadova (TCH)
1991	K. Alami (MAR)/G. Rusedski (CAN)	C. Barclay (AUS)/L. Zaltz (ISR)
1992	S. Baldas/S. Draper (AUS)	M. Avotins/L. McShea (AUS)
1993	S. Downs/J. Greenhalgh (NZL)	L. Courtois/N. Feber (BEL)
1994	B. Ellwood/M. Philippoussis (AUS)	E. DeVilliers (RSA)/E. Jelfs (GBR)
1995	M. Lee/J. Trotman (GBR)	C. Black (ZIM)/A. Olsza (POL)
1996	D. Bracciali (ITA)/J. Robichaud (CAN)	O. Barabanschikova (BLR)/A. Mauresmo (FRA)
1997	L. Horna (PER)/N. Massu (CHI)	C. Black (ZIM)/I. Selyutina (KAZ)
1998	R. Federer (SUI)/O. Rochus (BEL)	E. Dyrberg (DEN)/J. Kostanic (CRO)
1999	G. Coria/D. Nalbandian (ARG)	D. Bedanova (CZE)/M. Salerni (ARG)
2000	D. Coene/K. Vliegen (BEL)	I. Gaspar (ROM)/T. Perebiynis (UKR)
2001	F. Dancevic (CAN)/G. Lapentti (ECU)	G. Dulko (ARG)/A. Harkleroad (USA)
2002	F. Mergea/H. Tecau (ROM)	E. Clijsters (BEL)/B. Strycova (CZE)
2003	F. Mergea/H. Tecau (ROM)	A. Kleybanova (RUS)/S. Mirza (IND)
2004	B. Evans/S. Oudsema (USA)	V. Azarenka/V. Havartsova (BLR)
2005	J. Levine/M. Shabaz (USA)	V. Azarenka (BLR)/A. Szavay (HUN)

US Junior Championships

Boys' Singles

Year	Champion	Runner-up	Score
1973	B. Martin (USA)	C. Dowdeswell (ZIM)	46 63 63
1974	B. Martin (USA)	F. Taygan (USA)	64 62
1975	H. Schoenfield (USA)	C. Lewis (NZL)	64 63
1976	R. Ycaza (ECU)	J. Clerc (ARG)	64 57 60
1977	V. Winitsky (USA)	E. Teltscher (USA)	64 64
1978	P. Hjertquist (SWE)	S. Simonsson (SWE)	76 16 76
1979	S. Davis (USA)	J. Gunnarsson (SWE)	63 61
1980	M. Falberg (USA)	E. Wilborts (NED)	67 63 63
1981	T. Hogstedt (SWE)	H. Schwaier (FRG)	75 63
1982	P. Cash (AUS)	G. Forget (FRA)	63 63
1983	S. Edberg (SWE)	S. Youl (AUS)	62 64
1984	M. Kratzmann (AUS)	B. Becker (FRG)	63 76
1985	T. Trigueiro (USA)	J. Blake (USA)	62 63
1986	J. Sanchez (ESP)	F. Davin (ARG)	62 62
1987	D. Wheaton (USA)	A. Cherkasov (URS)	76 60
1988	N. Pereira (VEN)	N. Kulti (SWE)	61 62
1989	J. Stark (USA)	N. Kulti (SWE)	64 61
1990	A. Gaudenzi (ITA)	M. Tillstroem (SWE)	62 46 76
1991	L. Paes (IND)	K. Alami (MAR)	64 64
1992	B. Dunn (USA)	N. Behr (ISR)	75 62
1993	M. Rios (CHI)	S. Downs (NZL)	76 63
1994	S. Schalken (NED)	M. Tahiri (MAR)	62 76
1995	N. Kiefer (GER)	U. Seetzen (GER)	63 64
1996	D. Elsner (GER)	M. Hipfl (AUT)	63 62
1997	A. Di Pasquale (FRA)	W. Whitehouse (RSA)	67 64 61
1998	D. Nalbandian (ARG)	R. Federer (SUI)	63 75
1999	J. Nieminen (FIN)	K. Pless (DEN)	67 63 64
2000	A. Roddick (USA)	R. Ginepri (USA)	61 63
2001	G. Muller (LUX)	Y. Wang (TPE)	76 62
2002	R. Gasquet (FRA)	M. Baghdatis (CYP)	75 62
2003	J. Tsonga (FRA)	M. Baghdatis (CYP)	76 63
2004	A. Murray (GBR)	S. Stakhovsky (UKR)	64 62
2005	R. Sweeting (BAH)	J. Chardy (FRA)	64 64

Girls' Singles

Year	Champion	Runner-up	Score
1974	I. Kloss (RSA)	M. Jausovec (YUG)	64 63
1975	N. Chmyeva (URS)	G. Stevens (RSA)	67 62 62
1976	M. Kruger (RSA)	L. Romanov (ROM)	63 75
1977	C. Casabianca (ARG)	L. Antonoplis (USA)	63 26 62
1978	L. Siegel (USA)	I. Madruga (ARG)	64 64
1979	A. Moulton (USA)	M. Piatek (USA)	76 76
1980	S. Mascarin (USA)	K. Keil (USA)	63 64
1981	Z. Garrison (USA)	K. Gompert (USA)	60 63
1982	B. Herr (USA)	G. Rush (USA)	63 61
1983	E. Minter (AUS)	M. Werdel (USA)	63 75
1984	K. Maleeva (BUL)	N. Sodupe (USA)	61 62
1985	L. Garrone (ITA)	A. Holikova (TCH)	62 76
1986	E. Hakami (USA)	S. Stafford (USA)	62 61
1987	N. Zvereva (URS)	S. Birch (USA)	60 63
1988	C. Cunningham (USA)	R. McQuillan (AUS)	75 63
1989	J. Capriati (USA)	R. McQuillan (AUS)	62 63
1990	M. Maleeva (BUL)	N. Van Lottum (FRA)	75 62
1991	K. Habsudova (TCH)	A. Mall (USA)	61 63

Year	Champion	Runner-up	Score
1992	L. Davenport (USA)	J. Steven (USA)	62 62
1993	M. Bentivoglio (ITA)	Y. Yoshida (JPN)	76 64
1994	M. Tu (USA)	M. Hingis (SUI)	62 64
1995	T. Snyder (USA)	A. Ellwood (AUS)	64 46 62
1996	M. Lucic (CRO)	M. Weingartner (GER)	62 61
1997	C. Black (ZIM)	K. Chevalier (FRA)	67 61 63
1998	J. Dokic (AUS)	K. Srebotnik (SLO)	64 62
1999	L. Krasnoroutskaya (RUS)	N. Petrova (RUS)	63 62
2000	M. Salerni (ARG)	T. Perebiynis (UKR)	63 64
2001	M. Bartoli (FRA)	S. Kuznetsova (RUS)	46 63 64
2002	M. Kirilenko (RUS)	B. Strycova (CZE)	64 64
2003	K. Flipkens (BEL)	M. Krajicek (NED)	63 75
2004	M. Krajicek (NED)	J. Kirkland (USA)	61 61
2005	V. Azarenka (BLR)	A. Glatch (USA)	63 64

	Boys' Doubles	**Girls' Doubles**
Year	**Champions**	**Champions**
1982	J. Canter/M. Kures (USA)	P. Barg/B. Herr (USA)
1983	M. Kratzmann/S. Youl (AUS)	A. Hulbert (USA)/B. Randall (AUS)
1984	L. Lavalle (MEX)/M. Nastase (ROM)	M. Paz/G. Sabatini (ARG)
1985	J. Blake/D. Yates (USA)	A. Holikova/R. Zrubakova (TCH)
1986	T. Carbonell/J. Sanchez (ESP)	J. Novotna/R. Zrubakova (TCH)
1987	G. Ivanisevic (YUG)/D. Nargiso (ITA)	M. McGrath/K. Po (USA)
1988	J. Stark/J. Yancey (USA)	M. McGrath/K. Po (USA)
1989	W. Ferreira/G. Stafford (RSA)	J. Capriati/M. McGrath (USA)
1990	M. Renstrom/M. Tillstrom (SWE)	K. Godridge/N. Pratt (AUS)
1991	K. Alami (MAR)/J. De Jager (USA)	K. Godridge/K. Sharpe (AUS)
1992	J. Jackson/E. Taino (USA)	L. Davenport/N. London (USA)
1993	N. Godwin/G. Williams (RSA)	N. London/J. Steven (USA)
1994	B. Ellwood (AUS)/N. Lapentti (ECU)	S. De Beer (RSA)/C. Reuter (NED)
1995	J. Lee (KOR)/J. Robichaud (CAN)	C. Morariu (USA)/L. Varmuzova (CZE)
1996	B. Bryan/M. Bryan (USA)	S. De Beer/J. Steck (RSA)
1997	F. Gonzalez/N. Massu (CHI)	M. Irvin/A. Stevenson (USA)
1998	K. Hippensteel/D. Martin (USA)	K. Clijsters (BEL)/E. Dyrberg (DEN)
1999	J. Benneteau/N. Mahut (FRA)	D. Bedanova (CZE)/I. Tulyaganova (UZB)
2000	L. Childs/J. Nelson (GBR)	G. Dulko/M. Salerni (ARG)
2001	T. Berdych (CZE)/S. Bohli (SUI)	G. Fokina/S. Kuznetsova (RUS)
2002	M. Koning/B. Van Der Valk (NED)	E. Clijsters/K. Flipkens (BEL)
2003 not played		
2004	B. Evans/S. Oudsema (USA)	M. Erakovic (NZL)/M. Krajicek (NED)
2005	A. Clayton/D. Young (USA)	N. Frankova (CZE)/A. Kleybanova (RUS)

World Junior Tennis

International Team Competition for players aged 14 and under, launched by the ITF in 1991. Sixteen boys' teams and 16 girls' teams qualify for a place in the final, held at one venue over a week.

Boys' Championships

1991 Final: Spain d. Italy 2-1, Yamanakako, Japan: J. Saiz (ESP) d. P. Tabini (ITA) 62 61; A. Martin (ESP) d. C. Zoppi (ITA) 62 76; A. Ciceroni/P. Tabini (ITA) d. A. Martin/J. Vicente (ESP) 57 64 86.

1992 Final: Austria d. USA 2-1, Yamanakako, Japan: C. Trimmel (AUT) d. K. Brill (USA) 46 62 62; M. Hipfl (AUT) d. G. Abrams (USA) 64 60; G. Abrams/B. Bryan (USA) d. M. Hipfl/C. Trimmel (AUT) 61 63.

1993 Final: France d. Slovenia 2-1, Yamanakako, Japan: J. Lisnard (FRA) d. A. Krasevec (SLO) 76 63; A. Di Pasquale (FRA) d. M. Gregorc (SLO) 61 61; M. Gregorc/A. Krasevec (SLO) d. A. Di Pasquale/V. Lavergne (FRA) 75 75.

1994 Final: Italy d. Belgium 2-1, Yamanakako, Japan: O. Rochus (BEL) d. N. Fracassi (ITA) 76 36 63; F. Luzzi (ITA) d. X. Malisse (BEL) 63 76; N. Fracassi/F. Luzzi (ITA) d. X. Malisse/O. Rochus (BEL) 64 16 63.

1995 Final: Great Britain d. Germany 3-0, Yamanakako, Japan: M. Hilton (GBR) d. P. Hammer (GER) 63 46 64; S. Dickson (GBR) d. B. Bachert (GER) 75 62; S. Dickson/A. Mackin (GBR) d. B. Bachert/R. Neurohr (GER) 75 61.

1996 Final: Argentina d. Sweden 3-0, Nagoya, Japan: G. Coria (ARG) d. F. Prpic (SWE) 61 61; D. Nalbandian (ARG) d. J. Johansson (SWE) 63 63; G. Coria/A. Pastorino (ARG) d. J. Johansson/F. Prpic (SWE) 61 63.

1997 Final: South Africa d. Czech Republic 2-1, Nagoya, Japan: A. Anderson (RSA) d. M. Kokta (CZE) 75 64; D. Stegmann (RSA) d. J. Masik (CZE) 63 60; D. Karol/J. Masik (CZE) d. A. Anderson/R. Blair (RSA) 61 60.

1998 Final: Austria d. Argentina 3-0, Nagoya, Japan: J. Ager (AUT) d. J. Monaco (ARG) 64 64; S. Wiespeiner (AUT) d. B. Dabul (ARG) 46 64 61; J. Ager/C. Polessnig (AUT) d. B. Dabul/J. Ottabiani (ARG) 64 75.

1999 Final: France d. Chile 2-1, Prostejov, Czech Republic: J. Tsonga (FRA) d. G. Hormazabal (CHI) 64 63; R. Gasquet (FRA) d. J. Aguilar (CHI) 76 36 64; J. Aguilar/G. Hormazabal (CHI) d. J. Robin/J. Tsonga (FRA) 75 63.

2000 Final: Spain d. Russia 3-0, Prostejov, Czech Republic: B. Salva (ESP) d. A. Sitak (RUS) 63 63; R. Nadal (ESP) d. N. Soloviev (RUS) 63 62; M. Granollers/R. Nadal (ESP) d. D. Matsoukevitch/A. Sitak (RUS) 46 61 64.

2001 Final: Germany d. Yugoslavia 2-0, Prostejov, Czech Republic: J. Schottler (GER) d. D. Bejtulahi (YUG) 36 61 63; A. Thron (GER) d. N. Djokovic (YUG) 64 06 62; doubles not played.

2002 Final: USA d. Spain 2-1, Prostejov, Czech Republic: J. Garrapiz (ESP) d. D. Arnould (USA) 62 63; M. Fugate (USA) d. R. Bautista (ESP) 61 64; D. Arnould/M. Fugate (USA) d. R. Bautista/J. Ramos (ESP) 64 63.

2003 Final: USA d. Japan 2-1, Prostejov, Czech Republic: K. Nishikori (JPN) d. L. Rosenberg (USA) 76 26 62; D. Young (USA) d. F. Kita (JPN) 62 63; L. Rosenberg/D. Young (USA) d. F. Kita/K. Nishikori (JPN) 61 61.

2004 Final: Great Britain d. Czech Republic 2-0, Prostejov, Czech Republic: L. Barnes (GBR) d. J. Trocil (CZE) 63 75; D. Cox (GBR) d. E. Rehola (CZE) 75 76; doubles not played.

2005 Final: France d. Argentina 2-1, Prostejov, Czech Republic: G. Andreozzi (ARG) d. C. Belot (FRA) 62 64; A. Puget (FRA) d. J. Vazquez (ARG) 64 75; C. Belot/A. Puget (FRA) d. N. Pastor/J. Vazquez (ARG) 63 76.

Girls' Championships

1991 Final: Czechoslovakia d. Australia 3-0, Yamanakako, Japan: A. Havrlikova (TCH) d. A. Venkatesan (AUS) 61 62; L. Cenkova (TCH) d. A. Ellwood (AUS) 75 62; L. Cenkova/A. Havrlikova (TCH) d. A. Ellwood/E. Knox (AUS) 62 76.

1992 Final: USA d. Australia 3-0, Yamanakako, Japan: A. Basica (USA) d. R. Reid (AUS) 36 76 64; M. Tu (USA) d. A. Ellwood (AUS) 64 64; A. Augustus/A. Basica (USA) d. S. Drake-Brockman/R. Reid (AUS) 62 75.

1993 Final: Germany d. USA 2-1, Yamanakako, Japan: S. Halsell (USA) d. C. Christian (GER) 60 63; S. Klosel (GER) d. K. Gates (USA) 64 76; C. Christian/S. Klosel (GER) d. K. Gates/S. Halsell (USA) 36 63 75.

1994 Final: Germany d. Czech Republic 2-1, Yamanakako, Japan: J. Wohr (GER) d. J. Schonfeldova (CZE) 75 60; S. Kovacic (GER) d. M. Pastikova (CZE) 62 75; M. Pastikova/J. Schonfeldova (CZE) d. S. Losel/Wohr (GER) 64 61.

1995 Final: Slovenia d. Hungary 2-1, Yamanakako, Japan: T. Pisnik (SLO) d. S. Szegedi (HUN) 76 63; Z. Gubacsi (HUN) d. K. Srebotnik (SLO) 46 63 64; T. Pisnik/K. Srebotnik (SLO) d. Z. Gubacsi/I. Szalai (HUN) 63 63.

1996 Final: Slovak Republic d. Great Britain 3-0, Nagoya, Japan: S. Hrozenska (SVK) d. S. Gregg (GBR) 61 62; K. Basternakova (SVK) d. H. Collin (GBR) 63 61; S. Hrozenska/Z. Kucova (SVK) d. H. Collin/H. Reesby (GBR) 64 62.

1997 Final: Russia d. Slovak Republic 2-1, Nagoya, Japan: L. Krasnoroutskaya (RUS) d. D. Hantuchova (SVK) 62 64; E. Bovina (RUS) d. M. Babakova (SVK) 64 61; D. Hantuchova/L. Kurhajcova (SVK) d. G. Fokina/L. Krasnoroutskaya (RUS) 62 26 62.

1998 Final: Czech Republic d. Russia 2-1, Nagoya, Japan: E. Birnerova (CZE) d. V. Zvonareva (RUS) 63 64; P. Cetkovska (CZE) d. G. Fokina (RUS) 62 26 64; E. Birnerova/P. Cetkovska (CZE) d. G. Fokina/R. Gourevitch (RUS) 75 16 63.

1999 Final: Russia d. Slovak Republic 2-1, Prostejov, Czech Republic: D. Safina (RUS) d. M. Zivcicova (SVK) 63 61; A. Bastrikova (RUS) d. K. Kachlikova (SVK) 63 62; L. Smolenakova/M. Zivcicova (SVK) d. A. Bastrikova/N. Brattchikova (RUS) 63 64.

2000 Final: Russia d. Czech Republic 3-0, Prostejov, Czech Republic: D. Tchemarda (RUS) d. L. Safarova (CZE) 76 62; V. Douchevina (RUS) d. B. Strycova (CZE) 46 61 62; I. Kotkina/D. Tchemarda (RUS) d. N. Freislerova/L. Safarova (CZE) 64 60.

2001 Final: Czech Republic d. Russia 2-1, Prostejov, Czech Republic: A. Tchakvetadze (RUS) d. R. Kucerkova (CZE) 61 60; L. Safarova (CZE) d. M. Kirilenko (RUS) 61 75; R. Kucerkova/L. Safarova (CZE) d. M. Kirilenko/E. Kiriyanova (RUS) 64 64.

2002 Final: Netherlands d. Poland 3-0, Prostejov, Czech Republic: B. Schoofs (NED) d. M. Lesniak (POL) 75 63; M. Krajicek (NED) d. M. Kiszczynska (POL) 61 61; M. Krajicek/B. Schoofs (NED) d. M. Kiszczynska/M. Lesniak (POL) 64 36 62.

2003 Final: Czech Republic d. Russia 2-1, Prostejov, Czech Republic: R. Kulikova (RUS) d. S. Novakova (CZE) 62 61; N. Vaidisova (CZE) d. E. Rodina (RUS) 61 61; E. Kadlecova/N. Vaidisova (CZE) d. R. Kulikova/E. Rodina (RUS) 64 76.

2004 Final: Belarus d. Austria 2-1, Prostejov, Czech Republic: M. Klaffner (AUT) d. I. Bohush (BLR) 76 75; K. Milevskaya (BLR) d. N. Hofmanova (AUT) 61 75; I. Bohush/K. Milevskaya (BLR) d. N. Hofmanova/M. Klaffner (AUT) 60 61.

2005 Final: Russia d. Japan 3-0, Prostejov, Czech Republic: E. Kulikova (RUS) d. C. Takayama (JPN) 61 76; A. Pavlyuchenkova (RUS) d. K. Nara (JPN) 60 61; A. Pavlyuchenkova/M. Sirotkina (RUS) d. M. Doi/K. Nara (JPN) 62 62.

Junior Davis Cup

International Team Competition for boys aged 16 and under. Launched by the ITF in 1985 as the World Youth Cup, renamed the Junior Davis Cup in 2002. Sixteen boys' teams qualify for a place in the final, held at one venue over a week.

1985 Final: Australia d. USA 2-1, Kobe, Japan: F. Montana (USA) d. R. Fromberg (AUS) 62 62; S. Barr (AUS) d. J. Falbo (USA) 64 64; S. Barr/J. Stoltenberg (AUS) d. J. Falbo/F. Montana (USA) 46 76 75.

1986 Final: Australia d. USA 2-1, Tokyo, Japan: M. Chang (USA) d. R. Fromberg (AUS) 64 64; J. Stoltenberg (AUS) d. J. Courier (USA) 62 64; J. Stoltenberg/T. Woodbridge (AUS) d. J. Courier/D. Kass (USA) 76 62.

1987 Final: Australia d. Netherlands 3-0, Freiburg, West Germany: J. Anderson (AUS) d. F. Wibier (NED) 60 61; T. Woodbridge (AUS) d. P. Dogger (NED) 75 36 62; J. Morgan/T. Woodbridge (AUS) d. P. Dogger/F. Wibier (NED) 63 62.

Junior Davis Cup (continued)

1988 Final: Czechoslovakia d. USA 2-1, Perth, Australia: J. Kodes (TCH) d. R. Leach (USA) 76 62; M. Damm (TCH) d. B. MacPhie (USA) 62 67 64; W. Bull/R. Leach (USA) d. M. Damm/L. Hovorka (TCH) 64 64.

1989 Final: West Germany d. Czechoslovakia 2-1, Asuncion, Paraguay: G. Paul (FRG) d. P. Gazda (TCH) 64 64; L. Thomas (TCH) d. S. Gessner (FRG) 75 75; D. Prinosil/P. Prinosil (FRG) d. P. Gazda/L. Thomas (TCH) 75 61.

1990 Final: USSR d. Australia 2-1, Rotterdam, Netherlands: D. Tomashevich (URS) d. T. Vasiliadis (AUS) 63 62; G. Doyle (AUS) d. A. Medvedev (URS) 06 64 75; Y. Kafelnikov/A. Medvedev (URS) d. G. Doyle/B. Sceney (AUS) 76 63.

1991 Final: Spain d. Czechoslovakia 2-1, Barcelona, Spain: G. Corrales (ESP) d. D. Skoch (TCH) 75 75; F. Kascak (TCH) d. A. Costa (ESP) 64 75; G. Corrales/A. Costa (ESP) d. F. Kascak/D. Skoch (TCH) 64 62.

1992 Final: France d. Germany 2-1, Castelldefels, Spain: R. Nicklisch (GER) d. N. Escude (FRA) 26 63 63; M. Boye (FRA) d. A. Nickel (GER) 75 06 63; M. Boye/N. Escude (FRA) d. A. Nickel/R. Nicklisch (GER) 67 60 63.

1993 Final: France d. New Zealand 2-1, Wellington, New Zealand: T. Susnjak (NZL) d. O. Mutis (FRA) 61 16 63; J. Bachelot (FRA) d. S. Clark (NZL) 46 64 64; O. Mutis/J. Potron (FRA) d. S. Clark/M. Nielsen (NZL) 63 64.

1994 Final: Netherlands d. Austria 2-1, Tucson, AZ, USA: C. Trimmel (AUT) d. P. Wessels (NED) 46 63 75; R. Sluiter (NED) d. M. Hipfl (AUT) 76 61; R. Sluiter/P. Wessels (NED) d. M. Hipfl/C. Trimmel (AUT) 63 64.

1995 Final: Germany d. Czech Republic 3-0, Essen, Germany: T. Messmer (GER) d. P. Kralert (CZE) 63 75; D. Elsner (GER) d. M. Tabara (CZE) 63 64; D. Elsner/T. Zivnicek (GER) d. P. Kralert/P. Riha (CZE) 67 64 64.

1996 Final: France d. Australia 2-1, Zurich, Switzerland: J. Haehnel (FRA) d. N. Healey (AUS) 64 62; J. Jeanpierre (FRA) d. L. Hewitt (AUS) 63 75; N. Healey/L. Hewitt (AUS) d. J. Haehnel/O. Patience (FRA) 75 46 76.

1997 Final: Czech Republic d. Venezuela 2-0, Vancouver, Canada: J. Levinsky (CZE) d. E. Nastari (VEN) 60 62; L. Chramosta (CZE) d. J. De Armas (VEN) 76 62; doubles not played.

1998 Final: Spain d. Croatia 2-1, Cuneo, Italy: M. Lopez (ESP) d. R. Karanusic (CRO) 63 36 36; T. Robredo (ESP) d. M. Radic (CRO) 64 64; M. Lopez/T. Robredo (ESP) d. R. Karanusic/M. Radic (CRO) 64 62.

1999 Final: USA d. Croatia 3-0, Perth, Australia: R. Redondo (USA) d. I. Stelko (CRO) 76 64; A. Bogomolov (USA) d. M. Ancic (USA) 76 63; R. Redondo/T. Rettenmaier (USA) d. M. Ancic/T. Peric (CRO) 76 76.

2000 Final: Australia d. Austria 2-0, Hiroshima, Japan: R. Henry (AUS) d. S. Wiespeiner (AUT) 57 64 86; T. Reid (AUS) d. J. Ager (AUT) 64 75; R. Henry/T. Reid (AUS) d. J. Ager/S. Wiespeiner (AUT); doubles not played.

2001 Final: Chile d. Germany 3-0, Santiago, Chile: G. Hormazabal (CHI) d. S. Klor (GER) 62 64; J. Aguilar (CHI) d. M. Zimmermann (GER) 60 61; G. Hormazabal/C. Rios (CHI) d. B. Koch/M. Zimmermann (GER) 62 16 76.

2002 Final: Spain d. USA 3-0, La Baule, France: T. Salva (ESP) d. P. Simmonds (USA) 62 63; R. Nadal (ESP) d. B. Evans (USA) 62 62; M. Granollers/R. Nadal (ESP) d. S. Oudsema/P. Simmonds (USA) 76 63.

2003 Final: Germany d. France 2-1, Essen, Germany: M. Dehaine (FRA) d. M. Bachinger (GER) 76 26 63; M. Zverev (GER) d. J. Chardy (FRA) 63 64; M. Bachinger/M. Zverev (GER) d. J. Chardy/J. Drean (FRA) 62 61.

2004 Final: Spain d. Czech Republic 2-1, Barcelona, Spain: M. Navratil (CZE) d. R. Bautista (ESP) 61 64; P. Riba (ESP) d. D. Lojda (CZE) 61 64; R. Bautista/P. Riba (ESP) d. D. Lojda/F. Zeman (CZE) 63 64.

2005 Final: France d. Czech Republic 2-0, Barcelona, Spain: J. Inzerillo (FRA) d. R. Jebavy (CZE) 57 64 61; K. Botti (FRA) d. M. Konecny (CZE) 46 63 62; Doubles not played.

Junior Fed Cup

International Team Competition for girls aged 16 and under. Launched by the ITF in 1985 as the World Youth Cup, renamed the Junior Fed Cup in 2002. Sixteen girls' teams qualify for a place in the final, held at one venue over a week.

1985 Final: Czechoslovakia d. Australia 3-0, Kobe, Japan: J. Pospisilova (TCH) d. S. McCann (AUS) 64 64; R. Zrubakova (TCH) d. N. Provis (AUS) 76 75; J. Pospisilova/R. Zrubakova (TCH) d. W. Frazer/N. Provis (AUS) 75 64.

1986 Final: Belgium d. Czechoslovakia 2-1, Tokyo, Japan: S. Wasserman (BEL) d. P. Langrova (TCH) 64 75; A. Devries (BEL) d. R. Zrubakova (TCH) 63 64; P. Langrova/R. Zrubakova (TCH) d. A. Devries/C. Neuprez (BEL) 64 62.

1987 Final: Australia d. USSR 2-1, Freiburg, West Germany: R. McQuillan (AUS) d. E. Brioukhovets (URS) 36 62 63; N. Medvedeva (URS) d. J. Faull (AUS) 46 62 62; J. Faull/R. McQuillan (AUS) d. E. Brioukhovets/N. Medvedeva (URS) 63 61.

1988 Final: Australia d. Argentina 3-0, Perth, Australia: K. Guse (AUS) d. F. Haumuller (ARG) 76 64; L. Guse (AUS) d. C. Tessi (ARG) 76 16 62; K. Guse/K. Sharpe (AUS) d. I. Gorrochategui/C. Tessi (ARG) 60 62.

1989 Final: West Germany d. Czechoslovakia 2-1, Asuncion, Paraguay: M. Skulj-Zivec (FRG) d. K. Matouskova (TCH) 60 75; A. Huber (FRG) d. K. Habsudova (TCH) 60 63; K. Habsudova/P. Kucova (TCH) d. K. Duell/M. Skulj-Zivec (FRG) 63 60.

1990 Final: Netherlands d. USSR 2-1, Rotterdam, Netherlands: P. Kamstra (NED) d. I. Sukhova (URS) 61 76; T. Ignatieva (URS) d. L. Niemantsverdriet (NED) 60 16 64; P. Kamstra/L. Niemantsverdriet (NED) d. T. Ignatieva/I. Sukhova (URS) 63 46 61.

1991 Final: Germany d. Paraguay 2-1, Barcelona, Spain: L. Schaerer (PAR) d. H. Rusch (GER) 76 63; M. Kochta (GER) d. R. De Los Rios (PAR) 63 61; K. Freye/M. Kochta (GER) d. R. De Los Rios/L. Schaerer (PAR) 57 63 63.

1992 Final: Belgium d. Argentina 3-0, Castelldefels, Spain: L. Courtois (BEL) d. L. Montalvo (ARG) 61 63; N. Feber (BEL) d. M. Reynares (ARG) 16 64 61; L. Courtois/S. Deville (BEL) d. M. Diaz Oliva/L. Montalvo (ARG) 16 75 64.

1993 Final: Australia d. USA 2-1, Wellington, New Zealand: S. Drake-Brockman (AUS) d. S. Nickitas (USA) 62 57 62; A. Ellwood (AUS) d. A. Basica (USA) 62 61; C. Moros/S. Nickitas (USA) d. A. Ellwood/J. Richardson (AUS) 26 75 60.

1994 Final: South Africa d. France 3-0, Tucson, AZ, USA: J. Steck (RSA) d. A. Cocheteux (FRA) 75 63; S. De Beer (RSA) d. A. Castera (FRA) 64 63; doubles not played (walkover for South Africa).

1995 Final: France d. Germany 2-1, Essen, Germany: S. Kovacic (GER) d. K. Jagieniak (FRA) 64 63; A. Mauresmo (FRA) d. S. Klosel (GER) 60 63; K. Chevalier/A. Mauresmo (FRA) d. C. Christian/S. Kovacic (GER) 63 75.

1996 Final: Slovenia d. Germany 2-1, Zurich, Switzerland: K. Srebotnik (SLO) d. S. Kovacic (GER) 61 63; J. Wohr (GER) d. P. Rampre (SLO) 62 61; P. Rampre/K. Srebotnik (SLO) d. S. Kovacic/J. Wohr (GER) 61 64.

1997 Final: Russia d. France 2-0, Vancouver, Canada: A. Myskina (RUS) d. S. Schoeffel (FRA) 63 26 86; E. Dementieva (RUS) d. S. Rizzi (FRA) 62 46 64; doubles not played.

1998 Final: Italy d. Slovak Republic 2-1, Cuneo, Italy: R. Vinci (ITA) d. S. Hrozenska (SLO) 62 26 68; D. Hantuchova (SLO) d. M. Camerin (ITA) 64 62; F. Pennetta/R. Vinci (ITA) d. D. Hantuchova/S. Hrozenska (SLO) 64 61.

1999 Final: Argentina d. Slovak Republic 2-1, Perth, Australia: L. Dlhopolcova (SVK) d. G. Dulko (ARG) 63 63; M. Salerni (ARG) d. L. Kurhajcova (SVK) 63 64; E. Chialvo/M. Salerni (ARG) d. L. Dlhopolcova/L. Kurhajcova (SVK) 63 62.

2000 Final: Czech Republic d. Hungary 2-1, Hiroshima, Japan: E. Birnerova (CZE) d. D. Magas (HUN) 76 63; V. Nemeth (HUN) d. P. Cetkovska (CZE) 75 46 86; P. Cetkovska/E. Janaskova (CZE) d. D. Magas/V. Nemeth (HUN) 75 57 61.

2001 Final: Czech Republic d. Poland 3-0, Santiago, Chile: P. Cetkovska (CZE) d. O. Brozda (POL) 61 63; B. Strycova (CZE) d. M. Domachowska (POL) 62 62; P. Cetkovska/L. Safarova (CZE) d. M. Domachowska/A. Rosolska (POL) 63 62.

2002 Final: Belarus d. Czech Republic 3-0, La Baule, France: D. Kustava (BLR) d. A. Hlavackova (CZE) 63 61; A. Yakimava (BLR) d. K. Bohmova (CZE) 63 64; D. Kustava/A. Yakimava (BLR) d. K. Bohmova/A. Hlavackova (CZE) 62 63.

2003 Final: Netherlands d. Canada 2-1, Essen, Germany: E. Shulaeva (CAN) d. B. Schoofs (NED) 61 63; M. Krajicek (NED) d. A. Wozniak (POL) 60 75; M. Krajicek/B. Schoofs (NED) d. A. Wozniak/K. Zoricic (POL) 61 64.

2004 Final: Argentina d. Canada 2-0, Barcelona, Spain: B. Jozami (ARG) d. V. Tetreault (CAN) 61 63; F. Molinero (ARG) d. S. Fichman (CAN) 36 64 62; doubles not played.

2005 Final: Poland d. France 2-0, Barcelona, Spain: U. Radwanska (POL) d. E. Guisard (FRA) 62 61; A. Radwanska (POL) d. A. Cornet (FRA) 76 63; Doubles not played.

ITF Sunshine Cup

International Team Competition for boys aged 18 and under. Established in 1958, the event was originally known as the Orange Bowl Junior Cup. The ITF took over its organisation in 1997.

Winning nations 1958-1990

1958 Brazil	1963 Mexico	1968 Australia	1973 USA	1978 Spain	1981 Sweden	1986 Spain
1959 Spain	1964 Australia	1969 USA	1974 USA	1979 USA	1982 France	1987 USSR
1960 USA	1965 USA	1970 USA	1975 USA	1980 Sweden	1983 Spain	1988 France
1961 USA	1966 USA	1971 Spain	1976 USA	1980 Sweden	1984 USA	1989 Canada
1962 USA	1967 USA	1972 USA	1977 France	1981 Sweden	1985 Argentina	1990 USSR

1991 Final: Spain d. France 2-1, Weston, FL, USA: S. Matheu (FRA) d. J. Martinez (ESP) 64 16 63; A. Berasategui (ESP) d. L. Rioux (FRA) 64 76; A. Berasategui/J. Martinez (ESP) d. S. Matheu/L. Rioux (FRA) 62 76.

1992 Final: Spain d. USA 2-0, Delray Beach, FL, USA: A. Costa (ESP) d. V. Spadea (USA) 63 75; F. Mantilla (ESP) d. J. Jackson (USA) 61 63; doubles not played.

1993 Final: Brazil d. Chile 2-1, Delray Beach, FL, USA: M. Carlsson (BRA) d. J. Gamonal (CHI) 63 63; M. Rios (CHI) d. G. Kuerten (BRA) 61 64; M. Carlsson/G. Kuerten (BRA) d. J. Gamonal/M. Rios (CHI) 62 67 64.

1994 Final: Argentina d. Spain 2-1, Delray Beach, FL, USA: J. Diaz (ESP) d. M. Zabaleta (ARG) 63 61; F. Browne (ARG) d. C. Moya (ESP) 64 16 64; F. Browne/G. Cavallaro (ARG) d. C. Moya/F. Vicente (ESP) 46 76 61.

1995 Final: USA d. Argentina 2-1, Delray Beach, FL, USA: R. Wolters (USA) d. M. Puerta (ARG) 63 26 62; M. Zabaleta (ARG) d. J. Gimelstob (USA) 63 61; J. Gimelstob/R. Wolters (USA) d. G. Canas/M. Zabaleta (ARG) 75 46 76.

1996 Final: France d. Germany 2-0, Delray Beach, FL, USA: O. Mutis (FRA) d. T. Messmer (GER) 76 62; S. Grosjean (FRA) d. D. Elsner (GER) 61 62; doubles not played.

1997 Final: France d. Germany 2-1, Delray Beach, FL, USA: J. Jean-Pierre (FRA) d. T. Zivnicek (GER) 64 67 64; A. Di Pasquale (FRA) d. B. Phau (GER) 60 76; T. Messmer/B. Phau (GER) d. A. Di Pasquale/J. Jean-Pierre (FRA) w/o.

1998 Final: France d. Russia 3-0, Key Biscayne, FL, USA: J. Haehnel (FRA) d. I. Kounitsyn (RUS) 64 64; J. Jean-Pierre (FRA) d. K. Ivanov-Smolenski (RUS) 61 75; J. Haehnel/J. Jean-Pierre (FRA) d. A. Derepasko/I. Kounitsyn (RUS) 64 63.

1999 Final: France d. Argentina 2-0, Key Biscayne, FL, USA: J. Benneteau (FRA) d. J. Acasuso (ARG) 62 64; N. Mahut (FRA) d. G. Coria (ARG) 76 26 62; doubles not played.

2000 Final: USA d. Spain 2-0, Key Biscayne, FL, USA: R. Ginepri (USA) d. C. Cuadrado (ESP) 61 62; A. Roddick (USA) d. M. Lopez (ESP) 64 67 64; doubles not played.

2001 Final: Russia d. Argentina 2-0, Key Biscayne, FL, USA: I. Andreev (RUS) d. L. Vitullo (ARG) 36 62 40 ret; P. Ivanov (RUS) d. B. Dabul (ARG) 61 76(4); doubles not played.

2002–2005: Competition not played.

ITF Connolly Continental Cup

International Team Competition for girls aged 18 and under. Established in 1976, the event was originally known as the Maureen Connolly Brinker Continental Players Cup. The ITF took over its running in 1997.

Winning nations 1976-1990

1976 USA	1979 Peru	1982 Italy	1985 Argentina	1988 Argentina
1977 USA	1980 USA	1983 USA	1986 Czechoslovakia	1989 USA
1978 USA	1981 USA	1984 USA	1987 USSR	1990 Spain

1991 Final: USA d. Spain 2-0, Plantation, FL, USA: P. Nelson (USA) d. L. Bitter (NED) 62 75; L. Davenport (USA) d. L. Niemantsverdriet (NED) 62 64; doubles not played.

1992 Final: USA d. Italy 2-1, Delray Beach, FL, USA: J. Stevens (USA) d. R. Grande (ITA) 64 36 62; F. Bentivoglio (ITA) d. N. London (USA) 63 63; N. London/J. Stevens (USA) d. F. Bentivoglio/R. Grande (ITA) 76 60.

1993 Final: Argentina d. Poland 3-0, Delray Beach, FL, USA: M. Diaz-Oliva (ARG) d. K. Bulat (POL) 61 61; L. Montalvo (ARG) d. K. Malec (POL) 63 62; M. Landa/L. Montalvo d. M. Grzybowska/K. Malec (POL) 85.

1994 Final: Italy d. Hungary 2-1, Delray Beach, FL, USA: K. Nagy (HUN) d. A. Canepa (ITA) 62 62; F. Lubiani (ITA) d. P. Mandula (HUN) 46 62 63; A. Canepa/F. Lubiani (ITA) d. P. Mandula/K. Marosi (HUN) 76 62.

1995 Final: Russia d. Spain 2-1, Boca Raton, FL, USA: A. Alcazar (ESP) d. E. Koulkikovskaia (RUS) 64 63; A. Kournikova (RUS) d. P. Hermida (ESP) 75 64; E. Koulkikovskaia/A. Kournikova (RUS) d. A. Alcazar/P. Hermida (ESP) 64 64.

1996 Final: Spain d. USA 3-0, Boca Raton, FL, USA: L. Pena (ESP) d. L. Osterloh (USA) 57 63 76; A. Alcazar (ESP) d. C. Morariu (USA) 76 63; A. Alcazar/L. Pena (ESP) d. L. Osterloh/T. Singian (USA) 60 ret.

1997 Final: Slovenia d. Russia 2-1, Delray Beach, FL, USA: T. Pisnik (SLO) d. E. Dementieva (RUS) 63 75; K. Srebotnik (SLO) d. E. Syssoeva (RUS) 36 64 63; E. Dementieva/A. Myskina (RUS) d. M. Matevzic/T. Pisnik (SLO) 64 61.

1998 Final: Russia d. Spain 2-1, Key Biscayne, FL, USA: M. Marrero (ESP) d. A. Myskina (RUS) 36 76 62; E. Dementieva (RUS) d. L. Dominguez (ESP) 76 76; E. Dementieva/A. Myskina (RUS) d. M. Marrero/M. Martinez (ESP) 36 63 61.

1999 Final: Russia d. Spain 2-0, Key Biscayne, FL, USA: N. Petrova (RUS) d. M. Martinez (ESP) 64 61; L. Krasnoroutskaia (RUS) d. A. Medina (ESP) 76 63; doubles not played.

2000 Final: USA d. Estonia 2-1, Key Biscayne, FL, USA: A. Harkleroad (USA) d. M. Ani (EST) 64 76; K. Kanepi (EST) d. M. Middleton (USA) 62 64; A. Harkleroad/B. Mattek (USA) d. M. Ani/K. Kanepi (EST) 76 64.

2001 Final: Russia d. Croatia 2-0, Key Biscayne, FL, USA: V. Zvonareva (RUS) d. K. Sprem (CRO) 75 62; S. Kuznetsova (RUS) d. M. Mezak (CRO) 36 75 75; doubles not played.

2002–2005: Competition not played.

Wheelchair Tennis Masters

The premier event on the ITF's wheelchair tennis circuit, this tournament invites only the top eight men and women, and four quad players to participate. Played every year in Eindhoven, Netherlands, until 1999, the event moved to Amersfoort, Netherlands, in 2000, and a doubles tournament was added.

Singles

Year	Event	Champion	Runner-up	Score
1994	Men	R. Snow (USA)	S. Welch (USA)	62 64
	Women	M. Kalkman (NED)	C. Vandierendonck (NED)	61 64
1995	Men	L. Giammartini (FRA)	R. Snow (USA)	75 46 64
	Women	M. Kalkman (NED)	C. Vandierendonck (NED)	61 62
1996	Men	S. Welch (USA)	L. Giammartini (FRA)	64 26 64
	Women	C. Vandierendonck (NED)	D. Di Toro (AUS)	64 63
1997	Men	K. Schrameyer (GER)	S. Welch (USA)	46 75 60
	Women	M. Smit (NED)	M. Kalkman (NED)	63 46 75
1998	Men	R. Molier (NED)	L. Giammartini (FRA)	75 75
	Women	E. Vergeer (NED)	M. Smit (NED)	60 76
1999	Men	R. Ammerlaan (NED)	M. Legner (AUT)	75 61
	Women	E. Vergeer (NED)	M. Smit (NED)	60 61
2000	Men	R. Ammerlaan (NED)	R. Molier (NED)	76 61
	Women	E. Vergeer (NED)	D. Van Marum (NED)	61 63
2001	Men	R. Molier (NED)	R. Ammerlaan (NED)	60 67 61
	Women	E. Vergeer (NED)	M. Smit (NED)	62 63
2002	Men	D. Hall (AUS)	R. Ammerlaan (NED)	26 63 64
	Women	E. Vergeer (NED)	S. Peters (NED)	46 64 76
2003	Men	R. Ammerlaan (NED)	S. Welch (USA)	63 64
	Women	E. Vergeer (NED)	S. Walraven (NED)	61 63
2004	Men	D. Hall (AUS)	M. Jeremiasz (FRA)	62 64
	Women	E. Vergeer (NED)	J. Griffioen (NED)	62 60
	Quad	D. Wagner (USA)	B. Van Erp (NED)	63 62
2005	Men	R. Ammerlaan (NED)	M. Jeremiasz (FRA)	62 63
	Women	E. Vergeer (NED)	F. Gravellier (FRA)	64 62
	Quad	D. Wagner (USA)	N. Taylor (USA)	61 62

Doubles

Year	Event	Champions	Runners-up	Score
2000	Men	R. Molier (NED)/S. Welch (USA)	R. Ammerlaan/E. Stuurman (NED)	63 62
	Women	D. Di Toro (AUS)/M. Smit (NED)	E. Vergeer/S. Peters (NED)	64 64
2001	Men	M. Brychta (CZE)/M. Legner (AUT)	T. Kruszelnicki (POL)/J. Mistry (GBR)	63 62
	Women	E. Vergeer/M. Smit (NED)	B. Klave/D. Van Marum (NED)	75 75
2002	Men	K. Schrameyer (GER)/S. Welch (USA)	M. Legner (AUT)/S. Saida (JPN)	26 63 62
	Women	M. Smit/E. Vergeer (NED)	B. Klave/D. Van Marum (NED)	76 63
2003	Men	M. Legner (AUT)/S. Saida (JPN)	M. Jeremiasz (FRA)/J. Mistry (GBR)	63 76
	Women	M. Smit/E. Vergeer (NED)	J. Griffioen/S. Walraven (NED)	62 62
	Quad	P. Norfolk (GBR)/S. Hunter (CAN)	R. Draney/D. Wagner (USA)	64 61
2004	Men	M. Legner (AUT)/S. Saida (JPN)	M. Jeremiasz (FRA)/J. Mistry (GBR)	61 36 63
	Women	J. Griffioen/K. Homan (NED)	B. Ameryckx (BEL)/S. Walraven (NED)	64 62
	Quad	S. Hunter (CAN)/P. Norfolk (GBR)	G. Polidori/A. Raffaele (ITA)	61 63
2005	Men	M. Jeremiasz (FRA)/J. Mistry (GBR)	M. Legner (AUT)/S. Saida (JPN)	62 62
	Women	J. Griffioen/E. Vergeer (NED)	F. Gravellier (FRA)/M. Smit (NED)	61 62
	Quad	N. Taylor/D. Wagner (USA)	G. Polidori/A. Raffaele (ITA)	63 67 75

World Team Cup

The official ITF wheelchair tennis team event. Men and women play on a knock-out principle, with a playoff system to determine the ranking of all participating teams. Quads and Junior events, added in recent years, are played in a round robin format. Winning nations in each category are listed.

Year	Venue	Men	Women	Quads	Juniors
1985	Irvine, CA, USA	USA			
1986	Irvine, CA, USA	USA	NED		
1987	Irvine, CA, USA	USA	NED		
1988	Irvine, CA, USA	USA	NED		
1989	Irvine, CA, USA	USA	NED		
1990	Irvine, CA, USA	USA	NED		
1991	Irvine, CA, USA	USA	NED		
1992	Brussels, Belgium	FRA	NED		
1993	Villach, Austria	FRA	NED		
1994	Nottingham, Great Britain	AUS	USA		
1995	Roermond, Netherlands	USA	NED		
1996	Melbourne, VIC, Australia	AUS	NED		
1997	Nottingham, Great Britain	USA	NED		
1998	Barcelona, Spain	GER	NED	USA	
1999	New York, NY, USA	NED	AUS	ISR	
2000	Paris, France	AUS	NED	ISR	USA
2001	Sion, Switzerland	NED	NED	GBR	NED
2002	Tremosine, Italy	AUS	NED	GBR	NED
2003	Sopot, Poland	JPN	NED	USA	SWE
2004	Christchurch, New Zealand	NED	NED	ISR	NED
2005	Groningen, Netherlands	NED	NED	USA	BEL

Paralympic Wheelchair Tennis Event

Wheelchair tennis has been a medal sport at the Paralympic Games since 1992.

1992 Barcelona, Spain

Men's Singles	Gold:	Randy Snow (USA)
	Silver:	Kai Schrameyer (GER)
	Bronze:	Laurent Giammartini (FRA)
Women's Singles	Gold:	Monique van den Bosch (NED)
	Silver:	Chantal Vandierendonck (NED)
	Bronze:	Regina Isecke (GER)
Men's Doubles	Gold:	Brad Parks/Randy Snow (USA)
	Silver:	Thierry Caillier/Laurent Giammartinin (FRA)
	Bronze:	Stefan Bitterauf/Kai Schrameyer (GER)
Women's Doubles	Gold:	Monique van den Bosch/Chantal Vandierendonck (NED)
	Silver:	Nancy Olson/Lynn Seidemann (USA)
	Bronze:	Oristelle Marx/Arlette Racineux (FRA)

1996 Atlanta, GA, USA

Men's Singles	Gold:	Ricky Molier (NED)
	Silver:	Stephen Welch (USA)
	Bronze:	David Hall (AUS)
Women's Singles	Gold:	Maaike Smit (NED)
	Silver:	Monique Kalkman* (NED)
	Bronze:	Chantal Vandierendonck (NED)
Men's Doubles	Gold:	Chip Parmelly/Stephen Welch (USA)
	Silver:	Mick Connell/David Hall (AUS)
	Bronze:	Ricky Molier/Eric Stuurman (NED)

* Née Monique van den Bosch

Paralympic Wheelchair Tennis Event (continued)

1996 Atlanta, GA, USA (continued)

Women's Doubles	Gold:	Monique Kalkman*/Chantal Vandierendonck (NED)
	Silver:	Hope Lewellen/Nancy Olson (USA)
	Bronze:	Oristelle Marx/Arlette Racineux (FRA)

* Née Monique van den Bosch

2000 Sydney, NSW, Australia

Men's Singles	Gold:	David Hall (AUS)
	Silver:	Stephen Welch (USA)
	Bronze:	Kai Schrameyer (GER)
Women's Singles	Gold:	Esther Vergeer (NED)
	Silver:	Sharon Walraven (NED)
	Bronze:	Maaike Smit (NED)
Men's Doubles	Gold:	Robin Ammerlaan/Ricky Molier (NED)
	Silver:	David Hall/David Johnson (AUS)
	Bronze:	Scott Douglas/Stephen Welch (USA)
Women's Doubles	Gold:	Maaike Smit/Esther Vergeer (NED)
	Silver:	Daniela Di Toro/Branka Pupovac (AUS)
	Bronze:	Christine Otterbach/Petra Sax-Scharl (GER)

2004 Athens, Greece

Men's Singles	Gold:	Robin Ammerlaan (NED)
	Silver:	David Hall (AUS)
	Bronze:	Michael Jeremiasz (FRA)
Women's Singles	Gold:	Esther Vergeer (NED)
	Silver:	Sonja Peters (NED)
	Bronze:	Daniela Di Toro (AUS)
Men's Doubles	Gold:	Shingo Kunieda/Satoshi Saida (JPN)
	Silver:	Michael Jeremiasz/Lahcen Majdi (FRA)
	Bronze:	Anthony Bonaccurso/David Hall (AUS)
Women's Doubles	Gold:	Maaike Smith/Esther Vergeer (NED)
	Silver:	Sakhorn Khanthasit/Ratana Techamaneewat (THA)
	Bronze:	Sandra Kalt/Karin Suter-Erath (SUI)
Quad Singles	Gold:	Peter Norfolk (GBR)
	Silver:	David Wagner (USA)
	Bronze:	Bas Van Erp (NED)
Quad Doubles	Gold:	Nick Taylor/David Wagner (USA)
	Silver:	Mark Eccleston/Peter Norfolk (GBR)
	Bronze:	Monique De Beer/Bas Van Erp (NED)

ITF Seniors and Super-Seniors World Individual Championships

The International Vets World Championships were renamed ITF Seniors World Championships (formerly Group A) and ITF Super-Seniors World Individual Championships (formerly Group B) in 2004. The winner of each category is shown below:

1981 Sao Paulo, Brazil

MEN: 45 Singles: Sven Davidson (SWE). **45 Doubles:** Sven Davidson (SWE)/Hugh Stewart (USA). **55 Singles:** Straight Clark (USA). **55 Doubles:** Straight Clark (USA)/Torsten Johansson (SWE).

WOMEN: 40 Singles: Estrella de Molina (ARG). **40 Doubles:** M. A. Plante/Nancy Reed (USA). **50 Singles:** Amelia Cury (BRA).

1982 Portschach, Austria

MEN: 45 Singles: Istvan Gulyas (HUN). **45 Doubles:** Jason Morton/Jim Nelson (USA). **55 Singles:** Robert McCarthy (AUS). **55 Doubles:** Adi Hussmeller (GER)/Laci Legenstein (AUT). **60 Singles:** Torsten Johansson (SWE). **60 Doubles:** Torsten Johansson (SWE)/Albert Ritzenberg (USA). **65 Singles:** Fritz Klein (USA). **65 Doubles:** Jean Becker/Fritz Klein (USA) (FRA).

WOMEN: 40 Singles: Renate Drisaldi (GER). **40 Doubles:** Charleen Hillebrand/Nancy Reed (USA). **50 Singles:** Eva Sluytermann (GER). **50 Doubles:** I. Burmester/Eva Sluytermann (GER).

1983 Bahia, Brazil

MEN: 45 Singles: Istvan Gulyas (HUN). **45 Doubles:** Klaus Fuhrmann/Folker Seemann (GER). **55 Singles:** Robert McCarthy (AUS). **55 Doubles:** Adi Hussmuller (GER)/Laci Legenstein (AUT). **65 Singles:** Ricardo San Martin (CHI). **65 Doubles:** Federico Barboza/Hector Hugo Pizani (ARG).

WOMEN: 40 Singles: Helga Masthoff (GER). **40 Doubles:** Helga Masthoff/Heide Orth (GER). **50 Singles:** Ines de Pla (ARG). **50 Doubles:** Gladys Barbosa/Julia Borzone (ARG).

1984 Cervia, Italy

MEN: 35 Singles: Juergen Fassbender (GER). **35 Doubles:** Gene Malin/Armistead Neely (USA). **45 Singles:** Istvan Gulyas (HUN). **45 Doubles:** Klaus Fuhrmann/Folker Seemann (GER). **55 Singles:** Giuseppe Merlo (ITA). **55 Doubles:** Jason Morton/Hugh Stewart (USA). **65 Singles:** Gardnar Mulloy (USA). **65 Doubles:** Fritz Klein/Gardnar Mulloy (USA).

WOMEN: 40 Singles: Helga Masthoff (GER). **40 Doubles:** Helga Masthoff/Heide Orth (GER). **50 Singles:** Clelia Mazzoleni (ITA). **50 Doubles:** Hana Brabenec (CAN)/Pam Warne (AUS).

1985 Melbourne, VIC, Australia

MEN: 35 Singles: Juergen Fassbender (GER). **35 Doubles:** Juergen Fassbender (GER)/Federico Gadoni (ITA). **45 Singles:** Ian Barclay (AUS). **45 Doubles:** Bob Duesler/Jim Nelson (USA). **55 Singles:** Hugh Stewart (USA). **55 Doubles:** Jason Morton/Hugh Stewart (USA). **65 Singles:** Jim Gilchrist (AUS). **65 Doubles:** Fritz Klein/Albert Ritzenberg (USA).

WOMEN: 40 Singles: Heide Orth (GER). **40 Doubles:** Judy Dalton (AUS)/Heide Orth (GER). **50 Singles:** Ilse Michael (GER). **50 Doubles:** Anne Fotherington/Helen Polkinghorne (AUS).

1986 Portschach, Austria

MEN: 35 Singles: Robert Machan (HUN). **35 Doubles:** Juergen Fassbender/Hans-Joachim Ploetz (GER). **45 Singles:** Jorge Lemann (BRA). **45 Doubles:** Jorge Lemann/Ivo Ribeiro (BRA). **55 Singles:** Lorne Main (CAN). **55 Doubles:** Bob Howe (AUS)/Russell Seymour (USA). **65 Singles:** Torsten Johansson (USA). **65 Doubles:** Gardnar Mulloy/Verne Hughes (USA).

WOMEN: 40 Singles: Helga Masthoff (GER). **40 Doubles:** Helga Masthoff/Heide Orth (GER). **50 Singles:** Shirley Brasher (GBR). **50 Doubles:** Shirley Brasher/Lorna Cawthorn (GBR).

1987 Garmisch-Partenkirchen, Germany

MEN: 35 Singles: Robert Machan (HUN). **35 Doubles:** Jurgen Fassbender (GER)/Robert Machan (HUN). **45 Singles:** Giorgio Rohrich (ITA). **45 Doubles:** Hans Gradischnig/Peter Pokorny (AUT). **55 Singles:** Istvan Gulyas (HUN). **55 Doubles:** Istvan Gulyas (HUN)/Hugh Stewart (USA). **60 Singles:** Bob Howe (AUS). **60 Doubles:** Laci Legenstein (AUT)/Andreas Stolpa (GER). **65 Singles:** Alex Swetka (USA). **65 Doubles:** Bernhard Kempa/Walter Kessler (GER). **70 Singles:** Fritz Klein (USA). **70 Doubles:** Verne Hughes/Gardnar Mulloy (USA).

WOMEN: 40 Singles: Marie Pinterova (HUN). **40 Doubles:** Gail Lovera (FRA)/Marie Pinterova (HUN). **50 Singles:** Shirley Brasher (GBR). **50 Doubles:** Shirley Brasher/Lorna Cawthorn (GBR). **60 Singles:** Dorothy Cheney (USA). **60 Doubles:** Dorothy Cheney/Cortez Murdock (USA).

1988 Huntingdon Beach, CA, USA

MEN: 35 Singles: Alvin Gardiner (USA). **35 Doubles:** Lajos Levai (GER)/Robert Machan (HUN). **45 Singles:** Keith Diepram (USA). **45 Doubles:** Friedhelm Krauss/Gunter Krauss (GER). **55 Singles:** Istvan Gulyas (HUN). **55 Doubles:** Sven Davidson (SWE)/Hugh Stewart (USA). **60 Singles:** Robert McCarthy (AUS). **60 Doubles:** Bob Howe/Robert McCarthy (AUS). **65 Singles:** Tom Brown (USA). **65 Doubles:** Lee Hammel/ Bob Sherman (USA). **70 Singles:** Fritz Klein (USA). **70 Doubles:** Glen Hippenstiel/Geoff Young (USA).

WOMEN: 40 Singles: Marie Pinterova (HUN). **40 Doubles:** Rosie Darmon/Gail Lovera (FRA). **50 Singles:** Dorothy Matthiessen (USA). **50 Doubles:** Jane Crofford/Dorothy Matthiessen (USA). **60 Singles:** Virginia Glass (USA). **60 Doubles:** Dorothy Cheney/Cortez Murdock (USA).

1989 Vina del Mar, Chile

MEN: 35 Singles: Alvaro Fillol (CHI). **35 Doubles:** Lajos Levai/Robert Machan (GER). **45 Singles:** Harold Elschenbroich (GER). **45 Doubles:** Gunter Krauss/Bodo Nitsche (GER). **55 Singles:** Istvan Gulyas (HUN). **55 Doubles:** Chuck de Voe/John Powless (USA). **60 Singles:** Robert McCarthy (AUS). **60 Doubles:** Bob Howe/Robert McCarthy (AUS). **65 Singles:** Armando Vieira (BRA). **65 Doubles:** Sergio Verrati (FRA)/ Armando Vieira (BRA). **70 Singles:** Albert Ritzenberg (USA). **70 Doubles:** Fritz Klein/Albert Ritzenberg (USA).

WOMEN: 40 Singles: Marie Pinterova (HUN). **40 Doubles:** Heide Orth (GER)/Marie Pinterova (HUN). **50 Singles:** Ilse Michael (GER). **50 Doubles:** Barbel Allendorf (GER)/Nancy Reed (USA). **60 Singles:** Betty Pratt (USA). **60 Doubles:** Dorothy Cheney/Cortez Murdock (USA).

1990 Umag, Yugoslavia

MEN: 35 Singles: Robert Machan (HUN). **35 Doubles:** Lajos Levai (GER)/Robert Machan (HUN). **45 Singles:** Harald Elschenbroich (GER). **45 Doubles:** Dick Johnson/Jim Parker (USA). **55 Singles:** Istvan Gulyas (HUN). **55 Doubles:** Lorne Main/Ken Sinclair (CAN). **60 Singles:** Sven Davidson (SWE). **60 Doubles:** Sven Davidson (SWE)/Hugh Stewart (USA). **65 Singles:** Robert McCarthy (AUS). **65 Doubles:** Oskar Jirkovsky/Josef Karlhofer (AUT). **70 Singles:** William Parsons (USA). **70 Doubles:** Albert Ritzenberg/Alex Swetka (USA).

WOMEN: 40 Singles: Marie Pinterova (HUN). **40 Doubles:** Louise Cash/Barbara Mueller (USA). **50 Singles:** Margit Schultze (ESP). **50 Doubles:** Jan Blackshaw/Kay Schiavinato (AUS). **60 Singles:** Louise Owen (USA). **60 Doubles:** Lurline Stock/Dulcie Young (AUS).

1991 Perth, WA, Australia

MEN: 35 Singles: Paul Torre (FRA). **35 Doubles:** Yestedjo Traik/Atet Wijono (INA). **45 Singles:** Don McCormick (CAN). **45 Doubles:** Bruce Burns/John Weaver (AUS). **55 Singles:** Peter Froelich (AUS). **55 Doubles:** Herman Ahlers/Gordon Davis (USA). **60 Singles:** Lorne Main (CAN). **60 Doubles:** Frank Sedgman/Clive Wilderspin (AUS). **65 Singles:** Robert McCarthy (AUS). **65 Doubles:** Bob Howe/Robert McCarthy (AUS). **70 Singles:** Robert Sherman (USA). **70 Doubles:** Verne Hughes/Merwin Miller (USA).

WOMEN: 40 Singles: Carol Bailey (USA). **40 Doubles:** Carol Bailey/Barbara Mueller (USA). **50 Singles:** Charleen Hillebrand (USA). **50 Doubles:** Jan Blackshaw/Betty Whitelaw (AUS). **55 Singles:** Carol Wood (USA). **55 Doubles:** Margaret Kohler/Carol Wood (USA). **60 Singles:** Betty Pratt (USA). **60 Doubles:** Ruth Illingworth/Ann Williams (GBR).

1992 Palermo, Italy

MEN: 35 Singles: Ferrante Rocchi-Landir (ITA). **35 Doubles:** Stanislav Birner (CZE)/Paul French (GBR). **45 Singles:** Rolf Staguhn (GER). **45 Doubles:** Ben de Jell (NED)/Gary Penberthy (AUS). **50 Singles:** Jorge Lemann (BRA). **50 Doubles:** Peter Fuchs/Gerhard Schelch (AUT). **55 Singles:** Klaus Fuhrmann (GER). **55 Doubles:** Les Dodson/Hugh Stewart (USA). **60 Singles:** Werner Mertins (GER). **60 Doubles:** Lorne Main/ Ken Sinclair (CAN). **65 Singles:** Robert McCarthy (AUS). **65 Doubles:** Bob Howe/Robert McCarthy (AUS). **70 Singles:** Robert Sherman (USA). **70 Doubles:** Mario Isidori (ITA)/Robert Sherman (USA). **75 Singles:** Gaetano Longo (ITA). **75 Doubles:** Tiverio de Grad (ROM)/Georg Hunger (GER).

WOMEN: 35 Singles: Sally Freeman (GBR). **35 Doubles:** Luisa Figueroa (ARG)/Oliveira Villani (BRA). **40 Singles:** Marilyn Rasmussen (AUS). **40 Doubles:** Lesley Charles (GBR)/Marilyn Rasmussen (AUS). **45 Singles:** Marie Pinterova (HUN). **45 Doubles:** Shirley Brasher (GBR)/ Marie Pinterova (HUN). **50 Singles:** Charleen Hillebrand (USA). **50 Doubles:** Jacqueline Boothman (GBR)/Charleen Hillebrand (USA). **55 Singles:** Nancy Reed (USA). **55 Doubles:** Belmar Gunderson/Nancy Reed (USA). **60 Singles:** Beverley Rae (AUS). **60 Doubles:** Astri Hobson/Beverley Rae (AUS).

1993 Barcelona, Spain

MEN: 35 Singles: Fernando Luna (ESP). **35 Doubles:** Tony Luttrell/Steven Packham (AUS). **45 Singles:** Robert Machan (HUN). **45 Doubles:** Robert Machan (HUN)/Miodrag Mijuca (GER). **50 Singles:** Jorge Lemann (BRA). **50 Doubles:** Jim Parker/Ken Robinson (USA). **55 Singles:** King Van Nostrand (USA). **55 Doubles:** Juan Manuel Couder (ESP/King Van Nostrand (USA)). **60 Singles:** Lorne Main (CAN). **60 Doubles:** Lorne Main/Ken Sinclair (CAN). **65 Singles:** Jason Morton (USA). **65 Doubles:** Laci Legenstein (AUT)/Hugh Stewart (USA). **70 Singles:** Tom Brown (USA). **70 Doubles:** Buck Archer/Tom Brown (USA). **75 Singles:** Gordon Henley (AUS). **75 Doubles:** Mirek Kizlink (GBR)/Albert Ritzenberg (USA).

WOMEN: 35 Singles: Jutta Fahlbusch (GER). **35 Doubles:** Dagmar Anwar/Jutta Fahlbusch (GER). **40 Singles:** Maria Geyer (AUT). **40 Doubles:** Carol Campling/Elizabeth Craig (AUS). **45 Singles:** Marie Pinterova (HUN). **45 Doubles:** Tuija Hannuakainen (FIN)/Marie Pinterova (HUN). **50 Singles:** Cathie Anderson (USA). **50 Doubles:** Siegrun Fuhrmann/Brigitte Hoffmann (GER). **55 Singles:** Roberta Beltrame (ITA). **55 Doubles:** Belmar Gunderson/Nancy Reed (USA). **60 Singles:** Nancy Reed (USA). **60 Doubles:** Ana Maria Estalella/Marta Pombo (ESP). **65 Singles:** Betty Pratt (USA). **65 Doubles:** Betty Cookson/Betty Pratt (USA).

1994 (Group A) Buenos Aires, Argentina

MEN: 35 Singles: Jose Luis Clerc (ARG). **35 Doubles:** Jose Luis Clerc (ARG)/Victor Pecci (PAR). **45 Singles:** Jairo Velasco (ESP). **45 Doubles:** Thomaz Koch (BRA)/Jairo Velasco (ESP). **50 Singles:** Jimmy Parker (USA). **50 Doubles:** Jimmy Parker/Ken Robinson (USA).
WOMEN: 35 Singles: Jutta Fahlbusch (GER). **35 Doubles:** Marcela de Gregorio/Beatriz Villaverde (ARG). **40 Singles:** Renata Vojtischek (GER). **40 Doubles:** Tina Karwasky (USA)/Susan Stone (CAN). **45 Singles:** Louise Cash (USA). **45 Doubles:** Carol Campling/Elizabeth Craig (AUS).

1994 (Group B) Los Gatos, CA, USA

MEN: 55 Singles: Gil Howard (USA). **55 Doubles:** Leslie Dodson (USA)/Klaus Fuhrmann (GER). **60 Singles:** King Van Nostrand (USA). **60 Doubles:** Whitney Reed/Russell Seymour (USA). **65 Singles:** Jason Morton (USA). **65 Doubles:** William Davis/Jason Morton (USA). **70 Singles:** Oskar Jirkovsky (AUT). **70 Doubles:** Francis Bushmann/Vincent Fotre (USA). **75 Singles:** Alex Swetka (USA). **75 Doubles:** Verne Hughes/Dan Walker (USA).
WOMEN: 50 Singles: Petro Kruger (RSA). **50 Doubles:** Ellen Bryant/Barbara Mueller (USA). **55 Singles:** Rosie Darmon (FRA). **55 Doubles:** Lynn Little/Dorothy Matthiessen (USA). **60 Singles:** Ilse Michael (GER). **60 Doubles:** Belmar Gunderson/Nancy Reed (USA). **65 Singles:** Louise Owen (USA). **65 Doubles:** Liz Harper/Louise Owen (USA).

1995 (Group A) Bad Neuenahr, Germany

MEN: 35 Singles: Thibaut Kuentz (FRA). **35 Doubles:** Thibaut Kuentz (FRA)/Stephan Medem (GER). **45 Singles:** Robert Machan (HUN). **45 Doubles:** Armistead Neel/Larry Turville (USA). **50 Singles:** Giorgio Rohrich (ITA). **50 Doubles:** Richard Johnson/Jody Rush (USA).
WOMEN: 35 Singles: Regina Marsikova (CZE). **40 Singles:** Renata Vojtischek (GER). **40 Doubles:** Tina Karwasky (USA)/Renata Vojtischek (GER). **45 Singles:** Marie Pinterova (HUN). **45 Doubles:** Carol Campling/Elizabeth Craig-Allan (AUS).

1995 (Group B) Nottingham, Great Britain

MEN: 55 Singles: Len Saputo (USA). **55 Doubles:** Leslie Dodson (USA)/Klaus Fuhrmann (GER). **60 Singles:** James Nelson (USA). **60 Doubles:** Leonard Lindborg/James Nelson (USA). **65 Singles:** Lorne Main (CAN). **65 Doubles:** Lorne Main/Ken Sinclair (CAN). **70 Singles:** Oskar Jirkovsky (AUT). **70 Doubles:** Neale Hook/Brian Hurley (AUS). **75 Singles:** Robert Sherman (USA). **75 Doubles:** Mirek Kizlink/Tony Starling (GBR).
WOMEN: 50 Singles: Charleen Hillebrand (USA). **50 Doubles:** Elly Blomberg (NED)/Jacqueline Boothman (GBR). **55 Singles:** Renate Mayer-Zdralek (GER). **55 Doubles:** Sinclair Bill/Carol Wood (USA). **60 Singles:** Jennifer Hoad (ESP). **60 Doubles:** Ruth Illingworth/Rita Lauder (GBR). **65 Singles:** Betty Pratt (USA). **65 Doubles:** Elaine Mason (USA)/Louise Owen.

1996 (Group A) Velden, Austria

MEN: 35 Singles: Greg Neuhart (USA). **35 Doubles:** Mike Fedderly/Greg Neuhart (USA). **40 Singles:** Julio Goes (BRA). **40 Doubles:** Julio Goes/Harry Ufer (BRA). **45 Singles:** Jairo Velasco (ESP). **45 Doubles:** Robert Machan (HUN)/Jairo Velasco (ESP). **50 Singles:** Peter Pokorny (AUT). **50 Doubles:** Ted Hoehn/Richard Johnson (USA).
WOMEN: 35 Singles: Regina Marsikova (CZE). **35 Doubles:** Jutta Fahlbusch (GER)/Regina Marsikova (CZE). **40 Singles:** Renata Vojtischek (GER). **40 Doubles:** Tina Karwasky (USA)/Renata Vojtischek (GER). **45 Singles:** Marie Pinterova (HUN). **45 Doubles:** Heide Orth (GER)/Marie Pinterova (HUN). **50 Singles:** Eva Szabo (HUN). **50 Doubles:** Carol Campling/Elizabeth Craig-Allan (AUS).

1996 (Group B), Vienna, Austria

MEN: 55 Singles: Giorgio Rohrich (ITA). **55 Doubles:** Hans Gradischnig/Peter Pokorny (AUT). **60 Singles:** King Van Nostrand (USA). **60 Doubles:** Bob Duesler/Jim Nelson (USA). **65 Singles:** Lorne Main (CAN). **65 Doubles:** Lorne Main/Ken Sinclair (CAN). **70 Singles:** Fred Kovaleski (USA). **70 Doubles:** Bob Howe/Fred Kovaleski (USA). **75 Singles:** Robert Sherman (USA). **75 Doubles:** Verne Hughes/Merwin Miller (USA). **80 Singles:** Dan Miller (USA). **80 Doubles:** Irving Converse/Dan Miller (USA).
WOMEN: 55 Singles: Charleen Hillebrand (USA). **55 Doubles:** Sinclair Bill/Dorothy Mattiessen (USA). **60 Singles:** Ilse Michael (GER). **60 Doubles:** Nancy Reed (USA)/Inge Weber (CAN). **65 Singles:** Ines de Pla (ARG). **65 Doubles:** Ruth Illingworth/Rita Lauder (GBR). **70 Singles:** Betty Pratt (USA). **70 Doubles:** Elaine Mason/Betty Pratt (USA).

1997 (Group A) Johannesburg, South Africa

MEN: 35 Singles: Greg Neuhart (USA). **35 Doubles:** Chris Loock/Kobus Visagie (RSA). **40 Singles:** Pierre Godfroid (BEL). **40 Doubles:** Pierre Godfroid (BEL)/Bruce Osborne (AUS). **45 Singles:** Frank Puncec (RSA). **45 Doubles:** Max Bates/Andrew Rae (AUS). **50 Singles:** Jairo Velasco (ESP). **50 Doubles:** Luis Flor/Jairo Velasco (ESP).

WOMEN: 35 Singles: Tracy Houk (USA). **35 Doubles:** Alexi Beggs/Vikki Beggs (USA). **40 Singles:** Renata Vojtischek (GER). **40 Doubles:** Sherri Bronson/Helle Viragh (USA). **45 Singles:** Rita Theron (RSA). **45 Doubles:** Kerry Ballard/Wendy Gilchrist (AUS). **50 Singles:** Marie Pinterova (HUN). **50 Doubles:** Carol Campling/Elizabeth Craig-Allan (AUS).

1997 (Group B) Newcastle, NSW, Australia

MEN: 55 Singles: Bob Howes (AUS). **55 Doubles:** Maurince Broom/Max Senior (AUS). **60 Singles:** Klaus Fuhrmann (GER). **60 Doubles:** Robert Duesler/Jim Nelson (USA). **65 Singles:** Russell Seymour (USA). **65 Doubles:** William Davis/Chuck de Voe (USA). **70 Singles:** Laci Legenstein (AUT). **70 Doubles:** Laci Legenstein (AUT)/Fred Kovaleski (USA). **75 Singles:** Robert Sherman (USA). **75 Doubles:** Robert Sherman/Ellis Williamson (USA). **80 Singles:** Alex Swetka (USA). **80 Doubles:** Gordon Henley (AUS)/Alex Swetka (USA).

WOMEN: 55 Singles: Heide Orth (GER). **55 Doubles:** Lyn Wayte/Margaret Wayte (AUS). **60 Singles:** Judith Dalton (AUS). **60 Doubles:** Lorice Forbes/Peg Hoysted (AUS). **65 Singles:** Beverley Rae (AUS). **65 Doubles:** Ruth Illingworth/Rita Lauder (GBR). **70 Singles:** Twinx Rogers (RSA). **70 Doubles:** Deedy Krebs/Elaine Mason (USA).

1998 (Group A) Nottingham, Great Britain

MEN: 35 Singles: Nick Fulwood (GBR). **35 Doubles:** Nick Fulwood (GBR)/Brad Properjohn (AUS). **40 Singles:** Pierre Godfroid (BEL). **40 Doubles:** Pierre Godfroid (BEL)/Bruce Osbourne (AUS). **45 Singles:** Wayne Cowley (AUS). **45 Doubles:** Benson Greatrex/Philip Siviter (GBR). **50 Singles:** Frank Briscoe (RSA). **50 Doubles:** Keith Bland/Richard Tutt (GBR).

WOMEN: 35 Singles: Tracy Houk (USA). **35 Doubles:** Susanne Turi (HUN)/Kathy Vick (USA). **40 Singles:** Ros Balodis (AUS). **40 Doubles:** Ros Balodis/Kaye Nealon (AUS). **45 Singles:** Marlie Buehler (USA). **45 Doubles:** Elizabeth Boyle/Pauline Fisher (GBR). **50 Singles:** Marie Pinterova (HUN). **50 Doubles:** Carol Campling/Elizabeth Craig-Allan (AUS).

1998 (Group B) Palm Beach Gardens, FL, USA

MEN: 55 Singles: Bob Howes (AUS). **55 Doubles:** Stasys Labanauskas (LTU)/Peter Pokorny (AUT). **60 Singles:** Bodo Nitsche (GER). **60 Doubles:** Henry Leichtfried/Leonard Lindborg (USA). **65 Singles:** Jim Perley (USA). **65 Doubles:** Lorne Main/Kenneth Sinclair (CAN). **70 Singles:** Jason Morton (USA). **70 Doubles:** Fred Kovaleski/Jason Morton (USA). **75 Singles:** Robert Sherman (USA). **75 Doubles:** Fran Bushmann/George Druliner (USA). **80 Singles:** Alex Swetka (USA). **80 Doubles:** Irving Converse/Dan Miller (USA).

WOMEN: 55 Singles: Heide Orth (GER). **55 Doubles:** Rosie Darmon (FRA)/Heide Orth (GER). **60 Singles:** Judith Dalton (AUS). **60 Doubles:** Belmar Gunderson/Katie Koontz (USA). **65 Singles:** Clelia Mazzoleni (ITA). **65 Doubles:** Lorice Forbes/Peg Hoysted (AUS). **70 Singles:** Betty Eisenstein (USA). **70 Doubles:** Phyllis Adler/Elaine Mason (USA).

1999 (Group A) Amsterdam, Netherlands

MEN: 35 Singles: Ned Caswell (USA). **35 Doubles:** Ned Caswell/Mike Fedderly (USA). **40 Singles:** Maris Rozentals (LAT). **40 Doubles:** Pierre Godfroid/Maris Rozentals (BEL). **45 Singles:** Andrew Rae (AUS). **45 Doubles:** Rob Prouse/Andrew Rae (AUS). **50 Singles:** Lito Alvarez (AUS). **50 Doubles:** Lito Alvarez/Peter Rigg (AUS).

WOMEN: 35 Singles: Klaartje van Baarle (BEL). **35 Doubles:** Jackie Reardon (GBR)/Jackie van Wijk (NED). **40 Singles:** Anna Iuale (ITA). **40 Doubles:** Gerda Preissing (GER)/Beatriz Villaverde (ARG). **45 Singles:** Renata Vojtischek (GER). **45 Doubles:** Mary Ginnard/Lilian Peltz-Petow (USA). **50 Singles:** Maria Pinterova (HUN). **50 Doubles:** Carol Campling/Elizabeth Craig-Allan (AUS).

1999 (Group B) Barcelona, Spain

MEN: 55 Singles: Giorgio Rohrich (ITA). **55 Doubles:** Giorgio Rohrich/Bepi Zambon (ITA). **60 Singles:** Roberto Aubone (ARG). **60 Doubles:** Bob Duesler/Henry Leichtfried (USA). **65 Singles:** Jim Perley (USA). **65 Doubles:** Lorne Main/Kenneth Sinclair (CAN). **70 Singles:** William Davis (USA). **70 Doubles:** Kingman Lambert/Jason Morton (USA). **75 Singles:** Oskar Jirkovsky (AUT). **75 Doubles:** Francis Bushman/Newton Meade (USA). **80 Singles:** Alex Swetka (USA). **80 Doubles:** Nehemiah Atkinson/Gardnar Mulloy (USA). **85 Singles:** Gardnar Mulloy (USA). **85 Doubles:** Edward Baumer/David Carey (USA).

WOMEN: 55 Singles: Heide Orth (GER). **55 Doubles:** Petro Kruger/Marietjie Viljoen (RSA). **60 Singles:** Jan Blackshaw (AUS). **60 Doubles:** Jan Blackshaw/Mary Gordon (AUS). **65 Singles:** Nancy Reed (USA). **65 Doubles:** Belmar Gunderson/Nancy Reed (USA). **70 Singles:** Ines de Pla (ARG). **70 Doubles:** Amelia Cury (BRA)/Ines de Pla (ARG). **75 Singles:** Dorothy Cheney (USA). **75 Doubles:** Julia Borzone (ARG)/Carmen Fernandez (MEX).

2000 (Group A) Buenos Aires, Argentina

MEN: 35 Singles: Jaroslav Bulant (CZE). **35 Doubles:** Ricardo Rivera/Gustavo Tibert (ARG). **40 Singles:** Patrick Serrett (AUS). **40 Doubles:** Mike Fedderly/Paul Smith (USA). **45 Singles:** Victor Pecci (PAR). **45 Doubles:** Michael Collins/Wayne Pascoe (AUS). **50 Singles:** Bruno Renoult (FRA). **50 Doubles:** Max Bates (AUS)/Xavier Lemoine (FRA).

WOMEN: 35 Singles: Raquel Contreras (MEX). **35 Doubles:** Beatrix Mezger-Reboul (GER)/Cora Salimei (ARG). **40 Singles:** Gabriela Groell-Dinu (GER). **40 Doubles:** Ros Balodis (AUS)/Kaye Nealon (AUS). **45 Singles:** Elly Appel (NED). **45 Doubles:** Ann Brown/Pauline Fisher (GBR). **50 Singles:** Heidi Eisterlehner (GER). **50 Doubles:** Carol Campling/Elizabeth Craig-Allan (AUS).

2000 (Group B) Cape Town, South Africa

MEN: 55 Singles: Hugh Thomson (USA). **55 Doubles:** Ben de Jel (NED)/Hans-Joachim Ploetz (GER). **60 Singles:** Robert Howes (AUS). **60 Doubles:** Bodo Nitsche (GER)/Peter Pokorny (AUT). **65 Singles:** Joseph Mateo (FRA). **65 Doubles:** Abie Nothnagel/Neville Whitfield (RSA). **70 Singles:** Lorne Main (CAN). **70 Doubles:** Lorne Main/Kenneth Sinclair (CAN). **75 Singles:** Vincent Fotre (USA). **75 Doubles:** Neale Hook/Brian Hurley (AUS). **80 Singles:** Robert Sherman (USA). **80 Doubles:** Nehemiah Atkinson/Alex Swetka (USA). **85 Singles:** David Carey (CAN). **85 Doubles:** Edward Baumer (USA)/David Carey (CAN).

WOMEN: 55 Singles: Ellie Krocke (NED). **55 Doubles:** Charleen Hillebrand/Suella Steel (USA). **60 Singles:** Rosie Darmon (FRA). **60 Doubles:** Sinclair Bill (USA)/Rosie Darmon (FRA). **65 Singles:** Lee Burling (USA). **65 Doubles:** Patricia Bruorton/Jackie Zylstra (RSA). **70 Singles:** Louise Owen (USA). **70 Doubles:** Louise Owen/Louise Russ (USA). **75 Singles:** Elaine Mason (USA). **75 Doubles:** Twinx Rogers/Amy Wilmot (RSA).

2001 (Group A) Velden, Austria

MEN: 35 Singles: Jeff Greenwald (USA). **35 Doubles:** Stefan Fasthoff/Stefan Heckmanns (GER). **40 Singles:** Patrick Serret (AUS). **40 Doubles:** Mike Fedderly (USA)/Patrick Serret (AUS). **45 Singles:** Trevor Allan (FRA). **45 Doubles:** Sal Castillo (USA)/Ferrante Rocchi Lonoir (ITA). **50 Singles:** Andrew Rae (AUS). **50 Doubles:** Max Bates/Andrew Rae (AUS).

WOMEN: 35 Singles: Klaartje Van Baarle (BEL). **35 Doubles:** Olga Shaposhnikova (RUS)/Klaartje Van Baarle (BEL). **40 Singles:** Ingrid Resch (AUT). **40 Doubles:** Gerda Preissing (GER)/Beatriz Villaverde (ARG). **45 Singles:** Patricia Medrado (BRA). **45 Doubles:** Patricia Medrado (BRA)/Carmen Perea Alcala (ESP). **50 Singles:** Elizabeth Craig-Allan (AUS). **50 Doubles:** Kerry Ballard/Elizabeth Craig-Allan (AUS).

2001 (Group B) Perth, WA, Australia

MEN: 55 Singles: Hans-Joachim Ploetz (GER). **55 Doubles*:** Jerry Kirk/Hugh Thomson (USA). Keith Bland/Richard Tutt (GBR). **60 Singles:** Len Saputo (USA). **60 Doubles:** Derek Arthurs/Bob Howes (AUS). **65 Singles:** Peter Froelich (AUS). **65 Doubles*:** Peter Froelich (AUS)/King Van Nostrand (USA). Ross Jones/John Whittaker (AUS). **70 Singles:** Lorne Main (CAN). **70 Doubles:** Charles Devoe/Russell Seymour (USA). **75 Singles:** Laci Legenstein (AUT). **75 Doubles:** Oskar Jirkovsky (AUS)/Laci Legenstein (AUT). **80 Singles:** Nehemiah Atkinson (USA). **80 Doubles:** John Benn/Charles Roe (AUS). **85 Singles:** Gardnar Mulloy (USA). **85 Doubles:** David Carey/Gardnar Mulloy (USA).

WOMEN: 55 Singles: Trish Faulkner (USA). **55 Doubles:** Carol Campling (AUS)/Frances Taylor (GBR). **60 Singles:** Heather McKay (AUS). **60 Doubles:** Rosie Darmon (FRA)/Suella Steel (USA). **65 Singles:** Dorothy Matthiessen (USA). **65 Doubles:** Ann Fotheringham/Margaret Robinson (AUS). **70 Singles:** Ruth Illingworth (GBR). **70 Doubles*:** Louise Owe/Louise Russ (USA). Ruth Illingworth/Rita Lauder (GBR). **75 Singles:** Elaine Mason (USA). **75 Doubles:** Elaine Mason/Virginia Nichols (USA).

* not played due to rain – two winning pairs.

2002 (Group A) Fort Lauderdale, FL, USA

MEN: 35 Singles: Franck Fevrier (FRA). **35 Doubles:** Ned Caswell/Orlando Lourenco (USA). **40 Singles:** Pablo Arraya (PER). **40 Doubles:** Peter Doohan/Patrick Serret (AUS). **45 Singles:** Harold Solomon (USA). **45 Doubles:** Sal Castillo/Larry Schnall (USA). **50 Singles:** Andrew Rae (AUS). **50 Doubles:** Tom Smith/Hugh Thomson (USA).

WOMEN: 35 Singles: Rene Simpson (CAN). **35 Doubles:** Suzanne Hatch/Rene Simpson (CAN). **40 Singles:** Ros Balodis (AUS). **40 Doubles:** Ros Balodis/Brenda Foster (AUS). **45 Singles:** Diane Fishburne (USA). **45 Doubles:** Vicki Collins/Kaye Nealon (AUS). **50 Singles:** Elisabeth Appel (NED). **50 Doubles:** Kerry Ballard/Elizabeth Craig-Allan (AUS).

2002 (Group B) Velden, Austria

MEN: 55 Singles: Hugh Thomson (USA). **55 Doubles:** Peter Blaas/Nico Welschen (NED). **60 Singles:** Peter Pokorny (AUT). **60 Doubles:** Alan Carter/Geoff Grant (USA). **65 Singles:** Klaus Fuhrmann (GER). **65 Doubles:** Peter Froelich (AUS)/King Van Nostrand (USA). **70 Singles:** Kenneth Sinclair (CAN). **70 Doubles:** Lorne Main/Kenneth Sinclair (CAN). **75 Singles:** William Tully (USA). **75 Doubles:** Douglas Corbett/Harward Hillier (AUS). **80 Singles:** Cornelis Marre (NED). **80 Doubles:** Bernhard Kempa/Hans Wendschoff (GER).

85 Singles: Alex Swetka (USA). **85 Doubles:** Donal Barnes (RSA)/Alex Swetka (USA).
WOMEN: 55 Singles: Carol Campling (AUS). **55 Doubles:** Carol Campling (AUS)/Frances Taylor (GBR). **60 Singles:** Heide Orth (GER). **60 Doubles:** Charleen Hillebrand/Suella Steel (USA). **65 Singles:** Dorothy Matthiessen (USA). **65 Doubles:** Dori de Vries/Belmar Gunderson (USA). **70 Singles:** Louise Russ (USA). **70 Doubles:** Mary Boswell/Louise Russ (USA). **75 Singles:** Elaine Mason (USA). **75 Doubles:** Elsie Crowe/June Farrar (AUS).

2003 (Group A) Hannover, Germany

MEN: 35 Singles: Guido Van Rompaey (BEL). **35 Doubles:** Girts Dzelde (LAT)/Torben Theine (GER). **40 Singles:** Anders Jarryd (SWE). **40 Doubles:** Tom Coulton (USA)/Anders Jarryd (SWE). **45 Singles:** Fernando Luna (ESP). **45 Doubles:** Pierre Godfroid (BEL)/Heiner Seuss (GER). **50 Singles:** Radovan Cizek (CZE).
WOMEN: 35 Singles: Rene Simpson (CAN). **35 Doubles:** Heike Thoms (GER)/Lucie Zelinka (AUT). **40 Singles:** Regina Marsikova (CZE). **40 Doubles:** Mary Dailey/Diane Fishburne (USA). **45 Singles:** Patricia Medrado (BRA). **45 Doubles:** Ros Balodis/Vicki Collins (AUS). **50 Doubles:** Max Bates/Andrew Rae (AUS). **50 Singles:** Eugenia Birukova (ITA). **50 Doubles:** Kerry Ballard/Elizabeth Craig-Allan (AUS).

2003 (Group B) Antalya, Turkey

MEN: 55 Singles: Jiri Marik (CZE). **55 Doubles:** Lito Alvarez/Peter Rigg (AUS). **60 Singles:** Peter Pokorny (AUT). **60 Doubles:** Stasys Labanauskas (LTU)/Peter Pokorny (AUT). **65 Singles:** Bodo Nitsche (GER). **65 Doubles:** Robert Duesler/Jim Nelson (USA). **70 Singles:** Lorne Main (CAN). **70 Doubles:** Donald Dippold/James Perley (USA). **75 Singles:** Clement Hopp (USA). **75 Doubles:** Jack Dunn/Graydon Nichols (USA). **80 Singles:** Robert Sherman (USA). **80 Doubles:** Neville Halligan/Frank Pitt (AUS). **85 Singles:** Federico Barboza (ARG).
WOMEN: 55 Singles: Carol Campling (AUS). **55 Doubles:** Carol Campling (AUS)/Frances Taylor (GBR). **60 Singles:** Heide Orth (GER). **60 Doubles:** Charleen Hillebrand/Suella Steel (USA). **65 Singles:** Jeannine Lieffrig (RSA). **65 Doubles:** Lynn Little/Dorothy Matthiessen (USA). **70 Singles:** Margaret Robinson (AUS). **70 Doubles:** Mary Boswell/Louise Russ (USA). **75 Singles:** Elaine Mason (USA). **75 Doubles:** Olga Mahaney/Elaine Mason (USA).

2004 (Seniors) Antalya, Turkey

MEN: 35 Singles: Sander Groen (NED). **35 Doubles:** Hubert Karrasch (CAN)/Pete Peterson (USA). **40 Singles:** Marcos Gorriz (ESP). **40 Doubles:** Egan Adams/Tom Coulton(USA). **45 Doubles:** Mike Fedderly (USA)/Paul Smith (NZL). **50 Singles:** Radovan Cizek (CZE). **50 Doubles:** Michael Collins/Andrew Rae (AUS).
WOMEN: 35 Singles: Lucie Zelinka (AUT). **35 Doubles:** Karim Strohmeier (PER)/Lucie Zelinka (AUT). **40 Singles:** Klaartje Van Baarle (BEL). **40 Doubles:** Brenda Foster (AUS)/Sylvie Mattel (FRA). **45 Singles:** Diane Fishburne (USA). **45 Doubles:** Beatriz Villaverde (ARG)/Susana Villaverde (SUI). **50 Singles:** Sherri Bronson (USA). **50 Doubles:** Lynette Mortimer/Susanne Walter (AUS).

2004 (Super-Seniors) Philadelphia, PA, USA

MEN: 55 Singles: Tomas Koch (BRA). **55 Doubles:** Neal Newman/Larry Turville (USA). **60 Singles:** Jimmy Parker (USA). **60 Doubles:** Peter Adrigan/Hans-Joachim Plötz (GER). **65 Singles:** Gene Scott (USA). **65 Doubles:** Henry Leichtfried/George Sarantos (USA). **70 Singles:** King Van Nostrand (USA). **70 Doubles:** Richard Doss/John Powless (USA). **75 Singles:** Jason Morton (USA). **75 Doubles:** William Davis/Edward Kauder (USA). **80 Singles:** Fred Kovaleski (USA). **80 Doubles:** Fred Kovaleski/Robert Sherman (USA). **85 Singles:** Alex Swetka (USA). **85 Doubles:** Irving Converse/Howard Kuntz (USA).
WOMEN: 55 Singles: Anne Guerrant (USA). **55 Doubles:** Kerry Ballard/Elizabeth Craig-Allan (AUS). **60 Singles:** Heide Orth (GER). **60 Doubles:** Susan Hill/Jenny Waggott (GBR). **65 Singles:** Rosie Darmon (FRA). **65 Doubles:** Janine Lieffrig/Audrey Van Coller (RSA). **70 Singles:** Yvonne Van Nostrand (USA). **70 Doubles:** Mary Boswell/Belmar Gunderson (USA). **75 Singles:** Louise Russ (USA). **75 Doubles:** Louise Owen/Louise Russ (USA).

2005 (Seniors) Perth, WA, Australia

MEN: 35 Singles: Chris Wilkinson (GBR). **35 Doubles:** Matthias Huning/Frank Potthoff (GER). **40 Singles:** Mario Tabares (USA). **40 Doubles:** Glenn Erickson/Mario Tabares (USA). **45 Singles:** Patrick Serret (AUS). **45 Doubles:** Mike Fedderly/Val Wilder (USA). **50 Singles:** Alan Rasmussen (DEN). **50 Doubles:** Bruce Osborne/Andrew Rae (AUS). **55 Singles:** Bob Litwin (USA). **55 Doubles:** Neal Newman/Larry Turville (USA).
WOMEN: 35 Singles: Florence Boucard (FRA). **35 Doubles:** Mary Dailey/Renata Marcinkowska (USA). **40 Singles:** Rene Plant (RSA). **40 Doubles:** Rosanne Duke (AUS)/Rene Plant (RSA). **45 Singles:** Ros Balodis (AUS). **45 Doubles:** Ros Balodis/Kaye Nealon (AUS). **50 Singles:** Elisabeth Appel (NED). **50 Doubles:** Lyn Mortimer/Susanne Walter (AUS). **55 Singles:** Elizabeth Craig-Allan (AUS). **55 Doubles:** Kerry Ballard/Elizabeth Craig-Allan (AUS).

2005 (Super Seniors) Antalya, Turkey

MEN: 60 Singles: Jimmy Parker (USA). **60 Doubles:** Jimmy Parker/Ken Robinson (USA). **65 Singles:** Peter Pokorny (AUT). **65 Doubles:** Henry Leichtfried/George Sarantos (USA). **70 Singles:** King van Nostrand (USA). **70 Doubles:** Gordon Davis/Richard Doss (USA). **75 Singles:** Lorne Main (CAN). **75 Doubles:** Lorne Main/Ken Sinclair (CAN). **80 Singles:** Graydon Nichols (USA). **80 Doubles:** Anthony Franco/Graydon Nichols (USA). **85 Singles:** Gerry Ells (GBR). **85 Doubles:** Gerry Ells (GBR)/Franz Kornfeld (AUT).

WOMEN: 60 Singles: Petro Kruger (RSA). **60 Doubles:** Charleen Hillebrand (USA)/Frances Maclennan (GBR). **65 Singles:** Donna Fales (USA). **65 Doubles:** Susanne Clark/Dori de Vries (USA). **70 Singles:** Margaret Robinson (AUS). **70 Doubles:** Mary Boswell/Belmar Gunderson (USA). **75 Singles:** Louise Russ (USA). **75 Doubles:** Diane Hoffman/Louise Russ (USA).

King Van Nostrand (USA)

ITF Seniors and Super-Seniors World Team Championships

The International Vets World Team Championships were renamed ITF Seniors World Team Championships (formerly Group A) and ITF Super-Seniors World Team Championships (formerly Group B) in 2004.

Suzanne Lenglen Cup (Women's 35)

Year	Venue	Winner	Runner-up	Score
2001	Velden, Austria	GER	FRA	2-1
2002	Naples, FL, USA	NED	USA	2-1
2003	Hamburg, Germany	GER	FRA	2-1
2004	Manavgat, Turkey	USA	NED	3-0
2005	Perth, WA, Australia	FRA	GBR	2-0

Young Cup (Women's 40)

Year	Venue	Winner	Runner-up	Score
1977	Malmo, Sweden	ARG	GER	3-0
1978	Ancona, Italy	ITA	GER	3-0
1979	Cannes, France	GER	USA	3-0
1980	Bad Wiessee, Germany	GER	ITA	3-0
1981	Bad Wiessee, Germany	FRA	ITA	2-1
1982	Brand, Austria	FRA	ITA	3-0
1983	Cervia, Italy	GER	FRA	2-1
1984	Cervia, Italy	USA	FRA	3-0
1985	Portschach, Austria	GER	FRA	3-0
1986	Brand, Austria	GER	USA	2-1
1987	Venice, Italy	FRA	USA	2-1
1988	Bagnoles de l'Orne, France	GBR	GER	3-0
1989	Portschach, Austria	FRA	GER	3-0
1990	Keszthely, Hungary	FRA	USA	3-0
1991	Brisbane, QLD, Australia	AUS	GER	2-1
1992	Malahide, Ireland	GBR	AUS	2-1
1993	Bournemouth, Great Britain	USA	GBR	2-1
1994	Montevideo, Uruguay	USA	GER	2-1
1995	Dortmund, Germany	USA	GER	2-1
1996	Bad Hofgastein, Austria	USA	GER	2-1
1997	Pretoria, South Africa	USA	GER	3-0
1998	RAF Halton, Great Britain	USA	RSA	3-0
1999	Gladbeck, Germany	USA	ARG	3-0
2000	Mar del Plata, Argentina	GER	ARG	2-0
2001	Velden, Austria	FRA	ITA	2-1
2002	Naples, FL, USA	AUS	FRA	2-1
2003	Gladbeck, Germany	USA	NED	2-0
2004	Manavgat, Turkey	AUS	GER	2-1
2005	Perth, WA, Australia	USA	FRA	2-1

Margaret Court Cup (Women's 45)

Year	Venue	Winner	Runner-up	Score
1994	Perth, WA, Australia	FRA	USA	2-1
1995	Gladbeck, Germany	USA	AUS	3-0
1996	Seeboden, Austria	USA	RSA	3-0
1997	Pretoria, South Africa	USA	FRA	3-0
1998	Warwick, Great Britain	USA	RSA	2-1
1999	Hoofddorp, Netherlands	GER	AUT	3-0
2000	Montevideo, Uruguay	USA	NED	3-0
2001	Bad Hofgastein, Austria	AUT	NED	2-1
2002	Ballenisles, FL, USA	USA	BRA	2-0
2003	Erfurt, Germany	AUS	USA	2-0
2004	Manavgat, Turkey	USA	FRA	2-1
2005	Perth, WA, Australia	AUS	USA	2-1

Maria Esther Bueno Cup (Women's 50)

Year	Venue	Winner	Runner-up	Score
1983	Portschach, Austria	GBR	USA	2-1
1984	Le Touquet, France	USA	GBR	2-1
1985	Bremen, Germany	USA	GBR	3-0
1986	Brand, Austria	USA	GBR	2-1
1987	Helsinki, Finland	USA	GBR	2-1
1988	Itaparica, Bahia, Brazil	USA	CAN	2-1
1989	Bournemouth, Great Britain	USA	GBR	2-1
1990	Barcelona, Spain	AUS	ESP	2-1
1991	Perth, WA, Australia	USA	FRA	2-1
1992	Bagnoles de L'Orne, France	USA	FRA	2-1
1993	Barcelona, Spain	USA	GER	2-1
1994	San Francisco, CA, USA	USA	GER	3-0
1995	Velden, Austria	NED	USA	2-1
1996	St Kanzian, Austria	AUS	GER	2-1
1997	Pretoria, South Africa	AUS	GER	2-1
1998	Dublin, Ireland	USA	AUS	2-1
1999	Hoofddorp, Netherlands	USA	GER	3-0
2000	Sao Paulo, Brazil	FRA	USA	2-1
2001	Bad Waltersdorf, Austria	GER	USA	2-1
2002	Ballenisles, FL, USA	GER	FRA	2-1
2003	Eisenach, Germany	USA	AUT	3-0
2004	Manavgat, Turkey	USA	NED	2-1
2005	Perth, WA, Australia	NED	AUS	2-1

Maureen Connolly Cup (Women's 55)

Year	Venue	Winner	Runner-up	Score
1992	Tyler, USA	AUS	GBR	2-1
1993	Corsica, France	USA	FRA	3-0
1994	Carmel, CA, USA	USA	FRA	2-1
1995	Le Touquet, France	FRA	RSA	2-1
1996	Eugendorf, Austria	FRA	USA	2-1
1997	Canberra, ACT, Australia	USA	FRA	3-0
1998	Pompano Beach, FL, USA	GER	GBR	3-0
1999	Murcia, Spain	USA	NED	3-0
2000	Durban, South Africa	RSA	USA	2-1
2001	Perth, WA, Australia	USA	GER	2-1
2002	Vienna, Austria	HUN	AUS	2-1
2003	Belek, Turkey	USA	GER	3-0
2004	Philadelphia, PA, USA	AUS	USA	2-1
2005	Perth, WA, Australia	AUS	USA	2-1

Alice Marble Cup (Women's 60)

Year	Venue	Winner	Runner-up	Score
1988	Portschach, Austria	USA	GER	3-0
1989	Brand, Austria	USA	GER	2-1
1990	Paderborn, Germany	USA	GER	2-1
1991	Perth, WA, Australia	USA	GER	3-0
1992	Keszthely, Hungary	GBR	USA	2-1
1993	Portschach, Austria	USA	GBR	2-1
1994	Carmel, CA, USA	USA	GBR	2-1
1995	Worthing, Great Britain	USA	ESP	2-1
1996	Bad Hofgastein, Austria	USA	ESP	3-0
1997	Adelaide, SA, Australia	USA	CAN	3-0
1998	Boca Raton, FL, USA	AUS	USA	2-1

Year	Venue	Winner	Runner-up	Score
1999	Sabadell, Spain	FRA	RSA	2-0
2000	Sun City, South Africa	AUS	RSA	2-1
2001	Adelaide, SA, Australia	AUS	RSA	3-0
2002	Bad Hofgastein, SA, Austria	FRA	USA	2-1
2003	Manavgat, Turkey	GER	FRA	3-0
2004	Philadelphia, PA, USA	GBR	AUS	2-1
2005	Antalya, Turkey	FRA	GER	2-1

Kitty Godfree Cup (Women's 65)

Year	Venue	Winner	Runner-up	Score
1995	Bournemouth, Great Britain	USA	CAN	2-1
1996	Brand, Austria	GBR	USA	2-1
1997	Melbourne, VIC, Australia	GBR	USA	2-1
1998	Ft. Lauderdale, FL, USA	GBR	USA	2-1
1999	Palafrugell, Spain	USA	GBR	2-0
2000	Cape Town, South Africa	USA	RSA	2-1
2001	Perth, WA, Australia	USA	CAN	2-1
2002	Velden, Austria	USA	CAN	2-1
2003	Belek, Turkey	RSA	USA	2-1
2004	Philadelphia, PA, USA	FRA	AUS	2-0
2005	Antalya, Turkey	AUS	FRA	2-1

Althea Gibson Cup (Women's 70)

Year	Venue	Winner	Runner-up	Score
1998	Palm Beach Gardens, FL, USA	USA	GER	Round Robin
1999	Barcelona, Spain	GBR	USA	2-1
2000	Cape Town, South Africa	USA	RSA	2-1
2001	Melbourne, VIC, Australia	GBR	NZL	2-0
2002	Portschach, Austria	USA	GBR	2-1
2003	Manavgat, Turkey	USA	GBR	2-0
2004	Philadelphia, PA, USA	AUS	USA	2-0
2005	Antalya, Turkey	USA	AUS	2-1

Queen's Cup (Women's 75)

Year	Venue	Winner	Runner-up	Score
2002	St Kanzian, Austria	USA		Round Robin
2003	Manavgat, Turkey	USA		Round Robin
2004	Philadelphia, PA, USA	USA	GBR	3-0
2005	Antalya, Turkey	USA	CAN	2-1 (RR)

Italia Cup (Men's 35)

Year	Venue	Winner	Runner-up	Score
1982	Cervia, Italy	ITA	USA	2-1
1983	Cervia, Italy	GER	USA	2-1
1984	Brand, Austria	GER	FRA	2-1
1985	Reggio Calabria, Italy	USA	ITA	2-0
1986	Bagnoles de L'Orne, France	GER	USA	3-0
1987	Grado, Italy	USA	AUT	2-1
1988	Bol, Yugoslavia	GER	USA	3-0
1989	Mainz, Germany	GER	USA	3-0
1990	Glasgow, Great Britain	ESP	AUS	2-1
1991	Melbourne, VIC, Australia	AUS	ESP	3-0
1992	Ancona, Italy	ITA	FRA	2-1
1993	Barcelona, Spain	ESP	FRA	2-1
1994	Rosario, Argentina	GER	USA	2-1

Year	Venue	Winner	Runner-up	Score
1995	Dormagen, Germany	GER	USA	2-1
1996	Rome, Italy	USA	ITA	2-1
1997	Johannesburg, South Africa	USA	GBR	2-1
1998	Winchester, Great Britain	GBR	ITA	2-1
1999	Velbert, Germany	GBR	GER	2-1
2000	Buenos Aires, Argentina	GER	USA	3-0
2001	Portschach, Austria	FRA	USA	3-0
2002	Hallandale, FL, USA	GBR	GER	2-1
2003	Berlin, Germany	GER	FRA	3-0
2004	Manavgat, Turkey	GER	FRA	2-1
2005	Perth, WA, Australia	FRA	GBR	2-0

Tony Trabert Cup (Men's 40)

Year	Venue	Winner	Runner-up	Score
2000	Santa Cruz, Bolivia	USA	GER	3-0
2001	St Kanzian, Austria	GER	USA	2-0
2002	Naples, FL, USA	USA	GBR	3-0
2003	Hamburg, Germany	GER	USA	3-0
2004	Manavgat, Turkey	ESP	AUT	3-0
2005	Perth, WA, Australia	USA	NED	2-0

Dubler Cup (Men's 45)

Year	Venue	Winner	Runner-up	Score
1958	Monte Carlo, Monaco	ITA	GER	3-1
1959	Bad Ischl, Austria	SUI	ITA	4-1
1960	Bad Gastain, Austria	ITA	SUI	5-0
1961	Ancona, Italy	ITA	AUT	4-1
1962	Merrano, Italy	ITA	FRA	3-2
1963	Merrano, Italy	ITA	BEL	4-1
1964	Merrano, Italy	ITA	GER	5-0
1965	Merrano, Italy	ITA	SWE	3-0
1966	Florence, Italy	SWE	ITA	4-1
1967	Avesta, Sweden	FRA	SWE	3-2
1968	Paris, France	USA	FRA	5-0
1969	St. Louis, MO, USA	USA	SWE	4-1
1970	Cleveland, OH, USA	USA	SWE	4-1
1971	Le Touquet, France	USA	FRA	4-1
1972	Le Touquet, France	USA	FRA	4-1
1973	London, Great Britain	AUS	USA	3-1
1974	New York, USA	USA	AUS	3-2
1975	London, Great Britain	AUS	USA	5-0
1976	Alassio, Italy	ITA	CAN	3-2
1977	Barcelona, Spain	USA	FRA	4-1
1978	Le Touquet, France	USA	AUS	4-1
1979	Vienna, Italy	AUT	USA	3-2
1980	Cervia, Italy	SWE	AUT	2-1
1981	Buenos Aires, Argentina	USA	GBR	2-1
1982	Athens, Greece	USA	GBR	2-1
1983	New York, USA	USA	GER	2-1
1984	Bastad, Sweden	GER	USA	3-0
1985	Perth, WA, Australia	GER	AUS	2-1
1986	Berlin, Germany	GER	SUI	3-0
1987	Portschach, Austria	ITA	AUT	2-1
1988	Huntingdon Beach, CA, USA	USA	GER	3-0
1989	Montevideo, Uruguay	USA	GER	2-1

Year	Venue	Winner	Runner-up	Score
1990	Bol, Yugoslavia	GER	USA	2-1
1991	Sydney, NSW, Australia	USA	GER	3-0
1992	Portschach, Austria	GER	ESP	2-1
1993	Barcelona, Spain	ESP	FRA	2-1
1994	Santiago, Chile	USA	CHI	2-1
1995	Saarbrucken, Germany	USA	GER	2-1
1996	Velden, Austria	USA	AUS	3-0
1997	Pretoria, South Africa	AUS	RSA	2-1
1998	Dublin, Ireland	USA	ESP	2-1
1999	Arquebusiers, Luxembourg	BRA	ESP	2-1
2000	Asuncion, Paraguay	USA	FRA	2-1
2001	Vienna, Austria	FRA	USA	3-0
2002	Ballenisles, FL, USA	FRA	USA	2-1
2003	Bielefeld, Germany	GER	FRA	3-0
2004	Manavgat, Turkey	USA	GER	3-0
2005	Perth, WA, Australia	USA	GER	2-1

Fred Perry Cup (Men's 50)

Year	Venue	Winner	Runner-up	Score
1991	Bournemouth, Great Britain	GER	GBR	3-0
1992	Berlin, Germany	GER	USA	3-0
1993	Royan, Germany	GER	USA	2-1
1994	Buenos Aires, Argentina	FRA	USA	2-1
1995	Luchow, Germany	FRA	GER	2-1
1996	Portschach, Austria	GER	AUT	3-0
1997	Sun City, South Africa	ESP	GER	2-1
1998	Glasgow, Great Britain	USA	ESP	2-1
1999	Amstelveen, Netherlands	USA	ESP	3-0
2000	Santiago, Chile	USA	CHI	2-1
2001	Velden, Austria	USA	AUS	2-1
2002	Ballenisles, FL, USA	ESP	AUS	2-0
2003	Bielefeld, Germany	GER	AUS	2-1
2004	Manavgat, Turkey	AUS	USA	2-1
2005	Perth, WA, Australia	AUS	USA	3-0

Austria Cup (Men's 55)

Year	Venue	Winner	Runner-up	Score
1977	Baden, Austria	GBR	AUT	2-1
1978	Brand, Austria	USA	SWE	2-1
1979	Brand, Austria	USA	SWE	3-0
1980	Brand, Austria	USA	SWE	2-1
1981	Portschach, Austria	USA	SWE	3-0
1982	Cervia, Italy	AUS	USA	2-1
1983	New York, USA	AUS	USA	2-1
1984	Portschach, Austria	USA	AUS	2-1
1985	Perth, WA, Austria	AUS	USA	3-0
1986	Portschach, Austria	AUS	CAN	2-1
1987	Umag, Yugoslavia	CAN	AUS	3-0
1988	Huntingdon Beach, CA, USA	CAN	GER	2-1
1989	Buenos Aires, Argentina	CAN	USA	2-1
1990	Portschach, Austria	CAN	USA	3-0
1991	Sydney, NSW, Australia	USA	AUS	3-0
1992	Monte Carlo, Monaco	GER	USA	2-1
1993	Murcia, Spain	USA	AUS	2-1
1994	Carmel, CA, USA	AUS	USA	2-1

Year	Venue	Winner	Runner-up	Score
1995	Dublin, Ireland	GER	AUT	2-1
1996	Portschach, Austria	AUT	USA	2-1
1997	Canberra, ACT, Australia	AUT	GER	2-1
1998	Naples, FL, USA	USA	NED	3-0
1999	Barcelona, Spain	FRA	GER	2-0
2000	Pietermaritzburg, South Africa	USA	FRA	2-1
2001	Perth, WA, Australia	FRA	AUS	2-1
2002	Vienna, Austria	ESP	FRA	3-0
2003	Belek, Turkey	USA	NED	2-1
2004	Philadelphia, PA, USA	ESP	USA	2-1
2005	Perth, WA, Australia	AUS	ESP	2-1

Von Cramm Cup (Men's 60)

Year	Venue	Winner	Runner-up	Score
1989	Kempten, Germany	AUS	NZL	3-0
1990	Ontario, Canada	USA	AUT	2-1
1991	Adelaide, SA, Australia	USA	NZL	2-1
1992	Bournemouth, Great Britain	CAN	USA	2-1
1993	Aix les Bains, France	USA	FRA	3-0
1994	Burlingame, CA, USA	USA	GER	3-0
1995	Portschach, Austria	USA	GER	3-0
1996	Velden, Austria	USA	FRA	3-0
1997	Hamilton, New Zealand	USA	AUS	3-0
1998	Ft. Lauderdale, FL, USA	GER	USA	2-1
1999	Tarragona, Spain	FRA	GER	2-1
2000	Cape Town, South Africa	AUT	AUS	2-1
2001	Adelaide, SA, Australia	GER	USA	2-1
2002	St Kanzian, Austria	AUT	ITA	3-0
2003	Manavgat, Turkey	AUT	AUS	3-0
2004	Philadelphia, PA, USA	USA	GER	2-0
2005	Antalya, Turkey	USA	GER	2-1

Britannia Cup (Men's 65)

Year	Venue	Winner	Runner-up	Score
1979	London, Great Britain	USA	GBR	3-0
1980	Frinton-on-Sea, Great Britain	USA	SWE	3-0
1981	London, Great Britain	USA	SWE	3-0
1982	New York, USA	USA	CAN	3-0
1983	Portschach, Austria	USA	AUS	3-0
1984	Portschach, Austria	USA	AUS	3-0
1985	Portschach, Austria	USA	AUS	3-0
1986	Bournemouth, Great Britain	USA	NOR	3-0
1987	Bastad, Sweden	USA	SWE	2-1
1988	Huntingdon Beach, CA, USA	USA	FRA	3-0
1989	Umag, Yugoslavia	USA	FRA	3-0
1990	Bournemouth, Great Britain	USA	AUS	2-1
1991	Canberra, ACT, Australia	AUT	AUS	2-1
1992	Seefeld, Austria	AUS	AUT	2-1
1993	Le Touquet, France	USA	ITA	2-1
1994	Portola Valley, CA, USA	USA	AUT	2-1
1995	Glasgow, Great Britain	USA	CAN	2-1
1996	Warmbad Villach, Austria	USA	CAN	2-1
1997	Hamilton, New Zealand	USA	CAN	2-1
1998	Palm Beach Gardens, FL, USA	CAN	USA	3-0
1999	Palafrugell, Spain	USA	CAN	2-1

Year	Venue	Winner	Runner-up	Score
2000	Cape Town, South Africa	AUS	USA	2-1
2001	Perth, WA, Australia	USA	AUS	2-1
2002	Velden, Austria	USA	GER	3-0
2003	Belek, Turkey	GER	MEX	3-0
2004	Philadelphia, PA, USA	USA	AUS	2-0
2005	Antalya, Turkey	AUT	USA	2-1

Jack Crawford Cup (Men's 70)

Year	Venue	Winner	Runner-up	Score
1983	Brand, Austria	USA	SWE	3-0
1984	Helsinki, Finland	USA	GBR	3-0
1985	Brand, Austria	USA	AUT	3-0
1986	Seefeld, Austria	USA	FRA	3-0
1987	Portschach, Austria	USA	GBR	3-0
1988	Keszthely, Hungary	USA	GBR	3-0
1989	Bol, Yugoslavia	USA	BRA	3-0
1990	Brand, Austria	USA	BRA	3-0
1991	Canberra, ACT, Australia	GER	USA	2-1
1992	Le Touquet, France	USA	GER	3-0
1993	Menorca, Spain	USA	FRA	3-0
1994	Oakland, CA, USA	AUS	FRA	2-1
1995	Aix les Bains, France	USA	AUS	2-1
1996	Seeboden, Austria	AUT	USA	2-1
1997	Adelaide, SA, Australia	AUT	USA	2-1
1998	Pompano Beach, FL, USA	USA	AUT	2-1
1999	Barcelona, Spain	USA	AUS	3-0
2000	Cape Town, South Africa	CAN	USA	2-1
2001	Melbourne, VIC, Australia	CAN	USA	2-0
2002	Portschach, Austria	CAN	USA	3-0
2003	Manavgat, Turkey	USA	CAN	2-1
2004	Philadelphia, PA, USA	USA	JPN	3-0
2005	Antalya, Turkey	USA	FRA	2-0

Bitsy Grant Cup (Men's 75)

Year	Venue	Winner	Runner-up	Score
1994	Mill Valley, USA	USA	MEX	3-0
1995	Bournemouth, Great Britain	USA	SWE	3-0
1996	Bad Waltersdorf, Austria	USA	GER	3-0
1997	Hobart, TAS, Australia	USA	AUS	3-0
1998	Boca Raton, FL, USA	USA	AUS	3-0
1999	Barcelona, Spain	USA	MEX	3-0
2000	Cape Town, South Africa	USA	GBR	3-0
2001	Perth, WA, Australia	AUT	AUS	3-0
2002	Bad Waltersdorf, Austria	AUS	AUT	2-1
2003	Manavgat, Turkey	USA	FRA	3-0
2004	Philadelphia, PA, USA	FRA	USA	2-1
2005	Antalya, Turkey	CAN	USA	2-1

Gardnar Mulloy Cup (Men's 80)

Year	Venue	Winner	Runner-up	Score
1996	Seefeld, Austria	USA	MEX	Round Robin
1997	Melbourne, VIC, Australia	USA	AUS	Round Robin
1998	Naples, FL, USA	USA	AUS	Round Robin
1999	Murcia, Spain	USA	AUS	3-0
2000	Cape Town, South Africa	USA	AUS	2-1

Year	Venue	Winner	Runner-up	Score
2001	Perth, WA, Australia	USA	GER	Round Robin
2002	St Kanzian, Austria	AUS	USA	3-0
2003	Manavgat, Turkey	USA	AUS	2-1
2004	Philadelphia, PA, USA	USA	AUS	2-0
2005	Antalya, Turkey	USA	GBR	3-0

Nations Senior Cup

The ITF-sanctioned Nations Senior Cup was first held in 1999, and became the first nations senior tournament to bring together the most successful elite tennis players, retired from the ATP Tour and Davis Cup play.

Year	Champion
1999	Sweden
2000	France
2001	Spain
2003	**Spain d. Germany 2-1:** Carlos Costa (ESP) d. Patrik Kuhnen (GER) 64 63; Boris Becker (GER) d. Sergi Bruguera (ESP) 76 75; Emilio Sánchez/Carlos Costa (ESP) d. Michael Stich/Boris Becker (GER) 16 64 10(7).
2004	**Russia d. USA 2-1:** Andrei Cherkasov (RUS) d. Aaron Krickstein (USA) 76(4) 64; Jim Courier (USA) d. Andrei Chesnokov (RUS) 64 62; Andrei Cherkasov/Andrei Olhovskiy (RUS) d. Jim Courier/Jonathan Stark (USA) 63 46 119
2005	**USA d. Spain 2-1:** Sergi Bruguera (ESP) d. Aaron Krickstein (USA) 62 63; John McEnroe (USA) d. Emilio Sanchez (ESP) 61 76(5); John McEnroe/Jonathan Stark (USA) d. Carlos Costa/Sergi Bruguera (ESP) 63 64.

National Associations

Correct as at 22 December 2005

INTERNATIONAL TENNIS FEDERATION (ITF)
Bank Lane
Roehampton
London SW15 5XZ
Great Britain
President: Mr Francesco Ricci Bitti
Executive Vice President: Mr Juan Margets
Telephone: 44 20 8878 6464
Fax: 44 20 8878 7799
Email: reception@itftennis.com
Website: www.itftennis.com

Class B (Full) Members With Voting Rights (144)

ALGERIA – ALG
Fédération Algerienne de Tennis
CNOSAOS
Rue Ahmed Ouaked
Dely Ibrahim Alger, Algeria
President: Dr Mohamed Bouabdallah
Secretary: Mr Hakim Fateh
Telephone: 213 21 79 13 70/71
Fax: 213 21 79 13 71
Email: fatehkim@yahoo.fr
Website: www.multimania.com/tennisdz

ANDORRA – AND
Fed Andorrana de Tenis St. Antoni
C/Verge Del Pilar 5
3er Desp. No 10
Andorra La Vella, Andorra
President: Mr François Garcia Garcia
Secretary: Mrs Assumpcio Lluis
Telephone: 376 861 381
Fax: 376 868 381
Email: tennisfat@andorra.ad

ANGOLA – ANG
Federacao Angolana de Tenis
Cidadeia Desportive
PO Box 6533
Luanda, Angola
President: Mr Manuel Gomes Maiato
Secretary: Mr Joao M N Junior
Telephone: 244 222 261494
Fax: 244 222 261496
Email: fatennis@hotmail.com

ANTIGUA & BARBUDA – ANT
Antigua & Barbuda Tennis Association
PO Box 2758
St John's, Antigua & Barbuda
President: Ms Eleanor Mourilon
Secretary: Mr Peter Quinn
Telephone: 1 268 560 5575
Fax: 1 268 462 4811
Email: a_btennis@hotmail.com

ARGENTINA – ARG
Asociacion Argentina de Tenis
Maipu 471 – 3er piso
1376 Capital Federal
Buenos Aires, Argentina
President: Mr Enrique Morea
Secretary: Dr Hériberto A. Raggio
Telephone: 54 11 4322 0059
Fax: 54 11 4328 9145
Email: secconsejo@aat.com.ar
Website: www.aat.com.ar

ARMENIA – ARM
Armenian Tennis Association
Hrazdan Sport Complex
Kilikia
Yerevan 375082, Armenia
President: Mr Harutyun Pambukian
Secretary: Mr George Karamanoukian
Telephone: 3741 0 529 429
Fax: 3741 0 529 429
Email: tennisarmenia@mail.com

AUSTRALIA – AUS
Tennis Australia
Private Bag 6060
Richmond South
Victoria 3121, Australia
President: Mr Geoff Pollard
Secretary: Mr David Roberts
Telephone: 61 392 861 177
Fax: 61 396 502 743
Email: tennis@tennisaustralia.com.au
Website: www.tennisaustralia.com.au

AUSTRIA – AUT
Osterreichischer Tennisverband
Eisgrubengasse 2-6
2331 Vösendorf, Austria
President: Dr Ernst Wolner
Secretary: Mr Peter Teuschl
Telephone: 43 1 865 4506 0
Fax: 43 1 865 45 06 85
Email: info@tennisaustria.at
Website: www.asn.or.at/oetv/

AZERBAIJAN – AZE
Azerbaijan Tennis Federation
67 Tbilisi Ave – ap. 206
Baku 1012, Azerbaijan
President: Mr Oktay Asadov
Secretary: Mr Ilham Kuliyev
Telephone: 99 412 4314767
Fax: 99 412 4313355
Email: tennisfed@azeronline.com

BAHAMAS – BAH
The Bahamas Lawn Tennis Association
National Tennis Centre
PO Box N-10169
Nassau, Bahamas
President: Mrs Mary Shelley
Secretary: Mr Kevin Major
Telephone: 1 242 323 3933
Fax: 1 242 323 3934
Email: president@blta.net
Website: www.blta.net

BAHRAIN – BRN
Bahrain Tennis Federation
PO Box 26985, Bahrain
President: H H Shaikh Ahmed Al Khalifa
Secretary: Mr Matter Yousuf Matter
Telephone: 973 17 687 236
Fax: 973 17 781 533
Email: btennisf@batelco.com.bh

BANGLADESH – BAN
Bangladesh Tennis Federation
Tennis Complex
Ramna Green
Dhaka 1000, Bangladesh
President: Mr Toufiq M Seraj
Secretary: Mr Sanaul Hoque
Telephone: 880 2 862 6287
Fax: 880 2 966 2711
Email: btf@bttb.net.bd

BARBADOS – BAR
Barbados Lawn Tennis Association
PO Box 615C
Bridgetown, Barbados
President: Dr Raymond Forde
Secretary: Mrs Eleanor Brown
Telephone: 1 246 426 6453
Fax: 1 246 429 3342
Email: blta@sunbeach.net

BELARUS – BLR
Belarus Tennis Association
Pobeditelei Avenue 63
Minsk 220033, Belarus
President: Mr Mikhail Pavlov
Secretary: Mr Simon Kagan
Telephone: 375 17 226 9374
Fax: 375 172 269 823
Email: beltennis@yahoo.com

BELGIUM – BEL
Fédération Royale Belge de Tennis
Galerie de la Porte Louise 203/3
1050 Bruxelles, Belgium
President: Mr Pierre Paul de Keghel
Secretary: Mr Franz Lemaire
Telephone: 32 2 548 0304/513 2920
Fax: 32 2 548 0303
Email: info@rbtf.be
Website: www.rbtf.be

BENIN – BEN
Fédération Beninoise de Lawn Tennis
BP 2709
Cotonou I, Benin
President: Mr Edgar-Yves Monnou
Secretary: Mr Leopold Somissou
Telephone: 229 315 153
Fax: 229 311 252
Email: fbtennis@netcourrier.com

BERMUDA – BER
Bermuda Lawn Tennis Association
PO Box HM 341
Hamilton HM BX, Bermuda
President: Mr Ross Hillen
Secretary: Mr Scott Wheeler
Telephone: 1 441 296 0834
Fax: 1 441 295 3056
Email: blta@northrock.bm
Website: www.blta.bm

BOLIVIA – BOL
Federación Boliviana De Tennis
Calle 21 Esquina
Avenida Costanera No. 1999
Edificio Amy & Abril
Casilla Correo 3-12080
La Paz, Bolivia
President: Lic. Edgar Aguirre
Secretary: Ms Maria Eugenia Oporto
Telephone: 591 2 279 7092
Fax: 591 2 279 7092
Email: secfbt@fbtenis.org.bo
Website: www.fbtenis.org.bo

BOSNIA/HERZEGOVINA – BIH
Tennis Assn. of Bosnia & Herzegovina
Bulevar Kulina Bana 30
Zenica, Bosnia/Herzegovina
President: Mr Ratko Stamenic
Secretary: Mr Milenko Rimac
Telephone: 387 32 409 161
Fax: 387 32 411 077
Email: tsbih@yahoo.com

BOTSWANA – BOT
Botswana Tennis Association
PO Box 1174
Gaborone, Botswana
President: Mr Judge Mookodi
Secretary: Mr Nelson Amanze
Telephone: 267 3973 193
Fax: 267 3973 193
Email: bta@it.bw

BRAZIL – BRA
Confederacao Brasileira de Tenis
Av. Arnolfo Azevedo, 182 – Pacaembu
Cep: 01.236-030
Sao Paulo SP, Brazil
President: Mr Jorge Lacerda
Secretary: Mr Paulo Moriguti
Telephone: 55 11 3868 0160
Fax: 55 11 3 864 2141
Email: cbt@cbtenis.com.br
Website: www.cbtenis.com.br

BRUNEI – BRU
Brunei Darussalam Tennis Association
Hassanal Bolkiah Sports Complex
PO Box 859, Gadong Post Office
Bandar Seri Begawan, Negara
BE 3978, Brunei
President: Mr Pg Kamaruddin Pg Hj Radin
Secretary: Mr Hj Zuraimi Hj Abd Sani
Telephone: 673 2 381 205
Fax: 673 2 381 205
Email: bdta@brunet.bn

BULGARIA – BUL
Bulgarian Tennis Federation
Bul. Vasil Levski 75
Sofia 1040, Bulgaria
President: Mr Plamen Minchev
Secretary: Mr George Donchev
Telephone: 359 2 951 5696
Fax: 359 2 951 5691
Email: bft@bgtennis.bg
Website: www.bgtennis.bg

BURKINA FASO – BUR
Fédération Burkinabe De Tennis
01 BP 1306 Ouagadougou 01
Burkina Faso
President: Mr Christian Yves Zongo
Secretary: Mr Souleymane Yameogo
Telephone: 226 70 22 82 22
Fax: 226 50 31 03 40
Email: fbt_burkina@yahoo.fr

CAMEROON - CMR
Fédération Camerounaise de Tennis
BP 1121
Yaounde, Cameroon
President: Mr Edouard Akame Akame
Secretary: Dr Jean-Michel Fotso
Telephone: 237 993 8615
Fax: 237 222 4694
Email: jmfotso63@yahoo.fr

CANADA - CAN
Tennis Canada
1 Shoreham Drive
Toronto
Ontario M3N 1S4, Canada
President: Mr Michael Downey
Secretary: Ms Kim Ali
Telephone: 1 416 665 9777
Fax: 1 416 665 9017
Email: compcoord@tenniscanada.com
Website: www.tenniscanada.com

CHILE - CHI
Federacion de Tenis de Chile
Jose Joaquin Prieto No. 4040
San Miguel
Santiago, Chile
President: Mr Mario Pakozdi Piko
Secretary: Mr Juan Honorato
Telephone: 56 2 554 0068/0154
Fax: 56 2 554 1078
Email: ftch@tie.cl
Website: www.ftch.cl

CHINA, PEOPLE'S REPUBLIC OF - CHN
Chinese Tennis Association
5' Tiyuguan Road
Beijing 100763, China, P.R.
President: Mr Lu Zhenchao
Secretary: Ms Sun Jin Fang
Telephone: 86 10 67180176
Fax: 86 10 6711 4096
Email: cta@tennis.org.cn

CHINESE TAIPEI - TPE
Chinese Taipei Tennis Association
Room 705, 7th Floor
No. 20, Chu-Lun Street
Taiwan 104, Chinese Taipei
President: Mr Chen-Yen Yeh
Secretary: Mr Jesse Wu
Telephone: 886 2 2772 0298
Fax: 886 2 2771 1696
Email: ctta@tennis.org.tw
Website: www.tennis.org.tw

COLOMBIA - COL
Federacion Colombiana de Tenis
Centro De Alto Rendimiento
Calle 63 No 47-06
Bogota D.C., Colombia
President: Dr Gabriel Sanchez Sierra
Secretary: Mr Armando Gonzalez
Telephone: 571 314 3885
Fax: 571 660 4234
Email: fct@etb.net.co
Website: www.fedetenis.com

CONGO - CGO
Fédération Congolaise de Lawn Tennis
BP 550
Brazzaville, Congo
President: Mr Germain Ickonga Akindou
Secretary: Mr Antoine Ouabonzi
Telephone: 242 411 222
Fax: 242 810 330
Email: g_ickonga_akindou@hotmail.com

COSTA RICA - CRC
Federación Costarricense de Tenis
Apartado 575 1000
San José, Costa Rica
President: Mr Ricardo Castro
Secretary: Mr Jurgen G Nanne-Koberg
Telephone: 506 524 2400
Fax: 506 524 2433
Email: fedtenis@racsa.co.cr
Website: www.fctenis.com

COTE D'IVOIRE - CIV
Fédération Ivoirienne de Tennis
01 BPV 273
Abidjan 01, Cote D'Ivoire
President: Mr Georges N'Goan
Secretary: Mr Athanase Kakou
Telephone: 225 22 441 354
Fax: 225 22 442 707
Email: fede_ivoirtennis@yahoo.fr

CROATIA - CRO
Croatian Tennis Association
Gundulieeva 3
HR-10 000 Zagreb, Croatia
President: Mr Radimir Cacic
Secretary: Miss Suzana Knezevic
Telephone: 385 1 4830 756
Fax: 385 1 4830 720
Email: hts@hts.hr
Website: www.hts.hr

CUBA - CUB
Federacion Cubana de Tenis de Campo
Calle 13 Nr 601 Esq Ac
Vedado Habana 4, Cuba
President: Mr Rolando Martínez Pérez
Secretary: Mr Juan Baez
Telephone: 53 7 951694/973011
Fax: 53 7 952 121
Email: fctennis@inder.co.cu

CYPRUS - CYP
Cyprus Tennis Federation
Ionos Str. 20
PO Box 3931
Nicosia 1687, Cyprus
President: Mr Philios Christodoulou
Secretary: Mr Stavros Ioannou
Telephone: 357 22 666 822
Fax: 357 22 668 016
Email: cytennis@spidernet.com.cy

CZECH REPUBLIC - CZE
Czech Tenisova Asociace
Ostrov Stvanice 38
170 00 Prague 7, Czech Republic
President: Mr Ivo Kaderka
Secretary: Mr Josef Nechutny
Telephone: 420 222 333 444
Fax: 420 222 311 327
Email: cts@cta.cz
Website: www.cztenis.cz

DENMARK - DEN
Dansk Tennis Forbund
Idraettens Hus
Broendby Stadion 20
DK-2605 Broendby, Denmark
President: Mr Henrik Klitvad
Secretary: Mr Niels Persson
Telephone: 45 43 262 660
Fax: 45 43 262 670
Email: dtf@dtftennis.dk
Website: www.dtftennis.dk

DJIBOUTI - DJI
Fédération Djiboutienne de Tennis
BP 728, Djibouti
President: Mr Houmed Houssein
Secretary: Mr Ibrahim Ali
Telephone: 253 352 536
Fax: 253 352 536
Email: oned@intnet.dj;medseg_8@yahoo.fr

DOMINICAN REPUBLIC – DOM
Federacion Dominicana de Tenis
Calle 1ra. #18 Res. ABDY
Arroyo Hondo I
Santo Domingo, Dominican Rep.
President: Mr Persio Maldonado
Secretary: Mr Rafael Castillo
Telephone: 1 809 483 8882
Fax: 1 809 483 8883
Email: fedotenisoffice@hotmail.com

ECUADOR – ECU
Federacion Ecuatoriana de Tenis
Edificio de la FET
Lomas de Urdesa
Tres Cerritos
Guayaquil, Ecuador
President: Mr Manuel Carrera del Rio
Secretary: Mr Daniel Canizares
Telephone: 593 42 610 467
Fax: 593 42 610 466
Email: fetenis@gye.satnet.net

EGYPT – EGY
Egyptian Tennis Federation
13 Kasr El Nile Street
Cairo, Egypt
President: Mr Ismail El Shafei
Secretary: Mr Mohamed Abdel Haleem
Telephone: 202 576 3522
Fax: 202 575 3235
Email: etf@urgentmail.com

EL SALVADOR – ESA
Federacion Salvadorena de Tenis
Apartado Postal (01) 110
San Salvador, El Salvador
President: Mr Enrique Molins Rubio
Secretary: Mr Miguel Irigoyen
Telephone: 503 2289 5169
Fax: 503 2278 8087
Email: fedetenis_esa@integra.com.sv

ESTONIA – EST
Estonian Tennis Association
1-5P Regati Ave
11911 Tallinn, Estonia
President: Mr Jaanus Otsa
Secretary: Ms Ilona Poljakova
Telephone: 372 6 398 637
Fax: 372 6 398 635
Email: estonian.tennis@tennis.ee

ETHIOPIA – ETH
Ethiopian Tennis Federation
PO Box 3241
Addis Ababa, Ethiopia
President: Mr Bezuayehu Tesfaye
Secretary: Mrs Werkeye Ferede
Telephone: 251 1 639170/186009
Fax: 251 1 513 345
Email: werkeyeetftennis.com

FINLAND – FIN
Suomen Tennisliitto
Varikkotie 4
SF – 00900 Helsinki, Finland
President: Mr Jukka Roiha
Secretary: Mr Mika Bono
Telephone: 358 9 3417 1533
Fax: 358 9 323 1105
Email: mika.bono@tennis.fi
Website: www.tennis.fi

FRANCE – FRA
Fédération Française de Tennis
Stade Roland Garros
2 Avenue Gordon Bennett
75016 Paris, France
President: Mr Christian Bimes
Secretary: Mr J Dupre
Telephone: 33 1 4743 4800
Fax: 33 1 4743 0494
Email: fft@fft.fr
Website: www.fft.fr

GABON – GAB
Fédération Gabonaise de Tennis
PO Box 4241
Libreville, Gabon
President: Mr Samuel Minko Mindong
Secretary: Mr Marcel Desire Mebale
Telephone: 241 247 344
Fax: 241 703 190
Email: minkomindo@yahoo.fr
Website: rdd.rdd-gabon.gouv.ga.fegaten

GEORGIA – GEO
Georgian Tennis Federation
K Marjanishvili St 29
Tbilisi, Georgia
President: Ms Leila Meskhi
Secretary: Mr Zurab Katsarava
Telephone: 995 32 952 781
Fax: 995 32 953 829
Email: gtf@gol.ge

GERMANY – GER
Deutscher Tennis Bund EV
Hallerstrasse 89
Hamburg 20149, Germany
President: Dr Georg von Waldenfels
Secretary: Mr Reimund Schneider
Telephone: 49 40 411 782 60
Fax: 49 40 411 782 33
Email: dtb@dtb-tennis.de
Website: www.dtb-tennis.de

GHANA – GHA
Ghana Tennis Association
PO Box T-95
Sports Stadium Post Office
Accra, Ghana
President: Mr Jeffrey Abeasi
Secretary: Mr Charles Kudzo Attah
Telephone: 233 21 667 267
Fax: 233 21 236 788
Email: gtennis@africaonline.com.gh

GREAT BRITAIN – GBR
The Lawn Tennis Association
The Queen's Club
Palliser Road
London W14 9EG, Great Britain
President: Mr Stuart Smith
Secretary: Mr John Crowther
Telephone: 44 20 7381 7000
Fax: 44 20 7381 5965
Email: info@lta.org.uk
Website: www.lta.org.uk

GREECE – GRE
Hellenic Tennis Federation
267 Imitou Street
11631 Pagrati
Athens, Greece
President: Mr Spyros Zannias
Secretary: Mr Dimitris Stamatiadis
Telephone: 30 210 756 3170/1/2
Fax: 30 210 756 3173
Email: efoa@otenet.gr

GUATEMALA – GUA
Fed. Nacional de Tenis de Guatemala
Section 1551
PO Box 02-5339
Miami. FL 33102-5339, USA
President: Ms Marissa Maselli de Gabriel
Secretary: Mr Mario España Estrada
Telephone: 502 2385 1224
Fax: 502 2331 0261
Email: fedtenis@terra.com.gt

HAITI – HAI
Fédération Haitienne de Tennis
PO Box 1442
Port Au Prince, Haiti
President: Mr Frantz Liautaud
Secretary: Mr Hulzer Adolphe
Telephone: 509 45 1461/46 2544
Fax: 509 49 1233/46 1259
Email: tennis_haiti@abhardware.com

HONDURAS – HON
Federacion Hondurena de Tenis
P.O. Box 30152
Toncontin
Tegueigalpa MDC, Honduras
President: Mr Humberto Rodriguez
Secretary: Mr Rodulio Perdomo
Telephone: 504 2 396 890
Fax: 504 2 396 889
Email: fedtenishon@123.hn

HONG KONG CHINA – HKG
Hong Kong Tennis Association Ltd
Room 1021, Sports House
1 Stadium Path
So Kon Po, Causeway Bay
Hong Kong China
President: Mr Kenneth Tsui
Secretary: Mr Joelle Ho
Telephone: 852 2 504 8266
Fax: 852 2 894 8704
Email: info@tennishk.org

HUNGARY – HUN
Magyar Tenisz Szovetseg
Istvanmezei Ut 1-3
Budapest H-1146, Hungary
President: Dr Janos Berenyi
Secretary: Mr Attila Deak
Telephone: 36 1 460 6807
Fax: 36 1 460 6809
Email: tennis@interware.hu
Website: www.mtsztenisz.hn

ICELAND – ISL
Icelandic Tennis Association
Kurland 4
108 Reykjavik, Iceland
President: Mr Skjoldur Vatnar Bjornsson
Secretary: Mr Raj Bonifacius
Telephone: 354 820 0825
Fax: 354 514 4001
Email: shrb@simnet.is
Website: www.isisport.is/tennis/

INDIA – IND
All India Tennis Association
R K Khanna Tennis Stadium
Africa Avenue
110029 New Delhi, India
President: Mr Yashwant Sinha
Secretary: Mr Anil Khanna
Telephone: 91 11 2617 9062
Fax: 91 11 2617 3159
Email: aita@aitatennis.com
Website: www.aitatennis.com

INDONESIA – INA
Indonesian Tennis Association
Gelora Senayan Tennis Stadium
Jakarta 10270, Indonesia
President: Mrs Martina Widjaja
Secretary: Mr Soebronto Laras
Telephone: 62 21 571 0298
Fax: 62 21 570 0157
Email: pelti@vision.net.id

IRAN, ISLAMIC REPUBLIC OF – IRI
Tennis Fed. of Islamic Republic of Iran
Niayesh Highway/Valiasr Ave
Enghelab Sports Complex
Tehran, Iran
President: Mr Ali Reza Khorooshi
Secretary: Mr Nasser Mirzaei
Telephone: 98 21 2203 8189/2203 9096
Fax: 98 21 2203 71 11
Email: info@tennisiran.org
Website: www.tennis.ir

IRAQ – IRQ
Iraqi Tennis Federation
PO Box 440
Baghdad, Iraq
President: Mr Ghazi Al-Shaya'a Hamel
Secretary: Mr Khalid Saeed Al-Sultani
Telephone: 964 1 774 8261
Fax: 964 1 772 8424
Email: Iraqitenfed2003@yahoo.com

IRELAND – IRL
Tennis Ireland
Dublin City University
Glasnevin
Dublin 9, Ireland
President: Mr David Nathan
Secretary: Mrs Jan Singleton
Telephone: 353 1 8844 010
Fax: 353 1 8844 013
Email: info@tennisireland.ie
Website: www.tennisireland.ie

ISRAEL – ISR
Israel Tennis Association
2 Shitrit Street
Hader Yosef
69482 Tel Aviv, Israel
President: Dr Ian Froman
Secretary: Mr Yoram Baron
Telephone: 972 36 499 440
Fax: 972 36 499 144
Email: igutenis@netvision.net.il

ITALY – ITA
Federazione Italiana Tennis
Stadio Olimpico
Curva Nord, Scala G, Primo Piano
00194 Rome, Italy
President: Mr Angelo Binaghi
Secretary: Mrs Felicetta Rossitto
Telephone: 390 636 858 406
Fax: 390 636 858 166
Email: internazionali@federtennis.it
Website: www.federtennis.it

JAMAICA – JAM
Tennis Jamaica
68 Lady Musgrave Road
Kingston 10, Jamaica
President: Mr Ken Morgan
Secretary: Mrs Joycelin Morgan
Telephone: 1 876 927 9466
Fax: 1 876 927 9436
Email: tennisjam@cwjamaica.com

JAPAN – JPN
Japan Tennis Association
C/o Kishi Memorial Hall
1-1-1 Jinnan, Shibuya-ku
Tokyo 150-8050, Japan
President: Mr Masaaki Morita
Secretary: Mr Hiroshi Suzuki
Telephone: 81 33 481 2321
Fax: 81 33 467 5192
Email: office@jta-tennis.or.jp
Website: www.tennis.or.jp

JORDAN – JOR
Jordan Tennis Federation
Sport City/Gate 4 or 5
PO Box 961046
11196 Amman, Jordan
President: Eng. Hazem Adas
Secretary: Mr Nidal Lutfy
Telephone: 962 6 568 2796
Fax: 962 6 568 2796
Email: tennisfed@tennisfed.org.jo

KAZAKHSTAN – KAZ
Kazakhstan Tennis Federation
Central Sports Club of the Army
480051 Almaty, Kazakhstan
President: Mr Pavel Novikov
Secretary: Mr Valery Kovalev
Telephone: 7 3272 640 469
Fax: 7 3272 640 469
Email: kovalev2001@pochtamt.ru

KENYA – KEN
Kenya Lawn Tennis Association
PO Box 48620-00100
Nairobi, Kenya
President: Mr Francis Mutuku
Secretary: Mr Kepha Otieno
Telephone: 254 20 582646
Fax: 254 22 725672
Email: otienok@wananchi.com

KOREA, REPUBLIC OF – KOR
Korea Tennis Association
Room 108, Olympic Gym No. 2
88-2 Oryun-Dong, Songpa-Gu
Seoul 138-151, Korea, Rep.
President: Mr Dong-Kil Cho
Secretary: Mr Yeong-Moo Huh
Telephone: 82 2 420 4285
Fax: 82 2 420 4284
Email: kortennis@hanmail.net

KUWAIT – KUW
Kuwait Tennis Federation
PO Box 1462
Hawalli 32015, Kuwait
President: Sheik Ahmed Al-Sabah
Secretary: Mr Abdul-Ridha Ghareeb
Telephone: 965 539 7261
Fax: 965 539 0617
Email: info@kuwaittennis.com
Website: www.kuwaittennis.com

KYRGYZSTAN – KGZ
Kyrgyzstan Tennis Federation
Moskovskey Str 121/58
Bishkek 720000, Kyrgyzstan
President: Mr Tanaev Nikolai Tanaev
Secretary: Mr Valentin Akinshin
Telephone: 996 312 664 713
Fax: 996 312 664 713
Email: tfkr@elcat.kg

LATVIA – LAT
Latvian Tennis Union
Oskara Kalpaka Pr.16
LV 2010 Jurmala, Latvia
President: Mr Juris Savickis
Secretary: Mr Janis Pliens
Telephone: 371 775 2121
Fax: 371 775 5021
Email: teniss@parks.lv

LEBANON – LIB
Fédération Libanaise de Tennis
1st Floor – Beirut-Lebanon & Kuwait Bdg
Dora Main Street
Beirut, Lebanon
President: Mr Riad Haddad
Secretary: Mr Nicolas Haddad
Telephone: 961 1 879 288
Fax: 961 1 879 277
Email: lbtf@elbarid.net

LESOTHO – LES
Lesotho Lawn Tennis Association
PO Box 156
Maseru 100, Lesotho
President: Mr Khoai Matete
Secretary: Mr Mokhali Lithebe
Telephone: 266 22 321 543
Fax: 266 22 321 543
Email: tennis@ilesotho.com

LIBYA – LBA
Libyan Arab Tennis & Squash
Federation
PO Box 879-2729
Tripoli, Libya
President: Mr Murad Husen Halal
Secretary: Mr Khaled Zankouli
Telephone: 218 214 780 481
Fax: 218 214 780 510
Email: libyan_tennis_fed@hotmail.com

LIECHTENSTEIN – LIE
Liechtensteiner Tennisverband
Rheingau 15
9495 Triesen, Liechtenstein
President: Mr Daniel Kieber
Secretary: Ms Vanessa Schurte
Telephone: 423 392 4440
Fax: 423 392 4418
Email: tsv@strub.lol.li
Website: www.ltv.li

LITHUANIA – LTU
Lithuanian Tennis Association
Azuolyno 5
Vilnius, LT-07171, Lithuania
President: Mr Liutauras Radzevicius
Secretary: Ms Edita Liachoviciute
Telephone: 370 680 23868
Fax: 370 5246 0829
Email: LTS@TAKAS.LT
Website: www.tenisosajunga.lt

LUXEMBOURG – LUX
Fédération Luxembourgeoise de Tennis
Boite Postale 134
L-4002 Esch-sur-Alzette
Luxembourg
President: Mr Yves Kemp
Secretary: Mr Francois Dahm
Telephone: 352 574 470
Fax: 352 574 473
Email: fltennis@pt.lu
Website: www.flt.lu

MACEDONIA, F. Y. R. – MKD
Macedonian Tennis Federation
Gradski Park Bb
1000 Skopje, Macedonia, FYR.
President: Mr Risto Guskov
Secretary: Mrs Biljana Dimovska
Telephone: 389 2 3118530
Fax: 389 2 3118530/2735745
Email: mtf@unet.com.mk or
inteko@mol.com.mk

MADAGASCAR – MAD
Fédération Malgache de Tennis
BP 4370
6, rue Indira Gandhi
Immeuble Vitasoa Analakely
101 Antananarivo, Madagascar
President: Mr Mamiharilala Rasolojaona
Secretary: Ms Emma Lisiarisoa
Rabodomalala
Telephone: 261 20 22 330 66
Fax: 261 20 22 297 96
Email: isi@wanadoo.mg

MALAYSIA – MAS
Lawn Tennis Association of Malaysia
National Tennis Centre
Jalan Duta
50480 Kuala Lumpur, Malaysia
President: Datuk Abdul Razak b. Latiff
Secretary: Mr David Siew
Telephone: 603 620 161 73
Fax: 603 620 161 67
Email: ltam@first.net.my

MALI – MLI
Fédération Malienne de Tennis
IFA-BACO
425, Avenue de L'Yser
Quartier du Fleuve
Bamako, Mali
President: Mr Mohamed Traore
Secretary: Ms Amedine Traore
Telephone: 223 222 48 05
Fax: 223 222 23 24
Email: ifabaco@cefib.com

MALTA – MLT
Malta Tennis Federation
PO Box 50
Sliema, Malta
President: Mr Anthony Cilia Pisani
Secretary: Dr David Faruggia Sacco
Telephone: 356 9942 3049
Fax:
Email: mark.camilleri@atlas.com.mt; tcp@icm.com.mt

MAURITIUS – MRI
Mauritius Tennis Federation
National Tennis Center
Petit Camp
Phoenix, Mauritius
President: Mr Jean-Michel Giraud
Secretary: Mr Akhtar Toorawa
Telephone: 230 686 3214
Fax: 230 686 3231
Email: mltate@intnet.mu

MEXICO – MEX
Federacion Mexicana de Tenis
Miguel Angel de Quevedo 953
Col. El Rosedal
Mexico City 04330 DF, Mexico
President: Mr Francisco Maciel
Secretary: Mr Antonio Vargas
Telephone: 52 55 5689 9733
Fax: 52 55 5689 6307
Email: direccion@fmt.com.mx
Website: www.fmt.com.mx

MOLDOVA – MDA
Moldova Republic Tennis Federation
bul. Decebal 72
Chisinau, MD-2038 Moldova
President: Mr Jury Drozd
Secretary: Mr Serghei Zaicenco
Telephone: 37322 72123
Fax: 37322 568 312
Email: ftenis@mdl.net
Website: www.angelfire.com/vt/mtennis

MONACO – MON
Fédération Monegasque de Lawn Tennis
BP No 253
98005 Monaco Cedex, Monaco
President: Mrs Elisabeth De Massy
Secretary: Mr Alain Manigley
Telephone: 377 93 255 574
Fax: 377 93 305 482
Email: info@monaco-tennis.com

MONGOLIA – MGL
Mongolian Tennis Association
PO Box 522
Ulaanbaatar 44, Mongolia
President: Mr Ch. Ganzorig
Secretary: Mr Janchiv Batjargal
Telephone: 976 11 350 071
Fax: 976 11 343 611
Email: mta@magicnet.mn

MOROCCO – MAR
Fédération Royale Marocaine de Tennis
BP 50171
Casa Ghandi
Casablanca 20007, Morocco
President: Mr Mohamed M'Jid
Secretary: Mr Hachem Kacimi My
Telephone: 212 22 981 266/262
Fax: 212 22 981 265
Email: frmt@casanet.net.ma
Website: www.frmtennis.com

MYANMAR – MYA
Tennis Federation of Myanmar
Thien Byu Tennis Plaza
Mingalar Taung Nyunt
Yangon, Myanmar
President: Mr U Zaw Zaw
Secretary: Mr Tin Aung Lynn
Telephone: 951 372 360/513 009
Fax: 951 527 797
Email: reservation@maxmyanmar.com.mm

NAMIBIA – NAM
Namibia Tennis Association
PO Box 11393
Windhoek 9000, Namibia
President: Mr Bob Mould
Secretary: Ms Birgit Hacker
Telephone: 264 61 227 764
Fax: 264 61 237 078
Email: mouldwhk@iafrica.com.na

NETHERLANDS – NED
Koninklijke Nederlandse
Lawn Tennis Bond
PO Box 1617
3800 BP Amersfoort, Netherlands
President: Mr Klaas Rijpma
Secretary: Mr Evert-Jan Hulshof
Telephone: 31 33 454 26 00
Fax: 31 33 454 26 45
Email: knltb@knltb.nl
Website: www.knltb.nl

NETHERLANDS ANTILLES – AHO
Netherlands Antilles Tennis Assn.
PO Box 3644
Willemstad
Curacao, Netherlands Antilles
President: Mr Kenneth Hennep
Secretary: Ms Shariselle Gonet
Telephone: 599 9 737 8086
Fax: 599 9 738 3486
Email: president@natf.an
Website: www.natf.an

NEW ZEALAND – NZL
Tennis New Zealand
PO Box 18 308
Vodafone Tennis Park
69 Merton Road, Glen Innes
Auckland, New Zealand
President: Mr Jim Martin
Secretary: Mr Don Turner
Telephone: 64 9 528 5428
Fax: 64 9 528 5789
Email: info@tennisnz.com
Website: www.tennisnz.com

NIGERIA – NGR
Nigeria Tennis Federation
National Stadium Complex
PO Box 7956
Surulere, Lagos, Nigeria
President: Mr Sanni Ndanusa
Secretary: Mr Opeyemi Aminu
Telephone: 234 1 472 2006
Fax: 234 1 585 0530
Email: nigtennisfederation@yahoo.com

NORWAY – NOR
Norges Tennisforbund
Haslevangen 33
PO Box 287 – Okern
0511 Oslo, Norway
President: Mr Per Wright
Secretary: Mr Jarle Aambo
Telephone: 47 22 72 70 00
Fax: 47 22 72 70 01
Email: tennis@nif.idrett.no
Website: www.nif.idrett.no/tennis/

OMAN – OMA
Oman Tennis Association
PO Box 2226
Ruwi 112, Oman
President: Mr Khalid Md Al Zubair
Secretary: Mr Imad Kamal Sultan
Telephone: 968 751 402
Fax: 968 751 394
Email: tennis@omantel.net.om
Website: www.omantennis.com

PAKISTAN – PAK
Pakistan Tennis Federation
39-A Jinnah Stadium
Kashmir Highway
Islamabad, Pakistan
President: Mr Syed Dilawar Abbas
Secretary: Major Abdul Rashid Khan
Telephone: 92 519 212 846
Fax: 92 519 212 846
Email: pktenfed@isb.comsats.net.pk

PANAMA – PAN
Federacion Panamena de Tenis
Apartado 6-4965
El Dorado
Panama City, Panama
President: Mr Michael Bettsak
Secretary: Mr Guillermo Saez
Telephone: 507 263 6422
Fax: 507 263 7590
Email: bal43c@ventas.net

PARAGUAY – PAR
Asociacion Paraguaya de Tenis
Centro Nacional de Tenis
Direccion Gral. de Deportes
Avda Eusebio Ayala km 4 y 1/2
Asuncion, Paraguay
President: Dr Ruben Meilicke
Secretary: Mr Atilio Pereira
Telephone: 595 21 446 855
Fax: 595 21 524 880
Email: apt@cmm.com.py
Website: www.apt.com.py

PERU – PER
Federacion de Tenis de Peru
Cercado Campo de Marte S/N
Casilla Nro. 11-0488
Lima 11, Peru
President: Mr Edmundo Jaramillo
Secretary: Mr Javier Tori Guerrero
Telephone: 511 424 9979
Fax: 511 431 0533
Email: tenisperu@terra.com.pe
Website: www.perutenis.com.pe

PHILIPPINES – PHI
Philippine Tennis Association
Rizal Memorial Sports Complex
Pablo Ocampo Sr. Street
Manila, Philippines
President: Mr Manuel D Misa
Secretary: Mr Raymundo N Suarez
Telephone: 63 2 523 6415
Fax: 63 2 525 2016
Email: philta@info.com.ph

POLAND – POL
Polski Zwiazek Tenisowy
Frascati Street 4
00-483 Warsaw, Poland
President: Mr Waldemar Dubaniowski
Secretary: Mr Tomasz Polgrabski
Telephone: 48 22 629 2621
Fax: 48 22 621 8001
Email: pzt@pzt.pl

PORTUGAL – POR
Federacao Portuguesa de Tenis
Rua Actor Chaby Pinheiro, 7A
2795-060 Linda-a-Velha, Portugal
President: Mr Manuel Valle-Domingues
Secretary: Mr Jose Costa
Telephone: 351 21 415 1356
Fax: 351 21 414 1520
Email: fptenis@mail.telepac.pt
Website: www.fptenis.pt

PUERTO RICO – PUR
Associacion de Tenis de Puerto Rico
1611 Fernandez Juncos Avenue
Santurce
PR 00909, Puerto Rico
President: Dr Pedro Beauchamp
Secretary: Mr Fernando Figueroa
Telephone: 1 787 982 7782
Fax: 1 787 982 7783
Email: rodriguez@cta.usta.com

QATAR – QAT
Qatar Tennis Federation
Khalifa Int. Tennis Complex
Majlis Al – Taawon St
Al Dafna – PO Box 4959
Doha, Qatar
President: Sheikh Mohammad Bin Faleh Al-Thani
Secretary: Mr Tariq A Al-Siddiqi
Telephone: 974 4 409 666
Fax: 974 4 832 990
Email: qatartennis@qatartennis.org

ROMANIA – ROM
Federatia Romana de Tennis
Bd. Pierre de Coubertin 11
70139 Bucharest, Romania
President: Mr Ilie Nastase
Secretary: Mr Dimitru Haradau
Telephone: 4021 324 5330
Fax: 4021 324 5329
Email: frtenis@mcit.ro

RUSSIA – RUS
Russian Tennis Federation
Lutzhnetskaya Nab 8
119871 Moscow, Russia
President: Mr Shamil Tarpischev
Secretary: Mr Boris Fomenko
Telephone: 7 095 923 2137
Fax: 7 095 924 6427
Email: arta@russport.ru

RWANDA – RWA
Fédération Rwandaise de Tennis
Stade National Amahoro
BP 3321
Kigali, Rwanda
President: Dr Charles Ruadkubana
Secretary: Mr Freddy Somayire Rubona
Telephone: 250 574521
Fax: 250 574074
Email: ntwalit@hotmail.com or frttennis@yahoo.fr

SAINT LUCIA - LCA
St Lucia Lawn Tennis Association
PO Box 189
20 Micoud Street
Castries, Saint Lucia
President: Mr Stephen Mcnamara
Secretary: Mrs Pauline Erlinger-Ford
Telephone: 1 758 452 2662
Fax: 1 758 452 3885
Email: mcnmara.co@candw.lc

SAN MARINO - SMR
San Marino Tennis Federation
Strada di Montecchio 15
47890 San Marino
President: Mr Christian Forcellini
Secretary: Mr Marino Guardigli
Telephone: 378 0549 990 578
Fax: 378 0549 990 584
Email: fst@omniway.sm
Website: www.fst.sm

SAUDI ARABIA, KINGDOM OF - KSA
Saudi Arabian Tennis Federation
Saudi Olympic Complex
PO Box 29454
Riyadh 11457, Saudi Arabia
President: Dr Ahmad Al Senany
Secretary: Mr Rasheed Abu Rasheed
Telephone: 966 1 482 0188
Fax: 966 1 482 2829
Email: sf@sauditenfed.gov.sa
Website: www.sauditennis.com

SENEGAL - SEN
Fédération Senegalaise de Tennis
km 7,5 Boulevard du Centenaire
de la Commune
BP 510
Dakar, Senegal
President: Mr Issa Mboup
Secretary: Mr Ousseynou Kama
Telephone: 221 832 0267
Fax: 221 832 0496
Email: fst@arc.sn

SERBIA & MONTENEGRO - SCG
Serbia & Montenegro Tennis Federation
Aleksandra Stanboliskog 26
11000 Beograd
Serbia & Montenegro
President: Mr Petar Ivanovic
Secretary: Mr Dusan Orlandic
Telephone: 381 11 367 0787
Fax: 381 11 367 0509
Email: yugtenis@verat.net.

SINGAPORE - SIN
Singapore Tennis Association
Unit 10 National Stadium
15 Stadium Road
397718, Singapore
President: Mr Edwin Lee
Secretary: Mr Ha Kie Tjoeng
Telephone: 65 6348 0124
Fax: 65 6348 2414
Email: info@singtennis.org.sg
Website: www.singtennis.org.sg

SLOVAK REPUBLIC - SVK
Slovak Tennis Association
Prikopova 6
831 03 Bratislava, Slovak Rep.
President: Mr Tibor Macko
Secretary: Mr Igor Moska
Telephone: 421 2 49209 877
Fax: 421 2 49209 879
Email: stz@stz.sk
Website: www.stz.sk

SLOVENIA - SLO
Slovene Tennis Association
Vurnikova 2/vi
1000 Ljubljana, Slovenia
President: Mr Andrej Polenec
Secretary: Mrs Marjeta Smodis
Telephone: 386 1 430 63 70
Fax: 386 1 430 66 95
Email: info@teniska-zveza.si
Website: slotenis.megahit.si

SOUTH AFRICA, REPUBLIC OF - RSA
South African Tennis Association
PO Box 521022
Saxonwold 2132, South Africa
President: Mr Johann Koorts
Secretary: Mrs Sandra Delport
Telephone: 27 11 442 0500/01
Fax: 27 11 442 0503
Email: satennis@mweb.co.za
Website: www.supertennis.co.za

SPAIN - ESP
Real Federación Española de Tenis
Avda Diagonal 618 2-B
08021 Barcelona, Spain
President: Mr Pedro Muñoz
Secretary: Mr Victor Barreira
Telephone: 34 93 200 5355
Fax: 34 93 202 1279
Email: riba@rfet.es
Website: www.rfet.es

SRI LANKA - SRI
Sri Lanka Tennis Association
45 Sir Marcus Fernando Mawatha
Colombo 7, Sri Lanka
President: Mr Suresh Subramaniam
Secretary: Mr Maxwell de Silva
Telephone: 94 11 533 7161
Fax: 94 11 268 6174
Email: sltennis@sltnet.lk

SUDAN - SUD
Sudan Lawn Tennis Association
PO Box 3792
Africa House
Khartoum, Sudan
President: Mr Khalid Talaat Farid
Secretary: Mr Ahmed Abuelgasim Hasim
Telephone: 249 1 837 95473
Fax: 249 1 837 70246

SWEDEN - SWE
The Swedish Tennis Association
Box 1064
269 21 Bastad, Sweden
President: Mr Jan Carlzon
Secretary: Mr Tony Wiréhn
Telephone: 46 431 783 90
Fax: 46 431 756 84
Email: info@tennis.se
Website: www.tennis.se

SWITZERLAND - SUI
Swiss Tennis
Solothurnstrasse 112
2501 Biel, Switzerland
President: Mrs Christine Ungricht
Secretary: Mr Daniel Monnin
Telephone: 41 32 344 0707
Fax: 41 32 344 0700
Email: daniel.monnin@swisstennis.com
Website: www.myTennis.ch

SYRIA - SYR
Syrian Arab Tennis Federation
Al Faihaa Sport City
Mazraa
Damascus, Syria
President: Mr Samer Mourad
Secretary: Miss Safa Sarakbi
Telephone: 963 11 441 1972
Fax: 963 11 441 1972
Email: sytennis@scs-net.org

TAJIKISTAN – TJK
National Tennis Federation of
Republic of Tajikistan
Tennis Palace/A/b 308
Dushanbe 734001, Tajikistan
President: Mr Amircul Azimov
Secretary: Mr Vazirbek Nazirov
Telephone: 992 372 246342
Fax: 992 372 246342
Email: ttf@tojikiston.com

THAILAND – THA
Lawn Tennis Association of Thailand
327 Chartpattana Party Building
Sukhothai Road
Dusit District
Bangkok 10300, Thailand
President: H.E. Suwat Liptapanlop
Secretary: Admiral Banawit Kengrian
Telephone: 662 668 7624
Fax: 662 668 7435
Email: ltat@ksc.th.com
Website: www.ltat.org

TOGO – TOG
Fédération Togolaise de Tennis
BP 7160
Lome, Togo
President: Mr Kouassi Luc Dofontien
Secretary: Mr Koffi Galokpo
Telephone: 228 227 43 53
Fax: 228 222 02 72
Email: fttennis@togo-imet.com

TRINIDAD & TOBAGO – TRI
Tennis Assn. of Trinidad & Tobago
21 Taylor Street
Woodbrook
Port of Spain, Trinidad & Tobago
President: Mr Vincent Pereira
Secretary: Mr Nicholas Gomez
Telephone: 1 868 628 0783
Fax: 1 868 628 0783

TUNISIA – TUN
Fédération Tunisienne de Tennis
B.P. 350, Cite Nationale Sportive
El Menzah
1004 Tunis, Tunisia
President: Mr Tarak Cherif
Secretary:
Telephone: 216 71 844 144
Fax: 216 71 798 844
Email: ftt@ati.tn

TURKEY – TUR
Turkiye Tenis Federasyonu
Ulus Is Hani
Ankara, Turkey
President: Mr Azmi Kumova
Secretary: Mr Naci Dumanoglu
Telephone: 90 312 310 7345
Fax: 90 312 3107345
Email: tenis@ttf.org.tr
Website: www.ttf.org.tr

TURKMENISTAN – TKM
Turkmenistan Tennis Association
Azadi Str, 44/app 4
744000 Ashgabat, Turkmenistan
President: Mr Berdimurad Redjepov
Secretary: Mr Bjashimov Serdar
Telephone: 993 12 35 1819
Fax: 993 12 35 1819
Email: olimpya@online.tm

UGANDA – UGA
Uganda Tennis Association
Mosa Court Offices
Plot 12 Shimoni Road
PO Box 2186
Kampala, Uganda
President: Mr Simon Kisasa
Secretary: Mr Cedric Babu
Telephone: 256 41 236 688
Fax: 256 41 230 310
Email: cedricb@iconafrica.com

UKRAINE – UKR
Ukrainian Tennis Federation
A/C B-2
PO 01001
Kiev, Ukraine
President: Mr Andriy Medvedev
Secretary: Mr Volodimir Gerashchenko
Telephone: 38 044 224 8782
Fax: 38 044 234 8782
Email: ftu@rql.net.ua

UNITED ARAB EMIRATES – UAE
United Arab Emirates
Tennis Association
PO Box 22466
Dubai, United Arab Emirates
President: Sheikh Hasher Al-Maktoum
Secretary: Mr Mohammed Al-Merry
Telephone: 971 4 269 0393
Fax: 971 4 266 9390
Email: tennis@emirates.net.ae

UNITED STATES OF AMERICA – USA
United States Tennis Association
70 West Red Oak Lane
White Plains – New York
N.Y. 10604-3602, USA
President: Mr Franklin R Johnson
Secretary: Mr Lee Hamilton
Telephone: 1 914 696 7000
Fax: 1 914 696 7167
Email: Hamilton@usta.com
Website: www.usta.com

US VIRGIN ISLANDS – ISV
Virgin Islands Tennis Association
P.O. Box 303408
St Thomas, USVI 00803
United States Virgin Islands
President: Mr William F McComb
Secretary: Ms Deborah Davis
Telephone: 1 340 774 8547
Fax: 1 340 776 1558
Email: wfmccomb.eng@attglobal.net

URUGUAY – URU
Asociacion Uruguaya de Tenis
Galicia 1392
CP 11.200
Montevideo, Uruguay
President: Sr Gilberto Saenz
Secretary: Mr Elbio Arias
Telephone: 598 2 902 9391
Fax: 598 2 902 1809
Email: aut@montevideo.com.uy

UZBEKISTAN – UZB
Uzbekistan Tennis Federation
1 Assaka Pereulok
House 14
Tashkent 700035, Uzbekistan
President: Mr R Inoyatov
Secretary: Mr I Shepelev
Telephone: 99 871 137 2554
Fax: 99 871 133 5503
Email: uztennis@intal.uz
Website: www.uzbektennis.uz

VENEZUELA – VEN
Federacion Venezolana de Tenis
Complejo Nacional de Tenis
Calle A – Apartado 70539
Urb Santa Rosa de Lima
Caracas 1070-A, Venezuela
President: Mr Rene Herrera
Secretary: Mr Deva de Gonzalez
Telephone: 58 212 979 2421
Fax: 58 212 979 2694 or 7462
Email: gerencia@fvtenis.com
Website: www.fvtenis.com

VIETNAM – VIE
Vietnam Tennis Federation
175 Nguyen Thai Hoc Street
Ba Dinh District
Hanoi, Vietnam
President: Mr Dang Huu Hai
Secretary: Mr Tran Ngoc Linh
Telephone: 844 733 0036
Fax: 844 733 0036
Email: vtf@fpt.vn

ZIMBABWE – ZIM
Tennis Zimbabwe
PO Box A575
Avondale
Harare, Zimbabwe
President: Mrs Ann Martin
Secretary: Ms Patricia Mavunduke
Telephone: 2634 740 509
Fax: 2634 740 351/753 992
Email: teniszim@africaonline.co.zw

Class C (Associate) Members Without Voting Rights (59)

AFGHANISTAN – AFG
Afghanistan Tennis Federation
c/o Ahmad Shaheer
British Embassy
Kabul, Afghanistan
President: Mr Abdul Azim Niazi
Secretary: Mr Ahmad Shaheer Shahriar
Telephone: 93 70 274 772
Email: afghantennisfederation@yahoo.co.uk

ALBANIA – ALB
Albanian Tennis Federation
Rruga Myslym Shyri
Pallati 46, Ap.10/1
Tirana, Albania
President: Mr Avni Ponari
Secretary: Mr Tonin Mema
Telephone: 355 42 74 361
Fax: 355 42 54 750
Email: albanian_tennis_federation@yahoo.com

AMERICAN SAMOA – ASA
American Samoa Tennis Association
PO Box 2070
Pago Pago
AS 96799, American Samoa
President: Mr Dave Godinet
Secretary: Ms Elena Dworsky
Telephone: 684 699 9512
Fax: 684 699 2105

ARUBA – ARU
Aruba Lawn Tennis Bond
Fergusonstraat Nr 40-a
PO Box 1151
Oranjestad, Aruba
President: Mr Ling Wong
Secretary: Ms Mathilde Velazquez
Telephone: 297 5 833 506
Fax: 297 5 887 184
Email: arubalawntennis@hotmail.com

BELIZE – BIZ
Belize Tennis Association
PO Box 365
16 Regent Street
Belize City, Belize
President: Mr Edward Nabil Musa Sr
Secretary: Mr John Owen Longsworth
Telephone: 501 22 77070
Fax: 501 22 75593
Email: brodies@btl.net

BHUTAN – BHU
Bhutan Tennis Federation
PO Box 838
Thimphu, Bhutan
President: Mr Lyonpo Ugen Tschering
Secretary: Mr Chencho Norbu
Telephone: 975 232 2138
Fax: 975 232 6768
Email: btftennis@druknet.bt

BRITISH VIRGIN ISLANDS – IVB
British Virgin Islands LTA
PO Box 3169 PMB 259
Road Town
Tortola, British Virgin Islands
President: Mr Henry Creque
Secretary: Mr Clive Gumbs
Telephone: 1 284 494 9225
Fax: 1 284 494 4291

BURUNDI – BDI
Fédération de Tennis du Burundi
BP 2221
Bujumbura, Burundi
President: Mr Salvator Matata
Secretary: Mr Joseph Ngomirakiza
Telephone: 257 242 443
Fax: 257 222 247
Email: salmatfr@yahoo.fr

CAMBODIA – CAM
Cambodia Tennis Federation
c/o Power Investment Group
Office 14, Hotel Cambodiana
313 quai Preah Sisowath
Phnom Penh, Cambodia
President: Mr Cham Prasidh
Secretary: Mr Tep Ritivit
Telephone: 855 23 218 580
Fax: 855 23 218 580
Email: power_in@online.com.kh

CAPE VERDE ISLANDS – CPV
Federacão Cabo Verdiana de Ténis
Pavilhão Desportivo Váva Duarte
Chã de Areia – B.P. 584
Praia – Cabo Verde (Island)
Cape Verde Islands
President: Mr Hugo Almeida
Secretary:
Telephone: 238 2 613 309
Fax: 238 2 613 309
Email: fedcabtenis@cvtelecom.cv

CAYMAN ISLANDS – CAY
Tennis Fed. of the Cayman Islands
PO Box 2499 GT
Strathvale House
Grand Cayman, Cayman Islands
President: Mr Chris Johnson
Secretary: Mr John Smith
Telephone: 1 345 946 0820
Fax: 1 345 946 0864
Email: chrisjohnson@candw.ky

CENTRAL AFRICAN REPUBLIC – CAF
Fédération Centrafricaine de Tennis
S/c Dameca
B P 804
Bangui, Central African Republic
President: Mr I Kamach
Secretary: Mr Jean Ombi
Telephone: 236 61 18 05
Fax: 236 61 56 60
Email: fcat_cf@yahoo.fr

CONGO, DEMOCRATIC REPUBLIC OF – COD
Fédération Congolaise Démocratique de Lawn Tennis
BP 11 497 KIN 1
Kinshasa, Congo, Dem Rep.
President: Mr Ndombe Jacob
Secretary: Mr Georges Koshi
Telephone: 243 884 3469
Fax: 243 880 1625
Email: fecodelat@yahoo.fr or ndombepres@yahoo.fr

COOK ISLANDS – COK
Tennis Cook Islands
PO Box 806
Rarotonga, Cook Islands
President: Mr Brian Baudinet
Secretary: Mr Brendan Stone
Telephone: 682 26027
Fax: 682 26027
Email: brian@baudinet.co.ck
Website: www.baudinet.com

DOMINICA – DMA
Dominica Lawn Tennis Association
PO Box 138
Roseau, Dominica
President: Mr Thomas Dorsett
Secretary: Mr Simon Butler
Telephone: 1 767 448 8367
Fax: 1 767 448 7010
Email: tennisdominica@yahoo.com

EQUATORIAL GUINEA – GEQ
Equatorial Guinea Tennis Federation
PO Box 980 BN
Malabo, Equatorial Guinea
President: Mr Enrique Mercader Costa
Secretary: Mr Francisco Sibita
Telephone: 240 09 2866
Fax: 240 09 3313

ERITREA – ERI
Eritrean Tennis Federation
C/o Eritrean Olympic Committee
PO Box 3665
Asmara, Eritrea
President: Mr Fessahaie Haile
Secretary:
Telephone: 291 1 121 533
Fax: 291 1 120 967
Email: tesat@tse.com.er

FIJI – FIJ
Fiji Tennis Association
PO Box 453
Lautoka, Fiji
President: Mr John Shannon
Secretary: Mr Paras Naidu
Telephone: 679 666 6642
Fax: 679 666 8820
Email: otfagm2007@yahoo.com.au

GAMBIA – GAM
Gambia Lawn Tennis Association
PMB 664
Serrekunda, Gambia
President: Mr Sheriff Jammeh
Secretary: Mr Tunde Taylor-Thomas
Telephone: 220 4495 946
Fax: 220 4378 894
Email: jakes_r@hotmail.com

GRENADA – GRN
Grenada Tennis Association
PO Box 1202
St George's, Grenada
President: Mr Ricardo Charles
Secretary: Mr Earl Charles
Telephone: 1 473 440 1977
Fax: 1 473 440 0453
Email: rickyc@caribsurf.com

GUAM – GUM
Guam National Tennis Federation
PO Box 4379
Hagatna 96932, Guam
President: Mr Rick Ninete
Secretary: Ms Jane Aguon
Telephone: 1 671 472 6270
Fax: 1 671 472 0997
Email: ricn@ite.net

GUINEA-BISSAU – GBS
Fédération de Tennis de la Guinee-Bissau
Caixa Postal 387
Bissau, Guinea-Bissau
President: Mr José Rodriques-Santy
Telephone: 245 720 6030
Email: bissaumar@yahoo.fr

GUINEE CONAKRY – GUI
Fédération Guineenne de Tennis
B P 4897
Conakry, Guinee Conakry
President: Mr Kiridi Bangoura
Secretary: Mr Abdoulaye Conte
Telephone: 224 44 40 19
Fax: 224 41 19 26

GUYANA – GUY
Guyana Lawn Tennis Association
PO Box 10205
Olympic House
Church & Peter Rose Streets
Georgetown, Guyana
President: Mr Wilfred Lee
Secretary: Ms Grace McCalman
Telephone: 592 2 2 75501
Fax: 592 2 2 55865
Email: glta18@yahoo.com

KIRIBATI – KIR
Kiribati Tennis Association
PO Box 245
Tarawa, Kiribati
President: Dr Komeri Onorio
Secretary: Mrs Ahling Onorio
Telephone: 686 28271
Fax: 686 28271
Email: komeri@tskl.net.ki

KOREA, DEMOCRATIC PEOPLE'S REPUBLIC OF – PRK
Tennis Assocation of DPR of Korea
Kumsong
Mangyongdae Dist
Pyongyang, Korea, Dem. Rep.
President: Mr Kim Su Ik
Secretary: Mr Ko Yong Su
Telephone: 850 218 111 Ext. 8164
Fax: 850 2381 4403

LAO, DEMOCRATIC PEOPLE'S REPUBLIC – LAO
Lao Tennis Federation
PO Box 6280
Vientiane, Lao, D.P.R
President: H.E. Somphong Mongkholvilay
Secretary: Mr Phoukhong Nilaxay
Telephone: 856 21 218956
Fax: 856 21 218956/215274
Email: gcdnl@laopdr.com

LIBERIA – LBR
Liberia Tennis Association
PO Box 1742
Randall Street
Monrovia, Liberia
President: Cllr. Lloyd Kennedy
Secretary: Mr Manfred Jones
Telephone: 231 225 626
Fax: 231 226 253/225
Email: clemenceauurey@yahoo.com

MALAWI – MAW
Lawn Tennis Association of Malawi
c/o Wellcome Trust Research Labs.
PO Box 30096
Blantyre 3, Malawi
President: Mr Steve Graham
Secretary: Ms Barbara Halse
Telephone: 265 1 676 444
Fax: 265 1 675 774

MALDIVES – MDV
Tennis Association of the Maldives
PO Box 20175
Chaandhanee Magu
Male, Maldives
President: Mr Ahmed Aslam
Secretary: Mr Yusuf Riza
Telephone: 960 317 018
Fax: 960 310 325
Email: tennismaldives@avasmail.com.mv

MARSHALL ISLANDS – MSH
Marshall Islands Tennis Federation
PO Box 197
Marjuro
MH96960, Marshall Islands
President: Mr Wally Milne
Secretary: Mr Dwight Heine
Telephone: 692 625 5275
Fax: 692 625 3655
Email: wemilne@hotmail.com

MAURITANIA – MTN
Fédération Mauritanienne de Tennis
Office du Complexe Olympique
BP 3128
Nouakchott., Mauritania
President: Mr Isaac Ould Ragel
Secretary: Mr Cheickh Ould Horomtala
Telephone: 222 641 2092
Fax: 222 525 3787
Email: rimtennis2002@yahoo.fr

MICRONESIA, FEDERATED STATES OF – FSM
Federated States of Micronesia LTA
PO Box PS319
Paliker, Pohnpei
FM 96941, Micronesia, F.S.
President: Mr Sterling Skilling
Secretary: Mr Simao Ieshi
Telephone: 691 320 619
Fax: 691 320 8915
Email: fsmnoc@mail.fm

MOZAMBIQUE – MOZ
Federacao Mocambicana de Tenis
Caixa Postal 4351
Av Samora Mahel No. 11
Porta 38 Maputo, Mozambique
President: Mr Arao Nhancale
Secretary: Mr Armindo Nhavene
Telephone: 258 1 300473
Fax: 258 1 300473
Email: anhahaia@yahoo.com.br

NAURU – NRU
Nauru Tennis Association
PO Box 274
Aiwo District, Nauru
President: Chief Paul Aingimea
Secretary: Mr Preston Itaia
Telephone: 674 444 3118
Fax: 674 444 3231
Email: nta@cenpac.net.nr

NEPAL – NEP
All Nepal Tennis Association
PO Box 3943
Kathmandu, Nepal
President: Mr Siddheshwar K Singh
Secretary: Mr Ramji Thapa
Telephone: 977 1 426 002
Fax: 977 1 416 427
Email: anlta@mos.com.np

NICARAGUA – NCA
Federacion Nicaraguense de Tenis
Apartado Postal C-119
Managua, Nicaragua
President: Mr Ramon Sevilla
Secretary: Mr J Camilo Munoz
Telephone: 505 276 1954
Fax: 505 276 0948
Email: rsevilla@cablenet.com.ni

NIGER – NIG
Fédération Nigerienne de Tennis
Stade du 29 juillet 1991
Avenue du Zarmaganda
BP 10 788 Niamey, Niger
President: Mr Ahmed Ousman Diallo
Secretary: Mr Boubacar Djibo
Telephone: 227 735 893/734 286
Fax: 227 732 876
Email: nigerautennis@hotmail.com

NORFOLK ISLANDS – NFK
Norfolk Islands Tennis Association
Cheryl Tennis Club
PO Box 512
Queen Elizabeth Avenue
Norfolk Islands
President: Mr John Henderson
Secretary: Ms Julie South
Telephone: 6723 229 66
Fax: 6723 232 26
Email: cheryltennis@ni.net.nf

NORTHERN MARIANA ISLANDS – NMI
Northern Mariana Islands Tennis Assn.
PO Box 10,000
Saipan, MP 96950-9504
Northern Mariana Islands
President: Mr Jeff Race
Secretary: Mr Ed Johnson
Telephone: 1 670 234 8438
Fax: 1 670 234 5545
Email: race@saipan.com

PALAU, DEMOCRATIC REPUBLIC OF – PLW
Palau Tennis Federation
PO Box 44
Koror 96940
Palau, D.R.
President: Ms Christina Michelsen
Secretary: Ms Annabel Lyman
Telephone: 680 488 6267
Fax: 680 488 6271
Email: cmichelsen@boh.com

PALESTINE – PLE
Palestinian Tennis Association
Beit Sahour
PO Box 131, Palestine
President: Mr Issa Rishmawi
Secretary: Mrs Samar Mousa Araj
Telephone: 972 2 277 2833/4
Fax: 972 2 277 4677
Email: pta@p-ol.com
Website: www.paltennis.org

PAPUA NEW GUINEA – PNG
Papua New Guinea
Lawn Tennis Association
PO Box 1230
Boroko, NCD
Papua New Guinea
President: Mr David Toua
Secretary: Mr Sundar Ramamurthy
Telephone: 675 320 0633
Fax: 675 320 0611
Email: sundar@online.net.pg

SAINT KITTS & NEVIS – SKN
St Kitts Lawn Tennis Association
Cayon Street
Basseterre
Saint Kitts & Nevis
President: Mr Raphael Jenkins
Secretary: Ms Connie Marsham
Telephone: 1 869 465 6809
Fax: 1 869 465 1190

SAINT VINCENT & THE GRENADINES – VIN
St Vincent & The Grenadines LTA
PO Box 2395
Kingstown
Saint Vincent & The Grenadines
President: Mr Grant Connell
Secretary: Mrs Euchrista Bruce-Lyle
Telephone: 1 784 457 4090
Fax: 1 784 457 4080
Email: svgtennis@hotmail.com

SAMOA – SAM
Tennis Samoa Inc
PO Box 6402
Apia, Samoa
President: Mr Waikaremoana So'onalole
Secretary: Miss Fiaapia Devoe
Telephone: 685 22 115
Fax: 685 21 145
Email: lwsoonal@ipasifika.net

SEYCHELLES – SEY
Seychelles Tennis Association
PO Box 580
Roche Caiman
Seychelles
President: Mr Philip Brioche
Secretary: Mr Gian Carlo Lauro
Telephone: 248 323 252
Fax: 248 324 066
Email: tennisey@seychelles.net

SIERRA LEONE – SLE
Sierra Leone Lawn Tennis Association
National Sports Council
PO Box 1181
Freetown, Sierra Leone
President: Mr John Benjamin
Secretary: Mr E T Ngandi
Telephone: 232 22 226 874
Fax: 232 22 229 083
Email: johnben@sierratel.sl

SOLOMON ISLANDS – SOL
Solomon Islands Tennis Association
PO Box 532
Honiara, Solomon Islands
President: Mr Ranjit Hewagama
Secretary: Dr Morgan Wairiu
Telephone: 677 27 354
Fax: 677 25 686
Email: tennis@solomon.com.sb

SOMALIA – SOM
The Somali Tennis Association
C/o 5 Gabalaya Street
11567 El Borg
Cairo, Egypt
President: Mr Osman Mohiadin Moallim
Secretary: Mr Farah Ali Moallin
Telephone: 252 1 215 639
Fax: 252 1 216 516
Email: osmanmoallim@yahoo.com

SURINAM – SUR
Surinaamse Tennisbond
PO Box 2087
Paramaribo-Zuid
Surinam
President: Mr Michael Lutchman
Secretary: Mr Martijn de Haan
Telephone: 597 452 545
Fax: 597 471 047
Email: stb@cq-link.sr

SWAZILAND – SWZ
Swaziland National Tennis Union
PO Box 2397
Manzini, Swaziland
President: Mr L Nxumalo
Secretary: Mr J Mazibuko
Telephone: 268 408 2329
Fax: 268 505 8903
Email: tennisswaziland@realnet.co.sz

TANZANIA – TAN
Tanzania Lawn Tennis Association
c/o Royal Norwegian Embassy
PO Box 2646
Dar Es Salaam, Tanzania
President: Mr Dennis Makoi
Secretary: Mrs Inger Johanne Njau
Telephone: 255 22 741 291 864
Fax: 255 22 211 6564
Email: ijn@norad.no

TONGA – TGA
Tonga Tennis Association
PO Box 816
Nuku'alofa, Tonga
President: Mr Fuka Kitekeiaho
Secretary: Ms Kiu Tatafu
Telephone: 676 23933
Fax: 676 24127

TURKS & CAICOS ISLANDS – TKS
Turks & Caicos Tennis Association
PO Box 205
Providenciales
British West Indies
Turks & Caicos Islands
President: Mr Robert Smith
Secretary: Mrs Tanis Wake-Forbes
Telephone: 649 946 5918
Email: tcinoc@hotmail.com

TUVALU – TUV
Tuvalu Tennis Association
Private Mail Bag
Vaiaku, Funafuti
Tuvalu
President: Mr Levi Telli
Secretary: Mr Molotii
Telephone:
Fax: 688 20 304
Email: levi@tuvalu.tv

VANUATU – VAN
Fédération de Tennis de Vanuatu
B P 563
Port Vila, Vanuatu
President: Mr Cyrille Mainguy
Secretary: Mr Francis Bryard
Telephone: 678 24817
Fax: 678 26133/24817
Email: cmg@vanuatu.com.vu

YEMEN – YEM
Yemen Tennis Federation
PO Box 19816
Sana'a, Yemen
President: Dr Rashad Al-Alimi
Secretary: Mr Ahmed Al-Sadiq
Telephone: 967 1 271 857
Fax: 967 1 271 857
Email: ytf@y.net.ye

ZAMBIA – ZAM
Zambia Lawn Tennis Association
PO Box 40200
Mufulira, Zambia
President: Mr Robert Mwewa
Secretary: Mr Lazarus Pepala
Telephone: 260 241 1907/0439
Fax: 260 241 2301/2734
Email: pepalala@yahoo.com

Regional Associations

ASIAN TENNIS FEDERATION (ATF)
12F Manulife Tower
169 Electric Road
North Point
Hong Kong China
President: Mr Anil Khanna
Secretary: Mr Suresh Subramaniam
Telephone: 852 2512 8226
Fax: 852 2512 8649
Email: atf@i-wave.net.hk
Website: www.asiantennis.com

CONFEDERACION SUDAMERICANA DE TENIS (COSAT)
Avda. Providencia 2653
Oficina # 44
Santiago, Chile
President: Mr Sergio Elias
Secretary: Mr Edmundo Rodriguez
Telephone: 56 2 436 8111
Fax: 56 2 436 8114
Email: cosat@cosat.org
Website: www.cosat.org

CONFEDERATION OF AFRICAN TENNIS (CAT)
BP 315
El Mensah
1004 Tunis, Tunisia
President: Mr Tarak Cherif
Secretary: Mr Hichem Riani
Telephone: 216 71 84 77 85
Fax: 216 71 84 10 45
Email: rianihichem@yahoo.fr
Website: www.catennis.net

COTECC
C/O Federacion Salvadorena
Apartado Postal (01) 110
San Salvador, El Salvador
President: Mr Enrique Molins
Secretary: Mr Frantz Liautaud
Telephone: 503 2278 8850
Fax: 503 2278 8087
Email: cotecc@telesal.net
Website: www.cotecc.org.sv

OCEANIA TENNIS FEDERATION (OTF)
PO Box 13759
Johnsonville
Wellington, New Zealand
President: Mr Geoff Pollard
Secretary: Mr Patrick O'Rourke
Telephone: 64 4 478 0465
Fax: 64 4 477 0465
Email: patrick@oceaniatennis.com
Website: www.oceaniatennis.com

TENNIS EUROPE
Zur Gempenfluh 36
CH-4059 Basel
Switzerland
President: Mr John James
Secretary: Mrs Charlotte Ferrari
Telephone: 41 61 335 90 40
Fax: 41 61 331 72 53
Email: contactus@tenniseurope.org
Website: www.tenniseurope.org

ITF Recognised Organisations

The ITF recognises and works closely with the following three organisations.

International Tennis Hall of Fame

Officially sanctioned by the United States Tennis Association in 1954, the International Tennis Hall of Fame (ITHF) was recognised by the ITF in 1986. Situated at the historic Newport Casino, the site of the first US National Championships in 1881, the ITHF was founded by James Van Alen in 1954 as a tribute to the ideals of the game. It is a non-profit institution committed to preserving the history of the sport, enshrining tennis heroes and heroines, inspiring and encouraging junior tennis development, and providing a landmark for tennis enthusiasts worldwide. The ITHF is the world's largest tennis museum and owns the world's largest collection of tennis memorabilia. Since 1955, 190 people have been elected to the ITHF as a tribute to their outstanding contribution to the game. See the full list of the ITHF Enshrinees which follow.

In 2001 the ITHF and the ITF unveiled a new Award of Excellence for Davis Cup and Fed Cup. It was decided that, where possible, the candidate should come from the nation or region in which the host nation for the semifinals/final is located.

Contact details:
International Tennis Hall of Fame
194 Bellevue Avenue
Newport, Rhode Island 02840, USA
Telephone: 1 401 849 3990 Fax: 1 401 849 8780
Email: newport@tennisfame.com
Website: www.tennisfame.com

The International Club

The concept of a series of International Clubs was the idea of British tennis correspondent A. Wallis Myers in 1924. He said "We are seeking to cement the ties that bind us to all international players, to exchange greetings with them from time to time, to offer them hospitality when they come in our midst. Hands across the net, in fact, means hands across the ocean."

Membership of the clubs is limited to those who have played representative international tennis overseas. As a result many former Davis and Fed Cup players participate in competitive events and friendly matches arranged by individual clubs.

In 2005, 34 countries had International Clubs, reflecting the increasing globalisation of tennis. While the IC's traditional ideals remain relevant, Clubs are encouraging junior membership by holding junior competitions and often alongside senior matches.

Contact details:
Chairman – Barry Weatherill
Council of International Lawn Tennis Clubs
52 Bedford Row, London WC1R 4LR
Telephone: 44 20 7395 3160
Website: www.ic-tennis.org
Email: b.weatherill@btopenworld.com

Honorary Secretary – Peter McQuibban
c/o Paul Hutchins, IC Council
PO Box 400, Wimbledon, London SW20 0QZ
Tel: 44 20 8946 9374 Fax: 44 20 8944 6459
Email: tenconcept@aol.com

The Association of Centenary Clubs

In 1995 Juan-Maria Tintore, President du Real Club de Tenis Barcelona, had the idea of bringing together tennis clubs with over a hundred years of history. Since well over 300 clubs throughout the world are eligible to join the Association, it is hoped that the Association will expand gradually for the benefit of the game. Eligible clubs include 60 in Germany, 90 in the United Kingdom, 13 in Denmark, nine in France and Italy, six in the Netherlands, not to mention 50 in the US and 16 in Australia.

Recognised by the International Olympic Committee (IOC), the Association of Centenary Tennis Clubs headquarters is at the Olympic Museum in Lausanne. Founded on 11 June 1996 by eight European clubs, the aim of the Centenary Club is to continue the traditions of tennis through the activities of its members by staging sporting and cultural reunions, tennis meetings and by maintaining the spirit of fair play inherent in sport.

Contact details:
Juan M. Tintore, President, Real Club de Tenis Barcelona 1899
President, Centenary Tennis Clubs Association or/and
Carlos Merce General Manager, Real Club de Tenis Barcelona 1899
Secretary, Centenary Tennis Clubs Association
Bosch i Gimpera, 5-13, 08034 Barcelona/Spain
Telephone: 34 93 2037852 Fax: 34 93 2045010
Email: info@centenarytennisclubs.com
www.centenarytennisclubs.com

Official Tennis Championships Recognised by the ITF

a) The ITF officially recognises the following Championships know as "Official Tennis Championships of the International Tennis Federation:

i) Championships organised by National Associations or bodies associated with them

The Lawn Tennis Championships (Wimbledon)
The United States Open
The French Championships
The Australian Championships
(known as "The Grand Slam")

The Japan Open
The Italian Open Championships
The International Championships of Spain

ii) Championships organised by the ITF

Olympic Tennis Event
ITF Seniors World Individual Championships
ITF Super-Seniors World Individual Championships
The Wheelchair Tennis Masters

b) The ITF is a partner with other constituencies in the organisation of the following championships:

Tennis Masters Cup
WTA Tour Championships

Arthur Ashe Stadium

International Tennis Hall of Fame Enshrinees

Over 190 individuals have been enshrined into the International Tennis Hall of Fame representing 18 countries worldwide.

Name	Year
*#Adee, George – USA	1964
#Alexander, Fred – USA	1961
#Allison, Wilmer – USA	1963
#Alonso, Manuel – ESP	1977
Anderson, Malcolm – AUS	2000
#Ashe, Arthur – USA	1985
#Atkinson, Juliette – USA	1974
#Austin, H.W. 'Bunny' – GBR	1997
Austin, Tracy – USA	1992
*#Baker, Lawrence, Sr. – USA	1975
#Barger-Wallach, Maud – USA	1958
Becker, Boris – GER	2003
#Behr, Karl – USA	1969
Betz Addie, Pauline – USA	1965
#Bjurstedt Mallory, Molla – USA	1958
Borg, Bjorn – SWE	1987
#Borotra, Jean – FRA	1976
Bowrey, Lesley Turner – AUS	1997
#Bromwich, John – AUS	1984
#Brookes, Norman – AUS	1977
Brough Clapp, Louise – USA	1967
#Browne, Mary K. – USA	1957
#Brugnon, Jacques – FRA	1976
#Budge, Don – USA	1964
* Buchholz, Butch – USA	2005
Bueno, Maria – BRA	1978
#Cahill, Mabel – IRL	1976
#Campbell, Oliver – USA	1955
Casals, Rosie – USA	1996
#Chace, Malcolm – USA	1961
*#Chatrier, Philippe – FRA	1992
Cheney, Dorothy 'Dodo' – USA	2004
#Clark, Clarence – USA	1983
#Clark, Joseph – USA	1955
#Clothier, William – USA	1956
#Cochet, Henri – FRA	1976
* Collins, Arthur W. 'Bud', Jr. – USA	1994
#Connolly Brinker, Maureen – USA	1968
Connors, Jimmy –USA	1998
Cooper, Ashley – AUS	1991
Courier, Jim – USA	2005
Court, Margaret Smith – AUS	1979
#Crawford, Jack – AUS	1979
*#Cullman, Joseph F., 3rd – USA	1990
*#Danzig, Allison – USA	1968
*#David, Herman – GBR	1998
#Davis, Dwight – USA	1956
#Dod, Lottie – GBR	1983
#Doeg, John – USA	1962
#Doherty, Lawrence – GBR	1980
#Doherty, Reginald – GBR	1980
#Douglass Chambers, Dorothea – GBR	1981
#Drobny, Jaroslav – GBR	1983
duPont, Margaret Osborne – USA	1967
Durr, Francoise – FRA	2003
#Dwight, James – USA	1955
Edberg, Stefan – SWE	2004
Emerson, Roy – AUS	1982
+#Etchebaster, Pierre – FRA	1978
Evert, Chris – USA	1995
Falkenburg, Bob – USA and BRA	1974
Fraser, Neale – AUS	1984
Fry-Irvin, Shirley – USA	1970
#Garland, Chuck – USA	1969
#Gibson, Althea – USA	1971
#Gonzalez, Pancho – USA	1968
Goolagong Cawley, Evonne – AUS	1988
Graf, Steffi – GER	2004
#Grant, Bryan 'Bitsy' – USA	1972
*#Gray, David – GBR	1985
#Griffin, Clarence – USA	1970
*#Gustav V, King of Sweden – SWE	1980
#Hackett, Harold – USA	1961
#Hansell, Ellen – USA	1965
Hard, Darlene – USA	1973
Hart, Doris – USA	1969
Haydon Jones, Ann – GBR	1985
*#Heldman, Gladys – USA	1979
*#Hester, W.E. 'Slew' – USA	1981
Hewitt, Bob – AUS and RSA	1992
#Hoad, Lew – AUS	1980
#Hopman, Harry – AUS	1978
#Hotchkiss Wightman, Hazel – USA	1957
#Hovey, Fred – USA	1974
#Hunt, Joe – USA	1966
* Hunt, Lamar – USA	1993
#Hunter, Frank – USA	1961
#Jacobs, Helen Hull – USA	1962
#Johnston, Bill – USA	1958
*#Jones, Perry – USA	1970
* Kelleher, Robert – USA	2000
King, Billie Jean – USA	1987
Kodes, Jan – TCH	1990
Kramer, Jack – USA	1968
#Lacoste, Rene – FRA	1976
*#Laney, Al – USA	1979
#Larned, William – USA	1956
Larsen, Art – USA	1969
Laver, Rod – AUS	1981
Lendl, Ivan – USA	2001
#Lenglen, Suzanne – FRA	1978
#Lott, George – USA	1964
Mako, Gene – USA	1973
Mandlikova, Hana – AUS and TCH	1994
#Marble, Alice – USA	1964
* Martin, Alastair – USA	1973
*#Martin, William McChesney – USA	1982
*#Maskell, Dan – GBR	1996
McEnroe, John – USA	1999
McGregor, Ken – AUS	1999
#McKane Godfree, Kathleen – GBR	1978
#McKinley, Chuck – USA	1986
#McLoughlin, Maurice – USA	1957
McMillan, Frew – RSA	1992
#McNeill, Don – USA	1965
#Moore, Elisabeth – USA	1971
Mortimer Barrett, Angela – GBR	1993
Mulloy, Gardnar – USA	1972
#Murray, R. Lindley – USA	1958
*#Myrick, Julian – USA	1963
Nastase, Ilie – ROM	1991
Navratilova, Martina – USA	2000
Newcombe, John – AUS	1986
*#Nielsen, Arthur – USA	1971
Novotna, Jana – USA	2005
#Nuthall Shoemaker, Betty – GBR	1977
Olmedo, Alex – PER	1987
#Osuna, Rafael – MEX	1979
*#Outerbridge, Mary – USA	1981
#Palfrey Danzig, Sarah – USA	1963
#Parker, Frank – USA	1966
#Patterson, Gerald – AUS	1989
Patty, Budge – USA	1977
#Pell, Theodore – USA	1966
#Perry, Fred – GBR	1975
+#Pettitt, Tom – GBR	1982
Pietrangeli, Nicola – ITA	1986
#Quist, Adrian – AUS	1984
Ralston, Dennis – USA	1987
#Renshaw, Ernest – GBR	1983

International Tennis Hall of Fame Enshrinees (continued)

Name	Year
#Renshaw, William - GBR	1983
#Richards, Vincent - USA	1961
Richey, Nancy - USA	2003
#Riggs, Bobby - USA	1967
Roche, Tony - AUS	1986
#Roosevelt, Ellen - USA	1975
Rose, Mervyn - AUS	2001
Rosewall, Ken - AUS	1980
#Round Little, Dorothy - GBR	1986
#Ryan, Elizabeth - USA	1972
Santana, Manuel - ESP	1984
Savitt, Dick - USA	1976
Schroeder, Ted - USA	1966
#Sears, Eleonora - USA	1968
#Sears, Richard - USA	1955
Sedgman, Frank - AUS	1979
Segura, Pancho - ECU	1984
Seixas, Vic - USA	1971
#Shields, Frank - USA	1964
Shriver, Pam - USA	2002

Name	Year
#Slocum, Henry - USA	1955
Smith, Stan - USA	1987
Stolle, Fred - AUS	1985
#Sutton Bundy, May - USA	1956
#Talbert, Bill - USA	1967
#Tilden, Bill - USA	1959
*#Tingay, Lance - GBR	1982
*#Tinling, Ted - GBR	1986
* Tobin, Brian - AUS	2003
#Townsend Toulmin, Bertha - USA	1974
Trabert, Tony - USA	1970
*#Van Alen, James - USA	1965
#Van Ryn, John - USA	1963
Vilas, Guillermo - ARG	1991
#Vines, Ellsworth - USA	1962
#von Cramm, Gottfried - GER	1977
Wade, Virginia - GBR	1989
#Wagner, Marie - USA	1969

Name	Year
#Ward, Holcombe - USA	1956
#Washburn, Watson - USA	1965
#Whitman, Malcolm - USA	1955
Wilander, Mats - SWE	2002
#Wilding, Anthony - NZL	1978
#Williams, Richard, 2nd - USA	1957
#Wills Moody Roark, Helen - USA	1959
*#Wingfield, Major Walter Clopton - GBR	1997
Wood, Sidney - USA	1964
#Wrenn, Robert - USA	1955
#Wright, Beals - USA	1956
Yannick, Noah - USA	2005

Key

\# Deceased
* Enshrined for Contributions to Tennis
\+ Enshrined as a Royal Tennis Player

Eligibility was extended to include candidates worldwide in 1975

Golden Achievers

This award was first instituted in 1999 to recognise people, in addition to tennis players, who were contributing significantly to tennis worldwide.

Brian Tobin (AUS), ITF President 1991-99	1999
Gil de Kermadec (FRA)	2000
Pablo Llorens Renaga (ESP)	2001
Enrique Morea (ARG)	2002
J. Howard "Bumpy" Frazer (USA)	2003
John Curry (GBR)	2004
Eiichi Kawatei (JPN)	2005

ITF/ITHF Davis Cup Award of Excellence

Neale Fraser (AUS)	2001
Pierre Darmon (FRA)	2002
John Newcombe (AUS)	2003
Manuel Santana (ESP)	2004
Goran Ivanisevic (CRO) and Miloslav Mecir (SVK)	2005

ITF/ITHF Fed Cup Award of Excellence

Arantxa Sanchez-Vicario and Conchita Martinez (ESP)	2001
Virginia Wade (GBR)	2002
Larisa Savchenko-Neiland (LAT)	2003
Olga Morozova (RUS)	2004
Francoise Durr (FRA)	2005

AIVARAS BALZEKAS

Lithuanian Davis Cup player Aivaras Balzekas was tragically killed in a car accident on 9 October in Boca Raton, Florida. The 23-year-old, who had represented Lithuania in 19 Davis Cup ties between 1999 and 2004, was attending Lynn University. As a junior he competed at Junior Grand Slam events whilst part of the ITF Junior B team touring Europe in 1991, funded by the Grand Slam Development Fund.

IAN BARNES

The ITF's former Media & PR Administrator Ian Barnes passed away at the age of 70 on 13 December. He was the tennis correspondent for the Daily Express in London for over 10 years before working for the ITF from 1989 until 1996.

FRANCO BARTONI

ATP and WTA Tour Board member, and Chairman of European Tournament Directors Franco Bartoni passed away in Rome on 14 August after a long illness, he was 56. As a player Bartoni competed at Grand Slam events between 1969 and 1972 and was a member of the Italian Davis Cup team in 1970. He served as a Davis Cup coach in 1972-73. After working for the Italian Tennis Federation he went on to be tournament director of Italy's most prominent events, Rome, Bologna and Milan.

ROLAND CARTER

Former President of Vets Tennis Great Britain, Roland Carter, died on 9 March aged 86. Carter's career as a player was interrupted by World War II however he was in the post-war British Davis Cup squad and represented Great Britain on several overseas tours. He competed at Wimbledon from 1947 until 1951. Carter was involved in British Vets tennis almost from its inception. He took on the role of International Liaison Officer before becoming Chairman of Selectors with responsibility for sending British teams to take part in ITF competitions. This led to his election to the ITF Veterans Committee in 1980, a position he held until 1995.

CARLO HENRY GRANDE II

Broadcaster Carlo Grande died in New Haven, USA on 30 July aged 68. He had a distinguished and award-winning career in the broadcast industry which started in local radio and television. His creativity led to one of the first independent multi-faceted radio networks in the early 1970's. He originated, produced and anchored tennis programmes around the world for his TNT Productions, including coverage of Wimbledon, Roland Garros, Italian Open and US Open.

BUZZER HADINGHAM

Former Chairman of the All England Club, Buzzer Hadingham, passed away on 27 December 2004 at the age of 89. Following in the footsteps of his father he worked for Slazengers from the age of 18, retiring as Chairman and Managing Director in 1983. Soon after he took over the Chairmanship of the All England Club. During his tenure he established a rapport with the players that had not previously existed, improved facilities for media coverage, especially television, started the campaign to curb ticket touts and slimmed down the corporate side of the tournament. He was awarded a Commander of the British Empire (CBE) in 1987.

LES JENKINS

Les Jenkins passed away on 11 February at the age of 80. He served the USTA and Southern Section as a volunteer for over 35 years and was a former president of the Southern Section, a USTA Board of Directors member and USTA Secretary. He and his late wife, Jeanne, received the Samuel Hardy Award in 1990.

RAJ KUMAR KHANNA

The President Emeritus of the All India Tennis Association (AITA), Raj Kumar Khanna, passed away on 20 June aged 81. Born in Amritsar, North India in 1924 Khanna was a Chartered Accountant by profession. His interest in tennis started at school, and he continued to play tennis six days a week for the next 50 years. His involvement in tennis administration began when he was elected Hon. Secretary of the Delhi Lawn Tennis Association in 1959. He captained the 1966 Indian Davis Cup team when it reached the Davis Cup final for the first time. He became Secretary General of the AITA in 1966, a post he held until 1975, and again from 1988-92 after which he became President. During his tenure the game in India flourished, there were improvements to administration, finance, tournament structure, coaching, officials and a development infrastructure was also put in place. He served on the ITF Committee of Management from 1967 until 1977. Khanna was presented with the prestigious Padmabhushan Award by the Indian government in 1975 in recognition of his services to the game.

ALOIS KOVACS

Alois Kovacs, tournament director of the International Spring Bowl, lost his battle against cancer on 8 December. He was 56 years old. Austria's Spring Bowl has been part of the ITF Junior Circuit for over 20 years and offers vital competitive opportunities for future professional players.

CYNTHIA MARTIN

The daughter of Dwight F Davis, founder of the Davis Cup, Cynthia Martin died peacefully in Washington DC on 5 February after a lengthy illness. She was the wife of former Hall of Fame Chairman and Hall of Famer William McChesney Martin. The Davis/Martin family, along with Joseph Cullman, spearheaded the resurgence and renovation of the International Tennis Hall of Fame in the late 1970s.

DAVID MEEHAN

David Meehan, who oversaw the complete overhaul of the USTA National Tennis Center including the construction of the Arthur Ashe Stadium, died on 3 January from a brain tumour. Meehan was an employee of the USTA for more than 20 years. As director of facility operations he played a lead role in the $285 million refurbishment of the site at Flushing Meadows.

BERNARD NOAT

Monte Carlo Tournament Director, Bernard Noat, died in a cycling accident on 6 July at the age of 71. Noat served the Monte Carlo Country Club and the Monaco Tennis Association before taking over the Monte Carlo Tournament which he developed into a successful ATP Masters Series event. He also helped establish the ATP European headquarters in Monte Carlo in 1990, and the International Lawn Tennis Writers Association in 2001.

JAYAKUMAR ROYAPPA

India's Jayakumar Royappa died at his home in Chennai on 1 June following a heart attack, he was 51. He was a former member of the Indian Davis Cup squad, won a number of titles in Europe and USA, and competed at Wimbledon. After his retirement as a player he coached in Cyprus and Chennai.

JEREMY SHALES

ITF Gold Badge Chair Umpire and Referee Jeremy Shales died after a short illness on 8 September at the age of 62. Shales was one of the first two professional chair umpires hired by the Men's Tennis Council and one of the first professional umpires to travel the world officiating at Grand Slam and Grand Prix events. He umpired at 45 Wimbledon Championships including 11 finals, and at the Davis Cup Final in 1998. His last assignment was as referee of the India v Uzbekistan Davis Cup tie in April 2005.

MOEZ SNOUSSI

ITF Silver Badge Referee, Moez Snoussi, passed away on 18 February in Tunisia after a long struggle against cancer. He was 38 years old. Snoussi started his officiating career in 1995, working at many high profile events including the 2000 Sydney Olympics and Wimbledon. In 2001 he retired from being a chair umpire to concentrate on refereeing, a career move which led him to oversee Davis Cup ties and the African Junior Championships when it was held in Tunis. He also worked for the Tunisian Tennis Federation.

Country Abbreviations

AFG ....Afghanistan
AHO ....Netherlands Antilles
ALB ....Albania
ALG ....Algeria
AND ....Andorra
ANG ....Angola
ANT ....Antigua and Barbuda
ARG ....Argentina
ARM ....Armenia
ARU ....Aruba
ASA ....American Samoa
AUS ....Australia
AUT ....Austria
AZE ....Azerbaijan
BAH ....Bahamas
BAN ....Bangladesh
BAR ....Barbados
BDI ....Burundi
BEL ....Belgium
BEN ....Benin
BER ....Bermuda
BHU ....Bhutan
BIH ....Bosnia/Herzegovina
BIZ ....Belize
BLR ....Belarus
BOL ....Bolivia
BOT ....Botswana
BRA ....Brazil
BRN ....Bahrain
BRU ....Brunei Darussalam
BUL ....Bulgaria
BUR ....Burkina Faso
CAF ....Central African Republic
CAM ....Cambodia
CAN ....Canada
CAY ....Cayman Islands
CGO ....Congo
CHA ....Chad
CHI ....Chile
CHN ....China, People's Rep. of
CIV ....Cote d'Ivoire
CMR ....Cameroon
COD ....Congo, Democratic Rep. of (Zaire)
COK ....Cook Islands
COL ....Colombia
COM ....Comoros
CPV ....Cape Verde Islands
CRC ....Costa Rica
CRO ....Croatia
CUB ....Cuba
CYP ....Cyprus
CZE ....Czech Republic
DEN ....Denmark
DJI ....Djibouti
DMA ....Dominica
DOM ....Dominican Republic
ECA ....East Caribbean States
ECU ....Ecuador
EGY ....Egypt
ERI ....Eritrea
ESA ....El Salvador
ESP ....Spain
EST ....Estonia
ETH ....Ethiopia
FIJ ....Fiji
FIN ....Finland
FRA ....France
FSM ....Micronesia
GAB ....Gabon
GAM ....Gambia
GBR ....Great Britain
GBS ....Guinea-Bissau
GEO ....Georgia
GEQ ....Equatorial Guinea
GER ....Germany
GHA ....Ghana
GRE ....Greece
GRN ....Grenada
GUA ....Guatemala
GUI ....Guinee Conakry
GUM ....Guam
GUY ....Guyana
HAI ....Haiti
HKG ....Hong Kong, China
HON ....Honduras
HUN ....Hungary
INA ....Indonesia
IND ....India
IRI ....Iran
IRL ....Ireland
IRQ ....Iraq
ISL ....Iceland
ISR ....Israel
ISV ....US Virgin Islands
ITA ....Italy
IVB ....British Virgin Islands
JAM ....Jamaica
JOR ....Jordan
JPN ....Japan
KAZ ....Kazakhstan
KEN ....Kenya
KGZ ....Kyrgyzstan
KIR ....Kiribati
KOR ....Korea, Rep. of
KSA ....Saudi Arabia
KUW ....Kuwait
LAO ....Laos
LAT ....Latvia
LBA ....Libya
LBR ....Liberia
LCA ....St Lucia
LES ....Lesotho

Country Abbreviations (continued)

LIB ....Lebanon
LIE ....Liechtenstein
LTU ....Lithuania
LUX ....Luxembourg
MAD ....Madagascar
MAR ....Morocco
MAS ....Malaysia
MAW ....Malawi
MDA ....Moldova
MDV ....Maldives
MEX ....Mexico
MGL ....Mongolia
MKD ....Macedonia, Former Yugoslavian Rep. of
MLI ....Mali
MLT ....Malta
MON ....Monaco
MOZ ....Mozambique
MRI ....Mauritius
MSH ....Marshall Islands
MTN ....Mauritania
MYA ....Myanmar (Burma)
NAM ....Namibia
NCA ....Nicaragua
NED ....Netherlands
NEP ....Nepal
NFK ....Norfolk Islands
NGR ....Nigeria
NIG ....Niger
NMI ....Northern Mariana Islands
NOR ....Norway
NRU ....Nauru
NZL ....New Zealand
OMA ....Oman
PAK ....Pakistan
PAN ....Panama
PAR ....Paraguay
PER ....Peru
PHI ....Philippines
PLE ....Palestine
PLW ....Palau
PNG ....Papua New Guinea
POC ....Pacific Oceania
POL ....Poland
POR ....Portugal
PRK ....Korea, Democratic People's Rep. of
PUR ....Puerto Rico
QAT ....Qatar
ROM ....Romania
RSA ....South Africa
RUS ....Russia
RWA ....Rwanda
SAM ....Samoa
SCG ....Serbia and Montenegro
SEN ....Senegal
SEY ....Seychelles
SIN ....Singapore
SKN ....Saint Kitts & Nevis
SLE ....Sierra Leone
SLO ....Slovenia
SMR ....San Marino
SOL ....Solomon Islands
SOM ....Somalia
SRI ....Sri Lanka
STP ....Sao Tome and Principe
SUD ....Sudan
SUI ....Switzerland
SUR ....Surinam
SVK ....Slovak Republic
SWE ....Sweden
SWZ ....Swaziland
SYR ....Syria
TAN ....Tanzania
TGA ....Tonga
THA ....Thailand
TJK ....Tajikistan
TKM ....Turkmenistan
TLS ....Timor-Leste
TOG ....Togo
TPE ....Chinese Taipei
TRI ....Trinidad & Tobago
TUN ....Tunisia
TUR ....Turkey
UAE ....United Arab Emirates
UGA ....Uganda
UKR ....Ukraine
URU ....Uruguay
USA ....United States
UZB ....Uzbekistan
VAN ....Vanuatu
VEN ....Venezuela
VIE ....Vietnam
VIN ....Saint Vincent & Grenadines
YEM ....Yemen
ZAM ....Zambia
ZIM ....Zimbabwe

Historical Country Codes

FRG ....Germany FR (GER since 1990)
GDR ....Germany DR (GER since 1990)
BOH ....Bohemia (TCH from 1920)
TCH ....Czechoslovakia (SVK or CZE since 1994)
URS ....USSR (former Soviet Union)
EUN ....Unified Team (ex USSR)
RHO ....Rhodesia (Zimbabwe from 1968)
YUG ....Yugoslavia (Serbia and Montenegro from 2004)